CHRISTIAN COUNSELING

CHRISTIAN COUNSELING

A COMPREHENSIVE GUIDE

Gary R. Collins, Ph.D.

REVISED EDITION

WORD PUBLISHING
Dallas · London · Vancouver · Melbourne

CHRISTIAN COUNSELING: A COMPREHENSIVE GUIDE, revised edition

Library of Congress Cataloging-in-Publication Data

Collins, Gary R.
Christian counseling : a comprehensive guide / Gary R. Collins.—Rev. and expanded ed.
p. cm.
Bibliography: p.
Includes index.
ISBN 0-8499-0692-X
0-8499-3124-X (pbk.)
1. Pastoral counseling. I. Title.
BV4012.2.C56 1988
235.5—dc19 88-22076
CIP

8 9 0 QBP 14 13 12 11

Printed in the United States of America

In Memory of My Dad

Harold A. "Bus" Collins
1910–87

Contents

Preface

A wise author once told me that doing a revision is harder than writing a book. For more than a year I have spent hundreds of hours sitting in front of a word processor going over the first edition of this book, revising sentences, updating information, adding chapters, eliminating redundancies, rechecking Scripture references, and reevaluating what I had written before. Once again I have had to face the discipline, the long lonely hours, and the risk of expressing ideas in print where all can see, criticize, and perhaps at times applaud. My friend was right: it is easier and more fun to write a book than to work through a revision.

Nevertheless, the revision process has been challenging. I have been able to clarify some things that were not clear in the first edition, to deal with some of the questions raised by reviewers of the first book, and to incorporate suggestions that have come from students. My colleagues at Word sent a questionnaire to several thousand readers of the first edition, and those who responded gave helpful suggestions, many of which have been included in this revised edition. Letters from different parts of the world have alerted me to cross-cultural issues, and a few counselees have written to give their perspectives on the topics covered in the following chapters.

As with the first edition. I have tried in these pages to summarize much of what we know about counseling methodology and about the major problems that people face today. This book has been prepared as a resource tool for pastors and other Christian counselors, as a study guide for lay helpers, and as a textbook for use in colleges and seminaries. In my writing I have sought to be guided by the teachings of the Bible and to be sensitive to the constantly accumulating research in counseling and psychopathology. This new edition:

- Is a complete revision and rewriting of the earlier book.
- Includes case histories to illustrate the problems that are discussed.
- Has added new chapters on community counseling, young adulthood, violence (including abuse in the home), pregnancy issues, mental illness, addictions, and counseling the counselor.
- Discusses emerging topics such as eating disorders, abuse of the elderly, bitterness, and counseling people with AIDS.
- Makes reference to more than 1,500 books and journal articles, 80 percent of which have appeared since the first edition of this book was published and over half (53 percent) of which have been published within the past three years.
- Attempts to be clearly written, easy to read, and relatively free of technical, psychological, or theological jargon.

A project of this size draws on the help of many marvelous people. Some helped with the first edition and subsequently have gone to other places of service, but I still owe a debt of gratitude to the earlier assistance of Lawrence Tornquist, James Beesley, Charles Romig, Marlene Terbush, Kathy Cropp, Marilyn Secor, Lenore Scherrer, Sharon Regan, Nancy Fister, and Laura Beth Norton. Steve Brown, Paul Lightner, Scott Thelander, Sergio Mijangos, Ted Grove, Jim Thomas, Bill Secor, Tom Jensen, Kiel Cooper, Ron Hawkins, Sylvia Bacon, and Pam Lunde all helped in a variety of ways with the revised edition, as did a number of people at Word Books including Ernie Owen, Joey Paul, Laura Kendall, Ed Curtis, Carey Moore, Nancy Rivers, and Ed Stanley. Nöel Halsey and his colleagues in England worked to get the book into a Commonwealth edition, and I am grateful to those who labored to make the first edition available in Korean and Portuguese. As a result of these overseas editions, I have been able to get new insights to incorporate into the revision. Once again, the administration at Trinity Evangelical Divinity School, my colleagues in the psychology department, and my students have all shown great flexibility and have given freely of their encouragement as I worked to revise what has come to be known (affectionately, I hope) as the "big yellow book."

Without my family, however, this revision might never have been completed. My mother, whose failing eyesight will never allow her to read these pages, my daughters, Lynn and Jan, and my ever-supportive wife, Julie, have given constant encouragement and tolerated my long periods of retreat in my study. I am grateful to God and to them for their love and understanding.

Yet it is humbling to realize that in all of this, we write, we revise books, read, and counsel only because of the capacities, desires, and opportunities that God has given. Once again, therefore, this book goes forward with gratitude to God, with the prayer that it will bring honor to Jesus Christ, and with the hope that the Holy Spirit will use it to help many dedicated Christian counselors care more effectively for their counselees and for others who are in need.

Gary R. Collins

How to Use This Book

Christian Counseling: A Comprehensive Guide has been written to assist Christian leaders in their counseling work. The first five chapters of the book are designed to give an overview of counseling and probably should be read consecutively. The remaining chapters (except possibly the last) deal with specific problems. Because each chapter stands alone, they can be read in any order. Each chapter begins with a case example and introduction followed by a consideration of what the Bible says about the problem and a survey of the causes, effects, counseling considerations, and suggested ways to prevent the problem. All of this is intended to give relevant, up-to-date information that can be useful in counseling.

Experience has shown that the book is used as a resource guide for individual counselors including pastors, a textbook for students and their professors, a training tool for lay counselors, and a source of information for those who want a greater understanding of human behavior, a clearer perspective on the biblical basis of counseling, and a greater awareness of people-helping skills.

Certainly the book is intended to stand alone, but its effectiveness is extended when used in conjunction with the Christian Counselor's Library (revised edition). The library contains forty audio cassettes, a counselor's manual, counselee worksheets, and a copy of this book. It is available from the Educational Products Division of Word, Inc. (5221 N. O'Connor Blvd., Suite 1000, Irving, Tex. 75039) and is designed as a tool that counselors can use to extend their counseling proficiency.

If you use the Christian Counselor's Library as part of a training program (either for yourself or in a classroom or study group), we recommend that you begin by reading the first five chapters of this book. Pause after chapter 2 to listen to the tape by Dr. Louis McBurney that accompanies that chapter. Each of the remaining chapters can be studied in the following way:

First, read the appropriate chapter in *Christian Counseling.* Second, listen to the tape and complete the tape-worksheet. At times it will be difficult to complete the assignments on the tape. Young people, for example, may have difficulty imagining what it would be like to face retirement and the later years; single people may have difficulty completing the assignments on marriage and divorce. To complete as many assignments as possible, however, will give you a feel for the counselee and the problem being discussed. It is assumed that these two steps will be completed by individuals prior to meeting in the group.

The third step involves group discussion. The instructor may wish to give a brief lecture or comment on the subject matter in the book. It is recommended that the group members then do a role play based on the case history that begins each chapter. Assign one member of the group to serve as a counselor and ask others to play the role of the individual or individuals whose problems are described. After ten or fifteen minutes, stop the role play and discuss what was done. What was good about the sample counseling? How did the counselee and counselor feel in the role play? What would have made the counseling better? What was learned about counseling and about the problem area as a result of this exercise?

Whether or not you do a role play, it can be helpful to discuss the questions that follow. You can write answers to test your understanding of the chapter or you can discuss these questions as a group. These chapters are designed for use with chapters 6–38, although there may be a need for slight adaptation with some of the chapters.

1. What questions do you have about the chapter?
2. Can you summarize biblical teaching on the problem discussed in this chapter?
3. Summarize the causes and effects of this problem.
4. What have you learned about counseling people with this problem?
5. Can anyone give examples of people who have had this problem? (Be sure not to reveal the names of people involved or identifying details.) How could this person have been counseled?
6. Outline a program for preventing the development of this problem.
7. Summarize what you have learned from this chapter, from the tape, and from the role play.
8. What questions do you still have that have not been answered? To help find the answers, you may want to consult some of the books listed at the end of each chapter.

It is not always possible for an author or a publisher to enter into detailed correspondence with readers, but we would like to know if you have found the book and its supplementary materials to be of help in your counseling work. If a third edition is produced, do you have suggestions that would make this better? The author and publisher would like to hear your reactions. Please write to Dr. Gary R. Collins, c/o Word, Inc., Editorial Division, 5221 N. O'Connor Blvd., Suite 1000, Irving, Tex. 75039, or Department of Psychology, Trinity Evangelical Divinity School, 2065 Half Day Road, Deerfield, Ill. 60015.

Part 1

Introductory Issues

1 The Church and Counseling

I NEVER THOUGHT THERE COULD BE so many hurting people!" The young pastor was only a few years out of seminary. His little church was growing and he wanted to give the leadership that was desperately needed. But his days, and sometimes his nights, seemed to be filled with an unending stream of hurting people. Each was looking to him for guidance and counseling.

"In seminary, they never told us that so many people are needy," he continued. "They never warned us that a pastor might have to deal with mate beating, father-daughter incest, fear, confusion, threats of suicide, homosexuality, alcoholism, drug abuse, depression, anxiety, guilt, family problems, eating disorders, chronic stress, and a host of other problems. We had one counseling course and never suspected the depth and variety of problems that we could encounter following graduation."

Many years ago, Wayne Oates wrote, "The pastor, regardless of his training, does not enjoy the privilege of electing whether or not he will counsel with his people. They inevitably bring their problems to him for his best guidance and wisest care. He cannot avoid this if he stays in the pastoral ministry. His choice is not between counseling or not counseling, but between counseling in a disciplined and skilled way and counseling in an undisciplined and unskilled way."[1]

It isn't easy to counsel in a disciplined and skilled way, especially when the problems are so diverse, the needs are so great, and the available counseling techniques are often so confusing and contradictory.

Literally thousands of counseling methods are now in use. Books and articles on therapy and people helping roll off the presses with disturbing regularity. There seem to be as many theories and approaches to counseling as there are counselors. With all this advice and activity, even full-time professionals can feel overwhelmed.

It would be encouraging if these publications, theories, and counselor training aids all helped counselors to be more effective, but some of the counseling books and seminars are of questionable validity. Well-meaning but naive writers have proposed simplistic "new methods" that are claimed to be uniquely Christian but fail to be effective. Recent books have added confusion by attacking the counseling professions[2] and emotional sermons, some on national television, have misled many believers into thinking that counseling is never needed.

Sometimes counseling doesn't help. Even well-trained, experienced counselors who keep abreast of the professional literature and apply the best-proven techniques, find that counselees do not always improve. At times, individuals get worse as a result of counseling. It is hardly surprising, therefore, that some people give up and conclude that counseling is really a waste of time.[3]

If everybody gave up, however, where would people go with their problems? Jesus, who is the Christian's example, spent many hours talking to needy people in groups and in face-to-face contact. The Apostle Paul, who was very sensitive to the needs of hurting individuals, wrote that we who are strong must bear the weaknesses and help carry the burdens of those who are weaker.[4] Probably Paul was writing about those who had doubts, fears, and sinful lifestyles, but his compassionate concern extended to almost every problem that might be encountered by counselors today.

The biblical writers do not present people helping as an option. It is a responsibility for every believer, including the church leader.[5] At times, counseling may seem like a waste of time, but it is biblically mandated, and can be an effective, important, and necessary part of any ministry.

It should not be assumed that all pastors and other Christian leaders are gifted in this area, and called to counsel.[6] Because of their temperaments, interests, skills, training, or calling, some Christians avoid counseling, preferring instead to devote their time and gifts to other ministries. This is a legitimate decision, especially if it is made in consultation with fellow believers.

Each of us must be careful, however, not to quickly abandon a personally enriching, potentially powerful, and biblically based way of ministering to others. It isn't easy to counsel, but evidence is increasing that people from a variety of backgrounds can learn effective counseling skills.[7] God can use you as a counselor.

Care and Counseling

Counseling attempts to provide encouragement and guidance for those who are facing losses, decisions, or disappointments. Counseling can stimulate personality growth and development; help people cope more effectively with the problems of living, with inner conflict, and with crippling emotions; assist individuals, family members, and married couples to resolve interpersonal tensions or relate effectively to one another; and assist persons whose life patterns are self-defeating and causing unhappiness. The Christian counselor seeks to bring people into a personal relationship with Jesus Christ and to help them find forgiveness and relief from the crippling effects of sin and guilt. Ultimately, the Christian hopes to help others become disciples of Christ and disciplers of others.

Pastoral Care. Some have found it useful to make a distinction between pastoral care, pastoral counseling, and pastoral psychotherapy. Of the three terms, pastoral care is broadest. It refers to the church's overall ministries of healing, sustaining, guiding, and reconciling people to God and to one another.[8] Sometimes called "the care of souls,"[9] this includes the ministries of preaching, teaching, discipline, administering the sacraments, nurturing people, and caring in times of need. Since the time of Christ, the church has been committed to pastoral care.

Pastoral Counseling. This is a more specialized part of pastoral care that involves helping individuals, families, or groups as they cope with the pressures and crises of life. Pastoral counseling uses a variety of healing methods to help people deal with problems in ways that are consistent with biblical teaching. The ultimate goal is to help counselees experience healing, learning, and personal-spiritual growth.

As defined traditionally, pastoral counseling is the work of an ordained pastor. In view of the scriptural teaching that all believers are to bear the burdens of one another,[10] pastoral counseling can and should be a ministry of sensitive and caring Christians, whether or not they are ordained as clergy. In the pages that follow, pastoral counseling and Christian counseling will be used interchangeably.

Pastoral Psychotherapy. This is a long-term, in-depth helping process that attempts to bring fundamental changes in the counselee's personality, spiritual values, and ways of thinking. It is a form of help-giving that seeks to remove blocks, often from the past, that inhibit personal and spiritual growth. It is the work of a trained specialist and rarely will be mentioned in this book.[11]

What Makes Christian Counseling Unique?

Several years ago I led a seminar for a group of chaplains who challenged the idea that Christian counseling is unique. "There is nothing distinctively Christian about counseling," one of the class members argued. "There is no uniquely Christian form of surgery, Christian auto mechanics, or Christian cooking, and neither is there Christian counseling."

Christian counselors use many techniques that have been developed and used by nonbelievers, but Christian counseling has at least four distinctives.[12]

Unique Assumptions. No counselor is completely value free or neutral in terms of assumptions. We each bring our own viewpoints into the counseling situation and these influence our judgments and comments whether we recognize this or not.

Psychoanalyst Erich Fromm, for example, once stated that we all live "in a universe indifferent to our fate." Such a viewpoint would leave no place for belief in a compassionate, sovereign God. There would be no room for prayer, meditating on "the Word of God," experiencing divine forgiveness, or looking toward life after death. Fromm's assumptions must have influenced his methods of counseling.

Despite variations in theology, most counselors who call themselves Christian have (or should have) beliefs about the attributes of God, the nature of human beings, the authority of Scripture, the reality of sin, the forgiveness of God, and hope for the future. Read, for example, the first four verses of Hebrews. Won't our lives and counseling be different if we believe God has spoken to the human race, created the universe through his son, provided for the forgiveness of sins, and now holds everything together by the mighty power of his command?

Unique Goals. Like our secular colleagues, the Christian seeks to help counselees change behavior, attitudes, values, and/or perceptions. We attempt to teach skills, including social skills; to encourage recognition and expression of emotion; to give support in times of need; to teach responsibility; to instill insight; to guide as decisions are made; to help counselees mobilize inner and environmental resources in times of crisis; to teach problem-solving skills; and to increase counselee competence and "self-actualization."[13]

But the Christian goes further. He or she seeks to stimulate spiritual growth in counselees; to encourage confession of sin and the experience of divine forgiveness; to model Christian standards, attitudes, values, and lifestyles; to present the gospel message, encouraging counselees to commit their lives to Jesus Christ; and to stimulate counselees to develop values and live lives that are based on biblical teaching, instead of living in accordance with relativistic humanistic standards.

Some will criticize this as "bringing religion into counseling." To ignore theological issues, however, is to build our counseling on the religion of humanistic naturalism, to stifle our own beliefs, and to compartmentalize our lives into sacred and secular segments. No good counselor, Christian or non-Christian, forces beliefs on counselees. We have an obligation to treat people with respect and to give them freedom to make decisions. But honest and authentic people-helpers do not stifle their beliefs and pretend to be something they are not.

Unique Methods. All counseling techniques have at least four characteristics. They seek to arouse the belief that help is possible, correct erroneous beliefs about the world, develop competences in social living, and help counselees accept themselves as persons of worth. To accomplish these goals, counselors consistently use such basic techniques as listening, showing interest, attempting to understand, and at least occasionally giving direction. Christians and non-Christian counselors use many of the same helping methods.

But the Christian does not use counseling techniques that would be considered immoral or inconsistent with biblical teaching. For example, encouraging people to engage in extramarital or premarital sexual intercourse, using abusive language, or urging counselees to develop antibiblical values would all be avoided, regardless of their use by secular therapists.

Other techniques are distinctively Christian and would be used in Christian counseling with some frequency. Prayer in the counseling session,[14] reading the Scriptures, gentle confrontation with Christian truths, or encouraging counselees to become involved in a local church are common examples.

Unique Counselor Characteristics. In every counseling situation, the helper must ask at least four questions: What is the problem? Should I intervene and try to help? What could I do to help? Would someone else be better qualified to help?[15] It is important for Christian counselors to have an understanding of problems (how they arise and how they might be resolved), a knowledge of biblical teaching about the problems, and a familiarity with counseling skills.

There is evidence, however, that the counselor's personal characteristics are of even greater significance in helping. After writing an in-depth book on theories of counseling, psychologist C. H. Patterson concluded that the effective counselor must be "a real, human person" who offers "a genuine human relationship" to counselees. "It is a relationship characterized not so much by what techniques the therapist uses as by what he is, not so much by what he does as by the way he does it."[16]

Several years ago, research studies found that counseling techniques are most potent when used by helpers who are characterized by warmth, sensitivity, understanding, genuine concern, and a willingness to confront people in an attitude of love. Counseling textbooks stressed the importance of counselor qualities such as trustworthiness, good psychological health, honesty, patience, competence, and self-knowledge.[17] According to more recent research, helpers are most effective when they have these counselor traits, along with knowledge about human problems and good counseling skills.[18] Best intentions, suggests Jay Adams, are no substitute for knowledge and skills.[19]

Surely Jesus Christ is the best model we have of an effective "wonderful counselor" whose personality, knowledge, and skills enabled him effectively to assist those people who needed help. In attempting to analyze the counseling of Jesus, we must be aware that each of us could have a tendency, unconscious or deliberate, to view Christ's ministry in a way that reinforces our own views about how people are helped. The directive-confrontational counselor recognizes that Jesus was confrontational at times; the nondirective "client-centered" counselor finds support for this approach in other examples of Christ's helping ministry. Surely it is more accurate to state that Jesus used a variety of counseling techniques depending on the situation, the nature of the counselee, and the specific problem. At times he listened to people carefully and without giving much overt direction, but on other occasions he taught decisively. He encouraged and supported, but he also confronted and challenged. He accepted people who were sinful and needy, but he also demanded repentance, obedience, and action.

Basic to Jesus' style of helping, however, was his personality. In his teaching, caring, and counseling he demonstrated those traits, attitudes, and values that made him effective as a people helper and that serve as a model for us. Jesus was absolutely honest, deeply compassionate, highly sensitive, and spiritually mature. He was committed to serving his heavenly Father and his fellow human beings (in that order). He also prepared himself for his work with frequent periods of prayer and meditation. He was deeply familiar with Scripture. He sought to help needy persons turn to him so they could find ultimate peace, hope, and security.[20]

Jesus often helped people through sermons, but he also debated skeptics, challenged individuals, healed the sick, talked with the needy, encouraged the downhearted, and modeled a godly life style. In his contacts with people, he shared examples taken from real-life situations, and he sought constantly to stimulate others to think and act in accordance with divine principles. Apparently he believed that some people need an understanding helper to listen, comfort, and discuss before they can learn from confrontation, challenge, advice giving, or public preaching.

According to the Bible, Christians are to teach *all* that Christ commanded and taught.[21] This surely includes doctrines about God, authority, salvation, spiritual growth, prayer, the church, the future, angels, demons, and human nature. But Jesus also taught about marriage, parent-child interactions, obedience, race relations, and freedom for both women and men. He taught, too, about personal issues such as sex, anxiety, fear, loneliness, doubt, pride, sin, and discouragement.

All of these are issues that people bring to counselors today. When Jesus dealt with people he frequently listened to the inquirers and accepted them before stimulating them to think or act differently. At times he told people what to do, but he also used skillful and divinely guided questioning to help individuals resolve their problems. Thomas was helped with his problem of doubting when Jesus showed the evidence; Peter apparently learned best from reflecting (with Jesus) about past mistakes; Mary of Bethany learned by listening; and Judas learned by painful experience.

Teaching all that Christ taught includes instruction in doctrine, but it also involves helping people get along better with God, with others, and with themselves. These are issues that concern almost everyone. Some learn from lectures, sermons, or books; others learn from personal Bible study or from discussion; still others learn from formal or informal counseling; and perhaps most of us have learned from some combination of these approaches.

At the core of all true Christian helping, private or public, is the influence of the Holy Spirit. His presence and influence make Christian counseling truly unique. It is he who gives the most effective counselor characteristics: love, joy, peace, patience, kindness, goodness, faithfulness, gentleness, and self-control.[22] He is the comforter or helper who teaches "all things," reminds us of Christ's sayings, convicts people of sin, and guides us into all truth.[23] Through prayer, meditation on the Scriptures, regular confessions of sin, and daily deliberate commitment to Christ, the counselor-teacher becomes an instrument through whom the Holy Spirit may work to comfort, help, teach, convict, or guide another human being. This should be the goal of every believer—pastor or lay person, professional counselor or nonprofessional—to be used by the Holy Spirit to touch lives, to change them, and to bring others toward both spiritual and psychological maturity.[24]

The Church as a Healing Community

As we have seen, Jesus often talked with individuals about their personal needs and he met frequently with small groups. Chief among these was the little band of disciples whom he prepared to "take over" after his ascension into heaven. It was during one of these times with the disciples that Jesus first mentioned the church.[25]

In the years that followed it was this church of Jesus Christ that continued his ministry of teaching, evangelizing, ministering, and counseling. These activities were not seen as the special responsibility of "superstar" church leaders; they were done by ordinary believers working, sharing, and caring both for each other and for the nonbelievers outside the body. If we read Acts[26] and the Epistles it becomes clear that the church was not only an evangelizing, teaching, discipling community—it was also a healing community.

Healing communities are groups of people "characterized by intense commitment to the group and by a common interest in healing . . . psychological, behavioral, or spiritual maladies."[27] Within recent years, mental health professionals have come to see the value of therapeutic groups in which group members help each other by providing support, challenge, guidance, and encouragement that might not be possible otherwise. Of course such groups can be harmful, especially when they become uncontrolled encounters that seek to criticize and embarrass the participants instead of building them up or challenging them to openness and more effective behavior. If conducted by a sensitive leader, however, group sessions can be very effective therapeutic experiences for all people involved.

Such therapeutic groups need not be limited to counselees meeting with each other and with a trained counselor. Families, study groups, trusted friends, professional colleagues, employee groups, and other small bands of people often provide the help that is needed both in times of crisis and as individuals face the daily challenges of living. In all of society, however, the church has the greatest potential for being a therapeutic-healing community.[28] Local bodies of believers can bring a sense of belonging to the members,[29] support to those who feel weak, healing to troubled individuals, and guidance as people make decisions and move toward maturity.

It is sad that many contemporary churches seem to be little more than listless groups of rigid people who never admit to having needs or problems, who attend uninspiring services out of habit, and who leave most of the work to an overburdened pastor. Such a picture may be overstated, but for many people the local church is largely meaningless, not very helpful, and far from the dynamic growth-producing fellowship that Christ intended it to be.

Why was the church begun? Surely the answer lies in Jesus' final words to his followers before he went back into heaven: "Go and make disciples of all nations, baptizing them in the name of the Father and of the Son and of the Holy Spirit, and teaching them to obey everything I have commanded you. And surely I will be with you always, to the very end of the age."[30]

The church was created to fulfill the great commission of making disciples (this includes evangelism) and teaching. The early believers came together in a fellowship or *koinonia* that involved a community relationship with one another, a partnership that actively promoted the gospel and built up believers, and a mutual sharing of insights, experiences, worship, needs, and material possessions.[31] The true church has always been headed by Jesus Christ who showed us how to evangelize and teach, who by his life and instruction pointed us to the practical as well as the theoretical aspects of Christianity, and who summarized his teaching in two laws: to love God and to love others.

All of this is meant to take place within the confines of a group of believers, each of whom has been granted the gifts and abilities needed to build up the church. As a group, guided by a pastor and other chosen leaders, the believers direct their attention and activities upward through worship of God, outward through evangelism, and inward through teaching, fellowship, and burden bearing.[32] When one of these is missing the group is unbalanced and the believers are incomplete.

The remaining chapters of this book are written to assist counselors, pastors, church leaders, students, and other Christians in one important aspect of the church's work: burden bearing.[33] The topics discussed are among the most common issues faced by both Christians and nonbelievers: problems that interfere with worship, evangelism, teaching, fellowship, growth, meaningful relationships, individual maturing, and personal joy. For each of these topics we will consider what causes the problems, how people are affected by them, how the problems can be reduced or eliminated especially through counseling, how we can prevent their recurrence, and where we can get further information. The chapters will summarize biblical teaching about these issues and will draw on recent psychological research and insights.

CAN PSYCHOLOGY HELP?

To increase their counseling effectiveness, many church leaders have turned to the insights of psychologists and other mental health professionals. Psychology is a highly complex field of study that deals with both animal and human behavior. The college student who takes an introductory course in general psychology often encounters a mass of statistics, technical terms, and "scientific data" about a host of seemingly unimportant subjects. Seminary courses in pastoral counseling tend to be more people-centered and relevant, but even here the student (and sometimes the professor) may be lost in a maze of theories and techniques that are not very useful when one is face-to-face with a confused, hurting human being.

This has led some writers to reject psychology, including the field of counseling, and to conclude that a Bible is all the Christian people-helper needs to assist others. "True Christianity does not mix well with psychology," claims one recent author.[34] "God and His Word provide a completely sufficient foundation for mental-emotional health," writes another. "The Bible is the repository of the healing balm for all nonorganically based mental-emotional disorders."[35] Jay Adams argues that psychiatrists (and presumably psychologists) have usurped the work of preachers, and are in the dangerous occupation of trying to change people's behavior and values in an ungodly manner. Writing to pastors, Adams maintains that "by studying the Word of God carefully and observing how the biblical principles describe the people you counsel . . . you can gain all the information and experience that you need to become a competent, confident Christian counselor without a study of psychology."[36] Clearly these writers see little hope that psychology or related fields of study will be able to help the Christian counsel more effectively.

As you read the following pages, you will find frequent references to the Bible. God's Word *is* a healing balm for mental-emotional disorders. It speaks to people today. It has profound and lasting relevance to the counselor's work and to the needs of his or her counselees.

But the Bible never claims to be a textbook on counseling. It deals with loneliness, discouragement, marriage problems, grief, parent-child relations, anger, fear, and a host of other counseling situations, but it was never meant to be God's sole revelation about people helping. In medicine, teaching and other "people-centered" helping fields, we have been permitted to learn much about God's creation through science and academic study. Why, then, should psychology be singled out as the one field that has nothing to contribute to the work of the counselor?

As a field of study, scientific psychology is little more than a hundred years old. During the past century, God has permitted psychologists to develop careful research tools for studying human behavior and professional journals for sharing these findings. As perhaps hundreds of thousands of people have come for help, professional counselors have learned what makes people tick and how they can change. Our knowledge is far from complete and neither is it error-free, but careful psychological research and data analysis have led to a vast reservoir of conclusions that are known to help counselees and people who want to be effective people-helpers. Even those who would dismiss the field of psychology frequently use psychological terms in their writings and psychologically derived techniques in their counseling.

In the following chapters, the writings of social scientists are frequently cited on the assumption that all truth comes from God, including truth about the people whom God created. He has revealed this truth through the Bible, God's written Word to human beings, but he also has permitted us to discover truth through experience and through the methods of scientific investigation. Discovered truth must always be consistent with, and tested against, the norm of revealed biblical truth. But we limit our counseling effectiveness when we pretend that the discoveries of psychology have nothing to contribute to the understanding and solution of problems. We compromise our integrity when we overtly reject psychology but then smuggle its concepts in to our counseling—sometimes naively and without even realizing what we are doing.

Let us accept the fact that psychology can be of great help to the Christian counselor.[37] How, then, do we wade through the quagmire of techniques, theories, and technical terms to find the insights that truly are helpful? The answer involves our finding a guide—some person or persons who are committed followers of Jesus Christ, familiar with the psychological and counseling literature, trained in counseling and in research methods (so the scientific accuracy of psychologists' conclusions can be evaluated), and effective as counselors. It is of crucial importance that the guides be committed to the inspiration and authority of the Bible, both as the standard against which all psychology must be tested and as the written Word of God with which all valid counseling must agree.

The pages that follow, and the cassette tapes that accompany this book, have been prepared by guides who can assist Christian counselors in the joyful but demanding task of helping others. This is not meant to be a cookbook volume of never-fail recipes designed for producing master counselors. Human beings are far too complicated to always be changed, even through the intervention of the most skilled counselors. All counselors have failures, sometimes because of the counselor's inability, misperceptions, or error; often because the counselee cannot or will not change. But improvements are more likely when the counselor has some understanding of the problems and some knowledge of how to intervene. The following chapters have been written to help with this understanding and to provide some of the needed knowledge.

Before we begin our analysis, however, we need to have a closer look at ourselves, the counselors. What motivates us to be people-helpers, what are some dangers in counseling, and why do so many counselors wear out under the pressure of trying to help hurting people? These are the kinds of issues that we discuss in the next chapter.

SUGGESTIONS FOR FURTHER READING

Benner, David G. *Psychotherapy and the Spiritual Quest.* Grand Rapids, Mich.: Baker, 1988.

Bridges, Jerry. *True Fellowship.* Colorado Springs: NavPress, 1985.

Collins, Gary R. *Can You Trust Psychology?* Downers Grove, Ill.: InterVarsity, 1988.

Getz, Gene A. *Building Up One Another.* Wheaton, Ill.: Victor Books, 1976.

Kirwin, William T. *Biblical Concepts for Christian Counseling.* Grand Rapids, Mich.: Baker, 1984.

Miller, William R., and Kathleen A. Jackson. *Practical Psychology for Pastors.* Englewood Cliffs, N.J.: Prentice-Hall, 1985.

Trueblood, Elton. *The Incendiary Fellowship.* New York: Harper & Row, 1967.

2

The Counselor and Counseling

There is something innately attractive about being a counselor. Apparently, many people see counseling as a glamorous activity that involves giving advice, healing broken relationships, and helping people solve problems.

Counseling can be gratifying work, but it doesn't take long for most of us to discover that this also can be emotionally draining, difficult work. Counseling involves intensive concentration and sometimes brings pain when we see so many people hurting. When these people fail to improve, as often happens, it is easy to blame ourselves. We try harder and wonder what went wrong. As more and more needy people come for help, there is a tendency to keep increasing our counseling loads—pushing ourselves closer to the limits of our endurance. Sometimes the counselees' problems remind us of our own insecurities or conflicts and this can threaten the counselor's own stability or feelings of self-worth. Little wonder that counseling has been seen as both a fulfilling and a hazardous occupation. In this chapter we will discuss some of these hazards and consider ways to make the counselor's work more fulfilling and successful.

The Counselor's Motivation

Why do you want to counsel? Some Christian counselors, especially pastors, have been thrust into this work by people who have come spontaneously seeking help for their problems. Other counselors have taken special training and encouraged people to come for help, based on the valid assumption that counseling can be one of the most effective ways to minister to the needy. As we have seen, the Bible commands mutual caring and this surely involves counseling.

It always is difficult to evaluate our own motives. Perhaps this is especially true when we examine our reasons for doing counseling. A sincere desire to help people is a valid reason for becoming a counselor. Is there evidence from others that your counseling really has a positive influence? Do you find counseling to be personally fulfilling? These could be further indications of your potential effectiveness as a counselor.

But there are other issues, sometimes unrecognized, that can interfere with your effectiveness. When you counsel primarily to meet your own needs, you are not likely to be of much help to your counselees.[1]

1. *The Need for Relationships.* Everybody needs closeness and intimate contact with at least two or three other people. For some counselees, the counselor will be their closest friend, at least temporarily.[2] But suppose the counselor has no close friends apart from counselees. In such cases the counselor's need for a relationship

may hinder the helping. The counselor may not really want counselees to improve and terminate counseling since this would end some close relationships. If you notice that you are looking for opportunities to prolong the counseling, to call the counselee, or to get together socially, it may be that the relationship is meeting your needs for companionship as much (or more) as it is helping the counselee. At this point the counselor-counselee involvement has ceased to be a professional relationship. This isn't necessarily bad, but friends are not always the best counselors.

2. *The Need for Control.* The authoritarian counselor likes to "straighten out" others, give advice (even when it is not requested), and play the problem-solver role. Some dependent counselees may want this, but eventually most people resist controller-type counselors because they don't really help.

3. *The Need to Rescue.* The rescuer often has a sincere desire to help, but this counselor takes responsibility away from the counselee by showing an attitude that says "you can't handle this; let me do it for you." This may satisfy the counselee for a while, but it rarely helps permanently. When the rescue technique fails (as often happens), the counselor feels guilty, inadequate, and deeply frustrated.

4. *The Need for Information.* In describing their problems, counselees often give interesting tidbits of information that might not be shared otherwise. When a counselor is curious, he or she sometimes forgets the counselee, pushes for extra information, and often is unable to keep confidences. Curious counselors are rarely helpful and eventually people stop asking them for help.

5. *The Need for Personal Healing.* Most of us carry hidden needs and insecurities that could interfere with our people-helping work. This is one reason why graduate schools of psychology sometimes require students to get counseling for themselves before they start helping others. Counseling sessions are not likely to be effective if the counselor has a need to manipulate others, to atone for guilt, to please some authority figure, to express hostility, to resolve sexual conflicts, or to prove that he or she is intellectually capable, spiritually mature, and psychologically stable.

It is probable that every prospective counselor will experience these tendencies at times, but such needs must be dealt with apart from our work with counselees. When people come for counseling they take the risk of sharing personal information and committing themselves to the counselor's care. The counselor violates this trust and undermines counseling effectiveness if the helping relationship is used primarily to satisfy the helper's own needs.

The Counselor's Effectiveness

In his popular book *The Art of Loving,* Erich Fromm wrote, "[the] process of learning an art can be divided conveniently into two parts: one, the mastery of the theory; the other, the mastery of the practice." Even when we have all the theoretical knowledge, Fromm suggested, we still are not competent to practice an art. "I shall become a master of this art only after a great deal of practice, until eventually the results of my theoretical knowledge and the results of my practice are blended into one." If we apply this to counseling, there must be what Fromm called the "ultimate concern"—a deep-seated desire to learn the art of counseling and to do it well.[3]

Especially in the beginning, counselors often discover a gap between their formal academic learning and the actual experience of helping somebody with a real problem. Even experienced counselors sometimes find themselves struggling with doubts and feelings of inadequacy about the effectiveness of their counseling.[4] Many would agree with Fromm that if one wants to become a master in any art (including the art of counseling), "one's whole life must be devoted to it, or at least related to it."[5]

It is well known that some people are better counselors than others. This raises an important, basic question. Is it possible for every Christian to be an effective counselor or is counseling a gift, reserved for select members of the body of Christ? According to the Bible all believers should have compassionate concern for their fellow human beings, but from that it does not follow that all believers are or can become gifted counselors. In this respect, counseling is like teaching. Every parent has a responsibility for teaching children, but only some are specially gifted as teachers.[6]

Rom. 12:8 lists exhortation (*paraklesis*) as a spiritual gift that is given to some believers. The word means "coming alongside to help," and implies such activities as admonishing, supporting, and encouraging others. Those who have and are developing this gift will see positive results in their counseling as people are helped and the church is built up. If counseling seems to be your special gift, praise God and learn to do it better. If your counseling seems ineffective, perhaps God has gifted you in some other way. This does not excuse anyone from being a people-helper, but it may encourage some people to put their major efforts elsewhere and leave the art of counseling to those who are more gifted in that area.

To paraphrase 1 Cor. 12:14–18: "The body is not one member but many. . . . If the teacher should say, 'Because I am not a counselor, I am not a part of the body,' he or she is not for this reason any less a part of the body. If the whole body consisted of counselors, where would the formal teaching ministry be? If everyone was a teacher, who would do the deacon's work? But God has placed the members, each of them, in the body just as he desired. . . . The teacher cannot say to the evangelist, 'I have no need of you,' or again the preacher to the counselor, 'I have no need of you.'"

Clearly we need each other and counseling is a part—but only a part—of the functioning church. We help people by counseling, but we also help by evangelism, teaching, social concern, and other aspects of ministry.

The Counselor's Role

Counseling, especially pastoral counseling, sometimes becomes ineffective because the counselor does not have a clear picture of his or her roles and responsibilities. Building on the suggestions of pastor-psychologist Maurice Wagner, we could identify several potential areas of role confusion.[7]

1. *Visiting Instead of Counseling.* Visiting is a friendly activity that involves mutual sharing. Counseling is a problem-centered, goal-directed conversation that focuses primarily on the needs of one person, the counselee. All counseling will involve periodic visiting, but when visiting is prolonged and primary, counseling effectiveness is reduced.

2. *Being Hasty Instead of Deliberate.* Busy, goal-directed people often want to hurry the counseling process to a quick and successful termination. It is true that counselors should not waste time but it also is true that counseling cannot be rushed. "Much of any counselor's success rests upon his own quiet, thoughtful attention to what the counselee is saying."[8] When the pace is deliberate and relaxed, the counselor is less inclined to make hasty judgments and the counselee is more likely to feel the support and serious interest of the counselor.

Recent research has shown the effectiveness of brief, short-term approaches to counseling.[9] This type of counseling can be shorter because it limits its focus to specific problem areas instead of dealing with multiple issues. When a counselor attempts to do too much in one session, the counselee feels overwhelmed and often confused. Since it probably is true that counselees can only assimilate one or two major insights in each session, counseling should be paced and unhurried, even if this means shorter but more frequent sessions.

3. *Being Disrespectful Instead of Sympathetic.* Some counselors quickly categorize people (they may describe a counselee, for example, as a "carnal Christian," a "carefree bachelor," or a "phlegmatic type") and then dismiss individuals with hurried evaluations, quick confrontation, or rigid advice. No person likes to be treated with such disrespect. Few people are helped by counselors who fail to listen sympathetically.

4. *Being Judgmental Instead of Unbiased.* There are times when counselees must be confronted about the sin or unusual behavior in their lives, but this is not the same as condemning or preaching at people in the counseling office. When counselees feel attacked they either defend themselves (often in anger), adopt a resigned "what's the use?" attitude, or go along with the counselor temporarily and grudgingly. None of these reactions contributes to counselee growth, and all are in response to a counseling technique that often reflects the counselor's own anxiety, uncertainty, or need to control.

Jesus is described as one who was "touched with the feelings of infirmities." He never overlooked sin, but he understood sinners and always showed kindness and respect for those, like the woman at the well, who were willing to learn, repent, and change their behavior.

5. *Being Directive Instead of Interpretive.* This is a common error and, as we have seen, it may reflect the counselor's unconscious need to dominate and control. When counselees are told what to do, they confuse the Christian counselor's opinion with the will of God, feel guilty and incompetent if they don't follow the advice, and rarely learn how to mature spiritually and emotionally to the point where they can make decisions without the help of a counselor. The counselor and counselee must work together as a team in which the counselor serves as a teacher-coach whose eventual goal is to withdraw from the playing field.

6. *Being Emotionally Overinvolved Instead of Remaining Objective.* There is a fine line between caring and becoming too involved to be helpful. This is especially true when a counselee is deeply disturbed, confused, or facing a problem that is similar to the counselor's own struggles.

Emotional overinvolvement can cause the counselor to lose objectivity, and this in turn reduces counseling effectiveness. To some extent, compassionate people are not able to avoid emotional involvement, but the Christian counselor can resist this tendency by viewing the counseling as a professional helping relationship that clearly must be limited in terms of length or appointments, number of conversations, or schedule interruptions. These limitations are not designed to set the counselor apart. Instead, they are intended to keep the counselor objective enough to be helpful.

7. *Being Impatient Instead of Realistic.* Many counselors become discouraged and sometimes anxious when they don't see immediate positive progress in their counselees. Problems frequently take a long time to develop, and it is unrealistic to assume that they will disappear quickly and always in response to the counselor's interventions. Instant changes do happen, but these are rare. More often it takes time for counselees to give up their old ways of thinking or behaving and to replace these with something new and better.

8. *Being Artificial Instead of Authentic.* Counselors sometimes burden themselves with the belief that they must be perfect, must always know the appropriate thing to say or do, must never make mistakes, and must always have the knowledge and skills to let them handle any kind of counseling situation.[10] Such counselors are often reluctant to admit their own weaknesses or knowledge gaps. They are so anxious to be professional and successful that they appear artificial, aloof, and sometimes pompous. It is difficult, perhaps impossible, for a counselee to relax and share honestly with a counselor who gives the impression of being perfect, one who "has it all together."

In the history of this world, only one counselor ever reached perfection, never made mistakes, and always said the right things. We who are his followers need to relax, admit that we all make mistakes, quit hiding behind the professional role, and trust him to give us the words and the wisdom to counsel effectively.

9. *Being Defensive Instead of Empathic.* At times most counselors feel threatened in counseling. The ability to listen empathetically is hindered when we are being criticized, aware that we aren't helping, feeling guilty, or afraid of being harmed by a counselee.

When such threats arise it is helpful to ask yourself why. If you don't know the answer, consider discussing this with a friend or fellow counselor. The more we know and accept about ourselves, the less we are likely to be threatened by counselees.

The counselor must maintain a vigilant attitude if he or she is to avoid hazards such as these. As Christian helpers we honor God by doing the best job possible, by apologizing when we make mistakes, and by using our mistakes as learning situations and stepping stones to improvement.

When we slip into unhealthy counseling roles, we must restructure the relationship, at times even telling counselees how we intend to change (by setting firm counseling hours, for example, refusing to drop everything else when a counselee calls, or becoming less directive). This restructuring is always difficult because it involves taking back something that has been given. The alternative is further role confusion and ineffective counseling.

Mistakes and role confusions are not irreversible tragedies. Good rapport with counselees can cover a multitude of counseling mistakes, but we should not use this as an excuse for sloppy and incompetent counseling. "The most important concept to keep in mind is that Christ is really the Counselor; we are His agents doing His work, representing Him. His Holy Spirit is our Comforter and Guide and will lead us to deliver those He has brought to us for help."[11]

THE COUNSELOR'S VULNERABILITY

Counseling would be easier if we could assume that every counselee wanted help, was honest, and would cooperate fully in the counseling. Regretfully this does not always happen. Some counselees have a conscious or unconscious desire to manipulate, frustrate, or not cooperate. This is a difficult discovery for the counselor who wants to succeed and whose success chiefly comes when people change. It is always difficult to work with resistant and noncooperative people. By agreeing to help we are opening ourselves to the possibility of power struggles, exploitation, and failure.

There are three common ways by which people frustrate the counselor and increase his or her vulnerability.

1. *Manipulation.* Some people are masters at getting what they want by controlling others. The story is told of an insecure young counselor who wanted to be helpful. Not wishing to be labeled like the "previous counselor who didn't care," the new counselor was determined to please. The counseling sessions lengthened and became more frequent. Before long the counselor was making phone calls, running errands, giving small loans, and even shopping for the counselee, who constantly expressed gratitude and mournfully kept asking for more.

Manipulated counselors are rarely helpful counselors. People who attempt to manipulate the counselor often do this subtly and well; for them, manipulation may have become a way of life. The counselor must challenge these tactics, refuse to be moved by them, and teach more satisfying ways of relating to others.

It can be wise to ask continually: "Am I being manipulated?" "Am I going beyond my responsibilities as a counselor?" "What does this counselee really want?" Sometimes people ask for help with a problem, but they really want your attention and time, your sanctioning of sinful or otherwise harmful behavior, or your support as an ally in some family conflict. Sometimes people come because they hope concerned mates, family members, or employers will stop complaining about the counselee's behavior if it appears that counseling is taking place. When you suspect such dishonesty or manipulation it is wise to raise this with the counselee, expect that the counselee may disagree, and then structure the counseling in a way that will prevent manipulation or exploitation of the counselor in the future. It probably is true that "people who are genuine in their desire for help are seldom demanding," dishonest, or manipulative.[12]

2. *Countertransference.* According to Freud, who first suggested the term, countertransference occurs when the counselor's own needs interfere with the therapeutic relationship. When the counseling session becomes a place for solving your own problems, counselees are not likely to be helped, and you could be tempted to make statements or act in ways that would be regretted later.

Suppose, for example, that you have strong sexual or romantic feelings toward your counselee, that you are tempted to hover over and protect the counselee, that you fantasize about the counselee between sessions, that you find ways to avoid clients whom you dislike but spend extra time and longer sessions with others, that you have a constant need for a counselee's love and approval, or that you feel so close to a counselee that you cannot separate your own feelings from those of your client. These can all be indications that your own needs and problems are intruding on your work as a counselor.[13] Perhaps you have become so emotionally entangled with the counselees that your objectivity, and hence your counseling effectiveness, has been lost.

At times, all counselors see such tendencies in themselves. To recognize the dangers is a first step for avoiding entanglement and vulnerability. It can also be helpful to discuss this with a perceptive friend or other counselor. This person can help you keep things in perspective and help you see issues in your own life that may be interfering with your people-helping activities.[14]

3. *Resistance.* People often come for help because they want immediate relief from pain but when they discover that permanent relief might require time, effort, and greater pain, they resist counseling. Sometimes problems provide benefits that the counselee is reluctant to give up (personal attention from others, for example, disability compensation, decreased responsibility, or more subtle gratifications such as self-punishment for wrongdoing or the opportunity to make life difficult for others).[15] Since successful counseling would take away these benefits, the counselee does not cooperate. Then there are people who get a sense of power and accomplishment by frustrating the efforts of others, including professional counselors. These people often convince themselves, "I'm beyond help—but then that counselor who couldn't succeed with me isn't much good either." So the counselor continues to counsel, the counselee pretends to cooperate, and nothing changes.

When counseling begins, the counselee's psychological defenses may be threatened. This could lead to anxiety, anger, and noncooperation that sometimes may not even be conscious. If the resistance persists, more in-depth counseling may be needed. When counselees are relatively well-adjusted, however, resistance can be discussed gently and openly. Let the counselee know that he or she (not the counselor) is responsible ultimately for improvement or nonimprovement. The counselor provides a structured relationship, avoids getting on the defensive, and must recognize that one's effectiveness as a counselor (and as a person) is not always correlated with the improvement rate of counselees.

As counselors, we can remain alert to potential problems when we frequently ask ourselves (and each other) questions such as the following:[16]

- Why do I say this is the worst (or best) person I have ever counseled?
- Is there a reason why I or the counselee always arrive late?
- Is there a reason why I or the counselee wants more (or less) time than we had agreed previously?
- Do I overreact to statements this counselee makes?
- Do I feel bored when I am with this person? Is this because of the counselee, me, or both of us?
- Why do I always disagree (or agree) with this counselee?
- Do I find myself wanting to end this relationship or to hold on to it even though it should end?
- Am I beginning to feel too much sympathy for the counselee?

- Do I think about the counselee frequently between sessions, daydream about him or her, or show an unusual interest in the person or the problem? If so, why?

The Counselor's Sexuality

Whenever two people work closely together on a common goal, feelings of camaraderie and warmth often develop between them. When these people have similar backgrounds and especially when they are of the opposite sex, the feelings of warmth frequently have a sexual component.[17] This sexual attraction between counselor and counselee has been called "the problem clergyman don't talk about."[18] Whether we talk about it or not, this is a problem that almost all counselors encounter, at least periodically.

Counseling often involves the discussion of intimate details that would never be discussed elsewhere—especially between a man and a woman who are not married to each other. This can be sexually arousing to both the counselor and counselee. The potential for immorality is even greater if:

- The counselee is attractive and/or tends to be seductive.
- The counselor is not having emotional and sexual needs met elsewhere.
- The counselee indicates that he or she really needs the counselor.
- The counseling involves detailed discussions of sexually arousing material.

Many years ago, Freud wrote that subtle influences such as these "bring with them the danger of making a man forget his technique and medical task for the sake of a fine experience." Perhaps almost every reader of this book knows of counselors, including pastoral counselors, who have compromised their standards "for the sake of a fine experience." Their ministries, reputations, counseling effectiveness, and sometimes their marriages have been destroyed as a result—to say nothing of the adverse effects this can have on the counselee.[19] Sexual feelings toward counselees are common, and the wise counselor makes a special effort to maintain self-control.

1. *Spiritual Protection.* Meditation on the Word of God, prayer (including the intercession of others), and reliance on the Holy Spirit to protect us are all crucially important. In addition, counselors should watch what they do with their minds. Fantasy often precedes action and the alert counselor makes a practice of not dwelling on lustful thoughts. Focus instead on that which is true, honorable, right, pure, lovely, and good.[20]

There is also value in finding another believer to whom you can regularly be accountable for your actions. This can have a powerful impact on your own behavior. Finally, be careful not to fall into the dangerous trap of thinking, "It happens to others but would never happen to me." This is the kind of pride that can make any of us especially vulnerable to temptation. It is a notion that ignores the biblical warning: let the one who thinks he (or she) stands, take heed lest he fall.[21]

And what if you do fall? We serve a God who forgives[22] even though the scars—in the form of guilt feelings, a ruined reputation, or a marriage breakdown—may remain a lifetime. If we confess any sin we are forgiven, but then we have the obligation to change our subsequent thinking and behavior, making them more consistent with scriptural teaching.

2. *Awareness of Danger Signals.* Christian psychiatrist Louis McBurney suggests that "anywhere along this flower-strewn path to destruction we can back off and escape if we recognize the danger and understand the disastrous consequences" of yielding to sexual temptations in counseling.[23] The warning signs can be external (coming from others) or internal (lurking within).

External danger signs include:

- Growing dependence—the counselee's increasing requests for time and attention.
- Affirmation and praise—the counselee's continuing and increasingly frequent expressions of appreciation for the counselor.
- Complaints about loneliness—sometimes accompanied by statements about the counselor's compassion and desires to help ease the pain.
- The giving of gifts—these often indicate increasing emotional involvement and sometimes create a subtle sense of obligation.
- Physical contact—often starting with brief touches but moving to more and more physical involvement.
- Other seductive behavior. Notice, for example, "how a woman dresses, whether she wears perfume, makes subtle suggestions or jokes about (your) irresistibility as a man, sends messages about her availability when her husband is away, or increasingly talks about sexuality in the counseling sessions." These, writes McBurney,[24] are red flags that the counselor needs to spot and resist.

Similar signs may arise within the counselor. These internal danger signs include:

- Thinking about the counselee between sessions and admiring his or her personality traits.
- Comparing the counselee with your spouse, forgetting that the counselee is new, different, nondemanding, and possibly very impressed with you.
- Finding excuses to be with the counselee, perhaps in social gatherings or prolonged counseling sessions.
- Beginning to have sexual fantasies about the counselee.
- Wanting to share your own problems with this person who seems so sensitive and caring.

All of this is more dangerous if the counselor's own marriage has grown cold or unstable.

3. *Limit Setting.* By setting and maintaining clear limits, we can avoid some of the sexual dangers in counseling. Clearly decide on the frequency and length of counseling sessions, then stick with these limits; refuse to engage in long telephone conversations; be careful of physical contact;[25] meet in a place and seat yourself in a way that discourages wandering eyes or an opportunity for personal intimacies; and discourage lengthy detailed discussions of sexual topics. Avoid

every appearance of evil[26] and never forget that each of us must take care to avoid falling into temptation.[27]

4. *Examining Attitudes.* There is nothing to be gained by denying your sexual feelings. These are common, sometimes embarrassing, often arousing, but clearly controllable. Remember the following:

(a) Social Consequences. Yielding to sexual temptation can ruin one's reputation, marriage, and counseling effectiveness.

(b) Professional Implications. Sexual intimacies with counselees never help those with problems and never advance the counselor's professional image. Remember that you are a professional counselor. Seek also to be a maturing man or woman of God.

(c) Theological Truth. Sexual involvement outside of marriage is sin and must be avoided. The person, writes psychiatrist Viktor Frankl, "is *not* fully conditioned and determined; he determines himself whether to give in to conditions or stand up to them. . . . Every human being has the freedom to change at any instant."[28] We may complain that "the devil made me do it," but the devil only tempts. He never makes us do anything. We choose to sin by deliberating and acting contrary to the promptings of the Holy Spirit, who resides within the believer and is greater than Satan (1 John 4:4). Present circumstances or past influences may make you more vulnerable to temptation, but this does not remove responsibility. Each of us is responsible for our own behavior.

5. *Support Group Protection.* Effective coping involves honestly admitting the sexual attraction. There can also be value in discussing this with one or two trusted confidants.

First on the list is one's spouse. A good marriage does not prevent one's being sexually attracted to a counselee, but marriage has a significant influence on the counselor's ability to cope.[29] Sometimes because of fear, embarrassment, or a desire not to hurt, the counselor never discusses this issue with his or her mate. As a result we miss a good opportunity for in-depth marital communication, support, and reassurance. If a counselee becomes a serious threat to the counselor's marriage, it is probable that there were underlying problems in the marriage before the counselee came along.[30]

There also is value in discussing one's feelings with another trusted counselor or close friend. In this way the problem can be kept in perspective, the Christian friend can pray for protection, and the counselor has someone to whom he or she can be accountable.

Should the sexual attraction be discussed with the counselee? On occasion this may be appropriate since it could contribute to the counselee's self-understanding and growth. But the risks involved in such discussions are very high. Some counselees may interpret such discussions as an invitation to greater intimacy. Others, especially immature or flattered counselees, may talk to others about your discussion, and this could have professionally disastrous consequences. Before mentioning one's sexual feelings to a counselee, it would be wise to discuss this with another friend or professional consultant.

Whether or not you decide to share your feelings, try to apply the suggestions given in the previous paragraphs. Avoid all flirting and seriously consider referring your counselee to another counselor if you notice continuing anxiety in yourself during the counseling sessions, poor concentration interrupted by sexual fantasies, fear of displeasing the counselee, preoccupation with thoughts and fantasies about the counselee between sessions, and obvious anticipation of the next session coupled with fears that the session may be canceled or the counseling will be terminated.[31]

The Counselor's Ethics

Most professional counseling organizations (such as the American Psychological Association, the American Association of Marriage and Family Therapy, or the American Association of Pastoral Counselors) have developed ethical codes to protect the public from unethical practices and to guide counselors in ethical decisions. In general, Christian professionals seek to comply with these ethical codes, but since we view the Bible as God's Word, we accept the Scripture as the ultimate standard against which all ethical decisions are tested.

The Christian counselor respects each individual as a person of worth, created by God in the divine image, marred by mankind's fall into sin, but loved by God and the object of divine redemption. Each person has feelings, thoughts, a will, and freedom to behave as he or she chooses.

As a people-helper, the counselor sincerely seeks what is best for the counselee's welfare and does not attempt to manipulate or meddle in the counselee's life. As a servant of God, the counselor has a responsibility to live, act, and counsel in accordance with scriptural principles. As an employee, the counselor attempts to fulfill his or her responsibilities and perform duties faithfully and competently. As a citizen and member of society, the counselor tries to obey governmental authorities and contribute to the good of the culture.

When everyone has similar assumptions and values, the counselor's work can proceed smoothly. Ethical problems arise when values conflict or when difficult decisions have to be made. Many (but not all) of these decisions involve issues of confidentiality. Consider the following as examples:

- A counselee, in confidence, reveals that he has broken the law or that he intends to harm another person. Do you tell the police or the intended victim?
- The unmarried daughter of your church chairman reveals that she is pregnant and planning to have an abortion. What do you do with this information?
- A young man comes requesting help in gaining self-confidence around women so he can more comfortably encourage his girlfriends to have sexual intercourse with him. What is your responsibility as a counselor who believes premarital sex is wrong? Assume that you work in a church counseling center. Would your answer be different if you were employed in a secular setting?
- A seminary graduate currently seeking pastoral placement reveals in counseling that he is a practicing homosexual. Do you reveal this or say nothing when you are asked to complete a recommendation form?

These questions have no easy answers. The counselor is committed to keeping information confidential, but what do you do when the welfare of the counselee or some other person is at stake? At such times the counselee should be encouraged to share information directly with the people involved (police, employers, parents, or others), and as a general rule, information should not be shared by the counselor without the counselee's knowledge.[32]

In addition, the ethical counselor refrains from giving medical and legal advice or otherwise offering services for which he or she is neither trained nor qualified. In states and countries where counselors are licensed or certified, the counselor advertises his or her services accurately and in accordance with the law.[33] The person who counsels frequently may also want to consult a lawyer concerning the prospects of being sued for counseling malpractice and the wisdom of malpractice insurance.

In every ethical decision the Christian counselor seeks to act in ways that will honor God, be in conformity with biblical teaching, and respect the welfare of the counselee and others. When difficult decisions must be made, counselors have an obligation to discuss the situation in confidence with one or two other Christian counselors and/or with a lawyer, physician, or pastor who can help in making ethical decisions. Often these consultations can be done without your having to reveal the counselee's identity. When difficult ethical decisions must be made, the Christian counselor gets as much factual data as possible (including biblical data), sincerely trusts that God will lead, and then makes as wise a decision as possible based on the best evidence available.[34]

The Counselor's Burnout

Counseling students sometimes assume that the act of helping people will provide a lifetime of satisfaction and vocational fulfillment. At some time after graduation, however, most of us discover that counseling is hard work, that many counselee's do not get better, and that constant involvement with the problems and miseries of others is psychologically, physically, and sometimes spiritually draining. All of this contributes to counselor "burnout"—a condition described by one writer as "a progressive loss of idealism, energy, and purpose" that comes to people in the helping professions because of their work.[35] Often burnout is accompanied by feelings of futility, powerlessness, fatigue, cynicism, apathy, irritability and frustration. Counselors who believe in the importance of warmth, genuineness, and empathy, instead become cold, aloof, unsympathetic, detached, worn-out helpers. In a subtle and sometimes unconscious effort at self-protection, the professional dons such thick armor that no one can get through.[36]

Burnout is common in all helping professionals, including the ministry. It occurs most often in perfectionist people who are idealistic, deeply committed to their work, reluctant to say no, and inclined to be workaholics.

To prevent burnout, we first need the spiritual strength that comes through regular periods of prayer and meditation on the Scripture. Second, we need support from a few others who accept us for who we are rather than for what we do. Each of us needs at least one loving and understanding person with whom we can cry; one person who knows our weaknesses but can be trusted not to use this knowledge against us. Third, each of us must constantly evaluate the underlying drive to achieve. We need to remind ourselves that personal worth comes from God and not from the need to achieve and produce.[37]

Fourth, we need to take time off—regular periods away from demanding people and work schedules. Jesus did this and so must his followers if we are to remain efficient and capable helpers. Fifth, it helps to improve our ministry skills, learning to manage conflict, counsel better, or learn how to say no. Finally, we can share the load by encouraging other believers to be sensitive lay counselors and burden-bearers. The church leader or other Christian counselor who seeks to do all of the helping alone is heading for ineffectiveness if not eventual burnout. Louis McBurney adds that there is value, too, in keeping a sense of humor about life and trying to refrain from taking yourself too seriously.[38]

And what about the helper who is burned out already? As soon as possible take your phone off the hook and get away for at least a brief period of reevaluation. Consider how you can apply the suggestions listed in the preceding paragraph. Then think about your leisure activities. How can these lighten your load and add self-fulfillment and relaxation? The counselor needs to find balance in his or her activities, a time for rest or play, and an opportunity to laugh. Otherwise life becomes boring, routine, and lackluster. This isn't pleasant for the counselor and it certainly does nothing to improve your ability to help counselees cope with the stresses of life.

The Counselor's Counselors

Many professional training programs require counseling students to have supervised practice, sensitivity group training, personal therapy, or similar educational experiences. Each of these is designed to increase self-awareness, facilitate self-acceptance, and remove those emotional and psychological blocks that hinder counseling effectiveness. While these exercises are often helpful and highly recommended, they frequently overlook the greatest available source of strength and wisdom for Christian counselors—the Holy Spirit who guides and dwells in the life of each believer.[39] Christians can become so involved in the theories and technicalities of counseling that they forget the source from which all lasting help comes—the Lord himself. "The Spirit-filled counselor's ultimate assistance does not come from the latest thought of leaders in the counseling or psychological field, but is anchored in 'Thus saith the Lord.'"[40]

The Bible describes Jesus Christ as the Wonderful Counselor.[41] He is the counselor's counselor—ever available to encourage, direct and give wisdom to human people-helpers. It bears repeating that the truly effective Christian counselor is basically a skilled and available instrument through whom the Holy Spirit works to change lives. When the counselor's work brings anxieties and confusion, these can be cast on God himself, who has promised to sustain and help.[42] Daily prayer and Bible reading keep us in active communication with the one who is our own adviser and helper.

Throughout the Bible we see that God also works through other human beings. In the early church, believers devoted themselves to "fellowship," sharing together and sharing with one another in close spiritual relationships.[43] God often helps his children, counselors included, through other people with whom we can share, maintain perspective, relax, pray, and sometimes cry. Without the support, encouragement, and viewpoint of a trusted Christian friend,[44] the counselor's work is likely to be more difficult and less effective. Often two or more counselors can meet regularly to read Scripture, sustain, and pray for each other. If you lack such a relationship, ask God to help you find a colleague or two with whom you can share.

Several years ago a group of counselors was asked: How would you spend the rest of your life if you had the financial means to do anything you wanted? Of more than a hundred counselors surveyed, only three persons said they would spend their lives doing counseling work and of these, one person preferred to do counseling as a spare-time leisure activity.[45] Counseling can be fulfilling work, but it isn't easy. If you can recognize this and face it honestly, your helping ministry will be more satisfying and you likely will be more effective as a Christian counselor.

SUGGESTIONS FOR FURTHER READING

Corey, Gerald, Marianne Schneider Corey, and Patrick Callanan. *Issues and Ethics in the Helping Professions.* 3d ed. Monterey, Calif.: Brooks/Cole, 1988.

Guy, James D. *The Personal Life of the Psychotherapist.* New York: Wiley, 1987.

Kennedy, Eugene. *On Becoming a Counselor: A Basic Guide for Non-Professional Counselors.* New York: Seabury, 1977.

McBurney, Louis. *Counseling Christian Workers.* Waco, Tex.: Word, 1986.

3

The Core of Counseling

THE BIBLE CONTAINS many examples of human need. Its pages tell us about anxiety, loneliness, discouragement, doubt, grief, sadness, violence, abnormal sex, bitterness, poverty, greed, sickness, interpersonal tension, and a variety of other personal problems—sometimes seen in the lives of the greatest saints.

Job, for example, was a godly man, famous, wealthy, and highly respected by his contemporaries. Then things suddenly fell apart. He lost his wealth and his health. His children all died in a tornado, plunging him into intense grief and despair. Instead of giving support, his wife preferred to nag and complain. His three friends offered little help and God must have seemed far away.

Then, along came Elihu. He was a young man who listened to Job and heard his struggles. Elihu was critical of those well-meaning but insensitive counselors who had lectured Job and given advice in their attempts to be helpful. In contrast, Elihu showed acceptance and concern, a humble willingness to be on the same level as Job (without any holier-than-thou attitude), a courage to confront, and an unswerving desire to point the counselee to God who alone is sovereign and able to help in times of need. Elihu was the one counselor who succeeded where others had failed.[1]

Several years ago a former president of the American Psychological Association estimated that even today, three out of four counselors are ineffective. Recent research has shown that most pastors feel underprepared for their counseling responsibilities and most are not very competent as counselors.[2] Some evidence suggests that a majority of counselors are ineffective and perhaps even harmful.[3]

Others do succeed, however, and they counsel very effectively. These people are characterized by a personality that radiates sincerity, understanding, compassion, and the ability to confront in a genuine and constructive manner. These counselors are skilled in the use of techniques that help counselees move toward specific goals.[4]

In this chapter we will begin with a consideration of these counseling goals, discuss the counseling relationship, summarize some basic counseling techniques, give an overview of the counseling process, and conclude with a look at theoretical approaches to counseling.

THE GOALS OF COUNSELING

Why do people come for counseling? What do they want to accomplish? What is your reason for trying to help with their counseling problems? These are difficult questions. Each can have a variety of answers, depending on both the counselee and the counselor.

Christian counselors might expect their clients to bring problems concerning prayer, doubt, doctrine, spiritual growth, or guilt over sinful behavior. One survey found, however, that only 10 percent of pastoral counseling deals with religious issues such as these.[5] More often, people came with marriage tensions, crises, depression, interpersonal conflicts, confusion, and other problems in living.

Jesus was concerned about these kinds of problems. He stated that he had come to give life in abundance and in all its fullness.[6] In what is surely the most famous verse in Scripture, Jesus had told God's purpose in sending his Son—"that whoever believes in him shall not perish but have eternal life."[7] Jesus, therefore, had two goals for individuals: abundant life on earth and eternal life in heaven.

The counselor who follows Jesus Christ has the same ultimate goals of showing people how to have abundant lives and of pointing individuals to the eternal life that is promised to believers. If we take the Great Commission seriously we will have a strong desire to see all of our counselees become disciples of Jesus Christ. If we take the words of Jesus seriously we are likely to reach the conclusion that a fully abundant life only comes to those who seek to live in accordance with his teachings.

It is well known, however, that there are many sincere Christians who will have eternal life in heaven but who are not experiencing a very abundant life on earth. These people need counseling that involves something other than evangelism or traditional Christian education. Such counseling, for example, might help counselees recognize hidden harmful attitudes, teach interpersonal skills and new behaviors, guide those who are making decisions or changing their lifestyles, or show how to mobilize one's inner resources to cope with a crisis. At times such counseling, guided by the Holy Spirit, can free a counselee from persisting hang-ups, past memories, or present attitudes that prevent him or her from growing toward maturity. For the nonbeliever, such counseling can serve as a kind of "pre-evangelism"[8] which clears away some of the obstacles to conversion. Evangelism and discipleship, therefore, are the Christian counselor's ultimate goals, even though they are not the only goals.[9]

What are some other goals? Many counselees have only vague notions about what they want from counseling—except to understand themselves or feel better. If their counselors are equally vague, the therapy is likely to be aimless and ineffective. Specific counseling goals will depend largely on the counselee's problems, but any list is likely to include at least the following.

1. *Self-Understanding.* To understand oneself often is a first step in healing. Many problems are self-imposed, but the one being helped may fail to recognize that he or she has biased perspectives, harmful attitudes, or self-destructive behavior. Consider, for example, the person who complains, "Nobody likes me," but fails to see that the complaining annoys others and is a major reason for the rejection. One counseling goal is for an objective, perceptually alert helper to assist those being helped to get a true picture of what is going on within themselves and within the world that surrounds them.

2. *Communication.* It is well known that many marriage problems involve a breakdown in husband-wife communication. The same is true apart from marriage. Many people are unable or unwilling to communicate. The counselee must

be encouraged to communicate feelings, thoughts, and attitudes both accurately and effectively. Such communication involves clearly expressing oneself and accurately receiving messages from others.

3. *Learning and Behavior Change.* Most, if not all, of our behavior is learned. Counseling, therefore, involves helping counselees unlearn ineffective behavior and learn more effective ways of doing things. Such learning comes from instruction, imitation of a counselor or other model, and the experience of trial and error. At times it also will be necessary to analyze what went wrong when there was failure. Then the counselee must be encouraged to try again.

Assume, for example, that you are counseling a young man who feels insecure about dating. Dating is learned behavior. If you reread the previous paragraph you will be able to think of ways to help your date-fearing counselee.

4. *Self-Actualization.* Some writers have stressed the importance of helping individuals learn to achieve and maintain one's optimal potential. This is termed "self-actualization" and is proposed by some counselors as a goal for all human beings whether or not they are in counseling. For the Christian, a term like "Christ-actualization" might be substituted to indicate that the goal in life is to be complete in Christ, developing one's greatest potential through the power of the Holy Spirit who brings us to spiritual maturity.[10]

5. *Support.* Often people are able to meet the above goals and to function effectively, except for temporary periods of unusual stress or crisis. These individuals can benefit from a period of support, encouragement, and "burden bearing" until they are able to remobilize their personal and spiritual resources to meet effectively the problems of living.

6. *Spiritual Wholeness.* In his textbook on counseling, Howard Clinebell writes that the heart of pastoral care and counseling is helping people deal with their spiritual needs and find spiritual wholeness.[11] Although talk about religion can sometimes be a counselee's way of hiding personal-psychological problems, the reverse is also true. Counselees frequently fail to see or admit that there is a spiritual dimension to all human problems.[12] Many would agree with Carl Jung's oft-quoted conclusion that among his patients who are over thirty-five, "there has not been one whose problem in the last resort was not that of finding a religious outlook on life."[13] The Christian counselor, therefore, becomes a spiritual leader who guides spiritual growth, helps counselees deal with spiritual struggles, and enables them to find meaningful beliefs and values. Instead of dialogue between counselor and counselee, the Christian strives for a "trialogue" that acknowledges the presence of God at the heart of effective people helping.[14]

Counseling is rarely effective if counselors impose their own goals on clients. It is better if the counselor and counselee work together in setting goals.[15] Such goals should be specific (rather than vague), realistic, and (if there are several) organized into some logical sequence that identifies the goals to be worked on first and, perhaps, for how long.

The Relationship in Counseling

Many people are reluctant to come for counseling. It isn't easy for any of us to admit that we need help. Some individuals are in awe of counselors or afraid of what they might ask. Other people may have problems that are too embarrassing or too personal to discuss without feeling uncomfortable. Christians sometimes feel that they shouldn't have overwhelming problems so the need for counseling is seen as an indication of personal and spiritual failure.

The good counselor is aware of these insecurities and tries to help counselees relax. This can be done by counseling in a "therapeutic climate"[16] where the counselee feels comfortable and where there are few distractions and interruptions. This may be in an office or counseling center, but effective helping can take place almost anywhere. For some people, a quiet corner of some restaurant can sometimes be less threatening than the more formal setting of a counseling office.

More important than location, however, is the relationship between the helper and counselee. Many counselors would agree with the writer who called relationship "the heart of helping people."[17]

How is this therapeutic relationship built? Many years ago, in a four-year study conducted with hospital patients and a variety of counselors, it was found that relationships grew and patients improved when the therapists showed high levels of warmth, genuineness, and accurate empathic understanding.[18] When these counselor qualities were lacking, the hospital patients grew worse. Of course it is important to be sensitive and to use whatever techniques you can to set counselees at ease, but the heart of the helping relationship appears to center on the characteristics of the counselor.

1. *Warmth.* This word implies caring, respecting, or possessing a sincere, nonsmothering concern for the counselee regardless of his or her actions or attitudes. Jesus showed this when he met the woman at the well. Her morals may have been low, and he certainly never condoned sinful behavior. Jesus nevertheless respected the woman and treated her as a person of worth. His warm, caring attitude must have been apparent wherever he went.

2. *Genuineness.* The genuine counselor is "for real"—an open, sincere person who avoids phoniness or the playing of some superior role. Genuineness implies spontaneity without impulsiveness and honesty without insensitive confrontation. It means that the helper is deeply himself or herself—not thinking or feeling one thing and saying something different.

3. *Empathy.* What does the counselee think? How does he or she really feel inside? What are the counselee's values, beliefs, inner conflicts, and hurts? The good counselor is continually sensitive to these issues, able to understand them, and effective in using words and gestures to communicate this understanding to the counselee. The ability to "feel with" the counselee is what we mean by accurate empathic understanding. It is possible to help people, even when we don't completely understand, but the counselor who can empathize (especially near the beginning of counseling) is most likely to be effective as a people-helper.

Although warmth, genuineness, and empathy are among the most frequently mentioned attributes of a good counselor, there are other important characteristics. Effective helpers tend to be able to handle their own problems, for example. They are relatively free of immobilizing conflicts, insecurities, or personal hang-ups. The effective counselor is also compassionate, interested in people, alert to his or her own feelings and motives, more self-revealing than self-concealing, trustworthy, liked by people, and knowledgeable about the field of counseling. The Christian might summarize all of this by stating that the counselor's life must show evidence of the Holy Spirit's fruit[19]: joy, peace, patience, kindness, goodness, faithfulness, gentleness, self-control, and what probably is the most important—love.[20]

This was emphasized by a former president of the American Psychological Association who called love "incomparably the greatest psychotherapeutic agent . . . something that professional psychiatry cannot of itself create, focus, nor release."[21] Might it be, the writer suggested, that Christianity offers an approach to life that is based wholly upon love and thus is able to help where secular counseling fails? This raises a thought-provoking challenge to the Christian counselor: a basic way to help is to love—asking God to love needy people through us and praying that he will make us more loving.

For some people the experience of love is all they need to bring change, but for many others something more is needed. Many years ago a famous child psychiatrist wrote a book titled *Love Is Not Enough.* Often there is a need for discipline, structure, and other therapeutic influences.[22] The effective Christian helper seeks to develop counseling relationships based on love, but he or she also strives to become proficient in the knowledge and use of basic counseling techniques.

The Techniques of Counseling

In many respects, the counselor and counselee become friends who work together at problem solving.[23] Unlike more casual discussions between friends, however, the helping relationship is characterized by a clear purpose—that of helping the counselee. The helper's needs are mostly met elsewhere, and he or she does not depend on the counselee for love, affirmation, or help. Counselors lay aside their own conflicts, seek to become aware of counselee needs, and communicate both understanding and a willingness to help.

There is no simple formula to summarize how this help is given. The help-giving process can be complicated and it isn't easily summarized in a few paragraphs. Even so, some basic techniques are used in most counseling situations.

1. *Attending.* The counselor must try to give undivided attention to the counselee. This is done through (a) eye contact, looking without staring as a way to convey concern and understanding; (b) posture, which should be relaxed rather than tense and often involves leaning toward the counselee; and (c) gestures that are natural but not excessive or distracting. The counselor should be courteous, kind, and strongly motivated to understand.

As you counsel, recognize that your own fatigue, impatience, preoccupation with other matters, daydreaming, or restlessness can prevent you from giving careful attention to the counselee. People helping is demanding work that involves sensitivity, genuine expressions of care, and alertness to what the counselee may be trying to communicate.

2. *Listening.* This involves more than giving passive or half-hearted notice to the words that come from another person. Effective listening is an active process. It involves:

- Being able to set aside your own conflicts, biases, and preoccupations so you can concentrate on what the counselee is communicating.

- Avoiding subtle verbal or nonverbal expressions of disapproval or judgment about what is being said, even when the content is offensive.
- Using both your eyes and your ears to detect messages that come from the tone of voice, posture, gestures, facial expressions, and other nonverbal clues.
- Hearing not only what the counselee says, but noticing what gets left out.
- Waiting patiently through periods of silence or tears as the counselee summons enough courage to share something painful or pauses to collect his or her thoughts and regain composure.
- Looking at the counselee as he or she speaks, but without either staring or letting your eyes wander around the room.
- Realizing that you can accept the counselee even though you may not condone his or her actions, values, or beliefs. Jesus accepted the woman caught in the act of adultery even though he didn't approve of her behavior.[24] It can be helpful if you try to imagine yourself in the counselee's position and attempt to see things from his or her point of view.

It is easy to ignore all of this, to let your mind wander (especially if the counselee's story is boring or repetitious), or to slip into excessive talking and advice giving. When this happens, the counselee does not feel understood, and often there is reluctance to express hurts honestly or to share details. Counselors who talk a lot may give good advice but it is seldom heard and even less likely to be followed. In such situations counselees often feel that they have not been understood. In contrast, active listening is a way to tell counselees "I'm really interested and I sincerely care." When we don't listen but try instead to counsel by talking, this often expresses the counselor's own insecurity or inability to deal with threatening, vague, or emotional topics.

3. *Responding.* It should not be assumed that the counselor listens and does nothing else. Jesus was a good listener (consider his time with the perplexed pair on the road to Emmaus) but his helping also was characterized by action and specific verbal responses.

Leading is a skill by which the counselor gently directs the conversation. "What happened next?" "Tell me what you mean by . . . ?" are brief questions that can steer the discussion in directions that will give useful information.

Reflecting is a way of letting counselees know that we are "with them" and able to understand how they feel or think. "You must feel . . . ," "I bet that was frustrating," "That must have been fun" reflect what is going on in counseling. Be careful not to reflect after every statement; do it periodically. Try not to repeat word for word what the counselee says. That can be annoying to the counselee. Resist the urge to start almost every sentence with a stereotyped phrase such as "You must think . . . " or "I hear you saying . . . " A brief periodic summary of what has been going on can be one way of reflecting and stimulating more counselee exploration. The counselor may summarize feelings ("that must have hurt") and/or general themes of what has been said ("from all of this it sounds like you have had a whole string of failures"). Whenever you make a comment, give the counselee time and opportunity to respond to what you have said.

Questioning, if done skillfully, can bring forth a great deal of useful information.

The best questions are those that require at least a sentence or two to answer (e.g., "Tell me about your marriage." "What sorts of things are making you unhappy?") rather than those that can be answered in one word ("Are you married?" "Are you unhappy?" "What is your age?"). Beginning counselors tend to ask more questions than experienced counselors, and since too much questioning can stifle communication, students are often instructed to ask few questions. Also, questions beginning with *Why* are usually avoided. These tend to sound judgmental or they stimulate long intellectual discussions that keep the counselee from coming to grips with real feelings or hurts.

Confronting is not the same as attacking or viciously condemning another person. When we confront, we present some idea to the counselee that he or she might not see otherwise. Counselees can be confronted with sin in their lives, failures, inconsistencies, excuses, harmful attitudes, or self-defeating behavior. Confrontation is best done in a loving, gentle, nonjudgmental manner.

Sometimes counselees respond to confrontation with confession and a significant experience of forgiveness. Often, however, confrontation brings resistance, guilt, hurt, or anger. It is important to let counselees respond verbally to your confrontation. Give them time to discuss alternative ways of behaving.

Some Christians have suggested that counseling and confrontation are synonymous terms. This has neither biblical nor psychological support. Confrontation is an important and sometimes difficult part of counseling, but it is not the only skill that can be used in helping people.

Informing involves giving facts to people who need information. Try to avoid giving too much information at any one time, be clear, and remember that when people are hurting they respond best to information that is relevant to their immediate needs or concerns. This kind of informing is a common and widely accepted part of counseling; advice giving is much more controversial.

Advice givers often lack enough knowledge of a situation to give competent advice, their advice giving encourages the counselee to be dependent, and if the advice proves to be invalid it is the counselor who later is made to feel responsible for giving bad direction. Whenever you are asked for advice or inclined to give advice, be sure that you are well informed about the situation. Do you have enough information and expertise to advise another competently? Then ask yourself what might be the end results of this advice giving. Is it likely to make the counselee more dependent? Can you handle the feelings that might come if your advice is rejected or proven wrong? If you then do give advice, offer it in the form of a tentative suggestion, give the counselee time to react or talk through your advice, and follow up later to see the extent to which the advice was helpful.

Interpretation involves explaining to the counselee what his or her behavior or other events mean. This is a highly technical skill with great potential for enabling counselees to see themselves and their situations more clearly. But interpretations can also be harmful, especially if they are introduced before the counselee can handle the material emotionally, or if the interpretations are wrong. If you begin to see possible explanations for another person's problems or actions, ask yourself if the counselee is intellectually and emotionally ready to handle such an insight, keep the terms simple as you interpret, present your interpretations in a tentative way (e.g., "Could it be that . . . ?") and allow time for the counselee to respond.

As you discuss the interpretation, the counselee will often develop greater insights and be able to explore future courses of action with the counselor.

Supporting and *encouraging* are important parts of any counseling situation, especially at the beginning. When people are burdened by needs and conflicts they can benefit from the stability and care of an empathic person who shows acceptance and gives reassurance. This is more than holding up the downtrodden. Support includes guiding the counselee to take stock of his or her spiritual and psychological resources, encouraging action, and helping with any problems or failures that may come as a result of this action.

4. *Teaching.* All of these techniques are specialized forms of psychological education. The counselor is an educator, teaching by instruction, by example, and by guiding the counselee as he or she learns by experience to cope with the problems of life. Like other less personal forms of education, counseling is more effective when the discussions are specific rather than vague, and focus on concrete situations ("How can I control my temper when I am criticized by my wife?") rather than on nebulous goals ("I want my life to be happier").

A powerful learning tool is the *immediacy* response. This involves the ability of a counselor and counselee to discuss openly and directly what is happening in the "immediate" here-and-now of the relationship. "I feel very frustrated with you right now," someone might say, for example, or "I'm getting angry because I think you're not listening to me." Such honest, on-the-spot statements let individuals express and deal with feelings before they build up and fester. Immediate responses also help counselees (and counselors) better understand both how their actions affect others and how they respond emotionally to interpersonal relationships. This understanding is an important educational aspect of counseling.

5. *Filtering.* Good counselors are not skeptical people who disbelieve everything a counselee says, but it is wise to remember that counselees don't always tell the whole story and don't always say what they really want or need. Sometimes a counselee deliberately presents a distorted picture, leaving out embarrassing or potentially incriminating details. More often, counselees fail to see their problems in broader perspective. Sometimes they come for help with one problem but fail to see or are reluctant to raise other, deeper problems.

As you counsel, therefore, mentally try to sort through the counselee's words. What is he or she really asking? What does this person really want from us?[25] Are there problems other than the ones that are being presented? Sometimes people talk about one issue but really have little desire to change. Instead, they are looking for sympathy, attention, catharsis, another person's viewpoint, or a way to escape from some unpleasant situation. As you listen, you begin to suspect these underlying motives and you realize that often they aren't even recognized by the counselee.

In time you will want to raise these issues and talk about them in counseling. The counselor does not try to invent new issues or force counselees to consider topics they don't want to discuss. But your work will be more effective if you learn to listen with sensitivity and try not to accept everything at face value.

All of this points again to the counselor's need for wisdom and discernment. Some of this comes with experience, but Christians know that sensitivity more often comes when we pray, asking for the insights, guidance, and accurate perception that comes from the Holy Spirit.

The Process of Counseling

Counseling is not a step-by-step process like baking a cake or changing a tire. Each counselee is unique, with problems, attitudes, values, expectations, and experiences that are unlike any other. The counselor (whose own problems, attitudes, values, expectations, and experiences are also brought into the counseling situation) must approach each individual a little differently. The course of counseling will vary from person to person.

In every counseling relationship, however, there appear to be several steps or phases, some of which may be repeated several times as problems are considered and reconsidered.

1. *Connecting.* This involves initiating, building, and maintaining a relationship between the counselor and counselee. The counselor listens attentively and shows sincere concern and caring as the counselee begins, sometimes tentatively, to share feelings, concerns, or problems.

2. *Exploring.* Counselees need to "tell their stories"—revealing details of problem situations, missed opportunities, and frustrating experiences.[26] This is a time when counselees are encouraged to share their feelings, talk about their thoughts, and describe their actions. The counselor listens attentively, asks periodic probing questions, and responds with respect, empathy, and sensitivity. This exploration of issues lets the counselor and counselee build rapport and get a clearer understanding of the problem situation.

3. *Planning.* In time, the counselee begins to see the problem in a different light and discussion moves toward goals and actions that could be taken to find solutions. How could the counselee change? Are there things that can be done to make matters better? Must some things be accepted because they can't be changed? Are there sins to be confessed, actions to be taken, attitudes to be changed, goals to be reached, skills to be learned? Together, the counselor and counselee develop some plans for taking action.

Some counselors try to skip this and the previous two stages so they can move directly into the process of giving advice and challenging people to take action. This sometimes works but more often it is ineffective, like surgery done by a blindfolded physician who didn't take the time to make a diagnosis.

4. *Progressing.* Planning is not very useful unless it is followed by action. After people decide what needs to be done, they must be encouraged to start moving toward their goals. The counselor gives support, direction, encouragement, and sometimes gentle prodding. Sometimes counselees will take action and experience failure. The counselor then helps the counselee evaluate what went wrong and together they make plans to try again.

5. *Stopping.* Counseling does not last forever. In time, both the counselor and counselee back away from their more intense problem-solving relationship. Often there is a summarizing of what has been learned or accomplished. There may be discussion of ways in which the counselee can cope more effectively in the future. And the door is left open for future counseling contacts if they are ever needed.[27]

On paper all of this sounds straightforward and simple, but the process of counseling can be very complicated and demanding of one's time and energy. The stages of counseling are rarely identified so clearly or as easily as the previous paragraphs might imply. For example, the first step of connecting with counselees and building a relationship is especially important at the beginning when people might be nervous and apprehensive. Once a relationship has begun, however, it must be maintained. For this reason, the counselor must never lose sight of step one. As counseling progresses, there is continual vacillation between these stages as problems become clearer, solutions are found and tried, and counseling moves toward termination.

THE THEORIES OF COUNSELING

Sigmund Freud's famous system of psychoanalysis was one man's theory of counseling. It summarized Freud's views about human nature, the causes of personal problems, and the best methods for helping people change. Like every theorist since, Freud sought to build his theory on facts, objective information, good logic, and his own knowledge about human beings. Unlike other theorists, however, Freud did not seem to understand that every theory is also a reflection of its creator's personality, interests, biases, values, beliefs, goals, past experiences, culture, training, and perhaps even the country in which one lives.

It is impossible to give an accurate estimate of the number of counseling theories that currently exist. Adlerian theory, Jungian analysis, existential therapy, Rogers's person-centered therapy, Gestalt therapy, transactional analysis (TA), Glasser's reality therapy, the rational-emotive therapy (RET) of Albert Ellis, the various behavior therapies, social-learning theory, and family systems therapy are among those that are best known. In addition, a number of Christians have proposed biblically based approaches to counseling. These include Jay Adams's nouthetic counseling, Lawrence Crabb's biblical counseling, Charles Solomon's spirituotherapy, and the growth counseling of Howard Clinebell.

Some counseling theories are highly developed and presented in formal language; others are more speculative and informal. Some theorists emphasize feelings while others stress behavior change or counselee thinking. Some assume that counselees must take primary responsibility for helping themselves; others put more emphasis on the counselor's role. Many Christian approaches are built on the theorist's views of biblical teaching; other theories place greater emphasis on the findings of psychological insights and theory. Some theories are complicated and difficult to summarize; others are brief and much simpler. Although a summary of these various positions is beyond the scope of this book, good overviews and critiques are available for those who want further information.[28]

Why Bother with Theory? Some have argued that theories are of little importance, that they exist primarily to boost the egos of the theory builders, and that they don't have much influence on the actual experience of counseling. To some extent these arguments are true, but theories can also serve a useful purpose.

Theories are like systems of theology. They summarize what we know and believe, what we are seeking to accomplish, and how we go about reaching our goals. As the size of this book would indicate, there is a massive amount of information about the complexities of human behavior, the causes of human problems, and the ways that counselors can help. Theories help us to incorporate all of these facts into some kind of an integrated, understandable, and useful framework. Theoretical approaches guide as we seek to help people cope with their problems.

Which Theory Is Right? The answer is "none." Theories are human inventions, created by fallible human beings, and likely to be revised as our knowledge and understanding increases. Many professionals have their favorite theories (and theorists), but almost half of those who responded to a recent survey identified themselves as "eclectic."[29] This word describes those who prefer to draw concepts and techniques from a variety of approaches instead of being restricted to a single theory.

Eclecticism is not a haphazard, intellectually lazy collecting of ideas. Instead, this is an approach that draws from the various sources in a thoughtful manner and enables you, in time, to arrive at your own counseling style.

There is no one way to do this, just as there is no right way to counsel. Jesus used a variety of approaches, depending on the needs of the counselee. Christian counselors, even those who seek most diligently to be biblical, utilize a variety of approaches and sometimes disagree with the theoretical viewpoints of their Christian colleagues. It is helpful to understand the different theories, but ultimately each of us must trust the Holy Spirit to work through our own personalities and perspectives to enable us to help others most effectively.

The Law and Counseling

Several years ago, the pastor of a large evangelical church in California was sued for malpractice by the family of a young man who had committed suicide following pastoral counseling. The suit was resolved in favor of the pastor, but the case attracted national publicity and pointed to the frequency with which counseling and the law interact.

For many years, psychiatrists and psychologists have participated in the legal process by giving expert testimony in law courts, by helping courts determine if a defendant is psychologically competent to stand trial, by participating in commitment hearings, by giving psychiatric and psychological examinations, and by counseling with prisoners and their families. Since 1843, when a Scotsman named Daniel M'Naghten was accused of murder but found not guilty by reason of insanity, professional counselors have been used to help courts determine whether defendants were aware of the difference between right and wrong when they committed criminal acts. More recently, the interaction between psychiatry and the law was heightened following the controversial verdict that "by reason of insanity," John W. Hinckley, Jr. was not guilty of attempting to assassinate President Reagan.[30]

Of more immediate interest to the Christian counselor have been the passing of licensing laws and the increasing frequency of malpractice suits like the one brought against the California pastor. Laws in your area may determine who is legally competent to counsel, what titles the counselor may use, which counselors are exempt from revealing details about counseling in a court of law, the civil liberties of counselees, the conditions under which individuals can be involuntarily hospitalized for mental problems, the educational requirements for professional counselors, who can legally accept fees in return for counseling services, what constitutes counseling malpractice, and the conditions under which a counselor can be sued for professional negligence.

Laws covering these and other counseling issues vary from place to place and frequently the statutes change. If you counsel infrequently, informally, or within the confines of a church or educational institution, you probably are exempt from many of the laws that apply to professional counselors. If you counsel frequently, however, it would be wise to check with a lawyer to determine how local laws could influence and perhaps limit your counseling.[31]

This discussion of legal issues is a reminder that no counseling takes place in a vacuum. Counselors and counselees live as members of a society and community. Sometimes the community creates problems and restricts counseling effectiveness, but the opposite is also true. The community (including the Christian community) can greatly facilitate your work as a counselor. The role of these community influences will occupy our attention in the next chapter.

SUGGESTIONS FOR FURTHER READING

Benjamin, Alfred D. *The Helping Interview with Case Illustrations.* Boston: Houghton-Mifflin, 1987.

Brammer, L. M. *The Helping Relationship.* 2d ed. Englewood Cliffs, N.J.: Prentice-Hall, 1979.

Crabb, Lawrence J., Jr. *Understanding People: Deep Longings for Relationship.* Grand Rapids, Mich.: Zondervan, 1987.

Collins, Gary R. *How to Be a People-Helper.* Ventura, Calif.: Regal, 1976.

Egan, Gerard. *The Skilled Helper.* 3d ed. Monterey, Calif.: Brooks/Cole, 1986.

Welter, Paul. *Connecting with a Friend: Eighteen Proven Counseling Skills to Help You Help Others.* Wheaton, Ill.: Tyndale, 1985.

———. *How to Help a Friend.* Wheaton, Ill.: Tyndale, 1978.

Worthington, Everett L., Jr. *When Someone Asks for Help: A Practical Guide for Counseling.* Downers Grove, Ill.: InterVarsity, 1982.

4 The Community and Counseling

IN ONE OF HIS FIRST STATEMENTS about human beings, the Lord God declared, "It is not good for man to be alone."[1] So God created woman, and the human race began.

It wasn't long before people were in conflict with each other. The sibling rivalry between Cain and Abel led to murder. Then the earth was filled with violence.[2] After the great flood, the conflicts resumed,[3] and they have continued to this day. Throughout the centuries, a few hermits have sought to live solitary lives, far from the maddening crowd, but most of us can appreciate John Donne's oft-quoted statement that "No man is an island, entire of itself." Human beings may compete with one another and live in conflict, but we also need one another. It isn't good or healthy to exist in isolation.

Despite this conclusion, we who live in the Western world still tend to value independence and rugged individualism. We talk about cooperation and mutual support, but we admire the "self-made" man or woman and often assume that personal problems are best handled alone. At least until recently, counseling was usually a one-to-one relationship: one counselor, one counselee, one hour in duration, one session per week.

This type of counseling between individuals can be helpful, but the benefits are likely to be greater when the counselee is part of one or more supportive caring groups. Often the family gives this encouragement. It may come from friends or from colleagues at work. Ideally, the local body of believers should also be giving much of the fellowship, instruction, feedback, guidance, acceptance, and support that individuals need. Surely something is lacking when Christian counseling ignores the fellowship of believers and attempts to help people completely apart from the community of faith.

COMMUNITY COUNSELING

Many counselors would agree that most behavior, including problem behavior, is influenced by the social and physical environment of the counselee. This has been called the *ecological perspective* on counseling. Unlike the traditional views that look within the counselee to find the cause of problems, the ecological perspective proposes an interaction between each of us and our environments. Human problems are assumed to rise sometimes from inside the person, sometimes from the environment, and often from both.

None of this is meant to say that individuals have no responsibility for their actions. If a teenager in your church attempts suicide or becomes a problem drinker, the young person is responsible for his or her own behavior. The causes of this behavior may be found within the individual, perhaps the result of confused thinking, a low self-concept, or an unwillingness to avoid sin. But the counselor also looks outside of the counselee for the influence of family tension, peer pressure, or stresses coming from school, work, and dating relationships.

Effective counseling often has a diverse emphasis. The counselor and counselee still talk together in private, discussing inner struggles and insecurities, but sometimes family members or people from the community join in the problem-solving process. There is recognition that the community that sometimes creates problems can also be a source of support, a place for learning, and an environment for healing.

Community counseling is an approach to problem solving that may involve:

- *Teaching social skills* so people are more competent in coping with stress, relating to others, and managing their lives.[4]
- *Building social support* by promoting increased cooperation, communication, and unity in a family or community organization (including the church) so there is greater support and less isolation among the members.
- *Equipping lay people,* giving them training and encouragement so they can provide counseling, education, tangible assistance, self-help group support, and other aid to needy people in their communities.
- *Getting help from others* by calling on the assistance or expertise of people in the community who can contribute to the counselee's problem-solving efforts.
- *Preventing problems* by anticipating the future and helping both individuals and groups of people develop the skills and make the life changes that will prevent future problems from developing.
- *Changing the community,* sometimes by taking social, political, or other action to reduce poverty, stress, unemployment, pornography, violence, ignorance, sinful behavior, or other environmental problem-causing influences.

One textbook describes community counseling as an approach that seeks to improve the environment instead of concentrating solely on helping the victims of a community's shortcomings. "The community counselor must learn to deal with large groups as well as with individuals; to become an educator as well as a counselor; and to deal with the environment as well as the person being affected by the environment." This is an approach that requires an awareness of the social forces affecting individuals, a willingness to use new techniques and skills, a tendency to be socially active, a recognition that the counselor is only one positive resource among many, and a hope that someday there will be so much caring, support, and competence within the community that professional helpers will no longer be needed.[5]

It seems unlikely that we will ever reach this goal. Human problems are complex and many come from physiological influences that need the intervention of a trained expert. Community counselors do not resist individual counseling given in a private office, but they challenge the assumption that this is the only or even the best way to help people. Sometimes counseling has to reach out to include and intervene in the community.

The church is an important part of this community. The body of believers can give the love, hope, peace, challenge, and support that enables individuals to cope with life's pressures and complexities. Wayne Oates is correct when he contends that Christian counseling is flawed when it is done "apart from vital access to a community of faith."[6] Christian counseling is a contradiction in terms if it gives no heed to the body of believers who should exist to care for the needy, to welcome strangers, to do good to all people, to heal the broken-hearted, to forgive the repentant, to comfort the sorrowing, to hold up the weak, and to point all people to Christ. It may be difficult for one church to fulfill all of these responsibilities, but surely it is the Christian counselor's duty to work with others to make the local body of believers more caring and compassionate—in conformity to biblical teaching.

Systems and Social Networks

George is a sixty-eight-year-old man who lives in a high-rise condominium on the outskirts of a large metropolitan community. He and his wife have been married for more than forty years and have three grown children, all of whom have moved to other parts of the country. The family keeps in telephone contact and periodically there are visits, but since his retirement, George and his wife have spent most of their time watching television, visiting with friends, or attending church functions.

Not long ago, George had a heart attack. His wife called a neighbor who, in turn, called the paramedics and accompanied the stricken couple to the hospital. For almost three months, George remained hospitalized, receiving treatment not only for his heart condition but for a form of cancer that the doctors discovered as part of their examinations. When he came home recently, George was weak, barely able to walk, and constantly sustained by an oxygen supply that rarely left his side. His children have each visited during the crisis, but their families and work responsibilities have kept the visits brief. George and his wife have been forced to cope largely on their own. Their experiences illustrate what counselors mean by systems and social networks.

Systems are the social groups to which individuals belong. For most of us there are a number of these groups and often they overlap to form a *network* of groups. Each of us, for example, may be part of a family, a group of residents who live in the same apartment complex, a college community, a neighborhood, a church, a work setting, a Bible study group, a self-help group, or some other small band of people. You or your counselee may be part of an organization (like the company where you work, the school where you study, the union in which you participate, or the denomination to which you belong), a vocation (like the ministry or psychology), or an interest group (like a basketball team or a computer-users club).[7] Each of these systems can be the cause of stress and personal tension, but each can also give help in times of need.

In one study, researchers attempted to discover why some people are overwhelmed by major life changes but others appear to recover quickly. The best adjusters were those who had a variety of social relationships. When death or some other crisis disrupted one support group, the successful copers were those who could shift to get support and help from other relationships.[8] People who had boring jobs or difficult family lives could put up with these when they had rewarding and satisfying relationships in the other systems of life.

George and his wife were able to cope with his physical illness because they had emotional support from each other, from their children (even though these children were far away), from the neighbors in their condominium complex, from some extended family members (brothers and in-laws who lived nearby), from caring medical personnel at the local hospital, from some former work associates, from acquaintances who sent cards and called occasionally, and from the pastor and members of the church.[9] At different times during the crisis, these people provided the six forms of help that everybody needs on occasion:[10]

- Tangible aid, in the form of money, food, or other objects.
- Physical assistance that might include the providing of transportation, mowing a lawn, typing a paper, pushing a wheelchair, or sharing in other tasks.
- Guidance; offering advice or practical suggestions.
- Listening while feelings, personal concerns, frustrations, and fears are expressed.
- Feedback; giving people information about themselves.
- Social participation that involves informal conversation, relaxation, and temporary diversion from demanding and difficult conditions.

One psychiatrist argued recently that there is one major way for our society to make significant gains in providing mental health services. We must find, train, encourage, and use unpaid volunteers who can be community mental health workers.[11] George and his wife found these helpers among their wide circle of friends, but some people in the community do not have these supportive relationships. Individuals who are elderly or without families may have few social contacts. Others, like drug and alcohol abusers or some former prisoners, may have many social contacts, but all are part of pathological and problem-creating social networks. These people may not get support from the system unless willing people in the community can be found and encouraged to become helpers to those in need.

The Other Helpers

During the past two or three decades, counseling has become extremely popular. In colleges, universities, seminaries, and other educational institutions, counselor-training programs are flooded with applicants. Lay counseling has attracted considerable attention in schools, churches, crisis-telephone centers, businesses, and even prisons. A variety of training programs have appeared[12] along with a host of new theories, innovative techniques, professionally trained counselors and expanding counseling centers. At least in America, we appear to be in the midst of a counseling boom.

Despite all this activity (and perhaps because of it), we still hear about a continuing shortage of needed professional counselors, especially in smaller communities. To meet the demands for counseling and to fill in when professionals are not available, a large network of "other helpers"[13] has appeared. Some of these nonprofessionals have been around for decades, but now they are seen as important adjuncts to any counseling ministry.

The other helpers vary in the extent of their training, psychological knowledge, sensitivity, therapeutic skills, and ability to help. Despite good intentions, many probably do more harm than good. Some want to become people helpers because they hope this will help solve their own insecurities and unresolved conflicts. Others are manipulative, dogmatic, psychologically naive, and critical of other helpers, including professional counselors.

Even with these drawbacks, however, there is considerable evidence that nonprofessional counselors can be effective, sometimes even more effective than professionals.[14] Some people feel less threatened and more at ease when they can talk to a nonprofessional. Others prefer to get their help from magazine articles or radio talk shows. Some would rather talk with a pastor or with the members of a self-help group.

As a counselor, you may choose to ignore these community sources of help, but it is unlikely that they will be ignored by your counselees. Whether or not you think about this, most of your counseling probably will be accompanied by the less formal and sometimes unsolicited help-giving that comes from people in the community. Instead of ignoring or resisting these other helpers, the counselor should be aware of their existence. At times they can undermine what the counselor attempts to do, but they can also be a great source of help. Sometimes you may choose to enlist the assistance of these other helpers as you work with your counselees.

Medical Professionals. The counselor would be foolish to ignore the help that can come to counselees from doctors, nurses, clinics, and other community medical resources. These professional care givers have at least some training in psychiatry and their work often puts them in contact with patients who have severe emotional problems in addition to physical illnesses. Because of suspicion and mistrust, nonmedical and medical counselors may need to work at building rapport and mutual respect if they are to cooperate in helping those who need counseling.

Community Agents. These are the lawyers, school teachers, policemen, union leaders, clergy, athletic coaches, taxicab drivers, shopkeepers, funeral directors, youth workers, beauticians, bartenders, and others in the community who may have little or no training in counseling but who often are the first to see people in times of psychological crises. It probably is unrealistic to think that many cab drivers or bartenders would be willing to take courses in lay counseling, but in some segments of the community such training is being offered.[15] Police officers now get training in crisis management and mental health intervention because policemen are often the first and only outsiders to be present when there is domestic violence or the threat of suicide. Teachers, school officials, attorneys, and, of course, seminary students routinely get training in counseling and mental health management as part of their educational backgrounds.

Mutual Aid Groups. Nobody knows how many self-help groups meet on a regular basis to help members deal with their stresses. Alcoholics Anonymous (AA) and weight reduction programs like TOPS (Take Off Pounds Sensibly) or Weight Watchers are best known, but groups exist to deal with almost every common problem.[16] There are widows groups, groups of former mental patients, parents without partners, heart patients, compulsive gamblers, parents of retarded children, pregnant teenagers, disabled war veterans, and literally hundreds of others. Sometimes working with professional counselors, but more often on their own, these group members give mutual support, tangible assistance, pertinent information, opportunities to help others, social interaction, encouragement, protection, acceptance, and special help in times of crises. Many people who have stable families and caring churches still join mutual aid groups because of the closeness that comes from contact with others who share similar problems. In addition, one of the greatest benefits of these groups is the help they give to members as they reach out to assist others.[17]

Family Members and Friends. Most people probably talk about problems with friends or family members long before they seek help from a counselor. Parents, for example, are major sources of encouragement, behavior modification, confrontation, and guidance, even though we rarely view them as mental health counselors.[18] Numerous books have been written to help parents with these challenges,[19] and professionals have been encouraged to teach parents how to help their children.[20] Alcoholics can often be helped by their spouses, terminally ill patients get support from their families, and relatives often rally to help and give advice during times of need.

Sometimes this input from friends and family creates more harm than good. At some time, every counselor has the experience of working with a counselee and then having this work undermined by parents, other relatives, or friends, some of whom sincerely want to be helpful. By listening carefully, the counselor can be aware of these outside influences and sometimes you can help counselees cope with the harmful input from others.

It is also possible to get friends and family involved in the counseling, and you can show them how to be genuinely helpful. If you ignore the counselee's friends and family members, your work as a counselor may be much more difficult, and you may be cutting off a valuable additional resource for helping your counselee.

Media Help. During the days when I was writing this chapter, a series of teenage suicides rocked our community and were reported across the country. The method of death was always the same, and there were outcries against the media for reporting the suicides, drawing attention to the victims, and subtly teaching other distressed young people how to kill themselves successfully. Reporters replied that publicity can alert communities to serious problems that are being ignored.

This debate reminds us that television, radio, newspapers, books, and magazines may create human problems but can also contribute to their solutions. Although news stories and television programs may stimulate violence or arouse stress, these same media influences can provide information, give guidance, and show people where to get help.[21]

Exotic Helpers. Palm readers, fortune tellers, cult leaders, herb doctors, exorcists, magic faith-healers, spiritists, and other exotic "helpers" appear in almost every community. Most professionals regard these people as charlatans or quacks who prey on the fears, hopes, and superstitions of troubled people. Some counselors have suggested, however, that these community healers should be enlisted to practice their healing arts alongside more traditional counselors.[22] Since the exotic helpers are especially revered by uneducated and poorer people, it is suggested that these needy individuals will be more open to healing if their helper-heroes are part of the treatment process.

Christian counselors should not encourage counselees to talk with exotic helpers.

Many appear to be involved with occult practices and extreme care must be taken to keep such influences well away from your counseling.

TAKING COUNSELING HOME

All of these community influences suggest that helping does not need to be restricted to the counseling room. Learning that occurs in counseling can be practiced after the session is over and reinforced by helpful people in the community. Homework assignments help to accomplish this goal.

There is evidence that each of us has a special way of learning. Some people learn best through *hearing*—listening to the words of others. Some learn best through *seeing*—reading books, watching movies, and looking at diagrams. Others prefer to learn by *doing*—completing projects, doing role plays, or acting out their feelings.[23] Although there have been some recent exceptions,[24] traditional people helping has involved a talk-listen approach that involves one hour sessions separated by a week or more of other activities.

Homework assignments enable people to extend their learning beyond the counseling sessions and permit both seeing and doing in addition to hearing. Jay Adams writes that homework is the essence of good counseling. "Learning how to give good homework, homework that is biblical, homework that is concrete, and homework that creatively fits the situation, takes time and effort, but is worth both."[25]

Homework sometimes raises thoughts of dull busywork imposed upon an unwilling recipient.[26] It is better if the counselor and counselee can agree on useful and specific tasks that can be done between sessions. These tasks can help counselees keep aware of counseling goals, gain additional information (often through reading or listening to tapes), develop and practice new skills, eliminate harmful behavior, test what is being learned in counseling, and try out new ways of thinking and acting.

Homework assignments can be of various types and may include such specific behaviors as giving one compliment each day, refraining from criticism, reading in the Bible, spending time with a significant relative, keeping a record of time use, or making a list of one's values, goals, and priorities. At the end of each counseling session, you might ask, "Following our meeting today, how can you practice what you have learned or get new learning that might be of further help?" Try to help the counselee think of creative answers and useful homework assignments.

Despite the potential for diversity, several types of homework assignments are used most often:

1. *Testing.* This includes the use of questionnaires, sentence completion forms, standardized tests, and writing assignments (such as preparing a brief biography, listing life goals, making a list of what one likes or dislikes about a job, listing what might be good or bad about a contemplated change, recording successes and failures, or keeping a diary). These written responses are then taken back to the counselor where they are discussed.

2. *Discussion and Study Guides.* Although study guides sometimes appear only in the appendix of a book, many entire volumes are written to guide home study or promote small-group discussion. Sometimes these books are read by individuals who answer the author's questions and fill in the blanks but never discuss any of

this with another person. Others work on the books between counseling sessions and subsequently discuss the books with a counselor.

A variety of study guides and similar self-help programs can be found in most bookstores[27] and some materials are available through the mail. The quality of these programs and workbooks varies, however, and some recent research has suggested that the do-it-yourself treatment books may be of limited value, especially if they are used by people who are not discussing them with a counselor.[28]

3. *Behavior Assignments.* Counselees sometimes are encouraged to change their actions in some small but important ways between counseling sessions. Saying "thank you," giving periodic compliments, not complaining about some annoying practice in one's mate, getting to work on time, practicing a communication skill learned in the counseling session, attending a church service, reading the Bible for ten minutes daily, spending fifteen minutes playing with one's children are the kinds of specific behavior change suggestions that counselors give and discuss later with counselees.

4. *Reading.* Books and articles often contain helpful information that can supplement the counseling session. There is always the danger that counselees will misinterpret what has been written or that something will be pulled out of context. Few counselors have time to screen all potentially relevant books and it will be difficult to find a variety of written materials with which the counselor agrees totally. In spite of these limitations, articles and books can be a helpful adjunct to counseling, especially if the reading is discussed subsequently within the counseling session.[29]

5. *Recordings.* Music therapy—the use of music to help people with their problems—is at least as old as the soothing melodies that David played to calm the troubled Saul. Many people today relax by turning on the stereo after a busy day of work.

The widespread interest in audio and videocassette recordings and the availability of inexpensive playback equipment have given the counselor a potentially powerful resource. Literally thousands of tapes—especially audio tapes—are available on a wide variety of subjects. The quality of these tapes and the accuracy of the information is not always good, but these can be improved and used as a helpful supplement to personal counseling.[30]

Several years ago, for example, the staff at a university counseling center prepared a number of cassette recordings, each of which ran for seven to ten minutes and contained practical counseling advice plus information about where to get further help. Brochures were distributed on campus listing the tape topics (such as how to deal with depression, how to know if you are pregnant, how to study better) and students were invited to call a twenty-four-hour telephone service where they could listen to the tape of their choice. Research showed that the tapes were widely used, helpful, and able to encourage some people to get needed counseling.[31] More recently local hospitals and community counseling centers have offered similar services. Church dial-a-message numbers are a variation of the same concept.

Chapters 6–37 of this book include information to help counselors deal with a number of practical counseling issues. At the end of each chapter, suggestions are given for further reading—including books that could be helpful for counselees. In addition, each chapter has an accompanying cassette tape and assignment sheet prepared by a skilled Christian counselor who seeks to (a) give information to counselees that can supplement private counseling, and (b) suggest exercises to stimulate further thought and learning. When the tapes and assignment sheets are given to counselees, they can experience homework exercises that involve hearing, seeing, and doing—all in an attempt to help in the attainment of counseling goals.[32]

6. *Computer Assignments.* With the widespread use of personal computers, it is possible to give homework assignments that can be done in response to instructions on a screen. Computerized testing is now common,[33] educational and behavior modification programs can be presented by computer, and some simplified therapy programs have been designed for computer users. Research in this fascinating area is beginning to unlock new and previously unimagined opportunities that can be genuinely helpful to counselees and their counselors.[34]

The Environment and Counseling

Have you ever tried to counsel in a place that is noisy, cluttered, too hot, or filled with distractions? Have you considered the stress that could come from living in such an environment? The places where we live and work can contribute to personal problems and can interfere with counseling effectiveness. Sometimes the best way to help people or prevent further problems is to change existing conditions or remove counselees from a stressful environment.[35] Sometimes it is more realistic to help people understand and adapt to difficult circumstances. Four environmental influences are of special importance.

1. *Noise.* In urban areas especially, people constantly are bombarded by noise from traffic, airplanes, radios, construction, barking dogs, people talking, telephones, and other sources of noise pollution. While some sounds (such as desired music) can be soothing and relaxing, other noises can increase tension and irritability, prevent sleep, interfere with job performance and even lead to a reduction in sex drive or a loss of appetite.[36] People who live in noisy environments often find the perpetual sound to be annoying, disruptive, and stress producing.

2. *Crowding.* Most people enjoy a little—but not too much—distance between themselves and other human beings. We like stimulation from others but too much or too little can be distracting or harmful to our feelings of well-being. We like to be near people, but we don't like to be crowded. At times we need a quiet place where we can withdraw for a time of solitude. When such withdrawal is impossible (as often is true in crowded cities, campus dormitories, ships at sea, many work settings, and some mission compound situations) tensions develop, tempers often flare, and people can feel trapped.[37]

3. *Architecture.* Architects and interior decorators have long recognized that room shape, colors, type and arrangement of furniture, decorations (such as pictures, plants, or books), temperature, and lighting can all affect people psychologically. These architectural and design effects have a subtle bearing on work productivity, interpersonal relations, attitudes, emotions, and the extent to which people feel comfortable and relaxed.[38]

4. *Weather.* It is well known that weather can have a great influence on human behavior. Everyone knows that people feel sluggish and tired when the heat and

humidity are high. It has been shown that weather can influence suicide and accident rates, crime, academic performance, productivity, degree of participation in social activities, mood, subjective feelings, and attitudes.[39] When weather conditions are extreme—as in heat waves, blizzards, or intense storms—an additional stress is applied to everyone. People who are under stress already may see these weather pressures as the "last straw" which then produces dramatic change in behavior. Following a recent snowstorm in one large city, for example, travel was restricted, people were forced to stay home, frustration and domestic quarrels increased, and the number of family murders rose sharply.

These environmental influences affect counseling in two important ways. First, they can create stress and complicate counseling. In the midst of his busy life, Jesus moved away from the noise, crowds, and other environmental pressures to get alone with his Father.[40] Counselees and counselors at times need to do the same. The sensitive counselor keeps alert to environmental stresses that may intensify both the counselor's and the counselee's pressures and thus hinder counseling effectiveness.

This brings us to the second influence of environment on counseling. The place where we do our counseling is important. As we have seen, it is not necessary or always desirable to counsel in a formal office. When you do use an office, however, recognize that comfortable chairs, pleasant surroundings, neatness, warm colors (like beige, brown, yellow, red, or even blue—never white), soft floor coverings, comfortable temperatures, soothing music (or silence) can all reduce tension—providing the counselee feels comfortable in this kind of environment. If you are counseling in a restaurant or other public place, be alert to the potentially adverse influences of background music, commotion, architectural design, and other environmental influences.

Groups and Counseling

The early Christians probably did not meet under ideal environmental conditions, but they came together in small groups for the teaching, fellowship, eating, and prayer described in Acts 2:42. Undoubtedly there was mutual support, encouragement, sharing, and burden-bearing. For Christians, this was the beginning of group helping.

Modern group therapy has been traced to the beginning of this century when a Boston internist set up "classes" for his tuberculosis patients. Soon it became apparent that these gatherings were providing opportunity for the patients to share their struggles, encourage one another, and develop feelings of closeness and solidarity. The value of this mutual interaction became known to psychiatrists, and group counseling began to develop as a unique and specialized form of treatment. Originally developed as a form of psychoanalysis, group therapy soon embraced a variety of theoretical approaches and developed literally thousands of techniques. Perhaps the movement reached its peak of popularity during the encounter group era of the 1960s and 1970s, but group counseling is still widely used, sometimes to supplement and often in place of individual counseling.[41]

According to Irvin D. Yalom, one of the leaders in group psychotherapy, groups can provide a number of "curative factors."[42] Groups, for example, can:

- Instill hope and optimism.
- Decrease each participant's sense of feeling alone with his or her problem.
- Impart information about mental health, illness, and specific counselee problems.
- Create an altruistic climate where participants can give help, support, encouragement, and love.
- Give feedback so members can learn how they are perceived by others, including people outside the group.
- Teach new learning so people can change their behavior and learn to function more effectively.
- Help people acquire and practice social skills so they can learn to relate to others in positive and mature ways.
- Give models of effective behavior as the participants observe effective and mature behavior in the leader or other group members.
- Provide opportunity for expression of feelings.
- Give a sense of belonging, acceptance, and cohesiveness.
- Help people deal with significant issues such as personal responsibility, basic values, planning for the future, the meaning of life, or one's sense of self-worth.
- Provide opportunity for believers to pray, read scripture, and seek divine guidance together.

It is beyond the scope of this book to discuss issues such as how to select group participants, how to train leaders, how to maintain confidentiality, what to do with noncooperative or domineering group members, the stages through which developing groups evolve, how to terminate groups, what techniques to use, or the possible dangers of groups. In the hands of inexperienced or untrained leaders, group interaction can sometimes create more problems than are solved. The relaxed group atmosphere may encourage individuals to discuss their problems openly and then feel betrayed and hurt because they "told everything" but experienced no healing. Frustration can be intense if group members are insensitive to one another, inclined to explode in criticism or verbal abuse, unwilling to show respect or patience for other group members, or inclined to talk gossip away from the group.

All of this suggests that Christian counselors should be aware of both the unique benefits and the potential harm in small group counseling. If you want to work in this area, try to get further information about group techniques and attempt to get supervised training in the process of group counseling.[43]

Community Counseling and the Christian

Community counselors assume that we cannot really help people without, at the same time, dealing with and being aware of the community. Even as they discuss other issues, the counselor and counselee are aware of several basic questions about their relationship.[44]

1. To what extent can the problem be solved apart from the environment and largely through inner change in the counselee?

2. What resources are available in the community and environment that could help the counselee grow?
3. To what extent does the solution really rest in the environment instead of in the individual?
4. How can the counselor and/or the counselee act to bring the necessary changes in the environment?

In addition to personal counseling, community counselors are involved in activities such as finding or providing educational programs; giving training in self-help skills; assisting governments and social service agencies in planning social programs; identifying community support groups; working to establish telephone hot lines, rehabilitation centers and other community resources; and at times participating in political movements in an effort to improve the community.

Community counselors recognize that they are not alone in trying to improve the community. For this reason they work with a variety of professional, political, and other resource people to bring about change. By improving the community it is assumed that community residents will be enabled to cope with life and its problems.

It takes only a casual look at the literature to discover that the field of community counseling says very little about the church.[45] If we consider the helping ministry of Jesus, however, we might conclude that he was a community counselor. He tenderly and sensitively helped individuals with their doubts and struggles, but he also spoke against hypocrisy and poverty. He drove the moneychangers out of the temple, criticized the government, and spoke of a day when a kingdom would come and eliminate injustice.

In view of the recent trends in community counseling, it is exciting to ponder how Christian counseling might change in the future. As individuals who live in communities and seek to obey biblical teachings, Christians—including counselors—must have an active concern about hunger, poverty, injustice, crime, pornography, family violence, declining moral standards, and other social ills that give rise to many of the issues discussed in the following chapters. The church, as a community within a community, must ask how it can have an impact both on the unchurched and on church members. Following is the oft-quoted instruction that we should bear each other's burdens, Paul wrote: "Let us not become weary in doing good, for at the proper time we will reap a harvest if we do not give up. Therefore, as we have opportunity, let us do good to all people, especially to those who belong to the family of believers."[46]

Christian community counseling is a new territory, but it is clearly consistent with the teachings of the Bible.

SUGGESTIONS FOR FURTHER READING

Bloom, Bernard L. *Community Mental Health: A General Introduction.* 2d ed. Monterey, Calif.: Brooks/Cole, 1984.

Collins, Gary R. *Innovative Approaches to Counseling.* Waco, Tex.: Word, 1986.

Corey, Gerald, and Marianne S. Corey. *Groups: Process and Practice.* 3d ed. Pacific Grove, Calif.: Brooks/Cole, 1987.

Drakeford, John W. *People to People Therapy.* New York: Harper & Row, 1978.

Egan, Gerard, and Michael A. Cowan. *People in Systems*. Monterey, Calif.: Brooks/Cole, 1979.

Evans, Gary W., ed. *Environmental Stress*. Cambridge: Cambridge University Press, 1982.

Gershon, Michael, and Henry B. Biller. *The Other Helpers*. Lexington, Mass.: Lexington, 1977.

Heller, Kenneth, et al. *Psychology and Community Change*. Homewood, Ill.: Dorsey, 1984.

Schulberg, Herbert C., and Marie Killilea, eds. *The Modern Practice of Community Mental Health*. San Francisco: Jossey-Bass, 1982.

5

The Crises in Counseling

WALTER ANDERSON WAS a high school dropout who enlisted in the Marine corps as a teenager, served in Vietnam, and didn't go to college until after the war. In those days nobody could have predicted that this young veteran would be appointed editor of a national magazine before his thirty-sixth birthday. Writing later about this meteoric career rise, Anderson described his fears and the constant inner suspicion that he was "not good enough" to edit *Parade*.

Do all of us harbor insecurities like this? According to Walter Anderson, struggle is a universal experience and most of us feel insecure, at least periodically. The editor's contacts with successful and famous people have convinced him that many feel highly insecure and anxious. Few, if any, sail through life without setbacks, failures, or inner fears. Most have experienced anxieties and crises that slowed them down temporarily but then gave them the motivation to courageously pick up the pieces and go on.[1]

Briefly defined, a crisis is a turning point that cannot be avoided. Crisis situations may be expected or unexpected, real or imagined, actual (like the death of a loved one) or potential (like the prospect that a loved one will die soon). It has often been stated that the Chinese word for "crisis" involves two characters.[2] One means danger; the other means opportunity.

Crises are filled with *danger* because they disrupt life and threaten to overwhelm the people who are affected. As we grow toward adulthood, each of us develops a repertoire of problem-solving techniques based on our past experiences, training, and personality characteristics. There are emotional and spiritual ups and downs, of course, and at times we must exert extra effort to deal with emergencies or unexpected problems. Nevertheless, we learn how to cope and are able to meet the insecurities and challenges of life successfully.

At times, however, unusually severe or demanding situations arise. There might be the loss of someone or something significant, a sudden shift in one's role or status, or the appearance of new and threatening people or events. Because the new situation is so unique and intense, our customary ways of handling stress and solving problems no longer are effective. Often this leads to confusion and bewilderment, frequently accompanied by inefficiency, anxiety, anger, discouragement, sorrow, or guilt. Usually this intellectual, behavioral, and emotional turmoil is temporary, but sometimes it persists for several weeks or even longer.

Crises, however, present people with the *opportunity* to change, grow, and develop better ways of coping. Since people in crises often feel confused, they are more open to outside help, including the help that comes from God and from the counselor. Even when they get counseling, some individuals try to ignore and evade the crisis, withdraw into irrational fantasies, give up in despair, or respond in socially unacceptable ways. Others react in healthier ways. They reevaluate the situation and look for creative, socially acceptable, reality-based, problem-solving techniques that can help in the present crisis and add to the person's capacity to deal effectively with future difficulties.[3]

When doctors talk of a medical crisis they refer to a crucial time when there is a change, either toward improvement and recovery or toward decline and death. Emotional and spiritual crises likewise are unavoidable turning points in life. To live is to experience crises. To experience crises is to face turning points that bring either growth and maturation or deterioration and continuing immaturity. The Christian counselor is in a vital position to influence which direction the crisis resolution will take.

The Bible and Crisis Types

Much of the Bible deals with crises. Adam, Eve, Cain, Noah, Abraham, Isaac, Joseph, Moses, Samson, Jepthah, Saul, David, Elijah, Daniel, and a host of other figures faced crises that the Old Testament describes in detail. Jesus faced crises (especially at the time of the crucifixion) and so did the disciples, Paul, and many early believers. Several of the Epistles were written to help individuals or churches meet crises, and Hebrews 11 summarizes both crises that had happy endings and those that resulted in torture, incredible suffering, and death.

Contemporary writers have identified three types of crises, each of which has both modern and biblical examples. The first of these, *accidental* or *situational crises,* occurs when there is a sudden threat, intensely disruptive event, or unexpected loss. The death of a loved one, the discovery of a serious illness, the experience of rape or other violence, a pregnancy out of wedlock, social disruptions such as war or economic depression, the loss of one's job or savings, a sudden loss of respect and status are all situational stresses that affect both individuals and their families.

Someone has observed that stressful events originating outside of the family—persecution, natural disaster, a serious fire, or racial prejudice, for example—often solidify a family so that members pull together to resolve the crisis. When stress is internal—like a suicide attempt, infidelity, child abuse, or alcoholism—the crisis is more disruptive and inclined to tear the family apart.[4] More disruptive are the crises that come in sequence, one following quickly on the heels of another. For some people, the crisis that brings them to counseling is the last straw, the most recent in a series of stressful changes and losses.[5]

This was Job's experience. Within a short period of time, this religious man lost his family, wealth, health, and status. His marriage appears to have been strained and his counselors soon learned about Job's anger and inner turmoil. He was confused about why a caring God would let so many bad things happen to a good person.

Developmental crises, the second type, happen in the course of normal human development. Starting school, going away to college, adjusting to marriage and then to parenthood, handling criticism, facing retirement or declining health, or adapting to the deaths of one's friends can all be crises that demand new approaches to coping and problem solving. Abraham and Sarah, for example, coped with moving, criticism, many years of childlessness, family stress, and even the command of

God that young Isaac should be sacrificed. We might wonder how an elderly couple like Zacharias and Elizabeth handled a son as unique as John the Baptist, or how Mary and Joseph were able to raise so unusual and brilliant a boy as Jesus. Surely there were developmental crises—turning points that demanded prolonged periods of wise decision-making but which also led to increased growth.

Existential crises, the third type, overlap with the other two. There are times when all of us face disturbing truths, often about ourselves:

> I'm a failure.
> I'm going to graduate but haven't any idea what I will do next.
> I'll never be successful in my company.
> I didn't get the long-anticipated promotion.
> I'm now a widow—single again.
> My life has no purpose.
> My marriage has ended in divorce.
> My illness is incurable.
> I'm trapped in this town.
> I have nothing to believe in.
> My house and possessions are all gone in the fire.
> I've been rejected because of my skin color.
> I'm too old to reach my life goals.

These, and similar realizations, take time and effort to assimilate. They are changes in self-perception that can be denied temporarily but in time they must be faced realistically if life is to go on and be fulfilling.

After a great spiritual victory, Elijah was chased by Jezebel and ran to the wilderness where he concluded that his life was a failure. Jonah had similar thoughts as he debated with God. In the midst of his struggles, Job must have wondered "What will become of me and what will happen now?" Did the disciples feel the same in the hours following the crucifixion?

When people ask about the reasons for their crises, it is difficult and often impossible to give definitive answers. The Bible speaks about all three types of crises, but the scriptures do not give clear and complete reasons to explain why we suffer when and as we do. We may agree that every event has a divine purpose and ultimately is under God's control. We know that crises can be learning experiences that mold character, teach us about God and his resources, and stimulate growth. But the ultimate reasons for specific life crises may never be known while we live on this earth.

In the meantime, we can help counselees cope and grow through their crises. In the chapters that follow, different kinds of crises will be discussed in detail, but there are counseling techniques that apply to them all. These intervention methods should be understood by any Christian who wants to be a people-helper.

Crisis Intervention

Crisis intervention is a way of providing immediate, temporary, emotional first aid to victims of psychological and physical trauma. The intervener must react skillfully and quickly to deal with behavior that is often disorganized, confused, and potentially harmful.[6] Since they frequently appear suddenly and are of limited duration, crises are best treated as soon as possible after they arise. There are several counseling goals:

- To help the person cope effectively with the crisis situation and return to his or her usual level of functioning.
- To decrease the anxiety, apprehension, and other insecurities that may persist during the crisis and after it passes.
- To teach crisis-management techniques so the person is better prepared to anticipate and deal with future crises.
- To consider biblical teachings about crises so the person learns from the crisis and grows as a result.

Crisis counselors cannot treat every person (or group of people, including families) in the same way. There are individual differences in flexibility, customary ways of coping, ability to learn new adjustment techniques, physical and psychological strength, or level of emotional and spiritual maturity. Some people tend to be optimistic, even in the midst of crises; others are pessimistic and easily overwhelmed. Some are excessively dependent while others are very independent. Some counselees are able to discuss the crisis and understand its implications. Others are too distraught to think clearly or make rational decisions.

With these differences in mind, the counselor can intervene in several ways during times of crises. Think of the following as a checklist for giving psychological first aid in times of mental health emergencies.[7]

1. *Make Contact.* People in crises don't always come to a counselor for help. Often we must go to others and show our warmth, understanding, and genuine interest. Listen carefully so you can understand the counselee's concerns and point of view before making suggestions for action. If the person slips into daydreaming, fantasy, withdrawal, or deep thought, try to bring the discussion back to reality.

Eye contact can reassure the counselee and so can touching. Even when there are no words, touching and other forms of physical contact can communicate care and bring great comfort.

Remember, however, that some cultures and subcultures have strong taboos against touch. At least until recently, it was acceptable to shake hands in our society, to slap a friend on the back, or to hug athletes briefly after a team victory, but hugging, holding hands, or even putting your arms around a person in crisis has usually been discouraged in counseling. Some have suggested that counselees may misinterpret such physical contact and see it as having sexual overtones. Other counselees feel threatened by physical contact, are uncomfortable with touch because this was discouraged by their families, are suspicious that touch may be manipulative, or have a fear of intimacy.

For most people, however, touch can be comforting, therapeutic, and encouraging. As a counselor, you should realize the value and risks of physical contact, then decide whether your touch could be misinterpreted and whether it might help the counselee. As we have suggested earlier, it is also helpful to ask yourself about your reasons for touching. Is this more likely to meet your affiliation and sexual needs, rather than the needs of the counselee? Even though touching can be an excellent way to make contact and give support, for any individual (including you) it should be guided by this general rule: if in doubt—don't![8]

2. *Reduce Anxiety.* The counselor's calm, relaxed manner can help reduce anxiety in the counselee, especially when this calmness is accompanied by reassurance. Listen patiently and attentively as the counselee describes the situation. Encourage talk about the insecurities and other feelings that always accompany a crisis. Try to provide reassuring facts ("There *are* ways to deal with this problem"), state your approval when something is done well ("I think that was a good decision—it shows you are on the right track"), gently suggest other interpretations if the counselee's point of view appears to be overly pessimistic or distorted ("Maybe I could suggest another way of looking at this situation"), and when possible, offer a prediction about what will happen ("I know it's tough but I think you can handle this").[9] Try to answer questions honestly, but without raising the counselee's anxiety level unnecessarily. If a person is seriously injured, for example, you could say, "I don't know the extent of your injuries yet, but you are in the care of good medical people. They are checking out everything and you can be sure they will do whatever is needed to help you." This is an honest, reassuring statement that doesn't increase anxiety or raise false hopes.

Often there is value in removing the counselee from a stressful situation, at least temporarily. It may help, for example, to take an anxious relative away from the hustle of emergency room activities and into a quiet side room or down the hall for a cup of coffee. (Be sure to let the emergency room receptionist know where you have gone in case you are needed). Sometimes you may want to encourage counselees to take deep breaths, to go for brief walks, or to consciously tighten and then relax muscles. The calming effect of Bible verses such as 1 Cor. 10:13 can also be helpful. Each of these anxiety-reduction methods can be overused, causing the counselee to feel trapped or smothered, but each can reduce the effects of stress and make it easier to deal constructively with the crisis issues.

3. *Focus on Issues.* In times of crisis it is easy to be overwhelmed by what appears to be a mass of confusing facts, potential problems, and decisions that need to be made. As a somewhat objective outsider, you are in a good position to help the counselee decide what specific issues must be faced first and what immediate problems need to be solved. Try to focus on the present situation rather than discussing the past or pondering what might happen in the future.

At times, especially near the beginning, you may have to make decisions for the counselee. "Let's go and see another doctor," or "You need to get on a plane and go there tomorrow morning" are directive remarks that counselees sometimes need. Often this lets the crisis victim feel that something definite is being done to help. Be careful not to be manipulative, however. Always listen to the counselee's observations, and try to avoid taking actions that you could regret later.

4. *Evaluate Resources.* The counselor's willingness to help is one important resource for the counselee in crisis, but there are others. Even if you are multi-talented and have plenty of time, you should not try to be the hero who walks alone with the person in crisis. Counselees often feel isolated and in need of supportive acceptance

from a variety of people. Others' resources can supplement what you are doing and allow your crisis counseling to be more effective.[10]

Spiritual resources. The Christian counselor must never lose sight of the indwelling presence and guidance of the Holy Spirit, along with the comforting words and promises of Scripture. These can be sources of great strength and direction during crises. Some counselors use Scripture as a hammer to push or manipulate counselees into doing what the counselor thinks should be done. This is neither helpful nor ethical. Instead, Scripture should be presented as truth, along with the expectation that the Holy Spirit will use it as he desires, in the life of the counselee.

Personal resources. Counselees sometimes become overly dependent during times of crisis. For a while this reliance on others may be necessary, but it is good to emphasize the counselee's inner strengths early. Most people have intellectual abilities, skills, past experiences, helpful attitudes, or motives that can help them grow through the crisis. In pointing these out, try to be realistic. Remember that a simple listing of counselee strengths and reminders of past success in coping can be both reassuring and helpful.

Interpersonal resources. Often the person in crisis already has a network that needs to be activated. Family members, friends, business associates, church members, and people in the community would often help eagerly if they knew of the need. People can be asked to pray, give money, or provide other practical assistance during the time of crisis. If you don't know all the significant others in the counselee's life, ask who should be contacted.

Occasionally, counselees won't want to contact anyone. It is difficult for some people to accept help even when they know that social support has great therapeutic value. If the counselee doesn't want to bother others, try to point out the importance of mutual dependency and the satisfaction that comes *to* friends when they are able to help. Be sensitive to the fact that some people are embarrassed about the attention that comes with their crisis, threatened by the implication that they need help, and sometimes even angered by the counselor's attempt to involve others. It is important to discuss all of this with the counselee who, whenever possible, should be encouraged to seek help from others without the counselor's assistance. If a support network does not exist, try to help the counselee develop one. In crisis management, few influences can match the help that comes from other people who care and are concerned.

Despite its great value, sometimes outside support will be less helpful than you might expect. When there is too much dependency on others, counselees may develop a "do nothing" attitude that keeps them from growing. This is most likely when family members become overly involved in their attempts to be helpful. Try to encourage helpers to be supportive but not stifling.[11]

Additional resources. Every community has legal, medical, psychological, financial, educational, and other sources of help that are available in times of crisis. Sometimes the counselee needs money, a place to live temporarily, somebody who can watch young children, meals on wheels, or other tangible sources of relief. You can help counselees find these resources. If the local church is functioning as it should, these resources can often be found within the body of believers.

5. *Plan Intervention.* After evaluating the problem and considering available resources, it is helpful to decide on a course of action that asks "Specifically, what

will we do now?" Together, the counselor and counselee can look at the available facts and list alternative courses of action. How realistic is each one of these? Which should be done first, second, and subsequently?

Some counselees will have difficulty making these decisions. Our goal is not to put more pressure on the counselees by forcing them to make decisions, but neither do we want to encourage dependency and an attitude of letting someone else solve the problems. Gently, but firmly, the counselor can help the counselee make plans and, if necessary, think of better alternatives when an early plan is unsuccessful.

Psychiatrist Raymond E. Vath has stated what could be a golden rule for crisis intervention: "We must do for others what they cannot do for themselves, but we must not do for them what they will not do for themselves. The problem is finding the wisdom to know the difference."[12]

6. *Encourage Action.* It is possible for people to decide on some course of action but then be uncertain how to get started or afraid to move ahead with the plan. Taking action always involves risk. There is the possibility of failure and later regret, especially if the action involves major life changes such as moving or changing jobs. The counselor may need to encourage counselees in their actions. Help them evaluate progress and, if necessary, modify plans for taking further actions.

It may be helpful to keep the following checklist in mind:[13]

- Listen and learn about the problem.
- List alternatives for action (mentally or on paper).
- Decide on a course of action.
- Take action.
- Evaluate the results of action taken.
- Based on the evaluation, continue on the chosen course or repeat the above steps.

In some situations the crisis will never be resolved completely, even by taking action. When someone loses a loved one in death, discovers the existence of an incurable disease, or fails to attain an important promotion, the crisis may bring permanent change. The counselee then must be helped to face the situation honestly, acknowledge and express feelings, readjust one's lifestyle, realistically plan for the future, and rest in the knowledge that God, in his sovereignty, knows and cares about our pain. In all crises, but especially in times of permanent change, it helps if people are surrounded by sincere, concerned, helpful, praying friends who are available to assist whenever and however they are needed.

7. *Instill Hope.* In all counseling, improvement is more likely if counselees can be given a sense of realistic hope about the future. Hope brings relief from suffering because it is based on a belief that things will get better. Hope helps us avoid despair and releases energy to meet the crisis situation.

The Christian counselor can instill hope by using one or more of the following. First, we can share scriptural truths that give reassurance and hope that are based on the unchanging nature and Word of God. This is an approach that instills hope by stimulating faith in God. It is an approach that helps most when the counselor is familiar with Scripture and is growing in his or her own relationship with God. Second, counselees can be helped to examine their self-defeating logic. Ideas like

"I'll never get better" or "Nothing can be worse than this" may enter the counselee's thinking in times of crisis. Such ideas should be challenged gently. What is the evidence for the conclusion that "I'll never get better"? What is the evidence for a more hopeful outcome? Third, counselors can get the counselee moving and doing something. Even minimal activity gives the feeling that something is being done and that the counselee is not helpless. This, in turn, can arouse hope, especially if the activity accomplishes something worthwhile.

8. *Follow-up.* Crisis counseling is usually brief. After one or two sessions the counselee returns to the routines of life and may not come for counseling again. But was anything learned? Will the next crisis be handled more effectively? Is the person getting along satisfactorily now that the major point of crisis is past?

These issues should concern the counselor who can follow up with a phone call or visit. Often it is helpful to make contact on anniversaries. Sometimes people experience a flood of old feelings and insecurities on the birthday of a loved one who has died, the first time a divorced person faces Easter alone, or the one-month or one-year anniversary of the start of the crisis. Even when counseling is no longer needed, such follow-up interest can encourage the counselee and remind him or her that somebody still cares and remembers.

Referral

Sometimes we help counselees most by referring them to someone else whose training, expertise, and availability can be of special assistance. Referral does not mean, necessarily, that the original counselor is incompetent or trying to get rid of the counselee. No one person is skilled enough to counsel everyone, and referral is often a way to show your desire to have the counselee get the best help possible.

People should be referred when they are not showing signs of improvement after several sessions, have severe financial needs, need legal advice, are severely depressed or suicidal, show bizarre or extremely aggressive behavior, appear to be severely disturbed emotionally, stir strong feelings of dislike or sexual arousal in the counselor, or have problems that are beyond the counselor's felt area of expertise. People with eating disorders, drug dependency, physical problems, persisting emotional disorders, fears about unwanted pregnancy, or worries about the possibility of a disease like AIDS, are among those who need medical attention in addition to (and sometimes instead of) your counseling.

Counselors should be familiar with community resources and persons to whom counselees can be referred. These include private practitioners such as physicians, lawyers, psychiatrists, psychologists, and other counselors; pastoral counselors and other church leaders; private and public clinics or hospitals; service agencies such as the Retarded Children's Society or the Society for the Blind; government agencies including the welfare department in your community or the unemployment bureau; school guidance counselors and local educational institutions; private employment agencies; suicide or drug prevention centers; volunteer organizations like the Red Cross or those who deliver "meals on wheels"; and self-help groups such as Alcoholics Anonymous. Many of these are listed in the telephone book or you can talk to some other counselor who might know what is available. As you consider referral, do not overlook church groups that often can give support and practical help in time of need.

Ideally, it is best to refer your counselees only to helpers who are both competent and Christian. Regretfully, many communities do not have professional Christian counselors, and some Christians in the helping professions are not very competent. Many problems (medical issues, for example, or learning disorders) do not need to be treated by a Christian. Some psychological problems are far removed from Christian values and can be handled effectively by nonbelievers. Even when the counselee is struggling with deep personal issues, non-Christians are often sympathetic to religious values and not inclined to undermine a counselee's faith. If Christian help is not available in your community, you must decide—for each individual—whether to make a referral or whether to continue seeing the counselee yourself, even though you would prefer to make a referral.

Before suggesting referral to a counselee, it is best to know what sources of help are available. Check first with the referral group or individual to see if they really are able to give the needed assistance. (It can be devastating to counselees if they approach a source of help that you have recommended and get turned away.) In suggesting referral to the counselee, be sure to indicate your reasons for making this recommendation. Present this as a way to get the best possible help for your counselee. Some will resist the idea of referral and counselees may conclude that you think they are too disturbed or too much of a problem for you to treat. Take time to discuss these fears if they arise and try to involve the counselee in the decision to move to a different source of help.

It is best to let counselees make their own appointments with the new counselor. Sometimes these new counselors will request information about the counselee, but this should be given only if the counselee has granted his or her consent—preferably in written form. When the referral has been made, it is good to keep an interest in the counselee, but remember that somebody else is now responsible for the counseling.

Avoiding Extremes

People who read books on counseling often are surprised to discover that the field is filled with controversy. Advocates of different counseling techniques sometimes argue bitterly, criticize those who think differently, and proclaim the superiority of their favorite counseling theories or theorists. This debate seems to be as heated in some Christian circles as it is in the secular counseling field.

Some counselors believe that problems arise because of inner psychic conflicts and insecurities. A few have put the cause of all problems in the environment and others maintain that human problems come because of faulty learning.[14] Among Christian counselors, debate about the causes and cures of personal problems often centers around physiology, theology, and demonology.

Physiology. To what extent are personality problems and psychological disorders caused by chemical imbalances, glandular malfunctioning, genetic influences, disease, or other physical factors? This question cannot be answered without looking at each individual case, but for many years medical practitioners have argued that all problems have a physical component and many have a physical cause that can only be treated by someone with medical training. In this book we do not assume that all or even most personal problems are physiologically caused, but you will see frequent reference to the biological influences on behavior.[15]

Theology. Are all problems the result of individual sin in the counselee's life?

Many counselors and theologians hold this viewpoint. They argue that counseling must consist primarily of confronting people with sin, urging them to confess, and teaching them how to live in accordance with biblical teachings.

Most Christian counselors would agree, I suspect, that human problems began when sin entered the world millenniums ago. Frequently, people today have problems because they reject, ignore, or are ignorant of God's truth. Counseling is not likely to be effective if it ignores the pungent reality of sin, the need for forgiveness and the crucial importance of Christ-honoring behavior. The following chapters mention sin frequently and consider it seriously. But we do not assume that all or even most problems come primarily because of specific sinful behavior or thinking in the counselee.

Demonology. Within the church there have always been those who assume that problems arise from demonic influence and must be treated by exorcism and other forms of spiritual battle. These well-meaning people gather, sometimes regularly, to pray for deliverance and demand that demons of depression, lust, anxiety, anger, or confusion depart when they are commanded to do so.

Ephesians 6 clearly teaches that Christians are engaged in spiritual battle. The devil is described in Scripture as a schemer who masquerades as an angel of light but prowls around like a roaring lion looking for someone to devour.[16] His demonic forces are mentioned often in the Bible and there is no reason to think that the devil's agents are inactive today. Christians disagree about the extent to which demons are involved in personal problems; in this book we will assume that demonic forces at times create or complicate the lives of counselees and the work of their counselors.

Counselors might ponder the conclusion of C. S. Lewis who wrote that "There are two equal and opposite errors into which our race can fall about the devils. One is to disbelieve in their existence. The other is to believe and to feel an excessive and unhealthy interest in them. They themselves are equally pleased with both errors."[17] There are Christian counselors who fall into both of these extremes, undoubtedly to the detriment of their counselees. The following pages accept the reality of the demonic but assume that exorcism should be used rarely and only with the full support of spiritually mature and biblically astute church leaders.

Looking Ahead

Traditionally, counseling has been divided into three areas: remedial, preventive, and educative. Remedial counseling involves helping people deal with the existing problems of life. Preventive counseling seeks to stop problems from getting worse or prevent their occurrence at all. Educative counseling involves the counselor in teaching principles of mental health to larger groups. It is impossible to estimate the percentage of counselor involvement in each of these three areas, but it is probable that remedial counseling takes the vast majority of counselor time and energy. Graduate training programs have contributed to this lopsided emphasis, and professionals have discovered that it is much easier to make a living with rehabilitative counseling than with preventive and educative work. Many people will pay to get help with an existing problem; few will spend money or time to have a problem prevented.

Several years ago, a committee of the American Psychological Association recommended that these three counseling roles should be reversed.[18] We should put greatest emphasis on educative counseling, the committee concluded, secondary emphasis on prevention, and least emphasis on traditional remedial, rehabilitative helping. Such a change would broaden and vastly alter the field of counseling. In addition to focusing on individuals with problems, there would be greater emphasis on groups of people within the community. Rather than waiting for counselees to come to the office, helping would take place more often where people live, work, and interact. In addition to the current emphasis on counseling techniques, there would be a focus on the use of books, programmed and computer learning, audio and videocassette tapes, and other educational methods. None of this assumes that remedial counseling will fade or disappear. Probably it will always be present and needed. But the field of counseling is changing and Christian counselors are both feeling and contributing to the changes.

In many respects, Christians are ahead of these trends. Since the time of Christ, the church has been concerned with prevention and education. When the pastoral counseling movement arose, the church increased its emphasis on individual helping, but the larger role of educating people and helping them find spiritual and mental health has never been abandoned. Our educative and preventive efforts have not always been effective, and neither have our goals consistently been clear, but within the church there already exists a way of thinking that gives education a place of prominence, often surpassing the emphasis on remedial counseling.

In writing the following chapters, I have attempted to reflect both the traditional rehabilitative approach to counseling and the educative-preventive perspective. The chapters are written (1) to convey an understanding of each problem area, (2) to present guidelines for helping those who are experiencing problems, and (3) to suggest ways to educate Christians so the problems can be prevented in the future. Each of the following chapters is designed to stand alone—they need not be read in any special order. This allows the volume to be a handbook with chapters that can be used for general information and used for reference when specific counseling issues arise. Hopefully the book and accompanying audio cassette tapes also will be used as a training program for counselors and as a basis for the education of lay people.[19]

Christian counseling is a difficult but challenging task. It involves the development of therapeutic personality traits, the learning of skills, a sensitivity to people, an understanding of the counseling process, an alertness to the dangers involved, an in-depth familiarity with the Scriptures, and a sensitivity to the guidance of the Holy Spirit. Counseling can be discussed in a book but it cannot be learned completely from a book. We become good Christian counselors through commitment to Christ, through training under the supervision and guidance of a more experienced counselor, and through the experience of helping people with their problems. These problems are discussed in the pages that follow.

SUGGESTIONS FOR FURTHER READING

Aguilera, Donna C., and Janice M. Messick. *Crisis Intervention: Theory and Methodology.* 4th ed. St. Louis: Mosby, 1982.

Davis, Creath. *A Crisis Is for Climbing.* Grand Rapids, Mich.: Zondervan, 1987.

Strom, Kay Marshall. *Helping Women in Crisis: A Handbook for People Helpers.* Grand Rapids, Mich.: Zondervan, 1986.

Swihart, Judson J., and Gerald C. Richardson. *Counseling in Times of Crisis.* Waco, Tex.: Word, 1987.

Switzer, David K. *The Minister as Crisis Counselor.* Nashville: Abingdon, 1974.

Wright, Norman. *Crisis Counseling.* San Bernardino, Calif.: Here's Life Publishers, 1985.

———. *How to Have a Creative Crisis.* Waco, Tex.: Word, 1987.

Part 2

Personal Issues

6

Anxiety

Ron is twenty, healthy, handsome, and liked by his friends. Until recently, he was enrolled as a business major in a midwestern Christian college, but in the middle of his sophomore year, just a week before finals, he dropped out.

"I couldn't handle the anxiety," he told his family doctor after arriving home. "During tests, I would break out in a cold sweat, my mind would go blank, and I would forget everything I had studied. After being at school for a while I stopped going to lectures. They were too scary because I was afraid I might forget something that would be on the test. By the end of the quarter, I was uncomfortable even going into the academic building. Then I stopped going to the coffee shop because I was afraid I would meet one of my teachers. By the end of my time at school, I was almost too anxious to leave my room."

Ron is a Christian. He has a marker in his Bible at Philippians 4 and he has underlined verses 6 and 7: "Do not be anxious about anything, but in everything, by prayer and petition, with thanksgiving, present your requests to God. And the peace of God, which transcends all understanding, will guard your hearts and your minds in Christ Jesus."

But despite his prayers, Ron feels no peace. In contrast, he feels panic as he anticipates looking for a job, now that he is out of school. "What if nobody will hire me?" he wonders. "What if I find a job and can't do it?" "What if I get too anxious to go to work?"

The doctor prescribed some anti-anxiety medication for Ron and suggested he contact a counselor. The calming effects of the tranquilizers enabled Ron to make an appointment for counseling. Together, Ron and his counselor will try to understand the reasons for his intense anxiety. Probably they will consider ways to relax and to cope with stress—including the stress of a new job.

Ron's parents accept the idea of counseling, but they are impatient for improvement. His father is a highly successful, achievement-oriented businessman who likes to see things accomplished quickly. He has little patience with the idea of his son seeing "some kind of a shrink" and hopes that all of Ron's anxieties will be gone soon.

Ron believes that he is the cause of much of his own anxiety. He knows too that his anxiety could have a physical basis. But he also wonders if a lot of the problem comes from the pressure exerted by his well-meaning but impatient and insensitive father.

Anxiety, stress, fear, phobia, tension—technically these words have different meanings but they often are used interchangeably to describe one of this century's most common problems. Anxiety has been called "the official emotion of our age," the basis of all neuroses, and the "most pervasive psychological phenomenon of our time." It is as old as human existence, but the complexities and pace of modern life have alerted us to its presence and probably increased its influence.

Anxiety is an inner feeling of apprehension, uneasiness, concern, worry, and/or dread that is accompanied by heightened physical arousal. In times of anxiety, the body appears to be on alert, ready to flee or fight. The heart beats faster, blood pressure and muscle tension increase, neurological and chemical changes occur within, sometimes perspiration appears, and the person may feel faint, jumpy, and unable to relax. Anxiety can arise in response to some specific identifiable danger (many writers call this "fear" rather than anxiety), or it may come in reaction to an imaginary or unknown threat. This latter kind of anxiety has been termed "free-floating"; the anxious person senses that something terrible is going to happen but he or she does not know what it is or why.

Various types of anxiety have been identified including normal and neurotic, moderate and intense, state and trait.

Normal anxiety comes to all of us at times, usually when there is some real threat or situational danger. Most often, this anxiety is proportional to the danger (the greater the threat the greater the anxiety). It is anxiety that can be recognized, managed, and reduced, especially when circumstances change. *Neurotic* anxiety involves intense exaggerated feelings of helplessness and dread even when the danger is mild or nonexistent. Many counselors believe this anxiety cannot be faced squarely and dealt with rationally because it may arise from inner conflicts that are not conscious. To quote Rollo May's precise but technical observation, neurotic anxiety "is disproportionate to the objective danger because some intrapsychic conflict is involved."[1]

Anxiety can vary in its intensity and influence. *Moderate* anxiety can be desirable and healthy. Often it motivates, helps people avoid dangerous situations, and leads to increased efficiency. *Intense* anxiety, in contrast, is more stressful. It can shorten one's attention span, make concentration difficult, cause forgetfulness, hinder performance skills, interfere with problem solving, block effective communication, arouse panic, and sometimes cause unpleasant physical symptoms such as paralysis, rapid heartbeat, or intense headaches.

One psychological researcher has suggested that anxiety can also be a state or a trait.[2] *State* anxiety often comes quickly, may or may not be of high intensity, and has a short duration. This is an acute, relatively brief apprehensive reaction that comes to all of us from time to time. Usually it comes as a response to some threat, and at times it is experienced as excitement.[3] *Trait* anxiety, in contrast, is a persistent, ever-present, ingrained emotional tension. It is seen in people who appear to worry all the time. Often it causes physical illness because the body cannot function effectively when it remains in a perpetual state of tension and arousal.

Two other types of anxiety have attracted media and professional attention during the past several years: post-traumatic stress disorders (PTSD) and anxiety disease. Intense stress—like dangerous military conflict, rape, terrorist violence, involvement in a serious accident, kidnaping, or natural disasters such as a tornado or earthquake—can leave a lifelong legacy of anxiety. For years after the trauma, some people have nightmares, irrational fears, depression, worry, and loss of interest in activities that once were pleasant. For these people, anxiety has become a way of life that follows in the wake of an earlier stress experience. These post-traumatic stress disorders have been seen frequently in Vietnam veterans,[4] but they are persisting anxieties that can occur in any of us following a traumatic experience.

Anxiety disease is a term used to describe sudden, terrifying, intensely severe panic attacks that come to apparently normal people, often without warning, and frequently when they are least expected. An estimated 5 percent of the population, mostly women, experience these panic reactions. For many years this anxiety was assumed to be a psychological disorder but, as we will see, increasing evidence now indicates that the root is biological.[5]

THE BIBLE AND ANXIETY

In the Bible "anxiety" is used in two ways, as healthy concern and as fret or worry.

Anxiety in the form of realistic concern is neither condemned nor forbidden. Although Paul could write that he was not anxious (that is, worried) about the possibility of being beaten, cold, hungry, or in danger, he said that he *was* anxious (that is, concerned) about the welfare of the churches. This sincere care for others put a daily pressure on the apostle[6] and made Timothy "genuinely anxious" (concerned and interested) as well.[7]

Anxiety as fret and worry may have been in the psalmist's mind when he wrote that "anxiety was great within me," and that God's consolation brought joy.[8] In his Sermon on the Mount, Jesus taught that we should not be anxious (worrying) about the future or about life's basic needs, such as food and clothing. We have a heavenly Father, Jesus said, who knows what we need and will provide.[9] In the New Testament Epistles, both Peter and Paul echoed this conclusion. "Do not be anxious about anything," we read in Philippians. Instead, Christians are to bring their requests to God, with an attitude of thanksgiving, expecting to experience "the peace of God, which transcends all understanding."[10] We can cast all anxiety upon the Lord because he cares for us.[11]

Anxiety as fret and worry comes when we turn from God, shift the burdens of life on to ourselves and assume, at least by our attitudes and actions, that we alone are responsible for handling problems. Instead of acknowledging God's sovereignty and power, or seeking his kingdom and righteousness first,[12] many of us—both counselors and counselees—slip into sinful self-reliance and preoccupation with our own life pressures.

According to the Bible, there is nothing wrong with honestly facing and trying to deal with the identifiable problems of life. To ignore danger is foolish and wrong. But it also is wrong, and unhealthy, to be immobilized by excessive worry. Our persisting concerns must be committed in prayer to God, who can release us from paralyzing fear or anxiety, and free us to deal realistically with the needs and welfare both of others and of ourselves.

Everyone knows that it isn't easy to "banish anxiety,"[13] or to "not be anxious about anything."[14] It is difficult for people to "cast their burdens on the Lord," to trust that God will meet their needs, to wait for his help and to know when they should take some responsibility for meeting a difficult situation. Anxious people often are impatient people who need help in handling their pressures realistically and within God's perfect time schedule.

The Christian counselor can be an example of one who is calm and trusting in God to meet needs. The counselor also can help counselees see God's promises, recognize his power and influence in our daily lives, and take action when appropriate. For many counselees it also is helpful if they can understand the causes and effects of their persisting anxiety.

The Causes of Anxiety

Counseling textbooks describe several theories about the causes of anxiety. In a little book titled *The Problem of Anxiety,*[15] for example, Freud discussed this condition in terms of his view that personality has three parts: the *id* which consists of instincts that demand immediate gratification, the *ego* which is aware of the external world and keeps the personality in contact with reality, and the *superego* which is the moral sense of right and wrong. According to Freud, anxiety arises (a) when the ego sees a clear threat to the person (this was called realistic anxiety); (b) when the id begins to get so powerful that it threatens to overwhelm the ego and cause the person to act with socially aggressive and sexually unacceptable behavior (neurotic anxiety); or (c) when the superego gets too powerful, causing the person to be overwhelmed by guilt or shame (moral anxiety). Later writers shifted away from this Freudian view and saw anxiety as coming less from an internal instinctual struggle and more as the result of cultural pressures and threats from the world in which we live. Then came an emphasis on learning, with the proposal that anxiety is a condition that we acquire through conditioning.[16] More recent writers have focused attention on the biological basis of anxiety.[17]

Sifting through these and other theories we might conclude that anxiety arises from threat, conflict, fear, unmet needs, physiology, and individual differences.

1. *Threat.* Following an in-depth survey of the literature, psychologist Rollo May concluded that anxiety is always cued off by a threat to something that an individual considers important.[18] Sometimes anxiety arises because one's life is threatened. More often, we feel threatened (and therefore anxious) because of danger, loss of self-esteem, separation from others, the undermining of our values, or the impact of unconscious influences.

(a) Danger. Crime, war, violent weather, unexplained and unexpected illness, even visits to the dentist, can threaten individuals and create anxiety. At times, most people are anxious about applying for a job, giving a speech, or taking a test. This apprehension comes because the person is uncertain about what to expect and feels helpless to prevent or reduce the threat.

(b) Self-Esteem. Most people like to look good and perform competently. We feel threatened by anything that might harm the self-image or imply (to others or to ourselves) that we are not competent. Many self-conscious people sense a mild anxiety in new social situations because they aren't sure how to act or are threatened by the possible reaction of others. On a more serious level, some people avoid taking exams, accepting a promotion, or risking failure because the possibility of not succeeding is too threatening to their self-esteem.

(c) Separation. It never is easy to be separated from significant other people.

Being on your own can be confusing, and the pain is especially intense when we have been left or rejected by an important person. The death of a loved one, moving, divorce, the breakup of an engagement—these and other separations can leave us feeling uncertain about the future, saddened by a gaping inner emotional void, and threatened as we wonder "What do I do now?"

(d) Values. Many of us who live in democracies tend to take our political freedoms for granted. It can be threatening and anxiety-producing, however, when freedom and other things we value are in danger of being undermined or taken away. The employee who fails to get a valued promotion feels threatened by his or her inability to succeed and advance economically. The child who turns from the family religion or rejects traditional sexual standards is likely to create anxiety (and often anger) in parents whose values are being challenged and perhaps threatened. The politician who gets elected on a political platform that contrasts with our values can make any of us feel threatened and anxious.

(e) Unconscious Influences. Even counselors who reject many of Freud's theories often agree that unconscious influences may be the basis of some anxiety. There are so many (real and imagined) dangers in this world that most people ignore some potential stresses and push these out of their minds. This is not necessarily bad when it is done deliberately and temporarily, but according to Freud, threats and concerns that are pushed into the unconscious can fester while they remain out of sight. Later these unconscious ideas might move toward becoming conscious. That can be threatening because we then are forced to face difficult issues that we don't understand or know how to resolve.

Consider, for example, the case of a young man who was seized with intense anxiety one evening as he watched a ballet. He felt better upon leaving the theater but subsequently decided to go for counseling. As the incident was discussed, the counselor concluded that this man had strong unconscious homosexual tendencies that he was struggling to keep from becoming conscious. During the performance, he was attracted unconsciously to the male ballet dancers. The anxiety that followed was thought to be in reaction to the threat that his defenses might break down, allowing the homosexual tendencies to become apparent to himself and to others.

Such an interpretation is difficult for the counselor to see at first, and there is disagreement among counselors—both Christian and non-Christian—about whether the unconscious even exists.[19] Nevertheless, the young man's panic is a good example of anxiety that arises in response to a specific situation. By considering the times and places when anxiety has been aroused, the counselor often is able to get a clue concerning the specific issue that threatens the counselee.

2. *Conflict.* Conflict is another cause of anxiety. When a person is influenced by two or more pressures there is a sense of uncertainty that often leads to anxiety.[20] Most introductory psychology books suggest that conflicts come from two tendencies: approach and avoidance. To approach is to have a tendency to do something or to move in a direction that will be pleasurable and satisfying. To avoid is to resist doing something, perhaps because it will not be pleasurable or satisfying. There are three basic kinds of conflicts: approach-approach, approach-avoidance, and avoidance-avoidance.

(a) Approach-Approach Conflict. Here is a conflict over the tendency to pursue two desirable but incompatible goals. We may be faced with two dinner invitations on the same night, either of which would be pleasant. Often making such a decision is difficult and sometimes it arouses anxiety.

(b) Approach-Avoidance Conflict. Here is a desire both to do something and not to do it. For example, a person may grapple with the offer of a new job. To accept might bring more pay and opportunity (approach), but it also may bring the necessity of a move and the inconvenience of a training program (avoidance). Making such decisions can involve considerable anxiety.

(c) Avoidance-Avoidance. Here there are two alternatives, both of which may be unpleasant: like living with a painful illness versus having an operation that could also be painful.

Most conflicts involve a struggle between two or more alternatives, each of which may have both approach and avoidance characteristics. A young person may wonder, for example, whether to stay in the present job, shift to another position, or return to school. Each of these alternatives has both positive and negative aspects, and anxiety persists until the choice is made. Sometimes the anxiety lasts after the decision, while the person wonders if he or she made the right decision.

3. *Fear.* Even though some counselors distinguish fear from anxiety, a similar inner apprehension characterizes both.

Henri Nouwen has written that we who live in the twentieth century are a fearful people.[21] The issues that fill our newspapers and our minds are not about the perfect love that casts out fear. Instead, each of us tends to be concerned about our own list of fears. Different people are afraid of failure, the future, nuclear war, rejection, intimacy, success, taking responsibility, conflict, meaninglessness in life (this is sometimes called existential anxiety), sickness, death, loneliness, change,[22] and a host of other real or imagined possibilities. Sometimes these fears can build up in one's mind and create extreme anxiety even in the absence of any real danger.

According to one research study, anxiety often arises because people have irrational beliefs that create fear. When counselees conclude that "everything is sure to get worse," "nothing can be done to change my circumstances," or "I'll never be able to give a public speech," these beliefs create persisting fear. To help these people, the irrational beliefs need to be challenged.[23]

4. *Unmet Needs.* What are the basic needs of human beings? Each of us might have different answers, but one writer[24] suggests that six needs are fundamental:

- Survival (the need to have continued existence).
- Security (the need for emotional and economic stability).
- Sex (the need for intimacy).
- Significance (the need to amount to something and be worthwhile).
- Self-fulfillment (the need to achieve fulfilling goals).
- Selfhood (the need for a sense of identity).

If we fail to meet these or other needs, we can feel anxious, "up-in-the-air," afraid, and frustrated.

But what if all of these needs are met? Would life be complete, satisfying, and anxiety free? Probably not! There still would be questions that transcend life on earth: Where will I go after death? Does existence consist of only a few short years on earth? What is my purpose for living? These are sometimes called existential questions and often they lead to considerable anxiety. We can have no lasting freedom from this kind of anxiety until we are at peace with God, resting in his promises for eternity, and knowing the stability that comes when our sins have been confessed and we are completely forgiven.[25]

5. *Physiology.* Medical research has uncovered a variety of physical disorders that can bring anxiety and paniclike symptoms.[26] Mitral valve prolapse, for example, is a minor heart abnormality that is found in 5 to 15 percent of the adult population, especially women. Over half of these people experience no symptoms and need no treatment. Others, however, have symptoms associated with panic: chest pain, fatigue, dizziness, shortness of breath, rapid heartbeat, and intense anxiety.[27]

Psychiatrist David Sheehan has shown how such biologically produced "anxiety disease" has created terrifying, life-disrupting panic in thousands of people.[28] Sheehan has identified seven stages of anxiety:

- The individual has anxietylike physical symptoms (lightheadedness, for example, breathing difficulty, a racing heartbeat, chest pain, a choking sensation, or intense headaches) that occur without warning and for no apparent reason.
- In time, the symptoms get stronger and occur in the form of intense panic attacks that arise spontaneously and may come several times each week.
- It is not surprising that the person becomes intensely concerned about his or her health. Worried about what is happening to their bodies, patients begin to look like hypochondriacs. Friends and relatives tell them to "snap out of it," or "commit it to the Lord," but the panic and physical concerns persist.
- If panic attacks persist, the individual begins to develop phobias. One lady had a panic attack in an elevator. This was so frightening that she became afraid to get into elevators wondering "what if" the elevator could cause the panic to recur.
- Next, social phobias develop. Afraid of being near other people when panic occurs, the patients begin to withdraw.
- As the disorder gets worse, the person is afraid to go out. Every place or event associated with a prior attack or possible future attack is avoided.
- It is not surprising that all of this leads to depression, hopelessness, feelings of guilt, and sometimes thoughts of suicide.

Once this and other biologically produced anxiety have been diagnosed, medical treatment is often very effective, especially when it is combined with counseling.

6. *Individual Differences.* It is well known that people react differently to anxiety-producing situations. Some people are almost never anxious, some seem anxious most of the time, many are in between. Some people are made anxious by a variety of situations; others find that only one or two issues create apprehension. Free-floating anxiety—the kind with no clear cause—characterizes some; others are made anxious by clearly identified dangers. Then there are those with claustrophobia, hydrophobia, and other phobias—irrational fears of enclosed spaces, water, heights, or other situations, most of which are not in themselves dangerous.

Why do these differences exist? Perhaps the answer comes in terms of a person's past learning, personality, social environment, physiology, and theology.

(a) Learning. Most behavior is learned from personal experience, from watching people, and from the teaching of parents and others. These learning experiences can create anxiety. If a mother is anxious during a thunderstorm, her young child will learn to be anxious. If you are taught that being alone is dangerous, you will feel anxious when nobody else is in the house. The person who has failed an important exam will be anxious about trying again. If some person demands more than you can give, you feel anxious in that person's presence. Since we all have different experiences, we view the world differently and differ in the frequency and intensity of our anxieties.

(b) Personality. It appears that some people are more fearful and "high strung" than others. Some are more sensitive, insecure, hostile, self-centered, or worrisome than others. These personality differences arise from a combination of inherited and learning influences that, in turn, create individual differences in anxiety.

(c) Social Environment. Someone has suggested that most anxiety comes from society: political instability, economic trends, shifting values, mobility that disturbs our sense of rootedness, changing moral standards, or declining interest in religion. These are not the only reasons for anxiety, but the society and neighborhoods in which we live can either stimulate anxiety or give such a secure environment that anxiety is lessened.

(d) Physiology. As we have seen, the presence of disease can stimulate anxiety, and so can dietary imbalance, neurological malfunctioning, and internal chemical changes. The opposite can happen as well. Just as physiological changes can trigger anxiety, so can anxiety create physical reactions.

(e) Theology. Beliefs have a great bearing on one's anxiety level. If God is seen as all-powerful, loving, good, and in ultimate control of the universe (which is the biblical teaching), then there can be trust and security even in the midst of turmoil. If we believe that God forgives when we confess our sins, that he promises eternal life, and that he meets our needs on earth, then there is less cause for anxiety.

In his farewell address to the people of Israel, Moses listed anxiety as one of the consequences of disobedience to God. "The Lord will give you an anxious mind, eyes weary with longing, and a despairing heart. You will live in constant suspense, filled with dread both night and day, never sure of your life."[29]

From this we must not assume that anxiety always indicates disobedience or a lack of faith and neither can we conclude that believers will be less anxious than nonbelievers. The causes of anxiety are too complex for such simplistic explanations. Even so, if you want to understand why people differ in the ways they experience and handle anxiety, try to discover what they believe about God and his universe.

The Effects of Anxiety

Anxiety is not always bad. When there is no anxiety life can be boring, inefficient, and not much fun. A moderate amount of anxiety (not too little, not too much) motivates people and adds zest to life. When we are able to control the situations that create anxiety, it can even be a welcome experience. Perhaps this is one reason why some individuals line up for hours waiting to be "scared to death" by a horror movie or a ride on the "screaming eagle" roller coaster.

When anxiety is intense, prolonged, or uncontrollable, however, people begin to experience crippling physical, psychological, defensive, and spiritual reactions.

(a) Physical Reactions. It is common knowledge that anxiety can produce ulcers, headaches, skin rashes, backaches, and a variety of other physical problems. Almost everyone has experienced stomach discomfort ("butterflies"), shortness of breath, inability to sleep, increased fatigue, loss of appetite, and frequent desire to urinate during times of anxiety. Less conscious are changes in blood pressure, increased muscle tension, a slowing of digestion, and chemical changes in the blood. If these are temporary they cause little, if any, harm. When they persist over time the body begins to break under the pressure. This is the origin of psychosomatic (psychologically caused) illnesses.

Research on the effects of stress shows how busy people—those who have much to accomplish but feel pressured by limited time—often wear out their own bodies by the overproduction of adrenaline. In what has been termed "stress disease," some people push themselves to the point of collapse, and then wonder why their busy and anxious lifestyles lead them to feel worn-out, unable to sleep, and prone to sickness.[30]

(b) Psychological Reactions. Everyone who has taken an examination or applied for a hard-to-get job knows how anxiety can influence psychological functioning. Anxiety can reduce productivity (so we don't get much done), hinder interpersonal relations (so we have trouble getting along with others), stifle creativity and originality, dull the personality, and interfere with the ability to think or remember. The student whose mind goes "blank" during a test, or the actor who forgets his lines on stage, both show evidence of anxiety-produced memory failure. In extreme cases, anxiety so immobilizes an individual that he or she is unable to function independently as an adult.

(c) Defensive Reactions. When anxiety builds, most people unconsciously rely on behavior and thinking that dulls the pain of anxiety and makes coping easier. These defensive reactions are seen often in counseling.[31] They include ignoring the feelings of anxiety, pretending the anxiety-producing situation does not exist, convincing oneself that there is "nothing to worry about," rationally explaining away the symptoms, blaming someone else for one's problems, developing physical illnesses that distract from the anxiety, or slipping back into childish ways of responding. Sometimes people escape through alcohol, drugs, or withdrawal into various kinds of mental illness. All of these are ways of trying to cope.

(d) Spiritual Reactions. Anxiety can motivate us to seek the divine help that might be ignored otherwise. Although foxhole conversions were probably less common than we once thought, there is evidence that many people do turn to God in times of stress.[32]

But anxiety can also drive people away from God at a time when he is most needed. Fraught with worry and distracted by pressures, even religious people find there is little time for prayer, decreased desire or ability to concentrate on Bible reading, reduced interest in church worship services, bitterness about heaven's seeming silence in the face of crisis, and anger because God seems to let bad things happen to good people. The Christian counselor may be welcomed as a spiritual minister, or rejected because he or she represents a God who has permitted the stresses and left the impression that he doesn't care.

Counseling and Anxiety

It is not easy to counsel the anxious person, partially because it can be difficult to uncover and resolve the causes of anxiety, and partly because anxiety can be psychologically contagious. Anxious people often make others anxious, including the counselor who is trying to help. To counsel anxious people, therefore, the counselor must first be alert to his or her own feelings.

1. *Recognizing the Counselor's Own Anxieties.* When you, as a counselor, feel anxious in the presence of an anxious counselee, you might ask yourself several questions: What in this situation is making me anxious? Is the counselee anxious about something that makes me anxious too? What does my anxiety tell me about the counselee and about myself? By considering one's own anxiety it sometimes is possible to gain insight into the counselee's anxiety. These questions also enable the counselor to keep from confusing his or her own anxieties with those of the counselee.[33]

2. *Calming Tension.* Counseling is unlikely to be effective if the counselee is too tense to concentrate. To deal with this tension, let the counselee see that you are a calm, caring, and reassuring person. Encourage the counselee to sit quietly, breathe deeply, and try to relax the muscles. Sometimes it helps to tighten different groups of muscles, such as the fist or the shoulders, and then let the muscles relax as freely as possible. Some counselees find it helpful to close their eyes and imagine that they are relaxing on a beach or sitting in some other nonthreatening situation.[34] Try to reduce distracting influences such as clutter in the office or background music that has high volume or a fast pace.

None of this removes the underlying causes of anxiety, but by helping people feel more relaxed and in control, you direct attention away from the symptoms. Then counselees are better able to focus attention on the sources of anxiety.

3. *Showing Love.* Love has been called the greatest therapeutic force of all,[35] but nowhere is this more true than in the reduction of fear and anxiety. The Bible states that "perfect love drives out fear."[36] "The enemy of fear is love," writes one well-known counselor. "The way to put off fear, then, is to put on love. . . . Love is self-giving; fear is self-protecting. Love moves toward others; fear shrinks away from them. . . . The more fear, the less love; the more love, the less fear."[37] The counselor can help to drive out fear and anxiety when he or she shows love mixed with patient understanding. Counselees can be introduced to the love and help that comes from Christ,[38] and anxious people can also find relief when they are encouraged to reach out in loving acts to others.

4. *Identifying Causes.* Anxiety and fear are God-created emotions. They warn of danger or internal conflict and they rarely disappear solely in response to the counselor's reassurances or expressions of Christian love. The sensitive helper does not tell the counselee to "buck up" or "stop being anxious." Most of us get no help from the well-meaning but naive Christian who proclaims that worry is a sin that can be stopped at will. Instead, the effective counselor seeks to assist the counselee in the difficult task of uncovering the sources of anxiety. This can be done in several ways.

(a) Observation. In counseling sessions does the counselee show evidence of added anxiety (shifting position, deep breathing, perspiration) when certain topics are discussed? What are these topics?

(b) Reflection. Can the counselee suggest circumstances that have raised or currently raise anxiety? It might be helpful to ask, "When are you most anxious?" "When are you not anxious?" "When was the last time you felt really anxious?" "What was happening in your life at that time?" Never underestimate the counselee's insights into the reasons for his or her own anxiety.

(c) Contemplation. As a counselor, remind yourself of the causes of anxiety listed a few pages back. Ask yourself if any of these might be creating the counselee's anxiety. Raise some of these issues and watch for signs of anxiety as the counselee responds to your questions. Then discuss your hunches.

In all of this, remember the need for patience and understanding. By its very nature, anxiety often arises in response to threats that are vague and difficult to identify. By pushing the counselee to "snap out of it" or to "hurry and tell me what is wrong," we increase the anxiety, create more confusion, and risk losing or alienating the anxious person. Once again it is important to emphasize loving patience.

5. *Making Interventions.* Anxiety differs from person to person; each may have a unique set of symptoms and there may be different forms of treatment. The individual who fears giving a speech, for example, may not be similar to the person who is afraid of heights or another who has sudden and seemingly irrational panic attacks.[39]

In spite of these differences, anxiety-specialist David Sheehan suggests an approach to treatment that can be adapted to all individuals.[40]

(a) Biological Intervention. As we have seen, anxiety sometimes has a physical cause and needs to be treated medically. Often a physician will work in cooperation with a nonmedical counselor.

Should this cooperation include the giving of anxiety-reducing medications? Some psychiatrists and other physicians too quickly prescribe drugs when they may not be needed; some pastors and other Christian counselors too quickly criticize the use of medications when they could calm the counselee and facilitate counseling. Try to work with a physician who is cautious about the overuse of tranquilizers but who is willing to prescribe and monitor the use of such medication when anxiety seems high. Some counselees may need help in overcoming a resistance to or bias against the use of medications.

(b) Behavioral Intervention. Several years ago behavior therapy was introduced as a form of treatment that appeared to be especially effective with anxious and phobic individuals. Based on the assumption that anxiety responses frequently are learned, counselors attempted to teach people how to be more relaxed in the presence of anxiety-producing situations. Sometimes, for example, counselees would be taught to relax physically and then they would be exposed slowly to feared objects. At other times, counselees would be encouraged to act (pretend) as if they were in an anxious situation and the counselor would teach effective ways to cope. Techniques such as these are still used widely and successfully. They appear to be most effective when anxiety is known to be produced by a specific object or situation that the counselee can learn to control.[41]

(c) Environmental Intervention. Sometimes the best and most direct way to deal with anxiety is to change one's lifestyle, relationships, place of residence, or career direction. Consider, for example, the lawbreaker who is anxious about getting caught. His anxiety can be eliminated by becoming a law-abiding citizen. Are there other, perhaps less obvious, changes that the counselee could make to change anxiety-producing circumstances or situations? Such changes may need the encouragement and guidance that come from a supportive counselor.

6. *Encouraging Action.* The purpose of counseling is not to eliminate all anxiety. Instead, the goal is to assist counselees in discovering the sources of their anxiety. Then they must learn how to cope. Help counselees see that more is to be gained by facing and trying to overcome the anxiety—even though this can be risky—than by persisting in a state of inner tension that may be familiar but painful. Encourage counselees to admit their apprehensions but then to plan what must be done if they are to handle the anxiety-producing situations. Are there skills or pieces of information that the counselee needs before taking action? Try to avoid intellectual talk that may sound reassuring but does nothing to help people plan and take direct specific action in dealing with anxiety. At some time, you may want to suggest that real courage involves a willingness to move ahead even when we are fearful and anxious.

7. *Giving Support.* Earlier it was mentioned that anxious counselees get little help from counselors who are tense or impatient. Instead, the helper must be calm, supportive, and patient as he or she watches progress that may be very slow. Sometimes there seems to be nothing counselees can do to take action against the source of their anxieties. At such times they need to feel the caring support of a warm relationship with an understanding counselor.

8. *Encouraging a Christian Response.* The Bible gives unusually specific and clear directions for overcoming anxiety. In Phil. 4:6 we are instructed to stop being anxious about anything. As we have seen, however, it practically is impossible to stop worrying by an act of the will. Such deliberate effort directs our attention to the problem and can increase anxiety instead of decreasing it. A better approach is to focus on activities and thoughts that indirectly reduce anxiety. The Bible shows how this can be done and in so doing it gives a formula to be shared with counselees:

(a) Rejoice. This is a command, repeated twice in Phil. 4:4. When the world is dark and dreary, the Christian still can "rejoice in the Lord." This is because Jesus promised he would never leave us, that he would give us peace, that he would send his Holy Spirit (whom Jesus called the Counselor) to stay with us and remind us of truths we need to remember, and that he would come again to take believers to a place prepared for us in heaven. With this knowledge we can believe in God and not let our minds be troubled or fearful.[42]

(b) Be Gentle. The Greek word translated "gentleness" in Phil. 4:5 has no real equivalent in English. It means: let everybody see your kind, sweet, gentle, considerate, gracious attitude.[43] These qualities do not come naturally. They come with God's help and as we work to control our tendencies to condemn others or demand our rights. A negative condemning outlook on life builds anxiety; a gracious forbearing attitude reduces it.

(c) Pray. Phil. 4:6 gives instructions about prayer in times of anxiety. Such prayer is to be about everything (even small details), should include definite and precise petitions, and should involve thanksgiving for God's goodness. "If you do this," the Bible promises,[44] "you will experience God's peace, which is far more wonderful than the human mind can understand." Clearly prayer is a major antidote to anxiety.

(d) Think. Anxiety often comes when we think continually about human weaknesses, evil influences in the world, and things that might go wrong. Phil. 4:8 instructs us, instead, to let our minds dwell on positive ideas including that which is noble, right, pure, lovely, admirable, excellent, and praiseworthy. This is not suggesting that we deny problems or ignore dangers. In contrast, the scriptures are giving evidence for the power of positive, biblically based thinking.

(e) Act. The Apostle Paul sets himself up as a model for action. "Whatever you have learned or received or heard from me, or seen in me—*put it into practice.* And the God of peace will be with you."[45] The Christian's task is to *do* what the Bible teaches and not simply to sit listening.[46] Anxiety reduction involves obedience and godly behavior even in the midst of anxiety.

Preventing Anxiety

Philippians 4 gives a formula for preventing anxiety as well as an approach to counseling. When people can be helped to rejoice, be gentle, pray, think, and act in accordance with scriptural teachings, there is progress toward anxiety prevention and control.

A study of military personnel on combat duty in Vietnam revealed other ways by which people defend themselves against anxiety.[47] First, there is the development of self-confidence—a belief in one's abilities to meet the challenges and dangers of life. Second, there is involvement in work and other activities that expend nervous energy and distract from the anxiety-producing situation. This can be a healthy way to prevent excessive anxiety, unless the work becomes compulsive and a way to escape from the real dangers of life. Third, there is faith in the ability and confidence of leaders who can deal with the anxiety. Fourth, there is belief in God.

1. *Trust in God.* The person who learns to walk in daily contact with God comes to agree with the hymn writer who wrote, "I know not what the future holds, but I know who holds the future." This conviction can bring great security even when others are inclined to be anxious.

At times, however, such trust leads to a blind denial of reality, to a refusal to accept responsibilities, or to a rigidity of thinking that ultimately prevents the person from adapting to changing circumstances. In contrast, the Bible encourages realistic confrontation with problems and flexible decision-making. This lets people grow and adapt to change or danger, even as they maintain an underlying confidence in the sovereignty and wisdom of an all-powerful God.

2. *Learn to Cope.* Coping with the causes of anxiety, when and before they arise, can prevent the development of anxiety. Such coping involves the following, each of which can become part of a person's lifestyle:

- Admitting fears, insecurities, conflicts, and anxieties when they arise.
- Talking these over with someone else—on a regular basis if necessary.
- Building self-esteem.
- Acknowledging that separation hurts, attempting to maintain contact with separated friends, and building new relationships with others.
- Seeking help from God and others in meeting one's needs.
- Learning to communicate more effectively.
- Learning principles and techniques of relaxation.
- Periodically evaluating one's priorities, life goals, and time management.[48]

3. *Keep Things in Perspective.* Whenever we find ourselves in a threatening, challenging, or potentially dangerous situation, most of us ponder the circumstances and try to determine how well we might cope. This process, sometimes called "cognitive appraisal," helps to explain why two people may look at the same situation but respond in very different ways. How we evaluate a situation depends largely on one's perspective or point of view.

There is some evidence that personality characteristics influence these perceptions. Some people see the bad in everything; others are more optimistic and inclined to look on the bright side of life. To help prevent anxiety, we can encourage people (especially those who tend to be negative) to keep a realistic perspective that does not always conclude immediately that the worst is likely to happen.[49]

4. *Reach Out to Others.* People who care about others and reach out to give help tend to be the people who cope best with the pressures and anxieties of life.[50] People helping and the bearing of one another's burdens[51] may be one of the best ways to control and prevent anxiety.

Conclusions about Anxiety

Many counselors believe that anxiety is a basic part of all psychological problems; it goes along with most of the issues discussed in the following chapters.

Anxiety warns people of danger and motivates us to take action. When it creates panic or immobilizes individuals, the anxiety is harmful. When it challenges us to deal more effectively with the challenges of life, it can be helpful.

Jesus put all of this in perspective when he spoke about worry in the Sermon on the Mount. God knows about our needs and anxieties, Jesus said. If we give him first priority in our lives, we can rest assured that our needs will be supplied[52] and there will be no need to worry. This is a message that makes Christian counseling unique.

SUGGESTIONS FOR FURTHER READING

Beck, A. T., and G. Emery. *Anxiety Disorders and Phobias: A Cognitive Perspective.* New York: Basic Books, 1985.

Benson, Herbert. *Beyond the Relaxation Response.* New York: Times Books, 1984.*

* Books marked with an asterisk (*) are especially suited for counselees to read.

Gittelman, Rachel, ed. *Anxiety Disorders in Childhood.* New York: Guildord, 1986.
Last, Cynthia G., and Michel Hersen. *Handbook of Anxiety Disorders.* New York: Pergamon, 1987.
May, Rollo. *The Meaning of Anxiety.* Rev. ed. New York: Norton, 1977.
Osborne, Cecil. *Release from Fear and Anxiety.* Waco, Tex.: Word, 1976.
Sheehan, David V. *The Anxiety Disease.* New York: Charles Scribner's Sons, 1983.*
Wilson, R. Reid. *Don't Panic: Taking Control of Anxiety Attacks.* New York: Harper & Row, 1986.*

* Books marked with an asterisk (*) are especially suited for counselees to read.

7

Loneliness

DR. N. IS A BRIGHT YOUNG PROFESSOR at a university in Canada. She is well liked by her teaching colleagues, popular with her students, and competent as a researcher. Last year she got the outstanding teacher of the year award, and several people have predicted that she is well on the way to building a successful career, both as a scholar and as a researcher.

Few people know, however, that intense feelings of loneliness are hidden behind Dr. N.'s vivacious personality and intellectually competent manner. In a magazine article she read that one person in six doesn't even have a single friend with whom she or he can talk about personal problems and that 40 percent of the population feels shy and isolated. Dr. N. feels like this is a description of her life. Every day she is surrounded by people, but she doesn't know any of them personally, and most of them don't even call her by her first name. Her family is miles away, so at the end of each busy day she goes back to her apartment, talks to the cat, and reads by herself. There is not much else to do.

Dr. N. doesn't feel comfortable looking for friends in bars, and she feels like a misfit in church. The people there all seem to have their own friends, and nobody knows how to relate to a single woman—especially if they find that she is a university professor with a Ph.D. Last winter she went on a cruise and met some nice people, but they are scattered around the country and too far away to be friends.

Despite her professional competence, Dr. N. feels like a personal failure. She is an attractive person with good social skills and a bright mind. She knows that God accepts and cares for her, but she also knows of her need for human companionship—people with whom she can relax and be herself. Her loneliness makes her feel depressed, and recently she has been wondering if she should resign from her position and move someplace else. She knows, however, that the loneliness would still go with her.

Recently Dr. N. decided to talk with a counselor. "I've been wondering if something is wrong with me when I am surrounded by so many people but still feel lonely," she said.

This lady appears to have no deep-seated emotional problems. She needs another person's perspective and help in finding ways to overcome the feelings of loneliness that now appear to be interfering with her ability to concentrate at work.

Loneliness has been called "the world's most common mental health problem,"[1] "one of the most universal sources of human suffering,"[2] an "almost permanent condition for millions" of people, regardless of class, race, or sex.[3] It is an experience that hits all of us at times; a painful inner emptiness that may flee after a few minutes or persist for a lifetime.

Based on a landmark study of loneliness, sociologist Robert Weiss estimates that a quarter of the American population feels extremely lonely at some time during any given month.[4] It is a condition that effects people of all ages, including young children, but researchers agree that loneliness soars during the teenage years and reaches its highest peak in people between ages eighteen and twenty-five.[5] Although it is seen in all cultures, loneliness occurs most often in societies, like ours, that emphasize individualism.[6] Lonely people appear in all vocational groups, but there is evidence that highly ambitious, "fast-track," upwardly mobile people (including the much discussed yuppies and baby boomers) have an especially high incidence of loneliness.[7] The same is true among leaders who often feel alone at the top, workaholics consumed by activities that interfere with personal intimacy, and counselors who spend their lives giving to others but failing to build closeness in their own lives. One study found that pastors and their spouses experience significantly more loneliness (as well as burn-out and diminished marital adjustment) than a comparable group of Christian lay people.[8]

Loneliness is the painful awareness that we lack close and meaningful contact with others. It involves a feeling of inner emptiness, isolation, and intense longing. Even when they are surrounded by others, lonely people often feel left out, unwanted, rejected, or misunderstood. Frequently there are feelings of sadness, discouragement, restlessness, and anxiety, accompanied by a longing to be wanted and needed by at least one other human being. There may be an intense desire to reach out, but often the lonely person feels frustrated and unable to initiate, continue, or experience a close relationship.[9]

You may not find it surprising that many lonely people tend to look down on themselves. Weighted down with feelings of low self-esteem and worthlessness, the lonely often think, "nobody wants me so I guess I'm not worth anything." Sometimes there is a sense of hopelessness and a strong desire for almost any kind of relationship that might end the awful pain of involuntary aloneness. Many people try to find relief in bars, encounter groups, church meetings, or involvement with the billion-dollar "loneliness industry" that provides seminars, dating services, health spas, singles vacation trips, self-help books, and a variety of other promised antidotes to loneliness. Even when they do have human contact, many lonely people still are unable to build significant relationships or gain emotional satisfactions from others.

Loneliness can be transient and situational or chronic and long-lasting. Transient-situational loneliness lasts from a few minutes to a few months. Usually it arises because of some event, like moving from close friends, temporary separation from family members, a misunderstanding or disagreement, divorce or death, a young person's move to college, or graduation and the subsequent scattering of one's classmates. Chronic-persisting loneliness more often comes because of an individual's shyness, a poor self-image, self-condemnation, socially insensitive behavior that drives people away, or self-defeating thoughts such as "I must never be alone," "I've got to be the life of the party," or "I'm not worth anything unless I get into their group."

Most of us have had the experience of feeling lonely even when we are surrounded by people. At other times we may be by ourselves but feel no loneliness at all. This has led some psychologists to conclude that loneliness is primarily an inner feeling that doesn't always depend on whether or not others are present. The inner feeling of loneliness comes when we perceive ourselves to be isolated from others, fail in our efforts to find friends, or lack the social skills needed to relate to others. Often this sense of isolation is felt when the person is separated from God and feels that life has no meaning or purpose.[10] Such persons need a committed and growing relationship with God, preferably within the confines of a concerned community of believers.

It is important to distinguish loneliness from solitude. Loneliness comes when we are forced to be alone; solitude is a voluntary withdrawal from other people. Loneliness sweeps over us and hangs on in spite of our best efforts to cast it off; solitude can be started and terminated at will. Loneliness is painful, draining, and unpleasant; solitude can be refreshing, rejuvenating, and enjoyable. People talk to counselors about the problem of loneliness; solitude rarely gets mentioned in the counseling room.

The Bible and Loneliness

Shortly after Adam's creation, God declared: "It is not good for the man to be alone. I will make a helper suitable for him."[11] Adam and God had talked together in the garden, but the Creator knew that human beings need other humans if they are to get along effectively. So God created Eve and instructed the couple to "be fruitful and multiply and fill the earth." In fellowship with God and with each other, Adam and Eve were neither alone nor lonely.

When they fell into sin, the first married couple broke their communion with God and a wedge was driven between husband and wife. Selfishness and interpersonal tension came into their relationship and feelings of loneliness must, at that point, have entered the human race.

Loneliness is rarely discussed in the Scriptures,[12] but it is seen repeatedly, even in the lives of Bible heroes such as Moses, Job, Nehemiah, Elijah, and Jeremiah. David once wrote that he was "lonely and afflicted."[13] Jesus, who knows all of our infirmities, surely was lonely in Gethsemane. John ended his life alone (and perhaps lonely) on the Isle of Patmos, and the Apostle Paul apparently spent his last days in prison. Writing to Timothy, the aging Paul noted that his friends had left, that some had forsaken him, and that he needed his young colleague to "make every effort to come to me soon."[14]

The entire Bible focuses on our need for communion with God and for people, especially Christians, to love, help, encourage, forgive, and care for one another. A growing relationship with God and with others becomes the basis for any solution to the problem of loneliness. But how do individuals build a relationship with God or with others?[15] To begin, it is helpful if we consider the causes of loneliness.

The Causes of Loneliness

The many causes of loneliness could be grouped into five categories: social, developmental, psychological, situational, and spiritual.

1. *Social Causes.* Loneliness often increases during times of change and turmoil.[16] This may account for the higher reports of loneliness among young people in

the post-high school years. It also suggests that rapid social changes in our era of history may be creating more loneliness by isolating people from close contact with each other. Social influences that increase loneliness include the following:

(a) Technology. As government, business, and education get "bigger" and more impersonal, people feel smaller and less needed. As efficiency, productivity, and convenience have become more important, there is less time for developing deep, satisfying relationships. Complex technology increases the need for specialists, and these people sometimes have neither the time nor the ability to communicate with nonspecialists. As a result, relationships are shallow, understanding decreases, and loneliness becomes more prevalent.

(b) Mobility. Modern transportation that makes moving easier, the development of large corporations, and sometimes the lure of a better life elsewhere all contribute to widespread mobility, especially in the United States and Canada. This tears up friendships, separates families, eliminates neighborhood and community spirit, and causes people to avoid close friendships that could end later in painful separations.

(c) Urbanization. As people have moved close together, especially in cities, there has been a tendency to withdraw from others. Sometimes there is a fear of strangers or of inner city crime and this leads to suspicion and withdrawal. Living in the midst of crowds, noise, and commotion, some city people prefer to avoid additional close proximity to others, but this can lead to intense isolation and loneliness.

(d) Television. This modern invention enhances separation both by program content, that can promote superficiality and arouse fear, and by the viewing habits of people who sit in front of the screen, seldom communicating directly with each other. Caught up in the unreality of television productions, it is easy to live one's life through the people on the screen instead of interacting with neighbors and relatives. Swayed by the attractive presentations of some television religious leaders, it is easy to avoid the local church with the supportive relationships that come from the body of believers.

Along with its many benefits, our changing, dehumanizing, technological society has disrupted people, shattered many traditional sources of security, and created the potential for even greater isolation and greater loneliness.

2. *Developmental Causes.* Following his survey of the literature on loneliness, Ellison concluded that three basic developmental needs must be met if loneliness is to be avoided. These are the needs for attachment, acceptance, and the acquiring of social skills.[17]

(a) Attachment. An impressive body of literature has supported the conclusion that people, especially children, need to feel close bonds with other human beings.[18] When children are separated from their parents there is anxiety and an emotional aloofness. If one parent remains, or if the departed parents return, the child clings to the father or mother, apparently afraid that separation will occur again. When we consider the increasing divorce rate and the alarming prevalence of child abuse,[19] it is easy to recognize why many young people feel alienated and unattached. These people often grow up feeling lonely.

(b) Acceptance. Parents communicate acceptance in a variety of ways; by touching, by spending time with their children, by listening, by discipline, by showing affection. When these clues are missing, or when children are ignored or excessively criticized, they begin to feel worthless. They conclude that they don't belong and they either withdraw from others or force themselves on others in a way that brings more rejection. It then becomes difficult to trust people and this inability to trust prevents close relationships from forming.

We who are older respond in similar ways when we feel unaccepted. Parents who feel they are no longer accepted or wanted by their children, spouses who feel rejected by their mates, pastors who feel unappreciated by their congregations, or employees who feel shunned by their employers and coworkers—all are examples of people who feel unaccepted, not needed, and often lonely.

(c) Acquiring Skills. All of us know people who are social misfits. They are insensitive to the needs or attitudes of others, and they do not know how to build smooth interpersonal relationships. They may try to manipulate or force themselves on others but this only brings rejection, frustration, low self-esteem, and increased loneliness. Such people have never learned how to get along. They keep trying, fail continually, and remain in their loneliness.

These lonely feelings are accentuated if we grow up surrounded by social values that undermine closeness. "The intense emphasis on freedom in our society has promoted an emphasis on individualism and personal rights that militates against responsible long-term relationships in which intimacy can be developed."[20] Individuals in our society tend to value things more than people. We judge a person's worth by his or her achievements and outward appearance. People who aren't affluent or outwardly successful tend to be ignored and this can increase their loneliness.

3. *Psychological Causes.* To some extent loneliness depends on perceptions—the way we look at the world. Circumstances that make one person feel overburdened with human contacts, may leave another feeling lonely. The college student who is alone in the library on a Tuesday night may not feel lonely, but the same student who is left alone on Saturday night may feel rejected and lonely. One person may live alone and not feel lonely because she believes she has many friends. Another person may be surrounded by people but still feel lonely because "most people have more friends than I do." Chronically lonely people sometimes conclude that nothing can be done to improve the condition, so they sink further into their loneliness.

In addition, loneliness appears more often in people who have low self-esteem, inability to communicate, self-defeating attitudes, lack of control, hostility, and fear.

(a) Low Self-Esteem. When we have low opinions of ourselves, we underestimate our worth and either withdraw from others or overexaggerate our qualities so that we appear conceited. Both reactions interfere with our closeness to others. It is difficult to build friendships when we have little self-confidence. It is not easy to develop intimacy when we feel unattractive or afraid of being rejected.

According to one writer,[21] good self-esteem gives us the confidence to build close relationships which, in turn, decreases loneliness. In contrast, low self-esteem makes the person feel weak or shy. This results in a tendency to withdraw, accompanied sometimes by an excessive need to depend on others. When others are not available there is intense insecurity and deep loneliness.

(b) Inability to Communicate. Communication breakdowns are at the root of many interpersonal problems. When people are unwilling to communicate, or when they don't know how to communicate effectively, there can be a persisting isolation and loneliness even when these individuals are surrounded by others.

(c) Self-Defeating Attitudes. Shortly after the Second World War, a Swiss counselor named Paul Tournier wrote a penetrating book on loneliness.[22] Its message is surprisingly relevant today. Loneliness, wrote Tournier, comes because we have developed:

- Parliamentary attitudes by which we see life as a big tournament with success as the winner's prize and competition as a way of life.
- Independent attitudes that cause us to act as if we were each rugged individualists, absolutely autonomous, independent of God and of others.
- Possessive attitudes by which we are driven to get what we can for ourselves.
- Demanding attitudes that cause us to fight for our rights and demand "fairness."

All of this implies something that has not yet been mentioned. Loneliness, at least to some extent, may be one's own fault. People increase the potential for loneliness when they are intensely competitive, struggling for self-sufficiency, preoccupied with themselves and their successes, inclined to be critical or intolerant, holding on to grudges, or demanding attention from others. When such attitudes persist, other people are driven away and loneliness intensifies.

(d) Lack of Control. A voluntary walk by yourself in the countryside can be a pleasant and relaxing interlude, but to be abandoned in the same location can be a horrible anxiety-producing experience. The difference depends on the person's ability to be in control of a situation. Hermits, artists, or people on personal religious retreats can be productive and motivated even though they may be miles from other people. In contrast individuals who are widowed, divorced, abandoned, or isolated in prison cells can feel intensely lonely because of their forced isolation. This has led one writer to conclude that "having control over any given social situation decides the difference between feeling lonely and being alone. . . . Lack of control is the essence of loneliness."[23]

(e) Hostility. Have you ever noticed that some people appear to be innately angry? Even when they smile or make jokes, there is an underlying attitude of vengeance and hostility. The causes for this are complex[24] but sometimes angry people feel thwarted, frustrated, or resentful because of real or imagined injustice. On occasion the anger comes from self-hatred that is turned outward to others. When such thinking is accompanied by negative attitudes and constant complaining, others are driven away. This creates both loneliness and continuing unhappiness.

(f) Fear. I have a plaque that reads, "People are lonely because they build walls instead of bridges." This isn't the only cause of loneliness, but sometimes people do erect barriers to keep others out. Some hide behind facades, pretending to be competent, always unruffled or in control and never bothered by criticism or emotion. But behind the masks there is loneliness, a feeling of isolation, and fear: fear of intimacy, fear of being known, fear of rejection, fear of acting inappropriately in social situations, fear of having one's work or plans disrupted, or fear of being hurt.[25] This kind of loneliness is painful, but for these people it seems less painful than the fear and insecurity of contact with others.

4. *Situational Causes.* Some people are lonely because of the special circumstances in which they find themselves. Young people away from home for the first time,[26] affluent people who seem to be in a financial class all by themselves, leaders who have moved ahead of or away from their peers, extremely talented people, those who are intensely dedicated to a sport or artistic venture, foreigners and newcomers to an area, older people who live alone, individuals who have been recently widowed or divorced, compulsive workaholics—all have been identified as people who especially are prone to loneliness. We must not assume, however, that all of these people are lonely.

Some researchers have suggested that shyness, and the resulting tendency to withdraw from people, may have a genetic basis that could contribute to later loneliness.[27] People with diseased or deformed bodies can also be prone to loneliness. In our society these individuals tend to be rejected by healthy people who say, in effect, "You are different," or "I don't know how to act around you." As a result of this rejection, handicapped people tend to withdraw. Their physical conditions often prevent easy access to others and further loneliness can result.

5. *Spiritual Causes.* In a famous prayer Augustine once expressed our need for God: "Thou has formed us for Thyself and our hearts are restless till they find rest in Thee." God created human beings for himself, but he respected us enough to let us decide whether or not to rebel. This, of course, is what we have done, and ever since our hearts have been restless because we have been cut off from our Creator.

At the time of creation, Adam and Eve enjoyed intimacy with God and with each other, but when sin entered the human race, intimacy was replaced by misunderstanding, defensiveness, blaming, self-interest, and power struggles.[28] Loneliness often comes because sin has alienated us from God and from one another. Instead of turning to God in repentance and seeking restitution with fellow human beings, thousands of lonely people seek to escape from their loneliness through involvement with drugs, sex, encounter group experiences, work, sports, or a host of other activities that fail to remove the inner restlessness. When God is ignored and sin is unconfessed, loneliness is likely to persist.

The Effects of Loneliness

What does loneliness do to people? What are its symptoms? How can it be spotted by a counselor? Because of human uniqueness, each person will show loneliness in a different way.

Perhaps the most obvious indication of loneliness is *isolation* from people, often accompanied by periodic but futile attempts to reach out to others. Remember, however, that many "loners," older people, singles, and others who live by themselves are not lonely even though they appear to have little contact with others.

Low self-esteem and feelings of worthlessness can be symptoms as well as causes of loneliness. Failure in relationships or in activities can lower self-esteem and lead to greater loneliness. Unable to relate to others as they would like, lonely people sometimes withdraw into self-centered thinking, a poor-little-me attitude, a belief that nobody understands, and a conviction that things will never get better.

Depression is also common. Some chronically lonely people are not depressed and some depressed people are not lonely, but many are both.[29] Lonely people sometimes have a hopelessness that can lead to despair and even thoughts of suicide. When loneliness is too great, suicide becomes a "way out" that might also give a clear message to the people who didn't seem to care.

In contrast, some people resort to *exhibitionist behavior,* like becoming the class clown, wearing outlandish clothing that is likely to be noticed, or acting in attention-getting ways. A few cover their loneliness by workaholic behavior, frequent travel, or accumulating possessions.

Alcoholism and drug abuse are also ways to escape. Some people turn to these in an attempt to find friends among other drinkers or to dull the pain of being alone.

Others express their frustrations through *violence.* Based on a review of research reports, one writer concluded that "very lonely people, who get angry rather than depressed, will be prone to express their lonely frustration in destructive ways. I do not think it is mere coincidence that we are witnessing an unequaled rise in violence and at the same time loneliness is so pervasive and intense."[30] When loneliness is expressed in violence or delinquency, this may become a release from pain and a cry for attention.

Sometimes the loneliness is expressed physically. Evidence suggests that lonely people are more likely to suffer from *physical problems* such as heart disease or high blood pressure.[31] There now is convincing evidence that stress (including the stress of loneliness) affects the immune system and reduces the body's ability to resist disease.[32] Like most of the problems discussed in this book, loneliness can sometimes be hidden from the casual observer, but it influences the body and sometimes shows itself through physical illness.

Counseling and Loneliness

There are many suggestions for dealing with loneliness: get involved in busy activities, reach out to people in need, join a volunteer organization, find fulfillment in Christ, learn to be assertive, and a host of others. Many of these remedies can dull the pain of loneliness for a while, but they fail to deal with the problem at the deepest level and they rarely produce lasting solutions.[33]

How can the problem be handled more effectively?

1. *Admitting the Problem.* Loneliness has a negative connotation in our society. For many people, admitting that they are lonely is like admitting that they are social misfits, unattractive, or unable to relate to others. Counselees can be reminded, however, that everyone is lonely at times. When people feel lonely, the first steps toward recovery are to admit the loneliness, to acknowledge that it is painful, and to decide to do something about the problem.

2. *Considering the Causes.* Loneliness, as we have seen, can arise from a variety of causes. If these causes can be identified (through discussion with the counselee and through probing questions), then it is possible to work on the sources of the loneliness rather than trying to eliminate the symptoms. Prior to counseling, you might want to review the causes of loneliness listed earlier in this chapter. By keeping this information in mind, the counselor can be alert to possible causes in the counselee's life and thinking.

3. *Changing One's Thinking.* In considering the causes, try to remember that some things can be changed (such as a poor self-concept or inappropriate social

skills) but other issues are unchangeable. The lonely widow, for example, cannot bring back her husband, and neither can we stop the modern tendency of people to move frequently—with the alienation and loneliness that this produces.

Even when circumstances cannot be altered, however, counselees still can be helped to change their attitudes toward loneliness. Often there is self-pity, pessimistic thinking, and ruminations about the unfairness of life. All of this needs to be gently but firmly challenged. Loneliness is less likely to persist if people can be helped to see the bright side of life, even in the midst of disturbing personal and social change.

One counselor encourages lonely people to develop "a lifestyle of keeping in touch."[34] When individuals avoid relationships with others, hide behind social masks, or withdraw into lives of inactivity, then loneliness is intensified. In contrast, work, play, creative hobbies, awareness of the daily news, and church attendance are some of the activities that keep counselees in contact with people and events. This contact can pull any of us out of loneliness or a tendency toward self-centered brooding.

Reminders about the power, sovereignty, and compassion of God can also help people change their attitudes and see life in a more realistic perspective even when surrounding circumstances seem to be unchangeable and defeating. Sometimes it also helps to remind your counselees that loneliness rarely lasts forever.

4. *Developing Self-Esteem.* Lonely people must be helped to see and acknowledge their strengths, abilities, and spiritual gifts as well as their weaknesses. Most of us go through life talking to ourselves (usually not out loud), and often we convince ourselves that we are unattractive, incompetent or disliked by others.[35] At times, we compare ourselves to people who are more popular or successful, and in so doing we become convinced of our own inferiorities. As a result, individuals develop low self-esteem and there is little of the confidence needed to tackle new problems.

Counselees need to be reminded that in God's sight every human being is valuable and loved,[36] that every sin can be forgiven,[37] that each of us has abilities and gifts that can be developed, and that all people have weaknesses that can be lived with and for which we can make adjustments. Counselees can be helped to see that no person ever attains perfection in what he or she does, so we should quit striving for the impossible. Instead, we must learn to do the best we can with God's supernatural help and with the abilities and circumstances that we have been given.

Self-esteem is considered more fully in chapter 21. If this is a problem for the lonely counselee, it might be good to work on the self-esteem problem as an important first step in tackling loneliness.

5. *Encouraging Risk-Taking.* Even when someone does have a positive self-image it sometimes takes great courage to reach out to others. What if people criticize or reject us? What if they fail to respond? That can be embarrassing and threatening.

It is here that a counselor can provide the encouragement and support that the counselee needs as he or she makes contact with others. There can be ongoing consideration of questions such as "To whom can you reach out?" "In what specific ways can you reach out to contact others?" "What have you done (or failed to do) in the past to prevent close contact with others?" As counselees risk getting involved, the counselor can give encouragement and provide opportunities to discuss how this social outreach is working, where it might be failing, and how failure can be prevented.

6. *Teaching Social Skills.* Although some causes of loneliness cannot be changed, other causal situations can be altered, corrected, or removed. People can, for example, watch less television, spend more time in family activities, reevaluate their workaholic and self-centered lifestyles, or move into useful church activities. All of this may involve reaching out to others, but for some people this is very difficult because they lack the social and communication skills. Often, these individuals are social cripples who are insensitive to people and uncertain how to handle themselves in social situations.

Counselors can point out social errors, teach individuals how to relate to others, and help counselees evaluate the effectiveness of their attempts to interact. Chapter 16 of this book discusses interpersonal relationships and may be of further help to counselors who are working with those lonely people who lack basic communication skills and social finesse.

7. *Meeting Spiritual Needs.* A once-popular Christian song begins with the words: "Why should I be lonely? I have Jesus only." These lyrics may imply that true believers have no need of human companionship, but, as we have seen, God himself declared that people need each other if they are to avoid loneliness.

From this we should not conclude that human contact is the only solution to loneliness. Loneliness never disappears completely until an individual is introduced to Jesus Christ. He loves each of us unconditionally,[38] died for us, makes it possible for us to come to him by confession of our sins, welcomes us as adopted children,[39] and becomes a friend who sticks closer than a brother.[40] His Holy Spirit lives inside of every believer,[41] helps us, prays for us, and makes us more Christlike.[42]

God is real and his presence can be sensed. He communicates through his Word even though we cannot hear him with our ears. But God is also intangible; he cannot be touched or seen. This is where his tangible body, the church, enters the picture. The church should be a healing, helping community that radiates love, acceptance, and support. As a member of this community and a follower of Jesus Christ, the counselor should radiate this loving acceptance and point the counselee both to Christ himself and to the local church—which the Bible calls the "body of Christ" here on earth.

It would be wrong to assume that religious people never are lonely. On the contrary, one research study found no difference in reported loneliness between religious and nonreligious people.[43] The groups did differ, however, in the way they coped. Believers, especially theologically conservative Christians, were more likely to see God's hand in their loneliness and to seek divine help in facing the problem. For some, this became a reason to do nothing about their loneliness apart from prayer and waiting for God to act. For most of the believers, however, faith in God, prayer, and Bible study all helped make the loneliness more tolerable and became an additional way of coping.[44]

Preventing Loneliness

There are several ways by which the causes of loneliness can be attacked and the experience of loneliness be reduced.

1. *Strengthening the Local Church.* The local congregation can and should be the best antidote to loneliness. To prevent loneliness, people should be encouraged to

worship in the church, to participate in church activities, and to accept the fellowship of church members. Small Bible study or spiritual growth groups, informal potlucks, church-sponsored workdays or community projects, group attendance at local concerts, participation in the choir—these are among the church ministries that give opportunity for lonely people to build meaningful contacts with others.

Regretfully not all church members are open to receiving new people. Some churches are cold, indifferent, and cliquish. Regular attenders may fail to notice newcomers, may extend no welcome when visitors are noticed, or may embarrass nonmembers with well-meaning but insensitive expressions of welcome from the pulpit.[45]

In preventing loneliness, therefore, the church leader must stimulate individuals to be involved with the church and must stimulate church members to love, support, accept, forgive, care for, and welcome individuals into the fellowship. In an era when so many people are separated by distance from their natural families, the church can provide a network of substitute families. Encourage individuals and families to visit in each others homes. In addition, there must be opportunity for meaningful activities, especially on weekends, when lonely people so often drift into bars, casual sexual encounters, and intimate experiences with strangers, all in an effort to find love and companionship.

2. *Coping with Change.* In a book on loneliness published several years ago, Ralph Keyes wrote that most of us want a sense of community with others, but there are three things that we want more: privacy, convenience, and the freedom to move. Regretfully these are the three values that are most likely to prevent community closeness.[46] Is it possible to be people-centered and intimate with others in an age that prizes mobility, computer technology, urbanization, television, VCRs, and other dehumanizing influences? The answer probably is yes—but with qualifications. We can get really close to only a few people, and to do so we must make up our minds to give the time and effort needed for building relationships in these days when superficiality is convenient. Seminars, classroom presentations, and counseling sessions can all be used to help people manage their time or relationships and thus prevent loneliness.

3. *Building Self-Esteem and Competence.* Loneliness, as we have seen, sometimes arises because people are self-defeating in their attitudes or actions, immobilized by a poor self-concept, or lacking in effective social skills. By eliminating these problems, loneliness can often be prevented. When children and adults learn social skills, communication ability, and healthy realistic attitudes toward life, they are better able to relate to others and avoid loneliness.

These things can be taught in churches, schools, counselors' offices, or through seminars, sermons, books, articles, and tapes. Probably this teaching is most effective if it can be started and practiced in the home. Teaching family members to communicate openly, to respect and care for one another, to accept individual differences, to work, relax, and worship together are among the ways that counselors and church members can reduce loneliness and prevent its increase or recurrence.

4. *Stimulating Spiritual Growth.* Loneliness is reduced or prevented when individuals are helped to build intimate relationships with God as well as with other humans. As people are enabled to "understand their gifts and connect with the deep purposes of God for them, loneliness will be swallowed up in a life of giving

and loving. Emptiness will be filled with meaning."[47] Helping people to grow spiritually, therefore, becomes a significant way to prevent loneliness.[48]

CONCLUSIONS ABOUT LONELINESS

Most of us live in what appears to be a loneliness-producing society where rapid change and modern technology discourage intimacy and stimulate loneliness. Even in homes and churches, people avoid each other. In an attempt to find closeness and escape inner feelings of isolation, many individuals throw themselves blindly into open sharing with strangers (like casual sexual partners, fellow drinkers, or seatmates on airplanes).

Caring relationships with others will help to remove loneliness, especially when individuals can be free of hostility, poor self-esteem, social incompetence, and personal insecurity. But inner self-confidence and human togetherness, in themselves, will not give a permanent solution to the loneliness problem. We need to help people develop intimate relationships with God. We need to help them build strong involvements with at least a few people, including family members, where there can be mutual openness, acceptance and respect for each other's uniqueness.

SUGGESTIONS FOR FURTHER READING

Ellison, Craig W. *Saying Good-bye to Loneliness and Finding Intimacy.* San Francisco: Harper & Row, 1983.*

Gordon, Suzanne. *Lonely in America.* New York: Simon and Schuster, 1976.*

Natale, Samuel M., ed. *Psychotherapy and the Lonely Patient.* New York: Haworth Press, 1986.

Peplau, L. A., and D. Perlman, eds. *Loneliness: A Sourcebook of Current Theory, Research and Therapy.* New York: Wiley-Interscience, 1982.

Paul Tournier. *Escape from Loneliness.* Philadelphia: Westminster, 1962.*

* Books marked with an asterisk (*) are especially suited for counselees to read.

8 Depression

SYLVIA, AGE THIRTY-ONE, FIRST NOTICED the signs of depression after the birth of her second child. The pregnancy and delivery had gone well, and everyone was delighted with the arrival of a healthy baby boy.

When she came home from the hospital, Sylvia was tired, but she attributed that to the physical effects of the pregnancy, late-night feedings, and taking care of two small children, instead of one.

But the fatigue got worse as the months passed, and Sylvia's mood got blacker. She cried often, felt like a failure as a mother, and had difficulty coping with the children's demands. Her husband tried to be helpful and supportive, but he sensed that Sylvia had lost interest in almost everything: her friends, her spiritual life, the daily news, her home, her family, and even the career that she had so enjoyed prior to the second pregnancy. Sylvia claimed that she lacked the energy to go to church, to get together with friends, to have sex with her husband, or even to go to a doctor or a counselor.

Often she wondered how she could keep going, and at times, whenever she was alone, she thought about suicide. But she thought about how this would affect the children and her husband, wasn't sure how to kill herself, and had a vague discomfort that this might be displeasing to God. So she never attempted to take her life—but she longed for life to end.

When she finally got to a counselor, Sylvia learned that depression often persists for long periods of time and that progress is slow in pulling out of the valley of despair. Her doctor has looked for medical causes for the depression, and her counselor is helping her cope with the stresses. Most helpful, she thinks, has been the support of her husband. He has stayed with her throughout the depression, even though Sylvia's despair has put him under more stress than she will ever realize.

Vance Havner, a well-known Southern Baptist preacher, once wrote that Christian experience has three levels.[1] First there are "mountaintop days" when everything is going well and the world looks bright. These experiences are temporary: they can't go on forever. It is unrealistic to expect, as many people do, that we can spend life leaping from one mountain peak to another as if there were no plains or valleys in between. Instead, most of life consists of "ordinary days" when we work at our usual tasks, neither elated nor depressed. Then, third, there are "dark days" when we trudge heavily through confusion, doubt, despair, and discouragement. Sometimes these days string out into months or even years before we begin to experience a sense of relief and victory. When they persist, dark days are days of depression.

Depression (previously called "melancholia") has been recognized as a common problem for more than three thousand years. It is a worldwide phenomenon[2] that affects individuals of all ages (including infancy), appears to be increasing among teenagers and young adults, and disrupts the lives of an estimated 30 to 40 million people in the United States alone.[3] Some of history's greatest military leaders, statesmen, musicians, scientists, and theologians have been its victims, but depression is no respecter of persons. It is known as the "common cold" of mental disorders and has been called "the most widespread, serious, and costly psychiatric disease afflicting humankind today."[4] On occasion almost all of us experience depression, sometimes when we least expect it. In its milder forms depression may come as a passing period of sadness that follows a personal disappointment. More severe depression may overwhelm its victims with feelings of despair, fear, exhaustion, immobilizing apathy, hopelessness, and inner desperation.[5]

Probably no two people experience this common condition in the same way. The word "depression" covers a wide variety of symptoms that differ in severity, frequency, duration, and origin. The signs of depression may include (1) sadness, often accompanied by pessimism and hopelessness; (2) apathy and inertia that make it difficult to "get going" or face decisions; (3) general fatigue, along with loss of energy and a lack of interest in work, sex, religion, hobbies, or other activities; (4) low self-esteem, frequently accompanied by self-criticism and feelings of guilt, shame, worthlessness, and helplessness; (5) a loss of spontaneity; (6) insomnia and difficulties in concentration; and often (7) loss of appetite. In what is sometimes known as masked depression,[6] the person has many of the above symptoms but denies that he or she feels sad. The alert counselor may suspect that depression is present even behind a smiling countenance. In many cases the symptoms of depression hide anger that has not been expressed, sometimes isn't recognized and, according to one traditional theory, is often directed inward against oneself.

Depressive reactions have been classified in a variety of ways with terms such as reactive versus endogenous, primary versus secondary, and unipolar versus bipolar. *Reactive* depression (sometimes called exogenous or neurotic depression) usually comes as a reaction to some real or imagined loss or trauma, is accompanied with high levels of anxiety, is of short duration, and often is self-correcting. *Endogenous* (also called autonomous and sometimes psychotic depression) is more likely to arise spontaneously from within, involves intense despair sometimes accompanied by self-destructive tendencies, persists for a long period of time, is more resistant to treatment, and has a high recurrence rate. *Primary* depression occurs by itself while *secondary* depression comes as the side effect of some medication, the influence of one's diet, or the result of an illness like cancer, diabetes, or even influenza. *Unipolar* depression refers to a condition where there is one or more episodes of depression as the primary disorder. Less common is *bipolar* depression that involves periods of mania interspersed with the depressive behavior. Most professionals would distinguish all of this from *discouragement,* which is a mild, usually temporary, and almost universal mood swing that comes in response to disappointments, failures, and losses.[7]

All of this shows that depression is a common but complicated condition, difficult to define, hard to describe with accuracy, and not easy to treat.

The Bible and Depression

Depression is a clinical term that is not discussed in the Bible even though the condition appears to have been common. Psalms 69, 88, and 102, for example, are songs of despair, but notice that these are set in the context of hope. In Psalm 43 David expresses both depression and rejoicing when he writes:

> Why are you downcast, O my soul?
> Why so disturbed within me?
> Put your hope in God,
> for I will yet praise him,
> my Savior and my God.

Elsewhere in the Bible it appears that Job, Moses, Jonah, Peter, and the whole nation of Israel experienced depression.[8] Jeremiah the prophet wrote a whole book of lamentations. Elijah saw God's mighty power at work on Mount Carmel, but when Jezebel threatened murder, Elijah fled into the wilderness where he plunged into despondency. He wanted to die and might have done so except for the "treatment" that came from an angel sent by God.[9] Jesus in Gethsemane was greatly distressed, an observation that is poignantly described in the words of the Amplified Bible: "He began to show grief and distress of mind and was deeply depressed. Then He said to them, My soul is very sad and deeply grieved, so that I am almost dying of sorrow."[10]

These examples, accompanied by numerous references to the pain of grieving, show the realism that characterizes the Bible. It is a realistic despair contrasted with a certain hope. Each of the believers who plunged into depression eventually came through and experienced a new and lasting joy. The biblical emphasis is less on human despair and more on belief in God and the assurance of abundant life in heaven, if not on earth.[11] Paul's confident prayer for the Romans will someday be answered for all Christians: "May the God of hope fill you with all joy and peace as you trust in him, so that you may overflow with hope by the power of the Holy Spirit."[12]

The Causes of Depression

Depression can have a number of causes. Often several of these work together, and if you can uncover, understand, and help counselees deal with each of these, your counseling is likely to be better.

The Christian counselor's task is made more difficult by a number of myths about depression that are widely accepted and sometimes preached. It is *not* true, for example, that depression always results from sin or a lack of faith in God, that all depression is caused by self-pity, that it is wrong for a Christian to ever be depressed, that depressed feelings can be removed permanently by spiritual exercises, that happiness is a choice, or that a "depressed Christian is a contradiction of terms."[13]

Christians, like everyone else, get depressed and the causes can be grouped into two major categories: the genetic-biological causes and the psychological-cognitive causes.

1. *The Genetic-Biological Causes.* Depression often has a physical basis. At the simplest level, we know that lack of sleep, insufficient exercise, the side effects of drugs, physical illnesses, or improper diet can all create depression. Thousands of women experience depression as part of a monthly premenstrual syndrome (PMS) and some are victimized by postpartum depression following childbirth. Other physical influences, like neurochemical malfunctioning, brain tumors, or glandular disorders, are more complicated creators of depression.

There is evidence that some depression runs in families and may have a genetic basis. This is difficult to demonstrate conclusively; research reports are sometimes contradictory.[14] Other research has linked depression to brain chemistry that often can be altered by antidepressive drugs.

Archibald Hart has suggested that Elijah's depression following his encounter with the prophets of Baal[15] was probably an example of the physiologically based "postadrenalin depression" that frequently comes to those who have recently had an emotional "high."

> Whenever the body has experienced a period of high adrenalin demand, such as coping with an emergency, public speaking, or meeting a deadline, the adrenal system becomes exhausted and switches off when the demand is over. It is like the calm following a storm, except that the calm is more like a total switch-off. Most of us feel it as depression. It is the body's way of demanding rest; it turns you off to all interests and saps you of energy so that you are forced into a period of recovery. During this time the adrenal glands and other important systems are rejuvenated. The longer your system has been in a state of demand or energy, the longer it will take for it to rejuvenate. . . . The older we get, the less resilient is our adrenal system and the more depressed we become after an adrenalin high.[16]

Elijah rested and slept until his system was rejuvenated. Perhaps this was how God chose to lift the prophet's postadrenalin depression.

Research in the genetics and biochemistry of depression is both complex and moving at a rapid pace. Scientists still do not know if depressed thinking causes biochemical changes or if a chemical imbalance in the brain causes the depression. One former president of the American Psychiatric Association has predicted, however, that research in this area is where a Nobel Prize will one day be won.[17]

2. *Psychological-Cognitive Causes.* Depression is a significant mental health problem for between 4 percent and 9 percent of the general population, but these figures rise radically among some young adults. An estimated 25 percent of college students suffer from depression at one time, and 33 percent of college dropouts suffer from serious depression before leaving school.[18] Startling statistics like these have led to the conclusion that developmental, psychological, interpersonal, spiritual, and other nonphysical influences are at the basis of much depression.

(a) Background and Family Causes. Some evidence suggests that childhood experiences can lead to depression in later life. Many years ago a researcher named Rene Spitz published a study of children who had been separated from their parents and raised in an institution.[19] Deprived of continuing and warm human contact with adults, these children showed apathy, poor health, and sadness are indicative of depression that could continue into later life. Depression is more likely when parents blatantly or subtly reject their children or when status-seeking families set unrealistically high standards that children are unable to meet. When standards are too high or too rigid, failure is almost inevitable and depression often follows. This is especially likely when one of the parents is also struggling with depression.[20]

Teenagers in conflict with their parents, young adults having trouble becoming independent of their families, people from unstable homes, and college students with negative opinions about their families are more inclined to be depressed.[21] These experiences do not always lead to depression, but they may increase the likelihood of severe depression in later life.

(b) Stress and Significant Losses. It is well known that the stresses of life stimulate depression, especially when these stresses make us feel threatened[22] or when they involve a loss. Loss of an opportunity, a job, status, health, freedom, a contest, possessions, or other valued objects can each lead to depression. The same is true when there is loss of people. Divorce, death, or prolonged separations are painful and known to be among the most powerful depression-producing events of life.

(c) Learned Helplessness. One theory suggests that depression most often comes when we encounter situations over which we have little or no control.[23] It is easy to get depressed when we learn that our actions are futile no matter how hard we try, or that nothing can be done to relieve our suffering, reach a goal, or bring change. At such times we may feel helpless and give up trying. This could explain some of the depression in grieving people who can do nothing to bring back a loved one, in the student who is unable to relate to other students or succeed academically, or in the older person who is powerless to turn back the clock and restore lost physical capacities. When such people are able to control at least a portion of their environments, depression may subside or disappear.

(d) Cognitive Causes. How a person thinks often determines how he or she feels. This is a basic assumption of the cognitive views of depression. If we think negatively, for example, see only the dark side of life, maintain a pessimistic mindset, and overlook the positive, then depression is almost inevitable.

According to psychiatrist Aaron Beck, depressed people show negative thinking in three areas.[24] First, they view the world and life experiences negatively. Life is seen as a succession of burdens, obstacles, and defeats in a world that is "going down the drain." Second, many depressed people have a negative view of themselves. They feel deficient, inadequate, unworthy, and incapable of performing adequately. This in turn can lead to self-blame and self-pity. Third, some people view the future in a negative way. Looking ahead they see continuing hardship, frustration, and hopelessness.

Such thinking sometimes is used in an attempt to control others and influence how they respond. A comment like, "I'm no good," often is an unconscious way of getting others to say, "Oh, no, you really are a fine person." Self-condemnation, therefore, becomes a way of manipulating others to give compliments. Such compliments really are not satisfying, however, so the negative thinking and depression goes on. Additionally, if you keep thinking negatively, then you are less likely to be hurt or disappointed if some of your thinking comes true.

(e) Anger. An old and widely accepted viewpoint suggests that depression comes when anger is held within and turned against oneself.[25] Many children are raised in homes and sometimes sent to schools where the expression of anger is not tolerated. Some attend churches where all anger is condemned as sin. Other people are convinced that they shouldn't even feel angry, so they deny hostile feelings when these do arise. A widow, for example, may be angry at her husband who died leaving her to raise the children alone, but such anger seems irrational and is sure to arouse guilt. As a result, the anger is denied and kept within.

What happens then? If the anger is pushed out of our minds, it festers "under cover" and eventually affects us in some other way. The following diagram illustrates this process.[26]

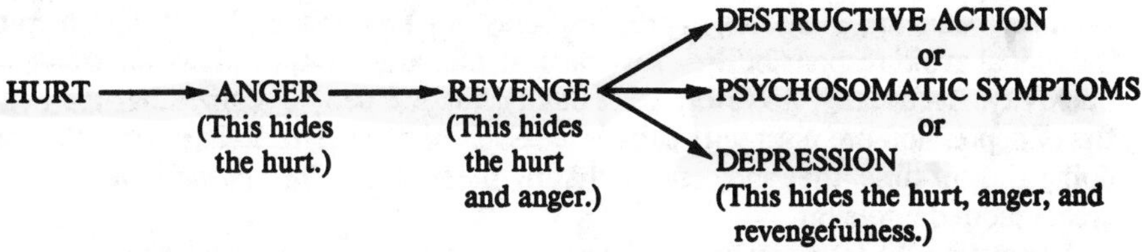

Perhaps most anger begins when we feel hurt as the result of a disappointment or because of the actions of some other person. Instead of admitting this hurt, the individual mulls it over, ponders what happened, and begins to get angry. The anger then builds and becomes so strong that it hides the hurt. If the anger is not admitted and expressed or dealt with, it then leads to revenge. This involves thoughts about hurting another person, either the one who caused the original hurt or someone else who is nearby.

Revenge sometimes leads to destructive violent actions, but this can get us into trouble, and violence is not socially acceptable, especially for a Christian. As a result, many people try to hide their feelings. This takes energy that wears down the body so that emotions may appear in the form of psychosomatic symptoms. Others, consciously or unconsciously, condemn themselves for their attitudes and become depressed as a result. This depression may be a form of emotional self-punishment that sometimes even leads to suicide. It is not difficult to understand why such people feel guilty, self-condemning, and unhappy.

Some people use depression as a subtle and socially acceptable way both to express anger and to get revenge. The depressed person seems to be saying, "I'm depressed and miserable, it isn't my fault, and if I don't get attention and sympathy, I may even get more depressed or do something desperate." One writer calls this "a kind of psychological blackmail."[27]

As the diagram shows, depression often hides underlying hurt, anger, and resentment which then may be forgotten. It should be emphasized that this explanation does not account for all depression, but undoubtedly it explains some.

(f) Sin and Guilt. It is easy to understand why sin and guilt can lead to depression. When a person feels that he or she has failed or done something wrong, guilt arises and along with it comes self-condemnation, frustration, hopelessness, and other depressive symptoms. Guilt and depression so often occur together that it is difficult to determine which comes first. Perhaps in most cases the guilt comes before depression, but at times depression will cause people to feel guilty (because they seem unable to snap out of their despair). In either case, a vicious cycle is set in motion. Guilt causes depression which causes more guilt, and the cycle continues.

The Effects of Depression

Most people don't enjoy having problems, but sometimes problems can serve a useful purpose. When we are physically sick, for example, we are excused from work, people shower us with attention or sympathy, others make decisions for us or take over our responsibilities, and sometimes we can enjoy a period of leisure and relaxation. The same thing is true when we are emotionally down or distraught. Neurotic behavior, including depression, may not be pleasant, but it does help an individual avoid responsibilities, save face, attract attention, and have an excuse for inactivity. Eventually, however, emotionally hurting people realize that the benefits of depression are not really satisfying. Such people begin to hate what they are doing and, in time, they may end up hating themselves. This, as we have seen can create more depression.

Depression leads to any or all of the following effects. In general, the deeper the depression the more intense the effects.

1. *Unhappiness and Inefficiency.* Depressed people frequently feel "blue," hopeless, self-critical, and miserable. As a result they lack enthusiasm, are indecisive, and sometimes have little energy for doing even simple things (like getting out of bed in the morning). Life thus is characterized by inefficiency, underachievement, and an increased dependence on others.

2. *Physical Illness.* Depression, including the sadness that comes with grief or loneliness, tends to suppress the body's immune system. As a result, the individual is more susceptible to illness and the body is less able to fight viruses and other disease. Depressed people, therefore, are more likely than others to get sick, and the reverse is true as well: whenever they have a psychiatric disorder of physical illness, they often develop depression as a result.[28]

3. *Low Self-Esteem and Withdrawal.* When a person is discouraged, unmotivated, and bored with life, there often is low self-esteem, self-pity, a lack of self-confidence, and the strong desire to get away from other people. Social contacts may be too demanding and the depressed person may not feel like communicating. Instead, the individual may daydream and escape into a world of television, novels, or alcohol or drug use. Some people dream of running away or finding a simpler job. A few do this, but more often the depressed person lacks the energy.

4. *Suicide.* There is no more complete way to escape than to take one's own life. Suicide and suicide attempts are often seen among teenagers, people who live alone, the unmarried (especially the divorced), and persons who are depressed. Many depressed people never even consider suicide but others do, often in a sincere attempt to kill themselves and escape life. For some, suicide attempts are an unconscious cry for help, an opportunity for revenge, or a manipulative gesture designed to influence some person who is close emotionally. While some suicide attempts are blatantly clear (as when a man leaves a note and shoots himself), others are more subtle and made to look like accidents. While some people carefully plan their self-destructive actions, others drive recklessly, drink excessively, or

find other ways to flirt with death. All of this illustrates the pervasive and potentially destructive influence of depression.

In some people, the depression is hidden even from themselves, but it comes out in other ways including physical symptoms and complaints (hypochondriasis), aggressive actions and angry temper outbursts, impulsive behavior (including gambling, drinking, violence, destructiveness or impulsive sex), accident proneness, compulsive work, and sexual problems, to name the most common. These are symptoms of *masked depression*[29] that occur in children and adolescents as well as in adults. The person may be hurting emotionally but expressing this hurt in ways that hide the real inner despair. Sometimes the hiding is so good that even close friends or counselors don't recognize the depression.

More often, however, the depression has a strong impact on others. People who live with a depressed person often feel burdened by the patient's worrying, fatigue, feelings of hopelessness, and lack of interest in social activities. According to one study, the burden of living with a depressed person is so great, that 40 percent of relatives need counseling themselves.[30]

Counseling and Depression

"You could not have picked a better time in human history to feel miserable," according to a recent book about depression. "At long last there are effective treatments and cures for depression."[31] Most of these treatments have been found to reduce symptoms, at least with some people, and frequently the depression can be eliminated completely.[32]

Depressed people often are passive, nonverbal, poorly motivated, pessimistic, and characterized by a resigned, what's-the-use? attitude. The counselor, therefore, must reach out verbally, taking a more active role than he or she might show with other counselees. Optimistic reassuring statements (but not gushiness), sharing of facts about how depression affects people, patiently encouraging counselees to talk (but not pushing them to talk), asking questions, giving periodic compliments, and gently sharing Scripture (without preaching) can all be helpful. Try to avoid confrontation, persistent probing questions or demands for action, especially in the beginning. These techniques often increase anxiety and this can create more discouragement and pessimism.

As the counselee talks about the depression, you should listen attentively. Watch for evidence of anger, hurt, negative thinking, poor self-esteem, and guilt, which you might want to discuss later. Encourage counselees to talk about those life situations that are bothersome. Avoid taking sides, but try to be understanding and accepting of feelings. Watch for talk about losses, failures, rejection, and other incidents that may have stimulated the current depression.

As you work with depressed people, try to be aware of your own feelings. Are you impatient when you have a negative, complaining counselee? Are you inclined to let your mind wander or be pulled into despondent negative thinking yourself? Counseling the depressed can be a demanding test for your helping skills. These counselees are likely to need special effort and attention.

For example, many depressed people have a strong need to be dependent. As you counsel, ask yourself, "Am I encouraging dependence in an already depressed person?" "If so, am I trying to build my own feelings of power or importance?" "Am I encouraging anger or negative thinking?" "Am I making so many demands that the counselee feels overwhelmed and thus inclined to cling?" When they are not aware of these tendencies, counselors sometimes increase depression instead of contributing to its relief.

In counseling the depressed, some combination of the following approaches can be helpful.

1. *Dealing with the Physiology.* In their enthusiasm to help the depressed, nonmedical counselors sometimes forget that many depressive reactions have a physical basis. One estimate suggests that 40 percent of depression may come as the direct result of physical illness, some of which may be undiagnosed.[33] Other depression may come from the counselee's poor eating habits. An approach to helping known as nutritional therapy assumes that depression sometimes is best treated by changes in one's diet.[34]

If there are persisting physical symptoms or if the depression does not yield to your initial counseling, it is important to refer your counselee to a competent and psychologically astute physician. The nonmedical counselor is not qualified to decide whether or not a counselee's symptoms are psychologically induced, and neither can the nonphysician make valid evaluations about whether or not the depression has physical causes.

Nonmedical counselors may also want to contact a psychiatrist or other physician who could prescribe antidepressant drugs. If the depression has a biological cause, this treatment may remove the problem. Often, however, the drugs bring temporary symptom relief that changes the counselee's mood and makes him or her more amenable to therapy. Counseling can then focus on the nonphysical sources of depression.

The most controversial treatment in psychiatry[35] is the use of electroconvulsive therapy (sometimes called ECT or shock treatment) in which a pulse of electrical energy is passed through the brain. This leads to convulsions and a period of confusion, followed by a brightening of mood. Widely used in the 1940s and 1950s, this treatment has been criticized because of its risks and possible adverse side effects. It still is used, however, especially with severely depressed or actively suicidal people who cannot take drugs or who fail to respond to pharmacological or other medical treatment.

2. *Dealing with the Causes.* Counseling will be easier if you can find the psychological and spiritual causes that produce the symptoms. Review the causes of depression listed earlier in this chapter and then try to discover through questioning and careful listening what might be producing the depression.

Background. Are there past influences or family pressures creating depression? If so, it may be helpful to discuss these, to help counselees see them in a different perspective and, if possible, to take remedial action. Counselees may need help in learning how to relate to their families in more effective ways. Family members can be urged to accept the counselee, to challenge negative thinking, to encourage action in place of inactivity, and to include the depressed person in family activities. When communication is good and when the family is accepting, interested, and involved, counselees often improve more quickly.

Stress. Is the counselee experiencing stress, especially the stress that comes from a loss? Encourage the person to share his or her feelings about this, discuss practical approaches to stress management, and help the counselee find ways to continue with life in spite of the loss.[36]

Learned Helplessness. Does the counselee feel that life is out of control? If so, discuss how things can be accomplished, starting with small tasks and moving on to the more difficult. You can discuss the inevitability of uncontrollable events, and can help counselees see that God is always in control, even when we are not.[37]

Thinking. Is there negative thinking? Ask the counselee to state some of these thoughts. Then ask, "Is this a valid conclusion? Could there be another way of viewing the situation? Are you telling yourself things about the world, yourself, and the future that are not really so?" All of this is designed to challenge the counselee's thinking and to teach ways of evaluating conclusions so we can learn to think more positively and more realistically. Without denying the depression-producing situation, the counselor and counselee must both be guided by the truth of Phil. 4:8: "Whatever is true . . . noble . . . right . . . pure . . . lovely . . . admirable—if anything is excellent or praiseworthy—think about such things."

Anger. Is there an attitude of revenge coming from anger or is there anger that comes from hurt? These emotions must be discussed and expressed, even if they seem irrational. Hurt can be deeply embedded and sometimes uncovered only after considerable probing and a lot of careful listening. Perhaps you will want to draw the diagram from a few pages back and show how hurt can lead so easily to depression.

Guilt. Has the person sinned or done something else to arouse guilt? Has there been confession to God and perhaps to others? Does the counselee know about divine forgiveness and about the importance of forgiving oneself? (See chapter 10.)

In discussing these issues, the counselee often gains insights into the problem and can think of ways to deal with the depression-producing influences. At times the counselor may want to give his or her own insights and observations, but there should be time for the counselee to respond to these interpretations. All of this contributes to better understanding and often this leads to change and improvement.

3. *Dealing with Thinking.* Most people do not snap out of depression. The road to recovery may be long, difficult, and marked by mood fluctuations that come with special intensity when there are disappointments, failures, or separations. Depressed people want to *feel* better, but feelings by themselves are difficult, if not impossible to change. Telling a person "You shouldn't feel depressed," does nothing to relieve the depression and often adds guilt since most of us cannot change our feelings at will.

To change feelings we must change thinking. When problems or disappointments come it is helpful to ask what the counselee thinks. Often he or she decides "this is terrible," "this proves I'm no good," "nobody wants me now," or "I never do anything right." These are self-criticisms that often are not based on solid fact. If a person fails, for example, it does not follow that he or she is "no good" or unwanted. Failure means, instead, that we are not perfect (nobody is), that we have made a mistake and should try to act differently in the future. Effective counseling must encourage counselees to reevaluate depression-producing thoughts and attitudes toward life.[38]

In a popular magazine article, one woman wrote that her depression came from a mind-set that said, "I should be a perfect hostess, parent, wife, and friend. I should not fail. I should contribute to the community by serving on committees and making contributions to everyone who asks." This lady had set up high expectations that were impossible to reach. When she failed, she became depressed.[39] Recovery did not come until she was helped to see her human frailty and was able to accept the fact that all of us fail at times.

Sometimes Christians convince themselves that we must always be spiritually alive and enthusiastic but never angry, lethargic, or discouraged. When failure or disappointment comes, as it inevitably does, these believers feel crushed because their unrealistic expectations have not been met.

The counselor tries to help counselees evaluate their expectations, attitudes, values, and assumptions. Help counselees see which of these are unrealistic, nonbiblical, and harmful. Since these kinds of thoughts often are well entrenched, sometimes coming from a lifetime of thinking, it may take repeated efforts to help people reevaluate and change their attitudes toward life and themselves.

4. *Dealing with Inactivity.* Even when they have some understanding of the depression, counselees often have difficulty in doing something about it. Inaction is common in depressed people. Often they lack the energy or the motivation to take actions that will deal with the problem. For many, it is easier to stay in bed or to sit alone brooding and thinking about the miseries of life.

Gently, but firmly, you may need to push the depressed person to take action, to get involved in daily routines, family activities, and recreation. Start by encouraging activities in which the counselee is likely to succeed. This increases optimism and interrupts the tendency to ruminate on negative ideas. When the counselee does take action, try to give encouragement and compliments.[40]

5. *Dealing with the Environment.* Depression is common in the winter months, especially among people who live in the north. Known as seasonal affective disorders (SAD), these periods of depression appear to come, at least in part, from a lack of sunlight. When they were exposed to bright fluorescent light, most of the seasonally depressed people in one research study improved substantially.[41]

Findings such as this suggest that a change in environment can sometimes reduce depression. Counselors may not be able to do much to change the depression-producing circumstances in a person's life, but it is possible to encourage counselees to modify routines, reduce work loads, attempt to avoid stress-inducing situations, or take periodic vacations. Counselees can also be encouraged to find groups of people who can help to create a supportive environment. The church, of course, is an excellent place to start this process.

6. *Dealing with the Potential for Self-Harm.* People can harm themselves in many ways, for example, by changing jobs, by quitting school, or by making unwise marriage decisions. The counselor must be alert to a tendency for people to make major long-lasting decisions when they are in the grips of depression. Helping counselees decide if they really want to do what they are proposing, helping them see the possible consequences of the decisions, and urging them to wait a while, can all prevent actions that could be harmful.

Suicide is one action that is contemplated by many depressed people. Since most people give prior clues about their intentions, the counselor should be alert to indications that suicide is being considered. Be alert, for example, to any of the following:[42]

- Talk of suicide.
- Evidence of a plan of action for killing oneself.
- Feelings of hopelessness and/or meaninglessness.
- Indications of guilt feelings and worthlessness.
- Recent environmental stresses (such as job loss, divorce, or death in the family).
- An inability to cope with stress.
- Excessive concern about physical illness.
- Preoccupation with insomnia.
- Evidence of depression, disorientation, and/or defiance.
- A tendency to be dependent and dissatisfied at the same time.
- A sudden and unexplainable shift to a happy, cheerful mood (which often means that the decision to attempt suicide has been made).
- Knowledge regarding the most effective methods of suicide (guns and carbon monoxide work best; wrist slashing is least successful; drug use depends on how much is taken and the type of drug).
- A history of prior suicide attempts (those who have tried before, often try suicide again).

Counselors should not hesitate to ask whether or not the counselee has been thinking of suicide. Such questioning gets the issue out into the open and lets the counselee consider it rationally. Rather than encouraging suicide (as is commonly assumed), open discussion often reduces its likelihood.

If a person is really determined to commit suicide the counselor may delay this action, but in time the counselee will try again. Even the most dedicated helper cannot prevent suicide forever. It is well to remember this when a suicide does occur. Otherwise, the counselor may wallow in guilt because he or she was unable to prevent the counselee's death. Suicide is discussed in more detail in chapter 31.

Preventing Depression

Can depression be prevented? The answer is "not completely." There is no evidence that we can prevent many of the biologically produced attacks of depression, and at times the pressures of life are certain to plunge each of us into deep sadness, if not depression. Disappointments, losses, rejections, and failures come to everyone and these lead to periods of unhappiness and discouragement. Even so, there are some ways by which we can prevent or soften the blows of depression.

1. *Trust in God.* Writing from prison, the Apostle Paul once stated that he had learned to be content in all circumstances. Knowing that God gives strength to his children and is able to supply all our needs, Paul had learned how to live joyfully, both in poverty and in prosperity.[43] Through his experiences, and undoubtedly through a study of the Scriptures, Paul had learned to trust in God and this helped to prevent depression.

The same can be true today. A conviction that God is alive and in control can give hope and encouragement, even when we are inclined to be discouraged and without hope. If modern people can learn this lesson and if church leaders and Christian counselors can teach it, then discouragements need not hit as hard as they might hit otherwise.

Regretfully, the teaching of some well-intentioned Christian leaders seems to make the depression worse, instead of relieving and preventing it. When people are told to "trust in God and the depression will go away," there can be guilt and deeper discouragement if the depression persists. When writers show little understanding of biological depression or when they present their lists of "Christian" rules for getting rid of depression, depressed people sometimes feel deeper despair and hopelessness if they can't seem to make the formulas work. Some (not all) of the self-help books "are very hard on many of the Christian patients whom I see who have deep depression," according to one Christian psychiatrist.[44] Much more helpful is the support that comes from a community that says "We are with you in this pain and are praying for you, even though we don't completely understand it."

2. *Expect Discouragement.* The second verse of a famous hymn[45] proclaims that "we should never be discouraged" if we take things to the Lord in prayer. This is a popular view for which there is no scriptural support. Jesus warned that we would have problems and the Apostle James wrote that trials and temptations would come to test our faith and teach us patience.[46] It is unrealistic to smile and laugh in such circumstances, pretending that we are never going to be discouraged.

Consider our Lord at the time of the crucifixion. He was "deeply distressed" and openly acknowledged his agony. One can hardly imagine him smiling in Gethsemane or on the cross, trying to convince everyone that he was rejoicing and bubbling over with happiness. Jesus trusted in his Father, but he expected pain and was not surprised when it came.

When we are realistic enough to expect pain and informed enough to know that God is always in control, then we can handle discouragement better and often keep from slipping into deep depression.

3. *Be Alert to Depression-Prone Situations.* Everyone expects the recent widow to be depressed and in need of special support during the months following her husband's death. We know that she may be especially down on the first birthday, the first Father's Day, or the first anniversary following the death. By anticipating these sad times, and by being present, each of us can prevent predictable depressions from being worse.

Most counselors are now aware that holidays can be depression-producing times for some people. Christmas, for example, may not be a time of joy and happiness for people who are separated from loved ones, without friends or the money to buy presents, worried about relatives who drink too much at the holiday celebrations, pressured by the demands of the season, or reminded of deaths or other traumatic experiences that took place in a previous December. People who are prone to the holiday blues may need special understanding and encouragement if they are to keep from slipping into deeper depression at times when most other people are celebrating joyfully.

4. *Learn to Handle Anger and Guilt.* Some people slide into depression because their minds dwell on past injustices or past failures. This may sound simplistic, but these people must ask God to help them forget the past, forgive those who have sinned against them, and forgive themselves. When people dwell on past events and wallow in anger, guilt, and the misery of discouragement, it would seem that such

thinking has some purpose. Is it an excuse for avoiding responsibility or seeking forgiveness? Churches can teach people to admit their anger or guilt and show how these can be overcome (see chapters 9 and 10). If individuals can learn to handle anger and guilt, much depression can be prevented.

5. *Challenge Thinking.* If it is true, as some have suggested, that we each talk silently to ourselves all day, then each of us should notice what we are saying to ourselves. This self-talk often is like a cassette tape that plays over and over, convincing ourselves of ideas that may be harmful and wrong. If, for example, I keep telling myself that I am incompetent, this can undermine my self-confidence and make me depressed. To challenge this thinking I need to ask, "What is the evidence for the view that I am incompetent?" "In what areas am I incompetent (and where am I more competent)?" "Is it OK to be incompetent in some things?" "How can I become more competent in the areas that matter?" When people learn to challenge their own thinking, and that of others, this can also prevent or reduce the severity of depression.

The Bible discusses meditation on the Word of God[47]and on things that are good, positive, and just.[48] Meditation is a form of self-talk that directs our minds away from thinking that is negative and inclined to produce depression.

6. *Learn Coping Techniques.* Several years ago, a report compared those who resist depression with those who succumb. The resisters, it was concluded, are people who have learned to master and cope with the stresses of life.[49] When they feel they have some control over their circumstances, individuals are less likely to feel the helplessness that leads to depression.[50]

Children and adults can be overprotected. This interferes with the ability to learn how to cope with or to master the stresses of life. If people can see how others cope, and can learn how to cope themselves, then circumstances seem less overwhelming and depression is less likely.

7. *Finding Support.* Emile Durkheim, author of a classic book on suicide,[51] concluded that religious people were less suicide-prone than those who were nonbelievers. The reason for this, Durkheim reasoned, was that religion integrated people into groups. Less lonely and isolated, these people were less inclined to get depressed or to attempt suicide. Churches and other social institutions, can become therapeutic communities where people feel welcome and accepted.

A concerned group of people who have learned to be caring can do much to soften the trauma of crises and provide strength and help in times of need. Aware that they are not alone, people in crises are able to cope better and thus avoid severe depression.

8. *Reaching Out.* Alcoholics Anonymous has shown conclusively that needy people help themselves when they reach out to assist others. This, as we have seen, is the helper-therapy principle.[52] It states that those who reach out to help others are the ones who benefit and are helped the most.

The principle doesn't always work; sometimes depressed people can pull one another down. Healing is also unlikely if the depressed helper selfishly concludes, "I don't care about others but I'll help grudgingly if this is what I have to do to feel better myself." In contrast, when there is a willing attempt to help others, including depressed people, then everybody benefits and depression may be reduced. Once again, therefore, we see that the creation of a caring community is an indirect way to prevent depression.

9. *Encourage Physical Fitness.* Since poor diet and lack of exercise can make people depression prone, individuals can be encouraged by word and by example to take care of their bodies. It would be simplistic to assume that this could completely prevent more serious physically based depression, but it is well known that a healthy body is less susceptible to mental as well as physical illness.

Conclusions about Depression

Vance Havner, the preacher mentioned earlier in this chapter, once hoped that his dying wife would be healed through some miracle. But she died, and he was plunged into grief. The old man did not understand why this had happened when it did. "Whoever thinks he has the ways of God conveniently tabulated, analyzed, and correlated with convenient, glib answers to ease every question from aching hearts has not been far in this maze of mystery we call life and death," Havner wrote. God has "no stereotyped way of doing what He does. He delivered Peter from prison but left John the Baptist in a dungeon to die. . . . I accept whatever He does, however He does it."[53]

This man was deeply saddened when his wife died, but I suspect he never became deeply depressed. He had a realistic perspective on life and death. This is a perspective that can do much to help both counselors and counselees to deal more effectively with the problem of depression.

Suggestions for Further Reading

Baker, Don, and Emery Nester. *Depression.* Portland, Oreg.: Multnomah, 1983.*
Beck, Aaron T., et al. *Cognitive Therapy of Depression.* New York: Guilford, 1979.
Hart, Archibald D. *Counseling the Depressed.* Waco, Tex.: Word, 1987.
Klerman, Gerald L., et al. *Interpersonal Psychotherapy of Depression.* New York: Basic Books, 1984.
McCoy, Kathleen. *Coping with Teenage Depression.* New York: New American Library, 1982.*
Papolos, Dimitri, and Janice Papolos. *Overcoming Depression.* New York: Harper & Row, 1987.
Rush, John A., ed. *Short-Term Psychotherapies for Depression.* New York: Guilford, 1982.
White, John. *The Masks of Melancholy.* Downers Grove, Ill.: InterVarsity, 1982.*
Williams, J. M. G., and G. Mark. *The Psychological Treatment of Depression.* New York: Free Press, 1984.

*Books marked with an asterisk (*) are especially suited for counselees to read.

9

Anger

PASTOR FRANK RECENTLY CELEBRATED an anniversary, his thirtieth year in the ministry. Now fifty-six, he has served in several churches during the past three decades and is respected by parishioners and denominational leaders alike.

Few of them know about Frank's anger. Most of the time he keeps it under control although he sometimes gets red-faced in his sermons and pounds the pulpit with a vehemence that looks more like an angry outburst than a preacher's indignation over sin. In church business meetings Frank often feels on the verge of exploding with tension, but thus far he has kept his cool and hidden his real feelings behind a pious facade and a sense of humor that sometimes barely conceals his cynicism and sarcasm.

His feelings, however, aren't hidden at home. Once inside the parsonage, Frank often shouts, pounds the furniture, proclaims the weaknesses of the church leaders, and sometimes swears. He has never harmed his wife or children physically, but they all have been stung by his verbal abuse, and their father's outbursts have convinced at least two of his children that they want nothing to do with his church or his religion.

Frank is bothered by his anger. He knows it isn't right, and after his outbursts he often apologizes to his family and asks God for forgiveness. After the anniversary celebration, Frank began to wonder if he was really a hypocrite, acclaimed by others but unable to control himself.

After a lot of deliberation and with considerable hesitation he decided to talk about his anger with an older pastor. As he shared his concerns, Frank was surprised how angry and frustrated he sounded. During all those years of ministry, he had never really talked about his feelings without shouting and losing his temper. As the hostility poured out, Frank began to recognize how he had passively accepted unfair criticism and harbored resentment because of the demands of others. Sometimes even innocent and well-meant requests had triggered hostile feelings that were taken out on his innocent family.

Throughout his ministry, Frank had spent many hours helping others. Now, at last, somebody was helping him. He was learning to cope with his frustrations and to handle his anger more effectively. He was also learning from a caring clergyman who knew firsthand about the pressures of the pastorate.

Far different is the tragic story of a quiet seventeen-year-old, a high school baseball star, who never complained about his parents, never got into trouble at school, and never showed anger—until the night of the murders! While most of the neighbors slept, he returned to the tree-lined suburban street where he lived, quietly entered the house, and brutally murdered his parents and brother in what police called a frenzied killing of bullets and multiple stab wounds.

Why would a likable small-town boy suddenly explode in an outburst of violence? His baseball coach couldn't answer that question, and neither could the police, the neighbors, the pastor, or anybody else who had known the teenager before news of his aggressive actions spread over the pages of newspapers nationwide.

Anger is an emotional state, experienced by everyone, but impossible to define precisely.[1] It occurs in varying degrees of intensity, from mild annoyance or aggravation to violent rage. It begins in infancy and continues to the later years. It may be hidden and held inside or expressed openly and freely. It can be of short duration, coming and going quickly, or it may persist for decades in the form of bitterness, resentment, or hatred. Anger may be destructive, especially when it persists in the form of aggression or revenge, but it can also be constructive if it motivates us to correct injustice or to think creatively. Anger is aroused when we feel threatened, demeaned, or blocked in our progress toward some desired goal. Usually we know when we are angry, and others know as well. Sometimes, however, anger is kept hidden behind a calm and smiling facade, or buried someplace in the recesses of our brains. It always involves a physiological arousal that the angry person may not recognize consciously.

Anger, openly displayed, deliberately hidden from others, or unconsciously expressed, is at the root of many psychological, interpersonal, physical, and spiritual problems. Along with hostility, anger has been called "the chief saboteur of the mind," and "the leading cause of misery, depression, inefficiency, sickness, accidents, loss of work time and financial loss in industry. . . . No matter what the problem—marital conflict, alcoholism, a wife's frigidity, a child's defiance, nervous or physical disease—elimination of hostility is a key factor in its solution."[2]

These are strong words but probably not an overstatement. Anger can interfere with our ministries[3] and hinder our counseling, especially when counselees make *us* angry.[4] Some have argued that the entire course of world history has been shaped by anger and the struggle for emotional control.[5] Despite its prevalence and importance, however, anger has tended to be overlooked by researchers. It is difficult to measure and rarely mentioned in counseling journals. Christian psychologist Neil Clark Warren calls anger "our most baffling emotion," and concludes that "anger management is a shockingly underdeveloped skill in our society."[6] An understanding of anger, including the counselor's own anger, is basic for effective Christian counseling.

The Bible and Anger

Divine wrath and human anger are mentioned repeatedly in the Bible. In the Old Testament alone there are almost six hundred references to wrath or anger, and this theme continues in the New Testament.[7] Anger is an attribute of God and a common, probably universal, experience of human beings.

In the Bible, God's anger, fury, and wrath are mentioned more frequently than his love and tenderness. Since anger is a part of God's nature, we cannot conclude that anger, in itself, is bad. God is completely good and holy, so we must conclude that divine wrath is also good. According to James I. Packer, "God's wrath in the Bible is never the capricious, self-indulgent, irritable, morally ignoble thing that human anger so often is. It is, instead, a right and necessary reaction to objective moral evil."[8] Divine anger is vigorous, intense, controlled, and consistent with God's love and mercy. It is anger directed both at sin and at people who are sinners. Repeatedly God was angry with the unfaithful Israelites, and Jesus (whose wrath clearly is seen in Mark 3) was angry at the "stubborn hearts" of the religious leaders in his day.[9]

Because all human beings are sinners,[10] we deserve to receive the full outpouring of God's wrath against sin. But God, who is just, is also forgiving and compassionate. For this reason, he at times restrains the full expression of his wrath to give human beings the time and opportunity to repent.[11] Rom. 1:18 speaks of a divine wrath that, at present, is being revealed "from heaven against all the godlessness and wickedness of men who suppress the truth by their wickedness," but the Bible also speaks of a wrath to come in the future.[12]

An understanding of the divine wrath of God is important if we are to comprehend the biblical teachings about human anger. The Bible never criticizes the anger of God, but it warns against human anger repeatedly.[13] This is not a double standard. Anger against injustice is right and good in both God and human beings. Because God is wise, sovereign, powerful, perfect, and all-knowing, he never misinterprets a situation, never feels threatened, never loses control, and is always angered by sin and injustice. In contrast, we humans misinterpret circumstances, make mistakes in judgment, react quickly when we feel threatened or hurt, and sometimes respond with vengeance and vindictiveness. As a result, human anger can be harmful and dangerous. The Bible cautions us about this because human anger can provide an opportunity for Satan to get a foothold that creates further problems.[14] When you are angry do not sin, we read in Eph. 4:26. "Do not let the sun go down while you are still angry."

From these and similar Bible passages, we can reach several conclusions about human anger.

1. *Human Anger Is Normal and Not Necessarily Sinful.* Human beings were created in the image of God and given emotions, including anger. This anger is a necessary and useful emotion. It was seen in Jesus[15] and is not sinful in and of itself.

2. *Human Anger May Result from Faulty Perception.* God is perfect, omniscient, and always completely accurate in the way he sees things. Because of this, divine anger is always a reaction of righteous indignation against some form of unrighteousness. Human beings, in contrast, are imperfect and we see each situation from our own perspectives. We are not always able to judge accurately between real injustice (as perceived accurately by an omniscient God) and apparent injustice. As a result, we sometimes become angry over issues that we think are wrong but which, in fact, would not be considered wrong if we had all the facts. Sinful self-interest often causes our perceptions to be distorted. Because we feel vulnerable, threatened, or inclined to be critical, we can misinterpret the actions of others and jump to angry, perhaps unjustified conclusions.[16]

3. *Human Anger Often Leads to Sin.* Like other emotions, anger can be constructive (serving a useful purpose) or destructive. It can be Christ-honoring or it can be sinful. Paul's warning, "in your anger do not sin," suggests that some expressions of anger are appropriate but others are morally wrong.[17]

Because it so easily leads to sin and harmful, destructive behavior, anger is often condemned in the Bible. Anger, we are warned, lies in the lap of fools. We should, therefore, "refrain from anger and turn from wrath," being careful to control our tempers.[18] When others are angry, we are reminded that "a gentle answer turns away wrath, but a harsh word stirs up anger."[19] In the Book of Proverbs alone, anger is accepted with qualifications in one reference, but soundly condemned nine times. Although it isn't wrong in itself, anger clearly can get out of control and cause problems.[20]

Sinful anger can be expressed in a variety of ways including vengeance, verbal abuse, dishonest sharing, and even a refusal to admit that one is angry.

(a) Vengeance. Bitterness, hatred, revenge, and an attitude of judgment all result from anger and all are condemned in Scripture.[21] Vengeance is God's responsibility alone. There can be no scriptural justification for human revenge or hostile attempts to get even.

(b) Verbal Abuse. Christians are responsible for controlling their words, but this is especially difficult when we are angry. In the Old Testament the person who ventilates verbally and loses his or her temper is described as a fool.[22] In the Book of James, the dangers of verbal abuse are clearly outlined and in the same sentence readers are urged to be "quick to listen, slow to speak and slow to become angry."[23] Some modern writers, concerned about anger-inspired *physical* abuse and violence in families, are now suggesting that anger-inspired *verbal* abuse also can be a powerful and prevalent form of mistreatment.[24]

(c) Dishonest Sharing. The Bible teaches that there is value in expressing anger if this will lead another person to repent and change for the better.[25] This is a proper use of anger. But what if we pretend to be concerned about the other person's own good but use this as an excuse for expressing our own hostility? What if we gossip about another (perhaps claiming that this sharing of information is really a prayer request)? Could this be a sinful expression of hostility? All of this is dishonest sharing, a form of subtle and sinful vengeance.

(d) Refusal to Share. Since we are instructed to express anger when it is for the good of another, then it is wrong to deny, ignore, distort, or refuse to share our feelings. It is not easy to express anger in a way that lets others know that we feel hurt. As a result, some people refuse to admit their anger or gloss over feelings in a well-intentioned attempt to maintain peace. The motivation may be commendable, but the effects can be harmful. The other person never realizes that he or she has made someone angry and never knows why. As a result, there is no opportunity to change for the better. In turn, the person who represses anger sometimes harbors a bitterness that can lead to depression.[26] The Bible even calls such repression a form of lying.[27]

4. *Human Anger Can Be Controlled.* It is unlikely that God would have instructed us to control anger if human anger control is impossible. Several Bible passages imply that control *is* possible and indicate how this can be done.

(a) Anger Must Be Acknowledged. Before we can put away our bitterness, wrath, anger, and malice, we must admit, at least to ourselves, that such feelings exist.

(b) Outbursts Must Be Restrained. The man or woman of God thinks before acting. There must be a quiet weighing of issues instead of a gushing forth of sinful verbal explosions.[28]

Sometimes it is helpful to share one's burden of anger with a friend; it is always good to pour out one's feelings to God. This verbal activity often leads to new perspectives that reduce or dissipate anger before it is expressed inappropriately and allowed to harm others or damage relationships.

This is seen clearly in Psalm 73. The writer got angry and embittered because the wicked seemed to be so happy and successful while the godly were having trouble. Instead of exploding in anger the psalmist came into the presence of God and began to get a fresh new perspective on the apparent injustice in the world. His anger, as a result, subsided and was replaced by praise.

(c) Confession and Forgiveness Must Be Utilized. This involves confession to God, confession to others, and a willingness both to forgive and to receive forgiveness (repeatedly if necessary).[29]

(d) Ruminating and Revenge Must Be Resisted. It might be assumed that when Jesus was persecuted he had every right to become angry. Nevertheless, "when they hurled their insults at him, he did not retaliate; when he suffered, he made no threats. Instead, he entrusted himself to him who judges justly."[30] People who are angry often enjoy ruminating on their difficulties, thinking vengeful thoughts and pondering ways to get even. This tendency must be resisted and replaced with an attitude of entrusting oneself and one's circumstances to God.

In summary, anger is seen in the Bible as an universal emotion that is good when expressed against real injustice, harmful when expressed for self-centered motives, and clearly an emotion to be controlled. "A man who controls his temper," wrote Solomon, "is better than a warrior who captures a city."[31]

The Causes of Anger

Forty-one counselors at a large university were asked recently to describe their own feelings of anger. "We get angry," some of the respondents replied, "when counselees are resistant to counseling despite our best efforts or when people impose upon us by making demands on our time and calling our homes when that isn't necessary." Most felt anger when they were attacked verbally or physically, and some said they got angry when people would try to manipulate them by demanding special attention or trying to make them feel guilty.[32]

For many people, anger seems to come more often because of the actions of others than because of circumstances or events.[33] The Bible gives several illustrations of this. Jonah was "greatly displeased and became angry" when the people repented and God spared Nineveh, largely because of Jonah's reluctant preaching.[34] Herod became indignant and angry when he saw that the wise men had tricked him.[35] The ten disciples were angry when James and John asked for special prominence in the kingdom.[36] Jesus, himself, got angry at the self-righteous attitudes of the religious leaders and at the disciples' impatience with the little children who wanted to see him.[37]

Counselors have different viewpoints about the origins of anger.[38] Some take an *instinct approach* and assume, with Freud, that anger comes from within the individual. Anger, this theory suggests, is an innate biological drive that can be aroused by a hostile environment, the actions of other people, or the restrictions that come from living in a society. The instinct view assumes that anger boils within and is likely to explode if it isn't released.[39] In contrast, the *frustration-aggression approach* assumes that anger and aggression always come in response to frustration. Since frustration is a universal experience, all of us get angry at times. More recent (and better documented by research) is the *social learning approach* that sees anger as an emotional state of arousal that comes because of frustration but can be expressed in a variety of ways, depending on the person's perceptions and past learning.

Perhaps there are as many causes of anger as there are situations and human actions that make people angry. Nevertheless, most of these causes can be summarized under a few headings.

1. *Biology.* In a popular book on anger,[40] Carol Tavris describes a boy who got along with everyone, except during a temper tantrum. Periodically, without apparent provocation, he would fly into a furious rage that looked like a seizure. After it was over, the boy would cry and apologize, saying he couldn't help himself.

The cause for these outbursts was found to be bananas. When the boy ate a banana, his brain chemistry reacted in a way that produced rage and aggression. When bananas were eliminated from his diet, the angry outbursts stopped.

This is an unusual case; anger rarely can be understood and treated so simply. There is evidence, however, that allergies, brain disease, disorders of the body's chemistry, and perhaps genetic abnormalities can cause anger or at least make some people more prone than others to become angry.[41]

2. *Injustice.* This, as we have seen, is the reason for divine wrath; as is the injustice should also arouse anger in believers. Consider, for example, the actions of Jesus when he drove the moneychangers out of the temple. The Bible does not state that he was angry, but his overturning their tables and his criticisms of their disrespect for God's house surely imply anger. This was anger in response to a wrong that was being done. Clearly, this is one of the most valid reasons for anger (perhaps the only valid reason), but it probably is one of the least mentioned.

3. *Frustration.* A frustration is an obstacle (an event, person, or physical barrier) that hinders our progress toward some goal. Frustration may come (a) because of what someone else has done or failed to do, (b) because of unwanted events or circumstances, or (c) because of our own failures or inabilities to reach some desired goal. The extent to which we feel frustrated will depend on the importance of the goal, the size of the obstacles, and the duration of the frustration. It is mildly frustrating to be late in arriving at work because you encountered a string of red stoplights. It is much more frustrating if you fail an important exam, are denied a promotion, or have an illness that does not get better. It does not follow that anger increases automatically as one's frustration level goes up, but the *potential* for anger probably increases as the severity, frequency, and length of the frustrations increase.

4. *Threat and Hurt.* Anger is often aroused when a person perceives that he or she is rejected, put down, ignored, humiliated, unjustly criticized, or otherwise threatened. Sometimes we feel that others demand too much from us, have unrealistic expectations, or treat us unfairly. Threats like these challenge our self-esteem, remind us of our imperfections or limitations, and make us feel so vulnerable that anger and aggression become ways to fight back. Sometimes the anger hides the fact that we are hurt or threatened and lets us feel better at someone else's expense. According to one psychologist, hurt and anger always go together. "Seconds after the event which arouses the hurt feeling, another feeling skyrockets into awareness—anger."[42] This anger comes so quickly and is so visible that it is easy to miss the hurt that comes first.

It is well known that a single event can make one person livid with anger but hardly seem to bother someone else. In part, these variations depend on personality differences or on the ways in which a situation is perceived. How do you respond when somebody cuts you off in traffic or races to get the parking space that you were approaching? Some drivers would respond with anger and a determination to get even because they view this as a challenge to their driving skills or a stealing of their rights to the parking space. Others might be annoyed but conclude "If that's the only way the other guy can boost his self-esteem and assert his superiority, then he's the one with the problem; not me." Whether or not we get angry will depend on how we look at the situation.

5. *Learning.* Anthropological studies[43] have shown that people from different cultures get angry over different issues and express their anger in different ways. By watching or listening to others (including what we see on television), we learn how to act when we are angry and we even learn what to be angry about. One counselor who works with angry teenagers concluded that "in nearly every situation, there was at least one parent who was also a very angry person."[44] By watching others, children and adults both learn when and how to be angry.

"Do not make friends with a hot-tempered man," we read in Prov. 22:24–25. "Do not associate with the one easily angered, or you may learn his ways and get yourself ensnared."

The Effects of Anger

People do not all respond to an anger-producing situation in the same way. Our reactions could depend on the attitudes and examples of our parents, the size of our family or neighborhood where we live, our personalities and level of maturity, and the way we perceive a situation. It is probable that stressful events in the environment are less likely to arouse anger than are our perceptions, background experiences, and interpretations of the events. This helps explain why the same situation that makes one person respond with strong anger will barely ruffle another. These individual differences also help to explain why one person can calm another or, in contrast, why one angry person can arouse another's anger. If we can persuade others to change their interpretations of an event or situation, we often can change their emotions.

Religion can also affect the ways in which we experience and express anger. One of the fruits of the Spirit is self-control and there is some evidence that deeply religious people are more inclined to repress than to express anger.[45] One's religious group also can have an influence. Quakers, for example, believe that violence is wrong and this could influence how a Quaker might respond to an anger-arousing situation.

One writer has suggested that anger influences people in four basic ways.[46] It can be repressed (so that we refuse to admit its presence), suppressed (deliberately hiding it from others), expressed (in either destructive or harmless ways), or confessed (to God and to others). Perhaps another way to summarize the effects of anger is to suggest that we can hold back and withdraw from an anger-producing situation, turn our feelings inward where others cannot see them, act out by attacking the source of anger or some substitute, or face and deal directly with the causes of the anger. These four approaches overlap and each of us may shift from one to another, depending on the individual, on our perceptions, and on the situation.

1. *Holding Back.* This is perhaps the easiest but least effective way to deal with anger. When we withdraw from a situation, we often can ignore our anger and hold back facing and expressing our frustrations. Withdrawal can take several forms:

- Leaving the room, taking a vacation, or otherwise removing oneself physically from the situation that stimulates anger.
- Avoiding the problem by plunging into work or other activities, by thinking about other things, or by escaping into a world of television or novels.
- Hiding from the problem by alcohol or drug abuse or other behavior that could be used to get back at the person who makes us angry.

Holding back anger can be healthy for a while. It gives the person time to reevaluate the situation and can prevent angry outbursts and the resulting guilt. When anger is ignored, however, it begins to affect us in other ways.

2. *Turning Inward.* Sometimes people force anger out of awareness and deny, consciously or unconsciously, that it even exists. This can be an unhealthy way to cope with the problem. At best the relief is only temporary and in time the pressure builds until it bursts out to create more difficulties.

When anger is kept within and not expressed there may be calmness and smiling on the outside but boiling rage inside. This internal anger is a powerful force that may express itself in:

- Physical symptoms ranging from a mild headache to ulcers, high blood pressure, or heart attacks.
- Psychological reactions such as anxiety, fear, or feelings of tension and depression.[47]
- Unconscious attempts to harm ourselves (seen, for example, in accident proneness, a tendency to make mistakes, or even suicide).
- Thinking characterized by self-pity, thoughts of revenge, or ruminations on the injustices that one is experiencing.
- Spiritual struggles that come because we wallow in bitterness, wrath, anger, and slander. This grieves the Holy Spirit because we are ignoring his spiritual guidance and direction in our lives.[48]

3. *Acting Out.* It can be helpful to remember that anger is not the same as aggression, even though the two frequently go together. Anger is an emotional response that includes both physical and mental arousal. Aggression is a type of behavior that inflicts pain or pressure on others. It is possible to be angry and not aggressive; we also can be aggressive without being angry.

When anger leads to aggression, the person is said to be acting out. This can be done in three ways: direct aggression, passive aggression, and redirected aggression.

(a) Direct Aggression. Violence has been called "as American as cherry pie,"[49] but direct aggression is seen in almost all societies. The most natural and immediate response to anger is to lash out, verbally or physically, against the person or situation that has made us angry. When an individual explodes in anger, he or she may feel better *for a short period of time.* Others, however, are hurt in the process. Often the person who exploded feels later embarrassment and guilt, relationships are damaged, friendships and jobs are sometimes terminated, property may be destroyed, and the direct expression of anger usually leads to more anger in the future rather than less.[50]

(b) Passive Aggression. Some people are pleasant and apparently cooperative in face-to-face situations, but they give vent to their anger in subtle ways. "My wife is a wonderful cook," a preacher said in his sermon. "She makes wonderful burnt sacrifices." Everybody laughed, including the wife, but beneath the humor she felt her husband's barb.

Passive-aggressive people may gossip and spread damaging stories, "forget" to do what they promised, refuse to cooperate, make "put down" or embarrassing comments when others can't respond, or leave another person's property where it "just happens" to be damaged or stolen. Drinking, failing in school, or an extramarital affair are examples of subtle ways that people use to attack or get even with parents, a mate, or some other person who has made us angry. The passive-aggressive person seems to have an exquisite talent for doing what hurts the most,[51] but often these actions can be excused, justified, or explained. This is an indirect form of aggression aimed at the source of one's anger.

(c) Redirected Aggression. Sometimes aggressive anger is aimed at somebody who is innocent. The man who is angry with his boss may stifle his anger at work (lest he be fired), but he takes it out on his wife or children at home in the evening because this is a safe place to ventilate. The family may not have caused the anger, but they bear the brunt of the angry person's feelings.

Anger is especially difficult to handle when we cannot identify who is to be blamed or when we cannot reach the person who created the situation that made us angry. If inflation decreases our spending power, whom do we blame? The supermarket may be charging higher prices, but the store manager alone is not responsible for inflation. If we decide that the real source of the problem rests with some government leader, this may be some aloof, distant politician who is difficult to contact and never available to hear our complaints or criticisms. As a result, we may verbally, physically, or cognitively attack some largely innocent but accessible person. Angry revolutionaries who burn and loot stores in an attempt to bring down a political leader, often do nothing to change the leader but, in giving vent to their anger, they destroy the property of innocent store owners.

All of these acting-out approaches are ultimately destructive. They are forms of the eye-for-an-eye, tooth-for-a-tooth, get-even philosophy that Jesus so clearly condemned.[52]

4. *Facing the Sources of Anger.* This is an approach that attempts to deal directly with the threatening, incapacitating, or fear-producing situation that is causing the anger. The individual admits the anger, tries to see its causes, sometimes looks at the situation in a different way, and then does whatever seems best to accept or change the anger-producing situation. This is a constructive approach to anger reduction that some people only learn with the help of a counselor.

Counseling and Anger

Anger, as we have seen, can lead to sinful behavior and can harm people physically, psychologically, spiritually, and socially. Why, then, do so many people seem to take delight in hostility and persist in harboring grudges? Is it possible that anger makes some people feel powerful, superior, and right? For some, trying to handle the anger maturely or turning the other cheek seem to imply that they are weak, inclined to back down, or willing to be pushed around. In the guise of maintaining self-esteem or standing up for their rights, some people refuse to take the actions that could change the anger-producing situations and eliminate misunderstanding.

All of this suggests that some of our counselees might enjoy being angry. Counseling doesn't help much because there is little desire for change. When such an attitude is encountered there can be value in stating your suspicion that the counselee really doesn't want to be different. Be prepared for the counselee to disagree, but remember that this can lead to further discussion about one's desires and motives for changing.

When there is a desire for change, counseling can take several forms.

1. *Help Counselees Admit Anger.* Anger that is denied will never be eliminated, but sometimes the most difficult challenge in counseling is to help people see and admit that they are angry. Such an admission can be threatening, especially for people who are angry at a loved one or who think that all anger is wrong. It may help to point out that anger is a common, God-given emotion that, for most people, gets out of control periodically. Point out some of the signs of hidden anger (depression, physical symptoms, criticism, a tendency to gossip or not cooperate, impatience, or similar behaviors). If the counselee persists in denying the anger even after hearing the evidence, perhaps he or she will admit the *possibility* that anger is present.

2. *Help Counselees Express Anger.* One of the greatest and most destructive myths about anger is the view that we need to get it out of our systems, let off steam, swear, holler, scream, pound a pillow, or find some other way to vent hostility in an effort to decrease feelings of anger. This idea is never suggested in Scripture and neither is it supported by psychological research. In contrast, there is evidence that ventilation, expressions of rage, tantrums, and continual talking about our anger all tend to *increase* anger instead of reducing it.[53]

How, then, can anger be expressed in more healthy ways? Sports and hobbies can sometimes be harmless ways to redirect our energies. Even better are some of the suggestions given by Christian psychologist Archibald Hart.[54] Try to deal with your hurts and anger as they arise, one at a time, he suggests. This keeps anger from building up. Ask yourself if the anger is justified and if it has come because you feel afraid or threatened. When someone has hurt you, tell the person and say why it has hurt and made you feel angry. "Blowing up at someone you love doesn't help much. But the articulation of anger does help. To tell someone you care about that he or she has hurt or angered you is to allow a rectification."[55] Recognize that the other person has feelings too, and try to understand these. Listen and accept any explanation or apology that may be offered and try to be forgiving. All of this can be helpful to counselees who have a tendency to explode first and talk later.

3. *Help Counselees Consider the Sources of Anger.* Even if the anger is denied,

there can be value in asking, "What kinds of things do make you angry?" From this general beginning, move to the specifics: "I'd like you to think of a time when you were really mad. Tell me about it." In discussing specific examples, the counselee and counselor can begin to see what caused the angry feelings, when they occurred, and how they were expressed and handled. In considering the sources of anger, watch for attempts to make excuses. Comments like "I'm Irish so how can I help being angry?" or "My father had ulcers from being angry so I guess it runs in the family" can be attempts to avoid facing the real source of the anger. When statements like these aren't challenged, the anger persists.

Counselees can be taught to ask themselves some basic questions whenever they feel angry. (Counselors can also make a practice of asking themselves these questions.)

- What is making me feel angry?
- Why am I feeling anger and not some other emotion?
- Am I jumping to conclusions about the situation or person who is making me feel angry?
- Is there something about this situation that threatens me and makes me feel afraid or inferior?
- Did my anger come because I had some unrealistic expectations?
- How might others, including the person who is angering me, view this situation?
- Is there another way to look at the situation?
- Are there things I can do to change the situation in order to reduce my anger?

Following a winter storm, one of my friends lost control of his car, slid into a ditch, and hit a fence that dented a fender. Although the driver was not hurt, he was angered by the inconvenience, the damage to the car, and the towing expense of having the vehicle pulled back on to the road. As soon as the tow truck jerked the car out of the snow and my friend walked over to scan the damage, a car horn sounded and the well-dressed middle-aged driver of a big car began shouting from his window. "Hurry up, son," he demanded in an annoyed tone of voice. "You're holding up traffic. I can't sit here all day!"

My friend, who doubtless showed more patience and control than the shouting driver, said nothing, but got into his car and drove away. "But I was really mad," he said later. "This stranger took it upon himself to put me down and order me around. That wasn't what I needed, especially when I was so frustrated already."

Here is an example in which anger was admitted. My friend pondered what was really making him angry, discussed these frustrations with his wife, and later evaluated the situation in terms of the questions listed above. He recognized that he had felt belittled by a driver who acted superior, but my friend became less tense as he thought about why the other driver was so tense, insensitive and impatient. The anger did not go away immediately, but neither did it persist or erupt into physical symptoms, sinful outbursts, or impatience at home. Anger that is acknowledged, considered, and reevaluated loses much of its power.[56]

4. *Focus on Humility, Confession, and Forgiveness.* Teaching people to admit and evaluate their anger may be good first steps in dealing with the issue, but these are not

permanent solutions. As we have seen, anger can lead to sinful thoughts, desires, words, and actions. Counselees must be helped to deal with these issues if anger is to be controlled. Humility, confession, and forgiveness are of basic importance.

(a) Humility. It can be a humbling experience to admit that we are angry or have lost self-control and acted aggressively. Some people apparently prefer to remain angry rather than risk admitting their weaknesses or failure. Others, however, are willing to acknowledge the reality of their anger along with any accompanying sinful side effects. This attitude must come before confession.

(b) Confession. The Bible emphasizes the importance and value of confessing to God and to others.[57] When we confess to God, telling him honestly that we are angry and admitting that we are sorry for our acts of aggression,[58] then we can know for certain that we are forgiven.[59] If we confess to one or more fellow believers, they can support, forgive, encourage and pray for us.

(c) Forgiveness. Some people know intellectually that they are forgiven, but since they don't feel forgiven, they continue in their guilt. Perhaps one way to feel forgiven is to remind ourselves repeatedly of 1 John 1:9. An additional technique is to be sure that we forgive others.

When Jesus was asked about this one day, he said that we should forgive repeatedly. Then he told a story about forgiveness and anger, concluding that people who refuse to forgive others in turn will not be forgiven. This has great relevance for those who hold grudges. Their anger is certain to continue with all the accompanying misery and tension.

Forgiveness can be very difficult, especially in situations that are unjust. Both counselees and counselors need to ask God for the ability to forgive. We need help in giving up feelings of revenge, in casting off all feelings of hatred, and in being open to the possibility of a restored relationship.[60] When we can accept forgiveness and learn to forgive others, then we are freed from many of the hurts and frustrations from the past. Memories of past injustices may not disappear; to forgive does not mean that we automatically forget. Yet giving and receiving forgiveness leaves us less bogged down by anger and better able to focus our energies on other, more wholesome activities. Forgiveness is an act of choice that can help people let go of their bitterness.[61] Forgiveness may be the most crucial step in dealing with anger.

5. *Teach Self-Control.* When a person gets angry, reason often gives way to feelings, and something is said or done that might be regretted later. You can give at least four ways to help counselees gain greater self-control over anger.

(a) Growing Spiritually. This, of course, is an ongoing process that doesn't suddenly start when something makes us mad. Self-control is listed in Gal. 5:23 as a fruit of the Spirit. Believers who sincerely want to be led by the Holy Spirit will discover a slow decline in strife, jealousy, outbursts of anger, and other "deeds of the flesh." With God's help we can learn love, patience, gentleness, and self-control.[62] Only the Christian counselor can share such teaching and model it in his or her own life. Self-control is not something that we each must do alone and without divine help.

(b) Slowing Reactions. The old idea of counting to ten before speaking sometimes helps one gain control before reacting.[63] Others have suggested the value of speaking slowly, not raising one's voice, pausing periodically (if possible), tensing the muscles and then letting them relax, and mentally telling oneself to calm down. Clearly, "a gentle answer turns away wrath, but a harsh word stirs up anger."[64]

(c) Avoiding an Angry Mind-Set. Some people look for the worst in almost every situation. They are perpetually critical, always negative, and invariably hostile. Sometimes these people are in positions of Christian leadership and too often they are counselors. Almost always they are basically unhappy.

Most people find themselves slipping periodically into a negative mind-set, and unless this is resisted, we can get caught in what has been called a "hostility trap."[65] The Scriptures instruct us to think about things that are right, pure, good, and praiseworthy.[66] It is impossible to think such thoughts repeatedly while, at the same time, we wallow in anger, bitterness, and hostility. Perhaps it is even harder to hold on to angry thoughts if we sincerely pray for those who cause our frustration and anger.[67] The Apostle Paul had a positive mind-set and an attitude of thanksgiving and praise to God. As a result he avoided ruminating in anger, even when circumstances were unjust and difficult.[68]

(d) Using "I"-Statements. Some counselees may need help in distinguishing between anger and aggression. Point out that we can be angry without hurting others or thinking hostile thoughts. Stress the importance of using "I"-statements. "I was hurt by what you did," "I feel frustrated," or "I felt angry and put down by what you said," are all clear, nonblaming statements that express feelings without aggression or loss of self-control.[69]

6. *Build a Healthy Self-Concept.* Hostility and anger, including prolonged hostility, often indicate that a person feels inferior, insecure, and lacking in self-esteem or self-confidence. Individuals who are made to feel inferior often react with anger and attempts to assert superiority. This can lead to arguments in which two people try to bolster themselves and each tries to make the other feel inferior.

Counselees are better able to control their anger when they are helped to develop a healthy self-esteem, based on their value as God's special creatures.[70] One psychologist has described a solid self-concept as the ultimate answer to anger management. "The stronger your self-concept becomes," he writes, "the easier it will be to manage your anger."[71]

Christians recognize that we are sinners, subject to pride and the dangers of exalted self-importance. Nevertheless, we recognize that God has redeemed us, made us his children, and given us the worth that we didn't deserve. This can be the basis for a healthy self-image and self-confidence.

All of these counseling suggestions are designed to help people deal with anger without venting it in a vain attempt to "clear the air." Dealing with anger can be an effective way to approach the problem. Venting it, especially when this is accompanied by overt aggression, is of no value and may intensify the very feelings that the counseling is attempting to control.

Preventing Anger

Anger is a God-given emotion that, in itself, cannot and should not be eliminated or prevented. There are several ways, however, in which the unhealthy, destructive, and nonbiblical aspects of anger can be prevented.

1. *Biblical Teaching.* The Bible, as we have seen, says a great deal about anger, but it seems that these teachings are not often shared in a theologically clear and practical, relevant way. In the absence of such instruction, Christians are confused

by the seeming contradictions between the anger of Jesus and the biblical admonitions to control anger. On a practical level there is uncertainty about one's own anger and how it can be handled. Repeated teaching about anger and self-control can help individuals to better understand these concepts, to distinguish between righteous anger and personal reactions, and to avoid the long-lasting destructive effects of anger and hostility.

2. *Avoiding Anger-Arousing Situations and People.* Problems are never solved if we avoid them in an attempt to maintain peace. Sometimes duty or wisdom demand that we face frustrating situations squarely or deal directly with difficult people. Even so, there are times when one can stay away from situations, events, or people who are likely to arouse unnecessary anger.[72]

3. *Learning to Reevaluate Situations.* Coaches sometimes encourage athletes to be angry, hoping that this will stimulate adrenalin and improve performance. Regretfully some athletes find it difficult to control physical aggression outside the sports arena,[73] and others find that anger destroys their concentration and interferes with athletic skill. Studies have found that the best athletes remain calm, undistracted, and unangered even when they are provoked by opposition players. These self-controlled athletes have learned to expect setbacks. In preparing mentally for the game, they have anticipated the potentially upsetting events and have rehearsed ways to handle them. As a result, the distractions have produced increased concentration instead of disruptive rage.[74]

It is difficult to control emotions, but we can control the thoughts that give rise to feelings.[75] In the home, but also in the church and school, people can be taught by words and by example to evaluate each anger-arousing situation. They can learn to see that anger often comes from hurt, frustration, and disappointment. They can learn to respond calmly, perhaps by using "I"-statements, and without blaming, overreacting, or saying things that might be regretted later. Instruction about these issues can be helpful, but lasting learning is not likely to come from a lecture or book. Most people will learn slowly, by watching others and by having experiences, including failure experiences, that in time can teach more about anger-control.

4. *Building Self-Esteem.* It has been said that we can no more insulate ourselves from irritating remarks, attitudes, and actions than we can hide from germs. We can, however, protect ourselves by maintaining the resistance that comes from a healthy self-respect.[76] Anger is less destructive and more easily controlled when a person is secure as an individual and not plagued by excessive feelings of inferiority and self-doubt. Chapter 21 discusses inferiority and self-esteem including ways to prevent a poor self-concept. When Christians have realistic pictures of themselves as persons of value, there is less need or inclination to get angry.

5. *Avoiding Ruminations.* When people get angry they often go through the day meditating on the causes of their anger. As this ruminating continues, the original causes often are blown up into false proportions. This can cause the anger to increase, especially when critical people associate with other critical people and share their criticisms. In this way some people develop a whole mind-set of negativism and bitterness that grows worse as they get older.

This kind of thinking may be fun, at first, because it lets the thinker fantasize about his or her own superiority. Because this thinking is destructive, it must be resisted and replaced with thinking that is positive and less critical.[77] This message should be taught and modeled in the church and at home. Such teaching can prevent the harmful buildup of anger.

6. *Learning to Confront.* Conflict and disagreement are a part of life that cannot be avoided. Nevertheless, people can be taught how to tell each other how they feel, what they want, and what they think. This need not be done with a critical confrontation that stimulates anger. Instead, the truth can be spoken gently and in love.[78] When we learn to communicate honestly and effectively there is a prevention and reduction of destructive anger.

7. *Spirit Control.* Uncontrolled anger, as we have seen, is listed in the Bible as one of the deeds of the flesh, but self-control is one of the fruits of the Spirit. As believers in Jesus Christ seek to avoid sin and sincerely desire to be led by his Holy Spirit, there can be a slow but predictable growth in self-control and a steady decline in anger and hostility. Committing one's life to the Spirit's control on a daily basis can be an effective approach to the prevention of destructive anger.

Conclusions about Anger

There can be no easy answers to explain completely why a young high school student would kill his family in a late-night fit of rage. Severe anger, like angry feelings that are less intense, can have a variety of causes and ways to be treated. As this chapter has shown, the Bible and psychology can combine to increase our understanding of anger, and can help counselors to be more effective in working with people who struggle with anger and self-control.

SUGGESTIONS FOR FURTHER READING

Cosgrove, Mark. *Counseling and Anger.* Waco, Tex.: Word, 1988.
Hart, Archibald D. *Feeling Free.* Old Tappan, N.J.: Revell, 1979.*
Tavris, Carol. *Anger: The Misunderstood Emotion.* New York: Simon & Schuster, 1982.*
Warren, Neil Clark. *Make Anger Your Ally.* Garden City, N.Y.: Doubleday, 1983.*
Wilkes, Peter. *Overcoming Anger and Other Dragons of the Soul.* Downers Grove, Ill.: InterVarsity, 1987.*

* Books marked with an asterisk (*) are especially suited for counselees to read.

10

Guilt

AL IS TWENTY-EIGHT YEARS OLD, single, and engaged to a young lady whom he loves very, very much. In spite of his relatively young age, he is a deacon in the small suburban church that he and his fiancée attend.

But Al has a problem with masturbation. He knows that this is common in single men of his age, but he feels guilty about the practice and unable to stop. Once when he was in college, Al went to a counselor who wasn't a Christian and wasn't very helpful.

"All college students masturbate," the counselor said. "Don't worry about it. Just relax and enjoy it."

That did nothing to solve the problem or to alleviate Al's guilt. But it did make him hesitant to talk about his problem again. So he wrote a letter to me—someone whom he had never met.

"Does masturbation every have a physiological or chemical origin?" he wrote, perhaps in hopes that the problem might be physically caused and beyond his control.

"I feel ashamed of some of the thoughts that go through my mind when I masturbate," the letter continued. "I don't want to tell my fiancée, but I'm afraid to get married lest we have sexual problems because I masturbated as a single man. People in the church keep asking when we are getting married, but I keep putting it off because I feel so guilty.

"And what about my church? Should I resign from being a deacon? I like to serve in the church, I am well respected, and people say I am doing a good job. If I resign, they would want to know why, but I don't know what I would tell them. And how would my parents respond? They are in the same church."

In my letter of reply, I tried to reassure him. I urged him to share the problem with some older male who would keep the discussion confidential. In time, he might want to talk it over with his fiancée—just as he would talk it over with the Lord.

Some people, like the university counselor, make light of both masturbation and guilt. But for Al, these were real issues. In his letter, he even used the word "suffering." This was not physical suffering; it was a mental and spiritual anguish that was making all of life miserable.

For centuries, theologians and philosophers have struggled with the problem of suffering. Why do people suffer? Does suffering serve any useful purpose? How can human suffering be reduced or eliminated?

The answers, like the questions, are complex.[1] While most creatures suffer physical pain, humans additionally experience the anguish of mental suffering. Because of our intellect, we can worry about the future, agonize over the past, consciously inflict physical or mental pain on others, and struggle with the problem of pain in ourselves. Sometimes suffering comes through no fault of our own, but often we suffer because of what we ourselves have done.

Guilt is at the basis of much human suffering. "I'll never get used to it," one counselor has said. "There is no box big enough to hold all the persons with guilt. They are all unique and need to be seen as individuals. It is not an easy task."[2] Perhaps no other topic so consistently pervades all of the problem areas discussed in this book. Talk with people who are depressed, lonely, grieving, members of violent families, homosexual, alcoholic, terminally ill, struggling with marriage turmoil, or facing almost any other problem, and you will find people who experience guilt as part of their difficulties. Guilt has been described as the place where religion and psychology most often meet.[3] It has been called *the* crucial factor in the problems that people bring to Christian counselors.[4] According to psychologist Bruce Narramore, an understanding of guilt feelings is central to any understanding of psychological maladjustment.[5]

Several types of guilt have been identified. These can be grouped into two broad categories: objective guilt and subjective guilt. Objective guilt occurs when a law has been broken and the lawbreaker *is* guilty even though he or she may not *feel* guilty. Subjective guilt refers to the inner feelings of remorse and self-condemnation that come because of our actions. Your counseling is likely to be more difficult if you fail to distinguish between the different types of guilt.[6]

1. *Objective Guilt.* This can be divided into four types. These overlap, merge with one another, and often are less distinctive than the following paragraphs might imply.

First, there is *legal guilt*—the violation of society's laws. A person who drives through a red light or steals from a department store is guilty, even if the person is never caught and regardless of whether he or she feels any remorse.

Theological guilt involves a failure to obey the laws of God. The Bible describes divine standards for human behavior, standards that we all violate at times by our actions or thoughts. According to the Scriptures, we are all sinners.[7] We are all guilty before God whether or not we feel remorse.

Many psychiatrists and psychologists do not admit the existence of theological guilt. To do so would be to admit that there are absolute moral standards. If absolute standards exist, there must be a standard setter; that is, a God. For many, it is easier to believe that right and wrong are relative, dependent on one's own experiences, training, and subjective values. As we will see, this has great practical implications for counseling.

A third type of objective guilt is *personal guilt.* Here the individual violates his or her own personal standards or resists the urgings of conscience. No laws have been broken and neither has the guilty person disobeyed God. If a father determines to spend each Sunday with the family, for example, he experiences guilt when business keeps him away from home over a weekend. His overweight wife may feel guilty when she indulges in a tempting dessert.

Social guilt comes when we break an unwritten but socially expected rule. If a person behaves rudely, gossips maliciously, criticizes unkindly, or ignores someone who has a need, no law has been broken and there may be no feelings of remorse.

Nevertheless, the guilty person has violated the social expectations of other people in the neighborhood, church, workplace, or society.

Most people feel uncomfortable when they break a civil law (legal guilt), deliberately resist or ignore God (theological guilt), violate a personal standard (personal guilt), and/or act contrary to social expectations (social guilt). It is possible to do all of these, however, and never feel guilty. The hardened criminal may act violently but feel no sadness or remorse. Millions of people, including professed Christians, forget God every day and thus sin against him. These people *are* guilty before God but they do not *feel* guilty about their actions.

2. *Subjective Guilt.* This is the uncomfortable feeling of regret, remorse, shame, and self-condemnation that often comes when we have done or thought something that we feel is wrong, or failed to do something that should have been done. Often there is discouragement, anxiety, fear of punishment, low self-esteem, and a sense of isolation, all tied together as part of the guilt feeling. These emotions may be strong or weak. Usually they are unpleasant but they are not always bad. They can stimulate us to change our behavior and seek forgiveness from God or from other human beings. Guilt feelings, however, can also be destructive, inhibitory influences that make life miserable.

Subjective guilt feelings can be appropriate or inappropriate.[8] *Appropriate guilt feelings* are present when we have broken a law, disobeyed biblical teachings, or violated the dictates of our conscience and feel remorse in proportion to the seriousness of our actions. *Inappropriate guilt feelings* are out of proportion to the seriousness of the act. Some people, for example, can steal and murder but feel little guilt while others may be immobilized with guilt in response to some minor act or unkind thought. Often these inappropriate guilt feelings come from within ourselves, but at times other people make comments or judgments that make us feel guilty. Sometimes these comments are made with no harm intended, but at other times they are designed to create guilt.

All of this shows that guilt is a big and complex subject. In counseling it is important to distinguish between objective and subjective guilt, although most counselees will be concerned about the latter. It also is important to understand the biblical teaching about guilt.

The Bible and Guilt

When people talk about guilt they usually are referring to subjective guilt feelings, but the Bible never uses guilt in this way. The three Greek words translated "guilt" or "guilty" refer to the theological guilt that was described earlier. A person is guilty, in the biblical sense, when he or she has broken God's law. In the Bible, there appears to be little difference between guilt and sin.[9]

This has significant implications for Christians. Since the Bible never talks about subjective guilt feelings, in no place does it imply that we should try to arouse guilt feelings in others. In spite of this, many well-intentioned parents, teachers, preachers, television evangelists, and counselors attempt to stir up guilt on the assumption that this will motivate others, stimulate Christian growth, punish wrongdoers, prevent pride, protect people from future sin, or stimulate financial contributions.

Non-Christians have been critical of such tactics, arguing (correctly, I believe) that they arouse unhealthy guilt feelings and tend to be manipulative.[10]

Is it possible to help people deal with their sin or objective guilt without creating unhealthy guilt feelings? To answer, let us consider the concepts of constructive sorrow and divine forgiveness.

Constructive sorrow, sometimes called godly sorrow, is a term used by Bruce Narramore[11] and based on 2 Cor. 7:8–10. In this passage, Paul contrasts worldly sorrow (this seems to be equivalent to guilt feelings) and godly sorrow that "brings repentance that leads to salvation and leaves no regret." Godly sorrow is constructive sorrow because it leads to constructive change.

Narramore illustrates this by describing a situation in which two people are in a cafe and one accidentally spills coffee on the other person's lap. A guilt feeling reaction would be, "How stupid I am. Look at the mess I've made because I'm so clumsy. I'm sorry." The coffee spiller feels foolish and is self-critical. Constructive sorrow is different. The individual might say, "I'm very sorry. Let me try to help you wipe it up," and later there is an offer to pay the cleaning bill. The first response, psychological guilt, is self-condemning and not biblical; the latter, constructive sorrow, is scriptural and healthy.

Narramore suggests that many Christians go through repeated cycles of sin, guilt feelings, confession, temporary relief, and then more sin. For some, 1 John 1:9 "has come to be used as a kind of psychological spot remover for emotional guilt,"[12] but there is no real change. This is because the confession really is based on a selfish motive: to get relief from guilt feelings. As soon as this relief is experienced, the person feels free to sin again and the cycle is repeated.

In contrast, Peter followed his denial of Christ by weeping bitterly.[13] He experienced deep remorse, sincere repentance, and a genuine desire to change. He confessed his sin, was freed from any feelings of guilt, and knew he was forgiven.

Divine forgiveness is a major biblical theme, especially in the New Testament. Jesus Christ came to die so sinful human beings could be forgiven and restored to complete fellowship with God.[14]

Although some passages of Scripture mention forgiveness without discussing repentance, other passages imply that at least two conditions must be met before God forgives. First, we must repent. "For Him to forgive without requiring repentance would be like condoning sin or being indifferent to it."[15] Second, we must be willing to forgive.[16] Jesus mentions this at least three times in the Bible. The person who seeks forgiveness must be genuinely repentant and willing to forgive others.[17]

Try to remember this emphasis on constructive sorrow and the promise of divine forgiveness as you seek to help both those who have objective guilt and those who experience subjective guilt feelings.

The Causes of Guilt

As we have seen, objective guilt comes when we have violated legal, theological, personal, and/or social laws and moral standards. It is rare for someone to come for counseling solely because of objective guilt. More often, the guilty person has been caught and is afraid of punishment, or the person is experiencing subjective feelings of guilt.

Why do people feel guilty? There can be several reasons.

1. *Past Experience and Unrealistic Expectations.* An individual's standards of what is right and wrong, good and bad, usually develop in childhood.[18] As thinking and reasoning abilities develop, children learn the standards of their parents and others. Each child comes to understand the difference between right and wrong, and soon there is an awareness of the punishments or other reactions that come when one disobeys.

In some homes the standards are so rigid and so high that the child almost never succeeds. There is little if any praise or encouragement because the parents are never satisfied. Instead, the child is blamed, condemned, criticized, and punished so frequently that he or she is made to feel like a constant failure. As a result, there is self-blame, self-criticism, inferiority, and persisting guilt feelings, all because the child has learned a set of standards that seem impossible to reach. While parents most often express these standards, sometimes they come from church leaders who believe individuals can live completely free of sin.[19] If the young person decides to rebel against his or her moral upbringing, there may be additional feelings of guilt, some of which may come from the words of parents or others who disapprove and condemn but make no effort to understand and give realistic guidance.

As they grow older, children usually come to accept the standards of their parents and religious leaders. When these standards are unrealistically rigid, the young people come to expect perfection in themselves, set up standards that never can be reached, and slide into feelings of guilt and self-blame following the inevitable failures. Guilt feelings are one of the ways by which we both punish ourselves and push ourselves to keep trying to do better. Some workaholics, for example, seem influenced strongly by feelings of guilt. Because of their past learning and experiences, these people fear that they are not producing enough or not "redeeming the time." As a result, they keep working in an attempt to accomplish more. Perhaps unconsciously there is hope that this will keep them from feeling guilty.

The best response to unrealistic standards is the adoption of realistic standards. God expects us to keep pressing on toward the goal of Christian maturity.[20] He disapproves of sin and disobedience, but he sent his Son so we could find forgiveness and life in abundance. Surely he does not want us to wallow in self-condemnation and guilt feelings. Such an attitude has no biblical basis.

2. *Inferiority and Social Pressure.* It is difficult to know whether a feeling of inferiority creates guilt feelings or whether guilt feelings produce inferiority. In a widely influential book, *Guilt and Grace,* Paul Tournier titled the first chapter "Inferiority and Guilt." He argued, in company with more recent writers,[21] that there can be no clear distinction between guilt and inferiority since "all inferiority is experienced as guilt."[22]

Why do people feel inferior? This is discussed more fully in chapter 21, but it appears that our self-perceptions are greatly influenced by the opinions and criticisms of others. "In everyday life we are continually soaked in this unhealthy atmosphere of mutual criticism, so much so that we are not always aware of it and we find ourselves drawn unwittingly into an implacable vicious circle: every reproach evokes a feeling of guilt in the critic as much as in the one criticized, and each one gains relief from his guilt in any way he can, by criticizing other people and in self-justification. . . . Social suggestion is then the source of innumerable feelings of guilt."[23]

3. *Faulty Conscience Development.* The word "conscience" does not appear in the Old Testament, and although it is used thirty-one times by New Testament writers, the word is never clearly defined.[24] Paul wrote that consciences are built on universal, divinely given moral principles that are "written in" human hearts,[25] and probably placed in us by God before we are able to even think about right and wrong. But the conscience can be "seared," dulled into insensitivity, by persistent involvement with sin, by abandoning biblical teachings, and by dabbling in demonic ideas.[26] Consciences can be weak, and they can be strengthened.[27] Clearly the conscience can be altered by the teachings and actions of others.[28]

Beginning with Freud, psychologists and psychiatrists have maintained that the conscience is molded early in life by the prohibitions and expectations of parents. The child learns how to act in ways that will bring praise and avoid punishment.

At this early stage in life, the child also learns about guilt. When parents are good models of what they want to teach, when the home is warm, predictable, and secure, and when there is more emphasis on approval and giving encouragement than on punishment and criticism, then the child knows what it means to experience acceptance and forgiveness. In contrast, when there are poor parental models, or moral training that is punitive, critical, fear ridden, and unrealistically demanding, then the child becomes angry, rigid, critical, and burdened by a continuing sense of guilt. In time there may be rebellion against parental teachings and acceptance of the alternate views that come from one's peers.

Regardless of their backgrounds, most children eventually shift away from the belief that something is right or wrong simply because of what parents, the church, or even one's peers say. As they mature, children move toward a personal commitment to ideals that they believe "in their hearts" to be right. This does not involve ridding oneself of parental instruction, much of which has instilled the moral values of the family and society. Instead, the maturing young person reflects on what has been taught, ponders the competing values of one's peers, and eventually comes to accept one's own standards. According to psychologist Lars Granberg, "A mature Christian conscience is furthered by sound instruction in the Bible, an open and supportive climate of inquiry which encourages honest expression of opinion and thoughtful appraisal of conscience, good adult models after whom to pattern oneself, and a grasp both of the reality of forgiveness and the proper fruit of repentance: getting up and going on without wallowing in self-recrimination."[29]

Many people do not reach this ideal. Trained to think rigidly about right and wrong, convinced of their own imperfections and incompetences, fearful of failures or punishment, and lacking in the awareness of God's complete forgiveness, these people are constantly plagued with guilt feelings. These guilt feelings come not because of sorrow for sin or regret over law breaking. They are signs that the person is preoccupied with a fear of punishment, isolation, or lowered self-esteem. To bolster themselves, such people often are rigid, critical of others, unforgiving, afraid of making moral decisions, domineering, and inclined to show an attitude of moral superiority. They are difficult to have at home or in the church, but because they so often are angry and unhappy, these are people who need understanding and help more than criticism.

4. *Supernatural Influences.* Before the Fall, Adam and Eve apparently had no conscience, no knowledge of good or evil, and no sense of guilt.[30] Immediately after their disobedience, however, they realized that they had done wrong and they tried to hide from God.[31] Objective theological guilt and subjective guilt feelings had entered God's creation.

As the rest of the Bible shows, God's standards are high and people fool themselves if they pretend to be without sin.[32] An awareness of objective guilt, therefore, can come from the promptings of the Holy Spirit who convicts men and women of sin.[33] This supernaturally produced awareness is for our own cleansing and growth.

Satan also attempts to intervene in our lives both before and after sin. We know that he tempts us and tries to make us stumble, and the Bible states that he accuses God's followers, at least before the Lord.[34] Adam and Eve would not have known guilt if Satan had left them alone and it seems likely that he creates many of our guilt feelings today. Perhaps he also stimulates believers to continue feeling guilty and unforgiven, even when we have done nothing wrong or when we have disobeyed and then been forgiven by God.

The Effects of Guilt

Objective guilt can have a variety of consequences. Breaking the law can lead to arrest and conviction, even in people who do not feel guilty. Social guilt may bring criticism from other people. Personal guilt often leads to self-criticism and condemnation. Theological guilt has consequences that are even more serious. God, who is just and holy, does not wink at sin and neither does he fail to notice our acts of disobedience. According to the Bible, the ultimate punishment for sin is death, although God pardons and gives eternal life when we put our faith in Jesus Christ, who died to pay for our sins.[35] Sometimes it appears that lawbreakers are avoiding their punishment, but God will bring justice in the end.[36]

As we have noted, most counselors do not see the effects of objective guilt. People come for counseling because of subjective guilt feelings. These influence us in several ways.

1. *Defensive Thinking.* As described in psychology textbooks, defensive mechanisms are ways of thinking that most people use to avoid or reduce feelings of anxiety, frustration, and stress. These thoughts tend to distort reality in some way and usually we are not consciously aware of their use.[37] To some extent, all defensive mechanisms protect us from feelings of guilt. If we look for ways to blame others (that is the defense mechanism known as projection), deny wrongdoing, withdraw from people, and rationalize and find excuses in an attempt to justify our actions, then we can avoid anxiety and keep from facing responsibility for our guilt-arousing thoughts or actions. Sometimes when guilt feelings begin to arise, we get angry at others, try to justify our behavior, deny any personal responsibility for what has happened, or even apologize profusely.

One Christian counselor has identified another way of thinking that appears to be used by Christians, especially when we feel guilty about sexual lusts. Convinced that mental or behavioral lapses in moral purity are part of the sinful nature, we continually sin with our minds (and sometimes with our bodies), admit that this is wrong, ask God to forgive, and freely rely on his grace to take away the guilt. Then, as we have seen earlier in the chapter, we are likely to repeat the cycle. Such thinking "minimizes the severity of sin, cheapens grace and fails to comprehend the meaning of a life lived under the lordship of Jesus Christ."[38]

2. *Self-Condemnation Reactions.* Guilt feelings almost always arouse anxiety and self-condemning feelings of inferiority, inadequacy, weakness, low esteem, pessimism, and insecurity. Sometimes there is self-punishment: the person acts like a martyr who is pushed around by others. At times there may be a poor-little-me-I-don't-deserve-to-be-treated-well attitude. For others there is an inability to relax, a refusal to accept compliments, sexual inhibition, an unwillingness to say no to the demands of others, or an avoidance of leisure activities because the person feels guilty and unable to accept forgiveness. Often there is anger that is held within and unexpressed. This can lead the person into depression, sometimes with thoughts of suicide. Some people continually "put themselves down" and then wonder why this alienates and drives away their friends who don't enjoy being with someone who wallows in self-condemnation. Even accident proneness can accompany guilt feelings.

3. *Physical Reactions.* Guilt feelings, like any other psychological reaction, can produce physical tension. Recent research has found that the physiological effects of self-blame accumulate over the years. If you blame yourself for a long-enough period, your body begins to deteriorate.[39] Whenever tensions build in a person and are not released, the body weakens and eventually breaks down. Some psychiatrists view this as an unconscious form of self-punishment. Psychologically and emotionally it may be easier to tolerate physical pain than to bear the burden of guilt that would otherwise attract our attention.

4. *Moral Pain.* Perhaps thousands of articles have been written about the war in Vietnam and the emotional scars that still plague so many veterans. Many of these people were scarcely out of their teens when they went to Southeast Asia, and their youthful eyes saw excessive brutality, cruelty, and violence, some of which they may have committed themselves. Is it surprising that perhaps one in five veterans has been severely affected by the stress?[40] Writing about his involvement with distressed veterans, Peter Marin concludes that "involvement in the excessive violence of Vietnam is a fundamental source of their inner turmoil, and . . . it expresses not just psychological stress but *moral pain*."[41]

> It is here that our collective wisdom fails the vets, here that our dominant approaches to human nature and our prevailing modes of therapy prove inadequate. We seem as a society to have few useful ways to approach moral pain and guilt; it remains for us a form of neurosis of a pathological symptom, something to escape rather than something to learn from, a disease rather than—as it may well be for the vets—an appropriate if painful response to the past. As if reading my thoughts, a VA psychologist told me that he and his colleagues never dealt with problems of guilt. Nor did they raise the question of what the vets did in the war: "We treat the vets' difficulties as problems in adjustment."[42]

But inner guilt cannot be dismissed so glibly. Because of their experiences with intense violence, many veterans still feel a guilt that is accompanied by shame, confusion, depression, anger, inner emptiness, a fear of intimacy, and an inability to trust others. Many experience a "profound moral distress, arising from the realization that one has committed acts with real and terrible consequences."[43] These people, like many of their civilian counterparts who come to us for counseling, have learned that suffering is real, that "one's actions can sometimes irrevocably determine the destiny of others; the mistakes one makes are often transmuted directly into others' pain; there is sometimes no way to undo that pain—the dead remain dead, the maimed are forever maimed, and there is no way to deny one's responsibility or culpability."[44] These realizations persist in the thinking of those who live in moral pain. Many try, in vain, to get help from counselors who know about stress management but have no idea how to help guilt-burdened people find forgiveness.

5. *Repentance and Forgiveness.* The effects of guilt feelings are not all negative. Some people have learned to accept mistakes, to grow from them, to confess to God and to others, and to rest content in the assurance that "if we confess our sins, he is faithful and just and will forgive us our sins and purify us from all our unrighteousness."[45]

Counseling and Guilt

In counseling those with guilt, the Christian counselor has an advantage over the nonbeliever. Guilt is a moral issue and guilt feelings arise from moral failures. Few secular counselor training programs discuss morals, and the counselor who does not believe in God must somehow deal with values, forgiveness, atonement, and related theological issues about which there may be little understanding and no formal training.[46] Psychological approaches are based on helping people to express anger, make restitution, lower their standards or expectations, improve performance, and get insight into their own behavior. At best, these are stopgap efforts that rarely seem to bring permanent change. It is unrealistic to assume that guilt is no more than "a symptom that can be happily removed" by naturalistic methods.[47]

In a controversial book, psychologist O. Hobart Mowrer once argued that individuals sicken "in mind, soul, and perhaps even body because of unconfessed and unatoned real guilt."[48] Mental illness, this author proposed, is really moral illness that can only be cured by confession to significant other people and by making restitution. Although Mowrer's book attacked some basic Christian doctrines (such as the substitutionary atonement and the concept of original sin), his work challenged both counselors and pastors, urging them to acknowledge the central place of sin and forgiveness in counseling. A decade later, psychiatrist Karl Menninger expressed similar ideas in a book with the intriguing title, *Whatever Became of Sin?*[49]

Regretfully, these books were written from a humanistic perspective. Even though they used theological language, they failed to acknowledge biblical truths about confession, forgiveness, and justification. These concepts must be in the thinking of every Christian counselor who attempts to help those with guilt feelings.

1. *Understanding and Acceptance.* People with guilt feelings frequently condemn themselves and expect to be condemned by others. As a result they may

come to counseling with either a self-defensive or a self-blaming attitude.

What is your attitude toward people who have fallen into sin? How do you feel when these people are repentant and determined to change? What is your response if there seems to be no awareness of wrongdoing and no sense of shame or sorrow? The attitude of Jesus must have surprised the woman caught in the act of adultery.[50] She was objectively guilty and perhaps she felt guilty, but Jesus was not like the others who wanted to condemn her. He did not condone her sin—it clearly was wrong—but he talked kindly to her and told her to sin no more.

Christian counselors should do likewise. We must not attempt to minimize the reality of sin, and neither do we take an attitude of moral superiority. All of us are tempted and any of us could fall into the sin or experience the moral pain that we see in our counselees.[51] Our task is not to condemn[52] or to expect that the counselee's guilt feelings can be stopped at will. Instead, we approach others with an attitude of love and a willingness to understand. To restate an old cliché: we accept the sinner, even though we do not accept the sin.

2. *Insight.* When the prophet Nathan confronted David with his sin, the issues were clear: gross immorality, murder, and deception.[53] The king immediately admitted his sin, confessed his wrongdoing, and found forgiveness. For the rest of his life, David lived with the consequences of his actions, but he was free of moral pain because he had repented and changed in response to Nathan's challenge.

Counseling the guilty is not always that easy. Some people don't know why they feel guilty. Others freely admit their wrong actions or attitudes, but the guilt feelings still persist. At times you will encounter those who have broken the law or hurt another person, but there are no feelings of sorrow or remorse.

Often these people can be helped if they have some understanding of the forces that influence them from within. You might discuss issues such as the following. Encourage people to deal with specific examples.

- Are there things in your life that are making you feel guilty? What are these?
- How have you dealt in the past with your guilt feelings?
- What things have been helpful? What has not helped?
- What were your parental expectations about right and wrong?
- Were your parents' standards so high that you could never succeed?
- What happened when you failed?
- Was blame, criticism, and punishment frequent?
- What did your church teach about right and wrong?
- Was there a clear biblical basis for the church's teachings?
- What are some things that make others feel guilty but don't seem to bother you?

Questions like these can help you understand why counselees feel guilty and can let you look for defensive reactions, self-condemnation, fear of punishment, physical reactions, and other responses to guilt. Counselees can be helped to recognize how their guilt feelings may have arisen from past moral training. Is the person striving to act in ways or accomplish goals that are impossible to reach? How would the person react and what might happen if the goals are not accomplished? Are one's standards consistent with biblical teaching? Does the counselee understand what the Bible says about forgiveness? It is here that insight merges into spiritual teaching.

3. *Moral Education.* Counselees must be helped to reexamine their standards of right and wrong. This may take a long time. Some people feel guilty about things the Bible doesn't call sin; others have moral values that clearly violate biblical standards. Some counselees are like the Vietnam veterans who struggle with moral pain and sense that there may be no hope for relief. Others may blithely try to accept what has been called "our great therapeutic dream in America": the erroneous belief that "the past is escapable, that suffering can be avoided, that happiness is always possible, and that insight invariably leads to joy."[54]

What does God *really* expect from us? He knows us perfectly. He knows that we are merely dust and he recognizes that we will sin so long as we are on earth.[55] God expects not perfection, but a sincere attempt to do His will as we understand it and as best we can. He who is compassionate also loves unconditionally and will forgive our sins without demanding personal atonement and penance. Atonement and penance are no longer necessary because Christ has already paid for human sins "once for all, the righteous for the unrighteous, to bring you to God."[56]

This is basic theology that is so relevant and practical that it can revolutionize and completely free human thinking. The ultimate solution to guilt and guilt feelings is to admit our pain, suffering, failures, and guilt; to confess sin to Christ and at times to other human beings;[57] to pray for forgiveness and a sincere desire to repent and change behavior; and then to believe with divine help that we are forgiven and accepted by the God of the universe. It is he who in turn helps us to accept, love, and forgive both ourselves and others.

4. *Repentance and Forgiveness.* It is possible for a counselee to understand what the Bible says about guilt and forgiveness, but problems like the following may still persist.

(a) I can't ask for forgiveness. It is not the counselor's task to force people to pray, to confess, and to ask God to forgive. For some counselees it may take a while to reach that point and the counselor must be content to pray for the counselee and continue to work at accepting and helping the guilt-ridden person to understand these principles more clearly. The view that we earn divine favor by good works and that we pay for our sins by undergoing punishment is so widespread that it dies slowly. The Bible teaches, however, that repentance and confession are all we need to obtain forgiveness. Failure to understand this basic tenet of Christianity has caused countless people, including Christians, to experience unhealthy guilt feelings that lead to worry, depression, loss of inner peace, fear, low self-esteem, loneliness, and a sense of alienation from God.

(b) I don't feel forgiven. When we ask others to forgive us, sometimes we don't feel forgiven because we haven't really been forgiven. This is not so with God. If we confess our sins and pain to him, he forgives in every case.[58] Guilt feelings may not disappear overnight, but our counselees can rest in the assurance that they *are* forgiven, even if they don't feel like it. This may have to be restated frequently and accompanied with prayer that the feelings of liberation will come.

(c) I know God has forgiven me, but I can't forgive others. Lewis Smedes has written that forgiving is hard work that seems almost unnatural. Most of us have to keep working at it, and often we forgive only with God's help. Perhaps your counselee will agree that "if you are *trying* to forgive; even if you manage forgiving in fits and starts, if you forgive today, hate again tomorrow, and have to forgive again the day after, you are (nevertheless) a forgiver. Most of us are amateurs, bungling duffers" when we try to forgive.[59] All of us need God to help us to forgive, especially when we don't feel like it.

(d) How can I forgive when I can't seem to forget? God alone is able to forgive and forget. We humans tend to remember past sins and injustices even when they have been completely forgiven. Sometimes it may not be wise to forget. By trying to ignore some past evils, we run the risk of their happening again.[60] In most situations, however, old memories are best abandoned. When there has been forgiveness, these memories may linger, but if we refuse to dwell on them, they will begin to fade. When an individual has sincerely forgiven others and genuinely been willing to accept God's forgiveness, then there is no reason to mull over life's injustices. The memories will return, sometimes when they are least expected, but these memories will have decreasing power. Forgiving must come first. Then complete or partial forgetting will follow.

Preventing Guilt

"Let your conscience be your guide," is a frequently quoted but not very wise principle for living. As we have seen, individual standards of morality differ from person to person, in part because early moral teaching and parental expectations can have such profound influence on an individual's later thinking about right and wrong. The place to start the prevention of unhealthy guilt feelings, therefore, is with the parents.

1. *Helping Parents Teach Values.* Children (like adults) learn both from what they hear and from the climate in which teaching occurs. If parents or other teachers are rigid, condemning, demanding, and unforgiving, children feel like constant failures. This does much to instill prolonged guilt feelings. Parents can be helped to prevent unhealthy guilt feelings and encourage conscience development in their children if the parents have some understanding of conscience development as outlined earlier in this chapter. Teach them to instill in their children a commitment to Scripture and stress discipline that points out failure but also includes abundant love, encouragement, and forgiveness. Since guilt feelings are tied so intimately with self-esteem, it can also be helpful to follow the prevention guidelines listed in chapter 21.

2. *Helping People Find Values.* In a perceptive commentary on modern life, one writer has suggested that many people reject or ignore traditional values, but have difficulty in finding ways to replace them. "We are surrounded by divergent and frequently changing value systems that compete for our allegiance," he writes. "Confusion or uncertainty about values is thus widespread, and this tends to increase interpersonal conflict and personal insecurity."[61] The culture may do the most to create the moral confusion and ethical uncertainty that so many of our counselees face, but it has been suggested that the church shares this value confusion and even makes it worse.[62]

Authoritarian religious groups may try, probably in vain, to reimpose the old ethical certainties that "worked" in the past. Often this leads to condemnation of nonconformists and intense guilt in people who fail to meet the imposed standards. More constructive, it would seem, is an approach that lets people express their confusion but seek—with the help of sensitive counselors and other Christian leaders—to find relevant ethical standards that are derived from and consistent with biblical teaching.[63]

3. *Helping Parishioners Understand Values.* In the church, Christians must be helped to understand God's high standards of morality. Each believer should realize, too, that God understands our weaknesses and is willing to forgive freely when we fall. Try to show the difference between guilt feelings and constructive sorrow.

There could be value in encouraging people to examine their own self-expectations and standards of right and wrong. Are any of these unrealistic and unbiblical? Remind others that two good ways to learn about forgiveness are to experience it and to practice it. If church people can seek God's help in forgiving one another[64] there can be a reduction in bitterness and in the refusal to understand or accept forgiveness from God.

Finally, there is the issue of obedience. When we attempt to obey the law, meet social expectations, and do what God wants, we are less likely to experience objective guilt. This in turn prevents the development of many subjective guilt feelings.

In themselves, guilt feelings may not all be bad. Sometimes they stimulate us to confess sin and to act more effectively. When these feelings persist as paralyzing influences, however, they are harmful. It is such harmful guilt feelings that we seek to prevent and eliminate.

Conclusions about Guilt

Jesus never relaxed his standards when he talked with the woman caught in adultery. God's standards are perfect and he never winks at sin or settles for imperfection. The woman was told to sin no more and hopefully her lifestyle changed radically.

It is unlikely that she every reached perfection. None of us do. Nevertheless we are accepted by God, forgiven unconditionally when we confess our sins, and assured that some day we will reach divine standards because of what Christ has done and is doing.

At times, most of the problems discussed in this book will involve people with guilt. Counselors can work to help people let go of their guilt,[65] but the ultimate answer to guilt is not found in psychology. It is found in the biblical teachings about forgiveness. Because God forgives, we can be forgiven, our guilt can be removed, and a way is provided to deal with guilt feelings.

SUGGESTIONS FOR FURTHER READING

Freeman, Lucy, and Herbert S. Strean. *Guilt: Letting Go.* New York: Wiley, 1986.
Narramore, S. Bruce. *No Condemnation.* Grand Rapids, Mich.: Zondervan, 1984.
Oden, Thomas C. *Guilt Free.* Nashville: Abingdon, 1980.*
Smedes, Lewis B. *Forgive and Forget.* New York: Harper & Row, 1984.*
Tournier, Paul. *Guilt and Grace.* New York: Harper & Row, 1962.
Wilson, Earl. *Counseling and Guilt.* Waco, Tex.: Word, 1987.

* Books marked with an asterisk (*) are especially suited for counselees to read.

Part 3

Developmental Issues

11

Child Rearing and Parental Guidance

THE TEACHERS CALLED HIM a troubled child. His parents called him unmanageable. His peers called him a variety of derogatory names. The neighbors called him a spoiled brat, and sometimes they called the police.

Although he was only thirteen and still had a boy-sized body, Kevin could swear like a trooper. He already had created more havoc than all the other kids in the neighborhood combined.

He was constantly at odds with his parents, in conflict with his teachers, and unable to get along with his peers. His three sisters hated him, and his presence in Sunday school always disrupted the class.

Kevin's mischief in the neighborhood was well known. Using a can of spray paint, he had scribbled graffiti on the side of the local supermarket. Twice he had been caught shoplifting, and once he was suspected of starting a fire in a neighbor's garage, though his guilt was never proven.

In an effort to reform their son, the parents sent him to boarding school one year. The discipline was strict, and Kevin seemed to respond well to the routine, but his behavior was even more out of control when he came home.

The school scheduled conferences. The juvenile authorities discussed his case. The family doctor prescribed some tranquilizers. The parents went for counseling. Kevin went to a different counselor. Eventually the whole family was involved.

The problem was accentuated by the prominence of his parents. Kevin's father was a successful gynecologist, and his mother was involved in local politics. Both were active in their church. The counselor wondered if the parents were neglecting their son; if Kevin's attention-seeking behavior was an attempt to be loved and to get noticed by his busy parents. But Kevin's behavior didn't seem to change, regardless of the amount of attention that came his way. The boy seemed sincerely sorry for his behavior and often vowed to change, but he seemed unable to do so. Some men in the church concluded that Kevin must be demon possessed, and they met with the pastor to discuss the possibility of exorcism.

One day Kevin's grandmother read an article about a chemical imbalance that sometimes leads to hyperactive childhood behavior. The parents were at their wit's end and not much interested in some new theory about their son's behavior. Secretly, the father had concluded that Kevin would become a juvenile delinquent and probably spend the rest of his life in jail.

Nevertheless, at the grandmother's urging, Kevin was taken to a well-known clinic where he was seen by a specialist in chemical disorders. The physician prescribed a treatment program consisting of a changed diet and the use of medication that would correct the imbalance in Kevin's system.

The change in this young man's behavior was radical. He and his family continued in counseling for a while, but before long Kevin was back in school trying to catch up on the things he hadn't learned. His behavior problems have largely disappeared and everybody was grateful, including the neighbors and the police.

While they were waiting for the birth of their first child, a young couple read a pile of books on child rearing and even wrote for advice to a well-known psychologist. "Read all the books carefully," the psychologist replied. "Then, when you are done, throw them all away and do what you were going to do in the first place."[1]

Probably this is good advice. In his infinite wisdom, God chose to entrust tender young lives to the guidance of adults (including some very immature adults) who have little or no experience in child rearing, but who face a variety of challenges and perhaps an even greater variety of child-rearing books. Some parents devour these books and even write to the authors, all in an attempt to be better mothers and fathers. Others ignore the advice givers and try to do "what comes naturally." Better, perhaps, is the approach that gathers information and encouragement from books and more experienced parents, but then tries *with divine help* to do the best possible job in the task of training up children in the ways they should go.

At times the Christian counselor will be involved in counseling with children directly, but more often the emphasis will be on *parental guidance.* This is the task of offering parents encouragement, information, advice, clarification, support, or other counsel that will help the child indirectly. Parental guidance recognizes that parents can influence children more profoundly than any counselor. It assumes a cooperative working alliance between the parents and counselor, who together are interested in the welfare and maturing of the child.[2]

Literally thousands of books have been written about children and child rearing. Freud, Erickson, Piaget, Fowler, Driekurs, Gesell, Spock, and numerous others have produced theories of child development. Christian writers like James Dobson, Kevin Leman, Grace Ketterman, and Ross Campbell are among the many writers and seminar speakers who have given guidance to help parents with their child-rearing problems.[3] Innumerable studies have investigated the abilities and psychological maturation of developing children, while other research has studied physical malfunctioning, psychological retardation, and childhood pathology. Pediatrics, the well-known medical speciality, has been paralleled by child psychiatry, child psychology, and related specialties. Clearly, in one chapter it is not possible to summarize the massive literature that has built up in this field, but some general principles are identifiable and helpful to the Christian counselor.

The Bible and Child Rearing

Shortly after the creation, God instructed Adam and Eve to "be fruitful and increase in number." Unlike most divine commands, this one was obeyed and the world quickly filled with people. In Old Testament times a large family was considered a source of special blessing from God and childlessness was regarded with reproach.[4] In our modern era of overpopulation, many people have chosen to limit the size of their families, but children are still very important. Jesus showed them special attention and he lauded their simplicity and trust.[5]

Biblical teaching on children and parental guidance can be divided into two categories: comments about children and comments about parents and parenting.

1. *Children.* In the Bible, children are seen as gifts from God that can bring both joy and sorrow. Young people are to be loved, honored, and respected as persons; they are important in God's kingdom and they are not to be harmed.[6] Children are also given responsibilities: to honor and respect parents, care for them, listen to them and be obedient.[7] "Children, obey your parents in the Lord, for this is right," we read in Eph. 6:1–3. "Honor your father and mother . . . that it may go well with you and that you may enjoy long life on the earth."

Elsewhere in his writings, Paul strongly criticizes childhood disobedience,[8] but it seems unlikely that children are expected to obey forever. If parents require compliance with something unbiblical it should be remembered that God's laws always take a higher priority than human instruction.[9] It would seem, further, that adults who leave their parents and cleave to a spouse have moved to establish new families, but these families are never freed from the responsibility of honoring older parents.

2. *Parents.* Mothers and fathers have a responsibility to model mature Christian behavior, to love their children, to care for their needs, to teach the young, and to discipline fairly.[10] "Do not exasperate your children," we read in Eph. 6:4, "instead, bring them up in the training and instruction of the Lord."

According to one commentator,[11] we exasperate children when we abuse them physically, abuse them psychologically (by humiliating them and failing to treat them with respect), neglect them, don't try to understand them, expect too much from them, withhold love unless they perform, force them to accept our goals or ideas, and refuse to admit our mistakes. In contrast, we "bring them up" by being examples to our children and by giving instruction and encouragement. All of this is more easily discussed than accomplished. Children, like parents, have different personalities and the biblical directives for child rearing are not as specific as many people might like.

In the Old Testament, however, there is one section that puts all the principles together and summarizes the biblical teachings about child rearing. Although this was written for the Israelites prior to their entrance into the promised land, these paragraphs have great practical relevance for modern child rearing and parental guidance.

> These are the commands, decrees and laws the Lord your God directed me to teach you to observe . . . so that you, your children and their children after them may fear the Lord your God as long as you live by keeping all his decrees and commands that I give you, and so that you may enjoy long life. Hear, O Israel, and be careful to obey so that it may go well with you and that you may increase greatly in a land flowing with milk and honey, just as the Lord, the God of your fathers, promised you.
>
> Hear, O Israel: The Lord our God, the Lord is one. Love the Lord your God with all your heart and with all your soul and with all your strength. These commandments that I give you today are to be upon your hearts. Impress them on your children. Talk about them when you walk along the road and when you lie down and when you get up.[12]

Christian parenting involves the following:

(a) Listening. The good parent wants to hear God's commandments and to understand them so well that these become "upon your hearts," a part of one's being. This learning comes through regular study of God's Word, the Bible, made clear to us by the Holy Spirit.

(b) Obeying. Knowledge is not enough. In addition to hearing, parents must be intent on keeping God's decrees and commands. It is possible that when parents show no apparent desire to obey God, their children, in turn, are less inclined to obey parents.

(c) Loving. We are to love the Lord and give ourselves to him wholeheartedly—heart, soul, and strength. Notice that the emphasis here is for the parents. In spite of their importance, children are not prominent in the Bible. Although we read that Jesus grew psychologically (in wisdom), physically (in stature), spiritually (in favor with God), and socially (in favor with others),[13] we know very little about his childhood. The early years are important, but children are with their parents temporarily and then they leave, as God intended. Parents, therefore, do not exist primarily for their children. Parents exist first as individuals who love and serve God. If we are given children, then raising them is part of our life purpose, but this is not our only purpose.

(d) Teaching. There are four ways by which teaching is to be done:

- Diligently. Even though child rearing is not a parent's sole task in life, it is an important responsibility that is not to be taken lightly.
- Repeatedly. Scripture indicates that teaching is not a one-time effort. It is to concern parents repeatedly through the day and night.
- Naturally. When we sit, walk, lie down, and rise up we are to look for teaching opportunities. Daily family devotions are valuable, but parents are to teach whenever the opportunity arises.
- Personally. What one says is rarely as influential as what one does. This returns us to the first part of the Deuteronomy passage. When parents listen, obey, and love, they provide a model for children that reinforces what is being said in the home.

Notice the words "in the home." Peers and teachers are important, but the most significant teaching and child rearing occurs at home.

Causes of Child-Rearing Problems

Generations of psychology students have heard about the wild boy who was found in the woods near Aveyron, France, at the end of the last century. The child was unable to communicate, behaved like an animal, and apparently had not had human contact for a number of years. With patience and determination, a psychologist named Itard undertook the task of trying (largely in vain) to rehabilitate the boy.

If he were living today, Itard might not be any more successful in his rehabilitative efforts, but he would have considerably more evidence to help him understand why children and their parents have problems during the child-rearing years. Complex theories of childhood development and psychopathology have described how young people mature and why problems develop. Specialists have analyzed the causal roots of diverse issues such as mental retardation, childhood depression, a variety of learning disorders, speech pathology, excessive rebellion, violence, childhood schizophrenia, and the difficulties many young people have in adjusting to frequent moves, parental divorce, periods of hospitalization, adoption, and other early stresses.[14] Some may question the conclusion that we have learned more about babies and older children in the past twenty years than we have learned in the previous two thousand,[15] but most will agree that the more we learn, the more complicated the problems seem to become.

At times, children and their parents do not even agree on what constitutes a problem. A parent may view disobedience as a source of family stress, but the child may not see this as a problem at all. An issue that might not be a problem at one age (for example, bed wetting) only becomes a major issue if it persists into later childhood or adolescence. Sometimes the neighbors or school officials may think a child has a problem, but the parents may disagree. Despite these differences, several themes appear repeatedly in discussions about the causes of child-rearing problems.

1. *Neglect or Abuse of the Spiritual.* Psychology textbooks almost never recognize the spiritual bases of child development, but this is important to biblical writers.[16] Ps. 78:1–8, for example, emphasizes that children should receive spiritual instruction so they will put their faith in God, remember his faithfulness, and not become unruly, stubborn, or rebellious. Perhaps there is no well-designed research comparing the adult behavior of children who had religious training with those who did not, but the Scriptures clearly teach that biblical education is beneficial to children; its absence is surely harmful. Equally harmful, no doubt, is a rigid indoctrination that crams religion into young minds, pictures God as a stern and boring disciplinarian, and leaves no room to let young people ask questions and grow into spiritual maturity.

2. *Instability in the Home.* When parents cannot cope with their stresses or when they do not get along with each other, children can feel anxious, guilty, and angry. They are anxious because the stability of the home is threatened, guilty because they suspect that they may have caused the strife, and angry because they often feel left out, forgotten, and sometimes manipulated into taking sides, which they do not want to do. Sometimes there is a fear of being abandoned physically or psychologically. To escape the pressures and often to express their anger, thousands of young people run away from home in an effort to find security elsewhere. Some youth counselors have used the term "throwaway kids" to describe children who are victims of parental instability.[17]

Instability in the home can lead to a variety of behavioral problems in children. Falling grades, conflict with other children, or petty crimes can all indicate problems at home and a cry for help. On a more serious level, researchers have found that children who deliberately set fires are frequently from homes where there is family conflict, communication breakdown, and parental psychopathology.[18] Although many children survive family stress and grow into normal, successful and well-adjusted adulthood,[19] it remains true that unstable homes tend to produce unstable children.

3. *Psychological Abuse.* The physical abuse of children (an issue that we discuss

more fully in chapter 20) has attracted much popular and professional attention within recent years. Less noticed are the actions of parents who never hurt their children physically but abuse them psychologically. When they are rejected subtly or overtly, nagged and criticized excessively, punished unrealistically (or not at all), disciplined inconsistently, humiliated persistently, shown love spasmodically (or never), or threatened periodically with abandonment, children often experience personal problems or show disruptive behaviors that in turn are annoying to parents. Child development experts have alerted us to the harmful effects of parental overprotection, overpermissiveness, overstrictness, and overmeticulousness that can arouse anxiety and create insecurity in children.

It should not be assumed that psychological mistreatment is always deliberate. Many parents are confused or overwhelmed by child behavior, insensitive to their children's needs, and unsure how to respond. Some are more tense and have a low tolerance for the essentially normal behavior of active children. These parents need encouragement and guidance so that psychological abuse and its harmful consequences can be prevented.[20]

4. *Unmet Needs.* Psychologists do not always agree on what to include in any listing of basic human needs. The needs for security, acceptance, discipline, or encouragement, are included in most lists,[21] and some counselors have noted that handicapped, retarded, or gifted children have special needs that differ from those of their peers.[22] Most important, however, is the need for love. When children are deprived of love and when their other needs are not met, maturation is hindered and problems frequently develop.

5. *Physical Influences.* Generations of parents and pediatricians have known that prolonged illness, hospitalization, and surgery can all be confusing and disruptive to children. The amount of disruption will depend on the nature of the illness, the organ systems affected, the types of treatment required, the reactions of parents or other significant adults, and the child's ability to cope. The stress of serious illness often leads to intense anxiety, negativism, withdrawal, resentment of parents, fear, and other psychological reactions.[23] Illness is difficult for any of us to handle; it is especially hard for children.

To illustrate how physical influences can lead to child-rearing problems, let us consider two examples.

(a) Mental Retardation. According to the somewhat formal language of the American Association of Mental Deficiency, mental retardation refers to "significantly subaverage intellectual functioning existing concurrently with deficits in adaptive behavior, and manifested during the developmental period." Most of these people are mildly retarded, show no obvious signs of their intellectual defects, are able to learn, and subsequently can hold simple jobs. Of the more severe forms of retardation, Down's syndrome is probably best known, largely because of the distinctive facial features of the children.

Mental retardation can have a variety of causes. Many children fail to develop normally because they live in impoverished environments where there is so little stimulation that brain development is slowed and intellectual functioning is hindered. Other retarded children, including those with Down's syndrome, are victims of physical malfunctioning. Genetic abnormalities, prenatal disease,[24] head injuries or other complications at the time of birth, infant infections or nervous system damage, and a variety of acquired childhood diseases have all been listed as causes of retardation.[25]

These physical influences often create irreversible mental conditions that counselors cannot eliminate. Nevertheless, you can help parents, family members, and retarded people adjust. Sometimes parents need help in facing the reality of the child's retardation and in answering questions about rearing a retarded child. In addition, counselors can give support, encouragement, accurate information, and guidance as parents struggle with their feelings of guilt and disappointment.

(b) Attention Deficit Disorder. It has been estimated that half of all children brought to mental health clinics, come because of what has come to be known as attention deficit disorders (or ADD).[26] The symptoms often persist throughout life, but they tend to be spotted first in grade-school children. Inability to concentrate or pay attention, distractibility, impulsivity, impatience, inability to relax, hyperactivity, disorganization, mood swings, feelings of low self-confidence, difficulty in getting along with peers, sleep disorders, and anxiety are among the symptoms of people who are "always on the go" and feel as if they are "driven by an internal motor."

Frustrated teachers and parents often urge these children to settle down and to stop being so "fidgety," but for many this is physiologically impossible. Although the causes of ADD are complex, it is widely recognized that the problem has a physical and probably a genetic basis. One theory proposes that ADD comes from a chemical deficiency in the brain; in many cases there is a startling change in behavior and a reduction of hyperactivity when the chemical dopamine is replaced.

6. *Other Influences.* Traumatic early experiences (such as accidents, a serious fire in the home, or a near drowning), peer rejection, the serious illness or death of significant persons (including a parent or sibling), and the frustration of failure can each lead to problems in later life. As a result of these and similar experiences, children can develop unhealthy self-concepts, preoccupation with danger, a fear of failure or rejection, continuing insecurity, or an attitude of bitterness and rebellion.

The previous paragraphs could be discouraging to counselors and parents who might wonder if it is ever possible to raise a child successfully and without the development of severe problems. Perhaps it *is* true that all of us are wounded on the way to adulthood.

Two facts need to be remembered when we consider these issues. First, it appears that most children grow up normally in spite of parental mistakes and failures. Even when the home has abusive, psychotic, or desperately poor parents, many children (sometimes called "invincibles" or "superkids") respond by developing extraordinary competence.[27] Poor home situations do not always produce problem children.

Second, there are times when problems arise through no fault of the parents. Many parents blame themselves when their children rebel or go wrong, but sometimes the problems arise from other sources. Peers can be very influential in leading each other astray, and sometimes the child's failures or rebellion are really attempts to assert independence. Even if parents could be perfect there still is the possibility of rebellion and problems because children have minds and wills of their own.

No one could be more perfect than God and yet Isaiah's prophecy begins with these words: "the Lord has spoken: 'I reared children and brought them up, but they have rebelled against me.'"[28] Parental failures are not always the cause of child problems. This realization can be a source of encouragement and challenge to the parents of problem children.[29]

The Effects of Child-Rearing Problems

Perhaps it was in Sunday School that you first heard about Samuel, the Old Testament prophet, who as a boy received a message from God concerning Eli the priest. Eli's sons had "made themselves contemptible, and he failed to restrain them." As a result, God announced that he would judge the family because of their sin and because of the father's failure to deal with the rebellious actions of his children.[30] Soon Eli and his sons died, and Samuel grew to a position of leadership. His own sons, however, were also a source of embarrassment. They did not walk in the ways of God but "turned aside after dishonest gain and accepted bribes and perverted justice" even though they were judges. The Bible does not say if Samuel had neglected his parental duties, but the children still turned from God and behaved dishonestly. When parent-child problems occur, this can influence both the parents and the children and sometimes childhood pathology results.

1. *Parental Effects.* It is difficult to have children "turn out" differently than parents had hoped. Fathers and mothers often feel—with or without good evidence—that childhood problems are a monument to the parents' incompetence. This can lead to frustration, conflict between the husband and wife, anger expressed toward the children, guilt, fear of what might happen next, and sometimes frantic attempts to assert authority and get back in control.[31] On occasion there may be attempts to defend or protect the child, but often this is mixed with anger because the young person needs defending or protection. Then there are parents who appear to be like Eli, unwilling or perhaps powerless to do anything about a deteriorating situation, so they watch as things get worse.

2. *Child Effects.* When there are parent-child problems, the children sometimes act in ways similar to parents. Anger, hostility directed toward parents and other family members, guilt, and fear can all occur. Unlike parents who can express themselves verbally, children often resort to nonverbal means of expression. Temper tantrums, rebellion, underachievement (especially in school), delinquency, fighting, silliness, excessive crying, dawdling, and other attention-getting behavior can all be ways of saying nonverbally, "Notice me. I'm hurting too!" Of course this is rarely conscious or deliberate, and we cannot always assume that such behaviors mean that the child senses something is wrong. Neither does the absence of such behavior mean that the child is oblivious to the problem. Such children may be afraid to express themselves. They may attempt to deny reality or they may quietly conclude that they are incompetent failures. The seeds of inferiority and low self-esteem are being planted, even though they may not bloom into prominence until much later in life.

3. *Pathological Effects.* Sometimes more severe disturbances develop, all of which indicate the existence of problems in the children, and some (but not all) of which imply that there are problems in the home. Even when parent-child relationships are good, these conditions put a strain on the family and often indicate a need for counseling.

(a) Psychophysiological Disorders. These physical reactions include asthma, ulcers, bed wetting, and headaches. Each may have physical causes or may come as a psychological reaction to severe stress, strict discipline, disappointments, loss of family members, or a smothering mother-child relationship. Children with these disorders should be seen by a physician, but often counseling can help both parents and children to handle stress better.

(b) Developmental Disorders. Sometimes speech, motor, social, thinking, or other abilities are slowed down by family pressures, frequent moves, or other stresses. Eventually most children catch up, but even temporary developmental slowdowns can be difficult for everybody in the family.

(c) Psychoneurotic Disorders. Psychological functioning is likely to be hindered when conflicts are held within or when aggressive and sexual impulses are denied or suppressed. Anxiety, irrational fears, excessive guilt reactions, sleeping disturbances, eating disorders, and compulsive behavior may all be clues that something is bothering the young person.

(d) Personality Disorders. Sometimes the child senses no conflict or anxiety[32] but develops a personality that is high strung, overly inhibited, isolated, excessively independent, or distrustful. All of this can reflect inner tension.

(e) Sociopathic and Delinquent Disorders. When a child is frustrated by the environment, he or she sometimes acts out with frequent temper tantrums, delinquency, and sometimes aggressive or sexually impulsive behavior.[33] Here the person is reacting to frustration by lashing out at others, often with no feelings of remorse or desire to change. Society, including parents, is burdened with the effects of aggression and with the challenge of attempting to rehabilitate the aggressor.

(f) Childhood Depression. Within recent years, childhood depression has become more noticeable and perhaps more common.[34] In addition to feelings of sadness and deep disappointment, depressed children often withdraw, refuse to eat, are apathetic, have physical complaints, and sometimes run away or show sullenness, aggression, or immobility. All children show each of these periodically, but their prolonged appearance indicates more troublesome underlying problems. With increasing frequency, it seems, some of these children are attempting to escape from their tensions by suicide.[35]

(g) Psychotic Disorders. This is the severely disturbed behavior that requires professional treatment. Like emotionally disturbed adults, psychotic children may show bizarre behavior, severe fears, extreme withdrawal, lack of self-control, and irrational thinking, to list a few symptoms. Sometimes very young children develop "infantile autism," a widely studied condition characterized by withdrawal, emotional blandness, repetitious behavior, and fascination with inanimate things (such as a chair) rather than with people.

(h) Brain Damage and Mental Retardation. Slow physical development, learning disabilities, and memory problems are among the results that might be expected when the brain is not functioning normally. Although brain damage and mental retardation rarely come as a result of faulty child rearing, these conditions greatly influence parents who often have difficulty adjusting to the reality and challenge of raising a mentally handicapped child.

(i) Hyperactivity. This common condition is characterized by excitability, short attention span, destructiveness, sleep disturbances, poor impulse control, and an overabundance of energy. Often this has psychological causes, but increasing evidence suggests that minimal brain damage, central nervous system malfunctioning, allergies, endocrine or dietary imbalances, or other physical issues may create or worsen the condition. Even when the major treatment is medical, parents and children can profit from counseling that helps them accept or adjust to the condition.

(j) Learning Disabilities. These are widespread and not necessarily the result of low intelligence or poor schooling. Sometimes learning problems are the result of hearing or visual difficulties, problems with speech, poor learning skills, or childhood fears and stress. When they learn slowly, children often experience ridicule by peers, criticism by parents, and pressure by teachers that can damage the child's self-concept and increase learning disabilities. If these children grow older without improvement, there can be failure at school, truancy, self-condemnation, delinquency, and subsequent adult irresponsibility and employment difficulties.

Each of the ten conditions described above will often concern parents and adversely affect child development. Usually these conditions are treated by physicians, psychologists, educators, and others who are specially trained in the problems of children. Unless the Christian counselor is a specialist in these areas, he or she should seek professional consultation or should refer the child and parents to some person who specializes in the disorders of childhood.

Counseling and Child-Rearing Problems

Christian counselors have three responsibilities in working with the problems of children: counseling the children, counseling the parents, and making referrals. In each case you may do one, two, or all three of these.

1. *Counseling Children.* Unlike adults, children (especially very young children) often lack the verbal skills or self-awareness to discuss their feelings and frustrations. Because of this, child counselors often observe children at home, ask them to make up stories, or watch as the young people play with doll families, draw pictures, model with clay, or play house. These techniques, along with the use of psychological tests, are used by child specialists to build rapport, elicit information, uncover childhood problems, and provide opportunity for giving help.

From this it should not be assumed that talking is never helpful. Children are spontaneous and sometimes share their worries and concerns openly. At times it is helpful to ask questions about what makes the child happy or unhappy, what is scary, what is the funniest or saddest thing he or she can think of, what the child would ask for if he or she had three wishes, or similar questions that have potentially revealing answers.

Although the goals of child counseling depend largely on the stated and identified problems, counselors often seek to reduce irrational fears and disturbing behavior, resolve conflicts, increase the child's ability to express feelings, improve interpersonal relationships at home or school, and teach skills. Counseling may involve instruction, play therapy, skills training, the demonstration of kindness and respect, and the giving or withholding of reinforcement. In working with children, most counselors probably use a variety of approaches in reaching their counseling goals.[36]

Child counselors should remember the obvious but easily forgotten fact that children are people. They have feelings, needs, and insecurities. At times they try to manipulate adults,[37] but children respond to love and firmness. They need to be treated with sensitivity, empathy, warmth, consideration, and a respect that does not treat them with disdain or convey a smug adult superiority. Remember too that the counseling of children almost always occurs in conjunction with the counseling of parents.

2. *Counseling Parents.* At times the Christian counselor will first come in contact with the "problem" child and then make contact with parents. More often, it is the parents who come seeking help and the child is seen later, with or without the parents being present. When counseling children it is very important to see parents since your counseling can be undermined quickly by uncooperative or uninformed parents. Sometimes helping the entire family to function better may be the best way to help the child.[38]

(a) General Issues. There are several general guidelines for working with parents regardless of the specific problem. These include the following.

Appreciate the parents' position. Child rearing can be frustrating, and in spite of their failures and mistakes it can be assumed that most parents really want to succeed in this task. It doesn't help, therefore, to blame, criticize, or demean the parents with whom you counsel. Try to discourage parents from condemning each other for the child's problems. Attempt to understand the parents' perspectives and express your desire to work together in helping the parents help their children.

Use various approaches. Some parents need simple information or a clearer understanding of the situation. Others may need advice, cautioning, support, encouragement, and/or suggestions for dealing with problems. Some parents have a good idea about what to do, but they need a counselor to give a little push and offer support once action is taken. At times it will be necessary to challenge parental myths (for example, "children should be seen and not heard," "all teenagers are rebellious," "boys are harder to raise than girls"). Frequently you may decide to break down a problem into smaller issues that can be dealt with more easily, one at a time. It is only after listening and observing for a while that counselors can decide on suitable guidance techniques.

Be sensitive to parental needs. In raising their children, many parents feel self-doubt, a sense of being overwhelmed, competition (perhaps with the child or with a spouse over the child's affections), jealousy, a fear of losing one's children, or a need to be in authoritarian control of the family. When these needs are intense or when they are unmet, tensions often result. In counseling, such needs should be identified, discussed, and reevaluated.[39]

Be aware of family dynamics. Family systems therapies are increasingly popular approaches that treat entire families, rather than focusing solely on individual family members. Whenever a child (or adult) has a problem, it is assumed that the whole family is dysfunctional in some way, and the whole family comes for treatment. As a simple example, consider the child who develops behavior problems and falling grades when his mother goes to work. Counseling the child alone may be helpful, but it probably would be better to involve the whole family in discussions about ways of adapting to the mother's dual career.[40] Whenever you counsel with children, try to learn about family issues that might be creating or complicating the child's problems.

Model the parental role. The counselor does not treat parents like they are children, but the counselor nevertheless models communication skills, a willingness to understand, and sometimes a kind firmness. If the counselor talks to the children in the parents' presence, this can be an example of adult-child respect and interaction.

Recognize that you are expendable. One goal in counseling is to promote maturing, Christ-centered relationships between family members. The counselor is a facilitator of this process. His or her ultimate plan is to withdraw from the situation. One psychiatrist has recommended two contrasting approaches to help you reach this goal.[41] When advising parents to do something the child won't like, such as being stricter or less inclined to give in to the child's demands, state this to the parents with the children present. This lets the counselor take the blame, helps the parents feel less guilty, and hooks them into carrying out the recommendation. In contrast, when encouraging the parents to do something the child will like, such as relaxing restrictions or spending more time together, tell the parents privately, without the children present. This lets the parents take full credit for the pleasant changes and does not put them in a position of being criticized by their children when the counselor's recommendations are forgotten or rejected.

Someone has said that an effective parent is the child's most important counselor. If this is true, then one very effective way to help children is to teach parents how to help their sons and daughters. This teaching is known as *filial therapy.* The counselor meets regularly with the parents, applies the principles described in this chapter, and serves as a consultant and coach. This works best when at least one parent is relatively well adjusted and when the children are free of severe internal conflict.

(b) Theological Issues. The Bible says relatively little about the family compared to what it teaches about the church. According to Gene Getz, this is because "the Christian home in the New Testament world was almost synonymous with the Church. . . . What was written to the Church was also written to individual families. . . . The family is really the *Church in miniature*."[42] Issues that concern the church (evangelism, Christian education, the teaching of moral standards and compassion, helping young people learn about the meaning of life and death) are issues that parents must also face in raising their children. Parents who are failing in these areas should be challenged and helped to make their homes more alert to the presence of Jesus Christ and the guiding power of the Holy Spirit. The Christian counselor must be willing to raise and discuss these and other theological or moral issues. This is a crucial aspect of effective Christian counseling with parents and children.

(c) Psychological Issues. Several psychological issues commonly arise as parents are counseled.

First, there is often a need for *understanding*. One way to help parents understand is to encourage them to think of the world and the family from the child's perspective. Remind parents that children have feelings and the need for significance, security, acceptance, love, praise, discipline, and faith in God. It can help to discuss specific examples of conflict or misunderstanding. What happened? Why? How could the situation have been handled better? Be careful to acknowledge that parents need understanding too.

At times, it also helps to suggest books that can help parents understand child behavior. Since readers sometimes tend to see and remember what they want to remember, it is wise to discuss such readings and be ready to correct misinterpretations after parents have had opportunity to read.[43]

Second, families should be helped with *communication.* The principles of good interpersonal relations that we discuss in chapter 16 can apply within the family and can be shared, modeled, and practiced in counseling sessions. If they want to communicate with their children, parents should model good husband-wife communication.[44] The family should establish a time for communication, perhaps over dinner. Children should know that their opinions, gripes and experiences are of interest to their parents and the parents should show a willingness to listen. Parents can also share their ideas, experiences, frustrations, and dreams. Although there should be no limits on the subject matter to be discussed, everyone should expect that there will be no disrespectful language or long nagging, Each family member should be encouraged to talk, but each should also have a right to privacy and personal opinions. Sometimes the family must agree on rules such as "no interruptions until the person who is talking has time to finish." When questions are raised, they should be answered honestly and fully. All of this takes time to learn and is difficult to put into practice. To teach these communications skills, however, is an important part of counseling.

Third, *behavior management* is of concern to many parents. Most know that punishment can be a way to curb undesired behavior, and it may instill some respect for authority. Yet punishment tends to lose its effectiveness if it is repeated too often, and it rarely brings permanent change. More efficient is the rewarding of desired behavior and the nonrewarding of undesired behavior. If the child's whining and temper tantrums are ignored, for example, they usually disappear. In contrast, little things like words of approval, stars stuck on a chart (for younger children), the reading of a story, or other reinforcers can help mold a child's behavior. Parents can be taught how to give such reinforcements immediately after desirable behavior. With the counselor's help, parents can decide what behavior they want to instill. Then they decide on the steps necessary to bring this about and reinforce each specific behavior that helps move the child toward the desired goal. Such a program sometimes can be taught by counselors who have only a small knowledge of reinforcement principles, but for more extreme cases there is value in making referrals to a specialist.

Behavioral principles like these appear to work best when there is general stability in the family and a high level of involvement between the father and the children. One recent research study on "taming tyrants" in the home, found that traditional individual counseling did not work well. More effective were programs that educated parents in how to interact with their children, how and when to give positive reinforcement (like praise and hugs), how to deal with undesirable behavior, and how to instruct children effectively.[45]

Much of your counseling will involve teaching parents how to be more skillful and effective in their child rearing. Parents often get discouraged because their children are not learning social skills such as politeness, good grammar, athletic capabilities, effective study habits, or remembering to pick up clothes that most often get left on the floor. Sometimes parents need encouragement, perhaps mixed with a little humor.[46] You can help parents understand that many of these childhood actions are common and will disappear in time. Point out that parents can help best when they give gentle reminders to their children, try to avoid nagging, praise desirable behavior, and sometimes lower their parental expectations a little.

(d) Special Problem Issues. Parents often express concern about special problems such as autism, bed wetting, stuttering, school phobia, aggressive behavior, excessive nightmares, intense fears, or reactions to traumas such as accidents, deaths, or hospitalization. Many of these problems are transitory and often they are evidences of anxiety. Fears that arise during the day or overstimulation from books and television programs at bedtime, for example, can lead to nightmares or expressions of terror during the night. Fears of hospitalization or worry over death often surface when a grandparent or other significant person dies. These fears reflect anxiety about the unknown or insecurities about being abandoned or rejected. Bed wetting and stuttering may indicate that the child feels pressure from parents and others, pressure that sometimes increases as the enuresis and stuttering persist. Parents should be helped to give reassurance, approval, acceptance, and support. Fears are best discussed openly in the home and overstimulation with anxiety-arousing movies or stories should be avoided. It often helps if parents are encouraged to discuss their concerns with other parents who have dealt successful with the offending problem. If none of these simple tactics relieve the symptoms, counselors may want to consult some of the books that deal in depth with these special problems of children.[47]

(e) The Issue of Disturbed Parents. Sometimes children are brought to counseling by parents who want help for themselves but are too embarrassed to ask. More often, parents are less aware of their own problems, but it becomes clear to the counselor that the child's symptoms largely result from parental problems. When these parents are helped to deal with their own hang-ups and insecurities, children often improve spontaneously as a result. The counselor must not impose counseling on parents who do not want it, but whenever children are brought for help it is important to be alert to parental problems, many of which can be dealt with in the context of discussing the child. For example, a parent might be asked "What could you do differently to help solve this problem?" From this there is opportunity to talk about parental frustrations, fears, and actions.

At times it will appear that parents are severely disturbed or so concerned about their own problems and difficulties that they are unable to meet their children's needs effectively. Child abusers, socially incompetent people, or alcoholic parents are examples. The counselor has the challenge of providing stability and strength for these parents and their children, while helping them deal with conflicts in themselves and in their homes. This is a difficult task that requires experience, resilience, and the capacity for "endless patience that can put up with interminable recitals of petty resentments, trivial preoccupations, obsessive questioning, repeated recriminations, the breaking of appointments without warning, prolonged telephone calls, unexpected disappearances from the therapeutic scene, and clamorous demands for help at all times of day and night."[48] Often these parents are threatened by counseling, afraid of change, or concerned that their children will be taken elsewhere as a safeguard. Thus, there may be denial of problems and an unwillingness or inability to cooperate in counseling. All of this suggests that counselors must be flexible and at times willing to make referrals or seek guidance from more specialized professionals.

3. *Counseling Referrals.* Child counseling is a specialty within the helping professions. The Christian counselor who mostly works with adults may wish to refer children and their parents, especially disturbed parents, to counselors who are more skilled or experienced in the treatment of children, families, or adult psychopathology.

Preventing Child-Rearing Problems

In all of society there is no institution that can match the church in its potential influence on childhood, parenting, and family development. Entire families come to church. They bring their infant children for dedication or christening and often they return consistently for church services, Sunday School classes, fellowship, and spiritual help in times of need. In a variety of ways the church can prevent family problems through its influence on child rearing.

1. *Spiritual Training.* Earlier in this chapter we discussed biblical teachings about the home and child rearing. Sermons, Sunday school classes, seminars, retreats, and small study groups[49] can all teach families how to build Christian homes. Parents can be helped to be example believers. They can learn to teach their children in accordance with the approach outlined in Deuteronomy 6, making spiritual issues a normal part of family discussions. The home is the backbone of society, and stable Christian homes are built on the guidance that comes from the Bible, often through the church.[50]

2. *Marital Enrichment.* When marriages are good and growing, this influences the children positively by creating stability and security at home. Problems with children can put a strain on the parents' marriage, just as marital problems can adversely influence the children. Stimulating good marriages, therefore, is one way to prevent child-rearing problems.

3. *Parental Training.* Parenting can be a difficult and sometimes overwhelming responsibility. On occasion almost all parents feel that they have failed, and most have periods of discouragement and confusion. At such times parents need understanding, encouragement, and guidance concerning the needs and characteristics of children. Christian leaders can give such help. Point to books or other helpful resources on child rearing. Alert parents to the child's need for security, love, discipline, self-esteem, acceptance, and an awareness of God's presence. Point out the dangers of overprotection, overpermissiveness, overrestrictiveness, and overmeticulousness. Emphasize that both parents need to be actively involved in child rearing; fathers should not neglect their responsibilities in the home.[51] Then, as part of parent training, it may be helpful to consider the principles of effective parent-child communication,[52] teach ways to discipline, talk about behavior management, and discuss how children's needs can be met. All of this may be discussed in church settings where parents can share with one another.

Be careful to emphasize that while child rearing is a serious responsibility, everyone makes mistakes and parents who are too rigid or uptight probably create problems because of their anxiety and inflexibility. Child rearing can be difficult and challenging, but it also can be fun, especially when parents can discuss their mutual concerns informally with other parents, including Christian counselors.

4. *Encouragement.* A man was invited to speak to a group of teenagers and asked his daughter what to say. "Tell them," the daughter replied, "that they should be patient because their parents are just learning how to raise kids."

This is a simple message that should be proclaimed to both parents and children. It is biblical to encourage one another,[53] and there are times when family members should be encouraged, prayed for, given verbal emotional support, and reminded that all of us are "just learning."

Conclusions about Child Rearing and Parental Guidance

It has been suggested that many people find it easy to give advice about parenting until they have children. Then favorite child-rearing theories tend to be discarded quickly as mothers and fathers begin an occupation for which they are largely unprepared and which they rarely master.

After raising his children, one former college president shared his "homemade, groping, amateur rules on how to learn to be a parent in this bewildering age." The rules are over ten years old, but in many respects they are timeless and worth sharing as we help parents deal with the challenges of parenthood.

- Accept the fact that being a parent is one of the most important tasks you will ever undertake and budget your time and energy accordingly.
- Think long and hard about the particular parental role you have to play now.
- Don't regard your child as an extension of yourself.
- Enjoy your children.
- Love and believe in them.
- Expect something of your children.
- Be honest with them.
- Let them go. We do not own our children. In the end, the best we can do for them is to free them into the hands of God.[54]

SUGGESTIONS FOR FURTHER READING

Arnold, L. Eugene., ed. *Helping Parents Help Their Children.* New York: Brunner/Mazel, 1978.

Byrd, Walter, and Paul Warren. *Counseling Children and Teen-agers.* Dallas, Tex.: Word, forthcoming.

Brenner, Avis. *Helping Children Cope with Stress.* Lexington, Mass.: Heath, 1984.

Dobson, James. *Dr. Dobson Answers Your Questions.* Wheaton, Ill.: Tyndale, 1982.*

———. *Love Must Be Tough: New Hope for Families in Crisis.* Waco, Tex.: Word, 1983.*

* Books marked with an asterisk (*) are especially suited for counselees to read.

Gordon, Sol, and Judith Gordon. *Raising a Child Conservatively in a Sexually Permissive World.* New York: Simon and Schuster, 1983.
Kesler, Jay, Ron Beers, and LaVonne Neff, eds. *Parents and Children.* Wheaton, Ill.: Victor Books, 1986.*
Ketterman, Grace H. *The Complete Book of Baby and Child Care for Christian Parents.* Rev. ed. Old Tappan, N.J.: Revell, 1987.*

* Books marked with an asterisk (*) are especially suited for counselees to read.

12

Adolescence

RICH IS IN HIS TWENTIES NOW. He is employed as an assistant manager in a supermarket that hires a lot of teenagers who work part time after school. Sometimes Rich looks at these kids and thinks of his own tumultuous teenage years less than a decade ago.

Rich's parents are active in a very conservative, fundamentalist church. They wanted the best for their children, took Rich and his sister to church regularly, and had family devotions in the home every night.

Too often, according to Rich, the parents imposed arbitrary rules that were held with rigid tenacity. Rock music was banned from the house. The children were forbidden to attend movies or to work on Sunday. The parents closely monitored their children's activities and often criticized their friends. There wasn't much laughter or informal interaction in the home, but there were a lot of arguments. Rich felt that his parents never listened to his point of view. Whenever there were disagreements the children were told to respect their parents' wishes, and there was little opportunity for discussion. The parents expected their children to obey without question.

Instead the children rebelled. Rich took delight in doing everything his parents forbade him—drinking, sex, drugs, pornographic movies. He even started his own rock band, singing songs with lyrics that even Rich described as filthy. His grades dropped in school, he quit going to church, he argued constantly with his parents, and eventually they kicked him out of the house.

After high school, Rich drifted from job to job and eventually started work in the supermarket. He lives in a dingy little apartment now, talks to his parents only occasionally, and wonders if he will always be working in his present job. He would like to go to school, dreams at times of becoming a lawyer, and silently envies many of those teenage part-time workers who seem to have such a bright future. Occasionally he sees kids in the throes of rebellion, like he was, and he wonders how life might have been different for him if he had coped better with the stresses of adolescence.

The chapters in this book deal with problems that many of us have never experienced. We have, however, all been adolescents, and most of us can remember those stressful but exciting years when we were moving through a time of life that one psychiatrist has called "the most confusing, challenging, frustrating, and fascinating phase of human development."[1]

The word "adolescence" means a "period of growth to maturity." It begins at puberty (the beginning of the growth spurt and sexual maturation) and extends to the late teens or early twenties. During this time of conflict and growth the young person changes physically, sexually, emotionally, intellectually, and socially.[2] He or she moves away from dependence and the protective confines of the family and toward relative independence and social productivity. Life for many (at least in our society) is filled with friends, television, sports, study, jobs, hobbies, and sometimes a lot of stress and reflective thinking. Internally, "teenage life consists of a multitude of emotional peaks and valleys, ranging from exhilarating highs to depressing lows."[3] The teenager's world is often confusing and changing so quickly that immature young people do not always adjust efficiently. This has led some to describe adolescence as a highly disruptive period characterized by rebellion, perpetual turmoil, and stormy periods of stress.[4]

This view is not always supported by the professional literature. Many research studies have confirmed that adolescence is a period of rapid growth and frequent change, but it probably is true that "taken as a whole, adolescents are *not* in turmoil, *not* deeply disturbed, *not* at the mercy of their impulses, *not* resistant to parental values, *not* politically active, and *not* rebellious."[5] One study of teenagers found that the vast majority were trouble free; only 15 percent were plagued by trouble and turmoil.[6] Nevertheless adolescents *are* going through a significant change period, characterized first by the need to adjust to a variety of physical changes, second by the influence of great social pressures, and third by the challenge of making life-determining decisions about values, beliefs, identity, careers, lifestyles, and relationships with others, including those of the opposite sex.

Adolescence often is divided into three overlapping periods: *preadolescence* (sometimes called "pubescence" or "early adolescence") beginning around age ten or eleven and continuing for at least a couple of years; *middle adolescence,* the period from ages fourteen to eighteen when the young person is in high school; and *postadolescence* (sometimes called "late adolescence" or the period of "youth") that includes the late teenage years and extends into the early twenties.[7]

Preadolescence. This period begins with a bursting of biological changes that can evoke simultaneous feelings of anxiety, bewilderment, and delight. In both sexes there is a spurt of growth, especially in the limbs (this creates clumsiness and a gangly appearance), a change in body proportions (boys widen in the shoulders and develop thicker muscles, girls expand in the hips and develop breasts), a lowering of the voice in males, an enlargement of the sexual organs, an increase in sex hormones, the growth of pubic hair, an increase in the size of skin pores with more active glandular activity (which often leads to acne), and the appearance of hair on the face and body which, of course, is generally heavier in boys. A need for new emotional adjustments comes with the beginning of female menstruation and the occurrence in young males of both ejaculations and a sharp increase in the frequency of erections. During the past hundred years there has been a steady decline in the age of first menstruation and first ejaculation of semen. This means that the onset of adolescence has been getting earlier in life.

These physical changes have social and psychological implications. Most adolescents have times when they feel awkward, self-conscious, and dissatisfied with their physical appearance. Often there is difficulty in handling emerging sexual urges, and people who develop quickly or slowly often feel embarrassed, especially in the locker room where their peers easily observe and sometimes comment freely about the differences. Girls who feel awkward about using sanitary pads or young males who have erections at the most unexpected and potentially embarrassing times are bothered by these preadolescent influences, especially if they were not anticipated.

Peer influences and pressures, the insecurities of shifting into junior high school, the development of close friendships, hero worship, and "crushes" on people of the opposite (or same) sex, all indicate social adjustments during this period. There is, in addition, a new spirit of independence from parents, sometimes accompanied by increased conflict in the home. The development of more abstract, self-critical, and reflective thinking leads to an initial questioning of parental values and an increased ability to worry and be anxious.

Middle Adolescence. This period has fewer physical changes but the adolescent must adapt to his or her new identity as a person with an adult body. Sexual urges become more intense, especially in boys, and control is difficult in view of peer pressures, strong needs for intimacy, and the temptations from a hedonistic society that no longer considers self-control to be important or even possible. The result has been an upsurge in the number of sexually active teenagers (including those associated with the church)[8] and a staggering increase in the number of teenage pregnancies.[9]

Peers who were of importance in preadolescence now become of even greater significance as adolescents seek to break away from parental influences, values, and controls. The family still provides money, transportation, and a place to live, but teenagers often criticize parental standards and have no desire to accompany parents to church, on vacations, or on shopping trips. Communication at home may be minimal, but daydreaming is common and long hours are spent talking with friends on the telephone. There is a great desire to be accepted and to identify with current teenage language, heroes, music, styles of dress, and forms of entertainment. Dating or other relationships with the opposite sex become of extreme significance and "breakups" are very painful.

During this period three influences become important: sex, drugs, and motor vehicles. Each of these relates to the peer pressures, physical changes, insecurities, and adolescent struggles for identity. The need for love and acceptance, the influence of sexual hormones, the sexual openness in our society, and the relative ease of finding privacy (often in a car) make sexual intercourse a common experience for adolescents, even though this often arouses guilt, self-criticism, and sometimes causes pregnancy. The use of drugs, including alcohol, has always characterized adolescence, especially those who are seeking an unusual experience, escape from anxiety and boredom, or acceptance with drug-using friends.[10] Cars and motorcycles also lead to greater acceptance from peers and provide a way to express power or bolster feelings of insecurity.

You may not agree completely with the following observations of Harvard psychiatrist Armand M. Nicholi, but they give a thought-provoking insight into the needs of middle adolescents.

> Charging through the streets on a motorcycle (or in a car) gives the adolescent a sense of moving ahead, of doing, and of exerting himself; but it is finally a false sense and a poor substitute for concentrated effort. Racing a motorcycle into the middle of the night relieves the anxiety of rejection or failure, but it

> effects little change in the conditions causing the anxiety. A fast, noisy, breathtaking ride tends to relieve apprehension over exams, but it helps little in preparing for them. The cycle stimulates sexual feeling and even helps the adolescent approach a girl, but it contributes little to forming a meaningful relationship with her. The cycle helps express anger, but the destructive tendencies of these adolescents make a machine that can travel 125 miles an hour, a less than adaptive means of doing so.[11]

Hidden behind the continuing interest in sex, drugs, vehicles, peers, and independence is the pressure to face some serious challenges about the future. These include choosing a college or finding a job, leaving home, shifting responsibility onto themselves, and coping with the subtle but often unconscious attempts of parents to keep their growing children dependent and close to home.

Postadolescence. This is the period that begins when high school ends. Neither child nor adult, the young person in this period is faced with the tasks of moving comfortably into adult society, assuming adult responsibilities, shifting to an independent status, and formulating a distinct lifestyle. Planning for the future, getting further education, choosing a mate, and moving into a career are all tasks that take time and energy. These challenges of early adulthood will be discussed in more detail in the following chapter.

To an outside observer or counselor, many adolescent behaviors may seem to make no sense. We may understand the vacillation between maturity and immaturity (most of us have seen that in ourselves), but we rarely begin to comprehend the nature of adolescence, especially later adolescence, until we recognize that young people need to answer at least four crucial questions during this time in life.[12]

First is the question of identity: "Who am I?" Early in life, children imitate and identify with their parents and family members. Later they model their behavior after admired adults, develop relationships with peers, and then struggle, at least in our society, to develop their own self-concepts, uniqueness, values, and identities.[13] For many this can be a time of self-searching, anxiety, confusion, experimentation with lifestyles, and drifting goalless behavior.

Second is the question of relationships: "How do I get along with others?" In addition to developing relationships with both sexes, adolescents must learn how to fit into society and how to shift the nature of the parent-child bond so there is less dependency on parents. Teenage crushes, conflicts with authority, gang behavior, sexual involvements, hero worship, "best friend" relationships, petty squabbles, resistance to adult suggestions, and yielding to peer pressure can all reflect adolescent attempts to learn social skills and build meaningful bonds with others.

Third, the adolescent is concerned about the future: "Where do I fit?" The answer to this question will depend somewhat on one's economic level, personality traits, opportunities, capabilities, values, and family expectations. Choosing a career can be a difficult decision and adolescents, like people in their twenties and thirties, often make a number of vocational "false starts." Because they are idealistic and sometimes overly optimistic, young people may move in unrealistic career directions. This can lead to frustration, pessimism, and the need to constantly reevaluate vocational choices.

Fourth, there is the question of ideology: "What do I believe?" This includes but goes beyond questions about religion. Adults may not be willing or able to give answers, but young people may wonder about a number of troubling issues: for example, why so many people in this world go hungry, why some people live in poverty while others can flaunt their affluence, why nuclear disarmament doesn't happen, whether their parents' religious or political views are really "right," what is wrong with premarital sex, why the Bible or the government should be sources of authority, or why anybody should go to church. In their attempts to find what they believe and why, young people have always asked hard questions to the generation that is now in control.[14] In the process of finding answers, adolescents develop their own values, religious beliefs, and life philosophies.

Too often, the society and people in the older generation give little in the way of clear values and practical help. Perhaps it is not surprising that many adolescents struggle with feelings of inner emptiness, confusion, interpersonal tension, and anxiety.

The Bible and Adolescence

The concept of adolescence, as we know it, did not appear in the literature on child rearing until late in the nineteenth century. The word "adolescent" does not appear anywhere in the Bible, and it may be that the biblical writers did not think of adolescence as a separate period of development. As we saw in the previous chapter, childhood and youth are mentioned frequently in Scripture, but we have no indication of when this period ends. The fact that biblical instructions were given to children implies that these young people were old enough to understand and comply. The Bible's teachings on children,[15] therefore, undoubtedly apply to "children" of adolescent age.

Scripture also speaks of "young men" and "young women." The writer of Ecclesiastes, for example, tells young men to be happy: "Young man, it's wonderful to be young! Enjoy every minute of it! Do all you want to; take in everything, but realize that you must account to God for everything you do. So banish grief and pain, but remember that youth, with a whole life before it, can make serious mistakes."[16]

Young people are portrayed in Scripture as visionaries who are strong, able to incorporate the Word of God into their lives, capable of overcoming Satan, expected to be submissive to elders, self-controlled, and instructed to humble themselves "under God's mighty hand, that he may lift you up in due time. Cast all your anxiety on him because he cares for you."[17] These few phrases, like the teachings of the entire Bible, can be helpful to counselors who work with young people struggling with adolescence.

The Causes of Problems in Adolescence

In describing modern adolescents, one expert concluded that "taken as a whole, the data do not present a picture of escalating woes. I stress this point because adolescents are extremely vulnerable to external influences. If we portray them in the media and in legislative hearings as pathological, spaced-out, drunk, and assaultive, we run the risk of alienating greater numbers of young people and of encouraging them unwittingly to fulfill our worst expectations."[18] If parents, teachers and counselors look for the worst in teenagers and expect the worst, it may be that we will see the worst and subtly encourage teenagers to engage in the very behaviors that we most fear and hope to have them avoid.[19]

Adolescent society changes quickly and most adults find themselves out of touch with contemporary teenagers. In spite of the changes, however, several issues persist and create problems for adolescents regardless of the times in which they live.

1. *Physical Changes.* The growth spurt, skin problems, excess fat, periodic decreases in energy, changes in body proportions, development of body hair, lowering of voice pitch, and other physical changes can each influence adolescents psychologically. Recent reports suggest that teenagers, as a group, are not in good health; many are out of shape, overweight, physically unfit, and victims of lack of exercise or poor nutritional habits.[20] At a time when it is important to look attractive, a teenager's physical development can bring embarrassment and dissatisfaction, especially if the biological changes are obvious to others or if maturation is slow in coming. Late maturers tend to be treated as children by both peers and adults. This can lead to problems in social adjustment and feelings of rejection. Although these effects of late maturation usually can be overcome, some young people carry their insecurities and adjustment problems into adulthood.

2. *Sexual Changes.* Even when they are expecting the sexual changes of adolescence, most young people experience anxiety over the physical changes in their bodies, the increasing erotic impulses within, and the confusion about sexual behavior. Sexual fantasies, masturbation, heavy petting, and adolescent intercourse can all produce guilt. Crushes on people of the same sex can lead to fears of homosexuality. Intimate contact with others can increase the fear of AIDS or venereal disease. Sudden physical growth can create confusion over one's identity and uncertainty about how to act appropriately as an adult male or female. Dating may be feared and desired at the same time. There is a sexual freedom in our society, an easy access to sexually explicit and erotically arousing video movies, a parental reluctance to give clear sex education,[21] and frequent opportunities to engage in impulsive sexual experimentation. All of this can lead to loss of self-control, guilt, pregnancies, and the emotional trauma that follows.

3. *Interpersonal Changes.* As we have seen, adolescence is a time when there are changes in relationships with parents, peers, and others in society. It is important to be liked and accepted by other adolescents, especially those of the opposite sex, but even as they move away from parental control, young people need to feel that their environments have stability. When there is no clear parental guidance, or when the inner and outer worlds both seem to be unstable, adolescents often feel confused, anxious, and angry.

4. *Changing Values, Morals, and Religious Beliefs.* Prior to adolescence, the young person may accept parental standards with little question or challenge. As they get older, however, adolescents begin to question parental viewpoints and peers have a greater impact on the molding of beliefs and values. Often, young people get no help with the process of values clarification except from equally confused and struggling peers. Religious doubt, a decrease in church-related activities, and a turning to some other faith (at least temporarily) are all common in adolescence, much to the distress of parents and church leaders.[22]

Studies confirm that the commonly accepted values and beliefs of one generation may differ greatly from the values of those who were adolescents a few years earlier.[23] Within the past several years, for example, attitudes toward sex have been changing (perhaps because of the fear of AIDS),[24] and there have been changes in beliefs about the roles of women, the use of drugs, and the importance of career success. Many of these and other value changes seem to be nationwide and many reflect changes in adult thinking and behavior. Recent studies have shown, for example, that the American family has "begun to divest itself of responsibility for the young, just as earlier it abandoned much of its responsibility for the elderly." Two-thirds of American parents want to "be free to live their own lives even if it means spending less time with their children."[25] If this trend continues, some experts fear that adolescents will no longer inherit a cohesive value system from their parents. Instead, young people will look to the mass media, peers, and other hit-and-miss resources for molding their future beliefs.[26] The resulting confusion could present counselors with a greater responsibility for helping people find and clarify values.

These issues are made more complex by the role of cultural differences. A recent comparison of "traditional" and Hispanic youth, for example, found a number of value differences. The mainstream culture glorifies youth, but the Hispanic culture traditionally respects age. Peer groups have a major influence in the larger culture; Hispanic young people are more influenced by family. Competition and individual achievement are rewarded in the mainstream; cooperation and interdependence are encouraged by Hispanic families. These and similar cultural differences can create further value confusion for minority adolescents who want to fit both cultures.[27]

Religious cultures also create tensions for young people. Many years ago, a denominational conference arranged a meeting to discuss the problems of today's teenagers. The topics for discussion were selected by adults and proved to be of little interest to the adolescent participants. When urged to express their real concerns, the young people expressed frustrations that probably still exist. Many felt that:

- Christian parents and church leaders fail to realize the intense pressures and problems facing teenagers today, including the pressures to turn on with drugs and sex.[28]
- Outward conformity to adult standards often is taken as evidence of spiritual maturity when, in fact, it may show a desire to not "rock" the family boat by asking questions or expressing doubts.
- Christian parents don't instill healthy and realistic attitudes toward sex.
- Adults fail to show the confidence in adolescents that would come by letting them undertake *real* responsibilities.
- Many church people take a lackadaisical attitude toward important economic, health, social, and political issues.
- There often is a disparity between the pat answers and the day-to-day Christian lives of older Christians.[29]

These conclusions are not based on scientific study, but they demonstrate some of the moral struggles of adolescents. Alert older Christians, including counselors, recognize that we may be ignoring pressing adolescent issues while we seek to answer questions that nobody is asking.

5. *The Move to Independence.* Adolescence, as we have seen, is a period of growth into maturity. Aware that they are no longer children, adolescents want freedom in large doses, but they handle it better in small and slowly increasing amounts. What young people want and think they can handle often differs from what parents are willing or think it wise to give. This can create tension, frustration, rebellion, and persisting power struggles. An old cliché says that parents often find it easier to give their children roots than to give them wings.

6. *Acquiring Skills and Building Self-Esteem.* According to James Dobson teenagers do not feel good about themselves unless they have physical attractiveness, intelligence (which sometimes translates into academic ability), and money.[30] Rarely are these all present and frequently there are feelings of self-condemnation, social incompetence, academic and athletic ineptness, and spiritual failure that are emphasized whenever there is criticism, social rejection, or the inability to succeed in some important task.

Self-esteem problems sometimes come because adolescents are lacking in social skills. Each of us must learn how to cope with stress, study effectively, manage time, interact smoothly with others, resist temptation, hold a job, mature spiritually, relate to the opposite sex, or handle money. These are some of the survival skills that individuals must learn if they are to get along smoothly in life.[31] When adolescents have limited opportunities to learn these skills, adjustments to life can be much more difficult.[32]

7. *Concerns about the Future.* Late adolescence has been called a period of "psychosocial moratorium" when young people are free to regroup psychologically and socially while they seek to find their niches in society.[33] Even during this time, however, many older adolescents feel pressure to make decisions about careers, college majors, values, lifestyles, and what to do with their lives. No decision is permanent at this age and it is possible to change later, at least in our society. Nevertheless some adolescent decisions can have lifelong implications. An awareness of this creates pressure and anxiety for people who want to make wise decisions.

The Effects of Problems in Adolescence

Even though most teenagers *do* grow up into a relatively normal adulthood (sometimes to the amazement of their beleaguered parents) the pressures of adolescence do take their toll. Teenage insecurities, feelings of guilt, inferiority, loneliness, and rejection can persist far into the adult years, and for many young people the problems of adolescence make their presence felt long before adulthood.

1. *Holding in the Problems.* Some adolescents struggle with their problems alone. There may be loneliness, daydreaming, alienation, or withdrawal from friends, apathy, a forsaking of usual interests and activities, or perpetual inner turmoil that sometimes appears in the form of psychosomatic illness, anxiety, scholastic failure, or more serious emotional and behavioral disorders. Depression, anxiety, and unexplainable changes in mood or behavior tend to be common in adolescence, but these are not pathological unless they are prolonged and intense. More common are the adjustment reactions of adolescence. These come in response to stress and are characterized by irritability, persisting depression, brooding, and temper outbursts.[34]

2. *Acting out the Problems.* Adolescents often act out their problems in socially disapproved ways that have the effect of resisting parents and asserting independence. Excessive drinking, drug abuse, lying, stealing, crime, "gang" behavior, and other forms of delinquency or rebellion give the adolescent a sense of power, a feeling of independence, a way of challenging authority, and a means for gaining and retaining the attention and acceptance of one's friends, most of whom also may be acting out.

Sometimes acting out takes other forms. Failing in school subjects or rejecting parental religious beliefs and moral standards can be ways of expressing independence. Suicide, murder, and automobile accidents (often the result of speeding or intoxicated teenage drivers) have become the major causes of death among adolescents and young adults. All of these acts of violence can be a way of "bucking the system" and expressing uniqueness.[35] In addition, sexual experimentation, including intercourse, sometimes becomes a way for adolescents to act like adults and gain peer acceptance.

Teenagers often feel intense social pressures to experiment sexually. Sometimes sexual behavior is not an acting out; instead, it becomes an attempt to overcome inhibitions, find meaningful relationships, prove one's virility, bolster self-esteem, or escape loneliness. According to one Harvard study, however, sexual permissiveness has led to "pervasive feelings of guilt," feelings of self-contempt and worthlessness, empty relationships, and persisting concerns among young people that they were using others or being used as sex objects. All of this was accompanied by an epidemic of venereal disease and a rapid increase in unwanted pregnancies.[36]

This increase in teenage pregnancies has become a serious national problem. Not only is there concern for the care and welfare of the babies, but there is clear evidence that, compared to their classmates, teenage parents get less education, earn less money in life, hold lower-prestige jobs, experience less vocational satisfaction, and have a higher than average rate of divorce and remarriage.[37] When compared to their peers, the children of teenage parents are poorer in cognitive development, school achievement, emotional development, and social skills.[38] Of course these unhappy results may not be due to teenage pregnancy alone, but the contrasts between adolescent childbearers and nonchildbearers is sharp enough to suggest strongly that teenage child bearing can radically change a young person's whole educational, occupational, social and marital future. This clearly is a long-term effect of adolescent acting out in response to sexual impulses.

3. *Running from the Problems.* Every year large numbers of adolescents (mostly females between the ages of fifteen and seventeen) run away from home. Many of these young people are frustrated at school, unable to communicate, in conflict with parents, lacking in self-esteem, victimized by abusive family members, impulsive, or having problems with peers. Many come from poorly functioning families and there is evidence that about one out of every seven has been kicked out of the house.[39]

Leaving home is not the only way to escape. Some withdraw from the world psychologically with or without the help of drugs and alcohol.[40] Others attempt to withdraw by taking their own lives. Within recent years there has been a sharp increase in the suicide rate among adolescents, and suicide, as we have seen, has become a leading cause of teenage deaths. Suicide attempts often indicate a real desire to die, but usually the young person is also crying for help. Social pressures, the example of peers who have attempted suicide, adolescent depression, problems with self-esteem, and sometimes even the pressures of being gifted[41] can all lead to suicide. In addition, according to psychiatrist Robert Coles, the cause may be moral and spiritual. Adolescence is a time for soul searching, Coles suggests, and when there are no opportunities to ponder the existential and ultimate issues of life, the individual despairs and attempts suicide.[42]

As we will see in chapter 31, self-destruction can sometimes be subtle. Young athletes, for example, sometimes build their entire identities and feelings of self-worth around their athletic skills and performances. If one of these players is dropped from the team, or if an injury prevents further participation in sports, the effects can be devastating. Depression, anger, confusion, low self-esteem, and feelings of rejection can all follow.[43] Sometimes the individual lashes out in anger or slips into self-destructive behaviors such as excessive drinking, drug use, or other forms of irresponsible running away.

4. *Sticking with the Problems.* Not all adolescents hold in, act out, or run away from their problems. Many face the challenges squarely, talk them over with friends or trusted adults, read about teenage stress, react to failures by trying harder next time, learn from their mistakes, and move through the era of adolescence in a relatively smooth fashion. These young people and their parents could benefit from preventive, educative, and supportive counseling, but they rarely come for help. Instead, Christian counselors tend to see people whose adjustment problems are more disruptive to the teenagers, their families, and society.

Counseling and the Problems of Adolescents

Adolescent problems can be approached in two ways, by counseling the adolescent and by helping parents. In both cases, the counselor must show that he or she has a broad understanding of the struggles of adolescents and a knowledge of the kinds of tensions that build up both inside the counselees and within their homes. Often, parents and teenagers are confused, disappointed, and hurt over the interpersonal tensions and adolescent pressures that have developed. Frequently there is anger, a loss of self-esteem, anxiety about the future, and feelings of guilt over the past. The counselor who understands and accepts such problems without taking sides can have a significant impact on both parents and teenagers. The impact can be even greater if the counselor is sensitive, calm, compassionate, and secure enough to tolerate criticism and adulation, sometimes in the same counseling session. Adolescents and their parents need a caring, wise, self-confident person who provides a haven of calm guidance in times of strong upheaval.

1. *Counseling Parents.* In chapter 11 we considered ways for helping parents cope with the problems of their children. Most of these principles also apply when you are counseling the parents of adolescents, but you might want to ponder several additional guidelines.[44]

(a) Support and Encouragement. When adolescent problems arise, parents often conclude that they are to blame, that they are not good parents, or that their children are headed for certain disaster. Counselors do not help if they ignore or explain away such feelings, but there is value in reassuring and encouraging parents. Almost all children—even the children of effective parents—go through periods of anger, rebellion, withdrawal, depression, and criticism. Earlier we noted that God, the only perfect parent, had children that rebelled against him.[45] It can be comforting for parents to know that he understands their struggles. It also is helpful to remind parents that they are not the only people who influence teenage and young adult behavior. At home, parents need to relax, listen, and try to understand their teenagers. Most important is the seeking of continual daily help and divine guidance from a God who guides and knows the best way to handle problems, even adolescent problems.

(b) Family Counseling. Parents should not be blamed for all teenage stresses, but this does not mean that parents are never at fault. When an adolescent or some other member of the family is having problems, the real root of the trouble often lies with a malfunctioning family. When parents have serious marriage problems, for example, children may act out, run away, or develop other noticeable behavior. This distracts the parents from their marriage difficulties, brings them together while they focus on the adolescent problem, and sometimes gives the teenager a way to escape an intolerable home situation.

Some counselors ask the whole family to come for counseling, even when an adolescent son or daughter is identified as the one with the problem. The problem person may really be reflecting deeper issues in the home. Sometimes if the family can be helped to function better, the adolescent's problems improve dramatically.[46]

(c) Limit Setting. Some of the home conflicts in adolescence come because young people push for more freedom than the parents are willing to give, at least initially. When adolescents react adversely to the setting of limits, parents may respond in different ways. Some parents begin to wonder if they are being rigid and unreasonable. Some feel threatened and overwhelmed. Others respond by tightening the rules and refusing to negotiate or yield. Many question their competence as parents.

Instead of giving in to adolescent demands (an action that will usually lead to more demands), parents can be helped to recognize that all family members have rights in the household. To ensure these rights, some limits must be set and maintained, regardless of adolescent and neighborhood pressures, but there also must be flexibility, communication, and discussion. By their own words and actions, parents can show love, acceptance, and respect for one another and for all other members of the family. This modeling is likely to be much more effective than nagging, criticizing, or advice giving. As the teenagers get older, they should be given greater freedom, but at all times there must be emphasis on the rights and interests of others. Counselors can help parents set limits that are practical, sensitive to the young person's needs, and conforming to biblical standards. Sometimes the parent knows what to do, but he or she needs an outsider to give support, especially in times of family stress.

(d) Spiritual Guidance. Merton Strommen is a researcher who has spent many years studying teenagers and their parents.[47] Some of this research has led to the conclusion that adolescents tend to forsake the family religion when the parents' faith is based on rules, rather than on the Christian virtues of acceptance and forgiveness. If the parents are rigid and legalistic, or if the family is greatly concerned about status, acceptance in the neighborhood, or competition, then the young people are more likely to rebel. At times, these parental attitudes are really a cover for underlying insecurity and anxiety. Counseling in these areas could be helpful, but there is also value in helping parents grow spiritually, develop biblical values, and live a consistent Christian lifestyle. This kind of counseling benefits both the parents and the family members who are helped indirectly.

2. *Counseling Adolescents.* Perhaps the most difficult task involved in counseling adolescents is to establish trusting relationships and to help the young counselees recognize the need for help. Some counselees come voluntarily for help, but often the adolescent sees no need for counseling and is sent by a parent, teacher, or judge. When this happens, the counselor is seen as the parent's ally and resistance is present from the beginning.

(a) Rapport Building. Honesty and respect, mixed with compassion and gentle firmness, are all important especially as counseling begins. If there is resistance, deal with it directly and give the counselee opportunity to respond. "Could you tell me what brought you here?" you might ask. If the counselee doesn't respond, ask "Well, somebody else must have wanted you to come. I'm sure you must have some ideas why." Show respect for the counselee and avoid asking questions in a way that implies judgment or criticism. This only serves to arouse resistance and increase the adolescent's defensiveness. Attempt to focus the discussion on specific concrete issues, listen carefully to what the counselee is saying, permit the expressing of feelings, and periodically point out what is happening emotionally during the interview. "You look like you're really mad," or "I sense that you feel pretty confused right now," are examples of comments that stimulate discussion of feelings. Try to keep all of this on a relaxed, informal, conversational level.

(b) Transference. As we noted earlier, this word refers to the tendency of some individuals to transfer feelings about a person in the past to a person in the present. For example, a young counselee who hates his father may transfer this hatred to the male counselor. The counselor must recognize that he or she often will be treated with hostility, suspicion, fear, or praise primarily because the counselor resembles some other adult. Counselors may want to discuss these transference feelings with their counselees. Sometimes this leads to helpful insights and behaviors that can be carried away from the counseling session.

As a counselor, try not to respond like the counselee's parent, hero or other individual with whom you are being compared. In addition, be alert to countertransference. This refers to the counselor's tendency to see similarities between the counselee and some other person. If the counselee reminds you of your own daughter, for example, or if you are reminded of the neighborhood troublemaker, your feelings for these other people may transfer on to the counselee and interfere with your objectivity as a helper. It is best not to disclose this to the counselee, but it can be helpful for you to discuss it with another counselor.

(c) Problem Identification. It is difficult to help if you cannot identify the problem. Since adolescent counselees sometimes deny that they have problems, counseling becomes a challenge. Instead of trying to classify or diagnose problems, it is more helpful to encourage adolescents to talk about issues such as school, leisure activities, interests, likes and dislikes, parents, friends, plans for the future, religion, dating, sex, worries, and similar issues. Start with relatively nonthreatening items (for example, "Tell me about your school or family"; "What has happened recently that interested you?") and move to more sensitive areas later. In all of this you should show that you really want to listen. Try to be a friend instead of an interrogator. Some general questioning may be needed to get the process started, but once the counselee starts talking and you show a willingness to understand, the adolescent counselee may begin to reveal his or her fears, feelings, attitudes, worries, impulses, interpersonal tensions, personal defenses, and other significant issues.

(d) Goal Setting. After you have built rapport, begun to identify the problems, and gained some insight into why earlier plans of action have not been working, it is good to set some goals. In an earlier chapter we considered the goals of self-understanding, building better communication with others, helping people acquire skills or change behavior, giving support, and stimulating spiritual growth. These apply to adolescents as well as to adults.

In any counseling situation, goals should be as specific as possible. If you and your counselee have differing goals, this discrepancy should be resolved. Then, when clear and mutually acceptable goals are established, the counselee must be helped to take action that will move toward reaching these goals. This has been called a crucial stage in counseling; a critical point where failure in the counseling process may be most likely to occur.[48] It can be easy for everyone to agree on goals, but it is much harder to make the changes that will move one toward attaining these ends.

Ultimately, the Christian counselor seeks to help young people grow into maturity and become adults who honor Christ with their lifestyles, beliefs, inner serenity, and interpersonal relationships. To help counselees reach this goal it is necessary to focus on present, more immediate problems. Sometimes this is done by guiding counselees as they change their thinking, perceptions, and behavior. At times you may want to encourage group counseling. This can be of special help to adolescents who have interpersonal problems, tendencies to withdraw, or problems that others share, such as family abuse, an alcoholic parent, or a terminally ill relative. The relationships and mutual sharing that comes in group counseling can give support and teach adolescents the important lesson of how to relate to others effectively. Often this frees them to move on to the spiritual growth that brings ultimate answers to the problems of life.

Preventing the Problems of Adolescence

It is well known that baby chicks struggle to peck their way through the shell of the egg. If a sympathetic observer tries to help by breaking the shell, the chick gets out faster, but it fails to experience the struggles and build the strength that would prepare it for the stresses of life.

Adolescents are somewhat similar to those baby chicks. It can be painful and difficult to break out from the restraints of childhood, but with each challenge the adolescent can gain in confidence, competence, and knowledge, even when there is failure. Parents and other sympathetic adults sometimes try to prevent all problems and protect teenagers from the stresses of life, but this is both impossible and poor child rearing. Instead, we should seek to help young people mature without the painful and unnecessary consequences that come when there is a breaking of the law, sexual immorality, severe emotional disturbance, inability to succeed academically, interpersonal conflict, or loss of faith. There are several ways by which counselors and other Christian leaders can help parents prepare for adolescence and can help young people mature without falling into many of the painful pitfalls of the teenage years.

1. *Building a Spiritual Foundation.* Someone has said that the best time to begin preparing for adolescence is at least ten years before it begins. By building communication skills, mutual respect, concern for others, and an open attitude about problems, parents help children learn how to deal honestly and immediately with issues when they arise.

This training is of special importance in the spiritual realm. Adolescents are not impressed by theological legalism or religion that has a lot of talk but little action. They are much more impressed when their parents *show* that theirs is a vital faith, characterized by a sincere commitment to Jesus Christ and a daily willingness to worship and serve him. When parents can be taught to grow spiritually, there is greater love, stability, acceptance, and forgiveness in the home. This creates a firm foundation on which adolescents can build lives, formulate values, solve problems, and plan for the future.

2. *Education.* A variety of school programs have been developed to educate teenagers about the dangers of teenage drinking, drug use, unrestrained sex, and related issues. This information can be helpful, but adolescents often know (or think they know) more about drugs and sex than their teachers. Frequently factual knowledge fades in the face of peer pressure or the excitement of taking a chance. Urging teenagers to say no to drugs is an admirable goal, but slogans like this are of little help if the person hasn't learned skills that teach *how* to say no when the pressures arise. Educational efforts to prevent teenage suicide can be constructive, but only if suicide is not made to sound glamorous, if students are given factual information about suicide, and if they are shown how to cope with their pressures in less destructive ways.[49]

Drugs, sex, and health education must not be abandoned, but some of this may be more effective if it is not given by professional teachers but comes instead from those who have experienced the pain of chemical abuse or sexual promiscuity. Even more important is the consideration of moral standards, values, and biblical teachings about right and wrong. These issues must be discussed openly and honestly, preferably at home and before they arise unexpectedly in the young person's experience. In addition, adolescents must be helped to find love and acceptance in life so there is less need to escape into chemical euphoria, immoral sex, or suicide attempts.

Christian parents and church leaders often assume that God will protect our children if we pray for them regularly. This is a valid conclusion, but sometimes it becomes an excuse that we use to ignore developing problems and do nothing about the pressures that teenagers face daily. Surely it is valid to conclude that God sometimes answers our prayers and protects our adolescents through the moral teaching and forewarning that come from parents and Christian teachers. This learning does not occur if issues like sexual intercourse, birth control, drinking, masturbation, teenage pregnancies, and drug abuse are never mentioned. When these are discussed openly before they arise, they can be discussed again when the temptations abound.[50]

3. *Family Example and Stability.* The example of parents is one of the most effective preventive influences in the adolescent's life. How do parents cope with stress, resolve differences, or respond to temptation? Is their marriage stable? Is the family able to provide a haven in times of stress or a place of certainty when the world around seems to be in turmoil? Stimulating better marriages is one crucial way by which the church can prevent teenage problems. Parents can also be encouraged to love their kids, to accept them as they are, to try to understand, to point out their good points, and to avoid constant nagging. Counselors can help parents realize that if they can overlook some minor irritations, they will have a better chance of being heard when they have to draw the line on issues that are of greater importance.

4. *Interpersonal Support.* Most churches are aware that peer support and encouragement is crucial in adolescence. Of course teenage rebellion, drug abuse, and immorality occur in church and parachurch groups; however, when friends and sensitive, concerned leaders are available to provide a place for discussion of real problems, give emotional and social support, help young people have fun, build self-esteem, and give both direction and spiritual teaching, then the church can have a great positive and preventive impact. Modeling, as we have noted, is one of the most important means of teaching adolescents. If older believers can be models who get to know the adolescents and gain their respect, this can have a significant influence on teenage development. No counselor should underestimate the importance of youth leaders and effective youth organizations.

5. *Guidance.* Choosing a career, finding one's place in life, learning to date, developing an identity, formulating values, and deciding what to believe are among the decisions that adolescents must face. No one else can make these decisions for them, although parents, Christian counselors, and leaders in the church can give guidance and encouragement as the decisions are being made. Sunday School classes, youth groups, and retreats can stimulate discussion and thinking about these issues—and so can parents.

Conclusions about Adolescence

It is not easy to be an adolescent or to help young people through their adolescent years, but surely the crisis nature of this period in life has been overrated. Considering the changes that occur and the adjustments that are required, most young people reach adulthood in remarkably good shape.

Immediately before his ascension into heaven, Jesus told his followers that they had one basic responsibility to complete in his absence: to make disciples.[51] Where could this be done more effectively than in the home? As children become teenagers, parental discipline should move into parental discipleship, teaching by word and example how to be a follower of Jesus Christ. Teenagers are too big to spank,[52] but they are old enough to respond to logic, persuasion, fairness, interest, positive reinforcement, love, parental example, and the power of prayer. Rather than trying to force adolescents into some parental mold, our task as counselors and parents is to help them grow into Christian personal maturity. Few tasks could be more challenging, fulfilling, or important.

SUGGESTIONS FOR FURTHER READING

Benson, Dennis C., and Bill Wolfe. *The Basic Encyclopedia for Youth Ministry.* Loveland, Colo.: Group Books, 1981.

Collins, Gary R. *Give Me a Break: The How-to-Handle-Pressure Book for Teenagers.* Old Tappan, N.J.: Revell, 1982.*

Dobson, James. *Preparing for Adolescence.* Ventura, Calif.: Regal, 1978.*

Kesler, Jay, ed. *Parents and Teenagers.* Wheaton, Ill.: Victor Books, 1984.*

McCoy, Kathleen. *Coping with Teenage Depression: A Parent's Guide.* New York: New American Library, 1982.

McDowell, Josh. *What I Wish My Parents Knew about My Sexuality.* San Bernardino Calif.: Here's Life Press, 1987.*

Olson, G. Keith. *Counseling Teenagers.* Loveland, Colo.: Group Books, 1984.

* Books marked with an asterisk (*) are especially suited for counselees to read.

13

Young Adulthood

BRENT AND MICHELLE ARE both in their twenties; he is twenty-six, she is twenty-one. They attend the same church. He has been attending for only a few months, but she has been in the same church for all of her life and most of her family still attends.

Brent grew up in a home that paid little attention to religion. His parents call themselves Christians, but they only attend church once or twice a year (usually around Christmas). For many years they had hoped that Brent, their only son, would enter the family business, but after college he decided instead to enroll in seminary. After some initial protests, they gave their blessing and have helped a little with tuition.

Now, graduation day is approaching and Brent has concluded that he might not fit very well into the pastorate. He wonders about a career in missions and has decided to spend a summer as a short-term missionary in Africa. His parents are not supportive of this idea. They think he has wasted his seminary years, has become too involved in religion, is foolish to consider missions, and is embarrassing them by trying to raise "support" money so he can "take a jaunt to Africa at somebody else's expense." Brent is confused about his own career direction. He doesn't know what he wants to do and he wonders, at times, if some of his parents' attitudes might be right.

Michelle is also confused vocationally. Her parents are enthusiastic about missions and would be delighted if their daughter went to the mission field. But she wants to be a fashion designer and spends a lot of her time designing clothes. She went to college for a year and dropped out because the courses were too dull. She is vaguely aware of ways to become a designer, but she hasn't done anything to make her dreams a reality and she isn't interested in schooling. Instead, she would like to travel, to meet interesting people and to earn more money than she gets from her job as a checker at the local supermarket.

Brent and Michelle are both discouraged because they have noticed that most of their friends are floundering too. A few have gone on to college and graduate school, and some are in successful jobs. These people seem to have clear directions. Individually, and sometimes together, Brent and Michelle pray about their careers, but sometimes they wonder (and so do their parents) if they ever will find clear direction for their lives.

The *Comprehensive Textbook of Psychiatry/IV* is a massive volume that weighs over seven pounds, is almost three inches thick, and contains more than two thousand pages of concisely written, technical information, arranged in double columns.[1] This impressive reference book includes detailed articles on childhood, adolescence, middle age, and the elderly, but it says very little about young adulthood. Young adults comprise a third of our population, most are the parents of young children. They are a large proportion of the labor force, and—as marketing analysts are aware—a group of people with massive political clout and buying power. Sandwiched between middle-aged or elderly parents and the adolescents who attract so much media attention, young adults have unique needs and problems of their own, but this is the age group that is most overlooked by writers of psychiatric or counseling psychology textbooks.

Young adulthood is a period in life that extends from the late teens to the late thirties. It has been called a time of rich satisfaction in terms of love, sexuality, family life, occupational advancement, creativity, and realization of one's major life goals, but it can also be a time of intense stress. "Early adulthood is the era in which we are most buffeted by our own passions and ambitions from within and by the demands of family, community, and society without. Under reasonably favorable conditions, the rewards of living in this era are enormous, but the costs often equal or exceed the benefits."[2]

According to Daniel Levinson and a team of research associates at Yale University, early adulthood can be divided into four overlapping periods, each of which lasts for about five to seven years.[3] As shown in Figure 13-1, the early adult era begins with the *early adult transition* that comes between ages seventeen and twenty-two. Moving from adolescence to adulthood, young people at this place in life are making decisions about the future. The choices are hard, the separations from parents may be painful, but for most this is a time in life that is challenging, exciting, difficult, and frightening—all at the same time.[4]

When they reach about age twenty-one, young adults find themselves entering the adult world with the need to make practical decisions. These years of the mid twenties are when most people decide about marriage, parenthood, occupations, and living arrangements. Often there are a variety of alternatives to explore and sometimes decisions are made too quickly or based on circumstances and regretted later.

The *age thirty transition* begins around age twenty-eight and extends into the early thirties. For many, this is a time of reappraisal when past choices are examined and sometimes modified. By this time, most of us have discovered talents, abilities, and interests that we missed earlier. Some people conclude that their idealistic, youthful values and dreams were unrealistic or unattainable. Those who have made few commitments during their twenties may feel fragmented, rootless, and inclined to think that their lives are drifting. Many attempt to change this pattern so the future can have greater stability. For some, this is a time of such upheaval that young men and women wonder if they are encountering a mid-life crisis ten years early.

Between the ages of thirty-three and forty, most individuals go through a period of *settling down*. According to Levinson, "life in the thirties is always different—whether the change is subtle or dramatic—from what it was a decade earlier."[5] Demands from one's family, community, and occupation are at a peak. In our society, at least, there is often competition for professional and economic advancement during this period, and many people have increasing concerns about achieving greater autonomy, independence, and self-sufficiency.

Figure 13-1
Stages in Adult Development

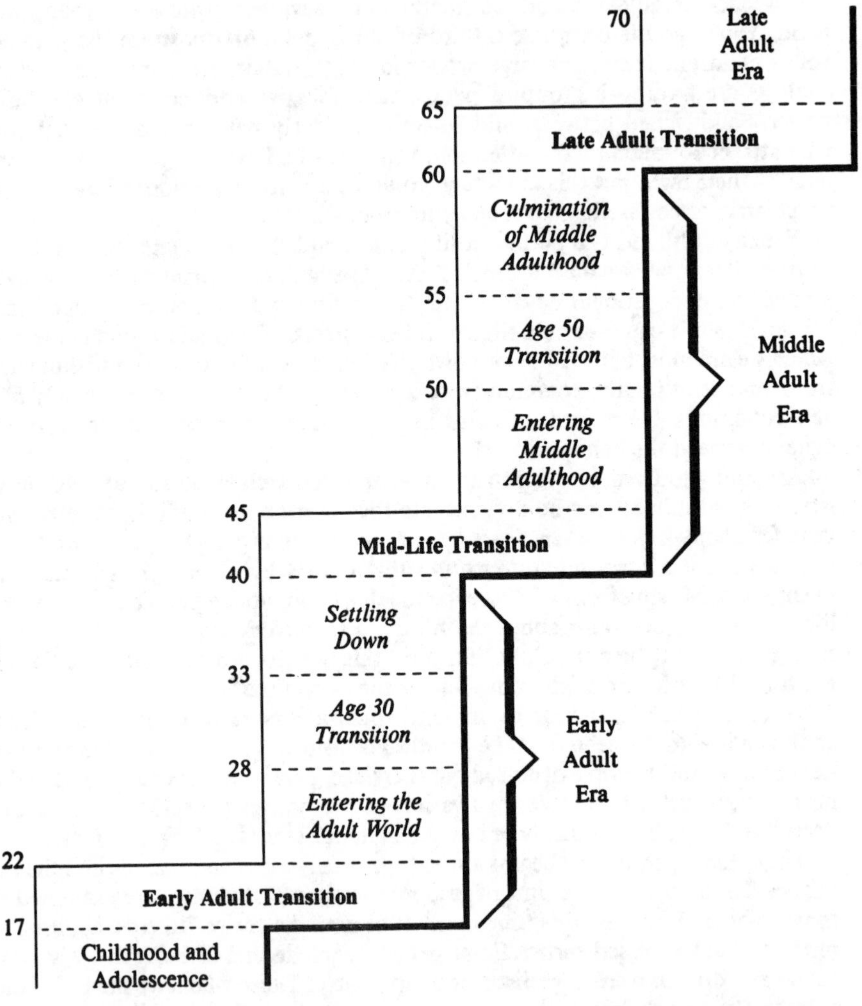

Reprinted with permission from Daniel J. Levinson et al., *The Seasons of a Man's Life* (New York: Knopf, 1978), 57.

At present, all of this is complicated by what has come to be known as the baby boom. Following the Second World War, in 1946, the worldwide birth rate experienced a sudden and expected upsurge. In most countries, this increase in pregnancies and childbirth soon dropped, but in four countries—Australia, New Zealand, Canada, and the United States—the birth rate stayed high for almost twenty years. This has created what one observer has called "the pig in the python"—a great population bulge that is moving through life, radically changing society, and greatly affecting the generations that are behind.[6] In the Western world, this is the first generation to be raised on television, to be free of infectious diseases like diphtheria or polio (but to know about AIDS), to be accustomed to the daily use of computers, to be familiar with space travel, and to experience limitless educational opportunities. It is a generation that has sought to reform society, liberate women, pursue affluence, change sexual values, tolerate diversity, and challenge established tradition. It is a generation that is proud of being open-minded but is criticized for being intellectually impoverished and culturally closed-minded.[7] It is also a generation with intense competition for the jobs, promotions, and affluence that many grew up learning to expect.[8]

Those who were born later may have mixed feelings about their older brothers and sisters who comprise the "biggest, richest, and best-educated generation" that has ever been produced, but who now are described as people of "uncertainty, unsure about what their expectations really are, unsure about their role in society, unsure about marriage and family, unsure even about reproducing themselves."[9]

It is well known that young adults often drop out of the church during their post-high-school years and return later when they become parents. Too often those of the baby-boom and post-baby-boom eras find churches that fail to understand their struggles or meet their needs. Like so many psychiatry books, many churches also tend to overlook the challenges of young adulthood.[10]

The Bible and Young Adulthood

Of all the people mentioned in the Bible, nobody appears more frequently than David. His life history is cited in four Old Testament books and throughout Scripture his name is recorded even more than the name of Jesus.[11] Sometimes we forget that David's mobile lifestyle, his struggles with Saul, his friendship with Jonathan, his spiritual growth, and perhaps his marriage difficulties,[12] all appear to have taken place before he was thirty.[13] Many of the Psalms must have been written while David was in the early years of young adulthood.

Unlike modern writers, the Bible does not identify young adulthood as a specific age period, but perhaps most biblical people made their mark on history when they were young adults like David. Jesus was a young adult when he carried out his whole ministry and changed the course of history. Many of the early church leaders appear to have been young people. They all had struggles, but many were used by God in mighty ways. "Don't let anyone look down on you because you are young," the Apostle Paul wrote to Timothy, perhaps when he was a young adult. "Set an example for the believers in speech, in life, in love, in faith and in purity."[14]

Even though young adulthood is not identified by name in Scripture, many of the concerns and problems of this age group are mentioned frequently. Anxiety, discouragement, marriage, sex, money management, careers, relationships with parents and children, temptation, and spiritual growth are among the issues mentioned in the Bible and are of special concern to people in the early years of adulthood.

The Causes of Young Adulthood Problems

An in-depth study of college students once suggested that many have a "lifeboat" mentality. Each feels like a sailor, alone in a boat that is far from harbor and caught in a terrible storm. As the boats begin to take on water, "each student must single-mindedly bail. Conditions are so bad that no one has time to care for others who may also be foundering."[15]

Is this picture—only a few years old—a valid description of college students and other young adults today? Some scholars suggest that students, like the rest of the population, follow cycles. One generation may be characterized by student activism, political consciousness, and concern for others. A few years later, the campuses are quiet as students focus on academics and the pursuit of personal and material success. Effective counselors are aware of these trends in society and realize that they influence the individual struggles of counselees. But even though cultural trends and conditions change, young adults of every generation feel alone in the world. Like solitary sailors in leaking boats, many are so concerned about their own safety and future survival that there is little energy left to worry about society or to care for others.

The challenges of these young adult years could be grouped into four major categories. Each can give rise to young adult problems.

1. *Competency.* Most of childhood is spent learning the skills we need to survive and get along with others. As we get older, we learn how to study, to solve problems, to handle stress, to deal with emotions like anger or anxiety, and to relate to parents and peers. Many personal failures come because we have not learned the skills needed to function well in this complex culture. If individuals are to live successfully as adults, they must continue to develop competence in several skill areas.[16]

(a) Physical Skills. By the time we reach adulthood, almost everybody has learned the importance of good grooming, regular exercise, and a balanced diet. But some young people punish their bodies with unhealthy eating, crash diets, lack of sleep, laziness, or excessive use of alcohol and other drugs. Young bodies rejuvenate quickly, so counselees may forget that tired, overweight, sluggish, poorly nourished, self-abused bodies do not function well or cope with stress efficiently. At times, complicated problems arise or worsen because people fail to take care of themselves physically.

(b) Intellectual, Problem-Solving Skills. Individuals must be able to learn efficiently, communicate effectively, and think clearly if they are to have success in handling stress, solving problems, and adapting to change. Regrettably many young people go through the educational system and graduate without the ability to think clearly. Our schools have put so much emphasis on creativity, tolerance, and "fun learning," suggest some critics,[17] that students don't know how to learn or think.

Basic problem solving involves clarifying the issues, setting goals, exploring possible solutions, trying out one or more of these alternatives, evaluating what happened, and sometimes repeating the process. On occasion problems arise or worsen because people fail to think clearly, don't know where to get helpful information, or have no concept of how to solve problems. It is then that the counselor becomes an educator, teaching intellectual and problem-solving skills.

(c) Self-Management Skills. Some wise person once said that many people want to be writers, but few people want to write. Being known as a writer carries prestige and sometimes fame,[18] but to write and write well an author must spend many lonely and sometimes frustrating hours putting words on paper. It is a task that demands rigid discipline and careful time management.

Some overly compulsive people live lives that are so disciplined that they become rigid and lacking in fun or spontaneity. More often, I suspect, counselors hear about wasted time, squandered money, missed opportunities, lack of self-control, and lazy lifestyles. Because they lack self-management skills, young adults may fritter away some of their best years. Only later do they awaken to discover that their lives are drifting without direction or purpose—and that other more disciplined people have passed them by.

The counselor may be faced with the challenge of teaching money-management skills, self-discipline, career planning, or ways to control time. Without these skills, young-adult problems are likely to persist throughout life.[19]

(d) Interpersonal Skills. Getting along with people is one of the most difficult challenges of life.[20] This is a task that requires determination, tact, hard work, sensitivity, and sometimes a lot of patience. The Bible tells us to live in peace with each other but implies that this isn't always possible, and sometimes the peace-making effort is one-sided.[21]

Many of the challenges of young adulthood require interpersonal skills. Getting launched in a career, finding a mate, building a marriage, starting a family, getting along in the community, becoming involved in a church involve such "people skills" as learning to listen, being able to communicate clearly, resolving disagreements, and acting appropriately in social situations. Each of these skills involves knowledge (knowing how to respond) and action (doing what is appropriate). Each takes time and effort to learn.[22] When learning does not occur, problems are likely to develop.

(e) Emotional Skills. Emotion, as everyone knows, is a part of human nature that sometimes appears when it is least expected. Disappointment, anxiety, anger, excitement, guilt, lust, enthusiasm, compassion, and a host of other emotions can affect our thinking and influence our behavior. Sometimes people squelch their emotions, ignore them, express them inappropriately, or even fail to recognize that they exist. All of this can lead to serious psychological and social difficulties.

Each of us must learn to be sensitive to our own feelings and to the feelings of others. Some counselees must be taught where to express their feelings and how to express them in ways that are socially appropriate. Some young men, for example, still do not realize that crying is normal and healthy. Much depends on where one cries, with whom, and when.

(f) Spiritual Skills. Within recent years the Western world has seen an upsurge of interest in Eastern forms of meditation, altered states of consciousness, and self-awareness programs. Much of this interest has been among young adults, many of whom are looking for greater meaning and purpose in life. Special classes teach the skills of relating to spiritual forces that are assumed to exist.[23]

Christians, instead, seek to relate to a person, Jesus Christ. For many young people, however, these are years of searching for a faith that is meaningful and fulfilling.[24] Most of us may dislike the idea of spiritual "skills," but even the disciples asked

Jesus how to pray, and the Bible is filled with examples and instructions of ways by which we grow in a relationship with God. It takes a lifetime to learn how to pray, how to study Scripture, how to select and benefit from devotional literature, how to worship, how to have genuine fellowship with other believers, or how to grow spiritually. Young believers (like those who are older) often encounter frustrations in their spiritual and personal lives if they lack a basic knowledge of these spiritual skills or never discipline themselves to put the skills into practice.

2. *Independence.* Young adults need to break away from home and develop a sense of autonomy. Often this takes time and effort; sometimes it involves frustration, tension, feelings of insecurity, periods of uncertainty, and struggles with a number of questions. Can I make it on my own? Can I find workable living and roommate arrangements? How can I get financially free from my parents? Is there a way to stay connected with my family without having to remain a child? How do I deal with the guilt and loneliness associated with my separation from the family?[25] For some, there is the problem of how to fit back into the family temporarily after tasting the independence of living away at college or elsewhere.[26]

The challenge of becoming independent involves at least four overlapping and ongoing tasks: developing self-sufficiency, building an identity, finding values, and coping effectively.

(a) Developing Self-Sufficiency. Self-sufficiency could be described as "a sometimes complicated balance between self-direction and sensitivity to the needs of others."[27] To be self-sufficient does not mean that we are stubborn about doing things "my way," totally independent from and insensitive to the feelings and opinions of others. For the Christian, self-sufficiency does not mean that we pull away from God and try to live solely on the basis of human strength. In contrast, the self-sufficient Christian trusts God to give direction and recognizes that other people—including parents, counselors, and mature Christian leaders—can give helpful guidance and valuable counsel. The move to greater independence involves self-initiated planning, a willingness to tackle problems and make decisions, taking responsibility for one's own choices and finances, admitting and learning from mistakes, and listening to the advice of others—even if this guidance subsequently is rejected.

One college senior has described how he faced the issue of self-sufficiency shortly after his arrival on campus: "It occurred to me not long after I arrived here that, with 15,000 students around, no one was going to be watching over me to see how I was doing. I'd really have to have a huge problem before anyone would notice. I made it a point to seek out my adviser, get to know her, and stay in touch. Last week, she wrote me a great letter of recommendation for a job."[28]

(b) Building an Identity. Identity has been defined as a fairly stable mental picture of who you are; a picture that seems to be shared by others who know you and whom you consider to be significant.[29] Identity development is a continuing process of seeking to answer such questions as "Who am I?" "What is unique about me?" or "Where do I fit in this world?" The questions come with special urgency in late adolescence and early adulthood. If there are not at least tentative answers, young people often experience confusion, helplessness, inner turmoil, a lack of direction, and a sense of quiet desperation as they go through what is known as an identity crisis.[30]

As they reflect on their goals, interests, beliefs, hopes, personality traits, interests, aptitudes, and abilities, most people begin to get a clearer picture of their self-identities. Sometimes there will be clarity in one area (a recognition of one's abilities, for example) while there is fluctuation in other areas (what one believes, for example, or what would be a good career). As their identities slowly become clearer—sometimes with the help of a counselor—young people are able to move more confidently into the future. Identity issues are likely to surface again, but this may not come until middle age.

(c) Finding Values. A value could be described as something an individual believes in, lives by, and is willing to express publicly. Values are important because they govern how we think and the way we act.

As they move into adulthood and are forced to make decisions about lifestyles, vocations, spending priorities, and time management, young people have to decide what they really believe—and why. They must determine to what extent they will keep the values that came from parents and teachers. Often the young adult is idealistic and accepts standards of right and wrong that may be unrealistic and impossible to follow. Some throw out traditional standards and try to live a "value-free" life, but even this decision reflects a value. Still others fail to give much thought to their values until they are presented with the opportunity to act in a way that society or one's family would consider immoral. At such times, one is forced to make value decisions, often without much time for reflection.

Values are reflected in how we spend our time and money, what we claim to believe, what we think about when our minds wander, the people we spend time with, or the things we read. Young people often struggle with values. This can create confusion and indecision about moral choices, about social behavior, and about plans for the future.

(d) Coping Effectively. Independent people can accomplish the tasks of day-to-day living and handle the hassles and stresses of life without seeking rescue and continual assistance from others. These people are willing to seek or accept help when necessary, and they are willing to help others. In the routine tasks of living, they function by themselves, with little or no assistance from others. In contrast, when people can't cope, they are more likely to have problems.

3. *Intimacy.* Nobody is totally independent and completely free of other human beings. The maturing individual instead seeks to develop a healthy interdependence. Confident of their abilities to function on their own, these people allow themselves to need and be needed by others.[31]

According to psychiatrist Erik Erikson, the greatest need in young adulthood is the need for intimacy. This, wrote Erikson, is the capacity to commit oneself "to concrete affiliations and partnerships and to develop the ethical strength to abide by such commitments, even though they may call for significant sacrifices and compromises."[32]

The people in our lives might be divided into three groups. Acquaintances are people whom we know only casually. Friends are closer. They are people who care for one another, spend time together, and have similar interests and viewpoints. Intimates have all the characteristics of friends, but they also share mutual concerns and personal struggles. Intimate friends understand each other and experience a closeness, acceptance, loyalty, vulnerability, accountability, caring, empathy, and love that is not present in mere friendship.

In marriage, intimacy includes sexuality, but it should not be assumed that all intimacy involves sex. David and Jonathan, Ruth and Naomi, Paul and Timothy—each had nonsexual intimate relationships.

Such relationships are rare, perhaps in part because they require a degree of commitment to others that is not common in our society. More often, there is competition, selfishness, personal status seeking, avoidance of friendships, and a resulting loneliness and sense of isolation. When young adults fail to develop intimacy, writes Erikson, the future is more difficult because people feel isolated and distant from other human beings.

4. *Direction.* In their studies of young adults, the Yale researchers found that many young men have a "Dream" of the kind of life they want to lead.[33] This Dream is an imaginary picture of what life could be like. At first the Dream is vague and unrealistic, but as one moves into the twenties the Dream gets clearer. Sometimes life circumstances and the pressures of parents or friends interfere with the Dream, but this Dream can also generate excitement, vitality, and life purpose. The Dream helps the young adult answer the question: Where am I going? Research has demonstrated that people who build their lives around a Dream in early adulthood have a better chance for personal fulfillment, even though there may be times of struggle in maintaining the commitment and working toward the Dream's fulfillment. When there is no Dream, people drift.

Often, Dreams are formed, clarified, and strengthened through a relationship with a mentor. A mentor is a teacher, model, adviser, guide, sponsor, or discipler who is several years older than the young adult and experienced in the world that the young person is entering. Some young adults have mentors whom they admire, respect, and seek to emulate, even though they have never met. More effective is a mutual caring relationship between two adults, eight to fifteen years apart in age. The older person guides the younger, until he or she is able to stand alone. Sometimes the closeness of this relationship makes it difficult to terminate, especially when the mentor's help is no longer needed.[34]

Two major choices must be made if young adults are to move smoothly through this period of time. They must choose an occupation and make a decision about marriage. Of course, these may occur simultaneously, and each may take several years. When a young person wants to choose carefully and wisely, there often is a period of exploring alternatives before making a serious choice. In our society and perhaps in most others, young people rarely are viewed as full-fledged adults until they are established in a career and marriage. Children may or may not follow. Unlike previous generations, many young adults now appear to be marrying later and postponing the decision to have children until their careers are successfully in place.[35]

These challenges of young adulthood—competence, independence, intimacy, and direction—can be exciting and at the same time the cause of problems. When counselors understand the challenges that young people face, we are better able to give the guidance and the help that people need during the third and fourth decades of life.

The Effects of Young Adulthood

What happens when someone starts down the long road of young adulthood and stumbles? Most people pick themselves up and keep going, but by the time they reach mid-life many are struggling with past failures, facing disillusions about life, and passing into a painful tumultuous time of life reevaluation.[36] Why do so many people seem to leave young adulthood with these kinds of scars and disappointments?

Part of the answer may come if we look at the life patterns that young people develop in their twenties. One popular writer has suggested that most young men tend to fit into one of three patterns.[37] *Transients* are those who are unwilling or unable to make any firm commitments in their twenties. These people try to prolong the period of youth, but around age thirty they feel an urgent push to establish some long-term goals and attachments. Men with a *locked-in* life pattern, have made solid commitments in their twenties without giving their decisions much thought. People who enter the family business, for example, those who take any available job and stay with it, or individuals who go to medical school so they can follow a parent's footsteps may all reach their thirties feeling secure but also stifled, in a rut, and angry with themselves because they never took the time earlier to decide what they really wanted.

Less common are the *wunderkind* men who are workaholics, hard-driving, goal-dominated, ambitious, and seemingly filled with energy. Most are also insecure, afraid to let others get close, insensitive, unwilling to let down their guards, and vaguely hoping that all insecurities will vanish when they reach the top of their professions.

More healthy are the *integrator* men who try to balance their ambitions with a genuine commitment to family. These men seek to combine "economic comfort with being ethical and beneficial to society."[38] It is a life pattern that rarely comes before the mid thirties, and it never comes unless one decides to work for it. This is a life pattern that would seem to be most consistent with the teaching of Scripture.

There are other male life patterns. These include the *never-married* men who are in a minority in our society and who may or may not be well adjusted; the *latency boys* who remain bound to their mothers throughout their adult lives; and the *paranurturers,* who devote themselves not to building careers but to serving others. Many missionaries, medical practitioners, teachers, and clergymen are paranurturers. Their dedication and achievements are often admired, but problems arise if they are not realistic enough to take care of their own needs as well as the needs of others.

Some of these patterns also apply to women. Transient and never-married women are assumed to be similar to their male counterparts, but there are also uniquely female life patterns. The *care giver* usually marries in her twenties and has little intention of going beyond the domestic role. Later many feel locked in to the homemaker role, taken for granted by their families, unable to be fulfilled personally, afraid of being dumped, and deeply threatened if a family crisis forces her to fend for herself. The *either-or* woman is one who felt pushed in her twenties to choose either to marry and have children or to work and build a career. Later there may be regret over decisions made earlier but often it is hard to make a change. The *integrator,* in contrast, seeks to combine all in the twenties—marriage, career, and motherhood.

Gail Sheehy is one who tried to be a young adult integrator but reached an interesting and disturbing conclusion.[39] "It rarely is possible for a woman to integrate marriage, career, and motherhood in her twenties, and it's about time some of us who have tried said so. It is quite possible to do so at 30 and decidedly possible at 35." When women (and many men) try to do everything in their twenties, usually something suffers at least for a while: one's career, one's marriage, one's family, one's health, or one's stability.

Is it possible for people of both sexes to be nurturers and achievers without running themselves ragged? As they move through young adulthood, perhaps individuals need to keep several options open, focus attention primarily on one or two, and leave the others for the future. Otherwise, the young person may be overwhelmed by the pressures and conflicts that seem to come with special intensity during this time in life.[40]

Counseling Young Adults

Professional journals often include articles on counseling college students (perhaps because most journal articles are written by college professors), but far fewer publications discuss counseling young adults who are beyond college age.[41] Often these counselees come with problems of depression, career uncertainty, anxiety, interpersonal conflicts, or other issues that are not limited to any one age group.[42] In dealing with these and other problems, counselors often experience the great satisfaction that comes in working with young adults. When compared with older people, young adults are often more flexible, enthusiastic, willing to change, and less threatened by the idea of counseling.

Like counselees of all ages, young adults often show the most improvement when they work with a counselor who is willing to build a caring relationship,[43] who understands the unique needs and struggles of this age group, and who is willing to serve at least temporarily as a mentor.[44] Frequently counselees need reassurance that their problems are common and not evidence of mental illness. Often there is a need for guidance in the making of decisions, help in choosing a career or forming an identity, support and encouragement during times of turmoil or uncertainty, counsel in resolving interpersonal conflicts or building intimacy, help in dealing with sexual feelings including struggles and fears about homosexuality, or assistance in coping with stress, anger, feelings of failure, depression, or thoughts of suicide.[45]

Despite the importance of these issues, perhaps the greatest challenge for counselors of young adults is to teach the life skills that will help people change. Although God sometimes works in mysterious ways to accomplish his purposes and to bring change, the Bible shows that he frequently uses human beings to accomplish his purposes. Christian counselors seek to make themselves available as channels through whom God works to bring healing and growth in other human beings. Often this healing growth comes as counselees are helped to learn skills that will help them change themselves and/or their environments.

William Miller and Kathleen Jackson are pastoral counselors whose three-part approach for helping people change could be applied in counseling with young adults.[46] First, there is *awareness*. Counselees are not likely to change until they have a clear awareness of the problem. Few are likely to work at learning new life skills until they see the need for skill development. Together, therefore, the counselor and counselee attempt first to specify the problems, to better understand what counselee behaviors might be creating the problems, and then to set a temporary goal or goals for change.

Next comes the stage of *alternatives* when an attempt is made to answer the question "What can be done to bring about change?" For a period of time they may brainstorm and develop a variety of ideas and alternative solutions (sometimes writing these down) without stopping to evaluate any of them. Then, together, they will review the list. What has been tried before and found not to work. What is new and might work? What skills need to be learned if the desired change is to come about? How could these skills be learned and practiced? Eventually, preferably after a time of prayer, there can be a selection of one or two strategies that could be tried and later evaluated carefully.

Throughout all of this there needs to be an emphasis on *acceptance.* When they are learning life skills, counselees often slip and fail. This can lead to self-castigation and increased frustration. The existence of a helping, mentoring relationship enables the counselor to show acceptance, empathy, understanding, encouragement, and the support counselees need as they learn new skills and, with God's help, work to bring about change.

The Stuck Syndrome. As an example, consider the young adult who feels stuck in an undesirable job, living situation, geographical area, relationship, or other obligation.[47] The older we get, the harder it is to change; the risks may be greater and the consequences that come with failure could be harder to repair. In young adulthood, however, change may be easier. When I was an unmarried college student, for example, I felt stuck in my hometown where I had been attending college classes. So I went to study in England without enough money to live or to get back across the Atlantic. If I did that today, my family could suffer, my mortgage wouldn't get paid, and people might be less tolerant of a jaunt overseas than they were when I was twenty-three.

Once a person becomes aware that he or she is stuck in a situation that needs to be changed, it helps to consider what behavior may be making the problem intolerable and what needs to be changed. With the counselor's help, the individual can consider the alternatives. What skills are needed to get unstuck? What actions can be taken? What is a viable plan for solving the problem? If a big change may be involved—like moving to a new location or going back to college—plan the change carefully, making a note of all that needs to be done and when.

The counselor can give acceptance, support, and guidance as these changes are being considered and implemented. Remember, however, that some people may choose not to change but to stay as they are. Sometimes even young people have gone through so many life changes that they lack the energy or the courage to attempt another change. Point out that it is all right to wait until later. The longer we wait and delay decision making, however, the less likely we are to attempt change or be successful.

Preventing Young Adult Problems

After completing their in-depth studies of young adult men, the Yale researchers concluded that "the twenties and thirties are perhaps the most abundant and the most stressful decades in the life cycle. Given the tremendously difficult tasks of adaptation and development a young man (or woman) must deal with, this era cannot be made easy or simple to traverse. Still, much can be done to reduce the excessive stress and facilitate work on the developmental tasks."[48] To begin, the researchers suggest, it helps to assist young people in finding work and living environments where their personal and career development will be stimulated and not hindered.

When I was working in a university counseling center, one of my counselees took ill. Since he didn't have a car, I offered to drive him home. When I saw the psychologically unhealthy family in which he lived, I had a new appreciation of the reasons why he was having trouble adjusting to young adulthood. Everything we tried to accomplish in counseling was being undercut by his family. If a young adult works or lives in a disorganized, fragmented, hypercritical environment, it is difficult to prevent problems from developing or getting worse.[49] At times, the best preventive therapy may be helping the young adult to move.[50] There are at least five other preventive approaches.

1. *Education and Encouragement.* Young adults are sometimes surprised and overwhelmed by the pressures of their age group. College orientation courses often give warnings and practical coping suggestions to incoming students, but this process can be extended. Sunday school classes, church discussion groups, clubs for young mothers or junior executives, home Bible study groups, or an occasional sermon might alert young adults to the stresses, give recommendations for handling pressure, provide opportunity for discussion, and give participants an opportunity to encourage one another. When church or other programs speak to real needs, the people come.

2. *More Mentoring.* It is a myth to conclude that people must have mentors to succeed, but there is abundant evidence to show that mentoring can be very helpful both to the mentors and to their young adult protégés. This may be true especially in cultures, like ours, where family closeness tends to be rare. It is also true for people entering new vocations. One large company discovered, for example, that the organization and individuals both benefited when there was voluntary mentoring, with genuine bonds between mentors and protégés, and maximum freedom for people to spend time together discussing whatever they found to be helpful.[51] Big brother and big sister programs provide similar preventive guidance and so do the various Christian approaches to discipling.

Mentoring programs for young adults do not always need to be formally organized. It is not simplistic to suggest that a valid approach is to pray about a mentoring relationship and then to be alert to finding some person who can mentor you, or to whom you can be a mentor.

3. *Dream Development.* The young adult's Dream—that imagined possibility that generates excitement and vitality—will be vague and ill-defined at first, but with time the idea becomes clearer. To translate that Dream into reality young adults must ponder, plan, and take step-by-step action to reach their goals. The process begins when one asks "What would I like to be doing in ten years?" "Is this what God wants me to do?" "What steps would I have to take to reach my Dream?" When they work toward fulfilling a Dream, young adults are less likely to develop self-defeating or frustrating life patterns.

4. *Parental Patience.* It isn't easy for parents of young adults to watch their grown children flounder as they struggle with the emerging issues of adulthood.

Sometimes parents make matters worse because of their intolerance, frequent criticisms, and well-intentioned advice giving. It is better if parents give encouragement, support, and a clear indication that they are available and willing to talk. Parents should be reluctant to rescue their adult children with offers of money or other provisions that would help the young adult avoid responsibility. It can be better to give gentle guidance when the needs arise. Sometimes the best help for young adults is the guidance that Christian counselors or other church leaders give to the parents.

5. *Spiritual Support.* A friend once described how she was kept from a potentially disastrous and impulsive marriage. "My parents didn't lecture me," she said. "I knew they didn't care for my fiancé, but I also knew they were praying. They had a tremendous faith that their God was powerful enough to guide their grown kids in making important life decisions. Shortly before the wedding, I realized what a mistake I was making. I am convinced that a tremendous problem was prevented by the deep faith and consistent prayers of my parents." This could be a slogan for all Christian counselors, including parents, who counsel their children: Prayer prevents potential problems.

Conclusions about Young Adulthood

John Morgan is a twenty-two-year-old circus performer who calls himself "Mercury Morgan." As a teenager he would autograph his friends' school yearbooks by signing his name and the letters IAUTGBSRITWT (standing for "I Am Unquestionably the Greatest Bicycle Stunt Rider in the World Today"). He now admits that this was cocky, but unlike most of his high school friends, the young Mercury Morgan had a Dream—to be the best stunt rider he could be. Whenever there was time, he practiced, often jumping over garbage cans in the backyard of his home.

One day, the teenager went to hear an evangelist who once had worked as a motorcycle stunt man. Soon Mercury had a mentor who also introduced the young man to Jesus Christ and became Mercury's discipler. Unlike many of his former classmates, the young circus stunt man has already reached his Dream of becoming a part of show business. Even more important, he has learned that a relationship with Jesus Christ is the constant force in his life and what he calls "a bottomless well of strength."[52]

This is an unusual story, but it illustrates some of the principles that have been stressed in this chapter. Young adulthood may be overlooked in many counseling books, but it is a crucially important stage in human development. There can be problems at this time in life, and there often is a need for counseling, but helping young adults can be among the Christian counselor's most rewarding experiences.

SUGGESTIONS FOR FURTHER READING

Bocknek, Gene. *The Young Adult: Development after Adolescence.* Monterey, Calif.: Brooks/Cole, 1980.

Collins, Gary R. *Getting Started.* Old Tappan, N.J.: Fleming H. Revell, 1984.*

* Books marked with an asterisk (*) are especially suited for counselees to read.

Egan, Gerard, and Michael A. Cowan. *Moving into Adulthood.* Monterey, Calif.: Brooks/Cole, 1980.*

Jones, Landon Y. *Great Expectations: America and the Baby Boom Generation.* New York: Coward, McCann and Geoghegan, 1980.

Levinson, Daniel J., et al. *The Seasons of a Man's Life.* New York: Alfred A. Knopf, 1978.

Parks, Sharon. *The Critical Years: The Young Adult Search for a Faith to Live By.* New York: Harper & Row, 1986.

* Books marked with an asterisk (*) are especially suited for counselees to read.

14

Middle Age

BEN MADE HIS DESIRES VERY CLEAR to the family. There was to be no party to celebrate his birthday. For years he had joked that life begins at forty and that he wanted a big bash to usher him into middle age. But when the time came, he had changed his mind.

Other things had changed as well.

His marriage had lost the spark that once was so obvious. He rarely complimented his wife any more but was free with his criticisms and sarcastic remarks. Even when they visited with other couples, Ben belittled his wife and displayed a generally sour attitude. Was it surprising that even some longtime friends seemed to be pulling away?

Things were no better at work. After graduating from college, Ben had gone to work for IBM. His career moved off to a good start, and he had been buoyed by some early promotions. Shortly before his fortieth birthday, however, Ben was passed over for the manager's position that he had long worked for and expected. He plunged into depression, condemned himself for his career failures, and defiantly announced that his two teenagers should forget about college because the "old man" didn't have the money to send them or the right connections in the company to get a decent promotion. When his son was found to be on drugs, Ben exploded in anger and refused at first to meet with the boy's counselor.

Ben would often jog in the mornings, usually by himself. On Sundays he seemed to delight in jogging past the church so everyone would notice that he no longer attended services with all those "hypocrites."

In response to his wife's urgings, Ben eventually met with the school counselor to talk about his son's drug problem. Ben said little about himself, but he did open up with a couple of old friends who were able to tolerate his griping, overlook his sarcasm, and understand his frustration. One day he had a long talk with his boss and decided to accept an offer to relocate in another part of the country. Selling his house, finding college financial aid for his kids, moving to a warmer climate, replacing the old car, getting into a new job—all of these seemed to give Ben a new lease on life. He started attending church again, slowly dropped the sarcasm, and began to build better relationships with his wife and children. To his surprise, he has even begun to encourage one of his coworkers who is just starting to face the struggles of middle age.

WHAT IS MIDDLE AGE?

Some say it is the prime of life. It is a time to feel fabulous, writes the enthusiastic author of a self-help book.[1] It is a cruel joke says another, a turning point, the end of youth, and the beginning of the end. It is a forgotten generation, according to one family physician, "ignored by social planners, neglected by educators, and forsaken by the fashion industry."[2] For many it is a time of crisis,[3] even though some experts claim that evidence for a midlife crisis does not exist.[4] For everyone it is a time of transition and change. Like all of life's changes, the movement into middle life is a time for adjustment and reevaluation. Some handle this smoothly and without difficulties; others feel the threat, instability, and uncertainty that makes this a time of moderate or severe crisis.[5]

Tom Mullen sees middle age in a lighter perspective:

> Turning forty for many men is a traumatic experience. . . . While the crisis is primarily psychological and not due to hormonal changes, it often is precipitated by a man's awareness of his physical deterioration. At forty, many men conclude that if they had known they were going to live this long, they would have taken better care of themselves. When they go to the beach with their families, they notice that young bathing beauties *look away* as they stride by, holding their breath and pulling in their stomachs until they look like contortionists. Their children do not add to their peace of mind, either, when they compare one's left leg with its varicose veins to a road map of Louisiana. Nor does anyone need to remind them of their middle-aged and medium-sized paunches which have gradually appeared and hair which is conspicuous by its absence.
>
> At about age forty men . . . may even attempt to flirt with young women, an event not unlike a dog chasing a car as it doesn't know what to do when it catches one either. . . .
>
> Women and children often demonstrate tender concern and love for middle-aged men, but their solicitations are frequently counterproductive. To warn a ten-year-old child that he shouldn't roughhouse with daddy because his father "isn't as young as he used to be" is about as ego-building as a hemorrhoid examination.[6]

How do we define middle age—this period that is humorous to some but a time of crisis for others? Many would answer in terms of years: middle age is a period that covers the time from the late thirties to the late fifties. Others might agree with Carl Jung, the famous Swiss psychiatrist, who described middle age as the time in life when we are free to move on to other things because we have pretty much completed such tasks as the "begetting of children . . . protecting the brood" and the "gaining of money and social position."[7] Some define the middle years as a time when there is a growing realization that all goals will not be reached, that time is running out, and that one must decide whether to keep moving in the same direction or to make changes before it is too late.

Middle age, therefore, means different things to different people. Beginning around age forty, there begins a period of life characterized by self-examination, reevaluation of beliefs and values, readjustment to physical change, and reconsideration of one's lifestyle, career direction, and priorities. For many men and women middle age *is* a time of crisis, but for most this is more than a mere time for survival.[8] It can be instead a time that launches us into the best half of life.[9]

All of this has relevance for Christian counseling. In churches, as in the society, middle-aged adults make most of the decisions, earn and disperse most of the money, fulfill most leadership positions, and appear to have most of the power. But middle-aged people also struggle with boredom, declining vitality, marriage disintegration, and shifting values. When one considers the prevalence of middle-aged people and the preponderance of middle-aged problems both in the community and in the church, it becomes clear that middle-age concerns are basic to much Christian counseling.

The Bible and Middle Age

Scripture says little about middle age, perhaps because relatively few people lived that long in Bible times in spite of the famous individuals who lived to be very old. It has been estimated that the life expectancy for people in the Bronze Age was eighteen years. In Greece it wasn't much longer, and by medieval times the average life span had risen only to thirty-seven years. Even in 1900, life expectancy was a relatively low fifty years, so there is little historical precedent, age-related biblical instruction, or theological insight to guide modern people through the middle years.

Of greater help for Christian counselors are those biblical passages that speak to the major problems encountered by middle-aged people—problems of good and bad marriages, self-esteem, life purpose, work, grief, interactions with children and older parents, spiritual maturity, impatience, physical illness, disappointment, and similar issues. When these are discussed in Scripture, there rarely is reference to age. Biblical teachings and principles for living apply universally, but individuals—including middle-aged persons—can be helped to see how Scripture is relevant to meeting one's unique personal needs.

The Causes of Middle-Age Problems

According to Jung, most people are wholly unprepared to embark on the second half of life. Often we reach middle age with its "storm and stress, not infrequently accompanied by all the tempests of passion," and fail to realize that we no longer face the same problems and neither can we rely on the same solutions that were effective earlier.[10]

Yale psychologist Daniel Levinson, whose work was discussed in the previous chapter (see Figure 13-1), sees adulthood as a series of phases, each with its own benefits and liabilities. The middle life phase begins around age forty and involves a period of self-examination and reevaluation. Levinson's observations reveal much about the causes of midlife problems:

> Middle age activates our deepest anxieties about decline and dying. The most distressing fear in early adulthood is that there is no life after youth. Young adults often feel that to pass thirty is to be "over the hill." . . . The

> middle years, they imagine, will bring triviality and meaningless comfort at best, stagnation and hopelessness at worst.
>
> Middle age is usually regarded as a vague interim period, defined primarily in negative terms. One is no longer young and yet not quite old. . . . The connotations of youth are vitality, growth, mastery, the heroic, whereas old connotes vulnerability, withering, ending, the brink of nothingness. Our overly negative imagery of old age adds greatly to the burden of middle age. It is terrifying to go through middle age in the shadow of death, as though one were already old; and it is a self-defeating illusion to live in the shadow of youth, as though one were still simply young.[11]

Approximately 80 percent of the people in Levinson's study experienced the transition into middle age as a time of crisis that came with the realization that time was getting short and that important life goals were not likely to be reached. But crises don't always come at midlife.[12] "I have come to believe that there is no single predictable, universal adult experience—there are many," writes one professor. As people face the changes and realities of middle age, there are four S's—situation, self, supports, and strategies—that determine whether or not this will be a time of crisis.[13]

Situation refers to the way one sees life. Are the transitions and changes of middle age seen as positive, expected, and challenging, or negative, unexpected, and dreaded? Are marriage, occupation, religion, family, leisure, or other areas of life satisfying or are they frustrating and inhibiting? Does the individual have hope and expectant optimism that things will get better, or is there despair and a feeling of being trapped?

Self-Perception is important in answering these questions. What is the middle-aged person like? Does he or she have the skills, experiences, and self-confidence to cope with the stresses of middle life? How has the person dealt with change in the past? Is he or she optimistic and able to handle uncertainty and ambiguity?

Supports refer to one's financial assets, job security, or religious beliefs, along with the encouragement of family, close friends, past mentors, and coworkers. Whenever we deal with transitions, including the changes of middle life, it is helpful to have people around us who are supportive. Too often, however, the comments and actions of others make the problems worse.

Strategies are the techniques people use to cope. The creative and successful coper uses a number of strategies. He or she realizes that there is rarely one magical, always-successful way to deal with change.

Research indicates that life changes appreciably between early and middle adulthood. Men, for example, tend to become more reflective and compassionate, less bothered by inner conflicts and external demands, more loving and gentle.[14] Women, in contrast, often become more interested in careers and successful involvement outside the home.[15] In both sexes, according to Erik Erikson, there will be stagnation unless the individual moves to the stage of "generativity"—an active involvement in encouraging and guiding the next generation.

Middle-life problems can have a variety of causes, but these can be categorized into four categories of change: physical, psychological, vocational, and marital-family.

1. *Physical Changes.* Living in a society that values youth, many of us are reluctant to see the physical changes that come with middle age. Gray hair, baldness, coarser skin, bags under the eyes, less resiliency in movements, a decrease in physical strength and stamina, the loss of youthful appearance, and changes in body build all occur in midlife and all are visible reminders that we are aging. Few people take these changes as lightly as the middle-aged movie actress who remarked that her bust and hip measurements were the same as ever except for the fact that within recent years "everything has slipped down about six inches." More often, middle-aged people recognize that they are developing a middle-age spread. Whereas body fat is only 10 percent of body weight in adolescence, it is at least 20 percent by middle age, and most of that settles around or below the waist. As the bust or chest gets smaller, the abdomen and hips get larger. All of this can lead appearance-conscious people to diet, exercise, and give more attention to clothing and cosmetics.

Many people in middle age reach a new awareness of the need to take better care of bodies. Some begin to realize that middle-age physical problems, feelings of stagnation, sexual lethargy, weakened bodies, and unattractive paunches, can all be one's own fault. All can appear or be made worse by drug and alcohol use or by middle-aged "sedentary living and gourmandizing."[16] Often, middle age is a time of discouragement over the perceived loss of youthfulness and attractiveness.[17] In women, the physical changes are combined with the anticipation and experience of menopause with the hormonal and emotional changes that come as a result. Some researchers believe that a similar, though less noticeable change may occur in men.

With both sexes, middle age brings a decline in vigor. For twenty or more years, most individuals have been actively involved in building a career and developing a family. It is not surprising that many reach middle age feeling tired and unenthusiastic about the fact that at least twenty more years must pass before retirement. Men and women who have not accomplished much may push themselves at this point in a concerted effort to prove their worth. Others have begun to succeed and must exert extra effort to keep up. All of this can cause some people to collapse physically or emotionally, while others begin to think of ways to withdraw or escape to get rest.

2. *Psychological Changes.* Someone has observed that middle age comes when we start counting the years backward from the time of retirement or death, rather than forward from birth.[18] Research suggests that learning is slower in middle age, memory is slightly poorer, and thinking is less flexible.[19] But the middle-aged person is also more experienced than he or she was in earlier years. For many, this is the prime of life when people are at the height of their influence, creativity, personal accomplishments, and earning capacity. Often the person feels overwhelmed by too many obligations, duties, and seemingly insignificant or trivial demands on one's time. The middle aged have many friends, work acquaintances, relatives, and religious associates, most of whom are active, in good health, and far removed from worries about retirement or terminal illness. Even so, middle age can be a time of both boredom and fear.

Boredom. In the middle years, the excitement and challenge of establishing a career and launching a marriage can give way to what has been called "middle-age blahs." Everyday routines at work or home, dull and uninspiring church services, duty-motivated visits with uninteresting relatives, the perpetuation of daily frustrations (such as a house that always needs work, monthly bills that must be paid, bosses that make continual demands) all of these can merge into a routine of boredom. The problem is greater in what have been called "constrained people" and "excitement addicts."[20] Constrained people are fearful, never-take-a-chance personalities who always abide by the rules and rarely allow themselves to have pleasurable or intellectually stimulating experiences. It is not surprising that their lives are boring. In contrast, the excitement addicts thrive on taking risks, but they get bored when declining physical strength or increasing responsibilities force them to slow down. For some, boredom leads to depression, inertia, excessive worry, or escape into a mindless addiction to television. Others try to escape their boredom through extramarital affairs, radical lifestyle or job changes, and unconventional or outlandish dress.

Fear. Middle-aged people feel afraid as they see physical changes within themselves, watch their aging parents, and observe the struggles of their middle-aged friends. For many this time in life brings the first major health problems or fears of death. Many are concerned about the empty nest that will come when the children leave home. Some fear that younger people will replace them at work, that life will become meaningless, or that physical limitations will dictate unwanted lifestyle changes. Others wonder if they will become rigid and unwilling or unable to change with the times. Then there is the fear of one's ability to remain sexually active and attractive. The evidence suggests that sexual drive and fulfillment persists in people whose sexual activity has been pleasurable and consistent during the formative years,[21] but fear of impotence, lack of privacy, a lifestyle that is too busy or rushed, marital tensions, and worry about decreased sex drive can all create tension in bed. It is then that the feared inability to perform becomes a reality.

All of this can stimulate middle-age reflection, reevaluation, dissatisfaction, and search for new purpose and self-esteem. Frequently this leads to struggles with the twin issues of vocation and marriage. According to one writer,[22] a person must work through these two issues if there is to be a successful resolution of midlife problems.

3. *Vocational Changes.* Whatever one's vocation, and regardless of one's degree of success or failure, it is good to remember that every line of work has its less attractive features. These become more obvious the longer we work at a job. If we feel bored, no longer challenged, taken for granted, pressured, or afraid of failure, it is easy to get angry, disappointed, and disillusioned.

As people mature, they appear to develop a greater inclination and capacity for inner dialogue, the talking to oneself about life experiences. When work is not satisfying, this inner dialogue may involve anger directed toward the job and self-criticism for being in such an undesirable vocation. Often there is an intellectual struggle about whether to hold on to a secure but unfulfilling job, or to let go and risk finding something better.[23]

Many individuals feel inadequate and self-critical even when they have been vocationally successful. *Fortune* magazine, for example, devoted a cover story to the problem of guilt among successful executives. According to a survey of the magazine's readers, the number-one cause of executives' guilt concerns their children—who is taking care of the children and how they will turn out.[24] As one moves up the ladder of success, responsibilities become greater, time with families may become scarcer, and competition may become stronger—all at a time when physical energies are declining. Some people are asked to train new workers who, in time, could take their jobs. Others, including executives with major responsibilities, lose their jobs in midlife. These people face lowered self-esteem and the psychological trauma of being unemployed and unable to find work that is consistent with one's capabilities, experience, or previous earning capacity. Homemakers, whose lives may have been busy and productive, now discover that the nest is emptying and there is less need for their services at home. All of this can lead to frustration, self-pity, and sometimes a temptation to leave and try a vocation that is new, different, and potentially more fulfilling.[25]

4. *Marriage-Family Changes.* Freud once said that the need of every person is *leben und arbeiten*—to love and to work. If we don't find fulfillment in these areas, our lives are incomplete. We have already discussed work, but what about middle-aged love? We will consider four aspects of this issue: love as it relates to children, parents, spouse, and sex.

(a) *Children.* When children leave home, parents may feel depressed, empty, and inclined to grieve. For some there is guilt over past failures, loneliness, a tendency to cling, and a feeling that one is no longer needed or useful. Some parents feel a sense of envy and competition as their children leave home, and often there is a type of mourning as mothers and fathers let go and feel increasingly excluded from the lives and activities of their maturing offspring.[26] The departure of children does not seem to be as painful when one or both parents work and find satisfaction outside the home. Nevertheless, the empty nest forces both parents to examine their roles in the home. Sometimes there is a sense of relief, freedom, and renewed vigor. With the children gone, both parents must face each other and realistically evaluate the status of their marriage.

(b) *Older Parents.* Caught up with the challenges of raising a family and then starting a career, young adults often fail to notice that their own parents are growing older. When we reach middle age, these parents often begin to lose their health, their freedom, their financial stability, and at some time their mates. Parents, therefore, become more dependent, often at the time when their grandchildren are facing the struggles of adolescence. Middle-aged adults find themselves in what has been called the "sandwich generation," a time of life when we feel caught and sometimes torn between two generations, one older and one younger, both of whom have needs for help and guidance.[27] This can create added pressure in middle age, along with the constant reminders that we all are growing older.

(c) *Marriage.* It is widely agreed that individuals go through a series of stages as they progress through life, but parenting and marriage also go through stages.[28] Middle age, for example, can be a stage of life when there is unusual marital stress. Bored with the family routines of middle life, well aware of the weaknesses of one's mate, no longer held together by dependent children, and tired of routine sex, many middle-aged husbands and wives conclude that their marriages are in a state of instability and marital midlife crisis.[29] Often there is a decline in intimacy, similarity of interests, and ability to communicate. As a result, the couple may resign themselves to marital boredom, decide on divorce, or find that one (or both) of the partners has slipped into a midlife affair. Affairs may give temporary excitement, the experience of being cared for, a new sense of closeness, and reassurance of one's sexual prowess or continuing attractiveness to the opposite sex. Long-term affairs, like short-term unfaithfulness, can create tension, arouse guilt, and put enough strain on a marriage that divorce often follows.[30]

(d) *Sex.* "Is there sex after forty?" Several years ago a few hundred university students were asked that question. Most replied that their parents probably never had oral-genital sex and the students thought that most people over forty rarely had intercourse.[31] Aware of their declining vigor and loss in attractiveness, some middle-aged people might conclude that their children are right; that satisfying sex after forty is rare. Conway describes the problem concisely. At midlife, he writes,

> a man's sexual capacity is his single greatest concern. Often he is afraid of losing his sexual ability. The drama goes something like this: a man is overextended at work. He is running out of energy. Younger men seem eager to take his place. He is on innumerable boards and committees for the community and the church. His family has giant financial needs, and there never seems to be enough money to go around. With that as a background, he crawls into bed at night. His wife is experiencing a new sexual awakening. Instead of being passive, she begins aggressive sexual moves on him. To his amazement, he finds he is extremely slow in being ready for the sex act. Part way through intercourse, he may lose his erection, and at that moment, he suddenly believes life is all over. He no longer is a man. It's exactly as he had heard—the middle years mean the end of sex.[32]

This attitude can lead people to give up on sex or plunge into an affair in order to prove their attractiveness and virility. The prevalence of such affairs shows that sex after forty and after menopause is not only possible—it can be better and more satisfying than it was in the earlier years.[33]

This emphasis on marriage and family must not ignore the fact that single people reach middle age too. Many of the special challenges of singleness, including divorce and the issue of being a single parent, come into the unmarried person's life and intensify his or her middle-life struggles. The middle-adult era, therefore, affects each person—married or single—in unique ways.

The Effects of Middle Age

Counseling books tend to focus on what is wrong with life without mentioning what is good. While some people struggle with the problems of "making it from forty to fifty,"[34] others are like a forty-seven-year-old lady who described her philosophy of living. "This is the best age to be," she exclaimed enthusiastically. "I don't want to be younger or older." She has kept that attitude throughout the years, although many stresses—including middle-age stresses—have invaded her life.

Even when our attitudes are positive, however, almost everyone is affected in some way by middle age and its pressures. These effects of middle age may be hidden within, shown in outward behavior, seen at work, or reflected in marriage and family relationships.

1. *Hidden Emotional Effects.* As they become aware of physical changes and their middle-aged status, many people experience anger, bitterness, frustration, a sense of failure, boredom, self-pity, and discouragement. Sometimes these come

and go, one or two at a time. Each swells up with brief intensity but then recedes into the background waiting for the opportunity to rise up again. There may be disenchantment with life, periods of sadness, the fears that were mentioned earlier, a sense of futility, and some envy of the freedom, exuberance, and potential in young people. For many this turmoil and emotional conflict may have been present for years, but the long-hidden problems come into focus when they encounter the pressures and realities of middle life.

Inner emotional struggles can be hidden from outsiders, at least for a while, but often they are apparent to one's family and usually to oneself. Sometimes there is a tendency to blame the problems on others. Frequently there is failure to see that even though outside circumstances may trigger tensions, many of life's problems still come from within.

2. *Outward Behavioral Effects.* When we try to keep feelings hidden, they appear in other ways. We may become irritable, impatient, complaining, preoccupied with things other than our work or family, less efficient, restless, and prone to overactivity. Some people try to escape by drinking, by excessive involvement with television or spectator sports, or by preoccupation with hypochondriacal physical symptoms. Many avoid contact with people, including longtime friends.

In addition, there may be the frequently noticed middle-age attempts to break out of one's routine by changing jobs or residence, altering lifestyles, or dressing in ways that are designed to create a new and more youthful image.

3. *Vocational Effects.* There are three ways in which a man or woman can react to the midlife disillusionment with work.[35] First, one may push harder in an effort toward greater success. Since many people measure their worth in terms of work, it becomes critically important to succeed at the job even if this means becoming a workaholic.

A second reaction is to give up in discouragement. Sometimes there is anger, resistance in the form of lowered productivity, or an attitude of resignation that says, "Why work hard since I'll never be appreciated or get anywhere here?" Often this dissatisfaction comes because the person's interests, values, goals, and abilities do not match what the job requires. This can be true of the frustrated employee as well as the frustrated housewife who is tired of her work as a homemaker.

A third reaction is to use one's dissatisfaction as a springboard for change. This may involve risk and often it takes courage. Some people change their jobs in an attempt to find new work that better fits their interests, abilities, and personality characteristics. Others choose to stay in the same unfulfilling vocations, but they reorganize other parts of their lives so there is more satisfaction in living.

In addition, there are those who lose their jobs. This is especially devastating at midlife when financial or family responsibilities are great, and when few well-paying, satisfying positions are available for middle-aged men and women.

4. *Marriage-Family Effects.* It can be difficult to live with a family member who is struggling through the issues of midlife. People in the home, especially the spouse, are greatly affected by the vacillating emotions, changing attitudes, and on-again-off-again planning that is sometimes seen in middle age. The family suffers most when there is an affair, an abrupt change in lifestyle, or the loss of work with its resulting influence on family finances and on the unemployed family member's self-esteem.

Counseling the Middle Aged

One psychiatrist has suggested that the American culture "conspires against sound mental and bodily hygiene in middle life." The society favors and encourages striving for pressured jobs and adaptation through the use of drugs (stimulants, tranquilizers, antidepressants) or alcohol (business lunches and cocktail parties). Doctors are willing to prescribe drugs, but there is little interest in personal lives and not much emphasis on diet or exercise. "Middle-aged housewives are left at home to fend for themselves in their loneliness; the divorced and widowed have few supports of any kind."[36]

Despite this somewhat gloomy appraisal, a number of popular self-help books and seminars on middle age have offered common sense, but often-forgotten, suggestions that might be shared at times with a counselee:

- Get periodic and regular physical check-ups.
- Get regular exercise and sufficient rest.
- Work to control your diet and keep down your weight.
- Get into the habit of saying no to the outside demands that so frequently crowd the schedules of middle-aged people.
- Try to eliminate some of your activities and make time for reading and contemplation.
- Consider taking on new challenges or activities that could add variety and change from regular routines—providing these activities don't add significant additional stress.
- Listen to music or make time for other activities that can be relaxing.
- Postpone major decisions, especially about your job, residence, or marriage, until there is time for reflection and discussion with a sympathetic friend or counselor.
- Take time to pray and cultivate your spiritual life and relationship with God.

Counseling the middle aged has been described as "a therapy of inventory and redirection." It involves helping counselees to take stock, to look again at their values and life direction, to see new potential for growth and fulfillment, to be educated about the pressures and opportunities of middle age, to reevaluate and sometimes change the nature of one's relationships with parents and children, and to learn about good health and prevention of illness.[37] All of this can be done in several ways.

1. *Build an Understanding, Accepting Relationship.* This, of course, is basic to all counseling, but it becomes especially important in working with someone who feels inadequate, unaccepted, and no longer valuable to family members or society. The counselor-counselee relationship gives the emotional support that enables the middle-aged person to express his or her frustrations and to slowly regain self-esteem and the courage to move in and through the middle-adult era. At times, there may be a strong dependency on the counselor. This may be needed for a while, but the middle-aged counselee should be helped to make decisions and take responsibilities that eventually will lead to greater self-reliance.

Try to build a collaborative let's-work-together-on-this attitude, rather than a manner that appears to look down on the counselee or shows criticism, moralizing, and condemnation. Instead, the counselor needs to model tolerance, patience, interest, understanding, and acceptance mixed with a strong dose of realistic thinking so that the counselee can keep things in perspective. It is not helpful or scripturally sound to imply that Christians should never have midlife problems, and neither is it helpful to avoid facing the practical but sometimes difficult decisions that must be made in middle life. Remind counselees that most midlife problems are temporary. Many people have no crisis at this time in life and most come through the period with no permanent damage. Middle life can be a time of great fulfillment and for those who struggle, it can be reassuring to know that prognosis for improvement is usually excellent.

2. *Work on the Specific Problems of Middle Age.* By careful listening and periodic questioning, seek to determine exactly what is bothering the middle-aged counselee. What are his or her feelings and what specifically is causing unhappiness? How much clear evidence is there to support the complaints? In practical ways, what can be done about the midlife problems?

Most problems of middle age do not come because of hormone defects of glandular secretions. Problems come because individuals fail to admit and deal with the threats and emotional strains of the midlife transition. The counselor's task, then, is to stimulate discussion of specific midlife complaints and help counselees reach realistic solutions. At times, counselees will need guidance as they make important decisions about life, values, vocation, marriage, and family issues. The counselee may need encouragement to slow down, to modify life goals, to talk about physical changes or the inevitability of death, to let grown children develop their own lives, to handle the stresses of midlife, and to discuss better ways to use one's time.

People in middle age often need help in making a distinction between courage and foolhardiness. It can be courageous and exciting to move into a new career, to launch an innovative project, or to build new relationships. It is foolhardy, however, to plunge ahead without taking the time to consider and reduce the risks involved.[38] Most of us know of men who, buoyed by the passion and excitement of a sexual affair, decide to divorce their wives and launch a new marriage—only to later conclude that they made a terrible and foolhardy mistake.

When they are tempted to make foolhardy decisions, people aren't always willing to listen to reason—especially that which comes from a spouse or counselor. Try not to condemn or ridicule a new idea, even if it clearly seems foolish. Attempt, instead, to encourage counselees to ponder the consequences and implications of their plans before making the plunge. Encourage them to get the perspective and guidance of others whom they respect. If the counselee is considering a residential, career, or job change, suggest that no action be taken until some homework is completed. When further information is available, the planned change may be less desirable than it appeared at first.

Although feelings are not always a reliable guide, it sometimes is wise to listen to one's intuition. Long ago I discovered (as have numerous other men) that it usually is unwise to move ahead if my wife feels uncomfortable about a decision. Invariably she is right.

In all things, encourage counselees to pray and seek God's guidance before making a change. Often there is an inner sense of peace when one is moving in the right direction.

Many of the specific problems in middle age are discussed in greater detail in other chapters of this book.[39]

3. *Work with the Family.* An understanding, supportive, and interested family can do much to help an individual through middle life. The Christian counselor can help the family, especially the spouse, understand the problems of middle age, give support and encouragement in the home, participate in and sometimes guide decisions, and help the middle-aged person discuss and do something about his or her boredom, fatigue, changing self-image, fears, vocational frustrations, and marital tensions. The spouses can help each other to work at maintaining and building better sexual relationships. Sometimes the counselor can suggest books that family members or the counselee might read to increase understanding.[40]

It should not be assumed that family members will have an easy task as they try to help someone face middle age. Since husbands and wives often face middle life together, it may be difficult for one to help the other. Spouses and other family members will need patience, a willingness to understand, and the courage to challenge the middle-aged person's thinking when this seems wise. Since the counselee may be moody and not easy to live with, family members may need periodic encouragement and coaching from an understanding counselor.

4. *Encourage Spiritual Awareness.* The Bible was written to teach us about God and ourselves. Its pages bring comfort and direction to any person who takes the time to read carefully. Such comfort and direction do not always come quickly and neither are they usually experienced as an emotional high. Instead consistent communion with God helps us remember that he is present with us and ministering through his Holy Spirit.

As he went through a midlife crisis, one pastor explained his feelings in a way that might be an encouragement to other middle-aged believers: "Early in the crisis I became deeply aware that God was my ally. I could tell him anything, even share with him the contradictory motives within my personality, and he would still love and accept me. As the crisis deepened and I came into the depression and withdrawal stages, I knew intellectually that God was still my friend, even though I did not feel it emotionally."[41]

Preventing Problems of Middle Age

Many years ago Carl Jung noted that we have schools and colleges to help people prepare for young adulthood, but there are no colleges for forty-year-olds who need to be educated into the intricacies of living as older adults.[42] If we did have such colleges, most people in middle age would be too busy to attend. Community institutions, especially the churches, can give the preparation and help that are needed to prevent serious midlife problems. This can be done in at least three ways.

1. *Anticipation.* When serious storms approach an area, there is less subsequent damage if the weather bureau issues a warning in time for the residents to get ready and take cover. It also can be helpful if people in their mid-thirties are warned that the midlife transition is coming. Such warnings need not be frightening, but they

need to be mentioned periodically and in conjunction with a positive attitude toward middle age.

Middle age can be a time of problems, especially during the early forties, but middle age is also a period filled with rewards and challenges. There is a sense of being settled, of having found one's place in life, and of being freed from the demands and responsibilities of raising small children. When compared with younger adults, middle-aged people often have more financial security, positions of prestige and leadership in the community, more opportunity to travel, and increased wisdom. Some of the striving and financial struggles of the twenties and thirties have passed, and often middle age presents the greatest opportunity for significant Christian service. It should not be assumed or implied, therefore, that there is nothing to live for after thirty-nine—or after one turns fifty.[43] People can be helped to anticipate both the positive and negative aspects of this period in life.

2. *Education.* Family conferences, couples' retreats, discussion groups, Sunday school classes, and occasional sermons can and should deal with the major issues of middle age. In many churches the pews are filled with middle-aged people and their families who fail to understand the turmoil that is building within and who do not recognize the universality of middle-life struggles. When the problems are identified and acknowledged they can be faced and discussed often among friends in an atmosphere of acceptance.

Churches are filled with middle-aged people, many of whom feel like moral, spiritual, emotional, and personal failures. The sermons talk about forgiveness, love, and acceptance, but too often the people seem to radiate success or stability, and there is little evidence of sensitive caring or in-depth conversation about significant issues. Many leave the church disillusioned and misunderstood.

This can be prevented when midlife problems are anticipated, accepted, and faced in an educated manner—especially within the confines of the local church.

3. *Outreach.* Shortly after his fiftieth birthday, Ray Ortlund gave some wise advice to his fellow church members who had passed the half-century mark. "Don't huddle around with people your own age all the time," he suggested. If we do, "when you die, everything you know will die too—because they'll be dying about the same time you do! Pour your knowledge into people twenty or thirty years younger than you. And when you're gone, everything you've taught them will be walking around this earth for another twenty or thirty years teaching others. Extend your life!"[44]

In a more formal way, Erik Erikson said the same thing. In order to avoid stagnation in middle age and move smoothly into the later years, we need to be strongly involved in working to establish and guide the next generation.[45] As we have seen, Erikson called this "generativity." Teachers have unusual abilities to reach out in this way, but so do youth leaders, counselors, parents, and any person who works in and through the church. When middle-aged people are involved in sharing with others, especially with those who are younger, benefits come to both the giver and the receiver. When they reach out to those who are younger or needy, middle-aged people experience the satisfaction of knowing that life can still be meaningful and useful to others.

Employers, book writers, magazine editors, government leaders, counselors, teachers, and broadcasters can all contribute to the prevention of middle-age problems, but the church can be most helpful of all. Its members know the healing power of love and can demonstrate the burden bearing that should characterize Christians. This caring can bring crucial support and guidance to people in middle age.

Conclusions about Middle Age

Readers of this book are likely to see themselves in its pages at times, but so does the writer. In preparing this chapter, for example, and in rewriting it for the revised edition of the book, I have been acutely aware of my own struggles and victories in passing through middle adulthood. It has been encouraging for me to realize afresh that the emotions and struggles of middle age are common, temporary, and ultimately able to contribute to spiritual growth and personal maturity.[46] With God's help, we can guide ourselves or our counselees through middle life. It is possible to face this and every other stage of life in ways that will enable us to grow and live lives that honor God and fulfill his purposes. Regardless of age, that should be the goal of all of us—the writer of this book, the readers, and the people to whom we minister and offer counsel.

SUGGESTIONS FOR FURTHER READING

Conway, Jim. *Men in Mid-Life Crisis.* Elgin, Ill.: David C. Cook, 1978.*
———, and Sally Conway. *Women in Midlife Crisis.* Wheaton, Ill.: Tyndale, 1983.*
Levinson, Daniel J., et al. *The Seasons of a Man's Life.* New York: Knopf, 1978.
Mickey, Paul A. *Marriage in the Middle Years.* Valley Forge, Penn.: Judson, 1986.*
Ortlund, Ray, and Anne Ortlund. *The Best Half of Life.* Ventura, Calif.: Regal, 1976.*
Wright, H. Norman. *Seasons of a Marriage.* Ventura, Calif.: Regal, 1982.*

* Books marked with an asterisk (*) are especially suited for counselees to read.

15

The Later Years

ALMOST ALL OF HER NEIGHBORS would agree: Mrs. R. is a remarkable lady.

She would be the first to admit that her eighty-three-year-old body has slowed down in the last few years. Her hearing isn't as good as it used to be. Her hands swell with arthritis, especially in the mornings and on damp days. She admits that she forgets things easily and doesn't have the energy and "zip" that she had only a few years ago.

Like most elderly people, at least in the United States, Mrs. R. likes to be independent. Since the death of her husband eight years ago, she has lived alone in a small apartment, near friends and neighbors who help her with grocery shopping, but further from her family than she might like. Her divorced son lives alone in another state. Her married daughter and son-in-law are missionaries in the Philippines. The one son who lives nearby is about half an hour's drive from Mrs. R.'s home. He is a busy professional with three teenage children and a wife with a career of her own. Most weekends, one of the family members drops by for a visit, and Mrs. R. keeps in contact by phone. She knows that the family would help out in an emergency, but she knows too that her children and grandchildren are busy and not always able to come visiting.

Most Sundays, Mrs. R. gets to church. She finds it hard to climb the stairs, is nervous about venturing outside in winter, can't always catch the words in the sermon, and is sad to be reminded of how many of her friends are physically feeble or gone.

She lives on a small pension that is sufficient for her needs, but she worries about how she would handle a major medical expense or what might happen if she couldn't live alone.

All in all, she tries not to worry too much. She prefers to keep her mind active through reading and contacts with her friends. Her house is filled with plants that she cares for tenderly, and she still has time for knitting and visiting with other people in her apartment building. The neighbors appreciate her cheerful manner and willingness to help when she sees a need.

"I decided many years ago that I could be a bitter, complaining old woman, or a woman who is sweet and nice to be around," she said recently. "Nobody wants to be around somebody who talks about aches and pains all the time, so I try to be cheerful."

Mrs. R. may not realize that her attitude does more than keep her cheerful. It makes old age a more fulfilling time of life and lets others agree that she really *is* a remarkable old lady.

A few days after the presidential inauguration that ushered him into the world's most strenuous job, Ronald Reagan celebrated his seventieth birthday. The former radio announcer and movie actor was starting a new career—joining the ranks of those who have made significant contributions to this world long after most of their peers have retired. Architect Frank Lloyd Wright created some of his best works when he was in his eighties and finished the impressive Guggenheim Museum when he was ninety-one. Douglas MacArthur became commander of the United Nations forces in Korea when he was seventy. Later, after telling Congress that "old soldiers never die, they just fade away," the general went on to become a successful businessman. Guitarist Andres Segovia was still giving classical concerts at age ninety-two. Bob Hope and George Burns failed to let old age slow down their entertainment schedules. Sir George Solti led his world-renowned Chicago Symphony Orchestra in a gala concert to celebrate his own birthday when the maestro turned seventy-five. Grandma Moses attained fame as an artist when she was in her eighties. Winston Churchill continued to influence the world as an elderly British statesman. After turning eighty, psychologist B. F. Skinner and psychoanalyst Erik Erikson each wrote books about the experience of growing old.[1]

It could be argued that these are exceptions. Men and women with unusual abilities are always exceptions, regardless of age,[2] but these famous people—and thousands like them who never became famous—show that the later years need not be times of misery, rigidity, and inactivity. French writer André Maurois once observed that "growing old is no more than a bad habit which a busy man has no time to form." Robert Browning might have agreed when he invited readers to "Grow old with me! The best is yet to be. . . ."

This optimism is not shared by everyone. Egyptian philosopher Ptah-hotep wrote in 2500 B.C. that "old age is the worst of misfortunes that can afflict a man." Ralph Waldo Emerson described the elderly as "rags and relics," while William Shakespeare wrote that the later years usher in a "second childishness and mere oblivion. Sans teeth, sans eyes, sans taste, sans everything."

Regardless of these assessments, the numbers and percentages of older people in the population have been increasing at a phenomenal rate. In the United States alone, perhaps because of better medical care, improved diet, and increasing interest in physical fitness, the number of people over sixty-five has doubled in the past thirty-five years. Every day the over-sixty-five population in this country increases by sixteen hundred people. Early in the next century, when the first baby boomers begin to retire, it is estimated that 20 percent of the population will be over sixty-five. More than a thousand professional articles on aging appear every year,[3] and it is not surprising that scholars, politicians, and journalists talk increasingly about the "graying of America" and of the rest of the world. Churches already minister to large numbers of older people, and as the years pass it seems likely that increasing numbers of senior citizens will seek counseling.

It is widely agreed (at least by younger people) that old age begins between sixty and sixty-five. Some call the next twenty-year period "young old age" and suggest that people over eighty-five are the "oldest old." Most professionals dislike such classifications[4] because they fail to recognize that people age at different rates, both physically and psychologically. Among sixty-five-year-olds, for example, there are wide differences in health, attitudes, abilities, beliefs, physical appearance, intellectual alertness, spiritual maturity, and capability for handling stress or managing one's life.[5] Some people seem to be old at forty while others—like Mrs. R.—seem youthful and vigorous even when in their eighties and beyond. For everyone, however, growing old and adjusting to the realities of old age can be the source of new problems and challenges. These challenges often can be met more efficiently with the help of a Christian counselor.

The Bible and Old Age

Old age, as we all know, is not something new. In previous generations their numbers were fewer, but there have always been aged people. Methuselah's 969-year age was unusual, but many of the Old Testament patriarchs lived well past 100, and this was not limited to biblical times.

Even in those times, however, older people apparently faced rejection and frustration. While it was recognized that wisdom often increased with age,[6] the psalmist still prayed "Forsake me not, O God, when I am old and gray."[7] Even in past generations, older people faced rejection.

Perhaps Ecclesiastes 12 is the clearest biblical picture of old age. Near the turn of the century, psychologist G. Stanley Hall called this the most pessimistic description of old age ever written,[8] but it also is realistic. People in their later years do not delight in their age, we read. Days can be cloudy, strength fails, often there is nothing to do, sight and hearing decline, fears increase, and there is a new realization of the nearness of death.

All is not, however, a modern "vanity of vanities." Every person, including those who are old, can find meaning in life when one fears God and keeps his commandments.[9] While young people have strength, the elderly should be respected for their wisdom and experience.[10] In turn, the elderly are to be temperate, dignified, sensible, sound in faith, loving, and willing to persevere, teaching what is good, and not malicious gossips or excessive drinkers.[11] This is a picture of hope, and nowhere should this be more apparent than in the community of believers. Christians are commanded to honor their parents "that it may go well with you and that you may enjoy long life on earth."[12] This is a promise that clearly is positive.

The Bible, therefore, is realistic in its portrayal of old age, positive in its attitude toward the value of old age, and specific in its commands concerning how we should treat persons in old age. Older persons are to be respected, cared for, and loved as human beings. Christians have no other options.[13]

The Causes of Problems in Old Age

Pat Moore was a twenty-six-year-old industrial designer who wanted to know what it was like to cope with the physical limitations of advanced age or to experience the attitudes that older people encounter. To find out, she enlisted the help of a professional makeup artist who applied makeup and provided a gray wig. To blur her vision, the young woman applied baby oil to her eyes. She wore splints and bandages under her clothes to stiffen her joints and put plugs in her ears to dull her hearing. Then, looking like a woman in her eighties, she ventured out onto the city streets. For three years, in more than a hundred cities, fourteen states, and two

Canadian provinces, whenever she went on one of her many business trips, the young woman rarely missed a chance to add a few hours when she would dress like an old woman and observe how people reacted.

These experiences put Pat Moore into contact with many caring people who were sensitive to the needs of the elderly. She found that older people have many concerns but concluded "that they generally whine and complain less, despite more valid reasons to do so, than any other group of people I have ever been around."[14] One day she was beat up by a group of twelve- and thirteen-year-old boys who ran off with her purse. To her surprise, she became so intimidated by the impatience and critical attitudes of others, that she found herself agreeing that the elderly are not important. On several occasions she went into the same stores and made identical purchases, once disguised as an old woman and once as herself. Invariably the clerks showed different attitudes. They were more impatient and negative with the "elderly" Pat Moore.

From this it should not be assumed that life is difficult for all older people. For many, the later years *are* a fulfilling and happy time of life. Despite rates of depression and suicide that are higher than the younger population, the incidence of psychopathology in the elderly appears to be low rather than high.[15] Not all persons over sixty-five are lonely, failing in health, bored, poverty stricken, depressed, intellectually dull, or exploited. These facts must be stated lest the following paragraphs be taken to imply that the later years are always plagued by problems.

The causes of problems that do arise could be grouped into several categories.

1. *Physical Causes.* As we get older our bodies run down, but some bodies decline sooner and more quickly than others. Physical decline tends to come sooner when bodies have been weakened by earlier disease or by breakdowns in the immune system. Other bodies wear out more quickly because they have been deprived of exercise or sufficient rest, permanently harmed by pollution or unhealthy work conditions, or abused by too much smoking, eating, or alcoholic consumption. Sometimes stress is the villain that hinders normal physical functioning, and we know that an individual's mental attitude can have an important impact on the type and speed of physical decline.[16] These physical changes can be viewed in at least four ways.

(a) Cosmetic Changes. Graying and thinning hair, loss of teeth, decreasing weight, wrinkling skin including bags under the eyes, dark spots on the hands and wrists are changes that begin long before a person turns sixty-five, but in the later years they can no longer be hidden or ignored. In a culture that prizes youth and physical attractiveness, these evidences of age can influence one's self-esteem and sense of security. The problem can be accentuated when older people stop taking care of their physical appearance and allow themselves to look "dumpy" and slovenly.

(b) Sensory Changes. It is well known that older people cannot see or hear as well as they once could. In addition there is a degeneration in the senses of taste and smell, a stiffness of joints so that movement is hindered, a decline in strength and energy level, a slower reaction time, changes in kinesthetic sensitivity so that balance is more difficult, and greater problems with memory. These changes come slowly and rarely appear as a "jolt," but as Pat Moore demonstrated so effectively they can greatly interfere with one's ability to get along and to get around.

(c) System Changes. Physiological degeneration and changes often are seen in the body's organs and systems. In the skeletal system, for example, bones become brittle, less able to resist stress, and much slower to heal. Rheumatoid arthritis often restricts movement and creates pain. Osteoporosis influences millions of women bringing pain, restricted movement, and shriveling of the spine.

Other changes occur in the muscular, reproductive, gastrointestinal, cardiovascular, respiratory, and central nervous systems. As they grow older, people learn to adapt to these changes. They avoid foods that upset the gastrointestinal system, for example, or they take precautions to prevent heart attacks and other cardiovascular illnesses.

Sometimes, however, the physical changes lead to elderly hypochondriacs. Most of these people complained about their health when they were younger as well, but in the later years people worry more about their bodies and the costs of health care. As a result they may talk more about symptoms and go to doctors when treatment isn't necessary.[17]

(d) Sexual Changes. Reproductive capacities diminish as one grows older, but it is not true that sexual interest and activity diminish as well. Older people need physical closeness and human contact, just like the young. Pleasurable sexual experiences are possible for both sexes well into the later years.[18]

It is true that older couples take longer to achieve orgasm and the intensity may be reduced, but for many older people, sexual activity and satisfaction increase as they grow older. Jokes about old age as "a time when a man flirts with girls but can't remember why," or about sex in adulthood as a progression from "tri-weekly, to try-weekly, to try-weakly" are all a mixture of humor with an attitude that dismisses sex in the elderly as something wrong or lecherous. Such attitudes are believed by many older people who then avoid sexual involvement, physical closeness, and physical expressions of love with one's mate.[19]

(e) Disease and Illness. For many years, old age was viewed as a time of inevitable physical decline, incapacitating illness, and immobility. This, however, is not a valid picture. According to several surveys, at least half of all people between seventy-five and eighty-four are free of health problems that require special care or curb their activities. Even in the oldest group, those above eighty-five, more than one-third report no limitations due to health. Most older people (an estimated 80 percent of those over sixty-five) have at least one of the four major chronic conditions of later life—arthritis, high blood pressure, hearing impairment, or heart disease—but these are physical impairments to which many people adapt without much decline in activity or change of lifestyle.[20]

This optimistic picture should not hide the reality of common physical problems that do come with age. Eventually most older people will suffer from diseases such as cancer or serious heart ailments, and in time internal organs begin to break down. All illness can arouse anxiety, diminish mobility, and create discouragement. When a person is healthy, the later years can be interesting and fulfilling, but when one is sick, this can be a terrifying and depressing time of life.[21]

2. *Mental Causes.* Thousands of research projects have attempted to determine the extent to which older people decline in terms of creativity, memory, intellectual ability, or capacity to learn new things.[22] It is well known that older persons take longer to respond, think more slowly, are less able to understand new ideas or develop new skills, and have difficulty with short-term memory. Yet older people often rely

on their wisdom and appearance to make up for these declining activities. With extra effort they can continue to be creative, intellectually astute, and able to learn in the later years.[23] In speaking to an overflow crowd at a professional convention, psychologist B. F. Skinner once shared his own methods for adapting to old age, then paraphrased the wise Samuel Johnson: "Sir, an aging lecturer is like a dog walking on his hinder legs. It is not done well; but you are all surprised to find it done at all."[24]

The decline in mental ability is most apparent when one has to make a quick decision, like stepping on the brakes or jumping out of danger. Aware of their slower reaction time, many people learn to act cautiously—as many younger drivers have discovered when they get behind an older person who is at the wheel.

It isn't always possible to compensate for declining mental abilities, however, and some people give up trying. Bored by the inactivity of retirement, saddened by the death of friends, and frustrated by the inability to move about, it is easy for an older person to daydream about the "good old days." The present is uncomfortable and the future offers little hope, so there is an escape into past memories that have become distorted both by the passage of time and by the human tendency to forget that which was painful or unpleasant. Such a retreat sometimes contributes to confusion and senility that may be more psychological in origin than physiological.

In the past counselors tended to ignore or dismiss the older person's seemingly endless supply of dull and oft-repeated stories about the past. More recently, however, gerontologists and others have concluded that reminiscences, especially those that are discussed and shared, can help older people reexamine the past and get a better perspective on the present and future.[25]

3. *Economic Causes.* Retirement brings a departure from work, but for many it also brings a low income, a reduced standard of living, and adjustment to a retirement pay scale that often fails to keep pace with the rate of inflation. In a Pulitzer-Prize-winning book on aging in America, one writer described the tragedy of millions of people who live in an affluent society but grow poor as they grow old.[26] This has led to an increase in crime among the elderly, many of whom steal because that seems to be the only feasible way to survive.[27]

This economic situation creates problems like finding an affordable place to live, meeting medical expenses, maintaining a balanced diet, being able to afford transportation costs to continue contact with friends, or facing the self-esteem problems that come when one has declining resources and may have to apply for public welfare assistance. Economic problems and needs in the elderly have been of special concern to social workers and sociologists who see the harmful effects of financial pressure in old age.[28]

4. *Interpersonal Causes.* To function adequately as human beings, we need people with whom we can socialize and exchange ideas. Other people challenge us, encourage us, keep us in contact with reality, and enable us to feel useful.

For many older people there is a devastating loss of such social contact. Retirement isolates one from the occupational world. Friends and relatives, including one's spouse, often die and leave surviving older people without peers to bolster morale. Declining health limits one's ability to get away from home, friends may change residence or move away, and adult children sometimes are too busy, too far away, or too critical to provide contact. All of this can contribute to the older person's withdrawal from social contact, to the feeling that he or she is no longer useful or needed, and sometimes to a self-centered mentality that can contribute to premature death. Even in retirement communities, where people are surrounded by other senior citizens, there can be a tendency to withdraw from others. In contrast, studies show that older persons who have one or more close, intimate relationships seem to be happier, better adjusted, and in better mental health than those without such confidants.[29]

Research evidence shows that many people in the later years are mentally, financially, and physically abused, often by their children and other family members. Most of these victims are too weak to defend themselves, unable or unwilling to report the abuse, and often in a position of dependency on the same people who inflict the pain and abuse. Few issues are more likely to arouse the compassion and anger of sensitive counselors.[30]

5. *Self-Esteem Causes.* Based on her experiences dressed as an older person, Pat Moore concluded that perhaps the worst thing about aging is the "overwhelming sense that everything around you is letting you know that you are not terribly important any more." People constantly seemed exasperated by the slow moving "old" woman and in time it was easy for her to conclude, "You're right; I'm just a lot of trouble. I'm really not as valuable as all these other people, so I'll just get out of your way as soon as possible so you won't be angry with me."[31]

The self-confidence and self-esteem of older people are undermined frequently by the misconceptions and prejudices of those who think the elderly are too old to make decisions, do useful work, create new things, accept responsibilities, or go out alone. When the elderly are treated like children and assumed to be incompetent, it is easy for an older person to feel useless and unimportant. Little wonder that many have a poor opinion of themselves and of their value as persons.[32]

Some evidence suggests that legislators, the media, professions such as psychology and medicine, people in communities, advertisers, merchants, employers, and even psychological researchers are all guilty of *ageism.* This is a form of prejudice that demeans old age, discriminates against the elderly, and assumes that "younger is better." Like sexism and racism, ageism creates problems for its victims and contributes further to the older person's decline in self-esteem.[33]

For some, one of the most influential blows to self-esteem is the reality of retirement. Eagerly anticipated and enjoyed by many people, retirement can also be a stark reminder that society considers us too old to work, and one's income and sense of self-worth often drop substantially.

Mildred Vandenburgh is a perky Christian lady who became a missionary in later life and once described three stages of retirement.[34] The *get-up-and-go-stage* is a time for enthusiastic involvement in the activities, projects, and travel that one has long wanted to do but which work and other responsibilities have prevented. Without realizing it, people gradually slide into a *why-bother-stage* in which comfort is important and there is less willingness to exert unnecessary effort. Then, writes Vandenburgh, "unless you pull up your bootstraps or someone rescues you from apathy and lethargy, you are on your way to the third and final stage: the *my-get-up-and-go-has-gone-stage.*"

This popular analysis points to a well-documented conclusion that there are great individual differences in the ways people adjust to retirement and to the self-esteem changes it brings. Depending somewhat on one's health, financial security, attitudes, and degree of life success, some people welcome retirement and are able to relax and enjoy their golden years. Others have less success in coping. Unable or unwilling to face the realities of age, these people react with anger, condemn themselves, and blame others for life's miseries and their failure to achieve goals. Such persons have a low self-esteem and often slide into depression.[35]

Once again, however, we find individual differences. The people who adapt best to old age appear to be those who were well adjusted before retirement, who have a realistic view of their strengths and weaknesses, who thought about and made some preparations for retirement before it occurred, and who had a positive self-concept during the younger years. One's adjustment, attitudes, and self-concept at forty or earlier may be the best predictor of what one will be like decades later.

6. *Special Causes.* What is the effect of technology on older people? How does rapid social change influence people who are slowing down but want to keep up to date? Do advances in technology create more problems for the elderly?[36] Recently a corporation executive described his frustration after almost thirty years in his company. "I have all this experience with the business," he reflected, "but in many respects the young college graduate who knows the latest about computers and information retrieval is probably more valuable to the company."

Technological change is only one of the special concerns[37] that complicate life for some older people. For many the adjustment to later life is complicated by racism, sexism, alcoholism, physical limitations including deafness and blindness, neighborhood decline, crime, political corruption or incompetence, cutbacks in government funding, the deterioration of one's home, or local prejudices against older citizens. These issues are often overlooked by counselors, but they have a profound effect on many older people.

7. *Spiritual and Existential Causes.* Old age, declining health, and the passing of friends all bring us face-to-face with the reality and inevitability of death. For many there also is a fear of death itself and a painful uncertainty about the existence or nonexistence of life after death. Some people reach old age with a burden of guilt and a sense of failure that they don't know how to handle. One retired person described how he reached a point of concluding "nothing out there really depends on me now." This led him to wonder why he should do anything and even if what he had produced during his lifetime would ever matter to anyone. All of this led to depression and a search to find meaning now that he had reached old age.[38]

This is a time when the church could help, but many older people are unable to attend worship services. When they do attend, sometimes they feel unwanted and unwelcomed in congregations that emphasize youth programs, family ministries, and the activities of couples clubs. Even the design of church buildings, many with high stairs and no basement washrooms, can subtly imply that older people (especially those with problems) are not welcome. Churches must strive to minister to the spiritual needs of older people without adding to their burdens.[39]

The Effects of Old Age

One effective way for a counselor to understand aging people is to imagine life from their perspectives. Ask yourself how you would feel to have declining health, no useful work, limited income, a loss of friends, and a declining ability to think or act quickly. Ponder how it would feel to be lonely, rejected by a society that has little respect for the elderly, and living in a neighborhood where the crime rate is high but you have neither the strength nor the agility to escape or to defend yourself. When we imagine how an older person might think or feel, we can better understand the effects of aging. This should enable us to be more sympathetic and effective counselors.

The effects of aging on one's self-concept, emotions, interpersonal relations, lifestyle, and intellectual capabilities have already been mentioned. With aging there may also come a new anxiety over the future, self-pity, worries about finances, depression, and sometimes attempted suicide. Suicide rates among the elderly, especially among elderly men, are high,[40] and within recent years there appears to have been an increase in mercy killings by family members who struggle with the emotional pain of watching loved ones suffer.[41]

In their in-depth study of older persons and the church, Robert M. Gray and David O. Moberg summarize some of the effects of aging:

> The lack of respect for our senior citizens, the growing emphasis upon youth, and the substitution of technology for manpower has left tens of thousands of older Americans with no role in society. These, along with the numerous other problems alluded to in this book and elsewhere, contribute to the despair that is found so frequently among the elderly. Faced with disappointment and disillusionment at reaching the "harvest years"; finding the "golden years" to be a period of relative poverty; feeling themselves to be on the shelf and not permitted to make the contributions they still are able to make to the economic life of our nation; frustrated with the reduction of income which usually comes with retirement, and living in unpleasant, inconvenient, and unhealthful dwellings; it is no wonder that so many older persons are seriously maladjusted. The church has a tremendous challenge to face in the problems related to the economic plight of so many of our older citizens.[42]

Counseling and Old Age

The majority of elderly people are able to carry out their daily activities with little or no help from others. Because of the stresses of aging, however, many people do encounter personal problems that could be reduced by effective counseling.[43] Regrettably, many people do not get this help, perhaps because this age group tends to avoid counseling, does not know where to get help in coping with their stresses or is unable to afford the counseling costs. More often the lack of help may result from ageism in professionals who hold the prejudiced and pessimistic view that older people can't change, are unpleasant to work with, and probably won't get better if they do come for counseling.[44] The best place to start our consideration of counseling, therefore, is with an examination of the counselor's own attitudes.

1. *Counselor Self-Examination.* What is your attitude toward the elderly? Do you harbor some of the common stereotypes that see older people as incompetent, useless, childish, rigid, cranky, and preoccupied with physical aches and pains? Do you resent older people, look down on them, or try to avoid them? Have you concluded that counseling the elderly will probably be a waste of your time?

These reactions must disappear before a counselor can be helpful. If you hold these negative attitudes, ask God to make you more compassionate and loving. Then spend some time talking with a few older people about their lives, problems, and needs. Nothing removes prejudice like face-to-face discussion with the people against whom we hold negative opinions. As you talk, your attitudes probably will change, and you will see the elderly for what they really are: worthwhile human beings who are loved by God. It is then that you will be able to be able to counsel more successfully with those who are old.

2. *Physical Examination and Counseling.* Many of the problems in old age come or are accentuated because of physical problems. Older people, therefore, should be encouraged to have regular physical checkups by a competent physician. These doctors can also give general advice on health care and other medical issues that are beyond the training and expertise of nonmedical counselors. When medical treatment helps people feel better, some of their psychological problems disappear and others can be dealt with more efficiently.

Among the elderly, Alzheimer's disease (AD) is the best known, most disturbing example of physical deterioration that can influence psychological functioning. At present the disease has no clearly identifiable cause and no known cure.[45] From its start until the time of death, the disease may last for ten or more years. Beginning with mild memory loss, impaired judgment, and a decreasing ability to handle routine tasks, AD patients later become disoriented and confused, inclined to wander (especially at night), agitated, uncoordinated, and in time completely dependent, often mute, and unable to control body functions. Initially, family members care lovingly for their older relatives with AD, but eventually the entire family is disrupted, hindered in functioning, financially drained, and often filled with anger, frustration, and guilt. In describing the demands on families, one book suggests that caring for AD patients is like living a thirty-six-hour day with no breaks or time for rest.[46] The counselor's help begins with the patient, but eventually the spouse and whole family are more likely to be the focus of counseling services.

3. *Individual Counseling.* Older people need the opportunity to talk about their problems, but apparently few make contact with professional counselors. More often, the elderly talk to their pastors, physicians, social workers, or other helpers who can visit in the home, "chat" on the phone, or meet in some place other than a counselor's office.[47] One estimate suggests that perhaps 15 to 20 percent of the over-sixty population discovers for the first time that they cannot cope without help.[48] When these people are involved in individual counseling, there can be several approaches.

(a) Supportive Counseling. Older people often feel encouragement and a greater ability to face the realities of advanced age when a counselor listens sensitively and gives reassurance. The goal is not to encourage complaining and self-pity. Instead, supportive counseling helps people feel worthwhile and accepted. It can help the elderly forgive themselves and know that God forgives and cares. When the counselor emphasizes the love of God, he or she can also discuss God's plan of salvation, his justice, and his provisions for believers after death. At times there will be a need to help the older person face the realities of sickness or deal with the pain of grief.[49] This type of counseling can be done by an individual or a pastor making an occasional call, but it is better if a group of believers, including the counselor, can consistently show care, support, and acceptance. This support network[50] often supplements face-to-face contact with periodic telephone calls and cheerful notes.

(b) Educative Counseling. Older people, like those who are younger, have many misconceptions about the later years. These can be discussed and true facts about aging can be taught. Such discussions can give reassurance, reduce anxiety, and in turn prevent defeatist attitudes and maladaptive behavior.

Consider, for example, the issue of sex after sixty. It is helpful for older people to recognize that this is not wrong, that physical satisfaction is both possible and common, that problems like impotence can be temporary, and that sexual satisfaction need not stop at the time of retirement. A very different subject is that of living accommodations in old age. For example, what are the costs, advantages, and other relevant issues involved in living alone, moving to a retirement village or home, or moving in with one's children? The counselor may have to consult with several senior citizens and community leaders to get accurate information that might be shared with counselees.

(c) Life Review Counseling. Reminiscing about the past appears to be a normal part of aging, but in doing this elderly people often focus on their past failures, guilt, fears, and feelings of inadequacy. In contrast, a life review can help people find satisfaction in their accomplishments, deal with past frustrations, and get a more balanced perspective on both the past and the future.[51]

Life review counseling ideally involves preparing a complete biography, often on paper. Sometimes people can be encouraged to write an autobiography,[52] and you might ask the older person to show you photographs, diaries, and other memorabilia. It can also be helpful to talk with family members. The goals of these activities are to help counselees express and resolve tensions about the past, discuss and accept failures, get rid of guilt feelings, look at life realistically, solve conflicts and behavior patterns that continue to create difficulty, learn new ways to cope with problems, and prepare realistically for a smooth transition to the coming years. This review must include discussions about the older person's spiritual life, relationship with Jesus Christ, and expectations about life after death. In addition, consider the person's marital and family history, earliest memories, education and work history, happiest and saddest memories, and plans for the future.

(d) In-Depth Counseling. People who are deeply depressed, withdrawn, or otherwise inclined to show severe or persisting personal problems, can often benefit from more long-term involvement with a counselor. I know of no evidence to suggest that older people are more difficult to treat than those who are younger. Prognosis is especially good in counselees who want to get better.[53]

In counseling with the elderly, the counselor often is younger than the counselee. This can be awkward, since young people usually are not thought of as counselors to the elderly. Sometimes the younger counselor treats an older person like a father or mother, and the older counselee in turn might view the counselor like a son or daughter. These perceptions must be recognized, especially by counselors, when they work with older counselees.

4. *Family Counseling.* Unlike some other age groups, when problems of the elderly surface, they almost always involve or affect family members. We have seen how the family is disrupted by advancing Alzheimer's disease in an older relative,

but families also are influenced by depression, financial problems, health decline, increased stress, and almost every other problem in the aged.

Counseling with the elderly, therefore, is likely to be most effective if other family members are involved. At times, the counselor may serve as a mediator, helping resolve intergenerational conflicts. Sometimes the counselor gives information to family members, including practical and tangible suggestions for managing unusual behavior, getting medical treatment, deciding on appropriate living accommodations, and handling finances. With the counselor's help, the family can make plans for the future, support and encourage one another, and cope with their own grief or guilt. When an older person is resistant to counseling or unable to benefit from counseling, the only way to give help may be through family members.[54]

5. *Group Counseling.* Often there is reluctance for people to discuss their problems in groups and this may be especially true for older persons who, unlike those who are younger, are less accustomed to being open about themselves before others. Groups, however, can be helpful to the elderly who need contact with others, acceptance, and assurance that their problems are not unique or abnormal. Such groups can consider adjustment problems, life crises, prejudice against the aged, and most of the other issues that concern the elderly.[55]

6. *Environmental Counseling.* Many older people feel that they are powerless victims in a society that treats the elderly with scorn or indifference. Although this goes beyond the traditional role of counseling, the helper can sometimes mobilize community resources, stimulate self-help and self-care in the elderly, help people get to available legal and medical services, or guide in money management.

It has long been recognized that one good way to change an individual is to change his or her environment. Attractive accommodations, adequate meals, recreational opportunities, the acceptance of even minor responsibilities, and contact with cheerful encouraging people—especially younger people—can all help to alter the older person's outlook and adjustment to later life. Often these changes are beyond the financial means of older people and their families, but some environmental changes are possible. Even within the church, youth groups and others can serve useful roles in brightening the lives of older people in the church or community.

Preventing Old-Age Problems

It is not always possible to delay the aging process, but we can help people cope more effectively and avoid the negative attitudes that often hasten the process of physical and psychological deterioration. Prevention of old-age problems involves motivating people in four areas.

1. *Stimulate Realistic Planning.* According to one financial adviser, it is never too soon to plan for retirement.[56] Most counselors probably would agree. The problems of age sometimes hit with spiraling intensity because they were unexpected and come without prior preparation. Within the church we can encourage people to evaluate their attitudes toward aging, discuss how to use leisure time, ponder relationships with aging parents and with grown children, talk about death, and help with plans for retirement. These discussions need not be morbid. Instead they can be positive, pleasant, and presented as a healthy, useful exercise. While this planning for the future could take place in a one-to-one counseling situation, it probably is better

when it is done in groups, such as a workshop, retreat session, or Sunday school class. Such group discussions can serve as an inoculation against the psychological traumas of aging.

As an example of realistic planning, consider how people might be helped to prepare for retirement. It is best to start with those in their forties or fifties. Try to clear up misunderstandings about retirement and encourage people to think about the future, even when they are physically healthy and hardly aware of even the gradual changes that come with advancing age.

As they prepare for retirement, several questions should be considered:

- When will I (we) retire?
- What does God want me (or us) to do after retirement?
- Where will I retire?
- Where will I live in retirement?
- How will I spend my time after retirement?
- How will I keep healthy after retirement?
- What will I do to keep my mind alert and active?
- How much money and financial resources do I have?
- What financial needs will I have in retirement?
- How will I pay for my health needs in retirement?
- Do I have enough insurance?
- Is my will complete and up to date?
- Specifically, what can I do now to prepare for retirement?

Discussion of questions like these prevents future problems and helps with present concerns about later life. Sometimes people will find assistance in some of the self-help books designed to prepare people for their later years.[57]

2. *Stimulate Realistic Attitudes.* From the pulpit, through small groups, and in other church meetings, stereotypes and myths about aging must be attacked. The Bible clearly respects the aged, and followers of Christ are expected to do likewise. If the whole church can care compassionately for the aging[58] and develop positive attitudes toward the elderly, the older person will do the same.

One way to develop good attitudes toward aging is to get the congregation in contact with the elderly and involved in helping. Gray and Moberg have listed some of the things that a church can do for older people.[59] The church, they suggest, can:

- plan specific programs for senior citizens; (try to keep these attractive and not something that looks patronizing or like "babysitting for older people")
- speak to the spiritual needs of the elderly, including their feelings of insecurity, insignificance, alienation from God, regret over past failures and fear of death
- educate people to help them cope better with the problems of life
- stimulate social, spiritual, and recreational contact with same age and younger persons
- help solve personal problems before they get worse
- help meet physical and material needs
- meet with people in nursing homes

- influence civic affairs and government programs for the elderly
- adapt physical facilities so older people can come to church without hardship
- create opportunities for older people to be involved in useful service—teaching, visiting, praying, or doing clerical, maintenance, or other useful service activities

A program like this shows everyone that the elderly are important. This can reduce fears and facilitate a smoother adjustment to the later years.

3. *Stimulate Education and Activity.* People can avoid some of the problems of aging if they can be encouraged to use their minds, to exercise their bodies, to plan their diets, to make good use of their leisure time, and to find creative ways of serving others. This conclusion is based on the assumption that mental and physical activity will do much to keep one from becoming apathetic, lethargic, and senile.

4. *Stimulate Spiritual Growth.* No person is ever too old to come to Christ or to mature spiritually. A growing relationship with Jesus Christ does not prevent life's problems, but the committed believer should be able to deal with stress more effectively because he or she has confidence in an all-powerful, sovereign God. Throughout life, even longtime Christians can learn more about the one with whom we will be spending eternity. People of all ages need encouragement to pray, read Scripture, worship regularly, fellowship with other believers, and become involved—insofar as this is possible—in active service. The believer who, with God's help, is able to rejoice in the earlier years will carry the same joyful attitude into later adulthood.

Conclusions about Old Age

Liz Carpenter served as press secretary to Lady Bird Johnson when her husband, Lyndon, was president of the United States. The press secretary's role was fulfilling and exciting, but one day, when she was in her fifties, Mrs. Carpenter was jarred with the news that her husband had died. "Old age came early," she wrote later. "I was instantly plunged into shock, abandonment, sadness, anger, loneliness, isolation—and then came the inevitable restlessness." The president's wife became her first counselor and soon Liz Carpenter was involved in facing her later years.

In thinking about her anxieties, five fears appeared to be basic: not feeling needed; losing a sense of purpose; losing control over her own destiny; not feeling loved; and not being touched. Instead of withdrawing into herself, she determined to keep as active as possible and to keep learning. "The lessons learned in maturity aren't simple," she concluded. They "go beyond the acquisition of information and skills. You learn to avoid self-destructive behavior. You learn not to burn up energy in anxiety. You learn to manage tension. You learn that self-pity and resentment are among the most toxic of drugs. You learn to bear the things you can't change. . . . You learn that no matter what you do, some people aren't going to love you—a lesson that is at first troubling, then relaxing."[60]

Some people never learn these kinds of lessons. It has been estimated that one-fifth of the American population suffers from "gerontophobia" (the fear of growing old).[61] This figure may be different in other parts of the world, but one conclusion is clear: many people recoil from thoughts of their own old age and attempt both to deny aging in themselves and to avoid others who are older. Often the young and old both believe common but unfounded myths about the disadvantages of the later years.

Preparations for the later years begin with the attitudes, lifestyle, activities, and spiritual maturing that comes when we are younger. Inactive, critical, bitter, nervous, self-centered young people usually carry these characteristics into old age. Plato recognized this. He wrote, "He who is of calm and happy nature will hardly feel the pressure of age, but to him who is of opposite disposition youth and age are equally a burden."[62] For counselees and their counselors, the time to begin pondering the later years is now.

SUGGESTIONS FOR FURTHER READING

Becker, Arthur H. *Ministry with Older Persons: A Guide for Clergy and Congregations.* Minneapolis: Augsburg, 1986.

Butler, Robert N., and Myrna L. Lewis. *Aging and Mental Health.* 3d ed. St. Louis: Mosby, 1982.

Gillies, John. *A Guide to Compassionate Care of the Aging.* Nashville: Thomas Nelson, 1985.

Gray, Robert M., and David O. Moberg. *The Church and the Older Person.* Rev. ed. Grand Rapids, Mich.: William B. Eerdmans, 1977.

Jarvik, Lissy, and Gary Small. *Parentcare: A Commonsense Guide for Adult Children.* New York: Crown, 1988.*

Knight, Bob. *Psychotherapy with Older Adults.* Beverly Hills, Calif.: Sage, 1986.

Kra, Siegfried. *Aging Myths: Reversible Causes of Mind and Memory Loss.* New York: McGraw-Hill, 1986.

Linkletter, Art. *Old Age Is Not for Sissies.* New York: Viking, 1988.*

Lowry, Louis. *Social Work with Aging.* 2d ed. New York: Longman, 1985.

Sherman, Edmund. *Counseling the Aging: An Integrative Approach.* New York: Free Press, 1981.

* Books marked with an asterisk (*) are especially suited for counselees to read.

Part 4

Interpersonal Issues

16

Interpersonal Relationships

SCOTT IS IN THE stereo business. Until recently, he worked as sales manager for a chain of stores that sells speakers, stereo components, and music systems. Everybody in the company recognized his competence as a salesman. Most months he sold more than anyone else and his commissions and bonuses contributed to a very healthy weekly paycheck.

Scott's customers appreciated his charm, knowledge of stereo products, and willingness to be helpful. He appeared to be genuinely interested in his customers and intent on providing good service.

But Scott didn't get along with people in the company. He was impatient with fellow employees who asked questions and critical when others made mistakes. As sales manager, he insisted on punctuality and would swear at anyone who arrived late, but sometimes he wasn't punctual himself. He insisted that customer credit ratings be rigidly checked and that company rules be followed without deviation, but he broke these same rules often in his own dealings with customers. Whenever he was given instructions by the company owner, he felt an inner anger and an urge to resist. Sometimes he secretly ignored the boss's directives and did things in his own way.

Recently he was fired. There were no suggestions that Scott had been dishonest or incompetent. He was released from his job because of an apparent unwillingness to cooperate and an inability to get along with the people at work.

Scott has always had difficulty getting along with others, especially those in authority. As a young man he clashed continually with his dad, often had conflicts with his teachers, and sometimes reacted to his frustrations by lording it over his younger brother and others whom he could control.

Someone suggested that Scott might profit from counseling, but he has decided to find another job and then work things out on his own. One of his friends thinks that Scott may be afraid of counselors. Does he think they might act like his dad?

Scott is a young man with sales ability, intelligence, good business knowledge, and the potential for building a successful career in retailing. But he can't get along with people unless he can be in control and able to do things in his way. Without some kind of help, he isn't likely to change.

Human beings are social creatures. At the time of creation, God said it was not good for human beings to be alone. He gave Adam a companion, instructed the human race to multiply, and has permitted us to expand into the billions of people who now occupy planet Earth.

Whenever two or more of these people get together, there are interpersonal relations. Sometimes these relationships are smooth, mutually supportive and characterized by clear, concise, and efficient communication. Often, however, interpersonal relations are strained and marked by conflict. Modern men and women take pride in their individualism, independence, and self-determination, but sometimes these traits cut us off from other people and make us more insensitive, lonely, and unable to get along with others. We live in the information age, with its many multimedia and mechanical devices to aid communication and interaction, but we still misunderstand one another, fail to get along, and often feel isolated and alone. Many years ago, psychiatrist Harry Stack Sullivan suggested that all personal growth and healing, as well as all personal damage and regressions, come through relationships with other people. All counseling, and almost all of the issues discussed in this book, deal directly or indirectly with interpersonal relations. How people get along with each other, including how they communicate, must be an issue of crucial concern to all Christian counselors.

THE BIBLE AND INTERPERSONAL RELATIONS

The Bible records a long human history of interpersonal problems and communication breakdowns. Adam and Eve, the first married couple, had a disagreement about the reasons for their sin in the Garden of Eden. Their first two sons had a conflict that led to murder. Then, as its population multiplied, the earth filled with violence.[1] A few years after the flood, the herdsmen of Abram and Lot began fighting, there were family disputes, and a whole succession of wars continued throughout Old Testament history.

Things were not much better in New Testament times. The disciples of Jesus argued among themselves about who would be greatest in heaven.[2] In the early church, Ananias and Sapphira lied to their fellow believers, the Jews and Greeks were at odds with each other, and there were disputes over doctrine.[3] Many times in his letters, the Apostle Paul commented on the disunity of the church and appealed for peace. In his own missionary activities he was involved in conflict,[4] and on one occasion wrote to the Corinthians expressing the fear that if he came to visit he might find "quarreling, jealousy, outbursts of anger, factions, slander, gossip, arrogance," disorder and other evidences of interpersonal tension and sin.[5]

Although the Bible records many examples of dissension, such interpersonal strife is never condoned or overlooked. On the contrary, strife is strongly forbidden, and principles for good interpersonal relations are mentioned frequently. The Book of Proverbs, for example, instructs us to hold our tongues and avoid slander, to tell the truth, to speak gently, to think before we talk, to listen carefully, to resist the temptation to gossip, to avoid flattery, and to trust in God.[6] Unrestrained anger, hasty words, personal pride, dishonesty, envy, the struggle for riches, and a host of other harmful attributes are mentioned as sources of tension. There is no book in the Bible that equals Proverbs in clear, consistent teaching about good relationships between people.

The teaching, however, does occur elsewhere. Much of the Sermon on the Mount concerns interpersonal relations.[7] Throughout his later ministry Jesus taught about conflict resolution and intervened in several disputes.[8] Paul warned Timothy not to be quarrelsome, especially over unimportant things. Other Bible passages offer instructions to live in harmony, to demonstrate love, and to replace bitterness and wrath with kindness, forgiveness, and tender-hearted actions.[9] After a warning against those who cause trouble because they do not control their tongues, James notes that quarrels and conflicts come because of personal lust and envy.[10] Then, in the midst of an exciting list of practical guidelines for living, we read Paul's instructions to avoid revenge, to "not repay anyone evil for evil," and to make every effort to live in peace with everyone.[11] Jesus and the biblical writers were peacemakers who, by their example and exhortation, expected modern believers to be peacemakers as well.[12]

As we ponder the many biblical statements about interpersonal relations, several themes are apparent.

1. *Good Interpersonal Relations Begin with Jesus Christ.* Every Christmas the carols and cards remind us that Jesus Christ is the Prince of Peace.[13] During his ministry he predicted that tension would arise between his followers and their nonbelieving relatives and friends,[14] but he is described as "our peace" who is able to break down interpersonal barriers and the walls of hostility that divide people.[15]

The followers of Jesus have been promised an inner, supernaturally produced peace[16] that gives internal stability, even in times of turmoil and interpersonal tension. Peace with God comes when we confess our sins, ask him to take control of our lives, and expect that he will give us the peace that the Word of God promises. This peace, in turn, should calm us in times of interpersonal dissension.

Why then do Christians so often appear to be in conflict with each other and with nonbelievers? Why do so many of us have trouble getting along?

2. *Good Interpersonal Relations Depend on Personal Traits.* There is nothing wrong with negotiations between individuals in conflict, political factions, protagonists in labor disputes, or between nations. Such efforts at peacemaking often can be helpful, but the Bible puts greater emphasis on the attitudes and characteristics of the persons involved in the disputes.

In his first letter to the Corinthians, Paul appears to divide people into three categories.[17] The first of these are the *nonbelieving people.*[18] There are individual differences, of course, but as a group these people are characterized by sexual immorality, debauchery, involvement in occult practices, hatred, discord, jealousy, uncontrolled anger, selfish ambition, dissensions, factions, envy, and various failures in self control.[19] These people may desire and strive for peace, but their basic alienation from God makes both inner peace and interpersonal peace unattainable. The second group, known as *worldly people,* have committed their lives to Christ, but they have never grown spiritually. They act like nonbelievers and often resort to jealousy and quarreling. Since many church members appear to be in this group, we have the sad spectacle of believers in conflict, sometimes in violent conflict, with their neighbors and with each other. Some of these worldly Christians read the Bible regularly and have a good understanding of theology, but their beliefs mostly are intellectual and seem to have had little influence in their lives and interpersonal relationships. In contrast, *spiritual people,* the third group, are Christians who are yielded to divine control and are seeking to think and live like Christ. Sometimes these people slip into their former worldly ways and actions, but more often their lives show increasing evidence of the "fruits of the Spirit" that involves love, joy, peace, patience, kindness, goodness, faithfulness, gentleness, and self-control.[20]

When people are transformed within, a slow process of change begins in their outward behavior. In time this enables them to build better interpersonal relationships. Christian counselors can remember an important principle: for real peace to be felt within or to occur between individuals, there must first be a peace with God. This comes when individuals commit their lives to Christ, have regular times of worship, prayer, and meditation on God's Word, followed by changed thoughts and actions.

3. *Good Interpersonal Relations Involve Determination, Effort, and Skill.* Good interpersonal relations do not always happen automatically, even among committed Christians. The Bible and psychology agree that good relationships depend on the consistent development and application of skills such as listening carefully, watching, understanding oneself and others, refraining from unkind comments or emotional outbursts, and communicating accurately. All of this is learned; all of it can be taught by a perceptive Christian counselor.

The Causes of Problems in Interpersonal Relations

Why can't people get along with each other? This has been debated for centuries, and the answers are likely to differ from situation to situation. Nevertheless, the causes can be summarized into several categories.

1. *Satanic Involvement.* Satan is described in the Bible as a deceiver and the father of lies, who disguises himself as an angel of light and goes around the earth tempting individuals and looking for people to devour.[21] Although many people deny or laugh away his existence, the devil and his legions are powerful, evil schemers whom Christians are instructed to resist in the name of Jesus Christ.[22]

According to one biblical scholar, the "greed and self-centered ambitions of the nations, the deceptive diplomacy of the political world, the bitter hatred and rivalry in the sphere of commerce, the godless ideologies of the masses of humanity, all spring out of and are fostered by satanic influence."[23] On a more personal level, Satan "takes an informed interest in all Christian relationships and schemes either to bring about their downfall or to pollute them."[24] At the core of interpersonal conflict there is always the subtle and manipulative hand of Satan.

But he is not all powerful. Believers know that God is greater than the forces of satanic evil. They have limited power and ultimately will be defeated,[25] but at present they are permitted to afflict God's people and to bring interpersonal tension and conflict into the world.

2. *Personal Attributes, Attitudes, and Actions.* Perfect people do not exist, even though some individuals are easier to get along with than others. Interpersonal tension often begins and escalates with people whose personality traits, attitudes, perceptions, feelings, mannerisms, and behavior create conflict and distrust. Jesus once was approached by a man who said, "Teacher, tell my brother to divide the inheritance with me." Instead of arbitration, Jesus gave a warning against greed.[26] Apparently the man's family conflict came because of his greedy attitude. At another time, Jesus warned us against finding fault in others when there are even worse faults in ourselves.[27]

The faults that hinder good interpersonal relations include:

- A self-centered need to be noticed, to be in control, to have one's own way, or to have money, prestige, and status.
- A nonforgiving, bitter attitude.
- A tendency to be hypercritical, judgmental, and angry.
- An insecurity that involves feelings of threat, fear of rejection, and a reluctance to trust others.
- Prejudice, often unrecognized or denied.
- An unwillingness or inability to "open up" and share one's feelings and thoughts.
- A failure or unwillingness to recognize individual differences (this is the erroneous idea that not everybody thinks, feels, and sees situations in a similar way).

It would be incorrect to assume that all of these are deliberate attempts to hinder smooth relationships. An unwillingness to forgive, holding grudges, or demands to have one's own way are sinful, but they can be avoided at will and without counseling assistance. In contrast, fear of getting close, innate shyness, or a reluctance to trust others may be ingrained attitudes that are more difficult to change without help from a friend or counselor.

Sometimes, however, people behave in ways that are intended to control others and create tension. Some people have the erroneous belief, for example, that the best way to motivate others is to put people under pressure. This is a tension-producing philosophy that says, "My job is not to get ulcers: my job is to give them!"[28]

One management consultant has noticed that interpersonal problems are more prevalent when difficult people are involved. These people are small in number, but they have a great impact and a large ability to create frustration in others. Difficult people include abrasive personalities who are arrogant, frequently cynical, insensitive, intimidating, and inclined to explode in anger when they don't get their way.[29] Somewhat different are the complainers who find fault with everything but never do anything about their complaints, either because they feel powerless or because they refuse to take responsibility. Some difficult people are silent, unresponsive individuals who are difficult because they say very little and rarely reveal what they are thinking or doing. Other people may be always agreeable and unwilling to offend, but they are difficult to work with because they overcommit themselves and then cannot follow through on their promises. Negative personalities, in contrast, are those who take the pessimistic attitude that whatever you propose won't work, so they refuse to cooperate or try. The know-it-all "experts" tend to be pompous, condescending, verbose, and unwilling to cooperate. Different from these are the indecisive people who never act or make decisions until they can be absolutely sure that a decision is correct. As a result they almost never act.[30] Most counselors have seen these traits in their counselees, colleagues, fellow Christians, or family members. Too often, however, we see these traits in ourselves.

3. *Conflict Patterns.* Conflict involves a struggle that occurs when two or more people have goals that appear to be incompatible, or when they want something that is scarce. Stated somewhat formally, people in conflict "face the problem of reconciling their individual needs for power, success, attainment, and winning with their relationship needs for trust, affection, collective benefits, and mutual growth."[31]

Although conflicts often are destructive and threatening, they also can serve a useful purpose in clarifying goals, unifying a group, and sometimes bringing previously ignored disagreements to a point of discussion and resolution.

Just as people have unique personalities, it appears that individuals and groups also have unique conflict styles that may be very rigid. This in turn contributes to furthering the conflict.[32] Some people throw adult temper tantrums, pouting and stomping away when they are in conflict. Others resort to such diverse approaches as shouting, interrupting frequently, attempting to intimidate or attack the opposition, ignoring the other side, trying to manipulate subtly or openly, attempting to bribe, or pretending to be disinterested in the issue being debated. More helpful are those who approach conflict by using the gentle answer that calms anger,[33] and by facing issues openly and honestly.

When there is conflict the counselor should attempt to discover the real issues involved (these may be different from the issues that are stated). Watch for the personality traits and conflict styles that may be making matters worse.

4. *Lack of Commitment.* Many people, at least in America, appear to be afraid of making commitments.[34] Loyalty to friends, family, church, business associates, and the nation is given only lip service and then discarded when it gets in the way of self-fulfillment or personal advancement.[35] Perhaps because they are too hedonistic, too cautious, or too threatened by commitment, many people refuse to pledge themselves to another person or to some cause. There is an unwillingness to make any pledges, or there is easy abandonment of verbal promises when something more attractive comes along. Many would feel uncomfortable with the words of an anonymous writer who urged us to consider the postage stamp: "Its usefulness consists in its ability to stick to one thing until it gets there."

There can be many reasons for interpersonal tension, but one common cause is an unwillingness to make commitments and to stick with them. Even when people try to avoid commitments they really are committing themselves to something else by default. When we fail to commit ourselves to another person, to some cause, or to God, or when we freely abandon our verbal commitments, then we are really committing ourselves to loneliness, lack of intimacy, personal failure, and a variety of interpersonal tensions or frustrations.

Lack of commitment is not always due to laziness or self-centered values. Sometimes people forget their earlier commitments, get busy with other things, or later question the wisdom of an earlier commitment. At times, commitment is severely shaken when we trust a mate or business partner but discover later that our trust has been violated. One research team suggests that we should not be surprised that "a relationship in which partners have difficulty trusting one another is a relationship in trouble."[36] Commitment is very difficult if there can be no trust.

5. *Communication Failure.* The essence of good interpersonal relations is good communication. When communication is inefficient or in danger of breaking down, interpersonal tensions often follow. But even when two people want to communicate there can be several reasons for failure. At the simplest level a *sender* tries to communicate a message to a *receiver.* This process is hindered if:

- The sender is unclear in his or her own mind about the message (if the sender doesn't think clearly, communication cannot be clear).

- The sender is afraid, ashamed, deceptive, or otherwise reluctant to send a clear message.
- The sender does not put the message into clearly understandable words or gestures.
- The sender says one thing but conveys a different message by behavior (for example, if the sender says "I'm sad" but at the same time is laughing and joking, the message is confused. When we say one thing with our lips but show something else with our actions, we are sending "double messages." These can be powerful hindrances to good communication.[37]
- The sender mumbles, yells, or in other ways distorts the message so it is not sent clearly.
- The sender is afraid, ashamed, unsure, or otherwise reluctant to send a clear message.
- The receiver is unable to understand the message.
- The receiver is distracted from listening, or does not want to listen, perhaps because of disinterest, mistrust, fear of being persuaded, or some other reason.
- The receiver adds his or her interpretation to the message, or misses ideas that are too threatening to hear.

Even when the communication process begins clearly, the receiver responds with facial features, gestures, and verbalizations, often before the whole message is sent. This in turn can interrupt the sender and cause him or her to change the words or tone of the message, even in mid-sentence.

When communicators do not know each other, communication will depend largely on words and widely understood gestures. When the communicators are in intimate contact (like two close friends or a married couple) they know each other so well that much is communicated by facial expression, tone of voice, a half-sentence, or even a grunt. These shortcuts speed up communication, but they also create the potential for misunderstanding. This is because intimates often are inclined to interpret what is being said in terms of past experience rather than concentrate on the message or the messenger.

6. *Social Irritants.* Events or conditions in society can prevent or hinder good interpersonal relations. It appears that tensions are more likely to erupt in crowded, uncomfortable urban areas, than in the more spacious suburbs or rural communities. Prolonged heat waves or inclement weather that forces people to stay indoors can wear down patience and contribute to strife (as any mother of squabbling, housebound young children knows). When there are economic problems in the community, shortages of essential supplies, strikes or layoffs, crime waves, political corruption or unpopular decisions by government officials, even disagreements between neighbors or supporters of rival football teams, the climate is ripe for further disagreements, racial or labor violence, student unrest, church splits, political disruption or even military uprisings, and sometimes war.

On a more personal level, daily hassles, those "irritating, frustrating, distressing demands and troubled relationships that plague us day in and day out,"[38] can wear us down and arouse anger, fear, jealousy, guilt, or other emotions. When there is no opportunity to get away from noise, from the demands of a difficult work setting, or from other people (including the family), tension frequently builds and interpersonal conflict results.[39]

THE EFFECTS OF POOR INTERPERSONAL RELATIONSHIPS

People react differently to interpersonal tension. Some resist it, others avoid it, many feel deeply distressed by it, some are overwhelmed by it, and there are those who appear to thrive on it. Such tension is potentially threatening, however, so we often act in ways that protect ourselves. We hide our true feelings and insecurities, for example, and subtly try to manipulate others or pretend to be something that we are not. All of these tactics take a toll and can influence us physically, psychologically, socially, and spiritually.

The *physical* effects of stress and interpersonal tension are well known. Fatigue, tense muscles, headaches, stomach upsets, ulcers, and a variety of other biological reactions develop especially when tensions are denied or kept hidden. When we try to hide our emotions or interpersonal tensions, wrote one perceptive observer, our stomachs keep score.

Psychologically, poor interpersonal relations can trigger almost every human emotion, and the actions of people in conflict can range from a mild inclination to be uncooperative all the way to murder. When there is tension, individuals sometimes feel depressed, guilty, put down, lacking in self-confidence, and anxious. At times there is anger, bitterness, cynicism, and attempts to dominate, manipulate, or get revenge. When they feel threatened or frustrated in their attempts to get along, people don't always think clearly. As a result things are said or done that are later regretted.

This leads us to the *social* effects of interpersonal stress, including verbal aggression, violence, withdrawal from others, and the breaking of previous relationships. This may be seen, for example, when two business associates abruptly terminate their partnership, a family stomps out of church, an employee quits without notice, a couple decides to separate, or two nations go to war over a minor issue. Actions like these escalate or maintain the conflict, but they rarely solve anything. They may satisfy one's desire for power and revenge, but these are destructive reactions that often lead to suffering, negative attitudes, loneliness, and later feelings of regret.

None of this helps people *spiritually.* In the Garden of Eden, the devil succeeded in creating interpersonal tension between the Creator and his creatures. When they ate the fruit, Adam and Even were alienated from God and soon were in conflict, blaming each other. In a broad sense, therefore, all interpersonal tension is a result and reflection of sin. When they are separated from God or from each other, people cannot mature emotionally and spiritually.

When conflict exists because of the immaturity or self-centered attitudes of individuals, then conflict is wrong and potentially harmful, even though the experience may also stimulate growth.

COUNSELING AND INTERPERSONAL RELATIONS

The prophet Isaiah once wrote about a time in the future when the wolf would live with the lamb, the leopard would lie down alongside the goat, the calf and the lion would feed together, and a little child would lead them.[40] Until then, we all will have to live with at least some interpersonal tension. Social conflict is inevitable in a world filled with deprived people who have limited resources, freedom of choice, and the need to be mutually dependent. According to one University of Michigan researcher,[41] we have a challenge to control escalation among nations and among individuals, so we are kept from destructive personal conflict and international wars.

Getting along with people involves the development of personal characteristics such as self-awareness, kindness, concern, sensitivity, and patience. Good interpersonal relationships also involve skills, including the abilities to listen, communicate, and understand. These effective interpersonal skills do not just appear magically. They are learned, often with help from a sensitive counselor.[42] This help may occur in several areas.

1. *Starting with the Basics.* Love is rarely mentioned in the counseling literature, but it dominates the New Testament. It was love that motivated God to send his son into the world to die for lost human beings. It is love that has been called the greatest of all attributes and a characteristic so crucial to Christianity that it becomes the distinguishing mark of believers.[43]

One goal in counseling is to help people become more loving. In any counseling situation we begin by listening and trying to understand the problem, but the counselor also demonstrates love and sometimes talks about this with the counselee. Try to determine if he or she is a believer. Point out that complete yielding to Christ can change our attitudes and thus our relationships with others. It would be wrong to imply that interpersonal problems disappear automatically when one yields to Christ. Skill acquisition is also important, but interpersonal skills are more effective when the skill user is characterized by a spirit of love, patience, self-control, and the other fruits of the Spirit.

The sensitive Christian counselor also recognizes that satanic involvement is at the basis of interpersonal tension. The devil's power does not yield to counseling techniques unless the helper is strengthened and guided daily by the Holy Spirit, familiar with the Word of God, and consistently praying "for all the saints," including one's counselees.[44]

2. *Changing the Individual.* Since interpersonal conflicts often result from the attributes, attitudes, and abrasive actions of people, there can be value in working to change individuals. Often counselees are unaware of the ways in which their mannerisms and behavior create or escalate interpersonal tension. Sometimes a counselee is quick to see fault in others but much slower to see his or her own weaknesses.[45] It can be helpful, therefore, to gently point out these personal flaws and self-defeating behaviors. Try to give specific examples to support your observations and invite the counselee to respond. At times you may want to encourage your counselee to talk about personal strengths and weaknesses to one or two others (in sharing), to themselves (in self-examination), and especially in honesty to God (in confession).

Change sometimes is stimulated by sharing and making oneself known to at least one significant other person to whom we are accountable, but such sharing can be overdone. We don't encourage counselees to reveal intimate details of their lives indiscriminately or with a variety of people. Yet when counselees share with one or two others, including the counselor, inner tensions can be relieved and individuals often find greater self-understanding. This understanding often leads to behavior changes that in turn contribute to smoother relationships with others. When there is better self-knowledge, there is greater freedom to look to the needs of others and to work at building interpersonal relations.

The Christian counselor knows that the most basic and lasting changes in individuals come from God. For counselees and counselors, a consistent and growing relationship with Jesus Christ can help to break down walls between people, can help them get rid of the bitterness and insensitivity that divide individuals, and can contribute to interpersonal peace and unity.[46]

3. *Modeling Good Relationships.* Some counselees have rarely experienced mutual respect or good relationships with another human being. The counselor-counselee interaction, therefore, can be a model of caring, respect, and positive interaction. So significant is this modeling that a number of counselors believe the caring relationship is basic to counseling effectiveness.[47]

These model relationships will sometimes involve confrontation and discussion of painful topics, but the counselor also seeks to give consistent encouragement. Usually this is only a start in building better relationships, but when people are encouraged by a counselor, they often are better able to work on problems and in time to experience the satisfaction of encouraging others.[48]

4. *Teaching Conflict Resolution.* According to David Augsburger, conflict is natural, normal, neutral, and sometimes even delightful. "It can turn into painful or disastrous ends, but it doesn't need to. . . . It is not the conflicts that need to concern us, but how the conflicts are handled. . . . How we view, approach and work through our differences does—to a large extent—determine our whole life pattern."[49] Augsburger adds that people can be helped to view conflicts as honest differences. These can be resolved by those who are willing to treat each other with respect and to confront each other with truth expressed in loving ways.

Ask counselees to describe specific recent disagreements. What were the issues, who was involved, and how was the conflict handled? What are the differences between conflicts that were handled efficiently and those that were not? Can you see conflict styles evolving? With answers to questions like these, you and your counselee can work on clarifying goals, reconciling differences, and finding ways to resolve conflicts.

(a) Clarifying Goals. When people are in conflict, they often share many of the same goals in spite of their differences. A college faculty, for example, may want quality education but be in conflict over how this is best attained in a curriculum. A husband and wife may both want a good marriage but be in conflict over details of lifestyle, money management, or child raising. Both sides may want to see the conflict resolved in a way that will be mutually agreeable, beneficial to both, and inclined to enhance the relationship so that future communication will improve.

In working with these people, try to discourage bargaining over positions. In theory, position bargaining occurs when each side takes a position, argues for it, and tries to reach a mutually agreeable solution. In practice, each side tends to adopt a rigid position, stubbornly hold to it, and argue. As a result, tempers often flare, compromise is interpreted as weakness or losing face, there is little budging, agreement is slow in coming, and when a solution is reached, there often is a residue of persisting anger.[50] To avoid this, ask disputants to consider what they each really want and whether they have similar goals. When goals are similar, conflict resolution is easier.

Often, however, the two sides have different goals. If a wife wants the marital discord to be mended, but the husband wants a divorce so he can marry his new girlfriend, then conflict resolution is more difficult. Talking about issues such as finances, lifestyle, or contrasting views of religion doesn't help to bring peace because the ultimate goals of the husband and wife are different.

In your counseling, remember that most conflicts involve both issues and relationships. A father and teenage daughter, for example, may argue about the merits of the girl's new boyfriend. That is the issue being debated, but underneath there may be a more pressing relationship question of who has more power in the family: the father or the daughter. The goals of these people may be seen in terms of issues (to reach some conclusion about the boyfriend) or in terms of relationships (to assert and maintain control over the other person). These differences will not always be recognized or stated, so the counselor must observe activities and attitudes in an attempt to determine if the stated goals are the real or most pressing goals.

When goals are identified and clarified, they can be attained, understood, and modified more easily. Sometimes, in counseling, two people first can be reminded of the goals they do share. Then there can be a discussion of differences.

(b) Reconciling Differences. In talking to his disciples, Jesus outlined a procedure for restoring relationships between Christians who are at odds with each other.[51] The principles may not apply to nonbelievers, but they are specific for Christ's followers. In counseling believers, the Christian counselor should encourage counselees to follow these guidelines.

Step one: Take the initiative and go to the person who has wronged you. The New Testament implies that this should be done in person and in private. In making this move, it is best if the person goes with a spirit of humility, with a willingness to listen, with a determination to be nondefensive, and with a desire to forgive.[52]

Step two: Call some witnesses. If the other person will not listen or change, there should be a return visit with one or two witnesses present. These people are to listen, evaluate, determine facts, and presumably try to arbitrate and bring a resolution to the dispute.

Step three: Tell it to the church. If the person who has been visited still refuses to listen, change, or cooperate in resolving the dispute, he or she may be excommunicated.

Does all of this sound old fashioned? Churches today, it seems, prefer to overlook sin in their members, and some Christians joke about the infighting in their churches. Perhaps there are few people today who would be distressed about excommunication. In one recent court case, a church member sued a congregation when they threatened excommunication. The suit charged that the church leaders had exposed the woman's lifestyle and invaded her privacy by telling the church about her immorality.

It is not easy to follow biblical guidelines for interpersonal living. To forgive seventy times seven, to turn the other cheek, to repay evil with good, to pray for those who persecute us—these and other guidelines in Table 16-1 are all difficult to implement in our modern culture.[53] Nevertheless, the believer should seek to follow biblical guidelines, even when they are difficult. Often counselees and

Table 16-1
Some Biblical Guidelines for Interpersonal Relations

DO:

be sympathetic, kind, and loving
(Gal. 5:22; Eph. 4:32; Col. 3:12, 14; 1 Pet. 3:8; 4:8; 1 John 3:11)

be gentle, mild, and tactful
(Gal. 5:23; Eph. 4:2; Col. 3:12; 4:6; 1 Tim. 3:3; Titus 1:8; 3:2; 1 Pet. 3:4)

be humble, meek, deferring to others
(Matt. 5:3–5; John 13:34; Eph. 4:2; Col. 3:12; 1 Pet. 3:8; 5:5)

be generous and willing to give
(Matt. 5:42; 10:42; 25:35–36, 42–43; Mark 12:41–44; Rom. 12:8, 13; 1 Pet. 4:9; 1 John 3:17)

be hospitable without grumbling
(Rom. 12:13; Heb. 13:2; 1 Pet. 4:9; 1 Tim. 3:2)

be self-controlled and temperate
(Gal. 5:23; 1 Tim. 3:2; Titus 1:8; 2:1, 5–6; 1 Pet. 5:8; 2 Pet. 1:6)

be willing to show mercy, even when it is undeserved
(Matt. 5:7; 18:33; Luke 6:36; Rom. 12:8; James 2:13; 3:17)

be a peacemaker, seeking to live in peace with everyone
(Matt. 5:4; Rom. 12:18; Gal. 5:22; 1 Thess. 5:13; 1 Pet. 3:8; 2 Pet. 3:14; James 3:17)

be patient, even when provoked
(1 Cor. 13:4–5, 7; Gal. 5:22; Eph. 4:2; Col. 3:12; 1 Thess. 5:14; 2 Tim. 2:24)

be content, not longing for what we don't have in terms of possessions, happiness, or relationships
(2 Cor. 12:10; Phil. 4:11; 1 Tim. 6:6–8; Heb. 13:5)

be strong, immovable, not wavering in faith
(Matt. 14:29–31; 1 Cor. 15:58; James 1:6–8)

be subject to one another
(Eph. 5:21; 1 Pet. 2:13, 18; 3:1; 5:5)

be forgiving, repeatedly
(Matt. 6:14; 18:21–22; Col. 3:13)

be consistently encouraging and inclined to build up others
(Eph. 4:29; 6:22; 1 Thess. 4:18; 5:11, 14; Heb. 3:13; 10:25)

be truthful, speaking the truth in love
(2 Tim. 2:15; 1 Pet. 2:15; 3:15–16; Eph. 4:15; 2 Cor. 6:7)

be praying, even for those who create problems for us
(Matt. 5:44; Luke 6:28)

DON'T:

be proud or arrogant
(Rom. 12:16; 1 Cor. 13:4; 2 Tim. 3:1–2, 4; Jude 16)

be angry or quick-tempered
(Matt. 5:22; Gal. 5:20, 23; Col. 3:8; 1 Tim. 3:2; Titus 1:7; James 1:19–20)

be selfish, insisting on your own way, self-indulgent
(John 3:14, 16; Rom. 12:10; 15:1–3; 1 Cor. 10:33; Phil. 2:3; 2 Pet. 2:3; Jude 12)

give offense
(1 Cor. 10:32; 2 Cor. 6:3)

swear, call other people names, or use abusive language
(Matt. 5:22; 12:36; Col. 3:8; James 5:12)

judge or point out faults in others
(Matt. 7:1–5; Luke 6:37; Phil. 4:8; Jude 16)

Table 16-1 (*continued*)

DON'T:

try to get even, repaying evil for evil
(Rom. 12:17–20; 1 Thess. 5:15; 1 Pet. 3:9)

gossip
(2 Cor. 12:20; 1 Tim. 6:20; 2 Tim. 2:16, 23; Titus 3:9)

complain or grumble
(John 6:43; 1 Cor. 10:10; 1 Pet. 4:9; James 5:9; Jude 16)

argue, be contentious, belligerent, or strong willed
(2 Tim. 2:24; Titus 3:2; 1 Tim. 3:3)

slander or malign
(2 Cor. 12:20; Eph. 4:31; Col. 3:8; 2 Tim. 3:3; Titus 3:2; 2 Pet. 3:3; Jude 18.)

---

counselors must ponder together what Jesus would do today if he were in the situation facing the counselee.[54]

(c) Resolving Conflicts. When individuals, groups, or nations are in conflict, they have four choices about the direction they will take. They may seek to avoid the conflict, maintain it at its present level, escalate it, or reduce it. As we have seen, people don't always want conflict reduction, and sometimes the participants may decide to go in different directions. One spouse, for example, may want to avoid facing the conflict in hopes that it might go away if it is ignored for a while. The other spouse may want to escalate the conflict, perhaps in an attempt to get power or to get the differences out in the open.

Conflict resolution will often involve the counselor in negotiation and mediation. It may not always be wise to get involved in some other person's conflict even when you are invited to do so. The intervener will feel pressure to take sides, will be required to make quick analytical decisions, and will be responsible for keeping communication open. If you do choose to get involved, as a counselor you should try to:

- Show respect for both parties.
- Understand both positions without openly taking sides.
- Reassure people and give them hope if you feel there is reason to do so.
- Encourage open communication and mutual listening.
- Focus on things that can be changed.
- Try to keep the conflict from escalating (since this can break down communication).
- Summarize the situation and positions frequently.
- Help the counselees find additional help if your mediation does not seem to be effective.

According to one team of negotiators,[55] conflict resolution is most likely to be successful if a four-step method is used.

Step one: Separate the people from the problem. This means treating one another with respect, avoiding all defensive statements, name calling, or character judgments, and giving attention instead to the issues. Each side should attempt to understand the other side's perceptions, fears, insecurities, and desires. Parties should think of themselves as partners in a hard, side-by-side search for a fair agreement advantageous to each.

Step two: Focus on the issues, not the positions. When a nineteen-year-old recently announced to her father that she was planning to buy a motorcycle, he disagreed immediately. Here were two conflicting positions that had potential for considerable family conflict: she said she would get the motorcycle; he said she would not. Some reflection revealed, however, that the real issue was a desire for the daughter to have safe, reliable, inexpensive transportation. When this common issue was identified, and when father and daughter each determined to work on this problem with open minds, they explored various options and reached a compromise (a small car that the father helped finance) without a war in the home. The conflict was resolved because the father and daughter focused on the real issue, transportation, and avoided defending rigid positions.

Step three: Think of various options that might solve the problem. In the beginning there is no attempt to evaluate the options or to arrive at a single solution. Each side makes suggestions in a brainstorming session or two. After a number of creative and perhaps new alternatives have been proposed, then each option can be evaluated.

Step four: Insist on objective criteria. Conflict is less likely to occur if both sides agree beforehand on an objective way to reach a solution. If both sides agree to abide by the results of a coin toss, a judge's ruling, or an appraiser's evaluation, the end results may not be equally satisfying to both parties, but everybody agrees on the solution because it was determined by objective, fair, mutually accepted methods.

Sometimes it will be necessary to break larger issues into smaller parts that can be dealt with one at a time. The counselor will attempt to understand both sides. Although he or she will try to stay objective, the Christian counselor must challenge decisions that are nonbiblical—even if both parties agree to a solution that is not consistent with the Bible's teachings.[56]

5. *Teaching Communication Skills.* Criticism (when one person makes unfavorable, unkind, faultfinding remarks about another) has "caused more unhappiness, shattered more marriages, destroyed more children, discouraged more people, and stopped more progress than any other weapon." This is the opinion of an experienced Christian counselor who, after forty years in his field, recently concluded that the number-one problem of his counselees has been their inability to cope with criticism. Criticism, this counselor adds, looks at what is wrong and then, with bitterness and sarcasm, calls this to the other person's attention.[57]

People who attack others verbally (perhaps that includes all of us at times) are using words to hurt and create tension. For some, the criticism comes because they have never learned to communicate effectively, to speak the truth in love, or to discuss issues honestly and with an attitude of respect. All of us need to be reminded periodically that there are principles for effective communication. Some of these are seen in Table 16-2. When these guidelines are followed consistently, communication and interpersonal relations tend to be smooth, differences are discussed honestly, destructive criticism is avoided, and conflicts can be resolved satisfactorily.

Often, however, people never learn the communication principles, never practice them, forget them in the heat of argument, or choose to cast them aside. The counselor has the responsibility to (a) learn these and similar principles, (b) practice them in his or her own life, (c) model them in talking with counselees,

Table 16-2

Guidelines for Communication*

1. Remember that actions speak louder than words; nonverbal communication usually is more powerful than verbal communication. Avoid double messages in which the verbal and nonverbal messages convey something contradictory.

2. Define what is important and stress it; define what is unimportant and deemphasize or ignore it. Avoid fault finding.

3. Communicate in ways that show respect for the other person's worth as a human being. Avoid statements which begin with the words "You never . . . ."

4. Be clear and specific in your communication. Avoid vagueness.

5. Be realistic and reasonable in your statements. Avoid exaggeration and sentences which begin with the words "You always . . . ."

6. Test all your assumptions verbally by asking if they are accurate. Avoid acting until this is done.

7. Recognize that each event can be seen from different points of view. Avoid assuming that other people see things like you do.

8. Recognize that your family members and close friends are experts on you and your behavior. Avoid the tendency to deny their observations about you—especially if you are not sure.

9. Recognize that disagreement can be a meaningful form of communication. Avoid destructive arguments.

10. Be honest and open about your feelings and viewpoints. Bring up all significant problems even if you are afraid that doing so will disturb another person. Speak the truth in love. Avoid sullen silence.

11. Do not put down and/or manipulate the other person with tactics such as ridicule, interrupting, name-calling, changing the subject, blaming, bugging, sarcasm, criticism, pouting, guilt-inducing, etc. Avoid the one-upmanship game.

12. Be more concerned about how your communication affected others than about what you intended. Avoid getting bitter if you are misunderstood.

13. Accept all feelings and try to understand why others feel and act as they do. Avoid the tendency to say "you shouldn't feel like that."

14. Be tactful, considerate, and courteous. Avoid taking advantage of the other person's feelings.

15. Ask questions and listen carefully. Avoid preaching or lecturing.

16. Do not use excuses. Avoid falling for the excuses of others.

17. Speak kindly, politely, and softly. Avoid nagging, yelling, or whining.

18. Recognize the value of humor and seriousness. Avoid destructive teasing.

*Adapted with permission from Sven Wahlroos, *Family Communication: A Guide to Emotional Health* (New York: Signet-New American Library, 1976).

(d) share them with counselees, and (e) discuss how they could be applied to the counselees' interpersonal relationships.

Look, for example, at the first guideline: *Remember that actions speak louder than words*; nonverbal communication usually is more powerful than verbal communication. Avoid double messages in which the verbal and nonverbal messages convey something contradictory. Ask your counselee to think of a recent specific conflict situation. Did anyone give a contradictory message? How could this have been avoided—and be avoided in the future? As a counselor, look for examples of double messages and point these out to the counselee. Perhaps as an assignment outside of counseling, the counselee could concentrate on avoiding double messages. Discuss this in a later counseling session.

The ability to communicate effectively and nonabrasively is a skill. Like all skills, this one is learned slowly and comes as the result of practice. It starts with some awareness of the communication guidelines summarized in Table 16-2, but true communication involves more than the use of techniques. Real communication, the kind that eases interpersonal tension and builds good relationships, only occurs when there is a genuine willingness to respect, accept, understand, and care for others. Important as they are, communication skills, by themselves, are of limited value without good will and sincerity in the communicators.[58]

6. *Changing the Environment.* Since the environment contributes to interpersonal tension, counselors and counselees should attempt to change stress-producing conditions. Whenever possible, discuss conflict resolution in a quiet, comfortable place, where crowding is minimal and noise is reduced. Some people like to discuss their conflicts in a restaurant while drinking coffee. This can be a nonthreatening, relaxing place except where there is loud music, distracting customers, eavesdroppers at a nearby table, or gaudy decorations. Environment makes a difference, even when we are counseling.

The place where conflicts are discussed can be less important than the environment in which people live. It is not easy to reduce neighborhood noise, eliminate poverty and violence in the street, improve working conditions, create more pleasant home atmospheres, or decrease crowding and other physical discomforts. The counselor, therefore, must have a concern for more than the counseling process. He or she must be committed to the elimination of the social and environmental conditions that stimulate and escalate interpersonal tensions. Each counselor must decide on the extent of this involvement.

Preventing Poor Interpersonal Relationships

Christianity is a religion of relationships. Its founder is the God of love, and love is its most distinguishing characteristic. This is not a sentimental, wishy-washy affection. It is a powerful, sacrificial, giving love that involves the characteristics described in 1 Corinthians 13 and reflects the love of God who sent his son to die for individuals in a sinful world. The church is failing in its duty if it does not preach and practice this love that is so central to the Christian message. Whenever such a message is preached and practiced, interpersonal tensions are reduced.

God has also given some more specific guidelines for showing this love.[59] Much advice is given in the pages of the Bible, and in addition he has allowed us to discover additional principles for getting along and communicating effectively. Interpersonal relationships can improve, and many interpersonal tensions can be prevented when people of all ages are taught and encouraged to practice consistently:

- The biblical teachings about good relationships (see Table 16-1).
- A daily walk with Jesus Christ—a walk characterized by prayer, meditation on Scripture, confession of sin, and a willingness to seek and obey divine leading.

- A self-examination that leads to the removal, with God's help, of bitterness, cynicism, and other personal attitudes or actions that could stimulate dissension.
- An understanding of conflict and a practice of those tactics that reduce conflict.
- The guidelines for effective communication as listed in Table 16-2.
- The reduction, avoidance, or elimination of conflict-producing environmental stress.

This is a major task but one that should be emphasized repeatedly, especially in the church. When Christian leaders, including counselors, are involved in preventing interpersonal tension, they are helping individuals to live in peace and harmony with one another, to avoid destructive conflict, and to experience something of the peace that comes from God.[60]

Conclusions about Interpersonal Relations

Human beings are complex creatures with individual personalities and strong wills. We are crowded on a planet that seems to be overpopulated with individuals whose sinful natures put them at odds with God and with each other. Many of us want to get along with others, but this isn't easy.

Perhaps the Apostle Paul was thinking like this when he wrote the following inspired directive: "If it is possible, as far as it depends on you, live at peace with everyone."[61] These words come near the end of a few paragraphs dealing with practical rules for getting along: love others sincerely, be devoted to one another in brotherly love, honor one another above yourselves, share with others, practice hospitality, live in harmony with others, be willing to associate with people of low position, do not be conceited, do not pay back evil for evil, do what is right in the eyes of everyone.

Surely it is interesting that the instruction to live in peace is preceded by two qualifiers: "If it is possible" and "as far as it depends on you." The first of these implies that sometimes it isn't possible to live in harmony with others. Even so, each person has the responsibility for his or her own attitudes and behavior. As much as it depends on each of us, we are to live in peace. With the help of the Holy Spirit, Christian counselors try to establish such peace, and prevent the strain that is characteristic of so many interpersonal relationships.

SUGGESTIONS FOR FURTHER READING

Bolton, Robert. *People Skills: How to Assert Yourself, Listen to Others, and Resolve Conflicts*. Englewood Cliffs, N.J.: Prentice-Hall, 1979.

Bramson, Robert M. *Coping with Difficult People in Business and in Life*. New York: Ballantine, 1981.*

Diehm, William J. *Criticizing*. Minneapolis: Augsburg, 1986.*

* Books marked with an asterisk (*) are especially suited for counselees to read.

Egan, Gerard. *You and Me: The Skills of Communicating and Relating to Others.* Monterey, Calif.: Brooks/Cole, 1977.

Fenton, Horace L., Jr. *When Christians Clash: How to Prevent and Resolve the Pain of Conflict.* Downers Grove, Ill.: InterVarsity, 1987.*

Fisher, Roger, and William Ury. *Getting to Yes: Negotiating without Giving In.* New York: Penguin, 1981.

Griffin, Em. *Making Friends and Making Them Count.* Downers Grove, Ill.: InterVarsity, 1987.*

Huggett, Joyce. *Creative Conflict: How to Confront and Stay Friends.* Downers Grove, Ill.: InterVarsity, 1984.*

* Books marked with an asterisk (*) are especially suited for counselees to read.

17

Sex Apart from Marriage

PAM'S WEDDING WAS NOT LIKE she had expected. Even as a young girl she had dreamed of a church wedding with lots of fresh flowers, several bridesmaids, a large number of guests, an impressive ceremony, and a big reception.

Never had she assumed that her marriage ceremony would be brief, in a court house, performed by a judge, and with none of her friends present. Never did she expect to be two months pregnant on her wedding day.

Pam grew up in a Christian home, attended church regularly, and accepted the high moral standards that were taught by her parents. In spite of her own behavior, she has never approved of sexual intercourse before marriage, believes that it is sinful for unmarried couples to live and sleep together, and maintains that sex is created by God for its fullest expression within marriage.

When she enrolled as a freshman in a Christian college, her outgoing vivacious personality made her popular with students of both sexes. She never seemed to be lacking in social contacts and she often dated. These dates were fun times that rarely involved much physical contact.

When she and Todd began dating in their junior year, they both fell in love and talked about marriage after graduation. At the beginning their physical involvements were minimal, but as the months passed they became more and more involved with each other. Hugging gave way to massaging each other's bodies. Massage through clothing gave way to massage of each other's genitals. In time, they got "carried away" with passion and had intercourse.

The guilt was intense, but they determined never to have sex again. Todd was unwilling to purchase condoms because they both rationalized that "if we have condoms, we will be more tempted to go ahead." But they went ahead anyway. Soon they were in a vicious cycle of sex, guilt, determination to stop, and more sex. The pregnancy came a few months before their graduation.

Pam and Todd live in a society where nonmarital sex is common, pregnancies are frequent, and abortion is widely accepted. But Pam and her new husband come from families and churches where premarital sex is considered wrong and abortion is not an option. It never occurred to either of them that abortion would be an alternative. They have decided that marriage and child rearing is the most honorable and biblical way to deal with the difficult situation in which they find themselves.

So they are now married, not really ready to become parents, wondering how they will finish college, and struggling with the shame, guilt, and disappointment that have permanently changed their lives.

"Sexuality, like everything else created, has fallen into trouble. We are more vulnerable than ever, living in a society that crowds sexual innuendoes into every available space, whether billboards or office conversations." This conclusion, from a Christianity Today Institute report on human sexuality, gets to the core of a major issue that is not limited to counselors. The whole society is reeling, according to the report. We are burdened by "ruined families, staggered by millions of abortions, and terrified by a sexual epidemic. The wide-eyed promises of the sexual revolution, that all would be well once Victorianism was uprooted, can hardly be made with a straight face anymore." For many, sex no longer is something that may be right or wrong; it is little more than a way for two people to be together. Instead of speaking forcefully and clearly about the issues, evangelical Christians tend to be "sounding an uncertain note on the ethics of sexuality."[1]

Sex apart from marriage is widely accepted in Western society and frequently tolerated within the church. Cohabitation, an unmarried male and female living together with full sexual relationships but with no intention of getting married, is so widespread that hardly anyone criticizes the practice today. Hedonistic philosophy, with its easy acceptance of both premarital and extramarital sexual intercourse, has become a part of the culture's values, reinforced by television, practiced by millions, and criticized by almost no one. Professor Allan Bloom once asked a college class why parents, who once would have criticized their sexually active daughters, now rarely protest even when boyfriends sleep over in their homes. A "very nice, very normal, young woman" responded that premarital sex is not criticized because "it's no big deal."[2]

Sexual intercourse apart from marriage is not the only issue that is "no big deal" for many people today. Homosexuality, a sexual orientation that has been practiced for centuries, recently has increased in prominence as gay liberation groups have become more visible and more active. A controversial government commission report on pornography has drawn attention to the dangers and also the widespread use of pornographic literature and films.[3] Masturbation, probably the most common sexual behavior apart from intercourse, is so prevalent that it hardly concerns sexual researchers, even though the practice brings guilt and anxiety among boys and young men. Then there are the rarer and more pathological forms of sexual expression including exhibitionism, rape, transvestism, bestiality (sex with animals), the sexual exploitation of children, and voyeurism, each of which continues to attract the periodic attention of reporters and psychiatrists.

Has our society become obsessed with sex? It is a central issue in much of television, magazines, advertising, music, literature, theater, movies, art, and popular conversation. It often appears in business, education, politics, and even the church. One would have to be a hermit to avoid the sexually arousing stimuli of contemporary culture. That which God created for enjoyment and intimacy has become perverted—*the* major example of the sin and moral sickness that characterizes modern human beings.

This chapter will limit our discussion to three of the four most common examples of sex outside of marriage: masturbation, premarital sex, and extramarital sex. Homosexuality is considered in chapter 19.

THE BIBLE AND SEX APART FROM MARRIAGE

Most people realize that sex is more than a physical instinct or biological attraction. Sexuality pervades all of life and ranges from mild feelings of pleasure about human relationships, to sensual lovemaking and stimulating orgasms. Sex involves in-depth intimacy and intense communication even in the absence of physical contact. "Sexuality throbs within us as movement toward relationship, intimacy, companionship," writes Lewis Smedes. It is "an exciting desire, sometimes a melancholy longing, to give ourselves in trust to another." It is an urge toward closeness and the expression of a deep personal relationship with someone else.[4]

The Apostle Paul was unmarried and inclined to favor singleness,[5] but this does not mean that he was unfulfilled or nonsexual. He understood lust and the passions of sensuality,[6] but surely he also appreciated his maleness and experienced both intimacy and personal wholeness without physical sex. Within Scripture, sexual intercourse is intended to be confined to marriage. It is true that the Bible does little to define marriage, but sex apart from the marital bond was condemned.[7] The well-known one-night stand of David and Bathsheba is only one illustration of the destructive nature of sex apart from marriage.

When it deviates from God's perfect plans for human beings, sex is destructive. It destroys intimacy and communication, is self-centered, and often expresses a desire to manipulate, control, or hurt another person. The experience is pleasurable; it dulls one's sense of loneliness, temporarily reduces anxiety, and gives a feeling of intimacy. All of this, however, is fleeting, dehumanizing, and ultimately unfulfilling.

Perhaps this is why the biblical writers so soundly condemned fornication (which usually refers to premarital sex), adultery (sexual relations with a person other then one's spouse), and other forms of sex outside of marriage.[8] These are sinful because they deviate from God's plan and commands. While sinful pleasures are enjoyable, the pleasure is only for a "season."[9] Within marriage (as we will see in the next chapter) sexual intercourse is good—created by God for reproduction, intimacy, and pleasure—but sexual abuse is condemned with great vehemence.

Consider, for example, what the Bible says about fornication and adultery. In the New Testament alone, the word "fornication" (*porneia*) occurs thirty-nine times[10] and often refers to general immorality.[11] Although it is used sometimes as a synonym for adultery,[12] the word "fornication" more often means voluntary sexual intercourse by an unmarried person with someone of the opposite sex (that is, premarital sex).[13] The word would include what today is known as casual sex, including sex with a prostitute.[14] In every case, fornication is presented as behavior opposed to the plan and will of God.[15]

"Adultery" is used two ways in the Bible. One meaning refers to idol worship and unfaithfulness to God;[16] the other concerns sexual intercourse by a married person with someone other than one's mate (that is, extramarital sex). In both cases, adultery is forbidden and strongly condemned.[17] Several times in the writings of Paul, lists of sinful behavior are given—lists that include adultery and fornication along with "immorality," "impurity," "sensuality," and "homosexuality."[18] It is significant that the wrath of God will come upon those who engage in such behaviors. Clearly God does not take a light view of sexual intimacies apart from marriage.

What then can we conclude from our discussion thus far?

1. *Sex Was Created by God and Is Good.*[19] This is the place to begin all considerations of sexuality. God created the human race with male and female bodies capable of sexual intimacy including genital orgasm. As with other parts of his creation, God called sexual human beings "very good" and instructed us to "multiply."[20] When the human race fell into sin, God's creation was marred and the potential for unhealthy sexuality came into being. Adam and Eve, who previously were not ashamed of their nakedness, suddenly became self-conscious about their bodies.[21]

2. *Sex Apart from Marriage Involves Sinful Behavior.* This is stated most firmly in 1 Corinthians 6 where sexual sin is described as something that affects the body, the place where the Holy Spirit lives. "The body is not meant for sexual immorality but for the Lord," we read in Scripture. "All other sins a man commits are outside his body, but he who sins sexually sins against his own body." We are implored, therefore to "flee from sexual immorality."[22]

Repeatedly, the Bible warns against the enslaving influence of sexual behavior apart from marriage.[23] There is nothing to even hint that sexually aroused persons are free to engage in sexual intercourse, even if they intend to marry. If you cannot restrain yourself, the Apostle Paul wrote, then get married because it is better to marry than to burn with passion.[24]

This kind of thinking is widely rejected today, even by many within the church. There is evidence that evangelical young people are almost as active sexually as their non-Christian classmates.[25] Many people violate God's laws of sexual behavior and appear to suffer little for their indiscretions, so there seem to be no logical reasons to abstain—especially when everyone else is "doing it" and seems to be getting along fine.[26] Some writers argue that this philosophy contributes to major social problems including the breakdown of the family, the increase in AIDS and other sexually transmitted diseases (STDs), the increase in one-parent families, the upsurge in teenage pregnancies, and the huge number of abortions, to cite the most apparent. Psalm 73 describes the personal end results of ignoring God's laws, and 1 Corinthians 6 would seem to suggest that immoral sex hinders the potential oneness that can come within marriage.

Allan Bloom writes as an educator when he observes that sexual looseness teaches people about the erotic but somehow leaves them "flat souled"—going through life devoid of imagination, with few ideals, afraid of both isolation and detachment, and with no real ability to form lasting commitments.[27]

3. *Sex Apart from Marriage Involves Sinful Thinking.* Some have maintained that no adultery occurs as long as the male does not let his penis enter the female's vagina. Such a legalistic view was challenged by Jesus in the Sermon on the Mount. Anyone who "looks at a woman lustfully has already committed adultery with her in his heart," Christ stated.[28] Clearly adultery, lust, and fornication can all take place in the mind without genital contact at all.

"Lust" is difficult to define accurately. Surely it does *not* refer to normal God-given sexual desires or feelings of attraction toward sexually stimulating people. It seems unlikely that God would give us sexual needs and interests and then condemn these as lust.[29] Lust is sometimes translated "strong desire," and the word is used in a positive and nonsexual sense elsewhere in the Bible.[30] In commenting on mental adultery, perhaps Jesus was referring not to fantasies but to mental desire.

According to one writer,[31] the Lord might have phrased his words in this way: "To want what is wrong sexually is just as evil as to do what is wrong sexually."

In a controversial book, one Christian writer has suggested that sexual fantasies, excitement in the presence of a sexually stimulating person, and even the viewing of sexual pictures is not necessarily lust, unless the excitement leads our minds to imagine or plan sexual involvement with the people we are thinking about.[32] Not all Christians would agree with this opinion. Even when they do not lead to subsequent genital contact, obsessive sexual fantasies can be harmful,[33] especially when the thinking involves fantasies about forbidden acts with specific people. At times, these fantasies can become a substitute for intimacy, especially when the fantasizing person is unable or unwilling to engage in sexual communication with a real person.

Engaging in sex before marriage leaves at least two people abused. Mental lusting primarily influences the one who lusts. According to Jesus, both are wrong.

4. *Sex Apart from Marriage Involves Sinful Talk.* The Bible condemns loose sexual talk. Among Christians there should not be "even a hint of sexual immorality, or of any kind of impurity, or of greed, because these are improper for God's holy people. Nor should there be obscenity, foolish talk or coarse joking, which are out or place. . . ."[34] Dirty language, jokes with sexual connotation, impropriety in terms of one's talk and behavior—all can undermine the Christian's reputation and raise questions about the believer's purity, even when nothing improper occurs. The believer must avoid even the appearance of evil and seek to maintain his or her good reputation.[35] This can quickly be undermined by sinful sexual talk.

5. *Sex Apart from Marriage May Involve Masturbation.* Unlike fornication and adultery, masturbation (the self-stimulation of one's genitals to the point of orgasm) is never mentioned in the Bible. Some have argued that the sin of Onan, described in Genesis 38, is a form of masturbation because he "spilled his semen on the ground." Even a casual reading of the text indicates, however, that Onan's sin involved disobedience to God by refusing to impregnate the wife of his deceased brother.

Is masturbation wrong? According to one survey of evangelical Christians, respondents were divided equally in their answers. Some maintain it is wrong but within recent years an increasing number of leaders have stated publicly that they see no necessary harm in the practice.[36] Even though their views differ, all believers agree that masturbation often is accompanied by lusting thoughts. Such thoughts, as we have seen, are wrong whether or not they are accompanied by genital stimulation.

6. *Sex Apart from Marriage Restricts Freedom.* Many things in this world are possible, but this does not mean that everything is wise. This conclusion is stated at the beginning of one important New Testament treatment of immorality.[37] In this world, everything has a design and function, and we get along best when we stay within these guidelines. A fish, for example, is designed to swim in the sea, and although it is free to jump onto the shore, the results would be tragic. In the same way, the Bible states that the human body is created for sex within marriage. We are most fulfilled when we stay within that divine guideline. We are free, of course, to engage in immorality, but such actions are unwise because they ultimately will have harmful aftereffects. The person who cannot resist sexual temptation is not free. He or she is

caught in the strangling hold of uncontrolled impulses[38] and often has trouble getting free without the help of a counselor.

The Causes of Sex Apart from Marriage

Almost everybody has experienced sex apart from marriage. It is widely agreed, for example, that at some time almost all men and most women masturbate to the point of orgasm. Various researchers have reported a disturbing increase in the number of persons (including Christians and even pastors[39]) who admit that they have been involved in premarital or extramarital sexual intercourse. The production, distribution, and selling of pornographic materials, including sexually explicit movies, is a big business, and various gay rights movements have shown the prevalence of homosexual involvements. There can be a variety of overlapping reasons for sexual behavior apart from marriage including environmental stimulation and internal pressure.[40]

1. *Environmental Stimulation.* Our sex-saturated culture stimulates people to think about sex and encourages us to seek hedonistic physical sexual gratification.

(a) Social Atmosphere. Modern society emphasizes the value of immediate, physical sexual pleasure. Many popular magazines, most films, numerous television programs, many commercial advertisements, and literally thousands of novels seem blatantly designed to arouse and play on our sexual urges and desires. Citizen attempts to clean up the media or reduce pornography are often met with resistance in the form of compelling arguments: "We shouldn't restrict the rights of others to view what they want." "What people see and do in private is their own business." "Although media stimulate sexual (and violent) urges, the media also reflect what most people really want—and are willing to pay for."

This sexually supercharged atmosphere is soaked up by the populace (including Christians) who in turn exude a powerful peer pressure. This is seen with special clarity in the young. At a time when sexual urges are most intense, and the need for peer approval is most pressing, adolescents often succumb to social pressures and enter into sexual encounters in an attempt to find acceptance and status.

Social pressure can also influence adults, including traveling business people, entertainers, speakers (even Christian speakers), and others whose work draws them away from home and repeatedly puts them into secluded motel rooms. Often pornographic materials are available to stimulate the mind and bring sexual arousal. These materials may appear harmless and entertaining, but they distort sexuality and portray sex as no more than a physical activity that dehumanizes and uses other human beings. "The sex of the pornographic trade is too slick, too wonderful, too ecstatic." It creates a make-believe fantasy world that is "genuinely destructive to both true sexuality and true spirituality."[41] It also influences thousands of people and stimulates unhealthy and immoral sexuality.

(b) Sexual Convenience. A newspaper report once described the difficulties faced by Russian couples who want privacy. Cars are scarce, motel rooms are difficult to rent, and apartments are usually crowded with relatives. Such is not the case in Western culture. As mobile people with cars, we can get to private locations easily. As affluent people with money, we can pay for secret lunches and motel rooms. As independent people who have less social and parental surveillance, we can be less anxious about sexual experimentation. As sexually open people with easily obtained contraceptive devices and condoms (which are advertised freely), we can be less worried about AIDS or pregnancy. "Convenient" adultery is becoming more and more accessible to teenagers and adults.

(c) Liberal Values. Sex apart from marriage is no longer a taboo subject. Our generation probably knows more about birth control, sexual intercourse, and masturbation than any previous generation. Cohabitation, mate swapping, unfaithfulness, and similar behaviors are openly discussed and widely tolerated, if not accepted. Sexual restrictions have lessened, sexual standards have loosened, and sexual expectations have become more liberal. Marriage vows are taken less seriously and when the sexual "thrill" is gone or when more attractive potential partners appear, then adultery or divorce are seen as alternatives. For many, loyalty is given only lip service and discarded when it stands in the way of self-fulfillment or self-advancement.[42]

Openness about sex is not necessarily bad, and some Victorian inhibitions are best discarded. Yet the changes in our sexual values have become a stampede to license and licentiousness. These new liberal values are hard for sexually vulnerable people to resist.

(d) Inappropriate Education. Many people, especially young people, enter sexual relationships with inaccurate or inadequate knowledge of the emotional and physical consequences. Novels and films often give a distorted picture of sexual love, and sex education classes teach the facts of biology without the stabilizing influence that comes with knowledge of the principles of morality. For many people the basis of their behavior is the still-prevalent ethic: "if it feels good, do it!"

2. *Internal Pressure.* The environment makes it easier to yield to sexual temptation, but the real source of trouble rests inside the individual's mind. Jesus indicated this clearly during one of his talks with the pious Pharisees. "The things that come out of the mouth come from the heart. . . . For out of the heart come evil thoughts, murder, adultery, sexual immorality."[43] These internal "heart" pressures include the following.

(a) Curiosity. With the present emphasis on sex, it is easy for anyone, married or single, to conclude: "I must be missing something that I'd like to try." Bored or dissatisfied with one's current sexual behavior (or lack of behavior), there is a desire to try something new and different. This increases the likelihood that we will take advantage of sexual opportunities when they become available.

(b) Uncontrolled Fantasy. Many people (one report says about 95 percent of males and 50 percent of females) engage in sexual fantasies.[44] This mental activity is sexually arousing and often occurs before and during intercourse to enrich the sexual experience. Some people fantasize to reduce anxiety about sex, to mentally explore taboo acts that they would not consider trying in real life, or to add sensual stimulation to a life that has little sexual excitement otherwise. Research evidence shows that some individuals are more aroused by fantasizing a sexual event than by viewing erotic pictures or reading pornographic materials.[45] Since nobody else can see what we fantasize or even knows if and when we have sexual fantasies, this mental sexuality often continues unchecked in the mind. When this fantasy is frequent and lustful, there is more likelihood that overt sexual acts will occur if and when the opportunity presents itself.

(c) The Search for Identity and Self-Esteem. Many people feel inferior, insignificant, insecure, and lacking in any real life purpose. On a partially unconscious level, some view sex apart from marriage as a way to be accepted, to prove oneself, to feel needed, and to bolster self-esteem. Many middle-aged and older people, fearing a loss of virility and attractiveness, have an affair in an attempt to convince themselves that they are still desirable sexually. Masturbation, accompanied by fantasies of sexual exploits, can give a passing feeling of self-acceptance and sexual capability, without the risks of real intimacy with another person. Regrettably, the transitory nature of such sexual behaviors often leaves the participants feeling more rejected and self-condemning than before. As a result, some run from relationship to relationship in an attempt to fill the emptiness and find a more stable self-identity.

(d) The Search for Intimacy and Closeness. As we have seen, sexuality involves more than genital contact. It can involve deep communication, acceptance, and sincere love. When people feel lonely, unwanted, unloved, and emotionally deprived, they often seek intimacy, tenderness, excitement, and fulfillment in sexual relationships apart from marriage.

(e) Escape or Rebellion. Sexual behavior, including masturbation, sometimes can be a way to escape boredom, relieve tension, and temporarily avoid the pressures of life. At other times, sexual behavior is an indication of rebellion against parental or church authority, a declaration of independence from one's past, or an expression of anger and defiance against one's mate or some other person.

(f) Distorted Thinking. It is easier to document the prevalence of sexual deviation than to uncover its causes. Past learning about sex, failures in earlier sexual encounters, fears that one is "different," neurotic and psychotic misperceptions, failure to anticipate the consequences of one's actions, an unconscious desire to be caught and punished, excessive daring and risk taking are among the many reasons people involve themselves in perverse sexual activities.

(g) Satanic Influence. Scripture states that Christians are in a spiritual battle against the forces of evil and the "devil's schemes."[46] Satan is alert and very wise. By masquerading as an "angel of light,"[47] he "prowls around" trying to devour and lead people into darkness. Since many people appear to be vulnerable in the area of sexual temptation, it is here that the attack often comes, and it is here that many fall. In a desire to be sexually liberated and free of hang-ups, we allow ourselves to enter potentially disastrous, compromising situations. Even Christians fail at times to rely on the protective power of the Holy Spirit. Satan is successful because believers try to fight the battle alone, failing to appreciate the truth of 1 John 4:4: "the one who is in you is greater than the one who is in the world." It is the Holy Spirit within believers who alone can give us power to resist satanic influences.

The Effects of Sex Outside of Marriage

It is impossible to understand or adequately describe the effects of sex apart from marriage. Much of this sexual activity is sin, and, according to the Bible, all sin that is not forgiven will be punished in a time of future judgment. The effects of sin, however, often come much sooner. For a while there is pleasure, but the harmful influences of nonmarital sex quickly become apparent to many people.

It would be inaccurate to imply, however, that sex outside of marriage always (or even frequently) leads to immediate guilt and remorse. A perusal of research in this area[48] indicates that many people report little or no guilt following nonmarital sex, especially if the participants feel a genuine affection for each other. As sex apart from marriage continues, initial qualms and insecurities often disappear.

A lack of remorse does not make such sexual activity morally right. Sometimes people develop an attitude that is hardened to biblical teaching and unable to sense inner promptings from the Holy Spirit.[49] In time, these people, some of whom may be highly respected and educated members of the church and society, "do not think it worthwhile to retain the knowledge of God," so he leaves them to their lust, sexual impurity, depraved minds, degrading behavior, and tendency to "not only continue to do these very things but also approve of those who practice them."[50]

The Christian counselor cannot ignore these biblical statements. The modern world, having rejected biblical teaching, largely is insensitive to the ultimate dangers and harms of the debauchery in which we live. Like the proverbial frog in the water pot whose temperature rises slowly as the surrounding water approaches the boiling point, many people are blithely unaware of the consequences of their attitudes or behavior until it is too late to jump.

Sex apart from marriage has the potential to cause harm in several areas.

1. *Emotional Effects.* Emotional turmoil, guilt, jealousy, fear, anxiety, insecurity, self-condemnation, anger, and depression are among the reactions that have been known to follow sexual behavior apart from marriage. Widespread belief in the benefits of sexual "freedom" may entice many people into what one psychiatrist has called a "freedom that enslaves."[51]

2. *Interpersonal Effects.* How does nonmarital sex (including masturbation and heavy petting) influence one's dating, family, marriage, and other relationships? To some extent the answer may depend on one's sex, educational level, attitudes, and ethnic group.[52] The so-called double standard that tolerates sexual looseness in men but not in women seems to be disappearing, but it is still strong in some levels and segments of society. Although there is some evidence that premarital and extramarital sex often do not influence marriages adversely,[53] there are many examples of situations in which marriages have disintegrated, careers and ministries have been wrecked, families have broken up, and personal relationships have been destroyed because of nonmarital sexual actions.

3. *Spiritual Effects.* As we have seen, fornication, adultery, lust, and other forms of nonmarital sex are condemned in Scripture and described as sin. The Christian is obligated to forsake sin and follow the teachings of Christ. Attempting to maintain a Christian witness while engaging in sinful sexual practices is a contradiction. If the sexual immorality continues, one's spiritual vitality and influence are certain to decline. Sin must be confessed and forsaken if one is to expect spiritual growth and avoid spiritual stagnation.

4. *Physical Effects.* It is well known that sex apart from marriage increases the prospects of illegitimate pregnancies, venereal disease, and AIDS—all of which are currently increasing at an alarming rate. There is also evidence that sexual intercourse within marriage is influenced by nonmarital sex. Some popular viewpoints maintain that the influence is usually good, others say the effects are neutral, some say the influence is harmful, and each view has research evidence to support its claim. The Christian counselor is convinced of the biblical teaching about the ultimate harmfulness of nonmarital sex. This harmfulness is most apparent when guilt, mistrust, emotional involvements in other relationships, comparisons with other

partners, anger, anxiety, or insecurity are brought to the marriage bed. In these circumstances, or when at least one partner finds major sexual fulfillment apart from marriage, it is difficult for a married couple to attain maximum physical satisfaction and sexual fulfillment.

As sexual standards continue to change, and especially as the AIDS epidemic gallops unchecked, it is probable that the debate will continue about the effects of sex apart from marriage. It is difficult for any researcher, writer, or counselor to maintain neutrality in evaluating such a sensitive and important issue as nonmarital sex. The Christian counselor should recognize that our ultimate authority is not scientific data, cultural mores, or the opinions of some respected leader or communicator. The Christian's ultimate authority is the Bible, God's Word. Scripture affirms what our own experiences show us; namely, the "real world of sexuality is very unlike *Playboy*: it includes tragedy, loss, and aloneness along with comedy, pleasure, and triumph. Vulnerable people need wisdom."[54]

Counseling and Sex Apart from Marriage

Sexual problems can have a variety of causes, including a lack of accurate information, unconscious avoidance of healthy sexuality, anxiety about sex, past traumatic experiences, or interpersonal tension between partners. Understanding the cause of one's problems or reading about healthy sexuality may bring some relief, but problems often remain unsolved until there are attitude and behavioral changes. Sometimes these only come with the help of a counselor whose goals might include the following.

1. *Look at Your Own Attitudes and Actions.* Someone has defined counseling as a relationship between two anxious people. Perhaps this is never more true than with sexual counseling. When counselors are embarrassed, ill at ease, and uncertain about how to proceed, they tend to express shock, discomfort, or a tendency to provide pat answers that may do nothing to help anxious, searching counselees. Some clinical evidence suggests that counselors tend to be more harsh and condemning when they are guilty of the same thoughts and behavior that bring their counselees for help.

Like everyone else, the Christian counselor is open to temptation and sexual arousal, especially when counselees talk in detail about their own sexual experiences and struggles. Each of us must seek to maintain a close personal walk with God, an accountability relationship with some other Christian, and sexual purity in our own lives. This enables us to show an understanding and compassionate attitude that acknowledges the reality of sin, the lure of temptation, and the healing power of forgiveness. To be outraged, embarrassed, vindictive, condemning, or ill-informed does nothing to help. Instead these attitudes can alienate the counselee when help is most needed. Even worse, a nonunderstanding counselor can batter self-esteem and communicate hopelessness. This in turn creates despair and sometimes pushes the counselee back into further immorality.

When we hear about sexual involvement apart from marriage, it is easy to feel angry or threatened. Showing a realistic, understanding attitude is difficult, especially if we know the individuals involved. The counselor needs divine help if he or she is to show love without compromising our biblical standards, compassion without denying reality, and directness without becoming vindictive. If sexual counseling is too threatening or too difficult, we must evaluate our attitudes (perhaps with the help of another counselor) and possibly avoid this kind of counseling, at least until our attitudes change.

2. *Listen with Sensitivity.* This is a basic starting point for all counseling, but it sometimes is forgotten when we hear about sexual issues. If we excessively exalt or trivialize sexuality, we convey the impression that sexual difficulties, including sexual sins, are somehow in a class by themselves and fundamentally different from other human problems.[55] In contrast, when we listen, we show a willingness to understand another human being's distress, and we convey a desire to help with the counselee's real problem. It is appropriate to ask clarifying questions, providing that these are intended to increase understanding and not meant to satisfy our own curiosity. Try to avoid giving advice, preaching, expressing opinions, or even quoting Scripture, at least until you have a clear perspective on the problem.

One sex counselor suggests that you should expect not to be surprised at anything.[56] At times, for example, you may hear about the sexual exploits of some person who is respected, even in the church. Initially this may come as a shock, but instead of reacting with anger or gossip, try to determine whether this information is important for helping your counselee and whether there is a need to verify if the information is correct. With a tinge of humor in his voice, a military chaplain once told me that he believes nothing that he hears and only about half of what he sees. Maybe this is a good guideline. Sometimes counselees and other informers will make allegations that are completely or partially untrue. In your mind, and with the counselee, try to explore why the counselee may be passing on the information that you are hearing.

3. *Examine Counselee Attitudes.* As we listen, we can begin to understand the counselee's values and attitudes toward sex. Such attitudes can greatly influence sexual behavior. As a counselor you will discover that values and attitudes often have to be changed before behavior will be different.

Be alert also to the counselee's knowledge about sex. Misinformation and misunderstanding frequently contribute to attitudes and sexual behavior that the counselee later regrets.

4. *Consider Counseling Goals.* My first counseling job was in a university counseling center. A few days after I began work, a female student came to my office and asked for my help in "finding somebody to go to bed with." The counselee's goals were clear—and clearly in conflict with *my* values. When you counsel in the area of human sexuality, try to determine what the counselee wants to accomplish. If this is not done, counseling may flounder because you have one set of goals (for example, helping the counselee avoid immoral sexual behavior apart from marriage), and the counselee may have another (such as reducing guilt over sexual behavior that he or she plans to continue). When goals are different, this should be discussed. The Christian counselor cannot work to help others pursue goals that are antibiblical and thus ultimately harmful to the counselee.

5. *Help with Practical Issues.* Counseling is always most effective when it deals with specifics. Sometimes counselees need support and practical suggestions for resisting sexual approaches, fleeing temptation,[57] terminating sexual relationships, or informing a mate or parents about illicit sex or an illegitimate pregnancy. It may also

be helpful for counselees to discuss their feelings about masturbation, premarital or extramarital intercourse, homosexuality, abortion, or related issues. Once again it is not helpful to give advice too quickly, but neither is it helpful to maintain a consistent nondirective approach that offers little practical guidance and ignores the clear teachings of the Bible.

In dealing with practical issues, remember that people always respond best when the desire and motivation to change come from within. Instead of telling counselees what to do, encourage them to think of different courses of action that might work. Point out the dangers or problems that counselees might not see, and encourage commitment to one of the alternatives that does not violate biblical teaching. If such action fails to resolve or reduce the problem, help the counselee find another biblically appropriate alternative and give guidance, support, and encouragement until the situation improves.

6. *Help Counselees Find Forgiveness.* At the heart of the Christian message is the issue of forgiveness. Because God forgives, we have freedom from guilt, abundant life on earth, and eternal life in heaven.[58] It is inconsistent and confusing to talk about forgiveness but never show it. As believers, we experience God's forgiveness, but we are expected to forgive others.[59] If Christian counselors model forgiveness, we help others forgive people who have participated in sexual acts apart from marriage, and we encourage counselees to forgive themselves, just as God and the counselor forgive.

In past decades, church members tended to be too condemning and not much inclined to forgive. Have we now gone in the opposite direction so that we forgive freely and with such ease that there is no spirit of repentance and no determination to change? When Jesus talked with the woman who had been caught in adultery, the theologians of his day were inclined to condemn. Jesus, in contrast, forgave the woman, but he followed this with a concise directive: "Go now and leave your life of sin."[60] Forgiveness doesn't mean much if the sinner has no desire to follow this with obedience and changed behavior.

7. *Stimulate Sound Attitudes, Christian Behavior, and the Securing of Accurate Information.* Christian counseling often is a specialized form of Christian education. At times the counselor must give accurate information or know where such information can be found.[61] Many counselees also need help in learning self-control, evaluating current sexual standards, forming a personal set of values that is consistent with biblical truth, determining appropriate dating behavior, evaluating the moral issues surrounding masturbation, and understanding biblical teachings on sex. Often these can be discussed openly, especially if counselees are encouraged to ask questions that are answered candidly and without shock or condemnation. Often the counselor's behavior and general comments will model an accurate and consistent picture of sex as God intended.

8. *Be Alert to the Need for Referral.* At times every counselor faces situations in which referral to another counselor would be most helpful for the counselee. Referral should be considered when counselees appear to have more complicated sexual problems than the counselor can handle, when sexual problems are accompanied by intense anxiety or depression, when there is great guilt or self-condemnation, when there is extremely disturbed behavior and thinking in the counselee, when sexual perversions are involved, when counselees need detailed sexual information that the counselor is unable to provide, when you suspect physiological disease or

malfunctioning, or when the counselor feels a strong and/or persisting sexual attraction to the counselee. In situations like these the counselor must decide whether to continue counseling, to terminate the relationship, or to make a referral. Remember that referral can be threatening to many people. These individuals need to be shown that referral is common, is not an indication of rejection by the present counselor, and ultimately is for the greatest benefit of the counselee.

Preventing Sex Apart from Marriage

While fornication, adultery, lust, and other forms of immorality clearly violate scriptural teaching, it should be emphasized that not all sexual behavior apart from marriage is wrong. Dating, for example, is sexual activity that we do not want to prevent, although the Christian counselor does want to help people avoid the immorality that sometimes comes with dating relationships.

Prevention of immoral sexual behavior can focus on three overlapping goals.

1. *Providing Sex Education.* Where should people learn about sex? Most educators and parents would agree that sex education should occur at home, and many agree that sex education can be taught in the schools. What role should the church play in this educational process?

The church can influence sex education in two ways: *indirectly,* by encouraging and instructing parents about what to teach at home, and *directly* through sermons, classes, discussion groups, and retreats. This teaching must involve giving factual information, but of equal importance is teaching biblically based principles of morality. This teaching must be honest, practical, and in good taste. To be sure it is accurate, do not hesitate to bring in resource persons such as a physician or psychologist who can give specialized information. To ensure the relevance of this information, encourage honest questioning and try to avoid pat answers. Written questions submitted anonymously can be one way to uncover real issues. For some, there is value in recommending books, including those listed at the end of this chapter.[62]

Perhaps there was a time when young people were naive about sex and unfamiliar with the facts of life. Today this is no longer true. According to theologian Kenneth Kantzer, the furor over whether sex ought to be taught in the public schools tends to overlook one fact: sex already is being taught to youngsters through the wide distribution of pornography.[63] While making no mention of pornography, some public schools have distributed contraceptives to students in an attempt to reduce teen pregnancies. The public reaction has been predictable.

The idea that people must be given contraceptives because they are not responsible or not capable of controlling their appetites is "simply lunatic," writes one commentator in a secular paper. People are expected to diet, to exercise, to stop smoking, and to be self-disciplined about the ways in which they live, but "only sexual gratification seems to have been granted a sacrosanct status for continued limitless indulgence—with, of course, the help of the condom."[64] Perhaps it is surprising that some young people are returning to an old birth-control method: abstinence. The church should be actively involved in helping young people say no to immoral sex.[65]

2. *Helping People Decide about Practical Issues.* Although issues such as premarital and extramarital sex are clearly discussed in the Bible, other practical sexual issues are not even mentioned. Let us consider two of these.

(a) Dating and Petting. Dating has changed radically in the past several decades. Chaperones are a thing of the past and so, for many people, are dates without heavy petting or sexual intimacies.

Dating, the relationship between two people of the opposite sex, provides mutual human companionship, better understanding of the opposite sex, greater self-understanding, sexual stimulation, and some sexual fulfillment. The rules and practices of dating vary geographically and change frequently. Often dating involves little physical contact except for periodic touching that conveys concern, interest, compassion, empathy, and affection. In many cases, however, touch is much more sensual in nature and intended to bring sexual arousal.

The term "petting" refers to sexual touching that does not involve intercourse. Petting may involve little more than hugging and kissing, but often it refers to conscious mutual physical stimulation and exploration designed to bring erotic arousal through the fondling of sexually excitable areas of the body. Considerable debate and confusion surround the issue of petting. For those who see no harm in nonmarital sex, petting is no problem. If it leads to sexual intercourse—as it often does—this is acceptable to the parties involved.

What should be the attitude and behavior of couples who believe that intercourse should be confined to marriage? Can there be "responsible" petting that expresses intimacy and exists for mutual discovery and sexual gratification apart from intercourse?[66] Some Christians say no and argue for abstinence, but most single Christians seem to show by their actions that their answer is yes. The church often gives no guidance in this significant area of prevention.

There are no easy answers to questions about dating and petting, but several preventive guidelines can be helpful:[67]

- Sexual attractiveness and sexual feelings have been created by God and should be considered good, not sinful.
- All persons, male and female, are created in God's image and each should be respected. To use another person is to violate his or her personality by making that person an object.
- God intends his people to live holy lives. Whatever they do should be done to the glory of God.[68]
- Christians must respect God's directions for expressing sexuality. The Bible warns against the misuse of sex;[69] sexual sin is anything done contrary to the revealed Word of God.
- From God's perspective, the only proper place for sexual intercourse is within the context of a mutual, lifelong commitment of a man and woman, in the form of marriage. God has our best interests in view when he commands us to wait for intercourse until we are married.
- Petting is a common activity among people who are not married to each other. Unlike foreplay, which is a tender preparation for sexual intercourse, petting is a tender exploration of one another by two people who do not intend to have intercourse.
- Petting has many risks, spiritual and psychological. One of the adverse effects of heavy petting is illustrated by the law of diminishing returns; the principle that with constant repetition over a period of time, the effect of a

stimulus on an individual tends to decrease. To keep the same effect, the stimulation must be increased. Petting is a physical stimulation that conforms to this law. After reaching a certain point of intimacy, a couple almost always finds that retreat to less intimate involvement is difficult. In contrast, petting creates the desire for more intimate sexual union. In advanced stages, petting is especially difficult to stop and may result in frustration, tenseness, irritability, and decreasing self-control.
- God, through his Holy Spirit, is the source of personal, practical power to help us guide and control our sexuality. Sex need not be a drive that enslaves, but it is an appetite we can feed, sometimes illicitly. For those who seek his help, God will cleanse us on a moment-by-moment basis to keep us from wrong attitudes and actions.[70]

These are preventive principles that the church can communicate, sometimes in public presentations, followed by discussion.

(b) Masturbation. The stimulation of one's own genitals to the point of orgasm is a very common form of sexual arousal apart from marriage—especially in males. The frequency of masturbation declines following adolescence and marriage, but it does not disappear. Apparently many married men and some married women continue to masturbate at times throughout their lives, and regular church attenders masturbate as frequently as nonattenders.[71]

There is no medical evidence to indicate that the practice is harmful to the body or that it interferes physically with subsequent sexual intercourse. In one survey of evangelicals, 31 percent of laypeople and 30 percent of pastors considered masturbation to be wrong, 32 percent of the laypeople and 35 percent of pastors said it was not wrong, and the remainder said it depends on circumstances.[72] Probably most would agree that masturbation is not wrong when, for example, a man masturbates when his wife is ill or recovering from a pregnancy or when a couple cannot have sexual intercourse because the husband is away on a business trip. Is masturbation wrong when practiced by a single college or seminary student whose sex drive is intense and who seeks to keep from engaging in nonmarital sexual intercourse? Masturbation often is accompanied by feelings of guilt, frustration, or self-condemnation. Many feel angry and discouraged because of its compulsive grip. In spite of a greater willingness to discuss the topic, it remains steeped in controversy, especially in Christian circles. There are numerous arguments against and some in favor of masturbation, but many of these are controversial and of questionable validity.[73]

How then does the church speak to what surely is the most universally practiced form of sexual behavior apart from sexual intercourse? It is difficult for Christian counselors to prevent the start, continuance, or increase of masturbation, but the following observations could be helpful if shared in small, same-sex groups.

- Masturbation is very common and of no harm physically.
- Masturbation is never mentioned in the Bible. This does not make it right, and theologians know that arguments from silence are weak. Nevertheless, when we consider the range of sexual behavior that is discussed in Scripture—homosexuality, bestiality, adultery, prostitution, rape, transsexuality, incest—it is difficult to think that masturbation is left out by accident. Clearly

masturbation does not seem to be one of God's great concerns; his Word says more about the mistreatment of animals.[74] We must be careful not to harshly condemn something that the Bible does not condemn.

- Masturbation can be helpful in relieving sexual or other tensions, and it is a substitute for sexual intercourse apart from marriage. Many singles and married people away from their spouses masturbate as sexual release.
- Christian counselors differ in their views of masturbation. It has been called "sin," "a gift from God," and an issue that is minor on God's list of priorities. Many would agree with J. Herbert Miles who argues that a "rigid condemnation of all masturbation as being sinful is rather arbitrary, unrealistic, and out of harmony with the creative plan of God." Instead Miles argues that an individual may "practice, without being sinful, a *limited, temporary program of masturbation*" for purposes of self-control.[75]
- Although it causes no known physical harm, masturbation can be harmful in other ways, especially if it becomes compulsive, excessive, or a way to retreat from contacts with others. It can increase self-centeredness, lower self-esteem, produce intense guilt, and both stimulate and be stimulated by sinful lust.
- Masturbators should understand the biblical perspective on sex and marriage. Masturbation clearly is a substitute activity.
- Masturbation is rarely stopped solely by a determination to quit. This focuses attention on the issue, sometimes increases anxiety, and makes failure more incriminating.
- Masturbation can be reduced by prayer, a sincere willingness to let the Holy Spirit control, an accountability relationship with some other Christian who prays and to whom one gives regular reports about masturbation activity. It also can help to keep busy, especially with activities that involve contact with others, to avoid sexually arousing materials (such as erotic movies or novels), and to resist the temptation to dwell on sexual fantasies.

Any person who teaches (or writes) about masturbation is likely to be criticized. In the absence of clear biblical guidance on this issue, we are left with a variety of conflicting opinions, often given by sincere, compassionate counselors whose views we should understand and respect. Surely masturbation is a sin when it is accompanied by a lusting for sexual relationships that God forbids, when it masters us, and when it hinders one's relationship with God. Masturbators need to know that God helps and forgives, and that open communication about masturbation helps to diffuse its destructive impact. For most people it will be replaced in time by more fulfilling sexuality within marriage.

3. *Providing Realistic Alternatives.* As we have seen, sex concerns more than genital stimulation. It includes issues of intimacy, communication, and interpersonal relationships. Like all topics discussed in this book, sex is best considered in the context of a caring, supportive Christian community. It is here that people can feel accepted and loved. Within the Christian community healthy and meaningful activities can be provided especially for young people and those adults who otherwise might find themselves bored, lonely, or lured into morally dangerous situations. The church should be a place where problems and questions can be discussed, where

values and sexual ethics can be formulated through counseling or group interaction, and where opportunities can exist for dating other believers.

Conclusions about Sex Apart from Marriage

At times every Christian counselor faces conflict between social pressure and the Bible, or between scientific data and Scripture. What does one do in such situations?

It is helpful, first, to examine the scientific, social, and scriptural data to see if the conflict can be resolved. Perhaps most of us would agree that the wisdom of this world, if it *really* is true, cannot be in conflict with the truth that comes through written revelation. If conflict persists, many Christians, including the author of this book, would agree that the Word of God must be accepted as the final authority to which other findings must be submitted.

This is not a popular view, but it raises questions that must be considered whenever sex outside of marriage is discussed. Society's values and some scientific data are in conflict with biblical teachings. Where then do we find principles that will guide our counseling and our own moral behavior? The Bible isn't always explicit on these issues, but the Christian people helper sees the Word of God as the only source of stability and certainty on morals. This then must be our guide in all counseling, not just in our dealing with issues of sex apart from marriage.

Suggestions for Further Reading

Mayo, Mary Ann. *A Christian Guide to Sexual Counseling.* Grand Rapids, Mich.: Zondervan, 1987.

McDowell, Josh. *What I Wish My Parents Knew about My Sexuality.* San Bernardino, Calif.: Here's Life Publishers, 1987.*

Miles, Herbert J. *Sexual Understanding before Marriage.* Grand Rapids, Mich.: Zondervan, 1971.*

Mylander, Charles M. *Running the Red Lights: Putting the Brakes on Sexual Temptation.* Ventura, Calif.: Regal, 1986.*

Penner, Clifford, and Joyce Penner. *A Gift for All Ages: A Family Handbook on Sexuality.* Waco, Tex.: Word, 1985.*

Smedes, Lewis B. *Sex for Christians.* Grand Rapids, Mich.: William B. Eerdmans, 1976.*

Trobisch, Walter, and Ingrid Trobisch. *My Beautiful Feeling.* Downers Grove, Ill.: InterVarsity Press, 1976.*

White, John. *Eros Defiled: The Christian and Sexual Sin.* Downers Grove, Ill.: InterVarsity Press, 1977.*

Wilson, Earl D. *Sexual Sanity: Breaking Free from Uncontrolled Habits.* Downers Grove, Ill.: InterVarsity Press, 1984.*

Zimbelman, Ernie. *Human Sexuality and Evangelical Christians.* Lanham, Md.: University of America Press, 1985.

* Books marked with an asterisk (*) are especially suited for counselees to read.

18

Sex within Marriage

BEFORE THEY WERE MARRIED, almost twelve years ago, Steve and Linda had petted heavily (to the point of orgasm), but they had never had sexual intercourse and neither had they undressed in each other's presence. They approached their wedding night as virgins and with great anticipation for their sexual relationship as husband and wife.

At first, they both felt a little awkward, perhaps even embarrassed. A little Vaseline helped in those early days when penetration was difficult, but soon this was no longer needed, and the newlyweds were finding increasing physical and emotional satisfaction in their love-making activities. Each tried to meet the other's needs, and there were frequent opportunities to enjoy sex without any need to hurry.

The twins arrived about a year later. Suddenly life was different, and the hectic pace of parenthood was complicated by Steve's increasing responsibilities in his business. Sex became less frequent and sometimes was interrupted by crying babies. At times, both husband and wife used the not-tonight-I'm-too-tired reasoning. Sometimes two weeks would pass with no intercourse. Steve rediscovered masturbation and occasionally would purchase a "men's" magazine to stimulate his fantasies while he stimulated himself sexually. As months and then years passed, intercourse became less frequent, more routine, and less fulfilling. One night the couple's love making was interrupted by one of the twins who had awakened and entered the parents' room to ask naively what they were doing. After that, Steve and Linda were even more inhibited about sex, lest they awaken the children. An occasional night away gave them a break, but Steve discovered that he ejaculated too quickly and then his penis went limp, leaving Linda feeling frustrated and unfulfilled.

Life, it seemed, had become hectic and filled with activity, including church work. Steve served on the deacon board, and one weekend he represented the church at a conference in another city. When one of the conference participants suggested dinner together, Steve agreed and a couple of hours later the conversation had shifted to sexual topics and talk about skipping the evening meeting and going to a motel.

"Suddenly I was jolted into what I was planning," Steve reported later. "It went against everything I believed." Feeling sexually aroused like he had not felt for several years, he was beginning to think of reasons to justify sexual intercourse with another participant at a church conference.

It didn't happen, but the conference experience alerted Steve to his sexual vulnerability and to the lack of sexual satisfaction within his own marriage. Steve decided to tell Linda about his near fall. They decided to seek counseling for their increasingly strained marriage relationship and, as a part of the counseling, they were helped to deal with their sexual problems. Together they learned how to enjoy each other again, they practiced exercises to deal with the ejaculation problem, and the sexual fulfillment that once was so central in their marriage returned with even greater intensity. Sex, they discovered, did not have to be abandoned as they grew older or got busier, and neither was it necessary to look for fulfillment in masturbation, pornography, or immoral relationships with someone outside of the marriage.

Sex has been described as only one strand in the cable that ties a husband and wife together, but sex is a central strand that is tied intimately with other aspects of the relationship. According to Masters and Johnson, at least 50 percent of marriages are flawed by some form of sexual maladjustment or dysfunction.[1] Sometimes the sex problems come first and produce marital discord. More often it seems the marital conflict or drifting apart comes first, and this generates so much anger, disappointment, resentment, fear, or tension that mutually satisfying sex no longer occurs. Regardless of which comes first, sex problems or marriage problems, it is clear that sex and marriage are so closely interwoven that problems in one area invariably influence the other.

In writing this chapter, I have been guided by two limitations. First, even though there is a close relationship between sex and marital adjustment, this chapter will focus primarily on sex. Marriage problems will be considered in chapter 27. Second, the following pages discuss sexual relations between a husband and wife within marriage. In our society, promiscuity is common and some see sex as little more than flesh rubbing against flesh for the purpose of achieving erotic experiences. Warmth, concern, love, trust, and especially commitment are all relegated to a position that is of secondary importance to the sensations that come from foreplay and orgasm. Although these pages draw on the research of writers who study sex between partners, the emphasis here will be on sex between marriage partners who have committed themselves to one another in a marriage relationship.

There still are people who believe that sex and sex problems are topics for physicians to discuss with patients but not issues for Christian counselors, especially pastors, to consider with their counselees. This narrow viewpoint isn't held by many who are actively involved in counseling. Issues of sex often arise in counseling, and they cannot be ignored. God created sex when he made the world and created human beings. Sex was part of his plan, something beautiful to be enjoyed by the human race, but something that has been marred and disfigured by the Fall. Helping people deal with sexual problems is an important and significant responsibility for any Christian counselor.

The Bible and Sex within Marriage

Sex is not a taboo subject in the Bible. Almost every book says something about sex, and some of the descriptions (for example, in Song of Solomon) are explicit and even sexually arousing. Not all of these references can be considered here, but several are major and represent clear biblical teaching about sex within marriage.

1. *Sex Was Created by God and Is Good.* When he created human beings, God made us male and female and declared that his creation was good. He instructed the first husband and wife to "be fruitful and increase in number"—instructions

that clearly involved nakedness and sexual intercourse.[2] This was not something considered shameful or at best tolerated by God, but rather sex is evidence of God's goodness. It is something for which we can express praise and gratitude.

2. *Sex Is for Propagation and Pleasure.* The first birth recorded in the Bible is described as a result of sexual intercourse plus "the help of the Lord."[3] Obviously sex is involved in the conception of children and in the divine command to multiply. But is sex also intended for pleasure?

Perhaps the clearest answer comes from the Song of Solomon. In vivid poetic language, this little book describes the pleasures of physical sex between married lovers. The descriptions are explicit but never offensive.[4] The same is true of Proverbs. "May you rejoice in the wife of your youth," we read. May "her breasts satisfy you always, may you ever be captivated by her love."[5]

In the New Testament, we read that a husband and wife are depriving one another when they refuse to give physical pleasure and satisfaction to each other. The only exception to this is when a married couple agrees to abstain from sex temporarily and for the purpose of retreating spiritually for a special time of prayer.[6]

3. *Sex Is for Marriage.* Whenever the Bible speaks approvingly about sex, it refers to married couples. Quoting Genesis, Jesus spoke with favor about the permanence and "one flesh" nature of marriage. Paul noted that marriage (not intercourse outside of marriage) is the desirable answer for a person who is struggling with sexual self-control. When marriage occurs, the husband and wife are to give their bodies freely to each other and not hold back sexually.[7]

4. *Sexual Immorality Is Condemned Strongly.* Sexual looseness may be tolerated in our society, but it is condemned with vehemence in the Bible. God, who created sex, has commanded us to abstain from sexual immorality. This is not because God wants to take away our fun. It is because the Creator knows the dangers of sexual abuse and wants to protect us from the misery that comes when we give in to lustful passions and accept the self-centered sexual values of people who neither know nor respect God's Word.[8] Adultery is pictured in the Bible as something very attractive that ultimately is destructive and foolish.[9]

In contrast, the biblical view of sex within marriage could be summarized in the prayer of one long-married couple: "Lord, help us think of sex as you first thought of it, a gift to celebrate, excellent in every way."[10] "Scripture enthusiastically affirms sex within the bonds of marriage," writes Richard Foster. "Frequency of sex and variations of sexual technique simply are not moral issues, except in the sense of consideration for one another. In other words, married couples are free in the Lord to do whatever is mutually satisfying and contributes to the relationship. There is nothing inherently wrong with oral sex or mutual masturbation or many other ways to give pleasure to each other if they are mutually agreed upon."[11] When the gift of sex is misused or abused, however, it ceases to be excellent. Instead it leads to problems, difficulties, and regrets that arise later if not immediately.

The Causes of Sexual Problems within Marriage

Probably most people approach marriage with enthusiasm about the sexual freedom that will follow. Many of these same people are disappointed when they discover (sometimes as early as the honeymoon) that sex within marriage is not as consistently exciting or pleasurable as they had hoped or expected. There are numerous causes for this.

1. *Misinformation.* Despite the modern openness about sex, counselors often are amazed at the ignorance and lack of accurate knowledge that is characteristic of many couples. Sex researcher William Masters has concluded that "the greatest cause of sexual problems is misinformation, misconception, and taboo."[12] In every other area we are taught knowledge systematically, but sex education is left to be gathered willy-nilly from a variety of sources including adolescent jokes in the locker room, television programs, sexually explicit movies, magazine articles, and sometimes from the much-criticized sex education courses in school. Is it surprising that so many people are left with confusion,[13] misinformation, unrealistic expectations, inhibitions about asking questions, distorted fantasies, and a failure to realize that male and female responses differ from each other? Sexual instinct and urges are inborn, but a knowledge of love making must be learned. When the learning is inadequate, sexual adjustment problems often arise.

2. *Cultural Attitudes.* The society in which one lives often molds sexual attitudes and behavior. In past decades sex was not discussed openly in our culture, and marital fidelity was the expected norm. Some people considered sex to be dirty, a taboo subject for polite society, something that interested men but was of little concern to women who were assumed to be passive and lacking in sexual interest or arousal. Attitudes like these may have contributed to the relatively low frequency of intercourse apart from marriage, but they also must have created misunderstanding and sexual frustration.

Then things began to change. Sex became a subject that could be discussed more openly. Old taboos began to break down, sexual intercourse outside of marriage became more accepted and frequent, and the media—especially television and popular magazines—began the long, continuing, and subtle process of challenging traditional views of marital fidelity and sexual responsibility. This prevalence of sexual discussion has created great public awareness about sex, has elevated our expectations about sexual enjoyment, has made us less tolerant of sexual problems in our own lives and marriages, has given cultural sanction to extramarital sex, and has led to a belief that sexual awareness, fulfillment, and participation are *the* signs of healthy adult maleness and femaleness.

Cultural expectations like these can generate anxiety and feelings of insecurity in people who do not conform. Young people, whose sexual urges are especially intense and difficult to control, frequently yield to temptation but feel guilty, afraid of getting caught, and pressured to experience orgasm as quickly as possible. Sexual fulfillment is often diminished when intercourse is hurried, primarily self-centered, or lacking in relaxed tenderness. People feel cheated and disappointed. Often there are feelings of shame, self-criticism, and the loneliness that many thought sex would take away.

Despite claims to the contrary, these early experiences can have adverse effects on later marriage. When initially high expectations have not been met in marriage, or when marital faithfulness has not been maintained, sexually experienced people may feel less of a willingness to work at solving sexual problems and more of an inclination to seek satisfaction elsewhere in a society that sanctions promiscuity. Later sexual problems, such as premature ejaculation or impotency, appear to be at least as often related to ingrained psychological and social attitudes as to physiological malfunctioning. Cultural standards, the explosion of sexual information in the media, changing sexual expectations, earlier unfulfilling sexual experiences, and previously learned attitudes can all contribute to later sexual problems.

3. *Stress.* Recently an experienced sex therapist was asked to list some sexual problems that have become more apparent during the past fifteen years. It is surprising perhaps that "lack of desire" came at the top of the list. "One big cause of lack of desire today is stress," the counselor added. Many people invest so much energy and time into their jobs that they feel drained and want to be left alone.[14] When work creates anxiety, concern over job security or fear of business reversals, interest in love making declines, partly because of physical reasons. In men, for example, prolonged stress sharply decreases the level of testosterone, the primary male hormone. Distracted by the problems and pressures of life and lacking both energy and sexual drive, many men would rather read a book or watch the late show than make love to their wives.[15] When one's stress level goes up, interest and involvement in sexual intercourse tends to go down.

4. *Fatigue, Haste, and Lack of Opportunity.* Fatigue is a common cause of unsatisfactory sex. Mutually pleasurable sexual intercourse takes physical and mental energy. It also takes a relaxed, unhurried attitude that is not greatly concerned about time.

When a young couple is first married, they can sleep late on weekends, and have no children to demand their attention, to interrupt their love making, or to interfere with sexual spontaneity. These couples often have a great deal of vigor and natural energy. As they grow older, the husband and wife may have an undiminished desire for sex, but they also have less energy, more responsibilities and demands on their time, increased mental or physical fatigue, and a need for more sleep. Growing children demand attention, and their presence often forces couples to reduce the frequency and spontaneity of sexual intercourse. When they are able to get alone in bed, there often is a desire to "hurry so we can get some sleep" or to "keep quiet so the kids won't wake up." It requires almost no sophistication for us to realize that common concerns like these can interfere with relaxed sexuality and can create sexual tensions within the marriage.

5. *Boredom.* After a couple has been married for a while, they get accustomed to each other. They run out of novel ways to have sex, foreplay becomes shorter, and coitus becomes routine. After several years, the sexual activities that once were so exciting have become monotonous. Partners spend little time stimulating each other sexually, and sometimes the husband and wife become less interested in their appearance. Sex under such circumstances is not very fulfilling to say the least, and the stage has been set for an extramarital experience with someone who is more exciting and novel than one's mate.

Some couples cope with their boredom by fantasy. During the act of intercourse, they fantasize about previous, desired, or exotic sexual involvements. As we have seen in an earlier chapter, fantasies are common and not always wrong. Sometimes they add variety to sex and increase its pleasure. They can also be guilt inducing and harmful for Christians who are seeking to avoid lustful thinking. In addition, fantasies can hinder intimacy if one individual can reach orgasm only by thinking of some person other than one's mate.

6. *Physical Causes.* Sometimes sexual problems have physical origins such as endocrine disturbances, obesity, diabetes, low energy level, or the weakening of vaginal muscles in women who have given birth. Sometimes a physical illness prevents sexual behavior, and at other times it may cause people to be afraid of intercourse. In one research study, for example, it was found that 80 percent of heart attack patients were afraid to resume sexual activity after their illness, and 42 percent of the men had difficulties attaining and maintaining an erection.[16] Almost always, when physiology creates sexual problems, psychological tensions come as well and a vicious circle develops: the physiological problem creates psychological tension that in turn hinders physical functioning. In some cases physiological malfunctioning (real or imagined) is used as an excuse for abstinence or sexual difficulties.

Perhaps the most common physical hindrance to sexual fulfillment is the use of drugs, including alcohol. Since alcohol relaxes people, minimizes anxiety, and makes them less inhibited, some couples drink before intercourse. In quantity, however, alcohol dulls sensations. It is one of the principle causes of impotence in males. Such impotence creates anxiety and a fear that one is sexually inadequate. These anxieties hinder further attempts at intercourse, especially if the man has a few more drinks to relax before "trying again."

7. *Psychological Blocks.* Herbert J. Miles has suggested four categories for grouping the psychological barriers to sexual fulfillment.[17] First, there may be conflict in the relationship between husband and wife. Misunderstandings, disagreements, anger, jealousy, or a distrust of one's mate can all hinder mutual feelings of love, confidence, and intimacy. Sexual intercourse is an expression of love, but real love cannot coexist with bitterness, perpetual conflict, and continuing anger. Second, there may be personal problems in the husband. Domineering men, men who feel guilty about compulsive masturbation or other sexual behavior apart from marriage, men who have a driven need to perform well, and those who lack tenderness, patience, or kindness can all have sexual problems. Third, the wife may have personal problems. These might include fears about pain during intercourse, the idea that sex is dirty, fear of pregnancy,[18] guilt about past sexual behavior, or feelings of inferiority, insecurity, or embarrassment. Fourth, there are miscellaneous reasons, including lack of accurate knowledge or privacy, a tendency to feel rushed, a belief that sexual fulfillment somehow undermines one's spirituality,[19] and the tension that arises because of the inaccurate idea that sex must always be easy, automatic, and intensely fulfilling. Other psychological blocks include the following.

(a) Doubts about One's Masculinity or Femininity. Apparently many people go through life wondering if they are really masculine or feminine. This concern is a special problem in our society where traditional male and female roles are breaking down and where there is confusion over the meaning of masculinity and femininity.

One place where these roles are clear is in bed. It is the male penis that enters the female vagina. If a couple, especially the male, cannot perform in bed, this is a great threat to his self-esteem and feelings of sexual adequacy. Even when male impotency has clear physical reasons, the inability to get an erection is for many a psychological trauma. For women, a common sexual problem is the inability to experience orgasm even when there is a strong desire to do so. This can be a threat to one's self-concept as a woman[20] and so too is the issue of hysterectomies.

These are difficult psychologically because women who know they can no longer bear children sometimes feel unconsciously that a part of their femininity is gone.

When problems in the genital area raise doubts about one's maleness or femaleness, this in turn can hinder sexual functioning. This leads to more doubts, and another vicious cycle begins.

(b) Fear. As we have seen, sexual fears are of various types. There can be fear of pregnancy, fear that sex will hurt, fear of not being able to perform adequately, fear of being compared with previous sexual partners, fear that one's sexual advances will be rejected, fear that the penis is too small or too large, fear of losing self-control, or fear of intimacy. Each of these can be sexually inhibiting since fear and love (including sexual love) are mutually exclusive.[21]

(c) Differences in Sexual Preferences. Sometimes there are differences in the frequency with which a husband and wife want intercourse (one may want it more frequently than the other), differences in the preferred time for intercourse (one person wants it in the morning; the other prefers to have sex at night), and differences concerning what is appropriate for a couple (one may want oral-genital contact, for example, but the other person does not; one likes to try a variety of positions or locations for sex, but the other does not). These differences, several of which seem minor, nevertheless can create serious blocks to sexual satisfaction.

(d) Guilt. This is one of the most common psychological blocks. Guilt over past sexual behavior, extramarital activities, homosexual tendencies, masturbation, or recurring fantasies can create sexual problems in marriage. When a person finds sexual satisfaction apart from marriage, sex with one's spouse can be less satisfying.

8. *Marital Conflict.* Sex can be a powerful weapon in marriage. Withholding sex or demanding it, can be ways by which some couples assert their authority and get favors or decisions from a partner. Sometimes this is discussed openly. More often sex is a passive way to react. "I'm too tired for sex" or "I don't feel well" may at times be ways of saying, "I'm going to get even with you by withholding sex."

9. *Miscellaneous Causes.* Other blocks to sexual fulfillment may include persisting depression, fatigue, inhibiting religious beliefs, distractions that come from worry about one's career or family finances, or a poor self-concept. "I'm so flat chested, I feel sexless," wrote one wife in describing her reluctance to have intercourse. Others gave equally revealing reasons: "I'm so fat, I can't enjoy myself"; "I can't stand his breath"; "He seems so selfish in his lovemaking that I feel used"; "My wife ridicules my ability to make love . . . I am somewhat clumsy"; "I just can't forgive him for the affair he had."[22] Clearly sexual problems can arise from a variety of circumstances and can have a profound influence on both individuals and marriages.

THE EFFECTS OF SEXUAL PROBLEMS WITHIN MARRIAGE

When sexual problems appear, some couples simply give up and don't try to resolve their difficulties. There may be fear of discussing the frustrations or a belief that things will never get better. Others develop physical symptoms—headaches, abdominal pain, fatigue, or emotional distress—all of which hide the sexual problem and provide an excuse for abstinence. In a surprisingly large number of young marriages, there is no sex at all.[23] This can be very difficult for a mate who wants sexual fulfillment.

In addition to the avoidance of intercourse, sexual difficulties in marriage can lead to several major effects:

1. *Inability to Perform.* Numerous books and research reports have described the symptoms and causes of the more common sexual problems in marriage. These include orgasmic dysfunction (more often known as frigidity, a condition in which the female is unable or unwilling to experience full sexual pleasure including orgasm), vaginismus (a condition in which the vaginal entrance closes tightly when penetration is attempted), erectile dysfunction (also known as impotence, the inability of a male to achieve or maintain an erection), premature ejaculation (the ejaculation of semen, with a resulting loss of erection, immediately before, just at, or shortly after insertion of the penis into the vagina), retarded ejaculation (the opposite of premature ejaculation this occurs when the penis remains erect but ejaculation does not occur), and dyspareunia (painful intercourse). While each of these may have a physical basis, the cause can also be psychological.

This gives another example of the vicious cycle that has been mentioned earlier in the chapter. Psychological blocks to sexual fulfillment usually come first. Because of these fears and attitudes, sex is not satisfying. The realization that intercourse is not satisfying then intensifies the fears and creates even stronger psychological blocks. This in turn makes sexual fulfillment even more unlikely. It then becomes difficult to distinguish the causes from the effects.

2. *Lowered Self-Esteem.* Self-esteem and sexual capability often go together, especially in men. If intercourse is not mutually satisfying, the husband and wife may both have doubts about their sexual competence, doubts that sometimes are accentuated by the joking of one's mate. If a man cannot maintain an erection or arouse his wife, for example, he is likely to experience a loss of confidence about his sexual and manly capabilities. If his wife jokes about the fact that he may be losing his virility, this is an even greater blow to his self-esteem, and his ability to perform sexually is hindered further.

3. *Selection of Substitutes.* When sex within marriage is not satisfying, husbands and wives often turn to substitute activities. These include masturbation, increased fantasies (these become a "second-best" substitute for the real thing), or extramarital sex. Affairs often come as a result of sexual problems within marriage, but instead of the hoped for fulfillment, affairs can often lead to guilt, concerns about secrecy, and further marital, sexual, and personal frustration.

4. *Deteriorating Relationships.* Sexual problems can create anger, resentment, interpersonal tension, impatience, and communication breakdowns. It would be overly simplistic to conclude that sexual problems lead to divorce, but it is accurate to conclude that sexual tensions, coupled with other marital pressures contribute to marriage breakups. It is difficult to have a really good marriage when there are also sexual dissatisfactions and incompatibilities.

5. *Increased Motivation.* Some couples (fewer than we might wish) face their sexual problems with a new determination to make sex better. Open to suggestions, disinclined to blame each other, and willing to work on the problems, these couples invariably see improvement both in their sexual relationships and in their marriages. These are the people with whom counselors most like to work.

Counseling and Sexual Problems within Marriage

Talking to others about the details of their sexual lives can be embarrassing and anxiety producing for counselors. Even though the Bible talks openly about sex, counselors sometimes feel that sexual counseling is spiritually inappropriate, that it violates the counselee's privacy, or that it might stimulate the counselor's own sexuality in an unhealthy way.

The counselor's insecurity may appear in a variety of disguises.[24] Some counselors ignore the subject and avoid any mention of sex. Others get rid of the issue with a comment like, "I suspect you don't have any sexual problems, do you?" The answer, not surprisingly, is usually no, and the counselor moves quickly to less threatening issues. Other counselors talk of sex in aloof intellectual or theological terms that keep the conversation emotionally detached and vague. Some ask a lot of specific questions that may even titillate the counselor but give no help to the counselees. Others announce that sexual problems are all psychological and quickly move to some supposed real problem that permits everyone to avoid talking about the sexual symptoms. All of these are avoidance tactics. To really help counselees, these tactics must be avoided and the counselor must be at ease with his or her own sexuality. If you prefer not to talk about sexual issues, it is quite acceptable (and probably preferable) to refer counselees to another counselor.

For those who are willing to counsel people in the area of sex, try to stay alert to the subtle sexual implications that sometimes occur in this type of counseling. When issues of sex are discussed openly and in detail, both the counselor and the counselee can be aroused erotically. At times this is complicated by sexual curiosity on the part of the counselor, seductive behavior in the counselee, or feelings of sexual attraction that sometimes are mutual. The counselor constantly must be alert to these issues. In no case will the counselor be effective if there is erotic involvement with the counselee. Acting on one's sexual impulses in counseling is both bad morals and bad therapy.

The counselor should maintain an interpersonal distance from counselees who are seductive or sexually arousing. If you continue to feel attraction for a counselee, it might be helpful to discuss this with another counselor. If your counselee is seductive, this should be raised in counseling and discussed directly. Ask yourself if the counselee's behavior can tell you anything about the ways in which he or she relates to a mate or to others apart from marriage.

Other counseling guidelines include the following.

1. *Listen with Acceptance and Understanding.* It is not easy for counselees to talk about their sexual problems and failures. Embarrassment, shame, guilt, and anxiety can all accompany such discussions and the sensitive counselor will help by showing an understanding attitude. Gently encourage the individual or couple to talk openly, compliment them for doing so, and state (if you think this would help) that difficulty in talking about sexual issues is common. Remember that counselees are more likely to discuss their problems openly when they see that the counselor is relaxed, accepting, not awkward or embarrassed, and wanting to understand and help.

In discussing sexual issues, remember that one reason for the awkwardness and embarrassment may be the counselee's difficulty in finding words to describe genitals and sexual activities. Your counselee may prefer pet terms or even slang that is not easy to express to a counselor, especially to one who is a Christian.[25] As a counselor, you should be accepting of such language but in general try to use correct terminology (for example, penis, vagina, intercourse, masturbation), making sure that the counselee knows what you are talking about. Recognize that there will be times when you may have to use terms that are more familiar to the counselee. For example, technically it is correct to ask, "Do you have problems with premature ejaculation?" but it may be clearer to ask, "Do you come too fast?"

2. *Gather Information.* It is easier to help when you understand the nature of the problem. You may not want to ask all of the following questions, but these are examples of the kinds of information you may need to help you uncover the causes and possible approaches to resolving the problem. Sometimes counselees are helped solely as a result of answering your questions.

- What are the sexual problems that the couple is having? Encourage them to be specific and honest.
- What did they expect from sex, and how have they been disappointed?
- How do they feel about such issues as oral-genital sex, masturbation, frequency of sex, or using a variety of sexual positions and locations?
- Who initiates sexual activities, and how is this done?
- How do they communicate about sex?
- Where and how did they first learn about sex?
- What are their attitudes about sex now?
- What do they think might be causing their sexual problems?
- Apart from sex, how does the couple get along with each other?
- What stresses do they currently face as a couple?

It is best if you can counsel with both the husband and wife, even though this is not always possible. Many counselors prefer to see the couple together. Do they answer questions in the same way? Does one partner condemn, dominate, or put down the other? Periodic private interviews with each may add additional information.

As information is gathered, you might form hunches about the causes of the problems. Further questioning in these areas will give additional information and help to confirm or disprove your guesses. These hypotheses can later be shared with the counselees.

3. *Recommend a Physical Examination.* Although many (probably most) sexual problems arise from psychological causes, you should not overlook the possibility of physiological malfunctioning. For this reason, couples with sexual problems should be urged to get a physical examination. If physical problems are found, the counselor can work with the physician in helping the counselees.

4. *Give Accurate Information.* This may not be the only or best solution to a sexual problem, but information giving is often very important. Such information can be of several types. The counselor, for example, can:

- Answer questions with factual information. This rests on the debatable assumption that counselees know what to ask.
- Explain details of physiology and the techniques of foreplay or intercourse. Such minilectures can be helpful, but they often are difficult for counselees to remember.
- Give counselees helpful books or articles to read at home and discuss later.[26]
- Encourage counselees to listen to cassette tapes dealing with sex within marriage.[27]
- Instruct couples in sexual exercises that can be done at home. Premature ejaculation, for example, can be treated with a very high degree of success when couples are taught and encouraged to practice the squeeze technique in which the woman manipulates the male penis in a way that permits ejaculatory control. A description of these techniques is beyond the scope of this book, but detailed information is easily available to counselors.[28]
- Provide information about the biblical teaching on sex and sexual fulfillment.

Whenever you give information, allow time for counselees to ask questions or otherwise clarify what you are sharing. Discuss practical ways in which the information can be used to improve sexual functioning.

5. *Deal with Related Problems.* As we have indicated, psychological blocks (such as fears, embarrassment, guilt, and anger); marital conflicts (including power struggles, disagreements, and communication breakdowns); inhibiting attitudes and memories of past sexual experiences; guilt over past or present sexual thoughts and actions; beliefs that sex is bad, dirty, or un-Christian; unrealistic expectations about sex; and a variety of other issues can hinder sexual satisfaction. When problems like these are present, the counselor must do more than give factual information.

The counselee must be encouraged to describe the problem fully. Its origins should be discussed, if possible, and strategies should be worked out so counselees can take practical steps to resolve the problems with the counselor's guidance and encouragement. At times counselees will have to face previous sexual sins and learn to experience the liberation of knowing that sins are forgiven when we confess to our loving Savior. When marital conflict is apparent, counselors must be careful not to take sides but rather to apply the principles discussed in the chapter on marriage counseling.[29] As these problems are resolved, sexual relations often improve.

6. *Be Alert to the Need for Referral.* Sexual counseling and the treatment of sexual dysfunction are parts of a highly skilled specialty for which some professionals have unique training. When counselees do not respond to counseling, when there continue to be sexual problems and dissatisfactions, when medical issues are involved, when a counselee is consistently seductive, or when it appears that there will have to be prolonged training and sexual exercises, then referral to an expert in sexual counseling is recommended. This is not an admission of counseling failure; it is a recognition of the need for more specialized treatment.

Preventing Sexual Problems within Marriage

Attitudes toward sex are changing. Intercourse apart from marriage is no longer considered immoral by many (probably most) people in the society; instead it is common to be guided by the premise that "we are absolutely entitled to the full satisfaction of our appetites, and we are, furthermore, so helpless before the lusts of the flesh that it is both foolish and wrong to expect us to resist temptation."[30] Actress Shirley MacLaine once told an interviewer that sex limited to one partner within marriage is not a "natural" function. This remark led one author to respond that it is more unnatural for "men and women to be governed by their passions. Sex is a wonderful servant but a terrible master."[31]

How can we teach people to view sex as a monogamous relationship that is both fulfilling and consistent with biblical morality when it is confined to the marriage relationship?[32]

1. *Sex Education.* Since misinformation is at the basis of many sexual problems it would appear that giving accurate information can do much to prevent sexual difficulties. This information can be in four areas: what the Bible teaches about sex, basic facts about male and female physiology, information about techniques of intercourse, and teaching healthy sexual attitudes.

Ideally this information should be given by parents in the home, long before marriage is ever contemplated. It is well known, however, that for many people there is no sex education at home. The church, therefore, can encourage and instruct parents in giving sex education and can provide this information directly to young people. (This is best done with prior parental approval.) Church meetings, including youth meetings, small group discussions of printed materials,[33] and presentations from the pulpit can all help to instill healthy and biblical perspectives on human sexuality.

2. *Moral Guidance.* Sex education often focuses on physiology and facts about sexuality, but this is not enough. Many people struggle with ethical choices about what is right and wrong, and too often they find little help in the church. How do people make decisions about birth control, artificial insemination, surrogate parents, the limits of biblically acceptable behavior between unmarried men and women, or even decisions concerning sexually oriented films and plays? Too often it seems our theological discussions of these issues remain in classrooms and scholarly books and never get down to help people in the pews. Ethics, including sexual ethics, need to be made practical and discussed in churches *before* rather than after immoral behavior occurs.[34]

3. *Premarital Counseling.* When sexual issues are discussed as part of premarital counseling, there can be a clearer understanding of physiology or love-making techniques, more realistic expectations about sex in marriage, and less likelihood of sexual problems, especially at the beginning of marriage. When a good counseling relationship has been established before the wedding, couples are more inclined to return for help if problems arise after the marriage begins. This is especially true if premarital counselors encourage postmarital checkups. When sexual problems or frustrations are discussed early, before they become complicated, then serious difficulties are less likely to develop.[35]

4. *Communication.* If people cannot communicate in general, it is not likely that they will be able to communicate about sex. Teaching people, especially couples, to communicate is one way to prevent sexual problems.

Some people feel uncomfortable talking about sex, even with their own mates. To improve communication, encourage husbands and wives to share their feelings and attitudes about sex. Males do not know automatically how to stimulate a female and neither do all females know how to turn on a man. The husband and wife can tell each other what is stimulating. This communication should be honest, gentle, and nonverbal as well as verbal. Taking the hand of one's mate and showing him or her how to stimulate can be an excellent communication technique.

Writing from a female perspective, one person commented that "it is amazing how silent we women are on something as important as the sex act in marriage. We *wish* in silence or we *suffer* in silence or we *hope* that this time it will be different, that this time he will think of doing that which we long for him to do. Why not just tell him?"[36] Why not just show him? Why not recognize too that men need to communicate just as much as women? When a couple is encouraged to communicate like this, many subsequent sexual problems will be prevented.

5. *Effort and Cleanliness.* Good sex, like good marriage, requires time, effort, and a willingness to work at making things better. If sex is to be satisfying and if serious sexual problems are to be prevented, a couple must always be alert to ways in which they can build a better relationship. This may involve reading about sex and trying new positions. It also involves an attitude that says "I will try to keep myself as attractive as possible, as clean, and at least as concerned about my mate as I was when we were first married."

Married people who get lax about personal hygiene, weight control, and physical appearance find that sex is less satisfying as they grow older. A young woman who once enjoyed sex with her clean-shaven, freshly bathed husband is not going to enjoy sex more if her middle-aged husband is sloppy in appearance, not inclined to shower before sex, and unwilling to shave on weekends. Cleanliness and a determination to improve sex are both preventive measures.

6. *Marriage Enrichment.* Within recent years, marriage enrichment and marriage encounter programs have been developed for the purpose of improving marriage (including sex within marriage) and preventing marital and sexual problems. Before recommending any of these to a couple, try to discover the moral and theological perspectives of the program designers and speakers. While some of these programs are based on humanistic values, others have a Christian orientation and can be recommended. Counselors and church leaders may, as an alternative, design their own marriage and sexual enrichment programs. Often there are counseling experts in the community who can help with this program development.[37]

Conclusions about Sex within Marriage

Many years ago, I had a teaching colleague who argued that sexual counseling was inappropriate for pastors and probably something that Christian counselors should avoid. My friend was aware of the dangers of erotic involvements between counselor and counselee, but he failed to see that sex involves much more than selfish, narcissistic, hedonistic pleasure between two individuals.

Sexual fulfillment not only is God's plan for married people, but it teaches about intimacy and closeness to him. "The theological and psychological parallel between letting go sexually, as in organismic release, and in accepting one's dependence upon God is quite apparent," according to two Christian sex counselors. "It appears that the finest, most sublime foretaste of heaven (overcoming separateness and attaining oneness) lies in sexual intercourse and that God wants us to experience this joyful foretaste of heavenly unity."[38]

Others have also commented on the link between sexuality and spirituality. Richard Foster, for example, writes that one of the "real tragedies in Christian history has been the divorce of sexuality from spirituality."[39] Tim Stafford would agree. In a discussion of marital problems, he writes that couples "who share each other's spiritual calling almost inevitably come to appreciate each other as more than mere sex partners—and that appreciation is likely to help them become better sex partners."[40]

Helping people deal with sexual problems in marriage need not be a distraction from spirituality or an advocating of self-centered hedonism. It is helping a husband and wife to relate more effectively to each other, to experience the marital closeness that God intended, and to be free of sexual hang-ups so they can reach out more effectively to love God and serve others.

SUGGESTIONS FOR FURTHER READING

Maier, Richard A. *Human Sexuality in Perspective.* Chicago: Nelson-Hall, 1984.

Mayo, Mary Ann. *A Christian Guide to Sexual Counseling.* Grand Rapids, Mich.: Zondervan, 1987.

Miles, Herbert J. *Sexual Happiness in Marriage.* Grand Rapids, Mich.: Zondervan, 1982.*

Penner, Clifford, and Joyce Penner. *A Gift for All Ages.* Waco, Tex.: Word, 1985.*

Smedes, Lewis. *Sex for Christians.* Grand Rapids, Mich.: Eerdmans, 1976.

Wheat, Ed, and Gaye Wheat. *Intended for Pleasure: Sex Techniques and Sexual Fulfillment in Christian Marriage.* Rev. ed. Old Tappan, N.J.: Revell, 1981.*

Zimbelman, Ernie. *Human Sexuality and Evangelical Christians.* Lanham, Md.: University Press of America, 1985.*

* Books marked with an asterisk (*) are especially suited for counselees to read.

19

Homosexuality

How does it feel to be homosexual and struggling? One student gave an account of his experiences:

"I never decided to be more attracted to men than to women. If I did have the chance to choose, I certainly would not have chosen to be the kind of person all the other kids considered to be a freak. I felt totally helpless when my sexual urges were toward boys and not girls. I had fantasies about men all the time. I can remember masturbating as early as age eight, but my fantasies at that time were not specifically sexual. It was when I hit puberty that the sexual fantasies began. I masturbated almost every day, sometimes more than once a day. Every time I thought about other boys rather than girls. When I tried to think of girls while masturbating, it didn't work.

"I dealt with this discovery alone. I never told anyone about my 'sexual identity.' I was so afraid of rejection. I remember rejection in seventh grade when all the other kids called me 'fag' and 'queer.' No one even knew about me at that time; I couldn't bear to think how they would react if they really did know. All through high school and most of college I kept my secret—and my pain—to myself.

"When I got to college, I fell in love with another guy. He was not homosexual, and I had to keep my secret from him. We were roommates for three years, and he never knew about me until just before graduation. What was hard for me in this situation aside from the terrible hurt that he could not love me back was the realization that it was more than my sex drive that was gay. I felt like I was perverted to the depths of my being.

"I had been a Christian since I was seven years old and had asked God to take away my homosexuality many times. He never did. It became hard to reconcile the fact that Scripture says homosexuality is wrong with my strong sexual and emotional attraction to men. It was at this time that I began to experiment a bit with the gay scene in the city. I went to gay bookstores and made phone calls to the gay hot line. There was so much promise of gratification and fulfillment in these places. I began to lead a double life. I was leading Bible studies back on campus and very much involved in the campus ministry, but every once in awhile I would go downtown to the bookstore. I always felt guilty and dirty when I left, but that did not stop me from going the next time. The promise of fulfillment was so strong!

"I finally told someone about my struggles. She was very understanding and did not reject me. After some time I was even able to tell my roommate. This did not stop me from going to bookstores right away, but it was the first step in a healing process. I couldn't handle this alone any longer.

"Since then God has put some wonderful people in my life who have helped me to have the courage not to fall to temptation. Some of these friends also struggle with homosexual temptation, but we are trusting in Christ's victory over sin to give us power over the sin of homosexuality. It took some people who were compassionate and caring to hear my struggles and help me understand them. I do not know when or if my temptation to engage in homosexual acts will go away, but I am no longer burdened by the belief that I am hopeless and that there is no power over these temptations. My identity is in Christ not in my temptations."

Several decades ago homosexuality was rarely mentioned in polite society. Viewed as something sinful, sick, or illegal, it was ignored by most heterosexuals (including church members), treated by psychiatrists who viewed it as sexual deviation, and hidden by perhaps millions of people who wanted to keep their homosexual tendencies from becoming known.

Then things began to change. Forty years ago, researcher Alfred Kinsey estimated that 4 percent of the American population was homosexual[1] and that 37 percent of the male population had participated in at least one homosexual act. In 1954 a government-sponsored report on homosexuality rocked Britain, and before long homosexuality had become a topic of government and media debate. Great numbers of homosexual persons who previously had been silent about their sexual orientation came out of the "closet" to declare their homosexuality, to form gay organizations, and to demand a stop to government, cultural, and media persecution. The American Psychiatric Association voted to drop homosexuality from its manual of mental disorders, concluding that homosexuality is a disorder only when it is subjectively disturbing to an individual.

With the outbreak of the AIDS epidemic, homosexuality was thrust into even greater public awareness. Controversy over homosexuality soon invaded every part of society: the military, local elections, government, the courts, schools, sports, science, professional societies, the entertainment world, business, industry, the media, and, of course, the church. Heated debate over the ordination of homosexuals continues to characterize several denominations. A string of gay churches has been established, and a growing and influential organization of evangelical homosexuals has been formed.[2] Within recent years there has been an increasing stream of articles and books on homosexuality written by both Christian and non-Christian authors.[3]

Some Christians still try to ignore homosexuality. Some make ill-informed and insensitive comments about homosexual individuals, others lash out in condemnation and anger against homosexuals, while still others seem intent on making "Christian homosexuality" a legitimate, God-approved way of life. Many believers, perhaps most, are not sure what they think.

This uncertainty is easy to understand. Homosexuality is not easily defined, and its causes are still debated. There are many unfounded but widely held assumptions about the characteristics of homosexuals, and it seems that change is difficult, even with counseling. "The wonder here is that after years of research we remain virtually ignorant of why some people become heterosexual, others homosexual," wrote the authors of a recent psychology text. "We can now discount some formerly popular theories, . . . but we have no reliable way of predicting—certainly not from knowledge of your relationships with your parents, your childhood sexual experiences, and so forth—whether you are primarily attracted to members of your own sex or the other sex. But on this much the researchers generally do agree: one's sexual orientation seems neither willfully chosen nor easily changed."[4] All of this is complicated by widespread fear within society and often within the church. Many people seem afraid both of the influence of gays and of the possibility that homosexual tendencies might be found in themselves. This fear even has a name: "homophobia"—the fear of homosexuals or homosexuality.

Because of the controversy and confusion surrounding this topic, it is almost certain that some readers will disagree with the following paragraphs. Please remember, however, that this chapter is not written to advocate any one theory or to stimulate insensitive debate. I have attempted instead to summarize what is known about homosexuality, to pinpoint the issues of controversy, and to cut through the emotional rhetoric so we can understand and help those homosexually inclined persons who seek our counsel.

Most of us, perhaps, will agree with Richard J. Foster who wrote:

> Because this issue has wounded so many people, the first word that needs to be spoken is one of compassion and healing. Those who are clearly homosexual in their orientation often feel misunderstood, stereotyped, abused, and rejected. Those who believe that homosexuality is a clear affront to biblical norms feel betrayed by denominations that want to legislate homosexuality into church life.
>
> There is a third group that has been hurt by the contemporary battle over homosexuality: I refer to those who agonize over their own sexual identity, those who feel torn by conflicting sexual urges and wonder if perhaps they are latent homosexuals. Perhaps this group suffers the most. They are cast into a sea of ambiguity because the Church has given an uncertain sound. On their right, they hear shrill denunciations of homosexuality, and, though they appreciate the concern for biblical fidelity, they have been offended by the brash, uninformed, pharisaical tone of the pronouncements. From their left, they hear enthusiastic acceptance of homosexuality and, though they appreciate the compassionate concern for the oppressed, they are astonished at the way the Bible is maneuvered to fit a more accommodating posture.
>
> All who are caught in the cultural and ecclesiastical chaos over homosexuality need our compassion and understanding.[5]

Broadly defined, homosexuality is an erotic attraction to persons of one's own sex.[6] Although homosexuality includes sexual thoughts, feelings, fantasies, and overt sexual acts with same-sex partners, the term usually is not applied to preadolescents, to individuals (usually young people) whose curiosity leads to brief experimental erotic involvement with a person of the same sex, or to people in prisons or other isolated same-sex environments who temporarily engage in homosexual behavior because opposite-sex partners are not available.

It is important to distinguish between homosexual *behavior* (engaging, at least periodically, in sexually stimulating actions with another person of the same sex) and homosexual *orientation* (feeling sexual attraction toward members of the same sex). Many people with a homosexual orientation never let others know of this same-sex preference and never engage in homosexual behavior with another human being. Sometimes counselors also refer to *latent* homosexuals. These people are sexually aroused by same-sex individuals, but latent homosexuals are unable to admit to themselves that their basic orientation is homosexual. There is no homosexual personality type (or types), and neither are there typical homosexual mannerisms. Homosexuals are of both sexes (female homosexuals usually are called lesbians; there is no comparable term for males). Homosexual people are of all ages, come from all occupations and socioeconomic levels, possess a variety of interests, are inside the church as well as outside, and are not always thinking about sex any more than heterosexuals think only about sex. While some homosexuals "cruise" in and out of gay bars looking for sexual partners (despite the increasing fears of AIDS), many more are respected and often married members of the community. Some are open about their sexual preferences; others keep their homosexuality well hidden. While many are lonely and insecure, it cannot be assumed that homosexuals as a group are mentally disturbed, socially incompetent, or even more lonely than heterosexuals. In fact, we cannot even assume that humans can be divided into two groups: homosexual and heterosexual. The Kinsey report suggested a scale with seven points in which zero represents a person who is exclusively heterosexual, three is midpoint, and six represents a person with exclusively homosexual tendencies and actions. The Kinsey researchers concluded that few people are at the zero- and six-point positions on the scale.

To help homosexuals we first must rid ourselves of the harmful stereotypes and misconceptions that so often are imposed on a group of people who, usually through no choice of their own, find themselves attracted to others of the same sex.

The Bible and Homosexuality

The Bible says little about homosexuality. It is mentioned in only seven passages, and in each case the reference is relatively brief.[7] Clearly homosexuality is never approved, but neither is it singled out as being worse than other sins.

In an attempt to clarify the biblical teachings about homosexuality, several Christian writers have written books and articles that sometimes reach conflicting conclusions.[8] At times it seems that many writers start with an opinion about homosexuality and then interpret Scripture in a way that supports their positions. Some, for example, have used Scripture to support sweeping condemnation of homosexuals[9] while others seek to explain away the sinful implications of homosexuality and conclude that it is a condition that comes from God.[10]

In the Old Testament, homosexual behavior is condemned, but some argue that this teaching is part of the law that was put aside when Christ came to die for our sins. Within the New Testament, however, there are three references to homosexuality, and in two of these the Greek word means "coitus with other males."[11] Homosexual behavior is condemned in these passages, along with idolatry, thievery, lying, murder, and other sins.

Rom. 1:26–27 is more explicit in its teachings about homosexuality. Some maintain that this passage condemns only former heterosexuals who have shifted to homosexuality, but this interpretation makes two highly debatable assumptions: (a) that people are attracted to the same sex by deliberate choice, and (b) that the verses do not apply to lifelong homosexuals. Others argue that the writer of Romans 1 is concerned not about homosexuality but about idolatry. Clearly the passage condemns people who worship something other than God, but Paul makes no attempt to say here that only idolatrous homosexuality is wrong. Instead he states that when people don't care about God, he lets them get into all kinds of sinful situations, including overt homosexuality.

Whenever homosexuality is mentioned in the Bible it is mentioned negatively. It seems clear, therefore, that erotic homosexual acts are wrong. If overt homosexuality is sinful, what about homosexual thoughts and feelings? What can be said about those persons who have sexual fantasies and impulses that are primarily homosexual but are kept well hidden? What can be concluded about people, including Christians, who appear to live normal lives, who have satisfying heterosexual marriages, but who are bothered by recurring homosexual tendencies that threaten one's masculinity or femininity and that might sometime slip out and become apparent to others?

To have homosexual tendencies, feelings, and desires is nowhere condemned in Scripture, but when one dwells on such thoughts and continually engages in sexual fantasy—either homosexual or heterosexual—then thoughts become lust, and lust clearly is sin. The Christian can expect to be tempted, even as Jesus was tempted,[12] but the Bible gives a message of hope. Scripture shows that we can avoid dwelling on lustful thoughts or giving in to sinful temptations of any kind, including homosexual temptations.[13]

The Causes of Homosexuality

Despite probably thousands of scientific studies, one conclusion seems clear: *There is no clearly identified single cause of homosexuality.* A number of competent researchers have investigated whether sexual orientation and homosexual behavior are the direct result of heredity or other biological influences. Some have concluded that "scientific evidence supports the view that hormonal and neurological variables, operating during gestation, are the main determinants of sexual orientation."[14] Others concluded, however, that "prenatal hormones do not rigidly determine sexual orientation."[15] Even medical and biological researchers conclude that "postnatal socialization" is more likely to influence sexual preference.[16] Stated in less technical terms, there is no solid evidence to support the view that homosexuality has only a physical or biological cause.

Most researchers do agree, however, that homosexuality is "no more chosen than a native language." According to investigators, sexual orientation should be considered under three terms: nature, critical period, and nurture. Concerning one's *nature* there may be some hormonal-congenital influences that have a bearing on later sexual orientation. At some *critical periods* in life, especially in early childhood, experiences will influence the person's later sexual preferences. Later sexual orientation and behavior will be influenced by *nurture,* the impact that comes from one's home and social environment. Stated in somewhat formal language, heterosexuality, homosexuality, "and bisexuality all have both prenatal and later causes, which interact during critical periods of development to create a long-lasting or even immutable sexuoerotic status."[17]

We are left then with the conclusion that homosexuality can arise from a variety of causes. Some inconclusive data suggest that biological influences, operating before birth, may play some role in the development of later sexual orientation, but there is even greater evidence that homosexual preferences and behaviors are determined by psychological development and social learning. Several theories describe how homosexuality is acquired.

1. *Parent-Child Relationships.* Psychoanalytic theories have been widely accepted and intensively studied.[18] Based on Freud's view that homosexuality is produced by arrested sexual development, psychoanalytic writers conclude that homosexual males usually are raised in families with a weak, passive, ineffective father and a domineering mother. This mother subtly teaches her son to be passive and dedicated to her. He has no strong male example to follow and soon discovers that he is less competent than his peers in relating to girls. As a result, the son loses confidence in his masculinity and dreads the thought of intimacy with women. Daughters in such families perceive their fathers as being unfriendly and rejecting, so the girls have little opportunity to relate to men. They relate better to women.

A thought-provoking and perhaps more believable variation of this view has been presented by a Christian writer, Elizabeth R. Moberly. Her research suggests that homosexuality comes, not from relationship problems with the opposite-sex parent, but because of a defect in relating to the same-sex parent. In normal development, needs "for love from, dependency on, and identification with, the parent of the same sex are met through the child's attachment to the parent," Moberly writes. If this relationship is lacking or disrupted, the individual unconsciously attempts to restore the attachment. The person who becomes homosexual has a need to make up for "earlier deficits in the parent-child relationship. The persisting need for love from the same sex stems from, and is to be correlated with, the earlier unmet need for love from the parent of the same sex."[19] One way to repair this deficit, to fulfill unmet needs, and to successfully treat homosexuals is to build a "good nonsexual relationship with a member of the same sex."[20] Homosexuals, according to this view, are helped best by caring, same-sex, heterosexual counselors.

While many homosexuals do experience disruptions in parent-child relationships, others do not. Children in the same family do not all become homosexual even though there may be similar parent-child relationships.[21] This has led some counselors to seek other explanations for homosexuality.

2. *Other Family Relationships.* Homosexuality has been found to result when:[22]

- Mothers distrust or fear women and teach this to their sons.
- Mothers distrust or fear men and teach this to their daughters.
- A son is surrounded by too many females (mothers, sisters, aunts), but he has limited contact with adult males, thus he learns to think and act like a girl.
- Parents who wanted a daughter but instead have a son subtly raise the boy to think and act like a girl (a similar situation arises when parents wanted a son but instead have a daughter); in both cases the child has great confusion about sexual identity and orientation.

- A son is rejected or ignored by his father and hence feels inadequate as a male and unsure how males relate to females.
- A daughter is rejected by her mother and hence feels inadequate as a female, thus she can't relate well to males.
- Both parents are afraid of sex, unwilling to discuss it in the home, or strong in their condemnation of sex; in all of the this the child gets a distorted view of sex and as a result struggles with heterosexual adjustment.
- A mother (or father) is so overindulgent that the child is overly attached to the parent, unable to break away, and convinced that no mate could ever compare with the opposite-sex parent.

A list like this could continue perhaps for several pages, but enough has been stated to show that the roots of homosexuality can be complex and often are embedded in the family setting.

In any society, a child learns what it means to be male or female. If there is no opportunity to learn healthy male or female roles, or if the society (like ours) has vaguely defined roles, then the child's behavior and attitudes become distorted. Such children reach adulthood not knowing what to expect or how to react to the opposite sex. Sometimes it is more comfortable to retreat into homosexuality, especially if the person already has begun to sense same-sex preferences.

3. *Other Early Experiences.* What happens to a young boy when his genitals are stimulated by an older male? It would be inaccurate and simplistic to conclude that homosexuality comes solely because of early sexual experiences. Nevertheless, these experiences can have an influence on adult sexual orientation.

One report suggests, for example, that homosexuality may be acquired in three stages. Stage one, the *egocentric stage,* occurs when a child or young adolescent has trouble relating to same-sex peers, feels inadequate and different (perhaps because the young person lacks athletic or other skills that peers possess), and/or experiences excitement or erotic arousal with a person of the same sex. Sometimes children feel so inadequate or uncomfortable with their sexual identity that they want to be members of the opposite sex. Most of these children become homosexual as adults.[23]

At stage two, the *sociocentric stage,* the individual begins to sense a same-sex orientation. Often there are attempts to deny this to oneself and efforts to hide it from others. Many struggle at this stage for their whole lives.

Some move to stage three, the *universalistic stage,* where they admit their homosexuality to themselves and to others despite the consequences.[24]

4. *Fear.* For various reasons, some people are afraid of the opposite sex. Lasting fears may arise from lack of frequent contact with opposite sex persons, rejection by those of the opposite sex, or traumatic and embarrassing experiences with someone of the opposite sex. Some have suggested that religious groups or same-sex schools inadvertently promote homosexuality. When heterosexual contact is prohibited, homosexuality becomes a less threatening alternative.

For some this fear of the opposite sex is accompanied by fear or awkwardness around members of the same sex. If one is attracted to same-sex people, there may be fears of rejection, uncertainty about how to react normally, or insecurities lest one's homosexual urges be detected.[25]

5. *Willful Choice of Homosexuality.* Some popular books suggest that homosexuality results from a deliberate choice, but this view is not held by experienced professionals or by most people who have a homosexual orientation. Sexual attraction to the members of one's own sex rarely if ever comes as a willful and conscious decision. At some time in their lives most homosexuals begin to realize that, through no deliberate choice of their own, they are attracted primarily to people of the same sex. Such a realization can be so disturbing that many individuals try to hide it even from themselves. The person often concludes that he or she must have been born as a genetically predetermined homosexual even though, as we have seen, this conclusion is not supported by the findings of research.

Homosexual tendencies are acquired often before one realizes what is taking place. Just as a predominantly heterosexual person is attracted by the opposite sex, so a predominantly homosexual individual has learned an attraction for the same sex. These attractions are not wrong. What is wrong, according to the Bible, is the willful decision to engage in homosexual *actions*.

Whenever a person experiences pleasure from sexual activities with someone of the same or opposite sex, the sexual activities become more appealing the next time. It doesn't matter how the behavior got started—as a result of seduction by another person, as an expression of curiosity, or as an attempt to release tension while one is in the military or confined to jail.[26]

More important is whether the sexual activities continue. According to one early writer, "lasting homosexual patterns tend to be established by *recurrent homosexual practices* beginning even before adolescence and continuing after it, especially if the homosexual partner—whether a contemporary or an adult—is someone the young person admires."[27] For many young people a passing sexual encounter, even with a same-sex person, isn't especially satisfying and is unlikely to be repeated. For people whose backgrounds and tendencies make them vulnerable, one sexual experience can lead to another, and a vicious cycle begins. Homosexual acts (including masturbation with homosexual fantasies) increase homosexual tendencies that in turn lead to more homosexual acts. Of course a similar cycle can begin when persons with heterosexual tendencies choose to engage in sexual activities with persons of the opposite sex. According to the Bible, this heterosexual cycle isn't wrong within marriage, but outside of marriage such physical involvement is sinful.

The Effects of Homosexuality

People in the Gay Rights movement emphasize the benefits of homosexuality and despite widespread promiscuity in the gay community, many same-sex couples are able to live together for a prolonged period of time.[28] This should not hide the fact that millions of people with homosexual tendencies are extremely unhappy.[29] Their homosexual orientation tends to cloud every area of their lives. Of course individuals are affected in uniquely different ways, but homosexuality influences four areas especially: one's lifestyle, self-concept, interpersonal relationships, and family relationships.

1. *Lifestyle Effects.* Media reports sometimes give a disturbing picture of gay communities and homosexual lifestyles. One report, for example, described

homosexual communities where the shops cater to gays, where the streets are "dominated by pairs of men holding hands or walking with their arms around each other's waists," where women and children are conspicuously absent, and where clothing styles reflect a way of dress currently favored by gays.[30] Newspaper reports sometimes describe school teachers or youth leaders who sexually molest young boys and lure them into homosexual acts. Others have described gay bars where both men and women come to seek other homosexuals who can give acceptance, friendships, and sexual involvement. Reports such as these undoubtedly describe only a minority of homosexuals and ignore the fact that many avoid gay bars and shun promiscuity, especially now when concern about AIDS is so prevalent.[31] Nevertheless, the media reports have aroused fear and revulsion in the minds of many people, including church members.

Counselors should remember that there is no typical homosexual lifestyle. It is inaccurate, insensitive, and unkind to conclude that most homosexuals are bar-hoppers, activists who march in favor of gay rights, child molesters, effeminate (in males; masculine in lesbians), psychologically maladjusted,[32] or constantly preoccupied with sex. Such stereotypes lead Christians to push homosexuals away and deny them the love and acceptance that should be found in the church community. Of course, each of these characteristics describes some homosexuals, but it also is true that many homosexual persons are law-abiding, accepted members of the community. Some live together in overt homosexual relationships; others, as we have seen, keep their homosexual tendencies hidden and controlled. It is estimated that 10 percent of the adult population in the United States is gay. If this is so, there probably are a number of homosexuals in your church, though their identities may be well hidden.

Homosexual tendencies clearly influence people and their lifestyles in different ways. Some are open about their sexual preferences; others give no hint of their tendencies but live with a quiet and persisting fear that the homosexual orientation might surface inadvertently and lead to the loss of friends, jobs, and acceptance from others.

2. *Self-Concept and Emotional Effects.* With the recent openness about homosexuality, some gays have concluded not only that gay is "good" but that to be gay is to be superior to others. More prevalent is the inner insecurity and lower self-esteem that comes to anyone who is different from the majority. Guilt over homosexual tendencies or actions, loneliness, fear that one's homosexuality might be detected, a sense of hopelessness (leading at times to drinking and sometimes to suicide), and an inner anger have all been seen in homosexuals. Others struggle with issues of identity and questions about their place in society.[33] For many persons, especially those who are unmarried, the flight to gay bars is an attempt to find love and support from understanding people who can bolster individual self-confidence and salve the inner pain.

3. *Relationship Effects.* While some homosexuals build supportive intimate relationships with other people of the same sex, these relationships are often temporary, and for many they never develop at all.[34] In a world that values youth, virility, and good looks, it is difficult to find intimacy and acceptance if one lacks these qualities. Married people who keep their homosexuality hidden (at times even from their mates) may discover that their sexual preferences, fantasies, or fears of

rejection can put a strain on their marriages and prevent them from getting close to others lest the hidden tendencies slip out and become obvious. Those who are open about their homosexuality tend to have less permanent, less diversified, and less fulfilling social relationships than do heterosexuals.[35]

Then there is one's relationship with God. Since homosexual behavior is sinful, involvement in this activity puts a barrier between the person and God. Many Christians fail to distinguish between homosexual behavior (including lust), which is sin, and homosexual tendencies and desires that in themselves are not sinful. Failure to recognize this distinction can lead to perpetual attempts to squelch one's gay tendencies. When this proves futile, there often is discouragement, guilt, a stifling of spiritual growth, or sometimes a flight to one of the gay churches that openly accept and even encourage homosexuality.

After reading this chapter, one young man wrote that he feels accepted by other people when they assume he is heterosexual, but he feels a barrier go up if anyone discovers that he struggles with homosexuality. "I want to be accepted as a fellow Christian who is like others in the church except that I struggle with homosexuality," he wrote. "Sometimes I wonder if the only place where a person like me can really feel accepted is in heretical gay churches instead of in the true church of Jesus Christ."

4. *Family Effects.* Homosexuals often regret their lack of children,[36] and those who have children from a previous heterosexual marriage often find that gay parents have some unique problems as parents. In custody cases, judges rarely give children to gay parents because there is fear (1) that the child will grow up gay if raised by a homosexual parent, (2) that the child might be molested sexually if raised in a gay home environment, or (3) that the child will be stigmatized by his or her peers if the parent's sexual orientation becomes known. No evidence exists to support the first two of these fears, and only minor data support the third.[37] Children of gay parents lack the example that comes from having both a male and female parent in the home, but the same is true of children who grow up in single-parent families when the parent is heterosexual.

Relating to children may be difficult for homosexuals, but for many it is harder to relate to their own parents. Many parents are crushed when they learn their child is homosexual, and these fears are greater as parents consider the prevalence of AIDS among gays. Confused, guilt ridden, and fearful, parents sometimes feel shunned by their friends and uncertain about how to react to one's gay children and their homosexual lovers.[38] Adult gay children in turn may feel guilt for the pain their homosexuality has inflicted on their parents' lives. All of this can create tension in the home.

COUNSELING THE HOMOSEXUAL

The place to begin counseling is with your own attitudes. If you are afraid of homosexuals, joke about them, condemn them, uncritically accept stereotypes, or are unfamiliar with the complexity of homosexuality and its causes, then you will be ineffective in helping. Jesus loved sinners and those who were tempted to sin. We who seek to follow in his steps should do the same. If we sense no inner compassion for overt homosexuals or for people with homosexual tendencies, then we must ask God to give us the compassion that we lack. We must examine our own attitudes toward gay people, must seek to understand the diversity of homosexuality, and should avoid counseling homosexually oriented people so long as our negative attitudes persist or we are unwilling to change.[39]

One idea that must change is the myth that homosexuality is a disease that cannot be cured. Homosexuality is not a disease; it is a tendency that often but not always leads to habitual fantasies or acts of homoerotic behavior. If homosexuality is primarily a learned condition, as the evidence suggests, then it can be unlearned. If homosexual behavior is sinful, as the Bible teaches, then forgiveness is available and so is divine help that can keep a homosexually oriented person from sexual sin.

Change is never easy for homosexuals and their counselors. The counselee dropout rate is high, and enthusiastic reports from ex-gay ministries often appear to be overly optimistic.[40] Nevertheless, change (even to heterosexual tendencies and behavior) is possible,[41] especially when some of the following are present (the more that are present, the better the chance for change):

- The counselee honestly faces his or her homosexuality.
- The counselee has a strong desire to change.
- The counselee is willing to break contact with homosexual companions who tempt the counselee into homosexual behavior.
- There is a willingness to avoid drugs and alcohol since these leave one more vulnerable to temptation.
- The counselee is able to build a close nonsexual intimate relationship with the counselor or other same-sex person.
- The counselee experiences acceptance and love apart from homosexual friends and contacts.
- The counselee is under thirty-five and/or is not deeply involved in homosexual attachments to others.
- The counselee has a desire to avoid sin and to commit his or her life and problems to the Lordship of Jesus Christ.

These preliminary considerations should be remembered and could be discussed with the homosexual who seeks help. Then the counselor can help in the following ways.

1. *Determine Counseling Goals.* When someone comes for help, what does he or she want: elimination of homosexual tendencies, knowledge of the biblical teaching on homosexuality, help in stopping gay behavior, sanction for continuing homosexual activity, help in relating better to a gay lover, or something else? Sometimes the counselee has no real desire to change but comes at the urging of a parent, youth leader, or spouse. Do not assume that you know what the person wants until you ask and discuss the counselee's answers.

2. *Instill Realistic Hope.* It is not easy to counsel with homosexuals. While homosexual actions can be stopped and completely forgiven by God, homosexual tendencies are much more difficult to eradicate. Sometimes a person will not change to a heterosexual orientation, but he or she can be helped to live a victorious, meaningful life free of homosexual entanglements and activity.

This seems to be the conclusion of Christian psychologists David Myers and Malcolm Jeeves:

> Homosexual people may struggle to ignore or deny their desires and may successfully avoid acting on their desires, but the desires seldom go away. If they try to change their sexual orientation—through effort, psychotherapy, or prayer—they find that the feelings are as persistent as those of heterosexual people. This has been the experience even of several of the founders of Christian "ex-gay" programs. . . .
>
> Accepting the limits on our capacity to change can be liberating. . . . It frees us from daily living with guilt and self-blame over not having accomplished whatever it is that we keep thinking we will do. To make peace with oneself is to be able to say that grace extends to me, just as I am. . . . whether my longings are heterosexual or homosexual. . . .
>
> But is there not a danger if we say no more? . . . If, indeed, one's sexual orientation is neither willfully chosen nor easily changed, are there not still ethical choices that are within one's power to make? Whether heterosexual or homosexual, one can choose to engage in promiscuous sex, to elect celibacy, or to enter into a committed, loving, long-term relationship. Sexual orientation per se does not dictate the choice, nor is it an excuse for sexual exploitation of anyone.[42]

Even though change is difficult, there is cause for real hope, especially when the person sincerely wants to change, but you may have to keep reminding your counselees (and yourself) of this. Sinful homosexual actions can be stopped with the help of God; innate homosexual predispositions may be changed, but if that doesn't happen, the sexual orientation can be lived with and life still can be fulfilling.

3. *Share Knowledge.* Homosexuals who come for counseling may believe some of the greatest myths about the problem. As counseling progresses, be alert to these myths and look for opportunities to challenge the misconceptions and to replace them with accurate information about homosexuality and about human sexuality in general. It can be encouraging for the counselee to know, for example, that people with homosexual feelings are not all incompetent, mentally ill, incurable, perverted, rejected by God, or unable to function effectively in society. At some time you probably will share the biblical statements about homosexuality, especially the distinction between homosexual tendencies and homosexual actions.

4. *Show Love and Acceptance of the Person.* In a courageous and insightful chapel address, a Christian seminary student once talked about his own homosexual tendencies and his ministry among the gay community:

> Come to one of the dozens and dozens of gay bars in Chicago with me tonight and at 3 A.M. I will show you some of the nicest people in the world who are crying out to be loved—hundreds and hundreds of them—and where are we who know of the love of Christ? Surely the search for love often takes on twisted and sinful expressions, but the hunger, the heart's cry, the vacuum seeking to be filled with the love of God is there and it is the same as yours and mine. Christian friends need to be there; not tract-wielding preachers, but listening compassionate friends. . . .
>
> More than anything else, a person who struggles with gayness, Christian or non-Christian, has a desperate need for love. He or she has been hurt by

> pathogenic family patterns, twisted environmental influences, or basically the sin which affects each of us. More than being a victimizer, the gay person has been a victim of sin. He has been hurt and usually has suffered greatly for his orientation which he did not inherit or choose, but rather learned long before the age of accountability. Often as a last resort in falling into gay sex the person has sought love which becomes eros defiled. So why does he or she need a Christian friend? Because we have Christ in us and we know the love of Christ—the redeeming, sanctifying, healing power of God's incarnate love. Our whole world has a desperate need to see this love of Christ, to feel it, to touch it, to experience it personally, and we are his instruments.[43]

According to this speaker, the Christian community should reach out, accept the counselee, and give the continuing love that makes individual counseling more effective. Christians also can demonstrate that it is possible to have close friends of both sexes without the necessity of sexual involvement. To break with one's gay friends is threatening and involves a real grief process as one loses people who have been supportive and accepting. If there is no supportive community of believers waiting and willing to accept the homosexual, then there can be an easy retreat back into the old lifestyle.

The experience of a close, nonsexual relationship with a counselor of the same sex is the basis of Moberly's approach to helping homosexuals. When there is acceptance and love from another same-sex human being, healing is most likely to come especially if the relationship is accompanied by prayer.[44]

5. *Encourage Behavior Change.* Even when there is love and acceptance, change will not come to the person who continues his or her sexual involvement with other homosexual persons. If this involvement has continued for a long time it may be especially difficult to stop. After a deliberate decision to change, the counselee may experience relapses and at times may resist the idea that change is desirable. Such resistance should be discussed in a straightforward, patient, kind, and firm manner.

One way to help change behavior is to avoid people, publications, and situations that are sexually arousing. This may lead to loneliness and a change in lifestyle, but this is a price that must be paid. Remind the counselee that Christ forgives[45] and that the Holy Spirit always is present to help us resist temptation and forsake sinful behavior. This will be much easier if there are other human beings to give continual encouragement and human contact.

At this point there also can be value in discussing the counselee's whole lifestyle. Sex is a part of life but so is worship, work, family, recreation, time management, exercise, and rest. One does not find fulfillment in life solely through sexual satisfaction and neither do problems all disappear if counseling considers only sex. Unless the counselee finds satisfaction and personal feelings of identity in nonsexual parts of life—such as in his or her relationship with Christ, church involvement, work, or recreational activities—there will be a tendency to slip back into homosexual relationships when the pressures build. A more balanced life is a common-sense remedy, especially for the many minor and fleeting homosexual feelings and actions.[46]

6. *Recognize That Counseling May Be Complex and Time Consuming.* Homosexuality is a complicated problem, often highly ingrained, and difficult to treat, especially by a counselor who has limited training or experience in working

with homosexuals. This is not meant to discourage you. Instead it should alert you to the complexity of your task and show that in some cases referral to another counselor may be the best way to help.

At the risk of oversimplification, we will mention only three of the many approaches to counseling homosexuals.

(a) The Psychoanalytic Approaches. Long, expensive, and in-depth, this approach aims at helping the homosexual gain insight into the causes of his or her orientation. There is much debate about whether or not homosexuals are really helped by this approach. Even if it could be shown that they are helped, it is unrealistic to think that most counselees could afford the 150–350 sessions of individual counseling that would be required for psychoanalytic treatment.[47]

(b) The Behavioristic Approaches. Based on principles of conditioning and learning, these approaches try to help counselees unlearn their preferences for the same sex and relearn a heterosexual orientation. Little or no emphasis is placed on consideration of the family interactions or fears that may have caused homosexuality. Although the method appears to be used with decreasing frequency, some counselors show sexually arousing (some would say pornographic) homosexual pictures to counselees, accompanied by mild electric shock. This is followed by the presentation of heterosexual pictures without shock. Other counselors encourage heterosexual behaviors apart from marriage in an attempt to stimulate heterosexuality. These practices are of limited effectiveness and, because of their sinful moral implications, should be avoided by Christians. Some behavioristic methods do tend to change behavior and reduce anxiety, but they may do little to alter homosexual tendencies and there is little evidence that the change in behavior is permanent.

(c) The Multiple-Phase Approach. As reported by John Powell, an evangelical counselor on the faculty of Michigan State University, this approach has two stages: the premultiple and the multiple. In the premultiple phase the counselee meets for several sessions with a same-sex counselor who shows acceptance, warmth, and support while there is discussion of the possible causes and implications of homosexuality in the counselee's life and a consideration of the counselee's homosexual behavior and goals for counseling. Then there is a shift to the multiple-phase. Here a male and female counselor work together with a counselee in an attempt to show how men and women relate in mutually satisfying ways, to help the counselee resolve persisting conflicts with parents, and to teach the counselee how to relate to males and females in mutually fulfilling ways.[48]

The approach of Powell and his associates emphasizes the value of helping counselees to reexamine the family background and other causes of their homosexuality, to help them learn how to relate in healthy ways to people of both the same and opposite sex. Such an approach also permits counselors to discuss the sinful nature of homosexual behavior and to challenge counselees to change their actions with divine help. Since it deals with more than current behavior, the approach (or one like it) can also help people change homosexual tendencies.

Preventing Homosexuality

As we have seen, there is strong evidence that homosexuality is primarily a learned condition that is affected mildly (if at all) by genetic, glandular, or physiological influences. If this is true, then homosexuality can be prevented by providing learning experiences that stimulate heterosexuality. This does not mean, of course, that we can give a lecture or reading assignment and expect that this will prevent homosexuality. The learning must start in the home even before the child knows how to read.[49]

1. *Building Healthy Home Environments.* Since homosexuality often appears to arise from undesirable parent-child relationships, the family is where prevention must begin. It is true, no doubt, that no parent who has a satisfying marriage turns to a son or daughter for a relationship that should be had with one's mate. No father rejects or ignores his children if he has a satisfying marriage, a career that does not dominate his time, and the feeling that he is secure in his masculinity and adequate as a male.[50] No child is likely to become homosexual if there has been a warm, emotional relationship, especially with both parents.

All of this suggests that the church prevents homosexuality when it stimulates biblically based family patterns in which the father and mother maintain clearly differentiated roles; the father is a leader in the home, the children are respected and disciplined, and the parents have a mutually satisfying relationship. Stable homes stimulate healthy heterosexual attitudes in the family members.

2. *Giving Accurate Information about Homosexuality.* It is sad to observe the condemnation and horror with which so many Christians react to homosexuality. Growing up in such an environment, young people learn to fear homosexuals and to suppress any gay tendencies within themselves. Instead of admitting and dealing with one's same-sex preferences, the young person keeps them hidden. Since he or she cannot get understanding and help from parents or church members, in time there may be a drift toward homosexual groups who are understanding, accepting, and loving. By its condemning attitude, therefore, the church sometimes pushes people into situations in which overt homosexual behavior is encouraged.

The alternative is not to develop liberal attitudes that deny the sinfulness of homosexual acts. The alternative is for churches to teach what the Bible says about sexual control, love, friendship, and sexuality (including homosexuality). Church leaders should demonstrate an attitude of compassion and encouragement rather than one of condemnation. Stereotypes about homosexuality (some of which are taught in popular Christian books about gays) should be exposed for what they are: untruths that alienate people, perpetuate ignorance, stimulate fear, push homosexuals away from Christian fellowship, and serve mainly to boost the critic's own sense of self-righteous superiority. All of this implies that issues like homosexuality should be discussed in the church instead of being denied. This is true now more than ever because of the high incidence of AIDS among homosexuals.[51]

Since overt homosexuality can become a habit in response to environmental stimulation, the church should emphasize the importance of sexual self-control. This comes through prayer, meditation on Scripture, avoidance of sexually arousing situations or people, deliberate decisions to avoid sinful actions, and the habit of being accountable to an understanding friend or counselor.

3. *Developing Healthy Self-Concepts.* Several years ago George Gilder pointed out that "there are millions of males who under the wrong conditions are open to homosexuality. A frequent catalyst is self-abasement. Failure in love or work may so deject a man that he feels incapable of rising to a relationship with a woman.

. . . To have a woman, a man must to some extent feel himself a man."[52] If a male feels inadequate or unmasculine, he may seek a safe relationship where he does not have to act like a male or prove his maleness. Perhaps a similar situation exists in women. A low self-concept contributes to the prospect of homosexual behavior.

Chapter 21 discusses the development of self-esteem. Churches and homes can help individuals build realistic and positive self-concepts and this, in turn, can contribute to the prevention of homosexuality.

Conclusions about Homosexuality

It is impossible to estimate how many people, including Christians, struggle with homosexual urges. Afraid of rejection or of being misunderstood, these people are reluctant to admit their tendencies. Often they struggle alone, grappling with guilt or self-condemnation, and seeking to find rationalizations that might explain or pardon their sexual thoughts or actions. People like this can be helped and the church can be a helping place. For the sensitive counselor who tries to understand homosexuality, counseling with gay people is not much different than other types of counseling. It involves "an application of the power of the gospel to heal and transform the lives of God's people within a counseling setting."[53]

At this time in history, there is widespread interest in homosexuals and openness about homosexuality. Never before, perhaps, has there been such an opportunity for church members and Christian counselors to make an impact on both the counseling and the prevention of homosexuality.

SUGGESTIONS FOR FURTHER READING

Lovelace, Richard F. *Homosexuality and the Church.* Old Tappan, N.J.: Revell, 1978.*

Moberly, Elizabeth R. *Homosexuality: A New Christian Ethic.* Greenwood, S.C.: Attic Press, 1983.

Tripp, C. A. *The Homosexual Matrix.* New York: Signet, 1975.

White, John. *Eros Defiled: The Christian and Sexual Sin.* Downers Grove, Ill.: InterVarsity, 1977.*

Wilson, Earl. *Counseling and Homosexuality.* Waco, Tex.: Word, 1988.*

Zimbelman, Ernie. *Human Sexuality and Evangelical Christians.* Lanham, Md.: University Press of America, 1985.

* Books marked with an asterisk (*) are especially suited for counselees to read.

20 Violence and Abuse

GINNY GREW UP OVERSEAS, the child of dedicated missionary parents who always sought to be diligent in their work and sensitive to the needs of their children.

Several years ago, when the family came home on furlough, Ginny found the courage to tell her mother about the sexual abuse that had been common in their overseas home. Unknown to the family, their male servant had frequently fondled and sometimes forced Ginny to have intercourse. He told her to never tell and promised to blame and hurt her if reports of this activity ever became known.

Ginny's parents were shocked to hear this news and eventually found a Christian counselor for their daughter. The counselor was an older Christian man with excellent credentials and a good reputation. In his meetings with Ginny, the young girl was helped greatly as she worked to overcome the trauma of sexual abuse.

One morning, to the shock of everyone in the Christian community, the radio announced that the counselor had been arrested for taking "indecent liberties" with a young patient in the psychiatric hospital where he worked. The family found another counselor for their daughter. This time they chose a well-respected female psychologist who has been understanding and sensitive but not very effective in helping Ginny with her hurts and anger.

"Never again will I be able to trust men," Ginny told her counselor recently. "I have been hurt too much. I don't want to date, and I'm not sure I even want to change."

The counselor is not as pessimistic. Ginny's emotional scars run deep. In spite of the loving support of her parents and other family members, Ginny has been greatly harmed by the self-centered actions of two insensitive men. For this young missionary kid, recovery and healing may take a long time.

Violence and abuse, especially in the home, appear to be increasing. It is possible, of course, that we are only now beginning to recognize the widespread prevalence of a problem that has been with us for centuries. Media attention and public outcries have riveted attention on child neglect and abuse, sexual violence, psychological maltreatment of children, rape, mate beating, and mistreatment of the elderly. Various observers have confirmed that these problems of abuse not only are getting more attention, they are getting worse.[1]

Abuse is difficult to define, perhaps because the term covers so many types of physical and psychological maltreatment. *Child abuse,* as defined by the formal language of the U.S. Child Abuse Prevention and Treatment Act, involves the "physical or mental injury, sexual abuse or exploitation, negligent treatment, or maltreatment of a child under the age of eighteen, by a person who is responsible for the child's welfare and under circumstances which indicate the child's health or welfare is harmed or threatened thereby."[2] *Mate abuse,* most often has the wife as the victim and includes deliberate physical assault, threats of violence, emotional abuse (including ridicule, demeaning behavior, and neglect), and forced involvement in sexual acts. *Elder abuse* is the maltreatment of older people and includes rough handling, beating, negligence, verbal condemnation, withholding of food or medication, financial exploitation, sexual mistreatment, and ignoring the person's needs for comfort and human contact. *Sexual abuse* may overlap with any of the above and includes exhibitionism, forced intercourse or other sexual behavior which the victim resists, or fondling the sex organs of a minor or other person who is naive or powerless to resist.[3] The National Center for Child Abuse and Neglect includes the use of children in the production of pornography, as an example of sexual abuse. To all of this we could add rape, criminal violence, physical assault of students by teachers, sexual exploitation of counselees by their counselors, harassment of neighbors by juveniles, the physical and emotional exploitation of employees by their employers, and most other behavior where one human being deliberately inflicts physical and emotional pain in an effort to harm a helpless and unwilling victim.[4]

Just as abuse is difficult to define, so is its incidence difficult to measure. Many victims are reluctant to report abuse, especially when the abuser is a family member. Children and the elderly often are unable to report abuse, and some people aren't even aware that the pain they experience is abuse. Many rape victims are embarrassed to report their experiences, and some say nothing because they fear reprisals if the rapist is identified or apprehended.

Even with these obstacles, the figures that do get reported are staggering. One study shows that during a one-year period, 1.7 million Americans faced a spouse wielding a knife or gun.[5] According to the FBI, between 50,000 and 200,000 rapes occur every year. Spouse abuse is estimated to occur in 3 to 6 million families in the United States, perhaps 12 to 15 million women were victims of incest,[6] between 2,000 and 4,000 child deaths occur annually because of child abuse or neglect,[7] an estimated 1.5 million children are victims of neglect,[8] and between 100,000 and 200,000 children are sexually abused.[9] One national estimate suggests that 4 percent of the elderly (that represents 1 million people) are victims of abuse, but the House of Representatives Select Committee on Aging estimates that only one in five or six cases of elder abuse is ever reported.[10] All of these figures will be different in other countries, of course,[11] but wherever the abuse is reported, most often the abuser is someone whom the victim knows, frequently a family member or friend.

There was a time when believers dismissed all of this as something that rarely occurs in Christian homes. No longer can we maintain such naiveté. Recent authors have begun to document the prevalence of abuse in Christian circles.[12] This is a problem that Christian counselors are likely to encounter with increasing frequency as people become more willing to talk about their experiences as victims of abuse.

THE BIBLE AND ABUSE

It could be argued that much of the Bible deals with violence. Accounts of biblical history frequently mention murder, military battles, and the blood of martyrs. Often the violence came because of the sinful acts of disobedient people whose lives were corrupt in the sight of God.[13] Violence also came as the result of wars that God had sanctioned in order to punish the wicked and administer justice. When "the rod of correction" is mentioned in Proverbs,[14] the emphasis is on discipline intended to rid the child of folly, to keep him or her from self-destructive behavior, to "impart wisdom," and to promote peace and good relationships in the family.[15]

Nowhere does the Bible sanction or approve of child, mate, elder, or sexual abuse. On the contrary, there is emphasis, especially in the New Testament, on behavior that is nonviolent. Jesus condemned not only murder but the harboring of angry thoughts toward another person.[16] "Do not judge," we are told in the Sermon on the Mount, or we likewise will be judged for our own faults and weaknesses.[17] In Colossians, husbands are told to love their wives and not be harsh with them.[18] Fathers are instructed to "not embitter your children, or they will become discouraged."[19] Employers are instructed to provide "what is fair and right." No room is allowed for employee abuse or harassment.[20] Believers are told to "get rid of all bitterness, rage and anger, brawling and slander, along with every form of malice." Instead we are to "be kind and compassionate to one another, forgiving each other, just as in Christ God forgave you."[21] Among believers there is to be "no hint of sexual immorality, or of any kind of impurity, or of greed, because these are improper for God's holy people. Nor should there by obscenity, foolish talk or coarse joking, which are out or place, but rather thanksgiving."[22] In 1 Timothy and James we read about the importance of treating elderly relatives and other seniors with care and respect. There is no place for elder abuse among believers.[23]

All of these examples describe divine ideals. Even though many fail to heed these instructions, they show clearly that God is opposed to abuse. His people must be opposed also.

What about the victims of abuse? Jesus told us to love our enemies and pray for our persecutors. "Do not resist an evil person," he said. "If someone strikes you on the right cheek, turn to him the other also." We are instructed to forgive those who sin against us, and to not be anxious about anything.[24] These instructions have led some Christian counselors to advise victims to submit passively to repeated beatings, harassment, and other abuse.

Surely Scripture does not instruct us to abandon self-defense or to stand by passively while our children or elderly parents are abused by family members. Commenting on Matt. 5:38–42, William Barclay writes that "time and time again life brings us insults either great or small; and Jesus is here saying that the true Christian has learned to resent no insult and to seek retaliation for no slight."[25] With God's help, people in time can learn to love their persecutors, pray for their enemies, forgive their abusers, and trust God for inner peace in the midst of difficult life situations. This does not prevent victims and their counselors from taking action to prevent further abuse, to protect victims from further harm, and to bring about the nonabusive ideals that Scripture clearly teaches.

The Causes of Abuse

Why would one human being physically and psychologically abuse another? The most basic answer is human sinfulness, but this does not explain why some people act in sinful abusive ways while most others do not. Once again we are confronted with behavior that has no simple nor single cause. The rapist's actions may have causes that differ significantly from the middle-age daughter who neglects and mistreats her elderly mother or the father who takes sexual advantage of his little girl. As we list some of the causes of abuse in the following paragraphs, remember that for each of your counseling cases, all, part, or none of the following may apply. Each situation is likely to have its own group of causes.

Before we look at these causes, it is important to dispel one misconception that victims and their families frequently believe. It is *not* correct to assume that victims of abuse usually ask for it by giving subtle hints to indicate that they would like to be mistreated. It is cruel and inaccurate to conclude, for example, that rape victims somehow really want to be raped and that they could prevent this personal sexual attack if they really wanted to escape. On rare occasions, victims may subtly invite the attacker's assaults, but this is unusual and certainly not the norm. Rape is a violent attack on a woman in which sex is used as a weapon.[26] For most victims it is a humiliating and often life-threatening experience. Rape victims, like all other recipients of abuse, do not encourage it to happen and neither do they secretly enjoy the experience.

What causes abuse to occur? The following are among the numerous, complex, and overlapping reasons that counselors have discovered.

(a) Environmental Stress. Many years ago, psychologists first identified frustration-aggression behavior. Whenever people get really frustrated, a common reaction is to respond to these feelings by verbally or physically lashing out at some other person or object. The pressured businessman who snaps at his secretary or the frustrated tennis player who throws his racket on the ground or the person who kicks the family dog are examples.

It is easy for parents to get frustrated with crying, whining children and to wish there was some way to "shut up that kid." It can be very frustrating to have older relatives who are getting more and more dependent and unable to care for themselves. If financial or work pressures begin to build, it is easy to take this out on family members, especially if the family members are weak, unable to help, or powerless to defend themselves. Sometimes even trivial stresses can trigger abuse, like the crying child who interrupts parents' sexual intercourse or the frustration of cleaning up after a messy feeding or soiling.[27] Stress in the life of the abuser, of course, is never an excuse for violence, even if the victim creates the stress. Nevertheless stress may help us understand why some people are abusive.

One writer[28] suggests that stress-induced violence often occurs in three stages. First is the tension-building stage where stress increases and coping techniques become less and less effective. In the second stage violence erupts. Often the outburst is irrational, and the abuser must be stopped physically. Third is the stage of remorse that follows the attack. The batterer apologizes profusely, expresses great feelings of remorse, promises never to let this happen again, and sometimes floods the victim with gifts and affection. This gives the victim hope that the violence will never be repeated. The victim is led to stay with the relationship, but when stresses build the cycle tends to be repeated.

(b) Learned Abuse. Children who are abused or who observe violence in their parents, often become abusers in later life.[29] One study of elder abuse found that one in four hundred children who are reared nonviolently attack their parents in later life, compared to one in two children who are abused by their parents.[30] Another report showed that children who are neglected never learn how to care for others, so they grow up to become neglecters of their own children.[31]

Other research supports this conclusion about prior learning. When older adults slap or hit their care givers, the care givers are more inclined to hit back. When children grow up in homes where fistfights and other physical contacts are common, these children learn to communicate violently. In related research, studies of some war veterans and secret police in totalitarian regimes have shown that ordinary people could be trained to inflict pain and torture on others with no follow-up feelings of guilt.[32] Abusive behavior—and criminal behavior as well—clearly can be learned and passed from one generation to the next.[33]

(c) Personal Insecurity. Studies often show that abusers are people who feel insecure, impulsive, and threatened; they generally hold low self-concepts. Sometimes wife beaters feel jealous, possessive, or intimidated by their wives, so the husband tries to boost his own feelings of inadequacy by being tough. Some child batterers feel inadequate as parents, so they attempt to manage their offspring with violence. Other parents have a low tolerance for the normal hyperactive behavior of their children, so violence becomes a way to gain control.[34] Studies of convicted rapists show that these often are angry men who release pent-up feelings of rage and bolster their feelings of sexual inadequacy by attacking women and using sex as a weapon.[35] Incest, in contrast, is less violent, but it often is seen in men who look to their daughters for tenderness and understanding. Some incestuous fathers (mother-son incest is very rare) get plenty of sexual fulfillment elsewhere, but they lack the emotional closeness that comes with father-daughter sex. Other men simply take selfish sexual advantage of children who are available but too naive or powerless to protest.[36]

There can be other causes of abuse. Sometimes there are ongoing power struggles between the abuser and the victim. Recent research has shown that sexually violent movies, pornographic materials, and television programs can and do promote violence, especially violence against women.[37] Then there is abuse that comes from people who are overwhelmed by family responsibilities.

When one sixty-eight-year-old lady recently died of starvation the community was outraged, but a newspaper reporter described the helpless feelings of her son. The mother had been confused, incontinent, blind, helpless, and uncooperative. She refused to eat and sometimes would take food from her mouth and hide it in her pockets. The son had a job, had no help in caring for his mother, and knew nothing about community social services that might have given assistance. He did not abuse his mother verbally or violently. He abused her by neglect because he simply did not know how to cope.[38]

All of this suggests the complexity and difficulty in trying to pinpoint causes of abuse. Unlike some other problems, however, in counseling the victims of abuse there may be less interest in why it happened and more of a need to consider ways to help people recover from the effects of abuse.

The Effects of Abuse

Newspaper columnist Bob Greene recently contacted a woman whom he had interviewed several years previously about her experience of being raped. The woman described her initial reactions, talks with a counselor, and life in the years that had passed since the rape.

"I was unlucky," she said. "It happened to me, and my life isn't the same because of it. I'm alive, but I'm not the same person, and I probably never will be. I can function, and I can have a good time, and I can sleep through the night now. I think it's asking too much to expect that I'll ever be exactly the way I was before, though. I've read that some women blame themselves. I never did that. But I think I'll always be different."[39]

The experience of this woman is not unusual. Abuse tends to affect victims deeply and often has a lifelong influence. In a *Los Angeles Times* nationwide poll of 2,627 randomly selected adults, 98 percent of those who had been sexually molested as children felt that the harm done by the abuse was permanent; 83 percent said the greatest damage was emotional.[40]

Depending on the age, personality, sex, type of abuse, and past experiences of the victim, the effects of abuse can influence people in a variety of ways. When compared with nonvictims, for example, incest victims are more inclined to show inability to trust others, low self-esteem, conflicts over sexual identity, feelings of guilt or shame, and isolation from others.[41] One counselor observed what he called the post-sexual-abuse syndrome, characterized by anxiety, sleep disturbances, anger, sexual dysfunction, substance addiction, and self-destructive tendencies.[42] A study at the University of South Carolina School of Medicine found that adult victims of child abuse tended to be overweight, depressed, and chronically anxious. Many had nightmares, almost all had problems with sex, and most had difficulties forming stable relationships. Some appeared to be intent on making themselves appear unattractive to others. [43] Another report found that teenagers who had been abused or neglected as children are more likely than the nonabused to be involved in delinquent behavior and to commit violent crimes.[44] Abused wives, as we might expect, feel afraid, angry, depressed, lacking in self-esteem, and often helpless. Rape victims are more likely than other women to suffer from anxiety, depression, sexual difficulties, family tensions, impaired work and social adjustment, withdrawal from others, self-condemnation, apathy, and inertia.[45] Victims of elder abuse often feel confused and helpless, but most don't complain or report the abuse even if they are able to do so. The fear of being abandoned, placed in an institution, socially isolated, or punished leads many to suffer in silence and sometimes even to find reasons to excuse the abusive actions of their adult children.

These diverse effects of abuse could be grouped into three general categories. Abuse influences the victim's feelings, thinking, and actions.

(a) Feelings. Victims often feel angry, afraid, ashamed, guilty, embarrassed, confused, and worthless. Many victims report feeling violated, dirty, vulnerable, and afraid to trust others. Depression is common and sometimes there is self-pity and self-blame.

(b) Thinking. People who have been abused often have low self-concepts and think of themselves as being unattractive, incompetent, inadequate, dependent, and unwanted by others. Often victims have low morale and impaired concentration. Abused children, battered wives, and mistreated older people sometimes blame themselves for the treatment they receive and think that they must deserve to be abused. Often there is a willingness to take the abuse without resisting because the victim feels so helpless and afraid of the consequences if the abuse is reported.

(c) Actions. Abuse sometimes leads victims to develop antisocial behavior, learning disabilities, interpersonal tensions, inefficiency at work, and, as we have seen, a tendency to become violent and abusive themselves. Often victims are afraid to venture outside, so they stay home. Many withdraw from people at a time when they most need social support. Some start drinking, a few withdraw into a world of mental fantasy, but many become like the lady interviewed in the Bob Greene column. They go on with life as best they can, but they recognize that because of the abuse, life will always be different than it might have been if the abuse had not occurred.

Where is God in all of this? For some victims there is theological confusion and questioning. Why, they wonder, would God allow this to happen? Could any good possibly come from such a painful situation? Many are angry at God and this may be directed toward the Christian counselor. Often there are struggles with doubt, the seeming inability to forgive, or questions about whether they can ever hope again or trust God to protect them.

In considering the effects of abuse, try to remember that the victim is not the only one who suffers. Family members, boyfriends, mates of rape victims, and close friends may all react with anger, confusion, prejudice, and feelings of helplessness, revulsion, and embarrassment. Male mates of rape victims sometimes feel personally violated because of what has happened to their wives. One husband felt "physically disgusted when approaching his 'unclean' wife sexually, immediately following her rape."[46] All of this can lead to marital tension, depression, and further stress on the victim.

Finally we should not forget the abuser. Often these people feel deep and lasting remorse, especially after their abusive behavior becomes public knowledge. Many are frightened, guilt-ridden, and confused, but they find little support or sympathy from others. Few attempt to understand abusers, and counselors seem reluctant to realize that many abusers need help as much as their victims.[47]

Counseling and Abuse

It can be difficult to counsel abusers and their victims. Compassionate counselors, even those with long experience, can be shocked and repulsed when they observe the physical and psychological pain that some human beings inflict on others, often repeatedly.[48] At times counselors have difficulty knowing if they should believe the reports of abuse that come from young children or old people; at other times we may suspect abuse but wonder what to do if the counselee denies it. Men, including male ministers, often find that female counselees are too ashamed or embarrassed to talk with a male about abusive sexual experiences, so counseling must be turned over to another.[49] A perusal of the counseling literature could indicate that counseling with abuse victims has not yet proven to be particularly effective,[50] and the challenge is complicated further by the fact that each victim or abuser is unique and needs to be treated somewhat differently from the others.

Despite these uniquenesses, recovery from abuse can be considered as a process having four overlapping stages.[51]

First, there is the *impact* stage. It lasts for a few hours to several days and is characterized by shock, disbelief, anxiety, and fear. Often victims are confused about whether to report the abuse and frequently there is fear that the abuse may recur. Sometimes the impact is made worse because the abuse victim feels overwhelmed by too many professionals or police officers asking questions.[52] At this stage, counselors can give support, guidance as decisions are made, or help in finding medical care and safety. Often none of this help is given because the victim is too afraid, confused, powerless, or embarrassed to report the abuse or to seek help.

Stage two involves *denial.* In order to cope with the stress, the victim tries to push aside the trauma of abuse and return to a precrisis stage of functioning. Victims at this time need to feel secure, organized, and in control. To others, and even to the victims themselves, it may appear that everything has returned to normal, but the hurt is still present and will need to be dealt with before complete healing occurs. The denial stage may be over within a few days, although for some it lasts for years.

Stage three, the *process* stage, begins when the experience of assault can no longer be suppressed. Often some crisis event or emotional distress may trigger the old feelings and the victim is flooded with anxiety, depression, nightmares, flashbacks, and constant thinking about the assault. This is a period when the victim needs to talk, to express feelings, to struggle with guilt and anger, and to feel counselor support. Many find comfort and help by joining support groups where sexual-assault victims help one another. Others find help through community or church support networks that give emotional support, understanding, and information.[53] If you have not had experience in counseling abuse victims, you might be wise to contact a local rape or sexual-assault center where experienced helpers can often give information and assistance as you work with victims and their families.

The final stage of *integration* comes as the individual begins to feel no longer controlled or dominated by the effects of the sexual assault or assaults. These are viewed as painful and significant events in the past, but the person has grown to a higher level of psychological and spiritual maturity and is able to move on with life.

Although everyone involved needs support, guidance, and help in coping with the stress and emotional reactions to abuse, much of your counseling will depend on the type of abuse and on the counselee's specific involvement.

Helping the Children of Abuse. A physician who had spent years trying to help abused children once described the difficulties of her work. "Those who try to assist sexually abused children must be prepared to battle against incredulity, hostility, innuendo, and outright harassment. Worst of all, the advocate for the sexually abused child runs the risk of being smothered by indifference and a conspiracy of silence. The pressure from one's peer group, as well as the community, to ignore, minimize, or cover up the situation may be extreme."[54] Children, as we have seen, rarely report sexual or physical abuse, sometimes because they don't know who to tell but often because they have been threatened with further harm if they talk to anyone about the abuse.

Sometimes you can suspect abuse or neglect by observing several of the following:

- The child seems unduly fearful, especially of parents.
- The child is poorly groomed or inappropriately dressed for the weather.
- The child appears undernourished or inappropriately fed.
- The child's injuries or sicknesses are inappropriately treated in terms of bandages or medication.
- The child is withdrawn and depressed or overactive and aggressive.
- The child seems disinterested, unable to concentrate, inclined to cling to adults other than the parents or unable to get along with other children.
- The parents are rigid, highly demanding of their children and inclined to punish harshly.
- The parents have experienced multiple stresses such as marital discord, divorce, debt, frequent moves, job loss, or other pressures.

Frequently the outside observer has few or no indications of abuse. There are no scars and the child looks healthy, but sometimes there will be inappropriate behavior such as aggression, altered sleep patterns, or inappropriate sexual behavior.

It is true that children have vivid imaginations and sometimes make up stories, but young children do not have the capacity to fantasize about something that they haven't experienced. Listen carefully if they give hints about abuse and, if you can, ask them to describe what they mean in more detail. When caring adults are bold enough to intervene, lifelong psychological damage can often be prevented.

Remember that abusers often demand that their young victims keep the abuse secret. Even those who do tell often retract the complaint when it becomes known. As they get older, children and adolescents begin to realize that most people won't believe that an apparently normal adult, like one's own father, could be capable of "repeated, unchallenged sexual molestation of his own daughter. The child of any age faces an unbelieving audience when she complains of ongoing incest. The troubled, angry adolescent risks not only disbelief, but scapegoating, humiliation, and punishment as well."[55]

Child abuse, including incest, is an issue that involves the whole family. The victim may be the person who suffers most and is noticed first, but other family members need help as well. For this reason, most counselors try to involve the entire family in the counseling process, especially when the abuse occurs within the home.[56]

Helping the Adult Victims of Incest and Abuse. It is not surprising that victims sometimes carry the pain of childhood abuse into adulthood and never share the secret with anyone. When we consider that perhaps 20 to 30 percent of college-age females have been sexually victimized as children, it is sobering to recognize how many silent victims of abuse may be in your church or may pass through your counseling office. After speaking on the radio about abuse, Karen Burton Mains reports that she was swamped with hundreds of letters from listeners who had been abused.[57] One psychologist put a small notice in a campus paper inviting readers to call if "you have been involved in sexual abuse and still have problems resolving this." Fifty-four calls came within the next twenty-four hours.[58]

If you suspect abuse in a counselee, do not hesitate to raise the issue gently. Mention that the problem is common, that victims do not deserve the abuse, and that people can get over their feelings of shame and hurt. Often the gentle, caring, nonjudgmental encouragement of a sensitive counselor is all the counselee needs to break a long-guarded secret and to deal, finally, with the bottled-up feelings and questions about abuse.[59]

Helping the Victims of Rape. Rape victims have been classified in three ways, depending on how they respond to the rape.[60] The majority show the rape trauma syndrome. This begins with acute stress immediately following the rape. There may be fear, anger, anxiety, shock, self-blame, and disbelief, often expressed by crying, sobbing, tenseness, nausea, or restlessness, but sometimes hidden behind a calm, composed exterior. At this point the victim may be flooded with feelings of terror, concern for her safety, and guilt because she did not struggle more. Some women wonder if the myth really is true which says that women secretly attract rapists.

At this point the counselee will probably be sensitive to someone who will listen, accept, and believe her, especially if she has faced subtle disbelief and rejection from family, friends, police, or medical personnel. The counselor can encourage the expression of feelings, can help the woman find competent medical and legal aid, can give support when she does encounter criticism, can help her and her friends recognize the myths about rape, can encourage the victim to discuss her fears for future safety, and can give assurance of continued support especially as the woman faces crisis situations in the coming weeks.

Two or three weeks after the rape, many women begin to experience nightmares, irrational fears, and restless activity. Often there is a decision to move, change a phone number, stay indoors at night, or spend more time with close friends. In all of this the victim is in the process of reorganizing her life following an experience that for many has been terrifying. Such women need support, freedom to express feelings, acceptance, an opportunity to talk with someone who considers them normal, and guidance as they make decisions. Many will want to discuss the issue of "Why me?" and will need to be reassured of God's continued care, love, and concern. Often it helps for a counselor to take the initiative in helping these women instead of waiting for the victim to seek more traditional counseling. It also is helpful to counsel with the families and mates if possible. These people can be very supportive to the victim, but, as we have seen, relatives often have feelings of their own that need to be expressed, attitudes that need to be changed, and misconceptions that need to be corrected.

A second general response to rape has been termed the "compound reaction." Victims with previous physical, psychiatric, or social difficulties sometimes develop more intense symptoms such as depression, psychotic or suicidal behavior, psychosomatic disorders, drug use, excessive drinking, or sexual acting out behavior. Such women need referral for help that is more in-depth than crisis counseling.

A third response to rape is the "silent rape reaction." These women, including some who were molested as children or adolescents, have not told anyone about the rape, have never talked about their feelings or reactions, and have carried a tremendous psychological burden. Later in life these women may develop anxiety, fear of men, avoidance of sexual behavior, unexplained fears of being alone or going outside, nightmares, and a loss of self-esteem. If these people are abused again, they often spend more counseling time talking about the pent-up emotions concerning the first rape than they do about the more recent situation.

Studies of rape victims report that women usually are able to reorganize their lives and protect themselves from further assault.[61] This is most likely when victims are helped to get the medical treatment, psychological help, and practical guidance they need after rape.

The victimization of women by rape or any other means is a gross deviation from God's intended plan, but there is no evidence to support the myth that rapists primarily are militants in a male battle against women. Some rapists are men who find themselves in a situation where rape appears convenient, so their action is a spur-of-the-moment decision. Often rapists are young, married, employed people whose family life is disturbed, who can't relate successfully to women, and who deny that they are a menace to society. In each case, rapists need more than supportive counseling. They need to know God's forgiveness, to experience the power of God to transform lives, and to participate in counseling designed to deal with those underlying issues that caused them to initiate the act of rape.

Helping the Victims of Mate Abuse. Most mate abuse is assumed to involve the physical and psychological mistreatment of a wife by her husband. Husband abuse by a wife is usually thought to be rarer, although emerging evidence suggests that domestic violence against men is increasing and in some places may even be more common than wife abuse. Because of their greater strength, men are better able to inflict injury on their wives, but women often do more physical harm because they tend to attack with something other then their hands.[62]

In both cases the victim often has low self-esteem and, in the case of wife abuse, there may be a distorted belief that the husband's role as head of the home gives him the right to tyrannize his family. Sometimes the victim is even made to feel that she, rather than the abuser, is the real cause of the problem. In other cases, the abusive mate may usually be loving and willing to provide for the family, except for periodic and often unpredictable explosions of rage and violence.

Once again most victims are reluctant to report the abuse. There is realistic fear that the abusing mate could explode in more violence if he (or she) discovers that the family aggression has been reported. A woman whose livelihood depends on her abusive husband is reluctant to risk being cut off from food and shelter, especially if this would make her solely responsible for the care of her children. Some Christian women believe (and are told by their pastors) that wives should be submissive to their husbands, even if the husband's behavior is intensely violent and life threatening.

Counselors, therefore, should be alert to nonverbal signs of spouse abuse. These include:[63]

- A history of miscarriages.
- Frequent visits to the emergency room for treatment of illnesses or injuries.
- Signs of ongoing stress, such as headaches, gastrointestinal ailments, vague "not feeling well" complaints, or excessive use of tranquilizers or alcohol.
- Withdrawal and isolation from friends, church, and family.
- Moody, discouraged, unpredictable, or depressive behavior, sometimes accompanied by periodic suicide attempts.
- Frequent absence from work.

- Reports from others, including neighbors or children, about conflict or disruption in the home.
- References to previous abuse or violence in the home.

If abuse is suspected, the counselor should not be reluctant to raise the issue. Pastors who can visit in the home have unusual opportunities to explore these issues with victims who might not voluntarily come for counseling.

Intervention is most effective if the family sees the violence as a crisis situation. Try to learn as much as you can about the home situation and seek to determine the likelihood of future harm or danger. Especially in this early stage, many victims need support, the calming effect that comes from a caring counselor and guidance in making practical decisions. Ultimately the Christian counselor wants to help the couple maintain and heal the marriage, but when the risk of further violence seems high, it may be wise to help the abused mate and children get away from the danger and withdraw, at least temporarily, to a place of security and safety. This could be the home of a church family, but it also may mean the use of a community emergency shelter for abused spouses and children. When this removal seems best, you would be wise to get the advice and guidance of community resources, such as a lawyer, law enforcement officials, or medical personnel. Many counselors lack experience in this kind of social intervention, so it is helpful to know what community assistance is available and what legal issues might be involved.[64]

Once the immediate danger is lessened, counseling is likely to focus on issues of guilt, low self-esteem, the biblical position on husband-wife relationships, the difficulty of learning to forgive, and the battered mate's feelings of guilt, anger, discouragement, hopelessness, and worries about coping in the future. Later the counselor may be involved in helping the husband and wife deal with issues of communication, conflict resolution, sexual adjustment, husband-wife roles, trust, and other issues of marriage counseling.

Helping the Victims of Elder Abuse. Maurice Chevalier once said that "growing old isn't so bad when you consider the alternative." For many older people, the alternative—death—would seem to be much better, especially if one's life is bombarded with physical or psychological abuse.

This abuse does not come only from younger family members. Sometimes the elderly are abused by hospital personnel, employees of nursing homes, neighborhood vandals, their own mates, or impatient workers in stores or government offices. Since few older people seek counseling, it is probable that the pastor may be the first to suspect elder abuse.

Whenever an older person talks about mistreatment, the counselor can listen with sympathy and sensitivity. Remember, however, that some older people are unable to think clearly,[65] and their reports of mistreatment may be more imagined than real. It is wise, therefore, to talk with care givers, including the older person's relatives. Abuse of the elderly is more probable when older people have needs that are great, but the care givers have limited resources or abilities to meet these needs.

Counseling will often involve support for the older person and help for the family as they learn to cope in ways that are compassionate and nonabusive. This may mean finding individuals or community and church groups who can provide emotional support for both the old person and the family, home nursing care, visitation, transportation, and other more tangible expressions of help. If the older person is in a living situation where abuse continues, he or she may need guidance and practical help in finding other accommodations.

Helping the Abusers. The victims of abuse are hurting people who often can get help from caring counselors. Abusers, in contrast, tend to be condemned, ignored, and incarcerated without treatment. Abusers need counseling too. Estimates vary, but some have suggested that between 35 and 80 percent of untreated abusers and sex offenders repeat the violence; the return to abuse is much less likely among those who have been treated.[66]

When confronted with their violent actions, many abusers deny what they have done, excuse their actions, or try to shift the blame onto the victim or somebody else.[67] Perhaps it is not surprising that recurrences of battering are reduced when abusers are arrested. The reality of fines, imprisonment, and social disgrace makes denial less possible and forces at least first-time abusers to get serious about counseling.[68]

Counseling abusers is often a long-term process dealing with the counselee's anger, low self-esteem, and lack of self-control. Many lack communication, problem-solving, conflict-resolution, and stress-management skills. Since many victimizers were earlier victims of abuse, it often is important to deal with attitudes and insecurities that have built up over a lifetime. Some abusive counselees have never learned how to express their feelings in nonviolent, socially appropriate ways. Some have rigid and domineering attitudes about leadership or the role of the husband or parent. Others are entrenched in erroneous beliefs—like the myths that victims enjoy the battering, that victims encourage it, or that violence is the macho way to assert authority. All of these attitudes must be challenged and changed if abuse is to cease. This is time-consuming work, best done by an experienced counselor.

Although individual counseling can be helpful with abusers, many published reports stress the value of group treatment.[69] By meeting with other abusers, the counselee sees people who understand because they have similar problems. As they interact in the group, counselees can learn to express feelings in ways that are nonviolent, can feel acceptance and support, and can be helped to develop needed communication, stress-management, and social skills. Old attitudes can be challenged, sometimes by victims of abuse who are invited to tell what it was like so abusers can see that victims do not enjoy the experience. Since many (some would say most) abusers lack the social skills needed for responsible community living, group counseling becomes an education in violence-free living.

Abusers also need to understand forgiveness, including the ability to forgive themselves. They need to see that abuse is not an unpardonable sin. The God who forgives can and will give help and guidance to those who sincerely want to rebuild their lives and live in ways that do not hurt others. To be a helper in this rebuilding process can be a demanding but highly fulfilling role for any counselor.

Some Disturbing Ethical Issues. Abuse is not limited to physical violence. Sometimes verbal battering, sexual harassment, expressions of racism or sexism, discrimination against the elderly (often known as ageism), homophobia (the fear and hatred of homosexuals), the creation of continual fear, hazing on college campuses, economic subjugation, or other nonviolent abuse can in time be as wearing as more blatant assault.[70] Sexual harassment, for example, has been compared to tiny drops of water. Each drop may be of minor importance and small effect, but months and years of regular droplets erode even the hardest of substances.[71]

It is difficult to intervene in this "droplet" kind of abuse, but whenever a counselor encounters more blatant violence, we are confronted with at least two important ethical issues.

The first concerns *confidentiality*. Effective counselors normally respect the privacy of their counselees and do not talk about the issues that are brought into a counseling session. What do you do if a counselee has been harmed physically and is in danger of being harmed again? How do we respond when we learn that innocent children are being victimized by abusive parents or other adults? What is the responsibility of a pastor or other counselor if he or she discovers that some innocent party is in danger of being harmed? Do we break confidentiality to warn the victim?

These are difficult ethical issues, but some of them have been resolved by the government. If you live in the United States, for example, counselors in most places are required by law to report suspected incidents of child abuse. Only in some states are clergy exempted from this requirement. In some places, laws also require the reporting of mate abuse or mistreatment of the elderly. This issue of mandatory reporting has raised what one writer has called a "clergy dilemma,"[72] but other counselors also are concerned. If you suspect abuse, for example, report it as the law requires, and then discover that your suspicions were wrong, are you likely to be sued?[73] According to one report, 60 percent of reported abuse incidents cannot be substantiated. This can leave an innocent but reported family feeling very angry, especially if the report has become public knowledge.[74] These issues are complicated by variations from one state to another in how abuse is defined, in what needs to be reported, and to whom.[75] It is important for counselors to get information about the laws in their own communities.

Most organizations of professional counselors have standards of ethics that emphasize the importance of confidentiality. When counselees threaten to harm themselves or others, however, professional counselors are ethically bound to warn or otherwise protect people (including counselees) who are in danger. Often, of course, the counselee has no intention to harm others despite his or her talk, but when the threat appears to be serious, the counselor has a legal and professionally responsible duty to warn and protect.[76]

It can be helpful to remember that confidentiality is not the same as secrecy. Secrecy is the absolute promise to never reveal information to anyone, regardless of the circumstance. Confidentiality is the promise to hold information in trust and to share it with others only if this is in the best interest of the counselee or sometimes in the interest of society. On occasion the counselor needs to break confidence in order to take action that is likely to prevent violence. This, rather than infringement on anybody's rights, surely is the intent of many professional statements of ethics and mandatory reporting laws.

A second and closely related issue concerns direct counselor *intervention* in a counselee's life. Assume, for example, that you are the pastor of a church who one night discovers a deacon's wife at the door begging for protection from her abusive husband. Most of us would agree that the woman should be taken in and not sent home, but the counselor's responsibility may also extend to getting victims to medical treatment facilities, helping abuse victims (including children and the elderly) to get out of an abusive home situation, calling the police when there appears to be no other way to stop domestic violence, or otherwise getting involved in helping those who cannot help themselves. For the Christian, the act of helping the abused and abusers cannot always be confined to a comfortable counseling office.

Preventing Abuse

Abuse and violence have become so prominent within recent years that a number of professional counselors and community groups have turned their attention to prevention. Some communities have developed telephone hot lines to give immediate, twenty-four-hour daily access to help for people who are victims of abuse. The development of self-help and support groups also can be helpful for both victims and abusers.

One observer[77] has urged churches to get involved by sponsoring educational events that will increase public awareness of abuse. Churches should be setting up peer-support groups, the writer suggested. We should be developing or participating in telephone crisis lines, helping to establish safe shelters for battered women and their children, and urging schools, police departments, and other community agencies to consider educative and preventive programs. All of this could be helpful, both for intervention in abuse and for prevention. The following are additional suggestions.

1. *Education.* Programs for preventing violence and sexual assault on college campuses have focused largely on providing information for both women and men.[78] Assault is less frequent when students know how to protect themselves, what to do in case of an attack, where to report violence or suspected abuse, what is myth and what is factual about abuse, or where to get further information. Throughout the community, including the Christian community, public awareness is good prevention.

2. *Stimulate Individual and Family Stability.* Abuse, as we have seen, often occurs in families where there is intense stress, misunderstanding of husband-wife or parent-child roles, or an inability to cope with family pressures. By helping people deal with the demands of child rearing, marital pressures, or the needs of elderly parents, we can reduce some of the underlying causes that lead to abuse. Research on delinquency prevention tends to support this conclusion. Children with close family bonds are less likely to experiment with delinquency. In contrast, violence, fighting, vandalism, and other forms of misbehavior most often come when children have been raised in homes where parents lack effective parenting skills. These may not be violent or unloving parents. Often they are parents who are overwhelmed by the demands of child rearing. When these parents get help, delinquency in their children is much less likely.[79]

3. *Teaching Interpersonal Skills.* The previous paragraphs have mentioned repeatedly that abusers often lack skills in effective communication, handling conflict, dealing with feelings, solving problems, negotiating when there are differences of opinion, managing stress, or coping with crises. Often the best way to prevent abuse is to help abusers and their victims handle life more effectively. Since victims

of abuse so often become abusers, it could be beneficial to give special attention to abuse victims, teaching them how to cope when stresses arise.

4. *Social Action.* Ultimately prevention will have to focus on ways to eliminate some of the psychological and social environmental issues that stimulate abuse and battering.

All of this may seem far removed from the work of Christian counselors or from the ministry of the local church. Throughout the Bible, however, there is an emphasis on helping the sojourner, the orphan, the widow, the poor, the helpless, and those who are in need. In today's society surely no person is more powerless than the victim of abuse. The follower of Jesus Christ has a responsibility to give help and protection to those who for a variety of reasons have become abused and abusers.

Conclusions about Abuse

When I was in the process of writing this chapter, the media and recording worlds were enamored by a nine-year-old, brown-eyed third grader who had recorded a song that suddenly become a hit record.

"Dear Mr. Jesus," sung by Sharon Batts, was written in 1985, from the viewpoint of a child reacting to a news report about child abuse. "Dear Mr. Jesus," the lyrics began, "I just had to write to you; something really scared me when I saw it on the news. A story about a little girl beaten black and blue." The song concluded with the words, "Dear Mr. Jesus, please tell me what to do. And please don't tell my daddy, but my mommy hits me too."*

All over the country, radio stations received requests to play the song. After playing it once, New York City's WHTZ began getting three thousand calls a day, many from callers who wanted to discuss their own experiences with abuse. Some radio stations followed the song with the telephone numbers of child-abuse hot lines and many of these counseling facilities suddenly were swamped with calls. When Sharon Batts was flooded with requests for personal appearances, her Christian parents humbly concluded that all of this came from God.

"You can go on with child-abuse announcements and public service all you want," suggested the program director of one Chicago radio station, "but this song causes an emotion in you that you really are not prepared for. People call to say thank you for playing the record. And that's never happened before."

By the time this book appears, the song and the story behind it may have been forgotten. Its spectacular rise to prominence surely illustrates, however, that family violence and abuse are big issues for many people. They are issues that no church or Christian counselor can ignore—least of all, people like us who have been alerted to the pressing needs of those who are the victims and the perpetrators of abuse.

---

*Lyrics to "Dear Mr. Jesus" reprinted by permission, all rights reserved, words and music by Richard Klender, © 1985 Klenco, Inc. (Klenco Music Group).

SUGGESTIONS FOR FURTHER READING

Baxter, Arlene. *Techniques for Dealing with Family Violence.* Springfield, Ill.: Charles C. Thomas, 1987.

Berry, Joy. *Sexual Abuse, Abuse and Neglect, and Kidnapping.* Waco, Tex.: Word, 1984.**

Brenner, Avis. *Helping Children Cope with Stress.* Lexington, Mass.: Lexington Books, 1984.

Courtois, Christine A. *Healing the Incest Wound: Adult Survivors in Therapy.* New York: W. W. Norton, 1988.

Hancock, Maxine, and Karen Burton Mains. *Child Sexual Abuse: A Hope for Healing.* Wheaton, Ill.: Harold Shaw, 1987.*

Kempe, Ruth S., and C. Henry Kempe. *Sexual Abuse of Children and Adolescents.* New York: Freeman, 1984.

Martin, Grant. *Counseling for Family Violence and Abuse.* Waco, Tex.: Word, 1987.

———. *Please Don't Hurt Me.* Wheaton, Ill.: Victor Books, 1987.*

Olson, Esther Lee, with Kenneth Petersen. *No Place to Hide: Wife Abuse: Anatomy of a Private Crime.* Wheaton, Ill.: Tyndale, 1982.*

Pellauer, Mary D., Barbara Chester, and Jane Boyajian, eds. *Sexual Assault and Abuse: A Handbook for Clergy and Religious Professionals.* San Francisco: Harper & Row, 1987.

Quinn, Mary Joy, and Susan K. Tomita. *Elder Abuse and Neglect: Causes, Diagnosis, and Intervention Strategies.* New York: Springer, 1986.

Schetky, Diane H., and Arthur H. Green. *Child Sexual Abuse: A Handbook for Health Care and Legal Professionals.* New York: Brunner/Mazel, 1988.

Sgroi, Suzanne M., ed. *Handbook of Clinical Interventions in Child Sexual Abuse.* Lexington, Mass.: D. C. Heath & C., 1982.

Van Hasselt, Vincent B., et al., eds. *Handbook of Family Violence.* New York: Plenum, 1987.

* Books marked with an asterisk (*) are especially suited for counselees to read.

** These are books for children in the Alerting Kids to the Danger Zones series. Each is illustrated in color and concludes with two pages of concise Important Information for Parents and Teachers.

Part 5

Identity Issues

21

Inferiority and Self-Esteem

SARAH WILL BE FIFTY on her next birthday. "I've been around for almost half a century," she told her husband recently, "And for all that time I've had an inferiority complex."

Sarah continually puts herself down in front of the family but feels hurt when her teenage daughters are in any way critical of her actions and attitudes. She is convinced that inferiority is "something some of us are born with" and refuses to believe that anything can be done to change.

Sometimes it seems Sarah uses her feelings of inferiority as an excuse to keep from helping in the church or to avoid social gatherings. "I can't do things as well as others," she has said frequently, and after turning down a number of social invitations because "I'm sure they really don't want us there," Sarah has discovered that invitations no longer come. This she accepts as further proof of her inferiority and lack of attractiveness to others.

Recently Sarah found an ally for her views when she heard a radio preacher who condemned what he called the "godless humanistic view that we should have good self-esteem." The preacher spoke against "feeling good about yourself," and criticized other preachers and counselors who speak well of self-love, self-acceptance, or a positive self-image. "These ideas are antibiblical," the preacher continued. "It is more biblical to put yourself down, to practice self-denial, and to emphasize your weaknesses. We are worthless, sinful creatures who should abhor ourselves."

Sarah has no desire to get counseling for her low self-esteem and feelings of inferiority. She doesn't see her attitudes as a problem. In contrast, she takes a secret pride in what she considers to be her more biblical view of self-condemnation. Thus she goes on, maybe for the rest of her life, feeling worthless, useless, and inferior.

Many years ago Alfred Adler, a European psychiatrist, wrote that everyone has feelings of inferiority. Sometimes these feelings stimulate us to healthy actions and achievements, but inferiority feelings also can be so overwhelming that they cause us to withdraw from others and develop what Adler called an "inferiority complex."

People who feel inadequate and inferior (one estimate suggests that this may include 95 percent of the population) tend to compare themselves unfavorably to others. Such comparisons can lead to a lot of human misery and feelings of inadequacy. Adler believed we can only escape this inferiority trap by stopping the comparison of ourselves with others and by giving up the common desire to be superior. More recent writers have argued that individuals overcome inferiority by developing a positive and healthy self-esteem.

The word "self-esteem" appears frequently in the counseling literature along with related terms such as "self-image" and "self-concept." Self-image and self-concept refer to the pictures we have of ourselves. Ask yourself or a counselee, "If you were a novelist describing yourself as the chief character in a book, what words would you use?" Probably the description would include a listing of character traits, strengths, weaknesses, and physical features. Self-image and self-concept include these thoughts, attitudes, and feelings we have about ourselves. Self-esteem means something slightly different. This term refers to the evaluation that an individual makes of his or her worth, competence, and significance. Whereas self-image and self-concept involve a self-description, self-esteem involves a self-evaluation.

Clearly these terms overlap, and often they are preceded by adjectives such as "good," "bad," "positive," or "negative." People who have good self-concepts, for example, tend to use desirable words like "competent," "confident," "understanding," or "patient" in describing themselves. People who have a positive self-esteem evaluate themselves as being worthwhile and capable. All of these self-perceptions are carried around in our minds, and often they change as the result of our experiences. Sometimes, however, they are maintained stubbornly in spite of contrary evidence, and almost always they influence how we think, act, and feel.

The development of a good self-image and positive self-esteem has become almost universally accepted by mental health professionals. Many modern approaches to counseling focus on the goal of helping counselees improve their self-concepts. In reality therapy, for example, William Glasser seeks to help people meet "the need to feel that we are worthwhile to ourselves and to others."[1] Family therapist Virginia Satir writes that "the crucial factor in what happens both inside people and between people is the picture of individual worth that each person carries around with him."[2] Carl Rogers, the most influential of the self-esteem psychologists, wrote often about self-worth and unconditional positive regard. These were ideas that theologian Robert Schuller developed further in a controversial book that called self-esteem "the greatest need facing the human race today," our "universal hope," and the basis for a "new reformation" that carries us forward from the Protestant Reformation of Luther and Calvin.[3] Overcoming inferiority and helping people build self-esteem have clearly emerged as significant issues in both secular and pastoral counseling.

The Bible and Self-Esteem

Within the past several years, many Christians have been locked in debate about the value of self-esteem. Well-known Christian counselor Jay Adams is highly critical of terms like "self-esteem," "self-love," and "self-image." He uses words like "paganism" and "a plague" to describe the self-esteem movement, and argues that Scripture focuses on human sinfulness and self-denial rather than on self-worth or self-affirmation. The Bible is not intended to "make us satisfied with ourselves as we are, but to *destroy* any satisfaction that may exist," Adams writes. "You must treat yourself like a criminal, and put self to death every day."[4] Psychologist Paul Vitz has taken a similar view in a book that criticizes our modern overemphasis on the self and calls psychology a new religion that is based on worship of the self.[5]

A different perspective comes from theologian Anthony A. Hoekema who wrote a book designed to "show that the Bible teaches us to have a positive image of ourselves because we are new creatures in Christ."[6] Counselor David Carlson would agree. Writing from a rich background of clinical experience, Carlson realizes how many people are devastated by a poor self-image. The solution is not, however, to give ourselves a pep talk designed to boost our self-image. Instead people need to be helped to find a biblical kind of self-esteem.

> Self-love, as I understand the concept biblically and psychologically, includes the following: (1) accepting myself as a child of God who is lovable, valuable, capable; (2) being willing to give up considering myself the center of the world; (3) recognizing my need of God's forgiveness and redemption. Christian self-esteem results from translating "I am the greatest, wisest, strongest, best" to "I am what I am, a person made in God's image, a sinner redeemed by God's grace, and a significant part in the body of Christ."[7]

Perhaps to the surprise of some, Schuller gave a somewhat similar answer when he was asked to define self-esteem. "Self-esteem comes when a person realizes that Christ, who died an atoning death for him, comes to live in him through the Holy Spirit." Self-esteem, according to this view, can be seen as "the sense of value that comes to me when I have been restored to a relationship with God as the Heavenly Father, and I have the assurance that I am worth a lot. Christ died on the cross for me. If he thinks that much of me, I had better start thinking something good about myself."[8]

As Christian counselors, we are likely to encounter many people who feel inferior and have a poor self-esteem. Some are confused when they learn about the debate over self-esteem, when they read popular books that condemn self-esteem,[9] or when they hear preaching that sometimes condemns and sometimes lauds self-worth. It is crucial, therefore, that we understand and share the biblical teaching about human worth.[10] It is then that we can be most effective in helping people overcome their feelings of inferiority. It is then that we can develop self-perceptions based on the truths of Scripture.

1. *The Biblical Teaching about Human Worth.* Throughout its pages the Bible constantly affirms that human beings are valuable in God's sight. We were created in God's image with intellectual abilities, the capacity to communicate, the freedom to make choices, a knowledge of right and wrong, and the responsibility to administer and rule over the rest of creation.[11] Even after the Fall, we are described as "a little lower than God" (and lower than the angels) but crowned with "glory and honor."[12] Because he loves us, God sent his own son to pay for our sins and to make possible our redemption and renewed communion with God the father.[13] He has sent angels to guard us, the Holy Spirit to guide us, and the Scriptures to teach us that we are the salt of the earth and the light of the world. Individuals who trust in God will spend eternity with him in a place prepared for us in heaven.[14]

Several years ago, Bruce Narramore suggested what this means for human self-acceptance:

> Compared with . . . secular perspectives, the Christian view of self-esteem is in a category by itself. It alone elevates man above the animals. It alone

> provides a solid foundation on which to build self-esteem. The biblical view of man acknowledges our sins and failures, but it doesn't demean our deepest significance as creations of the living God. . . . Because we are created in the image of God, we possess great worth, significance, and value. We are loved by God and deserving of the love of ourselves and others.[15]

2. *The Biblical Teaching about Human Sin.* The Bible teaches that as a result of Adam's sin, all people are sinners who have become alienated from God and condemned because of their sinful natures and actions.[16] Sin is rebellion against God. It represents a doubting of God's truthfulness and a challenge to his perfect will. Sin leads to interpersonal conflict, attempts at self-justification, a tendency to blame others for our weaknesses, psychosomatic problems, verbal and physical aggression, tension, and a lack of respect for God.[17] All of this surely influences the way we feel about ourselves, often producing guilt and undoubtedly lowering our self-esteem.

Even in our fallen state, God still loves and values us. He hates the sin but loves the sinner. He knows that we are ungodly and helpless, but this does not mean that we are unredeemable and worthless. Indeed because of his love and mercy, he sent his son to die so that we could be made righteous and be brought back into his family as fully forgiven sons and daughters.[18]

Sin breaks one's relationship with God, but sin does not negate the fact that in God's sight we still are human beings, the apex of divine creation, and of immense worth and value.

3. *The Biblical Teaching about Pride.* Some Christians who emphasize human depravity argue that self-esteem is a form of pride. Since pride is greatly abhorred by God,[19] these believers assume that self-condemnation and inferiority are attitudes that keep us humble.

Pride is characterized by an exaggerated desire to win the notice or praise of others.[20] It is an arrogant, haughty estimation of oneself in relation to others. It involves the taking of a superior position that largely disregards the concerns, opinions, and desires of other people. In essence, it is an attempt to claim for oneself the glory that rightly belongs to God.

In contrast, humility is characterized by "accurate self-appraisal, responsiveness to the opinions of others, and a willingness to give praise to others before claiming it for one's self."[21] The humble person accepts his or her imperfections, sins, and failures, but also acknowledges the gifts, abilities, and achievements that have come from God. Humility is not a self-negation or the rejection of all our God-given strengths and abilities. Humility involves a grateful dependence on God and a realistic appraisal of both our strengths and weaknesses.

The Apostle Paul, for example, was deeply aware of his sinful past and continuing imperfections, but he also recognized his considerable achievements.[22] He recognized that he had been redeemed and greatly used by God. His was a realistic self-image. It was characterized not by pride, but by a humble evaluation of what God had done and was doing through him. Self-esteem, a realistic self-appraisal, and humility go together.

4. *The Biblical Teaching about Self-Love.* The Bible assumes that we will love ourselves.[23] This conclusion is difficult for some Christians to accept because they

equate self-love with an attitude of superiority, stubborn self-will, or self-centered pride. Self-love, however, is not an erotic or ecstatic self-adoration. Self-love means to see ourselves as sinners who have been saved by grace, people who are created, valued, and loved by God, gifted members of the body of Christ (if we are Christians), and bearers of the divine image. We can love ourselves because God loves us, and we do not deny the abilities and opportunities that God has given. This biblical view of self-love must become the basis of self-esteem.

Perhaps some of the theological disagreement about self-esteem comes because basic terms are defined differently.[24] It has been suggested, for example, that self-worth must not be considered the same as self-worship, that self-love is not the same as selfishness, that self-affirmation is different from self-conceit, that we can be aware of ourselves without being absorbed in ourselves, that self-denial is not the same as self-denigration, that putting off the sinful nature is not the same as putting yourself down, that humility is not the same as humiliation, and that being unworthy is not the same as being worthless.[25] The Christian can have positive self-esteem, not because of human works and human nature but because of God's grace and divine redemption.[26]

The Causes of Inferiority and Low Self-Esteem

Biblical teachings and theological discussions on self-esteem are at the basis of many inferiority and self-concept problems. For each counselee, however, there can be different reasons for low self-esteem, including the following.

1. *Faulty Theology.* As we have seen, any of us will feel inferior if we assume that all humans are worthless, that sin makes us of no significance to God, and that the way to be humble is to condemn ourselves while we deny the gifts and abilities that the Lord God has given to each of his children. Each of these views is held by sincere people, many of whom apparently assume, incorrectly, that self-esteem is wrong or that feelings of inferiority should typify committed Christians.

A variation of this view is held by those sincere Christians who advocate a self-crucifixion approach to theology. This assumes that humans are worthless, that our desires, thoughts, and individual abilities should be denied or "crucified," that we should put down our human nature, and that Christ's thoughts and attitudes should completely engulf our lives. This view seems to be spiritual, but it denies (and therefore squelches) the individual gifts, abilities, personalities, and capacities that come to each of us from God and are intended to be used in his service. The self-crucifixion view fails to realize that Christians have been crucified with Christ (in the past), but nevertheless *we now live* as new creatures in vital fellowship with him. This does not mean that we are to become robots who reject our abilities and squelch our personalities. Instead we are to submit these to divine control and trust that God will work through the unique individual differences he has given to each person.

In talking to his disciples, Jesus once said "If anyone would come after me, he must deny himself and take up his cross and follow me."[27] Christians are not to live self-centered, self-gratifying, self-affirming lives. Instead we are to abandon selfish personal ambition so we can serve Christ sacrificially.[28] To deny oneself is to "make God the ruling principle, more, the ruling passion, of life. The life of constant self-denial is the life of constant assent to God."[29]

It does not follow, however, that the person who denies selfish ambition or the drive for personal gratification, must also deny his or her God-given gifts. Believers have been forgiven, adopted into God's family, and endowed with special gifts and responsibilities that enable them to serve Christ and the church more effectively.[30] When we deny the existence of these gifts, we are engaging in self-deception rather than self-denial.

2. *Sin and Guilt.* When God created human beings, he gave us a standard of right and wrong, guidelines for living in accordance with his universal principles. When we violate these principles, we are guilty and as a result we feel remorse and disappointment in ourselves. This contributes to our feelings of inferiority and undermines self-esteem.

3. *Past Experience.* In a society that values success, it is difficult to experience failure, rejection, and criticism. If we have failed frequently or are belittled often, it is easy to conclude, "I'm no good. Look at what people think of me. Look how I mess things up."

Researchers at Taylor University studied the self-esteem levels of more than fifteen hundred people, including a number of evangelical Christians. There was no difference in self-esteem between believers and non-Christians, but there was a significant difference between those who were highly educated and successful in contrast to those with fewer educational attainments. This is consistent with other findings that people who achieve in this life tend to have more positive self-esteem than those who do not.[31]

Sometimes failure comes, not because we have tried and failed, but because others expect us to fail. In situations like this it is easy for a person to conclude, "Nobody expects me to succeed or be liked so why should I try?" When we don't try, failure is assured and self-esteem is eroded further.

4. *Parent-Child Relationships.* Counselors generally agree that the basis for a child's self-esteem is formed during his or her early years.[32] Inferiority and low self-esteem, therefore, often arise in the home.

Most parents are inconsistent in their child rearing and feelings about children. Even the most patient parent explodes in criticism at times or withholds acceptance and warmth. Children rarely, if ever, are damaged by such minor parental fluctuations, but real feelings of inferiority do come when parents:

- Criticize, shame, reject, and scold repeatedly.
- Set unrealistic standards and goals.
- Express the expectation that the child probably will fail.
- Punish repeatedly and harshly.
- Imply that children are a nuisance, stupid, or incompetent.
- Avoid cuddling, hugging, or affectionate touching.
- Overprotect or dominate children so they fail later when forced to be on their own.

5. *Unrealistic Expectations.* As we grow up, most of us develop expectations for the future and ideals that we would like to attain. When these expectations and ideals are unrealistically high, we have set ourselves up for failure and for the feelings of inferiority that often follow.

One perceptive writer suggests that there are three common "enemies of self acceptance."[33] These are assumptions that many people have learned to accept even though they tend to undermine self-esteem. The three enemies are the false but widely held beliefs that:

> "I must meet other people's standards and expectations if I am to be accepted and loved."
>
> "Whenever I fail to reach my goals and expectations (or those of other people) I need to be pressured, shamed, frightened, or punished."
>
> "I must seek to master my world, to be in charge, to be smart, to be the center of my environment, and to make my own decisions."

Whenever a person holds unrealistic beliefs or assumptions like these, it is common to find failure, feelings of inferiority, and low self-esteem.

6. *Faulty Thinking.* Sometimes we assume that high achievers and successful people rarely have doubts about their abilities and competency, but this is not necessarily true. There is evidence that many high achievers reach their goals but feel insecure in their positions of success. Many wonder if they really are as competent as others assume. Few high achievers ever measure up to their own standards of excellence. Some even wonder if their successes came not as a result of competence but because of chance. "I got the lead in the play," said one actress, "because the director's first choice dropped out." "I only got into graduate school because the dean knew my dad," confessed another. Even though others view them as being bright and talented, many of these people feel like impostors. They have successful careers but inferiority feelings because of the way they think about themselves.[34]

It is common for each of us to believe and sometimes to make up statements about ourselves that have little or no basis in reality. "Nobody likes me" or "I'm no good" are ideas that may contain more fantasy than realism. If it is not to control us, such thinking must be challenged, perhaps by some realistic self-talk. Where, one might be asked, is the real evidence to support the conclusions we hold about ourselves?

7. *Community Influences.* Every society has values that are emphasized by the mass media and demonstrated in homes, schools, governments, businesses, and social settings. It is widely assumed, for example, that a person's worth depends on one's intelligence, physical attractiveness, education, money, powers, and achievements. People are encouraged to manipulate circumstances and each other to attain and retain these symbols of success.[35] It is thought that the possession of these symbols increases one's self-esteem, that their loss or nonattainment increases one's sense of inferiority. This is a cultural myth that motivates many people but leads to lowered self-esteem when the status symbols are not attained, when they are attained and found to be meaningless, or when they are acquired and then lost.

The Effects of Inferiority and Low Self-Esteem

Libraries, commencement addresses, and many sermons are filled with inspiring stories of people who faced handicaps or other great obstacles but, with unflinching determination, rose to overcome the deficiencies. Whenever he ran for public office, Abraham Lincoln lost, but he persisted until he was elected president. Theodore Roosevelt, a nearsighted and sickly child, learned boxing and horseback riding in order to toughen himself. Franklin Roosevelt overcame the effects of polio. Helen Keller couldn't see or hear, but she learned to communicate. Winston Churchill failed at school but became a great statesman and communicator. For many people, it seems, difficult life experiences become a prod that pushes them to overcome their inferiorities.

Less admirable, perhaps, but more apparent are those who try to hide their inferior feelings and boost sagging self-esteem by acquiring the trappings of power or success. Insecure men who act tough, people from poor environments who go into debt so they can buy big cars or wear flashy clothes, frustrated workers who stage violent strikes that give them feelings of power over company management, poorly educated people who use big words in an effort to impress others are methods that people try in order to deal with inferiority by showy overreactions.

There are other ways to react. Researchers have shown, for example, that people with feelings of inferiority may:[36]

- Feel isolated and unlovable.
- Feel too weak to overcome their deficiencies and lack the drive or motivation to defend themselves.
- Be angry, but afraid of angering others or drawing attention to themselves.
- Have difficulty getting along with others.
- Be submissive, dependent, and so sensitive that their feelings are hurt easily.
- Have lower curiosity or creativity.
- Be less inclined to disclose themselves to others.

Lowered self-esteem and inferiority also may contribute to:

- A lack of inner peace and security.
- Low self-confidence.
- Social withdrawal.
- Jealousy and criticism of others.
- Interpersonal conflict.
- Self-criticism, self-hatred, and self-rejection.
- Depression.
- A drive to gain power, superiority, or control over others.
- A tendency to be complaining, argumentative, intolerant, hypersensitive, and unforgiving.
- An inability to accept compliments or expressions of love.
- An inclination to be a poor listener or a poor loser.

All of this shows that low self-esteem can have a wide influence. Everybody feels inferior at times, but when the inferiority feelings are intense or long-lasting, virtually all human actions, feelings, attitudes, thoughts, and values are affected.

Counseling People with Inferiority Feelings and Low Self-Esteem

Feelings of inferiority and low self-esteem build up over many years. It is unrealistic, therefore, to expect that change will come quickly, but over a period of time counselors can help in a variety of ways.

1. *Give Genuine Support, Acceptance, and Approval.* People who feel inferior have a tendency to "back off" and respond negatively to expressions of approval or affirmation that are unrealistic, abrupt, or ungenuine. If a counselor is too enthusiastic in giving praise or approval, counselees don't believe what they are hearing and at times may even decide to avoid the counselor. It is more helpful to give continuing support, gentle encouragement, and mild but sincere approval for achievements that clearly can be evaluated as good. A back-slapping attitude that says, "Buck up, you really are a significant person," rarely does anything to help a person shed feelings of inferiority.

2. *Seek to Develop Understanding.* Insight into one's behavior is not easy, and sometimes it isn't very helpful. Introspection causes some people to become more self-condemning, to overlook significant facts, and to lose objectivity. You can help the counselee search out the sources of his or her poor self-concept. Start by looking at past experiences that were affirming or condemning. As you do this, remind the counselee (often if necessary) that we need not be prisoners of the past. As we understand the past roots of behavior and thinking, we are better able to change.

3. *Share the Biblical Perspective on Self-Esteem.* Counseling will not be very successful if the counselee has heard or is convinced that inferiority is the same as humility or that a healthy self-esteem is equivalent to sinful pride. Christians must be helped to see the biblical teachings about human worth and self-esteem. They must be urged to give up self-condemnation and shown that such condemnation is both destructive and wrong in the sight of God who has redeemed us and given us a new nature. It may take a long time before ideas such as these will be accepted, but their acceptance is important, especially for believers who want to overcome feelings of inferiority.

4. *Encourage Self-Disclosure and a Realistic Self-Evaluation.* Sharing often helps build self-esteem. When a person shares his or her self-concept, others can give their feedback. As these others show acceptance, counselees can begin to accept themselves.

Try to be aware that such sharing can lead counselees to attempt a subtle, often unconscious manipulation of others. If I say, for example, "I'm no good; I'm such a failure," other people are made to feel that they should deny this evaluation with a comment like, "Oh, that's not true!" Counselees should be shown how their own self-condemning comments sometimes are used to pull expressions of praise from other people. Praise and affirmation that come through manipulation are not really affirming. As a result the inferiority feelings persist.

It is better to help the counselee list his or her good traits, strengths, and assets as well as weaknesses, inabilities, and less desirable characteristics. As the list is developed, preferably on paper, ask "What is the objective evidence (for example, in the form of past experiences or other people's opinions) that each item on the list (both positive and negative) should be there?" Remember to emphasize the counselee's strong points, special talents, or gifts and consider how each of these can be put to better use. People often focus so much on their weaknesses that they inhibit or deny their God-given talents and abilities.

At times you probably will notice that some people are reluctant to acknowledge their strengths, often because this can be threatening. When a person is convinced of his or her inferiority, there may be no effort to succeed and no motivation to risk failure. "After all," these people reason to themselves, "since I'm probably going to fail, why should I bother to try anything?" Some individuals even seem to delight in their assumed inferiorities. Once they admit that they have strong points, the pressure is on to develop and use these positive traits and take responsibility for their actions. That takes effort, and there is a new realization that failure is possible. For persons with a poor self-concept, the risk may seem too great. It is safer to wallow in one's inferiorities.

5. *Stimulate a Reexamination of Experiences, Goals, and Priorities.* There can be two kinds of goals: long-range and short-term. Long-range goals are often major (like getting a college degree, buying a house, or earning a promotion) while short-term goals are more immediate and more easily attained (like reading this chapter, passing a test, finishing a do-it-yourself project, or introducing yourself to a new neighbor). Long-range goals often seem overpowering and unattainable so the person who feels inferior declines to tackle them. Counselees can be reminded, however, that long-range goals can be broken down into short-term projects. As each short-term goal is reached, we experience a sense of accomplishment and edge slightly toward our long-term aspirations.

Consider, for example, the writing of this book. At first the project seemed overwhelming, especially when I heard the publisher talking about deadlines. I keep reminding myself, however, that a task like this moves along one sentence at a time. Every day I block out time to write and set up (short-term) daily goals. These are challenging enough to motivate me but realistic enough to ensure that on most days I will succeed in meeting my expectations.

Counselees can be encouraged to write down their long-range goals and priorities. Then they should be helped to break these down into much smaller, attainable goals. As the smaller goals are reached the individual can experience a feeling of success, with a resulting boost in self-image. There even may be value in rewarding oneself whenever a goal is reached. (Whenever I work on a book, I sometimes reward myself with a break or a cup of coffee whenever I finish typing a specific number of pages.)

In all of this, the counselor can stimulate realistic goal planning (which will ensure some successes), can give encouragement as the counselee attempts new activities, can help the counselee evaluate what went wrong when there is failure, can encourage the person to try again, and when necessary can point out that periodic failure is not proof of one's innate inferiority.

At times there also is value in examining motives. Why does the counselee want to attain certain specific goals? What are his or her motives? Be sure to remind people that it is important to do what one believes to be right (even if this leads to criticism from others). It is unlikely that one can experience real self-esteem unless this is done.

Counselors and their counselees can remember that no human being is completely alone. God gives strength and guidance to those who seek his help. He directs individuals in the development and attainment of goals and priorities. He also helps us to develop new skills.

6. *Teach New Skills.* Sometimes counselees need to learn new skills or improve old ones. This in turn can help them attain goals or reach vocational objectives. Part of your work as a counselor may involve encouraging someone to attend school or enroll in a training program.

Many skills, however, can be learned in counseling and practiced between sessions. For example, you can teach counselees to:

- Avoid dwelling on the negative; that is, the tendency to think hypercritical thoughts or to make negative, argumentative comments. These alienate others, arouse hostility within the critic, and undermine the critical person's own self-esteem.
- Give frequent encouragement, compliments, and respect to others. Respecting people whom God has created helps us to respect ourselves.
- Meditate regularly on God's Word. He loves us and communicates with us through the Bible. This book can help individuals keep a realistic perspective when there is a tendency instead to slip into thoughts of one's own inferiorities and incompetence.

7. *Help Counselees Avoid Destructive Tendencies.* In a book on building an adequate self-concept,[37] one experienced Christian counselor noted that we all have destructive tendencies that can alienate us from people, prevent spiritual growth, and lower self-esteem. These include the tendencies to:

- Treat other people as objects to be manipulated.
- Resent and dwell on circumstances that are painful, unpleasant, or humiliating.
- Become angry and resentful when we lose control of a situation.
- Give up or react with anger when we are shown to be wrong.
- Become paralyzed and unwilling to act whenever we are afraid.
- Dread problems instead of accepting them as challenges.

When these are seen in a counselee, they should be pointed out, discussed, and changed if possible since each can hinder self-esteem.

8. *Stimulate Group Support.* Being accepted by a group of people can do much to stimulate self-esteem and help an individual feel worthwhile. Group counseling is often a helpful way to build self-esteem, providing the group members are supportive, wanting to help, and not inclined to use the group as a vehicle for criticizing and tearing down each other.[38] Sometimes an active involvement in a church or other religious group can also boost self-esteem.[39]

9. *Teach Counselees to Deal with Sin.* It is impossible to feel good about ourselves when we deliberately disobey God's principles for our lives. Sin ultimately creates guilt, self-condemnation, depression, and a loss of self-esteem. Counselees must be helped, therefore, to honestly face their sin, to confess it to God and sometimes to one or two others, and to remember that God forgives and forgets.[40]

The inability to forgive, especially the inability to forgive oneself, can also undermine self-esteem. There is a need to remember that vengeance and the administration of justice are God's responsibilities, not ours.[41] We must ask him to help us forgive, to give up our grudges, and to really accept the fact that wrongs and injustice can be committed to God who will both forgive those who are sorry and will bring justice to unrepentant wrongdoers. At times your greatest contribution to a counselee's self-esteem may be to help him or her accept forgiveness and learn to forgive.[42]

Preventing Inferiority and Low Self-Esteem

Ideally the local church is a body of believers with a commitment to worship and world evangelism along with a determination to teach, care for, build up, and do good deeds for one another, all free from the power struggles, manipulation, and status seeking that characterize so much of our society. Of course, most churches fall short, often far short, of this ideal. Even so the Christian community can have a powerful influence in changing self-concepts and preventing individual feelings of inferiority. This can come through teaching, support giving, and parental guidance.

1. *Prevention through Teaching.* We have seen that many people develop low self-esteem because they have been taught that spiritual people should constantly put themselves down and feel inferior. Some are taught that God is either a harsh judge who is waiting to pounce on our misdeeds so he can condemn us or a being who delights in squelching our personalities and taking the fun out of life. These harmful and distorted views need to be challenged and replaced with the biblical teachings on human worth, forgiveness, pride, and the importance of self-love.

A person's self-concept cannot depend on human goals and achievements alone. Each person's sense of belonging, worth, and competence comes because we are loved and held up by the sovereign, almighty God who teaches us about sin and divine forgiveness, endows us with unique abilities and gifts, makes us into new creatures, and gives the true reason to have a healthy self-esteem because we have been redeemed by Christ.

Within the church, Christians should learn that we can love ourselves because God loves us and has made us his children. We can acknowledge and accept our abilities, gifts, and achievements because they come from God and with his permission. We can experience the forgiveness of sins because God forgives unconditionally, and believers can praise God for what he is doing in and through our lives. There is no institution that comes closer than the biblical church in educating people toward a more realistic self-concept. In addition to biblical teaching from the pulpit and classrooms, this education might include group discussion of books similar to those listed at the end of this chapter.

2. *Prevention through Christian Community.* It is comforting and self-esteem building to know that one is an accepted, valued member of a group. The church can provide this acceptance and give support especially in times of need. Church members should be encouraged to show care and concern for each other[43] without smothering or overwhelming newcomers or reluctant participants.

The church can also help people acquire new practical skills, and within the church we can reject much of the materialism and trappings of success that are so common in society. We can learn to love each other as brothers and sisters, each of whom has important gifts and contributions to make to the body of Christ.[44] Of course this is idealistic, at least in part. People's dress, bearing, and speech reveal their social status. The variety of cars in the parking lot show that the congregation is divided economically. Nevertheless since God is unimpressed with these status symbols, we should attempt to keep them from influencing our interpersonal relationships and values within the body of Christ.

3. *Prevention through Parental Guidance.* Since many self-esteem problems begin in the home, it is there that the problems are most effectively prevented. Surely it is within the confines of Christian education to teach parents how to build a loving Christian home and how to communicate acceptance to their children. With younger children there is need for physical contact and spontaneous expressions of pleasure, including times for play. With older children there must be encouragement, consistent discipline, praise, and time spent in communication. Since there is evidence that parents with high self-esteem tend to have children with high self-esteem,[45] it also is important to help mothers and fathers overcome their inferiorities and build more positive self-concepts.

Conclusions about Inferiority and Self-Esteem

Walter Trobisch must have been a remarkable man. His books have touched millions of readers throughout the world, and even after his early death this remarkable man of God still has an influence on new generations of young people who struggle with issues of dating, sex, marriage, and personal growth.

Trobish was not a psychologist, but he was a remarkably perceptive observer of human behavior. "Self-love is the foundation of our love for others," he wrote,[46] and when we lack self-love a host of personal problems result. This does not mean that we deny scriptural teachings about self-denial and self-sacrifice. The life of Jesus shows that we can accept ourselves without being selfish; we can deny and sacrifice ourselves without denying the work of Christ in our lives or casting aside the spiritual gifts he has given.

For the nonbeliever who sees human beings as little more than well-developed animals, there is no ultimate reason for human dignity and worth. The Christian, however, believes that human worth comes from the love, words, and actions of God. It is sad that many Christians have misunderstood and misapplied biblical teaching so that feelings of inferiority have built up in themselves and in others. In contrast, it is encouraging to realize that the church and church-related counselors can play a vital role in the understanding, counseling, and prevention of self-esteem problems.

Suggestions for Further Reading

Carlson, David E. *Counseling and Self-Esteem.* Waco, Tex.: Word, 1988.

Ellison, Craig W. *Your Better Self: Christianity, Psychology and Self-Esteem.* San Francisco: Harper & Row, 1983.

Smith, M. Blaine. *One of a Kind: A Biblical View of Self-Acceptance.* Downers Grove, Ill.: InterVarsity, 1984.
Wagner, Maurice E. *The Sensation of Being Somebody: Building an Adequate Self-Concept.* Grand Rapids, Mich.: Zondervan, 1975.*
Wilson, Earl D. *The Discovered Self: The Search for Self-Acceptance.* Downers Grove, Ill.: InterVarsity, 1983.*

*** Books marked with an asterisk (*) are especially suited for counselees to read.**

22

Physical Illness

THE CRISIS CAME suddenly. If you had asked about his health a few days before that December morning, Harold would have replied, "I don't feel the best, but overall I'm still in pretty good shape." Apart from high blood pressure and some shortness of breath, he seemed to be in reasonably good health for a man of seventy-seven. During his whole life he had almost never seen a doctor, and his one hospitalization was brief (to have a cataract removed).

All of this changed quickly. After breakfast on that life-changing morning, he found himself gasping for breath. He thought he should lay down, but couldn't get out of his chair. "This is the end," he told his alarmed wife. "I'm not going to make it!"

The paramedics arrived within minutes and began to administer oxygen. By the time they got Harold to the hospital his heart had stopped, but an alert and skilled medical team got it going again.

While they worked, Harold's anxious wife sat with a neighbor and a hospital chaplain away from the flurry of activity in the emergency room. The words "cardiac arrest" didn't sound very encouraging and neither was the prognosis that he might not make it through the day.

But Harold did survive. Within a few weeks he was able to go home, but his life for the next several months seemed to revolve around medicines and hospitals. The doctors discovered evidence of a previous heart attack, and the patient was diagnosed as having a form of blood cancer. His kidneys began to fail, his strength and energy waned, and his sagging skin began to develop bed sores.

Harold vacillated between times of thinking that he could and would recover, and periods of sadness because death seemed so near. He talked for long hours with his wife and family, reviewing their lives together and preparing for the time when he would be gone. Faithfully he followed his doctor's orders, but often he struggled with sleeplessness and stomach upsets because of the medications he was taking. To the surprise of many, he kept his sense of humor and uttered remarkably few complaints during his long illness.

One morning the doctor pulled up a chair next to Harold's bed and told the patient, "I have to be honest. We have done all we can do. You aren't going to get better. All we can do now is make you as comfortable as possible." The doctor knew that Harold and his family wanted to let him die peacefully. In the event of another heart attack, there were to be no heroic attempts to keep the patient alive on life-support systems.

One summer afternoon Harold died peacefully in his sleep after eight months of fighting a losing battle with his increasing physical problems.

Unlike some of the other case histories that begin the chapters in this book, the story of Harold is well known to the author. Harold Collins was my father. I watched him suffer through his physical illness while I was working on the revision of this book.

As everybody knows, the human body is a remarkable organism. Consisting of billions of cells, numerous chemicals, hundreds of muscles, miles of blood vessels, and a variety of organs, the body can grow, heal itself, fight disease, adapt to temperature changes, react to environmental stimulation, and survive a host of physical abuses. Centuries ago the psalmist praised God because we are "fearfully and wonderfully made."[1] And the more we learn about the amazing human body, the more we can stand in awe of both the body's complexity and the Creator who made us.[2]

But the body does not last forever, at least in this world. Sometimes it is injured beyond repair. It can break down if it isn't cared for, and eventually bodies begin to wear out.

We don't think much about this when we are healthy. When there are no physical problems, we take the body for granted. Colds and periodic bouts with the flu are annoying but usually only temporary interruptions to the activities of life. When sickness is more serious, painful, or long-lasting, however, we are forced to recognize our own limitations. Physical suffering vividly confronts us with the stark reality that each of us inhabits a body that is destined to die. Since most of us try to avoid thoughts of illness and sometimes even ignore symptoms, it becomes more difficult to tolerate or accept sickness when it does come. Sickness inhibits our activities, slows us down, makes life more difficult, and often seems to have no meaning or purpose. If the illness persists, we start to ask hard, largely unanswerable questions like "Why me?" or "Why is this happening now?" Often the sickness is accompanied by anger, discouragement, loneliness, hopelessness, bitterness, and confusion. Counseling the physically sick and their families, therefore, is a major challenge for Christian counselors.

The Bible and Physical Illness

Sickness is an issue that runs through the pages of Scripture. The physical illnesses of Miriam, Naaman, Nebuchadnezzar, David's newborn child, Job, and a variety of others are described with clarity in both the Old and New Testaments. When Jesus came to earth his concern for the sick was so important that almost one-fifth of the Gospels is devoted to the topic of healing.[3] The disciples were expected to carry on this healing ministry,[4] and the Book of Acts records how the early church cared for those with physical illnesses.

This biblical emphasis on physical illness points to several conclusions that can be helpful for the Christian counselor.

1. *Sickness Is a Part of Life.* Few people, if any, go through life without experiencing at least periodic illness. It seems likely that sickness entered the human race as a result of the Fall, and since that time people have known what it is like to be unhealthy. The Bible makes no attempt to diagnose, categorize, or systematically

list the symptoms of mental and physical illness, but it does mention symptoms in passing and refers directly or indirectly to alcoholism, blindness, boils, deafness, muteness, dysentery, epilepsy, fever, hemorrhaging, indigestion, infirmity, inflammations, insanity, leprosy, palsy, speech impediments, and a number of other illnesses. It is implied that each of these causes psychological as well as physical stress, and all seem to assume that sickness is an expected part of life in this world.

2. *Care, Compassion, and Healing Are Important for Christians.* By his words and actions, Jesus taught that sickness, while common, also is undesirable. He spent much of his time healing the sick,[5] he encouraged others to do likewise, and he emphasized the importance of compassionate caring for those who were needy and unhealthy. Even to give someone a drink of water was considered praiseworthy, and Jesus indicated that helping a sick person was the same as ministering to himself.[6] Elsewhere believers are instructed to pray for the sick and to help them in practical ways.[7] Clearly, therefore, the Christian has a responsibility to care for those who are not well.

3. *Sickness, Sin, and Faith Are Not Necessarily Related.* When Job lost his family, possessions, and health, a trio of well-meaning but ineffective comforters argued that all these problems resulted from the victim's sin. Job discovered, however, that sickness does not always come as a result of individual sin—a conclusion that Jesus clearly taught in John 9.[8] All sickness comes ultimately because of the Fall. Sometimes physical illness and personal sin *are* related, but we cannot conclude that individual cases of sickness are necessarily the result of the sick person's sin.[9]

This becomes clearer as we examine the healing miracles of the New Testament. Sometimes people improved because they personally believed that Christ would heal. The woman with the issue of blood is a good example.[10] There were other times, however, when a person other than the patient had faith. Several parents came to Jesus, for example, told about their sick children, and saw the children healed.[11] Then in the Garden of Gethsemane a servant's ear was healed even though no person had faith except Jesus. In contrast, there was Paul, a man who had great faith in Christ but whose "thorn in the flesh" never left. Still others had no faith and no healing.[12] From these examples it surely is clear that to be sick is not necessarily a sin or a lack of faith.[13]

The Bible gives no support to those Christians who proclaim that sick people are always out of God's will or lacking in faith. God has never promised to heal all of our diseases in this life, and it is both incorrect and cruel to teach that instant health always will come to those whose faith is strong.

4. *Sickness Raises Some Difficult and Crucial Questions about Suffering.* In a classic little volume on pain,[14] C. S. Lewis summarized two basic questions that face anyone who suffers. These questions often occur in counseling. If God is good, why does he permit suffering? If he is all powerful, why doesn't he stop suffering? Entire volumes have been written to grapple with these questions,[15] but it seems probable that our finite minds will never completely comprehend the reasons for suffering.

For most of us, pain and suffering do not make any sense. We do what we can to reduce pain in ourselves or others, and we pray for the pain to go away. The Bible lifts the veil of confusion slightly when it teaches that suffering keeps us humble, refines our faith, conforms us to Christ's image, teaches us about God, and produces patience, maturity, perseverance, and character. Suffering also teaches us to be more compassionate and caring.[16]

I have a friend and former student whose seminary career was interrupted by a diagnosis of terminal cancer. To the surprise of his physicians and the gratitude of those who prayed, my friend recovered and eventually became chaplain of a large hospital where he counsels with suffering patients and their families every day. My friend's own suffering has enabled him to better understand and counsel with others who suffer now.

Suffering doesn't always serve such a clear and noble purpose. More often counselors are called to understand and give help to those whose pain we cannot know and have never felt.

5. *Serious Illness Often Raises Issues about the Right to Die.* For reasons that are not clearly understood, some people seem to reach a time when they let go of life and die even though they have not been sick. For these individuals, it seems, a healthy cardiovascular system is less important than their conclusion that life is no longer worth living, so they die.[17]

More common, however, are those who develop such severe, painful, and lingering illnesses that they want to die but can't. These are people who sometimes beg to die and urge their doctors and relatives to withdraw all support systems, including food. These increasing requests for "assisted suicide" and the willing compliance of some compassionate relatives and medical personnel have thrown the legal and medical professions into great debate. It is a debate that some Christians try to ignore and that some theologians find frustrating because they find no unequivocal guidance in Scripture. The problem is complicated by confusing laws. At present few countries have adopted the position of one European nation that lets medications be given to hasten death, with legal impunity and immunity for all concerned, but many would argue that the United States and other countries are moving in that direction.[18]

The Christian counselor needs to grapple with issues such as these. Christians believe that all of life comes from God and is taken from us as he wills. Euthanasia—a word that the current debate tends to shun—is opposed by those who value human life. Surely there can be no biblical support for an attitude that hastens death because the patient wants to die, that condones starving someone to death because they are difficult to care for, or that withholds health care from someone who is comatose or brain dead. Yet do we use every technical and medical means available to keep someone alive and in pain who in past years would have died of natural causes? These questions have no simple answers, but Christian counselors need to be aware of these and related health-care issues that arise in times of serious physical illness.

The Causes of Sickness and Related Problems

Sickness, as everybody knows, comes from a variety of causes: contact with viruses and disease-carrying plants or animals, poor diet, lack of exercise or good body care, injury, hereditary defects, the ingestion of harmful substances (like drugs or poisons), the wearing out or degeneration of body organs, and contact with extreme heat or cold to name some of the most obvious. These are the causes that physicians seek to discover and treat, especially when symptoms are present.

Sickness involves much more than physical malfunctioning. It brings a variety of psychological and spiritual reactions that concern physicians and nonmedical counselors as well.[19] Many of these psychological-spiritual influences, including the following, accentuate the physical illness and delay or prevent recovery.

1. *The Experience of Pain.* There are great individual differences in how people experience pain, in how they respond to it, and in the intensity and duration of pain. Pain that is intense and brief—such as that experienced in the dentist's chair—is different from the gnawing, never-ending pain of some cancer patients. Pain that is understood and known to be short term—like a headache—is handled differently than pain that is long-lasting or undiagnosed.

Medical research has demonstrated that people show differences in their awareness and tolerance of pain, and there is evidence that these psychological responses largely are unrelated to the severity of the illness. One researcher found, for example, that soldiers injured in battle complained less of pain (some with serious wounds reported no pain at all) and required less pain medication than civilians who experienced similar injuries. The difference appeared to be in how the injury was perceived. The civilians were annoyed because of their unwanted injuries. The soldiers, in contrast, were relieved to still be alive and safe.[20]

Some people feel little pain even with a major illness; some feel great pain even when there is no discernible organic disease. Some deny their pain and pretend that it doesn't exist; others almost seem to enjoy the suffering. While these differences may in part have biological causes, many of the individual differences in pain tolerance result from a person's attitudes about pain, cultural and family backgrounds, past experiences with pain, personal values, and religious beliefs. Some people, for example, stoically believe that pain is a sign of weakness or that it should be accepted as something permitted by God. Others discover that the degree of pain depends on one's level of anxiety. When people are anxious about pain, this in turn can intensify both the illness and the pain that is felt.

These differences are not necessarily good or bad. A high ability to tolerate pain, for example, is no more a sign of strength or weakness than is a low level of tolerance. Counselors must recognize and accept these differences. They influence a sick person's emotions, reactions, prognosis for recovery, and response to counseling.

2. *Stress and the Feeling of Helplessness.* It is not easy to be sick, especially when routines are disrupted, when we do not understand what is wrong with our bodies, or when we don't know when or if we will get better. If we are sick enough to seek medical attention we must submit ourselves to the care of strangers, some of whom are more aloof and scientific than they are compassionate and sensitive.[21]

People who are physically ill, especially those who are hospitalized, experience several psychological stresses.

(a) A Loss of Control. It is threatening to experience even a temporary loss of one's physical strength, intellectual alertness, bowel or bladder control, speech, control of limbs, or the ability to regulate one's emotions. More disruptive is the realization that these losses often come when we are on semipublic display in a hospital room.

All of this tends to undermine the widely accepted but irrational belief that "we are always capable, independent and self-sufficient; that our bodies are indestructible; that we can control the world around us and are masters of our own destiny."[22] People are forced to change these views whenever they get sick. The patient is expected to comply with doctor's orders. He or she is told what medication to take and when to take it. The physically ill person is expected to submit passively to a variety of diagnostic and treatment procedures, even if this means exposing private body parts for others to view and touch. In the hospital the individual is told when to go to sleep, when to wake up, when and what to eat. Sometimes the person even needs help in going to the bathroom. In short, the patient is treated like an infant and sometimes even has to wear diapers and be "changed" by a nurse. Adults aren't supposed to act like infants, so it isn't acceptable for the sick person to make excessive demands or "just be terribly upset."[23]

(b) Submission to Strangers. When we are sick enough to need medical treatment, we are expected to put our lives and our bodies into the hands of strangers with whom we have no close personal ties and whose competence we may not be able to judge. This can be frightening and embarrassing. It can also be threatening to have these strangers manipulating, drugging, operating on, or removing parts of one's body.

(c) Fear of Losing Love, Approval, and Closeness to Others. Sickness separates us from friends and from customary routines. During hospitalization, the patient is separated from familiar people and things at a time when they are needed most. If the sickness or injury leaves one physically deformed, forced to slow down, or passively dependent on others, there is a fear that loved ones will no longer show love or respect. Sometimes there is a desire to have visitors who show that they care, mixed with the hope that "nobody will come and see me looking like this."

(d) Guilt and a Fear of Punishment. Sickness or accidents often lead people to think that their suffering is punishment for previous sins or failures. As we have seen, this was the view of Job's comforters, and it has been accepted by thousands of people ever since. When a person lies in bed for long hours wondering *why,* there can be overwhelming feelings of guilt, especially if there is no recovery.

3. *Fear and Depression.* Fear of pain or further complications, confusion about one's illness and prognosis for recovery, distress about an uncertain future, worry about what one might say when under the influence of an anesthetic are among the emotions that lead many people to experience fear and depression as part of the sickness. At times there is anger at oneself, at the illness, at one's doctors, at others (including family members or the counselor), and at God. With some illnesses, these feelings may be accentuated by physically produced chemical changes that alter one's mood.[24]

Medical personnel have long known that there are wide individual differences in how people react to their illnesses and the accompanying feelings. Some become very depressed, guilty, self-condemning, embarrassed, or frustrated because they feel so helpless. Others become angry and hypercritical, especially of doctors. All of this slows recovery and sometimes makes the patient more susceptible to further illness. In contrast, those who cheerfully make the best of a difficult situation often feel better and recover faster. When the counselor is aware of conclusions such as these, he or she is better able to understand and help patients and their families.

4. *Family Influences.* When a person gets sick, his or her family is affected and the awareness of this in turn influences the patient.[25] Changes in family routines as the result of an illness, financial hardships, difficulties in scheduling hospital visits, and even the loss of opportunity for sex between a husband and wife can all create tension that sometimes leads to fatigue, irritability, and worry. Visits from family members are supposed to make the patient feel better, but sometimes these contacts create more tension and worsen the illness.

In an attempt to reassure one another and prevent worry, the patient and family sometimes refuse to discuss their real fears or feelings with each other and as a result each suffers alone, fearing the worst but pretending that all is well, that "everything will be OK," and that recovery is on the way. This well-intentioned deception is a game that everybody plays but almost nobody admits or feels comfortable discussing.

In reflecting on the illness and death of his mother, Henri Nouwen once wrote a letter to his father in Holland and expressed some feelings that we often see in our counselees. "Isn't it true that it is much harder to say deep things to each other than to write them?" Nouwen observed. "I am quite familiar with my own inclination, and that of others, to avoid, deny, or suppress the painful side of life, a tendency that always leads to physical, mental, or spiritual disaster."[26]

This denial can lead to disaster within the whole family. If the illness is terminal, subsequent grief becomes much harder because family members missed the opportunity for anticipatory grieving, an open discussion of intimate feelings before the loved one died.[27]

These conclusions are not meant to paint a bleak picture of physical illness. Some families never have the problems we have mentioned. They appear frequently in other cases and sometimes are noticed by the counselor even though they are not seen by the patient or the patient's family. Once again you may observe how fears and threats can affect the course of treatment, influence the patient's attitudes toward the illness, and have a bearing on the speed or likelihood of recovery.

The Effects of Physical Illness

In many respects it is difficult to separate the effects of sickness from the causes. Pain, feelings of helplessness, emotions, and family reactions to an illness can all be as much the effects of sickness as they are causes of additional physical and adjustment problems. Many reactions, such as guilt or anger, can complicate the sickness and cause the physical illness to get worse. This leads to more guilt or anger, and a vicious circle develops.

It is easy to focus on the negative effects of an illness but fail to see the more positive benefits. One study of 345 male heart-attack victims showed that when men grumbled about their illnesses and blamed others (citing problems with the family, for example, or stress at work), there was a much greater likelihood of morbid thinking and another heart attack. Things were much different in men who could see some benefits in their heart attacks. These people often changed their life values and religious views, worked to improve interpersonal relationships, made an effort to reduce stress, and took better care of their bodies. As a result there were "fewer reinfarctions and lower morbidity."[28] The effects of an illness, therefore, need not always be negative.

Regretfully, however, the effects are often more negative than positive. For example, the following reactions to illness are seen frequently and may have to be dealt with by a sensitive counselor.

1. *Defense and Denial.* Since sickness is so unwelcome, there is a tendency to deny its seriousness and sometimes its presence. This is true if the illness is serious or likely to be terminal. At least for a while (and with some patients right up to the time of death) there is the attitude that says, "It can't be me. I'm sure the diagnosis is wrong. God surely will heal me."

Readers of introductory psychology textbooks are familiar with defense mechanisms—ways of thinking that enable us to deny reality and pretend that a frustration or conflict is of little importance. Such thinking is very common. It is used automatically, usually without prior deliberation, and often without our even being aware that it is taking place. Its purpose is to protect us from anxiety.

A number of defense mechanisms have been identified and many are seen in sick people and their families. Rationalization, for example, is the tendency to make excuses ("They've probably misinterpreted the test results"). Projection lets us blame our feelings of anger, fear, or helplessness on someone else ("My problem is with the doctor who is trying to make my life miserable"). Reaction formation is the tendency to display, in excess, the opposite of what one feels ("Look at how well I am and how much I'm improving day by day.") Magical thinking lets us pretend ("The doctor surely will find a new cure before long"). Repression is an unconscious forgetting, and suppression is a deliberate forgetting, both of which are used to push unpleasant reality out of our minds. Such gimmicks can be helpful if they give us time to gather strength and acquire the knowledge needed to cope more realistically with reality. When the defenses and denial persist, however, the patient or family member is being unrealistic and may be rudely awakened later.

2. *Withdrawal.* When we are sick, we need to let others help and love us. For many people, however, this is not easy. They feel threatened by their dependence on others, weak and misunderstood. As a result they withdraw, sometimes in an attitude of self-pity and subsequent loneliness.

3. *Resistance and Anger.* Some patients come out fighting. Since it isn't easy to fight disease, they direct their anger to doctors, nurses, family members, and others including counselors. Criticism, complaining, noisy protests, and demands for relief often characterize such patients and create frustration in the lives of others.

4. *Manipulation.* Some people go through life attempting to control and manipulate others by subtle or more blatant steam-rolling tactics. When such persons become ill, it is not surprising that they use the sickness to control others or to get attention and sympathy.

5. *Malingering and Hypochondriasis.* Sickness sometimes brings benefits, like attention and sympathy from others, an opportunity to do nothing, freedom from responsibility, and socially sanctioned permission to stay home from work and get up late. Some people enjoy the benefits of being sick. As a result they never get better or they experience a series of physical symptoms for which there is no organic basis and little relief.

Malingering has been defined as a "voluntary fabrication or exaggeration of physical or psychological symptoms in order to achieve a tangible goal distinct from the gain of being in the patient role."[29] Sometimes malingering is brief (such as the student who pretends to be sick so he or she can stay home from school and avoid a big test). At other times it may be more long-lasting (as with the worker who fakes an injury in order to get workman's compensation). Suspicion of malingering often angers doctors and family members, but there is no really effective way to prove that the "patient" is malingering, and physicians sometimes fear lawsuits if they fail to treat a supposed malingerer who really does have an illness or injury.

Hypochondriasis is also an assumed illness, but there is no conscious effort to appear sick. Hypochondriacs tend to be preoccupied with disease or illness, so they look for physical symptoms and assume that even the most minor physical changes are indicators of sickness. When doctors can find nothing wrong, these people get angry and sometimes look for a new doctor. "I don't know what's wrong with the medical profession," a man complained in a cartoon that appeared recently. "I've been to twenty-three doctors this year and everybody tells me there's nothing wrong with me."

According to one medical team,[30] these people can be of different types. The masochistic-hostile person, for example, tends to be angry at oneself and others. Some of these people have sacrificed themselves to care for another person. When that person dies or leaves, the care giver can only maintain equilibrium by caring for his or her own supposed illnesses.[31] The clinging-dependent type, in contrast, is less angry and more passive. This person often uses symptoms to get attention, relationships, feelings of importance, and guidance from authority figures.

Regardless of the causes or characteristics, it is helpful to recognize that sickness is a way of life for some people. This may (or may not) be pleasant for the patient, but some find being sick easier than living life without any physical complaints.

6. *Hope.* Sometimes illness has the effect of stimulating hope in patients and their families. In her well-known book, *On Death and Dying,* psychiatrist Elisabeth Kübler-Ross reported that whenever a patient stops expressing hope, death soon follows.[32] Even seriously ill people who have realistic views of their condition find that hope sustains and encourages them, especially in difficult times. Medical and nonmedical counselors have found that patients get along better when there is at least a glimmer of hope. This does not mean that doctors and others must lie about the patient's condition. It means, writes Kübler-Ross, that "we share with them the hope that something unforeseen may happen, that they may have a remission, that they may live longer than expected."[33] For the Christian there is even greater hope in the knowledge that the loving sovereign God of the universe is concerned about us both now and for eternity.

Counseling and Physical Illness

"Isn't it interesting," Charles Colson has observed, "that Jesus didn't set up an office in the temple and wait for people to come to Him for counseling? Instead, He went to them—to the homes of the most notorious sinners, to the places where he would most likely encounter the handicapped and sick, the needy, the outcasts of society."[34]

In counseling the sick, it often will be necessary to go to them. As we move away from the office, it is good to remember the basic principles that apply to all counseling: the importance of counselor warmth, empathy, and genuineness; the value of listening patiently and encouraging the patient (without pushing) to talk abut fears, anxieties, anger, the illness, one's family, the future, and similar issues; the need for confidentiality; and the importance of showing acceptance, understanding, and compassion without being gushy or condescending. In contrast to the physically healthy, sick people often are more sensitive to these counselor characteristics.

In addition to general counseling guidelines there are specific issues to remember when you counsel the physically ill person or those who give them care.

1. *Evaluate Your Own Attitudes and Needs.* When a person is found to have a terminal illness, doctors, nurses, clergymen, and even family members tend to withdraw and leave the patient to face the problem alone. It has been found that some of the best counseling in these situations is done by cleaning women who are cheerful, regular visitors, willing to both listen and talk.

This sad observation points to the fact that most of us don't like to face sickness, especially serious illness, so we avoid people who are ill. Perhaps we are threatened because these people remind us that we all are susceptible to illness. Maybe we are uncomfortable because we don't know what to say, are not sure how to react to the patient's anger and discouragement, or feel incapable of dealing with difficult questions such as "Why me" or "Do you think I'm going to die?" The sight of severely injured persons, perhaps with physical deformities or tubes and machines attached to their bodies, can create discomfort in the counselor and sometimes involuntary reactions of shock that the patient is quick to detect.

For some counselors, the more they face sickness, the easier it becomes to deal with the sick. If the counselor has been ill in the past, he or she may have greater understanding of patients now. This does not always happen, however, and some of us never become accustomed to hospitals or sickness. If this is so, the counselor should take some time—perhaps right now before you read further—to ponder the reasons for this discomfort in the presence of sick people. An understanding of our own attitudes toward sickness and physically ill people can help us become more effective. Central to all of this is the issue of prayer and spiritual preparation for counseling. Since Christians are instructed to care for one another,[35] surely we can ask a compassionate God to give us the ability and sensitivity to be compassionate in turn.

2. *Learn Some Guidelines for Visiting the Sick.* Sometimes it is easier to counsel when we are in familiar territory, for example, in our own offices. Because of physical limitations counselees cannot always come to us, so we may have to go to the sick person. In visiting the physically ill there are some generally accepted guidelines that the counselor should know and remember. These are summarized in Table 22-1.[36]

3. *Deal with the Specific Feelings and Concerns of the Sick Person.* When calling on somebody who is sick, visitors sometimes avoid sensitive topics on the assumption either that an appearance of cheerfulness will drive away worry or that the physically ill person cannot handle emotional issues. Some visitors talk about everything other than the patient and the sickness, often because the visitor is uncomfortable and feels better directing attention elsewhere. Other visitors take an isn't-it-terrible attitude that turns the visit into morbid introspection. Still others talk enthusiastically of miracles or healing and apparently ignore the realities of the present sickness.

Table 22-1
Guidelines for Visiting the Sick

For All Patients

Visit frequently but keep the visits brief.
Let the patient take the lead in shaking hands.
Stand or sit where the patient can see you easily—the side of the bed is more suitable than the foot of the bed.
Give the patient freedom to talk freely, and listen carefully as he does so.
Use your resources as a Christian: prayer, Scripture, encouraging comments, etc. Whether you pray audibly should be determined by the Holy Spirit and the situation—the patient, his spiritual background, the people present, etc. Suggest prayer rather than ask if it is desired, and keep it short.
Take appropriate precautions against contagious diseases.
Leave some devotional material.
Evaluate each visit to determine how they could be improved in the future.

For Patients at Home

Telephone the home before the visit to make sure you call at a convenient time.
Try to call when there will be time for private discussion.

For Hospital Patients

Upon arrival, check at the reception desk, introduce yourself and make sure that a visit at this time is acceptable.
Do not enter a room that has a closed door or a "no visitors" sign.
Try to call when there are not a lot of other visitors present.

Do:

Be friendly and cheerful.
Be reassuring and comforting.
Help the patient relax.
Recognize that anxieties, discouragement, guilt, frustrations and uncertainties may be present.
Give reassurance of divine love and care.
Promise to pray for the patient during his illness—and act on your promise.

Don't:

Speak in an unnatural tone of voice.
Talk about your own past illnesses.
Force the patient to talk. Your silent presence can often be very meaningful.
Promise that God will heal them. Sometimes in his wisdom God permits illness to persist.
Visit when you are sick.
Talk loudly.
Sit, lean on, or jar the bed.
Visit during meals.
Whisper to family members or medical personnel within sight of the patient.
Share information about the diagnosis.
Question the patient about the details of the illness.
Tell the family how to decide when presented with medical options (but help them to decide).
Criticize the hospital, treatment or doctors.
Spread detailed information about the patient when you complete your visit.

Counselors should avoid all of these extremes. Recognize that patients sometimes want to discuss their feelings and concerns, while at other times they prefer to talk about something else. As with all other types of counseling, you have to earn the right to be a helper. Sometimes you will raise a sensitive issue and get a cold or evasive response, clearly indicating that the person does not want to share personal issues with you. At times like this, nothing is gained by pushing the person to talk. It is better to show your continued interest, be available, respect the individual's privacy, and be sensitive to the following issues that you or the patient may choose to bring up later.

(a) Fear. Does the physically ill person or some family member experience any of the fears described earlier in this chapter? Are there additional fears that he or she may share? Are the fears based on real facts or are they unfounded? Fears should be expressed, discussed, evaluated, and not discounted, even when the counselor thinks they are irrational. Pray with counselees about their fears, asking God to bring an inner sense of peace even in the midst of physical disability.

(b) Self-Pity. When a person is sick, forced to slow down and sometimes be alone, there is more time to think about present circumstances. Often the mind drifts to thoughts of what is bad about the illness or about life in general, and this can lead to self-pity. That in turn can create additional problems. When boredom, loneliness, and physical illness lead to self-pity, the self-pity can lead to anger, anger leads to discouragement, and this creates both more self-pity and a slowdown of one's physical recovery.

Self-pity and brooding may be pleasant for a while. Such attitudes may elicit sympathy from others or feelings of self-righteous indignation about the unfairness of life. If this attitude persists, however, the person becomes bitter,[37] and this can drive other people away.

When a person is entangled in self-pity, point this out gently. The patient may respond with anger, but the counselor must be accepting and understanding, yet firm. Help the counselee think about the positive as well as the negative things in life. Can anything good come from this illness?[38] Can there be a more realistic view of the present situation? Encourage the counselee to pray, confessing bitterness and asking for divine forgiveness and direction. Then it may be helpful to ponder what one can *do* to make the best of one's illness. Recognize that the best solution for the present may be rest that gives the body time to experience physical rejuvenation, reevaluation of one's life, and time spent in communication with God.

(c) Anger. Anger is not always wrong or destructive, but when it accompanies illness, it often affects the patient's condition even when he or she doesn't recognize that it exists. Withdrawal from others, criticisms of one's family or the hospital staff, ignoring others, demanding attention or special treatment, whining and constant complaining, depression, refusal to pray, and persisting questions of "Why me?" can all be veiled evidences of anger against God, oneself, and others. When anger is suppressed or denied, it cannot be resolved. After asking for divine help, you can encourage the counselee to face his or her anger honestly, admit that anger is present, talk about it, confess it to God, and ask for his help so the anger can be controlled and not allowed to control the patient.

(d) Discouragement. An old hymn proclaims that Christians should never be discouraged if we "take it to the Lord in prayer." This correctly teaches that discouraging situations are a reason for prayer and for recognizing "what a friend we have in Jesus," but as we noted in chapter 8, the hymn has also reinforced the questionable conclusion that discouragement is wrong. Many people are unwilling to admit their discouragements and don't want to talk about the things that make them discouraged. Here again, the counselor can show that "it's all right to be discouraged for a while." Help counselees to understand and to do what they can to deal realistically with the sources of the discouragement.

(e) Guilt. Patients should be encouraged to express their guilt, to confess sins or failures to God and to others,[39] and to experience the joy of knowing that God forgives. With some people it will be necessary for the counselor to show that the guilt feelings, while real, are based on faulty conclusions and assumptions about past behavior or about God's dealings with human beings.

(f) Pain. According to one estimate, in the United States alone, as many as 80 million people suffer from chronic pain.[40] As we would expect, much of this persisting, constant pain is caused by chronic illness that some people must learn to accept and live with for the rest of their lives.[41] Research is accumulating that shows that pain has a strong psychological component. Anxiety, for example, is known to stimulate pain, and a number of pain-reduction clinics[42] have demonstrated that chronic sufferers can often learn to control and sometimes eliminate their pain by changing their attitudes, perceptions, and behavior.[43]

(g) Difficult Questions. Although they may not always say what they are thinking, many sick people struggle with questions like "Why am I experiencing this?"; "Why is this happening to me and not to somebody else?"; "What will happen to me and my family if I don't get better?"; "Do these doctors really know what they are doing?"; "Does the staff in this hospital really look after old people like me, or do they ignore us and conclude there isn't much hope for recovery in patients who are elderly?"; "While I have this serious illness, what do I do about my sexual desires and frustrations?"[44]

These are questions that counselors and family members often think about but are less inclined to discuss. They are questions that need not be brought up frequently unless the patient keeps raising them. In contrast, if the counselee never mentions issues such as these, the counselor should raise them—preferably when there is time for discussion without interruption. Of course these questions are not always answered easily. As we have seen, the Bible gives some answers, but it also teaches that God's ways often are beyond the capacity of our ability to understand.[45]

Also difficult to understand and talk about is the issue of death. Billy Graham writes about a "conspiracy of silence" that leads most people—medical personnel included—to avoid even mentioning the possibility of death, lest this destroy the patient's morale or raise topics that are too uncomfortable to discuss. Graham quotes one writer who concluded that "most hospitals in this country share at least two characteristics: they do their best to conceal from the patient the fact that he might be dying, and when the fateful time draws near they isolate him from family and friends."[46] Sometimes the patient is engulfed in a forced cheerfulness that prevents an honest discussion of death and avoids consideration of how the family will cope with their loss or where the patient will spend eternity.

Sometimes a family member may ask you if a patient should be told the truth about a serious or terminal diagnosis. This question has been debated often, but many doctors would agree with Kübler-Ross that most patients pretty much sense the truth even before they are told. A frank, honest, and caring description of the diagnosis does much to retain the patient's trust. When this is followed by unhurried discussions of the situation, the counselee can express his or her feelings, be helped to put practical and financial affairs in order, say good-bye to loved ones, resolve interpersonal tensions, and ensure that there is a peace with God.

4. *Encourage Decision Making.* It is possible for the physically ill person to develop a what's-the-use? attitude of inactivity and melancholy brooding. This hinders recovery and makes life miserable. The counselor can gently challenge these attitudes, help people develop a more balanced perspective on the present, and guide them as they make realistic decisions about the future. Some patients will be faced with permanent limitations and handicaps, but life can still be lived fully with the mental abilities, opportunities, and physical capacities that remain.

5. *Instill Hope.* The Christian recognizes that serious illness and even death are not the end of meaningful living. Hope is at the basis of our Christian faith. It is more than the wish that God will perform a miracle. It is the confidence that God, who is living and sovereign, also controls all things and can be expected to bring to pass that which ultimately is best.[47] Often that means recovery; sometimes it means long years of suffering or incapacity; eventually it means passing through death and, for the believer, into eternal life with Christ. Anger, frustration, and disappointment almost always are present with serious illness, but these can be countered by the hope that we have as Christians; not a hope in some emotionally based fantasy of what might happen, but a hope that is based solidly on the Bible's teachings about God and his creation.

6. *Help the Family and Staff.* When an individual has a problem, the family almost always is affected. This is especially true when a family member is ill since most of the issues that concern patients also concern their families. In addition, home routines tend to be disrupted, finances are strained, and at times there is the struggle of facing and coping with an approaching death. Families, therefore, need counseling too,[48] but this in turn can help the patient deal with the illness more effectively.

You can also help patients indirectly by working with those who give treatment. One experienced hospital chaplain notes that while patients and families pass through the hospital doors, the hospital staff remains, "continually immersed in a sea of human suffering." Many of these people are overworked, underpaid, frequently criticized, and emotionally drained by their constant contact with pain and sadness. Some health care professionals entered their fields with a desire to bring hope and healing, but they discovered too late that much treatment has changed emphasis from "the art of healing to the science of healing. In effect, sophisticated procedures and complicated tests have distanced health care professionals from the patient and the healing touch of life has been replaced by a pill or some cold, stainless steel object." If we add to this the frequent reports of disillusionment among care givers and the struggles that many face in trying to balance their personal and professional lives, we begin to understand why doctors, among others, have higher-than-average rates of suicide, alcoholism, drug abuse, and divorce.[49]

Hospital personnel may not often request the counselor's help, but you should be alert to what may be a pressing but unexpressed need for counseling. Sometimes it is best to start by giving casual, sensitive, supportive encouragement that helps staff people deal with their emotions and unanswered questions. Often when a counselor shows concern on the ward, this leads to later more in-depth counseling with medical personnel.

7. *Help the Malingerer and Hypochondriac.* For some counselees the sickness goes on despite medical treatment. It rarely helps to ignore the symptoms or to confront the patient by stating that the illness has an emotional basis. Medical treatment doesn't help much either. Someone has stated that no medication will cure a psychologically based illness and no surgery will cut it out. The illness ultimately must be treated at its cause; namely, the underlying anxiety and inability to cope with a symptom-free life.

Nonmedical counselors must first ensure that the illnesses are in fact nonorganic. This can be determined only by a physician and, as we have seen, sometimes even doctors have difficulty in deciding if a reported illness really is psychologically based. If the medical report concludes that there is no apparent physical basis for the symptoms, the counselor can proceed along the lines suggested in the chapter on anxiety. Although the symptoms may have no organic basis, remember that they nevertheless are very real and uncomfortable to the counselee. The counselor should show an understanding of the discomfort but attempt, in addition, to discover and help the counselee deal with underlying anxieties. Try also to determine what needs are being met by the symptoms (for example, the needs to be noticed, to control others, to get attention, or to be dependent). Can the counselee learn to meet these needs in a healthier way?

Prevention and Physical Illness

Within recent years the medical profession has given considerable attention to ways in which disease and injury can be prevented or avoided. When people are prevented from getting sick, the problems discussed in this chapter do not arise. Even before or when sickness does come, however, many illness-related problems can be reduced and sometimes prevented.

1. *Encourage People to Ponder and Discuss Their Attitudes toward Sickness and Death.* Since healthy people often avoid thinking about these issues, the realities of sickness and death hit with greater impact when we are forced to face them. Perhaps this trauma could be lessened if we would (a) maintain contact with people who are sick and suffering because they often need our help, (b) give deliberate thought to one's own possible sickness, death, and funeral (this is realistic planning), and (c) openly discuss sickness and death with family members while everyone is well. This need not be morbid or imply wishful thinking. It is an acknowledgment of the mortality that we all have on this earth. It is a way to prepare for the future and to open lines of communication before crises arise.

2. *Help People to See Meaning in Sickness and Suffering.* Josef Tson is a remarkable man. President of the Rumanian Missionary Society and former pastor of a large Baptist church in Rumania, he has been persecuted for his faith and spent time as a prisoner in communist labor camp. Tson's Bible study and painful experiences with suffering have convinced him that persecution, discomfort, pain, and hurt should be welcomed because they can honor Christ and advance the church. He writes that "suffering and dying for the Lord" is a privilege and not a calamity.[50]

To be arrested and incarcerated for one's faith seems a different kind of suffering than the painful and weary experience of living with a debilitating sickness. Often we see sickness as harmful and bad, but this is not necessarily so. Physical illness can bring us face-to-face with our own limitations, give us a clearer perspective on life and eternity, and teach us more fully about the love and forgiveness of God. Illness is often what people need to slow them down so they can get better, if not physically, then at least emotionally and spiritually. When a counselee can see sickness in this more meaningful light, it sometimes is easier to live with unanswered and perhaps unanswerable (from a human perspective) questions about why people get sick, stay sick, and suffer.

3. *Stimulate People to Face Concerns Realistically.* Fear, anger, guilt, confusion, concern about the family, thoughts about death and other concerns should be raised and discussed realistically. The sooner this is done, the better, otherwise the concerns can fester and complicate both the illness and the recovery process. If people can learn to share and pray about their concerns and emotions as a way of life, then issues such as these are less likely to be kept hidden when sickness comes.

4. *Give People Information.* Many years ago researchers discovered that surgical patients recover faster and experience less pain when they are told before treatment what to expect during and after the surgery.[51] When the patient and family know what is coming, the discomfort and anxiety can be handled much more effectively.

5. *Strengthen People's Christian Commitment.* Learning to walk with God through prayer, meditation, Bible study, and worship can prepare us for the crises of life. Scripture never teaches that believers are exempt from illness or that we should bear problems alone. When we are in the habit of "bearing one another's burdens" and casting our burdens on God in prayer, then we are better prepared for facing illness and death when they come. The physical and psychological pain will be present still, but underneath is the assurance that God is in control.

Conclusions about Physical Illness

Prior to World War II, Paul Tournier, the Swiss physician, first proposed his concept of medicine of the whole person. When an individual is sick, Tournier believed, his or her whole being is affected—the physical, psychological, and spiritual. Jesus demonstrated this concern for whole persons when he ministered to spiritual needs, but he also had a deep and practical concern about individual suffering, social conditions, mental struggles, and physical illness. We who are his followers must have a similar compassionate concern for whole persons. To divorce the physical, psychological, social, and spiritual parts of a person from each other is both unbiblical and impossible. It also prevents us from counseling effectively with the physically ill and their families.

SUGGESTIONS FOR FURTHER READING

Bittner, Vernon J. *Make Your Illness Count.* Minneapolis: Augsburg, 1976.*
Ecker, Richard E. *Staying Well.* Downers Grove, Ill.: InterVarsity, 1984.*

* Books marked with an asterisk (*) are especially suitable for counselees to read.

Gatchel, Robert J., and Andrew Baum, eds. *An Introduction to Health Psychology.* Reading, Mass.: Addison-Wesley, 1983.

Graham, Billy. *Facing Death and the Life After.* Waco, Tex.: Word, 1987.*

Koop, Ruth. *When Someone You Love Is Dying.* Grand Rapids, Mich.: Zondervan, 1980.*

Kübler-Ross, Elisabeth. *On Death and Dying.* New York: Macmillan, 1969.

Lawrence, Roy. *Christian Healing Rediscovered.* Downers Grove, Ill.: InterVarsity, 1980.

Nichols, Keith A. *Psychological Care in Physical Illness.* Philadelphia: Charles Press, 1984.

Yancey, Philip. *Where Is God When It Hurts?* Grand Rapids, Mich.: Zondervan, 1977.*

*** Books marked with an asterisk (*) are especially suitable for counselees to read.**

23

Grief

MILDRED AND HELEN ARE both widows. They live in the same neighborhood, attend the same church, and are only four years apart in age. Both of their husbands died within the past year.

Mildred's husband had cancer. His illness was discovered about a year before his death and, despite surgery and the best medical treatment available, his condition grew steadily worse as the months passed. Mildred devoted herself to caring for the man to whom she had been married for more than forty years. When he was hospitalized, she visited everyday. When he was at home, she cared for him tenderly, even at the end when she was exhausted. He couldn't feed himself and was unable to get out of bed to go to the toilet.

With reluctance and only at the urging of her children and doctor, Mildred finally agreed to let her husband return to the hospital where he spent the last days of his life. In the year of his illness, this couple had talked openly and often about death, about heaven, about their life together, about the things they regretted, and the pleasant memories they shared. They even talked about the coming funeral and how Mildred would cope as a widow.

Helen and her husband had no similar conversations. During a vacation trip to Florida, within weeks of retirement from his company, he collapsed in a restaurant and was dead on arrival at the local hospital. A massive heart attack had taken his life and jolted Helen into widowhood.

Months later these two Christian ladies continue to grieve, but it is clear to others that they are handling their grief differently. Mildred seems to be picking up life and is learning to live as a widow. Helen remains cloistered in her apartment. She is unwilling to go out, often refuses to answer the phone, and doesn't even want to see the grandchildren that she once doted over. Helen cries a lot, spends a lot of time in self-pity, continually reviews that fateful trip to Florida, and wonders what she or the paramedics might have done to save her husband's life. Helen keeps telling herself and anyone else who will listen that life for her will never be worth living again—ever.

When their husbands were alive, Mildred and Helen were good friends who often would chat after church. Now as they both mourn the deaths of their husbands these two widows seem to be going in different directions. Each is handling grief in a way that differs from the other.

Grief, writes Billy Graham, is a certainty—something most of us will experience at some time in life. "When death separates us from someone we love there is a time when we think no one has suffered as we have. But grief is universal." It is the method of handling grief that is unique and personal.[1]

Even though grief has gripped people for centuries, careful studies of the bereavement process are relatively recent. In 1917, for example, Freud published one of the most careful studies on grief.[2] Almost thirty years later Erich Lindemann, a Harvard professor, wrote a highly acclaimed paper based on his interviews with 101 grieving relatives.[3] Soon a number of books and articles began to appear. Among the best known was a book titled *On Death and Dying,* written by a previously unknown Chicago psychiatrist named Elisabeth Kübler-Ross.[4] Probably more than any other publication, this book stimulated development of a whole new body of literature and a field of study known as "thanatology"—the branch of knowledge that deals with dying and the bereaved.[5]

Grief is a normal response to the loss of any significant person, object, or opportunity. It is an experience of deprivation and anxiety that can show itself in one's behavior, emotions, thinking, physiology, interpersonal relationships, and spirituality. Any loss can bring grief: divorce, retirement from a job, amputation, the departure of a child to college or of a pastor to some other church, moving from a friendly neighborhood (or watching a good neighbor move), selling one's car, losing a home or valued possession, the death of a pet or plant, loss of a contest or athletic game, health failures, and even the loss of one's youthful appearance, confidence, or enthusiasm. Sometimes desirable and long-anticipated events—like the move to a better job and new neighborhood or graduation from college—can bring grief (mixed with happiness) because valuable memories or relationships are being lost and left behind. Doubts, the loss of one's faith, the waning of one's spiritual vitality, or the inability to find meaning in life can all produce sadness and emptiness that indicate grief. Clearly whenever a part of life is lost or taken away, there can be grief.

Most discussions of grief, however, concern losses that come when a loved one or other meaningful person has died. This grieving is never easy. We may try to soften the trauma by dressing up the corpse, surrounding the body with flowers or soft lights, and using words like "passed away" or "departed" instead of "died," but we cannot make death into something beautiful. As Christians we take comfort in the certainty of the resurrection, but this does not remove the emptiness and pain of being forced to let go of someone we love. When we encounter death, we face an irreversible, unalterable situation that we are powerless to change. Even though "death has been swallowed up in victory,"[6] the loss of a loved one can be devastating and grief can be overwhelming. Eventually each of us will die,[7] but in the meantime most of us will grieve at least periodically. Grieving gives counselors a difficult but rewarding challenge, to help people deal with death.

The Bible and Grief

The Bible describes the deaths and subsequent grieving of many people. In the Old Testament, for example, we read descriptions of Jacob mourning over the loss of Joseph and refusing to be comforted, David grieving over the anticipated loss of his infant son and the death in battle of his grown son Absalom, and Jeremiah lamenting the death of King Josiah.[8] The Psalms tell of God's presence and comfort as we "walk through the valley of the shadow of death";[9] we learn that the Word of God strengthens those who are "weary with sorrow."[10] Isaiah introduces us to the Messiah—"a man of sorrows and acquainted with grief"—who took up our own griefs and carried our sorrows.[11]

In the New Testament, the many passages on death and grief might be grouped into two categories. Each deals with the influence of Jesus Christ.

1. *Christ Has Changed the Meaning of Grieving.* There are many nonbelievers who grieve without any hope for the future. For them death is the end of a relationship—forever.

The Christian does not believe that. In the two clearest New Testament passages on this subject[12] we are given reason to hope, even in times of sorrow. "We believe that Jesus died and rose again and so we believe that God will bring with Jesus those who have fallen asleep in him."[13] We can comfort and encourage one another with these words,[14] convinced that in the future "the dead will be raised imperishable, and we will be changed. . . . When the perishable has been clothed with the imperishable, and the mortal with immortality, then the saying that is written will come true: 'Death has been swallowed up in victory.'"[15]

For the Christian, death is not the end of existence; it is the beginning of life eternal. The one who believes in Christ knows that Christians will always be with the Lord. Physical death will still be present as long as the devil is allowed to have the power of death, but because of the crucifixion and resurrection, Christ has defeated death and promised that the one who lives and believes in Christ "will never die."[16]

This knowledge is comforting, but it does not eliminate the intense pain of grief and the need for solace. In a discussion of death, Paul encouraged his readers to take courage and not lose heart since the believer who is absent from the body is present with the Lord.[17] Christians are encouraged to stand firm, to "let nothing move you," and to give ourselves to the work of the Lord because we know that this labor is "not in vain"[18] as we look forward with confidence to the resurrection.

2. *Christ Has Demonstrated the Importance of Grieving.* Early in his ministry, Jesus preached his Sermon on the Mount and spoke about grieving. "Blessed are those who mourn," he said, "for they will be comforted."[19] When Lazarus died, Jesus was troubled and deeply moved. He accepted, without comment, the apparent anger that came from Mary, Lazarus's sister, and he wept with the mourners. Jesus knew that Lazarus was about to be raised from the dead, but the Lord still grieved.[20] He also withdrew by himself (perhaps to grieve) when he learned that John the Baptist had been executed.[21] In the Garden of Gethsemane, Jesus was "deeply grieved,"[22] perhaps with an anticipatory grief, more intense but similar to that experienced by David as he watched his infant son die.[23]

Even for the Christian then grief is normal and healthy. It also can be pathological and unhealthy. As we will see, this difference is of special concern to any Christian counselor.

The Causes of Grief

Simply stated, grief arises because something or someone of value has been lost and the griever is faced with the emptiness and difficult task of readjusting. According to William Worden, the griever encounters four often difficult and time-consuming tasks: to accept the reality of the loss, to feel and consciously admit the pain of the loss (this includes untangling oneself from the ties that bind one to the deceased), to adjust to an environment in which the deceased person is missing, and to form new relationships. The last stage seems to be the most difficult because people feel both guilty and insecure about reinvesting their energies in new relationships.[24]

Nobody can say how long the mourning process will last. For some it may take only a few weeks or a few months, but studies of widows show that most need at least three or four years to reach stability in their lives.[25] Even then life is never like it was before the loved one died. All of this takes work. "It isn't for the moment that you are struck that you need courage," wrote Anne Morrow Lindbergh. Grievers need strength "for the long uphill climb back to sanity and faith and security."[26]

Sometimes that difficult uphill climb goes smoothly. Although some writers have tried to identify different stages of normal mourning, more recent studies suggest that "there is no uniform and orderly succession of stages through which all grieving must pass."[27] Normal grief usually involves intense sorrow, pain, loneliness, anger, depression, physical symptoms, and changes in interpersonal relationships. Often there is denial, fantasy, restlessness, disorganization, inefficiency, irritability, a desire to talk considerably about the deceased, an unconscious adoption of the lost person's mannerisms, and a feeling that life no longer has meaning. In all of this there are great individual differences. How one grieves depends on one's personality, background, religious beliefs, relationship with the deceased, and cultural environment. Even though the mourner may never recover completely from the loss, most people eventually return to a state of productivity and the restoration of mental and physical well-being. Grief counselors sometimes refer to this process of normal grief as "uncomplicated mourning."

At times, however, the grief is abnormal, pathological, and complicated. This is grief that is intensified, delayed, prolonged, denied, or otherwise deviating from the more normal expressions of sorrow. It is a grief that keeps the mourner in bondage to the deceased person and prevents one from coping and moving on with life. Often there are no symptoms unique to pathological grief. Instead the behavior seen in normal grieving appears with greater intensity and longer duration. There may be deep feelings of dejection, lack of interest in the outside world, a diminished capacity to love, withdrawal, and greatly lowered self-esteem.[28] For some there is hyperactivity, a giving-up attitude of helplessness and hopelessness, intense guilt, a strong self-condemnation, extreme social withdrawal or moodiness, impulsivity, antisocial behavior, excessive drinking, and veiled threats of self-destruction (sometimes followed by serious attempts at suicide).

Why is some grief normal while other grief is pathological? Although it rarely is possible to identify one cause for pathological grief, several influences seem to determine how one will react to a loss.

1. *Prior Anticipation.* There is some evidence that grief is more difficult when a loss is unexpected, untimely (when, for example, a person dies in the prime of life), traumatic (involving violence or an accident), and sudden.[29] Less certain is whether grief will be easier when the death was anticipated.

Studies of anticipatory grief are still inconclusive, but most evidence indicates that a period of anticipation and prior preparation can make the grief process smoother, especially if the deceased person and the survivors had opportunity to absorb gradually the reality of the impending death, were able to express their feelings including sorrow, had opportunity to complete "unfinished business" (such as expressing love or asking for forgiveness), were able to say good-bye, and could make plans for the future. Sometimes anticipatory grief grows more intense when the death does not occur when it was expected or if there is ambivalence in the participants who vacillate between wanting it to be over but dreading when that time will come.[30] When the survivor has taken the opportunity to visit and help the dying patient, there often is less guilt, self-condemnation, or regrets after the death does occur.

2. *Type of Loss.* Each type of loss appears to bring its own kind of suffering and reaction. In adult life, the death of a parent is the most common type of bereavement, the loss that is handled best (especially when the parent is older)[31] and the type of grief that is least likely to be pathological. Loss of a wife or husband is much more difficult. Burdens that previously were shared must now be borne alone, and that can be very stressful.[32] Even more difficult is the loss of a child. Parents often feel guilty, angry, depressed, self-condemning, and incompetent because they failed to protect the child from death (even when there was nothing they could have done to prevent the death). For parents, the death of a child is "one of life's most devastating losses."[33] For many couples, a child's death may dangerously weaken a shaky marriage. When a relationship is already under stress, the loss of a child may be more than the marriage can bear. In contrast, the experience may strengthen a marriage that is sturdier.[34] Couples that relate well to each other draw closer as they help one another cope.

According to one study, "it is almost axiomatic that the intensity of grief is determined by the intensity of love." The closer the relationship between the griever and the deceased, the greater the grief. Grief is also more intense (and more likely to become pathological) if the griever was very dependent on the deceased. In addition, if the relationship had involved at the same time both love and strong negative feelings, then the survivor is left with both guilt and anger. This makes grieving harder.[35]

3. *Beliefs.* In an attempt to help others (and often in an unconscious effort to help themselves), many grieving people have written books about their own sorrows and struggles with readjustment.[36] Often these writings describe the turmoil and deep pain involved in grieving, but many also point to the sustaining power of religious beliefs. There may be periods of doubt, confusion, and even anger with God, but in time the healing power of one's faith becomes evident. Religion gives support, meaning, and hope for the future. Christians believe, in addition, that the Holy Spirit who lives in each believer gives supernatural comfort and peace in times of mourning.

One study of grieving parents found that 70 percent turned to religion for answers and comfort. Even those who previously had drifted away from the church and many who claimed to be agnostic eventually sought solace in religion and remained with their new beliefs long after the initial pain of death had softened. In comparison with those who ignored religion, the study found that people who turned to God were better able to deal with their losses.[37]

When a griever has no religious beliefs or refuses to consider the claims of Christ, there is no hope. As a result, the pain is greater, the grieving may be more difficult, and presumably there is greater potential for pathological grief.

4. *Background and Personality.* Probably most psychologists would agree that "the best predictor of future behavior is past behavior." One indication of how grief will be handled in the future is how the mourner reacted to separations and losses in the past. If previous separations were difficult and problem producing, then present grieving is also likely to be difficult. Handling grief may also be more difficult for people who are insecure, dependent, anxious, unable to control or express feelings, prone to depression, or living under stress.

Again it should be emphasized that grief is so unique and individualized that we cannot list typical grief reactions that apply to everyone. Grievers differ in their personal needs, typical ways of handling stress, willingness to admit and express feelings, abilities to face the reality of loss, closeness to others who can give support, personal views about life after death, degrees of flexibility, and skills in coping with crises. Grieving is always difficult, but it seems to hit some people harder than others.

Even so a few people try to prolong their grieving because they enjoy the attention that comes from others. If this continues for too long, however, there may be a reverse effect. Once-sympathetic friends see what is happening, get annoyed, and pull away.

5. *Social Environment.* Most if not all cultures have socially sanctioned ways of meeting needs at the time of bereavement. These social mores are built around both religious beliefs and practices and the racial or ethnic backgrounds of the grievers. In a city like Chicago, for example, Polish Americans may express their grief in ways that differ from the customs in Black, Hispanic, Irish, or Jewish neighborhoods. Cultural and religious groups also differ in the extent to which they allow, discourage, or encourage the overt expression of sorrow. There are different practices concerning the wake and the social behavior that is expected of visiting friends and relatives. Even funerals differ, although it appears that in every culture the funeral offers group support to the bereaved, opportunity to express religious beliefs and rituals, and visual confrontation with the dead body. In most cultures the funeral ends with a procession which, in the opinion of some writers, symbolically pictures a final journey.[38]

In spite of these social, cultural, and religious variations, there are also some commonly held values. In American, Canadian, and British societies, for example, there has tended to be an intolerance of prolonged grieving. These countries value efficiency, intellectualism, rationalism, and pragmatism, so death often is seen as an inconvenience or embarrassment. Emotional expressions are discouraged and grief is viewed as something that, while inevitable, should end as quickly as possible. Since most of us will die in hospitals, away from our families, and since the society—especially American society—encourages a mobility and independence that separates us from close contact with others, it is easier to deny or ignore the reality of death. This can make the loss more traumatic for close relatives of the deceased, and there are fewer intimate people nearby who can give continual in-depth support. Instead we have encouraged ourselves and one another to deny death[39] and to respond to the bereavement of others with little more than cards, cut flowers, or casseroles. Of course, this description is not true of everyone and neither does it apply to all communities, but surely many of us will recognize that our modern social attitudes toward death greatly influence how mourners are able to experience, express, and work through the grieving process.

6. *Circumstances Accompanying Death.* The death of a revered and respected leader can bring grief to thousands of people, especially if the leader symbolized the hopes and expectations of those who mourn. This mass grieving differs from the grief experienced by the spouse or child of the deceased. If the dead person was elderly and sick for a long time, the grief of relatives is less likely to be prolonged or pathological than when the loss is sudden or the deceased is a child. When a brother or sister dies, there often is a sense of personal threat and a there-but-for-the-grace-of-God-go-I feeling that can make mourning more difficult.

Closeness to the deceased, suddenness of death, and age of the dead person are only some of the issues that influence the grieving process. One psychiatrist has listed almost fifty such complicating issues.[40] For example, grieving may be prolonged and more difficult when:

- The death is considered exceptionally untimely, such as the death of a successful adult "in the prime of life, at the beginning of a promising career."
- The mode of death is considered incomprehensible, senseless, or tragic, as in suicide, murder, or auto accidents.
- The survivor feels a sense of guilt because he or she participated in the event that caused the death (for example, the driver of a car involved in a wreck that killed one of the passengers).
- There was such extreme dependency on the lost person that the mourner had little other basis for self-confidence, identity, or meaning in life.
- There was so intimate a relationship with the deceased that close relationships with others did not exist.
- The mourner's work, family, or other environmental circumstances disallow the expression of grief.
- The dead person extracted a promise that the survivor would never grieve, be sad, remarry, or move.
- There is excessive attachment and proximity to the deceased person's possessions, allowing the survivor to pretend that the deceased person is still alive.
- There is excessive and premature "jumping back" into normal activities without allowing time to acknowledge and assimilate the loss.
- The griever believes, contrary to biblical teaching and the example of Jesus,[41] that Christians should so rejoice that they never grieve; this is the sincere but harmful view that grieving is a sign of spiritual immaturity.

The Effects of Grief

Grieving often begins with a period of shock, numbness, denial, intense crying, and sometimes collapse. It moves into a prolonged period of sorrow, restlessness, apathy, memories of the past, loneliness, and sleep disturbances. Then comes a slow waning of the grief symptoms and a resumption of normal life activities.

Despite these general trends, many counselors resist attempts to identify specific stages of grieving. Probably you can be more helpful if you know some common effects of grieving. Even these don't always appear, and they cannot be put into any rigid expected order of appearance.

1. *Physical Effects.* Bereavement can be bad for your health. It is true, at least in the United States, that widows and widowers do not seem to visit doctors or enter hospitals any more frequently than married people of the same age.[42] Several studies have shown that grief hinders the body's immune system so that viruses and other disease-causing organisms are more difficult to resist, especially during the first six months of mourning.[43] The death rate increases significantly during the first few years of widowhood and there are marked increases in congestive heart failure, high blood pressure, strokes, and cancer. In one Scandinavian study of 95,647 widowed persons, the death rate during the first five years of bereavement was 6.5 percent higher than expected. The suicide rate was 242 percent higher than expected, and the rate of traffic deaths was 153 percent higher.[44]

Grief can put a lot of stress on the body at a time when people are least able to resist the onslaught of illness. There is ample evidence to show that intense or prolonged stress disrupts the body and can lead to numerous ailments, including some that are serious.[45] In addition, stress can lead to exhaustion, weakness, headaches, indigestion, shortness of breath, loss of appetite, and inability to sleep. For many people, therefore, the first months of bereavement are physically difficult.[46]

2. *Emotional-Cognitive Effects.* Grief affects both how the person feels and how he or she thinks. Depression is common following the death of a loved one and often there are feelings of anxiety, inner emptiness, guilt, anger, irritability, withdrawal from others, forgetfulness, declining interest in sex, dreams about the deceased, nightmares, errors in judgment, and feelings of loneliness. For many there is a loss of zest, disorganization of routines, and a realization that even the most simple activities that once were automatic now require great effort and the expending of considerable energy. At a time when the grieving person feels least able to handle extra pressure, there usually is an increase in things that have to be done, including the submission of claims for insurance, consolidating and changing names on bank accounts, paying extra bills connected with funeral and hospital expenses, meeting with lawyers concerning the deceased person's will, changing names on legal documents such as the mortgage or car title, informing the providers of pensions or the Internal Revenue Service, and even handling daily hassles like the tap that starts leaking or the lawn that isn't mowed. All of this can create considerable frustration and put additional stress on the grieving person.

As C. S. Lewis observed,[47] these symptoms of grief come in waves, and rarely are they all present at the same time. As the months pass they tend to fade, but sometimes they come back with renewed intensity when they are least expected. Throughout all of this, most grieving people experience a persisting painful loneliness.

Some survivors take on and begin to show the characteristics of the deceased person; almost all survivors experience anniversary reactions. The first Christmas, Easter, birthday, or wedding anniversary after the loss can be especially difficult emotionally, as can the anniversaries of the death. These anniversary reactions may continue for a number of years. On specific significant days or in the presence of outstanding reminders of the loss (such as on subsequent visits to the hospital where the person died), many of the old grief feelings and reactions sweep over the person with new intensity. If this continues for several years there may still be uncompleted or pathological mourning. Sometimes, when people are not free to mourn immediately after the death, a full grief reaction will be triggered by a later anniversary or other reminder of the loss.

3. *Social Effects.* The death of a loved one is a major social disruption. When a spouse dies, the surviving mate must learn to relate to others as a single adult. Grown children and other family members find new demands on their time. Relationships between the surviving spouse and the dead person's family often show new and sometimes unexpected tension, particularly if the survivor starts dating. Old friends may not know how to relate to the survivor, and a widow may feel awkward to be the only unaccompanied person at a gathering of couples with whom she and her husband had socialized.

To avoid some of these social tensions, grieving people often withdraw from others, get busy so they won't have to face their anxieties, or start traveling. In themselves, none of these is harmful, but each can also become a way to deny the reality of one's new, unfamiliar, and uncomfortable social status.[48]

4. *Pathological Effects.* Pathological grief reactions occur when grief is denied, delayed, never ending, or distorted so there is intense fear, guilt, helplessness, withdrawal, or other evidences of pathology. This most often occurs when the death has been sudden or unexpected; the mourner has been excessively dependent on the deceased; there was an ambivalent relationship (love mixed with hatred) between the mourner and the lost one; there was unfinished business between the mourner and the deceased (such as siblings who hadn't talked for years, family conflicts that hadn't been resolved, confessions that hadn't been made, or love that hadn't been expressed); the cause of death was violent, accidental, or suicidal; and/or the loss left the mourner with new and difficult challenges such as raising children alone or making business decisions.[49]

When grief is pathological, the survivor may show several of the following behaviors, few or none of which were apparent before the death occurred. Be alert for mourners who show:

- Unwillingness to talk about the deceased, this accompanied by intense sadness whenever the dead person's name is mentioned.
- A tendency to speak of the deceased person in the present tense (for example, "He doesn't like what I am doing").
- Open or subtle threats of self-destruction.
- Persisting and deep depression, often accompanied by guilt and low self-esteem.
- Antisocial behavior.
- Excessive hostility, moodiness, or guilt.
- Excessive drinking or drug abuse.
- Withdrawal and refusal to interact with others.
- Impulsivity.
- Persisting psychosomatic illnesses.
- Veneration of objects that remind one of the deceased and the link the mourner had with the dead person.
- Refusal to change the deceased person's room or to dispose of his or her clothing and other possessions.
- Resistance to offers of counseling or other help.

- Stoic refusal to show emotion or to appear affected by the loss (this usually indicates denial and avoidance of grief).
- A happy, almost euphoric attitude (sometimes explained as "rejoicing in the Lord").
- Intense busyness and unusual hyperactivity.

It is generally agreed that the most intense grieving will be completed within a year or two. If the grief continues longer, especially when some of the above symptoms are present, this is a strong clue that there is pathological grieving.

Counseling and Grief

In future years, C. Everett Koop may be remembered as the United States Surgeon General who served as the country's chief medical officer when the AIDS epidemic began. Koop, however, first established his reputation as a highly regarded pediatric surgeon whose work frequently brought him into contact with dying children and grieving parents. One day the famous physician learned that his own son had died as he was climbing in the mountains of New Hampshire. In a moving and inspiring portrayal of their grief, young David Koop's parents wrote about their sadness and the faith that sustained them throughout life. "Our family life never will be the same," they wrote, "but we are trusting in the Lord to help us accept the empty place in our family circle and to keep us constantly aware that David is in heaven—which is far better for him." Like the hundreds of parents whom he had counseled, Koop and his wife found a permanent void in their lives after David's death. "In an effort to be comforting, so many Christians glibly say, 'God will fill the void,'" they wrote. "Instead, we found that the void is really never filled, but God does make the void bearable."[50]

In their grief, the Koop family discovered what some well-meaning counselors have failed to realize: the grieving are not looking for pat responses from people who come to talk rather than to listen. Instead grief-filled people need understanding, reassurance, and contact with sensitive individuals who care.

1. *Counseling and Normal Grief.* Normal grief is a difficult, long-term process of healing that "needs no special help; it takes care of itself and with time the mourner heals and recovers."[51] The most widely available sources of help are family members, friends, ministers, and physicians. These people can help in several ways.

- Encourage discussions about death before it occurs. When dying persons and their families feel free to express their feelings and discuss death before it happens, the anticipatory grief may make grieving more normal after the loss occurs.
- Be present and available. "There is a sort of invisible blanket between the world and me," wrote C. S. Lewis after his wife died. "I find it hard to take in what anyone says. Or perhaps, hard to want to take it in. It is so uninteresting. Yet I want the others to be about me. I dread the moments when the house is empty. If only they would talk to one another and not to me."[52] The presence of people can be important, even if they are talking to one another. Try to be available after the funeral. If the mourner is a special

friend, phone periodically to touch base, and be alert to giving support or expressing concern on holidays and anniversaries.
- Make it known that expressing feelings is good and acceptable, but do not pressure the griever to show feelings.
- Do not be surprised at outpourings of crying, frustration, or withdrawal, but still let it be known that you are available and accepting.
- Be a careful listener. Recognize that grieving people need, at their own time, to talk about issues such as the feelings and symptoms that are being experienced, the details of the death and funeral, details of past contacts with the deceased, the ultimate reasons for the death ("Why did God allow this now?") and thoughts about the future. Guilt, anger, confusion, and despair will all be expressed at times and need to be heard by the helper, rather than condemned, squelched, or explained away.
- Try not to push. It is best if you make yourself available, be willing to listen and respond when the counselee wants to discuss issues related to grief, but also be willing to back off if the griever wants to be alone for a while or wants to talk about something else. All of this implies that the counselor should be sensitive to the grieving person's fluctuating needs and feelings.
- Help the grieving person make decisions and gently try to discourage the making of major decisions (such as the sale of a house or a move to another state) at least until a few months have passed.
- Gently challenge pathological or irrational conclusions, then give the grieving person opportunity to respond and discuss the issues.
- Provide practical help like meal preparation or baby sitting. This frees the person to grieve, especially at the beginning.
- Do not discourage grieving rituals. Participation in a wake, funeral, memorial service, and religious ritual can help make the death more real, demonstrate the support of friends, encourage the expression of feelings and stimulate the work of mourning.
- Pray for the bereaved and comfort them with words of Scripture without preaching or using religious clichés as a means for stifling the expression of grief.

In all of this, remember that our desire is to support the mourner and not to build unhealthy dependency, to avoid reality, or to stimulate denial. In time the support and care of friends will help the bereaved work through the grief process and resume the normal activities of life once again.

2. *Counseling and Pathological Grief.* Counselors are most often called to work with people who are showing pathological grief reactions. These people often resist help, but the counselor's task is to bring a transformation of abnormal grief into more normal grieving. There are several ways that will help to accomplish this goal.

- Encourage discussion of the counselee's relationship with the deceased. This may involve detailed exploration of the past, including the highlights and low points in the relationship and the events that lead to the death. You can promote this by gentle encouragement and showing interest in the deceased. Sometimes this process is facilitated by looking, with the counselee, at photographs and treasured possessions of the deceased person.

- Encourage the expression of feelings and attitudes. As you listen, try to avoid the clichés, exhortations, and insensitive quoting of Bible verses that may have come previously from friends. When the bereaved person is disturbed by the presence, duration, or intensity of grief, anger, guilt, or other feelings, encourage discussion of these issues, and if these emotions are not extreme give reassurance that these are natural and a part of the healing process.
- Help counselees understand the grief process. Some people may find it helpful to read books, especially if the contents are discussed later in counseling.[53] Try to put the counselee into contact with others who can give support and realistic perspectives. Widows, for example, often can benefit from contact with other widows who are further along in the grief process.
- Encourage talk about the future. Gently challenge irrational thoughts or plans that appear to be unrealistic or made in haste. Look for opportunities to encourage discussion of practical issues, such as raising children, meeting financial needs, or dealing with loneliness and sexual frustrations. Remember that your goal is to help counselees avoid denial and deal instead with the reality of the loss.

Within recent years, some Christian counselors have stressed the benefits of helping people "heal" memories from the past. At times, grief cannot be overcome because the counselee has unresolved and deeply buried guilt, anger, hurt, or attachments to the deceased person that can no longer be discussed with the person who has died.

Healing of memories is an approach that is based on prayer. Together the counselor and counselee seek the Holy Spirit's guidance as they remember (and sometimes "relive" in memory) past memories or attitudes, then ask for divine forgiveness and healing. Some have criticized the Freudian overtones in this approach, and a number of extreme healing-of-memories books have advocated methods that could be harmful. There are responsible practitioners in this field, however,[54] and their work has demonstrated how the power of Christ can help people to deal with grief and other painful issues from the past.

Despite your best efforts, there may be times when a counselee requires the help of a more specialized counselor, such as a psychiatrist or clinical psychologist. When you make such a referral to a specialist, discuss this with the counselee so he or she can understand why you are suggesting another counselor.

3. *Counseling When Children Grieve.* In the midst of grieving, relatives sometimes try to protect children from the realities and sadness of death. It should be remembered, however, that children also have a need to grieve and to understand as best they can.

To really understand death, children must be able to distinguish between themselves and others, between living and nonliving, between thought and reality, and between past, present, and future. Whether or not the child has this understanding, he or she must be helped to comprehend the finality of death, to express emotion, and to ask questions. It is important to reassure children (repeatedly by words and actions) that they are loved and will be cared for. Children often interpret death, especially the death of a parent, as a form of rejection. When a sibling dies there often is guilt, confusion, feelings of isolation, and fear that "I may be next."[55] Children are sensitive to any signs of adult insecurity and need to know that they will not be forsaken. Many counselors would agree that, with the possible exception of the very young, children should be present at the wake and/or funeral since young people need emotional support and opportunity to accept the reality of the loss, just as do adults.

4. *Counseling When Children Die.* Death is always difficult for survivors to handle, but when the deceased is a child the experience is especially upsetting. Sudden Infant Death Syndrome (SIDS), for example, takes the lives of more than seven thousand infants every year in the United States. The cause is not completely understood and since the babies are strong and healthy before death, the loss comes as a rude jolt. Childhood accidents and terminal illnesses can also create grief that one writer describes as being "beyond endurance,"[56] and parents of those children who are stillborn or lost through miscarriages often grieve with almost equal intensity.[57] Even when children are weak or malformed before death, it is difficult for parents to accept the reality of death after a life that was so short. Guilt, self-condemnation, anger, despondency, and unanswered questions abound.

Often the grief leads to tension, parental conflict, and miscommunication in the home. The wife, for example, may feel that her husband doesn't care about the death because he doesn't cry as much as she does. The husband, in turn may be hiding his feelings because he doesn't want to upset his wife.[58] The counselor should be aware that the break-up rate for grieving parents is high. Part of counseling, therefore, should focus on the marriage and how the couple's relationship is surviving throughout the grief process.

As with other forms of grief, those who have lost children must be helped to express feelings, accept the loss, and learn to readjust. Often this help comes from neighbors and friends, from church members, and from the support of other parents who understand because they have experienced similar losses in the past.[59]

Prevention and Grief

Grief, of course, cannot and should not be prevented. When survivors show no grief it is possible that there was no close relationship with the deceased, but it also is possible that the grieving process is being denied or avoided. This can lead to pathological grieving, the kind of abnormal grief that we want to prevent.

1. *Before the Time of Death.* The prevention of unhealthy grief reactions should begin long before a death occurs. Predeath prevention can include the following:

(a) Developing Healthy Attitudes in the Home. When parents are open and honest about death, children learn that this is an issue to be faced honestly and discussed openly. Misconceptions then can be corrected and there is natural opportunity to answer questions. It probably is true that a child (or adult) can never fully be prepared for death, but an open attitude at home facilitates communication and makes later discussion of death more natural.

(b) Clarifying Family Relationships. Grief sometimes is complicated by guilt, anger, jealousy, bitterness, competitiveness, and other issues that never were resolved before the death. This can be prevented, and subsequent grief made smoother if before death family members could:

- Learn to express and discuss feelings and frustrations.
- Verbally forgive and accept forgiveness from each other.
- Express love, appreciation, and respect.
- Develop a healthy interdependence that avoids manipulation or immature dependency relationships.

To build better families is an important way to prevent pathological grief. This, of course, is an ideal that many families cannot reach unless they are helped through training and counseling.

(c) Building Friendships. Grieving is harder when there is no established network of supporting friends who can give intimate support in times of sorrow. Each of us needs a group of people with whom we can build quality relationships instead of putting exclusive dependence on one or two individuals. In all of society, the church should be the best example of a community with caring, affirming, accepting friends. Next to the immediate family, the church and its pastor become the first line of support in times of bereavement. When people are involved in the church before the loss, this community support is more meaningful and readily available at the time of a death and afterward.[60]

(d) Keeping Active. People who are involved in a variety of recreational, worship, work, or other activities find that they have fulfilling involvements that help soften the pain of death and other losses.

(e) Stimulating Mental Health. Well-adjusted people who have learned to handle little crises successfully usually handle grief with success. Such people have learned to express emotions freely, to face their frustrations openly, and to admit and discuss their confusions and problems.

(f) Anticipating and Learning about Death. Death education is a relatively new but growing field of study. In schools, colleges, churches, and elsewhere, people are learning to talk about death (including their own deaths) and to discuss issues such as how the terminally ill face death, how people grieve, and how to make a will and plan for the needs of our families should we die first.[61] It is difficult to talk about one's own death, funeral, place of burial, and afterlife, but it is easier to consider these issues when all those involved are healthy. Later, when death does occur, survivors are spared additional pain if the initial decisions about the funeral have already been made and with the deceased person's help. Hospice is a relatively recent movement[62] that exists to enhance the quality of life for dying patients and seeks to help both the terminally ill and their families prepare for death. A major objective is to make it possible for patients to die at home in familiar surroundings and with loved ones close by. Since this isn't always possible, Hospice volunteers and medical personnel sometimes try to create homelike settings within the confines of a hospital, sometimes in a specially designed inpatient unit.[63] When trained volunteers, medical personnel, and professional counselors all work together, family members can be helped to make a smoother transition from terminal illness to death and into the initial months of the bereavement.

Hospice provides a specialized form of anticipatory grieving. When people develop terminal illnesses, families and friends frequently pretend that all will be well, and often there is no talk of "leave taking." In contrast, when patients and their families are able to talk about the possibilities of imminent death and can be honest about their sadness, the subsequent grief process is less likely to be pathological. Such honesty, it has been found, is also important when talking with dying children.[64]

(g) Theological Understanding. After the funeral is not the time to start asking about eternal life and the reality of heaven or hell. The Bible says a great deal about death, the meaning of life, the reality and promise of eternal life for believers, and the pain of mourning. These biblical truths can be comforting, especially if they are taught and understood before the grieving process begins.

2. *At the Time of Death.* The hours and days following a death can have a strong influence on how grief is handled.

(a) Communicating the News. It is not easy to announce a death (especially when the death was sudden and unexpected) and for this reason medical personnel, policemen, and others often carry out this task as quickly and explicitly (that sometimes means as abruptly) as possible.

It is much better to communicate the news gently, somewhat gradually, and if possible in a location private enough to permit the free expression of emotion. Give the survivor time to respond, to ask questions, and to be surrounded by two or three friends who give continuing initial support.

(b) Giving Support. Some people face their grief alone, with no one present to give immediate support and help in making decisions. This makes grieving harder. In our society the pastor or chaplain is the one designated to give immediate care to the bereaved, but the church leader's task is much easier and more effective if church members give additional support. This would seem to be especially important when the circumstances of death were unexpected, unusual or violent, such as suicide, murder, or the accidental death of a child.

When one family lost their son, a church member came almost immediately to offer condolences. The grief-stricken family declined this man's offer of help, so he went back to his car and sat there. Several hours passed before the family became aware of their friend's continued presence outside. Later they reported that this quiet support more than anything else sustained them through the difficult months that followed.

(c) Planning Funerals. Within recent years, funeral practices have come under considerable criticism. Long-established customs have been discarded or changed to fit our changing lifestyles. These changes are not necessarily bad, but it should be remembered that funeral rituals do serve such useful functions as helping survivors accept the reality of death, receive the support of friends, get practical help during the time of readjustment, and experience the peace and presence of God. Funerals should develop a balance between a realistic acknowledgment of grief and sincere rejoicing over the fact that believers who are absent from the body are present with the Lord. A carefully planned, worshipful funeral service can facilitate the grieving process and help prevent pathological grief.

(d) Using Drugs. In an effort to sedate the grief-stricken, caring physicians sometimes give sedatives and other prescribed medications to survivors at the time of death. Although there may be nothing wrong with this as a temporary measure, there is a real danger that chemicals can dull the pain and inhibit the grief process. In general, therefore, the use of drugs does not contribute to the prevention of pathological grief.

3. *After the Time of Death.* The continuing presence of supportive care givers, including pastoral counselors, can help the griever during the months following the death. It is during this period that the counseling procedures described earlier in this chapter can help counselees adjust without developing pathological grief.

4. *The Church and Preparation for Death.* The preceding paragraphs have assumed that death preparation and the prevention of pathological grief often take place in and through the church. Help can come through pastoral counseling (including anticipatory grief counseling), the preaching of periodic sermons on the subject of death and related topics, Sunday school classes or study groups that give education about death, encouraging church members to read a book or two on dying and bereavement, and stimulating believers to pray and care for the spiritual, emotional, and practical needs of the grieving.

There also can be indirect preparation through the strengthening of family communication, the stimulation of loving honesty, encouraging people to express their feelings, and showing a freedom to talk about death. When death is talked about in the church, this is more likely to be discussed in the home. Church members may also be encouraged to develop a philosophy of life that is built on biblical teaching and that incorporates the reality of death into the person's way of thinking.

5. *Strengthening the Care Giver.* Should a grief counselor ever cry? If we are sensitive human beings, there will be times when we cannot and probably should not hold back the tears. Counselees often are helped by such empathy, unless the counselor appears to lose control so that he or she no longer gives the appearance of being able to help.

The loss of a loved one is an intensely painful experience that can also be difficult for those who watch and want to help. The bereavement counselor often is reminded of his or her own past losses, of bereavements that are still to come, or of the inevitability of one's own death. Often these pressures can create added stress and lead to counselor burn-out.

Three guidelines have been suggested to help grief counselors deal with their own needs.[65] First, you should know your limitations in terms of the number of people with whom you can work at any one time. This number varies from person to person, but often the pastor has no control over the number of funerals that must be conducted. This is draining work, however, and there must be some time away if the counselor is to avoid burn-out.

Second, give yourself permission to grieve. Admit your sadness after someone dies and try not to feel guilty if you do not grieve in the same way or with the same intensity after each death. This diversity is normal, even for grief counselors.

Third, get into the practice of reaching out to get support and help from others. Care givers are reluctant to ask for help, but we all need the support that comes both from God and from our fellow human beings. Richard Exley is a pastor who has written that we all need balance in life: time to work, rest, worship, and play.[66] Without this balance, any of us—but especially grief counselors—can be so overwhelmed by the pain and suffering of others that we lose our effectiveness as helpers.

Conclusions about Grief

Grief is a universal experience. Few escape it, some are trapped by it, and those who come through it often feel that they have had a painful refining experience. Grief is not something that we seek or grasp eagerly. It comes sometimes without warning, is received reluctantly, and can only be conquered when it is faced honestly with divine help and with the support of other human beings. It is a pain that God often uses to mature us and to make us more equipped for the Master's use.

Walter Trobisch was a godly man whose writings were used to help millions of readers.[67] One clear October morning he died of heart failure in his little home in the foothills of the Austrian Alps. "My whole world stopped the day he died," his widow wrote later. "I can now recognize the stages of grief as similar to what John Steinbeck describes: 'After seeming cut off and alone, you will be able to pick up a thread and draw in a string and then a rope leading back to life again.' After a close partnership and marriage of twenty-seven years, learning to walk alone again was no easy task."[68]

Counselors also know that it is no easy task to help the grieving walk alone again. Perhaps we can help our counselees grow through this experience, like Ingrid Trobisch grew.

> It took me many years to learn that no man on this earth can satisfy the deepest longings of a woman's heart. Only One can do that. He is also the only one who can help me live with that deep hole, that deep pain in my heart. . . . The pain is still there. He hasn't filled it up yet, but he has made a bridge over it. I can live with it now and I can stand on this bridge and reach out to others.[69]

SUGGESTIONS FOR FURTHER READING

Davidson, Glen W. *Understanding Mourning.* Minneapolis: Augsburg, 1984.

Graham, Billy. *Facing Death and Life After.* Waco, Tex.: Word, 1987.*

Kalish, Richard A. *Death, Grief, and Caring Relationships.* 2d ed. Monterey, Calif.: Brooks/Cole, 1985.

Lewis, C. S. *A Grief Observed.* New York: Bantam Books, 1961.*

Parkes, C. M., and Robert S. Weiss. *Recovery from Bereavement.* New York: Basic Books, 1983.

Rando, Therese A. *Loss and Anticipatory Grief.* Lexington, Mass.: Lexington Books, 1986.

Rowley, Carol A., and William J. Rowley. *On Wings of Mourning: Our Journey through Grief and Recovery.* Waco, Tex.: Word, 1984.*

Shuchter, Stephen R. *Dimensions of Grief: Adjusting to the Death of a Spouse.* San Francisco: Jossey/Bass, 1986.

Worden, J. William. *Grief Counseling and Grief Therapy.* New York: Springer, 1982.

* Books marked with an asterisk (*) are especially suitable for counselees to read.

24

Singleness

MOST OF HIS BOYHOOD FRIENDS WERE probably married by the time they had reached thirty, but not him. He had friends of both sexes, but no wife or children. He was able to relax in other people's homes, but he had no home of his own. He knew what it was like to care for an aging parent, but he never knew the joys and challenges of being a parent himself. He knew who he was, where he was going, and how he wanted his career to develop, but he also knew what it was like to be considered different, a threat to other people, and a misfit. He was a healthy young man with all the sexual urges and temptations that human beings experience, but he never had a wife with whom he could be sexually intimate. He knew how to laugh, how to hold his own in heated debates, and how to play with little children, but there were times when he cried and sometimes he felt very lonely and alone. Usually we don't think of him in this way, but Jesus was a single adult.[1]

So was the unmarried lady who wrote about her status at the conclusion of a Christian single's retreat. "There is nothing special about being single," her note began. "Everybody is single at least once and often single again. Only the duration and quality of singleness differ.

"Single or married, we all live in the same world. We are all part of a family, whether present or removed, and shouldn't we have common interests and concerns? Though I may not have my own children, shouldn't I be concerned with the success my friends have in raising theirs? Ultimately, that success or lack of it will influence every area in the lives of all of us.

"Singles as well as married couples can be very narrow in their perspectives—all wrapped up in their own concerns and with little interest in the world around them. The single person should have a greater incentive to aggressively reach out and take part in all of life. We singles tend to be too timid! Whether you are married or single is incidental; the point is, you can control the quality of your life. For the Christian this should have special meaning.

"To want others to 'do things' for me is a waste of my thinking and abilities. I can 'do' for other people. I can be involved and participate in wider concerns. I can love and care in all kinds of ways. I can make a difference at least in my part of the world.

"One of the 'formerly married' members of our singles' group says that many who are in her situation never accept their singleness and waste their energies resenting their status. That is a terrible waste of a life."

The number of single adults is astronomical, and their ranks are swelling rapidly. Fueled by a high divorce rate and a trend toward later marriage, the exploding singles boom is altering the nation's housing markets, changing our values, and inspiring scores of new services and products ranging from video dating to specially packaged foods that come in single servings.[2] This increasing percentage of our population includes the never married and those who were formerly married but have lost a spouse through death or divorce. The group includes parents without partners, widows (there are over 10 million in the United States), celibate priests and nuns, most college students, many homosexuals, separated people who are still married but are living apart from their mates, those who have chosen not to marry, and others whose lives are spent waiting for the day when they will walk to the altar. The figures do not include husbands and wives whose marriages have grown so cold and distant that the spouses coexist under the same roof but live isolated lives that in practice could be classified as single.

Sometimes singleness is seen as a swinging, no-strings-attached, carefree lifestyle. For many singles nothing could be further from the truth. In our society people walk in pairs. If you are alone, many will see you as a misfit, an embarrassment to married friends who don't always trust you and aren't sure how or whether to include you in their activities. Plagued by loneliness, insecurity, low self-esteem, and sometimes rejection, many singles face frequent reminders that they are out of step with society. Single people tend to pay higher taxes and often have difficulty getting credit, insurance, loans, job promotions, or even decent seating in a restaurant.

Meeting other singles can also be a problem. Contacts in singles bars or night spots can be fleeting and destructive, so some people turn to the church. Many find, however, that they are unwelcome or at best tolerated by church members who don't understand, don't know how to relate to singles, and sometimes blatantly reject unmarried people, especially if they are divorced. Of course many singles live fulfilled, meaningful, productive lives. Consider Jesus, for example, or the lady whose note appears at the beginning of this chapter. Many others, however, find it difficult to be single, and for them counseling can be helpful.

The Bible and Singleness

Adam was the first person to experience singleness, but this didn't last long. God declared that it was "not good for the man to be alone,"[3] so woman was created, and Adam became the first married man. Clearly marriage was God's intention for the human race. He expected that a man and woman would unite together for companionship, sexual fulfillment, perpetuation of the human race, and partnership in their use and control of the environment.

God knew that in our sinful state a happy blissful marriage would not be everyone's experience. The tendency for men to die earlier than women and the influence of wars that often reduce the male population both ensure that there never will be enough men for all the women in the world. In addition, many people fear intimacy with the opposite sex or find it difficult to make commitments.[4] Some lose spouses to death, others experience marital breakups, and still others choose not to marry.

These people are not unnatural because they are unmarried. Two passages of Scripture support this conclusion. Both indicate that the single state is a special gift that God bestows on selected people, including some who aren't enthusiastic about having the gift bestowed.

In Matthew 19, Jesus was asked about marriage and divorce. He emphasized God's high view of marriage, but he realistically acknowledged that marriages sometimes end in divorce. Then he pointed out that singleness is a gift that is given to certain people.[5] This does not imply that only those "gifted" people should be single. Many well-adjusted individuals are single even though they don't feel that their unmarried state is a gift.

Paul elaborated on this in more detail in 1 Corinthians 7. This section of Scripture discusses sex and presents a high view of marriage, but the writer also considers singleness. Once again singleness is called a gift[6] and the apostle, who indicates that he himself was unmarried, writes in positive terms about the single lifestyle. Marriage, he says, is fine, but singleness is even better.

> If you do marry, you have not sinned; and if a virgin marries she has not sinned. But those who marry will face many troubles in this life, and I want to spare you this. . . . I would like you to be free from concern. An unmarried man is concerned about the Lord's affairs—how he can please the Lord. But a married man is concerned about the affairs of this world—how he can please his wife—and his interests are divided. An unmarried woman or virgin is concerned about the Lord's affairs: Her aim is to be devoted to the Lord in both body and spirit. But a married woman is concerned about the affairs of this world—how she can please her husband. I am saying this for your own good, not to restrict you, but that you may live in a right way in undivided devotion to the Lord.[7]

Free of the greater responsibilities and financial pressures that often come with marriage, Paul here elevates the single life as a way of living in which the person can give undivided devotion to Christ.

Yet how many Christian singles view life like this? Instead of "undivided devotion to the Lord," many put far more emphasis on bemoaning their fates, wondering how to fit into society, struggling with feelings of inadequacy, trying with "undivided devotion" to find a mate, and sometimes resisting the pressures that come from parents who are critical of their unmarried adult children. This brings us to the problems of singleness.

The Causes of Singleness Problems

Why are some people unmarried? What is there about singleness that causes problems? To answer these questions, we can look at five major groupings of single people. Each has a somewhat unique set of challenges connected with being unmarried.

1. *Some Have Not Yet Found a Mate or Have Decided to Postpone Marriage.* Within recent years there has been a growing trend for young adults to postpone marriage. The woman's movement has helped make it acceptable and financially feasible for women to live on their own and experience independence before settling into a marriage. Often young people want to travel, to get established in their careers, or to otherwise experience the freedoms of adulthood before taking on the responsibilities of a mate and family. Changing social attitudes about sex have led many to conclude that there is no need to marry or remain faithful to one sexual

partner.[8] The Apostle Paul wrote that people who cannot control themselves should marry,[9] but today most people in our society reject that kind of teaching, concluding instead that people who cannot control themselves should give in to their urges and have sexual intercourse without bothering to marry.

Students in long training programs, young military personnel, individuals whose work involves traveling, or people getting started in the business world or other careers are among those who may have every intention of getting married but decide to wait a few years. These singles face many of the problems that concern all unmarried people, but those who have chosen to postpone marriage often have a healthy outlook. For them singleness is not seen as a tragedy that has come as the result of unwanted circumstances. Instead singleness is viewed as a choice that can be changed later.

For others, however, there is frustration and a waiting mentality that says, "I can't make any plans on my own and I shouldn't make any major decisions because I might have to change if I get married to somebody whose ideas and goals are different." Such an attitude may be strengthened by well-meaning but sometimes insensitive friends who imply that life isn't complete until one has a mate. This is an attitude that can immobilize single people so that they are always living in the future and waiting for that time when marriage will make life complete. This is an attitude that leads some people to jump at the first opportunity for marriage and discover later that they have landed in marital chaos. "I would rather be single and wish I was married," said one more-cautious person, "than to be married and wish I was still single."

2. *Some Choose Not to Marry.* This may be a deliberate decision to remain single or it may come as a gradual awareness and acceptance of the fact that marriage is unlikely. Often there are very good reasons for choosing to remain single: for example, a conviction that this is God's calling, a desire for continuing freedom, a sincere lack of interest in marriage, a preference for living alone, or a shortage of eligible marriage partners. Others may conclude that singleness is preferable because they have had bad experiences with marriage, have watched their friends go through painful divorces, feel shy and self-conscious with the opposite sex, or are afraid of intimacy.

One study found that 12 percent of women born in the mid-1950s will never marry, in contrast to 4 percent of women born twenty years earlier. According to the researchers, there are several reasons for this change. Women, for example, now have better job opportunities with increasing eligibility for promotions, especially if they are free to move or to work long hours at the office without worrying about families at home. Others prefer cohabitation, so they choose not to marry. (The number of couples living together outside of marriage has more than quadrupled in the past two decades.) Increasing numbers of women, the survey showed, are content *not* to marry—and this is becoming more acceptable in our society for both sexes.[10]

That one should choose singleness, however, may not be understood by onlookers, including church members (and probably a lot of mothers). Sometimes observers conclude that the single person must have problems (for example, "He's probably gay" or "She's afraid to leave her mother"). At times a single person may feel so much pressure to get married that he or she enters into a relationship that is not wanted and for which the individual may feel unsuited. Even without such pressures, people who are single by choice sometimes wonder if the conclusions of others might be true. "Perhaps I *am* afraid, gay, too choosy, or a social misfit," these people may think. Such possibilities must be considered honestly and evaluated realistically, otherwise they can quietly bother the unmarried person for years.

3. *Some Have Had Marriages Break Up.* If a marriage has been unhappy for a long time, its ending may bring at least a temporary sense of relief. Life is not easy for people who are "single again" because of separation or divorce.[11] Many experience loneliness, struggles in adjusting to the transition from marriage back to singleness, intense feelings of failure and guilt, bitterness, and difficulties with self-image. All of this can be made worse by criticism or social ostracism that comes from others, including family members or intolerant, unforgiving church members.

4. *Some Have Lost a Mate.* This can bring pain, loneliness, and so great a sense of loss that only those who have had similar experiences can really understand. When death occurs, relatives and friends reach out to offer support and sympathy (which is something that divorced people often do not get), but the grief persists long after the funeral is over and the friends have gone back to their regular routines. There is continuing sadness, emptiness, and the pressures of learning to live alone or to make decisions that previously were shared. This may be especially difficult for those who are older.[12]

5. *Some Have Other Reasons for Singleness.* Overlapping with the above categories are situations that reduce the likelihood of marriage. These include:

- Chronic illness and handicaps, both physical and mental, that reduce the person's potential for marriage and could hinder a satisfying relationship with someone of the opposite sex.[13]
- Unrealistic views of what members of the opposite sex are like.
- Immaturity, including an inability to give and an unwillingness to accept responsibility or to make commitments.
- A belief that cohabitation is better than marriage (even though some recent legal decisions have shown that common-law marriages have a number of traps and potential problems).[14]
- Homosexuality, real or imagined, that sometimes motivates people to spend life alone and at other times leads them into same-sex relationships that have no legal or economic ties, little social sanction, and a great potential for breakup with subsequent pain and loneliness.

The Effects of Singleness

It is important to emphasize that singleness in itself is not a problem for all unmarried people. Just as some married people have marriage problems while others do not, so some singles have singleness-related problems that do not bother others.

On occasion I have asked participants at singles' conferences to list their greatest sources of stress and frustration. The lists often have nothing to do with singleness. Like married adults, singles also have problems with job stress, finances, getting along with difficult people, managing time, controlling weight, and finding one's direction in life. Some issues appear more frequently with singles; issues that are likely to arise in counseling sessions.

1. *Problems with Loneliness.* Intense feelings of loneliness often engulf single people, especially those who live alone and those who have lost or been rejected by mates. "It's hard to create things to do when you're alone," one young person wrote in a seminar for singles. "My major stress is loneliness and the feeling that somehow I might never be able to cultivate an intimate relationship." "I lack fulfilling companionship," commented another, "It's lonely to come home to an empty apartment and have nobody there with whom I can share joys, hurts, or events of the day." One young person said it differently. "The pressures in my life are greater because I don't have a shoulder to cry on, somebody to laugh with, or even someone to say 'I understand. It's OK.'"

John R. W. Stott once was asked about the problems of being single. He replied that the first problem is "the tendency to personal loneliness. Any single person knows more about loneliness than somebody who is sharing his life with a wife and family. This has meant that I have needed to cultivate friendships and force myself to spend time in the company of others."[15]

Stott went on to identify another difficulty: "Singleness limits one's ministry in terms of acceptance. There are some people who distrust one's ministry because they feel you don't understand their problems if you're not married."[16] This brings us to the issue of self-esteem.

2. *Problems of Self-Esteem.* If other people distrust you, wonder if something is wrong with you, don't accept you, dismiss your opinions, or do not want to date you or have you as a marriage partner, it is easy to conclude "Apparently I'm not very attractive or worth much."

Several singles' seminar participants wrote that they so much fear rejection that they lack the courage to reach out to others. "When people learn that I'm not married, they must wonder if something is wrong with me," noted one young woman. "I have a terrible lack of self-worth since I failed at my marriage," said another. "Is there something wrong with me? I'm afraid others won't accept me." Few comments were sadder than those of the person who wrote "It is hard for me to feel that anyone would want to talk about anything other than work. Whenever I have tried to reach out to make friends, I have realized how much I am hurting. After a while, it hurts too much to try anymore."

Many years ago a song proclaimed "You're nobody 'til somebody loves you." Its concluding line, "So find yourself somebody to love," became a philosophy that has led many singles into transient relationships, often sexual in nature, that frequently end in further rejection and lowered self-esteem. When there are attempts to bolster one's sagging self-worth through socially abrasive behavior, heavy dating, or ill-advised marriage, the result is often failure, guilt, self-pity, discouragement, and further feelings of low self-esteem.

3. *Problems with Identity and Direction.* Many singles might identify with the person who wrote, "As a single adult, I don't know how to fit into a world where, if you are not part of a couple, it is hard to be accepted socially, in a job, or even at church." It is common for young people to lack direction, to feel confused about the future, or to have no purpose in life. Many struggle with questions of "Who am I?" or "Where am I going?"

Since society assumes that most people will marry, it is easy for the single person to conclude that life can have no purpose for the person who is alone. Disappointment and further frustration are likely to come to the single person who is unhappy with life, confused about the future, and waiting to build his or her identity on somebody else. Whenever one's happiness, purpose in life, and self-esteem primarily depend on some other person, an unhealthy dependency relationship can develop that may be dangerous and destructive if the other person fails, dies, or leaves. It is healthy, of course, to build mutual relationships and interdependency between a husband and wife. Our more complete identities are formed as we determine our God-given purposes in life, develop our abilities and gifts, and build relationships with a variety of people. Feelings of aimlessness and lack of identity are likely to remain in the single person who is self-absorbed or waiting inactively for a hoped-for marriage that, it is assumed, will give life a purpose.

"My biggest stress is that I don't know where I'm going—even at my age," wrote a single woman on her fifty-first birthday. "I want God to direct me totally in every aspect of my life, but I have just resigned from my job and I plan to start all over." Lack of direction and problems of identity concern people of every age regardless of one's marital status.

4. *Problems with Sex.* When God created male and female, he made us with hormones. He made sex a part of human experience and planned that men and women, within marriage, would enjoy each other's companionship and bodies. But what does the single person do with these God-given sexual urges? "Why can't I just have sex and have it now?" one seminar participant wrote. Others expressed similar concerns. "I'm having trouble waiting." "I have a lot of sexual frustration but no sexual outlet." "It's especially hard for me to adjust to being celibate when all my life I had planned on getting married." Margaret Evening wrote that "next to the problem of inner loneliness comes the problem of how to cope with sexual gifts and energies, and the finding of a proper outlet for them. No one can presume to give all the answers for no one knows them!"[17]

Some people engage in promiscuous relationships in an attempt to find instant intimacy, to feel loved, to bolster self-esteem, to give feelings of sexual potency, and sometimes to express anger and frustration. Others move into homosexual relationships. Undoubtedly many singles, including Christians, fantasize and masturbate at least periodically. These behaviors often are followed by guilt that complicates but does not solve the problem of sex for singles.

5. *Problems with Emotions.* Whenever people have problems that cannot be solved to their satisfaction, there is a tendency to get angry. Sometimes this hostility is directed toward God, "fate," or other people who may be innocent bystanders. According to the Bible, such bitterness can cause trouble and lead to impure actions.[18] Still for many singles the bitterness persists as an angry response to the question, "Why is it that I'm not married?" In addition to anger, some singles have guilt over their thoughts, attitudes, hostilities, and actions.

Fear is also common in singles: fear of being alone, fear of rejection, fear that singleness is evidence of God's displeasure, fear of making unwise decisions since there is nobody with whom to discuss plans. Seminar participants listed some others: fear of gaining weight that would make one less attractive to the opposite sex, fear of never having intimate friends, and even fear "of getting so used to being single that I will start to like it and retreat from others."

It should be emphasized again that these emotions, while common, are not limited to singles and neither are they characteristic of all or even a majority of unmarried people.

6. *Miscellaneous Problems.* Some studies suggest that singles, especially single men, may be more unhappy, less satisfied with their lives, more prone to mental illness, and generally less well adjusted than their married counterparts. Involvement with a church may not eliminate such differences.[19]

Some of these differences may be due to the unique stresses that some singles face. It is not easy, for example, to be a single parent who must make the decisions about raising children without the help and support of a mate.[20] Some single adults feel the pressure of living at home and trying to get along with parents who persist in treating their offspring like little children. Others feel pressure from married people who become matchmakers, who criticize or envy the single lifestyle, and who at times are threatened and unsure how to act in the presence of a single adult, especially a single person of the opposite sex or one who is divorced. Some singles struggle—often alone—with the pain of broken engagements, desired relationships that never developed, or the worry that one's "perfectionist attitudes" or "high standards" may ensure that marriage never occurs. Older singles face the difficulties of trying to build a social life when there are constrictions caused by loss of friends or failing health. Then there are the previously mentioned problems of social prejudice that make it difficult for singles to get housing, insurance, credit, or job promotions.

Counseling Singles

"Singleness once was looked upon as unusual, unfortunate, unnatural and even undesirable," wrote the enthusiastic author of one article. Now, she continued, things have changed. Singleness is "no longer a social stigma. In fact, singles enjoy greater social acceptance than ever before. . . . The state of singleness has been exalted to equality with the state of marriage, making marital status purely a matter of personal preference."[21]

For some this happy sense of equality exists, but more often, I suspect, singles struggle with many of the issues that are discussed in other chapters of this book—loneliness, anger, guilt, interpersonal relations, self-esteem, sex apart from marriage, and homosexuality, to name a few.[22] In addition, the counselor might consider the following.

1. *Evaluate Your Own Attitudes toward Singles.* Recently a large suburban church hired a minister to singles who privately expressed his reaction to the appointment. "I needed a job," he said. "This is only temporary because I really want to be a senior pastor." Such an attitude is likely to be picked up quickly, especially by single people who are accustomed to "second-class" treatment. No counselor is likely to be effective if he or she has a negative attitude toward singles, thinks that they are in some way inferior, or feels either envy or threat in the presence of single people.

Singles, as we have seen, often feel like misfits in the church. Many feel unwanted, tolerated at best, or sometimes the objects of subtle prejudice and not-so-subtle pressures. Remember that it is *not* true that most single adults are excessively lonely, frantically looking for a mate, bad credit risks, social misfits, afraid of intimacy or responsibility, spiritually immature, seething with anger, or wallowing in self-pity. Each single, like every married person, is a unique human being with individual strengths and needs. Some have a lot of problems because of their singleness; most do not.

2. *Help with Acceptance.* Single counselees need supportive acceptance, a listening ear that will hear their stories, and sometimes a person who can understand the pain, bitterness, and struggles without condemning. When a single counselee experiences such acceptance, he or she may be able to more honestly face the frustrations of singleness. In addition they may be more open to ponder the biblical teaching that the single life is God's special calling for some people. Help the counselee see that to be single is not necessarily to be second best or to be doomed to a life of misery and incompleteness. Be realistic enough to acknowledge that loneliness and single-person frustrations are likely to persist. In contrast you may occasionally remind counselees that the single individual avoids some of the equally frustrating problems that married couples must face. As these issues are discussed, be sure to give the counselee ample time to express his or her feelings and ideas. Remember, we don't solve problems *for* people; we solve problems *with* them.

3. *Stimulate Realistic Life Planning.* In addition to facing problems and dealing with them honestly, singles can learn to make clear plans for the future. It is not wrong to hope for marriage or to recognize that marriage is a possibility for the future, but it is not healthy to build our lives around events that are uncertain. Instead, individuals, especially Christians, must learn both to prepare for the future and to live fully in the present. For singles, this involves facing the fact that marriage (or remarriage) may or may not be a possibility. It involves a consideration and development of one's abilities and gifts, a prayerful pondering of God's will for one's life now, the formulating of long-range and short-term goals, and movement into a plan of action that will make these goals attainable. The counselor can help with these deliberations, guiding counselees in their thinking and encouraging realism. At times singles will need help with tangible issues such as finding a job, balancing a budget, or running a household. This may be a special need for young adults, parents without partners, or people who recently have lost a mate. In all of this, the goal is first to accept and deal with the problems, then to move in the direction of helping people to be single and satisfied.

Unmarried counselors might ponder the unique impact that their own singleness could have on their single counselees. Within recent years, several publications have noted the importance of mentoring.[23] Usually this refers to the role of older and more successful business and professional people who guide younger people in their careers. Mentors can also be helpful in noncareer areas as well. Earlier, for example, we mentioned John R. W. Stott, a well-known theologian and Bible scholar from England, who has been open in discussing both the difficulties and the benefits of serving in the church as a single minister. It is interesting to ponder how many single seminary graduates have been encouraged by Stott's example and have persisted in finding places of service, despite the tendency in many churches to distrust and not hire single pastors. Stott no doubt has been a single mentor for many young unmarried theologians whom he has never met.[24]

4. *Guide Interpersonal Relationships.* Since the single person has no mate, he or she must be helped to build intimate relationships apart from marriage. On paper this looks easy. In practice it is very difficult.

John Fischer has suggested two principles for helping singles build good relationships: accepting other people as they are without trying to change them, and committing yourself to others in an attempt to learn from and share with them.[25] When a single man and woman communicate like this, however, something that Fischer calls "weirdness" may develop. This is a subtle pressure that creeps in and hinders the relationship because the people involved begin to wonder, "Is this the one?" "Is this 'that special relationship'?" "What if I 'blow it'?" When there is a fear or unwillingness to discuss such thinking openly, both people get uncomfortable, conversation gets difficult, and one person (usually the man) backs away. To avoid this, Fischer suggests that the fears be acknowledged, that the couple openly agree to forget worrying about marriage and that they go on with their nonromantic relationship.[26]

For Christians this can be helped by an attitude that consistently places the relationship in God's hands and is willing to have him lead, even if this means that couples go their separate ways. Counselors must help singles deal not only with "weirdness" but also with the challenges of getting along effectively with a variety of people in different situations.

Some counselees may also need help in meeting new friends. Singles bars and encounter groups are not the best places to make these contacts, but those who look in the church find that some congregations (especially those that are small) don't have many single adults. As we have seen, many church members (and even some pastors)[27] are reluctant to have singles in the congregation, but these same people may be annoyed when an unmarried person leaves their church and begins attending a Christian singles group that meets elsewhere.

Some of this resistance can be broken down by singles who establish roots in their communities. This involves becoming established in a home or community, volunteering for activities and responsibilities in the church, showing a sincere interest in others of all ages (rather than talking mostly about one's own concerns or sticking only with other single people), and remembering that it is best to develop a variety of friendships, if possible, rather than searching for a "best friend."

The counselor can also help people recognize the differences between friendship and romantic love. According to one research study,[28] friendship is a relationship characterized by enjoyment of each other's company, mutual acceptance, respect, a willingness to assist one another, mutual understanding, a sharing of experiences and feelings, spontaneity, a comfortable feeling when friends are in each other's presence, and trust (the central characteristic of friendship). Romantic love may have some of the same features, but the relationship is most characterized by mutual fascination, a strong desire for sexual and other physical intimacy, and such exclusiveness that the love relationship takes precedence over all others. Clearly it is possible to have good friendships without romantic love. Presumably the best marriages are those that have both.

5. *Give Assistance to Single Parents.* Most parents, at times, feel overwhelmed and frustrated in the task of child rearing, but singles must experience the frustrations and make the decisions alone. Some evidence suggests that the stresses of

being a parent are especially intense among single mothers. Many have inadequate incomes, low standards of living, and excessive demands on their time. The strain is lessened when coworkers and friends give support or encouragement, but single mothers are four times more likely than married mothers to seek mental health services.[29] The single parent needs to understand and express his or her feelings about coping without a partner and often there is a need for practical guidance in making decisions.

Single parents sometimes need to be reminded that life with only one parent can be difficult for the children too. Statistics vary from country to country, but in the United States about one-fourth of all young people under the age of eighteen live with a single parent.[30] These children need understanding, love, contact with adults of both sexes, and opportunity to have some involvement with two-parent families that can give a broader perspective on adult and family life. Then there should be honest, open, genuine, loving communication within the home. As far as possible the missing parent should be described realistically, not torn down or put on a pedestal.

All of these suggestions apply equally to the parent in the home and to the parent who has visiting rights. The children can be appreciated and enjoyed by both parents, but the visiting parent especially should try to avoid frequent fantasy trips, overpermissiveness, or overindulgence. Help visiting parents see that these behaviors deny reality, create further tension, and often are unhealthy attempts to buy affection or to create a contrast between the two parents. These behaviors may reflect parental frustration or bitterness, but they can be harmful to the children who too often become unwilling pawns in a mother-father struggle.

Harold Ivan Smith once met a pastoral counselor who announced that he didn't want divorced people and single parents in the church. "Let them go to someone else's church," the pastor declared, and then he listed some problems in working with single parents. Of course there are problems.[31] Sometimes churches and Christian counselors attract singles who are neurotic, afraid to build relationships, complainers, or inclined to use the church to find a mate, free babysitting, or temporary bed partners. Working with singles, especially single parents, can take a lot of time, and success is not always guaranteed. It is helpful to remember that issues like these are not confined to counseling singles. Helping people always involves time and risk, but the rewards can be great—for the counselee, the counselor, the church, and the kingdom of Christ.

Sometimes it is helpful to put a single parent in contact with other parents who can engage in parent-to-parent support and encouragement. If you make these informal referrals to married couples, try to find people who are not threatened by close contact with single parents. In this, as in all counseling with singles, the goal is to help counselees put their confidence in God, meet their own needs effectively, and learn to raise their children with love, discipline, and understanding.

6. *Help People Wait.* Waiting is not easy, especially in this era of speed, efficiency, and impatience with inconvenience. When things are not happening quickly it may seem easiest to dash out, make decisions, and take independent action. The Christian, however, has volunteered to be under the Lordship of Christ, and he, who is in no hurry and wants our own good, often makes us wait. By waiting we can learn patience, deal with unconfessed sin or with personal problems, and work

to change our attitudes. Waiting does not imply that we sit and do nothing. We act carefully and in accordance with God's will so far as this can be determined. Then we trust that God's plans for us will become apparent, in his timing.

How does this apply to singles? Some sit and wait for God to provide a mate, assuming that if they have enough faith and please God enough, he will provide the reward of a perfect husband or wife. God does not conform to that kind of thinking. Single counselees, like people who are married, must be encouraged to trust God's goodness, to wait on him daily, and to seek his help in accepting his best for each of our lives.

Preventing Singles Problems

"If happiness is being single, why do these people look so sad?" This question was raised by a counselor who has spoken to thousands of singles.[32] Many have "Happiness Is Being Single" written on their bumper stickers but "I'm miserable and unhappy" written on their faces. How can unhappiness such as this be prevented?

1. *Change Church Attitudes.* Something is wrong with a church that sees single adults as misfits, has no place in the body for unmarried people, lacks programs to meet the needs of singles, and shows no understanding (or desire to understand) their struggles (especially if the single person is divorced).

These attitudes can be challenged from the pulpit. Married persons can be encouraged to welcome singles into the church and into their homes. It may be helpful to remind people that Jesus and Paul were single. They might not be welcome in some churches today. Certainly they would be unacceptable to many pulpit committees who maintain a strong prejudice against single pastors.

As Christians we find ultimate security in Christ and not in a local congregation, but believers do need one another. Many would agree that for singles especially, our "home is the church, our family the body of believers. No definition of 'family' can be called Christian which does not include single people."[33]

There may be a place in the church for sweetheart banquets, couples clubs, and family-related church programs, but too often these exclude, overlook, or put down singles. Probably most organizers of these activities have no intention of excluding the unmarried; more often there is a nonawareness of the singles in the congregation.

Christian counselors, pastors, other church leaders, and members of the congregation should all remember that single people are significant and equal members of the body of Christ. Unmarried adults should have full acceptance in the church community.

2. *Seek to Build Stable Marriages and Families.* Many singles are afraid to marry and others live difficult lives as single parents and divorced people because believers often have distorted and nonbiblical views of marriage. Teaching about healthy marriage and families may be an indirect and effective way to prevent problems that singles and married people both face.

To reduce the increasing incidence of divorce among believers, to cut down the number of unfulfilling and status-quo marriages, and to help singles get a more balanced perspective on family relationships, the church can:[34]

- Restate its commitment to the family and to the institution of marriage.
- Give strong, clear, biblical teaching and preaching on marriage, the family, and singleness.
- Encourage fathers to be more active in parenting and couples to be more involved in marriage building.
- Discourage thinking that creates unrealistic ideals about marriage and the family, or that encourages child-centered marriages.
- Teach communication and conflict resolution skills.

3. *Encourage Singles to Make Decisions and to Be Active.* Singleness problems can be prevented when unmarried people are helped to trust God for their present and future needs, to honestly face and attempt to deal with their personal problems and struggles, to reach out to others in a spirit of giving and friendship, to evaluate their life goals periodically, and to work on developing a balanced life that combines worship, work, play, rest, and periods of both socializing and solitude. Often when people are active and involved in meaningful activities, there is less time or reason to dwell on problems.

4. *Stimulate Ministries to Singles.* While single adults should be integrated into the mainstream of the church, there also can be programs to meet their unique needs. Singles groups in the church (or groups combining singles from several smaller churches) are most helpful when they reach out to newcomers, avoid an emphasis on matchmaking or dating, provide for and at times involve the children of singles in social gatherings, are sensitive to the personal and spiritual needs of group members, and are lead by mature, sensitive, preferably unmarried leaders. Programs must appeal to the interests and needs of singles, must recognize individual differences (older singles such as widows, for example, do not have the same needs as unmarried college students), and must focus on teaching, discipling, worship, social activities, and service. This kind of outreach has potential for preventing many singles problems and providing ways for handling existing problems before they get worse.

Conclusions about Singleness

Singleness is not a disease and neither is it a blight for the many unmarried people who live fulfilling and productive lives. Millions of adults in the world are single—never married and formerly married—and many will remain that way. These people struggle with the same issues and face most of the same problems that married persons encounter, but there are unique challenges in being single. These problems must be understood and faced honestly—both by married and single individuals and by their counselors.

Within recent years many churches have become more accepting and involved in ministering to singles. This is an encouraging sign, especially in view of the scriptural teaching that elevates singleness. To be single is not to be second class or second best. Singles have every potential for developing full, meaningful, Christ-centered lifestyles. The church and individual counselors can make this possibility a reality.

SUGGESTIONS FOR FURTHER READING

Bustanoby, Andre. *Being a Single Parent.* Grand Rapids, Mich.: Pryanee Books/ Zondervan, 1985.*

Cargan, L., and M. Melko. *Singles: Myths and Realities.* Beverly Hills, Calif.: Sage, 1982.

Olson, G. Keith. *Counseling Singles.* Waco, Tex.: Word, forthcoming.

Smith, Harold Ivan. *Pastoral Care for Single Parents.* Kansas City: Beacon Hill Press, 1982.

———. *Single and Feeling Good.* Nashville: Abingdon, 1987.*

Smoke, Jim. *Suddenly Single.* Old Tappan, N.J.: Revell, 1982.*

Witte, Kaaren. *Flying Solo.* Nashville: Abingdon, 1988.*

* Books marked with an asterisk (*) are especially suited for counselees to read.

25

Choosing a Marriage Partner

MURRAY IS TWENTY-NINE, white, a recent graduate from law school, and unmarried. When he was in college, Murray dated a little, but he tended to be shy around girls, uncomfortable in dating relationships, and more concerned about getting an education than getting a wife.

After graduation, he applied for a short-term missionary assignment and spent two years in Africa. The time overseas was exciting; an adventurous opportunity for both service and travel. Most of his friends were like Murray—single, enjoying their mid-twenties, and not much inclined to think about marriage.

Back home Murray launched enthusiastically into his studies in law school. Finances were tight and there wasn't much time for dating, so when Murray met a Christian girl at church they were "just friends." After several months, the friendship had become more serious and talk of marriage turned into an engagement. The couple agreed to marry as soon as Murray finished law school.

The wedding never took place. Murray's fiancée abruptly broke the engagement after she began seeing an old boyfriend who had returned from college. Murray was deeply disappointed and angry, but he turned his attention away from women, forgot about marriage, and devoted his attention fully to his law school training.

Now Murray is a lawyer, but he has no wife. Most of his friends are married, and some of his high-school colleagues even have teenage children. Recently Murray has been dating an attractive, vivacious, intelligent twenty-six-year-old who is a committed believer. "She will be a fine wife for some lucky guy," somebody said recently, but Murray feels insecure and has some uncertainties about whether he is or wants to be the "lucky guy."

"Will this relationship fall apart like my earlier engagement?" he wonders. "Is this girl the one that God wants me to marry?" "How can I be sure that a marriage with this girl wouldn't end in divorce?" "Should I wait a little longer?" "Have I waited so long that all the best girls are gone and now I'm getting anxious?"

The problem is complicated by the fact that Murray's female friend is Oriental. Even though her parents are Christians and glad that Murray is an active church member, they are reluctant to have their daughter marry a Caucasian. It has never occurred to Murray that he might talk these issues over with a counselor or caring friend. Instead this young lawyer is struggling alone with questions that can all be reduced to one big issue. How does one choose a mate?

Many Christians would agree that the most important decision in life is whether to accept or reject Jesus Christ as one's Savior and Lord. Second only to this is the choice of a life partner.

In some cultures the decision is easy. Marriages are arranged by the parents who sometimes enlist the aid of a marriage broker. This professional matchmaker considers family histories and proceeds to negotiate the best exchange in terms of bride price or dowry. The young couple may have no say in the matter and may not even meet each other until the day of the marriage.

How different this is from our society! For many marriage is no longer considered sacred or permanent. Living together out of wedlock, entering marriages casually, and dissolving marriages freely are all accepted parts of the Western way of life. For many people the careful choice of a life partner and the commitment to live with one's chosen mate "for better or for worse" have been replaced with a self-centered attitude that sees marriage as a convenient living arrangement that can always be terminated if love grows cold.

Christians, in contrast, still acknowledge the permanence of marriage, at least in theory if not in practice. Divorce, while common, is not encouraged, and single people take the choice of a mate very seriously. Some religious groups teach that God has one special person for each of us and that it is important not to miss God's best for your life. This attitude creates great anxiety in young people who are never told how to be sure if a choice is right, but who fear they might be sinning and missing God's blessing if one's choice is wrong. The problem is complicated when parents are led to believe that one person is the divinely chosen mate, but the young person feels God leading in a different direction.[1]

In attempting to choose a mate wisely, many unmarried people seek guidance from a friend, older couple, pastor, or professional counselor. Books on counseling tend to overlook this subject, but helping another person in the choice of a life partner can be one of the counselor's most fulfilling tasks.

The Bible and Mate Selection

The Bible says little about mate selection. Jesus gave his sanction to marriage and so did Paul, but neither discussed how a marriage partner should be chosen. This silence may reflect the fact that in biblical times choosing a mate was not a responsibility for the couple. Consider, for example, the choice of a wife for Isaac. His father sent a servant on a long journey to find a suitable candidate. The servant sought divine guidance in this process, and God gave a sign from heaven. When Rebekah was chosen, her parents were consulted and they asked the girl if she was willing to leave her family (perhaps forever) and travel to marry a man whom she had never met. Nobody ever talked about love or dating. Everybody assumed that the Lord was guiding in this choice, but personality, compatibility, sexual attraction, love, or the bride and groom's preferences were not part of the decision-making process.[2] With Jacob the situation was different. He was away from his parents when he fell in love, so the groom went directly to Rachel's father, although not to the bride.[3]

Isaac and Jacob married later in life, but apparently many people in biblical times married young—sometimes as early as age twelve or thirteen. The parents usually made the decision, just as they do in parts of the world today, but the young person could make his or her wishes known and sometimes even refuse to go along with the parental choice. After a marriage had been arranged there often was a period of unbreakable betrothal or engagement followed by a ceremony of marriage.[4] It appears that sometimes the groom didn't even see the bride's face until they were in bed together after the marriage. Even the thought of such a prospect can send shivers of anxiety up and down the spines of most contemporary single people.

Do we have biblical guidelines for choosing a mate today? Some have suggested that there is only one—believers are to marry only other believers; the Christian should not marry a non-Christian. "Do not be yoked together with unbelievers," Paul wrote. "For what do righteousness and wickedness have in common?" What has the believer in common with the unbeliever?[5] This is a warning: the Christian and non-Christian cannot pull together either as business partners or as marriage partners. A similar idea is emphasized in 1 Corinthians[6] and specifically applied to marriage when Paul states that the unmarried woman is free to marry whomever she wishes "but only if she marries a Christian."[7]

What about divine guidance? Just as Abraham's servant expected and experienced divine leading in selecting a wife for Isaac, perhaps most Christians would agree that we still can expect God's leading in mate selection. In writing about marriage, Paul instructed his readers to "be sure . . . that you are living as God intended, marrying or not marrying in accordance with God's direction and help."[8] This may apply more to general lifestyle than to mate selection, but several other biblical passages[9] teach that believers can expect divine leading—even though this may not come in dramatic or seemingly miraculous ways.

Christians are divided over the issue of whether God has only one choice for a person who is seeking a life partner. In his controversial and widely discussed book, *Decision Making and the Will of God,* Garry Friesen argues convincingly that there is no biblical support for the idea that in all the universe God has only one person for each of us, that the identity of this person will be revealed in time, and that life will be miserable if you marry someone else.[10] According to scriptural teachings, writes Friesen, marriage and singleness are both acceptable to God and the choice of a mate is governed only by the requirement that Christians must marry Christians. Beyond that Christians are free to choose a marriage partner based on one's own careful thinking and the thoughtful input of sensitive other people, including a Christian counselor.

Causes of Good and Poor Mate Selection

Choosing a marriage partner has been called "one of the most rewarding" of all the choices in life; "it is also one of the most difficult."[11] Many people appear to make unwise choices and their lives, as a result, are miserable. Because of this, some people are afraid or unwilling to take the risks of choosing a mate and building a marriage.

To help people choose wisely and lessen the risk of making a mistake, counselors might consider answers to five important questions.

1. *Why Do People Choose a Marriage Partner?* Some might answer that most people marry because they are in love. "Love" may be one of the most confusing and ambiguous words in the English language. To fall in love is to feel an exhilarating, exciting closeness and intimacy with another human being. This emotional high, however, cannot last by itself forever. For deep love to persist and grow there must be

a giving, other-centered relationship similar to that described in 1 Corinthians 13.[12] It may be that for most people deep and secure love comes *after* marriage rather than before. To *be* in love, therefore, is to experience a state of emotional exhilaration; to *grow* in love is to involve oneself deliberately in acts of giving and caring.

A feeling of being in love is not in itself a solid basis for marriage (and neither is the fact that "we don't love each other any more" a basis for divorce). The biblical marriages, like marriage in many countries today, were based on issues other than feelings, and even in our society it is probable that people really marry for reasons other than love. These reasons may be diverse, but often they center around the idea of needs. One theory of mate selection, for example, claims that opposites attract and that single people are drawn to potential partners who can meet one's needs by supplementing one's areas of weakness. A dominant person, therefore, might be attracted to someone who is less dominant, or an introvert may choose a person who is extroverted.

More accepted is the broader view that marriage meets mutual needs for companionship, security, support, intimacy, and sexual fulfillment. In addition, some marry because of premarital pregnancy, a yielding to social pressure, the desire to escape from an unhappy home environment, a fear that one will be left alone, a "rebound" reaction to the breakup of a prior engagement, or a compulsion to rescue some unfortunate single person. Each of these reasons for marriage meets some need, although none in itself can be the basis for a mature and stable relationship.

Perhaps you have noticed that some of these reasons for selecting a mate are immature and self-centered; others are more rational and may result from mutual deliberation and respect. In all of this it is wise to remember that people marry, ultimately, because God created us male and female, instituted marriage for companionship, mutual support, and sexual expression, and declared in his Word that marriage is honorable.[13] This must not be forgotten as we help people struggle through the choice of a marriage partner.

2. *Why Do Some People Not Choose a Marriage Partner?* The same God who created marriage apparently did not expect that everyone would find a mate. Jesus never had a wife. An unmarried Paul wrote that singleness should be considered a superior state since the unmarried person can be free for "undistracted devotion to the Lord."[14] Some people remain single, therefore, because they believe that this is the will and calling of God for their lives.

There are other, probably more common reasons why some people do not marry. First, there is the failure to meet eligible partners. Since there are more women than men, it follows that there simply are not enough potential husbands to go around. In addition, most people want a mate who has similar interests or education, but many people who desire marriage may not be able to find such compatible prospects. Consider, for example, the believer who wants a Christian mate but lives in an area where there are few eligible Christians. The desire for marriage may be strong, but the prospects are not.

Second, some people fail to take advantage of the opportunities that are present. Busy with education, building a career, travel, or other activities, these people decide to postpone marriage and eventually the prospects disappear. Others, with high expectations, keep waiting for someone better and discover too late that they have passed by some excellent opportunities for marriage.

There is always hope, suggested one woman in a somewhat humorous article. The key for finding a mate, she wrote, is to "drop your notions of finding Mr. Right who will solve all your problems." One forty-two-year-old woman, for example, "after many years of searching for the right man, finally wound up with a shy, sweet, loving fellow who made her very happy but was far from her usual dynamic, intellectual charmer type." The lady listed the characteristics she wanted in a husband and then broke her list into four categories (in declining order of importance): What I can't live without, absolute musts, extremely important traits, and what would be nice to have. Then she "dropped the last three categories and cut the first in half."[15] Not everybody is this anxious to find a mate!

Even if they write down lists of desirable traits for a mate, people in a third category still remain single because they are unattractive to those of the opposite sex. This may result from mental or physical defects, but more often psychological characteristics drive others away. People who are excessively timid, afraid of the opposite sex, too aggressive or loud, insensitive, socially inappropriate in their dress and mannerisms, or self-centered often cannot relate well in dating. The individual who is overly concerned about getting married can also scare off and drive away potential mates.

Fourth, there is a failure of some people to achieve emotional independence. An unusually strong dependence upon one's parents or guilt over leaving a parent can cause some to remain single. In addition, there are responsible people who make a mature and deliberate choice to remain single because of a duty to care for needy family members. Sometimes, however, this can be an excuse to keep from taking the risks involved in entering a marriage and building intimacy.

Fifth, some people prefer to find intimacy apart from traditional marriage. Living together secretly or openly in what used to be called common-law marriages, joining a commune, participating in a trial marriage or group marriage, or forming a homosexual relationship are alternatives to marriage that lead some people to remain single.[16]

Finally, some persons simply do not want to marry. This group includes homosexuals, those who have been burned in previous relationships, and people who are afraid of the opposite sex, of sexual relationships, of intimacy, and/or of losing independence. Then there are others, mature, well-adjusted people, who decide that they would prefer to remain single in spite of social pressures that might push them toward marriage.

3. *Where Do People Find Mates?* Several decades of research have confirmed that most people select mates from similar social classes, economic and educational levels, occupations, age groups, race, religious backgrounds, and areas of residence.[17] People often cross some of these barriers, of course, and many are able to build successful marriages despite their different backgrounds. Crossovers can also bring pressure that makes marital adjustment more difficult. Within recent years, for example, increasing numbers of women have been marrying younger men. Often these are good relationships except for the issue of children. Older women tend to be involved in careers and are less willing to have children; their husbands, however, are more inclined to want families. This can create tension.[18]

In looking for a mate, therefore, most people try to find someone who is of similar background and social-religious-educational level. Within this broad category the choice is often narrowed by one's personal standards, parental approval or disapproval, and by the single person's mental image of an ideal mate. Since few people can measure up to these great expectations, there often must be a relaxing of one's standards, a willingness to accept the less desirable characteristics in a potential mate, or a decision to remain single until the ideal person comes along.

All of this—background, age, socioeconomic and educational level, parental and personal expectations—resides in the minds of single people who contemplate marriage. With the entire opposite-sex population of single people thus narrowed, the unmarried person keeps alert to the people who are seen, met, or befriended at school, work, church, social and athletic gatherings, conferences, or in the neighborhood. It is well known that one person often may be attracted to another who has no desire to respond romantically. Sometimes a couple will meet first as friends or work associates with no thought of marriage, but then a more personal relationship begins to build. Other relationships start with feelings of sexual attraction, but before there can be a successful marriage, the couple must discover at least some similarities in their viewpoints and a mutual ability to meet each other's needs. For the Christian there is, in addition, the absolute essential that the two persons are believers.

4. *Why Do Some People Choose Unwisely?* Although choosing a mate is one of life's most important decisions, rarely is it done in a logical, analytical manner. Subtle influences, parental and society pressures or unconscious desires, often edge people into relationships that may be unhealthy. In addition some people may have unrealistic expectations about how their needs might be met in marriage.

Several years ago a survey attempted to discover what unmarried people were hoping for in a marriage. This list might be different if the survey could be repeated today, but perhaps many people still hope to find someone to "love me, confide in, show affection, respect my ideals, appreciate what I wish to achieve, understand my moods, help make my decisions, stimulate my ambition, look up to, give me self-confidence, back me in difficulty, appreciate me just as I am, admire my abilities, make me feel important, and relieve my loneliness."[19] While each of these is realistic and most are found in mature marriages, the satisfaction of these needs only comes when each mate gives to the other. When people expect to receive without giving they are headed for disappointment. When single people choose a mate solely on the basis of what one can receive from marriage, they are preparing for future marital tension.

This lopsided desire to receive, without giving, is a mark of immaturity and sometimes of neurosis. Other issues that reflect immaturity and lead to unwise marital decisions are a desire to prove one's adulthood, to escape from a difficult home situation, to rebel against parents or a former partner, to escape the stigma of being single, to find a substitute for a previous relationship (marrying on the rebound), to get a sexual partner, to improve one's economic-social status, or to bolster one's self-esteem and masculinity or femininity. Other "circumstances that warrant special caution"[20] and signal possible difficulties include wide age differences, recent mental illness in one or both individuals, no evidence of financial security, serious drug involvement, a pregnant bride, divergent religious traditions, wide cultural or obvious racial differences, or participants who have never dated anyone other than the intended mate. Good marriages can occur despite these obstacles, but when several are present or when a couple appears to have unhealthy motives for choosing a mate, the choice is likely to be regretted later.

5. *Why Do Some People Choose Wisely?* Despite all of the potential for failure, some people make a wise choice of a marriage partner. What are the reasons for this?

(a) Christian Convictions. In Western cultures, most mates are known first through dating. Since one never knows when a dating relationship may lead to marriage, it is a wise policy for unmarried Christian persons to limit their dating to other believers. Christians who choose wisely often pray about mate selection, at first alone and later as a couple.

(b) Similar Backgrounds and Complementary Needs. Christians, like nonbelievers, are unique and at different levels of emotional maturity. It does not follow that a marriage will be successful and stable simply because both people are followers of Jesus Christ. As we have indicated, marriage selection is best when the man and woman are similar in variables such as age, interests, values, socioeconomic level, and education. In addition, it is helpful if the couple can meet each other's needs.

Try, however, to distinguish between complementary and contradictory needs. Complementary needs fit so well together that a relationship is smooth and compromise is rarely needed. Contradictory needs clash and require frequent resolution. If both people enjoy social contacts but one person is outgoing and the other is a little shy, this can be complementary. In contrast, if one person loves parties and the other prefers to remain at home, these contradictory needs make conflict almost inevitable.

(c) Emotional Resonance. As single people, many of us have had the experience of asking, "How can I know when 'the right one' comes along?" To hear someone reply, "You'll just know!" is a common but not very satisfying answer. Some relationships are felt to be harmonious and right. With others, the "spark" just isn't there. To choose a mate on the basis of such feelings alone would surely be unwise, but to ignore one's feelings or to overlook the fact that there are no feelings of attraction would also be a mistake.

(d) Marriageability Traits. In his creative theory of "marriage personalities,"[21] Christian counselor David Field identified seven characteristics that appear in healthy marriages: time spent together, mutual spiritual interests, negotiating ability, maturity, play and humor, intimacy (including expressions of appreciation and the sharing of inner thoughts and feelings), and the willingness to make commitments. When characteristics such as these are present before marriage, it seems likely that there will be wiser mate selection and subsequently greater marital satisfaction and stability.

Other traits that could contribute to wise mate selection might include:[22]

- Adaptability and flexibility (the ability and willingness of persons to adjust to change, to accept differences in a partner, and to adapt if necessary).
- Empathy (a sensitivity to the hurts and needs of others and a willing attempt to see and experience the world from the other person's perspective).
- Ability to work through problems (the recognition of emotions and a willingness to define the issues and work toward solutions).
- Ability to give and receive love (elements that are both necessary).

- Emotional stability (accepting one's emotions, controlling them, and expressing them without tearing down another person).
- Communication ability (learning to talk frequently to one another about a wide range of subjects, to convey the feeling that one understands and is sensitive to the other, to keep communication opportunities open, and to express oneself personally, clearly, and at times nonverbally).
- Commitment (the willingness to yield oneself to a lifetime of adventure including the risks, joys, and sorrows, plus a commitment to work together even when difficulties, obstacles, and challenges interfere with a smooth relationship).

Counselors and single people can be discouraged when they see lists like these. Almost nobody can meet all of these expectations. The lists show, however, that for mate selection, a feeling of love or a strong urge to get married cannot be the sole basis for making a wise choice. The outside perspective and guidance of a friend or counselor can be helpful and important if one is to attain subsequent marital stability and happiness.

Effects of Good and Poor Mate Selection

Good choices do not always lead to good marriages, but careful selection of a mate does give a solid foundation on which to build a husband-wife relationship. Marriage involves effort, risk, and sometimes disappointment. These never are easy experiences, but it is more pleasant and motivating to work with a compatible teammate in life than with someone who apparently was the wrong choice.

Many people, however, make choices that in retrospect seem to have been unwise, but the couple determines nevertheless to build the best relationship possible considering the circumstances. These people discover that loving actions often create loving feelings. In time relatively good marriages can result.

In contrast other people never recover from poor mate selection. Unhappiness and conflict characterize the marriage, and the relationship is dissolved emotionally if not legally through separation and divorce. Counseling people in the selection of a marriage partner has the goal of preventing such unhappy endings to marriage.

Counseling and Mate Selection

Despite its importance, the selection of a marriage partner is seldom done carefully, objectively, and rationally. When people fall in love they tend to overlook the faults in each other, to ignore danger signals, and to dismiss the counsel of more objective persons. Few are likely to come for counsel until after a potential mate has been chosen, and most do not even come then. The counselor's help is most likely to come through informal talks with young people before they fall in love, through devotionals and other public speaking to singles groups, through side discussions with counselees who have come to get help for other problems, or through counseling with the never-married and formerly married who come for help in evaluating the wisdom of their mate choices. There are several goals for this counseling, goals that apply equally to young unmarried persons and to older individuals, including widows and divorced persons, who would like to get married or remarried.

1. *Spiritual Evaluation.* Since the Bible is so clear in its teaching that believers should marry only believers, this must be emphasized repeatedly. Even when they believe this, people often look for excuses to justify their dating of non-Christians. "We don't plan to get serious," they say, or "If we date, I could lead my friend to Christ." Statements like this usually are made with sincerity, but they signal a sidestepping of biblical teaching about the unequal yoke. Although Christians sometimes do lead potential mates to Christ, the reverse is also true and perhaps more likely—nonbelievers cause Christians to stumble spiritually or to lose spiritual vitality. This needs to be stated clearly at some time in counseling. Dating nonbelievers is risky and in general should be avoided.

When a potential marriage partner is being considered, encourage the counselee to ask questions such as the following and suggest that the answers be discussed with the counselor:

- Is my potential mate a believer?
- Does his or her life show evidence of the fruits of the Spirit (Gal. 5:22–23)?
- Have my partner and I ever discussed our spiritual lives, struggles, and goals?
- Have we ever prayed together? If not, why not?
- Do we agree on a church, on our basic standard of living, on our views about right and wrong, and on our perspectives about a Christian home?

2. *Reassurance.* Sometimes people come to a counselor with the fear that they never will get married. They may wonder if something is wrong or if God has let them down by not allowing them to get married.

Encourage these people to admit and express their feelings—including feelings of anger and frustration—and give the reassurance that God always cares and wants the best for us. Openly discuss the realities and discouragements of the single life, but point out too that singleness can be a special calling. Is the counselee willing to remain single? If not, why not?

By observing and by asking, try to determine (a) if the person shows traits (like overeagerness, timidity, or insensitivity) that may be driving away members of the opposite sex, and (b) if the counselee's life is so bound up in the desire to marry that little else seems to matter. Many people live in the future. They assume that life will be better when they earn more money, graduate from college, get a better job, or find a mate. While they wait, their lives are largely meaningless, nonproductive, and stagnant. Such people should be encouraged to live life to the fullest now. If a mate is found, this will be great. If no mate is found, life can also be worthwhile and fulfilling.

3. *Giving Direction in Mate Selection.* Some people need practical guidance in finding eligible partners. This involves two issues: finding places where there are other single people and learning how to relate.

It is an obvious but frequently overlooked fact that one does not find a mate by sitting at home watching television and waiting for God's gift of marriage to arrive at the door. To meet people, including potential marriage partners, one must go where others are. For some this means singles bars, but for many people, including believers, this is not considered a suitable place to find a mate. More desirable are churches, study courses, vacation trips, sports events, Christian single adult groups, and Christian conferences. Yet if one goes to these places primarily to find a marriage partner, this soon becomes apparent to everyone. Nothing drives people away like a single person's overanxious desire to latch on to potential mates. It is better to get involved in groups that are interesting, knowing that in so doing one may or may not find a potential partner.

Sometimes counselees may need to be reminded that they should look neat and attractive, learn how to ask questions about others, and try to be good listeners who are interested in other people. It is important to be oneself instead of pretending to be something we are not. The counselor can gently point out failings in these areas and, if necessary, do some role playing in which the counselor and counselee pretend to be strangers so they can practice relating to one another.

4. *Evaluating Motives, Ideals, and Maturity.* Why does the counselee want to find a mate (or why does he or she not want to marry)? The counselee's answers to these questions sometimes are not what counselors expect. It can be helpful, therefore, to ask, "Why do you want to get married?" Try to determine, sometimes by raising tentative questions, if there are unhealthy reasons for wanting marriage—like social and family pressures, the desire to escape an unpleasant home situation, the need to prove that one is an adult, or the feeling that marriage is now or never. If the person has chosen to remain single, ask yourself if there are also unhealthy reasons for this. Is there a fear of marriage, of sex, or of the opposite sex? Is the person homosexual? Is he or she rebelling against something, including traditional forms of marriage? Ask the counselee to discuss these attitudes. Talk about their implications and the possible reasons for their presence. If there is a desire for change, discuss how this might be done. Try to focus attention on specific issues and talk about how the counselee could take action to change.

At some time it may be good to ask a counselee to describe his or her ideal mate. Then, discuss this expectation. Is it unrealistic? Is it causing the counselee to overlook or reject potentially good marriage partners who do not fit the ideal? Can parts of the ideal be changed without lessening one's moral standards?

As these issues are discussed, try to assess the counselee's level of maturity. Immature single people make immature marriage partners and this can lead to problems in dating and marriage. The spiritually maturing Christian shows a desire to be like Christ, accompanied by some evidence of the fruits of the Spirit in his or her life.[23] As one matures there is also:

- A tendency to behave according to one's age (and not like somebody older or younger).
- A capacity to assume responsibility.
- An ability to look at oneself and one's problems objectively.
- An ability to acknowledge but control emotions.
- An understanding of other people's feelings and a sensitive ability to respond to these emotions.
- A growing independence from the control of family and friends.

- A willingness to postpone immediate gratification so that greater satisfaction can be attained in the future.
- A responsible attitude toward sex.
- An ability to laugh and see the humorous side of life without tearing others down or resorting to cynicism.
- A realistic and essentially positive self-image.
- An ability to make choices and live with the consequences of one's decisions.[24]

In counseling you may want to discuss some of these issues. In which does the person succeed and where does he or she fail? How could these traits and attitudes be developed? The more of these that are present, the greater the likelihood of successful mate selection and marital stability.

5. *Teaching about Mate Selection.* In many respects, counseling is a specialized form of education. Nowhere is this more true than when one is helped to choose a mate. Earlier we discussed the reasons why some people choose wisely. The contents of that section could be shared with the counselee, but it may be best to do this slowly and at different times throughout counseling. In this way, the counselee is not overwhelmed with information that may not be easy to handle.

6. *Encouraging Patience.* In all of this, encourage counselees to be patient, to pray regularly about a marriage partner, to trust in God's leading and timing, and to be alert for opportunities to meet potential mates. Pray for and with your counselees, asking for patience, for purity and protection for both the counselee and his or her potential mate, and for the willingness to accept singleness joyfully if this is God's plan.

PREVENTING POOR MATE SELECTION

In the selection of a marriage partner, to be forewarned is the best protection against mistakes. Information from the first parts of this chapter could be presented to singles privately or to singles groups, Sunday school classes, youth groups, special interest groups, or weekend conferences. If this or similar material is presented, be sure that there is opportunity for people to discuss what they hear, to ask questions, and to ponder how (in practical ways) this learning can be applied to their own lives.

The sooner such information is presented and discussed, the better. As we have noted, facts about mate selection tend to lose significance and influence after one has fallen in love. If facts and warnings can be given *before* emotional bonds are allowed to develop, it is more likely that error will be avoided. Thus single people should learn to evaluate relationships intellectually (this could steer them away from potentially harmful involvements) before getting into a situation where they might fall romantically and emotionally in love. When all of this is understood and practiced, much progress has been made toward the prevention of poor mate selection.

With some counselees, prevention will start long before a prospective mate appears. Immature or self-centered people, for example, can often profit from individual or group counseling that helps them cope more effectively with life in general. This can remove some of the unhealthy attitudes and behaviors that can lead to an unwise selection of a marriage partner.

Conclusions about Mate Selection

Erich Fromm, the famous psychoanalytic writer, once described mate selection as an exercise in bargaining. He wrote:

> Our whole culture is based on an appetite for buying, on the idea of a mutually favorable exchange. Modern man's happiness consists in the thrill of looking at the shop windows, and in buying all that he can afford to buy, either for cash or on installments. He (or she) looks at people in a similar way. For the man an attractive girl—and for the woman an attractive man—are the prizes they are after. "Attractive" usually means a nice package of qualities which are popular and sought after on the personality market. What specifically makes a person attractive depends on the fashion of the time, physically as well as mentally. During the twenties, a drinking and smoking girl, tough and sexy, was attractive; today the fashion demands more domesticity and coyness. At the end of the nineteenth and the beginning of this century, a man had to be aggressive and ambitious—today he has to be social and tolerant—in order to be an attractive "package." At any rate, the sense of falling in love develops usually only with regard to such human commodities as are within reach of one's own possibilities for exchange. I am out for a bargain, the object should be desirable from the standpoint of its social value, and at the same time should want me, considering my overt and hidden assets and potentialities. Two persons thus fall in love when they feel they have found the best object available on the market, considering the limitations of their own exchange values.[25]

This is a blunt humanistic analysis, but it contains an element of truth. Striking a marriage bargain may be more overt in other cultures where dowries and bride prices are part of a deal, but it surely is true that mate selection in our culture also includes some exchanges.

The Christian recognizes, however, that marriage involves more. It is the joining of two individuals so that they become one and yet remain unique and interlocking personalities. Probably it is untrue that within this world there is only one, perfect, God-ordained person for each of us, but it surely *is* true that God can and often does lead individuals to marriage partners who will meet their needs and with whom they can blend their lives. Often he leads through counselors who are willing to give guidance as single people make the choice of a mate.

SUGGESTIONS FOR FURTHER READING

Friesen, Garry, with J. Robin Maxson. *Decision Making and the Will of God.* Portland, Oreg.: Multnomah, 1980.*

* Books marked with an asterisk (*) are especially suitable for counselees to read.

Phillips, Bob. *How Can I Be Sure?—A Pre-Marriage Inventory.* Eugene, Oreg.: Harvest House, 1978.*

Rinehart, Stacy, and Paula Rinehart. *Choices: Finding God's Way in Dating, Sex, Singleness, and Marriage.* Colorado Springs: NavPress, 1982.*

Wright, Norman, and Marvin A. Inmon. *A Guidebook to Dating, Waiting, and Choosing a Mate.* Eugene, Oreg.: Harvest House, 1978.

*** Books marked with an asterisk (*) are especially suited for counselees to read.**

Part 6

Family Issues

26

Premarital Counseling

RICH AND ANDREA WERE READY to get married. Both in their early twenties, they met in the cafeteria of the state university where Rich was finishing his degree in biology and Andrea was a sophomore, still searching for a major.

It was love at first sight and the couple admitted to the pastoral counselor that their three-month relationship had been characterized mostly by starry-eyed infatuation and too much physical involvement. "We haven't gone all the way yet," Rich stated, "But we've come close and I'm not sure I can wait much longer."

Andrea came from a Jewish home. Her parents had never been very religious, but she knew they would object if she chose to marry a Gentile. Rich thought that his fundamentalist parents might be less resistant, especially since Andrea was attending church regularly and had become a Christian. Andrea, however, knew little about the Christian faith, in contrast to Rich who was almost raised in the church.

There were other differences in Rich and Andrea's past. One set of parents was well educated and both mother and father were successful professional people. The other parents were high school graduates of modest means. Both had worked most of their adult lives in secure but relatively low-paying jobs.

Rich and Andrea approached marriage with dreams about the bliss they would experience as husband and wife, but the couple didn't have very realistic plans for the future nor did they have money in the bank or jobs. When they approached the campus pastor during the university's spring break about a wedding, they were surprised and annoyed when he failed to share their enthusiasm. Instead the pastor recommended a few sessions of premarital counseling before making further plans. Rich and Andrea weren't sure they needed any of this and wondered instead if it would be wiser and easier if they eloped.

One night Rich got word that his father had been hurt badly in a car accident. The young student hurried home and eventually had to drop out of classes for a quarter while his dad recovered. In this case, absence did *not* make the heart grow fonder. After a time of telephone calls and letter writing, Rich and Andrea both concluded that their romance had been a passing fling. Eventually they both finished their degrees and went their separate ways.

"I have often wondered," Rich said recently. "If my dad had not had that accident, would Andrea and I have entered into a difficult and perhaps disastrous marriage? The pastoral counselor forced us to pause and consider the step we were intent on taking, but would premarital counseling have prevented later problems or stopped us from marriage?"

Psychologist Carl Rogers once gave a sobering perspective on marriage. "If 50–75 percent of Ford or General Motors cars completely fell apart within the early part of their lifetimes as automobiles," Rogers wrote, "the public outcry would be overwhelming and drastic steps would be taken to correct the situation."[1] But this happens to many marriages and hardly anyone raises a complaint. Divorce is frequent, fewer than half of the marriages that persist could be considered successful, and often couples seem unable or unwilling to correct the situation.

There are many reasons for the present instability of marriages, but one cause may be the lack of care with which many marriages are put together. Built primarily on sexual attraction, the desire to escape from a difficult home situation, a vague feeling of love, or some equally fleeting motive, many marriage relationships are too flimsy to survive the pressures, challenges, and storms of daily living. Unprepared for the stresses or for the effort and determination required to make marriage work, many people prefer to give up and bail out. That which was meant to be meaningful and fulfilling thus becomes frustrating and personally devastating.

Modern societies, especially in the West, do not demand or seem to expect much from marriage. In many places a marriage permit is easier to obtain than a driver's license. It is more difficult to get into a Rotary club than to get into a marriage—and the Rotarians expect more of their members. A prospective bride and groom may know nothing about a marriage. Often nobody says anything to a couple who seem to have made unwise decisions about mate selection. The same people who may spend hours planning vacations, careers, major purchases, wedding receptions, and honeymoons, sometimes resist the suggestion that they could benefit from a little guidance in preparing for marriage.

In the church we leave premarital counseling (perhaps "preceremonial" counseling is a more accurate term) to the pastor while the relatives and church members are content to remain smiling spectators. They come to the wedding, bring their gifts and cards, attend the showers, and have cake at the reception, all the time hoping that the marriage will last and that somebody has been guiding the couple in preparing for this crucially important step in life. The same dedicated church members who encourage prayer meetings before selecting a pastor or launching a new community outreach program hardly give a thought to praying for divine guidance for couples who are moving toward the beginning of a Christian marriage.[2]

Unlike most of the issues in this book, premarital counseling is primarily preventive. It focuses on education and information. It is less concerned about healing wounds that exist than about building a union that will survive future attacks. Since few people are enthusiastic about preventive counseling (most assume that "problems happen to others but will never happen to us") there is a tendency to resist and sometimes to resent this help. Counselors often become disillusioned with premarital counseling. Many wonder if it is worth the effort. One experienced counselor concluded that premarital counseling was futile because most of the couples in his church approached the counseling with "amused tolerance." So in that church the prospective brides and grooms promised only to seek a competent marriage counselor or minister at the first sign of problems.

When a couple resists premarital counseling, however, it seems unlikely that they would seek counseling at the first sign of marital difficulty. Wisely, therefore, many churches and religious leaders insist on premarital counseling before a church wedding is permitted. The benefits of this counseling have been acknowledged later by many grateful and happily married couples. Perhaps there are others who never think back to their premarital counseling but who nevertheless experience marital fulfillment that in part is due to the premarital counseling that came formally or informally before the wedding.

The Bible and Premarital Counseling

Every Christmas we are reminded of the engagement of Mary and Joseph.[3] If they acted according to the custom of the time, a written contract of engagement was signed under oath, and then the bride went home to learn the duties of a good wife and mother. If she was unfaithful during that time, the husband-to-be could have her stoned to death or he could give her a bill of divorce (even before their marriage). When Joseph learned that Mary was pregnant, he decided to divorce her quietly, but he changed his mind when an angel appeared and announced that Mary was to be the mother of the Messiah.

What did Mary and Joseph learn about marriage during this period of engagement? Was there any premarital counseling for the couple? The Bible does not say and neither does it give any direction about how people should prepare for marriage today.

In all of Scripture the closest we come to premarital counseling is Paul's advice in 1 Corinthians 7. He encourages people to remain single, but acknowledges that it is better to marry than to burn with lust.[4] He warns that marriage will bring challenges and pressures, and he notes that it is difficult for married people to serve the Lord wholeheartedly.[5] Elsewhere in the New Testament we read what an ideal marriage should be like, what roles the husband and wife should fulfill, and how they should function as parents.[6] In summary, therefore, the Bible warns of marital stress and gives God's portrait of ideal marriage as a goal toward which every couple can strive. Beyond that there are no specific instructions for premarital guidance.

Reasons for Premarital Guidance

In our society we tend to spend more time getting ready for the wedding than preparing for the marriage. As a result many beautiful wedding days are followed by years of misery or, at best, minimal happiness. For several reasons, therefore, it is important that we help people prepare for marriage.

1. *Unrealistic Expectations That Can Lead to Disillusionment.* When they approach marriage, perhaps most people assume that they have unique relationships. Most think it unlikely that their marriage would be destroyed by the pressures that lead others to divorce courts. Coupled with this optimistic outlook is our modern belief that marriage will be blissful and pleasure centered. In an older book that still is a standard on premarital counseling, Aaron Rutledge wrote that many couples expect marriage to provide self-development and fulfillment; mutual expressions of affection; satisfaction of sexual urges; a sharing of child-rearing responsibilities; a mutual experience of status, belongings, and security; and shared interest in friends, recreation, worship, and creative work. In the history of the human race, Rutledge wrote, never have "so many expected so much from marriage and family life."[7]

Perhaps these expectations are changing now that marriage failures are so much taken for granted. Still many people apparently fail to realize that meaningful marriages grow slowly and only with effort. Often there is impatience, insensitivity, self-centered attitudes, inadequate skill in relating, and great disappointment and disillusionment when one's expectations for marriage are not met quickly.

Premarital counseling lets couples express, discuss, and realistically modify their expectations for marriage. Conflicting expectations can be seen and hopefully resolved. With the counselor's help the couple can learn that dreams for a good marriage only become reality when there is mutual giving and consistent effort. Learning like this comes slowly, but it can help couples anticipate and sometimes avoid the disillusionment that clouds the anticipated brightness in many marriages.

2. *Personal Immaturity That Can Lead to Insensitivity.* Recently the police in Chicago found a seven-month-old baby girl abandoned in a pile of garbage on a cold January morning. When the teenage mother was apprehended later she reported that she didn't want the responsibilities of child rearing. She preferred to hang around the streets like she had done before she got pregnant.

It is not surprising that one's attitudes and behavior within a marriage differ little from the characteristics that were brought to the relationship. If one or both of the participants are self-centered, hypercritical, impatient, competitive, or striving for status—that is, immature—before marriage, these traits will put a strain on marital stability later. People who are irresponsible before marriage tend to be irresponsible after the wedding.

When a couple is dating there often is high anticipation about the future. Differences tend to be overlooked as plans are being made. After the wedding, however, when they settle into daily routines, each person's attitudes, mannerisms, and sometimes troublesome characteristics begin to surface. If these are expressed (even with emotion), discussed, understood, and in some way resolved or accepted, then the marriage builds and grows. When the differences are ignored or denied, the marriage begins to weaken.

Immature people tend to be self-centered. At different times these individuals may be manipulative (overtly or in subtle ways), exploitive, or competitive with their mates, all in an attempt to satisfy their own neurotic needs. These tactics strain a marriage, but the partners often are insensitive both to each other and to the ways in which their self-centered behaviors are destroying the relationship.

Premarital counseling should seek to uncover and discuss the self-centered tendencies that put strain on a marriage. The couple must be taught how to resolve differences, and they must develop both sensitivity and a willingness to accept and meet each other's needs. This involves giving freely to one's mate just as Christ gave to us.[8]

3. *Changing Roles That Can Lead to Confusion.* There was a time when the roles of husband and wife were clearly defined and widely accepted in this society. This has changed. Even within the church there is debate over the meaning of Bible passages like Eph. 5:21–33. This change and debate is not necessarily bad, but it does create some problems. Confusion and conflict may follow when a man and woman each come to marriage with unclear roles and vague expectations about their own and each other's responsibilities. Differing assumptions and views about who is supposed to do what can lead to tension unless the couple has learned to communicate honestly, nondefensively, and in a loving way.

Premarital counseling provides an opportunity for a couple to begin this type of communication. Together they can learn to discuss their different expectations and decide on areas of responsibility. "It is imperative that the spouses deliberately and mutually develop rules to guide their behavior," wrote Lederer and Jackson in their widely acclaimed book on marriage.[9] "Omission of this procedure can destroy a marriage. Husband and wife should operate in ways which mutually assist each other—regardless of custom or tradition."

Such role clarification must not ignore biblical teachings. According to Scripture, both the Christian husband and wife must be filled with the Spirit: daily confessing sin, giving thanks, and praying for the Holy Spirit to control each of their lives.[10] There also must be an attitude of mutual submission to each other, but the more stringent requirements are laid on the husband. He must love his wife unselfishly, discipline his children fairly, and lead the family wisely. The wife in turn is instructed to submit to her husband and respect him.[11] In no way does this give men the right to harm, dominate, ignore, or be insensitive to one's wife or children. In no way does this imply that women are inferior. The husband and wife are equally valuable and equally important in the building of a good marriage, but they have different responsibilities. These broadly defined scriptural roles for husbands and wives cannot be changed or ignored in order to accommodate the trends in a culture. Nevertheless there is room for variation as individual couples decide on their specific duties and behaviors, providing these decisions are considered within the broad guidelines outlined in the Bible.

4. *Alternative Styles of Marriage That Can Lead to Uncertainty.* Within recent years many have criticized the traditional family structure of one husband, who is the primary provider, legally married to one wife, who in turn bears one or more children. Criticisms of the traditional family are sometimes bombastic, hostile, more emotional than logical, and contrary to biblical teaching. The arguments, however, do contain some truth. The traditional family *does* have problems, and our rigid attitudes could be one of the causes. Many of the alternatives to traditional marriage—like marriages in which both husband and wife work to build careers or contribute to the family income, marriages in which the couple decides to have no children, or communal living (as experienced by some religious groups) in which everything is shared—can all be consistent with biblical teaching. Other alternatives, like trial marriage, open marriage, or gay marriage, are unbiblical and cannot be condoned by Christians.

All of this leaves some couples confused and uncertain. Can there be alternatives to traditional marriage that might be healthy and supported biblically? Is traditional marriage unrealistic in these years approaching the twenty-first century? Is it possible or wise to resist premarital sex? The counselor may have no problem in answering questions like these, but many couples need to think them through carefully in light of Scripture and with the guidance of a counselor who is patient, gentle, and not inclined to lecture.

5. *Loosening Sexual Standards That Can Lead to Immorality.* Sex before marriage is not new and neither is it rare, even among Christians. What is new is the increasing approval and acceptance of premarital sex, the widespread involvement of so many people in sex apart from marriage, and the flood of arguments that are used, often in a casual way, to justify behavior that clearly is condemned in Scripture.[12]

Parents and church leaders often look on in dismay and repeat scriptural injunctions, but these statements go unheeded, even by many Christians. "Everybody's doing it," one person concluded. "Surely it can't be wrong when it feels so right and pleasant."

As a result of these more liberal attitudes, dating for many has become a time for exploring each other's bodies and genitals instead of each other's mind, feelings, beliefs, values, and expectations. Love is reduced to sex, and there is a deemphasis on respect, responsibility, understanding, care, and developing interpersonal relationships with people other than one's partner. What is assumed to be increasing sexual freedom really is increasing bondage to one's physiological drives. By ignoring divine standards that free us for maximum life fulfillment, many have cast away their freedom and settled for a biological enslavement. Sexual standards are loosening and premarital sex, even among Christians, appears to be more prevalent. Nevertheless the Bible still calls this immorality—a violation of God's best for our lives. Issues like this should be discussed honestly, faced compassionately, and examined biblically.

6. *Previous Experiences That Can Lead to Overconfidence.* Books on premarital counseling often assume that most couples are young, inexperienced, and entering their first marriage. This is not always true. Many prospective brides and grooms have been previously married. Some have had unhappy past experiences and now hope for something better. Others have lost a much-loved mate and are hoping that the new marriage will restore some of the lost happiness. Older widows and widowers at times resist the cautions of their children and assume that older couples know all about marriage because of their years of experience.

Some previously married people recognize the need for new adjustments and appreciate the help that can come from a sensitive counselor. More often, it seems, people approaching remarriage resist premarital counseling and assume that it is unnecessary and only for those who have had no prior marital experience. Even so, writes one experienced counselor of singles, "we should insist on adequate counseling" for people who are approaching a second or third marriage.[13] The counselor can challenge unrealistic attitudes, help the couple see potential problems that even previously married people might miss, and guide them to resolve issues that may have been unresolved following the previous marriage. Perhaps nothing can create chaos in a new marriage like overconfidence in one's past marital experiences.

7. *Circumstances That Can Lead to Later Misery.* When they come to marriage, some people bring what one counselor calls red-flag situations that need special scrutiny and evaluation.[14] Some of these circumstances were mentioned in the previous chapter—a pregnant bride, one or both participants on the rebound from a previous marriage or engagement, serious drug involvement, emotional problems or mental instability, serious mental or physical handicaps, no financial security, contrasting cultural backgrounds or religious beliefs, wide gaps in education or age differences, and knowing each other for a very short time. Couples may not see these as obstacles to a good marriage and for some these differences can and will be overcome. The counselor, however, needs to urge caution and thorough discussion of issues such as these before the couple moves ahead with marriage. In this way a lot of potential misery may be avoided.

8. *High Divorce Rates That Can Lead to Unhappiness.* It is well known that

many marriages do not survive. Some of the reasons for this are listed elsewhere,[15] but part of the problem may stem from modern attitudes toward marriage. If a couple views marriage as a temporary relationship that lasts "until divorce do us part," then there is little real commitment and willingness to persist in times of pressure. Divorce is always painful, so the premarital counselor seeks to help couples build stable attitudes and behaviors that will undergird new marriages and help them endure.

Premarital counseling should not be viewed as a painful procedure designed to snatch unsuspecting couples from the grips of marital misery. Most premarital counseling is done, not with pathological people, but with relatively healthy individuals who can be helped to enhance and enrich a growing relationship. Research data shows that this relationship most likely will lead to a growing and stable marriage when four characteristics are present:

- Similarity in social and background influences (such as religious affiliation, age, education, intelligence or socioeconomic level).
- Personal-emotional stability and social skills (including an ability to communicate, positive self-concepts, and good emotional and physical health).
- Good parental models (including a good relationship with parents).
- Support from significant others.

In summarizing their work, the researchers concluded (in somewhat academic language) that "the greater the likelihood that motivation to marry is independent of problematic circumstantial factors, including internal or external pressures, the higher the marital quality."[16]

The Effects of Premarital Counseling

Does premarital counseling really improve marriages and reduce the incidence of family disintegration and divorce? Our immediate tendency may be to answer yes, but apart from the enthusiastic testimonies of some counselors and couples, there is little conclusive research evidence to demonstrate that premarital counseling really does prevent later difficulties and contribute to the building of more stable marriages. To some extent this lack of scientific data reflects the difficulties of trying to measure something as vague as the effectiveness of premarital counseling. The little research that has been reported tends to have been done poorly.[17]

In a study of 151 Christian couples, for example, Herbert J. Miles concluded that premarital counseling was followed by good sexual adjustment in marriage.[18] The questionnaire results were tabulated carefully, but the sample consisted only of college students in one institution. How can we know that it was the premarital counseling (and not something else) that contributed to the sexual happiness in marriage? Without a larger sample and a comparison control group who had no premarital guidance, how can we be sure that the counseling really made a difference?

Married individuals often report that their premarital counseling was beneficial, but we cannot reach solid conclusions based on personal testimonies. Some couples are unhappy in spite of their premarital counseling, and others have good marriages even though they never had premarital guidance.

Some research studies have compared one instructional method with another in an effort to determine if one approach is better than another,[19] but this doesn't consider if the instruction contributes to better marriages. David Mace, founder of the American Association of Marriage and Family Therapy, reports that, according to repeated studies, premarital counseling without follow-up after marriage does little good when a couple has problems at the start.[20] Apparently premarital counseling is most effective with couples whose adjustment is relatively good. Nobody has shown, however, that couples who participate in premarital counseling have better marriages and lower divorce rates.

Should we agree then with the pastor who describes premarital counseling as futile? Not yet! During counseling, engaged couples may be confronted with problems that they had not noticed previously. Such knowledge leads some to work on problem issues or to get further counseling. As a result of the counseling, others may decide to break the engagement or to delay marriage until the difficulties are resolved. Even though we lack definitive data about the effectiveness of premarital counseling, we may assume that this type of guidance may help couples detect and avoid potential marital trouble spots.

Even if the research support is never conclusive, the Christian counselor has a responsibility before God to help couples live fulfilled and God-pleasing lives. When people find fulfillment in their marriages and families, they are better able to serve the Lord effectively and to raise and nurture children in Christ-honoring ways.

True premarital counseling is something much broader than a few preceremonial meetings with a pastor. When viewed in its broader context, premarital counseling is a part of Christian discipleship. This broader education for marriage has not been studied empirically, but it has been mandated biblically.

Premarital Counseling

As we have seen, couples often approach premarital counseling with mixed feelings. While many recognize its potential value, there also is the feeling that "our love is so unique that we don't need this—especially now when we are so busy." Others may come with trepidation and defensiveness, afraid that the counselor will suggest that the marriage is unwise. As counselors, we should be alert to these attitudes. If we are to be helpful and effective, we must be convinced that premarital counseling serves some useful purposes.

1. *Purposes.* Premarital counseling seeks to help individuals, couples, and groups of couples to prepare for and build happy, fulfilling, Christ-honoring, and successful marriages. There are several goals.

(a) Assessing Readiness for Marriage. This involves observation and discussion of several issues. Why does the couple really want to get married? What do they expect from marriage? How similar are their backgrounds in terms of education, place of residence, religious beliefs, age, race, or socioeconomic level? Have they discussed their views of the husband and wife roles in marriage? In discussions of these and other issues the counselor can watch for signs of immaturity, rigidity, tension, and communication breakdown.

(b) Teaching the Biblical Guidelines for Marriage. The Bible makes a number of statements about marriage and the God-ordained roles for the husband and wife. The family is modeled after the relationship that Christ had with his church, and although no two marriages are alike (since each individual and each couple is unique) every marriage should reflect the influence of Christ in the home. Sometimes a couple will have little interest or knowledge of spiritual matters, but the Christian counselor must gently raise such issues. Scriptural passages such as 1 Corinthians 13; Eph. 5:21–6:4; Col. 3:16–21; 1 Corinthians 7; and 1 Pet. 3:1–7 should be read, discussed, understood, and applied to the couple's relationship.

(c) Guiding Self-Evaluation. The realities of marriage sometimes cause people to grow up quickly, but it is better if there is a strong element of psychological and spiritual maturity prior to the wedding. One experienced pastoral counselor has concluded that "no marriage will survive the pressures of life and the stresses of our age unless the bride and groom are both truly mature. Signs of maturity would include (1) an ability to forgo an immediate gratification in order to receive a greater benefit in the future, (2) an ability and willingness to share and compromise, (3) a concern for the well-being of others, (4) an ability to look at life realistically, and (5) a willingness to face problems and seek solutions."[21]

With the counselor's encouragement, couples should consider their own and each other's strong and weak points, values, prejudices, beliefs, attitudes about the husband-wife roles in marriage, and expectations or plans for the future. During the engagement period there often is a tendency to camouflage injured feelings and hide differences of opinion in order to keep the relationship running smoothly. These differences need to be acknowledged and discussed so the counselees learn to better understand themselves and each other.

To help with this evaluation, some couples find it helpful to work through one of the several premarital counseling manuals that are designed to prepare individuals for marriage. After completing each chapter in the manual, the couple can discuss their responses together and with the counselor.[22]

In addition, some counselors have found it helpful to administer psychological tests to help in the self-evaluation process. There are hundreds of these tests, but some are not very reliable or valid and many are difficult to get, especially if you are not a licensed professional counselor. At times tests are misinterpreted by people (including counselors) who may not be familiar with what the test is designed to show.

Table 26-1 lists some tests that are used by premarital counselors. Before you choose any of these, get a sample copy from the publisher and read the manual carefully so you know how to administer and interpret the test. Take it yourself and give it to one or two people whom you know well before you start using the test in counseling. If you do assign any tests, be sure to allow sufficient time to discuss the results with the prospective bride and groom.

(d) Stimulating Effective Communication Skills. It is well known that a failure or inability to communicate is one of the most fundamental problems in troubled marriages. Before they marry, couples must be shown the value of spontaneous, honest, sensitive communication. As they are encouraged to discuss their feelings, expectations, differences, attitudes, and personal hurts, they can learn to communicate about significant issues, to listen carefully as they try to understand each other, and to talk through problems without putting down each other or hiding what they feel.

Table 26-1
Some Useful Tests for Premarital Counseling

The following is a list of several assessment tools that counselors have used and found helpful. These are not listed in any order of importance, and neither should it be assumed that the tools listed here are the best or the only devices that premarital counselors might use. In most cases, the man and woman take the tests separately then discuss their results together—often with the help of a counselor.

Caring Relationship Inventory has male and female forms, takes about 40 minutes to complete, and yields seven scores: nurturing love, peer love, romantic love, altruistic love, self-love, being love, and deficiency love. Useful for discussing couple differences and similarities. Available from Educational and Industrial Testing Service, P.O. Box 7234, San Diego, Calif. 92107.

Interpersonal Behavior Survey is a carefully designed test with 272 items, designed to measure both assertive and aggressive behaviors. Eighteen scales include the test-taker's tendencies to show physical aggressiveness, verbal aggressiveness, disregard for the rights of others, frankness, willingness to request help, shyness, and conflict avoidance. Available from Western Psychological Services, 12031 Wilshire Boulevard, Los Angeles, Calif. 90025.

Marital Expectation Inventory has a form for engaged couples. Fifty-eight questions call for written answers that focus on expectations in nine areas: love, communication, freedom, sex, money, selfishness, religion, relatives, and children. Available from Family Life Publications Incorporated, P.O. Box 427, Saluda, N.C. 28773.

Premarital Counseling Inventory does not give a numerical score, but it asks questions that focus on several areas that couples can discuss later, including family background, past marital history, history of the present relationship, agreement on marital roles, and expectations for 20-years from now. Available from Research Press Company, 2612 North Mattis Ave., Champaign, Ill. 61820.

Prepare-Enrich is a series of three highly regarded and widely used inventories, each with 125 items. "Prepare" is for premarital couples, "Prepare-MC" is for premarital couples with children, and "Enrich" is for married couples. Each gives useful information in categories such as personality issues, sexual relationship, realistic expectations, and conflict resolution. Available from Prepare-Enrich, P.O. Box 190, Minneapolis, Minn. 55440.

Sex Knowledge and Attitude Test gives an indication of attitudes and knowledge in five areas. Available from The Center for the Study of Sex Education in Medicine, University of Pennsylvania, 4025 Chestnut Street, Suite 210, Philadelphia, Penn. 19104.

Sex Knowledge Inventory has two forms, each designed to assess individual knowledge of basic sex vocabulary, anatomy, and the function of anatomy. The inventories are published in five language. Available from Family Life Publications Incorporated, P.O. Box 427, Saluda, N.C. 28773.

Taylor-Johnson Temperament Analysis is a 180-item questionnaire designed to measure nine personality traits, including dominant-submissive, hostile-tolerant, and self-disciplined-impulsive. Easy to administer and score, the TJTA allows couples to compare themselves with their prospective mates. Available from Psychological Publications, Inc., 5300 Hollywood Boulevard, Los Angeles, Calif. 90027.

As you counsel, watch for and point out behaviors that could hinder communication. There could be problems, for example, if one person does most of the talking while the other remains silent and seemingly passive, if one shares feelings but the other talks on a more cognitive level, or if one responds spontaneously and openly but the other seems guarded and more introverted.

(e) Anticipating and Discussing Potential Stress. There are certain to be adjustment problems when two people of different sex and family backgrounds come together to share life intimately. How does a couple plan to handle finances, different values, in-law pressures and expectations, differences in interests, conflicts over choice of friends, preferences about recreation, vocational demands, political differences, and variations in spiritual beliefs or maturity? Then there is the issue of sex. Are there fears, unhealthy attitudes or different expectations for the honeymoon? Couples should be encouraged to discuss potential stresses such as these, although all of the discussion does not have to be in the counselor's presence.

In spite of their feelings of enthusiasm, many couples approach marriage with anxiety. Often there is worry about details of the ceremony or honeymoon. Frequently there is concern about whether or not the marriage will turn out OK, or whether it will become like the problem-plagued marriages of their friends or parents. In premarital counseling, couples can be encouraged to talk about their anxieties and inhibitions. By discussing their fears and insecurities together, they can relieve some of the anxiety and learn how to deal with potentially threatening situations.

(f) Providing Information. It is easy to assume that people know more than they do. A pastor's son may know less about spiritual things than you expect. A nurse may know little about family planning. A banker's son may have no idea about how to set up a budget or handle the financial aspects of marriage. Despite the free discussion of sex in our society, premarital counselors often discover that young people (and some who are older) know little about the basics of human sexuality.

In counseling, therefore, watch for knowledge gaps. If it appears that a couple needs information, this can be provided through the counselor's instruction, the distribution of books or pamphlets,[23] or putting counselees into contact with others (such as more experienced couples, a family physician, or a financial planner) who can give accurate and helpful information.

(g) Planning the Wedding. The counselor, especially the pastoral counselor, may play a major role in the wedding by performing the ceremony. Premarital counseling can be a time for (1) making sure that all legal requirements are met (such as obtaining a license and getting blood tests), (2) going over details of the service, and (3) urging the participants to take it easy on the expenses and activities of the wedding. There may be limited success with the latter goal since families in our culture often use weddings to impress others with their status and financial success. It is important to help people recognize that for Christians a wedding can be a service of praise and witness to the couple's mutual commitment to Christ. Too often this message gets lost in the midst of flowers, attendants, photographers, lengthy guest lists, and expensive meals and refreshments.

(h) Getting Experience with Counselors. Many people are anxious about counselors and reluctant to seek counseling help. Premarital counseling provides a relatively nonthreatening situation in which problems and issues are discussed and counselees get exposure to the counseling process. Hopefully this experience will make it easier for individuals to return if they need help in the future.

2. *Format.* It should be obvious that a counselor cannot accomplish all of these purposes in one brief interview. Most writers recommend that there be at least five or six one-hour sessions prior to the wedding. This of course can be demanding. It is easy for time pressures and counselee busyness to combine in convincing the counselor that a briefer period of premarital counseling would suffice. Try to resist that temptation. There is much to be discussed if a marriage is to be built on a solid foundation.

Each counselor should think through his or her own format for premarital counseling. Try to start several months prior to the planned wedding date and be adaptable. Nothing is more likely to kill healthy premarital counseling than a rigid format that requires everyone to conform to the counselor's prearranged course. Some couples will need more time, others will need less. If several marriages are being planned, you may want to begin by meeting once or twice with each couple alone and then see several couples together for group premarital counseling. The following is only one of several formats that you could use.[24]

Session one. Encourage the couple to talk about themselves, their backgrounds and interests. Listen carefully and resist the tendency to begin dealing with problem areas. Ask why they want to get married and listen to their expectations about marriage.

Discuss the premarital counseling. What would they like to accomplish? Share your policies about this kind of counseling—its purposes and goals, its benefits, its length, and how you will proceed. If you plan to give homework assignments, talk about these and the importance of this work being done. If you plan to use tests, these might be administered at the conclusion of the session or you might ask counselees to complete the tests at home and bring them back at the next session.

Ask about spiritual interests and the relationship that each has with Jesus Christ. Are they both believers? Does Christ have a central place in their relationship? What are they doing alone and together to build their Christian lives? Do they pray together?

Session two. Discuss the biblical view of marriage: its origins (Gen. 2:18–24), its purposes (such as companionship, sexual union, child rearing, or a reflection of God's relationship with the church), its permanence (Matt. 19:3–9). Look at the major biblical passages that deal with marriage and discuss how these apply to the counselees. Be practical and specific. Do not let this become a lecture, but include the counselees, getting their observations, questions, and discomforts. If you have given tests, try to get these scored after the second session.

Sessions three and four. Consider some of the practical issues of day-to-day living, including the following.

- What do they expect to get out of marriage that single life would not provide?
- In what ways are they different from each other? How are they the same? How can they live with these differences? (The test results may help with this discussion.)

- What are the parents' attitudes toward the marriage? How do the man and woman each anticipate dealing with in-laws after marriage? What are some good and bad things about the in-laws? Where will the couple spend Christmas?
- Do they like each other's friends? How will they form friendships after marriage?
- What do they like to do for recreation, hobbies, or vacations?
- Where will they live? How did they make that decision? How will they make decisions about furniture and housing?
- Do they have a budget? How will they decide on major purchases? Who will buy what? What are their attitudes toward credit cards? Have their past spending habits, including use of credit cards, shown potentially troublesome attitudes toward money and possessions?
- What are their attitudes toward children? Are they agreed on how many they want and when?

Issues such as these may take more than two sessions to discuss, especially if you are meeting in a group in which each member is encouraged to answer some of the questions. The discussions can continue apart from the counseling, however, and any major differences can then be considered in later counseling sessions.

As these issues are discussed, you can describe and have counselees practice the principles of good communication. Can they listen and express their feelings or ideas honestly and without being hostile and critical? Communication is an art that is best learned by discussing sensitive and important issues. A counselor can facilitate this process.

Session five. Discuss the meaning of love (see 1 Cor. 13:4–8) and its relationship to sex. What questions and concerns do they have about sex? If questions are slow in coming, you might raise the following issues that one study of Christian couples found to be of major importance.[25] The issues are listed in decreasing order according to the number of times each was mentioned by the couples surveyed.

- How to stimulate and arouse a wife to orgasm.
- The use of contraceptives.
- The methods of sexual intercourse.
- Suggestions on what to do and expect on the honeymoon.
- The nature of the clitoris.
- The different sexual timing of men and women.
- How to meet the husband's sexual needs.
- The spiritual and moral interpretation of the sexual relationship in marriage.
- The elimination of fears and misconceptions.
- The responsibility of husband and wife in meeting each other's sexual needs.
- How to purchase contraceptives.
- The nature of the hymen.
- The amount of time needed for good sexual adjustment.

The counselor who discusses these issues must be well-informed, comfortable in discussing sex, and able to get more help if necessary. A physician, for example, may be more helpful than a nonmedical counselor in dealing with specific sexual questions.[26] Even when they are well informed, some counselors may choose to have sexual issues discussed by another counselor. This decision may come because you feel uncomfortable talking so freely about sex or because (especially if you are a pastor) you may feel that such detailed discussion of sexual intimacies might hinder or conflict with your pastoral role.

If you do discuss these issues with counselees, remember that the couple may be either more naive than you think or more experienced sexually than you had assumed. Instead of giving a lecture, try first to discover the level of their knowledge. At times you may have to ask embarrassing personal questions, but if you do this, be sure that you are asking for some purpose other than to satisfy your own curiosity.

Session six. This involves discussion of the wedding ceremony, the legal requirements, the reception and its costs, and plans for the honeymoon. Remind the couple that you would like to have another session two or three months after the wedding so you can discuss how things are going, including the problems and joys of their young marriage. Make a note in your appointment book to call the couple when it is time to meet after the wedding.

3. *Variations.* As we have tried to emphasize, premarital counseling must not be rigid. Some couples are older, are more mature, have been married previously, have read books or attended seminars on marriage, are personally sensitive to others, and are spiritually alert. These men and women may need a different number of sessions and may be concerned with different issues than those that interest a young couple in their early twenties. Some couples will show clearly that they are ready for marriage and that their choice of a marriage partner is good. With others counseling may show that the proposed marriage is a poor risk. Some will resist this conclusion, but others may agree that it is wise to delay the marriage or break the engagement. Counselees need support, encouragement, and guidance as they make these kinds of difficult decisions.

In addition to the use of tests, you may want to encourage couples to read and discuss some books or to listen to cassette tapes.[27] At times you may see value in bringing a group of couples together and asking a physician, financial expert, or other resource person to share his or her expertise. Each of these approaches supplements the counseling and stimulates couples to communicate with each other about important issues.

PREVENTION

Each of the issues discussed in previous chapters has been presented in the form of a problem that we can try to understand, resolve through counseling, and prevent. This chapter is different because its whole emphasis is on prevention. Premarital counseling seeks to prevent marital problems and personal conflicts that could make life miserable, difficult, unfulfilled, and unproductive after marriage. All of this assumes that good marriages start before the wedding.

Good marriages also start long before the preceremonial counseling that we have discussed in the preceding pages. By observing parents and older adults, young people learn what to expect in marriage, what they want in their own marriages, and what they do not want. By watching television, many people—including young people—get a distorted, unrealistic, and nonbiblical view of marriage that can lead to problems later in life.

It is wise, therefore, to start premarital education with children.[28] Informal discussions with flower girls and ring bearers can provide a good opportunity for teaching, especially when we remember that weddings often make a great impact on children. Sunday school classes, children's camps, or junior high meetings can be opportunities for impressing young minds with healthy attitudes and biblical truths about marriage. According to one writer, "the senior high years are too late to begin this instruction; attitudes are formed and crystallized much earlier."[29]

The whole church should be involved in this educational process. Guided by the pastor's example, church leaders and parents can correct popular misconceptions about marriage and can build a realistic and biblical view of the family long before marriage becomes a possibility. Family conferences, Bible studies, meetings of youth groups, discussions in singles groups, sermons, viewing films and videos, or encouraging the reading of good books or articles are common ways to instill healthy attitudes toward marriage. High school students may have little interest in housing, finances within marriages, or in-law relationships, but they are interested in sex, male-female roles, home life, and ways in which they can evaluate themselves as potential mates. College students should be encouraged to take a course in marriage and family although it is wise to recognize that some professors and textbooks fail to take the biblical view into account. In the church, discussions of dating can point out that each date is a learning experience that helps unmarried people learn to respect, communicate with, and relate to the opposite sex.

The building of better marriages and families is a lifelong process. It begins in the home, continues in the church and society, is emphasized in premarital counseling, and must be practiced daily as a man and woman build their relationship together.

Conclusions about Premarital Counseling

Counselors usually are busy people. They have a demanding and difficult job helping people get untangled from problem situations and teaching them how to function more effectively. Surrounded by so many cries for help, it is easy for the counselor to ignore or casually dismiss those who do not have pressing problems. As a result prevention is overlooked and new problems continue to develop, problems that must be handled later.

For many years medicine has focused on preventing disease or injury and helping people maintain their health. The first mention of premarital counseling came more than sixty years ago in a medical journal,[30] and since that time counselors have shown increasing interest in prevention. In no area is preventive counseling and education more possible, more accepted by the society, and more important than in the area of preparation for marriage. In no counseling area is the church more experienced and more respected. Christian counselors have a responsibility to *show* that premarital counseling really works and *how* it can be done. This involves helping people anticipate difficulties in marriage and family living, teaching them how to communicate and resolve problems effectively, and showing them how to build marriages that are lived in accordance with God's plan as revealed in the Bible.

SUGGESTIONS FOR FURTHER READING

Crabb, Lawrence, J., Jr. *The Marriage Builder.* Grand Rapids, Mich.: Zondervan, 1982.*

Phillips, Bob. *How Can I Be Sure?* Eugene, Oreg.: Harvest House, 1978.*

Penner, Clifford, and Joyce Penner. *The Gift of Sex.* Waco, Tex.: Word, 1981.*

Smith, Harold Ivan. *Pastoral Care for Single Parents.* Kansas City, Mo.: Beacon Hill Press, 1982.

Stahmann, Robert F., and William J. Hiebert. *Premarital Counseling.* Lexington, Mass.: Lexington Books, 1980.

Wright, H. Norman. *Premarital Counseling.* Rev. ed. Chicago: Moody, 1981.

* Books marked with an asterisk (*) are especially suitable for counselees to read.

27

Marital Problems

TWENTY YEARS HAVE PASSED since Curt and Diane exchanged vows in a little country church and began their married life. At times both of them have wondered if their troubled relationship would survive, but they still live together, sometimes in an uneasy truce, in the same community where they were both born almost forty-two years ago.

Diane's parents were Christians who went to church regularly and lived as respected members of the community. Curt came from a home where religion was ignored, and the family of four boys seemed to be always in trouble with the neighbors and police. At the age of eighteen, Curt married his pregnant girlfriend, but the marriage was filled with conflict and ended in divorce after two years.

He met Diane at work and began attending church with her shortly after they started dating. In response to an evangelist's appeal, Curt became a Christian and throughout their married life, the couple has attended church along with their two children. There is little interest in spiritual things and apart from the Sunday-morning services, religion has tended to be forgotten during the week.

Early in their marriage, Diane did spend some time talking with the pastor about Curt's abusive behavior. Often he would stop at a bar with his friends after work, come home drunk, erupt in a rage over some minor issue, and beat his wife. The next morning he would deny Diane's descriptions of what had happened the night before—even when she showed her bruises as evidence.

Diane often considered leaving Curt, but she had no place to go with her two young children and knew that Curt would find her if she moved in with her parents. The pastor tried counseling with Curt, but he denied that a problem existed and later exploded in anger, accusing Diane of "waving our dirty laundry in front of the whole church."

As the situation deteriorated, help came from an unexpected source—Curt's employer. One day the personnel manager informed Curt that everyone knew he was drinking before work. He was given a choice: either lose his job or enter a company-sponsored alcoholic rehabilitation program. Curt chose the latter. He and Diane went to counseling together, and both the drinking and mate abuse stopped.

Now, after almost twenty years of marriage, Curt and Diane "get along OK." Neither would consider the marriage to be happy, and at times there is a lot of griping and mutual put downs. They have learned, however, to tolerate each other and to live together as companions. Most evenings are spent watching television, but there is little in-depth communication. Neither seriously thinks any more about separation or divorce. Instead they live together in what might be called a tired marriage.

Could Curt and Diane benefit from marriage counseling? Probably, but it is unlikely that either will ever seek help from a counselor. They may never know what a truly fulfilling marriage can be like.

Marriage is not a very stable institution—at least in the Western world. In the United States, the average duration of a marriage is only 9.4 years. More than a million couples are divorced every year. Many who stay together have marriages like that of Curt and Diane—tolerable but not especially happy.

Some marriages *are* happy. In our efforts to help troubled relationships we sometimes forget that many people do have lasting and mutually satisfying marriages. Researchers recently surveyed three hundred couples who had been married for at least fifteen years and who described themselves as "happily married." The respondents showed remarkable agreement in their views of what makes a marriage happy. Most frequently mentioned was "having a generally positive attitude toward one's spouse" and viewing the partner as one's best friend. In essence the couples said, "I am married to someone who cares about me, who is concerned for my well-being, who gives as much or more than he or she gets, who is open and trustworthy and who is not mired down in a somber, bleak outlook on life."

The second key to successful marriage was a belief in the importance of commitment. Marriage was viewed as something people should stick with and work to develop in spite of difficult times. In addition, happily married people agreed about aims and goals in life, had a desire to make the marriages succeed, and were able to laugh a lot. To the researcher's surprise, fewer than 10 percent of the happily married people mentioned good sexual relations as an important ingredient for good marriages.[1]

Even though happy marriages like these do exist and are possible, we live in a time when marital unhappiness is more common and where many see divorce as a convenient and ever-present fire escape should marital conflicts get too hot to handle. "Irreconcilable differences" become reasons for marriage breakups, and no-fault divorce allows marriage to be terminated legally when one or both spouses simply lose any desire to stay together. Marriage, the permanent union created by God, is treated more and more as a temporary arrangement of convenience.

These social attitudes, coupled with the stresses that put pressure on modern marriages, often create problems that come to the counselor's attention. Research during the past several years has shown consistently that more people seek counseling for marriage problems than for any other single issue.[2] It is not easy to help couples resolve marital conflict and build better marriages, but this can be one of the most rewarding of all counseling experiences.

The Bible and Marital Problems

Marriage is one of the first topics discussed in the Bible.[3] It is mentioned throughout the pages of Scripture and considered in depth in the New Testament. The purposes of marriage, the roles of husband and wife, the importance of sex, and the responsibilities of parents are all discussed,[4] sometimes more than once. Marriage failure is mentioned in the Old Testament law and treated in more detail by Jesus and Paul in their discussions of divorce.[5]

What does the Bible say about marital problems and ways to help troubled marriages? Almost nothing! Believers are encouraged to enjoy interpersonal and sexual relationships with their spouses,[6] and finding a mate is described as a good thing.[7] In contrast, the Book of Proverbs picturesquely decries the difficulties of living with a contentious, quarrelsome marriage partner. Sharing a house with such a person is like listening to a "constant dripping on a rainy day." Trying to control such a person is as futile as "restraining the wind or grasping oil with the hand."[8] Although the Bible describes some good marriages, there is evidence that Lot, Abraham, Jacob, Job, Samson, David, and a number of others had marital tensions at least periodically.[9] These are acknowledged honestly, but marital problems per se are not analyzed.

It should be remembered that marital conflict often is a symptom of something deeper, such as selfishness, lack of love, unwillingness to forgive, anger, bitterness, communication problems, anxiety, sexual abuse, drunkenness, feelings of inferiority, sin, and a deliberate rejection of God's will. Each of these can cause marital tension, each can be influenced by husband-wife conflict, and each *is* discussed in the Bible. Thus while the Scriptures deal with marital conflict only indirectly and in passing, the issues underlying marriage problems are considered in detail. Many of these issues are discussed elsewhere in this book.

The Causes of Marital Problems

In Gen. 2:24, we read that in marriage a man "will leave his father and mother and be united to his wife, and they will become one flesh." Three verbs in this verse—"leaving," "being united," and "becoming one"—indicate three purposes of marriage.

Leaving involves a departure from parents and implies a public and legal union of husband and wife into a marriage. Walter Trobisch once wrote that couples who ignore this legal element have a "stolen marriage." There may be love and sex, but they have no real reason to give themselves to responsible marriage building.[10]

Being united comes from a Hebrew word that means to stick or glue together. "If you try to separate two pieces of paper which are glued together, you tear them both. If you try to separate husband and wife who cleave together, both are hurt."[11] Ideally the couple is dedicated to loving, drawing together, and remaining faithful to each other. When such uniting is absent, they have an empty marriage that may be legal but is devoid of love.

Becoming one involves sex, but it goes beyond the physical. It means, writes Trobisch, "that two persons share everything they have, not only their bodies, not only their material possessions, but also their thinking and feelings, their joy and suffering, their hopes and their fears, their successes and failures."[12] This does not imply that two personalities are squelched or obliterated. The uniquenesses remain, but these are combined with those of one's mate to make a complete relationship. When the one-flesh relationship is lacking the couple has an unfulfilled marriage.

This kind of thinking is neither common nor popular today. People want happiness, the opportunity to realize one's potential, or having a full life,[13] but they fail to see that these contemporary and somewhat self-centered goals rarely come to marriages that ignore the biblical guidelines. Instead marriage problems often arise because a husband and wife have deviated from the biblical standards outlined in Gen. 2:24 and elaborated on in later portions of Scripture. Modern psychology, sociology, and related disciplines have clarified some of the ways in which people deviate from these biblical standards for marriage.

1. *Faulty Communication.* In the professional literature, this probably is the most commonly mentioned cause of marital discord. Citing James 4:1–3, psychologist Lawrence Crabb notes that communication problems inevitably result when people pursue self-centered goals,[14] but sometimes problems also come because individuals have not learned how to communicate clearly and efficiently.

Communication involves the sending and receiving of messages. Messages are sent verbally (with words) and nonverbally (with gestures, tone of voice, facial expressions, words on a paper, images on a computer screen, actions, gifts, or even periods of silence). When the verbal and the nonverbal contradict, a double message is sent. This leads to confusion and communication breakdown. Consider, for example, the woman who says verbally, "I don't mind if you go on the business trip," but whose slumping posture, resigned tone of voice, and depressionlike lack of enthusiasm says, "I *really* don't want you to go." In contrast, a wife gets a confused double message when her husband says, "I love you and like spending time with you," but never is home, never takes his wife out to dinner, or never does anything to show his love and appreciation. In good communication the message sent verbally is consistent with the message sent nonverbally.

Good communication also demands that the message sent is the same as the message that is received. Assume, for example, that a man buys his wife a new dishwasher because he loves her. The wife, however, concludes that she isn't loved because her husband never says the words "I love you." She begins to wonder if the dishwasher was given because the husband feels guilty about something. Clearly there is miscommunication here because the message being sent (love expressed by the gift of a dishwasher) is not the message that is being received.

Most of us would agree that occasional miscommunication between spouses is inevitable. When miscommunication is more common than clear communication, however, the marriage begins to have serious problems. Poor communication tends to breed more of the same.[15] Try to remember that communication is a *learned* interaction. Even when it is not good, people can learn to make it better.

2. *Underintegrated or Overintegrated Relationships.* Getting close to another person is risky. We open ourselves to criticism and possible rejection when we let another person know us intimately, become aware of our insecurities, or see our weaknesses. Since most of us have learned the value of fending for ourselves, it is not easy to trust another person—even when that other person is a marriage partner.

In a book on stress management, one writer suggests that problem marriages tend to be underintegrated or overintegrated.[16] In underintegrated marriage, the husband and wife appear to grow apart over the years. There is little willingness to share confidences, to be vulnerable, or to develop mutual life goals. Instead each seems to be moving through life independently of the other, with differing needs and goals. There is a tendency to be defensive, to criticize and put down each other or to manipulate subtly. Defensive, self-centered attitudes create tension and push the husband and wife apart.

In contrast, overintegrated marriage occurs when a relationship has become so engulfing that both partners have lost their identities and feel trapped. If you suggest that one person's harshness may be creating marital difficulties, the response might be, "That could be right, but I'm not the only one who is guilty." Both partners blame the other for their problems and neither is able to stand back, look at individual needs, and evaluate one's own faults that may be contributing to the tension. In time there may be a verbal or physically violent reaction as both partners try to tear away from the confinement of such a stifling relationship.

3. *Interpersonal Tension.* When two people marry, each comes to the marriage with approximately two or more decades of past experiences and ways of looking at life. Each has perspectives that are not shared by the other and sometimes, even when there is a sincere desire for compromise or synthesis, couples still have difficulty resolving their differences.

What happens if there is unwillingness to change, an insensitivity to the other person's viewpoints, or a refusal to acknowledge the differences? Often there is tension that frequently centers on one of the following issues.

(a) Sex. At times most couples have sexual problems. In an earlier chapter[17] we discussed some causes of sexual difficulties in marriage. These include lack of accurate knowledge, unrealistic expectations, fear of not being able to perform adequately, differences in sexual drive, inhibiting attitudes about sex, and insufficient opportunities for privacy. Impatience, frigidity, and infidelity (perhaps the three most common sex problems) in turn create more tension, and this further hinders smooth sexual functioning. Exceptional busyness, insensitivity in one or both of the partners, or nonsexual marital conflicts can also interfere with sexual functioning. When these problems are not resolved, marriages almost always suffer.

(b) Roles. We live at a time when traditional male-female roles are being reevaluated. This often leads to conflict over what it means to be a husband or wife. The society gives little guidance because opinions seem to be changing so rapidly.

The Bible, in contrast, is much more explicit,[18] but Christians differ in their interpretations of the scriptural passages that outline husband-wife roles. As a result there is disagreement, accompanied at times by both competition and feelings of threat. Often this tension centers on the nature and extent of the wife's work or career goals.

(c) Inflexibility. When a man and woman marry, each brings a unique personality to the marriage. Sometimes these personality differences complement each other and blend into a mutually compatible relationship. Often marriages take on personalities of their own, each of which can have strengths and weak points.[19] There can be difficulties, however, if one or both of the partners is rigid, unwilling to give, or strongly resistant to change.

When a couple first marries there often is a time of excitement, enthusiasm, and youthful idealism. As the partners grow older and the months turn into years, the marriage must also change and mature if it is to stay healthy. According to Christian counselor H. Norman Wright, marriages must grow through stages if they are to remain stable and fulfilling.[20] When couples are too busy or too rigid to work at building and enriching their marriages, problems are likely to develop.

(d) Religion. The Bible warns of problems when a believer and an unbeliever try to live together in marriage.[21] Counselors have observed tensions when a husband and wife differ from each other in their denominational preferences, degree of commitment to spiritual things, interest in religion, or expectations about the religious education of children. Sometimes these differences create tension in other areas such as choice of friends, views of ethics, whether and to whom charitable donations will be given, or the use of time on Sundays. Religion can be a binding, strengthening force in a marriage, but when a husband and wife have different viewpoints, religion can also be a destructive focus for marital tension.

(e) Values. What is really important in life? How should we spend our time and money? What are our goals? These questions concern values. When a couple has similar values, the marriage is often healthy and growing. When values are in conflict, however, the relationship may be one of tension, power struggles, and mutual criticism. Value conflicts are at the heart of many marital problems.

Consider, for example, how some of the following value alternatives could create potential for conflict.

- "Credit cards should never be used" versus "Credit cards can be used on occasion to get us over a financial crisis."
- "Divorce is never right" versus "Sometimes divorce is the best solution to marital problems."
- "We should never miss church on Sunday" versus "Sometimes it is OK to skip worship services."
- "Succeeding in one's career is of major importance in life" versus "Building a family is more important than building a career."
- "Abortion is always wrong because it is murder" versus "In some circumstances abortion is OK."
- "Children should be taught spiritual beliefs and values" versus "Children should be given the freedom to find their own beliefs."

Many of these views are held firmly. They influence how we act or relate to other people. In addition, values sometimes become the basis for intense conflict, especially if cherished beliefs are attacked or challenged by one's mate.

(f) Conflicting Needs and Personality Differences. For almost a century psychologists have debated about the existence of human needs. Most agree that we each need food, rest, air, and freedom from pain, but there also are psychological needs such as the need for love, security, and contact with others. In addition it seems that most people have unique personal needs (such as the need to dominate, to control, to possess, to achieve, or to help and rescue others). If one spouse has a need to dominate while the other wants to be controlled, then there may be compatibility. If both husband and wife have a need to dominate, this creates potential for conflict. If both are devoted to career building, there can be conflict, especially if one spouse wants to accept a career advancement that will involve a family move and the other spouse resists.[22]

Personality differences also can create tension. When one spouse is open (freely sharing about one's needs, temptations, attitudes, and feelings) but the other spouse tends to hold things in, these differences can create problems.[23] In one long-term study of several hundred marriages, researchers found that neurotic traits, especially impulsivity in the husband, frequently led to marital instability, distress, and divorce. Often these traits were noticed (and ignored) at the time of engagement, but they led to misery in the years that followed.[24]

(g) Money. How are the family finances to be earned? Who controls the money? How is it to be spent? What things are really needed and which are merely desirable? Is a budget necessary? How much should be given to the church? What happens when there is a shortage of money?

Answers to questions like these reflect one's financial values and attitudes. When a husband and wife have different answers to these kinds of questions, there is potential for conflict. Once again it is difficult to determine whether financial tensions cause other problems or whether the reverse is more accurate. It is true, however, that a harmonious financial relationship is essential if there is to be a harmonious marriage.

4. *External Pressures.* Sometimes marital tensions appear or are made worse because of the pressure that comes from other people or from stressful situations.[25] These external sources of pressure include:

- In-laws who criticize or otherwise make demands on the couple.
- Children whose needs and presence often interfere with the depth and frequency of husband-wife contacts, and sometimes drive a wedge between the spouses.
- Friends, including opposite sex friends, who make time demands on the couple and sometimes involve one or both spouses in infidelity.
- Crises that disrupt family stability and create stress for all who are involved.
- Vocational and career demands that put pressure on the husband and/or wife, create fatigue, and take time from the marriage.
- Financial reverses that put pressure on the family budget and lead to worry and sometimes disagreements about spending patterns.

Most of these pressures can be resisted, but each can be a powerful threat to marital harmony.

5. *Boredom.* As the years go by, husbands and wives settle into routines, get accustomed to each other, and sometimes slip into self-absorption, self-satisfaction, or self-pity, each of which can drain any remaining excitement from a marriage and make life boring. When marriage is dull and routine, couples sometimes begin to look elsewhere for variety and challenge. This in turn creates further marital tension.

THE EFFECTS OF MARITAL PROBLEMS

Bookstores and library shelves are filled with books describing the experiences of once-happy marriages that grew cold, distant, and unhappy.[26] Even as they tell their own stories, the authors of these books show how difficult it can be to separate the effects of marital distress from the causes. For example, sexual and financial difficulties can cause marital tension, but marital tension can also lead to problems in bed or in balancing the checkbook. Although there is a circular relationship between cause and effect, the counselor can observe several specific effects of marital tension.

1. *Confusion, Despair, and Hopelessness.* Caught in the middle of conflict and watching one's marriage disintegrate, the husband and/or wife often feels overwhelmed and confused about what to do next. Sometimes there are frantic, frequently futile, attempts to make amends. Sometimes there is despair and a resigned attitude that says, "Things will never get better, so why try?"

"Every marriage is built on hope," suggests one Christian marriage counselor. "People marry because they hope that life together will be more effective, satisfying, and purposeful than life alone." Nearly every marriage goes through periods of disillusionment. When this happens, hope is often replaced by sadness, hurt, and anger. The partners feel hopeless, and hopeless feelings are contagious. One goal of counseling, therefore, must be the recovery of hope.[27]

2. *Withdrawal.* It is impossible to estimate the number of people who are legally married, living together, and sometimes sleeping in the same bed, but who are emotionally and psychologically divorced. The husband and wife may even engage in similar activities and go places together, but there is little warmth, concern, communication, intimacy, love, or interest in one's mate. By withdrawing emotionally from each other, the partners avoid the pain and social stigma of divorce. Conflicts remain but there are few battles, and the marriage persists as an uneasy truce that may extend for a lifetime.

3. *Desertion.* When the marital and family pressures get too intense, some people simply leave. It is difficult to compile statistics on the incidence of desertion,[28] but there is evidence that thousands of mates desert their families each year and leave hurt feelings, confusion, uncertainty, financial pressures, and one-parent families behind. The courts can decree that a deserting spouse must return or meet family financial obligations, but these people are difficult to find and many ignore the court orders. Since most deserters are from lower-class families, the deserted mate often cannot afford the costs of bringing legal action against the spouse who has left.

4. *Separation or Divorce.* Divorce might be viewed as the legal termination of a once-promising, hope-filled, and satisfying relationship that has been coming apart socially and emotionally. Even though it is common, divorce is never a happy solution to marital problems. It is used too often and too quickly as a way to escape marital difficulties. Even Christian couples sometimes ignore the biblical guidelines for dissolving a marriage.[29] Nevertheless there are times when divorce may seem to be the most feasible alternative to a problem-plagued marriage.

Counseling and Marital Problems

Counseling one person is a difficult task; counseling a husband and wife is even more difficult and requires special skill and alertness in the counselor. Frequently one or both of the spouses come with skepticism about the value of counseling, and sometimes there is an attitude of resistance or hostility. Someone has called marriage counseling "one of the most difficult and sensitive of therapies—filled with psychological traps and surprises." Before starting (and frequently thereafter) counselors should look at themselves to clarify some of their own attitudes, prejudices, motivations, and vulnerabilities.

1. *Be Alert to Yourself.* What is your attitude toward marital problems? Are you critical of those who have marital difficulties, inclined to condemn, prone to take sides, annoyed because these problems take so much time from your schedule, afraid that marital counseling might arouse anxieties about your own marriage? Are you nervous lest your counseling be a failure?

Perhaps we need to remind ourselves that one's reputation as a counselor never rests on one case. Even though there are literally hundreds of how-to-do-it books and articles on marriage counseling, no one person can master all of the techniques. Your job is to be available to the couple, as technically skilled as possible, and sincerely willing to have the Holy Spirit work through you as an instrument of healing. Your help will be most effective if you can commit the counseling to God, relax, and try to provide an atmosphere where constructive discussion is possible. In addition, try to understand both sides of the situation from the perspectives of the people involved.

Intimate discussions about marriage can arouse sexual and other feelings in the counselor, feelings that must be admitted to oneself and handled, often with the help of others.[30] Sometimes a counselee will remind you of some person that you have known elsewhere. Unless you are alert and careful, your feelings and attitudes about this other person will become imposed on the counselees. This can hinder counseling.

Be aware too that some counselees may cast you into a role that you may neither recognize nor want. A woman, for example, might see her male counselor as "a kind, understanding man—so different from my insensitive, noncaring husband."[31] The husband in turn may think of the male counselor as a threat to the marriage and one who really doesn't understand the wife. In situations like these, try not to react in accordance with your feelings. Be careful not to let the counselee's expectations mold your behavior so that you overreact or become the kind of person that the counselee expected. When counselors have colleagues with whom they can discuss issues like these, the dangers are greatly reduced.

2. *Be Alert to Special Issues.* Within the past two or three decades, literally hundreds of marriage and family therapy techniques have been proposed and sometimes touted by enthusiastic advocates. Sculpting, for example, is a procedure where family members move around the room and position themselves in terms of how close or how far they feel from each other. Diagramming involves drawing a picture with the names of family members and other people set in boxes. Then lines are drawn between the boxes to show how the different people relate. (Solid lines, for example, may mean a good relationship, double lines mean a close relationship, a dotted line signifies a distant relationship, and a wavy line indicates conflict.) Other counselors use role playing, drama, or even choreography in counseling.[32]

Unless you have special training in marriage counseling you may not wish to use these somewhat unusual techniques, but even if your approach is more traditional you are likely to discover that marriage counseling raises procedural questions that may not be present in other types of counseling.

(a) Should the Couple Be Seen Alone or Together? Many counselors would say "both." Sometimes, after an initial joint session, counselors will see the husband and wife separately for a few minutes or a few sessions. Often this gives new information and different perspectives on the problem. At times you will find that each spouse has a different opinion about what the major problem is and who is primarily responsible. Sometimes you will discover that one of the partners wants counseling and the other does not. In some cases you will discover that one or both of the spouses have problems that will benefit from individual counseling. Marriage, however, is a relationship, and marital problems involve conflicts between two people. If these can be observed and discussed together (sometimes with the children present), progress may be greater and faster. Whether you see the couple separately or together, be careful to strive for impartiality. Taking sides can often hinder your counseling effectiveness.

(b) Should There Be Time Limits for Counseling? In his excellent book on Christian marriage counseling, psychologist Everett V. Worthington suggests three stages of counseling: assessment, intervention, and termination.[33] At the beginning, Worthington asks the couple to agree to three sessions for assessment and evaluation of their difficulties. After that the couple and the counselor decide whether or not they should continue. If they continue, the counselor suggests that eight to sixteen sessions should be sufficient to complete the counseling intervention stage followed by termination.

This is not a rigid approach; sometimes the counseling stops after a few sessions and at times it goes longer. Within the past decade or two, however, there has been a strong movement in the counseling field toward short-term, time-limited counseling. Increasing evidence suggests that the briefer approaches tend to be more effective than counseling that continues for months and years.[34]

(c) Is Group Counseling Desirable? Sometimes couples with similar problems can benefit from counseling that takes place in a group with other couples. In general this should not be considered or suggested until the counselor has had time to get some perspectives on the major issues involved in each marital dispute.[35]

(d) Should the Counselor Work Alone or with Another Counselor? Sometimes a man and woman, often a husband and wife, can work together as a counseling team.[36] This lets the couple have a male and female perspective, and the co-counselors can model good communication and interpersonal relationships. Such an arrangement can be time consuming, however, and can put pressure on the counselors, especially if they are married and subject to some of the same stresses that face the counselees. Nevertheless, mature couples who work together smoothly often are able to counsel other couples with special effectiveness.

3. *Assess the Marriage.* Why has the couple come for help? This question may not be as easy to answer as you might expect. Sometimes the husband and wife have different answers to this question. Often the answer is vague (for example, "We're not getting along," or "We're arguing a lot"), and you may have to ask for specific examples. Gently probe for more details and try to raise questions that will give more information and a better understanding of the problem. By asking the husband and wife to describe specific incidents of conflict, the counselor is enabled to understand not only the sources of dissension but also the accompanying feelings of rejection, anger, hurt, frustration, and fractured self-esteem. Some counselors also ask each spouse to fill out a paper-and-pencil inventory that will help clarify the areas of conflict.[37] Some couples have difficulty defining their problems in words and others may be embarrassed. Responding to a survey or questionnaire is easier and may offer more complete initial information.

Problems will vary considerably, of course, and here as in all counseling, the stated problem may not be the only or the major source of difficulty. Often there are concerns about loss of intimacy, communication breakdowns, frequent conflict, sex, money, husband-wife roles, religion, physical abuse, drinking, conflicting values, and a variety of similar issues. Counselees can be asked how they feel about each problem, how they have tried to solve the problems in the past, what has worked, and what has not.

In making your initial assessment, two issues are of great importance. First, try to discover where the couple is spiritually. Are they both believers? Are they growing spiritually or has religion become what William James once called a "dull habit"? The Christian counselor is likely to use different terminology and take a more overtly Christian approach when it is clear that the husband and wife are believers. Second, be careful not to spend all of your initial time in discussing the problems. When they come for counseling a couple already feels defeated and well aware of the pain and conflict in their marriage. If the whole session is spent in a listing of problems, the counselees may feel so discouraged that they are reluctant to return for the next session. Even as you gather information, therefore, remember that one of the main purposes of the early sessions is to "build positive expectancies, establish a commitment for change, and begin the process of change."[38] From the start, it is important that the couple be given hope.[39]

4. *Determine Counseling Goals.* The counselor, the husband, and the wife each approach marriage counseling with expectations and goals. These goals may be either vague or clearly defined. Some will be realistic, others will not. Some counselees will come with high expectations and a determination to work at healing the troubled marriage; others may have little hope or motivation to change. When the goals are clear, realistic, and accepted by everyone, marriage counseling starts with a high potential for success. When the goals are vague or in conflict (for example, the husband wants a smooth separation, but the wife wants a reconciliation), then counseling will be more difficult.

(a) Recognize and Formulate Counselor Goals. It is unlikely that you, the counselor, will approach marriage counseling with complete neutrality. Most of us have goals (some of which we may not have thought about clearly) that give direction to our counseling. These goals may include:

- Identifying and understanding the specific issues that are creating the marital problems.
- Teaching the couple how to communicate constructively.
- Teaching problem-solving and decision-making techniques.
- Helping the counselees understand the counseling relationship.
- Helping them express their frustrations, disappointments, and desires for the future.
- Keeping the husband and wife together.
- Instilling hope.
- Teaching the couple how to build a marriage based on biblical principles.

What are your goals in counseling? When these are recognized clearly, counseling can be more effective. The counselor knows where he or she is going and, with one's own goals in mind, it is easier to concentrate on the counselee goals.

(b) Determining Counselee Goals. Sometimes the counselees' goals are similar to those of the counselor, but often there is a discrepancy. Questions like "What would you hope to get out of counseling?" or "How would you like your marriage to be different?" often can initiate discussion that clarifies, for the counselees as well as for the counselor, what the husband and/or wife hope to achieve through counseling.

One experienced counselor[40] tries to determine the answers to four goal-related questions as the counseling begins:

- How does each partner experience the relationship?
- What does each yearn for?
- What can be done?
- What is each willing to do now?

(c) Setting Mutually Acceptable Goals. Many people have vague and distant goals (for example, to have a happy Christian marriage), but these are reached best through a series of more specific, more attainable, more immediate goals. Some counselors work on a contract approach in which the husband and wife each agree to change behavior in some specific way during periods between counseling sessions.[41] He, for example, agrees to take out the garbage nightly, she agrees to let him read the paper alone before dinner. When a couple sets such goals with the counselor's help, there is increased motivation to attain these goals, and the couple can learn about communication and problem solving in the process. As goals are reached, the couple is encouraged because they see specific progress.

At times, however, there is disagreement about goals. Counselees sometimes want help in attaining goals that the counselor considers unrealistic or immoral. If, for example, a wife complains that her husband has been unfaithful, but the husband wants the freedom to have occasional sexual contacts during business trips, the Christian counselor is faced with a goal conflict. The counselor realizes the value of not taking sides, but the husband wants permission to continue behavior that clearly is sinful, according to the Bible. In a noncondemning but honest way these differences in goals and values must be discussed. The counselor's goal is not to manipulate or force people to change, but neither should people be helped to act in ways that the counselor considers morally wrong, psychologically harmful, or detrimental to the marriage. If counselor-counselee goal conflicts persist, even after continued discussion, then withdrawal from the counseling and referral may be the best options.

If counselees have goals or values that differ from those of the counselor, or if the husband and wife have conflicting goals, all of this should be discussed openly. Usually there are at least some goals that everyone accepts, and it is possible to start there. Sometimes as counseling continues and as goals are clarified, the differences are not as divergent as they first appeared.

(d) Reaching the Goals. Each marriage is unique and every marital problem is in some ways different from all others. It is not possible, therefore, to give a step-by-step recipe for successful marriage counseling. As we have seen, a great number of counseling techniques have been proposed, but most of these are intended to help counselors focus on the persons, the problems, and the processes in counseling.[42]

5. *Focus on Persons.* Popular books on marriage often give practical advice on issues such as handling money, dealing with in-laws, improving communication, changing abrasive personal habits, or resolving sexual problems. Many of the

suggestions are practical and helpful, but marriage counseling involves more than solving practical problems. Even when they analyze their problems carefully and reach mutually agreeable conclusions, couples often discover that tensions still persist. This has been called the fallacy of the reasonable solution; it is the view that reasonable solutions often fail, even when they are accepted by reasonable people. This is because many problems are more emotional than rational. Logic and rational analysis fail to help because emotional and personality issues get in the way and prevent people from taking action to reach practical conclusions.[43]

The counselor must seek to understand persons, their feelings, and their frustrations as well as we understand problems. Sometimes helpers are so intent on solving problems and finding how-to-do-it answers that they become insensitive to the pain and personalities of the people with whom they are working. The basic counselor qualities of empathy, genuineness, and warmth are crucial in marriage counseling.

6. *Focus on Problems.* Once you have built rapport and shown that you care for the counselees as people, there is greater freedom to focus on the problem issues.

As you listen and ask some information-gathering questions, try to be supportive. Slowly move the counseling toward tentative solutions. Guide in the consideration of attitude change, behavior changes, confession, forgiveness, or reexamination of perceptions. Discuss alternative courses of action for the future, encourage and teach counselees how to try out these solutions, and take time to evaluate what works and what does not.

7. *Focus on Processes.* When they come for counseling, most people focus on a "content" issue: the husband wants a divorce, the wife is depressed, the couple can't agree how to handle a rebellious teenager. Professional counselors, however, are more inclined to focus on process issues. The counseling literature sometimes calls this the process/content distinction.

Assume, for example, that a husband and wife disagree about finances. It is helpful to learn *what* each spouse is thinking (content), but often it is even more helpful to learn *how* they talk about their differences (process). If they can learn new ways to talk and interact, they often can apply this learning to resolve the content differences.[44] During counseling, therefore, ask yourself questions such as the following:

> How does the couple communicate?
> How do they interact in public and in private?
> How do they handle disagreements?
> How do they interact when each perceives a problem in a different way?
> Do they criticize each other?
> Do they attack each other's integrity or use put downs and subtle (or not so subtle) criticisms?
> Do they build up one another?
> Does one person dominate the other?
> Does one or both partners withdraw when there are disagreements?

According to the dictionary, a process refers to the changes or continuous actions that are taking place during a period of time. In counseling, the word "process" often is used to describe the continuous ways in which people relate to each other or interact with the counselor during the counseling sessions.

Carefully watch the couple as they interact with you and with each other in counseling. Listen to their descriptions of how they relate to others. Try to point out how the couple is relating,[45] and then talk about ways that they could relate better. Are there different ways of relating that could be practiced between sessions? Be sure to discuss all of this when the couple returns.

Eventually, as you move toward termination, you may want to help counselees review what they have learned. Encourage them to launch out more and more on their own. Remind them that marriage counseling, like all other Christian counseling, is intended to help people grow personally, interpersonally, and spiritually. As counselors, our greatest successes come when couples learn to build marriages that are yielded to Jesus Christ, based on biblical principles, characterized by a commitment to each other, and growing as the husband and wife constantly work at skillful communication, goal attainment, and conflict resolution.

Preventing Marital Problems

Media people are often criticized, but perhaps television, newspaper, magazine, and radio reports have served a useful purpose in alerting us to the high divorce rates, frequent family violence, and widespread marital tensions that many people face. Within recent years, there has been a dramatic increase in the number of graduate-level marriage and family counseling courses.[46] Seminaries have developed courses in family life education, and churches are becoming aware of the need for more teaching about marriage and family issues. Some professionals and church leaders have begun to emphasize the unique needs of stepfamilies and single-parent families.[47] Others have noted that crisis intervention often provides opportunities to work with families, helping them both to deal with the present problems and to avoid long-term destructive patterns of problem solving. A perusal of the chapter titles in this book will point to a number of problem areas that could create or worsen existing marital difficulties. Dealing with these problems as they arise and working to prevent them can in turn prevent their becoming a cause for marriage tensions.

In addition there are several other preventive actions that may be taken, especially by church or parachurch groups, including discussion groups and Sunday school classes.

1. *Teach Biblical Principles of Marriage.* Christians believe that God, who created both male and female and who initiated marriage, also has given guidelines for marriage in the pages of Scripture. These guidelines need to be taught clearly at home and church and modeled consistently by Christian leaders. We live in a society that propagates nonbiblical values about sex and marriage, so the biblical teachings about sex and the meaning of love need to be reinforced frequently.

2. *Stress the Importance of Marriage, Marriage Enrichment, and Marital Commitment.* For most people life consists of a number of demands, commitments, and responsibilities. Often in the midst of these pressures one's marriage and family are slowly shunted to a lesser order of priority. Work, church, community responsibilities, and other activities take precedence over time spent with one's spouse. Marriage takes time, effort, and commitment if it is to grow and develop. This needs to be emphasized in churches and elsewhere. Encourage people to make marriage a high priority item in terms of the expenditure of time and effort. Marriage enrichment seminars can help and so can discussion groups, the reading of helpful books,

videotape programs that discuss marriage, and biblical sermons dealing with marriage. Try to stimulate couples to do things together and for each other. Help them establish priorities, work toward mutual goals, and think of ways to bring variety into their marriages.[48]

3. *Teach Principles of Communication and Conflict Resolution.* Married people are not the only members of the congregation who need help in learning how to communicate and deal with conflict. When there is gossip, backbiting, insensitivity, and stubbornness, there also will be tension and conflict. By teaching Christians how to get along with one another, we help them build better relationships within the family and without. Married people, for example, should be shown the importance of listening, self-disclosure, mutual acceptance, and understanding. Empathy, warmth, and genuineness do not need to be limited to counseling sessions. These attributes can be learned and practiced in marriage and throughout the church.[49]

4. *Encourage Counseling When Needed.* Like individuals, couples often are reluctant to seek counseling. For some this is embarrassing and may be seen as an admission of failure. In contrast it can be emphasized from the pulpit and elsewhere that going for counseling can be a sign of strength. Often the counseling is most effective when it is sought early, not after the problems have grown progressively worse.

Conclusions about Marital Problems

Marriage is the most intimate of all human relationships. When this relationship is good and growing, it provides one of life's greatest satisfactions. When it is poor or even static and routine, it can be a source of great frustration and misery. God surely wants marriages to be good, a model of the beautiful relationship between Christ and his church.[50] The Christian counselor who understands biblical teaching and who knows counseling techniques is best qualified to help couples attain the biblical ideal for marriage.

SUGGESTIONS FOR FURTHER READING

Dobson, James C. *Love for a Lifetime: Building a Marriage That Will Go the Distance.* Portland, Oreg.: Multnomah, 1987.*

Guernsey, Dennis, and Lucy Guernsey. *Real Life Marriage.* Waco, Tex.: Word, 1987.

Mason, Mike. *The Mystery of Marriage: As Iron Sharpens Iron.* Portland, Oreg.: Multnomah, 1985.*

Sherman, Robert, and Norman Fredman. *Handbook of Structured Techniques in Marriage and Family Therapy.* New York: Brunner/Mazel, 1986.

Thompson, David A. *Five Steps toward a Better Marriage.* Minneapolis: Bethany Fellowship, 1980.*

Worthington, Everett L., Jr. *Marriage Counseling with Christian Couples.* Downers Grove, Ill: InterVarsity, forthcoming.

Wright, H. Norman. *Marital Counseling: A Biblically Based Behavioral, Cognitive Approach.* Denver: Christian Marriage Enrichment, 1981.

* Books marked with an asterisk (*) are especially suited for counselees to read.

28

Pregnancy Issues

I'M IN SHOCK," Lois blurted when she told her twin sister. "George can't believe it, and we haven't gotten around to telling the kids." Forty-six years old, newly embarked on a long-delayed career, and finally free from the demands and restraints of child rearing, Lois had never intended to get pregnant again. She and her husband had raised two daughters. One was a college student, the other would soon graduate from high school, and neither ever expected to have a baby brother or sister. But Lois was expecting.

This was a child who wasn't wanted. "We've done our duty raising children," George complained to his business partner. "We're ready to have grandchildren. We aren't up to dirty diapers, ear infections, messy eating, and the junior high years all over again."

In the weeks that followed, George and Lois talked about abortion. They had always maintained a pro-life stance, but that was easy before. Would abortion really be wrong for somebody in their circumstances? What kind of an example would such a decision be to their daughters? Didn't God understand their momentary lapse when they had failed to use a condom because pregnancy at their age seemed so unlikely? What if the baby was carried to full term and found to have Down's Syndrome or some other handicap because the mother was older? Was it possible that God really wanted them to have another child?

As they pondered these issues, George was inclined to favor abortion; Lois felt it was wrong. Eventually they agreed to go through with the pregnancy, and in time they became the parents of a healthy baby boy.

"We decided not to name him Isaac!" Lois joked after the child was born, "and I don't like it when George calls me 'Sarah'—even in fun!"

The child is now almost five and ready to start school. He is loved by his parents, the darling of his older sisters, and doted over by most of his parents friends. Someday perhaps he will joke to his friends that he was an "accident," and his parents will admit, at least to each other, that this is true. Raising another child has been a delight at times, but Lois and George both admit that their lives would have been simpler and easier if they had avoided the unwanted pregnancy that came so unexpectedly and late in life.

Children can be a joy when they are planned and wanted, but sometimes pregnancies create sorrow and stress. For others the sorrow comes because a couple desperately wants children but there is no pregnancy.

Nobody knows, with certainty, how many couples try in vain to have children but are unable either to get pregnant or to bear a child to full term. Statistics vary about the frequency of unwanted pregnancies or the numbers of abortions that occur worldwide every year. Few issues arouse more controversy than debates about abortion, what to do about teenage pregnancy, how to give accurate sex education, or whether high-school students should be given free contraceptives.[1] Each of these issues may come up in counseling; each is in some way related to pregnancy.

Pregnancy problems could be divided into two broad categories: (1) the inability to bear children among couples who do want to have a child and (2) the pregnancies of those who do not want to have a child. Couples who want to bear children but are unable to do so either cannot get pregnant even after repeated attempts or they may conceive only to have their pregnancies end in repeated miscarriages. In contrast, unwanted pregnancies come to people, unmarried or married, who don't want children now. Included are those who have no desire for children at all, who had planned to start their families later, who wanted to stop childbearing because their families are already big enough, or who have had too many children too close to each other. The circumstances differ, but in all of these cases, the pregnancy issues can lead to frustration, anger, anxiety, embarrassment, discouragement, and confusion.

THE BIBLE AND PREGNANCY ISSUES

The Old Testament story of Hannah has been told in many Sunday school classes. She was married to a sensitive and caring man named Elkunah, but the couple had no children. Year after year they went to the temple to worship God, and Hannah would spend time in prayer asking for a child. "Oh Lord Almighty," she prayed one year, "if you will only look upon your servant's misery and remember me, and not forget your servant but give her a son, then I will give him to the Lord for all the days of his life."[2] In a time when childlessness was seen as an indication of God's displeasure, Hannah described herself as a woman who was "deeply troubled" and with "great anguish and grief" because of her infertility. Elkunah tried to be comforting, but his wife remained downhearted and sometimes too depressed to eat.[3] We can only guess at the depth of her joy when Hannah conceived and gave birth to Samuel.

The Bible does not give a lot of direct teaching about pregnancy issues; much comes from stories like that of Hannah. Nevertheless several conclusions are clear.

1. *Children Are Valuable and Gifts from God.* As gifts, children come from the Lord and are not the mere result of virility and fertility. Psalm 127 states this concisely:

> Sons are a heritage from the Lord,
> children a reward from him.
> Like arrows in the hands of a warrior
> are sons born in one's youth.
> Blessed is the man
> whose quiver is full of them.[4]

2. *Childlessness Is Cause for Sadness.* Hannah was not the only woman who grieved because she was barren. Sarah, Rebekah, Rachel, the Shunammite woman,[5] Elizabeth, and others felt disgrace, distress, and shame when they were unable to

bear children. In contrast, one of the biblical hymns of praise describes how God "settles the barren woman in her home as a happy mother of children. Praise the Lord."[6] Infertility can bring sadness. Children can make our lives happy and give us reason to praise God.

3. *Pregnancy Apart from Marriage Is Wrong.* We are reminded of this every Christmas when we hear again the story of Mary's pregnancy before her marriage. Because Joseph, her intended husband, "was a righteous man and did not want to expose her to public disgrace, he had in mind to divorce her quietly."[7] He changed his mind only after an angel appeared and explained that Mary's pregnancy was unique among all others before or since—she was "found to be with child through the Holy Spirit." Throughout its pages the Bible condemns immorality,[8] including rape and sexual intercourse with a variety of partners.[9]

4. *Human Life Begins Long before Birth.* Much of the debate surrounding abortion concerns the question of when the merger between an egg and a sperm becomes a person. The Bible does not tell us when we start to be humans, but it seems clear that the developing fetus already is human in God's eyes. When he was called to serve the Lord, Jeremiah heard some strange words:

> Before I formed you in the womb I knew you,
> before you were born I set you apart;
> I appointed you as a prophet to the nations.[10]

Apparently God considered Jeremiah to be a person long before he was born. The same conclusion might be reached about John the Baptist. When his mother Elizabeth was greeted by Mary, the baby "leaped in the womb." It could be argued, of course, that the child was only responding physically to an upsurge of adrenaline in the mother, but Elizabeth assumed that "the baby in my womb leaped for joy."[11] Apparently this was a real life that was able to experience joy even before birth.

Other Bible passages would support this conclusion. The psalmist wrote that he was "sinful at birth, sinful from the time my mother conceived me."[12] Ps. 139:13–16 praises God who "knit me together in my mother's womb" and "saw my unformed body." The fetus was not considered to be merely some impersonal biological organism. Human life was assumed to start before birth. It must start at some time during the gestation (prenatal development), most likely it starts at conception.

5. *Pregnancy Is Not Always a Cause for Rejoicing.* Jacob and Rachel had one of the most touching love stories in the Bible. For seven years Jacob worked for his future father-in-law in return for Rachel, but "the time seemed like only a few days to him because of his love for her."[13] Finally the wedding day approached and Jacob waited expectantly. With unembarrassed honesty he told his future father-in-law, "I want to lie with her." Imagine the shock that followed when evening came and Jacob found himself married to Leah instead.

"It is not our custom here to give the younger daughter in marriage before the older one," Jacob was told, so he worked another seven years. When he finally got the wife for whom he had waited so long, she was found to be barren. Eventually she gave birth to Jacob's favorite son, Joseph, but when she got pregnant a second time, Rachel died in childbirth.[14] It was not a happy time.

Pregnancies are not always happy occasions, and neither is there rejoicing when a couple wants to have a baby but cannot. Because of the physical implications, medical consultation will always be a part of pregnancy issues. Often there is also a need for counseling from a sensitive Christian counselor.

The Causes of Pregnancy Problems

At the most basic level, pregnancy problems have a physical cause. Infertility, for example, is defined most often as an inability to conceive after twelve to eighteen months of attempted conception, when intercourse has been timed midcycle and when no types of contraception have been used.[15] Sometimes pregnancy does not occur because sperm is absent or the male sperm count is low. In other cases the female does not ovulate normally, blockage may prevent the sperm from reaching the egg, the body produces antibodies that kill the sperm, or other physical problems may interfere with pregnancy. Infertility strikes about 10 to 15 percent of married couples, and the rate has been increasing partly because many people now choose to postpone childbearing until after thirty when fertility tends to decline. Most infertility problems can be diagnosed accurately and treated successfully.

When a woman does get pregnant, she has about a 20 percent chance of having a miscarriage (the spontaneous abortion of the fetus). Most often this occurs early in the pregnancy. If it happens beyond the fifth month of pregnancy, it is termed a stillbirth. This is nature's way of saying that something is abnormal about the pregnancy. In time most women who miscarry will get pregnant again and carry the baby to full term. Some women, however, have repeated miscarriages. Like couples who are infertile, these people remain childless.

Unwanted pregnancies, in contrast, occur when contraceptives were not used or were inefficient. It is then that many people are confronted with the practical question about whether or not to have an abortion.

Like all physical conditions, each of these pregnancy issues has a strong psychological impact that can complicate life further. One major study followed a group of three hundred married men whose wives could not get pregnant.[16] All of these men turned to activities that substituted for parenting while they kept trying to have a child. Some of the men (about 25 percent) devoted their attention to other people's children: spending time with nieces or nephews, coaching Little League, or leading a church youth program. These men had relatively few marriage or personal problems and many of them chose later to adopt.

Other men, however, turned their attention to nonhuman activities like developing a hobby or making home improvements. A minority (about 12 percent) focused attention on themselves: lifting weights, body building, or pursuing other macho activities that could increase their feelings of masculinity. These men were the most poorly adjusted. Many had marital problems and over half got divorces by the time they reached midlife. With both husband and wife, the infertility created depression, marital tension, anger, anxiety, frustration, and spiritual struggles.

From this it cannot be assumed that all childless couples have physical and/or psychological problems. Some people make a logical, prayerful, carefully considered decision to have no children, at least for the present. Both husband and wife may feel called to serve God in special careers, for example. They may decide that their work or ministry might be hindered by the presence of children, or might in turn interfere with the healthy development of children. In other cases, however, the decision not to have children may reflect insecurity, fear of intimacy, a desire to avoid responsibility, fear of sex, or some other internal or interpersonal conflict.

The inability to have a child when one is wanted has been called one of life's "low blows." Even though the cause is physical and often temporary, the way people respond can influence personal mental health, happiness in middle age, the stability of a marriage, and whether they eventually have children, adopt, or remain childless.[17]

Psychological issues like these also accompany unwanted pregnancies. In addition to the anger, frustration, regret, confusion, anxiety, fear, and depression, there may be an increase in substance abuse (drugs or alcohol) and often there is conflict between partners or with parents about whether or not to have an abortion. These might be considered effects of the pregnancy, but they also cause further conflict and tension. The problem is worse when a pregnant woman feels little support from others. (Parents, church people, and sexual partners sometimes show little care or concern, especially to unwed mothers.) In addition, the emotional issues that swirl around the topic of abortion sometimes leave pregnant women and their partners feeling both confused and pressured to make immediate, life-changing decisions.[18]

THE EFFECTS OF PREGNANCY PROBLEMS

Childlessness and unwanted pregnancies arouse similar emotional reactions, but the effects also differ depending on the circumstances.

1. *Childlessness.* Whenever a couple begins to realize that pregnancy is not forthcoming, even after repeated attempts to get pregnant, or when there is a medical confirmation that either the husband, wife, or both are unable to contribute to a pregnancy, there first comes a period of surprise. This tends to be followed by grief, anger ("Why us?"), and isolation from friends who might ask questions. Some couples find it too painful to be around children. One childless woman, for example, wanted to avoid Christmas because it was too difficult to see delighted nieces and nephews showing their excitement about the holidays.[19] These kinds of reactions are likely to be replaced by denial and a reluctance to admit the problem, followed finally by acceptance, a willingness to pursue all medical treatment that might be helpful, and a decision to find alternative sources of satisfaction (such as greater devotion to one's work, a decision to adopt or become foster parents, or involvement with other people's children).[20]

When their infertility is discovered, women especially feel guilty and inadequate. Many experience family and social pressure to bear children and there can be a sense of failure or a feeling of sexual incompetence when pregnancy does not occur. Sometimes there is constant worry and concern about the problem, accompanied at times by story swapping with other infertile couples.[21] According to one counselor, the whole world looks pregnant to the woman who can't conceive. "Everywhere she goes she sees babies and bellies."[22] One study of four hundred couples found that most were caught in a "hope-despair cycle." At the start of each month there is hope that "this time it might be different," followed by increasing pressure, anxiety, and despair when pregnancy does not occur.[23] This creates tension that can disrupt marital stability, influence bodily cycles, and delay conception even further.

The hope-despair cycle is a little different in couples who are childless because of repeated miscarriage. Each time the woman gets pregnant, there is hope that this time the baby will be carried to full term. When the miscarriage (or stillbirth) occurs, hopes are dashed again and the couple has a fresh experience of disappointment and grief. Often there are attempts to assign blame for the loss, frequently there are great feelings of helplessness, and almost always there is a need to work through the grief with supportive friends or relatives. Sometimes, however, family members and others feel uncomfortable talking about these issues, and the couple is left to cope pretty much alone. According to one grief expert, counselors need to recognize that a real loss, a death, has occurred. This should not be minimized or replaced by an upbeat focus on the future or the possibilities of other pregnancies.[24]

Counselors at fertility clinics have noted that many couples are reluctant, even ashamed, to admit their infertility or problems with repeated miscarriages. Some tend to feel that childlessness is an indication of one's inadequacy as a male or female. Many feel uncomfortable discussing sex even with a medical counselor. Others may resist genital examination by physicians, and some may fear that they will be told, "It's all psychological, so go home, relax, and try again to get pregnant."

The counselor should be aware of this reluctance to talk about infertility. If a married couple remains childless after several years of marriage you may wish to gently raise the issue, but try not to fall into the pressuring attitude of well-meaning relatives or friends. If the couple does not wish to talk about their childlessness, assure them of your availability to talk at any future time and do not press the issue further.

2. *Unplanned and Unwanted Pregnancies.* Christian psychologist Everett L. Worthington divides unplanned pregnancies into two broad categories: those that come too early and others that are too late. The too-early pregnancies include teenage pregnancy, pregnancies in unmarried couples who live and/or sleep together, pregnancies that occur immediately before or after a wedding, or back-to-back children (pregnancies that occur too closely together). The too-late pregnancies include those that come after a planned family is complete, accidental unexpected pregnancies, and pregnancies that occur in midlife. Each affects people somewhat differently.[25]

Consider, for example, the struggles faced by an unwed mother. The number of illegitimate pregnancies, especially among teenagers, has been rising at an alarming rate. Although sexual intercourse apart from marriage is becoming widely accepted in our society, this does not make it right. The Bible, as we have seen, condemns intercourse apart from marriage, and illegitimate pregnancies are still socially disapproved. Of course the male, whose sperm impregnates the woman, is as much a part of the problem as the unwed mother, but the father's identity is sometimes unknown even to the woman. Males can hide their involvement since they do not show evidence of the pregnancy, and sometimes the father flees, leaving the unwed mother (and sometimes her family) to face the problem alone.

Unwed mothers often try to keep the pregnancy hidden for as long as possible. Anxiety, fear of parental reaction, concern about social judgment, guilt, self-condemnation, and sometimes anger all serve to keep the unwed mother preoccupied and away from sources of help and prenatal care. When the pregnancy is confirmed there often are outbursts of anger, condemnation, fear, panic, and general confusion, especially if the pregnancy involves teenagers. All of these emotions may be brought to the counselor's office where the emphasis should not be on moral exhortations, theological discussions, or intellectual debates about why the girl became pregnant. The counselee needs help in coping with the crisis and making decisions about the immediate and long-range future.

3. *Abortion.* In January 1973, the United States Supreme Court granted women the absolute right to abortion on demand during the first six months of pregnancy and an almost unqualified right to abortion (that is, for health reasons—with "health" including psychological, physical, social, and economic well-being) during the final three months. Suddenly abortion ceased to be a crime and became a right. It ceased to be a privilege of the affluent and became available to all, sometimes subsidized by taxpayer dollars. The resulting shouts of approval and cries of disapproval have continued to the present and have been heard both in North America and beyond.[26] In the meantime, the number of legal abortions has increased drastically.

As we noted earlier, much of the debate about abortion centers on the question of when human life begins. The Supreme Court concluded that it did not need to resolve the difficult question of when life begins. Since "those trained in the respective disciplines of medicine, philosophy and theology are unable to arrive at any consensus, the judiciary, at this point in the development of man's knowledge, is not in a position to speculate as to the answer."[27] The answer, however, is crucially important. If life begins at birth, then abortion is not terminating a human being's existence. If human life begins earlier, especially at the time of conception, then abortion is murder.[28] It is ironic that the same legal code makes it a crime to destroy a baby born prematurely but makes it all right to destroy another child of identical age not yet been born. The same doctors who spend anxious hours and thousands of dollars fighting to save the life of a baby born prematurely will, with hardly a thought, arrange for the death of a same-age, unborn child. The same law that stresses civil rights denies these rights to the unborn.

The Christian counselor must grapple with these issues preferably before he or she counsels people concerning abortion. There is little or no convincing biblical, theological, physiological, medical, or other evidence to support the view that human life really begins at some specific time during the nine months between conception and birth. Many people conclude, therefore, that life must start when the male sperm and female egg unite at conception. If this is true, then abortion is wrong. It is not merely a medical procedure, legal issue, or counseling problem. It is a violation of the commandment, "You shall not kill."

Not all counselors will agree with this conclusion, and the issue is complicated by other ethical concerns such as the rightness or wrongness of abortion when the fetus is deformed, pregnancy as a result of rape, or the mother's life and health would be endangered if the pregnancy continues.

Abortion is now relatively (although not always) safe, common, easy to obtain, and widely accepted as one way to solve the pregnancy problem efficiently, quietly, and quickly. Intense debate surrounds the question of how the woman is affected by abortion. Case histories, some very moving and traumatic, are cited by those who counsel with women following abortions.[29] In contrast, a body of research and the writings of many pro-abortion advocates suggest that abortions may not be psychologically harmful.

It is important to note, however, that most of this research has used poor methodology and grossly substandard research design. Because of these weaknesses, the research findings are of questionable validity.[30] One study that *is* carefully conducted tends to support the arguments of those who cite frequent trauma after an abortion.[31] Counselors confirm that there *is* a postabortion syndrome in which women—and a surprising number of their male partners—feel guilt, grief, feelings of detachment, depression, emotional aloofness, and inner psychological pain following an abortion.[32]

"Post abortion trauma is more the rule than the exception," wrote one counselor in response to an earlier edition of this book. "The aftermath of abortion is not simply a little guilt or sadness or a wondering about the moral implications of one's actions. It generally goes far beyond that and involves deep grieving, self-destructive actions, broken relationships, sexual dysfunction, low self-esteem, increase in self-abuse, child abuse, suicide, alcoholism and drug involvement . . . and a crying out to a God they fear can never forgive them for 'murdering' (their word) their own children." These reactions, seen in a counseling center, may not be true of all women who have abortions, but the fact that many do experience postabortion trauma suggests that the risk of a severe psychological reaction is high.

What is the effect on infants when their mothers are denied an abortion? It depends on the attitudes of the mothers or on the home environment of the children. Unstable mothers or those who resent their unwanted children tend to have maladjusted children.[33] When mothers accept their unplanned children and raise them in loving homes, or when the children of unplanned pregnancies are placed in caring adoptive homes, the young people can be happy and normal.

4. *Infant Death.* Technically this is not a pregnancy issue, but when a child dies at birth or shortly thereafter, the parents are plunged into intense grief, even when they have been warned that the child may not survive. Children born with physical or mental deformities may continue to live, but the parents struggle with frustration, anger, discouragement, guilt, and sadness because many of their hopes for the child's future have died even as the infant has been born.

Sudden Infant Death syndrome (SIDS) is especially difficult for parents and other family members. Thousands of babies die this way each year.[34] The deaths come without warning, usually within the first six months of life. Although a viral infection may be involved, the cause is unknown. In addition to the grief accompanying the infant's death, parents sometimes are subjected to police interrogation because child abuse and neglect are so common in society. Often family members experience self-blame and sometimes suspicion from relatives, even though nothing could have been done to prevent the death. Siblings, who often resent the coming of a new brother or sister, frequently respond to the death with intense inner guilt.

Tension and misunderstanding between parents is often high following SIDS, and divorce frequently follows. Sometimes, as we have seen, a wife will feel that her husband doesn't care because he doesn't cry much. He, in turn, stifles the tears because he doesn't want to upset his wife. This type of misunderstanding puts tremendous strain on the relationship, and illustrates the communication breakdowns that can occur as parents grieve.[35]

COUNSELING AND PREGNANCY PROBLEMS

The previous paragraphs have made several references to grief, sorrow, anxiety, anger, depression, confusion, and guilt. These emotions are common in most pregnancy problems, along with communication breakdowns and interpersonal tension. All of these may be expressed in counseling along with the unique struggles that accompany childlessness, unplanned pregnancies, abortion decisions, and infant death.

1. *Childlessness.* Only a few years ago, it was logical to assume that childless couples must have some physical or psychological problem that prevented childbearing. Today this is no longer a valid assumption. Since many couples decide to delay or avoid starting a family, the counselor must not assume that childlessness is a problem.

When it is a problem, couples sometimes will show visible signs of depression or aloofness at family-centered gatherings. If you suspect some concerns about childlessness, you may wish to raise simple, nonthreatening questions like "How are things going at home?" or "Do you ever miss having kids around the house?" Be alert to casual comments that invite further questions or exploration of the childlessness issue.

When you are involved in helping a childless couple, try to remember the following guidelines.

- Childlessness may have several causes. Do not assume that you know why the couple has no children. As you talk together, raise a question about the reason for the childlessness.
- When there is a desire for children but an inability for the wife to get pregnant, make sure that they are seeing a competent physician. Often the family doctor will refer the couple to a specialist in infertility issues.
- Do not condemn, probe into areas of sexual intimacy that need not be discussed, assume that all couples should have children, use trite platitudes, or even hint that you find the problem amusing.
- Focus on the theological issues involved. These include the common but erroneous idea that God is punishing a couple by preventing pregnancy or that he doesn't care. There is no scriptural basis for either view,[36] and couples should be helped to discuss these concerns, including the question of "why?"
- Guide discussion of ethical issues. When they are unable to initiate or maintain a pregnancy, couples sometimes begin to wonder about artificial insemination by the husband, artificial insemination by an anonymous donor, in vitro fertilization,[37] embryo transfer, and the increasingly controversial issue of surrogate motherhood.[38]
- Help the couple find alternatives to bearing children. Realistically discuss adoption, foster parenting, or adapting to life without children. Discuss meaningful activities that can give purpose to life apart from children.
- Recognize that many couples need consistent support, especially during the down times of the hope-despair cycle or whenever a new medical or other procedure has been tried and found to fail. Some of this support can

come from the local church, but many couples have found help in support groups where there is mutual encouragement, sharing of information, learning about options, and expression of feelings. Sometimes these groups can sensitize the church to issues of infertility and often there is prayer and spiritual growth. National organizations such as Resolve, Inc.,[39] can provide information and help local groups get started, but many Christian couples have formed their own support groups drawn from one or several local churches.

It is encouraging to know that most of those who are involuntarily childless are able to have children following medical diagnosis and treatment. Of those who stay childless, a few will remain to mourn and be comforted,[40] but most will learn to accept their childless state and will make healthy adjustments, sometimes as the result of a counselor's help.

2. *Unplanned and Unwanted Pregnancies.* The forty-five-year-old married woman who is unexpectedly pregnant clearly has needs and problems that differ from those of a seventeen-year-old unmarried teenager. These differences must not be forgotten, but some similarities apply to almost all unplanned pregnancies.

First, there may be initial fears and insecurities. Do not discourage these initial expressions of emotion, but try to show acceptance, understanding, and a quiet confidence. Remember that a loving, wise, forgiving God will guide as we counsel.

Sometimes the initial fears are expressed through a strong resistance to counseling. The unmarried girl, for example, may resist because she has been brought or sent for counseling against her will, she may never have learned to trust people, or she may view the counselor as a condemning, unforgiving authority figure. Unwed fathers may have similar insecurities and resistances.

During the first session try to give calm reassurance that you will help (but avoid gushy or pious clichés). Attempt to find out what help is needed and what the counselee(s) and the family members see as immediate courses of action. Although you should encourage a physical examination for the mother, try to discourage quick decisions (such as abortion or immediate marriage) at least for a day or two and until the original emotions have been expressed. Prayer can be especially calming, helpful, and reassuring.

Second, you often can give help with practical decisions. The major questions involve "How do I respond to this pregnancy?" and "What will I do with this baby?" For some, abortion seems the immediate and logical choice. Others soon decide to keep the baby and begin to make life adjustments. For unmarried couples this may involve plans to marry. These hasty marriages often fail, but not always. A marriage immediately after pregnancy can be successful if the couple shows some evidence of maturity and if they have had a good and growing relationship prior to the pregnancy.

Some unmarried mothers decide to remain single and bear the child to the time of birth. Many find maternity homes, go to live with distant relatives or foster parents, or, in an increasing number of cases, stay at home where they continue with work or schooling and openly bear the child. Each of these alternatives should be discussed along with the issue of the baby's future.

Keeping the baby or making it available for adoption are alternatives that should both be considered. In deciding these issues, counselors are not alone with their counselees. Family members have opinions, and everyone can draw on the advice and expertise of others in the community, including local physicians, social agencies, adoption centers, and lawyers. Remember that unwed fathers are not always willing to leave the child's future in the hands of the mother or her family. Increasingly, unwed fathers want to be as involved as the mother in making decisions about the child's and the parent's immediate future.

Third, there often may be need for continued counseling. After the prenatal decisions have been made, either or both of the unwed parents may experience continuing guilt, insecurity, a lowered self-image, or similar emotional struggles. Married couples may have difficulties adjusting to the new child. The counselor can help, especially if he or she has been accepting, noncondemning, and helpful from the beginning. Early in counseling you might want to suggest that further sessions could be helpful, if not before the baby's birth, then shortly thereafter.

The mother may need someone with whom she can share the details of childbearing or the grief that comes if the baby is given up for adoption. Ideally, family members are the best people to give this kind of support, but sometimes this isn't done. When a child is born out of wedlock, for example, the young mother's parents may be unwilling or unable to listen compassionately or discuss anything concerning the new grandchild. The counselor can be available to the entire family to help with the discussion of feelings, moral questions, and plans for the future. If the child is stillborn or deformed, this can create additional guilt, grief, and confusion—all of which should be talked through.

Unwanted pregnancies, including illegitimate pregnancies, can be traumatic experiences, even in this age of sexual laxity and moral decline. The Christian counselor can use this experience to demonstrate and point people toward the love, compassion, and forgiveness that is found in Jesus Christ. Sometimes married couples can be helped to rethink their views on contraception. Unwed parents can be helped to reach new conclusions about responsibility and moral choice. In the church, believers can be encouraged to show compassion, acceptance, and forgiveness, instead of gossip, criticism, and rejection. In these ways the pain of unwanted pregnancies can be turned into a learning and personal growth experience that can help individuals and couples live more Christ-honoring lives in the future.

3. *Abortion.* Several years ago, two thousand Evangelical church leaders gathered in St. Louis for a congress on the family. As program director of this meeting, one of my duties was to oversee the preparation of an Affirmation of the Family that would be distributed following our meeting. After many hours, we prepared statements on marriage, parenting, childhood, divorce, sexuality, and other family issues. A battle arose over our one-paragraph statement on abortion.[41] Clearly Christians are among those who hold very strong positions on this subject and, in spite of some refreshing exceptions, there is rigidity and insensitivity on both sides of the debate.

As a Christian counselor, it is important to think through this issue *before* a counselee appears raising issues about abortion.[42] In general, the psychological and professional counseling literature maintains that abortion has no risks and that keeping the baby may create greater problems than terminating a pregnancy.[43] This conclusion is persuasively contested by those who work every day with women who bear the pain and trauma of the abortion experience.[44]

When a woman talks with you about abortion, initially it is best to let her discuss feelings and alternatives openly while you serve as a supportive, caring, and understanding counselor. If the father is available, he should be involved in the counseling as well. It may be helpful to discuss how abortions are performed and questions should be referred to a competent physician, preferably a gynecologist. Alternatives to abortion (such as adoption or keeping the child) should be discussed. You may want to enlist the help of an experienced crisis pregnancy counselor.[45] Counselors are rarely able to hide their own views on abortion, and probably you shouldn't try. Ultimately, however, the woman must decide what to do. The counselor is there to help.

What do you do if the woman decides to get an abortion, but you, the counselor, think this is morally wrong? It has been suggested that the counselor can either help the woman find competent medical care or graciously withdraw from counseling and refer her to a counselor who is not opposed to abortion. Is this really a wise course of action for the counselor who believes that abortion is sin? Nobody would suggest that a drug-abuse counselor should send a strong-willed drug abuser to another counselor who is neutral on the issue or to someone who believes that drug abuse should be a free choice. If the counselor believes that abortion is as self-destructive and as sinful as drug abuse, then we owe it to the woman, to her family, to the unborn child, and to the Lord to demonstrate our caring concern while we lovingly urge that abortion be avoided.[46] *When clear sin is involved, Christian counseling cannot be neutral.*

After abortion, many counselees can profit from individual or group counseling that focuses on issues such as feelings about the surgery, guilt, forgiveness, attitudes toward sex, contraception, the meaning of femininity, and biblical teachings about life, death, and sex. The goal here is not to condemn or to instill guilt. Instead you should try to help the counselee experience God's cleansing and forgiveness, express feelings, and work through the grief process that often follows abortion, reevaluate the meaning of sexuality, consider the biblical teachings about sex and life before birth, and help counselees grow beyond the abortion. Help them move into a future where they can begin or continue serving God and others as true disciples of Jesus Christ.

4. *Infant Death.* The loss of a child, either before or shortly after birth, is no less a grief experience than the death of an adult. Sometimes couples are expected to get over it quickly, and caring but insensitive friends sometimes urge them to quickly get pregnant again.

Instead, the couple needs support and sensitive grief counseling. Encourage the parents to agree to an autopsy. This lets them understand what happened and helps to relieve some of the guilt. Funerals and memorial services are important, especially since these can bring comfort from friends and an increasing awareness of God's presence in this time of crisis.[47]

Preventing Pregnancy Problems

Some conclusions about prevention are self-evident and may even seem simplistic. To prevent infertility, a couple needs expert medical diagnosis and treatment, sometimes accompanied by counseling. Medical intervention and good prenatal care can help to prevent many (but not all) miscarriages, stillbirths, birth defects, and infant deaths. To prevent premarital pregnancies, young people need sex education that includes moral guidelines and practical help in learning self-control. To prevent unwanted pregnancies, couples may need information or reminders about effective contraception and healthy sexuality. To prevent abortion there needs to be better education about abortion procedures, postabortion trauma, and alternative ways to cope with an unwanted pregnancy. If prevention is to be effective, each of these general suggestions must be adapted to individuals.

There also can be broader programs for prevention. These may focus on sex, support, and suffering.

Sex. This has caused intense pleasure and incredible misery since the beginning of the human race. One poignant Old Testament drama concerns a young man named Ammon, David's son, who was so much in love that others noted his haggard look. Through a series of shrewd moves (including deception), Ammon was able to get alone with the woman for whom he had so much attraction, but when she resisted his sexual advances he raped her. Almost immediately "Ammon hated her with intense hatred. In fact, he hated her more than he had loved her."[48] The young man's intense sexual urges had led to forced intercourse, followed by regret, family problems, and death.

Are things much different today? We live in a society where sex is paraded before us in advertising, in entertainment, and even in business, education, and religious circles. Perhaps it is not surprising that so many people fall into sexual sin followed by personal regret and increasing numbers of unwanted pregnancies—many of which end in abortion.

In part, at least, this must be countered by realistic and sensitive sex education that includes accurate information, clear teaching about biblical morality, and practical guidance to help people maintain self-control. The focus of this education may be on the young, but older people, including parents and even senior citizens, could benefit from a clearer understanding of healthy sexuality as opposed to the more popular, self-centered sexuality.

Support. When the human race was created, the Lord God said, "It is not good for man to be alone," so Adam was given a partner.[49] From that time until the present, human beings have looked to one another for love, support, help, and encouragement.

Many people try to handle life's problems alone. A few take pride in their rugged individualism and withdraw from people. For many there may be an insecurity or reluctance to get close to other human beings; for some there may be nobody with whom to relate. Whatever the cause, individuals are likely to have more difficulty when they try to handle problems and stresses without God and the support of other people.

This chapter has shown that support groups (for example, for infertile couples, for parents whose children have died, for unwed mothers, for women who suffer from postabortion syndrome, for parents with young children) can give the encouragement and love that enables participants to cope better with present stress and avoid future problems.[50] When the church provides some of this support,[51] stresses are reduced and future problems can be prevented.

Suffering. The professional counseling literature says very little about suffering except to suggest ways that suffering can be escaped or avoided. Nobody likes to suffer and most counselors, including Christian counselors, strive to help people cope with and grow beyond their suffering. Suffering, however, isn't always bad. Sometimes it can't be avoided, and often it is a prerequisite for personal and spiritual growth.[52] Jewish psychiatrist Viktor Frankl saw this while a prisoner in a Nazi concentration camp and later built his theory of counseling around the value of suffering.[53] When people complain about their suffering, see no meaning in their pain, or develop attitudes of bitterness, there is misery that may have a psychological as well as a physical basis.

Few experiences are more painful than the loss of a child near the time of birth. Parents or those who plan some day to be parents have no real understanding of the silent suffering that many couples feel because of their inability to bear children. Pregnancy crisis counselors, as we have seen, often describe the suffering that comes to some women following the abortion of an unwanted child. Each of these experiences can be glibly passed off by insensitive relatives and church members. Still the victims of pregnancy problems often retain the pain, holding their frustrations and feelings within and wondering why they fail to recover. When Christians can be helped to understand the meaning and value of suffering, continuing spiritual and psychological problems can often be prevented.

Conclusions about Pregnancy Issues

There are many books and articles on pregnancy issues, but few of these could match the lesson that many of us learned from a former student and his wife who discovered that they were expecting their first child. The joy of this news turned to sorrow when the couple learned that the baby would be born without a brain.

When they decided against abortion, their doctor dropped them as patients and they had difficulty finding another physician. The wife carried the baby for nine months and followed all the principles of good prenatal care. When the child was born, formed perfectly from its eyes down but brainless, the couple held their little girl, gave her a name, cried until there were no more tears, and then made arrangements for her funeral.

When the mother recovered physically, the couple determined to have another pregnancy, but they appear to be infertile. Now they know about the hope-despair cycle and have spent many hours going through the long process of adoption. As these words are being written, they still are childless. Are they sad about this? Yes. Has it curtailed their spiritual growth, forced them to withdraw from others or led to psychological problems? Absolutely not.

Perhaps hundreds have been helped personally and encouraged spiritually by the example of a couple who have experienced several pregnancy problems but have grown nevertheless.

SUGGESTIONS FOR FURTHER READING

Borg, S., and J. Lasker. *When Pregnancy Fails: Families Coping with Miscarriage, Stillbirth, and Infant Death.* Boston: Beacon, 1981.

Fowler, Paul. *Abortion: Toward an Evangelical Consensus.* Portland, Oreg.: Multnomah, 1987.

Love, Vicky. *Childless Is Not Less.* Minneapolis: Bethany House, 1984.*

Speckhard, Anne. *Post Abortion Counseling: A Manual for Counselors.* Falls Church, Va.: Christian Action Council, 1987.

Spring, Beth. *The Infertile Couple.* Elgin, Ill.: David C. Cook, 1987.*

Stanford, Susan. *Will I Cry Tomorrow? Healing Post-Abortion Trauma.* Old Tappan, N.J.: Revell, 1987.*

Stephenson, Linda. *Give Us a Child.* New York: Harper & Row, 1987.*

Stigger, Judith A. *Coping with Infertility: A Guide for Couples, Families, and Counselors.* Minneapolis: Augsburg, 1983.*

Stout, Martha. *Without Child: A Compassionate Look at Infertility.* Grand Rapids, Mich.: Zondervan, 1985.*

Strom, Kay Marshall. *Helping Women in Crisis.* Grand Rapids, Mich.: Zondervan, 1986.

Worthington, Everett L. *Counseling for Unplanned Pregnancy and Infertility.* Waco, Tex.: Word, 1987.

Young, Curt. *The Least of These: What Everyone Should Know about Abortion.* Chicago: Moody, 1983.*

* Books marked with an asterisk (*) are especially suited for counselees to read.

29 Family Problems

CHRIS RECENTLY CELEBRATED her sixteenth birthday—but nobody gave her a party. Her mother gave her a present but didn't want the house disrupted by "a bunch of teenagers who would make a mess." Chris's dad called to wish her a happy birthday, but he was too busy at the office to get away for any celebrating. Cheri, who is twelve, doesn't like her family, so she stays away from home as much as possible. One other sister, Cindy, is now twenty-three, but she is in no mood to celebrate birthdays—especially this year. After three rocky years of misery and mate beating, Cindy recently divorced her husband and is trying now to put her life back together.

The members of Chris's family all claim to be Christians. On any Sunday morning, two or three of them are likely to be in church, but they never sit together and usually they come in different cars. Religion is never mentioned in the home and Christ doesn't seem to be very important in the daily lives of the family members.

Chris belongs to a family where everybody sleeps in the same house, but where each person lives a life that is largely independent of the others. The family never eats together, even at Thanksgiving or Christmas, and it is rare to find all five family members in the house at the same time.

This family, however, is not as splintered at it looks; Chris's mother holds it all together. Her strong, opinionated personality is difficult to resist—which may explain why her husband is gone from home most of the time. She has a great ability to manipulate family members, often by making them feel guilty and dependent on her approval.

Chris looks forward to the time when she will be eighteen and able to leave home to attend college. Those people who know the family wonder if the girls will ever be able to break away. The family members all seem to need each other, but they get along best by avoiding one another and keeping mother happy. Unless they encounter a major crisis, it is unlikely that the family will ever come for counseling.

Robert Coles is a Pulitzer-Prize-winning Harvard psychiatrist whose professional career has focused on the study of children. "I was brought up in a family," Coles recently told a group of professional family therapists. "Many of the children who became my teachers also came from families. Yet, I was not trained to *think of the family as a means by which people pull together, learn from one another, gain mutual strength, and sometimes collectively fail, but still nevertheless persist*." Instead Coles' psychiatric training emphasized individuals filled with "defenses working against impulses and struggling with a superego."[1]

Many counselors have had similar experiences. Trained to see counselees as individuals, we have tended to ignore the family or to see it as a frequently disruptive influence in the lives of the people with whom we work. Influenced by the media or by reports from our counseling sessions, it is easy to conclude that families today are most often characterized by conflict, verbal and physical abuse, incest, infidelity, crises, selfish individualism, insensitivity, and instability.

Dolores Curran would challenge this conclusion. While she freely admits that many families have problems, this educator and columnist decided several years ago that we need to look at the positive side of family life. Based on a survey of five hundred people who work with families, Curran found that healthy families can and do exist. According to Curran's research, the healthy family:

- Communicates and listens.
- Affirms and supports one another.
- Teaches respect for others.
- Develops a sense of trust.
- Has a sense of play and humor.
- Exhibits a sense of shared responsibility.
- Teaches a sense of right and wrong.
- Has a strong sense of family in which rituals and traditions abound.
- Has a balance of interaction among members.
- Has a shared religious core.
- Respects the privacy of one another.
- Values service to others.
- Fosters family table time and conversation.
- Shares leisure time.
- Admits to and seeks help with problems.[2]

Many families lack these characteristics, however, and sometimes these families come to counselors for help. Within recent years, family counseling has become an increasingly complex and diversified speciality within the counseling field. There are a number of well-developed theories of family therapy,[3] perhaps several hundred widely used family intervention techniques,[4] and various counseling goals. At the core of this diversity, however, there is general agreement that family counseling exists to improve the functioning of dysfunctional families, to teach families how to cope with their stresses, and to build healthy family relationships.

The Bible and Family Problems

Families are mentioned often in the Bible, and the pages of Scripture give many examples of family tensions. The first family, that of Adam and Eve, was disrupted by murder when Cain killed his brother. Abraham had family problems when his wife Sarai had continuing conflict with Hagar, a maidservant, and her son, Ishmael, whom Abraham had fathered. Jacob and Esau were twin brothers whose lifelong conflict was complicated when their mother, Rebekah, sided with Jacob in the dispute. When he had a family of his own, Jacob mourned because his favorite son Joseph was rejected by his jealous brothers and sold into Egyptian slavery. Many years later, David's children were at odds with each other, and the king himself had to flee from his own son, Absalom. Subsequent rulers had similar problems; 1 and 2 Kings, for example, gives a history of numerous royal families where murder and family conflict were common.

Especially poignant is the Old Testament account of Eli, the high priest who raised young Samuel. Eli was a faithful servant of the Lord, but he failed as a father, perhaps because he was more involved in his ministry than in his duties as a parent. Eli's sons were worthless men who had little respect for spiritual things and engaged openly in sexual immorality.[5] Their father was rebuked and ultimately died because he failed to do anything about the behavior of his irresponsible children.

Despite family conflicts such as these, the Bible says relatively little about how families should function.[6] In the New Testament, for example, Paul never mentions the family in six of his letters, and neither are families mentioned in Hebrews, James,[7] the three epistles of John, Jude, or Revelation. In Colossians, the family is mentioned in only four verses out of ninety-five, and the statements are succinct: "Wives, submit to your husbands, as is fitting in the Lord. Husbands, love your wives and do not be harsh with them. Children, obey your parents in everything, for this pleases the Lord. Fathers, do not embitter your children, or they will become discouraged."[8] A parallel passage in Ephesians is only a little longer,[9] and in the other epistles family issues are mentioned only briefly.[10]

Even though the references are sparse and brief, the biblical teaching on the family appears to support several conclusions. The father is the head of the home, whose responsibilities include loving his wife in a way that demonstrates Christ's love for his children.[11] Within this home there is to be mutual submission and commitment between the husband and wife. The parents in turn are responsible to discipline their children[12] in such a way that they learn obedience but are not made bitter and discouraged.

Why doesn't the Bible say more about family issues and ways to solve problems in the home? Gene A. Getz has given a thought-provoking suggestion:

> Since so many problems in the world—from time immemorial—originate in the home, why hasn't God given us a guidebook for the home? Why aren't larger portions of the New Testament devoted to this important institution? . . .
>
> If we interpret the lack of references to the family per se as elevating the Church above the home in importance, we miss the significant fact that the Christian home in the New Testament world was almost synonymous with the church. . . .
>
> What was written to the Church was also written to individual families. Most of the New Testament, then, can be applied directly to individual family units. We *do* have a guidebook for the family unit! The Church simply becomes an umbrella concept that includes the home. The family is really the *Church in miniature.* True, on occasions the New Testament writers zero in on special needs that are uniquely related to family living. But in the most part, what was written to believers as a whole applies directly to Christian living in the smaller context of the home.[13]

This leads to the conclusion that biblical teachings about interpersonal relations, love, forgiveness, conflict resolution, self-denial, personal integrity, caring, the teaching of biblical principles, maturity, and spiritual growth must all be applied to the family.[14] Perhaps it is valid to conclude that "the whole of the New Testament, and particularly the New Testament correspondence, serves as a guideline for family living."[15]

The Causes of Family Problems

Family members who come for counseling usually need help with a crisis that they can't handle. These crises may be viewed as an $abc = x$ equation where a refers to the stressful event or situation, b equals the family's resources, and c is the way family members view the situation. Together these three influences determine the severity of the crisis x. According to this view,[16] family counseling involves (*a*) helping people reduce the stress, (*b*) learn better coping skills, and/or (*c*) learn to see the situation from a new or different perspective. Each family has to be approached differently since each stress is unique. Each family has its own ability to learn new coping skills, in part because family members differ in their levels of spiritual and emotional maturity.[17]

Because of these uniquenesses it is difficult to summarize the causes of family problems in a few sentences. With most families, however, you are likely to see one or more of the following.

1. *Lack of Interpersonal and Coping Skills.* In their attempts to deal with transition and crisis, many families have trouble coping because they lack the knowledge, skills, and flexibility to change. According to one experienced counselor, families that have difficulty adapting often get entangled in family "snag points"—attitudes and behaviors that impede flexibility and hinder readjustment. These snag points can be of different types:[18]

Snag points about communication come when family members don't know how to share feelings or express themselves clearly. Some families have taboo topics. They never talk about money, sex, spiritual issues, or feelings. Other family members never laugh when they are at home, rarely say what they think, fail to listen, or never communicate without yelling or the use of sarcasm and other destructive forms of communication. Some family members give double messages: their words say one thing but their actions say something different. It is difficult for a family to cope with a crisis if the family members can't communicate effectively.

Snag points about intimacy characterize families that have little closeness. Sometimes the family members are afraid of intimacy. They don't spend time together, may not trust or respect one another, rarely share problems, and have difficulty handling crises because they have never learned to work together closely.

Snag points about rules are unwritten, often unspoken, but generally accepted laws about who can't do what. Some families have almost no rules; this can be confusing especially to the children. Other families have rigid rules that stifle the growth of individual family members. Religious families, families that are attempting to advance socially, families that have at least one prominent member, military families, and some minority group families have all been identified as often having tight rules that can prevent flexibility, exclude outside sources of help, and hinder coping in times of stress.

Snag points about family history include secrets that no family member is supposed to reveal or issues that "our family doesn't discuss." Sometimes family members keep secrets from each other—like an illegitimate pregnancy, a retarded child who was given up, a previous marriage and divorce, or a debt not reported. This deception keeps some family members always on guard and others suspicious about what they suspect but don't know. Sometimes the family members all know about family secrets but keep these hidden because of family honor. All this can hinder honest coping in times of crisis when honesty is important.

Snag points about goals deal with the economic, academic, social, political, or other goals that some family members set for themselves or for other family members. One Christian pastor decided that all three of his sons would enter the ministry. When one of the sons rebelled openly against this goal and another resisted passively, the father repeatedly reacted with outbursts of anger. It can be healthy to have family goals and ambitions, but when these are held rigidly or when one family member sets the goals for another, there can be trouble, especially when things don't turn out as expected. Life rarely proceeds smoothly and families that can't readjust their goals often have problems.

Snag points about values are ways of thinking that often are just accepted until one or more of the family members begins to think otherwise. "Everybody in our family goes to college," "women in our family never work outside the home," "nobody in our family ever drinks," "everybody in our family is Presbyterian," can be examples of strongly held values that some, often younger, family members may challenge. When families aren't willing or able to adapt to changes, conflict often follows.

To this list, we might add snag points related to triangulation and detouring. These two technical words describe behavior that often appears in families.[19] A triangle is a group of three people in which two exclude the third. A mother and daughter may form a coalition against the father, for example. One of the parents may enlist a child as an ally in struggles with the other parent. Sometimes a husband and his mistress are aligned against the wife. Triangulated families rarely (if ever) function smoothly.

Detouring is another word for scapegoating. By criticizing a rebellious son, a daughter who refuses to eat, or a school teacher whom they call incompetent, parents are kept too busy to argue with each other. More basic problems, like a marriage conflict, are ignored or pushed aside so the couple can battle against a common enemy. It would appear that these kinds of detours appear often in church families. By fighting sin, or getting involved in church politics, family members temporarily are spared the pain of dealing with serious problems within their own homes.

2. *Lack of Commitment to the Family.* It is difficult to build family togetherness and to deal with problems when one or more members of the family have no desire or time to be involved. Some career-motivated people work for companies that expect 100 percent commitment from their employees. The job requires a willingness to work long and hard for the company "family." Employees often have little energy or desire to build rapport at home or to deal with evolving problems.[20]

Family counselors sometimes struggle with the ethical issues of trying to force unwilling family members to participate in problem solving.[21] Often an unwilling or busy family member can be persuaded to come for at least one session, and at times this can be a means of getting longer commitment to family issues. Often, however, you will have to work with willing family members, realizing that coping will be more difficult when some members of the family are too busy or unmotivated to be involved.

3. *Lack of Role Clarity.* Each family assigns roles to its members.[22] Some of these roles involve activities; like who takes out the garbage, writes the checks, cooks the meals, or takes the kids to the dentist. Other roles are emotional; some family members become encouragers, jokers, problem solvers, or etiquette advisers. Usually these roles evolve slowly at the beginning of a marriage but sometimes there are conflicts over who does what. These conflicts are especially acute when roles are held rigidly or when there is role confusion.

Psychologist Paul Vitz recently reviewed sixty social studies textbooks that are used in elementary schools. In the almost fifteen thousand pages of these books, religion was never mentioned and families were described vaguely. One textbook defined the family as "a group of people," and within the books, the words "husband" or "wife" were never used, "marriage" was mentioned only once, the word "homemaker" did not occur, and there wasn't one mention of the family with clearly traditional sex roles.[23]

The family, of course, is changing. The old model of one woman married for a lifetime to the same one man, who works together with his spouse to raise two or three children, is an increasingly rare family picture in our culture. More often we see single-parent families; marital instability that leads to divorces, remarriage, and the formation of stepfamilies; parent-child role reversals where the young person adopts parental behaviors (such as caretaking, supporting, or nurturing) and the parent seeks to please the children or to gain the child's approval; parent-child coalitions in which each parent sides with one or two children against the other parent and his or her family allies; or parent-child overinvolvement where parents become enmeshed in their children's activities, schoolwork, and lifestyles.[24] It hardly is surprising that some family members, including young children, are confused about their roles and immobilized when a crisis creates pressure and nobody knows who is supposed to do what.

4. *Lack of Environmental Stability.* Problems in the family often come from outside the home. Already we have mentioned the crises, changing social views about the family, and work pressures that create chaos in some homes. Television has stifled communication in many homes, replaced togetherness, and presented programs that paint a generally negative view of the family.[25] In addition, there are frequent moves, company mergers, unexpected job losses, or economic trends that throw some families out of their homes and places of employment.[26] In addition, there may be the discovery of AIDS in a family member, the decision of one family member (sometimes the father) to run away and desert the family, the emergence of domestic violence, one family member's use of drugs or alcohol, or the interference of in-laws and others who can disrupt family stability.

The Effects of Family Problems

More than 2,300 years ago, Plato suggested that newborn children communicate with their care givers by crying and screaming. This idea is now widely accepted, but less common is the view that older children and adults also communicate at times through unusual or antisocial behavior.[27] When a family has problems or comes for counseling, often there is concern about one individual, such as an alcoholic mother, an abusive father, a runaway teenager, or a rebellious and uncontrollable ten-year-old. The attitudes and disruptive behaviors of these problem family members often are signals to indicate that instability exists in the whole family. Like a baby's crying communicates that something is wrong, so the older family member's misbehavior can be a clue that all is not well within the home.

Family problems can influence people in a variety of ways. Despair, frustration, sadness, anger, anxiety, or feelings of helplessness are often mentioned in family counseling sessions. Family violence or verbal abuse may reflect frustration over family problems, and sometimes more than one family member will withdraw physically or try to escape from problems with the help of alcohol or other drugs. Sexual immorality, adjustment difficulties, negativism, delinquency, academic problems, depression, psychological withdrawal, communication breakdowns, declines in work efficiency, career indecision, and even incest have all been observed as an outgrowth of family tensions.[28]

Sometimes family problems are kept well hidden from outsiders. Only within the privacy of the home is there evidence of family pressure. In addition to the communication breakdowns that have been mentioned earlier, members of dysfunctional families may avoid or ignore one another, physically or sexually abuse one another, attempt to manipulate or control one another, blame each other for the family problems, or hurt one another verbally with critical, judgmental, sarcastic, or put-down comments. Often there is a lack of trust, feelings of low self-esteem, noncooperation, bickering, and sometimes placating—handling each other with "kid gloves"—in an attempt to maintain peace within a volatile home situation.[29]

Spiritual growth is possible but surely difficult in an environment such as this. It is not easy to be a maturing Christian when one's home life is filled with conflict and destructive interpersonal behaviors and attitudes.

Counseling and Family Problems

Counselors tend to focus on the negative. People come to us with stories of misery and conflict, so it is easy to miss the bright side of family life today. A report from the American Psychiatric Association has suggested, however, that the changing family may not all be negative. In spite of high divorce rates, the duration of marriage has increased within recent years. Three-fourths of first marriages are expected to last twenty years, half will continue past thirty, and one in five couples will celebrate their golden anniversary. Despite the high rates of teenage pregnancy and the large numbers of latchkey kids, smaller families have given many children more intimate contact with their parents, educational opportunities are better, and many women have been able to combine careers and parenthood successfully.[30]

At times, however, even the best families have problems, and some may come to you for counseling. As a family counselor you could use one of several theoretical approaches to family therapy. Many of these are summarized in Table 29-1 and most are described in greater detail by the authors of family therapy books.[31] Many of the frequently used approaches are identified with the names of their developers: Bowen's Family Systems Therapy, Satir's Conjoint Family Therapy, Haley's Problem-Solving Therapy, Minuchin's Structural Therapy, Patterson's Social Learning Therapy, and Ackerman's Biopsychsocial Therapy are among the best known.

Table 29-1

Approaches to Marriage and Family Counseling

Approach	*Special Features*
Classical	This is the traditional psychoanalytic approach. One family member who is viewed as the patient enters long-term counseling with the therapist who uses therapeutic methods to treat individual problems. As the individual improves, it is assumed that the marriage and family will be affected positively.
Collaborative	In this approach a husband and wife, or two or more other family members are seen individually by different counselors. Counselors may confer periodically, comparing notes and sharing information that can be mutually beneficial.
Concurrent	Here different family members are seen separately but by the same counselor. This gives one counselor the perspective of different family members, but some critics have wondered about favoritism or the counselor's ability to remain neutral and refrain from taking sides. A variation of this is consecutive counseling in which one mate or family member is seen for counseling and then, following termination, another family member is seen.
Conjoint	Here the family is seen together. The counselor assumes that the family operates as a social system. Counseling teaches everyone in the system to act differently so there is greater understanding, better communication, and less harmful behavior.
Changed Behavior	These are learning approaches to Behavior counseling. Problems are defined in terms of behavior that one or more family members would like to see terminated, decreased, increased, modified, or developed. In counseling harmful behaviors are unlearned and new skills and behaviors are learned.
Crisis	Here the counselor assumes that whole families will come for help in dealing with their crises. The family is seen together and helped in several ways: • Giving immediate aid—the counselor is available when needed; • Defining the problem as a family need, rather than as an individual problem, even though one family member may be showing the major symptoms; • Focusing on the present, rather than analyzing the past; • Reducing family tensions by psychological and sometimes pharmacological means; • Helping to deal with the crisis-producing stress: this also teaches families how to solve problems; and • Identifying sources of referral where families can be helped in the future.
Conflict Resolution	Working with whole families, the counselor attempts to teach conflict resolution and problem-solving skills. Sometimes there is an attempt to change the entire family structure by assigning new tasks, teaching new roles, changing rules, or teaching new communication skills.
Contract	Here married couples and family members are helped to make and keep family agreements in which there are agreed-upon *performances* or behaviors that lead either to special *privileges* (as rewards for something accomplished) or to *punishment*. This is a form of behavior change therapy in which all participants agree on the behavior to be changed and everybody agrees on the consequences to follow if there is change or no change.
Combined	This is a combination of two or more of the above. This is a "catch-all" approach that may be difficult to apply in practice.

Apart from these theories, there are two major ways that we can view the family in counseling. The family can be a support system in which the members *give* help and guidance to one another, or the family as a unit can be viewed as a therapy system that can *receive* counseling help and treatment.

1. *The Family as a Support System.* Although many families are scattered geographically or split by disagreements and tension, the extended family (which includes grandparents, aunts, uncles, and cousins) nevertheless provides help in a variety of ways.[32] Ideally the family:

- Collects and disseminates information about the world.
- Gives values and guides in the development of religious beliefs and ethical standards.
- Provides a place where individuals can get feedback about their behavior.
- Teaches basic skills, including human relations and conflict resolution skills.
- Gives guidance in solving problems.
- Provides information about outside sources of help.
- Mediates disputes.
- Gives practical assistance when needs arise.
- Is a haven for rest, recuperation, and recreation.
- Gives people an identity and a place to feel accepted.
- Controls behavior when it gets out of line.
- Helps individuals master emotions such as anxiety, depression, guilt, doubt, or feelings of helplessness.
- Gives support during crises and through the much longer periods involved in adjusting to loss and separation.

Like individuals, families change and go through cycles. The preschooler, for example, has a different family experience than he or she will encounter as a college student, a newly married adult, or the parent of two or three children. When our children become teenagers, when they leave the home and get married, and when we reach later life, our experiences as family members change further. If there is divorce, remarriage, serious sickness, or the death of family members, the whole family experience changes again.[33]

As these changes occur, the family members often support, help, guide, and encourage one another. Even in dysfunctional families where strife and bickering are common, family members tend to hold up one another in times of change and crisis.

Frequently the family members are helped by neighbors, friends, coworkers, and fellow church members. Professionals refer to this network of relatives and friends as a support system.[34] Most of us get help from the system of people who back us up, and most of us are part of several systems that help and support others. In addition to giving care and guidance, support systems provide acceptance, training in social and coping skills, encouragement during times of change, help with will power or self-control, and a reason to hope. There is evidence that people who have well-developed support systems tend to have less mental and physical illness and are better able to cope with stress.[35]

Although many people think of the family as their major support system, at times whole families need support. Often this support comes from individuals and other families in the community, and often the help comes from the church. Working together, families in the church can help other families and individuals meet crises and cope with the realities of life. As adjuncts to Christian counseling, including family counseling, supportive families within the church and community are without parallel.

2. *The Family as a Therapy System.* There are times, however, when the family is part (sometimes a major part) of the counselee's problems. Even when family members sincerely want to be helpful, they sometimes interfere with counseling and create more stress than they relieve. Because of these influences, many counselors prefer to work with whole families, even when only one family member is assumed to have a problem.

Family counselors often assume that an individual's problems *never* exist in isolation. As we have seen, the family does much to shape human behavior, provide values and beliefs, and teach people how to deal with crises. If an individual family member is having problems, this may indicate as much or more about the counselee's family attitudes and communication as it does about the counselee. The person who comes for counseling, then, may be a symptom bearer whose highly visible problems signal that something is amiss in the family. Treating the counselee will not help much if he or she continues to live in an unhealthy family. Indeed if the counselee starts to change behavior and improve, this could create confusion and even chaos in a family's ways of operating. The family confusion in turn could create more problems for the counselee.

Consider, for example, a three-person family with an alcoholic father. As long as the father is drinking, the mother and child may have a clear purpose: to protect and provide for themselves and to work at changing the alcoholic's drinking behavior. Let us assume, however, that the alcoholic goes for treatment, stops drinking, and determines to assume his role as head of the family. Suddenly the child, but especially the mother, may feel that there is less purpose for living. As a result she may get depressed, so the father and child team up to care for the mother. In one family (and probably in many more) a seesaw arrangement like this continued for years. Whenever the husband was drinking, the wife complained but otherwise was fine. When he stopped drinking, she became depressed and so hard to live with that he started drinking again. When this happened, she improved, and the cycle continued. In the meantime, the child grew up in a perpetually unstable home.

Clearly this family could benefit from help and that is the goal of the systems approach to counseling. An individual's problems do not exist in social isolation, according to systems theorists. "Given that the family is crucial in shaping human behavior, it follows that for all human relations to improve, families must change their ways of functioning so they will not nurture harmful modes of interaction and perpetuate ineffective or damaging models of behavior."[36] The systems counselor attempts to help families replace old behavior with new and better ways to cope.

While the individual counselee may be seen alone occasionally, it is more common for family members to come together for counseling as a unit. The counselor watches the family interact, points out their characteristic ways of relating, mediates their disputes, and teaches them more effective ways to communicate and relate to one another. The family members learn how to listen, to express their thoughts and feelings, to be flexible, to understand one another, to deal more effectively with conflict, and to develop a greater sense of mutual awareness and support. Occasionally a family will discover that something simple, like initiating family celebrations, can help to reduce tension and stimulate family togetherness.[37] Sometimes as they work together, family members come up with problem solutions of their own, solutions that they can try and discuss in later counseling sessions. In many respects, therefore, family counseling is a specialized form of group counseling in which all the group members are related to one another.[38]

As with other forms of counseling, family approaches work best if there is at least minimal direction. One highly experienced therapist suggests a seven-step process.[39]

Step 1: Responding to an Emergency. Families most often request counseling in response to a crisis or emergency. The counselor's first task is to give reassurance and express a willingness to help. Sometimes you can make immediate suggestions that enable the family to hang on until there is time to meet for an appointment. That initial appointment should come soon; on occasion you may decide to meet with the family immediately. Even in this time of crisis, however, try not to take over or allow family members to become dependent on you. Your job is to give direction without taking control.

Step 2: Finding a Family Focus. Often the family concludes that one member is the source of the problems. Everybody encourages you to work with that problem person. They may be surprised when you suggest that the whole family should be involved in counseling. Sometimes you may have to start with the problem person and slowly pull in the other family members.

"I see whoever comes," writes family therapist Frank Pittman. If somebody is important but absent, this counselor calls or writes a note to explain why the whole family should be seen together. Children are not always encouraged to be present since they tend to be disruptive. "The group to be assembled is not based on biology or proximity or fault, but on power. Whoever has the power to sanction or prohibit change must be included."[40]

Step 3: Defining the Crisis. As you listen to family members describe the problem, try to find answers to several questions. What brought on this crisis? Why did it happen now? When was the last time there was peace in the family before the crisis? Has something like this ever happened before?

It may take several sessions before you begin to make sense of the situation. Sometimes you will have to keep probing until you get a clear picture of the family's problems and ways of interacting. You may have to admit repeatedly "I don't understand" or "Tell me more about that" until things do make sense to you. One therapist periodically holds private consultations with different family members,[41] based on the assumption that one or two people in the family, including children or grandparents, may be able to give a clearer picture of the family dynamics.[42]

Step 4: Calming Everyone Down. Before the family can work to improve the situation, it may be necessary to give reassurance, to model calmness, and to instill hope. At this point you may want to share some of your initial conclusions about what is creating problems in the family.

Step 5: Suggesting Change. This involves making suggestions and gently guiding as people decide what changes should be attempted. You may want to help the family negotiate some contracts—behaviors that each family member will agree to do after the counseling session. You may spend time discussing communication or pointing out how the family members miscommunicate when they are together. There may need to be a reconsideration of family rules, roles, unrealistic expectations, limits, or better ways to get along with one another. Parents may need help in learning to be more assertive.[43] The problem family member may need guidance in changing behavior, and the family may need help in adjusting to this change. The family may need help in learning to relate to each other in ways that are consistent with biblical principles. All this will take time for discussion and practice of new behaviors both within the counseling room and between sessions.

Step 6: Dealing with Resistance to Change. After you begin making suggestions, you quickly discover who cooperates and who resists change. Often the person who most resists is not the previously identified problem family member.[44] Sometimes one or more people will get critical, try to withdraw from counseling, or attempt (perhaps unconsciously) to manipulate other family members so that change is prevented. At times you may need to point out how triangulation and detouring are hindering counseling progress.

At this point you have moved from the stress that created the crisis and are dealing with cherished family snag points. "Negotiating the family's inflexibilities may be a long difficult process—and a threatening one for the family."[45] Here a counselor needs considerable people skills[46] that enable you to keep people motivated to change, even when they feel threatened, guilty, angry, or impatient.

Step 7: Termination. The crisis that brought the family to counseling is likely to disappear in a short time. Your task as a counselor is to help the family cope with the immediate situation and learn how to get over their snag points. This will better equip them for relating to one another and learning how to handle crises in the future. When you or they feel that no further progress is being made, it is time to terminate the counseling. In doing so, try to leave the door open so family members can return for further help if they choose to do so in the future.

Preventing Family Problems

Bill Cosby is a professional entertainer with a doctorate in education and impressive success as a comedian and best-selling author. When his book on fatherhood appeared,[47] thousands of people hurried to bookstores to buy it. Perhaps for many this was the first book they had purchased in years. It is a humorous book that is easy to read, but interspersed with the anecdotes are some genuine guidelines for being an effective parent.

Professionals who write about the family often give more direct guidelines for preventing problems. In his excellent volume on family ministry, for example, Charles Sell writes about the usefulness of church-sponsored seminars and family life conferences, teaching about the family in Sunday school classes and sermons, training couples in marriage enrichment and parenting skills, stimulating family devotions, encouraging regular family nights especially in homes where there are young children, initiating programs of family camping, or developing family clusters in which several families meet together periodically to encourage each other and share their concerns and problems.[48]

Many people, however, avoid these kinds of programs. Since most are centered in the local church, nonattenders may miss opportunities for training and family enrichment that come through local congregations. Is it possible that radio or television programs and more popular books like Cosby's are the only preventive help that some people will get?

The Christian counselor must learn to be creative in preventing family problems. In addition to church-based prevention programs, it may be wise to work with schools, parent-teacher organizations, community service clubs (like Rotary or Kiwanis), government agencies, the media, or established family ministries.[49] The secular agencies may have values and views on the family that differ from those of Christians,[50] but unless we can penetrate the community with guidelines for family living, we are likely to see a continuation of the problems that bring so many people for family counseling.

Conclusions about Family Problems

Some families have problems or unique experiences that are shared by only a few others. Military families,[51] families of the mentally ill,[52] families of professional counselors,[53] minister's families,[54] families of famous people, families of professional athletes, homeless families,[55] the families of alcoholics,[56] families with young children,[57] families of the terminally ill, prisoner's families,[58] or families of AIDS victims[59] are among those who have unique needs and stresses that may require special counseling expertise.

No one counselor can be familiar with all of these groups. Each of us can listen, however, and each of us can learn from families even as we work with them. The counselor's goal is to be available, willing to be used by God to touch lives, and sensitive to the Holy Spirit's guidance as we seek to bring healing into the families who need help.

In spite of our best efforts, however, some families break up and marriages end in divorce. This is the topic to which we turn in the next chapter.

SUGGESTIONS FOR FURTHER READING

Boyer, Patricia A., and Ronnald J. Jeffrey. *A Guide for the Family Therapist.* New York: Jason Aronson, 1984.

Curran, Dolores. *Traits of a Healthy Family.* Minneapolis: Winston, 1983.*

Figley, Charles R., and Hamilton I. McCubbin. *Stress and the Family.* New York: Brunner/Mazel, 1983. Vol. 1: Coping with Normative Transitions. Vol. 2: Coping with Catastrophe.

Pittman, Frank S., III. *Turning Points: Treating Families in Transition and Crisis.* New York: Norton, 1987.

Rekers, George A. *Counseling Families.* Waco, Tex.: Word, 1988.

———, ed. *Family Building: Six Qualities of a Strong Family.* Ventura, Calif.: Regal, 1985.*

Sell, Charles M. *Family Ministry: The Enrichment of Family Life through the Church.* Grand Rapids, Mich.: Zondervan, 1981.

Sherman, Robert, and Norman Fredman, *Handbook of Structured Techniques in Marriage and Family Therapy.* New York: Brunner/Mazel, 1986.

Welter, Paul. *Family Problems and Predicaments: How to Respond.* Wheaton, Ill.: Tyndale, 1977.

* Books marked with an asterisk (*) are especially suited for counselees to read.

30 Divorce and Remarriage

EVER SINCE HE WAS a teenager, Jim has wanted to go into the ministry. His parents, devout Christians and active church members, have supported their son's vocational goals from the beginning and have contributed as much as they can to help pay the costs of tuition and other educational expenses.

After graduating from high school, Jim enrolled at a well-known Christian college where he majored in communications and took a minor in psychology. It was there that he met and married Sue. Also from a Christian family, Sue was enthusiastic about being a pastor's wife. The young couple talked about missions and wondered if God would lead them to serve overseas. Both musicians, they sang together in a Christian musical group and eagerly anticipated their ministry together.

The problems started after Jim began seminary. The academic program was heavy and finances were tight. Communication was less frequent than it had been in the early days of their marriage, and there seemed to be less and less time for sex. After a year working in an insurance office, Sue began to talk about wanting to quit so they could start a family—but this seemed impossible in view of the two years remaining in Jim's seminary program.

Jim still finds it hard to talk about what happened next. One night he came home from the library and discovered that Sue had moved out of their little campus apartment. In a short, somewhat curt note taped to the refrigerator, Sue wrote that she had moved in with her "boyfriend" and added that she was pregnant with his baby. "Don't bother to look for me," she added. "I'm not coming back!"

The next weeks were a nightmare for Jim. His parents and in-laws appeared to be as distressed as he was, but it soon became clear that Sue had no intention of returning to her husband. Jim couldn't concentrate on his studies and his grades went down. His friends, faculty adviser, and pastor all tried to be supportive, but Jim sunk deeper into depression. He felt rejected, betrayed, guilty, a failure. He was angry with Sue, angry with himself, and even angry with God. His career seemed to be on the rocks; he was well aware that his denomination would not ordain anyone who had been divorced.

Jim is still in seminary, but his heart isn't in his studies. Preparing for "some kind of ministry," Jim wonders if he will ever find a place of service. He isn't sure if the Scriptures permit remarriage for a man like him. He wonders if he ever will be able to trust a woman again, or if any woman would want a man whose marriage has failed.

Divorce is never easy. Even when a couple agrees to terminate their marriage, it hurts to separate. Guilt, anger, resentment, fear, and disappointment often dominate the divorced person's thinking. Frequently there is loneliness, confusion, lowered self-esteem, insecurity, a sense of rejection, and the haunting concern about who was at fault. When children are involved, the pain is even greater as sensitive parents watch innocent young people suffer because their families have been torn apart. Somebody has suggested that no one wins in a divorce. Everybody loses: the couple, their children, their parents, and the community at large.

It is well known that divorce is common, especially in the United States, Canada, and Western Europe. Television dramas, soap operas, and Hollywood films often dismiss the idea of marriage as a lifelong commitment. Divorce is portrayed as a welcome route to freedom or a convenient escape hatch from the difficulties of marriage. Millions of people, including Christians, may disapprove of these views, but we have learned to accept infidelity, illegitimacy, and divorce as a way of life for many in modern society.

Sermons, intellectual discussions, and divorce recovery workshops may deal honestly with the issues, but these rarely remove the pain that so often accompanies a broken marriage. "When I conduct coping-with-divorce seminars," said the minister of counseling at a large midwestern church, "the people don't just sit there and listen. Many of them cry!"

The Bible and Divorce

The difficulties of marriage and the pain of divorce have led some compassionate Christians to reinterpret or deemphasize biblical teachings in an effort to make divorce and remarriage seem easier and more acceptable theologically. Ignoring or deemphasizing biblical teaching, however, is neither compassionate nor helpful. If we are to be effective, Christian counselors must have a clear understanding of the scriptural statements about divorce and remarriage.

Regrettably biblical scholars themselves are divided in their conclusions. Most writers tend to fall into one of four categories,[1] each of which has strong advocates. First, there are those who conclude that marriage is for life, that divorce is never permitted on biblical grounds, and that remarriage of a divorced person always is adultery.[2] Second, some conclude that there are legitimate biblical grounds for divorce and that remarriage is permitted under these circumstances.[3] Third, another group contends that some circumstances arise in marriage that defy solution. Divorce then becomes necessary for the sake of the mental, emotional, or physical health of one of the spouses or their children. This conclusion is based less on specific biblical teaching and more on general biblical principles.[4] Fourth, a view held mostly by Roman Catholic writers, allows for a church court to annul a marriage and pave the way for remarriage.[5]

1. *The Teachings of the Old Testament.* The Bible clearly presents marriage as a permanent, intimate union between a husband and wife.[6] This is God's unchanging ideal, but since the fall, human beings have lived on a subideal level. The Bible recognizes this, and so in Deut. 24:1–4 there are brief guidelines that govern the practice of divorce—a practice that is tolerated but never commanded or divinely encouraged.

According to the Old Testament, divorce was to be legal (with a written document), permanent, and permissible only when "uncleanness" was involved.

Regrettably, the meaning of "uncleanness" became a subject for debate. Some maintained that it included any inappropriate behavior; others restricted the term and argued that uncleanness referred only to sexual infidelity. Jesus seems to have agreed with this second view.[7]

2. *The Teachings of Jesus.* In the New Testament, Jesus reaffirmed the permanent nature of marriage, pointed out that divine permission for divorce was only given because of human sinfulness (and not because it was God's ideal), stated that sexual immorality was the only legitimate cause for divorce, and clearly taught that the one who divorces a sexually faithful spouse and marries another commits adultery (and causes the new mate to also commit adultery).[8]

Like the Jewish leaders who questioned the meaning of uncleanness, some modern scholars have debated the meaning of "except for marital unfaithfulness" in Matt. 5:32 and 19:9. The Greek word for unfaithfulness is *porneia,* which refers to all sexual intercourse apart from marriage. This behavior violates the one-flesh concept that is so basic to biblical marriage.

Even when unfaithfulness is involved, divorce is not commanded, it merely is permitted. Forgiveness and reconciliation still are preferable to divorce. Nevertheless, if divorce does occur under these circumstances, it is the opinion of many evangelical biblical scholars that the innocent party is free to remarry.

3. *The Teachings of Paul.* In responding to a question from the Corinthians, the apostle echoes Christ's teaching and then adds a second permissible cause for divorce: desertion by an unbelieving mate.[9] This same passage deals with religious incompatibility—when a believer and an unbeliever are married. These theologically mixed marriages are not to be ended in divorce (except when the unbeliever deserts), even though the differences in religious beliefs may create tension in the home. By staying married, the believing mate sanctifies the marriage, Paul writes, and in time the nonbelieving mate may be brought to Christ.

4. *The Teachings on Remarriage.* The controversy over divorce in Jewish circles, at least until the time of Christ, centered on the causes of divorce. Some in the Jewish community never questioned the right to remarry once divorce occurred. In contrast, the focus of modern evangelical discussion has centered on the question of remarriage.

According to one team of writers,

> Deuteronomy 24:2 proves that divorce dissolves a marriage and gives the right to remarry. It does not require remarriage but grants the right if the party wishes to do so. . . .
>
> The exceptive clause of Matthew 5:32 and Matthew 19:9 clearly indicates that where the mate has practiced fornication (porneia) and a divorce occurs, the faithful partner has the right to remarry. Jesus seems to teach here that while divorce dissolves the contract, habitual immorality dissolves the covenant and therefore gives the faithful partner an opportunity to remarry. Jesus does not command remarriage. However, it is clear from Matthew 19:9 that Jesus assumes that a remarriage will take place. . . .
>
> In 1 Corinthians 7:15 . . . since it is the unbelieving partner who determines to go and initiates a divorce, . . . the believer is set free to marry if he or she so chooses. Again, remarriage is not commanded.[10]

Even if remarriage is permitted, it isn't always wise. Paul urged the unmarried (this could include the formerly married) to remain single,[11] and many would agree with a modern writer who suggested reasons for not remarrying.[12] If past problems have not been corrected or resolved, if the individual does not have a clear conscience about remarriage, or if there is no strong desire to enter a second marriage, then it is best to stay single.

4. *The Teachings Summarized.* Most Bible-believing Christians agree that God intended marriage to be a permanent and exclusive union between a man and woman who find their sexual fulfillment within marriage. Divorce is nowhere commanded in Scripture and neither is it encouraged.

Divorce is permissible on only two grounds. First, when one's mate is guilty of sexual immorality and unwilling to repent and live faithfully with the marriage partner.[13] Second, when one of the mates is an unbeliever who willfully and permanently deserts the believing partner.[14]

"No Christian should aggressively seek the dissolution of his or her marriage bond," wrote Charles Swindoll, but "in certain extreme cases, against the wishes and efforts of the committed mate, the marriage bond is destroyed beyond any human ability to restore it." God, in his grace and as a "divine concession to human weakness," then allows divorce. In the opinion of many biblical scholars, the Christian divorced person has the right and freedom to remarry "in the Lord," if that divorced person attempted reconciliation without success, and ended the marriage in accordance with biblical guidelines.[15]

5. *Three Lingering Issues.* To this must be added three additional comments. First, the Bible says nothing about the divorce of two nonbelievers. Clearly this is undesirable since it violates God's one-flesh ideal and often involves adultery, a behavior that is always sinful regardless of a person's beliefs. Nevertheless there are no specific divine guidelines for non-Christian divorce. Many would agree that an individual who was married and divorced prior to salvation is free to remarry after becoming a Christian.[16]

Second, we must emphasize the importance of forgiveness. God hates divorce[17] and forbids adultery,[18] but these are not unpardonable sins. God forgives and expects his followers to do the same.[19] It is wrong (and surely sinful) for Christians to treat the divorced as if they are second-class people, forbidden to participate in public services or to take any leadership positions.[20] Whenever sin is forgiven, we are to stop dwelling on the past and instead must focus our attention on living in ways that are pure and free from further sin.[21]

Third, all of this seems to overlook those marriages where there is no infidelity or desertion, but where homes are filled with violence, physical and mental abuse, deviant forms of sexual behavior (including forced incest), foul language, failure to provide for a family's physical needs, alcoholism, a refusal to let other family members worship, or a variety of other destructive influences. Emotional and physical harm, along with the fear and mental anguish that they create, can make home a hell rather than a heaven. Some mates try to defend themselves and their children, believing that to stay in a marriage and home where there is violence is better than trying to survive and raise children alone in a hostile world. Often, however, there comes a time when the victim either responds with violence in return or decides to separate from the marriage. Is divorce justified in these circumstances?

Here Scripture appears to be silent and the scholars disagree. Few would encourage the victims of abuse to stay put and suffer in silence. Submitting meekly to physical and mental attack seems to be neither right nor healthy. The abuser is psychologically and spiritually unhealthy. He or she is also sinning and, while such behavior must be forgiven, it cannot be condoned by a mate who passively stands by, says nothing, and lets various family members get hurt.

In itself abuse does not appear to be an accepted biblical cause for divorce (although some divorces occur because of this). The Bible discourages separation but recognizes that this does indeed happen.[22] In many cases a temporary separation may be necessary for the physical, psychological, and spiritual well-being of the abused mate and family members. Sometimes as a result of separation, the recalcitrant, hard-hearted person comes to a place of repentance and reconciliation is possible.[23]

The Causes of Divorce

There is no one cause of divorce. Every marriage is different, and each divorce comes because of a unique combination of causes and circumstances. In previous chapters we have considered some of the causes of marital problems.[24] When these problems are not resolved, divorce is more likely. In addition, the following influences sometimes motivate one or both of the spouses to initiate divorce action. We begin with the two biblically sanctioned reasons for divorce.

1. *Sexual Unfaithfulness.* Infidelity has been called the most common disruptive force in families, the most devastating, and the most universally accepted justification for divorce.[25] It has been estimated that infidelity takes place in at least 70 percent of all marriages, although most unfaithfulness is brief and sometimes a one-time-only, spur-of-the-moment occurrence. Even when the infidelity is confessed and discussed with one's mate, the marriage is likely to be affected.[26]

As we have seen, Jesus cited unfaithfulness as a legitimate reason for divorce. Although both parties may contribute to the adultery in some way, one partner frequently is involved in the actual offense. According to one biblical writer, such adultery "has the effect of aborting or dissolving a marriage union in the eyes of God. . . . This being true, the other partner is not guilty of adultery when getting a divorce."[27]

While divorce is permitted biblically under such circumstances, forgiveness and reconciliation are to be preferred. This is difficult because the innocent partner often feels betrayed, rejected, and hurt. It becomes more difficult to believe that one's spouse can be trusted in the future. Often there is anger, threat, and lowered self-esteem. Yet separation and divorce can be even more painful. The believer knows that all things are possible with God, even the restoration and growth of a marital relationship that has been ruptured by infidelity.

2. *Desertion.* To the words of Moses and Jesus, Paul added desertion as a second legitimate reason for divorce. When an unbelieving partner leaves, the believer is free to divorce.

But what if a believer forsakes the marriage? The New Testament word for "depart" (*koridzetai*) is used thirteen times and in no case does it imply divorce. The word means to depart or separate. If the departed spouse has been involved in sexual immorality or if the departure is so prolonged that there is little prospect of reconciliation, then, writes Stanley Ellison, "a *de facto* divorce will have taken place, whether or not it has been sought or granted. . . . Although God's desire is always for reconciliation, where that is impossible because of the partner's recalcitrance, there is no useful purpose served in refusing to acknowledge dissolution. Desertion in that sense becomes divorce."[28]

3. *Escalating Incompatibility.* Following a whirlwind romance, one couple married within a month and soon began having problems. He enjoyed sailing; boats made her seasick. She liked to socialize with other couples; he wanted her company alone. He liked to have sex in the morning; she preferred evenings. Their relationship had genuine good times with laughter and happiness, but as the months passed there were more arguments, disagreements, and misunderstandings. The counselor described this couple's deteriorating relationship as evidence of their growing incompatibility. Each was willing to work on the marriage, but they had almost nothing in common, so eventually they decided to get a divorce.[29]

While there is no biblical basis for separations such as this, many couples reach the point of being fed up with their dull, unrewarding, and seemingly incompatible relationships. Within recent years there has been a sharp increase in the numbers of people who get divorces after ten, twenty, or more years of marriage.[30] Perhaps some of these people waited until the children were older before leaving the mates with whom they felt so incompatible.

4. *Social Sanctions.* Recent changes in social attitudes and values have made divorce easier and more acceptable. Legal barriers to divorce have been lowered, the media has become more supportive of infidelity, some segments of academia and the women's liberation movement have become more verbal in encouraging divorce, the church has become more permissive, and many people have become less inclined to accept the sanctity and permanence of marriage. Monogamy may have come back into fashion,[31] but some people maintain the view that self-realization, career advancement, and personal fulfillment are such major goals in life that everything else—including a commitment to marriage—must take second place. These social attitudes combine to make divorce a more viable option when marital tensions arise.

5. *Immature Attitudes.* Sometimes divorce comes because of immaturity in one or both of the partners. Immaturity is difficult to define, but it surely includes an unwillingness to make and keep commitments, a disinclination to assume responsibility, a tendency to dominate, an insensitivity to the needs or interests of other people, and a self-centered view of life that insists upon the fulfillment of one's own wishes and rights. Attitudes like these stimulate conflict and work against attempts both to resolve difficulties and to avoid divorce.

Good relationships are built on dedication, persistence, sensitivity, communication skills, and a willingness to forgive. These marks of maturity are traits that some people never develop and for this reason their marriages are unstable.

6. *Persisting Stresses.* Almost any stress, when it is severe enough or if it lasts long enough, can put sufficient pressure on a marriage that the couple may drift apart and/or begin thinking about divorce. The demands of a time-consuming vocation, physical or psychological abuse, continuing financial pressures, boredom, alcoholism or drug abuse in one of the partners, the instabilities of middle age, or the rigidities and resentments that can build up over the years have all led

to divorce, especially when the spouses have also seen their parents' marriages end, sometimes for similar reasons. It is difficult to be the first one in a family to get a divorce, but when other family marriages have broken up, there is less resistance to subsequent divorces when stresses build.

THE EFFECTS OF DIVORCE

Every Tuesday evening, a little group of middle-aged men and women gathers at a restaurant north of Chicago for their weekly meeting of Divorce Anonymous. "We're here to share our feelings," said a woman who has been attending the group for three years. "This isn't a place to find sex or a new mate. It's a time for people to talk about their pain and their concerns, without having to be on guard."[32] Like most people who are divorced or in the process of ending a marriage, these members of Divorce Anonymous know that a marriage breakup can thoroughly disrupt one's life, routines, feelings of self-worth, and sense of security. Divorce can affect people physically, psychologically, and spiritually. Often it leads to emotional upheaval. irrational decisions, and interpersonal tensions. It affects the two people involved, but its influence can extend to children, parents, other family members, fellow employees, friends, neighbors, and people in the church.

Each divorce is unique, but some counselors have noticed common patterns as couples begin to separate. In most cases, one spouse is ahead of the other in deciding to end the marriage. When the issue is finally mentioned, the spouse who hears the news often feels helpless and devastated.[33] Although this pattern appears in many marriage breakups, it may apply equally to an individual who is breaking away from home, leaving a long-term employment situation, quitting college, or deciding to change roommates.

In this preseparation period[34] there are tensions and adjustment difficulties that lead to an emotional divorce. The one spouse—sometimes termed the initiator—realizes that the relationship is going down and begins to wonder, privately at first, if the marriage can be saved. Sometimes without much conscious awareness, the initiator begins to withdraw his or her emotional investment from the relationship. There is a gradual gathering of information: could I make it on my own, how would the kids or my mate respond, would I be lonely, could I find someone else, what would divorce do to my career?

During this period, unhappiness is communicated indirectly but there may be no mention of separation because the initiator is still pondering the idea and doesn't want to arouse arguments or possible retaliation. As time passes, the signals get bolder, the discontent is expressed more openly, and sometimes the initiator tries to provoke the other partner into declaring first that the marriage is over. Often, however, it is the initiator who announces the break. The spouse who hears the news may be shocked and deeply hurt, but the initiator has had time to think about the separation and to find some secure niches elsewhere.[35]

Sometimes the couple comes for counseling at this time, but often one or both of the spouses have made the decision that counseling won't work and that the marriage is over. The preseparation period is often so stressful that it leaves deep scars in the form of depression, anxiety, low self-esteem, anger, guilt, or self-doubt, especially in the partner who wants the marriage to continue.[36]

The litigation period is a time when the couple may become adversaries, each trying to work out the best deal for themselves with the help of their lawyers. This can be a period of tension, insecurity, anger, and considerable expense. Each of the partners may admit to some fault in the marriage breakup, but more often there is blame and criticism of the mate. Slowly there comes a change in thinking from "I'm married" to "I'm getting divorced." This takes time to settle in.

Like the people in the Divorce Anonymous group, one experienced counselor has described divorce as "an awful thing to go through, an even more awful thing to inflict on one's children." The divorce process, he adds, is at best unpleasant. "More often it is downright devastating for everyone in the family. It is usually distressing for relatives and disturbing for friends. It is probably more traumatic than a death in the family, since it tears family members apart rather than bringing them together. Few family crises produce such profound changes in so many lives."[37]

Divorce almost always involves a period of mourning. This includes positive mourning (which involves the experience of remembering the good and happy times in the marriage), negative mourning (which involves the experience of confusion or self-pity), and assembling the pieces (slowly picking up the demands of life and learning to live without a mate).[38]

In time the growth period begins. Here people honestly face the reality of their new status in life; set time aside for meditation, reading, prayer, and personal reflection; get involved with new friends; deliberately resist the tendencies to blame themselves or others; fight self-pity; and seek God's guidance in making realistic plans for the future.

In each of these stages, the counselor may observe emotional, behavioral, social, and spiritual effects of the divorce.

1. *Emotional Effects.* As we have seen, divorce is accompanied by an almost endless range of emotions including anxiety, guilt, fear, sadness, depression (sometimes accompanied by thoughts of suicide), anger, bitterness, and frustration. Most couples experience periods of indecision, confusion, or vacillation, but sometimes there is a sense of hyperalertness, as if the person is waiting expectantly for something else to go wrong. The body of course cannot maintain a continuing state of tension and vigilance, so psychosomatic illness often follows.

Divorce involves the loss of a love and the death of a relationship. It is valid, therefore, to think of divorce as a grief reaction with all of the emotions that grieving involves. Like all grief reactions, the pain seems greater at Christmas, Thanksgiving, anniversaries, and other special times of the year.

2. *Behavioral Effects.* Divorce affects how one feels, but it also influences what one does. Eating, paying the bills, solving daily problems, taking care of one's property, and other routine activities must continue, but they are continued without the help of a mate. If there are children, the divorced person must adjust to becoming a single parent either living apart from the children or with the children present in a one-parent family. Often the divorced parent must cope with the behavioral, academic, and emotional effects of the divorce on the children.[39] Preoccupied with problems like these, one's work often suffers. Quality and quantity of output may decline, efficiency drops, and sometimes there is high accident proneness.

3. *Social Effects.* It probably is true that no one ever gets divorced alone.[40] When a marriage breaks up, the couple is affected and so are:

- Family members including children (especially boys),[41] parents and other relatives whose reactions range from shock, rejection, rage, and fear to support and encouragement.
- Allies such as personal friends, lawyers, some fellow church members or coworkers, and supportive relatives who encourage but sometimes complicate the situation with their advice and opinions.
- Critics (some of whom may be in one's church or family) who reject, condemn, blame, and sometimes treat divorced persons judgmentally.
- Married friends, some of whom feel threatened and many who are not sure how to react in the presence of the newly divorced person.
- Other single people, including many who may be understanding, some who are critical, and a few who could be potential dating partners.

Divorced people often experience loneliness, insecurity, confusion about whether they should date or remarry, and concerns about identity or self-confidence. Most struggle with the issue of sex and self-control. In a minority of cases, the divorced person reacts to people as he or she has done in the past, remarries into a similar situation, repeats the same mistakes, and experiences another divorce. More often the difficulties of a disastrous first marriage are avoided in a subsequent marriage,[42] but this rarely enters the thinking of people who are newly divorced. Since at first they did not succeed, they may have initial fears of trying again.

4. *Spiritual Effects.* How does all of this affect the Christian's spiritual life? As with any crisis, divorce can pull some people closer to Christ for strength and guidance. Others may get angry at God and spiritually rebellious, especially if there is rejection and criticism from the church. More common, perhaps, is the tendency to withdraw spiritually. Worship becomes less important, personal times of prayer and Bible study become less frequent, and in the midst of all the other pressures there is a gradual drifting away or letting go of spiritual interests and activities.

Counseling and Divorce

Christian marriage counseling attempts to keep marriages together by helping couples develop smoother, more fulfilling, Christ-centered marital relationships. This type of counseling can be difficult, but it also can be challenging especially when the counselor is successful and the marriage improves.

It is more difficult to work with couples who have decided to separate and who have no mutual desire for reconciliation. These people nevertheless need counseling, and this is the purpose of Christian divorce counseling. It attempts to help an individual or couple separate from a marriage (a) in a way that is consistent with biblical teachings, (b) with a minimum of pain or destruction to themselves or to others, including their children, and (c) with a maximum of growth and new learning.

1. *Clarifying the Counselor's Attitudes.* Divorce counseling is rarely easy. If you feel frustrated, saddened, angry, or resistant to the concept of divorce, then it is unlikely that you will be able to listen carefully, understand, avoid condemning, or be able to withstand the pressures or your own inclination to take sides.

The effective helper must take time for personal reflection on his or her attitudes toward divorce, divorced persons, and people who are going through divorce. Can you in good conscience help people face a divorce that is acceptable biblically? What if the proposed divorce has no biblical justification? Can you forgive, support, and help even those who are clearly in the wrong? (If you abandon them, where will they get straightforward honest answers?) As a follower of Jesus Christ, what is your responsibility to people who are frustrated, confused, angry, and despondent because of marital breakdown? No one can answer these questions for you. Before God, each counselor must consider some difficult questions before getting enmeshed in the demanding, sometimes heart-rending work of divorce counseling.

2. *Determining Goals.* In divorce counseling, goal setting is not easy. Reconciliation and the development of a fulfilling, Christ-honoring marriage certainly are to be preferred, but often a couple has no such desire. When this is true, you can strive for a logical, respectful, mutually agreeable resolution of problems, but sometimes counselees have no desire to be logical. A psychologist once described a couple who fought so vociferously in the counseling sessions that he had difficulty restraining them.[43] "There is something you don't understand about divorce," the wife explained. "You are trying to be logical, but divorce is neither a civilized nor logical matter."

Not all divorce counseling is like this, however, and it is possible to reach a number of goals, including the following:

- Helping counselees evaluate their marital situation realistically, including consideration of the prospects for avoiding divorce.
- Discussing biblical teachings on divorce and remarriage, and helping counselees make application of these teachings to their own marital situation.
- Discovering and discussing the counselees' expectations and desires for counseling, and evaluating whether these are (a) feasible, (b) consistent with the counselor's own moral and ethical standards, and (c) goals that you can, without hesitation, help the counselees achieve.
- Helping couples admit, confess (to God and to each other), and change attitudes and actions that are sinful.
- Assisting those who need help in finding competent legal assistance.
- Helping counselees reach mutually acceptable agreements concerning such practical issues as the division of property, alimony, or child custody and support.
- Encouraging couples to calm down from vindictive or self-centered hostile ways of relating.
- Helping counselees formulate ways of explaining the situation to children (sometimes this may mean including the children in some counseling sessions).[44]
- Encouraging the couple to avoid belittling, blaming, and criticizing each other, especially in the presence of children.
- Helping the spouses understand the effects of divorce on children (including grown children) and encouraging counselees not to use children in manipulative ways, either to force children into taking sides or to get messages to the former spouse.
- Helping the couple (together, but more often separately) to cope with the emotions of divorce, including feelings of rejection.[45]

- Guiding in the adjustment to postdivorce, single life.
- Encouraging counselees in their spiritual growth and in their involvement with other people, including church people and Christian divorce recovery groups, where there is support, encouragement, friendship, and spiritual nourishment.

Unlike participants in marriage and family counseling, divorcing couples may be less willing to come together, especially if they have made a firm decision to separate. Try to emphasize, however, that some mutual sessions could be helpful, especially when there is need to make decisions about life after the divorce. Some counselees will prefer to leave those negotiations to meetings when their attorneys can be present. If so, express a willingness to see whomever will come. If they won't come together, see them separately or meet with the one spouse who wants counseling.

3. *Work on Practical Issues.* Since divorce is a crisis, counselors should seek to give the support, guidance, and practical help that people in crises need.[46] In addition you may want to discuss some of the following practical issues.

(a) Handling Emotions. It is difficult to make an emotional separation, even from a relationship that no longer is intimate. As we have noted, anger, anxiety, frustration, depression, and a host of other feelings flood the counselee, sometimes when they are least expected. Often there is a vacillation of feelings. Relief at being free, for example, may occur along with deep feelings of loneliness.

Most counselees will find it helpful to admit and express their emotions, but try to encourage growth beyond this emotional expression stage. Several guidelines may help counselees with this growth. Encourage them to:

- Admit and express emotions honestly as they arise.
- Ask God to help them resist hatred, resentment and bitterness. In a poignant farewell address to his staff, Richard Nixon made a powerful statement: "Those who hate don't win until you hate them back—and that will destroy you." No matter how much one has been hurt, nothing is gained by revenge.
- Forgive, with God's help, and pray for those who have created pain and disappointment.
- Deliberately avoid the emotional traps of the past.[47] These include making sweeping and unwarranted generalizations about oneself or others; developing unrealistic expectations; self-fulfilling prophecies (like deciding, for example, that life will now be miserable—an attitude that, in turn, may make life miserable); courting disaster (always being on the defensive and expecting the worse); wallowing in one's problems; blaming others perpetually (especially one's mate); rushing to new jobs, new locations, or new churches in an attempt to start fresh; living through others (finding satisfaction only in one's children or in the achievements of others); and assuming that life can only be meaningful again when there is another marriage.

Feelings often follow thinking; if you change your thinking, this often leads to changed feelings. Encourage counselees to logically accept what may not be changeable (in this case divorce), and then learn to resist dwelling on thoughts that can arouse painful feelings.

(b) Guiding Mediation. Until recently, divorcing couples almost always turned to lawyers for help in resolving such practical issues as child custody, division of property, alimony, or tax preparation. Within the past fifteen years, however, divorce mediation has become a fast growing profession among counselors and others who understand legal issues but may not be lawyers.[48]

Mediation seeks to avoid the combative, adversarial approach. Instead it is a more cooperative approach to conflict resolution. It is a system based on the needs of the parties and on their abilities to support themselves. There are no penalties for past conduct or awards given to one at the expense of the other. People use it to get on with the business of living and to let go of the past.[49] Any divorce counselor is likely to be involved in some mediation, but if you lack special training in this area, you may want to help couples find some competent and impartial person who can mediate successfully.

Even when a nonlegal mediator is involved, couples often will want to consult with lawyers. Counselors are not always qualified to know how a lawyer can be chosen and evaluated, although in time the names of competent lawyers become known. Encourage counselees to select attorneys carefully, to hire someone who specializes in divorces, to refrain from signing anything until one's attorney is consulted, and to avoid do-it-yourself divorce. It is best to select competent Christian lawyers if these are available. Such men and women are more likely to have an appreciation for the sanctity of marriage and be less inclined to stimulate hostility between the separating spouses.

(c) Finding a New Identity. Divorce plunges the formerly married person into singleness again. The individual is now alone, often a parent without a partner, and labeled with a new description: "divorced." It is easy to think about better times in the past and to worry about life in the future. "Will I be accepted in my church?" the newly divorced person may wonder. "How will I fit in society?"

Encourage counselees to discuss these insecurities and to talk about life again as a single person. Many may need help with self-esteem, learning to accept themselves as God accepts them.[50] Remind your counselees that it isn't easy to change our identities and it takes time to shift in the ways we think about ourselves.

(d) Building New Relationships. It can be difficult to form new relationships following a divorce. The person may look for new friends, but he or she also must redefine relationships with the former spouse, the children, old friends and relatives, or people in the church.

The Former Spouse. When a couple has shared the same bed, goals, joys, trials and hopes, it is difficult to separate, to watch a former mate remarry, to become the brunt of the former spouse's anger, to deal with one's own feelings of anger or rejection, to be comfortable in talking to or about one's former partner, and to avoid striking out or showing excessive curiosity about the former mate's present life. Getting along with a former mate requires patience and understanding, especially at the beginning when feelings are strong. Later, as time passes and new relationships are formed, the conflict level subsides. This may take many months, during which regular talks with a counselor or understanding friend can be helpful. In most cases it also is best if the counselee can make a clean break with the former mate. Seeing a former mate reminds one of the past that has gone and often delays both healing and the beginning of a new life.

The Children. Every year in the United States more than a million children watch their parents go through a divorce. This can be very painful, especially during the first twelve to eighteen months following the divorce and especially for children under six and older than fourteen or fifteen. (The children in between seem to have fewer adjustment difficulties.)[51] Confused, afraid, and insecure, these young people often express their frustrations in truancy, fighting with siblings, running away, school problems (including frequent absences), sickness, nightmares, or regression to more childish behavior. The problems are greater when the child doesn't get along with the custodial parent or when contact with the father is significantly reduced.[52]

Problems are also greater when the children become unwilling weapons used by the husband and wife to attack and manipulate each other or when children become prisoners of war to be lured from one camp into the other and subjected to brainwashing. At first these children are hurt and confused. Later they become angry, especially with the parent who is the greater manipulator.[53]

The separating parents also have difficulties. The parent who is given custody of the children often feels overwhelmed with the responsibility to care for the children alone and to meet their needs at a time when everyone is vulnerable emotionally. The other parent may feel guilty, lonely, sad, angry because of the separation, but sometimes happy to be relieved of the child-rearing responsibilities.

Based on his many years of work with divorced couples, Jim Smoke has suggested some guidelines for single parents. These can be shared and discussed with counselees.

- Don't try to be both parents to your children.
- Don't force your children into playing the role of the departed parent.
- Be the parent you are (without trying to be a buddy, big brother, or big sister).
- Be honest with your children.
- Don't criticize your former spouse in front of the children.
- Don't make your children undercover agents who report on the other parent's current activities.
- Recognize that the children of divorce need both a mother and a father. Don't deny them this right.
- Don't become a Disneyland Daddy or a Magic Mountain Mommy. (These are parents who act like a weekend Santa Claus, showering their children with good times and gifts, then sending them back to the realities of daily living with the other parent.) Children need to see and spend time with the departed parent in a real-life setting.
- Be open with the children about your dating life and social interests.
- Help the children keep alive their good memories of the past marriage.
- Work out a child care and management arrangement with your former spouse. If necessary, seek a mediator who can help the former partners agree on ways that lead to the best growth and development of the children.
- If possible, try not to disrupt the many areas in your children's lives that offer them safety and security.

- If your child does not resume normal development and growth within a year or eighteen months of the divorce, consider consulting a counselor or school psychologist.[54]

It should not be assumed that divorce only affects younger children. Some couples live together in misery, avoiding divorce until the children are grown and have left home. We can admire the dedication of these parents and their concern for the children, but many fail to realize that adult children also can be hurt deeply by a parental divorce.

Other Adults. Some friends may be supportive at the time of divorce, but others are critical, unsure how to help, threatened by the divorced person's new status, uncertain about what to say, or inclined to withdraw. Grandparents are often confused, angry, hurt, and uncertain about how to act, especially if the grandchildren are in the custody of the former son-in-law or daughter-in-law. Often the divorced person doesn't know how to relate to the couples with whom the husband and wife formerly related. The counselor can encourage talk about these issues and give support and guidance as new relationships are formed and former relationships are redefined.

The Church. The local congregation should be a place where people find support, caring, and love. More often, however, church members are inclined to show criticism, subtle rejection, and sometimes avoidance of anyone who is divorced. When confronted with these attitudes counselors can assist in two ways: (1) by helping church members understand, accept, and (if necessary) forgive the divorced people in their midst and (2) by helping counselees to face and cope with church rejection.

(e) Facing the Future. The divorced person cannot live in the past or bemoan the future. Bills must be paid, work must be completed, life must go on. The counselee can be helped to identify and learn from past mistakes, make immediate decisions about such practical issues as housing and finances, reestablish life priorities, set goals for the future, and move ahead to accomplish God's purpose for one's life.

(f) Building Another Marriage. The Christian must determine whether or not remarriage is permitted biblically. Christian counselors will differ in their views on this issue, but at some time the possibility of remarriage should be discussed with counselees.

Divorced persons often resent the need to start dating "like teenagers." Some fear that they will never find a spouse and others wonder if they will repeat earlier mistakes. At times there are fears about how the children would react to another marriage, especially if the new mate also has children that would be part of a blended family.

The counselor can help with these fears. Discourage people from marrying too quickly and help them choose another mate cautiously and wisely. Before marrying again, divorced persons could be encouraged to ponder what they learned from their past failed marriage and how mistakes can be avoided in the future. Premarital counseling should be considered essential.

If children are involved, it may be helpful to discuss some of the problems found in blended families: intrusions from previous spouses, fears that the new marriage will fall apart (like the previous ones), wrangling over finances (previously divorced people often want to keep their money separate from one another), children moving in and out, problems arising from the husband and wife having different authority over different children, the possibility of unequal financial realities for children in the same household, children's efforts to break up the marriage, parental jealousy of children's allegiances, increased danger of sexual involvement with the new spouse's children, and unclear relationships with grandparents.[55] Often, especially at the start of a new marriage, there is closer bonding between each biological parent and child than between the spouses. This makes it easier to relate more comfortably to the child rather than to the spouse. That creates increased tension, especially in times of stress.[56] None of this makes successful remarriage impossible, but it is helpful to know that blended families encounter unique difficulties as they try to combine old loyalties with new ties.[57]

In all of this, remind yourself and your counselees that God wants the best for his children. He forgives those who confess and guides those who want his leading. Divorced persons and their counselors are not left alone to fend for themselves. The Holy Spirit is the constant guide and companion of committed divorced believers and their Christian counselors.

Preventing Divorce

The most obvious way to prevent divorce is to build stronger marriages—marriages based on scriptural principles and characterized by love, commitment, and open communication. What can be done to prevent divorce when a couple has already decided to separate?

1. *Counseling.* Before a couple decides to separate they have a responsibility before God, to themselves, and to their families to do whatever is possible to avoid divorce and bring renewal into the marriage. This assumes a calm and reasoned approach to marriage problems; an approach that often is lacking. Nevertheless, if both husband and wife are sincerely willing to work at resolving conflicts and building a relationship, there is a good possibility that divorce can be prevented.

2. *Self-Examination.* With or without counseling, each spouse must ask, "What am I doing (or failing to do) that contributes to the problems in my marriage?" Often there is constant criticism, unrealistic expectations, attitudes of bitterness, refusal to forgive, sexual infidelity, unwillingness to work at building the marriage, or equally harmful attitudes that contribute to the marital tension. Jesus instructed his followers to look at (and presumably to remove) the faults in themselves before criticizing others.[58] It isn't always possible to see ourselves clearly, but if we ask God to enlighten our understanding, he surely will, perhaps through the observations of a counselor or through the insights of one's mate. Then couples should seek divine and human help to forsake these harmful behaviors.

3. *Reconciliation.* After filing for divorce, only one couple in eight tries reconciliation, but half of these attempts are permanent.[59] Most often reconciliation only comes after hours of realistic discussion of the problems involved. Reconciliation, however, surely is the desire of a God who never wants divorce.

4. *Divine Guidance.* Only God can really mend and bind a broken marriage. Separately and together, couples must seek divine wisdom, strength, and guidance as they strive to keep their spiritual lives alive and growing and as they work to prevent divorce. Daily Scripture reading and prayer are powerful forces that open

couples to the healing power of God. After almost fifty years of living together and conducting marriage seminars, Charlie and Martha Shedd concluded that there are only two ways to ensure *absolutely* that a marriage will last: praying together and studying the Bible together.[60]

This brings us to the influence of the church. Believers are instructed to bear one another's burdens, care for one another and pray for each other. For Christians, prayer, concern, caring, and support are not optional. These are commanded by God. To prevent divorce, therefore, believers should be instructed to pray for married couples, even when their marriages are healthy. Effective prayer and compassionate caring can accomplish much, including healing,[61] and perhaps even the healing of unhealthy marriages.

Conclusions about Divorce

It has been mentioned frequently that a marriage license, unlike most other licenses, is not granted on the basis of competence.[62] A driver's license implies that the recipient knows how to drive a car. A license to practice medicine means that the person has mastered a body of knowledge about the body's functioning and cures. Schools teach driver's education, but they rarely give courses in marriage competence, and church family life programs often do no better. Perhaps it is not surprising that so many marriages break down and disintegrate into painful divorces.

Building a good and lasting marriage is rarely easy. It is romantic for a couple to think that their love is strong enough to resist problems, but stable marriages more often build on persisting commitment, knowledge, sensitivity, interpersonal skills, and a willingness to live in accordance with biblical teaching. The Christian counselor, like others in the local congregation, can help to ensure that good marriages are built, cared for, and repaired when there are signs of breakdown. Backed by prayer and the support of others, marriages can grow, broken relationships can be restored, and divorce can be prevented.

Suggestions for Further Reading

Ellison, Stanley A. *Divorce and Remarriage in the Church.* Grand Rapids, Mich.: Zondervan, 1977.*

Pittman, Frank S., III. *Turning Points: Treating Families in Transition and Crisis.* New York: Norton, 1987.

Richards, Sue Poorman, and Stanley Hagemeyer. *Ministry to the Divorced: Guidance, Structure, and Organization That Promote Healing in the Church.* Grand Rapids, Mich.: Zondervan, 1986.

Richmond, Gary. *The Divorce Decision: What It Can Mean for Your Children, Your Finances, Your Emotions, Your Relationships, Your Future.* Waco, Tex.: Word, 1988.

Smoke, Jim. *Growing through Divorce.* Eugene, Oreg.: Harvest House, 1976.*

———. *Recovering from Divorce.* Minneapolis: Bethany, 1982.*

Thompson, David A. *Counseling and Divorce.* Waco, Tex.: Word, forthcoming.

* Books marked with an asterisk (*) are especially suited for counselees to read.

Part 7

Other Issues

31

Mental Disorders

DOUG IS A COLLEGE STUDENT majoring in business. He is also a mental patient. When his family lived in Atlanta, Doug had no unusual problems. Friends called him a loner, but he got along with others, maintained a "B" average in school, and held a part-time job where he was well liked. His father is a successful businessman who tends to be a workaholic, but this didn't seem to bother Doug or his two younger sisters. Each member of the family has always tended to be pretty independent.

When the father's career led to a cross-country move, Doug had some trouble adjusting, but he was planning to go away to college soon, so he never tried to fit into the new community. Everybody assumed that he would go to college, get a business degree, and follow in his father's footsteps.

During his freshman year, Doug became more and more withdrawn. He didn't bother going to church, even though his family always attended Sunday services at home. He rarely went to campus social events, and as the year progressed, he began skipping classes with increasing frequency. When Doug started missing meals, some of the other students expressed concern about this withdrawn behavior, but Doug stated often that he liked to be alone. Eventually the other students quit trying to get him involved.

One morning, when the dorm was quiet and most of the students were in class, Doug tried to hang himself in one of the shower stalls. He was found by a college employee and rushed to the hospital. When they heard the news, his family was confused. Doug's parents wondered if they had done something wrong. His sisters were embarrassed and didn't want their friends to know why Doug was in the hospital or that he was on the psychiatric ward. Nobody in the family could understand why a young, handsome college student would want to die by his own hand, and the family members had no idea what to expect next.

"Will he get better?" Doug's anxious father asked the college counselor. "Will he try to kill himself again?" "Is there any hope for his future?" Doug's family had been forced to encounter the world of mental illness and they were not sure where to turn for clear guidance, encouragement, and help.

Jack and Jo Ann Hinckley faced a worse dilemma on March 30, 1981. Their twenty-five-year-old son was in the nation's capital, far from the family home in Colorado, standing in a crowd outside the Washington Hilton. Nervously he fingered a gun in his pocket. When the intended victim emerged from the hotel and walked briskly toward his waiting limousine, John Hinckley took quick aim, pulled the trigger, and tried to assassinate the president of the United States. The events surrounding that tragic morning are history. Ronald Reagan and several others were felled, but they recovered. The would-be assassin was wrestled to the ground, taken into custody, and sent eventually to a psychiatric hospital where he has remained ever since.

In the meantime his parents struggled to understand. They had never known anyone who was mentally ill, and they wondered why two of their children had turned into outstanding students and leaders but another had attempted murder. The months following the assassination attempt were a nightmare of anguish and frustration. The family's private life was exposed to public scrutiny in Hinckley's much publicized trial. When the jury returned its verdict, not guilty by reason of insanity, there was a national outcry.

Jack and Jo Ann Hinckley did not retreat following their tragedy. Instead they established the American Mental Health Fund to support research and to provide public education about mental illness. These parents were determined to let others know about the prevalence and reality of serious mental illness. Unselfishly they have sought to stimulate research that would increase understanding of the causes and treatment of mental disorders. They have become dedicated to preventing mental disorders so other families can be spared the turmoil and tragedy that jolted their lives when an emotionally disturbed son tried to kill the president.[1]

What Is Mental Illness? This term describes a broad variety of symptoms that produce distress and or disability in one's personal, social, or occupational life. The distress and disability may be mild and minimally annoying, but they also can be more disruptive and sometimes of intense severity. In mild disorders the symptoms are hardly noticed. The person functions well in all areas, is interested and involved in a wide range of activities, gets along well with others, is generally satisfied with life, and has no major worries or problems in life. At the other extreme are persons whose thinking may be distorted, whose communication may be faulty, whose contact with reality is impaired, who have difficulty getting along with others, who often cannot function in society, and who may be in persistent danger of self-harm or of harming others.

What some call mental illness, insanity, or nervous breakdown, professional counselors are more likely to call psychopathology, emotional disturbance, or mental disorders. The latter term is used by the American Psychiatric Association in its classification manual (known popularly as DSM-III-R),[2] and this is the term that will be used most often in this chapter.

Mental disorders are not all the same. Several hundred disorders have been identified and classified into categories according to symptoms and severity of impairment. Schizophrenia, for example, is a disorder that strikes approximately one out of every hundred Americans sometime during their lives. It can be mild, moderate, or severe in intensity. It has a variety of causes and can be divided into several types, each of which has its own list of symptoms, only some of which may be present in any one person. It is beyond the scope of this book for us to describe even the major mental disorders, but Table 31-1 gives an overview based on the American Psychiatric Association's DSM-III-R classification. Although they may not be familiar with all of the disorders, counselors can be aware of the major symptoms of psychopathology, can understand some broad causes of mental disorder, and should know how to help mental patients and their families.[3]

Table 31-1
Major Mental Disorders

1. Disorders Usually First Evident in Infancy, Childhood, or Adolescence
    - Disruptive Behavior Disorders
    - Anxiety Disorders of Childhood or Adolescence
    - Eating Disorders
    - Gender Identity Disorders
    - Tic Disorders
    - Elimination Disorders
    - Speech Disorders Not Elsewhere Classified
    - Other Disorders of Infancy, Childhood or Adolescence
2. Organic Mental Syndromes and Disorders
    - Dementias Arising in the Senium and Presenium (This includes Alzheimer's Disease and Senile Dementia)
    - Psychoactive Substance-Induced Organic Mental Disorders (This includes brain damage associated with alcoholism and other forms of intoxification with substances such as amphetamines, cocaine, hallucinogens, and other toxic substances)
    - Organic Mental Disorders Associated with Physical Disorders or Conditions, or with Etiology that is Unknown.
3. Psychoactive Substance Abuse Disorders
    This includes dependence and abuse of alcohol, caffeine, cocaine, hallucinogens, inhalants, nicotine, sedatives and other substances.
4. Schizophrenia
    This includes catatonic, disorganized, paranoid, undifferentiated and residual types.
5. Delusional (Paranoid) Disorder
    This includes erotomanic, grandiose, jealous, persecutory, somatic and unspecified types.
6. Psychotic Disorders Not Elsewhere Classified
7. Mood Disorders
    - Bipolar Disorders (including mixed manic-depressive and manic disorders)
    - Depressive Disorders
8. Anxiety Disorders
    This includes panic disorders, phobias, obsessive-compulsive disorders, and post-traumatic stress disorder.
9. Somatoform Disorders
    These are disorders concerning the body including hypochondriasis and conversion disorders.
10. Dissociative Disorders
    These include multiple personality disorder, psychogenic amnesia, and depersonalization disorder.
11. Sexual Disorders
    - Paraphilias (including exhibitionism, fetishism, predophilia, sexual masochism, sexual sadism, transvestism, and voyeurism)
    - Sexual Dysfunctions (including hypoactive sexual desire, sexual aversion, sexual arousal disorders, orgasm disorders and sexual pain disorders)
12. Sleep Disorders
    These include insomnia, disorders in the sleep-wake schedule, nightmares, sleep terror disorder, sleepwalking and parasomnia.
13. Factitious Disorders
    These are disorders in which physical and psychological symptoms are feigned.

Table 31-1 *(continued)*

14. Impulse Disorders Not Elsewhere Classified
    These include kleptomania, pathological gambling, pyromania and impulse control disorders.
15. Adjustment Disorders
    Includes adjustment difficulties associated with
    - anxious mood
    - depressed mood
    - disturbance of conduct
    - physical complaints
    - withdrawal
    - work or academic inhibition
16. Psychological Factors Affecting Physical Condition
17. Personality Disorders
    These include paranoid, schizoid, antisocial, borderline, and narcissistic personalities.
18. Conditions Not Attributable to a Mental Disorder but the Focus of Attention or Treatment
    - Academic Problem
    - Antisocial Behavior
    - Malingering
    - Marital Problem
    - Noncompliance with Medical Treatment
    - Occupational Problem
    - Parent-child Problem
    - Other Interpersonal Problem
    - Other Specified Family Circumstances
    - Phase of Life Problem or Other Life Circumstance
    - Uncomplicated Bereavement

THE BIBLE AND MENTAL DISORDERS

The Bible says little about mental disorders, but psychopathology was recognized and perhaps common, especially when there were no psychotherapeutic drugs or modern treatment methods. David once pretended to be insane. His behavior was feigned, but it gives a brief insight into some of the symptoms of psychopathology that were recognized in Old Testament times. David "pretended to be insane in their presence; and while he was in their hands he acted like a madman, making marks on the doors of the gate and letting saliva run down his beard."[4]

Many years later, Nebuchadnezzar of Babylon had a dream that was interpreted by Daniel:

> This is what is decreed for you, King Nebuchadnezzar: Your royal authority has been taken from you. You will be driven away from people and will live with the wild animals; you will eat grass like cattle. Seven times will pass by for you until you acknowledge that the Most High is sovereign over the kingdoms of men and gives them to anyone he wishes.
>
> Immediately what had been said about Nebuchadnezzar was fulfilled. He was driven away from people and ate grass like cattle. His body was drenched

> with the dew of heaven until his hair grew like the feathers of an eagle and his nails like the claws of a bird.[5]

In the New Testament, Festus interrupted Paul's presentation of the gospel and shouted "You are out of your mind, Paul! . . . Your great learning is driving you insane."[6] Elsewhere we read that Jesus healed people who were "possessed by demons, or were insane, or paralyzed."[7]

The word translated "insane" in one version of the Bible is given different English words elsewhere. The King James Version, for example, used the term "lunatic" rather than "insane," but some modern translations refer to seizures. The New International Version states that Jesus healed "those suffering severe pain, the demon possessed, those having seizures, and the paralyzed," but the New American Standard Bible uses "epileptics" in place of "having seizures."

Modern psychiatry would view epilepsy as a physiological brain disorder that leads sometimes to seizures but should not be equated with insanity. (In modern usage, insanity is a legal term used to describe people like John Hinckley, Jr., who are considered not guilty of criminal actions because of insanity. These people are assumed to have an inability to fully grasp the meaning of their actions.) Most Christian counselors who believe in demon possession[8] would agree that physical illness, epilepsy, mental disorders, and demon possession are terms that refer to different conditions, even though many of the symptoms are similar.

The Bible does not claim to be a diagnostic textbook, but it gives several examples of suicide (including the deaths of Saul, who fell on his sword, and Judas, who hanged himself)[9] and it makes reference to many of the emotions that form the basis of psychiatric disorders: anxiety, anger, discord, jealousy, envy, lust, dissension, selfish ambition, impatience, lack of self-control, idolatry, orgies, marital infidelity, gluttony, drunkenness, strife, lying, violence, and a host of others.

From this it does not follow that mental disorders always involve or come from deliberate sin in the afflicted person's life. A few are like David who took on some symptoms of abnormality for his own purposes. More people are like Nebuchadnezzar whose psychopathology came because of a deliberate refusal to obey God. Others are like Job. He was a morally upright, God-fearing man whose physical and emotional problems came for reasons other than personal sin. Ultimately all physical and mental disorders come because sin entered the world centuries ago. Scripture teaches that all of us are sinners, but from this it does not follow that psychopathology necessarily results from the victim's own personal sinful actions.

The Causes of Mental Disorders

According to a multimillion dollar study by the National Institute of Mental Health, at any given time nearly one out of every five adults suffers from a psychiatric disorder. The severity of these disorders ranges from mildly disabling anxiety to severe schizophrenia. The rates vary from place to place, and there are some age differences. (When compared with older adults, people under forty-five have about twice the rate of mental disorders). Overall, mental illness is about equally divided between men and women although there are differences in the type of problem.

Women more often suffer from depression and phobias; men have more problems with drug and alcohol abuse or antisocial personalities.[10]

The causes of these disorders differ from person to person and are related to type of disorder. If we were to visit a psychiatric hospital we might find two patients with similar diagnosis but different life histories leading to the hospitalization. Just as a heart attack and appendicitis have different causes, so do the various psychiatric disorders.

Even though each case is unique, mental disorders arise from a combination of present stresses and past predisposing influences.

1. *Present Stress.* Is life more stressful now than it was a century ago? It could be argued that pressures are greater at this time in history because of the present pace and complexity of life, the technological changes that demand constant adjustment, and communication capabilities that give us immediate information about international tensions or problems in the neighborhood.

The stresses that lead to mental illness could be divided into at least three categories: biological, psychological, and social. Biological stresses include disease, the influence of drugs, toxins or pollutants in the air, brain damage, or physical deprivations such as a lack of nutrients or insufficient sleep. Get overly tired and you are likely to be impatient and depressed. Get exhausted and the signs of abnormality are even greater, at least until you have time to rest.

Psychological stresses include personal frustrations, inner conflicts, fears, and feelings of insecurity. With some frequency, newspaper reports describe the suicides of students who get distraught over an inability to pass important examinations. In a society that values success and achievement, it is very difficult for some people to face failure, especially if they set high standards for themselves or feel pressure from teachers, employers, and family members.

Family pressure can be one of the social stresses that push some people toward mental disorders. When there is economic uncertainty, widespread unemployment, or political instability, some people cannot handle the tension and uncertainties. Even the physical environment has an effect. Prolonged periods of heat, darkness, crowding, noise, or other stressful circumstances can make coping more difficult and increase the likelihood of mental disorders.[11]

2. *Predisposing Influences.* Although the stresses may be similar, individuals respond in different ways. Newspaper reports sometimes describe the aftermath of a tornado or other destructive weather conditions. The same loss that leaves one person depressed and immobilized may stimulate another to acts of compassion and determination to overcome the loss.

Differences like this often reflect one's background and past experiences. Like present stress, these predisposing influences can be of several types. Biological predispositions include the effects of heredity, past physical health, congenital defects, glandular malfunctioning, and other physical influences. Severe depression, for example, may be triggered by stress, but the condition is likely to be worse in some people because of genetic influences and neurochemical imbalances.[12]

Psychological predispositions include the effects of early family disharmony, childhood losses, past traumas, parental neglect or abuse, faulty learning, previous rejection, or an upbringing that was so demanding and rigid that the person always felt like a failure. One study of posttraumatic stress disorders (PTSD) compared

Vietnam veterans who showed no evidence of the disorder with those who did. In contrast to their nonaffected colleagues, PSTD veterans reported more time in combat, more friends killed, greater involvement in killing others, closer relationships with those who died, more combat injuries, and more negative experiences at home after their discharge. Many of these veterans had favorable preservice attitudes toward the war, but their traumatic experiences in Vietnam followed by a lack of support when they came home combined to create anxiety, depression, and other evidences of abnormality long after the war had ended.[13]

Mental disorders also can depend on sociological predispositions. These include one's social class, place of residence, marital status, socioeconomic level, religious affiliation, or membership in a minority group. When compared to the wealthy, for example, poor people tend to have higher rates of psychopathology. The poor have less control over their circumstances, and because of their lack of resources they must wait for treatment until their problems get severe. People with more money or access to insurance payments get counseling earlier and are less likely than the poor to be hospitalized or listed in the statistics about those who have mental disorders.

3. *Sin and Responsibility.* Some Christian writers and counselors assume that mental disorders result mostly from personal sin and that counseling involves urging people to confess their sins and change their behavior. This simplistic and naïve viewpoint fails to appreciate both the complexity of mental disorders and the deeply penetrating influence of sin.

Sin could be viewed from two perspectives: conscious deliberate sins that individuals commit and the innate sinfulness that is part of human nature. In a similar way, responsibility can be viewed from two perspectives: either I am responsible or somebody else is responsible. When a person is mentally ill, therefore, the problem may come from one's sinful acts and/or one's sinful nature; the ultimate responsibility for the problem may come from the counselee and/or from another person. This can be shown in a simple diagram (adapted from the work of Christian psychologist Bruce Narramore).[14]

The causes of mental disorders arise from all four quadrants and treatment will have to consider all four as well.

(a) Quadrant I. Here the person has problems because of something sinful (or foolish) that he or she has done. Responsibility for both the problem and the

Figure 31-1

Type of Sin		Responsibility for the Pathology: Oneself	Responsibility for the Pathology: Others
	Specific Deliberate Conscious Sins	I	II
	Inner Sinful Human Nature	III	IV

treatment rests largely with the individual. Confession, changed behavior, and relearning are among the most appropriate treatments.

(b) Quadrant II. This involves sinful or other harmful behavior that originates with someone different from the counselee. A person with great feelings of inferiority and low self-esteem, for example, may have developed these attitudes because of the constant sinful put-down criticisms that came from a teacher, parent, or hypercritical spouse. Adult children of alcoholics often suffer because of the drinking excesses of one or both parents. Treatment may involve helping individuals forgive, change perceptions, and deal with longstanding hurts, bitterness, and painful memories.

(c) Quadrant III. This presents a more complicated picture. Some people develop mental disorders not because of specific sins, but because they are pulled down by deeply felt fears, insecurities, immaturities, ignorance, past traumas, inherited physical influences, harmful attitudes, or other aspects of the personality that come because we live in a fallen world and are all deeply affected by sin. The Pharisees in the time of Jesus were models of righteous proper behavior, but inside they were full of greed, self-indulgence, hypocrisy, wickedness, and probably a lot of confusion and self-deception.[15] Help for these people could come only with increased insight and understanding, confession, and willingness to let God work to cleanse, change, and bring maturity to the inner life. This is a process that might take a lot of time and more in-depth treatment.

(d) Quadrant IV. Many personal problems come because we live in a world where sin permeates the culture: where there is conflict, stress, poverty, inequality, war, disease, and widespread injustice. Until Christ returns to bring perfect justice and an end to sin, these pathological conditions will persist to create both social havoc and personal mental disorders. Even though the battle will never be won completely prior to the return of Christ, Christians are responsible to resist social injustice, work for peace, and strive to create a better world. Counselors seek to change circumstances that give rise to pathology, teach people how to cope with stress, and help counselees overcome the persisting effects of painful past experiences.

Mental disorders rarely rise from only one of these four quadrants. Most often the influences come from several quadrants. This presents a greater challenge in our efforts to find causes and give treatment.

4. *Suicide.* Sometimes the pressures of life get too intense and individuals decide to take their own lives. Most have thought about the idea for weeks or months before.[16] Their suicidal acts are rarely sudden, impulsive, or random (although there are tragic cases such as teenage suicide epidemics where the attention that comes following one suicide leads other teenagers to try something similar). It is probable that most people who attempt or successfully commit suicide are *not* mentally ill.[17] Why, then do some people turn to acts of self-destruction? There can be various reasons:[18]

- To escape from loneliness, hopelessness, parental problems, depression, academic or work difficulties, financial pressures, or conflicts with other people.[19]
- To punish survivors who are likely to feel hurt and guilty.
- To gain attention.

- To manipulate others (often this can be best accomplished by the threat of suicide).
- To join a loved one who has died.
- To avoid punishment.
- To punish oneself for something that has created guilt.
- To prevent oneself from becoming a burden on others.
- To avoid the suffering and other effects of some dread disease.
- To seek martyrdom.

Some of the reasons on this list do not seem very logical. There is no guarantee, for example, that suicide will enable the victim to join a deceased loved one. Gaining attention or becoming a martyr isn't very satisfying if you kill yourself and aren't present to enjoy the pubic reaction.

When people try to kill themselves, however, their thinking at the time is usually not logical. When we function normally, we perceive the world accurately, tend to think logically, and have a healthy sense of reality. In times of crisis, however, thinking may be clouded by anxiety, hopelessness, and maladaptive self-defeating behavior. Even those occasional Russian roulette types of suicide are not logical, although we might be able to understand the victim's thinking. Young people like to flirt with danger. Because death seems so remote and unlikely, many might play with partially loaded guns or initiate high-speed automobile races because of the excitement.

This example of suicide raises the important issue of perception. We cannot really begin to understand the causes of another person's behavior until we have tried to see the world from his or her point of view. What seems illogical and foolish from the viewpoint of an outside observer may be much more rational and clearly understood when we see the situation from the perspective of the person who acts.

The Effects of Mental Disorders

Mental illness is a major social problem that consumes millions of tax dollars; costs billions in lost wages, absenteeism, inefficiency, criminal behavior, and expensive treatment; characterizes half or more of the homeless who wander the streets of America;[20] brings continual misery to the millions of people who are in the clutches of mental disorders; and causes incredible stress on families, many of whom fail to understand or know how to help their distraught relatives. "There are tens of millions of emotionally handicapped children and adults in our society who need help, aren't getting it and, as things stand, never will get it," according to a former president of the American Psychological Association.[21] Professional and government agencies are trying to combat the prejudice and discrimination that mentally ill people face,[22] while a relatively few hospital employees are working long hours in jobs that demand "the wisdom of Solomon, the patience of Job, the caring of Florence Nightingale—all for the wages of a janitor."[23] In most of this the role of the church is minimal or nonexistent.

Although the effects of mental disorders can be measured in dollars, numbers of cases, and other statistics, the counselor is more likely to see how individuals are affected and how their families suffer or struggle to cope.

1. *Effects on Individuals.* Sylvia Frumkin is a paranoid schizophrenic. At times she hears voices telling her to do illogical things. She dresses in a bizarre fashion, says things that don't make sense to others and sees things that aren't there. Sometimes she gets violent, hostile, and dangerous to herself, but at other times she is lucid, aware, and able to carry on an intelligent conversation. Frumkin has drifted in and out of mental institutions during most of her adult life, just as she drifts in and out of contact with reality. Her story has been told in an award-winning book, written by a sensitive journalist who sought to portray the effects of mental illness.[24] The detailed portrayal of this one life clearly illustrates the complexity and confusion that characterize people with mental disorders.

No two persons show identical effects, but there are several commonly seen symptoms. (Professional counselors might prefer to call these "clinical manifestations of psychiatric disorders."[25]) Some are biological, but nonmedical counselors more often notice psychologically unusual emotion, sensation, perception, thinking, and behavior.

(a) Emotion. It is well known that mental disorders often are characterized by intense anxiety, depression, anger, guilt, and other painful emotions. These feelings are so common that some counselors refer to mental disorders as affective or emotional disorders.

The emotional variations can be of several types. *Emotional variability* refers to extreme and sometimes unpredictable emotional ups and downs. Some people are up all the time, showing a euphoria that others would consider unrealistic; others are emotionally down and perpetually depressed. *Inappropriate affect* describes emotional reactions that are unusual and often without apparent cause: giggling in response to a sad story, for example, crying uncontrollably when one isn't sad, or exploding in anger when there is no apparent reason to do so. *Flat affect* is the tendency of some people to remain emotionless, perhaps because they neither feel nor can express feelings.

(b) Sensation and Perception. It is difficult to function well if we fail to receive and respond appropriately to stimulation from the world around. Some mental patients have *enhanced sensitivity.* Their hearing may be especially acute, colors are brighter, or sometimes the person is unable to relax or concentrate because he or she feels overwhelmed by the flood of data that seems to be bombarding the senses. In contrast, others experience *blunted sensitivity,* including a reduced ability to feel pain, see clearly, or hear well. At times these people have difficulty sorting out and synthesizing sensations. Some schizophrenics have difficulty watching television, for example, because they can't watch the screen and listen at the same time.[26]

More common perhaps is *distorted sensitivity* in which the person misinterprets stimuli and misperceives the world. Delusions (false ideas believed by the individual but not by anybody else), hallucinations (perceptions that a person experiences even though there is no external stimulation), and illusions (misinterpreting sensations) are all seen in mental patients. Often these are held with strong conviction and the person doesn't change when presented with evidence. Families experience great frustration when they try to convince a disturbed relative that his or her delusions of persecution are without foundation or that the voices one hears are not real.

(c) Thinking. Some psychiatrists suggest that thought disorders are the most obvious indications of mental illness. Often, for example, there is *faulty thought content* in which the person does not think clearly, logically, or consistently.

At times this may be true of everybody; we reach conclusions that aren't completely rational or realistic. Individuals who suffer from phobias may have unfounded fears of heights, enclosed spaces, or thunderstorms. The phobic person knows that these thoughts are irrational, even though they may be difficult to ignore or resist.[27] The mentally ill person, in contrast, may not even recognize that his or her thinking does not make sense, and there is no willingness or ability to change in response to arguments or evidence.

A different kind of thinking concerns *faulty thought progression*. This may include rambling disconnected thoughts, easily interrupted thinking, obsessive thinking, or an inability to think abstractly. In addition, some people appear to be confused, uncertain who or where they are, unable to appreciate the consequences of their behavior, unable to remember, and/or are easily distracted. All of these can show that the person is out of contact with reality.

(d) Behavior. It is not surprising that the person with faulty sensation, perception, emotions, and thinking is also likely to act in ways that are odd or socially inappropriate. This is so common that mental disorders are frequently known as behavior disorders. Ritualistic compulsive activity, hyperactivity, withdrawal, childlike behavior, lack of self-control, religious or political fanaticism and other unusual behaviors can indicate that something is wrong.

Some people, especially young children and the severely disturbed, are not sure how to express their inner turmoil in words. As a result they try to communicate behaviorally, sometimes acting out the confused feelings that they feel inside. The good counselor tries to understand what the behavioral message may mean.[28]

2. *Effects on Families.* Most people are able to think logically, experience emotion appropriately, and cope with life's stresses more or less effectively. When another person lacks these abilities, communication and interaction become extremely difficult. We realize that young children will act in immature and inappropriate ways, but most adults accept this because we know that young people are learning and we can have some influence on their behavior. When immature and inappropriate behavior is seen in one's spouse, parents, or grown children, it is much more difficult for family members to be understanding and to cope.

This difficulty was expressed in one popular article that called schizophrenia "a family nightmare."[29] Entire books have been written to help the families of mental patients cope,[30] and there is evidence that mentally disordered individuals sometimes drag down their more stable relatives. One study found, for example, that when family members live with a depressed person, 40 percent show sufficient distress to warrant counseling themselves. Relatives feel burdened by the depressed person's worrying, fatigue, feelings of hopelessness, and lack of interest in social activities.[31]

Unlike mental patients, who frequently get professional help, families are often left alone to face the uncertainty, confusion, mental stigma, financial pressures, guilt, self-blame, changes in family responsibilities, and tensions that may follow a relative who is found to have a mental disorder.

Families differ in their efforts to cope, but many move through a series of overlapping phases.[32] First the family tries to ignore or explain away the family member's strange behavior. Then comes the first shock of recognition when something happens that is too bizarre or disruptive to be ignored. Next comes a period of withdrawal and reevaluation when the family hopes that things will somehow get better. When this fails to happen, the family starts looking for causes and trying to get treatment. Eventually theirs is a collapse of optimism, sometimes accompanied by the acceptance, distancing, and limit setting shown in Figure 31-2. With difficulty, family members mourn the loss of the hopes and dreams that they had for the afflicted family member. If no improvement comes, the family tries to pick up the pieces and learns to adjust to living with a mentally disabled family member.

Since mental disorders influence so many people, the counselor's work rarely is limited to the mental patients themselves. At times counseling must also extend to families and to the many others who are affected.[33]

Figure 31-2*

How Families Cope with Mental Illness

Families cope in three general ways: Acceptance, Distancing and/or Setting Limits.

Acceptance

- acknowledging the reality of the disability and the likelihood that it will be around for a long time,
- being able to move from a reactive toward a more responsive form of coping,
- being able to work toward what is possible in their situation rather than maintaining unrealistic expectations for themselves or their disabled family member,
- being able to feel the pain, move through it, and move on to other feelings and options,
- becoming less intense,
- knowing that whatever they are doing is the best they can do at the time,
- knowing that they are not the only ones who can make a difference.

Distancing

- separating themselves from behaviors that they cannot change or should not be trying to change,
- tolerating behaviors that may be a little strange to them but that are not dangerous or harmful,
- not assuming responsibility where it does not need to be assumed,
- letting other family members' lives unfold more naturally,
- letting go of what is not possible and focusing on what is possible,
- being selective in their helping.

Setting Limits

- being firm around behaviors they do not like,
- being firm around behaviors they do like,
- knowing their limits and not waiting until they are pushed over the edge,
- living with the upset their limits cause and getting through it,
- knowing that structure can communicate caring,
- caring enough not to let their loved ones do something that is harmful to themselves or others and encouraging their loved ones to do things that are in their own best interests.

*Reproduced by permission. From LeRoy Spaniol, "Coping Strategies of Family Caregivers," in *Families of the Mentally Ill: Coping and Adaptation,* ed. Agnes B. Hatfield and Harriet P. Lefley (New York: Guilford, 1987), 213–14.

Counseling and Mental Disorders

The treatment of mental disorders can be a complex process, best accomplished by professionals working together in teams. Usually the process begins with a complete physical and psychological examination. This may be followed by traditional medical treatment, chemotherapy (the administration of antipsychotic, antidepressant, antianxiety, or other therapeutic drugs),[34] psychotherapy, and sometimes hospitalization or the use of electroconvulsive shock therapy.[35]

Many years ago, long before modern treatment techniques were discovered, mental patients were cruelly treated: whipped, starved, chained, seared with hot irons, dunked into freezing water and otherwise tortured, often with church sanction. Clergy and others held the view that physical abuse would drive out the illness-causing demons. Not until the early 1800s were more humane treatment methods proposed and used, first in France and Britain, then in America.

Early American psychiatry used what was termed "moral treatment"—an approach characterized by kindness, self-respect, patience, and meaningful relationships. The therapist treated patients as if they were mentally well. Counseling consisted of resocialization through therapies that today might be called recreational, physical, occupational, industrial, musical, and physical. Moral treatment appears to have been a high point in the history of emotional disorders; a movement that got lost in the industrial revolution that followed.[36]

Because of advances in treatment techniques, most mental disorders are treated today by professionals, but the principles of moral treatment can still be helpful. The community, and especially the church, can provide the ongoing support, warmth, acceptance, caring, and contact with reality that busy professionals often have limited time to give. At times the pastor or other church leader can help the mentally ill person get professional help, and frequently the church becomes the greatest source of support for the mentally ill person's family.[37]

Helping Families. Life can be very difficult for those who must live with someone who is deeply depressed, suicidal, inclined to be violent, or seriously mentally disabled. Family members are often the primary care givers for the mentally ill, but this consumes time, energy, emotional stamina, and sometimes eats up the family's financial resources. Activities and interests that once were pleasant and daily routines that used to be habitual or uninterrupted may be changed forcibly. Individual lifestyles and goals are altered. Family togetherness is so often disrupted that a conscious effort is required if the family is to retain a sense of unity. Many have difficulty keeping sensitive both to the needs of the person with the disability and to the needs and goals of the other family members.[38] How can these families be helped?

(a) Support. A variety of support groups exist to give guidance and encouragement to families of the mentally ill. These groups, composed often of others who have a mentally ill family member, have names such as Families Together for Mental Health, County Mental Health Support Group, Relatives and Friends of the Mentally Disabled, Families of Adult Mentally Ill, or Schizophrenia Support Group. Sometimes they are listed in the phone book; more often their existence can be traced through community mental health clinics or private professional counselors.[39]

Family support and advocacy groups enable family members to find others who understand the stresses of living with a severely disturbed person. The groups help participants deal with the anger, guilt, self-blame, and stigma that are so common. Often these groups help families learn how to manage and live with relatives who may show bizarre attitudes and behavior, aggressive and other antisocial actions, unkempt appearance and poor hygiene, social withdrawal and isolation, self-destructive tendencies, and sometimes perpetual and unrealistic demands. Many of the more disruptive aspects of mental disorders can now be controlled by medications, but often these drugs must be administered by family members who feel insecure about this responsibility. When a mental patient comes home following a period of hospitalization, the family may need special support throughout the initial period of readjustment.[40]

Shouldn't this kind of support come from the church? The answer, of course, is yes, but in many churches the members have little or no understanding of mental disorders and few can comprehend the pressures that family members face. Nevertheless the local body of believers must be at the center of supportive care for those with mentally incapacitated family members.

(b) Education. Until a mental disorder strikes, many family members have no understanding of psychopathology. Education, therefore, becomes important. Family members need to understand the nature and treatment of mental illness, but they also need education in how to cope with the disturbed person, how to give care, and how to keep their own lives from being swallowed up by the disturbed family member.

If they are to cope successfully, family members need to involve themselves in activities, hobbies and interests that are personally satisfying but have nothing to do with mental illness. Involvement in the church, spending time with friends, finding meaningful work, pursuing educational or other goals, engaging in physical exercise, getting away periodically for lunch or for a minivacation can be therapeutic for family members. Without such diversions, life can get out of balance, and family members become drained and worn out.

Getting away can be difficult if a disabled person needs constant care, if the family member feels guilt about leaving, if the mentally ill person encourages this guilt, or if there appears to be nobody who can take over the care-giving duties temporarily. Once again, the church can give practical support to a hurting family, and the counselor sometimes can stimulate the church involvement.[41]

(c) Counseling. Sometimes support and education are not enough. Family members need more specialized help in coping with their own feelings of futility, guilt, worry, and insecurity. Since the strain can be so overwhelming, family members may themselves begin to show symptoms of emotional disturbance, and this in turn can lead to a relapse in the mentally ill person, especially when family members are critical, hostile, or impatient.

In contrast, family counseling can lower tension, give encouragement, promote tolerance, allow the expression of emotions, deal with conflicts in the home, and teach family members how to care for the patient. In one study of schizophrenics, family meetings in the first year following hospitalization reduced relapse sixfold. These meetings were most effective when they were held in the home, rather than at a clinic or counselor's office.[42] Such meetings give opportunity for families to see their strengths, to ask questions, to learn about community resources, to clarify goals, to acknowledge their limitations, and to learn practical ways to get away for a break without feeling guilty or shirking family responsibilities.[43]

Counseling and Suicide. "Epidemic" may be an overused word but it has been used with increasing frequency to describe the rise in suicide rates, especially during the past three decades. Suicide and suicide attempts appear to be increasing among children,[44] prisoners,[45] the elderly,[46] young adults,[47] and especially among teenagers.[48] The problem is not limited to mental patients or to nonbelievers. Suicide has become increasingly prevalent among believers, including evangelicals.[49]

In the chapter on depression[50] we listed some of the clues that are seen in people who contemplate suicide. Often these people are overwhelmed by feelings of hopelessness and many see no further options for dealing with their problems. Suicide may seem like the best way to escape a situation of intense suffering,[51] and some people are so relieved when they finally decide on this solution that they are able to mask their plans with smiles and expressions of false cheer.[52] More often, however, the subtle presuicide clues indicate a cry for help.

When a counselee gives indications of suicidal thinking, it is appropriate to ask gently if this is being considered. Sometimes counselees are relieved to have the issue out in the open where it can be discussed. In assessing risk, try to determine if the person has considered a method, has chosen a means that is likely to be lethal (guns are more lethal than bottles of aspirin), has tried suicide before, and has a history of severe problems or mental disturbance. All of these increase the likelihood of suicide.

Try to assess what brought the counselee to this point of crisis. What solutions were attempted and failed in dealing with this and similar crises in the past? What could be tried in the future? As you talk with the counselee, challenge the romantic ideas about death. Teenagers, for example, sometimes think friends will grieve forever and talk about the victim's wonderful and tragic qualities. Point out that this might not happen, that others will get on with their lives, and that suicide is a permanent solution to what might be a temporary problem. Try to show respect for the person, don't shame or belittle, avoid arguments if possible, and let the individual know that you care. In all of this, remember the importance of prayer, asking God to give you wisdom and sensitivity.

Often your care and interest will help to defuse the suicide idea, at least temporarily, but if the individual persists in his or her determination, try to contact the family physician, a close relative, a suicide prevention center, or a counselor who has special training in dealing with suicidal emergencies.

What do you do if the person commits suicide? Often counselors and families feel guilt, anger, and self-condemnation because the suicide was not prevented. At times the counselor may be involved in helping survivors, many of whom show grief mixed with remorse. Sometimes the suicide is rarely mentioned either by the survivors or by relatives, friends, and church members who want to express condolences to the family but aren't sure if they should mention the cause of death. Like any other problem, the pain of suicide is best discussed honestly and compassionately, without attempts to avoid the pain that survivors feel.[53]

For the survivors, suicide is a painful and deeply distressing experience. Taking a life, including one's own life, is sin, but it is not the unpardonable sin. Close friends and family members may criticize themselves for not preventing the loved one's death, but ultimately the responsibility for suicide rests with the victim who was unable or unwilling to cope with the pressures of life. Christian counselors and those who worship alongside us in church need to show compassion and sensitivity in the aftermath of suicide. We must take care not to glamorize the suicide, lest this give reason for others to follow the victim's example.

Preventing Mental Disorders

A few months after his arrest for attempting to kill the president, young John Hinckley tried to kill himself. It wasn't his only attempt, but this one nearly succeeded. Once again, his family faced the uncertainty, the long waits, the embarrassment, and the questions of "why?" Once again the family was faced with the pain of mental illness and long talks about how this might have been prevented.

The prevention of mental illness and suicide has become a topic of increasing importance during the past several years.[54] Efforts often focus on physical treatment, education, helping people in the community spot potential problems, and giving special support and guidance to high-risk groups such as the adult children of alcoholics or children from broken homes. Community hot lines, support groups, and suicide prevention centers have been established worldwide, but the effectiveness of these efforts is still uncertain.[55] It is difficult to motivate people to be involved in preventing a problem that has not yet appeared, and the effects of prevention are almost impossible to measure.

A concise discussion of prevention has been given by psychologist George Albee.

> Most of the great plagues that have afflicted humankind through the centuries have been eliminated by effective primary prevention—working with large groups of people not yet affected by a disease to eliminate sources of infection or contagion and to build up resistance to the disease. . . .
>
> In the case of mental disorders, the key elements are not bacteria, viruses or other noxious organic agents but a high level of current or past stress that may be engendered by many things, including serious marital problems; involuntary unemployment; sexual confusion and guilt; or a childhood history of serious neglect, physical abuse, sexual exploitation and lack of affection.
>
> To lessen the incidence of mental disorders through prevention, we must reduce problems in three areas—organic factors, stress and exploitation of various kinds—and increase resources in three others—coping skills, self-esteem and support groups. To give just a few of many possible examples in each area, we can: reduce organic problems by improving nutrition during pregnancy and by reducing lead in the environment; reduce stress through guaranteed employment and better care and housing for the elderly; lessen the abuse of children and exploitation of women and minorities of all kinds; improve competence through assertiveness training and courses on preparation for marriage; increase self-esteem through fairer press portrayals of the aged, the handicapped, women and minorities; and finally, and perhaps most important, encourage the further development of self-help movements and support groups such as home health care programs, Meals on Wheels, day care centers and Big Brother/Big Sister programs. . . .

> Research has made it very clear that individuals who have the support of such organizations are much better off emotionally than those who face their problems alone.[56]

This is a creative proposal, one that involves intervention at all levels of society, but a program that is beyond the capabilities, resources, and time available to most counselors. Even as he advocates "prevention through social change," Albee concludes that this is "a faint but persistent hope."[57]

No one person, counseling agency, community or church can do everything, but each of us can carve out some area of need and work to prevent problems from getting worse. Some will work in drug prevention programs or suicide prevention centers. Others will concentrate on marriage enrichment, preretirement counseling or divorce recovery. Some will stimulate development of support groups that help the survivors of suicide, parents of handicapped children, unmarried pregnant teenagers, children of alcoholics, or others who could develop more severe emotional disorders.

The church has a role to play in this effort. Jesus demonstrated compassion, caring, and social concern, even as he preached the gospel and called people to repentance. Can we too find ways to fulfill the Great Commission while we also care for the needy, including the mentally disabled and those who are especially susceptible to mental illness?

Conclusions about Mental Disorders

In the mid-1960s, federal authorities and mental health experts embarked on an ambitious program to phase out large mental hospitals and move the mentally disabled into more humane and convenient community treatment centers. This was a creative idea that seems to have failed. The hospitals were depopulated, but there was insufficient housing, transitional care, and job training that could integrate patients into society. As a result increasing numbers of mental patients spilled into the streets, and we appear to have created a new class of needy people: the homeless mentally ill.[58]

There *is* cause for hope, however. Despite the prevalence of mental disorders and limited treatment facilities, people do get better. In the late 1950s, researchers selected a sample of the most chronically ill (lowest third) patients in the Vermont State Hospital and assigned them to a rehabilitation program. Eventually, all were released into the community. Over thirty years later, 68 percent of the 168 former patients who were still alive were found to be functioning adequately and with no evidence of mental disorders. The researchers concluded that "contrary to the expected downward and deteriorating course for schizophrenia or for other severe and chronic psychiatric disorders, symptoms can be ameliorated over time and functioning can be restored."[59]

Jesus once predicted that the poor will always be with us. Perhaps the same could be said for people with mental disorders. However, just as the gospel can reach the poor (as well as the rich), so the Word of God can bring solace and guidance both to the mentally disabled and to those who are healthier. Helping the mentally ill and their families is one of the greatest challenges for the Christian counselor.

SUGGESTIONS FOR FURTHER READING

Bennett, George. *When the Mental Patient Comes Home.* Philadelphia: Westminster, 1980.*

Blackburn, Bill. *What You Should Know about Suicide.* Waco, Tex.: Word, 1982.*

Hatfield, Agnes B., and Harriet P. Lefley, eds. *Families of the Mentally Ill: Coping and Adaptation.* New York: Guilford, 1987.

Maxmen, Jerrold S. *Essential Psychopathology.* New York: Norton, 1986.

Torrey, E. Fuller. *Surviving Schizophrenia: A Family Manual.* New York: Harper & Row, 1983.*

Wolman, Benjamin B., ed. *The Therapist's Handbook: Treatment Methods of Mental Disorders.* 2d ed. New York: Van Nostrand Reinhold, 1983.

* Books marked with an asterisk (*) are especially suited for counselees to read.

32

Alcoholism

LOREN IS THIRTY-EIGHT, a Christian, and the owner of a moderately successful little business. He hasn't had a drink for eight years, but Loren still considers himself an alcoholic.

"I'm a drunk," he told a group of high school students recently. "God pulled me back to sobriety, with the help of a loving wife and some patient people in a clinic for alcoholics. But I know that if I take one drink—ever again—I'll be back where I was before."

As a child, Loren attended church every week with his family. The pastor sometimes condemned drunkenness, but nobody in the congregation ever admitted to drinking and alcohol was never seen in Loren's home.

Things were different at college where almost everybody drank, including the Christians. A drink or two helped Loren feel better, especially when there were academic pressures. Sometimes he would get drunk at weekend parties. Once he was arrested for drunken driving, but he managed to hide this from his parents and convinced himself that his increasing use of alcohol was "typical student behavior," an opportunity for him to live it up a little before settling down.

After graduation, Loren got married and settled into his new job at a stock broker's office. The work was challenging and sometimes stressful, but the future looked bright. Loren enjoyed the opportunity to have lunch with his clients, but some coworkers noticed that he drank more than anybody else and usually didn't think too clearly when he got back to work. Often he later would stop at a bar to unwind on the way home from work, and sometimes he would still be there at one or two in the morning. He looked somewhat scornfully at others who couldn't control their drinking, but he denied emphatically that he had an alcohol problem.

Loren's wife tried to help. Sometimes she found liquor hidden in the house; it was poured down the sink. When her husband was too drunk to go to work, she called the boss to explain that Loren was not feeling well. When his parents had a fortieth anniversary celebration, she went to the dinner alone and apologized because her husband was caught up in his work, when in reality he was drunk. In the evenings, when the kids would ask questions about their father, she brushed them aside and tried to get the children into bed and asleep before Loren would stagger in the door. When he complained about her appearance, she agreed that her extra weight must be the problem and went on a diet. None of this worked to stop Loren's drinking.

One night he caused a serious accident on the way home from work. A little boy was badly hurt, and Loren found himself in trouble with the law, with his employer, and—at last—with his own conscience.

No longer could he pretend that he didn't have a drinking problem. His career was gone, his family was deeply hurt, his spiritual life was in shambles, his health was declining, and the judge left him only two choices: go to jail or enter a rehabilitation program.

He chose the latter and now is glad he did. "If I hadn't stopped drinking and had somebody to help me," he admits freely, "I would have been dead by now."

Alcohol abuse is a serious social, health, and moral problem. It disrupts families, ruins careers, destroys bodies, tears apart friendships, and leads to untold human misery. Statistics vary from year to year and from place to place, but in the United States alcohol misuse is involved in at least half of all fatal traffic accidents, fire deaths, drownings, arrests, murders, and incidents of child abuse and other violence in the home. Alcohol is involved in 41 percent of assaults, 34 percent of rapes, and 30 percent of suicides. The Department of Justice estimates that nearly one-third of the nation's prison inmates drank heavily before committing the crimes that landed them in jail. A recent Gallup poll showed that one family in four is troubled by alcohol, a significant increase over previous surveys.

At present, about 10 million Americans and 600,000 Canadians are alcoholics. They come from every socioeconomic level, most ethnic groups, and almost every age group, including one in five teenagers and increasing numbers of elderly drinkers. Alcoholism is common among both men and women. It cripples individuals outside of the church as well as those inside, including evangelicals. It is a major killer, ranking third after heart disease and cancer. It results in twenty-five times more deaths than are claimed by cocaine, heroin, and other illegal drugs combined. The focus of a $1 billion alcoholism treatment industry, alcohol abuse costs the economy well over $100 billion a year in reduced work efficiency, absenteeism, property damage, treatment expenses, and premature deaths.[1]

The prevalence of drinking varies throughout the world. In some Middle Eastern Muslim countries alcohol use is almost nonexistent; in parts of Europe almost everybody drinks. In the United States two out of every three persons over the age of fifteen consumes alcohol on occasion. This includes 95 percent of college students, about half the ministers, and one-third of those who call themselves evangelicals.[2] Most drink in moderation and confine their consumption to social occasions, some become heavy drinkers who have problems because they drink too much and get drunk several times every month, and about 10 percent of all drinkers become alcoholics.

What Is an Alcoholic? Even the experts disagree. Pioneer researcher E. M. Jellinek called alcoholism a disease. A recent Gallup poll found that 87 percent of those interviewed would agree, as would most counselors and physicians.[3] According to one definition, alcoholism is a complex, chronic, progressive disease in which the use of alcohol increasingly interferes with one's health, social, and economic functioning. Others have challenged the disease concept,[4] preferring instead to see alcoholism as a social phenomenon, a behavior disorder, or clear evidence of sin. "At the same time we say through our lips that alcoholism is a chronic disease," one physician told a *Time* reporter "many of us feel in our guts that it's a moral or self-inflicted problem."[5]

The World Health Organization gives a definition that avoids any reference to disease or morality. According to WHO, alcoholics are "those excessive drinkers whose dependence on alcohol has attained such a degree that it shows a noticeable mental disturbance or an interference with their bodily or mental health, their interpersonal relations, and their smooth economic and social functioning." Although alcoholics differ in their symptoms and in the speed with which their condition develops, all show physical symptoms, psychological difficulties (including an obsessive desire to drink), and behavioral problems that disrupt one's social or work life.

Is Alcoholism a Sickness or a Sin? This question is not confined to Christians. Physicians and many insurance companies accept alcoholism as a disease because it is predictable, progressive, physiologically debilitating, and treatable. By calling alcoholism a disease, individuals are less likely to be condemned and more likely to get treatment that insurance companies will finance.

The disease concept tends to relieve the alcoholic of personal responsibility. At his perjury trial, a former White House aide argued that he was not guilty of illegal acts because he was suffering from the "disease" of alcoholism when he broke the law. Certainly it is true that some people are physiologically more prone to become alcoholics, but at some time every drinker makes the decision to take a first drink and, at least at the beginning, each person can decide whether to stop or continue. "The disease concept of alcoholism is out of tune with the facts and a serious obstacle to rational solutions," writes one psychiatrist in the *British Medical Journal*. "What determines whether a person becomes dependent on alcohol is how much he drinks and for how long, rather than his personality, psychodynamics, or biochemistry."[6]

Alcoholism is a progressive addiction that engulfs its victim psychologically and physically, but alcoholism is also a moral condition for which the drinker is at least partially responsible. It is both simplistic and extreme to conclude that alcoholism is *only* a disease or *only* a black-and-white case of sin.

In the pages that follow, we will assume that alcoholism is *both* a sickness and a sin. Both are involved in the development of alcohol addiction; both must be considered in treatment.

The Bible and Alcoholism

The Bible does not appear to teach abstinence, although it does teach temperance. In Psalm 104, wine is included among the blessings from God and described as something that "gladdens the heart of man." In his first miracle, Jesus made wine from water, wine apparently was taken at the last supper, and it appears that Jesus himself drank wine.[7] Paul showed no hesitation in urging Timothy to "use a little wine" because of his stomach problems and frequent illnesses.[8]

According to one writer, the wine in first-century Judea was mixed with water, probably on an average of three parts water to one part wine. Translated into modern terms, two present-day martinis would equal twenty-two glasses of Palestinian wine.[9] Even so, the early wine could produce drunkenness, and the headwaiter at the Cana wedding implied that people drank freely and at the end of the celebration were less able to tell good wine from bad.[10] Whether the wine was strong or diluted, the drinker had a responsibility to control his or her input.

Throughout the pages of Scripture, excessive drinking is condemned. "Wine is a mocker and beer a brawler; whoever is led astray by them is not wise," the writer of Proverbs warned.[11] "Do not join with those who drink too much wine or gorge themselves with meat, for drunkards and gluttons become poor, and drowsiness clothes them in rags."[12] Paul gave a similar warning. "Do not get drunk on wine," he wrote to the Ephesians. This "leads to debauchery. Instead, be filled with the Spirit."[13]

Perhaps no biblical passage is more powerful and more descriptive of alcohol abuse than Prov. 23:29–35:

> Who has woe? Who has sorrow? Who has strife? Who has complaints? Who has needless bruises? Who has bloodshot eyes?
>
> Those who linger over wine, who go to sample bowls of mixed wine.
>
> Do not gaze at wine when it is red, when it sparkles in the cup, when it goes down smoothly!
>
> In the end it bites like a snake and poisons like a viper.
>
> Your eyes will see strange sights and your mind imagine confusing things.
>
> You will be like one sleeping on the high seas, lying on top of the rigging.
>
> "They hit me," you will say,"but I'm not hurt! They beat me up but I do not feel it! When will I wake up so I can have another drink?"

Although the Bible warns against drunkenness and teaches moderation in drinking, abstinence was also considered favorably. John the Baptist was a special messenger from God who "drank no wine."[14] When a person took the Nazarite vow, "to dedicate himself to the Lord," this was marked by abstinence from wine and strong drink.[15]

Many Christians today would conclude that moderation is good, but abstinence is better, especially in view of the clear dangers inherent in drinking. Alcohol is a mind-altering drug that for some can become psychologically and physically addicting. While its moderate use is not condemned or forbidden by Scripture, drinking may fall into the category of an act that is permissible but not beneficial.[16] If questionable behavior such as drinking alcoholic beverages controls the drinker, hurts the body, numbs sensation, dulls the mind, makes one more susceptible to immorality and other sin, causes harm to other human beings, or makes another believer stumble and fall, then such practices should be abandoned or avoided.[17] Sometimes believers must choose to use self-restraint because this will be for the good and growth of the body of Christ, the church.

What if another believer falls, begins drinking heavily or becomes an alcoholic? Spirit-led Christians, including counselors, have a responsibility to restore people who fall into sinful patterns of behavior that harm themselves or others. In a spirit of gentleness, humility, and compassion the people-helper patiently seeks to do good, confronting the fallen one with his or her responsibilities, and trusting that at the proper time, there will be restoration if we do not give up.[18]

The Causes of Alcoholism

Several years ago, a group of experts from Europe, Australia, North America, and Southeast Asia gathered in Bangalore, India, to discuss a Christian response to the alcohol and drug problem. The participants agreed that alcoholism is not limited to any one part of the world and neither is it a problem of recent origin.[19] From the dawn of recorded history, alcohol has been abused. Research from around the world demonstrates that the causes of this abuse are complex. There is no one reason for alcoholism. In most cases a combination of the following makes some people especially prone to addiction.

1. *Physiology and Heredity.* An increasing body of research shows that some people tend to inherit a high vulnerability to alcoholism. When compared to the children of nonalcoholics, the sons and daughters of alcoholic parents are four times more likely to become alcoholics when they grow up. This is true, even when the children of alcoholics are adopted at birth and raised without knowledge of the real parents' alcoholism. In contrast, children of nonalcoholics show no greater than average evidence of alcoholism, even when they are raised by an alcoholic parent.[20]

It is unlikely that anyone inherits a gene or genes for alcoholism. More likely, because of genetically based biological influences, some people have a high risk of becoming alcoholics if they start drinking.[21] One recent study, for example, compared the influence of alcohol on two groups of males in their teens and early twenties. The groups were carefully matched in terms of age, race, religion, education, habits of drinking, and other characteristics, but one group had alcoholic fathers and the other did not. When these young men were given alcoholic drinks they responded differently. Even though everyone had identical blood alcohol levels, the children of alcoholics felt less intoxicated, and performed better on intellectual and motor tests. This confirms other research that people who become alcoholics initially have greater tolerance for alcohol and less awareness of its impact. As a result, they are less likely to adjust their alcoholic intake and more likely to become addicted.[22]

2. *Environmental Influences.* The family in which one was raised, the place where we live, or the society and ethnic group to which we belong can all increase or decrease the likelihood of addiction.

(a) The Home Environment. Within the past decade, counselors have given increasing attention to the children of alcoholics (known often at COAs). At present, 7 million Americans below the age of eighteen live in alcoholic homes. These children feel confused, angry, scared, and often guilty. Eventually they will join the 21 million adult children of alcoholics (ACOAs), many of whom go through life carrying the emotional scars of their early years in an alcoholic home.

Often these people are insecure, self-condemning, and afraid of intimacy. Children in alcoholic families learn three rules for survival: don't talk, don't trust, and don't feel. When these young people become adults, they continue to have problems with trust, dependency, self-control, and the identification and expression of feelings.[23] Some become depressed, some develop eating disorders, and many live in constant fear of becoming alcoholic like their parents.[24] Despite these fears, many children of alcoholics do slip into the clutches of alcoholism.

As we have seen, sometimes genetic influences help to create this fall, but the home environment and parental attitudes are also important. When parents don't care if the children drink or if there is no concern about the dangers of alcohol, misuse often follows. If parents are neglectful or excessively punitive, the children may withdraw or rebel, and alcoholism often follows.

This pattern can be prevented. Some children grow up in alcoholic homes and are able to escape the harmful influences. In one study of a thousand adult children of alcoholics, 10.7 percent reported that they were not affected by growing up in an alcoholic home, and 11.1 percent said that they had been moderately affected; however, the remaining 78.2 percent said that they had been highly affected by the experience.[25]

(b) The Cultural Expectations. If a culture or subcultural group has clear guidelines about the use of alcohol or other drugs, abuse is less likely. Among Jews, for example, young people are generally permitted to drink, but drunkenness is condemned and the rate of alcoholism is low. In contrast, cultures such as ours are more tolerant of drunkenness. Teenage and college drinking is winked at as a sign of growing up; inebriation becomes a topic for television and cocktail hour jokes. Since getting "high" is often the "in" thing to do, conditions are ripe for alcohol abuse.

Religious differences also have an influence on drinking patterns. One study found that groups like Episcopalians or Presbyterians had a high number of alcohol users but a low number of problem drinkers. In contrast, according to one study, only 48 percent of Baptists used alcohol at all, but 18 percent of those got into trouble. Some of these may have been Christians trying to throw off the restraints of their moral and religious backgrounds. In doing so, they developed drinking problems.[26]

In their highly acclaimed book on alcoholism, Anderson Spickard and Barbara R. Thompson conclude that groups with high rates of alcoholism and groups with low rates are not separated by biological or racial differences. "The two most important factors are attitudes toward public drunkenness and whether or not drinking takes place outside of meals." Nations and groups that drink only at the dinner table and do not tolerate public drunkenness do not have high rates of alcoholism.[27] In view of these findings, perhaps it isn't surprising that alcoholism is a major problem in America.

3. *Present Stress.* Alcoholism often begins in the stressful teenage years. Consider, for example, how a hypothetical teenage male might become addicted.[28] By "normal" we mean that he likes some things about himself and dislikes others. In some things he feels competent and in others he feels inadequate. Like most people of this age, he experiences anxiety, fears, guilt, disappointment, and insecurity in certain situations. Even if he comes from a good family, sometimes there will be tension at home. Having been raised in an affluent society, he may be accustomed to comfort and the immediate gratification of his needs and desires. Because of this comfortable childhood, adolescent stresses may hit with special intensity.

Let us suppose further that about this time the young person has the opportunity to take his first drink. (Recent evidence suggests that many people take their first drinks long before they reach high school.) If our hypothetical person is typical, he may have seen the joys of beer drinking lauded in the almost 100,000 television commercials that he has seen during his life.[29] He may experience pressure from his friends, a desire to see what it is like to drink and get drunk, identification with a group or hero who drinks, a belief that alcohol use will prove his manhood, or be a way of getting even with his parents. Although teenagers tend to drink to get drunk, some use drinking as a reason for friends to get together and to relieve their stresses by relaxing with one another.

When our hypothetical young person starts to drink he may feel a sense of euphoria. He feels tranquil, less nervous, more adequate, and socially at ease. His problems or stresses seem less severe and the world looks rosy. If the drinking continues, there may be periodic hangovers or remorse during times of sobriety, but the alcohol use persists because the mood change is so pleasant and the danger seems so minimal.

By the time the young man is into his early twenties, drinking has become a habit. When he reaches thirty, his use of alcohol may have become an integrated part of his lifestyle. He is now addicted both physically and psychologically. Unlike earlier times, his body needs larger and larger quantities of alcohol to create euphoria and to relieve anxiety. If alcohol is withdrawn, sickness results (only more alcohol can take away the symptoms), and sometimes there are severe withdrawal symptoms including delirium tremens, disorientation, hallucinations, or seizures.

When he reaches middle age, acquiring and consuming alcohol has become so important that his personal, family, social, and business life all suffer. The person who began drinking as a way of relaxation and stress management has now become addicted. As the addiction has built, the needs for the drug have increased, self-control has lessened, work has suffered, and so has one's health, psychological stability, and social relationships.

4. *Perpetuating Influences.* To understand alcoholism and other addictions, we must recognize what makes some people vulnerable (including genetic influences, personality, culture, and family background), what motivates people to start drinking (primarily stress or the influences of others), and what perpetuates or keeps the addiction going.

At some time in the addiction process, endocrine and biochemical changes occur that make withdrawal very difficult. Equally powerful are the psychological changes that have built up over the years. The alcohol has become increasingly important until it becomes the core around which life is organized. It may be the cause of one's problems, but the drinker may also see alcohol as the solution, a magic but tragic potion that dulls the stresses of life.

The members of Alcoholics Anonymous believe that no cure will come until the person reaches bottom, admitting that he or she is powerless over alcohol and unable to manage life without the help of a power greater than ourselves. Drinkers are transformed only after they are willing to surrender.[30]

Strange as it may seem, this transformation is often delayed by the people who most want change to occur; namely, the alcoholic's family. Few alcoholics live on skid row. Most live at home with their families. As the alcoholic addiction gets worse, each member of the household is affected. Often each tries to deny the reality of the situation. Each family member is both protective and critical of the drinker, but each also tries to hold the family together with as little additional strain as possible. First, there is an attempt to control or stop the family member's drinking. Then there is an effort to understand it and eliminate the causes. Often there is an effort to hide the drinking behavior from the community even while the drinker is being urged repeatedly to quit.[31]

Sometimes the family members slip into survival roles, which are sincere and sometimes unconscious efforts to keep the family together and to prevent it from buckling under the stress. The *enabler role,* for example, is taken by the person, usually the spouse, who seeks to take responsibility for meeting the family needs. The *family hero,* usually the oldest child, tries to make things better for the family, often takes responsibility for the younger siblings, and fills in as the nondrinking parent's confidant and helper. The *scapegoat* acts out the family stresses, gets into trouble and often distracts attention from the drinking problem. In contrast, the *mascot* tries to inject humor into a painful situation, while the *lost child* covers up his or her feelings and tries to be the one person whom the family does not have to worry about. Sometimes the lost child stays away from home as much as possible and often turns to other adults and families for support and closeness. All of this reflects the pain and pathos that infiltrate and characterize the alcoholic's family.[32]

Roles such as these keep the family going, but they also can support the alcoholic in his or her addiction. As long as the family seems to be getting along, there is less motivation to change. The family, therefore, is caught in a trap where winning is impossible. If they adjust to the addiction, the problem is perpetuated and the pain goes on. If the family doesn't adjust, everybody is hurt, and the pain still continues.

Many counselors agree that treatment will be delayed and improvement will be prevented, as long as family members perpetuate the problem by denying its reality, hiding it from others, and protecting the drinker from facing the consequences of his or her irresponsible and self-centered behavior. Most families of alcoholics eventually discover that overprotection of the drinker or accepting the addict's rationalizations and excuses doesn't help. The sooner everyone faces the reality of the situation, the better.[33]

The family, however, is not the only group that perpetuates the addiction problem. The problem persists when employers, the drinker's friends, or others overlook the problem and try to ignore its existence. Society as a whole also perpetuates the problem when people overlook the seriousness of addiction, laugh at inebriation, tolerate drunken driving, excuse crimes committed under the influence of alcohol, use terms like "happy hour" or "Christmas cheer" to describe alcohol use, permit the free advertising of alcoholic beverages without warnings about its dangers, and portray alcohol use as an effective way to relax and cope with stress.

5. *Spiritual Influences.* It probably is true that nobody starts out to be an addict. Circumstances, genetics, family background, continuing stress, and innocent choices can lead almost anyone into addiction.[34] The route to addiction is made easier when human beings lack spiritual, religious, and moral values.

Many people grow up in homes where there is a spiritual void because of the lack of religious beliefs and instruction. Materialism, personal pleasure, and vocational success become substitute gods. When these prove elusive or when they fail to satisfy, individuals sense increasing stress and a feeling of emptiness that drugs or alcohol seem able to fill, at least temporarily.

It could be argued that human beings have an inner need for a real and growing relationship with God. When this craving is denied, unrecognized, and unfilled, there is a search for something else that will fill the vacuum. This is stated clearly in the Bible. "Don't drink too much wine, for many evils lie along that path; be filled instead with the Holy Spirit, and controlled by him."[35] Here, in one sentence, is a warning, an implied cause, and an answer to the problem of alcoholic addiction.

The Effects of Alcoholism

Excessive use of alcohol does not affect everyone in the same way. It is well known, for example, that some people become charming and loquacious after a few drinks, others become nasty and aggressive. Some hide their alcoholic intake well, but others show almost immediate behavior changes.[36] Even with these differences, however, developing alcoholics show many similar physical and behavioral effects of the addiction.

Figure 32-1 shows the effects of alcohol addiction as one moves from the early stages of occasional social drinking through the crucial and chronic phases to the point where complete defeat is admitted and the alcoholic progresses through rehabilitation to recovery.

1. *Physical Effects.* Whenever a chemical substance is taken into the body there will be a physiological reaction. The nature of this reaction depends on the physical condition of the person, the type of drug taken, the amount, and the frequency with which it is used.

Alcohol is a toxin (poison) that affects most body cells. If taken rapidly, the alcohol content of the blood rises, the brain's functioning is impaired temporarily, and the drinker's balance, motor skills, thinking, and emotional responses are influenced. If alcohol is taken consistently and in large amounts, almost every body organ will be affected either directly or indirectly, and severe physical damage can result.

In about one-third of all heavy drinkers, for example, liver cells are destroyed and the organ is no longer able to process the nutrients in food. This liver disease, cirrhosis, is usually painless until the damage is too advanced to be treated successfully.

Heavy alcohol use can also permanently damage the brain and nervous system, lead to numerous gastrointestinal diseases, put extra pressure on the heart so that strokes or heart attacks are more likely, inhibit the manufacture of red and white blood cells, lead to impotence, and cause potentially serious risk to a developing fetus. Recent research suggests that long-term alcohol abuse can also increase the risk of liver, stomach, colon, or breast cancer.[37] Because of these physical aspects of addiction, medical intervention is a crucial part of treatment.

2. *Psychological-Social Effects.* Since alcohol abuse is so common, many people are familiar with its most obvious effects: dulled thinking, inappropriate behavior and emotional responses, self-neglect, withdrawal, and loss of social inhibitions. As the condition worsens, psychological defenses begin to build, most noticeably rationalizations (making excuses for drinking or the resulting behavior), repression (a spontaneous forgetting of shameful and painful memories), projection (blaming others for one's problems and unacceptable thoughts, feelings, or actions) and, perhaps most common of all, denial that a problem exists.[38] Later life is built around getting enough alcohol; all else is of secondary importance.

3. *Family Effects.* The family effects of alcohol abuse have already been mentioned. Families at first try to protect, control, and blame the drinker. Then they take over the alcoholic's responsibilities, all the while living with tension, fear, insecurity, and shame. Often there is embarrassment that leads the family to withdraw from others. As a result there may be loneliness and social isolation.

4. *Spiritual Effects.* It is impossible to grow spiritually when one is dependent on and controlled by a drug. Many alcoholics know this, but they seem powerless

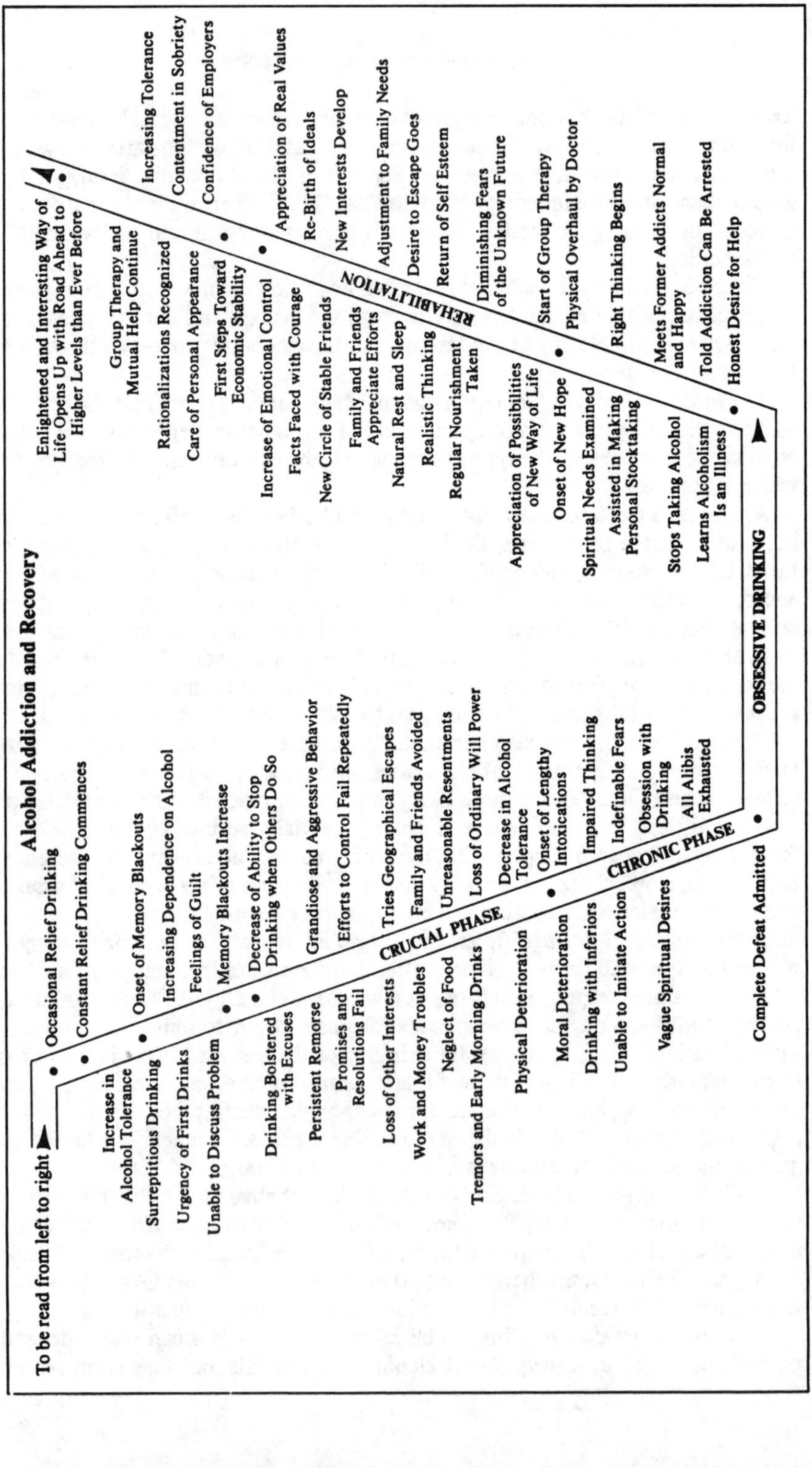

Figure 32–1

Alcohol Addiction and Recovery

To be read from left to right

Occasional Relief Drinking
Constant Relief Drinking Commences
Increase in Alcohol Tolerance
Onset of Memory Blackouts
Surreptitious Drinking
Increasing Dependence on Alcohol
Urgency of First Drinks
Feelings of Guilt
Unable to Discuss Problem
Memory Blackouts Increase
Decrease of Ability to Stop Drinking when Others Do So
Drinking Bolstered with Excuses
Persistent Remorse
Grandiose and Aggressive Behavior
Promises and Resolutions Fail
Efforts to Control Fail Repeatedly

CRUCIAL PHASE

Loss of Other Interests
Tries Geographical Escapes
Work and Money Troubles
Family and Friends Avoided
Neglect of Food
Unreasonable Resentments
Tremors and Early Morning Drinks
Loss of Ordinary Will Power
Decrease in Alcohol Tolerance
Physical Deterioration
Onset of Lengthy Intoxications
Moral Deterioration

CHRONIC PHASE

Drinking with Inferiors
Impaired Thinking
Unable to Initiate Action
Indefinable Fears
Vague Spiritual Desires
Obsession with Drinking
All Alibis Exhausted
Complete Defeat Admitted

OBSESSIVE DRINKING

Honest Desire for Help
Learns Alcoholism Is an Illness
Told Addiction Can Be Arrested
Stops Taking Alcohol
Meets Former Addicts Normal and Happy
Assisted in Making Personal Stocktaking
Right Thinking Begins
Spiritual Needs Examined
Physical Overhaul by Doctor
Onset of New Hope
Start of Group Therapy
Appreciation of Possibilities of New Way of Life
Diminishing Fears of the Unknown Future

REHABILITATION

Regular Nourishment Taken
Return of Self Esteem
Realistic Thinking
Desire to Escape Goes
Natural Rest and Sleep
Adjustment to Family Needs
Family and Friends Appreciate Efforts
New Interests Develop
New Circle of Stable Friends
Re-Birth of Ideals
Facts Faced with Courage
Appreciation of Real Values
Increase of Emotional Control
First Steps Toward Economic Stability
Confidence of Employers
Care of Personal Appearance
Contentment in Sobriety
Rationalizations Recognized
Increasing Tolerance
Group Therapy and Mutual Help Continue
Enlightened and Interesting Way of Life Opens Up with Road Ahead to Higher Levels than Ever Before

From E. M. Jellinek, *The Disease Concept of Alcoholism* (New Brunswick, N.J.: Hillhouse Press, 1960). Used by permission.

to change. As a result there is greater alienation from God. The alcohol becomes an idol of worship, the thing that matters most. This can have adverse spiritual influences on the family, although some families appear to draw closer to God during their time of crisis.

Counseling and Alcoholism

How does one help an alcoholic?[39] To begin, it might be useful to know some things that do *not* help. These include criticism, shaming, coaxing, making the person promise to stop, threats, hiding or destroying the alcohol, urging the use of greater will power, preaching, or instilling guilt. Most families try all of these, but they rarely work.

The treatment of alcoholism often is complicated by a number of parallel problems, each of which also needs to be treated. Alcoholics, for example, are often depressed or gripped by other psychiatric abnormalities.[40] Frequently there are physical illnesses that have come from excessive drinking and little eating. In an effort to treat themselves, some alcoholics begin taking barbiturates, amphetamines, and other drugs that complicate the alcoholic condition and make recovery more difficult.[41] Clearly early medical intervention is of great importance.

1. *Get the Alcoholic to Admit the Need for Help.* This is difficult because many alcoholics deny that there is any problem. Their thinking is dulled and the reality of the alcoholic's condition sometimes is hidden by the actions of well-meaning family members who cover for the drinker when he or she does something irresponsible. Most experts in alcoholic counseling agree, however, that without the drinker's cooperation, treatment is not likely to be effective.

How, then, can the alcohol abuser understand that help is needed? The members of Alcoholics Anonymous believe that the drinker needs to hit bottom in some way. Only then is the person willing to admit that he or she is powerless to control alcohol and unable to manage life without help. Regrettably some people die or damage themselves irreparably before they hit bottom. Is there some way to help the alcoholic accept the need for treatment before it's too late?

Many problem drinkers first come to the counselor's attention because of some problem that appears to have nothing to do with alcohol. A couple may ask for marriage counseling, for example, or there could be a problem with one of the children. At first the counselor (who may be guilty of thinking that alcoholics are all drunks who can't hold their jobs) fails to suspect that one of the well-dressed, seemingly relaxed counselees is really an alcohol abuser. The husband, for example, could be a successful business executive who anesthetizes himself with alcohol after work every evening while his family goes about the business of life without him.[42]

Even when you suspect alcohol abuse, the counselee is likely to deny that this is a problem. He or she may agree to complete one of the several alcoholism screening tests[43] or you may want to use the Drinking Indicators Checklist (DIC), developed by the alcoholism staff at the Boulder County Health Department in Colorado and shown in Figure 32-2. This is not a rigid screening test and there is no score. Instead it is more of a nonthreatening guide to be used in an interview to help you assess drinking patterns that might be evidence of early alcoholism.[44]

Figure 32-2
Drinking Indicators Checklist

____ Blackouts

____ Personality changes: ____________

____ Interpersonal difficulties: ____________

____ Vocational difficulties: ____________

____ Legal problems: arrested for ____________ Date: ____________

____________ Date: ____________

Maximum daily intake: ____________

____ Change in tolerance: ____ increasing ____ decreasing ____ no change

____ Loss of control over drinking

____ Physical addiction: ____ shakes, ____ hallucinations,

____ seizures, ____ history of DTs

Additional Clinical Information:

____ Previous attempts to stop drinking

____ Longest period of sobriety: ____________

____ Alcoholism in family: ____________

____ Diagnosis of live damage: ____ inflammation, ____ cirrhosis

From Michele A. Packard, "Assessment of the Problem Drinker: A Primer for Counselors," *Journal of Counseling and Development* 64 (April 1986): 520. Reproduced by permission.

As we have seen, developing alcoholism is characterized by the drinker's denial that a problem exists. Therefore, in a firm, factual, and nonjudgmental way, point out the nature of the drinker's actions. Present specific examples ("Last night around 11, you knocked over and broke the lamp") rather than vague generalities ("You're drinking too much!"). One writer has suggested that the message is best conveyed nonverbally. If the alcoholic collapses on the living room floor, for example, leave him there rather than helping him (or her) into bed. If something was broken or knocked over, don't pick it up. This makes it more difficult for the drinker to deny later that he or she passed out or damaged the house.[45]

One innovative approach for helping the alcoholic has been called the "intervention." This takes careful planning, usually involves rehearsal, and requires great commitment from the people who are distressed by the alcoholic's drinking. One person, often a professional counselor, chairs the group that may consist of the alcoholic's spouse, children, parents, business associates, best friends, employer, pastor, and other significant persons. At an appointed time and without giving the drinker prior warning, the group members all appear and, in a noncondemning way, give their perceptions and tell how each is being affected by the drinker's actions. Often this is a very emotional meeting. Sometimes the alcoholic gets angry and walks out; more often the person is faced with the reality of the drinking and agrees to enter a treatment program. This method (which is best used under the guidance of a professional) is one way to help the alcoholic face the need for help.[46]

Most addicts have high anxiety and low self-esteem. Try to be careful, therefore, not to criticize or condemn in a way that arouses anxiety or is threatening. Convey acceptance of the person but not of the behavior. Listen to the alcoholic but do not give reassurance. Recognize that addicts, including alcoholics, are dependent, often childish, manipulative, and specialists in evoking sympathy. The counselor must resist the tendency to give advice, preach, or act like a parent. Instead show a noncondescending, firm, sensitive attitude to imply that responsibility for recovery must remain with the alcoholic. In all of this remember that the best counselors are gentle but not soft hearted in their mannerisms.

2. *Stop the Drinking.* Detoxification is a procedure that must involve the intervention of a physician. Some alcoholics can withdraw on their own, but most need medical guidance, especially because the withdrawal symptoms (including tremors, nausea, sweating, weakness, anxiety, depression, and sometimes delirium) may be severe. Some physicians use sobering agents, other drugs that are assumed to counter the effects of withdrawal, but debate continues about the wisdom of using one drug to treat the effects of another.[47]

While detoxification usually can be accomplished safely and quickly, this is only the beginning of treatment. A larger problem is preventing relapse and keeping the individual free of further alcohol use. This involves counseling that has at least four goals: (1) getting medical treatment to repair the damage caused by alcoholism, (2) helping the counselee learn to cope with stress and function effectively without alcohol, (3) creating a new identity without alcohol, and (4) building or restoring self-esteem and dealing with guilt. The first of these goals involves medical treatment. The others can be goals for nonmedical counselors, preferably working with the family, support groups (like Alcoholics Anonymous), and other treatment specialists.

3. *Provide Support.* Alcoholics and other drug abusers are often lonely, immature people who are being asked to change a lifestyle that is well entrenched and to give up a substance that they depend on and value. This will not be accomplished in one or two hours of individual counseling each week.

Many addicts are best helped within the confines of hospitals or rehabilitation centers where help is available on a round-the-clock basis. Some can be assisted through group counseling where recovering addicts can help each other face the stresses of life, interact with people, and live life without chemical dependency.[48]

Probably the most effective group support comes from Alcoholics Anonymous (AA) and related groups (Al-Anon for spouses of alcoholics and Alateen for their children).[49] These organizations meet in cities and towns all over the world, are free of charge, listed in the phone book, and established as perhaps the most effective approach for helping alcoholics and their families. Although they are not specifically Christian, these groups use principles that in general are consistent with biblical teaching: acceptance of reality; faith in God; commitment of one's life to divine care; honesty with God, self, and others; desire and readiness to change one's way of life;

prayer; making amends; and sharing with others. Some have suggested that supportive group membership in an alcohol-free environment is likely to be more effective in treating alcoholism than efforts to provide psychological insights or better drugs.

Much of the supportive help should be provided by the church where members of the congregation are understanding, familiar with the facts about addiction, and available to give encouragement and practical assistance. Too often, however, church members are critical, condemning, or unwilling to help. Other believers are sympathetic, but their support may be limited because they are unfamiliar with the facts of alcoholism or unable to empathize with the struggles of alcoholics and their families. Some churches have developed Alcoholics Victorious[50] or similar groups that are based on the AA model but more openly Christian. If these are not available in your area, you may consider encouraging your counselees to be involved both in AA and in the broader, more diversified fellowship of a local church.

4. *Help with Stress Management.* In the past, alcoholics dealt with stress by escaping through the use of drugs. Counseling must show that there are better ways to meet the pressures of life. To show this, the counselee must learn that he or she can trust the counselor, who in turn must be patient and dependable. Stress in general can be discussed, but a better approach is to take each problem as it arises and help the counselee decide how it can be handled effectively. This will include considerations of interpersonal relations and how to get along with others apart from the use of alcohol.[51]

5. *Encourage Self-Understanding and a Change of Lifestyle.* When a trusting relationship has been established, there can be value in considering some of the reasons for the alcohol abuse. These discussions can lead to insight, but insight is of little value unless it is followed by practical, specific plans for changed behavior. Sometimes these plans may involve vocational counseling (see chapter 35), an evaluation of self-esteem (see chapter 21), a discussion of marital issues (chapter 27), or consideration of spiritual issues (chapter 36).

Then there is the issue of lifestyle. After the alcoholic has stopped drinking, how will life be different? One's style of life depends on making decisions concerning what will or will not be done now and in the future.[52] As you and the counselee consider life planning try to be sensitive to the unique needs that may be experienced, for example, by female alcoholics,[53] older alcoholics,[54] or teenagers.[55] In all of this, remember that decision making will involve both the counselee and the family.

6. *Counsel the Family.* Since alcoholism is a family problem, the whole family must receive support, understanding, and help. At times they must be encouraged not to withdraw, but to live as best they can despite the circumstances. Sometimes it is helpful to give factual information that better enables the family to understand the addiction. Often family members must be helped to see how they might be contributing to the addiction problem or how their protection of the drinker might prolong the condition. Before the drinker agrees to come for help, the family members may need your guidance and encouragement to confront the alcoholic relative with specific evidences of his or her alcohol-induced behavior.

As the alcoholism develops, family members are forced to take responsibility for running the household. When sobriety returns, the family must readjust to this change and learn to accept the recovering alcoholic as a responsible member of the home. This may be difficult either because of a fear, based on past experience, that the present dry spell is temporary, or because the family has grown accustomed to functioning smoothly around the drinker. Family change is risky for the family, important for the counselee, and accomplished best when there is encouragement from the counselor or outside support group.

7. *Be Prepared for Relapses.* AA has long maintained that one drink can plunge an alcoholic quickly back into addiction, although some professionals disagree.[56] Everyone agrees, however, that relapses are common among alcoholics. If these are followed by blame and condemnation from others, the alcoholic is inclined to give up and conclude "I'll never win, so why should I bother to try?"

It is not easy to work with chemically dependent people or their beleaguered families. The counselor can expect failures and after a relapse he or she must help the counselees pick up and keep working on the problem.

8. *Recognize That Evangelism and Discipleship Are Basic.* Professional books and articles about alcoholism almost never mention the role of the rescue mission in helping to free people from alcohol addiction.[57] It is true, perhaps, that these missions reach only a small number of alcoholics, but the approach is often effective. The mission leaders (who frequently are recovered alcoholics) are a rarely tapped but potentially very useful source of information and encouragement for the counselor of alcoholics.

If the counselee is to find new meaning and purpose in life, he or she must come to see that true and lasting fulfillment is found only in Jesus Christ. The counselor must depend on the Holy Spirit's guidance to determine when and how to present the gospel. Highly emotional preaching sometimes produces false decisions that later are rejected, although there are many examples of persons converted to Christ, freed from their alcoholism, and permanently changed through the preaching of evangelistic messages.

Counselees are most responsive to the gospel when they recognize that they have a need that can be met only by Christ. Alcoholics are masters at manipulating other people, but the counselor must be careful not to fall into the same pattern, attempting to manipulate individuals into the kingdom. The counselee should be presented with the facts of the gospel (presumably during times when he or she is sober enough to understand). Then urge, but do not coerce, the person into making a decision to commit his or her life to Christ.

In all of this, prayer is of central importance. Through the intercession of believers and the availability of concerned human helpers, God works to restore those who are controlled by alcohol or other chemical substances. He also helps to prevent alcoholism in others.

Preventing Alcoholism

The prevention of alcoholism has become a major concern of leaders in government, business, education, the military, and the church. Parent groups, service clubs, schools, medical and counseling professionals, media people, and a number of others recognize the importance of vigorous, long-term efforts aimed at changing public attitudes toward alcohol and other drugs. The National Council on Alcoholism, the federal Department of Education, the National Institute of

Alcohol Abuse and Alcoholism, and similar agencies have been joined, surprisingly perhaps, by the alcohol industry which has initiated TIPS (Training for Intervention Procedures by Servers of Alcohol), a program designed to educate bartenders, waitresses, and others who serve drinks. Despite these efforts, we still know more about treatment than about prevention. Even so, several preventive guidelines are likely to be helpful.

1. *Stimulate a Healthy Home Life.* Like most of the other issues discussed in this book, the prevention of alcoholism and other drug abuse begins in the home. When children are respected, loved, disciplined, and raised by sensitive, concerned, stable parents, there is greater opportunity for healthy maturing and less likelihood of chemical dependence. When emotional needs are met in the home, when children are helped to cope with stress, and when they are taught a clear set of values, there is a greater sense of security and self-esteem, accompanied by a greater ability to handle the problems of life without drugs.

In a major book on alcoholism, one Christian writer reports that parental example is the most influential issue in determining whether or not children will develop alcoholism or other chemical dependencies. When parents drink regularly, children learn to do the same. When parents rigidly prohibit and vehemently condemn the use of alcohol, children often react by experimenting with alcohol. A more effective approach is an open attitude about alcohol, a recognition of its dangers, an encouragement of moderation if not abstinence, and an example of parents who enjoy life without having to rely on alcohol to meet their problems or to enjoy fellowship with others.

It is well known that many homes do not fit this description. Children of alcoholics, for example, often live in families where there is inconsistent or inadequate parenting, frequently accompanied by denial of the reality and influence of alcohol abuse. As we have seen, many of these children feel confused, angry, guilty, afraid, unloved, and ill-equipped to face the demands of adult life. Some have no models of healthy adulthood. Research suggests that many of these young people suspect that they too will inevitably become alcoholics.[58] If this is to be avoided, the children of alcoholics need special encouragement and guidance from caring adults outside the home.

Shouldn't some of that caring come from the church?

2. *Instill a Healthy Religious Faith.* One survey of 5,648 university students revealed that habitual churchgoers and those who have a strong religious faith "are far less likely to be taking drugs than classmates who are shifting church affiliations in their search for the divine. And . . . drug use was highest among those for whom there was no spiritual search at all."[59] These conclusions about drug abuse in general may not apply to alcoholism specifically, and from this survey it does not follow that faith in God prevents alcoholism. Yet Christian counselors are aware that when one is filled with the Spirit, there is less likelihood or need of one being drunk with wine.[60]

3. *Provide Education on Alcoholism and Alcohol Abuse.* It is true that those who never take a drink will never become alcoholics. Emotional pleas for abstinence, however, rarely convince or influence people who are pressured by peers or by curiosity about the effects of alcohol. Neither is it helpful to ignore the subject of alcoholism on the assumption that discussion will arouse experimentation. When alcohol

abuse is considered in a frank, open discussion, this weakens the temptation to dabble with a dangerous drug, even when that drug is presented on television and elsewhere as a jovial and harmless way to relax.

Preventive education should (a) begin early, since most alcoholics start their long decline in the teenage years or sooner, (b) present accurate facts concerning the nature and effects of alcohol, (c) avoid emotional appeals that involve scare tactics but little factual information, (d) clearly discuss the biblical teachings about wine and drunkenness, (e) make young people aware of why people drink, (f) discuss how one can say no in an environment where one's peers may all be drinking, (g) encourage people to make a decision (to drink or not to drink) instead of drifting into the habit, (h) encourage abstinence as the best and most effective means of prevention, (i) describe the warning signs that indicate developing addiction, and (j) alert people to the availability, place, and nature of help for those with developing drinking problems.

4. *Teach People How to Cope with Life.* Table 32-1 is an example of helpful, practical advice for recovering alcoholics. It could be reproduced and shared with alcoholics and their families.

If we can assume that alcoholism and other misuse of drugs often reflect a failure in coping, then one approach to prevention is teaching people to openly face, discuss, and deal with the stress-related problems of life. "The key to prevention," concludes one report, "is to reduce exposure to stress where you can and to teach healthy means of coping with stress that can't be eliminated."[61]

Conclusions about Alcoholism

Every New Year's Eve the county courthouse in Northampton, Massachusetts, is transformed into a nightclub and becomes the scene of a party that has the blessings of the presiding judge. The partygoers invariably have a good time despite the complete absence of alcohol. Police officers drop by on breaks from duty, and many of the revelers volunteer to give rides home for people from other parties where abstinence is not practiced. The judge is pleased because people at the courthouse party won't appear later in his court for New Year's drunkenness, and the courthouse usually ends up cleaner the day after the bash than it was the day before.

When this story appeared in newspapers across the country, I wonder how many readers responded with criticism or cynicism? Theologian Reinhold Niebuhr once wrote that it is "no easy task to deal realistically with the moral confusion of our day, either in the pulpit or the pew and avoid the appearance, and possibly the actual peril, of cynicism."[62] Helping people face the reality and dangers of alcoholism can seem like an exercise in frustration and futility. One academic administrator described alcohol abuse as a blend of emotion, tragedy, personalities, complexity, desire, and lack of control. Add the competition between different community and governmental agencies, the heavy advertising of the alcohol industry, and the sometimes conflicting conclusions of researchers and other specialists, and we can understand why some describe the battle against alcoholism as an experience of taking two steps backward for every three steps forward.[63]

Table 32-1

Practical Advice for Recovering Alcholics

The following guidelines could be shared with the alcoholic who wants to change:

- The time to become drug-free is today. Drug-free means to be free of *all* drugs, including alcohol. This is impossible to do on one's own. You need to participate in a legitimate program of recovery.
- Recovery from alcohol addiction is a lifelong process and not just a one-time event. You must "work" your program in a step-by-step process. It will take time for your mind and body to heal and also time for God to change you.
- Get help from someone qualified. You shouldn't try to do it on your own.
- Don't give up if you should relapse. It is never too late to get back on the right track. God is the God of the second chance, and more.
- Don't struggle with alcoholism in your own strength. We must depend upon God's strength and power to stay drug-free. Read Gal. 5:16 and Phil. 4:13.
- You must stay away from all alcohol and alcohol-using friends. To associate with them is one of the easiest ways to relapse. As 1 Cor. 15:33 states: "Do not be misled: 'Bad company corrupts good character.'"
- Don't be surprised when you are tempted to use alcohol again. Temptation in itself is not sinful—it is what you do with it that matters (see 1 Cor. 10:13; James 1:13–15).
- Recognize that it is easier to lie to yourself than to anyone else you know. You must be aware of your ability to rationalize wrong attitudes and wrong behavior (see Jer. 17:9; Ps. 51:6).
- Don't become proud and self-sufficient once you become alcohol free, as you cannot claim credit for your recovery. "Pride goes before destruction, and a haughty spirit before a fall" (Prov. 16:18).
- Have confidence in God. He has your best interest at heart. Murphy's Laws do not control the life of the Christian (see Rom. 8:28).
- Walk with God one day at a time. He knows your problems and your needs (see Matt. 6:25–34; Phil. 4:6–7).
- Take time to pray every day. Prayer is the "glue" that keeps us close to God. It is through prayer that God changes us (read James 5:13–18).
- Read your Bible every day. God's Word has the answers for your problems and the direction you need (memorize Prov. 3:5–6).
- Attend church weekly. This is where you can worship and serve God. You will grow when you give yourself to others (read Heb. 10:24–25).
- Maintain a support system, a group of other Christians with whom you can share your struggles and receive encouragement. This will help you cope with the pressures of life (note Gal. 6:1–2).
- Memorize the following prayer:

  God, grant me the Serenity
  to accept the things I cannot change,
  Courage to change the things I can,
  and Wisdom to know the difference.

From Stephen Van Cleave, Walter Byrd, and Kathy Revell, *Counseling for Substance Abuse and Addiction*, Resources for Christian Counseling, No. 12 (Waco, Tex.: Word, 1987), 116–17. Used by permission.

Inactivity and cynicism, however, accomplish nothing. Like the people in Northampton, each community and each church must consider ways by which we can help people avoid or escape from the sickness and sin of alcoholism. The Christian counselor can be a leader in helping alcoholics and their families to overcome the alcoholism and to live their lives in obedience and submission to Jesus Christ. Only then is the difficult problem truly and effectively resolved.

SUGGESTIONS FOR FURTHER READING

Clinebell, Howard J., Jr. *Understanding and Counseling the Alcoholic.* Rev. ed. Nashville: Abingdon, 1968.

Martin, Sara Hines. *Healing for Adult Children of Alcoholics.* Nashville: Broadman, 1988.*

Metzger, Lawrence. *From Denial to Recovery: Counseling Problem Drinkers, Alcoholics, and Their Families.* San Francisco: Jossey-Bass, 1987.

Ohlemacher, Janet. *Beloved Alcoholic: What to Do When a Family Member Drinks.* Grand Rapids, Mich.: Zondervan, 1984.*

Spickard, Anderson, and Barbara R. Thompson. *Dying for a Drink: What You Should Know about Alcoholism.* Waco, Tex.: Word, 1985.*

Van Cleave, Stephen, Walter Byrd, and Kathy Revell. *Counseling for Substance Abuse and Addiction.* Waco, Tex.: Word, 1987.

* Books marked with an asterisk (*) are especially suited for counselees to read.

33 Addictions

MIKE IS A MIDDLE-AGED navy chaplain. Before joining the military twelve years ago, he pastored a little church in New England and watched it grow both in numbers and in the spiritual dynamic of the people. Military life has been radically different from the parish ministry. Long periods of sea duty and other frequent separations from his wife and children have not been easy, but Mike feels called to minister in the military, and his family is supportive. In spite of the pressures, there are advantages to navy life, and Mike continues to see this as an exciting mission field.

Recently, however, Mike has developed a habit that is genuinely disturbing. "Maybe it's all the talk I hear around me," he told a close friend recently. "Maybe it's because of the long separations from my wife." Whatever the reason, Mike's mind dwells almost constantly on sex. Hidden in his office are a number of pornographic publications, and whenever he can do so without danger of being caught the chaplain privately views sexually explicit movies.

"The problem is all in my mind," Mike told his friend. "I haven't been unfaithful to my wife. None of my colleagues in the Navy knows about my problem. But I think I've become addicted to sexual fantasy."

Mike has counseled often with addicted people: naval personnel who are controlled by drugs, alcohol, or gambling. At times he has counseled people who can't control their shoplifting, violent tempers, masturbation, or continual eating. As a counselor Mike knows that most of these behaviors begin in the mind. He recognizes that uncontrolled sexual fantasy often leads to uncontrolled sexual behavior. He has read the newspaper reports of well-known pastors whose ministries were destroyed when their sexual thoughts left them vulnerable to sexual temptations, and the temptations in turn led to their much publicized sexual sins.

Mike doesn't want to join these ministerial dropouts. He knows his wife would be devastated. His kids would be hurt and confused. He has pondered how his fall into sexual sin would shake the congregation that he left behind in New England. He wonders what might happen to his career in the chaplaincy. He knows that he has to escape his growing and ever-present fascination with sexual thoughts and pornographic materials. Even Mike, the respected chaplain-counselor, doesn't know how to get free of his secret addiction.

At our annual faculty retreat, the professors from the seminary where I teach were addressed recently by a local pastor. He is a young man whose creative ministry has attracted international attention and whose congregation has exploded from a few families to a huge church where thousands of worshipers pack each worship service.

In the question period that followed the pastor's talk, one of the professors asked a question that brought a surprising answer. "Based on your pastoral experience, what do you think is the most important course for us to give our seminary students?" The pastor didn't hesitate in giving an answer. "Require a course on addictions," he said. "That is one of the major problems facing people today."

In many societies, but especially our own, thousands of individuals are addicted to alcohol, drugs, television, compulsive spending, sexual immorality, smoking, overeating, and a host of other behaviors. Workaholism (the addiction to work) has almost become a badge worn proudly by those who want to be successful. Eating disorders, a specialized form of addictions, have become a major concern within the past decade. Some people seem addicted to politics, to physical fitness, and even to religion.

An addiction is any thinking or behavior that is habitual, repetitious, and difficult or impossible to control. Usually the addiction brings short-term pleasure, but there may be long-term consequences in terms of one's health and welfare. (Some have called this short-term gain with long-term pain.)

Addictions tend to be progressive conditions that slowly exert more and more power and control over the individual. With many addictions, the control is both psychological and physical. The addicted person may agree that the condition is harmful but stopping seems to be impossible. Even after difficult detoxification, the drug addict often returns to the needle. Even after repeated medical warnings, the smoker may continue to puff on two packs a day or the obese person continues to overeat and shun exercise. Even in the midst of increasing sickness and dehydration, the anorexic fails to eat. The workaholic continues a self-driving lifestyle even after a near-fatal heart attack.

Psychologist William Lenters has highlighted the complexity of addictive behavior: "The questions are many and puzzling. Addiction to *what*? Is addiction a disease? Is it a sin? Is it a psychological abnormality? Does it point to a personality anomaly? A genetic mix-up? Are addicts morally responsible for their frequent foul-ups? Is addiction a case of obsessive-compulsive behavior? Or is it just an excuse for antisocial behavior? What causes one person to become addicted to beverage alcohol while his biological brother does not? Is every addiction harmful? What about the so-called positive addictions?"[1]

In this chapter we will discuss some of these issues as we focus attention on three broad categories of addiction: substance abuse (sometimes called drug addiction), eating disorders (sometimes described as eating addictions); and addictive behaviors.

The Bible and Addiction

The Bible condemns drunkenness and alcohol abuse but makes no specific references to drug abuse, eating disorders, workaholism, or most other addictions that concern us today. Nevertheless, biblical principles such as the following can apply to the issue of addiction.

1. *Don't Be Mastered by Anything.*[2] It is possible to become enslaved even by actions that are permissible and not bad in themselves. In stating his determination not to be mastered by anything, Paul mentions food and sex, both of which are

good in themselves but sometimes abused. In addition, the apostle criticizes people who are sexually immoral, greedy, idolaters, drunkards, and in other ways mastered by behavior that they fail to control.

2. *Do Obey the Law.* The Bible instructs us to be law-abiding citizens.[3] It is wrong, therefore, to buy, sell, condone, possess, or use any drug illegally. Violence, drunken driving, criminal actions, and other illegal acts are wrong even if they are the actions of one who is addicted.[4]

3. *Don't Assume That Drugs or Other Addictions Resolve Problems and Reduce Tensions.* Stress is one of the major causes of addiction. When pressures build some people use alcohol or other drugs to hide the stress and give a feeling of euphoria and a sense that all is well. Others get involved in work, hobbies, or recreational pursuits that distract them from stress. Temporarily these behaviors may help a person avoid responsible stress management, but ultimately the stresses cry for attention and the developing addictions no longer provide relief. Instead the addictions create additional stress. People may try to escape from their problems through drugs, work, sexual fantasy, hyperactivity, compulsive eating, or other addictive behavior, but all of this fails to acknowledge the scriptural directive to bring our burdens to Christ[5] where we can face them squarely and deal with them directly.

4. *Do Keep the Body Pure.* The Holy Spirit dwells in the body of each Christian, and for this reason we must do whatever we can to keep our bodies free of pollutants, including drugs, excessive amounts of food, lustful thoughts, and immoral sexual behavior. Every human body was made by God, and the Christian body belongs to him both because of divine creation and because of divine redemption. Scripture and common sense tell us, therefore, that we should take care of ourselves so that we can glorify God with our bodies.[6]

5. *Don't Expect to Come to God through Drugs.* Several years ago a controversial book (written by a seminary professor) argued that psychedelic drugs can offer a superior route to discovering truth and entering into a meaningful religious experience.[7] This conclusion denies the fact that we come to God only by way of Jesus Christ,[8] and that we are to come with clear minds[9] rather than brains that are drugged by addictive substances.

6. *Do Practice Temperance, Self-Discipline, and Self-Control.* These characteristics are prominent in the list of qualifications for Christian leaders,[10] but they apply to nonleaders as well.[11] All believers are expected to say no to ungodliness and worldly passions, "and to live self-controlled, upright and godly lives."[12] Self-indulgence and selfish ambition are condemned;[13] self-control is commanded[14] and listed as one of the fruits of the Spirit.[15] Gluttony (which could involve addiction to eating), greed (which might involve addiction to possessions and material things), and lust (which could lead to sexual addiction) are all warned against and condemned.[16]

7. *Don't Get Drunk.* Drunkenness is clearly and explicitly condemned in Scripture and called a sin.[17] Would it be consistent with Scripture to extend this clear prohibition against alcohol and suggest that it could guide our response to other harmful addictions? We should not become drunk or addicted to any chemical substance or other addictive influence.

8. *Do Be Filled with the Spirit.* Eph. 5:18 instructs us to avoid drunkenness and be filled instead with the Holy Spirit. A life controlled by the Spirit is presented in

the Bible as superior to any alternative, including a life filled with chemical or other addictions.

The Causes of Addiction

There is nothing new about the problem of addiction and neither is this limited culturally. At different times and in a variety of geographical areas, addictions have enjoyed passing popularity. Alcohol abuse, for example, may be more prevalent now than it was a few years ago. Glue sniffing has ceased to be of great importance, but crack, a highly addictive and dangerous form of cocaine, has become a major source of addiction, especially when it is used in combination with alcohol.[18] Throughout recorded history and in countries all over the world, a percentage of every population has had serious problems with drug abuse and other types of addiction.

In chapter 32 we listed some of the causes of alcoholism: physiology and heredity, harmful environments (including one's home life, peer pressures, and cultural-ethnic mores), present stress, spiritual influences, and circumstances that keep the addiction alive and growing once it gets started. All of these influences can contribute as well to the nonalcoholic addictions.

In addition, substance abuse, eating disorders, and other addictive behaviors appear to have unique causes.

1. *Causes of Substance Abuse.* George Mann, medical director of the Johnson Institute in Minneapolis, a center for understanding and treating chemical addictions, has written that all addictive chemicals have one thing in common: they change moods. Some mood changes are very potent and highly addictive; others are much less powerful. According to Mann, and as shown in Table 33-1, drugs can be placed on a scale ranging from those with the highest potential for addiction to those with lowest potential.[19]

Almost any person can become psychologically and/or physically dependent on drugs if that person is exposed to a high dosage for a long enough period of time. With a drug like heroin the time may be short and the effects are both fast and very dangerous; with caffeine the time is longer and the effects are almost negligible.

Table 33-1
The Potential for Addiction

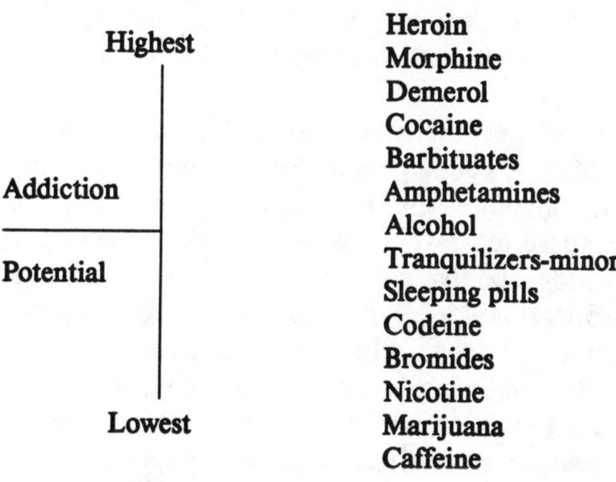

Life could be divided into four general categories: family life, social life, vocational life, and spiritual life. When a chemical interferes with the productivity, tranquility, efficiency, or well-being of any of these areas, and when a person is made aware that this is happening but still persists in using the chemical, then that person is addicted, at least psychologically. If one gets physically ill when the drug is withdrawn, then there is physical addiction as well.[20]

What causes this addiction? Perhaps there is a combination of several influences.

(a) Parental and Other Adult Examples. We live in a society of pill takers. Early in life most children become well acquainted with medicines that take away pain and make one feel better. Teenagers watch parents consume aspirin, cold tablets, sleeping medications, and a host of other drugs. Millions of people relax with coffee, a cigarette, or a drink before dinner. When problems arise, tranquilizers are available to calm our nerves. It isn't surprising that young people follow this adult example and, in turn, perpetuate the idea that drugs are the first line of defense against physical and psychological pain.

Few people would assume that drugs in themselves are bad. Their medicinal value is well known and even accepted by biblical writers.[21] Most people would see no harm in the occasional use of mild stimulants, pain relievers, or relaxation-producing drugs. Even mild drugs, however, can become addicting, sometimes as a result of parental example. If parents take a pill or a drink to calm down in times of stress, is it surprising that their children do the same? If the drug affects the children like it calms the parents, then drug use becomes reinforcing, and the substance is likely to be used again, perhaps with increasing frequency and in greater quantities.

Many substance abusers come from homes where drugs are not misused, but this does not deny the importance of parental example. A high percentage of teenage and adult addicts (especially those who use hard, highly addictive drugs) have grown up in homes where addiction and family instability are common.[22]

(b) Peer and Other Social Influences. Individuals in our society, especially young people, live in a world that is permeated by drugs. Why do some people use these drugs while others do not? Several theories try to answer this question and explain drug abuse.[23]

Disease-addiction theories maintain that otherwise healthy people experiment with a drug (perhaps in response to curiosity or peer pressure) and become addicted physically, so that drug abuse becomes a disease. There seems to be little evidence to support the idea that we inherit tendencies to become addicted to nonalcoholic drugs.[24]

Gateway theories suggest that use of one drug becomes a stepping stone to drugs that are more harmful. A young person, for example, may start with cigarettes and beer, then move to marijuana and on to more addictive drugs. The theory fails to say, however, why some make this progression and others do not.

Social theories conclude that race, age, socioeconomic status, the neighborhood where one lives, educational level, peer influences, and similar issues can combine to determine if one takes drugs, what drugs are likely to be used, how the habit is supported financially, and whether or not the drug use will continue.

Psychological theories look within the drug user to see if personality traits, psychological stresses, inner conflicts, hidden fears, or individual needs contribute to drug abuse. Many drug users do have inner tensions and frustrations. Some look for experiences, including drug experiences, that will bring excitement, stimulation, intoxication, and feelings of freedom from the worries and problems of life. Still, it is not clear why some distressed people turn to drugs but many others do not.

Psychosocial theories suggest that some people are problem prone because of personality, environment, stresses, or other influences. Many problem-prone people turn to drugs, especially if they are readily available, but others develop different problems.

Peer-Cluster theory draws from the above and assumes that when a young person uses drugs,

> it is almost always a direct reflection of the peer group. Friends, acquaintances, and siblings provide drugs and teach the young person how to use them. Peers shape attitudes about drugs, provide the social contexts for drug use, and, when young people share their ideas, help form the rationales that the youth uses to explain and excuse drug use. Eventually small groups form and the members use drugs together at particular times and places and share the same ideas, values, and beliefs about drugs. These groups are peer clusters; . . . tight, cohesive groupings—in which clearly defined attitudes and shared behaviors mark membership.[25]

Peer clusters are not limited to teenagers. When the neighbors get together for coffee or employees take a break from work, there often is pleasant conversation and relaxation, accompanied by eating, drinking coffee or soft drinks, and perhaps smoking. The consumption is reinforced by the accompanying social interactions. When the get togethers include drinking beer or hard liquor, or when nicotine is replaced by more addictive drugs, then pleasant peer interaction moves into more dangerous substance abuse.

All of this suggests that there are multiple causes of drug abuse: physical, familial, social, environmental, psychological, and spiritual. Each of these must be kept in mind when we begin counseling with substance abusers.

2. *Causes of Eating Disorders.* Many people, at least in some parts of the West, seem to have continual concerns about weight. It is impossible to know how many people are on diets, thinking about going on diets, or concerned because they are putting weight back on following a diet. Dozens and perhaps hundreds of diets, including some that have a Christian basis,[26] are embraced enthusiastically, tried with varying degrees of faithfulness, and most often found to be useless. According to one writer, "if 'cure' from obesity is defined as reduction to ideal weight and maintenance of that weight for five years, a person is more likely to recover from most forms of cancer than from obesity."[27]

Obesity and other eating disorders involve one's physical condition. For this reason, it is crucial to have medical diagnosis and treatment as part of the counseling. Nonmedical counselors are not qualified to treat people physically, but counseling is likely to be more effective when we have at least a minimal understanding of the physiological aspects of the three most often encountered eating disorders: obesity, anorexia nervosa, and bulimia.[28]

(a) Obesity. A person is obese, according to the most accepted definition, if his or her body weight is at least 20 percent greater than the weight listed in the standard height-weight tables. This is an approximate measure, and one physician suggests that the "eyeball test" is better: if a person looks fat, the person is fat.[29] The obese person accumulates fat by eating more calories than are used up through energy. Why does this happen to so many people? The answers are both physiological and psychological.[30]

Physiological causes are of at least two types. External influences are issues over which eaters have control, including what we eat, how much we eat, and how much exercise we get. All of these have a bearing on weight. In contrast, the internal influences are largely beyond one's control and include genetic variables, fat cell size or size of stomach and intestines.

Psychological causes center around habits and other learned behavior. Gregarious people who like to eat and drink when they get together tend to add weight. According to one study, the obese have a higher-than-average need to spend time with family and friends. When others aren't around, overweight people reward themselves with food.[31]

Many of us tend to eat more when we are under stress, feeling sorry for ourselves, angry, anxious, guilty, bored, depressed, or watching television. During withdrawal from smoking, people tend to crave and eat more carbohydrates. Such behavior may have both physiological and psychological causes.[32] Some evidence suggests that children who are told to clean their plates develop lifelong habits of overeating even when they have had enough or don't feel hungry. All of this suggests that overeating can result from a variety of learned and emotional influences.

(b) Anorexia Nervosa. The first report of this condition was published in 1689, but it was not until the 1980s that anorexia leapt into prominence. The condition, which appears most often in females,[33] is an eating disorder characterized by continual preoccupation with body weight and food. The anorexic often concludes that she is overweight, goes on a diet, and doesn't stop. As a result, there is dangerous weight loss (sometimes hastened by induced vomiting, abuse of laxatives, and excessive exercise), hyperactivity, an inaccurate perception of one's own body (the anorexic often considers herself fat despite considerable evidence to the contrary), and physical illness including menstrual irregularities, chemical deficiencies, weakening of the heart, and sometimes death.

(c) Bulimia. Closely related to anorexia, bulimia involves recurring episodes of eating (gorging or binging may be more accurate words) large quantities of food, followed by self-induced vomiting and feelings of guilt, depression, and self-disgust. Most bulimics are afraid of fat, many follow their binging with fasting or laxatives,[34] and in time there can be fluctuating weight and serious health problems. For reasons that are not completely understood, bulimics often come from families that have a history of alcoholism and many also have drug and alcohol problems.

Raymond E. Vath is a Christian psychiatrist and leading expert on eating disorders. His patients all tend to show, in greater or lesser degrees, eight common characteristics.[35] This list describes what the patients are like, but it also sheds light on the causes of anorexia nervosa and bulimia.

Perfectionism refers to the patients' unreasonable standards or expectations of themselves. Many of these young people come from homes where the standards are high, attractiveness (including a slim figure) is highly valued, overweight people are viewed negatively, weight is assumed to be under voluntary control, dieting is praised, achievement is prized, and the parents are often successful and expect the same in their children.

Eating disorders are more common among professions that emphasize trimness (dancers, figure skaters, models, gymnasts, or actresses) and in places, such as college dorms, where there is competition and emphasis on dating. Perhaps it is not surprising that many anorexics and bulimics exert unusual effort in their attempts to attain the high standards that they have seen in their families and set for themselves.

Low self-esteem often comes because the individual cannot meet the excessive standards and as a result feels worthless, unlovable, and like a failure.

Sexual identity confusion involves uncertainty about what it means to be a mature woman (or man). Often these people have poor sexual adjustment and sometimes there is a history of promiscuity.

Numerous women, including many bulimics, seem confused about the relative importance of professional success and personal beauty. The messages that come from parents, teachers, and the media are confusing: work hard at school but be popular and pretty, be a professional but show that you are feminine. Fascination with physical fitness and the desire to look trim and healthy can focus attention on one's body and create confusion about how this relates to purpose in life.

Recent writers have noted that this sex-role confusion and emphasis on both appearance and physical fitness is now becoming of greater importance to men. If this continues, more and more males may develop eating disorders.[36]

Depression results when people cannot reach their high ideals. The inability to achieve the aerobics instructor look, for example, may leave many people feeling defeated, ashamed, anxious, and depressed. Family example contributes to this depression. A high number of people with eating disorders come from families where one or more relatives have a history of depression.[37]

Deception is a way to hide one's failures and devious eating patterns. Often there is abnormal eating in private, sometimes food or laxatives are stolen, and induced vomiting is kept secret and often denied.

Power struggles come when the family discovers the illness and tries to force changes in eating patterns. Sometimes the family uses threats, criticisms, and punishment. This in turn meets with resistance and further deception.

Interdependency involves both the parents and the person with the eating disorder. The parents have high standards for their children and sometimes resist the normal process of separation. The children, in turn, want to break away but often are reluctant to leave. Many are exceptionally dependent on the parents for acceptance and affirmation.

Physiological problems come as a result of the eating disorder but also may be part of the cause. Women are genetically programmed to have a higher proportion of body fat than men. Differences in metabolic rate influence the efficiency with which calories are burned. These physical facts can create problems for people who live in a society that greatly values thinness.

3. *Causes of Behavior Addictions.* Alcoholism, substance abuse, and eating disorders get most of the media and counselor attention, but thousands of people struggle

with other, less common addictions. Many of these have no obvious physical cause. Instead they are behaviors that gain increasing prominence and are more and more difficult to control. Some people, for example, are addicted to work, physical fitness, sex, pornography, or stealing (kleptomania). Others have addictions to specific foods (such as chocolate), and many are addicted gamblers.

After the World Series of Poker at a casino in Las Vegas, the winner was asked what he planned to do with all the money. "Lose it," he replied without hesitation. The man was admitting his addiction to gambling. Like all compulsive gamblers, he is unwilling and perhaps unable to resist the urge to gamble, even if this leads to heavy debt, loss of work, family problems, and personal stress. Often gamblers are arrested for embezzlement, forgery, income-tax evasion, or other illegal activities that provide funds to pay gambling debts and feed the addiction.

Why do they do it? There is no known cause. Gamblers are frequently intelligent people who thrive on danger, excitement, and uncertainty, but these may be interspersed with periods of depression, anxiety, and stress. Organizations like Gamblers Anonymous (GA) are successful in helping the people who stay with the group, but most drop out of the program and return to their gambling.[38]

It is well known that addictions are not equally harmful. Alcoholism or anorexia nervosa are likely to be more dangerous that addiction to jogging, golf, or watching sports on television. Even so, any behavior that is compulsive and beyond the individual's ability to control can be harmful.

This includes one addiction that rarely is mentioned: addiction to religion. Some people it seems go to church regularly to get an emotional fix that keeps them high until the next service. What some observers have called "immature religion" or "sick religion," is marked by rigidity, narrow-mindedness, unwillingness to associate with or learn from others, self-justification, and magical thinking. "A defensive posture is built into the rabid religiosity of the addict. The typical alcoholic reflects a similar attitude: the world is all wrong, but I am all right."[39]

Again it is clear that addictions result from a combination of influences. These include family background, past experiences, personality, present stress, individual needs, physical makeup, and the reinforcement or rewards that come as a result of the addictive behavior.

THE EFFECTS OF ADDICTION

Addictions affect people in different ways; much depends on the individual, the circumstances, and the substance or behavior to which one is addicted. As shown in Table 33-2, for example, drug abuse and alcohol addiction have differing effects but both involve behavior change, physical deterioration, family stresses, financial problems, career destruction, and increasing psychological disintegration. Addiction to marijuana is much less destructive; however, the harmful effects of this drug have recently become more apparent.[40] Caffeine dependence is even less harmful.[41]

Although some people are able to withdraw from their addictions without help, most need professional guidance. Psychological and physical withdrawal symptoms can be very disruptive, but the effects of withdrawal depend on the addiction. It is easier to withdraw from caffeine than from nicotine; easier to quit smoking cigarettes than to stop using cocaine.[42]

Table 33-2
Symptoms of Chemical Dependency*

Alcoholism

I. Signs of:
   A. Growing preoccupation
      1. Anticipation of drinking
         a. During daytime activities
         b. Vacation times (fishing trips become drinking binges)
         c. Growing involvement in drinking activities (bar building, receipts)
      2. Growing need during times of stress
         a. On job
         b. Family and marriage problems
         c. Emergencies
   B. Growing rigidity in lifestyle
      1. Particular times for drinking during the day
      2. Self-imposed rules beginning to change—Saturday lunch
      3. Will not tolerate interference during drinking times
      4. Limits "social" activities to those which involve drinking
   C. Growing tolerance
      1. Increasing ability to hold liquor without showing it
      2. Ingenuity about obtaining the chemical without others being aware
         a. Gulping drinks
         b. Ordering "stiffer" drinks—doubles, martinis, etc.
         c. Self-appointed bartender at social gatherings
         d. Sneaking drinks
         e. Drinking prior to social engagements
         f. Purchasing liquor in greater quantities—cases instead of six-packs
         g. Protecting the supply
            (1) Purchasing more well before current supply is exhausted
            (2) Hidden bottles—at home, car, on the job

Drug Dependency

I. Signs of:
   A. Growing preoccupation
      1. Anticipation of drug usage
         a. Keeping track of prescribed times for dosage
         b. Growing number of physical complaints which would require more drugs to relieve them
      2. Growing need during times of stress
         a. Begins to attempt to prevent stress—"It's going to be a rough day so I'll take a couple just in case."
         b. Minor family and marriage problems
         c. Emergency situations
   B. Growing rigidity in lifestyle
      1. Has particular times during day for drug usage—example—can't sleep unless he/she takes a sleeping pill
      2. Cannot go anywhere without supply of medication
      3. Will not tolerate attempts to limit or change medication (drugs) times or amounts
   C. Growing tolerance
      1. Increasing dosage and/or number of different medication (drugs)
      2. Ingenuity about obtaining the drug without others being aware
         a. Seeking out a variety of physicians and dentists for prescriptions but not informing them about each other
         b. Attempting to get refillable prescriptions
         c. Use of several drug stores
         d. Using several drugs in combination for the synergistic effect—i.e., a barbiturate and an alcoholic drink
         e. Using the drug for longer than the original prescription called for
         f. Protecting the supply
            (1) Purchasing more before current supply is exhausted
            (2) Hiding bottles at home (suitcases), car, at work

*Reproduced with permission of The Johnson Institute, Minneapolis, Minn.

Table 33-2 *(continued)*

Alcoholism	*Drug Dependency*
D. Loss of control 1. Increasing blackouts 2. Unplanned drinking or larger doses and more frequent times 3. Binge drinking 4. Morning drinking 5. Repeated harmful consequences resulting from chemical use	D. Loss of control 1. Increasing blackouts and memory distortion 2. Larger and more frequent dosages, than prescription calls for—using another person's prescriptions 3. Continuous dosages—i.e., red pill every three hours, white pill every two hours, green capsule twice daily, etc. 4. Repeated harmful consequences resulting from drug usage
a. Family (1) Broken promises involving "cutting down" (2) Drinking during family rituals (Christmas, birthdays) (3) Sacrificing other family financial needs for chemicals (4) Fights (physical) or arguments about drug usage (5) Threats of divorce	a. Family (1) Frequent blackouts which lead to many "broken commitments" (2) Inappropriate behavior during family rituals (Christmas, birthdays) (3) Sacrificing other family needs for doctor appointments and prescriptions (4) Changing family duties due to physical incapacity (increase time in bed, lack of motivation and drive) (5) Drug-induced mood changes creates uncertainty and suspicion in family members
b. Legal (1) Traffic violations—DWI (Driving While Intoxicated), etc. (2) Drunk and disorderly (3) Suits—result of impaired judgment (4) Divorce proceedings	b. Legal (1) Buying and/or selling illegal drugs (2) Buying from illegal sources (3) Traffic violations (4) Disorderly conduct violations (5) Suits—result of impaired judgment (6) Divorce proceedings
c. Social (1) Loss of friendships because of antisocial behavior (2) Previous hobbies, interests and community activities neglected as a result of increased chemical use	c. Social (1) Loss of friendships because of past antisocial behavior (2) Previous hobbies, interests and community activities neglected as a result of increased drug usage
d. Occupational (1) Absenteeism (hangovers) (2) Lost promotions due to poor performance	d. Occupational (1) Absenteeism (2) Lost promotions due to poor performance

Table 33-2 *(continued)*

Alcoholism	*Drug Dependency*
(3) Threats of termination (4) Loss of job	(3) Demotions due to impaired and inappropriate behavior (4) Loss of job
e. Physical (1) Numerous hospitalizations (2) Medical advice to cut down (3) Using alcohol as medication (a) To get to sleep (b) Relieve stress	e. Physical (1) Numerous hospitalizations (2) Increasing number of physical complaints (3) Physical deterioration due to chemical use
f. Growing defensiveness (1) Vague and evasive answers (2) Inappropriate reactions to consequences of drug usage (3) Frequent attempts at switching to other areas of concern	f. Growing defensiveness (1) Vague and evasive answers (2) Inappropriate reactions to consequences of drug usage (3) Frequent attempts at switching to other areas of concern
II. Counselor should be: A. Direct but not prosecuting like a D.A. (District Attorney) B. Persistent but not threatening C. Aware of possible distortions due to sincere delusion D. Ready to seek out corroborating data from concerned person if alcoholic becomes highly defensive	II. Counselor should be: A. Direct but not prosecuting like a D.A. (District Attorney) B. Persistent but not threatening C. Aware of possible distortions due to sincere delusion D. Ready to seek out corroborating data from a significant other if drug user becomes highly defensive

As we have seen, addictions affect both the victim and his or her family. Families can be destroyed by an addict's behavior, but families also contribute to the condition and sometimes, in their efforts to help, family members can make the addiction worse.[43]

Similar conclusions could be reached about society. It is well known that drug abuse and crime often go together, causing pain to the victims and great detriment to local communities and the whole nation. On the national level addictions of all types contribute to the further loss of billions of dollars through absenteeism, declining work efficiency, failing health, and the high cost of treatment programs.

Most pathetic, however, are the shattered lives strewn in the paths that follow progressive addictions. Spiritual emptiness, broken bodies, destroyed relationships, ruined careers, dulled brains, and deep feelings of grief and guilt are all among the costs of addictions.

At times, even counselors get discouraged. "I have to limit my work with addicts," one psychiatrist said recently. "The emotional drain of treating them can be almost more than I can handle."

Counseling and Addiction

Various approaches have been used to treat addiction. These include family counseling, individual and group therapy, behavior therapy (to help people change and control behavior), and, of course, the medical treatment that helps individuals withdraw from the addictive substance and get treatment for the physical effects of the addiction. All of this takes large amounts of time and energy. Addicted people do get help and many escape from their addictions, but the failure rate is high and relapse is common.

According to one report,[44] treatment fails when counselors lack proper training and experience, try to explore the abuser's inner conflicts in the (mistaken) hope that this will end the abuse, and wait to begin counseling until detoxification is complete. It is better to be working with the family and significant other people along with the counselee, to encourage the counselee's participation in self-help group programs, and to be both supportive and active in helping the counselee stay away from the addiction. If you are a Christian counselor who lacks training or expertise in working with the victims of substance abuse, eating disorders, or other addictions, try to find a professionally trained counselor and/or physician with whom you can work in helping the addict and his or her family.

The following paragraphs assume that medical treatment is being given, when necessary, along with the nonmedical counseling. Many of the counseling suggestions presented in our discussion of alcoholism,[45] can also apply to the addictions discussed in this chapter.

1. *Counseling Substance Abusers.* Have Christian counselors been reluctant to enter the arena of substance abuse counseling? One government report showed that most help for addicts comes from medical personnel who tend to focus on detoxification and chemical interventions or from former addicts who understand street life but know little about the principles of counseling and behavior change. Less than 5 percent of treatment personnel are psychologists.[46] Despite the popularity of Teen Challenge, TOUCH,[47] and other Christian substance-abuse programs, relatively few Christian counselors appear to be involved in drug rehabilitation efforts.

Some counselors may feel inadequate to help. Many believe, incorrectly, that substance abusers are unmotivated to change, nonresponsive to treatment, and always difficult to manage.[48] In contrast, knowledgeable counselors find that treatment may be difficult, but it can also be successful. Often several approaches may be used. These include medical care, both individual and group counseling,[49] drug education, residential therapy (this often means hospitalization), family counseling, and after-care services such as halfway houses or outpatient clinics. Some have noted that detailed diagnosis is important if counseling is to be effective.[50] Others have emphasized the special needs of women substance abusers.[51] Then there are those who suggest that counselees, especially those who are young, are not likely to be helped until the counselor knows about one's peer clusters (where, when, and with whom drugs are used). Unless this influence can be changed, there may be little hope of changing drug involvement.[52]

Substance abusers are best treated by a team of specialists who combine their areas of expertise. In most cases, this combined treatment will include detoxification, education about abuse, support and counseling for the family, and helping the abuser live without drugs. Christians will be concerned about the counselee's spiritual growth and there may be interest in following the seven steps to recovery proposed by one group of experienced counselors:

- Help the person admit "I can't control drug use."
- Encourage the counselee to "give up control of his or her life and place it in God's hands."
- Guide in self-examination, making sure to consider feelings of guilt and regret.
- Encourage the abuser to "let God change you."
- Teach how one can live responsibly, without making excuses, but with accountability to others.
- Guide in spiritual growth.
- Show the person how to help others.[53]

2. *Counseling and Obesity.* The basics of weight loss are simple: reduce the intake of calories below what the body uses. To reach this goal, hundreds of diets have been developed. They appear in books, pamphlets, mimeographed sheets, and many women's magazines. Diets are a core part of self-help groups such as Weight Watchers and TOPS. Within recent years weight-control clinics have sprung up all over the country offering behavior modification, inspiration, encouragement, and a variety of nutritional programs. Hospitals, individuals, counselors, and other professionals are all involved in helping people lose weight. Yet most of these efforts fail.

The goals of weight-loss programs are the same, and often they do help people shed pounds, at least temporarily. The weight, however, usually comes back and with each return it gets harder to lose again. Very few people, including those who follow diets proposed by Christian writers, appear to retain their reduced weights for a period of two or more years after dieting.[54] Many will agree with the physician who called obesity "a chronic condition, resistant to treatment, and prone to relapse."[55]

In part, fighting obesity is difficult because the body resists weight loss and fights diets. If the caloric intake is too restrictive, the body (a) lowers its metabolism so that fewer calories are needed to maintain weight, (b) becomes more inactive in an effort to maintain body weight, (c) develops weight loss plateaus, and (d) causes the person to think more about food so consumption is harder to resist whenever food is available.[56]

Effective weight loss is likely to be less difficult and more permanent when:

- People understand the physiological and psychological aspects of weight loss (since understanding helps reduce depression and guilt).
- Counselees learn principles of sound nutrition (this will reduce craving for missing foods and help teach principles for weight control after the diet).
- Diets are not so restrictive that they deny all foods that are desirable (this sometimes encourages binging and quick weight gain after the diet ends).
- There is a program of regular exercise to accompany dieting.
- There is a program of reinforcement to reward the counselee as weight-loss goals are met.
- Others give constant encouragement and support (including prayer support) during and after the weight-loss program.
- Psychological issues that may contribute to excess eating are reduced, often through counseling.

Most weight-loss programs are self-imposed and self-terminated. Success is likely to be better if the weight loss is supervised by a physician, nutritionist, or competent weight-loss specialist. This is true, especially, when there are likely to be medical complications, if the counselee is not in good health, or if one must lose a lot of weight.

3. *Counseling People with Anorexia Nervosa and Bulimia.* Eating disorders are complex conditions that often resist treatment and rarely respond to the interventions of inexperienced counselors, even when their intentions are good. Most writers suggest a multimethod approach that may include some or all of the following.

(a) Medical Treatment. Eating disorders can do serious harm to the body; in time the physical changes can be life threatening. Competent medical treatment, therefore, is crucial.

People with eating disorders often do not see or accept the physical seriousness of the illness. Some will resist treatment or refuse to cooperate with the doctor. It is important to help these patients see that treatment will remove bothersome symptoms such as insomnia, fatigue, depression, and obsessive thoughts about food and weight.

(b) Behavior Change. The counselee needs to get control of the unhealthy eating behaviors, including the binge-purge cycles. Start by encouraging the counselee to keep a record of eating and binging behavior. Include information concerning what and how much is eaten. Where did the eating take place and when, and what emotions were experienced at the time?

Based on this foundation data, the counselee and counselor together can work out rules for behavior control. These might include eating only at planned mealtimes, eating in the same location, and agreeing on the quantities that will be eaten. Sometimes counselees are encouraged to spend some time in prayer or relaxation before eating since this can reduce anxious, tension-filled eating. Agree that all-or-nothing thinking must be resisted. (This is the idea that "since I blew it by eating this one chocolate, I might as well go ahead and finish the whole box.") These methods are designed to help the counselee control eating.

Often the counseling will reveal continuing stresses that lead one to lose control. When these are known, counseling can help people learn to cope with tensions and resist circumstances that might trigger unhealthy eating.[57]

(c) Individual Counseling. Since eating disorders often stem from unhealthy attitudes, these must be changed through counseling. Counselees may need to reconsider their beliefs that "thin is beautiful," that physical attractiveness is all important, or that perfectionism is desirable and attainable. Often counselees will need help with problems of sexual identity, parental relationships (including overdependency), depression, feelings of failure, or low self-esteem.[58] Disordered eating is not likely to change until there is a removal of the personal problems and conflicts that lead to the disorder.

(d) Family Counseling. Since many disorders begin with attitudes coming from the family, and since many anorexics and bulimics have family problems, the family is best brought into the treatment process.[59] Some research evidence shows that relapse is less likely when families are included in treatment and able to give support to people with eating disorders following the treatment.[60]

(e) Group Counseling. Some but not all counselors advocate the group approach as an adjunct to other treatment. Within the group, participants can work on issues of self-esteem, interpersonal relations, unhealthy attitudes toward weight or eating, and other shared issues.

(f) Spiritual Counseling. One Christian writer has described starvation as "an extreme, incorrect and unbiblical attempt to deal with various problems in life and is actually suicidal if it is not stopped." Often counselees need to learn biblically consistent ways to deal with parent-child relationships, sexuality, self-esteem, responsibility, worry, guilt, and similar issues. Eating disorders tend to reflect problems at a deeper level, and frequently this deeper level is spiritual.[61]

4. *Counseling and Behavioral Addictions.* Compulsive gambling, procrastination, workaholism, and other failures at self-control sometimes have a physical basis and need medical treatment. Attention-deficit disorders, for example, may result from chemical imbalances or neurological malfunctioning that make it difficult for some people to control behavior despite their best efforts and intentions.

More often, however, addictive behavior and lack of control have roots that are psychological, social, or spiritual. An old hymn urges Christians to "yield not to temptation, for yielding is sin. Each victory will help you some other to win." Every time we yield, it is easier to give in at the next opportunity. Sinful behavior can become addictive behavior.

As an example, consider addictions to pornography or erotic lustful thinking. Unlike mature expressions of love within marriage, pornography and mental lust (like sexual perversions in general) do not require an intimate relationship with another human being. Erotic thinking, with or without pornographic stimulation, is an individual mental experience. This is thinking done alone. Often it is unrealistic highly idealized thinking, and frequently it is characteristic of individuals who are unable or unwilling to establish intimate nonsexual relationships with persons of the opposite sex. Sometimes the mental adulterer has been hurt in the past, is afraid of the opposite sex, or fears his or her ability to perform sexually. Sometimes the fantasies occur in the minds of happily married individuals who are too busy for frequent sex with their spouses. Others may be bored with a lifetime of the same old thing in sex. As a result, the individual engages in mental self-stimulation, pondering erotic behavior that never would be attempted in real life. When the erotica is in the mind, nobody else knows about it, and the fantasies grow without much restriction.

Like all addictions, erotic thinking grows because some need is not being met in a more effective, less addictive way. The need for communication and close contact with other human beings, for example, may have been replaced with fantasy. This fantasy is pleasant and not considered harmful (at least at the beginning), so the individual doesn't try to stop. In time the lustful thoughts and/or use of pornography become increasingly frequent, there is greater withdrawal from others, and the person seems unable to abandon what has become a progressively compulsive habit.

What can be done to get out of this trap? Many behavioral addictions will yield to a three-part solution: determination, replacement, and need fulfillment.

(a) Determination. Addictive behavior will persist unless the individual determines to change. This is unlikely to be a one-time-only decision. Addictive behavior is pleasurable and relapse may be common even after repeated decisions to quit.

Despite these failures, the counselee must be motivated to change or there will be little progress.

(b) Replacement. Behavioristic psychologists have suggested several ways to find replacements for compulsive behavior and persisting thoughts. *Thought stopping* seems like a gimmick, but it works for many people. Whenever an unwanted thought comes to awareness, the individual thinks STOP and even says this out loud if nobody else is around. *Thought switching* follows. As soon as the undesired thinking is interrupted, quickly focus attention on something else. Sometimes this is accompanied by *success rehearsal* in which the person imagines that he or she will be successful instead of thinking about failure.[62]

The Bible gives similar guidelines. We are instructed to get rid of "whatever belongs to your earthly nature: sexual immorality, impurity, lust, evil desires and greed, which is idolatry."[63] It is not difficult to stop and throw out unhealthy thoughts or behaviors but it is hard to keep them from returning unless we bring in replacement thinking and actions. After we "put off the old self with its practices" we must "put on the new self" with its better ways of thinking and behavior.[64] Lustful thoughts must be replaced with other thinking that is healthy and Christ honoring. Christian counselors often suggest that whenever unhealthy thoughts appear, they should be replaced by mentally reciting a Bible verse.[65] None of this is likely to work, of course, if pornographic materials or other aids to addictive erotic thinking are still retained.

(c) Need Fulfillment. As we have seen, addictions often arise because some need is not being met in more healthy ways. Counseling may help the counselee ponder what needs are being met by the addiction and how these needs can be met in other ways. The compulsive television watcher, for example, may need contact with other human beings but lacks interpersonal skills or is afraid of intimacy. Counseling could help the individual relate to people in ways that are fulfilling and less threatening. The compulsive eater, in contrast, may eat whenever stress gets intense. This person needs help in learning more effective methods for managing stress.

Preventing Addiction

The widespread availability and abuse of drugs has led to repeated calls for mandatory drug testing. If an athlete takes drugs that increase strength or speed, it has been argued, this is unfair to the competitors who do not take drugs. If an airline pilot or bus driver uses drugs that could dull thinking, this can put many innocent lives in danger. If someone in the military uses drugs that might impair clear reasoning, this could have serious implications for the nation's defense. Opponents claim that drug testing invades privacy. Urinalysis is not always an accurate way to detect drugs, and some have argued that the whole idea is illegal.[66]

Even when drug testing is used, there is little evidence that this prevents substance abuse. Like most of the issues discussed in this book, prevention is often proclaimed but rarely practiced, in part because we don't really know how to prevent addictions.

The preceding chapter on alcoholism gave four preventive guidelines: stimulate a healthy home life, instill a healthy religious faith, provide education about substance abuse, and teach people how to cope with the stresses of life. Each of these, along with the suggestions that follow, can apply to the addictive behaviors that are discussed in this chapter.

1. *Just Say No.* These three words became the basis of a national drug-prevention program. The three-word slogan was creative and easily remembered, but it failed to acknowledge that some people want to just say no but are unable to do so. Swayed by peer pressure, inner conflicts, environmental stress, poor adult modeling, or family attitudes and tensions, many people need more than a good slogan if they are to avoid substance abuse, eating disorders, and behavioral addictions.

Nevertheless, the just-say-no prevention campaign has served some useful purposes. Parents, teachers, church leaders, and others in the society need to be aware of the signs of addiction. Educational programs increase this awareness, and sometimes sensitive adults are able to intervene early, before developing addictions get worse. In addition, when young people or other potential addicts are encouraged to say no, this helps increase the motivation to avoid or to stop addictive thoughts and actions.

2. *Skill Learning.* In their homes, schools, and churches, individuals should be taught how to resist peer pressures and harmful social attitudes. We don't learn to resist by pretending that problems don't exist. Instead, young people (and some who are older) need to think about peer pressures before they arise and ponder how these and other unhealthy influences are best avoided. One of the most successful programs for the prevention of substance abuse is built on the assumption that people will avoid drugs when they learn skills that enable them to cope with life's pressures without leaning on addictive substances or behaviors.[67]

Addictive problems should be less likely when young people are informed about addiction, feel loved and accepted without undue pressure to succeed, are given opportunities to find fulfilling activities without the need to rely on addictive behaviors, and have a healthy and supportive home life where parents are free of substance abuse or other addictive behaviors. All of this can help people cope without addiction.

3. *Meeting Needs.* As we have seen, addictive behaviors often arise because needs are not being met in more healthy ways. Substance abuse and other addictions are less common and less needed when people feel accepted, secure, loved, and capable. By stimulating maturity we weaken the need for addictions.

Conclusions about Addiction

Cherry Boone O'Neill, the eldest of singer Pat Boone's four daughters, was a beautiful, talented, and intelligent teenager. With her family, she performed before appreciative audiences all over the world—and she struggled with anorexia nervosa. In an effort to keep slim and attractive, she developed a lifestyle that involved rigorous fasting, long hours of grueling exercise, and regular binging. Slimness at first was a challenge, but it grew into a compulsion that almost led to her death. She was helped by a professional Christian counselor.[68]

Nobody knows how many people are held in the grip of addictions. Some, like Cherry Boone O'Neill, get help and are freed from their addictive cycles. Many do not. Some of these people may sit next to us in church or at work, struggling to control addictions that are still hidden. Helping people cope with addictive behavior is one of the major and most important challenges facing Christian counselors and the church.

SUGGESTIONS FOR FURTHER READING

Backus, William, and Marie Chapian. *Why Do I Do What I Don't Want to Do?* Minneapolis: Bethany House Publishers, 1984.*

Baucom, John Q. *Help Your Children Say No to Drugs.* Grand Rapids, Mich.: Zondervan, 1987.*

Bruch, Hilde. *The Golden Cage: The Enigma of Anorexia Nervosa.* New York: Vintage, 1979.*

Lenters, William. *The Freedom We Crave—Addiction: The Human Condition.* Grand Rapids, Mich.: Eerdmans, 1985.

O'Neill, Cherry Boone. *Starving for Attention.* New York: Dell, 1982.*

Orford, Jim. *Excessive Appetites: A Psychological View of Addiction.* New York: Wiley, 1985.

Van Cleave, Stephen, Walter Byrd, and Kathy Revell. *Counseling for Substance Abuse.* Waco, Tex.: Word, 1987.

Vath, Raymond E. *Counseling Those with Eating Disorders.* Waco, Tex.: Word, 1986.

Walters, Richard P. *Counseling for Problems of Self-Control.* Waco, Tex.: Word, 1987.

* Books marked with an asterisk (*) are especially suited for counselees to read.

34

Financial Counseling

RANDY WANTS TO BE a professional musician. He formed his first band when he was in high school. Now, almost three years after graduation, Randy and his group spend hours in practice every day. The effort seems to have been worthwhile. The band has been hired for a few local concerts and the audiences, though small, have been appreciative and enthusiastic.

Audience appreciation and enthusiasm, however, do not pay bills, and Randy is getting further and further into debt. The problem, he admits freely, is plastic money. Like millions of others, Randy discovered early that it is easy to get a credit card and even easier to use it. He has every intention of paying his bills, but when money is short or food is scarce, it is easy to rationalize his use of the card "just one more time." This attitude has put Randy over $8,000 in debt. Recently he even borrowed money using one card to pay the interest that was accumulating on another.

Getting a steady job and starting to pay off the debts would make sense, but this would mean at least temporarily abandoning his real love, music. Randy continues to practice and hopes that his big break will come soon, bringing with it success and the means to pay off the debt.

In the meantime the bills are accumulating and Randy is getting progressively worried about his financial problems. Sometimes the anxiety interferes with his music. Randy now knows what many others have learned: it is difficult to be relaxed and efficient at work when one is perpetually worried about finances.

Books on counseling almost never mention money. Scripture warns that "the love of money is a root of all kinds of evil,"[1] and counselors often discover that the abuse and mismanagement of money is at the root of all kinds of human problems. Yet this is rarely discussed in the professional journals, even though individual tension, family conflict, interpersonal strife, anger, frustration, driving ambition, worry, anxiety, suicide, and a host of other issues at times are all related directly or indirectly to the pursuit and management of money.

Money in itself is not the problem. We need money to trade and meet individual needs. Problems come because of our *attitudes* toward money and our *inefficiencies* in handling finances wisely. The Christian counselor discovers this frequently. Sometimes finances are listed as the basic problem; more often financial struggles are presented as a part of some broader problem, such as anxiety, marital conflict, or adjusting to retirement. Thus concerns about money often surface in counseling.

THE BIBLE AND FINANCES

The Bible says a lot about money, possessions, and the management of finances. These scriptural statements can be summarized in the form of several basic principles.

1. *Money and Possessions Must Be Viewed Realistically.* In one of his parables Jesus described a man whose life had been spent in the accumulation of wealth. Then the man died, unprepared to meet God and forced to leave his precious possessions to somebody else. Jesus called this man a fool.[2] He was rich in worldly wealth but poor in his relationship with God.

Things have not changed in modern times. Many people still live lives dominated by the love of money and the pursuit of affluence. The story has been told about several very successful American businessmen who met in 1921. The group included the most successful speculator on Wall Street, a cabinet member, and the presidents of the New York Stock Exchange, the Bank of International Settlements, the largest steel company in the United States, the largest utility company, and the largest gas company. A few years later, all of the men were dead. Three had committed suicide, three had been in prison, one had gone insane, and two died in bankruptcy. All had been ruined by the Great Depression of the 1930s. At a time when millions of common people tightened their budgets and went on living, these men had been destroyed because their lives centered on money. When the money was gone, there was little purpose in living.[3] Even sadder, perhaps, is the example of some modern preachers and television evangelists whose ministries and personal lives have been marred permanently by a preoccupation with fund raising and affluent lifestyles.[4]

According to the Scriptures, money is temporary.[5] Ultimately it does not satisfy or bring happiness and stability.[6] Perhaps this is one reason why we are warned to keep our lives free from the love of money and to be content with what we have.[7] If riches increase we are not to set our hearts on them.[8] Money in itself is not condemned in Scripture, but the love of money and dependence on riches clearly are wrong.

2. *Money and Possessions Are Provided by God.* He supplies all of our needs, expects us to trust him for our finances, and has shown that we need not be anxious or worried about having enough.[9] There are people who squander their money through mismanagement and others who confuse their real needs with their desired extras. In terms of the basic necessities, like food and clothing, God provides and often in great abundance.

Sometimes, however, he chooses to provide only the barest necessities. Despite the views of many believers, there is no biblical support for the idea that God consistently rewards faithful living and generous giving with affluence and abundance.[10] For reasons known only to him, God sometimes permits hunger and financial hardship, even among his faithful followers. Still he supplies what we need, even though he doesn't always give us what we want or think we need.

3. *Money and Possessions Can Be Harmful.* The rich young ruler who came to Jesus with a theological question walked away grieving when he heard the command to give all that he had to the poor.[11] Apparently a love for money prevented his spiritual growth. He was learning, as Jesus said on another occasion, that one can gain the whole world and lose one's soul.[12] Elsewhere Jesus taught that we cannot love both

God and money. Eventually we will come to the point of loving the one and hating the other.[13]

A love of money can prevent our turning to Christ and can stifle spiritual growth. Wealth can lead us to forget God, and sometimes a desire for things even leads people to steal.[14] Nowhere is this stated more clearly than in 1 Tim. 6:6–11, where the dangers of loving money are contrasted with an emphasis on godliness and a command to flee greedy attitudes:

> But godliness with contentment is great gain. For we brought nothing into the world, and we can take nothing out of it. But if we have food and clothing, we will be content with that. People who want to get rich fall into temptation and a trap and into many foolish and harmful desires that plunge men into ruin and destruction. For the love of money is a root of all kinds of evil. Some people, eager for money, have wandered from the faith and pierced themselves with many griefs.
>
> But you, man of God, flee from all of this, and pursue righteousness, godliness, faith, love, endurance and gentleness.

The Bible also shows that greed and the overemphasis on money can lead to interpersonal tension. A man once came to Jesus complaining about a family squabble, and the Lord blamed the problem on greed. Then he warned that even when we have abundance, real life consists of more than possessions.[15]

4. *Money and Possessions Should Be Managed Wisely.* In the parable of the talents, Jesus warns about the mismanagement of our resources and ends with the unfaithful servant being alienated from his friends.[16]

Kenneth M. Meyer suggests that several money management principles can be found in this parable.[17] We learn, for example, that

- God entrusts resources to us in many forms, especially financial.
- God gives these resources to his servants in different amounts.
- God expects us to plan and manage our resources with the goal of making a profit.
- God condemns laziness or anxiety in our planning (there was a harsh rebuke for the do-nothing manager).
- God holds each manager equally accountable even though some have more resources than others.
- God's work is advanced or hindered by the ways we plan our financial stewardship.[18]

Wisely managed resources should be:

- Gained honestly. Trying to make money quickly and dishonestly is condemned in the book written by Solomon, the richest man in the Bible.[19]
- Invested carefully. Returning to the parable of the talents we are reminded that the wise servants managed their money wisely. Clearly money is to be used carefully and not hoarded or mismanaged.[20]
- Spent realistically. This means keeping out of debt whenever possible. The

Bible gives little sanction for credit-card buying. In Romans we are instructed to pay our taxes honestly and then to "let no debt remain outstanding."[21] When we borrow, we are slaves to others and this can lead to a number of personal and interpersonal problems.[22]

- Shared joyfully. God loves a cheerful giver and throughout the Bible there is emphasis on giving to God, to the poor, and to each other.[23] Sometimes this giving is followed by material wealth and/or spiritual blessing[24] but, as we have seen, this doesn't always happen. It goes beyond biblical teaching to assume that "when we give, we also get." Believers should give joyfully in gratitude to God but without expecting or demanding immediate monetary returns.

As we ponder the above paragraphs, it is abundantly clear that the Bible speaks often about money. This is an issue that must concern every Christian. It is an issue that is certain to come up repeatedly in counseling.

The Causes of Financial Problems

Many people appear to live from payday to payday, financially flush at certain times of the month but flat broke at other times. Others manage to get along without great hardship, but saving seems impossible and there barely is enough cash to meet family needs. Some might argue that the pressures come because there is too little income and too many expenses. Financial difficulties, however, appear at all socioeconomic levels. For the wealthy, financial problems involve greater amounts of money, but the root causes are similar to those faced by less-prosperous people.

1. *Distorted Values.* The way one handles money can be a good indicator of one's values. Each of us spends money or wants to spend it on the things we consider important. Sometimes, however, what we consider important is what puts us into debt. Even Christians slip into accepting desires and values that are nonbiblical and harmful.

(a) Materialism. The dictionary defines this as an attitude of "devotion to material things rather than to spiritual objects, needs, and considerations." Materialism is an attitude that leads us to pursue money, possessions, pleasure, and the good things of life. It leads to impatience, overindulgence, and overspending on luxuries that are nice to have but are not really needed. It can lead even Christians to accept a hedonistic new morality that makes the pursuit of affluence a rival religion.[25] Money has a seductive power that is "capable of inspiring devotion, of giving a false sense of security, freedom and omnipotence. It takes on the very characteristics of a deity,"[26] and overlooks Jesus' statement that our lives do not consist of the abundance of those things that we possess.[27]

Some of the great spiritual leaders in biblical times had considerable wealth. Abraham, Solomon, and Job are examples. These people never gave evidence of pursuing riches. They accepted their wealth as God-given and sought to know and serve him better. Many wealthy people today have similar attitudes toward their possessions.

More common, it seems, is an attitude that finds reasons for the accumulation of things. We think, for example, that "as long as it doesn't hurt us or control us, why not have the best." "If we have more, we can give more to missions." This kind of reasoning can be legitimate, but often it is a veil to hide our materialism. "Although *other* people's material wants are often declaimed as materialistic and excessive in their cravings for luxuries, no one ever considers their own purchases as selfish, greedy or materialistic. In fact, if you listen to your own and others' justifications for their various purchases, it is need and not greed that is continually referred to. And not cynically, or tongue in cheek. You and they and I really mean it."[28] Maybe the rich young ruler had a similar attitude, but Jesus told him to give it all to the poor.

(b) Covetousness and Greed. These words imply a desire for more, even if others are made poorer as a result. This is an attitude expressed succinctly by an author who claimed to be a Christian but titled a book *How to Have More in a Have-Not World.* Such an attitude is soundly condemned in Scripture[29] but entrenched in our modern ways of thinking.

Shortly after his move from Russia, Alexandr Solzhenitsyn commented that "something which is incomprehensible to the human mind is the West's fantastic greed for gain which goes far beyond all reason, all limitations, good conscience." This has led one observer to conclude that covetousness and greed cause a variety of problems: inflation, unmanageable debts, and family arguments, to name a few.[30] In Western countries we don't worship idols of wood and stone, but many people, Christians included, seem to worship money and material things.

(c) A Desire to Get Rich Quickly. Perhaps people have always been impressed with the idea that one can earn a lot of money quickly and with little effort. The Scriptures warn against this,[31] but the itch for more urges some people to invest hard-earned funds into programs that, more often than not, fail to deliver what they promise.

(d) Pride and Resentment. The church at Laodicea took the proud attitude that it was rich and in need of nothing.[32] Even today such a superior attitude characterizes some wealthy and successful people who fail to realize that they are poor, needy, wretched, and miserable if they ignore God, rely on their wealth for security and happiness, or fail to admit that possessions and successes come as a gift from God. In contrast to the haughty rich, there are also the resentful poor who are angry at God because of their lack of wealth and envious of those who have more.

All of these values suggest that financial problems may be caused less by the possession or nonpossession of material things and more by the attitudes that we have toward money and possessions.

2. *Unwise Financial Decisions.* There are many ways to waste the money we can't afford to lose. Often the waste comes because of unwise financial decisions that include the following.

(a) Impulse Buying. This involves seeing and buying something without checking quality, prices, whether the purchase really is needed, or whether we can afford it. One place to resist this attitude is in the line at the checkout counter. It is a good policy to never buy anything while you are waiting in line.

(b) Carelessness. Without the limiting influence of a budget, some people spend money carelessly and then are surprised when their wallets are empty or their checking accounts are overdrawn.

At times perhaps all of us dream of being rescued by someone who will pay our bills. When people win lotteries or inherit large sums of money, however, the wealth often is gone within a year and there is little to show for the windfall. Apparently those who are careless with small sums of money are careless as well with large amounts.[33]

(c) Speculation. There is an old adage that many people ignore: if you can't afford to lose it, don't speculate with it, no matter how bright the prospects. The Bible warns against speculation[34] and so does common sense, but many people ignore these warnings and lose their money in attempts to get rich quick.

(d) Cosigning. This involves signing a statement to say that you promise to pay if someone else fails to remove a debt. Often cosigning is done for worthy motives (to help a friend get a loan, for example), but when the friend doesn't pay, the cosigner is left with the debt and the friendship disintegrates. Little wonder that the wise and wealthy Solomon, writing under divine guidance, warned against cosigning.[35]

(e) Laziness. When people are too lazy to work or to manage a budget, financial problems almost always follow.[36] In these days of government handouts for deserving people, the lazy and undeserving also come for money and in turn are encouraged not to work. This creates a financial strain for everyone and jeopardizes the continued existence of genuinely needed programs.

(f) Wasted Time. To a large extent we decide how to spend our time. For salaried employees this is less of a financial issue, but for the self-employed or for people who are paid according to productivity, time equals money. When a person is disorganized, undisciplined, or inclined to waste time, there is a resulting loss of income.

(g) Neglect of Property. When people fail to take care of property, there is faster deterioration, costly repairs, and the need to spend money that might have been used for something else.

(h) Credit Buying. In this day of easy credit and the proliferation of credit cards, buying on time is one of the major causes of financial problems. It is easy to fall into the credit-card trap. First, we purchase something we want and intend to pay for when the bill arrives at the end of the month. Then we see something else we want or a sale comes along, and we make one or two additional purchases on the assumption that we can spread the payments over a couple of months. If the minimum payment on the bill is a minor amount, we rationalize that an additional purchase will only raise the payment by a few dollars, so we buy more.

This is a process of slow financial self-strangulation. Using a credit card often doesn't seem like spending money, so we are tempted to buy more things than we might purchase otherwise. Impulse buying is encouraged, we are more inclined to buy when and where we can charge (that may not be where the prices are lowest), and we end up paying a large finance charge that adds to the cost of the item. In summary, credit-card buying becomes a license to spend money we don't have and can't spare for goods we often don't need.

All of this leads to increased debt that, in turn, is costly financially and binding psychologically. Caught in the credit-card trap, it is hard to get out. The stresses are greater when we are forced to use a limited salary to pay a high price for something that was charged originally but has been used or discarded already. As the pressure builds so do many family arguments and personal tensions. Undoubtedly it is true that credit cards in our pockets can be like time bombs with the potential to shatter peace, happiness, and mental stability.

3. *Lack of a Budget.* A budget is another term for a spending plan. When such a plan exists and is followed, there are controls on spending, less impulse buying, and fewer debts. When there is no financial plan, there is no control on spending. What we spend begins to exceed what we earn, and this leads either to a deficit at month's end or a turning to credit cards (or home equity loans) to make ends meet.

4. *Lack of Giving.* Hoarding is wrong and the person who refuses to give can hardly expect to receive God's blessing and financial guidance.[37] Believers are to give in three areas: to God,[38] to other believers[39] and to the poor.[40] There is no guarantee that givers will in turn receive abundant material things from God, but the believer who fails to follow the biblical directives to give is surely courting financial problems.

The Effects of Financial Problems

The previous paragraphs have mentioned several of the results that come with financial stress. These include:

- Worry about money or how to pay the bills (one national survey found that 70 percent of all worries concern money).
- Family and marital problems that arise or increase because of financial pressures, arguments over inheritances, or similar money issues.
- Guilt, envy, jealousy, resentment, or pride, each of which is sinful and each of which can be stimulated by financial issues.
- Emotional emptiness and unhappiness that come to those whose main interest in life is the accumulation of possessions.
- Spiritual deadness that follows when we get too concerned about money, have the wrong attitudes, or violate biblical principles for handling finances.

Sometimes there is a loss of friends because of money issues. Tensions may build if there is a sudden increase in money, but more often friendships disintegrate because a person becomes greedy, envious, embarrassed by debts, or intent on making loans from others. These are good ways to lose friends.

At times, financial problems put most of us under stress; stress that can bring physical illness, anxiety, discouragement, interpersonal tension, and inefficiency as a result. For some people there also can be uncontrolled, irresponsible spending especially if riches increase suddenly. For others there is bankruptcy with the resulting family pressures and psychological trauma. Clearly money and possessions, either too much or too little, can stimulate a number of the problems that people bring to a counselor.

Counseling and Financial Problems

There are several helpful books on financial management, some written by Christians.[41] These can be loaned to counselees who often are able to solve their financial problems without additional help. Others will benefit from counseling that may focus on one or more of the following issues.

1. *Help the Counselee Acknowledge the Problem and Determine to Solve It.* It is difficult, if not impossible, to counsel successfully with a person who fails to admit that a problem exists. It is equally difficult to help someone who claims things have always been this way and will never be different. Thinking like this can be an excuse to avoid problems and do nothing to bring solutions.

People with financial problems may think this way, but many also struggle with worry. They should be urged to face the reality of their situations and encouraged when this is done. Point out that God supplies our needs and that it *is* possible to get out of debt and to manage money efficiently. Try to emphasize, however, that the solution to financial problems depends less on the state of the economy than on the way individuals and families handle their financial attitudes and resources. Counselees need to experience hope. (Hope is a crucial ingredient in all successful counseling.) While this may not eliminate worry, hope gives encouragement and can motivate counselees to take action and to work on their financial problems.

The realistic counselor knows, however, that for some there is little hope because they don't want to change or are unwilling to work on financial problems. Such people may have to experience financial disaster before they are motivated to work on the problem. For some the motivation may never come.

2. *With the Counselee, Seek Divine Guidance.* In the midst of crises it is easy to be so distracted by circumstances that we take our eyes off God. Counselees should be reminded that God has abundant riches and knows our needs.[42] He has instructed us to cast our burdens and anxieties on him,[43] and surely this includes financial burdens. If someone asks for divine help and expects it, then God will meet the person's need. He also will help us to be content in any circumstances, including one's current financial state.

All of this implies that prayer should be an important starting point in financial planning. Pray with the counselee, asking God to lead as the practical details of financial planning are discussed. Then encourage the counselee and his or her family to pray together about this as they work together on their money problems.

3. *Teach Biblical Principles of Finance.* People with financial problems are in a hurry to get some relief. Rarely are they interested in sermons or in philosophical talks about finances, but they need to understand, nevertheless, that there are biblical guidelines for managing money. These principles must guide the Christian counselor and should be shared explicitly at various times as the counseling continues.

In addition to the concepts presented earlier, counselees should be helped to see the following:

(a) Everything Belongs to God. We are only stewards of God's possessions. In the psalm where God encourages people to "call upon me in the day of trouble; I will deliver you, and you will honor me," he also states that "the world is mine, and all that is in it."[44] A first step in financial planning is to recognize that ownership of everything must be transferred to God, who is the rightful owner.

(b) Stealing Is Wrong. Although God ultimately owns everything, he allows each of us to possess certain things. To take these things from another is to steal from God as well as from our fellow human beings. In times of need it is easy to cut corners on income tax, to borrow supplies that rightfully belong to an employer, or to get money in other questionable ways. This is stealing that ultimately does not help with our financial problems.

(c) Coveting Is Wrong. Like stealing, coveting is forbidden in the Ten Commandments.[45] To covet is to want something that we see others enjoying. It implies a dissatisfaction with the possessions and opportunities that God has given.

It is sad that our entire economy seems geared to helping people violate this principle. We are encouraged to engage in extravagant and wasteful spending even if this creates personal financial crisis, harms our national economy, or hinders the economics of less-developed nations. God can help us to be content with what we have and to avoid comparing ourselves with others who seem to have more.

In addition to coveting the goods of another, it also is possible to have a clinging, covetous attitude to our own possessions. If we assume that everything comes from God and rightfully is his, then there is no need to cling tenaciously to our goods or to be excessively distraught when something is lost, stolen, or broken. This involves a responsible but realistic attitude toward possessions.

(d) Giving Is Right. This is emphasized throughout the Bible. God expects us to give, even when we own little and have nothing to spare. Of course this does not mean that everything should be given away. In the Old Testament the people gave a portion of their possessions. We need a willingness to give, followed by acts of giving to God and to those in need.

(e) Money Management Is Right. In the parable of the talents,[46] the people possessed different amounts, but two managed their money carefully while the third did not. It was the poor manager whom Jesus criticized. God expects us to be good stewards of what he has given. He demanded this of Adam[47] and he has expected it of people ever since.

4. *Help Counselees Develop and Follow a Financial Plan.* Without a blueprint for money management, it is very difficult to control one's finances. A financial plan involves several elements that can be discussed in counseling. Some of the following steps can be initiated in the counseling session, completed by the counselees at home, and discussed subsequently in a later session.

(a) Get the Facts. This involves making a list on paper of one's assets and liabilities. Completing Table 34-1 is one way that this might be done. Getting an accurate picture of the current financial situation can be an important first step in solving financial problems. When one's net worth is increasing every year, the person is moving ahead financially. When the net worth is decreasing, the person is declining financially.

(b) Establish Goals. What are the counselee's financial hopes and plans? Begin with some general goals, like getting out of debt, being able to provide for the family, doing what we can to advance the cause of Christ, saving for the education of children and for retirement, having enough money to travel, or owning a home.

When these general goals have been written down, it is good to be more specific in listing long-range and short-term goals. What specifically does the counselee hope to have achieved in ten years, five years, and one year from now? Help counselees be realistic in terms of their educational level, present income and debts. A man who earns $15,000 annually, but has an $8,000 debt cannot realistically expect that all debts will be gone within a year. He can, however, set a goal to have a portion gone within the next twelve months.

In setting goals remember that these should fit within the scriptural guidelines about finances. Help counselees be honest and fair in all financial dealings

Table 34-1

Assets (what we own)		
Savings	$_____	
Checking Account	_____	
Value of Car	_____	
Value of House	_____	
Resale Value of Furnishings	_____	
Cash Value of Insurance	_____	
Other	_____	
	_____	
Total		_____
Liabilities (what we owe)		
Unpaid Balance on Car	$_____	
Home Loan	_____	
Other Debts (List)	_____	
	_____	
	_____	
	_____	
Total		_____
Net Worth (difference between Assets and Liabilities)		_____
Date _____		

including the payment of taxes. Encourage people to avoid selfish indulgence, to show a financial concern for others, and to avoid borrowing (except, perhaps, for major purchases such as a home or car and on occasion for bill consolidation). Emphasize that financial goals are best set after seeking God's guidance through prayer and study of the Bible.[48]

(c) Set Priorities. Few people can meet all of their financial goals immediately, so there must be decisions about what can be done now and what must wait until later. Tithing, paying off debts, and eliminating the misuse of credit cards must be high on the priority list.

One financial counselor has suggested that we need to distinguish between needs, wants, and desires.[49] *Needs* are the purchases necessary to provide food, housing, clothing, medical care, transportation, and other basics. *Wants* involve choices about quality: whether to get a used or a new car, or whether to eat hamburger or steak. *Desires* are choices for spending surplus funds after other expenses are met. A good used car would meet the need, a new car might be wanted, a sport's car might be desired. In establishing a financial plan and getting out of debt, needs must be met first, wants and desires can be met later. Each expenditure should be evaluated in terms of these categories. In setting priorities, remember once again that time management often is important financially. In many occupations, to waste time is to reduce income.

(d) Develop a Budget. A budget is a spending plan that enables us to manage and effectively control the expenditures of money. Such a budget includes keeping records that help determine where the money is going. "By keeping good records, having a plan and being honest with oneself, a person won't get into financial

Figure 34-1

10% of Gross Tithe	Taxes and Fixed Expenses	Working Income		
		10% Saving	70% Living Expenses	20% Debts
1	2	3	4	5

trouble," writes one counselor. "I seldom see financially successful people who don't keep good records."[50]

It is not easy to develop and stay within the guidelines of a budget. Some who claim they cannot keep a budget really don't want to take the effort to control their money carefully. Most people get along fine without budgeting, but in so doing they waste a lot of money that is spent more on whims than on one's priorities.[51]

One plan for saving and spending has been called the 10-70-20 plan for budgeting. As shown in Figure 34-1 above, each dollar is divided into five parts. Ten percent of one's total income goes to God in tithe, a second portion goes to the government, then the remaining portion is working income that is divided three ways. Ten percent of this is saved, 70 percent is for living expenses, and 20 percent goes to pay past debts. When the debts are gone, the 20 percent can be used for making purchases on a cash basis.

Table 34-2 gives a sample budget worksheet that counselees could use (with modifications for individual differences). This worksheet assumes the 10-70-20 plan and each month allows counselees to plan and evaluate how successfully they have been in keeping within the budget.

Remember that budgets should be tools to help manage spending and not strait jackets to bind spenders. If a budget is unrealistic or if one's financial status changes, then the budget should be altered accordingly. This should be done with care, however, and not in an attempt to cover up or justify reckless spending and deviations from the budget plan.

5. *Keep Track of Your Own Financial Affairs.* Everyone has heard sad stories about marriage counselors whose own marriages have ended in divorce, psychiatrists who have committed suicide, preachers who condemn sin then fall into sin themselves, or counselors of homosexuals who slip into gay love affairs. It is difficult to be an effective counselor if one's own life is not in order. The banker who goes bankrupt is not likely to be an effective financial counselor.

Before you encourage others to save, to tithe, to budget, or to follow a financial program similar to the 10-70-20 plan, it is helpful to pause and consider the management of your own resources. In addition to the embarrassment, your counseling effectiveness is likely to be undercut if you have to say no when a counselee asks if you are following your own advice.

6. *Conclusions.* Counselors who are accustomed to more in-depth problems may feel that detailed financial planning is beyond the scope of Christian

Table 34-2
Budget

Month of ____________________
Gross Income (before taxes) $____________*

Item	A Amount Allocated	B Amount Spent	C Difference (+ or −)
1. *Tithe* (10%)	$	$	$
2. *Fixed Expenses*			
Taxes			
Social Security			
Professional Dues			
Other			
Total	$	$	$
Total Tithe and Fixed Expenses	$____________**		
Working Income—Deduct Total Tithe and Fixed Expenses (**) from Gross Income (*)	$	$	
3. *Savings* (10% of Working Income)	$	$	$
4. *Living Expenses* (70% of Working Income)			
Mortgage or Rent			
Heat/Electricity			
Telephone			
Water/Sewage/Garbage			
Gasoline			
Car Repairs			
Insurance			
Medical			
Food/Household			
Clothing			
Home Expenditures			
Gifts			
Vacation			
Buffer			
Other			
Total	$	$	$
5. *Debts* (20% of Working Income)			
____________			
____________			
____________			
____________			
Total	$	$	$

6. *Summary of Allocations*

Gross Income (from * above)	$
Total Allocated (Total of 5 boxes in column A)	$
Difference (Balance or Amount Short)	$

7. *Summary of Amount Spent*

Gross Income (from * above)	$
Total Allocated (Total of 5 boxes in column B)	$
Difference (Balance or Amount Short)	$

counseling. Such counselors may wish to refer their counselees to a banker, accountant or other financial counselor. Be careful in making recommendations, however. Some who advertise themselves as financial counselors may lack training or qualifications and others may be concerned about getting investment money from their clients, but not much interested in helping people cope with their financial problems. Like every other field, professional financial planners include some among their numbers who are unethical, even though the majority have a sincere desire to help.

Helping people manage their money and possessions can be one of the most rewarding and visibly successful aspects of Christian counseling. When there is a resolution of financial difficulties, this often has a positive effect on a variety of other counseling problems.

Preventing Financial Problems

Most of the problems discussed in this book apply only to some people. Not everyone, for example, becomes alcoholic, is deeply depressed, or has marriage problems. Everyone, however, handles money, most of us have financial problems at least periodically, and the Christian counselor has a responsibility to help people handle their possessions better.

1. *Teach Biblical Values concerning Finances.* This can be taught from the pulpit, in group meetings (including youth meetings), in Sunday school classes, and in individual conversations. Such instruction should:

- Point to the many biblical passages that deal with money and possessions.
- Encourage people to thank God for what they have instead of making comparisons with others and lamenting their lacks and needs.
- Warn people of the dangers of credit buying and encourage them to live within their means.
- Emphasize the importance of saving and joyful giving.

2. *Teach Practical Guidelines for Managing Money.* This involves showing people how to budget (including tithing and saving), encouraging them to do so, and urging them to share their experiences with other believers. It can be exciting and encouraging for believers to see how God blesses and meets needs when his guidelines are followed.

The Christian counselor may not be an expert in insurance, banking procedures, the preparation of a will, or the best ways to save and invest money. Nevertheless the counselor can stress the importance of each of these issues and point Christians either to books or to people who can give practical advice. Within the body of Christ there often are persons with business and financial expertise. These people can be invited to meet with individuals or groups to help with financial planning. This involves members of the body sharing their knowledge and gifts to build up and encourage others.

3. *Emphasize Finances in Premarital Counseling.* When people get married they usually enter an entirely new financial picture. Two incomes and ways of handling money often merge into one, and there is potential for conflict over

finances. As they approach marriage, a couple sometimes needs reminders to look at their resources through the eyes of reality. What are their attitudes toward money, finances, saving, tithing, credit cards, or money management? What debts are they bringing to marriage and how will these be paid? Do the bride and groom have different spending patterns? Does one spend lavishly, for example, while the other is very frugal? By raising financial questions, premarital counselors can prevent future conflicts over issues of money and possessions.[52]

4. *Raise the Issue of Finances Whenever There Is a Crisis or Life Change.* Major changes in life—starting college, changing jobs, moving, retirement, prolonged sickness, death in the family—can each bring financial struggles. If these financial issues can be raised early and discussed informally, problems can often be faced and resolved before they become major difficulties.

Conclusions about Financial Problems

The Bible never condemns the possession of goods and money, but it does speak against hoarding, coveting, and money mismanagement. Satan has used financial pressures to enslave people, to plunge them into debt and to cause both worry and a turning away from God and from divine principles of money management. To help individuals get out of debt and into financial freedom can be a satisfying experience in counseling. For the counselor this can be a practical way to help people live more in accordance with the principles of Scripture, including the principles of sound money management.

SUGGESTIONS FOR FURTHER READING

Burkett, Larry. *Answers to Your Family Financial Questions.* Pomona, Calif.: Focus on the Family, 1987.*

———. *The Financial Planning Workbook.* Chicago: Moody, 1982.*

Dayton, Howard L., Jr. *Your Money: Frustration or Freedom? The Biblical Guide to Earning, Saving, Spending, Investing, Giving.* Wheaton, Ill.: Tyndale House, 1986.*

Haughey, John C. *Holy Use of Money: Personal Finance in Light of Christian Faith.* Garden City, N.Y.: Doubleday, 1986.*

Meyer, Kenneth M. *Minister's Guide to Financial Planning.* Grand Rapids, Mich.: Zondervan, 1987.*

Porter, Sylvia. *Sylvia Porter's New Money Book.* New York: Avon, 1986.*

Rushford, Patricia H. *From Money Mess to Money Management.* Old Tappan, N.J.: Revell, 1984.*

Watts, John G. *Leave Your House in Order: A Guide to Planning Your Estate.* Rev. ed. Wheaton, Ill.: Tyndale House, 1982.*

* Books marked with an asterisk (*) are especially suitable for counselees to read.

35

Vocational Counseling

BILL WAS FIFTY-TWO when he lost his job. "We're not unhappy with your work," Bill's employer stated with a coolness that reflected his discomfort in releasing a longtime and faithful employee. The company's merger with another firm had created an abundance of managers, and Bill was one of several whose jobs had to go.

The psychological effect was devastating. Bill felt useless, unwanted, a failure. Every morning when his wife and two grown children went off to work, Bill cleaned up the kitchen, perused the morning newspaper and half-heartedly went back to preparing résumés, trying to find another job that would draw on his managerial experience and pay something equal to his lost salary. Sometimes, when he sat alone, pondering his situation and realizing that his wife and kids were working extra to pay the family expenses, Bill would cry and wonder if he could ever again provide for his family.

Bill discovered that other men in his church had also lost good jobs at midlife. Some of them had formed a support group that would get together weekly for prayer, mutual encouragement, and breakfast. Bill felt he couldn't afford the breakfast, and he was too ashamed to let anybody know.

The story had a happy ending when Bill was hired by a competitor of his old company. He hasn't forgotten those sad days of unemployment, and Bill now is active in working with that breakfast support group. To make things a little easier, the breakfasts are now free for everyone who attends, paid for by a little fund that Bill and a couple of his reemployed friends have established.

Carol has a different kind of vocational problem. Twenty-one and a junior at college, she hasn't the remotest idea what to do vocationally. Carol has changed her major three times, doesn't care much for the major she has at present, and feels like her life is drifting. Others seem to have clear goals, but Carol is one year away from graduation and vocationally floundering.

The college counseling center has tried to help. They gave her a variety of tests that confirmed her areas of interest and abilities. Yet even with help, career planning is hard. There isn't much comfort in knowing that many other twenty-one-year-olds struggle with career indecision. The problem is complicated further by Carol's well-meaning and concerned parents who keep pushing her to decide what to do with her life.

There was a time when choosing a career was seen as a once-in-a-lifetime event that occurred in late adolescence or early adulthood. Little children were prepared for this ominous choice whenever they were asked, "What will you be when you grow up?" College students were forced to make an early choice of their majors and often it was assumed, especially by parents, that the primary purpose of education was to prepare students for successful careers and the making of wise vocational choices.

Vocational choices are crucially important, frequently difficult, and rarely once-in-a-lifetime events. They are important because career choices largely determine one's income, standard of living, status in the community, social contacts, emotional well-being, feelings of self-worth, use of time, and general satisfaction with life. Career choices frequently are difficult because of the many available careers, the staggering array of jobs, the great potential for making mistakes, and the misery that can come when we get into the wrong line of work. (According to one report, 24.3 percent of American workers are unhappy because they chose the wrong occupation or profession, one-third of middle managers wish they could work someplace else, and about half of all employees feel they are underpaid.)[1] Because most people learn through experience, career choices are rarely once-in-a-lifetime events.[2] Beginning in high school, or even before, people start making decisions about work. The decisions continue as educational courses, college majors, and further training are all considered. Vocational decisions also come whenever one applies for a job, is offered a position, is promoted or not promoted, changes work, is fired or laid off, reevaluates a career, or faces retirement. For the Christian, all of these are influenced by the belief that one's vocational choices should be in accordance with God's will.

The Bible and Vocational Choices

Why should people work? The Bible gives some remarkably comprehensive and penetrating answers that have little to do with meeting needs, finding fulfillment, becoming successful, or accumulating wealth.[3] Work is God-ordained. It is part of his original intention for human beings. Work, however, no longer is the pure joy that God intended it to be. Because of the fall, work has become a burden,[4] especially for employees of the rich who hoard their wealth and exploit their underpaid workers.[5] Some make work an idol and drive themselves in the vain accumulation of wealth and achievements.[6] Others pour their skills and efforts into work and anxious striving, only to wonder if all of their efforts are useless and without meaning.[7]

Work, however, has been redeemed from the curse by Jesus Christ.[8] He has given work a new dignity and made it a source of blessing. Work is to be done as a service to Christ. We do our jobs, not primarily to please our employers, "but with sincerity of heart and reverence for the Lord. Whatever you do, work at it with all your heart, as working for the Lord, not for men." According to Colossians, it is the Lord Christ we are serving,[9] even when we work for a non-Christian employer.

Work can bring glory to God but it also helps others and brings personal benefits as well. Stated concisely, work enables us to meet our needs. If we want to eat, most of us have to work.[10] Regrettably many Christians have lost the biblical perspective on work and have accepted secular thinking about vocations.

> The notion that a job should bring fulfillment is a dangerous half-truth, in that the Bible never indicates that our jobs should be "fun" or make us "happy." Fulfillment is more correctly understood in the sense of service,

> taking pleasure in the contribution that our work is making to the community. This implies that whenever possible we should choose work that benefits those in need and this should head the list of criteria by which a Christian chooses a career. . . .
>
> If we view decisions about our careers through the lens of self-satisfaction or self-interest, we are not being biblical people. . . . Disciples of Jesus Christ must view career decisions not through the lens of self-fulfillment but through the lens of the needs of God's people—indeed, of human needs whenever they are found.[11]

The Bible does not say much about what Adam did between the time of creation and the time of the fall. We know that he communicated with God, slept, and became a husband, but it also appears that he worked. He was given the job of naming all living creatures and was instructed to subdue the earth and rule over it. After the fall Adam, along with his wife, was banished from the Garden of Eden and sent to work the ground through painful toil and by the sweat of his brow.[12]

Throughout the Bible other examples of work appear frequently. Cain, the first child of Adam and Eve, cultivated the soil, and his brother Abel kept flocks. For at least part of his life Noah was a shipbuilder who later turned to farming. Abraham was a wealthy livestock owner. David was a shepherd who later changed careers and became a king. Prophets, priests, tent makers, hunters, political leaders, salespersons, homemakers, real estate dealers, carpenters, fishermen, all of these and more are mentioned in the Bible as occupations for both men and women. It appears, therefore, that work has always been part of God's plan for the human race. After the fall it became harder, but it has always been God-ordained and a human responsibility. Biblical descriptions of work lead us to several conclusions.

1. *Work Is Honorable; Laziness Is Condemned.* The early church was instructed to give suitable wages and honor, especially to those whose work involved preaching and teaching.[13] The wife of noble character is pictured as one who works diligently and is praised as a result.[14] In a psalm of praise to God for the work of creation, we read that "man goes out to his work, to his labor until evening,"[15] apparently with the approval of God. Surely we can see work as "something to which God calls us and something he can use to give divine order to our lives."[16]

In contrast, wise Solomon warned of the poverty and foolishness that would come to those who were lazy,[17] and Paul stated bluntly that if a man will not work, he shall not eat. None of this suggests that work is to be deified or worshiped as an end in itself. Some early advocates of the Protestant work ethic seemed to conclude that hard work and frugal living were good for the soul. Charles Spurgeon taught that labor was a shield against the temptations of the devil and noted that God often spoke to people when they were working.[18] (One theologian countered that Spurgeon conveniently forgot to mention the times when God appeared to people who were asleep.)[19]

2. *Work Is to Be Interspersed with Rest.* The Bible approves of diligence and quality in work, but it gives no sanction to the workaholic who never rests or takes a vacation. God rested after creating the world, and in the Ten Commandments he instructed human beings to rest one day out of every seven. Many modern believers do not regard one day as being any more special than another,[20] but we each have a

biblical precedent to follow the example of Jesus and the spiritual leaders in Judeo-Christian history who set aside one day each week for worship, rest, and relaxation.

3. *Work Is to Be of High Quality.* Employees and other workers have a responsibility to work honestly and diligently,[21] not merely to please others, but to honor Christ. The pursuit of excellence is a worthy goal; dishonest and shoddy workmanship are clearly unbiblical.[22] Employers are to be fair and just, recognizing that they too have a master in heaven.[23] Each of us must develop and show good stewardship of the talents and aptitudes that God has given.[24]

Summarizing the biblical principles we can conclude that the Christian's work is to be characterized by sincerity, enthusiasm, diligence, devotion to Christ, good will, discipline, quietness, cooperation, honesty, integrity, generosity, gratitude, and efficiency.[25]

4. *Work Is Unique and for the Common Good.* Like modern vocational counselors who emphasize the differences in human interests and abilities, the Bible points out that we each have unique capabilities and responsibilities. When a person becomes a Christian, he or she is given one or more spiritual gifts. These are to be developed, used for the common good, and applied to the building up of other believers in the body of Christ.[26] Our differences in abilities come from God, however, and it is he who allows some to become visibly successful. Because of this, the Christian has no reason for self-centered boasting about his or her accomplishments.[27]

5. *Work and Vocational Choice Are Guided by God.* Some people in the Bible had their life's work selected by God before birth. Isaiah, David, Jeremiah, John the Baptist, and Jesus are the clearest examples.[28] Could it be possible that God still chooses men and women to accomplish special tasks for him?

Many Christians would agree that God calls at least some people to special ministries and places of service. There is, however, disagreement about whether or not he has one specific career calling for each of his children. We know that he directs those who acknowledge him and seek his ways,[29] and we can be sure that he gives wisdom to those who ask.[30] For many, however, there remains an issue that is confusing to Christian job hunters—"What role does my effort play, and what role does God play?" Perhaps it is best to conclude that no one knows.[31] Each worker makes the dual assumption: "I must accept the fact that my unfolding vocational future is in God's hands and guided by his Holy Spirit," but, in addition, "I know that I have in my own hands the stewardship responsibility for developing my own talents, aptitudes, and abilities."[32]

The Christian vocational counselor uses modern techniques to help people choose or change careers. The Christian counselor goes about this work convinced that a sovereign God can and will guide the counselor and counselee who want divine leading in the making of vocational decisions.

Causes of Good and Poor Vocational Choices

Counselors have proposed a number of theories to explain career choice and guide vocational counselors.[33] Traditionally, however, vocational counseling has consisted of three parts: learning about the person, learning about vocations, and matching personal talents with job requirements. Sometimes the match is good, appropriate training and job openings are available, and the counselee is able to find a useful and satisfying career. Often, however, such a smooth process does not occur. High status, high prestige, and high-paying jobs are relatively scarce, but they are sought by numerous people. Many of the more attractive professional and entertainment careers require intellectual abilities, unique aptitudes, specialized training, and sometimes personal contacts that few people possess. Because of high demand, intense competition, and limited opportunities, many people are disappointed in their career choices and forced to settle for less desirable alternatives.

Others never have the opportunity to plan careers. In need of work, these people skim the classified section of the newspaper and slip into jobs that provide a paycheck and some security but are neither satisfying nor personally fulfilling. Some people stay in these jobs for their entire lives. They often are part of the 50 to 80 percent of the work force that is in the wrong type of work.[34] Most of these people are dissatisfied and unhappy. Some get laid off or shift from one position to another, none of which they enjoy or do well.

Even people who enjoy their work often make changes as they go through life. Government estimates suggest that ten years from now nearly half of the working population will be in jobs that have not yet been developed. Young people who are entering the work force can expect to change jobs twelve to fifteen times during their working lives, and most will change careers four or five times.[35] Clearly vocational guidance must be an ongoing process that involves everyone, not just professional counselors. With or without such guidance, some people make good vocational decisions while others decide unwisely. There are several reasons for this.

1. *Family and Social Influences.* In our society, teachers, friends, relatives, and especially parents tend to expect that career decisions will be made early.[36] At a time when they are immature, idealistic, inexperienced, and struggling with the problems of late adolescence, young people have the added responsibility of choosing from an almost unlimited number of career possibilities. Later in life, if one quits or is forced to leave a job there is financial and social pressure to find other work as quickly as possible. All of this prevents careful planning and encourages vocational choices that can lead to disappointment and frustration.

2. *Personality Influences.* An individual's personality affects both the selection of a vocation and the success or satisfaction that is experienced within one's career. One writer has suggested that most people can be categorized into six general vocational personality types: realistic (the person who prefers tangible, practical, skill activities), investigative (the one who is methodical, intellectual, curious, and scientific), artistic (the creative, aesthetically oriented person), social (he or she who is friendly, sensitive, and interested in people), enterprising (the aggressive, energetic, self-confident problem solver), and conventional (the person who prefers routine and orderly, practical, somewhat inflexible activities).[37] It never is possible to fit people into rigid categories. The theory suggests, however, that most people have one dominant personality type, which usually emerges between the ages of eighteen and thirty, plus one or two other types that are of lesser importance. These individual differences have a bearing on vocational choice and degree of career satisfaction and success.

According to the same theory, jobs also can be divided into six categories: realistic, investigative, artistic, social, enterprising, and conventional. If investigative people enter investigative work (such as scientific research) or if artistic people enter artistic occupations (like writing, painting, or acting), there will be a high degree of satisfaction. In contrast, if a socially inclined person gets into a realistic type of job, or if an enterprising person enters a conventional occupation, there is certain to be frustration and unhappiness.

3. *Interests.* In the field of vocational counseling it often is assumed that people will do best in those activities and occupations that interest them most. If a job is boring, it isn't likely to bring much personal fulfillment or sense of satisfaction, even if the salary is high.[38]

Why would someone choose a vocation for which there is no interest? Sometimes in their need and desire to find employment, people take whatever job is available whether or not they find it interesting. Often these people expect to change positions later, but frequently, because of insufficient training or lack of opportunities, they do not or cannot change. Others take a boring job because of the salary or fringe benefits. It appears that many of the least desirable jobs in our society have a high level of remuneration in order to attract and retain workers. Since many of these workers have little interest in their work, they look for fulfillment and satisfaction in leisure-time activities, including sports, social clubs, church work, or sometimes drinking.

4. *Aptitudes or Abilities.* A commercial airline has as part of its slogan, "doing what we do best!" When we have jobs "doing what we do best," there often is high vocational fulfillment, good work efficiency, and low rates of absenteeism and turnover. In contrast, workers feel frustrated and are poorer employees when they are unable to do what the job requires or when their work gives little opportunity for achieving one's greatest potential.

Technically there is a difference between an aptitude and an ability. Aptitude refers to the potential that one has for learning something in the future. Ability refers to skills that one has at present or other learning that has taken place in the past. A young student, for example, may have an *aptitude* (good potential and capacity) for learning music, but it is only after years of study and practice that he or she may demonstrate great *ability* (skill and knowledge) as a musician.

Careers are most satisfying when one's aptitudes and abilities relate to one's work. It has been estimated, however, that perhaps 80 percent of working people are underemployed; that is, working below their capacity and ability levels.[39] This is especially difficult for people who are gifted and unusually talented but forced to work in occupations where their skills and capabilities are not needed and rarely used.[40] Even highly intelligent people experience this frustration because they consider underemployment to be better than unemployment. As a result some spend their whole working lives feeling unhappy, unfulfilled, and dissatisfied with their work.

5. *Values.* What is most important in life? Succeeding generations tend to answer this question in different ways, but one study found that three values influence the career choices of many college students: helping people, having the opportunity to be creative, and succeeding in terms of money or status.[41] Others want to change society, attain independence, find the best working conditions, or have the greatest possible influence for Christ.

Values can be important in career choice and career satisfaction or dissatisfaction. The worker who values honesty, for example, works best for an employer who is also honest. The same worker likely will be intensely frustrated if he or she is employed by a company where dishonesty and shady business deals are common.

6. *Roadblocks.* Sometimes people have attitudes, beliefs, ways of thinking, or other roadblocks that impede good career choice.[42] These include incomplete information (sometimes because the person has failed to investigate opportunities carefully), a belief that no options are available, hasty and ill-informed decisions that later are regretted, unrealistic self-assessment or job expectations, a low frustration level, immobilizing fear of making the wrong vocational choice, an unwillingness to take risks, or equipotentiality (a situation where there are several good alternatives available but since no one stands out above the others, the individual makes no decision; in the meantime, the opportunities slowly disappear). Sometimes people are reinforced for indecisiveness. By not making a decision, the individual doesn't have to go to work and sometimes gets a lot of sympathy from relatives or friends. All of these roadblocks can keep people from making good choices; many of these may have to be discussed in counseling.

For some vocation seekers the roadblocks are more circumstantial than psychological. The problems of making wise vocational choices can be complicated when the job seeker is part of a two-career marriage (where one's own career development depends somewhat on the career of one's mate),[43] an exceptionally gifted[44] female (especially if she is wanting to be involved in male-dominated careers),[45] middle-aged,[46] or older.[47] People in rural areas sometimes have greater difficulty finding employment than do people in urban areas.[48] One report has described the difficulties that battered women face when they decide to move out of the home and face new life and career decisions.[49] Add to this the special challenges of career choice for released prisoners, recovering alcoholics, former mental patients, or the physically disabled,[50] and we begin to see the unique roadblocks that many people face in making career choices, finding work, and developing career decision-making skills.

7. *Divine Leading.* Most Christians believe that God guides in the lives of his children. Some people want and seek this guidance, others do not. When an individual seeks divine leading in career decisions, he or she can rest in the confidence that God is guiding. This does not eliminate work stress or dissolve vocational frustrations, but a conviction that God is leading and in control can often make a job more satisfying or at least more tolerable.

Jonah, for example, knew the experience of both ignoring and following divine leading. When God said "Go to the great city of Nineveh and preach against it," Jonah went elsewhere and the results were almost fatal. When Jonah "obeyed the word of the Lord and went to Nineveh," the results were more satisfying. Instead of rejoicing, however, Jonah was displeased, angry, and apparently depressed.[51] His obedience had been less than enthusiastic, and he was not happy in his work. Contrast this with the Apostle Paul. His work involved many hardships, but he ended life with a feeling of vocational satisfaction.[52]

It is probable that no one influence alone contributes to good or poor vocational choice. Social and family influences, personality traits, interests, aptitudes, abilities, values, roadblocks, circumstances, and sensitivity to God's leading all combine with job availability and training opportunities to influence the nature and direction of an individual's career. Because this issue can be so difficult and complex, many choose unwisely or drift into a vocation that is not satisfying. When this happens, all of life is affected.

The Effects of Good and Poor Vocational Choice

Whenever we meet strangers, one of the first questions we ask concerns the nature of their work. This may indicate more than personal interest or curiosity. When we learn about another person's work we often are able to make accurate assumptions about his or her education, social status, and economic level. One's income is determined largely by one's work. In turn, income can influence the person's lifestyle, place of residence, choice of friends, leisure activities, feelings of self-worth, and general satisfaction with life. People who like their work are often happy with life in general. When a person is not happy at work, this unhappiness can permeate all of life.

Sometimes the unhappiness comes near the start of one's career, but often it appears after several years. Some people move up corporate or professional ladders, only to conclude that they are bored, burned out, tired of the stress, and wanting a new challenge. Many wonder if they would be better suited, more satisfied, more successful, and a lot happier in some other occupation. People who feel euphoric on Friday afternoons and depressed on Sunday nights probably aren't happy in their careers, but for many thoughts of change go no further than restless dreaming. A few are willing to accept any new job that comes along. Most people lack the considerable courage to seriously review career goals and, if necessary, to uproot themselves or their families and change vocational direction. It is easier to accept the current situation and make the best of it.[53]

Those who do decide to change may consult professional counselors who specialize in vocational guidance. More often it seems people counsel themselves, sometimes getting help from the dozens of available life planning, self-help books.[54] Others talk with friends, a pastor, or some other person who can give guidance.

As he neared the end of his life, Paul wondered about the direction of his future. He knew that execution was a possibility, but he was willing to "live by faith, not by sight." Whatever might happen, he determined to make it his life goal to please Christ.[55] When contemporary Christians have a similar goal, we can be more content on the job and better able to handle the complexities of living. When we are committed to serving Christ in our vocations, our work becomes an opportunity for pleasing God and reaching out to touch the lives of others.

For the Christian counselor, vocational guidance is an area of special importance. For many of our counselees (and for we who are their counselors) career choice and degree of success can touch and influence almost every other area of life, including the spiritual.

Counseling and Vocational Choices

Within the counseling profession, career counseling has become a specialty with several theoretical approaches and a variety of vocational guidance techniques.[56] The goal of these approaches tends to be similar: helping people find fulfilling careers in which they can do well. This career education can occur at any time in life. It involves initial guidance for young career seekers, help with young or middle-aged adults who are seeking vocational changes, and postretirement guidance for senior citizens. The vocational counselor exposes people to information about careers (including the need for training), teaches people to evaluate themselves and their careers continually, and provides special support and guidance when career changes are being made.

Effective career counselors should have a knowledge of the world of work, a knowledge of the counselee, and an ability to gently guide those who are making specific decisions. All of this must be within the confines of seeking the will of God.

1. *Knowing the World of Work.* Vocational counselors sometimes administer a variety of tests that do little to prepare one for the realities of the job market. A counselee with musical talent and interests, for example, may show good qualifications to be a performer, but may not realize the difficulties of trying to make a living in a field that is highly competitive, filled with qualified people, demanding in terms of travel and scheduling, and not profitable except for a very few. When they meet people like this, perhaps some counselors do "live in a dream world with little understanding of the realities of life on the job."[57]

Unless you are a specialist in vocational guidance, it is unlikely that you can keep abreast of the literally thousands of available and ever-changing job opportunities. There are two ways by which a Christian counselor can help: sharing where to get information and suggesting ways by which such information can be used.

Public and college libraries often keep vocational information on file in the form of books, brochures, catalogs, and government publications such as the frequently updated *U.S. Dictionary of Occupational Titles* (DOT). Unions, professional organizations, businesses, and insurance companies often publish vocational information that is available free or at nominal cost. Sometimes local high schools or colleges may be willing to share vocational information with nonstudents. In addition, the yellow pages of a phone book can put you in touch with persons in specific vocations. Such persons may know where to write for further information, may be willing to give vocational information themselves, or may be able to arrange on-site visits for seriously interested career seekers.[58] When a person wants information about church-related vocations or about the field of counseling, the best source of relevant information may be you.

Most people are busy in their work, however, and there is a limit to the time available for information-giving interviews. More readily available, therefore, may be the specialists in libraries, government offices, private employment agencies, or local colleges. These people often can point to computer-based sources of career information that are accurate, constantly updated, and not difficult to locate or use.[59]

When one locates a source of information and is looking into one or more specific career possibilities, several questions can be asked, including the following:

- What is the nature of this work? What do people in this field do?
- What personal qualifications are needed (in terms of skills, abilities, interests, experience, or physical requirements)?
- What training is required, where is it available, how long does it take, and what does it cost?

- Can anyone enter the occupation or are there educational, age, sex, religious or other restrictions? (The law may decree that there must be equal opportunities and no restrictions, but the realities of the job may dictate otherwise.)
- What are the working conditions?
- What are the starting and potential salaries, including fringe benefits?
- How will the work influence one's personal life in terms of need for travel, overtime, Sunday work, or geographical moves?
- Will the work require the compromising of one's ethical principles or religious beliefs?
- What is the potential for the future in terms of available openings, opportunities for advancement, whether the career field will continue to exist, or preparing people for moves to other satisfying work?
- How could this work fit with the Christian's desire to serve Christ and to utilize one's God-given abilities and gifts?

In all of this, recognize that God seems to lead some people, but not all, into positions of full-time Christian ministry.[60] It should not be assumed that the committed missionary or pastor is more spiritual or more within God's will than the committed scientist or salesman.

2. *Knowing the Counselee.* Professional guidance counselors often begin with an initial interview that gathers personal and employment information, including the counselee's past work experiences, successes, frustrations, interests, goals, and dreams. Often this is followed by the use of psychological tests that can give concise information to help counselees in two ways: to increase self-understanding and to make predictions about the future. Psychological assessment tools include:

- Mental ability tests (that are designed to measure both general intelligence and competence in special areas such as abstract reasoning, mathematical capability, and verbal ability).
- Achievement tests (that measure skills and the amount of material that the counselee has learned).
- Aptitude tests (that measure one's potential for learning in areas such as music, art, manual dexterity, or skill acquisition).
- Interests tests (designed to measure not only expressed interests, but whether or not the counselee's general interests are the same as those of successful people in specific occupational groups[61]).
- Personality inventories (that can identify a variety of personality traits).
- Special tests (such as those designed to measure such diverse issues as creativity, flexibility, mental stability, or one's potential for learning a foreign language).

The use and interpretation of tests usually require special training that some counselors may not possess. It can be helpful, therefore, to refer counselees for testing to psychological clinics, college counseling centers, private employment agencies, or to Christian vocational guidance centers. Most of these resources will have computer-based testing capabilities that often allow a test to be taken, scored, and interpreted on a printout, all while the test taker is in the office. Before you recommend this testing, be sure to check the costs (they may vary greatly from place to place) and discuss with the counselee whether testing is even needed. Sometimes tests don't tell the person much that is new and they rarely take the marketplace into account. As a result, the test taker is left with interesting information about oneself, but information that may not be very practical in helping make realistic career decisions.

Even without test results, the counselor can get useful data from counselees themselves, information that can be supplemented and confirmed through observation and consultation with people who know the counselee. Through interviews it is possible to get accurate knowledge about the counselee's general mental ability, specific skills and abilities, educational level and potential for further training, personality traits, mental and physical health, personal appearance, interests (including those that are stated and some that are shown by the person's freely chosen leisure-time activities), level of spiritual commitment or maturity, and (for older counselees) dependability and efficiency as an employee. Of course, the counselor's observations may not always be accurate, but these observations can be discussed with each counselee and often altered as the vocational counseling process continues.

3. *Guiding Vocational Decisions.* It is not the counselor's responsibility to tell the counselee what to do vocationally. Instead the counselee must be helped to make and evaluate his or her own decisions based on the available information and personal reflection. It should not be expected that counseling will reveal the perfect job for each counselee. Instead counseling will narrow the list of career opportunities down to a few categories of potentially satisfying and realistically feasible kinds of work. Educational opportunities, counselee desires and motivation, job availability, and similar circumstances then help to determine the kind of career or job that will be chosen.

Since vocational education is a lifelong process, it is not surprising that many workers seek to make changes as they go through life. Some have suggested that vocational development occurs in stages, each of which has unique characteristics.[62] In the *childhood stage,* which lasts for the first twelve or fourteen years of life, the child thinks about many glamorous types of work, most of which will be abandoned later because they are unrealistic. In high school, the *exploratory* stage begins in which there is a tentative and more realistic self-appraisal and narrowing of career possibilities. Often there is considerable vacillation and floundering as the young person selects and discards a number of occupational plans. Sometimes this stage lasts well into the twenties, often to the frustration of the young adult and his or her parents. Eventually there comes a *realistic* stage. Here the individual seriously considers vocational possibilities and makes choices in terms of training and job selection. The *establishment* stage follows and often moves into a *maintenance* stage that may last for most of one's working life. If a person reaches his or her vocational goals, life can be satisfying and fulfilling. This can also be a time of frustration, especially if the person feels locked in to a boring and disappointing dead-end type of vocation. Many people go through a lengthy *reevaluation* stage (some go through this more than once) that may lead to career change and to the establishment and maintenance of a new vocation. Eventually one reaches a *retirement* stage when the individual leaves his or her major work setting but may move into a new postretirement career or involvement with nonwork activities. There are no clearly identifiable times when people move from one of these stages into another, but at every stage (except perhaps the first) many seek guidance from counselors.

How do individuals make vocational decisions? First, people must evaluate their qualifications and decide what they want to accomplish vocationally. You might encourage counselees to get a notebook and to write down their interests, gifts, or abilities, areas of experience or expertise, life goals and vocational objectives. Suggest that they take a page to list dreams, things that would be ideal vocationally. This process may take time and the lists may need to be revised and amended as the self-understanding process continues. Sometimes a mate or parent can help with the lists, and at times it may be necessary for the counselor to point out goals that are unrealistic.

Next, it can be helpful to gather information about potential job or career possibilities. Then one can list specific possibilities along with the positive and negative aspects of each alternative. Eventually the counselee should make a decision to pursue at least one alternative. This may be difficult for some counselees because decisions involve commitment and the risk of error or failure. Point out that the initial choice is not absolutely final, but stress that slow movement is better than no movement. Counselees can then be encouraged to (a) act on the decision by moving into a specific training program, seeking a job, or accepting an offer of employment and/or (b) reevaluate the job, at least periodically and if necessary repeat the whole process again. This is illustrated in Figure 35-1.

Whenever it occurs, vocational guidance could focus on one or more of four overlapping goals:[63]

Job or career placement. This involves helping people get information and training, helping them find positions, and sometimes helping potential employers find employees.

Job or career preparation. Prior to entry, counselees can be helped to ponder the good aspects of the intended job or vocation. This can occur whenever change is anticipated.

Job or career adjustment. Sometimes people find a desirable career but have difficulty adjusting. Consider, for example, the missionary who believes he or she is called to the mission field but has trouble adapting. Sometimes crisis counseling, helping to resolve interpersonal conflicts, or dealing with loneliness or anxiety may be among the ways of assisting these counselees as they adjust to new work situations. Often this counseling can make the difference between vocational satisfaction or stagnation.[64]

Job or career change. This includes discussion and guidance before, during, and after a forced or voluntary change. When people lose or are dismissed from a job, the stress can be intense, especially if the counselee has held the job for a number of years. Often there is grieving, low self-esteem, feelings of failure and despair, family tension, and frantic searches for work.[65] The stresses are not limited to job loss, however. When a company moves to a different location, the employee gets a promotion, or a new opportunity arises, there can be joy mixed with sadness, enthusiasm about the future mingled with reluctance to leave what is secure. In situations such as these, people often need support, encouragement, and guidance that most often will be informal.

Figure 35-1
The Vocational Decision-Making Process

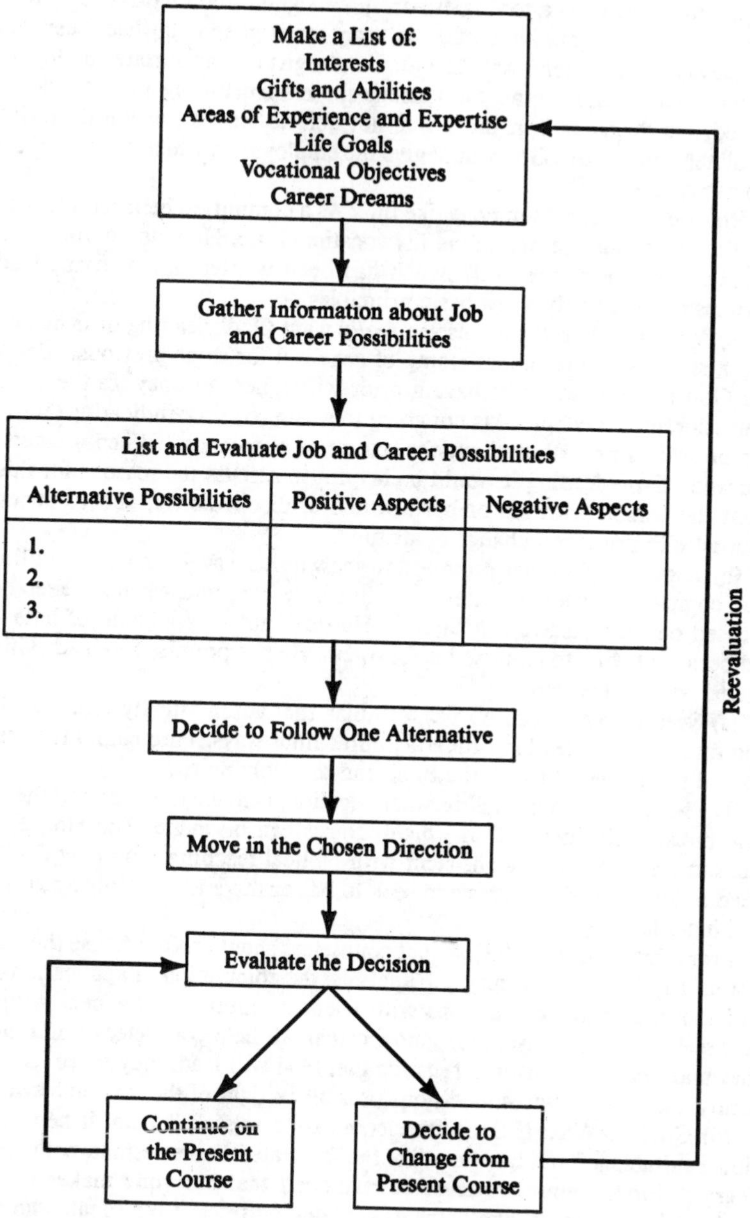

Make a List of:
Interests
Gifts and Abilities
Areas of Experience and Expertise
Life Goals
Vocational Objectives
Career Dreams

Gather Information about Job and Career Possibilities

List and Evaluate Job and Career Possibilities

Alternative Possibilities	Positive Aspects	Negative Aspects
1. 2. 3.		

Decide to Follow One Alternative

Move in the Chosen Direction

Evaluate the Decision

Continue on the Present Course

Decide to Change from Present Course

Reevaluation

4. *Knowing God's Will.* In an article published several years ago, a man with advanced academic degrees wrote that he could not find a suitable job and was employed, instead, as a tool salesman in a neighborhood hardware store. In evaluating his own disappointments, the man realized that he had been "holding a grudge against God for withholding . . . the gift of appropriate employment." The writer tried to understand the reasons for his frustrating job situation but concluded that "wish as I might, I was not able to find a portion of Scripture that absolutely guaranteed God would give me employment which allowed the extensive use of my talents."[66]

How do we counsel someone like this? As a committed believer, the man wanted God's will for his life, including his vocational life. How do counselees (or counselors) determine God's will? Much has been written about divine leading, but perhaps there are only a few basic principles.

(a) Want It. Does the counselee *really* want God's leading or is he or she seeking, instead, a divine rubber stamp of approval for some previously devised plan? For God to guide we must have a prior willingness to obey. In the words of one counselor, the Holy Spirit "is not going to waste His time indicating God's will to a person who is uncertain about the matter of obedience." When a counselee does not want divine leading it would be helpful to discuss the reasons for this, to confront the person with his or her attitude of disobedience, and to encourage the counselee to pray for a change of attitude.

(b) Expect It. God has promised to show us his way when we are willing to trust him completely, when we attempt to live holy lives and when we keep our minds focused on God-pleasing thoughts.[67] He does not play a game of hide and seek, deliberately trying to confuse his followers. He has promised to lead. This must be shared with counselees.

(c) Seek It. There are no pat formulas that automatically indicate God's will, and rarely does he lead in dramatic, miraculous ways. Throughout the centuries he has led most often through the Bible and the Holy Spirit.

The Scriptures do not tell us what vocational choice to make, but the Bible does give broad guidelines within which choices can be made. The Holy Spirit never leads in ways that are inconsistent with biblical teaching. To know God's will, we need to know the Scriptures and seek to be sensitive to the Holy Spirit's influence and inner leading.

From this it does not follow that counselees should refuse to use their God-given brains. Psychological testing, job analysis, the completion of application forms, vocational counseling, discussions with friends, mutual involvement with other career seekers,[68] and prayers for guidance can all help counselees find God's will as they make career decisions. Trusting that God will lead, they move forward confidently, making the wisest decisions possible in light of the available evidence.

(d) Cool It. What if the counselee makes a mistake? What if he or she cannot find a suitable job but becomes like the frustrated tool salesman with the graduate degrees? First, counselees must be reminded that everyone makes mistakes, but God forgives, restores, and helps us get back on track. Like Jonah who tried to go his own way, and Peter who denied Christ, individuals today can know that God always restores those who come back to him asking for further guidance.

Then remind counselees that God, in his wisdom and timing, allows us to be where he wants. He expects us to serve diligently, wherever and whatever the circumstances.[69] When there is anger or anxiety (both of which are common), believers should admit these feelings, perhaps discuss them with a friend or counselor, and bring them to God in prayer and ask that they be removed. In this way counselees can be helped, like Paul, to be content whatever the circumstances.[70]

Preventing Poor Vocational Choices

It's been called "the job nobody likes." There is no right way to do it, no formula that makes it easy, and no general agreement on its purpose. Everybody agrees that the job should be done, but often it gets delayed and sometimes forgotten. This undesirable job is reviewing and evaluating the work and performance of employees.[71] Positive evaluations are easy to give or get, but it isn't easy to tell an employee about his or her work weaknesses, and negative evaluations are difficult to receive.

Perhaps there will never be a way to make evaluation easy, but there can be ways to prevent people from getting into careers for which they are unsuited and likely to get poor evaluations. Prevention almost always is a specialized form of education. From the pulpit, in classrooms, in small groups, on weekend retreats, in Christian colleges and elsewhere, people can be taught and encouraged to apply some of the material presented in this chapter. This career education should be directed to people of all ages and could include consideration of:

- Biblical teachings about work.
- The causes of good and poor vocational choices.
- How to find God's guidance (want it, expect it, seek it, and cool it).
- How to get information about vocations and the world of work.
- How to know oneself better (including a knowledge of where to take psychological tests).

In this educational process, emphasize that vocational choice is not a once-in-a-lifetime decision. Most adults (including homemakers and others who are not included in the more traditional definition of the work force) struggle at times with career dissatisfaction, and this should be acknowledged. Encourage people to be open to further training and to evaluate their priorities, life goals and job satisfactions periodically, perhaps in accordance with Figure 35-1. Point out that as one gets older, it becomes increasingly more difficult and risky to change vocations. Nevertheless, there are things that can be done: changing employers or careers (the most risky alternative), changing jobs within the same company or vocation, learning how to handle and control work stress,[72] and/or changing one's attitude toward work. Even if little can be done to change the job situation, it is possible to stay with the present job (trusting that God either wants this and/or will bring a change in time), to do one's best "as to the Lord"[73] without complaining, and then to look for greater satisfaction and service opportunities in avocational, leisure-time activities that probably will occupy greater amounts of time as one gets older.

CONCLUSIONS ABOUT VOCATIONAL CHOICE

How does one do vocational counseling with people who are mentally retarded, psychologically unstable, physically handicapped, terminally ill, minimally educated, elderly, or unable to speak English? People such as these are rarely mentioned in vocational counseling literature, but all could benefit from meaningful, satisfying work that is within their capabilities. If the Christian counselor is unable to help, referral to a government agency or private counseling facility may be the best help you can give.

Vocational choices are among the most crucial decisions in life. To help people make these decisions wisely can be among the most satisfying and rewarding parts of the Christian counselor's own work.

SUGGESTIONS FOR FURTHER READING

Baldwin, Stanley C. *Take This Job and Love It.* Downers Grove, Ill.: InterVarsity, 1988.*

Bernbaum, John A., and Simon M. Steer. *Why Work? Careers and Employment in Biblical Perspective.* Grand Rapids, Mich.: Baker, 1986.*

Bolles, R. N. *What Color Is Your Parachute? A Practice Manual for Job-Hunters and Career-Changers.* Rev. ed. Berkeley, Calif.: Ten Speed Press, 1986.*

Brown, Keith, and John Hoover. *It's Never Too Late to Say Yes! Eleven Inspiring Accounts of People Who Made Mid-Life Ministry Commitments.* Ventura, Calif.: Regal, 1987.*

Dillard, John Milton. *Lifelong Career Planning.* Columbus, Ohio: Charles E. Merrill, 1985.*

Farnsworth, Kirk E., and Wendell H. Lawhead. *Life Planning: A Christian Approach to Careers.* Downers Grove, Ill.: InterVarsity, 1981.*

Laughlin, Rodney S. *The Job Hunter's Handbook: A Christian Guide.* Waco, Tex.: Word, 1985.*

Mattson, Ralph, and Arthur Miller. *Finding a Job You Can Love.* Nashville: Thomas Nelson, 1982.*

Osherson, Samuel D. *Holding On or Letting Go: Men and Career Change at Midlife.* New York: Free Press, 1980.

White, Jerry, and Mary White. *On the Job: Survival or Satisfaction?* Colorado Springs: NavPress, 1988.*

Yost, Elizabeth B., and M. Anne Corbishley. *Career: A Psychological Approach.* San Francisco: Jossey-Bass, 1987.

Zunker, V. G. *Career Counseling: Applied Concepts of Life Planning.* 2d ed. Monterey, Calif.: Brooks/Cole, 1985.

* Books marked with an asterisk (*) are especially suited for counselees to read.

Part 8

Concluding Issues

36

Spiritual Issues

MARILYN IS TWENTY-THREE, the youngest daughter of deeply religious parents who met in Bible school and who have always hoped that one of their four children would enter the ministry or become a missionary. Thus far they have been disappointed. One of their grown children is a shoe salesman with little ambition and no interest in the church. Another is married to a factory worker who has a steady job and provides well for his family but has only casual interest in spiritual things. A third child is divorced and struggling to get through college. Marilyn claims to be a Christian and once was active in the church youth group, but she has moved in with a middle-aged atheist lawyer who clearly is more interested in sex than in spirituality.

In the meantime the parents struggle. They wonder why none of their children go to church or show interest in spiritual things. They pray regularly for their children and boldly express their faith in God's sovereignty. Still they wonder if God has let them down. They tried to "bring up the children in the way they should go," but they wonder why God has not kept them in the faith.

The parents are distressed by Marilyn's criticisms of hypocrisy in the church, but sometimes they think she might be right. When their son went through his painful divorce, the people at church responded more with condemnation than with compassion. The church leadership offered little help; they seem to be interested only in people who are spiritually "alive" and involved actively and financially with the church programs.

Recently Marilyn's parents have become less faithful in their church attendance, and they have heard criticisms for that. Sometimes they wonder if they fit any more. Like several of their children, the parents are confused spiritually, and for the first time in either of their lives they have begun to harbor doubts about their own beliefs.

Should they go for counseling? They don't see the need to pay for professional counseling since their problems aren't that bad. They don't think a non-Christian professional would understand their struggles. They know their pastor wouldn't understand. He would be more inclined to preach about sin in the counseling sessions just like he condemns people from the pulpit.

So Marilyn's parents struggle alone. At times Marilyn also worries about her sinful lifestyle. Privately each of her siblings struggles spiritually as well, and there is nobody to offer help.

As a group professional counselors have not been sympathetic toward religious issues. Most don't understand religious terminology, few have had any training in helping people with spiritual struggles, many are unfamiliar with the ways religious people think, and some counselors still accept Freud's oft-stated view that religion is harmful and indicative of neurosis.[1] Secular counselors prefer to avoid religious issues, to give them naturalistic explanations, and sometimes to refer religious counselees to like-minded counselors.[2]

Christian counselors sometimes have difficulty with religious counseling as well. It isn't always easy to help people with their spiritual struggles. Sometimes there are no clear answers to the theological questions that counselees strive to answer.

To complicate issues further, believers tend to use terminology that can be confusing. We talk freely about love, for example, and we agree that love is *the* mark of a Christian,[3] but we don't always act in loving ways and we don't even agree on what the word means. Sometimes it seems we forget that the love basic to Christianity is not the transient, self-centered sentimentalism that forms the basis of many modern love songs or sexual liaisons. Christian love is giving, patient, other centered, Christ honoring, divinely bestowed, seen most clearly in the life of Jesus, and described throughout the pages of Scripture.[4]

It is sad that many Christians do not feel very loving; neither do their words or actions express a loving attitude. Many believers feel defeated by sin, internal conflicts, and the pressures of life. Some are frustrated because their growth seems to be so slow. Others are concerned because their lives seem so joyless, there is no sparkle in their worship, and they are caught in a net of spiritual "dryness." They read the Bible, but the words appear to be dull and irrelevant. They pray, more out of habit than desire, and their prayers seem to be unanswered. They want to do good and to love, but their actions aren't very loving and their consciences seem insensitive and blunted. They want their children to grow into godly men and women, but too often it seems young people leave the church, forsake the faith, and turn to lifestyles that allow them to "enjoy the pleasures of sin for a season."

This is not what God desires, but these are common experiences, perhaps even in the lives of the counselors or potential counselors who read these words. Counseling those with spiritual problems is a challenge at any time, but it is even more difficult when the counselor struggles with problems similar to those of the counselees. Walter Trobisch once wrote that "nobody knows what desperation really is" until he or she has faced another human being who craves help that the counselor cannot give because inside he or she feels "completely empty" and spiritually dry.[5] Unlike most of the previous chapters, this one speaks to the needs of counselors and counselees alike.

The Bible and Spiritual Problems

In a high-tech age of microchips and modems when people like to be progressive, computer literate, and able to get things done quickly and efficiently, it is difficult for many of us to realize that God, whose knowledge exceeds all the world's data banks, is never in a hurry. His goal is for each believer to mature into Christlikeness, but he knows that none of us will succeed completely this side of heaven. He wants us to be holy and to follow in Christ's steps, but he knows that nobody will ever do that totally.[6] He wants us to "put on the full armor of God," so that we can "stand against the devil's schemes," but the Lord realizes that we cannot fight life's battles alone.[7] He wants us to present our bodies to him "as living sacrifices, holy and pleasing to God,"[8] but he knows that this presentation will not be consistent or completely unselfish. He wants us to stop sinning and to flee from youthful lusts, but he realizes that we are fooling ourselves if we say we have no sin. So he tells us to confess our sins and to expect forgiveness when we do fall.[9] He sets up a high standard for our behavior because he is just and holy, but he has provided a savior to pay for our sins and failures since he is loving and merciful.[10] He has adopted us as his children and requires us to "act justly and to love mercy and to walk humbly," but he is compassionate, gracious, and "abounding in love" because he knows that we are nothing but dust so long as we remain in this world.[11]

God clearly has high standards. To expect anything less than perfection for his human creatures would be to lower his standards and to make him less than God. Yet in addition to his holiness, perfection, and greatness, he also emanates the divine attributes of love, mercy, and compassion. God is realistic. He knows that we are weak, so he has not left us to stand alone. Because of his great love, he sent his son to pay for our sins, and his Holy Spirit to live within, where he guides, strengthens, and teaches us.[12] We may think that God is far away at times, but he is ever near, sticking closer than a faithful brother.[13]

The goal of the Christian life is to be Christlike in worship, character, and service. In the Old Testament, *worship* included the offering of sacrifices to atone for sin. Now that Christ has died for our sins, "once for all, the righteous for the unrighteous,"[14] in a supreme and loving self-sacrifice intended to bring us to God, we are to offer our bodies "as living sacrifices, holy and pleasing to God." This continual commitment of self to God, along with verbal praise and faithful obedience, is how we worship.[15]

Worship, however, also involves a continuing change in *character*. We are not to conform to worldly standards. Instead we are to be transformed mentally and in terms of our actions. We are to disentangle ourselves from sin, to be holy as he is holy, to be like Christ, to walk in his steps, and to let the Holy Spirit mold us into individuals who are characterized by love, joy, peace, patience, kindness, gentleness, fruitfulness, and self-control.[16]

The Christian, however, must not be solely God-centered and self-centered. There must also be *service* to others. We please God when we "do not forget to do good and to share with others."[17] Indeed, the biblical view of success radically contradicts that of the world in which we live. "If you want to be great," Jesus said, then be a servant. We are warned not to compete against one another with envy and selfish ambition, but we are instructed instead to do good deeds, to humble ourselves, and to believe that in due time the Lord will lift us up to whatever acclaim we need.[18]

Christlike worship, Christlike character, and Christlike service—these are the goals of the Christian life. In one sense we press to reach these goals, like a runner straining toward the finish line. In another sense we grow not by effort but by yielding ourselves completely to divine control and direction. Christlikeness "is both the fruit of the Spirit as he works within us and the result of our personal efforts. We are both totally dependent upon his working within us and totally responsible for our own character development. This is an apparent contradiction to our either-or type of thinking, but it is a truth taught over and over again in the Scriptures."[19]

Throughout the centuries perhaps thousands of books have dealt with Christian growth, spiritual maturity, and the struggles of believers. The need for spiritual guidance and help with religious struggles is nothing new. Since the time of Christ (and before) believers have grappled with spiritual deadness, periods of stagnation, and the need for help in Christian growth. It could be argued that the entire Bible is written for such people, teaching us about God, his attributes, and his power to mold believers into instruments who are "useful to the Master and prepared to do any good work."[20]

The causes, effects, counseling, and prevention of spiritual problems are all discussed in the Bible. No other subjects are more Bible-based and less illuminated by psychology than the subjects of spiritual growth and solving spiritual problems. The Christian counselor is best equipped to help with such problems since only the believer has the mind of Christ that enables us to understand and to help others comprehend and accept the things that come from the Spirit of God.[21]

The Causes of Spiritual Problems

Religion is still popular in America. The statistics are different in other countries, but 40 percent of Americans attend religious services at least once a week, 60 percent are members of churches or synagogues, and 95 percent claim to believe in God.[22] Outwardly we are a religious people, but as Charles Colson has observed, "inwardly our religious beliefs make no difference in how we live. We are obsessed with self; we live, raise families, govern, and die as though God does not exist."[23] A widely acclaimed scholarly study of American life concluded that most people speak positively of religion, but our lives are guided, not by God, but by "the dream of personal success" and by "vivid personal feeling."[24] God is tolerated, but only when he is bland enough to pose no threat or challenge to our goals of the good life and good feelings.

In the midst of this environment, a number of deeply religious people sincerely want to serve God and to grow as Christians, but they struggle with spiritual deadness and despair. These are people who know that dynamic Christian living is possible, even in a culture that is only superficially religious. They long for a vital Christian spiritual life, even though many are unsure what that means and most have no idea how to get it.[25] To help these people, we need to understand some of the possible causes of spiritual problems.

1. *Where We Are.* For some people, problems come because of where they are spiritually. These individuals may attend services and do good deeds, but they are outside of God's kingdom. At its core, Christianity deals more with one's inner nature than with outer behavior. It is more concerned about what we *are* than with what we *do.* This is stated repeatedly in the Bible but nowhere with greater clarity than in Ephesians 2.

Prior to conversion we are "dead," controlled by the devil, and separated from God, regardless of our deeds. It is God who saves us and makes us his children. This salvation comes not because of our own efforts, but because he gives us salvation when we completely yield ourselves to him. "For it is by grace you have been saved, through faith—and this not from yourselves, it is the gift of God—not by works."[26] When we accept God's gift of salvation, he begins to work in our lives, molding us into the kinds of persons he wants us to be. Since he created us and knows us intimately, his plan is best for our lives.

Some people have spiritual struggles because they are not believers; they have never accepted God's free gift of salvation and are trying in vain to earn divine favor by their works. Others have committed their lives to Christ, but they have not grown spiritually because they have little real interest in spiritual issues. These people may be longtime Christians but they are still infants in Christ, not much different and spiritually no more mature than nonbelievers.[27] Still others have deliberately turned their backs on Christ and chosen to ignore or reject the religious training that they had in the past. These people may harbor some guilt over their actions (and many in time will return to their spiritual roots), but at present they are far away from Christ and spiritually dead. All of this suggests that spiritual problems are related closely to where we are in terms of a relationship with Jesus Christ.

2. *What We Do.* Have you ever considered what most disturbed Jesus during his time on earth? It was not pornography, violence, racism, abortion, political corruption, the misuse of church funds, or the other issues that concern us today. Jesus reserved his strongest attacks to condemn sin and to fight what perhaps angered him the most: pious legalism. Both of these can cause spiritual problems.

(a) Sin. Throughout the church's history, Christians have struggled with three major problems that seem more than any others to undermine or stifle spiritual growth: greed and the abuse of money, lust and the abuse of sex, and pride and the abuse of power. Spiritual revivals throughout history and the ancient monastic vows of poverty, chastity, and obedience were a direct response to the misuse and abuse of money, sex, and power.[28]

Important as these issues are, however, the biblical meaning of sin involves something more. Sin is any action or attitude that violates or fails to conform to the will of God. We sin by what we think, by what we do or fail to do, and by what we are. Sin is a powerful, pervasive, and penetrating force that can master and enslave us, especially when we fail to repent or admit and confess our faults. Sin is *the* major cause of spiritual problems, stagnation, and loss of vitality.[29]

(b) Legalism. When Jesus walked the earth, the Pharisees were religious purists who believed that spiritual maturity came as a result of observing rules. This view has been common in religious circles for centuries and is held today by many fundamentalists, evangelicals, Catholics, Protestants, liberals, and others. Often seen in people who sincerely want to please God and maintain a good testimony, this legalistic mentality maintains that there are rules and regulations to determine what a good Christian does not do (drink, attend the theater, watch R-rated movies, dress in certain ways, or shop on Sunday) and what the good Christian does do (read the Bible daily, witness to someone every week, or attend a specified number of religious services). The psalmist, prophets, Jesus, and Paul all condemned legalistic attitudes such as these (see Ps. 50:8–15; Isa. 1:11–17; Hos. 6:6; Matt. 23:23–24; Col. 2:23; Gal. 3:2; 5:1). These can lead to sinful pride and they contradict the very heart of the biblical message. The theme of the Bible is redemption, and we are saved through faith plus nothing.[30]

What about spiritual growth? Does this come from following rules? Jesus' condemnation of the Pharisees clearly indicates that the answer is no. True spirituality comes when we walk humbly before God with an attitude of thanksgiving and praise, a deep determination to be obedient, an awareness of our tendencies to sin, and acknowledgment of our need for his continued grace and mercy. This does not mean that we take a passive do-nothing attitude toward our spiritual lives. The Christian must be alert to the devil's schemes, and spiritual growth is closely related to prayer, meditation on the Bible, fellowship with other believers, and a sincere attempt to refrain from sin.

Yet the power and even the desire for holy living must come from God[31] and not from our determination to follow man-made rules. The Scriptures condemn both legalism (the strict keeping of rules) and its twin partners: gnosticism (the belief that spirituality is gained by superior knowledge) and asceticism (the conscious denial of pleasures, experiences, and material things).[32]

3. *What We Think.* Most human problems it seems begin in the mind.[33] It is our thinking that leads to self-sufficiency, pride, bitterness, and non-Christian values, each of which can create or accentuate spiritual problems.

(a) Self-Sufficiency. This is common in a culture that lauds self-made men and universally admires rugged individualism. Even in the church we praise perseverance and advocate possibility thinking that gives little or no thought to the will and power of God. Self-sufficiency, however, is the mark of lukewarm Christianity. To the believers who boasted "I am rich; I have acquired wealth and do not need a thing," the Scriptures urged repentance and noted that such self-sufficient people really are wretched, pitiful, poor, blind, naked, and neither hot nor cold spiritually.[34] Self-sufficiency is the absolute antithesis of spiritual maturity.

(b) Pride. Self-sufficiency and pride go together. Pride involves a trust in one's own power or resources and a tendency to derive satisfaction from the contemplation of one's status, capabilities, or accomplishments, especially as these are compared with others who seem to have less. Pride is more easily seen than defined and more easily detected in others than in oneself. Pride is self-centered, self-satisfied, and ultimately self-destructive.[35]

(c) Bitterness. According to the writer of Hebrews, bitterness can spring up to cause trouble and create defilement that apparently includes immoral and godless behavior.[36] Bitterness is a powerful and subtle source for spiritual problems.[37]

(d) Distorted Values. What really is important in life? The answer to this question is often seen in the ways people spend their money, their time (including spare time), and their mental energies, especially when their minds are free to wander. Often people value money, selfish pleasures, business success, acclaim, and other issues that are important in the society but potentially destructive to Christian growth.[38] Values such as these are subtle. They draw us away from God and create a false sense of security.[39]

In contrast to self-sufficiency, pride, bitterness, and distorted values, the spiritually maturing person is transformed mentally so that his or her thinking seeks and intends to do the "good, pleasing and perfect" will of God.[40]

4. *What We Lack.* Physical problems and deterioration both come when there is a lack of food, air, rest, and other physical necessities. In a similar matter, spiritual problems are caused by a lack of those basic ingredients that are needed for Christian health and growth.

(a) Lack of Understanding. Perhaps it would be distressing if we really knew how much spiritual pain and turmoil comes because people lack clear biblical knowledge and understanding of the Scriptures. Consider, for example, the biblically unsupported ideas that we are saved by good works, that Christian growth depends entirely on ourselves, that doubt or our sexual urges will arouse God's wrath, that God's love depends on our personal actions, that God refuses to forgive acts of sin and disobedience, that financial or family problems come as God's way of punishing us, or that God really doesn't know about or care about our needs and concerns. These and a host of similar misconceptions can create restlessness, uncertainty, spiritual doubt, and apathy.

(b) Lack of Nourishment. Just as a baby never grows without food, so a Christian never develops without continued prayer and reading of the Bible, God's Word.[41] Spiritual problems come to some people because they never spend much time taking in spiritual nourishment. For others there is so much "giving out" that the giver becomes spiritually depleted and empty. It is a spiritual law, wrote Walter Trobisch, that "the one who gives out much must also take in much. . . . If he gives out continuously without taking in, he will run dry."[42]

(c) Lack of Giving. People who eat too much become fat and in time uncomfortable. A similar condition can occur in our spiritual lives. Overfeeding on sermons, Bible studies, devotional reading, Christian radio programs, and weekend retreats can lead to spiritual bloating. Christians are not to be like sponges, soaking up and retaining everything. Instead we are to be vessels used by God to bring instruction and blessing to others. The essence of Christian love is giving and sharing so we don't grow fat.

(d) Lack of Balance. During his three-year ministry, Jesus lived a balanced life. He ministered, interacted with individuals, rested, spent time in prayer and worship, and relaxed with friends. He had a purpose in life, sought God's help in daily living, and took care of himself spiritually, physically, intellectually, and socially.

Many modern people lack this balance. They run themselves ragged, fail to get proper rest or exercise, do not eat a balanced diet, and are so busy—even while doing the Lord's work—that their efficiency and spiritual vitality run down. A balanced life requires planning, discipline, and a realization that no person in the body of Christ is so important that he or she is indispensable.[43]

(e) Lack of Commitment. To be a disciple, Jesus taught, one must be willing to take up a cross and follow him. True Christian growth must be preceded by a commitment to let Jesus Christ be Lord and controller of one's life. Any holding back interferes with spiritual maturing and contributes to lusterless Christianity.

For twenty-five years, one Christian leader watched as hundreds of Christian men and women dealt with the complexities of living. "Some flourished spiritually; others floundered. Some made an impact; others made no mark whatsoever. Some grew in Christ; others dried up spiritually and withered away. Some rejoiced and offered encouragement; others complained and griped. Some deepened and softened; others became more shallow and hardened." What made the difference? Commitment! "Ordinary people who make simple, spiritual commitments under the lordship of Jesus Christ make an extraordinary impact on their world. Education, gifts, and abilities do not make the difference. Commitment does."[44]

(f) Lack of Simplicity. Everybody knows that life is complex. We live in a world of stress, change, demands, and busyness. To complicate matters, contemporary culture is plagued by the passion to possess. Even some spiritual leaders preach that God wants us to be rich, and their messages proclaim that spirituality and material blessings go together. This is not a biblical message. The Bible consistently speaks against greed and covetousness.[45] There is emphasis on caring for the poor and a recognition that material goods are not to be hoarded. According to Richard Foster, the Old Testament "almost without exception" promised material blessings for the community rather than for the individual. "The idea that one could cut off a piece of the consumer pie and go off and enjoy it in isolation was unthinkable."[46]

Lives that are controlled by greed, concern about possessions, and the itch for more are not lives that are growing spiritually. "The love of money is the root of all kinds of evil," we read in the Bible. "People who want to get rich fall into temptation. . . . Some people, eager for money, have wandered from the faith."[47]

(g) Lack of the Holy Spirit's Power. The Holy Spirit lives in the life of every believer,[48] but the Spirit can be quenched and pushed aside. When that happens, spiritual lethargy is certain. In contrast, when the Holy Spirit is in control, our lives develop strength, spiritual understanding, unity with others, love, joy, peace, self-control, and the other spiritual fruits,[49] all of which are designed to bring glory to Christ.

(h) Lack of Body Life. The Christian is part of a group or body that consists of other believers, all of whom are important and gifted, all of whom love Christ, and each of whom should seek to know, love, pray for, help, encourage, challenge, exhort, teach, and minister to others. When Christians attempt to grow on their own, to build their personal empires, or to rise on some ladder of Christian status, they are out of God's will. He has placed us in the body and expects us to grow there, not forsaking true fellowship[50] with other brothers and sisters.[51]

5. *What We Experience.* Counseling textbooks rarely mention suffering and when they do, the emphasis is on ways that suffering can be reduced or avoided. Any mention of the good that might come from suffering tends to be dismissed as rationalization or distorted thinking. Christians, in contrast, often believe that personal and spiritual growth can come as a result of suffering, although we still have a responsibility to work diligently to reduce pain and other forms of human misery.

Throughout the centuries, Christian writers have struggled to understand the meaning and mystery of suffering. Some claim that any person who has enough faith will be released from the trials that come to the rest of humanity. This is an attractive idea that has no biblical support. Suffering builds patience, strength, and spiritual growth. It is an experience rooted in the human condition. It was the experience of Jesus and, despite its pain, we are told that it should be cause for joy and praise.[52] "For the Christian, suffering is not an evil. It is simply a pain-filled good, and we are to learn to express thanks to God for suffering and the good we trust it will bring."[53] Without suffering, there may be no spiritual growth. When we complain about suffering, we undermine one of God's major methods for molding believers.[54]

6. *What We Fight.* Whether or not we consciously recognize this, the Christian is in a battle. Jesus was tempted when he began his ministry and perhaps at other times thereafter. The giants of the faith, both those mentioned in the Bible and others, battled the forces of evil, and the struggle continues today. In this continuing world war there are no islands of neutrality. We are either fighting the devil or aligned on his side—in attitude if not in activity.

At times the battle is in the intellectual arena where confusion, doubt, nonbiblical thinking, and overt heresy are at issue. Sometimes the battle is physical as we struggle with disease and injury. Often the conflict centers around psychological discouragement, anger, anxiety, guilt, and other internal conflicts. Occasionally the battle seems mild, but the attack is more intense at other times, especially when we are tired, not feeling well, emotionally or intellectually drained, fresh from a spiritual retreat, or basking in (and distracted by) the gratifying and satisfying warm light of success.

Within the past few years a number of Christians have emphasized that spiritual battle often involves the devious and destructive influence of demons. In his ministry on earth, Jesus encountered the work of demons that created personal injury, psychotic-like symptoms, and intense distress in the lives of individuals and their families. In Acts and the Epistles we see less emphasis on the demonic, but during the Middle Ages demon possession and exorcisms were at the core of treatment for deviant or unusual behavior. In this century, the demonic has tended to be ignored or dismissed as bygone superstition, despite the actions of a few, sometimes sensational, preachers and exorcists.

More recently, however, interest in the demonic seems to be increasing. In an earlier chapter[55] we noted that C. S. Lewis, with characteristic wisdom and insight, began his *Screwtape Letters* with a sobering observation. "There are two equal and opposite errors into which our race can fall about the devils," he wrote. "One is to disbelieve in their existence. The other is to believe, and to feel an excessive and unhealthy interest in them. They themselves are equally pleased with both errors."[56] Today there still are those who disbelieve in the demonic, but increasing numbers of people, especially Christians, seem to be taking an excessive and unhealthy interest in demons. As a result, many believers are confused and distracted from competent counseling.[57]

There is a limit, however, to Satan's power and influence. The Bible tells us how to prepare for spiritual battle, warns us against satanic (and demonic) tactics, assures us that the Holy Spirit in us is greater than the devil's forces, and declares that Satan in time will be banished forever.[58] In the meantime, the fight continues and some people crumble spiritually because they are unprepared and not alert for the battle.

7. *What We Must Accept.* When we can identify the causes of spiritual and other problems, we often have some direction for our counseling. The ways of God, however, are not always comprehensible to the human mind. Sometimes we must stand with Job, shake our heads, wonder why, and yield ourselves to the sovereign Lord whose ways are not our ways and whose thoughts are not our thoughts.[59] It is not easy to accept what God permits, but at times that may be our best, most realistic, and only alternative.

The Effects of Spiritual Problems

Sometimes it is difficult to separate causes from effects. The spiritual issues that we discussed in the preceding paragraphs can have the effect of creating more spiritual problems. An attitude of pride often leads to more pride. Sin stimulates more sin. Legalism breeds more of the same. Self-sufficiency, distorted values, misunderstandings, selfishness, theological error, and nonbiblical thinking are like creeping vines that keep getting larger and better able to squeeze out the vestiges of spiritual life that are struggling to stay alive. How do they affect us?

1. *Spiritual Effects.* When spiritual problems are left unchecked they can lead to compromising sinful behavior, an increasing tendency to miss worship services and personal devotions, spiritual naïveté, a decreasing sensitivity to the Holy Spirit's leading or control, hypocrisy and phoniness, a boredom with religious activities and a greater tendency toward self-reliance. The fruits of the Spirit—love, joy, peace, patience, kindness, goodness, faithfulness, gentleness, and self-control—are experienced less and shown to others with decreasing frequency.

These spiritual effects may not be evident immediately. Many spiritually dry or dying people are good actors, especially if they know and can use the accepted theological jargon. Even Moses, whose face once shone as it reflected God's glory, kept a veil over his face so the Israelites could not see that the spiritual glory was fading away.[60] Many do something similar today. They try to hide their fading spirituality behind a veil of clichés or pious (but hypocritical) actions that others may or may not notice. Real change only comes to those who turn to the Lord so the veil is taken away and they become more Christlike.[61]

2. *Physical Effects.* It is well known that psychological tension and conflicts can influence the body physically, but can there also be a spiritually produced sickness and even death?[62] Not all illness comes from sin in the patient's life,[63] but sometimes sin does produce sickness.

3. *Psychological Effects.* Guilt feelings, self-condemnation, discouragement, anger, fears, defensiveness, insecurities, and misplaced values are all reactions that can result from spiritual deadness or waning spiritual vitality.

4. *Social Effects.* Christian fellowship can be a beautiful experience, but Christian fighting can be vicious. In describing spiritual immaturity, the Apostle Paul mentioned two issues of special significance: jealousy and strife. When there is spiritual growth, the barriers between people disintegrate;[64] when there are spiritual problems, then unkind criticism, cynicism, and interpersonal tension (jealousy and strife) are among the first and clearest signs of trouble.

5. *Evangelism Effects.* From the confines of a Roman prison, Paul once wrote about people who were preaching the gospel, not from motives of good will, but out of selfish ambition, and with the hope of stirring up trouble.[65] The same situation exists today. Some men and women seem so intent on building followers or converting others to their own points of view, that the person of Christ is forgotten even though his name may be mentioned often. The true disciple points people to Christ and seeks to have a part in building a body of believers who are Christ-centered, not centered on human beings.[66] When Christ is pushed behind the glory of some human leader, even a Christian leader, there is certain to be insensitivity, distorted values, and spiritual deadness in the leader and/or the followers.[67]

Counseling and Spiritual Problems

The approach and course of any counseling largely depends on the nature of the counselee's problem. If a person raises theological questions, for example, the counseling will probably differ from the help given to a defiant and unrepentant individual who is involved in deliberate sin. If a counselee is sincerely concerned about spiritual lethargy, our approach will differ from that taken with someone who is bitter and angry with God. As with every other type of counseling, therefore, helpers must listen carefully, show acceptance and empathy, and try to determine the nature and causes of the real problem. Your counseling is likely to involve some of the following.

1. *Prayer.* Before, during, and after counseling, the counselor must seek divine guidance. More than any other form of helping, spiritual counseling can involve us in conflict with satanic forces. This is one major reason why Christian counselors need to pray for special strength, wisdom, and direction. At times you may choose to pray directly with the counselee. Always you should spend at least some time alone in prayer concerning each counselee.

Does prayer have a psychological effect on the people who come for help? Some research would suggest that it does. When combined with meditation, for example, prayer has been shown to increase psychological well-being and decrease anxiety. Although researchers have difficulty measuring spirituality, there is some empirical evidence that prayer enhances spirituality and contributes to the effectiveness of psychotherapy.[68]

2. *Modeling.* People imitate and follow people. This is the basis of social learning theory and a principle reflected in the New Testament.[69] Jesus served as an example for the disciples. Paul instructed the believers to "follow my example as I follow the example of Christ." Peter urged church leaders to be examples to the flock.[70] Whether or not we want this role, Christians, including Christian counselors, are examples of Christian living. The counselor who is not seeking to imitate Christ or to grow as a Christian will not be effective in spiritual counseling. The counselor who wants to be effective in helping those with spiritual problems must recognize that he or she is a model that counselees will follow (and occasionally react against).

3. *Exhorting.* As used in the Bible, this word does *not* mean to preach at someone, to use sharp words, or to demand obedience. Exhortation involves a God-given ability to come alongside to help, to strengthen those who are spiritually weak, to reassure those who are wavering in their faith, to support those who are facing adverse circumstances, and to encourage those who lack assurance or security. At times the helper will point out sin, gently challenge the counselee's thinking or conclusions, encourage the counselee to change, guide as decisions are made, and give support as new behavior is tried and evaluated.

4. *Teaching.* Beginning counselors (and some who are more experienced) tend to be advice givers. Sometimes this reflects the anxiety of counselors who want to provide immediate answers that ease their own discomforts and briefly relieve the counselee's suffering. Too often, however, advice giving puts the counselor into "a superior, all-knowing position—one that some of them can easily come to enjoy—and it isn't difficult for them to delude themselves into thinking that they do have the answers."[71]

Counselees rarely grow or learn to solve problems based on advice that is given by others. Spiritual growth and renewal is a much slower process of soul care that frequently involves traveling through times of difficulty and spiritual darkness with the gentle instruction of a wise guide.[72]

Spiritual counseling often is a gentle, sensitive form of guidance and instruction, frequently conducted on a one-to-one basis. This teaching may involve giving information, answering questions, making suggestions, stimulating thinking, pointing out errors, and *sometimes* giving advice that can be discussed together. The teaching may involve a variety of issues, including one or more of the following.

(a) Knowing and Loving God. Confusion and spiritual problems often come to those who understand and ponder one or two of God's attributes while overlooking or forgetting the others. To emphasize the wrath of God without seeing his mercy is to plunge one into fear and guilt. To stress his mercy and love without his holiness and justice can lull us into a false sense of security and a lack of concern about spiritual issues and responsibilities.

God wants us to know him.[73] This is a continuing challenge that no human mind will ever complete. It is a process that comes first by listening to God's Word and by seeking to understand and apply it to our lives with the help and guidance of the Holy Spirit. Second, we know God by thinking about his character as revealed in the Bible and in the world, and by expressing thanks for his love and fellowship.[74] Third, we know God by obeying his commands.[75] Finally, we know God through participation and service in his body, the church.

In spiritual counseling, the counselor has the challenge of helping counselees to know and love God. We don't accomplish this by giving lectures or sermonettes. Instead the counselee must see God in the counselor's lifestyle, conversation, attitudes, and periodic references to Scripture. Such teaching places considerable responsibility on the counselor. We cannot teach others to know God unless we ourselves are growing in this knowledge and spiritual walk. Helping counselees to know God, therefore, requires an awareness and spiritual depth that far exceed the teaching of any book on counseling or psychotherapy.

(b) Christian Love. The giving, sacrificial, unconditional Christlike love described in 1 Corinthians 13 has been called "incomparably the greatest psychotherapeutic agent; something that professional psychiatry cannot of itself create, focus, nor release."[76] Love is the attribute of God that led him to send his son to earth so that we might personally become acquainted with the Lord of the universe.[77] Counselees need to hear about God's love. Even more, they need to experience and observe this love as it flows from God, through the dedicated counselor (and other Christians), and into the lives of counselees who feel unloved, unaccepted, guilty, confused, and spiritually needy.

(c) Sin and Forgiveness. The Bible never covers over sin or denies its prevalence and destructiveness. God hates sin and eventually punishes unrepentant sinners. In contrast, those who are in Christ Jesus are not condemned. God's son, Jesus Christ, came to pay for our sins. When we sin, therefore, we can be forgiven completely. "If we confess our sins, he is faithful and just and will forgive us our sins and purify us from all unrighteousness." This can be a liberating realization. God doesn't want sacrifices and penance. He wants confession and a willingness to change. When he hears our confession he forgives and completely forgets.[78]

The Bible also instructs us to confess our sins to one another. This is not done to get divine forgiveness. God forgives when we confess to him directly. Confession to others, however, can be therapeutic. Often it stimulates others to forgive us and sometimes it helps us to forgive ourselves. Confession to others can also be accompanied by the healing power of prayer.[79]

The counselor must share this biblical perspective on sin and forgiveness. At times, it will be necessary to confront counselees with their sin. In so doing, the counselor must show a forgiving, nonjudgmental attitude. We cannot talk about forgiveness and refuse to demonstrate it.[80]

(d) Holy Spirit Control. Christian counselors must never underestimate the role of the Holy Spirit in counseling. Often he gives counselors discernment and wisdom and supplements our training and experience so that we are more effective in the counseling role. According to one counselor, the Holy Spirit "offers incalculable resources for healing" as he leads counselees to a recognition of sin, teaches them about forgiveness, gives encouragement, and lives within as a quiet guide.[81]

In Eph. 5:18 Christians are commanded to "be filled with the Spirit," a process that involves:

- Self-examination (Acts 20:28, 1 Cor. 11:28).
- Confession of all known sin (1 John 1:9).
- Complete voluntary submission to God (Rom. 6:11–13).
- Asking in prayer for the Holy Spirit's filling (Luke 11:13).
- Believing that we then are filled with the Spirit and thanking God for this (1 Thess. 5:18).

Spirit filling is not a once-in-a-lifetime event. It is a daily process of breathing out sin through confession and breathing in the fullness of the Holy Spirit. Such repeated filling is not always accompanied by emotional highs or ecstatic experiences (although these do come at times), but it does lead to joyful thanksgiving, to mutual submission, and to the development of love, peace, patience, self-control, and the other fruits of the Spirit.[82]

Many of the spiritual problems discussed in this chapter arise and persist because believers attempt to solve the problems and grow on their own. It is the Holy Spirit who teaches, strengthens, and empowers us to meet and overcome the spiritual problems of life. Counselees must be aware of this foundational truth.

(e) Discipleship. In the Great Commission, Jesus instructed believers to make disciples—a process that involves evangelism and Christian education.[83] At times, the counselor will want to evangelize, sharing the good news of the gospel, although care must be taken not to violate counselor ethics by pushing religious teaching on to counselees who resist such teaching or who want to focus on other issues. The counselor and counselee also may discuss the meaning and importance of Bible study, prayer, trust in God, meditation, discipline in our devotional lives, and reaching out to others.

In two sentences, Paul once stated his ultimate purpose in life: "We proclaim him, admonishing and teaching everyone with all wisdom, so that we may present everyone perfect in Christ. To this end I labor, struggling with all his energy, which so powerfully works in me."[84] Can you write a two- or three-sentence statement to summarize your ultimate goals as a counselor? This can be a worthwhile and helpful exercise. For many Christian counselors the goal statement may be similar to Paul's: to proclaim Christ and to admonish and teach others so that they will move toward spiritual perfection and maturity.

Sometimes well-meaning but insensitive counselors are too hasty in presenting the gospel or urging counselors to make a commitment to Christ. We might hope to see all of our counselees grow spiritually, but growth is often slow and spiritual issues sometimes are raised too abruptly, too quickly, and too enthusiastically.

Seeking the Holy Spirit's leading must be a constant goal for Christian counselors. With his guidance, the effective and sensitive counselor moves gently into discussions of spiritual matters, aware that it is the Holy Spirit who (in his timing and in his ways) convicts people of sin and brings them to repentance and growth as disciples. We must submit ourselves to being divine instruments in this process.

(f) Balance. Counselees with spiritual problems need to be alerted to the importance of such nonspiritual influences as proper diet, rest, recreation, and exercise. Help counselees develop a balanced lifestyle that avoids legalism and self-sufficiency; deals with pride and bitterness (through discussion, understanding, and prayer); reexamines values, goals, and priorities; eliminates theological misunderstanding; and is free from the twin problems of spiritual undernourishment and overfeeding.[85]

(g) The Body. Christianity, as we have stated earlier, is not a do-it-yourself religion. God made us to be social creatures and declared that it is not good for humans to be alone.[86] In the Bible the church clearly is pictured as a body that has many parts.

Each person in the body is important. Each has been given one or more special gifts (such as teaching, counseling, hospitality, or evangelism). Each is expected to develop these gifts in order to serve and care for one another,[87] and to build up the church so that "in all things God may be praised through Jesus Christ," to whom belongs "the glory and the power for ever and ever."[88]

The effectiveness of Christian counseling will be weakened if it exists apart from the body of Christ, the church. Believers are instructed to help one another and to bear one another's burdens. When counselees experience this acceptance and support, they are better able to work with their counselors in handling spiritual and other problems.

5. *Exorcising.* At times, and in some Christian circles, the devil seems to get more credit and attention than he deserves. Satan is blamed for all problems and annoyances. Rebuke and exorcism are the preferred methods (and in some churches the only methods) of problem solving and there is little place for compassion, understanding, and sensitive Christian counseling.

In an overreaction to such distorted teaching, it is possible to forget that Christians are in a spiritual struggle and that each of us should constantly be alert to satanic influences in our own lives and in the lives of our counselees. Ephesians 6 warns that we are in a struggle that is "not against flesh and blood, but against the rulers, against the authorities, against the powers of this dark world and against the spiritual forces of evil in the heavenly realms." We are not instructed to battle these forces in highly dramatic exorcisms and confrontations. Instead we are to "be strong in the Lord and in his mighty power. Put on the full armor of God so that you can take your stand against the devil's schemes. . . . With this in mind, be alert and always keep on praying for all the saints." We are to stand firm against the devil, not trying to resist him with our own strength, but relying instead on Christ's mighty power.[89]

Should the Christian counselor engage in exorcism? The answer to this question is controversial, in part because it is so difficult to distinguish between psychopathology and demonology, between the need for psychotherapy and the need for spiritual warfare.[90] Recent years have seen a sharp increase in occult activity, however, and there appears to be new interest and involvement in spiritism, Eastern mysticism, seances, fortune telling, witchcraft, black magic, and even Satan worship. Many professional counselors and theologians agree that this involvement is dangerous.[91] It can open individuals to control by evil spiritual forces that may sometimes resemble but often go beyond the symptoms of psychopathology. These spiritual forces are unmoved by traditional methods of counseling.

On occasion, therefore, the Christian counselor will conclude that counseling is ineffective because of powerful satanic influences within the counselee's life. Be careful that this conclusion is not used as excuse to cover and explain away either your own incompetence and lack of skill or the counselee's lack of cooperation. If you decide (preferably after consultation with a colleague) that there could be demonic involvement, then it is wise to consider exorcism—in the name of Jesus Christ, commanding that the demonic forces leave the individual and never return. The methods of exorcism are varied and depend in part on one's theology.[92] Dealing with the demonic should be done cautiously and reluctantly, only by the spiritually mature,[93] and by those whom the church recognizes as being specially gifted as "discerners of spirits."[94]

It appears that some enthusiastic but ill-informed people have no understanding of the causes and treatment of abnormality, attribute all problems to demon involvement, and use exorcisms as a way to avoid the work of counseling or to inadvertently hide their ignorance about human behavior. This can create far more problems than it solves. Counselees can misinterpret comments about Satan, sometimes develop paranoid fears of the demonic and often have their problems made worse when they hear they are demon possessed. The problems are accentuated when exorcisms fail to bring any change, but the counselee is left to struggle both with the original problem and with the belief that he or she is possessed by demonic forces.

Counselors, therefore, should use discretion in mentioning Satan and should be alert to potential counselee misconceptions about the devil. His influence and power should be clearly understood, alertly recognized, and firmly resisted with determination and the Holy Spirit's power. Most Christian counselees will be able to understand both the devil's influence and the resounding truth that the Holy Spirit who resides in us is greater than the devil who is in the world.[95]

Preventing Spiritual Problems

Spirituality is a word used in various ways and by people in different religions. Most of us yearn for a "vital spiritual life," according to Lawrence Richards, but we don't know what that means, how to get it, or how to keep from losing it. Many writers have viewed spirituality as some kind of mystical union with God. Others have taken a more down-to-earth perspective that sees spirituality as living human life in continual harmony with God.[96] Stated differently, spirituality involves Christlikeness.

Spirituality also involves discipline. The spiritual life does not come automatically. It must be nurtured. "Only by affirming both that God is totally the source of our spiritual life and that human beings are totally responsible for their spiritual progress" can we hope to grow spiritually and in accordance with biblical teaching. Spiritual growth and change are the outcomes of a disciplined life.[97]

Spirituality and the movement toward spiritual well-being[98] are not easily attained and neither should the believer assume that spiritually maturing individuals will be free from trials, tribulations, and temptations. Jesus called us to take up a cross in following him. His life on earth was not easy and he never promised that we would be free of problems. Instead we are told that difficulties will come and can help us grow.[99]

This does not mean that we can forget about prevention. Through counseling, but especially through the church, the Christian can be taught how to prevent some of the spiritual problems of life. The preventive measures, surely well known to most Christian leaders, include:

- Committing one's life to Christ and accepting him as Lord and Savior.
- Developing the practice of regular, consistent prayer and Bible study.
- Regularly confessing sin and asking for God's forgiveness.
- Yielding to the Holy Spirit's control and expecting that Holy Spirit's filling.
- Becoming involved actively in a local body of believers.
- Reaching out to others in evangelism, service, and fellowship.
- Being alert to the devil and resistant to his influences.

This is not presented as a simplistic formula to prevent all spiritual problems. It is a basic foundation upon which the church's preventive and discipleship program must be built.

Conclusions about Spiritual Problems

Of all the topics discussed in this book, perhaps none is more familiar to Christian leaders and counselors than the spiritual problems considered in this chapter. These problems have concerned godly men and women for centuries, and the Bible deals with these in more detail than any of the other issues considered in this volume.

Since the Bible speaks so frequently about spiritual problems, some believers have concluded that *all* of our problems are really spiritual and that all can be solved through the discovery and application of some biblical principle. We may admire the dedication of many who hold such views, but this is difficult to apply in practice.

Spiritual problems have causes and solutions that most often are described in the Scriptures. The Bible, however, never claims to be a psychiatric diagnostic manual and textbook of counseling. While all problems ultimately stem from the fall of the human race, not all human problems are spiritual in that they involve the counselee's specific relationship with God. Some problems, for example, may be caused by faulty learning, misinformation, early traumas, environmental stress, physical illness, misperception, confusion over decision making, or other issues that may not be discussed by biblical writers. Counseling people with these problems may involve using techniques derived from the Scripture. More often the counselor will use methods that are *consistent with the Bible's teachings and values* but discovered and developed by social science and common sense.

Christian counseling then is deeply concerned with the issues discussed in this chapter, but it goes further. It recognizes that all truth, including psychological truth, comes from God—sometimes through secular psychology and psychiatry books. The Christian evaluates such secular findings carefully and discards what is inconsistent with the Bible. That which remains is used along with and in submission to biblical teaching. The counselor, so equipped, then seeks to be used by God to touch lives and change them so that people can be helped to live with greater meaning, stability, fulfillment, and spiritual maturity.

SUGGESTIONS FOR FURTHER READING

Benner, David G. *Psychotherapy and the Spiritual Quest.* Grand Rapids, Mich.: Baker, 1988.

Bufford, Rodger K. *Counseling and the Demonic.* Waco, Tex.: Word, 1988.

Foster, Richard J. *Celebration of Discipline: The Path to Spiritual Growth.* Rev. ed. New York: Harper & Row, 1988.*

———. *Money, Sex & Power: The Challenge of the Disciplined Life.* New York: Harper & Row, 1985.*

Lovelace, Richard F. *Dynamics of Spiritual Renewal.* Downers Grove, Ill.: Inter-Varsity, 1979.

MacDonald, Gordon. *Ordering Your Private World.* Nashville: Oliver-Nelson, 1984.*

Richards, Lawrence O. *A Practical Theology of Spirituality.* Grand Rapids, Mich.: Zondervan, 1987.

Shuster, Marguerite. *Power, Pathology, Paradox: The Dynamics of Evil and Good.* Grand Rapids, Mich.: Zondervan, 1987.

Stafford, Tim. *Knowing the Face of God: The Search for a Personal Relationship with God.* Grand Rapids, Mich.: Zondervan, 1986.*

* Books marked with an asterisk (*) are especially suited for counselees to read.

37

Other Problems

Brad is a professional counselor, thirty-six years old, with a doctorate in clinical psychology from an eastern university. Following the rigors of graduate school and his one-year psychological internship, Brad spent two semesters at a theological seminary where he supplemented his counselor training with courses in theology and biblical studies. When this work was completed seven years ago, Brad joined a private counseling practice where he works with several other professionals in psychology, psychiatry, and social work. Brad, however, is getting tired.

"I'm not even forty," he said recently, "But I feel drained, pressured, and bored with counseling. I'm exhausted when I go home at night. I dread the sound of the phone, and I tend to be impatient with my wife and kids. About every couple of months, we have to get away for a break."

Brad is a good counselor, highly regarded by his colleagues and counselees. Yet he feels overwhelmed at times because "the world is filled with so many hurting people." Many have gotten better with Brad's help, but progress is almost always slow. Few of Brad's clients realize that counseling people, hour after hour, day after day, can be draining, demanding, and difficult.

Brad knows about burnout, about the need for counselors to get away periodically, about the challenge of keeping up with the field. Often he attends seminars to learn about AIDS, counseling minorities, recent techniques in marital therapy, emerging research about psychopathology, or ongoing developments in counseling ethics and insurance plans. Brad reads professional journals and tries hard to keep abreast of his field.

Unlike many of his professional colleagues who leave the field after a few years, Brad has no plans to shift careers. Every day brings him into contact with some new problem that he has never encountered before. The work is challenging and often interesting—but it isn't always easy.

Your education about counseling is never likely to be complete. The pages of this book may have considered the most common problems that people bring to counseling, but no book or book series can deal with every counseling topic.[1]

Frequently problems are combined. The person with marriage difficulties may also be depressed, anxious, and struggling to make ends meet financially. The couple who comes for help in handling a rebellious child may feel trapped between generations; their worry may be greater because they also have elderly parents with adjustment problems. The man who seeks help with vocational decisions may also struggle with interpersonal conflicts, discouragement, low self-esteem, and a drinking problem.

Sometimes the presenting problems are colored by unique circumstances. Even if you have no prejudice, you may need extra understanding to counsel with people who are not of your race, cultural background, sexual orientation, or socioeconomic level. You may want to treat all people equally, but your work cannot ignore the unique problems that come to people who are physically handicapped, mentally retarded, unable to speak your language, or tied to a relative who needs constant care. Counseling in a private practice is likely to differ from counseling that occurs in a church, a prison, a military community, or a psychiatric hospital. In all of these situations, the counseling principles may be the same, but they need to be adapted to each individual and to each setting. Counselors are not robots; they need to be responsive, sensitive, and flexible.

Part of the flexibility comes when we are aware of issues like those presented in the following pages. These are not listed in any special order of importance, but each may be encountered at some time in your counseling work.[2]

Counseling and the Physically Handicapped

How would you counsel with someone who has impaired hearing? Communication could be difficult, especially if the counselee uses sign language and you do not. The presence of a translator could help, but this interferes with confidentiality and may inhibit the counselee from sharing concerns that are intimate or embarrassing. Lip reading, face-to-face contact, and visual communication may be more important than in other types of counseling, but could this hinder your counseling style or maybe invalidate some of our assessment procedures? People who are hearing impaired often have problems with depression, loneliness, or relationships, but these are difficult to discuss if communication is blocked by faulty hearing. Some people encounter prejudice or misunderstanding, even from sensitive counselors. Several years ago, one psychiatric textbook reported that deaf persons have a high rate of mental illness, particularly paranoia, but more recent studies have challenged this conclusion. When hearing is impaired it is normal to wonder what others are saying and sometimes to reach unfounded conclusions that an insensitive counselor might label as paranoid.[3]

Hearing impairment is one example of a *disability*. The word refers to any mental, physical, or emotional condition (defect or impairment) that can hinder a person's ability to function normally. People whose disabilities[4] interfere with optimal life adjustment usually are described as handicapped persons. These handicaps may range from minor issues that are almost unnoticed to disabilities that are severely inhibiting. The handicaps may be physical, mental, or both. They may be temporary (such as the loss of mobility following surgery) or permanent. They can result from congenital impairment, injury at birth or during childhood, or loss of some capacity later in life.

It is rare to find completely handicapped people. While there are things that the handicapped person *cannot* do, there also are many things that he or she *can* do. Medical treatment is designed to assist the disabled person as much as possible in the physical area, and the rehabilitation task is to help the individual live with the disability and reach maximum effectiveness.

(a) Helping Families. It is extremely difficult for parents to discover that their child is disabled or impaired. Parental guilt, rejection of the handicapped person, overprotection, criticism of physicians or schools, impatience with other family members, unrealistic expectations, feelings of embarrassment, and anger with God are all common. Many families with a handicapped child show increased levels of anxiety and depression, lowered self-concepts and self-esteem, feelings of frustration, and decreased marital and personal satisfaction.[5]

These families need understanding, support, and sometimes practical assistance (like help with child care or household chores) as they cope with their unique stresses. They need help in learning to live fulfilling lives with a disabled person. Siblings need to express their frustrations or feelings of rejection and then learn coping skills. Often there is value in putting the family in contact with other families of handicapped children. Mutual aid groups can do much to give support, encouragement, and practical guidance as families cope together.[6]

(b) Helping Handicapped People. Children who are born with handicaps learn to accept these as they adjust to life. If the handicap comes later, however, the adjustment usually is much more difficult. "I've lost the ability to walk," said one man whose injury in a car accident had left him paralyzed from the waist down. "I can't control my bowels and bladder. I can't have sex like I did before. I can't ride my motorcycle or play football. I've lost a lot of my freedom."

When we lose a limb, go blind, or lose control over some part of the body, we suffer grief reactions. Often there is shock, denial, anger, sometimes unrealistic hope, and often depression. People wonder *why* and sometimes expect that God will heal. When healing doesn't come, there may be despair, thoughts of suicide, sadness about being a burden to others, and a sense of hopelessness about the future.[7]

How does one escape from this emotional trap? The process will take time, but often it comes as the disabled person is helped to express feelings and to consider possibilities for living as fulfilling a life as possible. Sometimes this involves learning to live with physical limitations, overcoming transportation barriers, learning to cope with society's stereotypes, building a positive self-concept, finding a suitable vocation,[8] and developing a willingness to accept help with those things that can no longer be done without assistance.

The life story of Joni Eareckson Tada is well known. After an accident left her paralyzed from the neck down, she went through long periods of depression and rehabilitation, but eventually she learned to live with her limitations, got married, and developed a significant helping ministry to other handicapped people.[9] Less familiar perhaps is the example of psychologist B. F. Skinner who struggled with the disabilities of old age. Instead of moping about memory losses and physical limitations, Skinner wrote an entire book to help people cope by planning ahead and adjusting to their losses.[10]

In helping people cope and adjust to their losses, the counselor is unlikely to work alone in traditional one-to-one interaction. Helping often involves cooperative work with physical therapists, educators, physicians, and other specialists. It may involve cooperation with the counselee's friends and sometimes it will involve counseling the whole family.

At times it may involve looking at your own attitudes. If you jump to invalid conclusions about the physically disabled, are uncomfortable in working with handicapped persons, or have biases about their supposed moods or attitudes, then you are not likely to be effective as a counselor.[11] Regardless of your attitudes, *learn from your handicapped counselees* and your whole counseling work is likely to be enriched.

Jesus was much concerned about handicapped people: the lame, blind, deaf, epileptic, and deformed. He accepted them completely and met their needs. The Christian counselor must do likewise. Counseling may require creative approaches, forsaking some favorite techniques, and creating a network of helpers. This can be rewarding work, however, especially if one sees the disabled person growing in skills, psychological stability, and spiritual maturity.

COUNSELING AND THE MENTALLY HANDICAPPED

Jean Vanier grew up in Canada before moving overseas where he was shocked to discover that mentally retarded people in the small town where he lived were institutionalized along with the mentally ill. Seeking to form a Christian community, Vanier[12] invited two of the mentally retarded men to come and live with him. There was no intention of doing anything beyond this, but others heard of Vanier's life, came to see what he was doing, and left to start homes elsewhere. The result has been the worldwide expansion of L'Arche (a French word that means "the ark"). These are residential group homes for retarded people who learn to live together and care for one another, often with the help of local professionals, including counselors.[13]

Mental retardation is "below average intellectual functioning that becomes evident before age eighteen" and seriously interferes with a person's ability to "attain a level of personal independence and social responsibility appropriate for one's age and culture."[14] Mental retardation begins in infancy or childhood, persists indefinitely, and seriously hinders both the ability to learn and the capacity to live independently. Sometimes the cause is genetic, but mental retardation also may result from brain damage or childhood disease. Some physically normal children grow up retarded because they have not had sufficient sensory or intellectual stimulation.

Mental retardation, a condition that originates in childhood, is different from mental handicaps that may come later in life. Chemically induced disorders, diseases such as Parkinson's or Alzheimer's, brain tumors or head injuries, arteriosclerosis, strokes, AIDS,[15] cardiovascular disorders, and even faulty nutrition can all interfere with clear thinking. Many of these mental handicaps are permanent, but some are reversible.[16] Most handicapped people can be helped to cope with life despite their limitations.

Depending on the degree of impairment, mentally handicapped people can often be given at least some self-management skills and many are able to find simple and satisfying careers.[17] A few may profit from counseling if they can avoid overdependency and are able to comprehend what the counselor is saying. Medications often help; in some cases medical treatment can stop or even eliminate the mental handicap.

Parents, spouses, and other family members respond to mental handicaps in many of the same ways that they respond to physical handicaps. Often there is guilt, anger, depression, embarrassment, financial strain, and difficulties in coping. Most often the family must learn to live with the mentally handicapped person just as many learn to accept responsibility for aging or chronically ill relatives. These family care givers often need support and practical guidance to help them cope.

Counseling Minorities

Counselors have been criticized for acting as if their theories and techniques are universally applicable to people of all racial and ethnic groups. The criticisms may have some validity, but within recent years an expanding body of literature on cross-cultural counseling is showing that many counselors attempt to adapt their methods to the counselee's cultural background. This is true for missionaries or counselors who work in countries other than their own,[18] but cross-cultural issues are equally important in our own neighborhoods. North-American-born Orientals, native (American Indian) peoples, immigrants, Blacks, Hispanics, or Caucasians whose ancestors have been here for generations may all share the same citizenship, but they have different ethnic and cultural backgrounds or perspectives. These differences cannot be ignored in counseling.[19]

Consider, for example, your definition of normal. Often we assume that those who function best in our society do so on the basis of their own efforts and abilities. The best-adjusted people are assumed to be mature, independent, competent, and able to handle stress without great difficulty or dependence on others. If we need help we go to a counselor who is often a stranger. This person is seen by appointment, expects to be paid, usually meets us for fifty-minute sessions, and is not expected to be too directive. We openly express our most intimate concerns and expect that we will learn how to cope.

Some people don't think like this. People from some cultures and ethnic groups respect the wisdom of old age more than they value the training of a counselor with a doctoral degree. Problems tend to be hidden from strangers and confined to the family. Interdependence among family members is valued more than dependence. Time limitations are of little concern, counselors are expected to be directive, and nobody thinks that a helper should be paid.[20]

In addition, the stresses are different. Minorities in any culture are more likely to face prejudice, social isolation, fewer educational or employment opportunities, and lower self-concepts. Many feel powerless to control their circumstances or to change their lives. Depression is common because minorities feel helpless and without much hope.[21] Understandably some are reluctant to trust a counselor who is of a different race or ethnic group, could have different values, speaks a different language, and may not understand or appreciate cultural differences.

Nevertheless cross-cultural counseling is possible, especially when a counselor is aware of his or her own values, has a knowledge of minority group cultures and ways of thinking, is sensitive to individual differences and counselee expectations, is comfortable with the differences that exist between the counselor and counselee, is willing to be flexible in the use of counseling techniques, and has a real spirit of humility and willingness to learn.[22] The greater the mutual understanding, the greater the likelihood of counseling success. The more similar the values shared by the counselor and counselee, the better the communication. All of this suggests that Christians who counsel with other Christians cross-culturally are likely to have better rapport because there is a common devotion to Christ and acceptance of biblical authority.

Counseling and the Military

When I first began working with the military almost a decade ago, I quickly concluded that for civilians this is a form of cross-cultural counseling. Even though you may share the same citizenship as your counselees and may have grown up in the same community, life in the military is different than civilian living.

As a group, service personnel and their families may be unusually healthy. There is a camaraderie among military families, a willingness to help one another, and a sense of shared experiences. Despite reports of frequent substance abuse, poverty among lower-ranking personnel, harshness and insensitivity among some leaders, and pressures on military children,[23] many people function well in military environments.

The stresses, however, can also be great. Frequent moves, separations from family, continual competition for promotions, interpersonal tensions, assignments to remote duty or dangerous areas, uncertainty about the future, lack of control over one's life and circumstances, never-ending sensitivity to rank and protocol, high expectations that the whole family will conform to military norms, and the continual need for combat readiness can all take their toll in mental health. Some families have problems because an obsessive-compulsive, insensitive military husband-father tries to run his family like a platoon of soldiers or like the commander of a "tight" ship. The family learns to dread his presence and to be glad when his absences are frequent. Unlike civilian occupations, the military retires people sooner, and this can create unusual stress for longtime servicemen or women who are nervous about their abilities to function on the "outside." For some families there is also worry about the dangers of war, the continual possibility of terrorist attack, and the pain of waiting and wondering while a military family remains in captivity. Perhaps it is not surprising that some military people respond with family violence, incest, sexual promiscuity, and high rates of alcoholism and other forms of substance abuse.[24] Many stick it out but perform poorly at work because they are worried about their families and personal stresses. Others conclude that life apart from the service is better, so they go AWOL or resign at the earliest opportunity.

The military is concerned about personal problems so opportunities are provided for counseling. Each of the armed forces, for example, has family service centers that provide legal and financial counseling, relocation assistance, parenting courses, help with stress management, and referrals to community services. Professional counselors also are available, but many service people are reluctant to seek counseling because this information is recorded and could hinder future promotions. Some company commanders like to appear tough and insensitive to personal needs, so counseling tends to be discouraged even though it is never mentioned. Chaplains who sometimes bear the brunt of jokes also bear much of the counseling load. A visit to the chaplain is not recorded on anybody's record, but chaplains also have needs and some tend to burn out as they try to help people with their counseling needs.

Civilians, including church leaders and Christian counselors, often are involved in counseling service personnel, especially when one lives near a military base. Christian servicemen's centers exist worldwide to encourage, provide Christian fellowship, and counsel with service personnel.[25] Like all good counseling, the essence of working effectively with these people is to be sensitive to their stresses and willing to understand the uniqueness of military living.

Counseling Prisoners and Their Families

Charles Colson could never have predicted how his life would change. Following the Watergate crisis, the former aide to President Richard Nixon became a Christian, spent time in prison, and eventually founded Prison Fellowship, an international ministry to prisoners and their families.[26]

Like most of us who have never spent time behind bars, Colson had no prior awareness of the stresses that prisoners often face. Offenders frequently have adjustment, self-esteem, and relationship problems before they ever are arrested. Many have had unusually high levels of life stress before their incarceration, and the stresses of prison may increase anxiety, depression, and stress-related psychological and physical problems. Because the environment is "pervasive, intrusive, and inescapable,"[27] the prisoner-counselee has little freedom to make decisions, little opportunity for self-control, and frequent feelings of low self-worth. Lack of acceptance, sexual harassment, and threats of violence may be accompanied by worries about one's family or future. Some estimates suggest that half of all prisoners exhibit diagnosable psychological disorders, and a disturbing number of prisoners attempt suicide. Many succeed.[28]

Counseling prisoners involves unique approaches that do not apply elsewhere. The counselor must get permission to have access to the prisoner, privacy may be harder to find, and confidentiality may be more difficult to maintain (especially if the counselor learns of impending violence or disruption that could be prevented if it is reported). Techniques and counseling goals will have to be adapted to the needs of the individual prisoner and counselors will have to examine their own biases, prejudices, and fears before they attempt this kind of work. Some research suggests that counseling in prisons is not very effective,[29] but if we work on that assumption, our predictions are likely to come true.

Prison counselors are often specialists who work for the prison system and perform multiple roles including assessment, treatment, training, consultation, research, and education. There is a sizable literature on forensic psychology,[30] and the counselor who works in prisons will be aware of the special challenges of this type of work.

The nonspecialist is likely to have greater contact with the families of prisoners, with former prisoners, with offenders who are on parole or awaiting trial, sometimes with police officers (who often encounter stress and burnout in their work), or with the victims of crime.[31] These people are all under stress, but they have more freedom to control some of their own circumstances and to plan for the future. Once again, understanding of the counselees' unique circumstances is important if counseling is to be effective.

Counseling and Premenstrual Stress

Women have experienced it for centuries, some uninformed and insensitive people (usually males) have joked about it, and even some physicians dismiss it as being mostly psychological. Nevertheless there is increasing evidence that premenstrual syndrome (usually abbreviated PMS) is a real, biologically based condition that brings monthly misery to millions of women.

Many of the problems discussed in this book are accentuated and sometimes caused by physical disease or malfunctioning. Perhaps few physically produced conditions are more common, however, than the PMS disorder that one sufferer called "temporary insanity once a month."[32]

It is estimated that over 50 percent of women between the ages of fourteen and fifty don't have PMS at all and others have mild symptoms that are minimally disruptive. For some women, however, the days prior to menstruation can be severely debilitating and miserable both physically and psychologically. The wide range of symptoms may include mood swings, headaches, sinus problems, anxiety, dizziness, crying spells, forgetfulness, irritability, clumsiness, feelings of worthlessness or incompetence, craving for certain foods, abdominal bloating and cramping, panic, depression, poor judgment, difficulties in coping, and even thoughts of suicide. Some women get short-tempered and impatient; others feel that they are going crazy. For males who never experience these symptoms, a woman's PMS can create confusion, impatience, and frustration. Telling one's wife to snap out of it doesn't help. Instead this is likely to create more tension and make matters worse.

PMS is an organically based disorder that lasts from two to fourteen days prior to the menstrual period and usually disappears once the period begins. Despite its prevalence, there is no accepted diagnostic test, specific cause, or treatment. The problem is less common in teenagers than in older women, and it tends to increase in severity with age. Sometimes the condition first appears or is aggravated by pregnancy, reaching one's mid or late thirties, a tubal ligation or hysterectomy, or the start of menopause. Women who suspect PMS are often urged to keep a daily record of exactly when the symptoms occur. This is done for three or four consecutive cycles and then discussed with a physician.

Since PMS is a physical condition, a medical doctor should be consulted. Often he or she will suggest some commonly accepted (and medically supported) physical ways to reduce the symptoms: avoid caffeine, alcohol, and refined sugars (like those in candy bars or baked goods); eat more fruits, vegetables, poultry, and fish; avoid diuretics, tranquilizers, and medications that contain caffeine; eat five or six meals a day instead of two or three large ones (to help keep blood sugar at stable levels); take multiple vitamins with minerals at mealtimes; and exercise.

The counselor can encourage women to communicate about their symptoms and feelings. By listening to their wives, many husbands get a better understanding of PMS and its effects. Sometimes, for example, women experience a change in sex drive as a PMS symptom and the sensitive husband will want to be aware of his wife's feelings.[33]

The sensitive counselor should be aware of PMS and should recognize that this organically based recurring condition can make life miserable for both the sufferer and her family. This is one of many physical conditions that can have important counseling implications for people of both sexes.

Counseling and AIDS

Throughout the middle ages and before, plagues were common and the death rate was high. In 1665, for example, a plague in London killed seventy thousand residents (seven out of every forty people). Most of the wealthy citizens, many of the clergy, and almost all of the doctors left. A dwindling population made up mostly of poor people, remained to struggle with anxiety, depression, confusion, anger, pain, malnutrition, and death. Violence and crime were common as hungry and sometimes desperate people tried to find food and temporary relief from their misery.

With the advances of modern medicine, plagues largely have been eliminated, at least in the Western world. In 1979, however, the first cases of Acquired Immune Deficiency Syndrome (AIDS) were discovered, and what once appeared as a rare condition is now described with terms like "worldwide crisis," "epidemic," and even "plague."[34] Although most AIDS victims in North America have been homosexuals, the disease is spreading to others and in some parts of the world it is equally prevalent among both homosexuals and heterosexuals.[35]

AIDS is an infectious disease caused by a virus that attacks the immune system and reduces the body's ability to fight other diseases. When the immune system is damaged, the person with AIDS (often abbreviated PWA) is unable to resist otherwise harmless infections and some kinds of cancer. The virus also attacks brain cells and often causes *AIDS dementia complex,* a slowly progressing disorder that leads to impaired intellectual functioning, slowed motor activity, apathy, withdrawal, concentration difficulties, and reduced ability to solve problems. Sometimes these symptoms are followed by loss of coordination and mental disorder.[36]

The course of the disease is unpredictable and differs from person to person. Some show no symptoms, at least for a while. In other cases, the PWA may come down with transient flulike symptoms and then appear to recover without knowing that the virus remains dormant, sometimes for many years. Others develop *AIDS-related complex* (ARC), a milder form of the infection that leads to AIDS in about 30 percent of the cases. The most common AIDS symptoms include a persistent cough, weight loss, high fever, shortness of breath, low resistance to infections, and sometimes purplish blotches and bumps on the skin. Once AIDS has been diagnosed, the individual has only a few years to live, although some medical research is finding ways to prolong the life of AIDS patients.[37] At present there is no cure for AIDS and no vaccine to prevent spread.

Most researchers agree that prevention comes through education and changed behavior. Despite widespread rumors to the contrary, there is no evidence that AIDS is transmitted through social contact, by mosquitoes or pets, through toilet seats or by touching the possessions of a person with AIDS. In contrast, AIDS is transmitted in three ways: sexual contact (penis-vagina, penis-rectum, mouth-rectum, mouth-penis, and mouth-vagina), use of unsterilized needles or syringes that are contaminated with blood that contains the AIDS virus (most often this involves needle sharing by users of illicit drugs but occasionally a medical person is accidentally pricked by a dirty needle), or through heredity (a mother with the AIDS virus in her bloodstream can pass this to her unborn child). The disease also can be transmitted by blood transfusions, but this almost never happens, at least in advanced societies, because collected blood is always tested for AIDS virus.

According to the U.S. Surgeon General, "couples who maintain mutually faithful monogamous relationships (only one continuing sexual partner) are protected from AIDS through sexual transmission." More controversial are the calls for free distribution of condoms and sterile needles for people who continue to use a variety of sexual partners or illegal intravenous drugs. Yet even when they have accurate information or protective devices such as condoms, some people fail to take precautions. Swayed by their sexual passions or the throes of an addiction, few people stop to think about preventing the spread of disease.[38] So AIDS continues to infect increasing numbers of people.

(a) The Psychological Implications of AIDS. Since AIDS is an incurable, ultimately fatal disease, it is not surprising that its victims respond as they would to any other terminal diagnosis. Usually there is anxiety, depression, and intense feelings of hopelessness and helplessness. Thoughts of suicide are common and the fears are intensified by media reports or past contacts with friends who have died from AIDS-related illnesses.[39]

Unlike some other seriously ill individuals, people with AIDS have additional psychological stresses. Often there is guilt over past sexual behavior, promiscuity, or drug use.[40] It hurts to watch one's parents, other relatives, or friends suffer emotionally, both because of the illness and because they now know about the patient's past lifestyle and sexual behavior. Because of widespread fear and misinformation about the disease, people with AIDS often are avoided or rejected by others, including medical personnel, church members, and counselors. Insensitive Christians sometimes complicate this emotional pain by declaring that AIDS is God's judgment for immoral behavior.

According to Charles Brand, an experienced and sensitive Christian physician, sin causes spiritual tension and loss of fellowship with the Lord (at least until we confess our sin and experience divine forgiveness), but God rarely punishes people visibly and immediately. More often we harm ourselves and those around us by ignoring God's guidelines for living. The effects of these actions are often not observed immediately and are not always distributed fairly. Brand suggests that AIDS "is the *result* of breaking God's law, not His *judgment*. Thus many who break the law against sodomy do not catch AIDS, while some innocents . . . suffer as a result of what others have done."[41] Regardless of one's theological views about the causes of the AIDS epidemic, the Christian has a responsibility to treat the PWA with compassion, understanding, support, and love. The same attitudes must extend to the families, many of whom also suffer embarrassment, rejection, ostracism, and great emotional pain.

(b) Counseling Implications. AIDS counselors have identified several therapeutic issues that commonly surface in counseling the PWA.[42] First, there are feelings of anxiety, anger, fear, denial, and hopelessness. It is extremely difficult for a young person to face death and to accept the realities of the illness.

Second, there often is a sense of isolation and alienation. The PWA needs social support but tends instead to withdraw. The physical isolation required by medical treatment sometimes intensifies this sense of being alone, and many counselees feel that their families, friends, and neighbors do not want to have any contact. Withdrawal leads to loneliness, more depression, and sometimes greater withdrawal.

Third, there often is a severe drop in self-esteem, especially if the PWA feels guilt concerning the sexual behavior that led to the disease.

Fourth, some people jump to conclusions that are based more on rumor and misinformation than on fact. The news that one has been infected by the AIDS virus can lead some people to conclude that life is now over, that there never can be fulfillment or meaning in life, that God will never forgive, that the PWA will be rejected by everyone or that it never again will be possible to live independently. For some of course there will be immediate and severe limitations, but for many people these conclusions simply are not true. (While I was writing this section, I stopped for lunch and turned on the radio where a talk-show host was interviewing a PWA. The young man spoke freely about his disease and its serious implications but in addition told about his fulfilling work, his studies at a local university, and his continued enjoyment of attending plays and engaging in other socially enriching activities.)

Fifth, there is the issue of the family. It is not easy for a PWA to tell the family, relate to parents, and deal with the flood of emotions that often come to family members when they learn about the AIDS diagnosis.

How do we help these counselees? Start by looking at your own attitudes toward AIDS. This type of work can be emotionally draining and very stressful. Burnout is common. Someone has suggested that counseling the PWA is like riding a roller coaster: there can be one crisis after another. In dealing with these, you are likely to be ineffective if you are afraid of AIDS, unwilling to be face-to-face with pain or death, uninformed about AIDS, uncomfortable discussing sexual matters including homosexuality and sexual deviations, judgmental and nonforgiving, or afraid to get emotionally involved with a PWA and his or her family.[43]

For the counselor who does get involved, several counseling goals might be helpful.

- Encourage the PWA and the family members to express and openly discuss their fears and other emotions.
- Be aware of misperceptions and make every effort to give accurate information, or to show the counselee how to get this information.
- Help the PWA focus on the future. Often this will involve discussions about dying and death, divine forgiveness, salvation, saying good-bye, and other aspects of grief work. For many, especially those who are in the earlier stages of the disease, planning for the future involves finding as satisfying and fulfilling a lifestyle as possible before the disease takes control. Your work in this area will require some flexibility. "AIDS counseling diverges in many ways from therapy with healthy clients of a similar age. Instead of dealing with long-term concerns," writes one experienced counselor, you focus on "day-to-day issues, here-and-now kinds of things. You are not trying to restructure personality. There is neither the time nor the need. . . . You are focusing on ways to help this person live as completely and satisfyingly and meaningfully as possible given his (or her) particular resources."[44]
- Try to encourage involvement with other people. Social contact reduces the sense of isolation and alienation that people with AIDS often feel. Many counselors encourage group therapy for the PWA. Groups can be safe havens where there can be support, mutual understanding, and sharing of both feelings and effective coping strategies.
- Recognize that each counselee is unique. Each has distinctive features of the disease, each has a repertoire of past coping skills, and each copes with crises in unique ways. The counselor must be prepared to help with these crises frequently and whenever they arise.[45]

- Keep informed of the counselee's medical status. The counselor helps most when he or she works in close cooperation with medical personnel.
- Keep aware of prevention issues. Remind counselees about the ease with which their disease can be transmitted to others. Try to help them find sexual fulfillment in a way that is consistent with good health practices and biblical morality. At times the counselor will be the best resource for counteracting prejudice and misinformation about AIDS among church people.
- Make consistent use of your spiritual resources. Prayer, reading the Scriptures, sharing the good news of God's forgiveness and salvation, pointing the PWA to helpful devotional literature can help to reduce anxiety and help the counselee cope.

In all of this, try to be aware of your own feelings. "Those who care for AIDS victims often suffer right along with the patient. It is very draining to observe the rapid deterioration and death that follows. Counselors must recognize the importance of confidentiality, and acknowledge their own fears and attitudes toward homosexuality."[46] Some counselors fear contagion, are frustrated because they feel so helpless, overidentify with the patient, are uncomfortable facing death and dying, wonder about their own possible homosexual urges, want desperately to help the PWA get better, and even feel irrational anger when the counselee doesn't get well.[47] God can help us handle emotional pressures like this. The help comes in response to prayer, and it also comes through other counselors or friends who can give support and understanding when the counselor is involved in this very difficult but challenging area of work.

BITTERNESS AND THE QUESTION OF WHY

Bitterness is an attitude of anger and resentment over what appears to be a justified grievance. The bitter person often is intent on getting revenge, but instead he or she often gets ulcers, a hypercritical attitude, and rejection from others who don't enjoy being around bitter people. The writer of Hebrews warns against letting bitterness take root because this can "cause trouble and defile many."[48] Most often the person who suffers most from bitterness is the one who clings to this attitude and looks for opportunities to get even.

It is easy to be bitter when life appears to be unjust. When a friend dies of AIDS, a child is born handicapped, a woman suffers every month with PMS, or a bright young person is killed in a senseless accident, it is common to wonder *why.* "Why did this happen?" "Why did it happen now?" "Why did things not turn out like I expected?" "Why do bad things happen to good people?" "Why do some bad people seem to get away with their sinful actions, without getting caught or stopped?"

For centuries believers have struggled with questions like these and their answers, at best, are incomplete. Even the psalmist wondered if God had forgotten his people and let them almost slip away while arrogant nonbelievers appeared to have prosperity, health, callous attitudes of self-centered pride, and freedom from the burdens that most of us face.[49] In time there will be fair and perfect justice, but in the meantime we suffer—and our counselees ask us *why.*

We suffer in part because we belong to a fallen human race. God never promises that good Christians won't ever be murdered, that drunken drivers won't run into our children, or that missionaries in some primitive country will never be treated by a well-meaning doctor who makes an injection with a needle contaminated by the AIDS virus. As long as we live in a fallen world, we will suffer from its fallen condition. There are also times when pain comes because of our own actions. It is easy to be careless, irresponsible, or negligent in caring for our bodies and then experience the consequences.

Even when we don't feel personally responsible, suffering apparently comes to help us grow and mature. For Christians, problems refine our faith, make us more Christlike, teach us about God, and produce perseverance and character.[50] Suffering enables us to understand and care more effectively for others.[51] Does suffering also result from sin? All suffering results ultimately from the fall of humanity into sin, and it seems likely that many of our problems come because of the sufferer's specific sin. It must be emphasized, however, that the Bible explicitly refutes the idea that specific sin automatically brings resultant suffering.[52] People in need often conclude that "God must be punishing me," but such a conclusion is at best based on shaky theological evidence.

In a somewhat folksy illustration, one physician has talked about a man who buys a car and receives the owner's guide that tells about the car's care. The manual warns him against driving when a red light goes on telling him the engine is low on oil. Three months later, the red light comes on. But he is in a hurry, muttering to himself that he will not be restricted by rules imposed by the manufacturer. He will do it his way. The car breaks down because the overheated pistons become fused into the cylinder block. Is this the manufacturer's judgment on the owner of the car? Or is it a result the owner brought on himself by neglecting the manufacturer's warnings?

God's rules, concludes the doctor, are not arbitrary rules made to restrict us. They are designed to make our lives healthier, happier, and more fulfilling. When the laws are broken, people are harmed, including some innocent people. When the sin is confessed, the sinner is forgiven but often the results of that sin—the hurt lives, the maimed bodies, the destroyed property, the broken marriages, the pain in innocent victims—may continue to affect the sin's victims.[53]

From the human perspective, this isn't fair, and we cannot know for certain why people suffer. We do know, however, that bitterness and an attitude of revenge don't make things better. We know too that God is compassionate, all wise, all knowing, absolutely just and ever present. It is not wrong to struggle with *why* questions, and Christian counselors should expect to be involved often with counselees to grapple with these issues.

The ultimate answer, however, is not likely to be found in intellectual debate. It comes from a willingness of counselee and counselor alike to acknowledge the certain truth that the sovereign, compassionate God of the universe is aware of our problems and is in control. He knows why, and ultimately only that really matters.

SUGGESTIONS FOR FURTHER READING

Augsburger, David W. *Pastoral Counseling across Cultures.* Philadelphia: Westminster, 1986.

Crewe, Nancy M., and Irving Kenneth Zola. *Independent Living for Physically Disabled People.* San Francisco: Jossey-Bass, 1983.

Friedrich, JoAnn Cutler. *The Pre-Menstrual Solution.* San Jose, Calif.: Arrow Press, 1987.*

Hesselgrave, David J. *Counseling Cross-Culturally.* Grand Rapids, Mich.: Zondervan, 1984.

Kaslow, Florence W., and Richard I. Ridenour. *The Military Family: Dynamics and Treatment.* New York: Guilford, 1984.

Newman, Gene, and Joni Eareckson Tada. *All God's Children.* Grand Rapids, Mich.: Zondervan, 1987.

Schaeffer, Edith. *Affliction.* Old Tappan, N.J.: Revell, 1978.*

Sneed, Sharon M., and Joe S. McIlhaney, Jr. *PMS: What It Is and What You Can Do About It.* Grand Rapids, Mich.: Baker, 1988.*

Sue, Derald W. *Counseling the Culturally Different: Theory and Practice.* New York: Wiley, 1981.

Yancey, Philip. *Where Is God When It Hurts.* Grand Rapids, Mich.: Zondervan, 1977.*

*** Books marked with an asterisk (*) are especially suited for counselees to read.**

38

Counseling the Counselor

A YOUNG MAN, FILLED WITH ENTHUSIASM AND IDEALISM, once decided to list the good things in life. His tally was long and impressive. Health, love, beauty, talent, riches, fame—all were there, along with other less-obvious ingredients that would seem to make life complete. When the inventory was completed, its author proudly showed it to an older friend and spiritual mentor. "I was trying to impress him with my wisdom and the universality of my interests," the young list maker wrote later. In the corner of the friend's old eyes, however, there appeared some wrinkles of amusement.

"An excellent list," he said, reading it slowly and with care. "It is well digested in content and set down in not unreasonable order. But it appears, my young friend, that you have omitted the most important element of all." One ingredient was missing. Without it, according to the older man, the entire list would be a meaningless and intolerable burden.

As the young man watched, his friend took a pencil stub and crossed out the entire page. At the bottom he wrote three words: *peace of mind.*

"This is the gift that God reserves for his special protégés," he said. "Many have beauty, talent, wealth, and even fame. But most people wait, often in vain and sometimes through their whole lives, hoping to know a deep sense of inner peace."[1]

When he talked with his disciples before his crucifixion, Jesus gave no indication that his followers could expect wealth, beauty, economic security, or acclaim. He never promised freedom from suffering, persecution, sickness, discouragement, vocational uncertainty, or financial strain—but he did promise peace: "Peace I leave with you; my peace I give to you. I do not give to you as the world gives. Do not let your hearts be troubled and do not be afraid."[2]

Several years later, while incarcerated in an uncomfortable prison, Paul mentioned his contentment despite the circumstances.[3] In a setting that could have stimulated intense anxiety, discouragement, and self-pity, the apostle instead encouraged his fellow believers to rejoice and to experience the peace of God: "Rejoice in the Lord always. I will say it again: Rejoice! Let your gentleness be evident to all. The Lord is near. Do not be anxious about anything, but in everything, by prayer and petition, with thanksgiving, present your requests to God. And the peace of God, which transcends all understanding, will guard your hearts and your minds in Christ Jesus."[4]

Perhaps it is true that nothing in life is more valuable, more sought, and more often missed than God-given peace of mind. Trapped in the turmoil of their confusing conflicts and pressing problems, many of our counselees have no inner sense of peace. Yet even more tragic, many counselors fare no better.

Christian counseling can have a variety of goals, but at its core is the effort to help people find peace with God, peace with others, and peace with themselves. Sometimes this peace comes closer when people admit their problems and talk about their feelings, acquire better interpersonal and communication skills, change their attitudes and control harmful thought patterns, get insights into their own actions, and learn how to change their ways of doing things. "The pursuit of peace does not include an easygoing, peace-at-any-price kind of attitude; it does not include capitulating to wrong or injustice just for the sake of maintaining appearances."[5] Sometimes we courageously must face and cope with the conflicts that block or disturb our peace.

Ultimate peace, for the counselee and for the counselor, comes from God. It comes to those who cast their anxieties on the Lord, who present their requests to God with prayer and thanksgiving, who let their minds dwell on thoughts that are pure and Christ-honoring, who resist satanic influences, and who live in ways that would please Christ.[6] Lasting peace comes from the Holy Spirit, the comforter.[7] Like all traits of godliness, peace is acquired through spiritual exercise and discipline—"meditating upon and applying God's word under the direction of our teacher, the Holy Spirit."[8]

THE COUNSELOR'S SPIRITUALITY

In his work as a pastor, Richard Exley has helped many people through times of crisis. "There's nothing in life more meaningful than working with God in the reconstruction of a shattered life," he wrote. "Some call it *counseling*. I call it *ministry*, and it's always been a team effort among the three of us—God, the person and myself."[9]

Your perspective on counseling may be different, but most of us can identify with Exley's observation about people in crises.

> If you've lived for any length of time, you've probably had opportunity to see the different ways people respond to adversity, The same tragedy can make one person better and the other person bitter. What makes the difference? Resources. Inner resources developed across a lifetime through spiritual disciplines. If you haven't worshiped regularly in the sunshine of your life, you probably won't be able to worship in the darkness. If you haven't been intimate with God in life's ordinariness, it's not likely that you will know how or where to mind Him should life hand you some real hardships. But by the same token, if you have worshiped often and regularly, then you will undoubtedly worship well in the hour of your greatest need.[10]

Many counselors burn out because they give out. Hour after hour, day after day, we are asked to pour out our insights, sensitivity, compassion, healing skills, and inner energies. We see the needs and feel the pain. We want to heal and long to help. So we give repeatedly, with the noblest of motives, until we run dry. Sometimes overnight, almost without warning, we discover that there is nothing left to give. The Christian counselor, once filled with Christian compassion, finds that he or she is spiritually empty. There are no more inner resources.

Nevertheless needy people keep asking for our help. Like the poor who always will be with us,[11] there always will be those who are hurting, needy, and searching for peace. Most of us want to help. That may be why we are involved in counseling or have spent many hours working through the pages of a book like this.

No one person can do everything, and nobody can give indefinitely. Trying to do so leads to physical burnout and spiritual dryness. To prevent this or to help ourselves when the demands of others have left us empty, we need rejuvenation. It comes from several sources.

(a) Pulling Back. Several years ago a famous cardiologist was much in demand as a speaker. He traveled all over the country giving lectures on lifestyle and how to avoid heart attacks. One night his weary body gave out, and he collapsed with a heart attack in the middle of his speech.

How easily we give guidance to others but fail to heed our own words of advice. How quickly we spot hypocrisy in the lives of some Christian leaders but fail to notice our own double lives. How freely do we tell others to rest, to exercise, to avoid overeating or overwork, but despite our best intentions, we don't follow our own stress-reduction programs and then wonder why we collapse.

Henri J. M. Nouwen is a priest, professor, and counselor whose books contain a wealth of insight. In *The Genesee Diary* Nouwen describes how from the midst of a busy teaching, writing, and counseling schedule, he decided to retreat for a few months to a Trappist monastery. His desire to serve God had become a tiring job. He had become so much a prisoner of people's expectations that he felt weighed down and far removed from the inner freedom and peace of mind about which he had been writing. So Nouwen decided to step back.

Stepping back was not easy. "I had succeeded in surrounding myself with so many classes to prepare, lectures to give, articles to finish, people to meet, phone calls to make, and letters to answer, that I had come quite close to believing that I was indispensable." Was there a quiet stream underneath all the busyness of his world, Nouwen wondered. "Is there a still point where my life is anchored and from which I can reach out with hope and courage and confidence?"[12] Nouwen pulled back from his heavy schedule so he could ponder these questions and reestablish a closer communion with God.

In the midst of a busy ministry, Jesus took time to pull away.[13] At times he prayed on these miniretreats. Sometimes he apparently talked to his friends and perhaps there were times when he simply rested. People were looking for him and many needed healing, but he took time for the rejuvenation he needed.

(b) Priorities. When Simon and his companions found Jesus, they exclaimed "Everyone is looking for you!" The Lord's reply must have been surprising. "Let us go somewhere else," Jesus said.[14] He was not disinterested in the people who sought him, but he had thought through his priorities. He had come to preach in different locations and he was willing to say no to some demands so he could say yes to others.[15]

It isn't easy to make decisions about our priorities. Sometimes this involves saying no, and that can make us feel guilty, especially when fellow believers, prospective counselees, fund raisers, or others make us feel guilty. Once again, Exley has a healthy perspective.

> We must live God-centered, God-directed lives, not need-centered lives. Compassion born only out of sympathy for suffering humanity risks both the extremes of fanaticism and burnout. Healing compassion, on the other hand, combines the love and guidance of the Creator with a genuine concern for the hurting in our world. If our only motivation is need, we will be swallowed up, we will risk becoming part of the problem rather than part of the solution. Our only hope is to let God define our area of responsibility and then to live within our limits, both emotionally and physically. It's not easy to do, but it's the only hope we have. The alternatives—all consuming fanaticism or self-centered apathy—are not alternatives at all.[16]

It is liberating to admit that no one person can do everything and that God doesn't expect any of us to meet all the needs of humanity. Taped on my computer is a little note that says "I have all the time I need to do all God intends me to do." I can't identify the source of this wise statement, but it reminds me frequently to reevaluate my work. Each of us must seek the Holy Spirit's guidance in establishing our priorities. This involves using our God-given brains to ponder what we can and cannot do. Often it means seeking the wisdom and guidance of other dedicated believers who know us well.

(c) People. Those of us who work with people often want to get away from people at the end of a busy day. Retreat of course is healthy, but sometimes we make the mistake of retreating from those who are willing and able to help refurbish our dwindling supply of resources. Family members, close friends, colleagues, fellow believers can all be helpful, especially if they allow us to be ourselves without having to do off-the-job counseling. Some professionals take the time to teach, not because this is profitable financially, but because there is stimulation and refreshment from interacting with students.

Other people can also help with accountability. Christian spirituality, personal integrity, and mental stability rarely (if ever) survive in isolation. The Scriptures call us to live in union with others, spurring one another on "toward love and good deeds." We need to encourage each other,[17] but we also must hold one another accountable for our actions, lifestyles, and morals. The church is strewn with thousands of former Christian leaders (including a large number of counselors) who were accountable only to themselves and who fell into immoral, illegal, unethical, and foolish actions as a result. "So if you think you are standing firm, be careful that you don't fall."[18]

Sometimes, you may sense the need to find a counselor for yourself, but such a person may be hard to find. It is difficult and humbling to admit that "I, who am a counselor, needs counseling." You may know all of the other counselors in your area and it might be difficult to select one with whom you can talk about yourself. Some professionals look for a counselor who is some distance away, but you may want to start by discussing even this decision with a respected colleague who is closer to home. Over a decade ago, Louis McBurney wrote a book with the insightful title *Every Pastor Needs a Pastor.* Is it equally true at times that every counselor needs a counselor?

(d) Power. When Jesus trained the twelve disciples and sent them out for on-the-job training, he gave them power so they could speak and heal.[19] The disciples were not to serve in their own strength. They got their power and authority from the Lord himself.

There is no research evidence to support this conclusion, but it seems that many counselors who call themselves Christian try to find their greatest strength in counseling theories and techniques. Personal prayer and reflection on the Scriptures is of low priority. Corporate worship is of minor importance, and there is little time for uninterrupted confession and communication with God. It is not surprising that these counselors have little to give spiritually.

Several years after his sojourn in the Genesee Monastery, Nouwen reflected on the place of prayer in the helper's life. "You cannot consider yourself a witness for God's presence," he wrote,

> when your own life is cluttered with material possessions, your belly is overfull, and your mind crowded with worries about what to do with what you have. . . . In our utilitarian culture, in which we suffer from a collective compulsion to do something practical, helpful, or useful, and to make a contribution that can give us a sense of worth, contemplative prayer . . . is not useful or practical but a wasting of time for God. It cuts a hole in our busyness and reminds us and others that it is God and not we who creates and sustains the world. . . .
>
> Once we really know him in prayer then we can live in this world without a need to cling to anyone for self-affirmation, and then we can let the abundance of God's love be the source of all our ministry.[20]

Consistent prayer and daily meditation on the Word of God enable us to know God, to obey him, and to serve him more fully as his servants and counselors. The counselor draws consistently on his past training and experiences. We use a variety of techniques in our counseling and help people work toward a variety of goals. If counseling is to be Christian and maximally effective, we need to be servants who are guided and empowered by the Holy Spirit, and strengthened day by day with the insights of Scripture and persisting periods of prayer.

The Counselor's Lifestyle

The Book of James is intensely practical, but its message is sometimes disturbing: "If anyone considers himself to be religious and yet does not keep a tight rein on his tongue, he deceives himself and his religion is useless" (James 1:26). "Religion that God our Father accepts as pure and faultless is this: to look after orphans and widows in their distress and to keep oneself from being polluted by the world."[21] Perhaps there can be no better theme verse for counselors. Our lives are to be characterized by helping and holiness. We are responsible for caring actions and Christlike living.

Counselor training programs emphasize helping and caring skills. Often there is mention of warmth, empathy, and genuineness, three basic counselor characteristics. Rarely do we hear mention of personal holiness, the importance of keeping oneself from being polluted by the world.

Is this possible? Jesus did not expect that his followers would withdraw from the world,[22] but as long as we live on this polluted planet our minds and actions are likely to be affected. Christians who claim to be sinless are fooling themselves. On a consistent basis we need to confess our sins and to experience God's forgiveness.[23]

None of this lowers God's standards. "God did not call us to be impure but to live a holy life." Our lifestyles and characteristic behaviors should be exemplary and likely to win the respect of outsiders. We are to "make every effort to live in peace with all men and to be holy."[24] How can this be done? We can live this style of life if we strive for an attitude of humility and a determination to be obedient. We live holy lives by thinking and acting in conformity to the moral precepts of the Bible, but in contrast to the sinful ways of the world.[25] If we are to maximize our counseling effectiveness and counteract the barbs of our critics, we must strive for holiness, keeping control over our own lifestyles and ways of thinking.

The Counselor's Relevancy

During their years in college, seminary, or graduate school, students are surrounded by books and usually well acquainted with the library. Their professors (at least the good ones) strive to keep abreast of recent and emerging developments in their fields, and these new ideas often find their way into lectures and discussions with students. Then comes that happy day when the students graduate. Clutching their diplomas, these people scatter, are absorbed into the job market, and lose contact with the old alma mater.[26]

Unless we take precautions to prevent this, many of us get involved in our counseling and other work and lose contact with emerging developments in our fields. Some pastors get caught up in the challenges of ministry and rarely read. Counselors can get so busy in their therapeutic work that they become oblivious to professional issues or to current research that could have practical counseling implications. People whose work takes them to isolated communities or to some countries overseas feel far removed from the mainstream trends in their professions. How then does one keep up to date without wasting a lot of time and energy searching for resources that are relevant? There can be several answers.

(a) Conferences and Seminars. Attendance at a meeting for professional counselors, pastoral counselors, lay people, or others may consume a large block of time, but the formal presentations can be helpful and often there is great value in the informal interaction with other participants. Whenever you attend a conference, look to see if there is a display of books or other resources that might be helpful.

(b) Journals. Most of these are designed for professionals and many have a specific focus; for example, *Child Development, Journal of Personality and Social Psychology,* or *Journal of Experimental Psychology.* Others, such as *Journal of Psychology and Theology* or *Journal of Psychology and Christianity,* have a Christian orientation and deal more often with issues that interest counselors.

(c) Books. Every year more than fifty thousand new books appear in print. Most of course deal with issues other than counseling, but if we add all the self-help, counseling, and psychology-psychiatry books together there are more titles on the market than any one person can master. Even libraries have trouble keeping up to date. Books may have catchy titles and great promises on their covers, but every reader knows that many of these volumes are poorly researched, badly written, largely impractical, sometimes more sensational than accurate, and not worth buying or reading. It is difficult to plow through the new offerings to find the gems.

The search, however, is not hopeless. To find relevant titles, look at the advertisements in Christian magazines or professional journals. Skim the book reviews because these can alert you to other helpful titles. If there are no good bookstores in your area, write to one or two publishers and ask for a catalog so you can order books by mail. Whenever you are near a bookstore, take some time to browse.

As you look, remember that covers (including the descriptions on the covers) are designed to attract buyers; the old adage is still true—you can't judge a book by its cover. You can look for the author's qualifications, however. If the writer is a teacher, what is his or her institutional affiliation? Might that tell you something about the author's perspective? Has the book been endorsed by someone whom you respect? Who is the publisher? Publishers are not all the same. Some publish better quality books than others. Many have a theological orientation that will be reflected in the books. By asking other readers and by relying on some of your own experiences, you are likely to find publishers that tend to publish books that are most helpful for your work.

On occasion you will see a book in a library or hear an author interview that may interest you in purchasing a helpful book. Many professionals in the publishing industry agree, in addition, that word of mouth is the best advertising. Ask other counselors what they are reading and finding helpful. The books they read may be helpful to you as well.

(d) Other Resources. Audio cassettes, continuing education and correspondence courses (often available on videotape), newsletters, radio and television programs, and courses or lectures given by local educational institutions are among the ways that enable counselors to keep up.

Each of these resources can provide information. Many provide helpful contact with other counselors as well. Just as the spiritually dry counselor is not very able to help people spiritually, so the professionally outdated and emotionally drained counselor is unlikely to be effective in helping people cope with the various problems of life. The input of information from other people and resources can keep us mentally alert, professionally stimulated, and therapeutically more effective.

The Counselor's Legacy

"The dictionary is the only place where success comes before work." This statement, attributed to journalist Arthur Brisbane, recently appeared in bold letters across the top of a newspaper advertisement. The advertisers were business people, but the quotation could apply to almost every area of life, including counseling. In this world, if we want to be successful, we have to work—diligently and consistently.

Some workers can see the benefits of their labors almost immediately, but that isn't true of counselors. Often we work for many weeks without making any apparent progress and sometimes our counselees get discouraged (or threatened by the counseling process) and drop out. At times every counselor wonders if he or she is doing anything worthwhile.

The counselor's work and success is measured in changed lives. Sometimes we see these changes; often we do not. Sometimes we are encouraged by our work;

frequently we are not. Some professionals are acclaimed and affirmed publicly for their counseling successes; most of us are not. Instead we work day after day and hope we are making an impact on the lives of others—but we aren't always sure. One hundred years from now, if the world survives until then, most of us will have been forgotten by everybody except God. He knows our minds and is intimately acquainted with all our ways. He who is sovereign and omniscient, knows our motives, is familiar with our frustrations, forgives our failures and remembers our successes. In the light of eternity, his evaluation of our work is the only one that counts.

When James and John came to Jesus asking for positions of prominence in his kingdom, the Lord taught us all a valuable lesson.[27] In this world, he said, the most prominent people lord it over others and like to have authority. The believer, however, lives by a different standard. From God's perspective, the greatest people are those who are servants: humility comes before greatness and servanthood comes before success.

When we close the pages of this book and return to our counseling rooms, we will be involved with difficult and sometimes demanding work. As we grow older, hopefully each of us will leave a legacy of lives that have changed, not because of our efforts alone, but because God has allowed us to be his instruments in helping those with whom we counsel.

The ultimate legacy of any Christian counselor is to be a faithful servant—giving of ourselves to honor God and to serve him as we serve others. There can be no better goal for counselors and no greater mark of success.

Notes

Chapter 1 *The Church and Counseling*

1. Wayne E. Oates, ed., *An Introduction to Pastoral Counseling* (Nashville: Broadman, 1959), vi. In this quotation, the generic "he" is used in referring to pastors. I am well aware that many women are in the pastoral ministry. Apart from quotations like this one, the following pages will avoid masculine pronouns in referring to pastors.

2. See, e.g., Dave Hunt and T. A. McMahon, *The Seduction of Christianity* (Eugene, Oreg.: Harvest House, 1985); and Martin Bobgan and Deidre Bobgan, *Psychoheresy: The Psychological Seduction of Christianity* (Santa Barbara, Calif.: EastGate Publishers, 1987). I have tried to answer some of the criticisms of these authors; see Gary R. Collins, *Can You Trust Psychology?* (Downers Grove, Ill.: InterVarsity, 1988).

3. J. G. Swank, Jr., "Counseling Is a Waste of Time," *Christianity Today* (July 1977): 27. For an alternative point of view see David B. Jackson, "Counseling as Ministry," *Christian Counselor* (Winter 1986): 1–3.

4. Rom. 15:1; Gal. 6:2.

5. As an example of the need for helping, notice the number of times that the words "one another" appear in the New Testament epistles. We are instructed to build up, accept, admonish, be devoted to, be at peace with, serve, bear the burdens of, be kind to, teach, encourage, confess our faults to, pray for, and love one another (Rom. 14:19; 15:7, 14; 12:10, 18; Gal. 5:13; 6:2; Eph. 4:32; Col. 3:16; 1 Thess. 5:11; James 5:16; 1 John 4:7). While this activity extends beyond counseling, it also includes much of what is involved in the counseling process.

6. Timothy Foster, *Called to Counsel* (Nashville: Oliver-Nelson, 1986).

7. See J. A. Durlak, "Comparative Effectiveness of Paraprofessional and Professional Helpers," *Psychological Bulletin* 86 (1979): 80–92; and Gerard Egan, *The Skilled Helper: A Systematic Approach to Effective Helping,* 3d ed. (Monterey, Calif.: Brooks/Cole, 1986).

8. These are known as the four pastoral functions. For a historical overview, see William A. Clebsch and Charles R. Jaekle, *Pastoral Care in Historical Perspective* (Englewood Cliffs, N.J.: Prentice-Hall, 1964).

9. For more detailed discussions, see William E. Hulme, *Pastoral Care & Counseling* (Minneapolis: Augsburg, 1981); Thomas C. Oden, *Pastoral Theology* (New York: Harper & Row, 1983); and William B. Oglesby, Jr., *Biblical Themes for Pastoral Care* (Nashville: Abingdon, 1980).

10. See note 5 above.

11. For an excellent introduction to pastoral psychotherapy, see chap. 15 of Howard Clinebell, *Basic Types of Pastoral Care and Counseling* (Nashville: Abingdon, 1984); see also David G. Benner, *Psychotherapy and the Spiritual Quest* (Grand Rapids, Mich.: Baker, 1988); LeRoy Aden and J. Harold Ellens, eds., *The Church and Pastoral Care* (Grand Rapids, Mich.: Baker, 1988); and Richard Dayringer, *The Heart of Pastoral Counseling* (Grand Rapids, Mich.: Zondervan, 1988). A new *Journal of Pastoral Psychotherapy* began publication in 1987, published by Haworth Press, 28 East 22d Street, New York, N.Y. 10010-6194. It should be added, perhaps, that some writers have criticized the idea of pastoral psychotherapy; see, e.g., Richard A. Bollinger, "Differences between Pastoral Counseling and Psychotherapy," *Bulletin of the Menninger Clinic* 49 (1985): 371–86.
12. This discussion is adapted from chap. 17 in Gary R. Collins, ed., *Helping People Grow: Practical Approaches to Christian Counseling* (Ventura, Calif.: Regal, 1980).
13. Ibid., 325.
14. John R. Finney and H. Newton Malony, "Contemplative Prayer and Its Use in Psychotherapy: A Theoretical Model," *Journal of Psychology and Theology* 13 (Fall 1985): 172–81.
15. William R. Miller and Kathleen A. Jackson, *Practical Psychology for Pastors* (Englewood Cliffs, N.J.: Prentice-Hall, 1985).
16. C. H. Patterson, *Theories of Counseling and Psychotherapy* (New York: Harper & Row, 1973), 535–36.
17. These are among the characteristics listed by Michael E. Cavanaugh, *The Counseling Experience: A Theoretical and Practical Approach* (Monterey, Calif.: Brooks/Cole, 1982).
18. For a review of research on counselor characteristics, see Sol L. Garfield and Allen E. Bergin, eds., *Handbook of Psychotherapy and Behavior Change: An Empirical Analysis,* 3d ed. (New York: Wiley, 1986).
19. Jay E. Adams, *How to Help People Change* (Grand Rapids, Mich.: Zondervan, 1986), vii.
20. John 14.
21. Matt. 28:20.
22. Gal. 5:22.
23. John 14:16, 26; 16:7–15.
24. For a more detailed discussion of the Holy Spirit and counseling, see Marvin G. Gilbert and Raymond T. Brock, eds., *The Holy Spirit and Counseling: Theology and Theory* (Peabody, Mass.: Hendrickson Publishers, 1985).
25. Matt. 16:18.
26. See esp. Acts 2:42–47; 4:32–35.
27. Richard Almond, *The Healing Community: Dynamics of the Therapeutic Milieu* (New York: Jason Aronson, 1974), xxi.
28. Leigh C. Bishop, "Healing in the Koinonia," *Journal of Psychology and Theology* 13 (Spring 1985): 12–20.
29. For a discussion of belongingness in counseling, see William T. Kirwin, *Biblical Concepts for Christian Counseling* (Grand Rapids, Mich.: Baker, 1984).
30. Matt. 28:19–20.

31. For an in-depth consideration of Christian fellowship see Jerry Bridges, *True Fellowship* (Colorado Springs: NavPress, 1985).
32. For this threefold concept I am grateful to Theodore Olsen, who teaches practical theology at Trinity Evangelical Divinity School.
33. Gal. 6:2, 10.
34. William Kirk Kilpatrick, *Psychological Seduction: The Failure of Modern Psychology* (Nashville: Nelson, 1983), 23.
35. Martin and Deidre Bobgan, *The Psychological Way/The Spiritual Way* (Minneapolis: Bethany House, 1979), 11.
36. Jay Adams, *The Big Umbrella* (Philadelphia: Presbyterian and Reformed Publishing Co., 1972), 23–24.
37. I attempted to deal with some of the criticisms of psychology in Collins, *Can You Trust Psychology?*; see also, Mark R. McMinn and James D. Foster, "The Mind Doctors: Questions to Ask on the Road to Mental Health," *Christianity Today,* 8 April 1988, 16–20.

Chapter 2 *The Counselor and Counseling*

1. Paul Welter, *How to Help a Friend* (Wheaton, Ill.: Tyndale, 1978), 35–36.
2. Several years ago one writer wrote a book in which he suggested that in-depth counseling is really "the purchase of friendship" by people who need a "professional friend"; see William Schofield, *Psychotherapy: The Purchase of Friendship* (Englewood Cliffs, N.J.: Prentice-Hall, 1964.)
3. Erich Fromm, *The Art of Loving* (New York: Bantam, 1956), 4–5. I am grateful to Barry Estadt for applying this illustration to the art of counseling; see Barry K. Estadt, *Pastoral Counseling* (Englewood Cliffs, N.J.: Prentice-Hall, 1984).
4. For a further discussion of this issue see Gerard Corey, Marianne Schneider Corey, and Patrick Callanan, *Issues and Ethics in the Helping Professions,* 3d ed. (Monterey, Calif.: Brooks/Cole, 1988), 33–43.
5. Fromm, *Art of Loving,* 93.
6. Rom. 12:7; Eph. 4:11.
7. Maurice E. Wagner, "Hazards to Effective Pastoral Counseling, Part One," *Journal of Psychology and Theology* 1 (July 1973): 35–41; Part Two, 1 (October 1973): 40–47.
8. Ibid., pt. 1, 37.
9. For an overview of this method see chap. 7, "Brief Counseling," in Gary R. Collins, *Innovative Approaches to Counseling* (Waco, Tex.: Word, 1986). A more complete discussion is given by Richard A. Wells, *Planned Short-term Treatment* (New York: Free Press, 1982). For a more popular discussion see "Quick-Fix Therapy," *Newsweek,* 26 May 1986, 74–76.
10. Corey et al., *Issues and Ethics,* 38–39.
11. Wagner, pt. 2, 46–47. At this point Wagner quotes 2 Tim. 2:24–26.
12. William E. Hulme, "The Counselee Who Exploits the Counselor," *Pastoral Psychology* (June 1962): 31–35.
13. For an excellent discussion of these issues see Corey et al., *Issues and Ethics,* 46–53.

14. A. F. X. Calabrese, "Countertransference," in *Baker Encyclopedia of Psychology*, ed. David G. Benner (Grand Rapids, Mich.: Baker, 1985), 254–55.
15. Armand M. Nicholi, Jr., ed., *The Harvard Guide to Modern Psychiatry* (Cambridge, Mass.: Harvard University Press, 1978), 9.
16. Adapted from Eugene Kennedy, *On Becoming a Counselor* (New York: Seabury, 1977).
17. Nathaniel S. Lehrman, "The Normality of Sexual Feelings in Pastoral Counseling," *Pastoral Psychology* 105 (June 1960): 49.
18. Charles L. Rassieur, *The Problem Clergymen Don't Talk About* (Philadelphia: Westminster, 1976).
19. The adverse effects on counselees have been documented by Nicholi, *Harvard Guide to Modern Psychiatry*.
20. Phil. 4:8.
21. 1 Cor. 10:12. For further discussion of these issues see Randy Alcorn, "Strategies to Keep from Falling," *Leadership* 9 (Winter 1988): 42–47.
22. 1 John 1:9.
23. Louis McBurney, *Counseling Christian Workers* (Waco, Tex.: Word, 1986), 268–70.
24. Ibid., 269. These issues are discussed further by Andre Bustanoby, "Counseling the Seductive Female," *Leadership* 9 (Winter 1988): 48–54.
25. Touching and hugging in themselves can be therapeutic, but the counselor should ponder how the counselee might interpret this contact. Ask yourself if you tend to touch some counselees more than others. Why do you do this? Is touching a way of meeting your needs? For a popular book in defense of touching see John R. Hornbrook and Dorothy Fanberg Bakker, *The Miracle Touch* (Lafayette, La.: Huntington, 1985).
26. 1 Thess. 5:22 KJV.
27. 1 Cor. 10:12.
28. Viktor Frankl, *Man's Search for Meaning: An Introduction to Logotherapy* (New York: Pocket Books, 1963), 206–7.
29. 1 John 4:4.
30. Rassieur found this in his survey of pastors. Reported in *The Problem Clergymen Don't Talk About,* 32–34, and elsewhere; see also Michael E. Phillips, "What I Can, and Can't, Discuss at Home," *Leadership* 9 (Spring 1988): 52–56.
31. Ibid., 131.
32. Ibid., 116–17.
33. A letter to the state or provincial licensing office usually will bring you information about licensing laws. In some places, a person cannot use the term "psychologist" or "counselor" unless he or she has passed state licensing laws and/or been certified by the government. Such requirements differ widely.
34. For additional information on these issues see Corey et al., *Issues and Ethics,* and John C. Hoffman, *Ethical Confrontation in Counseling* (Chicago: University of Chicago Press, 1979). Neither of these books is written from a Christian evangelical perspective, but both are thought provoking and helpful.
35. Jerry Edelwich with Archie Brodsky, *Burnout: Stages of Disillusionment in the Helping Professions* (New York: Human Science Press, 1980), 14.

36. For more detailed information on burnout see Charles F. Warnath and John F. Shelton, "The Ultimate Disappointment: The Burned-Out Counselor," *Personnel and Guidance Journal* 55 (December 1976): 172–95; C. Maslach, *Burnout: The Cost of Caring* (Englewood Cliffs, N.J.: Prentice-Hall, 1982); Herbert Freudenberger and Geraldine Richelson, *Burnout: The High Cost of Achievement* (New York: Bantam, 1981); Charles Perry, *Why Christians Burn Out* (Nashville: Thomas Nelson, 1982); Raymond T. Brock, "Avoiding Burnout Through Spiritual Renewal," in *The Holy Spirit and Counseling,* ed. Marvin G. Gilbert and Raymond T. Brock (Peabody, Mass.: Hendrickson Publishers, 1985), 88–102; and Victor Savicki and Eric Cooley, "The Relationship of Work Environment and Client Contact to Burnout in Mental Health Professionals," *Journal of Counseling and Development* 65 (January 1987): 249–52.
37. McBurney discusses this further in *Counseling Christian Workers,* 179–81.
38. Ibid.
39. Rom. 8:9–10; 1 Cor. 3:16; 6:19.
40. Allen Groff, "The Devotional Life of the Counselor," in *The Holy Spirit,* 67.
41. Isa. 9:6.
42. Ps. 55:22; 1 Pet. 5:7.
43. For an excellent discussion of fellowship see Jerry Bridges, *True Fellowship* (Colorado Springs: NavPress, 1985).
44. One pastoral counselor has called this "collegiality"—close relationships with supportive colleagues; see in Estadt, *Pastoral Counseling,* 76–79. For a more theological perspective on spiritual friends see Kenneth Leech, *Soul Friend: The Practice of Christian Spirituality* (New York: Harper & Row, 1980); and Tilden H. Edwards, *Spiritual Friend* (New York: Paulist Press, 1980). The importance of soul friends is discussed from a more psychological perspective by David G. Benner, *Psychotherapy and the Spiritual Quest* (Grand Rapids, Mich.: Baker, 1988),
45. Sumner H. Garte and Mark L. Rosenblum, "Lighting Fires in Burned-Out Counselors," *Personnel and Guidance Journal* (November 1978): 158–60.

Chapter 3 *The Core of Counseling*

1. See Job 1–2, 32–37.
2. This research is summarized by Everett L. Worthington, Jr., "Religious Counseling: A Review of Published Empirical Research," *Journal of Counseling and Development* 64 (1986): 421–31.
3. For a summary of some of this research see Sol L. Garfield and Allen E. Bergin, eds., *Handbook of Psychotherapy and Behavior Change,* 3d ed. (New York: Wiley, 1986).
4. Ibid.
5. Reported in Howard Clinebell, *Basic Types of Pastoral Care and Counseling* (Nashville: Abingdon, 1984), 103.
6. John 10:10.
7. John 3:16.
8. This term was suggested by Francis A. Schaeffer, *The God Who Is There* (Chicago: Inter-Varsity, 1968).

9. It should be recognized, of course, that some counselees will accept our psychological help but reject our Christian gospel. Jesus must have experienced this with the ten lepers (Luke 17:11–19), only one of whom is described as coming to have faith in Christ.

It should also be added that in most secular counseling settings, the Christian counselor is forbidden to present a Christian message. In such cases the Christian's beliefs are likely to come out in more indirect ways. Sometimes the counselee will ask about religion and the Christian can discuss the meaning of discipleship. If even this is forbidden, some Christians feel they can no longer work under such limiting conditions. These are issues that pastors and counselors in Christian counseling centers rarely have to face.

10. Steven A. Hamon, "Beyond Self-Actualization: Comments on the Life and Death of Stephen the Martyr," *Journal of Psychology and Theology* 5 (1977): 292–99.

11. Clinebell, *Basic Types of Pastoral Care and Counseling,* 103–37.

12. Ibid., 106.

13. Carl Jung, *Modern Man in Search of a Soul* (New York: Harcourt, Brace & Co., 1933), 269.

14. Wayne E. Oates, *The Presence of God in Pastoral Counseling* (Waco, Tex.: Word, 1986); see also Alan A. Nelson and William P. Wilson, "The Ethics of Sharing Religious Faith in Psychotherapy," *Journal of Psychology and Theology* 12 (Spring 1984): 15–23.

15. Gerald Corey, Marianne Schneider Corey, and Patrick Callanan, *Issues and Ethics in the Helping Professions,* 3d ed. (Monterey, Calif.: Brooks/Cole, 1988), 116–18.

16. This term is used by Leroy G. Baruth and Charles H. Huber, *Counseling and Psychotherapy: Theoretical Analyses and Skills Applications* (Columbus: Charles E. Merrill, 1985), 171–98.

17. Helen Harris Perlman, *Relationship: The Heart of Helping People* (Chicago: University of Chicago Press, 1979); see also Lawrence M. Brammer, *The Helping Relationship* (Englewood Cliffs, N.J.: Prentice-Hall, 1979), C. H. Patterson, *Relationship Counseling and Psychotherapy* (New York: Harper & Row, 1974), Bernard G. Guerney, Jr., *Relationship Enhancement* (San Francisco: Jossey-Bass, 1977), and Arthur W. Combs and Donald L. Avila, *Helping Relationships: Basic Concepts for the Helping Professions,* 3d ed. (Boston: Allyn and Bacon, 1985).

18. C. R. Rogers et al., *The Therapeutic Relationship and Its Impact* (Madison: University of Wisconsin Press, 1967).

19. Gal. 5:22–23.

20. 1 Corinthians 13.

21. Gordon W. Allport, *The Individual and His Religion* (New York: Macmillan, 1950), 90.

22. Bruno Bettleheim, *Love Is Not Enough: The Treatment of Emotionally Disturbed Children* (Glencoe, Ill.: Free Press, 1950); see also James C. Dobson, *Love Must Be Tough* (Waco, Tex.: Word, 1983).

23. This is emphasized in two excellent books by Paul Welter, *How to Help a Friend* (Wheaton, Ill.: Tyndale, 1978), and *Connecting with a Friend: Eighteen Proven Counseling Skills to Help You Help Others* (Wheaton, Ill.: Tyndale, 1985);

see also Richard P. Walters, *How to Be a Friend: People Want to Be Friends With . . .* (Ventura, Calif.: Regal Books, 1981).

24. Adapted from A. M. Nicholi, Jr., "The Therapist-Patient Relationship," in *The Harvard Guide to Modern Psychiatry,* ed. A. M. Nicholi, Jr. (Cambridge, Mass.: Belknap Press of Harvard University Press, 1978), 12.

25. In his helpful little book, *When They Ask for Bread: Pastoral Care and Counseling in Everyday Places* (Atlanta: John Knox, 1978), George Bennett writes that the first principle in counseling is to find out what people are asking. What do they really want? What do they really mean by the words they are using?

26. The idea of "telling your story" is proposed in a book that has become a standard manual for counselor training; see Gerard Egan, *The Skilled Helper,* 3d ed. (Monterey, Calif.: Brooks/Cole, 1986).

27. Richard Walters is one of several writers who has proposed a similar series of goals. Walters calls his approach HELP: Hello (connecting with the counselee), Exploration (exploring and clarifying issues), Learning (establishing goals and planning for the future), and Progress (progressing toward one's goals). The fifth phase, Stopping, could be added; see Walters, *Practicing the Skills of Boldness* (Boulder, Colo.: Christian Helpers, 1982).

28. See, e.g., Raymond Corsini, ed., *Current Psychotherapies,* 3d ed. (Itasca, Ill.: Peacock, 1984); Gerald Corey, *Theory and Practice of Counseling and Psychotherapy,* 3d ed. (Monterey, Calif.: Brooks/Cole, 1986), or C. H. Patterson, *Theories of Counseling and Psychotherapy,* 4th ed. (New York: Harper & Row, 1986). For a survey of Christian approaches see Gary R. Collins, ed., *Helping People Grow: Practical Approaches to Christian Counseling* (Ventura, Calif.: Regal, 1980); also Everett L. Worthington, Jr. and Suzanne R. Gascoyne, "Preferences of Christians and Non-Christians for Five Christian Counselors' Treatment Plans: A Partial Replication and Extension," *Journal of Psychology and Theology* 13 (Spring 1985): 29–41.

29. D. Smith, "Trends in Counseling and Psychotherapy," *American Psychologist* 37 (1982): 802–9.

30. For a moving account of this issue, written by Hinckley's parents, see Jack Hinckley and Joan Hinckley, *Breaking Points* (Grand Rapids, Mich.: Zondervan, 1985).

31. For further information see Ralph Slovenko, "Law and Psychiatry," in *Comprehensive Textbook of Psychiatry/IV,* ed. Harold I. Kaplan and Benjamin J. Sadock, 4th ed. (Baltimore: Williams and Wilkins, 1985), 1960–90; Carl D. Swanson, "The Law and the Counselor," in *Being a Counselor,* ed. Jeannette A. Brown and Robert H. Pate, Jr. (Monterey, Calif.: Brooks/Cole, 1983), 26–46; Sara C. Charles and Eugene Kennedy, *Defendant: A Psychiatrist on Trial for Medical Malpractice* (New York: Free Press, 1985); and B. R. Hopkins and B. S. Anderson, *The Counselor and the Law,* 2d ed. (Alexandria, Va.: AACD Press, 1985).

Chapter 4 *The Community and Counseling*

1. Gen. 2:18.
2. Gen. 6:11.
3. See, e.g., Gen. 13:7.

4. This has been called a "competency model" for counseling; see G. W. Albee, "Preventing Psychopathology and Promoting Human Potential," *American Psychologist* 37 (1982): 1043–50. For a popular presentation of this approach, see Gary R. Collins, *Getting Your Life out of Neutral* (Old Tappan, N.J.: Fleming H. Revell, 1987).

5. Judith A. Lewis and Michael D. Lewis, *Community Counseling: A Human Services Approach* (New York: Wiley, 1977), 14–19.

6. Wayne E. Oates, *The Presence of God in Pastoral Counseling* (Waco, Tex.: Word, 1986), 60.

7. Howard Kirschenbaum and Barbara Glaser, *Developing Support Groups* (La Jolla, Calif.: University Associates, 1978).

8. Benjamin H. Gottlieb, ed., *Social Networks and Social Support* (Beverly Hills, Calif.: Sage Publications, 1981), 14.

9. For a consideration of the church as a social system, see E. Mansell Pattison, *Pastor and Parish—A Systems Approach* (Philadelphia: Fortress Press, 1977); see also Howard W. Stone, *The Caring Church* (San Francisco: Harper & Row, 1983). A more in-depth discussion of systems and networks is given by Gerard Egan and Michael A. Cowan, *People in Systems* (Monterey, Calif.: Brooks/Cole, 1979).

10. Gottlieb, *Social Networks,* 75.

11. Milton Greenblatt, "Volunteerism and the Community Mental Health Worker," in *Comprehensive Textbook of Psychiatry,* ed. Harold I. Kaplan and Benjamin J. Sadock, 4th ed. (Baltimore: Williams & Wilkins, 1985), 1893–97.

12. Some of these are summarized by David Larson, ed., *Teaching Psychological Skills* (Monterey, Calif.: Brooks/Cole, 1984).

13. This is the title of one of several books describing nonprofessional and paraprofessional counselors; see Michael Gershon and Henry B. Biller, *The Other Helpers* (Lexington, Mass.: Lexington Books, 1977).

14. Much of this research is summarized by Joseph A. Durlak, "Comparative Effectiveness of Paraprofessional and Professional Helpers," *Psychological Bulletin* 86 (1979): 80–92; see also John A. Hattie, Christopher F. Sharpley, and H. Jane Rogers, "Comparative Effectiveness of Professional and Paraprofessional Helpers," *Psychological Bulletin* 95 (1984): 534–41; A. Gartner and F. Riessman, eds., *The Self-Help Revolution* (New York: Human Sciences Press, 1984); and Sam Alley, Judith Blanton, and Ronald E. Feldman, eds., *Paraprofessionals in Mental Health* (New York: Human Sciences Press, 1979).

15. For a fascinating study of the counseling effectiveness and training of bartenders, hairdressers, industrial supervisors, and divorce lawyers, see Emory L. Cowen, "Help Is Where You Find It: Four Informal Helping Groups," *American Psychologist* 37 (April 1982): 385–95.

16. Of course groups such as these vary in their effectiveness. Much depends on local leadership. Some AA groups, e.g., are very helpful, but others seem to do more harm than good. For a discussion of pastoral use of self-help (mutual aid) groups, see Leonard Jason et al., "Clergy's Knowledge of Self-Help Groups in a Large Metropolitan Area," *Journal of Psychology and Theology* 16 (Spring 1988): 34–40.

17. This is known as the "helper-therapy" principle. The people who get most help are often those who are most inclined to reach out to others; see F. Riessman, "The

'Helper' Therapy Principle," *Social Work* 10 (1965): 27–32. For additional information on self-help mutual aid groups, see A. Gartner and F. Riessman, *The Self-Help Revolution* (New York: Human Sciences Press, 1984); Alfred H. Katz and Eugene I. Bender, eds., *The Strength in Us: Self-Help Groups in the Modern World* (New York: New Viewpoints, 1976); Herbert C. Schulberg and Marie Killilea, eds., *The Modern Practice of Community Mental Health* (San Francisco: Jossey-Bass, 1982), chap. 25; Richard J. Riordan and Marilyn S. Beggs, "Counselors and Self-Help Groups," *Journal of Counseling and Development* 65 (April 1987): 427–29; and Judith E. Pearson, "A Support Group for Women with Relationship Dependency," *Journal of Counseling and Development* 66 (April 1988): 394–96.
18. Gershon and Biller, *The Other Helpers,* chap. 9.
19. E.g., Sol Gordon and Judith Gordon, *Raising a Child Conservatively in a Sexually Permissive World* (New York: Simon & Schuster, 1983); or Grace H. Ketterman, *How to Teach Your Child about Sex* (Old Tappan, N.J.: Fleming H. Revell, 1981).
20. L. Eugene Arnold, *Helping Parents Help Their Children* (New York: Brunner/Mazel, 1978); and Larry B. Golden and Dave Capuzzi, *Helping Families Help Children* (Springfield, Ill.: Charles C. Thomas, 1986). More recently, several authors have turned to the other end of the age spectrum; see, e.g., Jane E. Myers, "The Mid/Late Generation Gap: Adult Children with Aging Parents," *Journal of Counseling and Development* 66 (March 1988): 331–35; and Lissy Jarvik and Gary Small, *Parentcare* (New York: Crown, 1988).
21. J. C. Bouhoutsos, J. D. Goodchilds, and L. Huddy, "Media Psychology: An Empirical Study of Radio Call-In Psychology Programs," *Professional Psychology: Research and Practice* 17 (October 1986): 408–14. For a slightly different perspective, see L. A. Jason, "Using the Media to Foster Self-Help Groups," *Professional Psychology: Research and Practice* 16 (1985): 455–64.
22. E. Fuller Torrey, *The Mind Game: Witchdoctors and Psychiatrists* (New York: Emerson Hall, 1972); Jerome D. Frank, *Persuasion and Healing,* rev. ed. (New York: Schocken Books, 1974).
23. Paul Welter, *How to Help a Friend* (Wheaton, Ill.: Tyndale, 1978).
24. Especially in some of the experience-oriented approaches to counseling.
25. Jay E. Adams, *The Christian Counselor's Manual* (Grand Rapids, Mich.: Baker, 1973), 343.
26. Welter prefers to use the term "task agreements" instead of the more negative term "homework," See Welter, *How to Help.*
27. See, e.g., John D. Adams, *Understanding and Managing Stress: A Workbook in Changing Lifestyles* (San Diego: University Associates, 1980); Kirk E. Farnsworth and Wendell H. Lawhead, *Life Planning: A Christian Approach to Careers* (Downers Grove, Ill.: InterVarsity, 1981); David A. Thompson, *Five Steps toward a Better Marriage* (Minneapolis: Bethany, 1980); David A. Thompson, *Recovering from Divorce* (Minneapolis: Bethany, 1982); and Waylon D. Ward, *The Bible in Counseling* (Chicago: Moody Press, 1977).
28. Gerald M. Rosen, "Self-Help Treatment Books and the Commercialization of Psychotherapy," *American Psychologist* 42 (January 1987): 46–51.
29. The use of reading as an adjunct to counseling is termed "bibliotherapy." For more information see J. M. Atwater and D. Smith, "Christian Therapists' Utilization of Bibliotherapeutic Resources," *Journal of Psychology and Theology* 10

(1982): 230–35; S. L. Jones, "Bibliotherapy," in *Baker Encyclopedia of Psychology,* ed. David G. Benner (Grand Rapids, Mich.: Baker, 1985), 117–18; and F. A. Schrank and D. W. Engels, "Bibliotherapy as a Counseling Adjunct: Research Findings," *Personnel and Guidance Journal* 60 (1981): 143–47.

30. For information on the creative uses of videotapes, see Ira Heilveil, *Video in Mental Health Practice: An Activities Handbook* (New York: Springer, 1983); and Edward A. Mason, "Audiovisuals in Mental Health Education: A Quantum Leap," in *The Modern Practice of Community Mental Health,* ed. Schulberg and Killilea, 633–49.

31. For more information contact CounseLine, University of Texas Press, Box 7819, Austin, Tex. 78712.

32. The tapes that accompany this book are part of the Christian Counselor's Library, available from Word, Inc., 5221 N. O'Connor Blvd., Suite 1000, Irving, Tex. 75039.

33. Michael J. Burke and Jacques Normand, "Computerized Psychological Testing: Overview and Critique," *Professional Psychology: Research and Practice* 18 (February 1987): 42–51.

34. Marc. D. Schwartz, ed., *Using Computers in Clinical Practice: Psychotherapy and Mental Health Applications* (New York: Haworth Press, 1984); Harvey A. Skinner and Andrew Paluka, "Challenge of Computers in Psychological Assessment," *Professional Psychology: Research and Practice* 17 (February 1986): 44–50; Scott T. Meier, "Software Counseling: What's Available," *Journal of Counseling and Development* 64 (April 1986); and Scott T. Meier, "Stories about Counselors and Computers: Their Use in Workshops," *Journal of Counseling and Development* 65 (October 1986): 100–103.

35. Paul M. Insel, *Environmental Variables and the Prevention of Mental Illness* (Lexington, Mass.: Lexington, 1980).

36. Rudolph H. Moos, *The Human Context: Environmental Determinants of Behavior* (New York: Wiley, 1976); Sheldon Cohen and Neil Weinstein, "Nonauditory Effects of Noise on Behavior and Health," in *Environmental Stress,* ed. Gary W. Evans (Cambridge: Cambridge University Press, 1982), 45–74.

37. Yakov M. Epstein, "Crowding Stress and Human Behavior," in *Environmental Stress,* ed. Evans, 133–48.

38. Albert Mehrabian, *Public Places and Private Spaces: The Psychology of Work, Play, and Living Environments* (New York: Basic Books, 1976).

39. Moos, *The Human Context.*

40. Mark 1:32–35.

41. W. G. Bixler, "Group Psychotherapy," in *Baker Encyclopedia of Psychology,* ed. David G. Benner (Grand Rapids, Mich.: Baker, 1985), 477–83.

42. I. D. Yalom, *The Theory and Practice of Group Psychotherapy,* 2d ed. (New York: Basic Books, 1975). All of the "curative factors" in the following list, except the last one, are adapted from Yalom's work.

43. For additional information see Gerald Corey and Marianne S. Corey, *Groups: Process and Practice,* 3d ed. (Monterey, Calif.: Brooks/Cole, 1987); G. M. Gazda, *Group Counseling: A Developmental Approach,* 3d ed. (Boston: Allyn & Bacon, 1984); and Jared Philip Pingleton, "Group Counseling in the Church: An Integrative Theoretical and Practical Analysis," *Journal of Psychology and Theology* 13 (Spring 1985): 21–28.

44. Lewis and Lewis, *Community Counseling.*
45. Exceptions include the work of Rodger K. Bufford and Trudi Bratten Johnston, "The Church and Community Mental Health: Unrealized Potential," *Journal of Psychology and Theology* 10 (Winter 1982): 355–62; Kelly O'Donnell, "Community Psychology and Unreached Peoples: Applications of Needs and Resource Assessment," *Journal of Psychology and Theology* 14 (Fall 1986): 213–23; and my own book on community counseling, Gary R. Collins, *Innovative Approaches to Counseling* (Waco, Tex.: Word, 1986).
46. Gal. 6:9–10.

Chapter 5 *The Crises in Counseling*

1. Walter Anderson, *Courage Is A Three Letter Word* (New York: Random House, 1986).
2. Glenn E. Whitock, *Understanding and Coping with Real-Life Crises* (Monterey, Calif.: Brooks/Cole, 1978).
3. Gerald Caplan, *Principles of Preventive Psychiatry* (New York: Basic Books, 1964), 43.
4. Rachel Callahan, "The Ministry of Crisis Intervention," in *Pastoral Counseling,* ed. Barry K. Estadt (Englewood Cliffs, N.J.: Prentice-Hall, 1983), 138–51.
5. Howard Clinebell, *Basic Types of Pastoral Counseling,* rev. ed. (Nashville: Abingdon, 1984).
6. J. L. Greenstone and S. Leviton, "Crisis Intervention," in *Concise Encyclopedia of Psychology,* ed. Raymond J. Corsini (New York: Wiley, 1987), 271. For one example of effective crisis intervention, see Pamela J. Kneisel and Gail P. Richards, "Crisis Intervention after the Suicide of a Teacher," *Professional Psychology: Research and Development* 19 (April 1988): 165–69.
7. This concept of mental first aid has been presented by Calvin J. Frederick, "Suicide Prevention and Crisis Intervention in Mental Health Emergencies," in *Clinical Practice of Psychology,* ed. C. Eugene Walker (New York: Pergamon, 1981), 189–213.
8. For a further discussion of touch in counseling, including a summary of research on this topic, see Beverly G. Willison and Robert L. Masson, "The Role of Touch in Therapy: An Adjunct to Communication," *Journal of Counseling and Development* 64 (April 1986): 497–500; see also, chap. 2, fn. 25.
9. Lawrence M. Brammer, *The Helping Relationship: Process and Skills* (Englewood Cliffs, N.J.: Prentice-Hall, 1973).
10. Judson J. Swihart and Gerald C. Richardson, *Counseling in Times of Crisis* (Waco, Tex.: Word, 1987), 155–61.
11. For a summary of research evidence showing the value of social support and the dangers of social overinvolvement, see Judith E. Pearson, "The Definition and Measurement of Social Support," *Journal of Counseling and Development* 64 (February 1986): 390–95.
12. Raymond E. Vath, *Counseling Those with Eating Disorders* (Waco, Tex.: Word, 1986), 178.
13. Adapted from David K. Switzer, "Crisis Intervention and Problem Solving," in *Clinical Handbook of Pastoral Counseling,* ed. Robert J. Wicks, Richard D. Parsons, and Donald E. Capps (New York: Paulist Press, 1985), 149.

14. These differences are discussed further in chap. 3.
15. In contrast to the first edition of this book, this edition puts greater emphasis on the biological bases of behavior.
16. 2 Cor. 2:11; 11:14; 1 Pet. 5:8.
17. C. S. Lewis, *The Screwtape Letters* (Glasgow: Collins-Fontana Books, 1942), 9.
18. Allen E. Ivey, *Professional Affairs Committee Report, Division 17—Counseling Psychology* (Washington, D.C.: American Psychological Association, 1976).
19. This was discussed more fully at the beginning of the book.

Chapter 6 *Anxiety*

1. Rollo May, *The Meaning of Anxiety,* rev. ed. (New York: Norton, 1977), 214.
2. Charles Spielberger, *Understanding Stress and Anxiety* (New York: Harper & Row, 1979).
3. Anxiety and excitement release the same hormones and turn on the same parts of the nervous system. Anxiety and excitement have been called "twin emotions, causing the same physical sensations." Sometimes the two are confused. Thinking they are excited when they really are anxious, some people proceed with abandon when they should be cautious. Thinking they are anxious when they really are excited, some people inhibit themselves and miss many of life's pleasures; see Martin Groder, "Excitement or Anxiety: Which Is Which?" *Bottom Line Personal* 8 (15 March 1987): 11–12.
4. See, e.g., Charles R. Figley, ed., *Stress Disorders among Vietnam Veterans* (New York: Brunner/Mazel, 1978); W. Kelly, *Post-traumatic Stress Disorder and the War Veteran Patient* (New York: Brunner/Mazel, 1985); and William P. Mahedy, *Out of the Night: The Spiritual Journey of Vietnam Vets* (New York: Ballantine, 1986).
5. Two excellent books discuss this in more detail: David V. Sheehan, *The Anxiety Disease* (New York: Charles Scribner's Sons, 1983); and R. Reid Wilson, *Don't Panic: Taking Control of Anxiety Attacks* (New York: Harper & Row, 1986).
6. 2 Cor. 11:28.
7. Phil. 2:20. The RSV uses the words "genuinely anxious"; the NASB states "Timothy . . . will genuinely be concerned about your welfare."
8. Ps. 94:19.
9. Matt. 6:25–34.
10. Phil. 4:6–7.
11. 1 Pet. 5:7; see also Ps. 55:22.
12. Matt. 6:33: "seek first his kingdom and his righteousness, and all these things will be given to you as well."
13. Eccles. 11:10.
14. Phil. 4:6.
15. S. Freud, *The Problem of Anxiety* (New York: Norton, 1936).
16. For further information on the causes of anxiety, see A. T. Beck and G. Emery, *Anxiety Disorders and Phobias: A Cognitive Perspective* (New York: Basic Books, 1985); R. Handley, *Anxiety and Panic Attacks: Their Cause and Cure* (New York: Rawson, 1985); and Wilson, *Don't Panic*.
17. See, e.g., D. B. Carr and David V. Sheehan, "Panic Anxiety: A New Biological Model," *Journal of Clinical Psychiatry* 45 (1984): 323–30.
18. May, *Meaning of Anxiety,* 205–6.

19. For a concise discussion of the unconscious by a Christian counselor, see David G. Benner, ed., *Baker Encyclopedia of Psychology* (Grand Rapids, Mich.: Baker, 1985), 1187–88.
20. For a discussion of conflict as it relates to stress and anxiety, see Susan Roth and Lawrence J. Cohen, "Approach, Avoidance, and Coping with Stress," *American Psychologist* 41 (July 1986): 813–19.
21. Fear and love are the themes of Henri J. M. Nouwen, *Lifesigns: Intimacy, Fecundity, and Ecstasy in Christian Perspective* (Garden City, N.Y.: Doubleday, 1986).
22. For a perspective on change and anxiety in women, see Carol Becker, *The Invisible Drama: Women and the Anxiety of Change* (New York: Macmillan, 1987).
23. J. L. Deffenbacher et al., "Irrational Beliefs and Anxiety," *Cognitive Therapy and Research* 10 (1986): 281–91.
24. Cecil Osborne, *Release from Fear and Anxiety* (Waco, Tex.: Word, 1976).
25. 1 John 1:9.
26. Wilson lists a number of these in *Don't Panic,* 13–14.
27. Ibid., 93–98.
28. Sheehan, *Anxiety Disease*.
29. Deut. 28:65–66.
30. Archibald D. Hart, *The Hidden Link between Adrenalin and Stress* (Waco, Tex.: Word, 1986).
31. For a more detailed discussion of defensive reactions, see any introductory psychology textbook.
32. For a discussion of conversions during combat, see Gordon W. Allport, *The Individual and His Religion* (New York: Macmillan, 1950), 52–57.
33. Eugene Kennedy, *On Becoming a Counselor* (New York: Seabury, 1977), 142–43.
34. Some Christian writers have criticized this "visualization" approach and called it "demonically inspired and unalterably hostile to Christianity"; see, e.g., Dave Hunt and T. A. McMahon, *The Seduction of Christianity* (Eugene, Oreg.: Harvest House, 1985), 140. I agree with those who see the Hunt-McMahon view as an overreaction. For a more balanced Christian perspective, see H. Norman Wright, *Self-Talk, Imagery and Prayer in Counseling* (Waco, Tex.: Word, 1986). For more detailed discussion of calming techniques, see Wilson, *Don't Panic*.
35. Allport, *The Individual*; he writes: "Love—incomparably the greatest psychotherapeutic agent—is something that professional psychiatry cannot of itself create, focus, nor release. . . . By contrast . . . the Christian religion—offers an interpretation of life and a rule of life based wholly upon love" (90, 92f.).
36. 1 John 4:18.
37. Jay E. Adams, *The Christian Counselor's Manual* (Nutley, N.J.: Presbyterian and Reformed, 1973), 414–15.
38. Note Heb. 13:6.
39. The differences are discussed briefly by Carol Turkington, "Panic and Anxiety," *APA Monitor* 17 (September 1986): 1, 5.
40. Sheehan, *The Anxiety Disease,* 113–18. In the following paragraphs I have retitled and revised Sheehan's "four target" approach to treatment.
41. For Christian perspectives on behavioral methods, see Rodger K. Bufford, *The Human Reflex: Behavioral Psychology in Biblical Perspective* (New York: Harper & Row, 1981); and Siang-Yang Tan, "Cognitive-Behavioral Therapy: A

Biblical Approach and Critique," *Journal of Psychology and Theology* 15 (Summer 1987): 103–12. See also Herbert Benson, *The Relaxation Response* (New York: William Morrow, 1975); Larry Michelson and L. Michael Ascher, eds., *Anxiety and Stress Disorders: Cognitive-Behavioral Assessment and Treatment* (New York: Guilford Publications, 1987); and selected chapters in Irwin L. Kutash, Louis B. Schlesinger, and Associates, eds., *Handbook of Stress and Anxiety* (San Francisco: Jossey-Bass, 1980). The entire January 1988 issue of *Counseling Psychologist* is devoted to congnitive-behavioral treatment of anxiety; see, e.g., Jerry L. Deffenbacher and Richard M. Suinn, "Systematic Desensitization and the Reduction of Anxiety," *Counseling Psychologist* 16 (January 1988): 9–30.

42. Everything in these sentences is taken from Jesus' teachings in John 14; see esp. vv. 1–3, 16–18, 25–28.

43. William Hendrickson, *Philippians* (Grand Rapids, Mich.: Baker, 1962), 193.

44. Phil. 4:7 LB.

45. Phil. 4:9, italics added.

46. James 1:22.

47. May, *The Meaning of Anxiety*, 366–67.

48. Relaxation methods, priority evaluation, and time management are all discussed on the cassette tape that accompanies this chapter. For more popular treatment of these issues, see Gary R. Collins, *Getting Your Life out of Neutral* (Old Tappan, N.J.: Revell, 1987). More technical discussion is given by Richard M. Suinn and Jerry L. Deffenbacher, "Anxiety Management Training," *Counseling Psychologist* 16 (January 1988): 31–49.

49. Theory and research in the area of cognitive appraisal is summarized by John J. Zarski, Donald L. Bubenzer, and John D. West, "Social Interest, Stress, and the Prediction of Health Status," *Journal of Counseling and Development* 64 (February 1986): 386–89; and Marvin R. Goldfried, "Application of Rational Restructuring to Anxiety Disorders," *Counseling Psychologist* 16 (January 1988): 50–68.

50. Zarski, "Social Interest."

51. Gal. 6:2.

52. Matt. 6:31–34.

Chapter 7 *Loneliness*

1. David D. Burns, "An End to Loneliness," *Bottom Line Personal* 6 (30 June 1985): 9–10.

2. Henri J. M. Nouwen, *Reaching Out* (Garden City, N.Y.: Doubleday, 1975), 15.

3. Suzanne Gordon, *Lonely in America* (New York: Simon and Schuster, 1976), 15.

4. Robert Weiss, *Loneliness: Emotional and Social Isolation* (Cambridge, Mass.: MIT Press, 1973).

5. This research is reported by Jeff Meer, "Loneliness," *Psychology Today* 19 (July 1985): 28–33. Allan Bloom has noted the loneliness of college students. This is a "new degree of isolation," he writes, "that leaves young people with no alternative to looking inward"; see Bloom, *The Closing of the American Mind* (New York: Simon & Schuster, 1987), 86.

6. Philip Slater, *Pursuit of Loneliness: American Culture at the Breaking Point* (Boston: Beacon Press, 1970).

7. Douglas LaBier, *Modern Madness: The Emotional Fallout of Success* (Reading, Mass.: Addison-Wesley, 1986).
8. Janelle Warner and John D. Carter, "Loneliness, Marital Adjustment and Burnout in Pastoral and Lay Persons," *Journal of Psychology and Theology* 12 (Summer 1984): 125–31.
9. C. W. Ellison, "Loneliness," in *Baker Encyclopedia of Psychology*, ed. David G. Benner (Grand Rapids, Mich.: Baker, 1985): 655–57.
10. This has been called existential anxiety; see Craig W. Ellison, "Loneliness: A Social-Developmental Analysis," *Journal of Psychology and Theology* 6 (1978): 3–17; and idem, *Loneliness: The Search for Intimacy* (Chappaqua, N.Y.: Christian Herald, 1980).
11. Gen. 2:18.
12. The word "lonely" appears only four times in the NIV. Two of these references (Mark 1:45 and Luke 5:16) refer to lonely places; the other references, both in Psalms (25:16 and 68:6) refer to people.
13. Ps. 25:16.
14. 2 Tim. 4:9–12.
15. These issues are discussed in more depth in chapters 16 (Interpersonal Relations) and 37 (Spiritual Issues).
16. Meer, "Loneliness."
17. Ellison, "Loneliness: A Social-Developmental Analysis."
18. See, e.g., J. Bowlby, *Attachment* (New York: Basic Books, 1969); and idem, *Separation* (New York: Basic Books, 1973).
19. See, e.g., Grant L. Martin, *Counseling for Family Violence and Abuse* (Waco, Tex.: Word, 1987).
20. Ellison, "Loneliness."
21. Elizabeth Skoglund, *Loneliness* (Downers Grove, Ill.: InterVarsity, 1975).
22. Paul Tournier, *Escape from Loneliness* (Philadelphia: Westminster, 1962).
23. D. F. Fisher, "Loneliness," in *Concise Encyclopedia of Psychology*, ed. Raymond J. Corsini (New York: Wiley-Interscience, 1987): 673–74.
24. See chapter 9.
25. Ira J. Tanner, *Loneliness: The Fear of Love* (New York: Harper & Row, 1973); see also the chapter on loneliness in Lewis M. Andrews, *To Thine Own Self Be True* (Garden City, N.Y.: Anchor/Doubleday, 1987).
26. C. E. Cutrona, "Transition to College: Loneliness and the Process of Social Adjustment," in *Loneliness: A Sourcebook of Current Theory, Research and Therapy*, ed. L. A. Peplau and D. Perlman (New York: Wiley-Interscience, 1982), 291–309.
27. Jules Asher, "Born to Be Shy?" *Psychology Today* 21 (April 1987): 56–64.
28. Ellison, "Loneliness."
29. Meer, "Loneliness."
30. W. A. Sadler, "Cause of Loneliness," *Science Digest* 78 (July 1975): 58–66.
31. Much of this research evidence is summarized by James M. Lynch in his two books, *The Broken Heart: The Medical Consequences of Loneliness* (New York: Basic Books, 1977); and *The Language of the Heart* (New York: Basic Books, 1985); see also Peplau and Perlman, *Loneliness: A Sourcebook*.
32. "Bereavement and Grief—Part I," *Harvard Medical School Mental Health Letter* 3 (March 1987): 1–4.

33. Richard Wolff, *The Meaning of Loneliness* (Wheaton, Ill.: Key, 1970).
34. Harvey H. Potthoff, *Loneliness: Understanding and Dealing with It* (Nashville: Abingdon, 1976).
35. This is basic to the rational-emotive therapy of psychologist Albert Ellis.
36. John 3:16.
37. 1 John 1:9.
38. John 3:16; Rom. 8:35–39.
39. Rom. 8:14–17.
40. Prov. 18:24.
41. Rom. 8:9; 1 Cor. 6:19; 1 John 4:13.
42. Rom. 8:26–31.
43. Brian D. Dufton and Daniel Perlman, "Loneliness and Religiosity: In the World but Not of It," *Journal of Psychology and Theology* 14 (Summer 1986): 135–45.
44. R. F. Paloutzian and C. W. Ellison, "Loneliness, Spiritual Well-Being and the Quality of Life," in Peplau and Perlman, *Loneliness: A Sourcebook*, 224–37.
45. Recently I visited a church where all "members of the congregation who attend this church all the time" were asked to be seated following the opening hymn, leaving the visitors (me included) standing. We were expected to give our names and then wear a bright "newcomers" ribbon. The church's intentions were good: to notice and acknowledge visitors, but this could be uncomfortable and threatening, especially for people who were shy or not wanting to be publicly acknowledged.
46. Ralph Keyes, *We, The Lonely People* (New York: Harper & Row, 1973).
47. Ellison, *Loneliness*, 234.
48. See chapter 37.

Chapter 8 *Depression*

1. Vance Havner, *Though I Walk through the Valley* (Old Tappan, N.J.: Revell, 1974). The book was written following the death of Havner's wife and the title is taken from Ps. 23:4.
2. The director of mental health for the World Health Organization has estimated that more than 100 million people in the world suffer clinical depression, and there is evidence that this number is increasing rapidly; A. J. Marsella, "Depression," in *Concise Encyclopedia of Psychology*, ed. Raymond J. Corsini (New York: Wiley-Interscience, 1987), 303.
3. These figures are reported by *Newsweek* in a cover story on depression, 4 May 1987, 48–57.
4. Heinz E. Lehmann, "Affective Disorders: Clinical Features," in *Comprehensive Textbook of Psychiatry/IV*, ed. Harold I. Kaplan and Benjamin J. Sadock, 4th ed. (Baltimore: Williams & Wilkins, 1985), 786–811. According to one report, 2 to 3 percent of men and 4 to 9 percent of women suffer from major depression at any given time; the lifetime risk may be as high as 10 percent for men and 25 percent for women; see "The Nature and Causes of Depression—Part I," *Harvard Medical School Mental Health Letter* 4 (January 1988): 1–4.
5. A number of first-person accounts have described depression; see, e.g., James W. Bennett, *A Quiet Desperation* (Nashville: Thomas Nelson, 1983); and Don Baker and Emery Nester, *Depression* (Portland, Oreg.: Multnomah, 1983).

6. Stanley Lesse, ed., *Masked Depression* (New York: Jason Aronson, 1974).
7. For an excellent discussion of the classification of depressive disorders, see Archibald D. Hart, *Counseling the Depressed* (Waco, Tex.: Word, 1986).
8. Job 3; Num. 11:10–15; Jon. 4:1–3; Exod. 6:9; Matt. 26:75.
9. 1 Kings 19.
10. Matt. 26:37–38.
11. See, e.g., Pss. 34:15–17; 103:13–14; Matt. 5:12; 11:28–30; John 14:1; 15:10; Rom. 8:28.
12. Rom. 15:13.
13. I have chosen not to identify the sources of these viewpoints, most of which have appeared in print; for a concise evangelical discussion of Christian myths about depression, see Hart, *Counseling the Depressed,* 21–35.
14. J. I. Nurnberger and E. S. Gershon, "Genetics of Affective Disorders," in *Neurobiology of Mood Disorders,* ed. R. Post and J. Ballenger (Baltimore: Williams and Wilkins, 1984; R. J. Cadoret et al., "Genetic and Environmental Factors in Major Depression," *Journal of Affective Disorders* 9 (September 1985): 155–64; and Svenn Torgersen, "Genetic Factors in Moderately Severe and Mild Affective Disorders," *Archives of General Psychiatry* 43 (March 1986): 222–26. According to one recent report, "the family transmission of depression is obvious, but upbringing is hard to distinguish from heredity"; see "The Nature and Causes of Depression—Part II," *Harvard Medical School Mental Health Letter* 4 (February 1988), 3.
15. 1 Kings 18–19.
16. Hart, *Counseling the Depressed,* 96–97; see also Archibald D. Hart, *The Hidden Link between Adrenalin and Stress* (Waco, Tex.: Word, 1986).
17. Keith Brodie, chancellor of Duke University, quoted in "New Hope for the Depressed," *Newsweek,* 24 January 1983, 39–42.
18. Frederick G. Lopez, "Family Structure and Depression: Implications for the Counseling or College Students," *Journal of Counseling and Development* 64 (April 1986): 508–11.
19. Rene Spitz, "Anaclitic Depression," *Psychoanalytic Study of the Child* 2 (1946): 312–42.
20. D. A. Cole and L. P. Rehm, "Family Interaction Patterns and Childhood Depression," *Journal of Abnormal Child Psychology* 14 (1986): 297–314.
21. Ibid.; see also Kathleen McCoy, *Coping with Teenage Depression* (New York: New American Library, 1982).
22. S. Folkman and R. S. Lazarus, "Stress Processes and Depressive Symptomatology," *Journal of Abnormal Psychology* 95 (1986): 107–13.
23. Martin E. P. Seligman, *Helplessness: On Depression, Development and Death* (San Francisco: Freeman, 1975). This theory has been challenged by some researchers. E.g., one comparison of nondepressed and depressed people found that the latter were more likely to feel in control of their stressful situations; see Harold A. Sackeim and Andrea Zucker Wegner, "Attributional Patterns of Depression and Euthymia," *Archives of General Psychiatry* 43 (June 1986): 553–60.
24. A. T. Beck et al., *Cognitive Therapy of Depression* (New York: Guilford, 1979).
25. This, of course, is really another cognitive theory. It assumes that angry thinking leads to feelings of depression.
26. This diagram is adapted from Paul Welter, *How to Help a Friend* (Wheaton,

Ill.: Tyndale House, 1978), 108, 224, and attributed to psychologist G. B. Dunning.
27. Roger Barrett, *Depression: What It Is and What to Do about It* (Elgin, Ill.: David C. Cook, 1977).
28. Steven E. Locke, "Depression and Immunity," *Harvard Medical School Mental Health Letter* 3 (October 1986); and "The Nature and Causes of Depression—Part III," *Harvard Medical School Mental Health Letter* 4 (March 1988): 1–4.
29. Stanley Lesse, ed., *Masked Depression* (New York: Jason Aronson, 1974).
30. J. C. Coyne et al., "Living with a Depressed Person," *Journal of Consulting and Clinical Psychology* 55 (1987): 347–52.
31. Mark S. Gold, *The Good News about Depression* (New York: Villard Books, 1987); see also Dimitri F. Papolos and Janice Papolos, *Overcoming Depression* (New York: Harper & Row, 1987).
32. J. Mervis, "NIMH Data Point Way to Effective Treatment," *APA Monitor* 17 (July 1986): 1, 13; this is a report of preliminary findings of a $10 million federally sponsored study of the treatment of depression.
33. Gold, *The Good News*.
34. Richard Carlton, "Nutritional Therapy, Traditional Psychiatry, and You," *Bottom Line Personal* 8 (30 January 1987).
35. This is how ECT is described in "Electro-convulsive Therapy," *Consensus Development Conference Statement* 5 (Washington, D.C.: U.S. Department of Health and Human Services, National Institutes of Health, 1985).
36. For a more detailed, ten-step approach to counseling those who have experienced loss, see Hart, *Counseling the Depressed,* 133–45.
37. Heb. 1:3; 13:5; Col. 1:16–17; John 14:1–4, 26–27.
38. A. John Rush, ed., *Short-Term Psychotherapies for Depression* (New York: 1982), 143–214.
39. Eda LeShan, "Pulling Out of a Depression," *Woman's Day* 42 (November 1978), 50–54, 246–48.
40. This is a simplified summary of behavioral counseling; see Ruch, *Short-Term,* 50–87; see also S. L. Jones, "Depression: Behavioral Perspectives," in *Baker Encyclopedia of Psychology,* ed. David G. Benner (Grand Rapids, Mich.: Baker, 1985): 301–3.
41. Carla Hellekson and Norman Rosenthal, "New Light on Seasonal Mood Changes," *Harvard Medical School Mental Health Letter* 3 (April 1987).
42. This list is adapted from the early, pioneering work of Farberow and Shneidman; see N. L. Farberow and E. S. Shneidman, eds., *The Cry for Help* (New York: McGraw-Hill, 1965); and E. S. Shneidman, *On the Nature of Suicide* (San Francisco: Jossey-Bass, 1969).
43. Phil. 4:11–13, 19.
44. R. Eugene Holeman, "A Psychiatric View of Depression," *Christian Counselor* (Summer 1986): 5–8.
45. "What a Friend We Have in Jesus."
46. John 16:33; James 1:2–3, 12.
47. See, e.g., Ps. 1:1–2; 119:9–16.
48. Phil. 4:8.
49. Seligman, *Helplessness,* 104.
50. S. C. Thompson, "Will It Hurt Less If I Can Control It? A Complex Answer to a Simple Question," *Psychological Bulletin* 90 (1981): 89–101.

51. Emile Durkheim, *Suicide* (1887; reprint, Glencoe, Ill.: Free Press, 1951).
52. F. Reissman, "The 'Helper-Therapy' Principle," *Social Work* 10 (1965): 27–32.
53. Havner, *Though I Walk through the Valley*, 66–67.

Chapter 9 *Anger*

1. For a discussion of the various definitions of anger, see Jeffrey Rubin, "The Emotion of Anger: Some Conceptual and Theoretical Issues," *Professional Psychology: Research and Practice* 17 (April 1986): 115–24.
2. Milton Layden, *Escaping the Hostility Trap* (Englewood Cliffs, N.J.: Prentice-Hall, 1977), 2.
3. Louis McBurney, *Counseling Christian Workers* (Waco, Tex.: Word, 1986).
4. Suzanne Fremont and Wayne Anderson, "What Client Behaviors Make Counselors Angry? An Exploratory Study," *Journal of Counseling and Development* 65 (October 1986): 67–70.
5. Carol Zisowitz Stearns and Peter N. Stearns, *Anger: The Struggle for Emotional Control in America's History* (Chicago: University of Chicago Press, 1986).
6. Neil Clark Warren, *Make Anger Your Ally* (Garden City, N.Y.: Doubleday, 1983), 15. The professional lack of attention to anger has been noted by J. R. Averill, "Studies on Anger and Aggression," *American Psychologist* 38 (1983): 1145–60; and Bruce S. Sharkin, "The Measurement and Treatment of Client Anger in Counseling," *Journal of Counseling and Development* 66 (April 1988): 361–65.
7. James M. Boice, *God the Redeemer* (Downers Grove, Ill.: InterVarsity Press, 1978), 95.
8. James I. Packer, *Knowing God* (Downers Grove, Ill.: InterVarsity Press, 1973), 136.
9. Mark 3:5.
10. Rom. 3:23.
11. Isa. 48:9; Ps. 130:3–4; Dan. 9:9; 2 Pet. 3:9; see also Psalms 10 and 73 where God's justice against the wicked is withheld temporarily.
12. Rom. 2:5; 1 Thess. 1:10; see also Revelation 6 and following.
13. E.g., Eccles. 7:9; Prov. 16:32; Matt. 5:22; Gal. 5:20; Eph. 4:26, 31; Col. 3:8; James 1:19–20.
14. Eph. 4:27.
15. Mark 3:5.
16. For a further discussion of these ideas see John T. Hower, "The Misunderstanding and Mishandling of Anger," *Journal of Psychology and Theology* 2 (Fall 1974): 269–75.
17. This view is expressed in the NIV Study Bible commentary on Eph. 4:26.
18. Eccles. 7:9; Ps. 37:8; Prov. 16:32.
19. Prov. 15:1.
20. Charles E. Cerling, Jr., "Anger: Musings of a Theologian/Psychologist," *Journal of Psychology and Theology* 2 (Winter 1974): 12–17.
21. Rom. 12:19; 14:4; Eph 4:31; Heb. 12:15; Matt. 7:1–5.
22. Prov. 14:29; 15:18; 29:11, 20, 22.
23. James 1:19; 3:3–14; 4:1–2.
24. James Garbarino, Edna Guttmann, and Janis Wilson Seeley, *The Psychologically Battered Child* (San Francisco: Jossey-Bass, 1987).

25. 2 Tim. 4:2; Luke 17:3–4; see also Paul's sharing that produced sorrow followed by change (2 Cor. 7:8–10).
26. See chapter 8.
27. Prov. 10:18; 26:24.
28. Prov. 15:28.
29. 1 John 1:9; James 5:16; Matt. 6:12; 18:21–22, 33–35.
30. 1 Pet. 2:23.
31. Prov. 16:32.
32. Fremont and Anderson, "Client Behaviors."
33. This was demonstrated many years ago in a study of anger that found other people to be the cause of anger in almost 80 percent of the reported cases; see G. S. Gates, "An Observational Study of Anger," *Journal of Experimental Psychology* 9 (1926): 325–26.
34. Jon. 4:1.
35. Matt. 2:16.
36. Matt. 20:24.
37. Mark 3:5; 10:14.
38. These and other theories of anger are described by David W. Augsburger, "Anger and Aggression," in *Clinical Handbook of Pastoral Counseling,* ed. Robert J. Wicks, Richard D. Parsons, and Donald E. Capps (New York: Paulist Press, 1985): 482–501; and R. E. Butman, "Anger," in *Baker Encyclopedia of Psychology,* ed. David G. Benner (Grand Rapids, Mich.: Baker, 1985), 58–60.
39. This viewpoint is basic to the theory of Konrad Lorenz, *On Aggression* (New York: Harcourt, Brace & World, 1966). According to one writer, instinct theory "is a blend of anecdote, analogical leaps, unsystematic journalism, and undefined concepts. . . . It is irresponsible, in the sense that, according to the theory, aggressive urges accumulate and must be expressed independent of the individual's choice. . . . But to accept an unknown and unknowable accumulation of unseeable and unmeasurable energy as the basis for aggressive behavior is to use a mythology almost totally unsupported, and in fact largely refuted, by scientific evidence" (A. P. Goldstein, "Aggression," in *Concise Encyclopedia of Psychology,* ed. Raymond J. Corsini [New York: Wiley-Interscience, 1987], 35).
40. Carol Tavris, *Anger: The Misunderstood Emotion* (New York: Simon & Schuster, 1982).
41. Ibid.; studies of family violence and abuse, many summarized by Dr. Grant Martin, have also found examples of biologically based aggression; see Grant L. Martin, *Counseling for Family Violence and Abuse* (Waco, Tex.: Word, 1987).
42. Paul Welter, *How to Help a Friend* (Wheaton, Ill.: Tyndale, 1978), 109.
43. Cited in Tavris, *Anger,* chap. 2.
44. Ray Burwick, *Anger: Defusing the Bomb* (Wheaton, Ill.: Tyndale, 1981), 19.
45. Mildred M. Batemen and Joseph S. Jensen, "The Effect of Religious Background on Modes of Handling Anger," *Journal of Social Psychology* 48 (February 1958): 140.
46. H. Norman Wright, *The Christian Use of Emotional Power* (Old Tappan, N.J.: Revell, 1974).
47. See chapter 8 where we discuss how depression often results from anger held within.
48. Eph. 4:30–31.

49. The quotation is attributed to H. Rap Brown; see Murray Scher and Mark Stevens, "Men and Violence," *Journal of Counseling and Development* 65 (March 1987).
50. Warren, *Make Anger Your Ally,* 40–54.
51. Martin Groder, "Passive Aggression," *Bottom Line Personal* 7 (30 April 1986).
52. Matt. 5:38–44.
53. Tavris, *Anger,* 120–50.
54. Archibald D. Hart, *Feeling Free* (Old Tappan, N.J.: Revell, 1979), 87.
55. Willard Gaylin, "Anger," *Bottom Line Personal* 7 (15 January 1986).
56. S. Feshbach, "Reconceptualizations of Anger: Some Research Perspectives," *Journal of Social and Clinical Psychology* 4 (1986): 123–32.
57. 1 John 1:9; James 5:16.
58. People who really aren't sorry can be encouraged to ask God to help them change.
59. 1 John 1:9.
60. Lewis B. Smedes, *Forgive and Forget* (New York: Harper & Row, 1984).
61. Warren, *Make Anger Your Ally,* 192; see also D. Hope, "The Healing Paradox of Forgiveness," *Psychotherapy* 24 (1987): 240–44.
62. Gal. 5:18–25.
63. This would be consistent with James 1:19–20.
64. Prov. 15:1.
65. Layden, *Escaping the Hostility Trap,* 34. Several research studies have shown the effectiveness of "cognitive treatment" including self-talk, in dealing with anger; see, e.g., J. L. Deffenbacher et al., "Cognitive-relaxation and Social Skills Interventions in the Treatment of General Anger," *Journal of Counseling Psychology* 34 (1987): 171–76; and S. L. Hazaleus and J. L. Deffenbacher, "Relaxation and Cognitive Treatment of Anger," *Journal of Consulting and Clinical Psychology* 54 (1986): 222–26.
66. Phil. 4:8.
67. Matt. 5:24.
68. Phil. 4:4–11.
69. C. F. Alschuler and A. S. Alschuler, "Developing Healthy Responses to Anger: The Counselor's Role," *Journal of Counseling and Development* 63 (1984): 26–29.
70. See chapter 21.
71. Warren, *Make Anger Your Ally,* 137–38.
72. Prov. 22:24–25.
73. S. R. Heyman, "Psychological Problem Patterns Found with Athletes" *Clinical Psychologist* 39 (1986): 68–71.
74. Edwin Kiester, Jr., "The Uses of Anger: Winning Athletes Turn Rage into Motivation and Concentration," *Psychology Today* 18 (July 1984): 26.
75. 1 Pet. 1:13; Phil. 4:8.
76. Layden, *Escaping the Hostility Trap,* 34.
77. Phil. 4:8. One recent book on interpersonal relations, written for women, suggests that venting anger does not make people feel less frustrated or more in control. Instead, there must be a redirection of anger into a constructive force; see Harriet Goldhor Lerner, *The Dance of Anger* (New York: Harper & Row, 1987).
78. David Augsburger, *Caring Enough to Confront: The Love-Fight* (Ventura, Calif.: Regal Books, 1973).

Chapter 10 *Guilt*

1. For more popular Christian considerations of this topic see C. S. Lewis, *The Problem of Pain* (New York: Macmillan, 1962); Philip Yancey, *Where Is God When It Hurts?* (Grand Rapids, Mich.: Zondervan, 1977); and Edith Schaeffer, *Affliction* (Old Tappan, N.J.: Revell, 1978). For a concise discussion of our faulty theoretical views of suffering, see Philip Yancey, "How Not to Spell Relief," *Christianity Today* 32 (19 February 1988): 64; see also David B. Jackson, "Suffering: The Core of Distress," *Christian Counselor* 2 (Winter 1987): 11–12.
2. Earl D. Wilson, *Counseling and Guilt* (Waco, Tex.: Word, 1987), 11.
3. G. Belgum, *Guilt: Where Religion and Psychology Meet* (Minneapolis: Augsburg, 1970); see also S. Bruce Narramore, "Guilt: Where Theology and Psychology Meet," *Journal of Psychology and Theology* 2 (1974): 18–25.
4. Howard Clinebell, *Basic Types of Pastoral Care and Counseling* (Nashville: Abingdon, 1984), 141.
5. S. Bruce Narramore, "Guilt," in *Baker Encyclopedia of Psychology,* ed. David G. Benner (Grand Rapids, Mich.: Baker, 1985), 486–88.
6. Ibid.
7. Isa. 53:6; Rom. 3:23.
8. In his classic book, *Guilt and Grace* (New York: Harper & Row, 1962), Paul Tournier used the terms "true guilt" and "false guilt." I tend to think Tournier's terms are more confusing than helpful so I have avoided them in the text.
9. L. R. Keylock, "Guilt," in *The Zondervan Pictorial Encyclopedia of the Bible,* ed. Merrill C. Tenney (Grand Rapids, Mich.: Zondervan, 1975), 2:852.
10. This is discussed further in Wilson, *Counseling and Guilt,* chaps. 2 and 6; see also S. Bruce Narramore, *No Condemnation* (Grand Rapids, Mich.: Zondervan, 1984), chap. 10. Narramore argues convincingly that guilt feelings never come from God. They "never motivate us to genuine repentance" but instead "motivate us to hide or offer our own self-punishments or solutions in the place of God's forgiveness" (p. 148).
11. Narramore, *No Condemnation*.
12. Ibid., 155; Narramore suggests that Protestants rely on 1 John 1:9 while many Catholics abuse the confessional in the same way—to give temporary relief from sin.
13. Matt. 26:75.
14. 1 Pet. 2:24.
15. 1 John 1:9; the quotation is from P. H. Monsma, "Forgiveness," in *The Zondervan Pictorial Encyclopedia of the Bible,* 2:599.
16. Matt. 6:14–15, 18:21f.
17. For an excellent and readable discussion of forgiveness see Lewis B. Smedes, *Forgive and Forget* (New York: Harper & Row, 1984).
18. Several writers have studied this in depth, including Lawrence Kohlberg, *The Philosophy of Moral Development* (San Francisco: Harper & Row, 1981); and James W. Fowler, *Stages of Faith* (New York: Harper & Row, 1981).
19. This view of sinless perfection is in contrast to 1 John 1:8–10.
20. Phil. 3:12–16.
21. Narramore, *No Condemnation,* 30–31, quotes Tournier and agrees that "subjective or psychological guilt or guilt feelings" all include "feelings of

self-rejection, self-punishment, and a loss of self-esteem." Narramore refers to the only experimental study comparing guilt and inferiority. The researcher found that "guilt and inferiority are operationally similar."

22. Tournier, *Guilt and Grace,* 24.
23. Ibid., 15–16, 18.
24. S. Bruce Narramore, "Conscience," *Baker Encyclopedia of Psychology,* ed. David G. Benner (Grand Rapids, Mich.: Baker, 1985), 220–21.
25. Rom. 2:15.
26. 1 Tim. 4:1–2.
27. 1 Cor. 8:10–12.
28. 1 Cor. 10:25–29.
29. L. I. Granberg, "Conscience," in *The Zondervan Pictorial Encyclopedia of the Bible,* 1:943–45.
30. Gen. 2:17; 3:4–5, 22; see also S. Bruce Narramore, "Guilt: Its Universal Hidden Presence," *Journal of Psychology and Theology* 2 (1974): 104–15.
31. Gen. 3:8.
32. 1 John 1:8–10.
33. John 16:8.
34. Job 1:9–11; Rev. 12:10.
35. Rom. 6:23.
36. Psalm 73.
37. See D. S. Holmes, "Defense Mechanisms," in *Concise Encyclopedia of Psychology,* ed. Raymond J. Corsini (New York: Wiley, 1987), 295–98.
38. Joel Johnson, "Desire, Guilt and Holiness," *Christian Counselor* 2 (Spring 1987): 6.
39. This research was done jointly at Harvard University, the University of Michigan, and Dartmouth College; reported by D. Goleman, "Research Affirms Power of Positive Thinking," *New York Times,* 3 February 1987, C1, 5.
40. This figure is suggested in the insightful article that I used in writing this section of the chapter; see Peter Marin, "Living in Moral Pain," *Psychology Today* 14 (November 1981): 68–80. Within the past several years a number of research articles have discussed posttraumatic stress disorder (PTSD); see, e.g., J. Fairbank, T. Keane, and P. Malloy, "Some Preliminary Data on the Psychological Characteristics of Vietnam Veterans with Posttraumatic Stress Disorders," *Journal of Consulting and Clinical Psychology* 51 (1983): 912–19; D. Foy et al., "Etiology of Posttraumatic Stress Disorder in Vietnam Veterans: Analysis of Premilitary, Military, and Combat Exposure Influences," *Journal of Consulting and Clinical Psychology* 52 (1984): 79–87; and K. Pearce et al., "A Study of Posttraumatic Stress Disorder in Vietnam Veterans," *Journal of Clinical Psychology* 41 (1985): 9–14.
41. Marin, "Living in Moral Pain," 71, italics added.
42. Ibid.
43. Ibid., 68.
44. Ibid., 74.
45. 1 John 1:9; the psychological benefits of forgiveness are discussed by D. Hope, "The Healing Paradox of Forgiveness," *Psychotherapy* 24 (1987): 240–44.
46. Marin ("Living in Moral Pain," 74) writes that many counselors "shy away from the question of moral pain simply because it is likely to open up areas of pain

for which there is really nothing like a 'cure.' As one therapist told me regarding the atrocities and attendant shame that were sometimes discussed in his rap group, 'That, my friend, is the hardest thing to deal with. When somebody brings it up, we all fall silent. Nobody knows how . . . to handle it.'"

47. Thomas C. Oden, *Guilt Free* (Nashville: Abingdon, 1980), 42; Oden argues that we show a "wholesale mishandling of guilt in our society" when we try to treat guilt without considering its theological aspects.

48. O. Hobart Mowrer, *The Crisis in Psychiatry and Religion* (Princeton, N.J.: Van Nostrand, 1961), 82.

49. Karl Menninger, *Whatever Became of Sin?* (New York: Hawthorn, 1973).

50. John 8:3–11.

51. 1 Cor. 10:12.

52. Matt. 7:1; Rom. 12:19–20.

53. 2 Sam. 12:1–14.

54. Marin, "Living with Moral Pain," 74.

55. 1 Sam. 16:7; Pss. 103:14; 139:1–4; 1 John 1:8.

56. 1 Pet. 3:18.

57. 1 John 1:9; James 5:16.

58. 1 John 1:9.

59. Smedes, *Forgive and Forget,* 12, 190.

60. This is the view of Lewis B. Smedes, "Secrets of Forgiving and Forgetting . . . But Not Necessarily," *Bottom Line Personal* 7 (30 June 1986): 1–2.

61. Geoffrey Peterson, *Conscience and Caring* (Philadelphia: Fortress Press, 1982), 41.

62. Ibid.; in *Understanding People* (Grand Rapids, Mich.: Zondervan, 1987), psychologist Lawrence Crabb argues that seminaries are partially at fault for this confusion. Overly impressed with the fine points of biblical exegesis and theological scholarship, seminary professors and their students are kept out of touch with the value conflicts and real life struggles of people we are trying to reach.

63. Much of Christian counseling deals with ethics: helping people to decide what is right and guiding them as they deal with guilt over past actions. For an excellent secular treatment of this, see Gerald Corey et al., *Issues and Ethics in the Helping Professions,* 2d ed. (Monterey, Calif.: Brooks/Cole, 1984). I know of no parallel volume dealing with ethics in Christian counseling. Such a book is much needed.

64. Eph. 4:32.

65. This is the theme of a book by Lucy Freeman and Herbert S. Strean, *Guilt: Letting Go* (New York: Wiley, 1986).

Chapter 11 *Child Rearing and Parental Guidance*

1. Cited by Judson Swihart in *Parents and Children,* ed. Jay Kesler, Ron Beers, and LaVonne Neff (Wheaton, Ill.: Victor Books, 1986), 24.

2. L. Eugene Arnold, ed., *Helping Parents Help Their Children* (New York: Brunner/Mazel, 1978); see also, Avis Brenner, *Helping Children Cope with Stress* (Lexington, Mass.: Lexington Books, 1984).

3. The following are some of the more complete books among those written from a Christian perspective: Grace H. Ketterman, *The Complete Book of Baby and*

Child Care for Christian Parents, rev. ed. (Old Tappan, N.J.: Revell, 1987); Leslie R. Keylock, ed., *The Encyclopedia of Christian Parenting* (Old Tappan, N.J.: Revell, 1982); and Kesler, Beers, and Neff, *Parents and Children*.

4. Ps. 127:3–5; Jer. 22:30; Gen. 30:22–23; Rachel, Sarah, Hannah, Michal, and Elizabeth were among biblical women whose childlessness caused considerable distress.

5. Luke 18:15–17.

6. Ps. 127:3; Matt. 18:10; Ps. 103:13; Titus 2:4; Matt. 18:1–6.

7. Exod. 20:12; Mark 7:10–13; Prov. 1:8; 4:1; 13:1; 23:22; Eph. 6:1.

8. Rom. 1:30; see also 2 Tim. 3:1–5.

9. Acts 5:29.

10. Titus 2:4; Deut. 6:1–9; Prov. 22:6; 2 Cor. 12:14; Col. 3:21.

11. Gene A. Getz, *The Measure of a Family* (Ventura, Calif.: Regal, 1976), 83–94.

12. Deut. 6:1–7.

13. Luke 2:52.

14. These and other issues are discussed in detail in Harold I. Kaplan and Benjamin J. Sadock, eds., *Comprehensive Textbook of Psychiatry/IV* (New York: Wiley, 1985); see also Jules R. Bemporad, ed., *Child Development in Normality and Psychopathology* (New York: Brunner/Mazel, 1980); Charles L. Thompson, *Counseling Children* (Monterey, Calif.: Brooks/Cole, 1983); and Steven Schwartz and James H. Johnson, *Psychopathology of Childhood: A Clinical-Experimental Approach,* 2d ed. (New York: Pergamon, 1985).

15. Robert J. Trotter, "You've Come a Long Way, Baby," *Psychology Today* 20 (May 1987): 34.

16. See, e.g., Deut. 6:1–9; Prov. 22:6; Ps. 78:1–8.

17. David Early, "Kicked Out: Children Become Castoffs When Parents Can't Cope," *Chicago Tribune,* 11 July 1984. According to this report, 27,000 new cases of homeless and runaway children are reported every year in the United States. Of the estimated 1.5 to 2 million "throwaway kids" who have left home, most are in late childhood or early adolescence.

18. A. E. Kazdin and D. J. Kolko, "Parent Pychopathology and Family Functioning among Childhood Firesetters," *Journal of Abnormal Child Psychology* 14 (1986): 315–29; see also, Wayne S. Wooden, "The Flames of Youth," *Psychology Today* 19 (January 1985): 22–28. Many fires are started accidentally by curious young children playing with matches. Of those who set fires deliberately, about 40 percent are children, many of whom appear to be crying for help. The United States has the highest arson rate in the world.

19. See Michael Rutter, "Resilient Children," *Psychology Today* 18 (March 1984): 56–65.

20. Psychological maltreatment has been called "a major threat to children's mental health"; see Stuart N. Hart and Marla R. Brassard, "A Major Threat to Children's Mental Health," *American Psychologist* 42 (February 1987): 160–65; see also James Garbarino, Edna Guttmann, and Janis Wilson Seely, *The Psychologically Battered Child* (San Francisco, Calif.: Jossey/Bass, 1987); and Diane H. Schetky and Arthur H. Green, *Child Sexual Abuse* (New York: Brunner/Mazel, 1988). The perceptions and characteristics of abusive parents are reported in research by J. B. Reid, K. Kavanagh, and D. V. Baldwin, "Abusive Parents' Perceptions of Child Problem

Behaviors: An Example of Parental Bias," *Journal of Abnormal Child Psychology* 15 (1987): 457–66.

21. For a readable discussion of the emotional needs of children, see Mary Vander Goot, *Healthy Emotions: The Emotional Development of Children* (Grand Rapids, Mich.: Eerdmans, 1987).

22. See, e.g., Roberta S. Myers and Terry M. Pace, "Counseling Gifted and Talented Students: Historical Perspectives and Contemporary Issues," *Journal of Counseling and Development* 64 (May 1986): 548–51.

23. Cynthia R. Pfeffer, "Children's Reactions to Illness, Hospitalization, and Surgery," in Kaplan and Sadock, *Handbook of Psychiatry,* 1836–42.

24. It is well known that mental retardation is common in children whose mothers contracted German measles during the first months of pregnancy.

25. For further information, see chapter 37 and Ludwik S. Szymanski and Allen C. Crocker, "Mental Retardation," in Kaplan and Sadock, *Handbook of Psychiatry,* 1635–71.

26. Richard W. Brunstetter and Larry B. Silver, "Attention Deficit Disorder," in Kaplan and Sadock, *Handbook of Psychiatry,* 1684–90.

27. Maya Pines, "Superkids," *Psychology Today* 12 (January 1979): 52–63; and E. E. Werner and R. S. Smith, *Vulnerable but Invincible: A Longitudinal Study of Resilient Children and Youth* (New York: McGraw-Hill, 1982).

28. Isa. 1:2.

29. Parents can also find help in books such as those by Joy P. Gage, *When Parents Cry* (Denver: Accent Books, 1980); and Guy Greenfield, *The Wounded Parent: Coping with Parental Discouragement* (Grand Rapids, Mich.: Baker, 1982).

30. 1 Sam. 3:11–13.

31. A more rational attempt to help parents is presented by Gregory Bodenhamer, *Back in Control: How to Get Your Children to Behave* (Englewood Cliffs, N.J.: Prentice-Hall, 1983).

32. Rachel Gittelman, ed. *Anxiety Disorders of Childhood* (New York: Guilford, 1986).

33. See, e.g., William N. Friedrich and William J. Luecke, "Young School-Age Sexually Aggressive Children," *Professional Psychology: Research and Practice* 19 (April 1988): 155–64.

34. It was not until 1980 that childhood depression was listed in the American Psychiatric Association's handbook of psychiatric disorders. Media interest in this condition has also increased. See Gloria Hochman, "Childhood Depression," *Chicago Tribune,* 22 March 1987; and Javad H. Kashani et al., "Current Perspectives on Childhood Depression: An Overview," *American Journal of Psychiatry* 138 (February 1981): 143–51; and Paul V. Trad, *Infant and Childhood Depression: Developmental Factors* (New York: Wiley, 1987).

35. Cynthia R. Pfeffer, "Suicidal Behavior of Children: A Review with Implications for Research and Practice," *American Journal of Psychiatry* 138 (February 1981): 154–59.

36. As examples, see Leonard T. Gries, "The Use of Multiple Goals in the Treatment of Foster Children with Emotional Disorders," *Professional Psychology: Research and Practice* 17 (October 1986): 381–90; Charles E. Schaefer et al., *Advances in Therapies for Children* (San Francisco: Jossey-Bass, 1986); and Nancy Taylor Mitchum,

"Developmental Play Therapy: A Treatment Approach for Child Victims of Sexual Molestation," *Journal of Counseling and Development* 65 (February 1987): 320–21.
37. For a discussion of "tactics used by children of all ages and ways parents can turn the tables," see Paul W. Robinson, *Manipulating Parents* (Englewood Cliffs, N.J.: Prentice-Hall, 1981).
38. Family counseling is discussed in chapter 29.
39. Some parents need to be more assertive with their children; training parents in this behavior may be the best way to help some children; see Terry Clifford, "Assertiveness Training for Parents," *Journal of Counseling and Development* 65 (June 1987): 552–54.
40. A popular discussion of working mothers is presented by Kathleen Gerson, "Briefcase, Baby or Bottle?" *Psychology Today* 20 (November 1986): 31–36. There are a number of books available on family therapy, including A. S. Gurman and D. P. Kniskern, eds., *Handbook of Family Therapy* (New York: Brunner/Mazel, 1981).
41. Arnold, *Helping Parents*.
42. Getz, *The Measure of a Family,* 13.
43. The market is flooded with these books, but the following are helpful volumes in addition to those listed above: Sol Gordon and Judith Gordon, *Raising a Child Conservatively in a Sexually Permissive World* (New York: Simon & Schuster, 1983); Grace H. Ketterman, *A Circle of Love* (Old Tappan, N.J.: Revell, 1987); Paul McKean and Jeannie McKean, *Leading a Child to Independence* (San Bernardino, Calif.: Here's Life Publishers, 1986); and Gary Smalley, *The Key to Your Child's Heart* (Waco, Tex.: Word, 1984). For a practical approach from a psychoanalytic perspective, see Bruno Bettelheim, *The Good Enough Parent* (New York: Knopf, 1987).
44. Someone has suggested that the best way for a father to love his children is to respect and love their mother.
45. G. C. Gard and K. K. Berry, "Oppositional Children: Taming Tyrants," *Journal of Clinical Child Psychology* 15 (1986): 148–58; see also Bodenhamer, *Back in Control.* For a summary of behavioral approaches to one common problem, bed wetting, see William G. Wagner, "The Behavioral Treatment of Childhood Nocturnal Enuresis," *Journal of Counseling and Development* 65 (January 1987): 262–65.
46. Remind parents that some kids never do learn to hang up their clothes. The parent works at this until the child leaves home; then the spouse can take over!
47. See especially, Arnold, *Helping Parents*; Brenner, *Helping Children Cope*; James Dobson, *Dr. Dobson Answers Your Questions* (Wheaton, Ill.: Tyndale, 1982); Kesler et al., *Parents and Children*; and Ketterman, *Baby and Child Care*.
48. E. James Anthony and Manon McGennis, "Counseling Very Disturbed Parents," in Arnold, *Helping Parents,* 339–40.
49. As a resource book for group discussion, see *Parents and Children: God's Design for the Family, Book 2* (Colorado Springs, Colo.: NavPress, 1980).
50. A complete and excellent practical resource for strengthening families has been written by Charles Sell, *Family Ministry: Enrichment of Family Life through the Church* (Grand Rapids, Mich.: Zondervan, 1981).
51. Gordon MacDonald, *The Effective Father* (Wheaton, Ill.: Tyndale House, 1977).
52. See chapter 16.
53. 1 Thess. 5:11; Heb. 3:13; 10:25.

54. Landrum Bolling, "Relaxing with Parenthood: Guidelines from a Veteran," *Eternity* (August 1975): 11, 23.

Chapter 12 *Adolescence*

1. Armand M. Nicholi, Jr., ed., *The Harvard Guide to Modern Psychology* (Cambridge, Mass.: Belknap Press of Harvard University Press, 1978), 519.
2. Mihaly Csikszentmihalyi and Reed Larson, *Being Adolescent: Conflict and Growth in the Teenage Years* (New York: Basic Books, 1984); see also Barbara M. Newman and Philip R. Newman, *Adolescent Development* (Columbus, Ohio: Charles E. Merrill, 1986); and M. Lerner and T. T. Foch, eds., *Biological-Psychosocial Interactions in Early Adolescence* (New York: Lawrence Erlbaum Associates, 1987).
3. Joshua Fischman, "The Ups and Downs of Teenage Life," *Psychology Today* 20 (April 1987): 56–57.
4. In 1904, G. Stanley Hall, one of the pioneers in American psychology and first president of the American Psychological Association, published a massive two-volume study of adolescence. He described the teenage years as a period of "storm and stress," and his work triggered literally thousands of research studies designed to help subsequent generations understand and counsel young people.
5. Joseph Adelson, "Adolescence and the Generalization Gap," *Psychology Today* 12 (February 1979): 33–37.
6. Anne C. Petersen, "Those Gangly Years," *Psychology Today* 21 (September 1987): 28–34.
7. American readers will recognize that these time frames correspond roughly to the junior high, high school, and college years.
8. Figures differ from country to country but in the United States it is estimated that a majority of teenagers are sexually active. Confidential surveys show that the percentage of sexually active Christian young people, including those from evangelical churches, is only slightly less than the national norms. See Josh McDowell, *What I Wish My Parents Knew about My Sexuality* (San Bernardino, Calif.: Here's Life Publishers, 1987).
9. Elizabeth Stark, "Young, Innocent and Pregnant," *Psychology Today* 20 (October 1986): 28–35.
10. E. R. Oetting and Fred Beauvais, "Peer Cluster Theory: Drugs and the Adolescent," *Journal of Counseling and Development* 65 (September 1986): 17–22.
11. Nicholi, *The Harvard Guide,* 532.
12. The first three of these have been called "the adolescent's developmental tasks"; see G. Keith Olson, *Counseling Teenagers: The Complete Christian Guide to Understanding and Helping Adolescents* (Loveland, Colo.: Group Books, 1984).
13. It is well known that Erikson suggested the term "identity crisis" to describe the major issue facing adolescents. Some critics have suggested that this is not a universal characteristic of youth, and for many it isn't even a crisis. E. H. Erikson, *Identity: Youth and Crisis* (New York: Norton, 1968).
14. "The Spirit of Youth," *Royal Bank Letter* [Canada] 66 (November/December 1985).
15. See chapter 11.

16. Eccles. 11:9–10 LB.
17. Acts 2:17; Prov. 20:29; 1 John 2:13–14; Titus 2:4–6; 1 Pet. 5:5–7.
18. These are the words of Joan Scheff Lipsitz, director of the Center for Early Adolescence at the University of North Carolina, testifying before the U.S. Congressional House Select Committee on Children, Youth and Families; quoted in Jeffrey Mervis, "Adolescent Behavior: What We Think We Know," *APA Monitor* 15 (April 1984): 24–25.
19. Charles Swindoll expresses a much healthier attitude in his views of the teen years: "I'm so thrilled with the teenage years, and I want to tell all the prophets of doom who say, 'Just wait until your kids are teenagers—you'll *hate* it': I've never hated a day of it! I'm sorry that kind of bad press gets around"; quoted in Jay Kesler, ed., *Parents and Teenagers* (Wheaton, Ill.: Victor Books, 1984), 20.
20. Ronald Kotulak, "America Awakens to Discover Its Teenagers Are Ill," *Chicago Tribune,* 11 January 1987.
21. "Incredible as it may seem, most opposition to sex education in this country is based on the assumption that knowledge is harmful"; this is the view of Sol Gordon, "What Kids Need to Know," *Psychology Today* 20 (October 1986): 22–26. Gordon argues that sexual problems in adolescence come, at least partially, because parents, schools, and churches have failed to give young people accurate advice and guidance about sex.
22. Cathryn I. Hill, "A Developmental Perspective on Adolescent 'Rebellion' in the Church," *Journal of Psychology and Theology* 14 (Winter 1986): 306–18.
23. See, e.g., Jerald G. Bachman, "An Eye on the Future" *Psychology Today* 21 (July 1987): 6–8; J. H. Bunzel, *Challenge to American Schools: The Case for Standards and Values* (New York: Oxford University Press, 1985); and Robert Coles, *The Moral Life of Children* (New York: Atlantic Monthly Press, 1986).
24. Virginia A. Sadock, "Adolescent Sexuality," *Harvard Medical School Mental Health Letter* 3 (March 1987), 8.
25. S. Preston, "Children and the Elderly in the U.S.," *Scientific American* 251 (1984): 44–49.
26. "The Values of America's Adolescents," *Search Institute Source* 2 (August 1986): 1–3.
27. Quest International Hispanic Advisory Committee, *Celebrating Differences: Approaches to Hispanic Youth Development* (Columbus, Ohio: Quest International, 1987).
28. This is clearly demonstrated by McDowell, *What I Wish My Parents Knew.* I have tried to summarize and give answers to some of these pressures in Gary R. Collins, *Give Me a Break: The How-to-Handle-Pressure Book for Teenagers* (Old Tappan, N.J.: Revell, 1982).
29. Don Booth, "What Christian Kids Don't Tell Their Parents," *Eternity* (November 1976): 32–33.
30. James Dobson, *Preparing for Adolescence* (Santa Ana, Calif.: Vision House, 1978).
31. Kearney B. Waites, "Survival Skills for Adolescents," *Christian Counselor* 2 (Spring 1987): 12–14.
32. A creative and highly successful program for training adolescents in life skills has been developed by Quest International (6655 Sharon Woods Boulevard, Columbus,

Ohio 43229-7019). Working in conjunction with Lions International, the Quest *Skills for Adolescence* program is now offered annually in thousands of school classrooms around the world.

33. Erikson, *Identity,* 156.

34. For further information on adolescent psychopathology see Carl P. Malmquist, *Handbook of Adolescence: Psychopathology, Antisocial Development, Psychotherapy* (New York: Jason Aronson, 1978); Sherman C. Feinstein, "Identity and Adjustment Disorders of Adolescence," in *Comprehensive Textbook of Psychiatry/IV,* ed. Harold I. Kaplan and Benjamin J. Sadock (Baltimore: Williams & Wilkins, 1985), 1760–65; and Kathleen McCoy, *Coping with Teenage Depression: A Parent's Guide* (New York: New American Library, 1982).

35. Eight out of ten deaths among adolescents and young adults are violent. These figures include those that are not intentional along with deaths caused by suicide and murder. Ronald Kotalak, "Violence," *Chicago Tribune,* 12 December 1986.

36. Nicholi, *The Harvard Guide,* 530.

37. Charlotte MacDonald, "The Stunted World of Teenage Parents," *Human Behavior* (January 1979): 53–55; see also "Teenage Pregnancy," *Search Institute Source* 1 (November 1985): 1–2.

38. W. Baldwin and W. Cain, "The Children of Teenage Parents," in *Teenage Sexuality, Pregnancy, and Childbearing,* ed. F. Furstenberg, R. Lincoln, and J. Menken (Philadelphia: University of Pennsylvania Press, 1981).

39. Colleen Cordes, "Runaways," *APA Monitor* 14 (April 1983). I am reluctant to cite statistics in this book, especially since many readers do not live in the United States. Some evidence suggests, however, that every year over a million American teenagers run away or are pushed out of home by their parents.

40. Drinking and drug use, as we have seen, can also be ways of acting out.

41. James R. Delisle, "Death with Honors: Suicide among Gifted Adolescents," *Journal of Counseling and Development* 64 (May 1986): 558–60.

42. Jon Anderson, "An Answer to Teenage Suicide: 'Soul Searching,'" *Chicago Tribune,* 3 May 1987; see also Jill M. Harkavy Friedman et al., "Prevalence of Specific Suicidal Behaviors in a High School Sample," *American Journal of Psychiatry* 144 (September 1987): 1203–6; and John Q. Baucom, *Fatal Choice* (Chicago: Moody, 1986).

43. S. R. Heyman, "Psychological Problem Patterns Found with Athletes," *Clinical Psychologist* 39 (1986): 68–71.

44. For more information, see Olson, *Counseling Teenagers*; Michael D. Stein and J. Kent Davis, *Therapies for Adolescents* (San Francisco: Jossey-Bass, 1982); Richard P. Barth, *Social and Cognitive Treatment of Children and Adolescents* (San Francisco: Jossey-Bass, 1987).

45. Isa. 1:2; for a discussion of teenage rebellion, written for Christian parents, see Truman E. Dollar and Grace H. Ketterman, *Teenage Rebellion: How to Recognize It, Deal with It, Prevent It* (Old Tappan, N.J.: Revell, 1979).

46. For a further discussion of family counseling see chapter 29.

47. Merton P. Strommen, *Five Cries of Youth* (New York: Harper & Row, 1974); and M. Strommen and A. I. Strommen, *Five Cries of Parents* (San Francisco: Harper & Row, 1985).

48. Olson, *Counseling Teenagers,* 159.

49. This is the opinion of Pamela Cantor, president of the National Committee of Youth Suicide Prevention, in "How Schools Should Treat Teen Suicide," *Chicago Tribune,* 23 March 1987; see also Joan Polly, *Preventing Teenage Suicide* (New York: Human Sciences Press, 1986).
50. Several years ago I wrote a book designed to stimulate such discussion in the church and family; see Gary R. Collins, *Family Talk* (Ventura, Calif.: Vision House, 1978).
51. Matt. 28:19–20.
52. This is the title of a book by the former president of Youth for Christ, Jay Kesler, *Too Big to Spank* (Glendale, Calif.: Regal Books, 1978).

Chapter 13 *Young Adulthood*

1. Harold I. Kaplan and Benjamin J. Sadock, eds., *Comprehensive Textbook of Psychiatry/IV* (Baltimore: Williams and Wilkins, 1985).
2. Daniel J. Levinson, "A Conception of Adult Development," *American Psychologist* 41 (January 1986): 3–13.
3. See Daniel J. Levinson et al., *The Seasons of a Man's Life* (New York: Alfred Knopf, 1978); and idem, *The Seasons of a Woman's Life* (New York: Alfred Knopf, 1988).
4. Daniel J. Levinson, "New Opportunities in Adult Development," *Bottom Line Personal* 8 (15 September 1987): 1–3.
5. Ibid., 2.
6. Landon Y. Jones, *Great Expectations: America and the Baby Boom Generation* (New York: Coward, McCann and Geoghegan, 1980).
7. This is the thesis of Allan Bloom, *The Closing of the American Mind* (New York: Simon & Schuster, 1987).
8. Landon Y. Jones, "The Baby Boomers," *Money* 12 (March 1983): 56–58.
9. Jones, *Great Expectations,* 1–2.
10. This is not universally true. On the day that I began this chapter, a brochure arrived in the mail announcing a conference for church leaders on the topic "Baby Boomers and the Church: A New Generation, A New Challenge."
11. Gene A. Getz, *David: God's Man in Faith and Failure* (Ventura, Calif.: Regal, 1978), 4.
12. 2 Sam. 6:16, 20–23.
13. 2 Sam. 5:4.
14. 1 Tim. 4:12.
15. Arthur Levine, *When Dreams and Heroes Died: A Portrait of Today's College Student* (San Francisco: Jossey-Bass, 1981), 22.
16. Some of the following discussion is adapted from a book that I wrote several years ago to help people adapt to young adulthood; see Gary R. Collins, *Getting Started: Direction for the Most Important Decisions of Life* (Old Tappan, N.J.: Revell, 1984).
17. E.g., Bloom, *The Closing of the American Mind*; the cover of the book has an interesting subtitle: "How Higher Education Has Failed Democracy and Impoverished the Souls of Today's Students."
18. I cannot resist inserting a personal footnote at this point. The prestige is less common than nonwriters might think, and the fame is even rarer!

19. For a self-help approach to life management skills, see Gary R. Collins, *Getting Your Life Out of Neutral* (Old Tappan, N.J.: Fleming H. Revell, 1987). Counselees might also find help in an excellent book by Gordon MacDonald, *Ordering Your Private World* (Nashville, Tenn.: Oliver-Nelson, 1984).
20. See chapter 16.
21. Rom. 12:18.
22. Collins, *Getting Started,* 39.
23. For balanced perspectives on some of these "spiritual" movements, see Paul C. Reisser, Teri Reisser, and John Weldon, *The Holistic Healers: A Christian Perspective on New-Age Health Care* (Downers Grove, Ill.: InterVarsity, 1983); and Douglas R. Groothuis, *Unmasking the New Age* (Downers Grove, Ill.: InterVarsity, 1986).
24. Sharon Parks, *The Critical Years: The Young Adult Search for a Faith to Live By* (New York: Harper & Row, 1986).
25. These are among the questions discussed in a group counseling approach designed to help young adults move from their homes, through college, and into their professional lives; see Karen M. Schwartz and C. Michele Ward, "Leaving Home: A Semistructured Group Experience," *Journal of Counseling and Development* 65 (October 1986): 107.
26. J. Kendall Lott, "Freshman Home Reentry: Attending to a Gap in Student Development," *Journal of Counseling and Development* 64 (March 1986): 456; see also Harold Ivan Smith, "When Jenny Comes Marching Home (Again)," *Christian Herald* 110 (September 1987): 47–51.
27. This is the definition of autonomy given by Gerard Egan and Michael A. Cowan, *Moving into Adulthood* (Monterey, Calif.: Brooks/Cole, 1980), 98.
28. Ibid., 97.
29. Ibid., 141.
30. Erik H. Erikson, *Identity: Youth and Crisis* (New York: Norton, 1968). For one discussion of identity formation in women, see Ruthellen Josselson, *Finding Herself: Pathways to Identity Development in Women* (San Francisco: Jossey-Bass, 1987).
31. Egan and Cowan, *Moving into Adulthood,* 110.
32. Erik H. Erikson, *Childhood and Society,* rev. ed. (New York: Norton, 1963).
33. Levinson, *Seasons of a Man's Life,* 91; Levinson and his associates refer to Dream with an initial capital letter to "identify and emphasize our special use of the word"; I have followed their example.
34. Mentoring has been discussed frequently in recent writings; see, e.g., L. Phillips-Jones, *Mentors and Protégés* (New York: Arbor, 1982); or Marilyn Haring-Hidore, "Mentoring as a Career Enhancement Strategy for Women," *Journal of Counseling and Development* 66 (November 1987): 147–48; see also, notes 44 and 51.
35. Carrie Tuhy, "What Price Children?" *Money* 12 (March 1983): 77–84; see also Kathleen Gerson, "Briefcase, Baby or Both?" *Psychology Today* 20 (November 1986): 30–36.
36. Anne Rosenfeld and Elizabeth Stark, "The Prime of Our Lives," *Psychology Today* 21 (May 1987): 62–72.
37. Gail Sheehy, *Passages: Predictable Crises of Adult Life* (New York: Dutton, 1976).
38. Ibid., 289.
39. Ibid., 340.

40. Gene Brocknek, *The Young Adult: Development after Adolescence* (Monterey, Calif.: Brooks/Cole, 1980), 189.
41. Apparently a similar discrepancy exists in terms of counseling services. A number of counseling centers seek to help college students make vocational decisions, but according to one report "most placement, counseling, and other services providing assistance . . . are not specifically aimed at the adult student (twenty-five years or older) whose employment needs are different from those of the traditional student"; Rosemary S. Arp, Kay S. Holmberg, and John M. Littrell, "Launching Adult Students into the Job Market: A Support Group Approach," *Journal of Counseling and Development* 65 (November 1986): 166–67.
42. In working with young adults who bring problems that are not age-related, you may want to consult the appropriate chapters elsewhere in this book.
43. The importance of relationships in counseling has been emphasized by a number of writers including Bernard G. Guerney, Jr., *Relationship Enhancement* (San Francisco: Jossey-Bass, 1977); and Helen Harris Perlman, *Relationship: The Heart of Helping People* (Chicago: University of Chicago Press, 1979).
44. M. Johnson, "Mentors—The Key to Development and Growth," *Training and Development Journal* 34 (1980): 55–57; Martin Gerstein, "Mentoring: An Age Old Practice in a Knowledge-Based Society," *Journal of Counseling and Development* 64 (October 1985): 156–57.
45. See, e.g., John S. Westefeld and Susan R. Furr, "Suicide and Depression among College Students," *Professional Psychology: Research and Practice* 18 (April 1987).
46. William R. Miller and Kathleen A. Jackson, *Practical Psychology for Pastors* (Englewood Cliffs, N.J.: Prentice-Hall, 1985), 144–67; see also, Allen Tough, *Intentional Changes: A Fresh Approach to Helping People Change* (Chicago: Follett, 1982).
47. The term "stuck syndrome" was suggested in an article by Martin G. Grober, "The Terrible Stuck Syndrome," *Bottom Line Personal* 20 (30 October 1985): 9–10.
48. Levinson et al., *Seasons of a Man's Life,* 337, parentheses added.
49. This theme is developed further by Frederick G. Lopez, "Family Structure and Depression: Implications for the Counseling of Depressed College Students," *Journal of Counseling and Development* 64 (April 1986): 508–11.
50. This less traditional type of people helping is emphasized by Eugena Hanfmann, *Effective Therapy for College Students: Alternatives to Traditional Counseling* (San Francisco: Jossey-Bass, 1978).
51. C. Farren, J. D. Gray, and B. Kaye, "Mentoring: A Boon to Career Development," *Personnel* 61 (1984): 20–24; see also M. Zey, *The Mentor Connection* (Homewood, Ill.: Dow Jones-Irwin, 1984); N. Collins, *Professional Women and Their Mentors* (Englewood Cliffs, N.J.: Prentice-Hall, 1983; and Felice A. Kaufmann et al., "The Nature, Role, and Influence of Mentors in the Lives of Gifted Adults," *Journal of Counseling and Development* 64 (May 1986): 576–78.
52. John "Mercury" Morgan, "The Kid Who Did," *Guideposts* 42 (September 1987): 2–6.

Chapter 14 *Middle Age*

1. Ruby MacDonald, *Ruby MacDonald's Forty Plus and Feeling Fabulous Book* (Old Tappan, N.J.: Fleming H. Revell, 1982).

2. Robert Taylor, *Welcome to the Middle Years* (Washington, D.C.: Acropolis Books, 1976), 2.

3. Jim Conway, *Men in Mid-Life Crisis* (Elgin, Ill.: David C. Cook, 1978); Jim Conway and Sally Conway, *Women in Mid-Life Crisis* (Wheaton, Ill.: Tyndale, 1983); Nancy Mayer, *The Male Mid-Life Crisis: Fresh Starts after Forty* (New York: Signet, 1978); and Eda LeShan, *The Wonderful Crisis of Middle Age* (New York: McKay, 1973).

4. Robert N. Butler, "Psychiatry and Psychology of the Middle-aged," in *Comprehensive Textbook of Psychiatry/IV*, ed. Harold I. Kaplan and Benjamin J. Sadock, 4th ed. (Baltimore: Williams and Wilkins, 1985), 1943–52.

5. David F. Hultsch and Francine Deutsch, *Adult Development and Aging: A Life-Span Perspective* (New York: McGraw-Hill, 1981).

6. Tom Mullen, *Parables for Parents and Other Original Sinners* (Waco, Tex.: Word, 1975), 128–30.

7. C. G. Jung, *Psychological Reflections*, ed. Jolande Jacobi (New York: Harper Torchbooks, 1961), 125.

8. Christopher Matthew, *How to Survive Middle Age* (London: Hodder and Stoughton, 1983).

9. Ray Ortlund and Anne Ortlund, *The Best Half of Life* (Ventura, Calif.: Regal, 1976).

10. Jung, *Psychological Reflections*, 121, 123.

11. Daniel J. Levinson et al., *The Seasons of a Man's Life* (New York: Knopf, 1978), ix–x.

12. One study of Protestant clergy, e.g., suggests that pastors fail to follow the Levinson stages; see Les Steele, "Adult Development Periods and Protestant Male Clergy: A Descriptive Framework," *Journal of Psychology and Theology* 16 (Spring 1988): 15–20.

13. Nancy K. Schlossberg, "Taking the Mystery out of Change," *Psychology Today* 21 (May 1987): 74–75.

14. Daniel J. Levinson, "A Conception of Adult Development," *American Psychologist* 41 (January 1986): 3–13.

15. Charlotte R. Melcher, "Career Counseling Tailored to the Evangelical Christian Woman in Midlife," *Journal of Psychology and Theology* 15 (Summer 1987): 133–43.

16. Butler, "Psychiatry and Psychology," 1945.

17. Lillian E. Troll, *Early and Middle Adulthood: The Best Is Yet to Be—Maybe* (Monterey, Calif.: Brooks/Cole, 1975).

18. B. L. Neugarten, ed., *Middle Life and Aging: A Reader in Social Psychology* (Chicago: University of Chicago Press, 1968).

19. N. R. Haimowitz, "Middle Age," in *Concise Encyclopedia of Psychology*, ed. Raymond J. Corsini (New York: Wiley, 1987): 717.

20. Martin G. Groder, "Boredom: The Good and the Bad," *Bottom Line Personal* 7 (15 March 1986): 9–10.

21. Haimowitz, "Middle Age," 718.

22. Conway, *Men in Mid-Life*, 105.

23. Samuel D. Osherson, *Holding On or Letting Go: Men and Career Change at Midlife* (New York: Free Press, 1980).

24. Fern Schumer Chapman, "Executive Guilt: Who's Taking Care of the Children," *Fortune* 115 (16 February 1987): 30–37.

25. For a further discussion of the problems of vocational change in middle age, see Peter Filene, *Men in the Middle* (Englewood Cliffs, N.J.: Prentice-Hall, 1981).
26. Carola H. Mann, "Mid-Life and the Family: Strains, Challenges and Options of the Middle Years," in *Mid-Life: Developmental and Clinical Issues,* ed. William H. Norman and Thomas J. Scaramella (New York: Brunner/Mazel, 1980), 128–48.
27. Gary R. Collins, "Caught between Parents and Children," *Christian Herald* 110 (February 1987): 51–53; see also J. E. Dobson and R. L. Dobson, "The Sandwich Generation: Dealing with Aging Parents," *Journal of Counseling and Development* 63 (1985): 572–74; Jane E. Myers, "The Mid/Late Life Generation Gap: Adult Children with Aging Parents," *Journal of Counseling and Development* 66 (March 1988): 331–35; Barbara Silverstone and Helen Kandel Hyman, *You and Your Aging Parent* (New York: Pantheon, 1983); Patricia H. Rushford, *The Help, Hope and Cope Book for People with Aging Parents* (Old Tappan, N.J.: Revell, 1985); and Lissy Jarvik and Gary Small, *Parentcare: A Commonsense Guide for Adult Children* (New York: Crown, 1988).
28. Ellen Galinsky, *Between Generations: The Six Stages of Parenthood* (New York: Times Books, 1981); H. Norman Wright, *Seasons of a Marriage* (Ventura, Calif.: Regal Books, 1982).
29. Paul A. Mickey, *Marriage in the Middle Years* (Valley Forge, Penn.: Judson, 1986).
30. For further discussion of affairs in midlife, see Conway, *Men in Mid-Life*; Wright, *Seasons*; Peter Kreitler with Bill Burns, *Affair Prevention* (New York: Macmillan, 1981); and J. Allan Petersen, *The Myth of the Greener Grass* (Wheaton, Ill.: Tyndale, 1983).
31. Ollie Pocs et al., "Is There Sex after 40?" *Psychology Today* 11 (June 1977): 54.
32. Conway, *Men in Mid-Life,* 124.
33. This can include oral-genital sexual contact which, says one leading Christian writer, is not sinful providing it is not offensive to either party and brings mutual pleasure and satisfaction; see Herbert J. Miles, *Sexual Happiness in Marriage* (Grand Rapids, Mich.: Zondervan, 1982).
34. This is the title of a highly anecdotal book by Joel Davitz and Lois Davitz, *Making It from 40 to 50* (New York: Random House, 1976).
35. Conway, *Men in Mid-Life,* 137f.
36. Butler, "Psychiatry and Psychology of the Middle-Aged," 1949.
37. Ibid.
38. Martin Groder, "The Fine Line between Courage and Foolhardiness," *Bottom Line Personal* 7 (30 September 1986): 11–12.
39. Look, e.g., at the chapters on anxiety, marital problems, sex, self-esteem, and vocational counseling.
40. Please see the list of suggested readings at the end of this chapter. Some of these books could be placed in church libraries.
41. Conway, *Men in Mid-Life,* 188.
42. Jung, *Psychological Reflections,* 121.
43. When I turned fifty, I wrote an article suggesting that this milestone was something to celebrate. I was surprised at the positive reaction and at the many people who have written—usually within months of their fiftieth birthdays—to share their feelings at reaching the half-century mark; see Gary R. Collins, "Something to

Celebrate," *Christian Herald* 106 (November 1984): 32–33; see also Herand Katchadourian, *Fifty: Midlife in Perspective* (San Francisco: W. H. Freeman, 1987); for a more humorous perspective, see Bill Cosby, *Time Flies* (Garden City, N.Y.: Doubleday and Co., 1987).

44. Ortlund and Ortlund, *The Best Half,* 116; this is practical discipleship that is not limited to the work of pastors or elders.

45. Erik Erikson, *Childhood and Society,* 2d ed. (New York: Norton, 1963).

46. In concluding this chapter, it perhaps should be noted that middle age is not a crisis for everybody; see Warren W. Wiersbe, "Mid-Life Crisis? Bah, Humbug!" *Christianity Today* 24 (21 May 1982): 26–27.

Chapter 15 *The Later Years*

1. B. F. Skinner and M. E. Vaughn, *Enjoy Old Age: A Program of Self-Management* (New York: Norton, 1983); and E. H. Erikson, J. M. Erikson, and H. Q. Kivnick, *Vital Involvement in Old Age: The Experience of Old Age in Our Time* (New York: Norton, 1986). The Swiss counselor Paul Tournier was a comparatively young seventy-three when he published his book on aging: Paul Tournier, *Learn to Grow Old* (New York: Harper & Row, 1982).

2. Jeff Meer, "The Reason of Age," *Psychology Today* 20 (June 1986): 60–64.

3. Jack C. Horn and Jeff Meer, "The Vintage Years," *Psychology Today* 21 (May 1987): 76–84, 89–90.

4. See, e.g., Carl Eisdorfer, "Conceptual Models of Aging: The Challenge of a New Frontier," *American Psychologist* 38 (February 1983): 197–202.

5. Some of these differences are discussed by B. F. Skinner, "Intellectual Self-Management in Old Age," *American Psychologist* 38 (March 1983): 239–44; Richard S. Lazarus and Anita DeLongis, "Psychological Stress and Coping in Old Age," *American Psychologist* 38 (March 1983): 245–54; and Susan Folkman et al., "Age Differences in Stress and Coping Processes," *Psychology and Aging* 2 (June 1987): 171–84.

6. Job 12:12.

7. Ps. 71:18.

8. Reported in C. Gilhuis, *Conversations on Growing Older* (Grand Rapids, Mich.: William B. Eerdmans, 1977), 19–21.

9. Eccles. 12:13.

10. Lev. 19:32; Prov. 16:31; 20:29.

11. Titus 2:2–3.

12. Eph. 6:3.

13. Tim Stafford, "The Graying of the Church," *Christianity Today* 31 (6 November 1987): 17–22; see also Robert M. Gray and David O. Moberg, *The Church and the Older Person,* rev. ed. (Grand Rapids, Mich.: William B. Eerdmans, 1977).

14. Pat Moore with Charles Paul Conn, *Disguised!* (Waco, Tex.: Word, 1985), 62.

15. David B. Larson, Alan D. Whanger, and Ewald W. Busse, "Geriatrics," in *The Therapist's Handbook: Treatment Methods of Mental Disorders,* ed. Benjamin B. Wolman, 2d ed. (New York: Van Nostrand Reinhold, 1983): 343–88.

16. For further consideration of this issue, see Molly S. Wantz and John E. Gay, *The Aging Process: A Health Perspective* (Cambridge, Mass.: Winthrop, 1981); and

Siegfried Kra, *Aging Myths: Reversible Causes of Mind and Memory Loss* (New York: McGraw-Hill, 1986).
17. Paul T. Costa, Jr., and Robert R. McCrae, "Hypochondriasis, Neuroticism, and Aging: When Are Somatic Complaints Unfounded?" *American Psychologist* 40 (January 1985): 19–28.
18. K. Ludeman, "The Sexuality of the Older Person: Review of the Literature," *Gerontologist* 21 (1981): 203–8; see also Edward M. Brecher, *Love, Sex, and Aging* (Boston: Little, Brown, 1983).
19. Barbara P. Payne, "Sex and the Elderly: No Laughing Matter in Religion," *Journal of Religion and Aging* 3 (Fall-Winter 1986): 141–52.
20. Anastasia Toufexis, "Older—But Coming on Strong" *Time,* 22 February 1988, 76–79.
21. Lewis Aiken, *Later Life* (Philadelphia: Saunders, 1978), 28.
22. Many of these studies are summarized in J. E. Birren and K. W. Schaie, eds., *Handbook of the Psychology of Aging,* 2d ed. (New York: Van Nostrand Reinhold, 1985); see also John W. Santrock, *Adult Development and Aging* Dubuque, Iowa: William C. Brown, 1985); Leonard W. Poon, ed. *Aging in the 1980s: Psychological Issues* (Washington, D.C.: American Psychological Association, 1980); and Kra, *Aging Myths*.
23. Increasing evidence suggests that cognitive functioning and problem-solving abilities in the later years depend little on chronological age but are influenced more by issues such as education, intellectual activity, verbal ability, and involvement with other people; see Tannis Y. Arbuckle, Dolores Gold, and David Andres, "Cognitive Functioning of Older People in Relation to Social and Personality Variables," *Psychology and Aging* 1 (March 1986): 55–62; and Steven W. Cornelius and Avshalom Caspi, "Everyday Problem Solving in Adulthood and Old Age," *Psychology and Aging* 2 (June 1987): 144–53.
24. From a report in the *APA Monitor* (October 1982).
25. Mark Kaminsky, *The Uses of Reminiscence: New Ways of Working with Older Adults* (New York: Haworth Press, 1984).
26. Robert N. Butler, *Why Survive? Being Old in America* (New York: Harper & Row, 1975).
27. Joan Wolinsky, "The Offender as Victim," *APA Monitor* (May 1982): 17, 32; this article reports on a first-of-its-kind conference on criminal behavior in the elderly.
28. See, e.g., Beth B. Hess and Elizabeth W. Markson, *Aging and Old Age* (New York: Macmillan, 1980); and Louis Lowry, *Social Work with the Aging: The Challenge and Promise of the Later Years,* 2d ed. (New York: Longman, 1985). A more recent analysis suggests that the social changes present both a paradox and a promise: A. Pifer and L. Bronte, *Our Aging Society: Paradox and Promise* (New York: Norton, 1986).
29. Dennis Pelsma and Mary Flanagan, "Human Relations Training for the Elderly," *Journal of Counseling and Development* 65 (September 1986): 52–53.
30. Select Committee on Aging, *Elder Abuse: A National Disgrace* (Washington, D.C.: U.S. Government Printing Office, 1985); Grant L. Martin, *Counseling for Family Violence and Abuse* (Waco, Tex.: Word, 1987); and Jane E. Myers and Barbara Shelton, "Abuse and Older Persons: Issues and Implications for Counselors,"

Journal of Counseling and Development 65 (March 1987): 376–80. Abuse and violence is discussed more fully in chapter 20 and in Mary Joy Quinn and Susam K. Tomita, *Elder Abuse and Neglect: Causes, Diagnosis, and Intervention Strategies* (New York: Springer, 1986).

31. Moore, *Disguised!* 76.

32. James A. Thorson and Bruce J. Horacek, "Self-Esteem, Value, and Identity: Who Are the Elderly Really?" *Journal of Religion and Aging* 3 (Fall-Winter 1986): 5–16.

33. The March 1988 issue of the *American Psychologist* included several articles on ageism; see, e.g.. Douglas C. Kimmel, "Ageism, Psychology, and Public Policy," *American Psychologist* 43 (March 1988): 175–78.

34. Mildred Vandenburgh, *Fill Your Days with Life* (Ventura, Calif.: Regal, 1975), 95.

35. Morton A. Lieberman and Sheldon S. Tobin, *The Experience of Old Age: Stress, Coping, and Survival* (New York: Basic Books, 1983). For a good overview of depression and several other major problem characteristics of the elderly, see Peter M. Lewinsohn and Linda Teri, *Clinical Geropsychology: New Directions in Assessment and Treatment* (New York: Pergamon, 1983).

36. This question is discussed by Gari Lesnoff-Caravaglia, "Liberation or Repression," *Generations: In-Depth Views of Issues in Aging* 11 (Fall 1986): 12–14.

37. This term is used in Robert N. Butler and Myrna I. Lewis, *Aging and Mental Health*, 3d ed. (St. Louis: Mosby, 1982).

38. Robert Kastenbaum, "The Search for Meaning," *Generations: In-Depth Views of Issues in Aging* 11 (Spring 1987): 9–13.

39. For discussions of the church's role in working with aging people, see Carl LeFever and Perry LeFever, eds., *Aging and the Human Spirit: A Reader in Religion and Gerontology* (Chicago: Exploration Press, 1981); and Michael C. Hendrickson, "The Role of the Church in Aging: Implications for Policy and Action," *Journal of Religion and Aging* 2 (Fall-Winter 1985–86): 5–16.

40. Nancy J. Osgood, "Suicide and the Elderly," *Generations: In-Depth Views of Issues in Aging* 11 (Spring 1987): 47–51; and Edward Paul Cohn, "Suicide among the Elderly: The Religious Response," *Journal of Religion and Aging* 3 (Fall-Winter 1986): 165–80.

41. Bruce Hilton, "As Funds for Elderly Dry Up, Mercy Killing Rises," *Chicago Tribune*, 25 January 1987.

42. Gray and Moberg, *The Church and the Older Person*, 35; used by permission.

43. A. G. Awad et al., eds., *Disturbed Behavior in the Elderly* (New York: Pergamon, 1987).

44. Butler and Lewis, *Aging and Mental Health*, 175–78; Edmund Sherman, *Counseling the Aging: An Integrative Approach* (New York: Free Press, 1981); Margaret Gatz and Cynthia G. Pearson, "Ageism Revised and the Provision of Psychological Services," *American Psychologist* 43 (March 1988): 184–88; and Melinda Dell Fitting, "Ethical Dilemmas in Counseling Elderly Adults," *Journal of Counseling and Development* 64 (January 1986): 325–27.

45. Numerous theories have proposed possible causes of Alzheimer's disease. One commonly held theory links AD with aluminum toxicity. Through pollution, acid rain, and a lifetime's use of aluminum pots and pans, the body ingests aluminum which, in some way and in some people, is assumed to lead to nerve cell degeneration

in the cortex of the brain; see Thomas H. Crook and Nancy E. Miller, "The Challenge of Alzheimer's Disease," *American Psychologist* 40 (November 1985): 1245–50; and Carol Turkington, "Alzheimer's and Aluminum," *APA Monitor* (January 1987): 13–14.

46. N. L Mace and P. Rabins, *The Thirty-six Hour Day* (Baltimore, Md.: Johns Hopkins University Press, 1981). For further information on Alzheimer's disease, contact Alzheimer's Disease and Related Disorders Association, Inc., 70 East Lake Street, Suite 600, Chicago, Ill. 60601. See also, Robert D. Nebes and David J. Madden, "Different Patterns of Cognitive Slowing Produced by Alzheimer's Disease and Normal Aging," *Psychology and Aging* 3 (March 1988): 102–4; and Thomas H. Crook and Nancy E. Miller, "The Challenge of Alzheimer's Disease," *American Psychologist* 40 (November 1985): 1245–51.

47. Satsuki Tomine, "Private Practice in Gerontological Counseling," *Journal of Counseling and Development* 64 (February 1986): 406–9.

48. Marilyn Nissenson, "Therapy after Sixty," *Psychology Today* 18 (January 1984): 22–26.

49. See chapters 22 and 23.

50. Jean E. Thompson, "Life Care Ministry: The Church as Part of the Elderly Support Network," *Journal of Religion and Aging* 2 (Spring 1986): 65–76; and Carolyn Cutrona, Dan Russell, and Jayne Rose, "Social Support and Adaptation to Stress by the Elderly," *Psychology and Aging* 1 (March 1986): 47–54; see also, Arthur H. Becker, *Ministry with Older Persons: A Guide for Clergy and Congregations* (Minneapolis: Augsburg, 1986).

51. Susan Malde, "Guided Autobiography: A Counseling Tool for Older Adults," *Journal of Counseling and Development* 66 (February 1988): 290–93: Kaminsky, *The Uses of Reminiscence*; and Robert L. Richter, "Attaining Ego Integrity through Life Review," *Journal of Religion and Aging* 2 (Spring 1986): 1–11.

52. James E. Biren, "The Best of All Stories," *Psychology Today* 21 (May 1987): 91–92.

53. These issues are discussed further by Bob Knight, *Psychotherapy with Older Adults* (Beverly Hills, Calif.: Sage, 1986).

54. For more detailed discussion of helping families of the elderly, see chapter 11, "Working with Families," in Lowry, *Social Work with the Aging*. Less practical, but also of interest, are works by Lee Hyer and Steven L. Hawthorne, "The Family of Later Life: Strategies and Interventions," *International Journal of Family Therapy* 4 (Winter 1982): 187–206; Jane E. Myers, "The Mid/Life Generation Gap: Adult Children with Aging Parents," *Journal of Counseling and Development* 66 (March 1988): 331–35; and S. Allen Wilcoxon, "Grandparents and Grandchildren: An Often Neglected Relationship between Significant Others," *Journal of Counseling and Development* 65 (February 1987). Family members might find guidance in Patricia H. Rushford, *The Help, Hope and Cope Book for People with Aging Parents* (Old Tappan, N.J.: Revell, 1985); or Lissy Jarvik and Gary Small, *Parentcare: A Commonsense Guide for Adult Children* (New York: Crown, 1988).

55. A number of books deal with the issue of group counseling among the elderly. These include Irene Burnside, *Working with the Elderly: Group Process and Techniques*, 2d ed. (Monterey, Calif.: Wadsworth, 1984); and Elizabeth B. Yost et al., *Group Cognitive Therapy: A Treatment Method for Depressed Older Adults* (New York:

Pergamon Press, 1986); see also, the chapters on group counseling in Lowry, *Social Work with the Aging*; and Sherman, *Counseling the Aging*. Christian psychologist Paul R. Welter has also written a helpful guide for people who work in nursing homes; see *The Nursing Home: A Caring Community* (Valley Forge, Penn.: Judson, 1981).

56. "Planning for Retirement? It's Never Too Soon," *U.S. News & World Report*, 24 January 1983, 51, 54.

57. An example is the book by Art Linkletter, *Old Age Is Not for Sissies: Choices for Senior Americans* (New York: Viking, 1988).

58. For help, see Arthur H. Becker, *Ministry with Older Persons: A Guide for Clergy and Congregations* (Minneapolis: Augsburg, 1986); and John Gillies, *A Guide to Compassionate Care of the Aging* (Nashville: Thomas Nelson, 1985).

59. Gray and Moberg, *The Church and the Older Person*, chap. 8.

60. Liz Carpenter, "The Silver Lining," *Milwaukee Journal Magazine*, 15 December 1985, 18–21, 46–47.

61. Joseph H. Bunzel, "Note on the History of a Concept—Gerontophobia," *Gerontologist* 12 (Summer 1972): 116, 203.

62. The Dialogues of Plato, vol. 2, *The Republic*, trans. Benjamin Jowett (New York: National Library, n.d.).

Chapter 16 *Interpersonal Relationships*

1. Gen. 6:11, 13.
2. Luke 22:24.
3. Acts 5; 6:1; 15:2, 7.
4. Acts 15:36–40.
5. 2 Cor. 12:20–21.
6. Prov. 10:18–19; 12:22; 13:3; 15:1, 28, 31; 16:24, 28; 17:9; 19:22; 24:26; 26:20; 28:23, 25.
7. Matthew 5–7 may take on a new perspective if you read these chapters as a commentary on interpersonal relations.
8. Matt. 18:15–35; 20:20–28; 22:36–40; Luke 12:13–15; 22:24–26.
9. Mark 9:50; 2 Tim. 2:14, 24; Phil 4:2; 1 Thess. 5:13; 1 Cor. 13:4–8; Eph. 4:31–32.
10. James 4:1–2.
11. Rom. 12:17–18.
12. Matt. 5:9; Prov. 12:20; Heb. 12:14.
13. Luke 2:14; Isa. 9:6.
14. Matt. 10:34.
15. Eph. 2:14–17.
16. John 14:27; Phil. 4:7.
17. 1 Cor. 2:14–3:3.
18. The Bible calls this "the man without the Spirit" (1 Cor. 2:14).
19. Gal. 5:19–21.
20. Gal. 5:22–23.
21. Rev. 12:9; John 8:44; 2 Cor. 11:13–15; Job 1:7; Matt. 4:3; 1 Thess. 3:5; 1 Pet. 5:8.
22. Eph 6:10–12; James 4:7; 1 Pet. 5:8.
23. D. E. Hiebert, "Satan," in *The Zondervan Pictorial Encyclopedia of the Bible*, ed. Merrill C. Tenney (Grand Rapids, Mich.: Zondervan, 1975), 5:283.

24. Joyce Huggett, *Creative Conflict: How to Confront and Stay Friends* (Downers Grove, Ill.: InterVarsity, 1984), 14.
25. 1 John 4:4; Matt. 25:41; Rev. 20:7–10.
26. Luke 12:13–15.
27. Matt. 7:3–5.
28. Rehoboam tried this approach when he first became king of Israel. This "hard line" failed and created long-term rebellion and interpersonal tension; see 2 Chronicles 10.
29. Barry Lubetkin, "How to Deal with Abrasive Personalities," *Bottom Line Personal* 7 (15 May 1986): 9–10; see also Thomas L. Quick, *Quick Solutions: 500 People Problems Managers Face and How to Solve Them* (New York: Wiley, 1987).
30. The personalities of these difficult people are described in detail, along with suggestions for coping with each, in Robert M. Bramson, *Coping with Difficult People* (New York: Random House, 1981).
31. Joyce Hocker Frost and William W. Wilmot, *Interpersonal Conflict* (Dubuque, Iowa: William C. Brown, 1978), 1.
32. Ibid.
33. Prov. 15:1.
34. This is one conclusion of Allan Bloom in his acclaimed critique of American students and higher education; Allan Bloom, *The Closing of the American Mind* (New York: Simon and Schuster, 1987), 122. Charles Colson has called commitment "a lost value in American life"; see the forward to Ted W. Engstrom, *A Time for Commitment* (Grand Rapids, Mich.: Zondervan, 1987).
35. Ibid., 8; see also Nancy Rule Goldberger, "Why It's So Hard to Make A Commitment: And What to Do about That," *Bottom Line Personal* 7 (15 November 1986): 9–10.
36. John K. Rempel and John G. Holmes, "How Do I Trust Thee?" *Psychology Today* 20 (February 1986): 28–34.
37. Albert Mehrabian, *Silent Messages,* 2d ed. (Belmont, Calif.: Wadsworth, 1981); see also Em Griffin, *Making Friends (And Making Them Count)* (Downers Grove, Ill.: InterVarsity, 1987).
38. Quoted by Bruce P. Dohrenwend and Patrick E. Shrout, "'Hassles' in the Compartmentalization and Measurement of Life Stress Variables," *American Psychologist* 40 (July 1985): 780–85.
39. For a discussion of environmental influences on behavior see Albert Mehrabian, *Public Places and Private Spaces* (New York: Basic Books, 1977); and Kenneth R. Pelletier, *Healthy People in Unhealthy Places: Stress and Fitness at Work* (New York: Delacorte Press, 1984).
40. Isa. 11:6.
41. Clyde H. Coombs, "The Structure of Conflict," *American Psychologist* 42 (April 1987): 355–63.
42. This is the basis of Egan's highly acclaimed approach to counseling; see Gerard Egan, *The Skilled Helper: A Systematic Approach to Effective Helping,* 3d ed. (Monterey, Calif.: Brooks/Cole, 1986).
43. 1 Cor. 13:13; 1 John 4:8; John 13:35.
44. Eph. 6:10–18.
45. Jesus addressed this issue in Matt. 7:3–5.

46. Eph. 2:14–16; 4:29; 5:1.
47. See, e.g., Helen Harris Perlman, *Relationship: The Heart of Helping People* (Chicago: University of Chicago Press, 1979); C. H. Patterson, *The Therapeutic Relationship: Foundations for an Eclectic Psychotherapy* (Monterey, Calif.: Brooks/Cole, 1985); and Bernard G. Guerney, Jr., *Relationship Enhancement* (San Francisco: Jossey-Bass, 1977).
48. Encouragement has been emphasized in a number of Christian books, including books on lay counseling; e.g., Bill G. Bruster and Robert D. Dale, *How to Encourage Others* (Nashville: Broadman, 1983); Lawrence Crabb, Jr., and Dan B. Allender, *Encouragement: The Key to Caring* (Grand Rapids, Mich.: Zondervan, 1984); Jeanne Doering, *The Power of Encouragement: Discovering Your Ministry of Affirmation* (Chicago: Moody Press, 1983); Gene A. Getz, *Encouraging One Another* (Wheaton, Ill.: Victor Books, 1981); and Michael Slater, *Stretcher Bearers* (Ventura, Calif.: Regal, 1985).
49. David Augsburger, *Caring Enough to Confront* (Ventura, Calif.: Regal, 1973), 3.
50. For a good discussion of position bargaining and its alternatives, see Roger Fisher and William Ury, *Getting to Yes: Negotiation Agreement without Giving In* (New York: Penguin, 1983).
51. Matt. 18:15–20.
52. These are the suggestions of Laurence Eck, "Blessed Are the Peacemakers: Resolving Business Conflicts, Part 2," *Bookstore Journal* (March 1987): 49–51; I have relied heavily on Eck's article in writing this section.
53. Table 16-1 was built on a mimeographed sheet of notes that I found in one of my files. I express my gratitude to the unnamed person who did the groundwork for this table and to Scott Thelander who refined and expanded it. For a Christian perspective on conflict resolution, see Horace L. Fenton, Jr., *When Christians Clash: How to Prevent and Resolve the Pain of Conflict* (Downers Grove, Ill.: InterVarsity Press, 1987).
54. Ibid., 49.
55. Fisher and Ury, *Getting to Yes*.
56. For more information on negotiation, see H. Raiffa, *The Art and Science of Negotiation* (Cambridge, Mass.: Harvard University Press, 1982); and D. G. Pruitt and J. Z. Rubin, *Social Conflict: Escalation, Stalemate, and Settlement* (New York: Random House, 1986).
57. William J. Diehm, *Criticizing* (Minneapolis: Augsburg, 1986), 18, 23, 123.
58. Robert Bolton, *People Skills: How to Assert Yourself, Listen to Others, and Resolve Conflicts* (Englewood Cliffs, N.J.: Prentice-Hall, 1979).
59. 1 John 4:16–19; John 13:35.
60. 2 Cor. 13:11; Phil. 4:5–6.
61. Rom. 12:18.

Chapter 17 *Sex Apart from Marriage*

1. Tim Stafford, "Great Sex: Reclaiming a Christian Sexual Ethic," *Christianity Today* 31 (2 October 1987): 25.
2. Allan Bloom, *The Closing of the American Mind* (New York: Simon & Schuster, 1987), 99.

3. U.S. Attorney General, *Final Report of the Attorney General's Commission on Pornography* (New York: Rutledge-Hill Press, 1986).
4. Lewis B. Smedes, *Sex for Christians* (Grand Rapids, Mich.: William B. Eerdmans, 1976), 20.
5. See 1 Corinthians 7.
6. Rom. 13:14; 1 Cor. 7:9.
7. See, e.g., Exod. 20:14, 17; Matt. 5:32.
8. Exod. 22:16–19; Leviticus 18; Matt. 5:27; 1 Cor. 6:9; Heb. 13:4.
9. Heb. 11:25 KJV.
10. Herbert J. Miles, *Sexual Understanding before Marriage* (Grand Rapids, Mich.: Zondervan, 1971), 204.
11. Acts 15:20, 29; 21:25; 1 Cor. 5:1; 6:13, 18; 2 Cor. 12:21; Eph. 5:3.
12. Matt. 5:32; 19:9.
13. 1 Cor. 7:2; 1 Thess. 4:3.
14. 1 Cor. 6:16–20.
15. Miles, *Sexual Understanding,* 206.
16. Isa. 57:3; Jer. 3:8–9; Ezek. 23:43; James 4:4; Rev. 2:20, 23.
17. Exod. 20:14; Lev. 18:20; Deut. 5:18; 22:22–24; Matt. 5:27–30; John 8:4.
18. 1 Cor. 6:9–10; Gal. 5:19–20; Col. 3:5.
19. This will be discussed more fully in chapter 18.
20. Gen. 1:27–28, 31.
21. Gen. 2:25; 3:9–11.
22. 1 Cor. 6:13, 18.
23. Prov. 5:1–8; 1 Cor. 6:9–10; 1 Thess. 4:3; Eph. 5:3–7; Col. 3:5–6.
24. 1 Cor. 7:9.
25. Josh McDowell, *What I Wish My Parents Knew about My Sexuality* (San Bernardino, Calif.: Here's Life Publishers, 1987).
26. Stafford has a good discussion of this issue; see "Great Sex," 33–34.
27. Bloom, *Closing,* 120, 143.
28. Matt. 5:28.
29. Ernie Zimbelman, *Human Sexuality and Evangelical Christians* (Lanham, Md.: University Press of America, 1985).
30. According to Stafford, "Great Sex," 43, Luke 22:15 should be translated, literally, "I have lusted [have a strong desire] to eat the Passover with you."
31. Ibid.
32. Smedes, *Sex for Christians,* 210.
33. For an in-depth discussion of sexual fantasies as obsessions, see Earl D. Wilson, *Sexual Sanity: Breaking Free from Uncontrolled Habits* (Downers Grove, Ill.: InterVarsity, 1984).
34. Eph. 5:3–4.
35. Luke 2:52; Acts 16:2; 1 Tim. 3:7; 1 Thess. 5:22.
36. Stafford, "Great Sex," 43.
37. 1 Cor. 6:12.
38. This appears to be the message of 1 Corinthians 6–7.
39. See, e.g., McDowell, *What I Wish*; and Stafford, "Great Sex."
40. This distinction is made by Smedes, *Sex for Christians,* 190–200; some of the discussion that follows is drawn from Smedes's analysis.

41. Richard Foster, *Money, Sex and Power* (New York: Harper & Row, 1985), 103; Foster argues convincingly that "one of the real tragedies in Christian history has been the divorce of sexuality from spirituality."
42. This is the view of Charles Colson in the forward to Ted W. Engstrom, *A Time for Commitment* (Grand Rapids, Mich.: Zondervan, 1987), 9.
43. Matt. 15:18–19.
44. Lonnie Barbach, "Sexual Fantasies," *Bottom Line Personal* 8 (15 January 1987): 13–14.
45. Reported in Richard A. Maier, *Human Sexuality in Perspective* (Chicago: Nelson-Hall, 1984).
46. Eph. 6:10–13.
47. 1 Pet. 5:8; 2 Cor. 11:14–15.
48. Some of this is summarized in James Leslie McCary, *McCary's Human Sexuality* (New York: Van Nostrand, 1978).
49. John 12:35–40; 1 Cor. 2:14.
50. Rom. 1:24–28, 32.
51. John White, *Eros Defiled: The Christian and Sexual Sin* (Downers Grove, Ill.: InterVarsity Press, 1977).
52. Ira L. Reiss, *Premarital Sexual Standards in America* (New York: Free Press, 1960).
53. David E. Shape, *Interpersonal Sexuality* (Philadelphia: Saunders, 1975).
54. Stafford, "Great Sex," 27.
55. Eugene Kennedy, *Sexual Counseling* (New York: Seabury, 1977).
56. Ibid.
57. 1 Tim. 6:9–11.
58. John 10:10; 3:16.
59. Matt. 6:12–15; Mark 11:25.
60. John 8:11.
61. Two good sources are both written by Cliff Penner and Joyce Penner; see *The Gift of Sex* (Waco, Tex.: Word, 1981); and *A Gift for All Ages: A Family Handbook on Sexuality* (Waco, Tex.: Word, 1985).
62. See also Grace H. Ketterman, *How to Teach Your Child about Sex* (Old Tappan, N.J.: Revell, 1981).
63. Kenneth S. Kantzer, "The Real Sex Ed Battle," *Christianity Today* 31 (17 April 1987); according to one member of the president's commission, the chief consumers of hard-core pornography are fifteen- to nineteen-year-old males.
64. Norman Podhoretz, "What Ever Happened to Self Restraint?" *Bottom Line Personal* 8 (15 May 1987).
65. Harold Smith, "Saying No," *Christianity Today* 31 (6 February 1987).
66. This view is argued persuasively by Smedes, *Sex for Christians*, 152–60; for a discussion of "the ethic of intimacy," see Tim Stafford, "Intimacy: Our Latest Sexual Fantasy," *Christianity Today* 31 (16 January 1987): 21–27.
67. These are adapted from a paper written by several of my students: Joan Barlett, Marty Hansen, Isolde Anderson, and Jay Terbush.
68. 1 Cor. 10:31b.
69. Prov. 5:1–20; Eph. 4:19–20; Col. 3:5; 1 Cor. 6:9–11.
70. 1 John 1:9; 1 Cor. 6:11; for a more detailed discussion of self-control, see

Richard P. Walters, *Counseling for Problems of Self-Control* (Waco, Tex.: Word, 1987).
71. This is the view of J. McCary and S. McCary, *McCary's Human Sexuality* (Belmont, Calif.: Wadsworth, 1982). In a 1987 survey by the Christianity Today Institute, 47 percent of pastors and 35 percent of *Christianity Today* readers reported that they masturbated at least once a month or more often.
72. Reported in Stafford, "Great Sex," 33.
73. For an excellent summary and biblically based critique of these arguments, see James R. Johnson, "Toward a Biblical Approach to Masturbation," *Journal of Psychology and Theology* 10 (Summer 1982): 137–46; see also, R. E. Butman, "Masturbation," in *Baker Encyclopedia of Psychology*, ed. David G. Benner (Grand Rapids, Mich.: Baker, 1985), 687–88; and Walter Trobisch and Ingrid Trobisch, *My Beautiful Feeling* (Downers Grove, Ill.: InterVarsity, 1976). Despite its somewhat archaic language, one of the best discussions of masturbation is still in Miles, *Sexual Understanding*, 137–77. My discussion of masturbation in the paragraphs that follow will doubtless provoke controversy—as it did in the first edition—but this reflects my present, far-from-rigid thinking.
74. Stafford, "Great Sex," 43–44.
75. Miles, *Sexual Happiness*, 147; Miles reaches this conclusion for "young men" but believes that masturbation is wrong for women because they do not have a build-up of sexual fluids similar to the male production of semen.

Chapter 18 *Sex within Marriage*

1. William H. Masters and Virginia E. Johnson, *Human Sexual Inadequacy* (Boston: Little, Brown, 1970).
2. Gen. 1:27–28; 2:24–25.
3. Gen. 4:1.
4. See, e.g., Song of Sol. 7:1–10.
5. Prov. 5:18–19.
6. 1 Cor. 7:2–5.
7. Matt. 19:4–6; 1 Cor. 7:1–9; 1 Thess. 4:1–8.
8. 1 Thess. 4:1–8; 2 Tim. 2:22.
9. Prov. 5:1–11, 20, 23; 6:23–33; 7:5–27.
10. Charlie Shedd and Martha Shedd, *Celebration in the Bedroom* (Waco, Tex.: Word, 1979), 11.
11. Richard Foster, *Money, Sex and Power* (New York: Harper & Row, 1985), 138–39.
12. Quoted in Eugene Kennedy, *Sexual Counseling* (New York: Seabury, 1977), 21; I assume Masters's use of the term "misconception" was not intended to be a pun. For an interesting list of these misconceptions, see Barbara E. Bess, "Those Silly But Sometimes Very Serious Misconceptions Men and Women Have about Each Other's Sexuality," *Bottom Line Personal* 8 (30 March 1987): 11–12.
13. See chap. 2 of Clifford Penner and Joyce Penner, *The Gift of Sex: A Christian Guide to Sexual Fulfillment* (Waco, Tex.: Word, 1981).
14. Shirley Zussman, "What's Changed in the Sex-Therapy Field?" *Bottom Line Personal* 6 (15 May 1985): 11–12. Inhibited sexual desire (ISD) is described in

an article by David Gelman, "Not Tonight, Dear," *Newsweek*, 26 October 1987, 64–66.

15. Karl Albrecht, *Stress and the Manager* (Englewood Cliffs, N.J.: Prentice-Hall, 1979).

16. C. B. Dhabuwala, A. Kumar, and J. M. Pierce, "Myocardial Infarction and Its Influence on Male Sexual Function," *Archives of Sexual Behavior* 15 (1986): 499–504.

17. Herbert J. Miles, *Sexual Happiness in Marriage* (Grand Rapids, Mich.: Zondervan, 1982).

18. In one study of a thousand wives who were physically able but psychologically afraid to have intercourse, almost half listed one or more of these three reasons for their abstinence; reported in James L. McCary, *McCary's Human Sexuality*, 3d ed. (New York: Van Nostrand, 1978), 326.

19. For a brief challenge to this idea, see Stanley J. Grenz, "What Is Sex For?" *Christianity Today* 31 (12 June 1987): 22–23.

20. This and other sexual dysfunctions are discussed in "Diagnosis and Treatment of Sexual Dysfunction—Part I: An Interview with Clifford and Joyce Penner," *Christian Journal of Psychology and Counseling* 2 (1987): 1–5.

21. 1 John 4:18.

22. These quotations are taken from Ernie Zimbelman, *Human Sexuality and Evangelical Christians* (Lanham, Md.: University Press of America, 1985), 243.

23. The most complete study of this was done in 1964. At that time sex was most often avoided because of the wife's fears and attitudes. This may not be equally valid today. See J. A. Blazer, "Married Virgins—A Study of Unconsummated Marriages," *Journal of Marriage and Family* 26 (1964): 213–14.

24. These disguises are discussed further by Kenneth Byrne, "Sexual Dysfunctioning," in *Clinical Handbook of Pastoral Counseling*, ed. Robert J. Wicks, Richard D. Parsons, and Donald Capps (New York: Paulist Press, 1985), 520–38; see also J. Edelwich, *Sexual Dilemmas for the Helping Professional* (New York: Brunner/Mazel, 1982); and Michele Bograd, "Behind the Mask: Sexuality in the Therapeutic Relationship," *Family Therapy Networker* 12 (March-April 1988): 31–34.

25. Kevin Leman discusses this in a thought-provoking and humorous chapter that describes the names we give to penises. His chapter is titled "Ying-Yangs, Weenies, Tallywackers, and 'The Thing'"; see Leman, *Sex Begins in the Kitchen* (Ventura, Calif.: Regal Books, 1981).

26. Most highly recommended are those by Cliff Penner and Joyce Penner, *The Gift of Sex*; and Ed Wheat and Gaye Wheat, *Intended for Pleasure*, rev. ed. (Old Tappan, N.J.: Revell, 1981).

27. Consider, e.g., the tape by David Seamands and Helen Seamands that is part of the series that accompanies this book. A more detailed treatment is given in two highly recommended tape packages by Ed Wheat, M.D. Each contains three hours of sexual information given by a Christian physician who specializes in sexual counseling. The tape packages, "Sexual Techniques and Sex Problems in Marriage," and "Love-Life," are both available from Bible Believer's Cassettes, 130 North Spring, Springdale, Ark. 72764. Christian counselors may want to keep these tapes available for loan to counselees.

28. See, e.g., the books listed at the end of this chapter. Also helpful may be F. Philip Rice, *Sexual Problems in Marriage: Help from a Christian Counselor* (Philadelphia: Westminster Press, 1978).
29. Chapter 27; see also G. Weeks and L. Hof, *Integrating Sex and Marital Therapy: A Clinical Guide* (New York: Brunner/Mazel, 1987).
30. This attitude is challenged by Norman Podhoretz, "What Ever Happened to Self Restraint," *Bottom Line Personal* 8 (15 May 1987): 1–2.
31. Michael Braun and George Alan Rekers, *The Christian in an Age of Sexual Eclipse* (Wheaton, Ill.: Tyndale, 1981), 26.
32. One popular secular book has discussed this issue; see Dagmar O'Connor, *How to Make Love to the Same Person for the Rest of Your Life—and Still Love It* (Garden City, N.Y.: Doubleday, 198).
33. Denominations often produce suitable materials.
34. For a secular view of one ethical issue, see Joseph Lederer, "Birth-Control Decisions: Hidden Factors in Contraceptive Choices," *Psychology Today* 17 (June 1983): 32–38; see also two books by Lewis B. Smedes, *Mere Morality* (Grand Rapids, Mich.: Eerdmans, 1983); and idem, *Choices: Making Right Decisions in a Complex World* (New York: Harper & Row, 1987).
35. Premarital counseling issues are discussed more fully in chapter 26.
36. Wheat and Wheat, *Intended for Pleasure*.
37. Sometimes it is best to arrange for small groups that can discuss relevant Bible passages or books. The books listed at the end of this chapter are good starting points; see also Mike Mason, *The Mystery of Marriage* (Portland, Oreg.: Multnomah, 1985). For an excellent discussion of family and marriage enrichment through the church, see Charles M. Sell, *Family Ministry* (Grand Rapids, Mich.: Zondervan, 1981).
38. James R. David and Francis C. Duda, "Christian Perspectives on Treatment of Sexual Dysfunction," *Journal of Psychology and Theology* 5 (Fall 1977): 332–36.
39. Foster, *Money, Sex and Power,* 91; see also, Dwight Hervey Small, *Christian: Celebrate Your Sexuality* (Old Tappan, N.J.: Revell, 1974); and Lewis B. Smedes, *Sex for Christians* (Grand Rapids, Mich.: Eerdmans, 1976).
40. Tim Stafford, "Great Sex: Reclaiming a Christian Sexual Ethic," *Christianity Today* 31 (2 October 1987): 23–46.

Chapter 19 *Homosexuality*

1. In a 1987 survey of evangelicals, The Christianity Today Institute found that 4 percent of pastors and 5 percent of laypersons admitted to having "homosexual tendencies."
2. Evangelicals Concerned, Inc., 30 East 60th Street, New York, N.Y. 10022.
3. One of the most controversial reports comes from researchers at the Kinsey Institute: Alan P. Bell and Martin Weinberg, *Homosexualities: A Study of Human Diversity* (New York: Simon & Schuster, 1978); see also William H. Masters and Virginia E. Johnson, *Homosexuality in Perspective* (Boston: Little, Brown, 1979); for more recent research, see Richard Green, *The "Sissy Boy Syndrome" and the Development of Homosexuality* (New Haven, Conn.: Yale University Press, 1987).
4. David G. Myers and Malcolm A. Jeeves, *Psychology through the Eyes of Faith* (New York: Harper & Row, 1987), 111.

5. Richard J. Foster, *Money, Sex and Power: The Challenge of the Disciplined Life* (New York: Harper & Row, 1985), 107.
6. This is the definition given by E. M. Pattison, "Homosexuality: Classification, Etiology, and Treatment," in *Baker Encyclopedia of Psychology*, ed. David G. Benner (Grand Rapids, Mich.: Baker, 1985), 519–26.
7. Gen. 19:1–11; Lev. 18:22; 20:13; Judg. 19:22–25; Rom. 1:25–27; 1 Cor. 6:9; 1 Tim. 9–10; five other passages refer to homosexuality in the context of male prostitution: Deut. 23:17; 1 Kings 14:24; 15:12; 22:46; 2 Kings 23:7.
8. E.g., Letha Scanzoni and Virginia Ramey Mollenkott, *Is the Homosexual My Neighbor?* (New York: Harper & Row, 1978); and Robin Scroggs, *The New Testament and Homosexuality* (Philadelphia: Fortress Press, 1983) write from a liberal perspective. A more traditional view is presented by Richard Lovelace, *Homosexuality and the Church* (Old Tappan, N.J.: Revell, 1978); and Earl Wilson, *Counseling and Homosexuality* (Waco, Tex.: Word, 1988); see also Richard A. Fowler and H. Wayne House, *Civilization in Crisis: A Christian Response to Homosexuality, Feminism, Euthanasia, and Abortion*, 2d ed. (Grand Rapids, Mich: Baker, 1988), pt. 2.
9. E.g., see Tim LaHaye, *The Unhappy Gays* (Wheaton, Ill.: Tyndale, 1978); and Ed Rowe, *Homosexual Politics: Road to Ruin in America* (Washington, D.C.: Church League of America, 1984).
10. Troy Perry, *The Lord Is My Shepherd and He Knows I'm Gay* (Los Angeles: Nash, 1972).
11. John F. Alexander, "Homosexuality: It's Not That Clear," *The Other Side* 81 (June 1978): 8–16; the two references are 1 Cor. 6:9 and 1 Tim. 1:10 (in the latter passage, the New International Version refers to "perverts" rather than "homosexuals").
12. Heb. 4:15.
13. 1 Cor. 10:13.
14. Lee Ellis and M. Ashley Ames, "Neurohormonal Functioning and Sexual Orientation: A Theory of Homosexuality-Heterosexuality," *Psychological Bulletin* 101 (1987): 233–58.
15. A. Ehrhardt and H. Meyer-Bahlburg, "Effects of Prenatal Sex Hormones on Gender-Related Behavior," *Science* 211 (1981): 1312.
16. John Money, "Sin, Sickness, or Status?: Homosexual Gender Identity and Psychoneuroendrocrinology," *American Psychologist* 42 (April 1987): 384–99; see also Jon K. Meyer, "Ego-Dystolic Homosexuality," in *Comprehensive Textbook of Psychiatry/IV*, ed. Harold I. Kaplan and Benjamin J. Sadock (Baltimore: Williams & Wilkins, 1985), 1056–65.
17. John Money, "The Development of Sexual Orientation," *Harvard Medical School Mental Health Letter* 4 (February 1988): 4–6.
18. For a classic study of the psychoanalytic view and related research, see I. Bieber and Associates, *Homosexuality* (New York: Basic Books, 1962).
19. Elizabeth R. Moberly, *Homosexuality: A New Christian Ethic* (Greenwood, S.C.: Attic Press, 1982): 5–6. It is neither possible nor fair to summarize Moberly's insightful theory in a few sentences. Her book is brief (only fifty-six pages) but worth reading by Christian counselors who work with homosexuals. Some support for Moberly's hypothesis is found in Green's book, *The "Sissy Boy Syndrome."* Green found that fathers of feminine boys recalled spending less time with their sons during the early

years as compared to fathers of masculine boys. It is interesting to note that mothers of feminine boys also recalled spending less time with their sons as compared with mothers of masculine boys.

20. Moberyly, 10.

21. Wainwright Churchill, *Homosexual Behavior among Males* (New York: Hawthorn, 1967).

22. These causes are among many listed by Lawrence J. Hatterer, *Changing Homosexuality in the Male* (New York: McGraw-Hill, 1970).

23. Susan Coates and Ethel Spector Person, "Extreme Boyhood Femininity: Isolated Behavior or Pervasive Disorder?" *Journal of the American Academy of Child Psychiatry* 24 (November 1985): 702–9; see also Green, *The "Sissy Boy Syndrome"*; and C. W. Roberts et al., "Boyhood Gender Identity Development: A Statistical Contrast of Two Family Groups," *Developmental Psychology* 23 (1987): 544–57.

24. This view is summarized by James Gumaer, "Understanding and Counseling Gay Men: A Developmental Perspective," *Journal of Counseling and Development* 66 (November 1987): 144–46; for a more complete discussion, see H. L. Minton and G. T. McDonald, "Homosexual Identity Formation as a Developmental Process," *Journal of Homosexuality* 9 (1983–84): 91–104.

25. An earlier draft of this chapter was read by three seminary students whose orientations are primarily homosexual. I am grateful to these students who read the manuscript so carefully. The paragraph about fear of same-sex contact was inserted at the suggestion of one of the students. Numerous other observations and suggestions have also been incorporated into the text.

26. John White, *Eros Defiled: The Christian and Sexual Sin* (Downers Grove, Ill.: InterVarsity, 1977), 117.

27. Hatterer, *Changing Homosexuality,* 45 (italics added).

28. C. Silverstein, *Man to Man: Gay Couples in America* (New York: Morrow, 1981); and J. Harry, *Gay Couples* (New York: Praeger, 1984). Homosexual promiscuity, especially as it relates to AIDS, is discussed by Nikki Meredith, "The Gay Dilemma," *Psychology Today* 18 (January 1984): 56–62. For a theological discussion of homosexual partnerships, see John R. W. Stott, "Homosexual Marriages: Why Same-Sex Partnerships Are Not a Christian Option," *Christianity Today* 29 (22 November 1985): 21–28.

29. Tim LaHaye discusses this in *The Unhappy Gays.* Regrettably some good conclusions in this book are overshadowed by the author's heavy-handed and insensitive treatment of homosexuals, most of whom need compassion and encouragement rather than criticism. In one widely quoted scientific study, 52 percent of white homosexuals said they regretted being homosexual and 50 percent claimed they would be upset if a child became homosexual; see A. P. Bell and M. S. Weinberg, *Homosexualities* (New York: Simon & Schuster, 1978).

30. "Gay Ghettos: A Search for Male Communities," *Human Behavior* (September 1978): 41.

31. Meredith, "The Gay Dilemma."

32. According to Pattison, "From a broad population standpoint, homosexuals do not demonstrate different rates of psychosis or neurosis from heterosexuals. Homosexual persons demonstrate as good adaptive and coping capacity as heterosexuals.

On the other hand, homosexuals do have a much higher rate of alcoholism, and probably drug abuse"; see "Homosexuality," 524.

33. R. R. Troiden, "Self, Self-Concept, Identity, and Homosexual Identity: Constructs in Need of Definition and Differentiation," *Journal of Homosexuality* 10 (1984): 97–109.

34. Meredith, "The Gay Dilemma."

35. P. Cameron, "Homosexuality: Social Psychological Consequences," in *Baker Encyclopedia of Psychology,* ed. David G. Benner (Grand Rapids, Mich.: Baker, 1985): 526–27.

36. This is one conclusion in a book based on lengthy interviews with "married" homosexuals; see Brenda Maddox, *Married and Gay* (New York: Harcourt Brace Jovanovich, 1982).

37. D. Hitchins, "Social Attitudes, Legal Standards, and Personal Trauma in Child Custody Cases," *Journal of Homosexuality* 5 (1980): 89–95; see also David Cramer, "Gay Parents and Their Children: A Review of Research and Practical Implications," *Journal of Counseling and Development* 64 (April 1986): 504–7. Cramer describes a study of more than five thousand gay men and women; 18 percent of the women and 13 percent of the men were parents.

38. Bryan Robinson, Patsy Skeen, and Lynda Walters, "The AIDS Epidemic Hits Home," *Psychology Today* 21 (April 1987): 48–52. For more popular treatment of this issue, see M. Borhek, *Coming Out to Parents: A Survival Guide for Lesbians and Gay Men and their Parents* (New York: Pilgrim Press, 1983); and D. K. Switzer and S. A Switzer, *Parents of the Homosexual* (Philadelphia: Westminster, 1980).

39. According to one report, counselors who work with gay men and lesbians need to be "relatively free of homophobia and knowledgeable" about homosexual lifestyles, struggles, and special problems; Barbara R. Slater, "Essential Issues in Working with Lesbian and Gay Male Youths," *Professional Psychology: Research and Practice* 19 (April 1988): 226–35.

40. There have been few careful studies of ex-gay ministries. One study did find, however, that eight out of eleven subjects had changed from exclusive homosexual orientation to exclusive heterosexual orientation through religious fellowship; see E. M. Pattison and M. L. Pattison, "'Ex-Gays': Religiously Mediated Change in Homosexuals," *American Journal of Psychiatry* 137 (1980): 1553–62. For a more anecdotal perspective, see Leanne Payne, *The Broken Image: Restoring Personal Wholeness through Healing Prayer* (Westchester, Ill.: Crossway, 1981).

41. Some of this is documented by Meyer, "Ego-Dystonic Homosexuality"; Moberly, *Homosexuality*; Hatterer, *Changing Homosexuality*; John E. Powell, "Understanding Male Homosexuality: Developmental Recapitulation in a Christian Perspective," *Journal of Psychology and Theology* 2 (Summer 1974): 163–73; Stanley R. Strong, "Christian Counseling with Homosexuals," *Journal of Psychology and Theology* 4 (Winter 1980): 279–87; and Wilson, *Counseling and Homosexuality*.

42. Myers and Jeeves, *Psychology,* 111–13.

43. I am grateful to a former student, Marty Hansen, for allowing us to quote from his chapel address at Trinity Evangelical Divinity School, 2 February 1978.

44. Moberly, *Homosexuality.* This approach also seems to underly much of the work of Wilson, *Counseling and Homosexuality,* who clearly has been influenced greatly by Moberly's work.

45. 1 John 1:9.
46. Eugene Kennedy, *Sexual Counseling* (New York: Seabury, 1977).
47. In an outdated but still oft-cited study, researchers reported that 27 percent of the bisexuals and homosexuals in treatment became exclusively heterosexual following 150–350 hours of psychoanalytic treatment; see I. Bieber and Associates, *Homosexuality: A Psychoanalytic Study of Male Homosexuals* (New York: Basic Books, 1962).
48. This approach is outlined by Powell in "Understanding Male Homosexuality."
49. These issues are discussed from a Christian perspective in two books by George Rekers, *Growing Up Straight: What Every Family Should Know about Homosexuality* (Chicago: Moody, 1982); and *Shaping Your Child's Sexual Identity* (Grand Rapids, Mich.: Baker, 1982).
50. Churchill, *Homosexual Behavior,* 290.
51. John E. Fortunato, *AIDS and Spiritual Dilemma* (New York: Harper & Row, 1987).
52. George Gilder, *Sexual Suicide* (New York: Quadrangle/New York Times Books, 1973), 227.
53. Strong, "Christian Counseling with Homosexuals," 286.

Chapter 20 *Violence and Abuse*

1. E.g., a recent conference sponsored by the New York Academy of Sciences, learned that sexual abuse is "very widespread"; see Carol Turkington, "Sexual Aggression Widespread," *APA Monitor* (March 1987): 15. "The neglect and abuse of children appears to be increasing and has become a major public health problem," according to Vincent J. Fontana, "Child Maltreatment and Battered Child Syndromes," in *Comprehensive Textbook of Psychiatry/IV,* ed. Harold I. Kaplan and Benjamin J. Sadock (Baltimore: Williams and Wilkins, 1985), 1816–24. Similar views on the prevalence and increase of abuse are reported by Ellen Greenberg Garrison, "Psychological Maltreatment of Children: An Emerging Focus for Inquiry and Concern," *American Psychologist* 42 (February 1987): 157–59; and Mary D. Pellauer, Barbara Chester, and Jane Boyajian, eds., *Sexual Assault and Abuse: A Handbook for Clergy and Religious Professionals* (New York: Harper & Row, 1987). A news magazine recently documented the increase of husband abuse; see Karen Diegmueller, "The Battered Husband's Case Shakes Up Social Notions," *Insight* (7 March 1988); and *Christianity Today* described wife-abuse as a "silent crime" that is overlooked by "the silent church"; see Kenneth W. Petersen, "Wife Abuse: The Silent Crime, the Silent Church," *Christianity Today* 27 (25 November 1983): 22–26.
2. Reported by Grant L. Martin, *Counseling for Family Violence and Abuse* (Waco, Tex.: Word, 1987), 131.
3. For in-depth consideration of these problems see Kathleen Coulborn Faller, *Child Sexual Abuse: An Interdisciplinary Manual for Diagnosis, Case Management and Treatment* (Irvington, N.Y.: Columbia University Press, 1987); idem, *Child Sexual Abuse: An Interdisciplinary Manual for Diagnosis, Case Management and Treatment* (Irvington, N.Y.: Columbia University Press, 1987); and Diane H. Schetky and Arthur H. Green, *Child Sexual Abuse* (New York: Brunner/Mazel, 1988).

4. There are exceptions; in the United States (although not in all countries) the spanking of children is not considered abuse. Incarceration in jails, the "toughening" of military recruits, the rigorous demands of athletic coaches, or medical and dental procedures that inflict pain but are intended to bring healing, usually are not considered abusive.

5. Reported by A. R. Denton, "Domestic Violence," in *Baker Encyclopedia of Psychology,* ed. David G. Benner (Grand Rapids, Mich.: Baker, 1985): 323–26.

6. These figures are reported by Virginia A. Sadock, "Special Areas of Interest," in *Comprehensive Textbook of Psychiatry*: 1090–96.

7. Reported by Fontana, "Child Maltreatment."

8. Avin Brenner, "Wednesday's Child," *Psychology Today* 19 (May 1985): 46–50.

9. National Center on Child Abuse and Neglect, *Executive Summary: National Study of the Incidence and Severity of Child Abuse and Neglect,* U.S. Department of Health and Human Services, December 1980.

10. U.S. House of Representatives Select Committee on Aging, *Elder Abuse: A National Disgrace—Introduction and Executive Summary* (Washington, D.C.: U.S. Government Printing Office, 1985), 1.

11. One report of a national survey in Canada—the only national study of its kind ever done—showed that 50 percent of the sample group described some kind of sexual abuse in childhood, ranging from exhibitionism or voyeurism to rape. According to Dr. Astrid Heger, director of the sexuality abuse program at the University of Southern California School of Medicine, the number of unreported cases of sexual abuse in the United States is "absolutely enormous"; see "Helping Molested Children," *U.S. News & World Report,* 10 March 1986.

12. See, e.g., Grant Martin, *Please Don't Hurt Me* (Wheaton, Ill.: Victor, 1987); Maxine Hancock and Karen Burton Mains, *Child Sexual Abuse: A Hope for Healing* (Wheaton, Ill.: Harold Shaw Publishers, 1987); and Esther Lee Olson with Kenneth Petersen, *No Place to Hide: Wife Abuse—Anatomy of a Private Crime* (Wheaton, Ill.: Tyndale House, 1982).

13. Gen. 6:11, e.g., describes a time before the flood when "the earth was corrupt in God's sight and was full of violence."

14. Prov. 29:15.

15. Prov. 22:15; 23:13–14; 29:15, 17.

16. Matt. 5:21–23.

17. Matt. 7:1–5.

18. Col. 3:19.

19. Col. 3:21.

20. Col. 4:1.

21. Eph. 4:31–32.

22. Eph. 5:3–4.

23. 1 Tim. 5:1–8, 17; James 1:27.

24. Matt. 5:39, 43; 6:14; Phil. 4:6.

25. William Barclay, *The Gospel of Matthew,* 2 vols. (Philadelphia: Westminster, 1975), 1:166.

26. For a more detailed discussion of crimes against women, including rape, family violence, household burglary, and fraud, see William J. Bopp and James J. Vardalis, *Crimes against Women* (Springfield, Ill.: Charles C. Thomas, 1987). Violence against

black women is discussed by Soraya M. Coley and Joyce O. Beckett, "Black Battered Women: A Review of the Empirical Literature," *Journal of Counseling and Development* 66 (February 1988): 266–70.

27. C. H. Kempe and R. Helfer, *The Battered Child,* 3d ed. (Chicago: University of Chicago Press, 1980); see also John H. Meier, ed., *Assault against Children: Why It Happens and How to Stop It* (San Diego, Calif.: College-Hill Press, 1985).

28. Denton, "Domestic Violence."

29. One study, e.g., found that 76 percent of abusers had been abused as children; see Linda L. Marshall and Patricia Rose, "Family of Origin Violence and Courtship Abuse," *Journal of Counseling and Development* 66 (May 1988): 414–18.

30. S. K. Steinmetz, "Battered Parents," *Society* 15 (1978): 54–55.

31. Hendrika B. Cantwell, "Psychiatric Implications of Child Neglect," *Harvard Medical School Mental Health Letter* 3 (December 1986): 5–6.

32. S. K. Steinmetz and D. J. Amsden, "Dependent Elders, Family Stress, and Abuse," in *Family Relationships in Later Life,* ed. T. H. Brubaker (Beverly Hills, Calif.: Sage, 1983), 178–92; Brenner, "Wednesday's Child"; Janice T. Gibson and Mika Hiritos-Fatouros, "The Education of a Torturer," *Psychology Today* 20 (November 1986): 50–58. Most psychology students at some time learn about the disturbing research by psychologist Stanley Milgrim who demonstrated convincingly that ordinary people will administer pain to someone else if told to do so by someone in authority; see S. Milgram, *Obedience to Authority* (New York: Harper & Row, 1974).

33. Sarnoff Mednick, "Crime in the Family Tree," *Psychology Today* 19 (March 1985): 58–61.

34. J. B. Reid, K. Kavanaugh, and D. V. Baldwin, "Abusive Parents' Perceptions of Child Problem Behaviors: An Example of Parental Bias," *Journal of Abnormal Child Psychology* 15 (1987): 457–66.

35. Sadock, "Special Areas of Interest."

36. Elizabeth Stark, "The Unspeakable Family Secret," *Psychology Today* 18 (May 1984): 38–46. A more detailed discussion is given by Diane H. Schetky and Arthur H. Green, *Child Sexual Abuse: A Handbook for Health Care and Legal Professionals* (New York: Brunner/Mazel, 1988).

37. Edward I. Donnerstein and Daniel G. Linz, *The Question of Pornography* (New York: Free Press, 1987); and N. Malamuth and E. I. Donnerstein, *Pornography and Sexual Aggression* (New York: Academic Press, 1984).

38. Paul Chance, "Attacking Elderly Abuse," *Psychology Today* 21 (September 1987): 24–25.

39. Bob Greene, "Media Move On, But Pain Remains," *Chicago Tribune,* 18 March 1987.

40. Lois Timnick, "22 Percent in Survey Were Child Abuse Victims," *Los Angeles Times,* 25 August 1985.

41. Gilda S. Josephson and Margaret L. Fong-Beyette, "Factors Assisting Female Clients' Disclosure of Incest during Counseling," *Journal of Counseling and Development* 65 (May 1987): 475–78.

42. J. Briere, "The Effects of Childhood Sexual Abuse on Later Psychological Functioning: Defining a Post-Sexual-Abuse Syndrome," paper presented at the Third National Conference on Sexual Victimization of Children, Children's Hospital National Medical Center, Washington, D.C., April 1984.

43. Kathleen Fisher, "Sexual Abuse Victims Suffer into Adulthood," *APA Monitor* 18 (June 1987): 25.
44. Susan Cunningham, "Abused Children More Likely to Become Teenaged Criminals," *APenn. Monitor* 14 (December 1983).
45. C. B. Meyer and S. E. Taylor, "Adjustment to Rape," *Journal of Personality and Social Psychology* 50 (1986): 1226–34. In one study it was found that rape victims frequently have subsequent sexual problems; see Barbara Gilbert and Jean Cunningham, "Women's Postrape Sexual Functioning: Review and Implications for Counseling," *Journal of Counseling and Development* 65 (October 1986): 71–73.
46. Daniel C. Silverman, "Sharing the Crisis of Rape: Counseling the Mates and Families of Victims," in *Sexual Assault and Abuse,* ed. Mary D. Pellauer et al., 140–50; see also Leslie L. Feinauer and Debbie L. Hippolite, "Once a Princess, Always a Princess: A Strategy for Therapy with Families of Rape Victims," *Contemporary Family Therapy* 9 (Winter 1987): 252–62.
47. See Michael Waldo, "Also Victims: Understanding and Treating Men Arrested for Spouse Abuse," *Journal of Counseling and Development* 65 (March 1987): 385–88; and D. Sonkin, D. Martin, and L. Walker, *The Male Batterer: A Treatment Approach* (New York: Springer, 1985).
48. A number of myths surround reports of violence and abuse. It is a myth to assume, e.g., that the sexual abuse of a child is usually a single incident. More often abusers repeat their actions, often with the same victim. For other myths, see Lynn W. English and Charles L. Thompson, "Counseling Child Sexual Abuse Victims: Myths and Realities," *Journal of Counseling and Development* 66 (April 1988): 370–73.
49. Cooper Wiggen, "The Male Minister and the Female Victim," in *Sexual Assault and Abuse,* ed. Mary D. Pellauer et al., 151–60.
50. John W. Fantuzzo and Craig T. Twentyman, "Child Abuse and Psychotherapy Research: Merging Social Concerns and Empirical Investigation," *Professional Psychology: Research and Practice* 17 (October 1986): 375–80.
51. This section is adapted from Chris Sevaty, "Support Counseling with Victims of Sexual Assault," in *Sexual Assault and Abuse,* ed. Mary D. Pellauer et al., 131–34.
52. Mary Ellen Elwell and Paul H. Ephross, "Initial Reactions of Sexually Abused Children," *Social Casework* 68 (February 1987): 109–16.
53. For further information, see Anu Sharma and Harold E. Cheatham, "A Woman's Center Support Group for Sexual Assault Victims," *Journal of Counseling and Development* 64 (April 1986): 525–27; Robin Sesan, Kristine Freeark, and Sandra Murphy, "The Support Network: Crisis Intervention for Extrafamilial Child Sexual Abuse," *Professional Psychology: Research and Practice* 17 (April 1986): 138–46; and Philip A. Mann, Michael Lauderdale, and Ira Iscoe, "Toward Effective Community-Based Interventions in Child Abuse," *Professional Psychology: Research and Practice* 14 (December 1983): 729–42.
54. Quoted by Ronald Summit, "Beyond Belief: The Reluctant Discovery of Incest," in *Sexual Assault and Abuse,* ed. Mary D. Pellauer et al., 172.
55. Summit, "Beyond Belief," 183. For helpful guidelines in helping children and adolescents cope with abuse and other issues, see Avis Brenner, *Helping Children Cope with Stress* (Lexington, Mass.: Lexington Books, 1984).

56. James Roberts, "Antidotes for Secrecy: Treating the Incestuous Family," *Family Therapy Networker* 8 (September-October 1984): 49–55.
57. Hancock and Mains, *Child Sexual Abuse,* x.
58. Reported by Ruth S. Kempe and C. Henry Kempe, *The Common Secret: Sexual Abuse of Children and Adolescents* (New York: Freeman, 1984).
59. Josephson and Fong-Beyette, "Factors Assisting Female Clients' Disclosure of Incest"; see also, Stephany Joy, "Retrospective Presentations of Incest: Treatment Strategies for Use with Adult Women," *Journal of Counseling and Development* 65 (February 1987): 317–19; and Christine A. Courtois, *Healing the Incest Wound: Adult Survivors in Therapy* (New York: Norton, 1988).
60. A. W. Burgess and L. L. Holmstrom, "Rape Trauma Syndrome," *American Journal of Psychiatry* 131 (September 1974): 981–86.
61. Ibid.
62. These are sad statistics, some based on a national study of 6,200 cases of domestic assault; see R. L. McNeely and Gloria Robinson-Simpson, "The Truth about Domestic Violence: A Falsely Framed Issue," *Social Work* 32 (November-December 1987): 485–90; and Karen Diegmueller, "The Battered Husband's Case Shakes Up Social Notions," 18–20.
63. Adapted from Martin, *Counseling for Family Violence and Abuse,* 51.
64. These issues are discussed in more detail by Martin; ibid.
65. Some of this is discussed by Siegfried Kra, *Aging Myths: Reversible Causes of Mind and Memory Loss* (New York: McGraw-Hill, 1986).
66. Robert E. Freeman-Longo and Ronald V. Wall, "Changing a Lifetime of Sexual Crime," *Psychology Today* 20 (March 1986): 58–64.
67. Denial is discussed by Martin in *Counseling for Family Violence and Abuse*; Martin's chapters on treating abusers (chaps. 5 and 9) are among the best available and perhaps are unique in that they discuss treatment from both a psychological and Christian perspective. Other useful sources are the chapters in M. Roy, ed., *The Abusive Partner: An Analysis of Domestic Battering* (New York: Van Nostrand Reinhold, 1982); and Suzanne M. Sgroi, ed., *Handbook of Clinical Interventions in Child Sexual Abuse* (Lexington, Mass.: D. C. Heath & Co., 1982).
68. L. W. Sherman and R. A. Berk, "The Specific Deterrent Effects of Arrest for Domestic Assault," *American Sociological Review* 49 (1984): 261–71.
69. See, e.g., Martin, *Counseling for Family Violence and Abuse*; Waldo, "Also Victims"; Freeman-Longo and Wall, "Changing a Lifetime of Sexual Crime"; Murray Scher and Mark Stevens, "Men and Violence," *Journal of Counseling and Development* 65 (March 1987): 351–55; and M. Waldo, "Group Treatment for Wife Battering Military Personnel," *Journal for Specialists in Group Work* 11 (1986): 132–38.
70. For a further discussion of this, see E. Santo, *Intimate Intrusions* (London: Rutledge & Kegan Paul, 1985).
71. Barbara Chester, "Sexual Harassment: Victim Responses," in *Sexual Assault and Abuse,* ed. Mary D. Pellauer et al., 164.
72. Marie M. Fortune, "Confidentiality and Mandatory Reporting: A Clergy Dilemma?" in *Sexual Assault and Abuse,* ed. Mary D. Pellauer et al., 198–205.
73. See "A Duty to Warn? Therapists Fear Rush to Suits," *American Bar Association: The Lawyer's Magazine* (January 1986): 28; see also Douglas R. Gross and Sharon E. Robinson, "Ethics, Violence and Counseling: Hear No Evil, See No

Evil, Speak No Evil?" *Journal of Counseling and Development* 65 (March 1987): 340–44.

74. This is discussed by Diane H. Schetky and Elissa P. Benedek, "Assessing Allegations of Child Sexual Abuse," *Harvard Medical School Mental Health Letter* 4 (November 1987): 4–6.

75. Even professionals are caught in the debate about the confused definitions of maltreatment; see, e.g., Gary B. Melton and Howard A. Davidson, "Child Protection and Society: When Should the State Intervene?" *American Psychologist* 42 (February 1987): 172–75.

76. This conclusion is controversial and may bring disagreement from some readers. For a more detailed discussion, please see Gerald Corey, Marianne Schneider Corey, and Patrick Callanan, *Issues and Ethics in the Helping Professions,* 3d ed. (Pacific Grove, Calif.: Brooks/Cole, 1988); chap. 6 is titled "Client Rights, Confidentiality, and Duty to Warn and Protect."

77. Peggy Halsey, "What Can the Church Do?" in *Sexual Assault and Abuse,* ed. Mary D. Pellauer et al., 219–22.

78. Karen Calabria Briskin and Juneau Mahan Gary, "Sexual Assault Programming of College Students," *Journal of Counseling and Development* 65 (December 1986): 207–8; Mary L. Roark, "Preventing Violence on College Campuses," *Journal of Counseling and Development* 65 (March 1987): 367–71; and Lucienne A. Lee, "Rape Prevention: Experiential Training for Men," *Journal of Counseling and Development* 66 (October 1987): 100–101.

79. Dan Hurley, "Arresting Delinquency," *Psychology Today* 19 (March 1985): 62–68.

Chapter 21 *Inferiority and Self-Esteem*

1. William Glasser, *Reality Therapy* (New York: Harper & Row, 1965), 9.
2. Virginia Satir, *Peoplemaking* (Palo Alto, Calif.: Science and Behavior, 1972), 21.
3. Robert Schuller, *Self-Esteem: The New Reformation* (Waco, Tex.: Word, 1982).
4. Jay E. Adams, *The Biblical View of Self-Esteem, Self-Love, and Self-Image* (Eugene, Oreg.: Harvest House, 1986), 79, 106.
5. Paul Vitz, *Psychology as Religion: The Cult of Self-Worship* (Grand Rapids, Mich.: Eerdmans, 1977); see also P. Brownback, *The Danger of Self-Love* (Chicago: Moody, 1982); and David Meyers, *The Inflated Self* (New York: Seabury, 1981).
6. Anthony A. Hoekema, *The Christian Looks at Himself* (Grand Rapids, Mich.: Eerdmans, 1975); see also idem, "The Christian Self-Image: A Reformed Perspective," in *Your Better Self,* ed. Craig W. Ellison (San Francisco: Harper & Row, 1983): 23–36.
7. David Carlson, *Counseling and Self-Esteem* (Waco, Tex.: Word, 1988), 12.
8. From "Hard Questions for Robert Schuller about Sin and Self-Esteem," *Christianity Today* 28 (10 August 1984): 14–21.
9. For an interesting and widely circulated example of this, see Dave Hunt, *Beyond Seduction: A Return to Biblical Christianity* (Eugene, Oreg.: Harvest House, 1987).
10. One Christian writer notes that confusion often results because we fail to distinguish "worthy" (which we are not) from "worthful" (which we are); see David K.

Clark, "Philosophical Reflections on Self-Worth and Self-Love," *Journal of Psychology and Theology* 13 (1985): 3–11.
11. Gen. 1:26–28.
12. Ps. 8:4–5.
13. John 3:16.
14. Ps. 91:11–12; Heb. 1:14; Luke 12:12; Matt. 5:13–14; John 14:1–3, 26.
15. S. Bruce Narramore, *You Are Someone Special* (Grand Rapids, Mich.: Zondervan, 1978), 29.
16. Rom. 3:25; 5:12, 17–19; 6:23a; 7:18.
17. Gen. 3:11–13; Ps. 32:1–5; Rom. 3:11–18.
18. See John 3:16; Rom. 5:1, 8–11, 14–17.
19. Prov. 16:18; James 4:6; 1 Pet. 5:5.
20. Craig W. Ellison, ed., *Self-Esteem* (Farmington Hills, Mich.: Christian Association for Psychological Studies, 1976).
21. Ibid., 5.
22. See Hoekema, *The Christian Looks,* chap. 1, "Paul's Self-Image."
23. Matt. 22:39; Eph. 5:28–29. Some of the theological debate about self-esteem concerns whether or not "as you love yourself" in Matt. 22:39 is a command or a statement of fact. There are arguments on both sides. I tend to agree with Stott that this is "not a command to love ourselves . . . self-love here is a fact." Further discussion concerns whether or not this fact of self-love is evidence of sin; see J. R. W. Stott, "Am I Supposed to Love Myself or Hate Myself?" *Christianity Today* 28 (1984): 26–28.
24. This is a major point in an article by Dale S. Ryan, "Self-Esteem: An Operational Definition and Ethical Analysis," *Journal of Psychology and Theology* 11 (1983): 295–302. In a radio discussion on self-esteem (recorded in 1987 on Chicago's WMBI and available as a cassette recording from the Moody Bible Institute Tape Ministry) Jay Adams and David Carlson clearly had different views, but when their terms were defined the two men appeared to be more in agreement than in disagreement.
25. These differences are discussed in detail by Carlson, *Counseling and Self-Esteem,* 25–30.
26. This point is made by Craig Ellison, "Self-Esteem," in *Baker Encyclopedia of Psychology,* ed. David G. Benner (Grand Rapids, Mich.: Baker, 1985): 1045–47.
27. Matt. 16:24.
28. See, e.g., James 3:13–16.
29. William Barclay, *The Gospel of Matthew,* rev. ed., 2 vols. (Philadelphia: Westminster, 1975), 2:151.
30. Rom. 12:4–8.
31. David W. Aycock and Susan Noaker, "A Comparison of the Self-Esteem Levels of Evangelical Christian and General Populations," *Journal of Psychology and Theology* 13 (1985): 199–208.
32. For a further discussion of this issue, see Dorothy C. Briggs, *Your Child's Self-Esteem* (Garden City, N.Y.: Doubleday-Dolphin, 1975).
33. S. Bruce Narramore, *You Are Someone Special* (Grand Rapids, Mich.: Zondervan, 1978), 29.
34. This is discussed further by Pauline Rose Clance, *The Impostor Phenomenon: When Success Makes You Feel Like a Fake* (Atlanta: Peachtree Publishers, 1985);

and by Clay F. Lee, "Extremes of Self-Esteem," *Christian Counselor* (1986): 6–7.
35. Consider, e.g., the title of a book by Edward de Bono, *Tactics: The Art and Science of Success* (Boston: Little, Brown, 1984).
36. This list is adapted from Ellison, *Self-Esteem,* and others.
37. Maurice E. Wagner, *The Sensation of Being Somebody: Building an Adequate Self-Concept* (Grand Rapids, Mich.: Zondervan, 1975).
38. Some of the research demonstrating the positive influences of growth groups on the development of self-concept, is cited by Michael Gilligan-Stierle and Harvey M. Rapp, "A Course in Religious Community and Its Effects on Self-Concept," *Journal of Psychology and Theology* 9 (1981): 359–63.
39. Ibid.
40. 1 John 1:8–9; James 5:16.
41. Rom. 12:19.
42. Counselors and counselees could both learn from Lewis B. Smedes's excellent book on forgiveness, *Forgive and Forget: Healing the Hurts We Don't Deserve* (New York: Harper & Row, 1984).
43. 1 Cor. 12:25.
44. 1 Cor. 12:4–25.
45. Ellison, *Self-Esteem,* 13–14.
46. Walter Trobisch, *The Complete Works of Walter Trobisch* (Downers Grove, Ill.: InterVarsity, 1987), 666. Shortly after I began work on the revision of this chapter, I was given a copy of this book. It is divided into three parts: dating and sex, marriage, and personal growth.

Chapter 22 *Physical Illness*

1. Ps. 139:14.
2. For some Christian perspectives on the human body, see Paul Brand and Philip Yancey, *Fearfully and Wonderfully Made* (Grand Rapids, Mich.: Zondervan, 1980); Paul Brand and Philip Yancey, *In His Image* (Grand Rapids, Mich.: Zondervan, 1984); Mark P. Cosgrove, *The Amazing Human Body* (Grand Rapids, Mich.: Baker Book House, 1987); and Gary R. Collins, *Your Magnificent Mind* (Grand Rapids, Mich.: Baker Book House, 1985).
3. Reported by Morton T. Kelsey, *Healing and Christianity* (New York: Harper & Row, 1963), 54.
4. Mark 6:7–13; Matt. 10:5–8; Luke 9:1–2, 6.
5. This healing proved both his power over Satan and his Messiahship.
6. Matt. 25:39–40.
7. James 5:14–16.
8. See esp. John 9:2–3 and Luke 13:1–5.
9. Matt. 9:2–6; 1 Cor. 11:29–30.
10. Matt. 9:20–21.
11. Mark 7:24–30; 9:20–27; Matt. 9:18–19, 23–26.
12. Matt. 13:58.
13. I realize that some may not agree with me here. For a somewhat different (and perhaps controversial) perspective, see John Wimber and Kevin Springer, *Power Healing* (New York: Harper & Row, 1987).

14. C. S. Lewis, *The Problem of Pain* (New York: Macmillan, 1962).
15. In addition to the book by C. S. Lewis, see Yancey, *Where Is God When It Hurts?*; Edith Schaeffer, *Affliction* (Old Tappan, N.J.: Revell, 1978); Billy Graham, *Till Armageddon: A Perspective on Suffering* (Waco, Tex.: Word, 1981); and Douglas John Hall, *God and Human Suffering* (Minneapolis: Augsburg, 1986).
16. 2 Cor. 2:7–10; 1 Pet. 1:6–7; Rom. 8:28; Heb. 12:11; Ps. 119:71; James 1:2–4; Rom. 5:3–5.
17. Robert Bobrow, "The Choice to Die," *Psychology Today* 17 (June 1983): 70–72.
18. Charlotte Low, "The Presumption of a Right to Die," *Insight* 3 (28 December 1987–4 January 1988); see also "The Right to Die," an entire issue of the *Journal of Christian Nursing* 2 (Fall 1985). For a more personal discussion, see Dorothea Marvin Nyberg, *Should We Allow Mother to Die?* (San Bernardino, Calif.: Here's Life, 1988).
19. Within recent years, e.g., psychologists have become increasingly involved in health care; see A. G. Burstein and S. Loucks, "The Psychologist as Health Care Clinician," in *Handbook of Clinical Health Psychology,* ed. T. Millon, C. Green, and R. Meagher (New York: Plenum Press, 1982): 175–89.
20. Reported by Troy L. Thompson, "Chronic Pain," in *Comprehensive Textbook of Psychiatry/IV,* ed. Harold I. Kaplan and Benjamin J. Sadock (Baltimore: Williams and Wilkins, 1985), 1212–15.
21. One pastoral counselor has noted that medical personnel often start their careers with an attitude of compassion, but in time they become distant and aloof, largely to protect themselves from the overwhelming effects of so much pain and suffering; see Gerald Fath, "Pastoral Counseling in the Hospital Setting," in *Clinical Handbook of Pastoral Counseling,* ed. Robert J. Wicks, Richard D. Parsons, and Donald E. Capps (New York: Integration Books/Paulist Press, 1985), 349–59.
22. James J. Strain and Stanley Grossman, *Psychological Care of the Medically Ill* (New York: Appleton-Century-Crofts, 1975), 25; see also, Keith A. Nichols, *Psychological Care in Physical Illness* (Philadelphia: Charles Press, 1984).
23. Ibid.
24. Jimmie C. Holland et al., "Comparative Psychological Disturbance in Patients with Pancreatic and Gastric Cancer," *American Journal of Psychiatry* 143 (August 1986): 983–86.
25. This is true regardless of the patient's age, but there is evidence that family disruption is especially intense when a child is seriously ill or deformed; see John Bales, "Entire Family Touched by Childhood Illnesses," *APA Monitor* 18 (August 1987): 38.
26. Henri J. M. Nouwen, *A Letter of Consolation* (San Francisco: Harper & Row, 1982), 28, 30.
27. Anticipatory grieving will be discussed further in the next chapter; it is considered in detail in Therese A. Rando, ed., *Loss and Anticipatory Grief* (Lexington, Mass.: Lexington Books, 1986).
28. G. Affleck et al., "Causal Attribution, Perceived Benefits, and Morbidity after a Heart Attack: An 8-Year Study," *Journal of Consulting and Clinical Psychology* 55 (1987): 29–35.
29. Stuart C. Yudofsky, "Malingering," in Kaplan and Sadock, *Comprehensive Textbook of Psychiatry,* 1862–65.

30. Strain and Grossman, *Psychological Care of the Medically Ill,* 83–91.
31. There is increasing evidence that long-term care givers need care too; see Tori DeAngelis, "Long-term Caregivers Need Some Care, Too," *APA Monitor* 18 (January 1988): 31.
32. Elisabeth Kübler-Ross, *On Death and Dying* (New York: Macmillan, 1969).
33. Ibid., 123.
34. Charles W. Colson, *Loving God* (Grand Rapids, Mich.: Zondervan, 1983), 192.
35. 1 Cor. 12:25–26.
36. See also, Dennis Saylor, *A Guide to Hospital Calling* (Grand Rapids, Mich.: Baker, 1983).
37. This in turn can create other problems; see Heb. 12:15.
38. This is the theme of a book by Vernon J. Bittner, *Make Your Illness Count* (Minneapolis: Augsburg, 1976).
39. 1 John 1:9; James 5:16.
40. Elizabeth Stark, "Breaking the Pain Habit," *Psychology Today* 19 (May 1985): 31–36.
41. For a consideration of how people can be helped to live with chronic illness and persisting pain, see Cheri Register, *Living with Chronic Illness: Days of Patience and Passion* (New York: Free Press, 1987); and Kenneth A. Holyroyd and Thomas L. Creer, *Self-Management of Chronic Disease: Handbook of Clinical Interventions and Research* (San Diego: Academic Press, 1987). For a more specialized treatment, see Paul Karoly and Mark P. Jensen, *Multimethod Assessment of Chronic Pain* (New York: Pergamon, 1987).
42. These are of differing quality and they use a variety of medical and nonmedical approaches. Encourage your counselees to ask their doctors to recommend a quality clinic. If you cannot locate one of these clinics, try writing for a recommendation to Emory Pain Control Center, 1441 Clifton Road, N.E., Atlanta, Ga. 30322; Pain Treatment Center, Johns Hopkins Hospital, Meyer Building, Room 279, Baltimore, Md. 55902; or Pain Treatment Center, Scripps Clinic and Research Foundation, LaJolla, Calif. 92037.
43. R. A. Sternbach, ed., *The Psychology of Pain* (New York: Raven Press, 1978); see also S. Y. Tan, "Cognitive and Cognitive-Behavioral Methods for Pain Control: A Selective Review," *Pain* 12 (1982): 201–28.
44. I had not thought about this last question until a book appeared discussing the sexual frustrations of the chronically ill; see Leslie R. Schover and Soren Buus Jensen, *Sexuality and Chronic Illness* (New York: Guilford, 1988).
45. Rom. 11:33.
46. Billy Graham, *Facing Death and the Life After* (Waco, Tex.: Word, 1987), 51.
47. Heb. 11:1.
48. Family counseling is discussed in more detail in chapter 29.
49. Fath, "Pastoral Counseling in the Hospital."
50. From an unpublished paper, "A Theology of Martyrdom," n.d., available from the Rumanian Missionary Society, P.O. Box 527, Wheaton, Ill. 60189.
51. Irving L. Janis, *Psychological Stress: Psychoanalytic and Behavioral Studies of Surgical Patients* (New York: Wiley, 1958); see also L. D. Egbert et al., "Reduction of Post-Operative Pain by Encouragement and Instruction to Patient," *New England Journal of Medicine* 270 (1964): 825.

Chapter 23 *Grief*

1. Billy Graham, *Facing Death and the Life After* (Waco, Tex.: Word, 1987), 164.
2. Sigmund Freud, "Mourning and Melancholia," in *Collected Papers of Sigmund Freud,* trans. J. Riviere (London: Hogarth Press, 1953), vol. 4. These papers appeared first in German and were published in English in 1925.
3. Erich Lindemann, "Symptomatology and Management of Acute Grief," *American Journal of Psychiatry* 101 (1944): 141–48. This paper is included in a book that brings together a number of Lindemann's significant articles on grief; see Erich Lindemann *Beyond Grief: Studies in Crisis Intervention* (New York: Jason Aronson, 1979).
4. Elisabeth Kübler-Ross, *On Death and Dying* (New York: Macmillan, 1969).
5. For a good overview of thanatology, see Avery D. Weisman, "Thanatology," in *Comprehensive Textbook of Psychiatry/IV,* ed. Harold I. Kaplan and Benjamin J. Sadock (Baltimore: Williams & Wilkins, 1985), 1277–86.
6. 1 Cor. 15:55; Hos. 13:14.
7. According to Heb. 9:27, "man is destined to die once." The only exceptions are Old Testament figures like Enoch and those believers who will still be alive when Christ returns. "After that, we who are still alive and are left will be caught up together . . . in the clouds to meet the Lord in the air" (1 Thess. 4:17).
8. Gen. 37:34–35; 2 Sam. 12:15–18; 18:33; 2 Chron. 35:25. Scripture also gives insight into some of the Old Testament mourning practices; see Jer. 16:6–8 and Ezek. 24:16–17. These issues are discussed briefly by Bill Flatt, "Old Testament Examples of Grief," *Christian Counselor* (Winter 1986): 3–5.
9. Ps. 23:4.
10. Ps. 119:28.
11. Isa. 53:3–4 NASB.
12. 1 Corinthians 15 and 1 Thessalonians 4.
13. 1 Thess. 4:14.
14. 1 Thess. 4:18.
15. 1 Cor. 15:52–54.
16. 1 Thess. 4:17; Heb. 2:14–15; 2 Tim. 1:10; John 11:25–26.
17. 2 Cor. 4:14–5:8.
18. 1 Cor. 15:58.
19. Matt. 5:4; some Bible scholars, including D. A. Carson, *The Sermon on the Mount* (Grand Rapids, Mich.: Baker, 1978); and D. Martyn Lloyd-Jones, *Studies in the Sermon on the Mount* (Grand Rapids, Mich.: Eerdmans, 1971); conclude that this statement about mourning is "a personal grief over personal sin" and has nothing to do with those who mourn and need comfort because a loved one has died. William Barclay gives the verse an even different interpretation but admits that the verse could be taken literally; see Barclay, *The Gospel of Matthew,* 2 vols. (Philadelphia: Westminster, 1975), vol. 1.
20. John 11.
21. Matt. 14:12–13.
22. Matt. 26:38.
23. 2 Sam. 12:15–23.

24. J. William Worden, *Grief Counseling and Grief Therapy: A Handbook for the Mental Health Practitioner* (New York: Springer, 1982).
25. C. M. Parkes, *Bereavement: Studies of Grief in Adult Life* (New York: International Universities Press, 1972).
26. Quoted by Betty Jane Wylie, *Beginnings: A Book for Widows,* rev. ed. (Toronto: McClelland and Stewart, 1985).
27. "Bereavement and Grief—Part I," *Harvard Medical School Mental Health Letter* 3 (March 1987): 1–4; see also Christopher Joyce, "A Time for Grieving," *Psychology Today* 18 (November 1984): 42–46. For a moving first-person account of one couple's "journey through grief and recovery" following the death of their daughter, see Carol A. Rowley and William J. Rowley, *On Wings of Mourning* (Waco, Tex.: Word, 1984).
28. These are among the characteristics listed by Freud; see Arthur C. Carr, "Grief, Mourning, and Bereavement," in *Comprehensive Textbook of Psychiatry,* 1286–93.
29. B. Raphael, *The Anatomy of Bereavement* (New York: Basic Books, 1983).
30. For an in-depth discussion of anticipatory grief, see Therese A. Rando, *Loss and Anticipatory Grief* (Lexington, Mass.: Lexington Books, 1986).
31. When the parent is younger, the death is more difficult to handle; see H. Finkelstein, "The Long-term Effects of Early Parent Death: A Review," *Journal of Clinical Psychology* 44 (1988): 3–9; see also Marc Angel, *The Orphaned Adult: Confronting the Death of a Parent* (New York: Human Sciences Press, 1987).
32. One recent book is devoted exclusively to the death of one's mate; see Stephen R. Schuchter, *Dimensions of Grief: Adjusting to the Death of a Spouse* (San Francisco: Jossey-Bass, 1986).
33. Ronald J. Knapp, "When a Child Dies," *Psychology Today* 21 (July 1987): 60–67; and Therese A. Rando, ed., *Parental Loss of a Child* (Champaign, Ill.: Research Press, 1986).
34. "Bereavement and Grief—Part I," *Harvard Mental Health Letter.*
35. Worden, *Grief Counseling,* 30.
36. See, e.g., Beatrice Sundbo, *Treasures in Heaven* (Beaverlodge, Alberta: Horizon House Publishers, 1977), on the death of four children; Joseph Bayley, *The View from a Hearse: A Christian View of Death* (Elgin, Ill.: David C. Cook, 1969), on the death of three sons; Joyce Landorf, *Mourning Song* (Old Tappan, N.J.: Fleming H. Revell, 1974), on the death of her mother; Vance Havner, *Though I Walk through the Valley* (Old Tappan, N.J.: Fleming H. Revell, 1974), on the death of his wife; and the most famous, C. S. Lewis, *A Grief Observed* (New York: Seabury, 1961), on the death of his wife.
37. Ronald J. Knapp, *Beyond Endurance: When a Child Dies* (New York: Schocken, 1987).
38. V. R. Pine, "Comparative Funeral Practices," *Practical Anthropology* 16 (1969): 49–62. For a more recent cross-cultural perspective, see Ken White, "Living and Dying the Navajo Way," *Generations* 11 (Spring 1987): 44–47. Other cultural differences are discussed by Elisabeth Kübler-Ross, *Death: The Final Stage of Growth* (Englewood Cliffs, N.J.: Prentice-Hall, 1975).
39. This was the topic of a Pulitzer-Prize-winning book by Ernest Becker, *The Denial of Death* (New York: Free Press/Macmillan, 1975).
40. David Barton, ed., *Dying and Death: A Clinical Guide for Caregivers* (Baltimore: Williams & Wilkins, 1977), 116–17.

41. John 11:33–36.
42. "Bereavement and Grief—Part I," *Harvard Mental Health Letter.*
43. M. Irwin et al., "Life Events, Depressive Symptoms, and Immune Functions," *American Journal of Psychiatry* 144 (1987): 437–41.
44. Jaako Kaprio, Markku Koshenvuo, and Heli Rita, "Mortality after Bereavement: A Prospective Study of 95,647 Widowed Persons," *American Journal of Public Health* 77 (March 1987): 283–87.
45. See, e.g., Archibald D. Hart, *The Hidden Link between Adrenalin and Stress* (Waco, Tex.: Word, 1986).
46. For more information, see Wolfgang Stroebe and Margaret S. Stroebe, *Bereavement and Health* (New York: Cambridge University Press, 1987).
47. Lewis, *A Grief Observed,* 66–67.
48. John F. Crosby and Nancy L. Jose, "Death: Family Adjustment to Loss," in *Stress and the Family: Volume II—Coping with Catastrophe,* ed. Charles R. Figley and Hamilton I. McCubbin (New York: Brunner/Mazel, 1983), 76–89.
49. V. D. Volkman, "The Recognition and Prevention of Pathological Grief," *Virginia Medical Monthly* 99 (1972): 535–40.
50. C. Everett Koop and Elizabeth Koop, *Sometimes Mountains Move* (Wheaton, Ill.: Tyndale, 1979), 40, 73.
51. Arthur Freese, *Help for Your Grief* (New York: Schocken Books, 1977), 48; see also, C. M. Parkes and Robert S. Weiss. *Recovery from Bereavement* (New York: Basic Books, 1983).
52. Lewis, *A Grief Observed,* 1.
53. Suggestions for reading are given at the end of this chapter.
54. Among the better books in this field are two written by Asbury Seminary professor David A. Seamands; see Seamands, *Healing for Damaged Emotions* (Wheaton, Ill.: Victor Books, 1981); and idem, *Healing of Memories* (Wheaton, Ill.: Victor Books, 1985).
55. Children who have lost a sibling have been called "the forgotten mourners." Often their grief is overlooked by mourners who focus most attention on grieving parents; see Helen Rosen, *Unspoken Grief: Coping with Childhood Sibling Loss* (Lexington, Mass.: Lexington Books, 1985).
56. Knapp, *Beyond Endurance.*
57. Diane Cole, "It Might Have Been: Mourning the Unborn," *Psychology Today* 21 (July 1987).
58. Worden, *Grief Counseling,* 87.
59. In many communities there are support groups for those who have lost children. Some of these groups may be located by contacting The Compassionate Friends National Headquarters, P.O. Box 3696, Oakbrook, Ill. 60522.
60. Larry Richards and Paul Johnson, *Death and the Caring Community* (Portland, Oreg.: Multnomah, 1980).
61. For a popular book in this area, see William L. Coleman, *It's Your Funeral* (Wheaton, Ill.: Tyndale, 1979). A more detailed discussion of issues such as these is found in the last three chapters of Rando, *Loss and Anticipatory Grief.*
62. In the United States, the first hospice program was established in New Haven, Connecticut, in 1974. Now there are more than a thousand hospices nationwide, and

the numbers are growing; see D. L. Kitch, "Hospice," in *Concise Encyclopedia of Psychology,* ed. Raymond J. Corsini (New York: Wiley, 1987), 529–30; and Vincent Mor, "Hospice," *Generations* 11 (Spring 1987): 19–21.

63. Jean Taylor, "Hospice House: A Homelike Inpatient Unit," *Generations* 11 (Spring, 1987): 22–26; see also, D. S. Greer et al., "An Alternative in Terminal Care: Results of a National Hospice Study," *Journal of Chronic Diseases* 39 (1986): 9–26; and Vincent Mor, *Hospice Care Systems: Structure, Process, Costs, and Outcome* (New York: Springer, 1987). It should be noted that hospice works with people of all ages; e.g., Susan Cunningham, "Hospice: A Place for Children," *APA Monitor* 14 (April 1983): 9–10.

64. Freese, *Help for Your Grief,* 122; and Constance Rosenblum, "Dying Children," *Human Behavior* 8 (March 1978): 49–50.

65. These suggestions are made by Worden, *Grief Counseling,* 111–12; see also J. W. Worden, *Personal Death Awareness* (Englewood Cliffs, N.J.: Prentice-Hall, 1976); and Ralph L. V. Rickgarn, "The Death Response Team: Responding to the Forgotten Grievers," *Journal of Counseling and Development* 66 (December 1987): 197–99.

66. Richard Exley, *The Rhythm of Life: Putting Life's Priorities in Perspective* (Rapid City, S.D.: Honor Books; Tulsa, Okla.: Harrison House, 1987).

67. See Walter Trobisch, *The Complete Works of Walter Trobisch* (Downers Grove, Ill.: InterVarsity, 1987).

68. Ingrid Trobisch, "Let the Deep Pain Hurt," *Partnership* (September-October 1985): 43–45.

69. Ibid.

Chapter 24 *Singleness*

1. Bob Vetter and June Vetter, *Jesus Was a Single Adult* (Elgin, Ill.: David C. Cook, 1978).

2. "19 Million Americans: Their Joys and Frustrations," *U.S. News & World Report,* 21 February 1983, 53–56; see also, J. Simenauer and D. Carroll, *Singles: The New Americans* (New York: Simon & Schuster, 1982).

3. Gen. 2:18.

4. Nancy Rule Goldberger, "Why It's So Hard to Make a Commitment," *Bottom Line Personal* 7 (15 November 1986): 9–10.

5. Matt. 19:11–12.

6. 1 Cor. 7:7.

7. 1 Cor. 7:28, 32–35.

8. Landon Y. Jones. *Great Expectations: America and the Baby Boom Generation* (New York: Coward, McCann and Geoghegan, 1980), esp. 175–82, "The Singles Society."

9. 1 Cor. 7:9.

10. The Yale-Harvard study of marriage patterns in the United States is summarized by one of the researchers, Neil G. Bennett, "The Real Reason Why Single Women Aren't Marrying," *Bottom Line Personal* 8 (15 October 1987): 7–8.

11. Some of these issues are discussed by Jim Smoke, *Suddenly Single* (Old Tappan, N.J.: Revell, 1982).

12. J. F. Gubrium, "Being Single in Old Age," *International Journal of Aging and Human Development* 6 (1976): 29–41.
13. Joni Eareckson Tada is one who married despite a physical handicap; she describes her marriage in *Choices . . . Changes* (Grand Rapids, Mich.: Zondervan, 1986).
14. Lynne Z. Gold-Bikin, "Living Together Is Getting Simpler . . . and More Complicated," *Bottom Line Personal* 6 (30 October 1985): 11–12.
15. A *HIS* interview with John R. W. Stott, *HIS* 36 (October 1975): 19.
16. Ibid.
17. Margaret Evening, *Who Walk Alone: A Consideration of the Single Life* (Downers Grove, Ill.: InterVarsity, 1974): 23–24.
18. Heb. 12:15–16.
19. Norman L. Thiesen and Benedict B. Cooley, "The Psychological Adjustment of the Single Male Adult Compared with Married Males and Single and Married Females Aged 25–34," *Journal of Psychology and Theology* 7 (Fall 1979): 202–11.
20. This is discussed in detail in a practical book by Andre Bustanoby, *Being a Single Parent* (Grand Rapids, Mich.: Pyranee Books/Zondervan, 1985).
21. Nancy DeMoss, "Don't Single Yourself Out," *Worldwide Challenge* (November 1981): 30–32.
22. Counselors are encouraged to consult the other chapters when issues such as these arise in counseling singles.
23. See, e.g., M. Zey, *The Mentor Connection* (Homewood, Ill.: Dow-Jones Irwin, 1984); and Felice A. Kaufmann et al., "The Nature, Role, and Influence of Mentors in the Lives of Gifted Adults," *Journal of Counseling and Development* 64 (May 1986): 576–78.
24. I have no research data to support these conclusions, but twenty years of teaching in a seminary has convinced me both of the prejudice against single seminary graduates in the churches and of the encouragement that many students have found in John Stott's example.
25. John Fischer and Lia Fuller O'Neil, *A Single Person's Identity* (Palo Alto, Calif.: Discovery Publishing, 1973).
26. Andre Bustanoby discusses these issues in *(Can Men and Women Be) Just Friends?* (Grand Rapids, Mich.: Zondervan, 1984).
27. Some of the pastoral resistance to singles, especially divorced singles, is discussed by Harold Ivan Smith, *Pastoral Care for Single Parents* (Kansas City: Beacon Hill, 1982).
28. Reported by Keith E. Davis, "Near and Dear: Friendship and Love Compared," *Psychology Today* 19 (February 1985): 22–30.
29. A. D'Ercole, "Single Mothers: Stress, Coping, and Social Support," *Journal of Community Psychology* 16 (1988): 41–54.
30. These figures are based on a report from the U.S. Census Bureau. In 1986, 24 percent of all American children lived in a one-parent situation; see "24 percent of Young Live with 1 Parent," *Chicago Tribune,* 21 January 1988.
31. The following list is adapted from Smith, *Pastoral Care,* chap. 4, "Risks."
32. Jim Smoke, *Suddenly Single*; see chap. 7, "If Happiness Is Being Single, Why Do These People Look So Sad?"
33. Nancy Hardesty, "Being Single in Today's World," in *It's O.K. to Be Single,* ed. Gary R. Collins (Waco Tex.: Word, 1976), 18.

34. The following list is taken, with slight adaptations, from Smith, *Pastoral Care,* chap. 9, "Preventing the Problem."

Chapter 25 *Choosing a Marriage Partner*

1. H. Klingberg, Jr., "Mate Choice," in *Baker Encyclopedia of Psychology,* ed. David G. Benner (Grand Rapids, Mich.: Baker, 1985), 688–90.
2. Genesis 24.
3. Genesis 29.
4. Merrill C. Tenney, ed., *The Zondervan Pictorial Encyclopedia of the Bible Vol. IV* (Grand Rapids, Mich.: Zondervan, 1975), 4:96–97.
5. 2 Cor. 6:14–15.
6. 1 Cor. 5:9f.
7. 1 Cor. 7:39 LB.
8. 1 Cor. 7:17 LB.
9. Ps. 32:8; Prov. 3:5–6; 16:3, 9.
10. Garry Friesen with J. Robin Maxson, *Decision Making and the Will of God: A Biblical Alternative to the Traditional View* (Portland, Oreg.: Multnomah, 1980).
11. Gerard Egan and Michael A. Cowan, *Moving into Adulthood* (Monterey, Calif.: Brooks/Cole, 1980), 36.
12. In the preceding chapter we suggested that lasting love in a marriage will involve both passion and friendship; see Keith E. Davis, "Near and Dear: Friendship and Love Compared," *Psychology Today* 19 (February 1985): 22–30.
13. Gen. 1:27; 2:18; 1 Cor. 7:9; Heb. 13:4.
14. 1 Cor. 7:35.
15. Abby Hirsch, "The Godmother's Formula to Find the Right Man," *Bottom Line Personal* 7 (15 November 1986): 11–12.
16. See John Scanzoni, "A Christian Perspective on Alternative Styles of Marriage," in *Making More of Your Marriage,* ed. Gary R. Collins (Waco, Tex.: Word, 1976), 157–68.
17. David M. Moss III, "Three Levels of Mate Selection and Marital Interaction," *Journal of Religion and Health* 16 (1977): 288–303.
18. Victoria Houston, "Older Women, Younger Men," *Bottom Line Personal* 9 (30 January 1988).
19. Ernest W. Burgess and Harvey J. Locke, *The Family* (New York: American Book Co., 1945), 420.
20. This term is used by John R. Compton, "Premarital Preparation and Counseling," in *Pastoral Counseling,* ed. Barry K. Estadt (Englewood Cliffs, N.J.: Prentice-Hall, 1983), 153–77; the following list is taken from Compton's chapter.
21. David Field, *Marriage Personalities* (Eugene, Oreg.: Harvest House, 1986).
22. This list is adapted from H. Norman Wright, *Premarital Counseling,* rev. ed. (Chicago: Moody, 1981).
23. Gal. 5:22–23.
24. This list is adapted from Cleveland McDonald, *Creating a Successful Chrtstian Marriage* (Grand Rapids, Mich.: Baker, 1975), 123–41; chap. 7, "Maturity in Mate Selection."
25. Erich Fromm, *The Art of Loving* (New York: Bantam, 1956), 2–3.

Chapter 26 *Premarital Counseling*

1. Carl Rogers, *Becoming Partners: Marriage and Its Alternatives* (New York: Delacorte, 1972), 11.
2. Harold Ivan Smith, *Pastoral Care for Single Parents* (Kansas City: Beacon Hill Press, 1982); see chap. 8 on premarital counseling. I first found the term "preceremonial counseling" here.
3. Matt. 1:18–25.
4. 1 Cor. 7:8, 26–27, 29.
5. 1 Cor. 7:28, 33.
6. Eph. 5:22–6:4; Col. 3:18–21; 1 Pet. 3:1–9.
7. Aaron Rutledge, *Pre-Marital Counseling* (Cambridge, Mass.: Schenkman, 1966), 25.
8. Eph. 5:25.
9. William J. Lederer and Don D. Jackson, *The Mirages of Marriage* (New York: W. W. Norton, 1968), 249.
10. Eph. 5:18–20.
11. Eph. 5:21–6:4.
12. Eph 5:3; for a sobering discussion of premarital sex, see Josh McDowell, *Teens Speak Out: What I Wish My Parents Knew about My Sexuality* (San Bernardino, Calif.: Here's Life Publishers, 1987). A much older but still widely consulted book is by Herbert J. Miles, *Sexual Understanding before Marriage* (Grand Rapids, Mich.: Zondervan, 1971).
13. Smith, *Pastoral Care,* 112.
14. John R. Compton, "Premarital Preparation and Counseling," in *Pastoral Counseling,* ed. Barry K. Estadt (Englewood Cliffs, N.J.: Prentice-Hall, 1983), 153–77.
15. Please see chapters 27, 29–30.
16. R. A. Lewis and G. B. Spanier, "Theorizing about the Quality and Stability of Marriage," in *Contemporary Theories about the Family,* ed. W. R. Burr et al. (New York: Macmillan, 1979); cited in Robert F. Stahmann and William J. Hiebert, *Premarital Counseling* (Lexington, Mass.: Lexington Books, 1980).
17. For an excellent summary and overview of studies in this area, see Dennis A. Bagarozzi and Paul Rauen, "Premarital Counseling: Appraisal and Status," *American Journal of Family Therapy* 9 (1981): 13–30.
18. Herbert J. Miles, *Sexual Happiness in Marriage* (Grand Rapids, Mich.: Zondervan, 1982).
19. See, e.g., Donald R. Fletcher, "A Comparison of the Effectiveness and Efficiency of a Premarital Counseling Program with and without an Audiovisual Aid," Ph.D. diss., International Graduate School, 1987.
20. Reported by Andree Brooks, "Premarital Counseling May Help Tie the Knot," *Chicago Tribune,* 9 May 1985.
21. Compton, "Premarital Preparation," 158.
22. Manuals include those by David A. Thompson, *A Premarital Guide for Couples and Their Counselors* (Minneapolis: Bethany, 1979); Wes Roberts and H. Norman Wright, *Before You Say 'I Do'* (Eugene, Oreg.: Harvest House, 1978); or Joan Hunt and Richard Hunt, *Preparing for Christian Marriage* (Nashville, Tenn.: Abingdon, 1981). The latter volume also has a companion manual for pastoral counselors:

Antoinette and Leon Smith, *Preparing for Christian Marriage: Pastor's Manual* (Nashville, Tenn.: Abingdon, 1982).

23. Some helpful books have been listed at the end of this chapter.

24. For others see Crompton, "Premarital Guidance"; or H. Norman Wright, *Premarital Counseling,* rev. ed. (Chicago: Moody Press, 1981).

25. Miles, *Sexual Happiness.*

26. In one community, a local physician agrees to see all couples from the church prior to the marriage. As part of the premarital counseling, the couple goes to this doctor who discusses sexual and other related issues.

27. Consider, e.g., the tape on premarital counseling in the Christian Counselor's Library that accompanies this book or Ed Wheat's two tapes, "Before the Wedding Night" (available from Scriptural Counsel, Inc., 130 Spring Street, Springdale, Ark. 72764).

28. This is the suggestion of Harold Ivan Smith, *Pastoral Care,* 91.

29. Ibid.

30. The first mention of premarital counseling was in a 1928 article in *The Journal of Obstetrics and Gynecology.*

Chapter 27 *Marital Problems*

1. Jeanette Lauer and Robert Lauer, "Marriages Made to Last," *Psychology Today* 19 (June 1985): 22–26.

2. In one highly acclaimed survey, e.g., 40 percent of respondents who had seen a counselor requested help for a marriage problem. The next highest problem area was 22 percent seeking help for "adjustment problems"; see Joseph Verloff, Richard A. Kulka, and Elizabeth Douvan, *Mental Health in America: Patterns of Help-Seeking from 1957 to 1976* (New York: Basic Books, 1981). More recently a survey of counselors reported that 63 percent of counselees came for help with marital difficulties. This figure may be high, however, because the sample consisted of readers of a family counseling journal; Douglas Rait, "Survey Results," *Family Therapy Networker* 12 (January-February 1988): 52–66.

3. Gen. 2:18–25.

4. See Eph. 5:21–33; Col. 3:18–25; 1 Pet. 3:1–7; Heb. 13:4.

5. Deut. 24:1–4; Matt. 5:31–32; 19:3–9; 1 Cor. 7:10–16. For more detailed discussion of divorce, please see chapter 29.

6. Prov. 5:18; Eccles. 9:9.

7. Prov. 18:22.

8. Prov. 27:15–16; see also Prov. 19:13; 21:9.

9. Richard L. Strauss has written an interesting critique of thirteen biblical marriages, including those of Abraham and Sarah, Jacob and Rachel, Boaz and Ruth, Ahab and Jezebel, Hosea and Gomer, Joseph and Mary, and Aquila and Priscilla; see *Living in Love: Secrets from Bible Marriages* (Wheaton, Ill.: Tyndale, 1978).

10. Walter Trobisch, "I Married You," in *The Complete Works of Walter Trobisch* (Downers Grove, Ill.: InterVarsity, 1987).

11. Ibid., 381.

12. Ibid., 383.

13. These were all listed as reasons for marriage in a woman's magazine; "If they

cannot find happiness with a man," the magazine said, many women "regard divorce as a reasonable alternative." This is cited in a theological discussion of the "one flesh" relationship; see Robert Roberts and Elizabeth Roberts, "Reconcilable Differences: In Marriage, Two Individuals Really Can Become One," *Christianity Today* 31 (12 June 1987): 17–20.
14. Lawrence J. Crabb, Jr., *The Marriage Builder: A Blueprint for Couples and Counselors* (Grand Rapids, Mich.: Zondervan, 1982), 64.
15. This is the conclusion of William J. Lederer and Don D. Jackson, *The Mirages of Marriage* (New York: Norton, 1968), 103.
16. Sidney Lecker, *The Natural Way to Stress Control* (New York: Grosset and Dunlap, 1978).
17. Please see chapter 18.
18. Eph. 5:21–33; Col. 3:18–25; 1 Pet. 3:1–7.
19. This view is presented in a book by Christian marriage counselor David Field, *Marriage Personalities* (Eugene, Oreg.: Harvest House, 1986).
20. H. Norman Wright, *Seasons of a Marriage* (Ventura, Calif.: Regal Books, 1982). A similar view has been applied to families by Elizabeth A. Carter and Monica McGoldrick, eds., *The Family Life Cycle: A Framework for Family Therapy* (New York: Gardner Press, 1980).
21. 1 Cor. 7:12–16; 2 Cor. 6:14–16.
22. For a discussion of the counseling implications of the two-career marriage, see G. Wade Rowatt, Jr., and Mary Jo Rowatt, *The Two-Career Marriage* (Philadelphia: Westminster, 1980). The dual-career family is the topic of the entire January 1987 (vol. 15) issue of *The Counseling Psychologist.*
23. Martin G. Groder, "Openness: Joys and Dangers," *Bottom Line Personal* 9 (15 February 1988): 9–10.
24. E. L. Kelly and J. J. Conley, "Personality and Compatibility: A Prospective Analysis of Marital Stability and Marital Satisfaction," *Journal of Personality and Social Psychology* 52 (1987): 27–40.
25. For an excellent treatment on stress and the family (including marriage), see the two-volume set edited by Hamilton I. McCubbin and Charles R. Figley, *Stress and the Family* (New York: Brunner/Mazel, 1983); vol. 1 is subtitled "Coping with Normative Transitions"; vol. 2 is subtitled "Coping with Catastrophe."
26. One of the most popular marriage stories within recent years has been the story of Pat and Jill Williams whose "perfect marriage" almost collapsed in failure. Sometimes these books can be enlightening to counselors and helpful to our counselees. See Pat Williams and Jill Williams (with Jerry Jenkins), *Rekindled* (Old Tappan, N.J.: Revell, 1985).
27. Robert J. Carlson, "Hope for Hurting Marriages," *Leadership* 7 (Winter 1986): 32–38.
28. Although others have given higher estimates, one marriage counselor estimates that there is at least one desertion for every four or five divorces; see Charles W. Stewart, *The Minister as Marriage Counselor,* rev. ed. (Nashville: Abingdon, 1970).
29. See chapter 29.
30. Please see chapter 3. For an excellent discussion of sexual temptation in counseling and how to keep from falling, see Randy Alcorn, "Strategies to Keep from Falling," *Leadership* 9 (Winter 1988): 42–47.

31. Sometimes there is a subtle or not-so-subtle seduction of the counselor. This can be very dangerous if the counselor doesn't spot what is happening. This is discussed by Andre Bustanoby, "Counseling the Seductive Female," *Leadership* 9 (Winter 1988): 48–54.
32. For more detailed discussions of these and similar techniques, see Jeannette R. Kramer, *Family Interfaces: Transgenerational Patterns* (New York: Brunner/Mazel, 1985); Dennis Bagarozzi, Anthony P. Jurich, and Robert W. Jackson, *Marital and Family Therapy* (New York: Human Sciences Press, 1982); Robert Sherman and Norman Fredman, *Handbook of Structured Techniques in Marriage and Family Therapy* (New York: Brunner/Mazel, 1986); and David M. Lawson, "Using Family Sculpting and Choreography in a Student Growth Group," *Journal of Counseling and Development* 66 (January 1988): 246–47.
33. Everett L. Worthington, Jr., *Marriage Counseling with Christian Couples* (Downers Grove, Ill.: InterVarsity, 1989).
34. See, e.g., Richard A. Wells, *Planned Short-term Treatment* (New York: Free Press, 1982); and Kenneth J. Howard et al., "The Dose-Effect Relationship in Psychotherapy," *American Psychologist* 41 (1986): 159–64.
35. Group counseling is a specialized form of helping that is not discussed in detail in this book. For a basic overview, see Marianne Schneider Corey and Gerald Corey, *Groups: Process and Practice,* 3d ed. (Monterey, Calif.: Brooks/Cole, 1987).
36. A good example is Louis and Melissa McBurney who work together in counseling with pastors and their wives. This work is described in a book by Louis McBurney, *Counseling Christian Workers* (Waco, Tex.: Word, 1986).
37. You may want to consider the following: "Marital Pre-Counseling Inventory," available from Research Press, 2612 N. Mattis Avenue, Champaign, Ill. 61820; "The Couple Communication Inventory," available from Interperson Press, 1103 Shore Drive, Twin Lakes, Wis. 53181; or "The Marital Communications Inventory," available from Family Life Publications, Inc., P.O. Box 427, Saluda, N.C. 28773; see also Mark T. Schaefer and David H. Olson, "Assessing Intimacy: The PAIR Inventory," *Journal of Marital and Family Therapy* 7 (1981): 47–60.
38. H. Norman Wright, *Marital Counseling: A Biblically Based Behavioral, Cognitive Approach* (Santa Ana, Calif.: Christian Marriage Enrichment, 1981), 62.
39. Carlson, "Hope for Hurting Marriages."
40. David L. Luecke, "Counseling with Couples," in *Pastoral Counseling,* ed. Barry K. Estadt (Englewood Cliffs, N.J.: Prentice-Hall, 1983), 178–200.
41. Contract therapy is more complex than I have indicated in the text. For more information, see A. D. Campaan, "Marital Contract Therapy," in *Baker Encyclopedia of Psychology,* ed. David G. Benner (Grand Rapids, Mich.: Baker, 1985), 674–75; and C. J. Sager, *Marriage Contracts and Couple Therapy* (New York: Brunner/Mazel, 1976).
42. Perhaps it is helpful to remember these (persons, problems, and processes) as the three P's of counseling.
43. Eugene Kennedy, *On Becoming a Counselor* (New York: Seabury, 1977), 219–20. The fallacy of the reasonable solution is not limited to marriage counseling. It applies to a number of situations, including parent-teen conflicts or political and theological discussions.

44. The content/process issue is discussed by Michael Nichols, *Family Therapy: Concepts and Methods* (New York: Gardner, 1984).
45. Some counselors videotape the earlier counseling sessions (with the counselees' prior permission) and later use the tapes to show counselees how they interact and to teach them how they could interact more effectively; see I. Alger, "Integrating Immediate Video Playback in Family Therapy," in *Family Therapy: Theory and Practice,* ed. P. J. Guerin, Jr. (New York: Gardner, 1976).
46. S. W. Peltier and S. O. Vale, "A National Survey of Counselor Education Departments: Course Offerings on Marriage and Family," *Counselor Education and Supervision* 25 (1986): 313–19; and Samuel T. Gladding, Margaret Burggraf, and David L. Fenell, "Marriage and Family Counseling in Counselor Education: National Trends and Implications," *Journal of Counseling and Development* 66 (October 1987): 90–92.
47. For a secular perspective see Emily B. Visher and John S. Visher, *Old Loyalties, New Ties: Therapeutic Strategies with Stepfamilies* (New York: Brunner/Mazel, 1988). For a Christian perspective, see Harold Ivan Smith, *Pastoral Care for Single Parents* (Kansas City: Beacon Hill Press, 1982).
48. For a practical and highly recommended guide to enriching family life through the church, see Charles M. Sell, *Family Ministry* (Grand Rapids, Mich.: Zondervan, 1981). A more recent book is Wallace Denton, *Marriage and Family Enrichment* (New York: Haworth Press, 1986). H. Norman Wright has devoted much of his professional life to marriage enrichment. For information about programs and materials write Christian Marriage Enrichment, 1913 East 17th Street, Suite 118, Santa Ana, Calif. 92701. Campus Crusade for Christ also offers marriage enrichment seminars. In addition, see G. L. Oliver, "Marital Enrichment," in *Baker Encyclopedia of Psychology,* 675–78; E. M. Lester and W. J. Doherty, "Couples' Long-term Evaluations of Their Marriage Encounter Weekend," *Journal of Marital and Family Therapy* 9 (1983): 183–88; and David Mace, *Close Companions: The Marriage Enrichment Handbook* (New York: Continuum, 1982).
49. Some of the principles outlined in chapter 16 also can be applied to prevent marital problems.
50. Eph. 5:23–30.

Chapter 28 *Pregnancy Issues*

1. The latter issue has been hotly debated especially in inner-city school districts where some have advocated the distribution of free contraceptives to prevent pregnancy and AIDS. Following publication of the first edition of this book, I received several letters (some accompanied by books, tapes, and articles) concerning my earlier two-page discussion of abortion. Christians, including evangelicals, have different (and sometimes conflicting) opinions on abortion, sex education, and other pregnancy issues. In preparing this chapter, I have read through most of the unsolicited materials that were sent to me and have tried to present a view that is more informed, balanced, and biblical.
2. 1 Sam. 1:11.
3. 1 Sam. 1:15–16; 8:1–22.
4. Ps. 127:3–5.
5. 2 Kings 4:17.

6. Ps. 113:9.
7. Matt. 1:19.
8. See, e.g., Eph. 5:3–5 and Col. 3:5.
9. Deut. 22:28; 2 Sam. 13:9–14; 1 Sam. 2:22.
10. Jer. 1:5.
11. Luke 1:44.
12. Ps. 51:5.
13. Gen. 29:20.
14. Gen. 35:16–19.
15. Judith Reichman, "Infertility and Miscarriage," *Family Life Today* (September 1986): 22–23.
16. John Snarey, "Men without Children," *Psychology Today* 22 (March 1988): 61–62.
17. Ibid.
18. The "highly antagonized debate over abortion in America," is discussed from a legal and moral perspective by James T. Burtchaell, "In a Family Way: Bearing Children in an Age of Abortion," *Christianity Today* 31 (12 June 1987): 24–27.
19. Reported by Beth Spring, "When the Dream Child Dies," *Christianity Today* 31 (7 August 1987): 27–31.
20. Merrill Rogers Skrocki, "Infertility: The Loneliest Problem," *McCall's* 105 (August 1987): 68–69.
21. One writer calls these "infertility tales," that are used in exchange for "old wives' tales"; Diane Cole, "Infertility Tales," *Psychology Today* 22 (March 1988): 64–65.
22. Skrocki, "Infertility."
23. This hope-despair continuum was one conclusion of an unpublished study by psychologist Betsy Haarmann reported by Beth Spring, *The Infertile Couple* (Elgin, Ill.: David C. Cook, 1987), 60–61.
24. J. William Worden, *Grief Counseling and Grief Therapy* (New York: Springer, 1982).
25. For an in-depth discussion of each of these pregnancies, see Everett L. Worthington, *Counseling for Unplanned Pregnancy and Infertility* (Waco, Tex.: Word, 1987).
26. In Canada, the abortion debate was largely dormant until early 1988. At that time, following a Supreme Court ruling, the prime minister of Canada called the future of abortion "the most complex issue that has confronted the Parliament of Canada probably in twenty-five years." Prime Minister Brian Mulroney's comments were reported in the Burlington (Ontario) *Spectator,* 7 March 1988.
27. *Roe et al.* v. *Wade,* 93 S.C. 705 1973, at 730.
28. A recent book that seeks to give a balanced perspective on the abortion question notes that people on both sides of the issue use emotional language which colors interpretation of the facts and influences the debate. "Murder" is a good example of a loaded word. Pro-abortion supporters almost never use the term; pro-life people use it much more often. See Hyman Rodman, Betty Sarvis, and Joy Walker Bonar, *The Abortion Question* (New York: Columbia University Press, 1987).
29. A good example is the book by Susan M. Stanford, *Will I Cry Tomorrow? Healing Post-Abortion Trauma* (Old Tappan, N.J.: Revell, 1987).
30. For a review of the studies, including an evaluation of the research design, see James L. Rogers, James F. Phifer, and Julie A. Nelson, "Validity of Existing

Controlled Studies Examining the Psychological Effects of Abortion," *Perspectives on Science and Christian Faith* 39 (March 1987): 20–30.

31. H. P. David, N. K. Rasmussen, and E. Holst, "Postpartum and Postabortion Psychotic Reactions," *Family Planning Perspectives* 13 (1981): 88–92.

32. Edward H. Fehskens, "Post-Abortion Syndrome: I Couldn't Shake the Nightmares," *Lutheran Witness* (January 1988): 2–4.

33. Judith E. Belsky, Livia S. Wan, and Gordon W. Douglas, "Abortion," in *Comprehensive Textbook of Psychiatry/IV,* ed. Harold I. Kaplan and Benjamin J. Sadock (Baltimore: Williams & Wilkins, 1985), 1052–56.

34. Worden, *Grief Counseling,* reports that 7,000 babies die of SIDS every year in the United States.

35. Ibid., 87.

36. See Ray S. Anderson, "God Bless the Children—and the Childless," *Christianity Today* 31 (7 August 1987): 28.

37. This is a complicated and expensive process in which the wife is given hormones to stimulate production of more than one egg, the eggs are "harvested" and then mixed in the laboratory with sperm from the husband or a donor before being returned to the woman's uterus. This and other alternatives to infertility are described and evaluated briefly by Beth Spring, "Alternatives to Infertility," *Christianity Today* 31 (7 August 1987): 30.

38. Laurie Denton, "Surrogate Parenting," *APA Monitor* 18 (April 1987): 6–10.

39. Resolve, Inc., 5 Water Street, Arlington, Mass. 02174, is a national nonprofit organization that provides support for infertile couples including telephone counseling, medical referrals, information about support groups, educational workshops, and publications.

40. William T. Bassett, *Counseling the Childless Couple* (Philadelphia: Fortress, 1963).

41. The final statement was accepted by most of the parties involved, but some accepted it reluctantly. The statement was as follows: "We acknowledge that Christians differ in their views concerning the time when personhood begins, but we agree that God has admonished us to choose life instead of death, and has set penalties for those who would, even accidentally, cause a pregnant woman to be injured in such a way that an unborn child is harmed. We believe that compassion for distressed mothers and families, and concern for unborn children, require us to offer spiritual guidance and material solace consistent with the teachings of God's Word. We urge the Church to influence the social-moral climate in which unintended pregnancies occur. We see no grounds on which Christians who are concerned for all human life and for the well-being of the family can condone the free and easy practice of abortion as it now exists in our society. At the same time, we exhort the Church to show compassion for those who suffer because of the abortion experience. (Exod. 21:22; Psalm 8; Ps. 139:13–18; Jer. 1:4–5; Luke 1:39–66; 10:30–37)."

42. To help with your thinking, see Curt Young, *The Least of These: What Everyone Should Know about Abortion* (Chicago: Moody Press, 1983); Paul E. Fowler, *Abortion: Toward an Evangelical Consensus* (Portland, Oreg.: Multnomah, 1987); and James K. Hoffmeier, ed., *Abortion: A Christian Understanding and Response* (Grand Rapids, Mich.: Baker, 1987).

43. See, e.g., Interdivisional Committee on Adolescent Abortion, "Adolescent Abortion: Psychological and Legal Issues," *American Psychologist* 42 (January 1987): 73–78.

44. For more information, write Christian Action Council, 701 West Broad Street, Suite 405, Falls Church, Va. 26046. This group has published two very helpful guidebooks for counselors: Anne Speckhard, *Post Abortion Counseling: A Manual for Christian Counselors* (1987); and Linda Cochrane, *Women in Ramah: A Post Abortion Bible Study* (1986). Information is also available from Lutherans for Life, 275 North Syndicate, St. Paul, Minn. 55104; and from Women Exploited by Abortion, P.O. Box 713, St. Louis, Mo. 63011.

45. Many communities have crisis pregnancy centers. The Christian Action Council (see note 44 above) is one organization that can help locate centers near you.

46. I am grateful to Gregory Jon Smith of Lutherans for Life who suggested this example in correspondence following the first edition of this book.

47. Karen Mohler, "Bringing Comfort When an Infant Dies," *Lay Leadership* 1 (1988): 58–64.

48. 2 Sam. 13:15.

49. Gen. 2:18.

50. There has been a recent surge of interest in self-help and mutual aid groups; see, e.g., Benjamin H. Gottlieb, ed., *Social Networks and Social Support* (Beverly Hills, Calif.: Sage, 1981); or Gary R. Collins, *Innovative Approaches to Counseling* (Waco, Tex.: Word, 1986), chap. 3.

51. Gal. 6:2 gives a biblical basis for the church's involvement in supportive burden bearing.

52. Job is an example. For a brief (four page) discussion of this issue see Josef Tson's paper, "A Theology of Martyrdom," published by the Rumanian Missionary Society, P.O. Box 527, Wheaton, Ill. 60189; see also Don Baker, *Pain's Hidden Purpose: Finding Perspective in the Midst of Suffering* (Portland, Oreg.: Multnomah, 1984).

53. Viktor Frankl, *Man's Search for Meaning* (New York: Pocket Books, 1963). Frankl's logotherapy is discussed from a Christian perspective by Paul R. Welter, *Counseling and the Search for Meaning* (Waco, Tex.: Word, 1987).

Chapter 29 *Family Problems*

1. Robert Coles, "Moral Purpose and the Family," *Family Therapy Networker* 11 (November-December 1987): 45–52, italics added.

2. Dolores Curran, *Traits of a Healthy Family* (Minneapolis: Winston Press, 1983). Similar conclusions were reached in the more systematic research of Nick Stinnett; reported in Nick Stinnett and John DeFrain, *Secrets of a Strong Family* (Boston: Little, Brown, 1985); and George Rekers, ed., *Family Building: Six Qualities of a Strong Family* (Ventura, Calif.: Regal, 1985); see also, Jerry M. Lewis, *How's Your Family? A Guide to Identifying Your Family's Strengths and Weaknesses* (New York: Brunner/Mazel, 1979).

3. Family counseling theories are summarized in several books, including those by Michael Nichols, *Family Therapy: Concepts and Methods* (New York: Gardner, 1984); and Irene Goldenberg and Herbert Goldenberg, *Family Therapy: An Overview* (Monterey, Calif.: Brooks/Cole, 1980).

4. For a good summary of techniques, see Robert Sherman and Norman Fredman, *Handbook of Structured Techniques in Marriage and Family Therapy* (New York: Brunner/Mazel, 1986); or L. L'Abate, G. Gahahl, and J. Hansen, *Methods of Family Therapy* (Englewood Cliffs, N.J.: Prentice-Hall, 1986).
5. 1 Samuel 2.
6. We should note, however, that many of the biblical passages that we have cited in this section appear to focus less on family dynamics and more on the ways in which God works through key men and women.
7. There is a brief mention of widows and orphans in James 1:27.
8. Col. 3:18–21.
9. See Eph. 5:22–6:4; Ephesians has 16 of 155 verses devoted to the family.
10. In 1 Thess. 2:7–12 Paul gives an illustration from the home. In 1 Corinthians and 1 Peter we have references to marriage issues. 1 Timothy mentions the care of widows and makes a statement about Timothy's home. In Titus, there is an exhortation to wives and mothers. That families are mentioned only briefly in the New Testament is a conclusion taken from Gene A. Getz, *Measure of a Family* (Ventura, Calif.: Regal, 1976).
11. Eph. 5:25.
12. Prov. 22:6, e.g., is one of a number of wisdom literature verses on child rearing.
13. Getz, *Measure of a Family,* 12–13.
14. This is a major theme in an article by Robert J. Salinger, "Toward a Biblical Framework for Family Therapy," *Journal of Psychology and Theology* 7 (Winter 1979): 241–50.
15. Getz, *Measure of a Family,* 20; I would add that much of the Old Testament can be applied to modern families as well.
16. First proposed following World War II by Ruben Hill, and summarized by R. P. Kappenberg, "Family Crises," *Concise Encyclopedia of Psychology,* ed. Raymond J. Corsini (New York: Wiley-Interscience, 1987), 419–20.
17. Dave Rice, "Counseling the Crisis Family," *Youthworker* 1 (Spring 1984): 20–26.
18. The following list of snag points (with the exception of the last one) are all suggested by Frank S. Pittman III, *Turning Points: Treating Families in Transition and Crisis* (New York: Norton, 1987). Pittman also lists "snag points about roles"; I have discussed this elsewhere in this chapter.
19. "Family Therapy—Part I," *Harvard Medical School Mental Health Letter* 4 (April 1988): 1–4. For a more in-depth discussion of family psychology and dynamics, see the two-volume work by Luciano L'Abate, ed., *Handbook of Family Psychology and Therapy,* 2 vols. (Homewood, Ill.: Dorsey, 1985).
20. "Effects of Work and Career on Family Life: An Interview with Dr. Paul Faulkner," *Christian Journal of Psychology and Counseling* 3 (1988): 5–8.
21. S. Allen Wilcoxon, "Engaging Non-Attending Family Members in Marital and Family Counseling: Ethical Issues," *Journal of Counseling and Development* 64 (January 1986): 323–24.
22. Pittman, *Turning Points,* 22.
23. Cited in *Cultural Trends and the American Family* (Washington, D.C.: Family Research Council, 1986).
24. Frederick G. Lopez, "Family Structure and Depression: Implications for the

Counseling of College Students," *Journal of Counseling and Development* 64 (April 1986): 508–11.

25. For a highly recommended analysis of the ways in which television has changed our ways of thinking, see Neil Postman, *Amusing Ourselves to Death: Public Discourse in the Age of Show Business* (New York: Penguin, 1984).

26. For several sobering articles on "homelessness in America," see the November-December 1987 issue of *Family Therapy Networker*.

27. Edward G. Carr and V. Mark Durand, "See Me, Help Me," *Psychology Today* 21 (November 1987): 62–64.

28. See, e.g., J. S. Wallerstein and J. B. Kelly, *Surviving the Break-up: How Children Actually Cope with Divorce* (New York: Basic Books, 1980); Patsy Skeen, Robert B. Covi, and Bryan E. Robinson, "Stepfamilies: A Review of the Literature with Suggestions for Practitioners," *Journal of Counseling and Development* 64 (October 1985): 121–25; and Frederick G. Lopez and Scott Andrews, "Career Indecision: A Family Systems Perspective," *Journal of Counseling and Development* 65 (February 1987): 304–7.

29. Patricia A. Boyer and Ronnald J. Jeffrey, *A Guide for the Family Therapist* (New York: Aronson, 1984).

30. E. James Lieberman, "The Changing Family," *Family Therapy Networker* 11 (November-December 1987): 13–16.

31. See, e.g., George A. Rekers, *Family Counseling* (Waco, Tex.: Word, 1988); Ray DeV. Peters and Robert J. McMahon, eds., *Social Learning and Systems Approaches to Marriage and the Family* (New York: Brunner/Mazel, 1987); A. Gurman and D. Kniskern, eds., *Handbook of Family Therapy* (New York: Brunner/Mazel, 1981); Nichols, *Family Therapy*; and David M. Allen, *Unifying Individual and Family Therapies* (San Francisco: Jossey-Bass, 1988); see also, Robert Simon, "Family Therapy," in *Comprehensive Handbook of Psychiatry/IV*, ed. Harold I. Kaplan and Benjamin J. Sadock (Baltimore: Williams and Wilkins, 1985): 1427–32.

32. The following list is adapted from Gerald Caplan, *Support Systems and Community Mental Health* (New York: Behavioral Publications, 1974).

33. For a more detailed consideration of family cycles, see Elizabeth A. Carter and Monica McGoldrick, *Family Life Cycle: A Framework for Family Therapy* (New York: Gardner, 1980).

34. For more information on support systems, see Benjamin H. Gottlieb, ed., *Social Networks and Social Support* (Beverly Hills, Calif.: Sage, 1981); Robert S. Weiss, "Relationship of Social Support and Psychological Well Being," in *Modern Practice of Community Mental Health*, ed. Herbert C. Schulberg and Marie Killilea (San Francisco: Jossey-Bass, 1982); and Gary R. Collins, *Innovative Approaches to Counseling* (Waco, Tex.: Word, 1986); see also Agnes B. Hatfield, "Social Support and Family Coping," in *Families of the Mentally Ill: Coping and Adaptation*, ed. Agnes B. Hatfield and Harriet P. Lefley (New York: Guilford Press, 1987), 191–207.

35. Gottlieb, *Social Networks*.

36. Virginia Satir, James Stachowiak, and Harvey A. Taschman, *Helping Families Change* (New York: Jason Aronson, 1975), 11–12; for an excellent overview of systems theory and counseling, see Gerard Egan and Michael A. Cowan, *People in Systems: A Model for Development in the Human-Service Professions and Education* (Monterey, Calif.: Brooks/Cole, 1979).

37. Even Imber-Black, "Celebrating the Uncelebrated," *Family Therapy Networker* 12 (January-February 1988): 60–66.
38. D. S. Becvar, "The Family Is Not a Group—Or Is It?" *Journal for Specialists in Group Work* 7 (1982): 88–95; see also Kathleen Y. Ritter, John D. West, and James P. Trotzer, "Comparing Family Counseling and Group Counseling: An Interview with George Gazda, James Hansen, and Alan Hovestadt," *Journal of Counseling and Development* 65 (February 1987): 295–300.
39. Pittman, *Turning Points*.
40. Ibid.
41. Jeannette R. Kramer, *Family Interfaces: Transgenerational Patterns* (New York: Brunner/Mazel, 1985).
42. For a discussion of the use of grandparents as adjuncts to counseling, see S. Allen Wilcoxon, "Grandparents and Grandchildren: An Often Neglected Relationship between Significant Others," *Journal of Counseling and Development* 65 (February 1987): 289–90.
43. This is the basis of an approach suggested by Terry Clifford, "Assertiveness Training for Parents," *Journal of Counseling and Development* 65 (June 1987): 552–54.
44. Pittman, *Turning Points,* 34.
45. Ibid., 35.
46. Robert Bolton, *People Skills* (Englewood Cliffs, N.J.: Prentice-Hall, 1979).
47. Bill Cosby, *Fatherhood* (New York: Doubleday, 1986).
48. Charles M. Sell, *Family Ministry: The Enrichment of Family Life through the Church* (Grand Rapids, Mich.: Zondervan, 1981); see also the Winter 1986 issue of *Leadership* (vol. 7) for an entire issue devoted to family ministry. Prevention is also discussed in Rekers, *Family Building,* and Howard Clinebell, *Basic Types of Pastoral Counseling,* rev. ed. (Nashville: Abingdon, 1984), chap. 11, "Family Enrichment and Counseling."
49. Such as James Dobson's Focus on the Family in Pomona, California, or The Family Research Council, 515 Second Street, Washington, D.C. 20002.
50. See the conclusions of Vitz, mentioned earlier in this chapter.
51. Florence W. Kaslow and Richard I. Ridenour, *Military Family* (New York: Guilford, 1984).
52. Hatfield and Lefley, *Families of the Mentally Ill*.
53. See Kramer, *Family Interfaces,* pt. 2, "The Therapist's Own Family."
54. Dean Merrill, *Clergy Couples in Crisis* (Carol Stream, Ill.: Leadership/Word Books, 1985).
55. Dick Anderson, "When the Bough Breaks," *Family Therapy Networker* 11 (November-December 1987): 18–29.
56. Lawrence Metzger, *From Denial to Recovery: Counseling Problem Drinkers, Alcoholics, and Their Families* (San Francisco: Jossey-Bass, 1987).
57. MOPS (Mothers of Preschoolers) is an educational, recreational, and spiritual program for mothers of small children. Write MOPS Outreach, 2269 W. Yale, Englewood, Colo. 80110.
58. Contact Prison Fellowship, P.O. Box 17181, Washington, D.C. 20041.
59. See "Family Therapy and AIDS: Four Case Studies," *Family Therapy Networker* 12 (January-February 1988): 33–43.

Chapter 30 *Divorce and Remarriage*

1. These categories are suggested in a helpful article by Cyril J. Barber, "Marriage, Divorce, and Remarriage: A Review of the Relevant Religious Literature, 1973–1983," *Journal of Psychology and Theology* 12 (Fall 1984): 170–77.
2. This view is held by J. Carl Laney, *The Divorce Myth* (Minneapolis: Bethany House, 1981).
3. Examples of this view include Jay E. Adams, *Marriage, Divorce and Remarriage* (Grand Rapids, Mich.: Baker, 1980); and Lawrence O. Richards, *Remarriage: Healing Gift from God* (Waco, Tex.: Word, 1981).
4. See, e.g., E. E. Joiner, *A Christian Considers Divorce and Remarriage* (Nashville: Broadman, 1983).
5. J. P. Zwack, *Annulment: Your Chance to Remarry within the Catholic Church* (New York: Harper & Row, 1983).
6. Gen. 2:18–25; Matt. 19:5; Mark 10:2–12; 1 Cor. 7:39.
7. Matt. 5:31–32; 19:3–9.
8. Matt. 19:9; Luke 16:18.
9. 1 Cor. 7:15.
10. "Marriage and Divorce: A Study by Evangelical Free Church Pastors," paper, 1980.
11. 1 Cor. 7:8, 32–38.
12. D. Hocking, *Marrying Again: A Guide for Christians* (Old Tappan, N.J.: Revell, 1983), 29–34.
13. Matt. 19:9.
14. 1 Cor. 7:15.
15. See Charles R. Swindoll, *Strike the Original Match* (Portland, Oreg.: Multnomah, 1980), 147–48; and John R. W. Stott, *Divorce* (Downers Grove, Ill.: InterVarsity, 1978).
16. This is true especially if the new believer has attempted reconciliation of the first marriage in light of the new relationship with Christ.
17. Mal. 2:16.
18. Exod. 20:14; Matt. 5:27–28.
19. 1 John 1:9; Matt. 6:14–15.
20. In 1 Tim. 3:2, 12 (and elsewhere) we read that the church leader ("overseer") must be "the husband of but one wife." Biblical scholars differ in their interpretations of this passage. Most agree that this is not intended to limit leadership positions to married men. Some have argued that remarried men are excluded from leadership, even if their first wives have died and they have remarried. Remarriage under such circumstances is not forbidden elsewhere, and in 1 Tim. 5:14 it is encouraged. Presumably, therefore, a person who remarries after the death of a mate can hold positions of leadership. As we have seen, under some circumstances, divorce and remarriage also appear to be permitted for believers. Surely these remarried believers are not to be excluded from leadership. I am inclined to agree with those commentators who conclude that "husband of one wife" means that the leader must be a loyal and faithful Christian husband. Presumably this includes some believers who have remarried following a divorce.
21. Rom. 6:1–2; 12:1–2; 13:14; 1 Pet. 2:11.

22. 1 Cor. 7:5, 10–11.
23. See Barber, "Marriage, Divorce, and Remarriage," 175.
24. See, esp., chapters 27 and 29.
25. Frank S. Pittman III, *Turning Points: Treating Families in Transition and Crisis* (New York: Norton, 1987), chap. 7, "Infidelity: The Secret Insanity."
26. Ibid.
27. Stanley A. Ellison, *Divorce and Remarriage in the Church* (Grand Rapids, Mich.: Zondervan, 1977), 52.
28. Ibid., 57–58.
29. Arnold A. Lazrus, "Divorce Counseling or Marriage Therapy? A Therapeutic Option," *Journal of Marital and Family Therapy* 7 (January 1981): 15–22.
30. H. A. Glieberman, "Why So Many Marriages Fail," *U.S. News & World Report,* 20 July 1981, 53–55.
31. This may be due in part to a fear of AIDS; see Anthony Astrachan, "The Joys of Monogamy," *Bottom Line Personal* 8 (30 November 1987): 7–8.
32. Eric Zorn, "Divorce Group Shares Pain of Untying Knot," *Chicago Tribune,* 19 February 1988.
33. Sarah Childs Grebe, "Mediation in Separation and Divorce," *Journal of Counseling and Development* 64 (February 1986): 379–82.
34. Several writers have attempted to divide the divorce process into stages; see, e.g., Constance Ahrons, "Divorce: Before, During, and After," in *Stress and the Family: Coping with Normative Transitions,* ed. Hamilton I. McCubbin and Charles R. Figley (New York: Brunner/Mazel, 1983), 1:102–15. For a more detailed discussion of divorce as "a normative developmental process," see Constance R. Ahrons and Roy H. Rodgers, *Divorced Families: A Multidisciplinary Developmental View* (New York: Norton, 1987). I have chosen to present a variation of the simple two-stage model (preseparation and litigation periods) proposed by A. C. Stylling in an article titled "Divorce," in *Baker Encyclopedia of Psychology,* ed. David G. Benner (Grand Rapids, Mich.: Baker, 1985): 318–22.
35. This process is described in more detail by Diane Vaughn, *Uncoupling: Turning Points in Intimate Relationships* (Fair Lawn, N.J.: Oxford University Press, 1987).
36. Stylling, "Divorce," 320.
37. Pittman, *Turning Points,* 129–30.
38. Jim Smoke, *Growing through Divorce* (Eugene, Oreg.: Harvest House, 1976), 18–19.
39. These changes have been discussed frequently in the counseling literature; see, e.g., Avis Brenner, *Helping Children Cope with Stress* (Lexington, Mass.: Lexington Books, 1984); J. W. Plunkett et al., "Perceptions of Quality of Life following Divorce: A Study of Children's Prognostic Thinking," *Psychiatry* 49 (1986): 1–12; or N. Long et al., "Self-Perceived and Independently Observed Competence of Young Adolescents as a Function of Parental Marital Conflict and Recent Divorce," *Journal of Abnormal Child Psychology* 15 (1987): 15–27.
40. H. S. Vigeveno and Anne Claire, *No One Gets Divorced Alone* (Ventura, Calif.: Regal, 1987).
41. One report indicates that boys generally suffer more from divorce than do girls, especially if contact with fathers is limited; see James Buie, "Divorce Hurts Boys More, Studies Show," *APA Monitor* 18 (January 1988): 32.

42. Robert S. Weiss, *Marital Separation* (New York: Basic Books, 1975), 309.
43. James L. Framo, "The Friendly Divorce," *Psychology Today* 11 (February 1978): 77.
44. Some of the issues facing children are described by William V. Arnold, *When Your Parents Divorce* (Philadelphia: Westminster, 1980). For a broader and more recent perspective, see William F. Hodges, *Interventions for Children of Divorce: Custody, Access, and Psychotherapy* (New York: Wiley, 1986).
45. See, e.g., Elizabeth Skoglund, *Growing through Rejection* (Wheaton, Ill.: Tyndale, 1983).
46. See Judson J. Swihart and Gerald C. Richardson, *Counseling in Times of Crisis* (Waco, Tex.: Word, 1987).
47. These are adapted from Mel Krantzler, *Creative Divorce: A New Opportunity for Personal Growth* (New York: M. Evans and Co., 1974), 103–16.
48. For good overviews of mediation, see Grebe, "Mediation in Separation and Divorce"; Sarah C. Grebe, ed., *Divorce and Family Mediation* (Rockville, Md.: Aspen, 1985); Craig A. Everett, ed., *Divorce Mediation: Perspectives on the Field* (New York: Haworth, 1985); Jay Folberg and Ann Milne, *Divorce Mediation* (New York: Guilford, 1988); D. T. Saposnek, *Mediating Child Custody Disputes* (San Francisco: Jossey-Bass, 1983); and J. Pearson and N. Thoennes, "Mediation and Divorce: The Benefits Outweigh the Costs," *Family Advocate* 4 (1982): 26–32.
49. Grebe, "Mediation in Separation and Divorce," 380.
50. See chapter 21 and David E. Carlson, *Counseling and Self-Esteem* (Waco, Tex.: Word, 1988).
51. Stylling, "Divorce," 321.
52. Ibid.; see also Thomas Oakland, *Divorced Fathers: Reconstructing a Quality Life* (New York: Human Sciences Press, 1983).
53. Edward Teyber, "How Divorced Fathers Can Stay Involved with Their Kids," *Bottom Line Personal* 8 (15 July 1987): 11–12.
54. Smoke, *Growing through Divorce,* 60–66; additional information on helping the children of divorce is presented by Marla Beth Isaacs, Braulio Montalvo. and David Abelsohn, *The Difficult Divorce: Therapy for Children and Families* (New York: Basic Books, 1986).
55. Pittman, *Turning Points,* 145–52.
56. To counter this potential cause of tension, there needs to be greater middle ground (shared experiences, shared values, and greater cooperation) built especially between the spouses. The issue of middle ground is discussed by P. L. Papernow, "Thickening the 'Middle Ground': Dilemmas and Vulnerabilities of Remarried Couples," *Psychotherapy* 24 (1987): 630–39.
57. Emily B. Visher and John S. Visher, *Old Loyalties, New Ties: Therapeutic Strategies with Stepfamilies* (New York: Brunner/Mazel, 1988); see also "Counseling Blended Families: An Interview with Dr. Tom Milholland," *The Christian Journal of Psychology and Counseling* 3 (1988): 5–9.
58. Matt. 7:3.
59. Weiss, *Marital Separation,* 121–23.
60. Charlie Shedd and Martha Shedd have written two books dealing with these issues: *Praying Together: Making Marriage Last* (Grand Rapids, Mich.: Pyranee Books

[Zondervan], 1987); and *Bible Study Together: Making Marriage Last* (Grand Rapids, Mich.: Pyranee Books [Zondervan], 1987).
61. James 5:16.
62. Lazarus, "Divorce Counseling."

Chapter 31 *Mental Disorders*

1. The story of the Hinckley family is told in a moving and fascinating book by Jack Hinckley and Jo Ann Hinckley, with Elizabeth Sherrill, *Breaking Points* (Grand Rapids, Mich.: Zondervan, 1985). For information about the American Mental Health Fund, write to P.O. Box 17389, Washington, D.C. 20041.
2. American Psychiatric Association, *Diagnostic and Statistical Manual of Mental Disorders DSM-III-R,* 3d ed. rev. (Washington, D.C.: American Psychiatric Association, 1987).
3. Readers who want more detailed discussion of mental disorders could consult one of the textbooks on abnormal psychology or psychiatry. Two of the better books are Theodore Millon, *Disorders of Personality* (New York: Wiley, 1981); and Jerold S. Maxmen, *Essential Psychopathology* (New York: Norton, 1986); see also Kurt Hahlweg and Michael J. Goldstein, eds., *Understanding Major Mental Disorder: The Contribution of Family Interaction Research* (New York: Norton, 1987).
4. 1 Sam. 21:13.
5. Dan. 4:31–33.
6. Acts 26:24–25.
7. Matt. 4:24 LB; see also Matt. 17:15.
8. This is discussed further in chapter 36.
9. Scripture does not give detailed teaching about suicide; see Thomas D. Kennedy, "Suicide and the Silence of Scripture," *Christianity Today* 31 (20 March 1987): 22–23.
10. Cristine Russell, "Mental Disorders May Afflict 1 in 5," *Washington Post,* 3 October 1984.
11. Gary W. Evans, ed., *Environmental Stress* (New York: Cambridge University Press, 1982).
12. "The Nature and Causes of Depression—Part I," *Harvard Medical School Mental Health Letter* 4 (January 1988): 1–4.
13. N. Solkoff, P. Gray, and S. Keill, "Which Vietnam Veterans Develop Posttraumatic Stress Disorders?" *Journal of Clinical Psychology* 42 (1986): 687–98.
14. Bruce Narramore, "The Concept of Responsibility in Psychopathology and Psychotherapy," *Journal of Psychology and Theology* 13 (Summer 1985): 91–96.
15. Matt. 23:25–38.
16. William L. Getz et al., *Brief Counseling with Suicidal Persons* (Lexington, Mass.: Lexington Books, 1983).
17. Erwin Stengel, *Suicide and Attempted Suicide* (New York: Jason Aronson, 1974), 59.
18. The following list is adapted from Bill Blackburn, *What You Should Know about Suicide* (Waco, Tex.: Word, 1982); see also John T. Maltsberger, "Determining Suicide Risk," *Harvard Medical School Mental Health Letter* 4 (January 1988): 8; and

Aaron T. Beck, Harvey L. P. Resnik, and Dan J. Lettieri, *The Prediction of Suicide* (Philadelphia: Charles Press, 1986).

19. These are the major reasons found in one study of suicide among college students; see John S. Westefeld and Susan R. Furr, "Suicide and Depression among College Students," *Professional Psychology: Research and Practice* 18 (April 1987): 119–23.

20. Colleen Cordes, "The Plight of Homeless Mentally Ill," *APA Monitor* 15 (February 1984): 1, 13.

21. George W. Albee, "The Answer Is Prevention," *Psychology Today* 19 (February 1985): 60–64.

22. Gary B. Melton and Ellen Greenburg Garrison, "Fear, Prejudice, and Neglect: Discrimination against Mentally Disabled Persons," *American Psychologist* 42 (November 1987): 1007–26.

23. Lowell Weicker, Jr., "Federal Response to Institutional Abuse and Neglect: The Protection and Advocacy for Mentally Ill Individuals Act," *American Psychologist* 42 (November 1987): 1027–28.

24. Susan Sheehan, *Is There No Place on Earth for Me?* (Boston: Houghton Mifflin, 1982).

25. Louis Linn, *Clinical Manifestations of Psychiatric Disorders,* in *Comprehensive Textbook of Psychiatry/IV,* ed. Harold I. Kaplan and Benjamin J. Sadock (Baltimore: Williams & Wilkins, 1985): 550–90.

26. E. Fuller Torrey, *Surviving Schizophrenia: A Family Manual* (New York: Harper & Row, 1983).

27. J. S. Mizes, B. Landorf-Fritsche, and D. Gross-McKee, "Patterns of Distorted Cognitions in Phobic Disorders: An Investigation of Clinically Severe Simple Phobics, Social Phobics, and Agoraphobics," *Cognitive Therapy and Research* 11 (1987): 583–92.

28. Edward G. Carr and V. Mark Durand, "See Me, Help Me," *Psychology Today* 21 (November 1987): 62–64.

29. Florence Hamlish Levinsohn and Jon Anderson, "Schizophrenia: A Family Nightmare," *Chicago Tribune,* 12 January 1986.

30. See, e.g., Torrey, *Surviving Schizophrenia*; Agnes B. Hatfield and Harriet P. Lefley, eds., *Families of the Mentally Ill: Coping and Adaptation* (New York: Guilford, 1987); see also I. R. H. Falloon, J. L. Boyd, and C. W. McGill, *Family Care of Schizophrenia* (New York: Guilford, 1984); and Carol M. Anderson, Douglas J. Reiss, and Gerard E. Hogarty, *Schizophrenia and the Family: A Practitioner's Guide to Psychoeducation and Management* (New York: Guildore, 1986).

31. J. C. Coyne et al., "Living with a Depressed Person," *Journal of Consulting and Clinical Psychology* 55 (1987): 347–52. It is possible, of course, that the mentally ill person is not the only or major cause of the relative's problems. Because many families are dysfunctional, the 40 percent who "show sufficient distress to warrant counseling themselves" may have needed help long before a family member got depressed.

32. Kenneth G. Terkelsen, "The Evolution of Family Responses to Mental Illness through Time," in *Families of the Mentally Ill,* ed. Hatfield and Lefley, 151–66.

33. For an detailed and in-depth analysis of the mental health needs and treatment in North America, see Joseph Verloff, Richard A. Kulka, and Elizabeth Douvan,

Mental Health in America: Patterns of Help-Seeking from 1957 to 1976 (New York: Basic Books, 1981).

34. For a good overview of the use of drugs in counseling, see Joseph G. Ponterotto, "A Counselor's Guide to Psychopharmacology," *Journal of Counseling and Development* 64 (October 1985): 109–15.

35. The effectiveness of electroconvulsive therapy, ECT, is still a much debated issue; see, e.g., "Electroconvulsive Therapy," *Harvard Medical School Mental Health Letter* 4 (December 1987): 1–4; and I. F. Small et al., "Electroconvulsive Treatment—Indications, Benefits and Limitations," *American Journal of Psychotherapy* 40 (1986): 343–56. For a discussion of more traditional therapies, see Benjamin B. Wolman, ed., *The Therapist's Handbook: Treatment Methods of Mental Disorders,* 2d ed. (New York: Van Nostrand Reinhold, 1983).

36. J. S. Bockoven, *Moral Psychiatry in American Psychiatry* (New York: Springer, 1963).

37. This is discussed further by William R. Miller and Kathleen A. Jackson, *Practical Psychology for Pastors* (Englewood Cliffs, N.J.: Prentice-Hall, 1985; see also Lewis B. Smedes, *Caring and Commitment* (New York: Harper & Row, 1987).

38. Spaniol, "Coping Strategies."

39. A state-by-state listing is given in appendix of Torrey, *Surviving Schizophrenia.* Information about groups may also be available from the National Alliance for the Mentally Ill (NAMI), 1234 Massachusetts Avenue, N.W., Washington, D. C., 20005. For a report on NAMI, see John Bales, "Schizophrenia: The Advocates: NAMI Grows in Size, Impact," *APA Monitor* 19 (March 1988): 8.

40. George Bennett, *When the Mental Patient Comes Home* (Philadelphia: Westminster, 1980); see also Ian R. H. Falloon, Jeffrey L. Boyd, and Christine W. McGill, *Family Care of Schizophrenia* (New York: Guilford, 1984).

41. Gal. 6:10 instructs believers to "do good" especially to those who are fellow Christians.

42. "Care and Treatment of Schizophrenia—Part II," *Harvard Medical School Mental Health Letter* 3 (July 1986): 1–4.

43. Some of these suggestions are discussed in more detail by Anthony M. Zipple and LeRoy Spaniol, "Current Educational and Supportive Models of Family Intervention," in *Families of the Mentally Ill,* ed. Hatfield and Lefley, 261–77.

44. Carol Turkington, "Child Suicide: An Unspoken Tragedy," *APA Monitor* (May 1983): 15.

45. Allen K. Hess, "The Self-Imposed Death Sentence," *Psychology Today* 21 (June 1987): 51–53.

46. Suicide among the elderly has been called "a devastating health problem," by Siegfried Kra, *Aging Myths* (New York: McGraw-Hill, 1986).

47. R. C. Fowler, C. L. Rich, and D. Young, "San Diego Suicide Study II: Substance Abuse in Young Cases," *Archives of General Psychiatry* 43 (1986): 962–65.

48. Numerous popular and scholarly articles document this increase; see, e.g., Cynthia R. Pfeffer, "Suicidal Tendencies in Children and Adolescents," *Medical Aspects of Human Sexuality* 20 (February 1986): 64–67; Diane Eble, "Too Young to Die," *Christianity Today* 31 (20 March 1987): 19–24; Ellen S. Zinner, "Responding to Suicide in Schools: A Case Study in Loss Intervention and Group Survivorship," *Journal of Counseling and Development* 65 (May 1987): 499–501; and Jill M. Harkavy Friedman et al., "Prevalence of Specific Suicidal Behaviors

in a High School Sample," *American Journal of Psychiatry* 144 (September 1987): 203–6.

49. See, e.g., Jim Whitmer, "Without Immunity," *Action* (November-December 1984): 4–6. The *Journal of Christian Nursing* devoted the entire Winter 1985 issue (vol. 2) to "Suicide: A Christian View."

50. Chapter 8.

51. After forty years of work with suicidal clients and analyzing suicidal notes, Shneidman concluded that all suicides are attempts to cope with some situation that is "generating intense suffering"; Edwin Shneidman, *Definition of Suicide* (New York: Wiley, 1985).

52. This is discussed further by John T. Maltsberger, *Suicide Risk: The Formulation of Clinical Judgment* (New York: New York University Press, 1986).

53. For a discussion of counselor reactions to a counselee's suicide, see Getz et al., *Brief Counseling with Suicidal Persons*, chap. 12, "When a Client Commits Suicide." Help for the family is discussed by John H. Hewett, *After Suicide* (Philadelphia: Westminster, 1980); and by Edward J. Dunne, John L. McIntosh, and Karen Dunne-Maxim, eds., *Suicide and Its Aftermath: Understanding and Counseling the Survivors* (New York: Norton, 1987).

54. Peter J. Valletuttif and Florence Christoplos, eds., *Preventing Physical and Mental Disabilities: Multidisciplinary Approaches* (Baltimore: University Park Press, 1979); Paul M. Insel, ed., *Environmental Variables and the Prevention of Mental Illness* (Lexington, Mass.: Lexington Books, 1980); Robert D. Felner et al., *Preventive Psychology: Theory, Research and Practice* (New York: Pergamon, 1983); Joan Polly, *Preventing Teenage Suicide* (New York: Human Sciences Press, 1986); Gary A. Crow and Letha I. Crow, *Crisis Intervention and Suicide Prevention: Working with Children and Adolescents* (Springfield, Ill.: Charles C. Thomas, 1987); and S. W. Johnson and L. J. Maile, *Suicide and the Schools: A Handbook for Prevention, Intervention and Rehabilitation* (Springfield, Ill.: Charles C. Thomas, 1987). For a concise overview of suicide prevention, see Calvin J. Frederick, "Suicide Prevention and Crisis Intervention in Mental Health Emergencies," in *Clinical Practice of Psychology*, ed. C. Eugene Walker (New York: Pergamon, 1981).

55. See, e.g., Mary Amanda Dew et al., "A Quantitative Literature Review of the Effectiveness of Suicide Prevention Centers," *Journal of Consulting and Clinical Psychology* 55 (March-April 1987): 239–44.

56. Albee, "The Answer Is Prevention," 64.

57. Ibid.

58. Lawrence D. Maloney, "Take Mental Patients Off Streets, Back to Hospitals?" *U.S. News & World Report*, 1 July 1985, 55–57; Ellen Bussuk, "Mental Health Needs of Homeless Persons," *Harvard Medical School Mental Health Letter* 3 (January 1987): 4–6.

59. C. M. Harding et al., "The Vermont Longitudinal Study of Persons with Severe Mental Illness: Methodology, Study Sample, and Overall Status 32 Years Later," *American Journal of Psychiatry* 144 (1987): 718–26.

Chapter 32 *Alcoholism*

1. These figures have been drawn from several sources, particularly Jan Ziegler, "Alcoholism: Seeking the Roots of Problem Drinking," *Chicago Tribune*, 8 July

1984; Lewis J. Lord, "Coming to Grips with Alcoholism," *U.S. News & World Report,* 30 November 1987, 56–62; and Edward W. Desmond, "Out in the Open," *Time,* 30 November 1987, 80–90.

2. "A Sickness Too Common to Cure?" *Christianity Today* 25 (18 September 1981): 12–13.

3. E. M. Jellinek, *The Disease Concept of Alcoholism* (New Haven: College and University Press, 1960); see also S. Peele, "The Dominance of the Disease Theory in American Ideas about Treatment of Alcoholism," *American Psychologist* 41 (March 1986): 323–24.

4. See, e.g., R. M. Dreger, "Does Anyone Really Believe Alcoholism Is a Disease?" *American Psychologist* 41 (March 1986): 322; and Herbert Fingarette, *Heavy Drinking: The Myth of Alcoholism as a Disease* (1988).

5. Desmond, "Out in the Open," 82.

6. Quoted in Russ Pulliam, "Alcoholism: Sin or Sickness?" *Christianity Today* 25 (18 September 1981): 22–25.

7. Ps. 104:15; John 2:9; Matt. 11:19; 26:27–29; Luke 7:33–34.

8. 1 Tim. 5:23.

9. Robert H. Stein, "Wine Drinking in New Testament Times," *Christianity Today* 20 (June 1975); it should be noted that some scholar's question the validity of Stein's conclusion about the strength of wine in New Testament times.

10. John 2:10.

11. Prov. 20:1.

12. Prov. 23:20–21.

13. Eph. 5:18.

14. Luke 7:33.

15. Num. 6:2–4.

16. 1 Cor. 6:12.

17. 1 Cor. 6:12; 8:9–13; Rom. 14:21.

18. Gal. 6:1–10.

19. According to one source, no period in recorded history is free from references to the production, consumption, and abuse of alcoholic beverages; see Robert O'Brien and Morris Chafetz, *The Encyclopedia of Alcoholism* (New York: Facts on File Publications, 1982). I learned about the Bangalore conference during a visit to India where I was given a copy of the conference report: J. Kenneth Lawton, Jonathan N. Gnanadason, and K. V. Mathew, eds., *The Christian Response to Alcohol and Drug Problem* (Bangalore: Ecumenical Christian Centre, 1983).

20. D. Goodwin, "Adoption Studies of Alcoholism," *Journal of Operational Psychiatry* 7 (1976): 7–8; and D. Goodwin, *Is Alcoholism Hereditary?* (New York: Oxford University Press, 1976).

21. This is the conclusion of a popular survey of the literature by Constance Holden, "Genes, Personality and Alcoholism," *Psychology Today* 19 (January 1985): 38–44; see also L. Volicer, B. Volicer, and N. D'Angelo, "Assessment of Genetic Predisposition to Alcoholism in Male Alcoholics," *Alcohol and Alcoholism* 20 (1985): 63–68; and Oscar A. Parsons, Nelson Butters, and Peter E. Nathan, eds., *Neuropsychology of Alcoholism: Implications for Diagnosis and Treatment* (New York: Guilford, 1987).

22. This research is reported by Marc A. Schuckit, "Why Are Children of Alcoholics

at High Risk for Alcoholism?" *Harvard Medical School Mental Health Letter* 3 (November 1986): 8; see also J. E. Helzer, "Epidemiology of Alcoholism," *Journal of Consulting and Clinical Psychology* 55 (1987): 284–92.
23. C. Black, "Innocent Bystanders at Risk: The Children of Alcoholics," *Alcoholism* 1 (1981): 22–26; see also Barbara L. Wood, *Children of Alcoholism: The Struggle for Self and Intimacy in Adult Life* (New York: New York University Press, 1987).
24. B. McFarland and T. Baker-Baumann, "The Food Fix in Some Alcoholic Homes," *Changes* 2 (1987): 16–18. I am indebted to Sandra D. Wilson for loaning me her excellent literature review and dissertation on ACOAs: Sandra D. Wilson, "A Comparison of Evangelical Christian Adult Children of Alcoholics and Nonalcoholics on Selected Personality and Religious Variables," Ph.D. diss., Union Graduate School, Columbus, Ohio, 1988; see also Sara Hines Martin, *Healing for Adult Children of Alcoholics* (Nashville: Broadman, 1988).
25. R. Ackerman, *Same House Different Homes: Why Adult Children of Alcoholics Are Not the Same* (Pompano Beach, Fla.: Health Communications, 1987).
26. Cited by Roy E. Hatfield, "Closet Alcoholics in the Church: A Conflict between Values and Behavior," *Christianity Today* 25 (18 September 1981): 28.
27. Anderson Spickard and Barbara R. Thompson, *Dying for a Drink: What You Should Know about Alcoholism* (Waco, Tex.: Word, 1985), 26–27.
28. The following is adapted from George A. Mann, *The Dynamics of Addiction* (Minneapolis: Johnson Institute, n.d.).
29. Lord, "Coming to Grips," 56; by age eighteen, a child in the United States will have seen 100,000 beer commercials in addition to whatever liquor advertisements he or she may have seen in magazines, billboard advertising, or elsewhere.
30. David Berenson, "Alcoholics Anonymous: From Surrender to Transformation," *Family Therapy Networker* 10 (July-August 1987): 25–31.
31. David Treadway, "The Ties That Bind: Both Alcoholics and Their Families Are Bound to the Bottle," *Family Therapy Networker* 10 (July-August 1987): 17–23.
32. Sharon Wegscheider, *Another Change: Hope and Health for the Alcoholic Family* (Palo Alto, Calif.: Science and Behavior Books, 1981).
33. This is the theme of several books including one by Ruth Maxwell, *The Booze Battle* (New York: Praeger, 1976).
34. This is the theme of chap. 1 in Stephen Van Cleave, Walter Byrd, and Kathy Revell, *Counseling for Substance Abuse and Addiction* (Waco, Tex.: Word, 1987).
35. Eph. 5:18 LB.
36. Claude M. Steele, "What Happens When You Drink Too Much?" *Psychology Today* 20 (January 1986): 48–52.
37. Donald W. Goodwin, "Alcoholism and Alcoholic Psychoses," in *Comprehensive Handbook of Psychiatry/IV*, ed. Harold I. Kaplan and Benjamin J. Sadock (Baltimore: Williams & Wilkins, 1985), 1016–26.
38. Notice the description of alcoholism in the title of a booklet by Joseph J. Kellermann, *Alcoholism: A Merry-Go-Round Named Denial* (New York: Al-Anon, 1969).
39. In preparing this chapter, I have been amazed at the large number of recent books dealing with the treatment of alcoholism; these include: Donald M. Gallant, *Alcoholism: A Guide to Diagnosis, Intervention and Treatment* (New York: Norton, 1987); J. Christopher Clarke, *Alcoholism and Problem Drinking: Treating*

Addictions or Modifying Behavior? (New York: Pergamon, 1988); and Reid K. Hester and William R. Miller, *Handbook of Alcoholism Treatment Approaches* (New York: Pergamon, 1988); see also Stephanie Brown, *Treating Adult Children of Alcoholics* (New York: Wiley, 1988).

40. Charles A. Dackis et al., "Evaluating Depression in Alcoholics," *Psychiatry Research* 17 (February 1986): 105–9.

41. In one study of the treatment of alcoholics, research demonstrated that drinkers who also abuse drugs have the worst rates of recovery. In general, psychopathology tends to inhibit the treatment of alcoholism; see B. J. Rounsaville et al., "Psychopathology as a Predictor of Treatment Outcome in Alcoholics," *Archives of General Psychiatry* 44 (1987): 505–13.

42. Treadway, "The Ties That Bind," 18.

43. For a review of these tests, see G. Jacobson, *The Alcoholisms: Detection, Diagnosis and Assessment* (New York: Human Sciences Press, 1976). For a concise, twenty-four-question test, you may want to use the Michigan Alcoholism Screening Test; it is reproduced in Van Cleave et al., *Counseling for Substance Abuse and Addiction*, 201–2.

44. The test is described more fully and the terms are defined briefly by Michele A. Packard, "Assessment of the Problem Drinker: A Primer for Counselors," *Journal of Counseling and Development* 64 (April 1986): 519–22.

45. Maxwell, *The Booze Battle*.

46. For more details of the intervention, see Vernon Johnson, *I'll Quit Tomorrow* (New York: Harper & Row, 1973); and Robert Forman, "Circle of Care: Confronting the Alcoholic's Denial," *Family Therapy Networker* 10 (July-August 1987): 35–41.

47. "Treatment of Alcoholism—Part I," *Harvard Medical School Mental Health Letter* 3 (June 1987): 1–4; see also, Gina Kolata, "New Drug Counters Alcohol Intoxication," *Science* 234 (5 December 1986): 1198–99.

48. For more information, see Baruch Levine and Virginia Gallogly, *Group Therapy with Alcoholics* (Newbury Park, Calif.: Sage, 1985).

49. A good overview of AA is provided by Berenson, "Alcoholics Anonymous"; see also, Norman K. Denzin, *Treating Alcoholism: An Alcoholics Anonymous Approach* (Newbury Park, Calif.: Sage, 1987). For a Christian perspective on AA, see Laird P. Bridgman and William M. McQueen, Jr., "The Success of Alcoholics Anonymous: Locus of Control and God's General Revelation," *Journal of Psychology and Theology* 15 (Spring 1987): 124–31.

50. For more information, write Alcoholics Victorious, 123 South Green Street, Chicago, Ill. 60627.

51. Professional counselors may also want to consider ways to help recovering alcoholics overcome the cognitive and intellectual losses that have come with the alcoholism; see J. Stephen Clifford, "Neuropsychology: Implications for the Treatment of Alcoholism," *Journal of Counseling and Development* 65 (September 1986): 31–34.

52. Counselees may find help in a popular-level book that I wrote to help people reevaluate their lifestyles and manage their lives more effectively; see Gary R. Collins, *Getting Your Life Out of Neutral* (Old Tappan, N.J.: Revell, 1987).

53. See, e.g., M. Sandmaier, *The Invisible Alcoholics: Women and Alcohol Abuse in America* (New York: McGraw-Hill, 1980); and Thomas E. DiMatteo and Thomas M.

Cesarini, "Responding to the Treatment Needs of Chemically Dependent Women," *Journal of Counseling and Development* 64 (March 1986): 452–53.

54. D. L. Sherouse, *Professional's Handbook on Geriatric Alcoholism* (Springfield, Ill.: Charles C. Thomas, 1983).

55. Tom Alihandi, *Young Alcoholics* (Minneapolis: CompCare Publications, 1978). In all of this, remember that decision making will involve both the counselee and the family.

56. E.g., Goran Nordstrom and Mats Berglund, "A Prospective Study of Successful Long-Term Adjustment in Alcohol Dependence: Social Drinking versus Abstinence," *Journal of Studies on Alcohol* 48 (March-April 1987): 95–103; and Charles G. Watson, "Recidivism in 'Controlled Drinker' Alcoholics: A Longitudinal Study," *Journal of Clinical Psychology* 43 (May-June 1987):404–12.

57. One exception is the excellent chapter entitled "How Religion Has Been Used to Help Homeless Alcoholics," in a book by Howard J. Clinebell, Jr., *Understanding and Counseling the Alcoholic,* rev. ed. (Nashville: Abingdon, 1968).

58. Wilson, "Selected Personality Characteristics."

59. Samuel Pearlman, "Religious Affiliations and Patterns of Drug Usage in an Urban University Population," presented to the First International Conference on Student Drug Surveys and reported in *Human Behavior* (May 1973): 44.

60. Eph. 5:18.

61. David F. Duncan, "Life Stress as a Precursor to Adolescent Drug Dependence," *Human Behavior* (February 1977): 52. A practical implementation of this concept is now used worldwide. Developed by Quest International (working with a team of fifty-seven experts on youth and education) and implemented in cooperation with Lions International and literally thousands of schools, the Skills for Adolescence program has demonstrated that education about drugs and training in coping skills significantly reduces substance abuse. For more information write Quest International, 537 Jones Road, P.O. Box 566, Granville, Ohio 43023-0566.

62. R. Niebuhr, *Leaves from the Notebook of a Tamed Cynic,* cited by Stephen J. Nelson, "Alcohol and Other Drugs: Facing Reality and Cynicism," *Journal of Counseling and Development* 65 (September 1986): 4–5.

63. Nelson, "Alcohol and Other Drugs," 4.

Chapter 33 *Addictions*

1. William Lenters, *The Freedom We Crave: Addiction—The Human Condition* (Grand Rapids, Mich.: Eerdmans, 1985), 5.

2. 1 Cor. 6:12.

3. Rom. 13:1–5; 1 Pet. 2:13–17.

4. As we noted in an earlier chapter, this issue was central to the defense of a former White House aide who admitted that he was guilty of perjury but argued that he should not be fined or imprisoned because he was addicted to alcohol and therefore unaware of the illegal nature of his actions.

5. 1 Pet. 5:7; Ps. 55:22.

6. 1 Cor. 6:19–20; Rom. 12:1.

7. Walter Houston Clark, *Chemical Ecstasy: Psychedelic Drugs and Religion* (New York: Sheed and Ward, 1969).

8. John 14:6; 1 Tim. 2:5.
9. This is implied perhaps in Col. 3:2; 1 Thess. 5:4–8; 1 Pet. 1:13; notice also Deut. 6:4–5. We are to love God with our minds and strength. This is impossible for one who is under the influence of drugs and some other addictions. Sorcery is also condemned in Scripture (Gal. 5:16–21; Rev. 9:20–21; 18:23; 21:8; 22:15). Sorcery comes from the Greek work *pharmakeia* and refers to one who prepares drugs for religious purposes.
10. 1 Tim. 3:2–3; Titus 1:7–8.
11. Titus 2:2–6; 2 Tim. 1:7 is written to Timothy, who clearly was a Christian leader, but self-discipline here appears to be a goal for all believers.
12. Titus 2:12.
13. Matt. 23:25; Phil. 2:3; James 3:14–16; 5:5.
14. 1 Thess. 5:6, 8; 1 Pet. 1:13; 4:7; 5:8.
15. Gal. 5:23.
16. Prov. 23:1–3; 28:7; Luke 12:15; 1 Pet. 5:2–3; Prov. 6:25; Col. 3:5; these are only some but not all of the many Bible verses that condemn gluttony, greed, and lust.
17. Prov. 20:1; 23:29–31; Isa. 5:11; Rom. 13:13; 1 Cor. 5:11; 6:10; Gal. 5:21; Eph. 5:18; 1 Pet. 4:3; 1 Thess. 5:7–8.
18. D. E. Smith, "Cocaine-Alcohol Abuse: Epidemiological, Diagnostic and Treatment Considerations," *Journal of Psychoactive Drugs* 18 (1986): 117–29; see also T. Morgantha, "Kids and Cocaine," *Newsweek*, 17 March 1986, 58–65; and "Crack: The New and Devastating Form of Cocaine," *Search Institute Source* 2 (December 1986): 1–3.
19. George A. Mann, *The Dynamics of Addiction* (Minneapolis: Johnson Institute, n.d.).
20. Ibid.
21. When Jesus was on the cross he refused to take the wine that would have dulled the pain as he died for the sins of the world. Elsewhere, however, he spoke approvingly of the Good Samaritan whose act of compassion included pouring wine on the wounds. It is well known that Timothy was encouraged to use a little wine for his ailing stomach; see Matt. 27:34; Mark 15:23; Luke 10:34; 1 Tim. 5:23.
22. In commenting on the family and abuse, one book presents a whole chapter to show that "addiction is a family affair"; see Stephen Van Cleave, Walter Byrd, and Kathy Revell, *Counseling for Substance Abuse and Addiction* (Waco, Tex.: Word, 1987).
23. E. R. Oetting and Fred Beauvais, "Peer Cluster Theory: Drugs and the Adolescent," *Journal of Counseling and Development* 65 (September 1986): 17–22. The authors list seven theories of drug use, plus their own. I have chosen not to summarize the political theories or lifestyle theories because these seem less plausible and have little research backing.
24. There is evidence, of course, that pregnant mothers who are addicted to drugs pass on this addiction to their unborn children. Some might argue that the newborn infants have an inherited addiction. The mother's addiction has been passed on biologically but not genetically.
25. Oetting and Beauvais, "Peer Cluster Theory," 19.
26. The most popular of these are reviewed by Mark R. McMinn and Stephen B. James, "Traditional and Biobehavioral Information in Dieting: The Anticipated

Effects of Christian Weight Loss Literature," *Journal of Psychology and Theology* 15 (Summer 1987): 132–40.

27. K. D. Brownell, "Obesity: Understanding and Treating a Serious, Prevalent, and Refractory Disorder," *Journal of Consulting and Clinical Psychology* 50 (1982): 820–40.

28. Professional books on eating disorders often deal with all three of these issues in one volume; see, e.g., W. Stewart Agras, *Eating Disorders: Management of Obesity, Bulimia and Anorexia Nervosa* (New York: Pergamon, 1987); and Kelly D. Brownell and John P. Foreyt, eds., *Handbook of Eating Disorders: Physiology, Psychology, and Treatment of Obesity, Anorexia, and Bulimia* (New York: Basic Books, 1987).

29. Albert J. Stunkard, "Obesity," in *Comprehensive Textbook of Psychiatry/IV*, ed. Harold I. Kaplan and Benjamin J. Sadock (Baltimore: Williams & Wilkins, 1985): 1133–42.

30. The following discussion is adapted from Susan I. Krieshok and Dennis H. Karpowitz, "A Review of Selected Literature on Obesity and Guidelines for Treatment," *Journal of Counseling and Development* 66 (March 1988): 326–30.

31. S. B. Jacobs and M. K. Wagner, "Obese and Nonobese Individuals: Behavioral and Personality Characteristics," *Addictive Behaviors* 9 (1984): 223–26.

32. Bonnie Spring, "Foods, Brain and Behavior: New Links," *Harvard Medical School Mental Health Letter* 4 (January 1988): 4–6.

33. One estimate suggests that only 4 to 6 percent of anorexics are male; see Katherine A. Halmi, "Anorexia Nervosa," in *Comprehensive Textbook*, ed. Kaplan and Sadock, 1143–48.

34. See J. E. Mitchell and L. I. Boutacoff, "Laxative Abuse Complicating Bulimia: Medical and Treatment Implications," *International Journal of Eating Disorders* 5 (1986): 325–34.

35. These are described in Vath's excellent book, Raymond E. Vath, *Counseling Those with Eating Disorders* (Waco, Tex.: Word, 1986); see also Paula R. Holleran, Joseph Pascale, and James Fraley, "Personality Correlates of College Age Bulimics," *Journal of Counseling and Development* 66 (April 1988): 378–81.

36. Ruth H. Striegel-Moore, Lisa R. Silberstein, and Judith Rodin, "Toward an Understanding of Risk Factors for Bulimia," *American Psychologist* 41 (March 1986): 246–63.

37. Depression in women with eating disorders has been documented in research by Mariette Brouwers, "Depressive Thought Content among Female College Students with Bulimia," *Journal of Counseling and Development* 66 (May 1988): 245–48.

38. George L. Ginsberg, "Adjustment and Impulse Control Disorders," in *Comprehensive Textbook*, ed. Kaplan and Sadock, 1097–1105.

39. Lenters, *The Freedom We Crave*, 92.

40. "Marijuana," *Harvard Medical School Mental Health Letter* 4 (November 1987): 1–4.

41. John F. Greden, "Caffeine and Tobacco Dependence," in *Comprehensive Textbook*, ed. Kaplan and Sadock, 1026–33.

42. Bruce J. Rounsaville and Herbert D. Kleber, "Untreated Opiate Addicts: How Do They Differ from Those Seeking Treatment?" *American Journal of Psychiatry* 42 (November 1985): 1027–77; John R. Hughes and Dorothy Hatsukami, "Signs and

Symptoms of Tobacco Withdrawal," *Archives of General Psychiatry* 43 (March 1986): 289–94; and F. H. Gawin, "Abstinence Symptomatology and Psychiatric Diagnosis in Cocaine Abusers," *Archives of General Psychiatry* 43 (February 1986): 107–13.
43. John D. West, Thomas W. Hosie, and John J. Zarski, "Family Dynamics and Substance Abuse: A Preliminary Study," *Journal of Counseling and Development* 65 (May 1987): 487–90.
44. M. Gallanter, "Treating Substance Abusers: Why Therapists Fail," *Hospital and Community Psychiatry* 37 (1986): 769.
45. Chapter 32.
46. National Institute of Drug Abuse, *Main Findings for Drug Abuse Treatment Units: Data from the National Drug and Alcoholism Treatment Utilization Survey*, ser. F, no. 10 (Rockville, Md.: NIDA, 1982).
47. TOUCH—Transforming Others Under Christ's Hand—is a rehabilitation program based in San Antonio, Texas.
48. Robert J. Craig, "Multimodal Treatment Package for Substance Abuse Treatment Programs," *Professional Psychology: Research and Practice* 16 (April 1985): 271–85; this is a concise and excellent overview of substance-abuse treatment.
49. For an overview of group approaches, see Philip J. Flores, *Group Psychotherapy with Addicted Populations* (New York: Haworth, 1987).
50. Robert J. Craig, "Diagnostic Interviewing with Drug Abusers," *Professional Psychology: Research and Practice* 19 (February 1988): 14–20.
51. Thomas E. DiMatteo and Thomas M. Cesarini, "Responding to the Treatment Needs of Chemically Dependent Women," *Journal of Counseling and Development* 64 (March 1986): 452–53.
52. Oetting and Beauvais, "Peer Cluster Theory," 21.
53. Van Cleave et al., *Counseling for Substance Abuse*, 105–10.
54. Many diets are acclaimed by their developers or a few "fans," but there are few systematic studies of long-term diet effectiveness.
55. Stunkard, "Obesity," 1138.
56. J. Rodin, "Obesity: Why the Losing Battle?" in *Psychological Aspects of Obesity: A Handbook*, ed. B. B. Wolman (New York: Van Nostrand Reinhold, 1982), 30–87.
57. These suggestions are among those given by Robert A. Mines and Cheryl A. Merrill, "Bulimia: Cognitive-Behavioral Treatment and Relapse Prevention," *Journal of Counseling and Development* 65 (June 1987): 562–64.
58. Pryor Baird and Judith R. Sights, "Low Self-Esteem as a Treatment Issue in the Psychotherapy of Anorexia and Bulimia," *Journal of Counseling and Development* 64 (March 1986): 449–51.
59. For a helpful book dealing with the treatment of bulimia and families; see Maria P. P. Root, Patricia Fallon, and William N. Friedrich, *Bulimia: A Systems Approach to Treatment* (New York: Norton, 1986); see also Merle A. Fossum and Marilyn J. Mason, *Facing Shame: Families in Recovery* (New York: Norton, 1986).
60. G. F. M. Russell et al., "An Evaluation of Family Therapy in Anorexia Nervosa and Bulimia Nervosa," *Archives of General Psychiatry* 44 (1987): 1047–56.
61. Bob Smith, "Anorexia Nervosa," *Journal of Pastoral Practice* 6 (1983): 20–32; the author gives some good scriptural perspectives on eating disorders, but he shows

a remarkable lack of compassion or awareness that counselees can't always change immediately and at will. Most counselors will be distressed at the author's threat to call a psychiatrist or "apply church discipline" if the anorexic doesn't change when instructed to do so. Insensitive confrontation, both within a Christian context and without, rarely changes behavior, especially behavior that is longstanding.

62. Marie Edwards Jacobson, "Behavioral Psychotherapy of Obsessional Checking: Treatment through the Relationship," in *Behavioral Psychotherapy: Basic Principles and Case Studies in an Integrative Clinical Model,* ed. Herbert Fensterheim and Howard I. Glazer (New York: Brunner/Mazel, 1983), 91–108.

63. Col. 3:5, 8.

64. Col. 3:9–10.

65. Thought stopping, displacement of unwanted thoughts, how to break habits, and scriptural references to replace unwanted thoughts are among the issues discussed with clarity and in detail by Richard P. Walters, *Counseling for Problems of Self-Control* (Waco, Tex.: Word, 1987).

66. Anne Marie O'Keefe, "The Case against Drug Testing," *Psychology Today* 21 (June 1987): 34–38.

67. This is the Skills for Adolescence program that was mentioned near the end of chapter 32. For information, write Quest International, 537 Jones Road, P.O. Box 566, Granville, Ohio 43023-0566; see also, Jean E. Rhodes and Leonard A. Jason, *Preventing Substance Abuse among Children and Adolescents* (New York: Pergamon, 1988).

68. This story is told in a best-selling book, Cherry Boone O'Neill, *Starving for Attention* (New York: Dell, 1982); the counselor was psychiatrist Raymond E. Vath whose book (*Helping Those with Eating Disorders*) has been mentioned earlier.

Chapter 34 *Financial Counseling*

1. 1 Tim. 6:10.

2. Luke 12:16–21; see also Prov. 28:20.

3. Cited in Malcolm MacGregor with Stanley Baldwin, *Your Money Matters* (Minneapolis: Bethany Fellowship, 1978), 14–15.

4. According to one writer, "the world looks upon Christians as either the biggest suckers or the worst crooks"; see John M. Montgomery, *Money, Power, Greed—Has the Church Been Sold Out?* (Glendale, Calif.: Regal, 1987).

5. Ps. 49:10–12; Prov. 23:4–5; 27:24; 1 Tim. 6:7.

6. Eccles. 5:10; Ps. 52:5–7.

7. Heb. 13:5.

8. Ps. 62:10.

9. Phil. 4:19; Mark 6:7–11; Matt. 6:25–34.

10. This health-and-wealth gospel has been critiqued by Bruce Barron, *The Health and Wealth Gospel* (Downers Grove, Ill.: InterVarsity, 1986). Heb. 11:32–40 is one example of God's sovereignty in treating the faithful. Some were protected and blessed of God while they lived on this earth; others were not. Some saw God work in remarkable ways; others were equally devoted but failed to receive what had been promised.

11. Matt. 19:16–24.

12. Mark 8:36.
13. Matt. 6:24.
14. Deut. 8:11–14; Ps. 52:7; Prov. 30:7–10; see also Luke 16:19f. and Job 31:24–25, 28.
15. Luke 12:13–15.
16. Matt. 25:14–30.
17. In passing it should be noted that money in this passage is a simile and not the main emphasis; see verse 13.
18. Kenneth M. Meyer, *Minister's Guide to Financial Planning* (Grand Rapids, Mich.: Zondervan, 1987), 17.
19. Prov. 28:20; 15:27; 10:9; 11:1; 17:23.
20. Matt. 25:14–30; Luke 12:16–21.
21. Rom. 13:6–8.
22. Prov. 22:7; see also Matt. 18:23–35, the parable of the unforgiving slave.
23. 2 Cor. 9:7; 8:14–15; Prov. 3:9; 19:17; 1 Cor. 16:2.
24. Prov. 3:9.
25. Tony Walter, *Need: The New Religion* (Downers Grove, Ill.: InterVarsity, 1985).
26. Stacy Rinehart and Paula Rinehart, *Living in Light of Eternity* (Colorado Springs: NavPress, 1986), 98.
27. Luke 12:15.
28. Walter, *Need,* 23.
29. Exod. 20:17; Rom. 13:9.
30. Waldo J. Werning, "Family Financial Planning," in *Living and Growing Together: The Christian Family Today,* ed. Gary R. Collins (Waco, Tex.: Word, 1976), 62–74.
31. Prov. 28:20, 22.
32. Rev. 3:17.
33. Cited in Dale E. Galloway, *There Is a Solution to Your Money Problems* (Glendale, Calif.: Regal, 1977), 94.
34. Prov. 21:5; Eccles. 5:15–17.
35. Prov. 11:15; 17:18; 22:26–27.
36. Prov. 19:15; 2 Thess. 3:10.
37. Luke 12:16–21.
38. Prov. 3:9; Mal. 3:10.
39. Gal. 6:10.
40. Luke 3:11; Prov. 14:21; 19:17.
41. See the listing at the end of this chapter.
42. Ps. 50:10–12; Matt. 6:25–34.
43. Ps. 55:22; 1 Pet. 5:7.
44. Ps. 50:12, 15.
45. Exod. 20:15, 17.
46. Matt. 25:14–29.
47. Gen. 1:28.
48. Some relevant biblical passages have been cited earlier in this chapter.
49. Larry Burkett, *Your Finances in Changing Times,* rev. ed. (Chicago: Moody, 1982).
50. Quoted in Haddon Robinson, *You Can Budget Your Money Successfully* (Grand Rapids, Mich.: Baker, 1978), 5.

51. Ibid.
52. The questions in this paragraph are adapted from a list of financial and economic questions suggested by John R. Compton, "Premarital Preparation and Counseling," in *Pastoral Counseling,* ed. Barry K. Estadt, Melvin Blanchette, and John R. Compton (Englewood Cliffs, N.J.: Prentice-Hall, 1983): 166–67.

Chapter 35 *Vocational Counseling*

1. Carol Kleiman, "Hate Your Job? Welcome to the Club," *Chicago Tribune,* 18 October 1987.
2. This is expressed succinctly in the title of a helpful guidebook on career planning; John Milton Dillard, *Lifelong Career Planning* (Columbus, Ohio: Merrill, 1985).
3. John A. Bernbaum and Simon M. Steer, *Why Work? Careers and Employment in Biblical Perspective* (Grand Rapids, Mich.: Baker, 1986).
4. Gen. 3:17–19.
5. James 5:3–5.
6. Eccles. 2:4–11.
7. Eccles. 2:17–23.
8. Bernbaum and Steer, *Why Work?* 4.
9. Col. 3:22–24.
10. 2 Thess. 3:10–12.
11. Bernbaum and Steer, *Why Work?* 5.
12. Gen. 3:17, 19, 23.
13. 1 Tim. 5:17–18.
14. Prov. 31:10–31.
15. Ps. 104:23.
16. Robert E. Slocum, *Ordinary Christians in a High-Tech World* (Waco, Tex.: Word, 1986), 155–56; see also, Doug Sherman and William Hendricks, *Your Work Matters to God* (Colorado Springs: NavPress, 1988).
17. Prov. 6:6–11; 12:24; 13:4; 18:9; 20:4; 24:30–34; 26:16.
18. As examples, Spurgeon cited God's speaking to Moses when he was tending the flock, Gideon when he was threshing corn, Elisha when he was plowing the field, and the disciples when they were fishing; cited in Bernbaum and Steer, *Why Work?* 29.
19. Ibid.
20. Rom. 14:5.
21. Eccles. 9:10.
22. Ted W. Engstrom, *The Pursuit of Excellence* (Grand Rapids, Mich.: Zondervan, 1982).
23. Eph. 6:5–9; Col. 3:22–4:1.
24. Matt. 25:14–30; Rom. 12:6–8.
25. This list is adapted from Garry Friesen, *Decision Making and the Will of God* (Portland, Oreg.: Multnomah, 1980), 337; and based on Eph. 6:5–7; Col. 2:22–23; 2 Thess. 3:8, 11–12; Titus 2:9–10; Eph. 4:28; 5:16; and Col. 3:17.
26. Rom. 12:3–8; 1 Cor. 12:4–31; Eph. 4:7–13.
27. Rom. 12:3; Jer. 9:23–24.
28. Isa. 49:1, 5; Ps. 139:13–16; Jer. 1:5; Luke 1:13–17, 30–33.

29. Prov. 3:5–6; Ps. 32:8.
30. James 1:5; see also Rom. 12:1–2.
31. Rodney S. Laughlin, *The Job Hunter's Handbook: A Christian Guide* (Waco, Tex.: Word, 1985), 14.
32. Slocum, *Ordinary Christian*, 162–63.
33. See, e.g., S. H. Osipow, *Theories of Career Development*, 2d ed. (East Norwalk, Conn.: Appleton-Century-Crofts, 1973); A. Collin and R. A. Young, "New Directions in Theories of Career," *Human Relations* 39 (1986): 837–53; and D. Brown and L. Brooks, eds. *Career Choice Development: Applying Contemporary Theories to Practice* (San Francisco: Jossey-Bass, 1984). One counselor suggests that theories must be tied to "ordinary language explanations of career behavior"; see Richard A. Young, "Ordinary Explanations and Career Theories," *Journal of Counseling and Development* 66 (March 1988): 336–39.
34. This estimate is suggested by Ralph Mattson and Arthur Miller, *Finding a Job You Can Love* (Nashville: Thomas Nelson, 1982).
35. These figures may be outdated; they are reported by Bernard Haldane, Jean Haldane, and Lowell Martin, *Job Power Now! The Young People's Job Finding Guide* (Washington, D.C.: Acropolis Books, 1976), 2.
36. According to one research study, "peers can exert very strong influence in certain areas of adolescent behaviors," especially in choice of lifestyles; however, "on matters relevant to future life goals, parents are clearly of greater importance than peers"; see M. Davis and D. B. Kandell, "Parental and Peer Influences on Adolescents' Educational Plans: Some Further Evidence," *American Journal of Sociology* 87 (1981): 363–87. For an approach to career counseling that places special emphasis on family background and influences, see Rae Wiemers Okiishi, "The Genogram as a Tool in Career Counseling," *Journal of Counseling and Development* 66 (November 1987): 139–43; and Frederick G. Lopez and Scott Andrews, "Career Indecision: A Family Systems Perspective," *Journal of Counseling and Development* 65 (February 1987): 304–7.
37. John I. Holland. *Making Vocational Choices: A Theory of Vocational Personalities and Work Environments* (Englewood Cliffs, N.J.: Prentice-Hall, 1985).
38. This conclusion was championed by E. K. Strong, an early pioneer in vocational counseling, who designed the most widely used interest test; see Jo-Ida C. Hansen, "Edward Kellog Strong, Jr.: First Author of the Strong Interest Inventory," *Journal of Counseling and Development* 66 (November 1987): 119–25.
39. R. N. Bolles, *What Color Is Your Parachute? A Practical Manual for Job-Hunters and Career Changers*, rev. ed. (Berkeley: Ten Speed Press, 1986).
40. Ronald H. Fredrickkson, "Preparing Gifted and Talented Students for the World of Work," *Journal of Counseling and Development* 64 (May 1986): 556–57.
41. Osipow, *Theories of Career Development*, 179.
42. The following list of roadblocks are suggested by Elizabeth B. Yost and M. Anne Corbishley, *Career Counseling: A Psychological Approach* (San Francisco: Jossey-Bass, 1987).
43. G. Wade Rowatt, Jr., and Mary Jo Rowatt, *The Two-Career Marriage* (Philadelphia: Westminster, 1980); see also Lucia Albino Gilbert and Vicki Rachlin, "Mental Health and Psychological Functioning of Dual-Career Families," *Counseling Psychologist* 15 (January 1987): 7–49.

44. Barbara A. Kerr, *Career Counseling for the Gifted: Assessments and Interventions* 64 (May 1986): 602–3.
45. Holly Hall, "A Woman's Place," *Psychology Today* 22 (April 1988): 28–29
46. Samuel D. Osherson, *Holding On or Letting Go: Men and Career Change at Midlife* (New York: Free Press, 1980); and Charlotte R. Melcher, "Career Counseling Tailored to the Evangelical Christian Woman at Midlife," *Journal of Psychology and Theology* 15 (Summer 1987): 113–23.
47. Edward F. Howard, "Jobs for Older People: Case Study of a Legislative Triumph," *American Psychologist* 38 (March 1983): 319–22.
48. K. F. Benesch, "The Displaced Farmer: Career Counseling Concerns," *Career Development Quarterly* 35 (1986): 7–13; and Mary J. Heppner, Joseph A. Johnston, and Julie Brinkhoff, "Creating a Career Hotline for Rural Residents," *Journal of Counseling and Development* 66 (March 1988): 340–41.
49. Farah A. Ibrahim and Edwin L. Herr, "Battered Women: A Developmental Life-Career Counseling Perspective," *Journal of Counseling and Development* 65 (January 1987): 244–47.
50. See, e.g., Richard T. Roessler, "Work, Disability, and the Future: Promoting Employment for People with Disabilities," *Journal of Counseling and Development* 66 (December 1987): 188–90.
51. Jon. 1:2; 3:3; 4:1, 3.
52. Phil. 4:10–13; 2 Tim. 4:6–8.
53. Berkeley Rice, "Why Am I in This Job?" *Psychology Today* 19 (January 1985): 54–59.
54. These include books by Bolles, *What Color Is Your Parachute?*; Dillard, *Lifelong Career Planning*; Laughlin, *The Job Hunter's Handbook*; J. L. Holland, *Self Directed Search: A Guide to Educational and Vocational Planning* (Palo Alto, Calif.: Consulting Psychologists Press, 1977); Richard J. Pilder and William F. Pilder, *How to Find Your Life's Work: Staying Out of Traps and Taking Control of Your Career* (Englewood Cliffs, N.J.: Prentice-Hall, 1981); and Kirk E. Farnsworth and Wendell H. Lawhead, *Life Planning: A Christian Approach to Careers* (Downers Grove, Ill.: InterVarsity, 1981). The Farnsworth and Lawhead book and the Laughlin volume are written from Christian perspectives.
55. 2 Cor. 5:7, 9.
56. For a summary of some approaches see Osipow, *Theories of Career Development*; John O. Crites, "Career Counseling: A Review of Major Approaches," *Counseling Psychologist* 4 (1974): 3–23; D. A. Jepsen and J. S. Dilley, "Vocational Decision-Making Models: A Review and Comparative Analysis," *Review of Educational Research* 44 (1974): 331–49; and Marianne M. O'Hare, "Career Decision-Making Models: Espoused Theory versus Theory-in-Use," *Journal of Counseling and Development* 65 (February 1987): 301–3. For a concise overview, see Yost and Corbishley, *Career Counseling*, 4–35.
57. Adele Scheele, "Career Counselors: Choosing Best/Using Best," *Bottom Line Personal* 8 (30 December 1987): 6.
58. Dennis Heitzmann, Amy K. Schmidt, and Frances W. Hurley, "Career Encounters: Career Decision Making through On-Site Visits," *Journal of Counseling and Development* 65 (December 1986).
59. James P. Sampson, Jr., Michael Shahnasarian, and Robert C. Reardon,

"Computer-Assisted Career Guidance: A National Perspective on the Use of DISCOVER and SIGI," *Journal of Counseling and Development* 65 (April 1987): 416–19; see also M. D. Jacobson and B. T. Grabowski, "Computerized Systems of Career Information and Guidance: A State-of-the-Art," *Journal of Educational Technology Systems* 10 (1982): 235–55.
60. Garry Friesen argues convincingly against the notion of a "call" to ministry. In no place does God require some kind of a mystical call to ministry. Requiring people to have a call, Friesen writes, "creates more problems than it purports to solve. Instead, believers should enter full-time Christian service for the reasons and with the qualifications established in the Bible. And decisions as to whether one should continue or change jobs should be made on biblical grounds as well"; see Friesen, *Decision Making,* 321. For a somewhat different view, see Bernbaum and Steer, *Why Work?* 33–44.
61. It may be discovered, e.g., that successful men in occupation *x* also enjoy sports, reading novels, and yard work. If a test taker scores high on these extracurricular interests, it is clear that he or she likes the same things that are liked by successful people in occupation *x*.
62. See, e.g., Dillard, *Lifelong Career Planning*; Robert E. Campbell and James V. Cellini, "Adult Career Development," *Counseling and Human Development* 12 (June 1980): 8–9.
63. These are suggested by J. C. Hansen, R. R. Stevie, and R. W. Warner, Jr., *Counseling Theory and Practice,* 2d ed. (Boston: Allyn and Bacon, 1977), 467–69.
64. This is discussed further by D. Brown, "Career Counseling: Before, After or Instead of Personal Counseling?" *Vocational Guidance Quarterly* (March 1985): 197–201.
65. William A. Borgen and Norman E. Amundson, "The Dynamics of Unemployment," *Journal of Counseling and Development* 66 (December 1987): 180–84; and Diane Cole, "Fired, But Not Frantic," *Psychology Today* 22 (May 1988): 24–26.
66. Meredith W. Long, "God's Will and the Job Market," *HIS* 36 (June 1976): 1–4.
67. Prov. 3:5–6; Rom. 12:1–2.
68. The group approach is described by Rosemary S. Arp, Kay S. Holmberg, and John M. Littrell, "Launching Adult Students into the Job Market: A Support Group Approach," *Journal of Counseling and Development* 65 (November 1986): 166–67.
69. Col. 3:2–24.
70. Phil. 4:11.
71. Berkeley Rice, "Performance Review: The Job Nobody Likes," *Psychology Today* 19 (September 1985): 30–36.
72. See Michael T. Matteson and John M. Ivancevich, *Controlling Work Stress: Effective Human Resource and Management Strategies* (San Francisco: Jossey-Bass, 1987).
73. Eph. 6:7.

Chapter 36 *Spiritual Issues*

1. Sigmund Freud's views about religion were expressed most succinctly in his book, *The Future of an Illusion* (Garden City, N.Y.: Doubleday Anchor Books, 1927); for a

fascinating and extremely well-documented critique of Freud's religious position, see Paul C. Vitz, *Sigmund Freud's Christian Unconscious* (New York: Guilford, 1988).

2. Some of the secular and religious attitudes toward religious counselees are documented in a carefully written and brilliant paper by Christian psychologist Everett L. Worthington, Jr., "Religious Counseling: A Review of Published Empirical Research," *Journal of Counseling and Development* 64 (March 1986): 421–31.

3. Francis A. Schaeffer wrote about this in a book based on John 13:34–35 and titled *The Mark of the Christian* (Downers Grove, Ill.: InterVarsity, 1970).

4. E.g., 1 Corinthians 13; Eph. 5:25–30.

5. Walter Trobisch, *The Complete Works of Walter Trobisch* (Downers Grove, Ill.: InterVarsity Press, 1987), 696.

6. 1 Pet. 1:14–16; 2:21.

7. Eph. 6:10–17.

8. Rom. 12:1.

9. Rom. 13:14; 1 Pet. 2:11; 1 John 1:8–2:2.

10. Eph. 2:4–9.

11. Rom. 8:15–17; Mic. 6:8; Ps. 103:8, 14.

12. John 14:16–17; Luke 12:12; 1 Thess. 4:8; 1 Pet. 5:10.

13. Matt. 28:20; Prov. 18:24.

14. 1 Pet. 3:18.

15. Rom. 12:1; Heb. 13:15; John 14:15, 21, 23.

16. Rom. 12:2; Heb. 12:1; 1 Pet. 1:14–16; 2:21–22; Gal. 5:22–23.

17. Heb. 13:16.

18. Matt. 20:26–27; James 3:13–14; 1 Pet. 5:6.

19. Jerry Bridges, *The Practice of Godliness* (Colorado Springs: NavPress, 1983), 257.

20. 2 Tim. 2:21.

21. 1 Cor. 2:14–16.

22. Theodore Caplow et al., *All Faithful People: Change and Continuity in Middletown's Religion* (Minneapolis: University of Minnesota Press, 1983).

23. Charles Colson, *Kingdoms in Conflict* (Grand Rapids, Mich.: Zondervan, 1987), 214.

24. Robert N. Bellah et al., *Habits of the Heart: Individualism and Commitment in American Life* (New York: Harper & Row, 1985), 281.

25. Lawrence O. Richards, *A Practical Theology of Spirituality* (Grand Rapids, Mich.: Zondervan, 1987).

26. Eph. 2:8–9.

27. 1 Cor. 3:1–3.

28. This is the conclusion of Richard Foster in his very fine book, *Money, Sex and Power: The Challenge of the Disciplined Life* (New York: Harper & Row, 1985).

29. Rom. 6:12, 16; Ps. 32:3–4.

30. Eph. 2:8–9.

31. Phil. 2:12–13.

32. Col. 2:8; 16–23.

33. I discussed this conclusion in detail in another book; see Gary R. Collins, *Your Magnificent Mind: The Fascinating Ways It Works For You* (Grand Rapids, Mich.: Baker, 1988).

34. Rev. 3:16–19.

35. Prov. 16:18.
36. Heb. 12:15–16.
37. This is discussed further in chapter 37.
38. 1 Tim. 6:10; Heb. 13:5; James 4:3, 13; Matt. 20:25–28.
39. 1 Tim. 6:10–21.
40. Rom. 12:1–2.
41. John 8:31; 2 Tim. 3:15–17; Heb. 4:12.
42. Trobisch, *Complete Works,* 697.
43. In an insightful and practical book, one writer argues that balance and release from our frantic lifestyles begins in the "private inner world that each of us possesses"; see Gordon MacDonald, *Ordering Your Private World* (Nashville: Oliver-Nelson, 1984).
44. Jerry White, *The Power of Commitment* (Colorado Springs: NavPress, 1985), 9; see also Ted W. Engstrom, *A Time for Commitment* (Grand Rapids, Mich.: Zondervan, 1987).
45. See, e.g., Luke 12:15; Eph. 5:3; Col. 3:5; Exod. 20:17.
46. Richard J. Foster, *Freedom of Simplicity* (New York: Harper & Row, 1981), 20.
47. 1 Tim. 6:9–10.
48. 1 Cor. 6:19.
49. 1 Thess. 1:6; Eph. 1:6; 3:16; 4:3; Gal. 5:22–23; Col. 1:29; 1 John 2:20, 27.
50. This is discussed in detail by Jerry Bridges, *True Fellowship* (Colorado Springs: NavPress, 1985).
51. Romans 12; 1 Corinthians 12; Ephesians 4; Heb. 10:24–25.
52. James 1:2–5; 2 Cor. 12:8–10; 1 Pet. 3:14; 3:17–4:6; 4:12–16.
53. Richards, *A Practical Theology,* 182.
54. Among the more recent discussions on suffering, see Ron Lee Davis, *Gold in the Making* (Nashville: Thomas Nelson, 1983); and Billy Graham, *Till Armageddon: A Perspective on Suffering* (Waco, Tex.: Word, 1981).
55. Chapter 5.
56. C. S. Lewis, *The Screwtape Letters* (London: Collins-Fontana, 1942), 9.
57. For two interesting perspectives on this problem, one from a psychiatrist and the other from psychologist-pastor, see M. Scott Peck, *People of the Lie: The Hope for Healing Human Evil* (New York: Simon and Schuster, 1983); and Marguerite Shuster, *Power, Pathology, Paradox: The Dynamics of Evil and Good* (Grand Rapids, Mich.: Zondervan, 1987).
58. Eph. 6:11–20; 1 Pet. 5:8–9; 2 Cor. 11:14; James 4:7; 1 John 4:3–4; Rev. 12:9; 20:3, 10.
59. Isa. 55:8.
60. 2 Cor. 3:7, 13; a footnote in the New International Version Study Bible notes that "the purpose of this veil was to prevent the Israelites from seeing the fading of the glory."
61. 2 Cor. 3:16–18.
62. 1 John 5:16–17.
63. Job in the Old Testament and Lazarus in the New Testament were men whose sicknesses apparently were not the result of personal sin; see Job 2:3 and John 11:4; also John 9:1–5.
64. 1 Cor. 3:3; Eph. 2:14.

65. Phil. 1:15–17.
66. 1 Cor. 3:4–23.
67. Following the demise of a famous television ministry, one of its leaders wrote: "A television camera can change a preacher quicker than anything else. . . . It turns good men into potentates." When this widely viewed television series was at the height of its popularity, "there was no time taken for prayer or for the family, because the show had to go on. We were so caught up in God's work that we forgot about God"; see Richard Dortch, "I Made Mistakes," *Christianity Today* 32 (18 March 1988): 47.
68. John R. Finney and H. Newton Malony, "An Empirical Study of Contemplative Prayer as an Adjunct to Psychotherapy," *Journal of Psychology and Theology* 13 (Winter 1985); 284–90; see also H. Norman Wright, *Self-Talk, Imagery, and Prayer in Counseling* (Waco, Tex.: Word, 1986).
69. A. Bandura, *Social Learning Theory* (Morrison, N.J.: General Learning Press, 1971); M. L. Marvin, "Social Modeling: A Psychological-Theological Perspective," *Journal of Psychology and Theology* 8 (1980): 211–21.
70. John 13:14–15; 1 Cor. 11:1; Phil. 3:17; 4:9; 1 Pet. 5:3.
71. Gerald Corey, Marianne Schneider Corey, and Patrick Callanan, *Issues and Ethics in the Helping Professions,* 3d ed. (Pacific Grove, Calif.: Brooks/Cole, 1988), 52.
72. For a discussion of soul care and psychotherapy, see David G. Benner, *Psychotherapy and the Spiritual Quest* (Grand Rapids, Mich.: Baker, 1988).
73. Jer. 9:23–24; Hos. 6:6; John 17:3.
74. James I. Packer, *Knowing God* (Downers Grove, Ill.: InterVarsity, 1973), 29, 32.
75. Obedience is a major theme of a popular book by Charles Colson, *Loving God* (Grand Rapids, Mich.: Zondervan, 1983). Some empirical evidence supports the idea that obedience to God is associated with higher levels of psychological and cognitive functioning; see David S. Zern, "Positive Likes among Obedience, Pressure, Religiosity, and Measures of Cognitive Accomplishment: Evidence for the Secular Value of Being Religious," *Journal of Psychology and Theology* 15 (Spring 1987): 31–39.
76. Gordon W. Allport, *The Individual and His Religion* (New York: Macmillan, 1950), 90.
77. John 3:16; 1 John 4:7–21.
78. Rom. 6:23; Matt. 13:41–42; Rom. 8:1; 1 Cor. 15:3; 1 John 1:8–10; Isa. 43:23–25; Jer. 31:34.
79. James 5:16.
80. Matt. 6:14–15; 7:1–5.
81. Francis J. White, "Spiritual and Religious Issues in Therapy," in *Baker Encyclopedia of Psychology,* ed. David G. Benner (Grand Rapids, Mich.: Baker, 1985), 1110–14; for a more detailed discussion of the role of the Holy Spirit in counseling, see Marvin G. Gilbert and Raymond T. Brock, eds., *The Holy Spirit and Counseling: Theology and Theory* (Peabody, Mass.: Hendrickson, 1985); see also Thomas C. Oden, *Pastoral Theology: Essentials of Ministry* (New York: Harper & Row, 1983), 206–19, chap. 14, "The Work of the Holy Spirit in Comfort, Admonition, and Discipline."
82. Eph. 5:18–21; Gal. 5:22–23.

83. Matt. 28:18–20.
84. Col. 1:28–29.
85. I have dealt with some of these lifestyle issues in an earlier book; Gary R. Collins, *Getting Your Life Out of Neutral* (Old Tappan, N.J.: Revell, 1987); see also Richards, *A Practical Theology of Spirituality.*
86. Gen. 2:18.
87. 1 Cor. 12:25; almost sixty references in the New Testament instruct Christians to do things for one another; we are urged, e.g., to show concern, pray for, help, encourage, love, strengthen, serve, and bear the burdens of one another.
88. 1 Pet. 4:10–11; other passages dealing with the body and spiritual gifts include Rom. 12:1–8; 1 Cor. 12–14; and Eph. 4:7–16.
89. Eph. 6:10–18; see also James 4:7–8 and 1 Pet. 5:8–9.
90. This is discussed in detail by Rodger K. Bufford, *Counseling and the Demonic* (Waco, Tex.: Word, 1988). Several years ago, a number of evangelical counselors, theologians, and Bible scholars spent several days considering this issue; their papers are available in John W. Montgomery, ed. *Demon Possession* (Minneapolis: Bethany Fellowship, 1973); see also Henry A. Virkler and Mary B. Virkler, "Demonic Involvement in Human Life and Illness," *Journal of Psychology and Theology* 5 (Spring 1977): 95–102; and Paul J. Bach, "Demon Possession and Psychopathology: A Theological Relationship," *Journal of Psychology and Theology* 7 (Spring 1979): 22–26.
91. Peck, *People of the Lie;* and Shuster, *Power, Pathology, Paradox.*
92. I have chosen not to deal with the methods of exorcism in this book; these are discussed by Bufford, *Counseling and the Demonic;* Kurt E. Koch, *Christian Counseling and Occultism* (Grand Rapids, Mich.: Kregel, 1965); and C. Fred Dickason, *Demon Possession and the Christian: A New Perspective* (Chicago: Moody, 1987).
93. Notice again the qualifications in Eph. 6:10–18; see also Matt. 17:19–21; Mark 9:18, 28–29.
94. 1 Cor. 12:10; 1 John 4:1–3.
95. 1 John 4:4.
96. According to Richards, spirituality is "living a human life in this world in union with God"; Richards bases this conclusion on John 17:20–23 and on the model of spirituality that we see in Jesus; see Richards, *A Practical Theology of Spirituality,* 53–57.
97. Ibid., 29, 67; see also Foster, *Celebration of Discipline.*
98. This term has been used by a number of Christian writers including Craig W. Ellison, "Spiritual Well-Being: Conceptualization and Measurement," *Journal of Psychology and Theology* 11 (Winter 1983): 330–40.
99. Heb. 12:5–11.

Chapter 37 *Other Problems*

1. Some of the issues are considered further and in greater depth in the ongoing Resources for Christian Counseling series of books that are published by Word Publishing Co., Inc. For more information, write to Word, Inc., 5221 N. O'Connor Blvd., Suite 1000, Irving, Tex. 75039.
2. Before work began on the revised edition of this book a questionnaire was sent to several hundred counselors asking for suggestions of topics to be included. Most

of the suggested topics have been incorporated. This chapter includes several topics that were requested but have not yet been discussed.

3. This paragraph has adapted some of the conclusions presented by Richard P. Halgin and Derek J. McEntee, "Psychotherapy with Hearing-Impaired Clients," *Professional Psychology: Research and Practice* 17 (October 1986): 466–72; this article includes a good bibliography and a listing of associations that work with and help others work with hearing-impaired people.

4. Joni Eareckson Tada has written that we no longer use words like "crippled" or "invalid" but some of the substitutes are worse. She tends to prefer "disabled people" or "people with handicaps." This puts the emphasis where it belongs—on the individuals and not on their handicaps; see Gene Newman and Joni Eareckson Tada, *All God's Children: Ministry to the Disabled* (Grand Rapids, Mich.: Zondervan, 1987).

5. Milton Seligman, "Handicapped Children and Their Families," *Journal of Counseling and Development* 64 (December 1985): 274–77; and Shirley Zeitlin, G. Gordon Williamson, and William P. Rosenblatt, "The Coping with Stress Model: A Counseling Approach for Families with a Handicapped Child," *Journal of Counseling and Development* 65 (April 1987): 443–46.

6. Judith E. Pearson and Abby Sternberg, "A Mutual-Help Project for Families of Handicapped Children," *Journal of Counseling and Development* 65 (December 1986): 213–15. Groups such as these may already exist in your community. Check with a doctor, hospital, or county agencies. If no support groups exist, it may be wise to start one.

7. Jan Cox-Gedmark, *Coping with Physical Disability* (Philadelphia: Westminster, 1980).

8. Edward M. Levinson, "A Vocational Evaluation Program for Handicapped Students: Focus on the Counselor's Role," *Journal of Counseling and Development* 65 (October 1986): 105–6.

9. Joni Eareckson Tada, *Choices . . . Changes* (Grand Rapids, Mich.: Zondervan, 1986).

10. B. F. Skinner and M. E. Vaughn, *Enjoy Old Age: A Program of Self-Management* (New York: Norton, 1983); a similar message is given by Nancy M. Crewe and Irving Kenneth Zola, *Independent Living for Physically Disabled People: Developing, Implementing, and Evaluating Self-Help Rehabilitation Programs* (San Francisco: Jossey-Bass, 1983).

11. One research study has shown, however, that expectations do not need to bias one's assessment of disabled counselees; Timothy R. Elliott, Robert G. Frank and Martha Brownlee-Duffeck, "Clinical Inferences about Depression and Physical Disability," *Professional Psychology: Research and Practice* 19 (April 1988): 206–10.

12. Canadian readers may be interested to know that Vanier is the son of former Governor General Georges Vanier.

13. George Harris, "L'Arche: Homes for People Who Are Mentally Retarded," *Journal of Counseling and Development* 65 (February 1987): 322–24; I first learned of L'Arche from the writings of Henri J. M. Nouwen, *Lifesigns: Intimacy, Fecundity, and Ecstasy in Christian Perspective* (Garden City, N.Y.: Doubleday, 1986).

14. "Mental Retardation—Part I," *Harvard Medical School Mental Health Letter* 3 (October 1986): 1–4.

15. Christopher Joyce, "Assault on the Brain," *Psychology Today* 22 (March 1988): 38–44; this article documents the common existence of ADC (AIDS dementia complex), a type of dementia that may strike as many as 90 percent of AIDS sufferers. According to one report, "people infected with the AIDS virus, suffer a surprisingly high level of neuropsychological impairment, including impaired coordination and memory and cognitive difficulties before they show any other symptoms"; A. J. Hostetler, "Behavior May Offer First Sign of AIDS," *APA Monitor* 19 (February 1988): 10.
16. Siegfried Kra, *Aging Myths: Reversible Causes of Mind and Memory Loss* (New York: McGraw-Hill, 1986); the title of this book is slightly misleading, the author deals with a variety of reversible brain disorders that are not limited to elderly people.
17. For a popular discussion of talent development in people with Down's syndrome; see Carol Turkington, "Special Talents," *Psychology Today* 21 (September 1987): 42–46.
18. David J. Hesselgrave, *Counseling Cross-Culturally* (Grand Rapids, Mich.: Baker, 1984); and David Augsburger, *Pastoral Counseling across Cultures* (Philadelphia: Westminster, 1986).
19. Some of these differences within our own culture are discussed in books by John M. Dillard, *Multicultural Counseling* (Chicago: Nelson-Hall, 1983); Elaine S. LeVine and Amado M. Padilla, *Crossing Cultures in Therapy: Pluralistic Counseling for the Hispanic* (Monterey, Calif.: Brooks/Cole, 1980); Derald W. Sue, *Counseling the Culturally Different: Theory and Practice* (New York: Wiley, 1981); and P. B. Pedersen et al., eds., *Counseling across Cultures,* 3d ed. (Honolulu: University of Hawaii Press, 1988).
20. Some of these differences were encountered by two American psychologists who tried to apply Western family therapy in Japan; see Joanna Biggar, "Meeting of the Twain," *Psychology Today* 46 (November 1987): 46–52. Japanese-American differences are highlighted more clearly by Peter N. Dale, *The Myth of Japanese Uniqueness* (New York: St. Martin's Press, 1986). For a fascinating Christian perspective on cultural differences, see Tim Stafford, *The Friendship Gap: Reaching Out across Cultures* (Downers Grove, Ill.: InterVarsity, 1984). Also helpful is a small volume by Sherwood G. Lingenfelter and Marvin K. Mayers, *Ministering Cross-Culturally: An Incarnational Model for Personal Relationships* (Grand Rapids, Mich.: Baker, 1986).
21. For more information, see J. A. Neff, "Race and Vulnerability to Stress: An Examination of Differential Vulnerability," *Journal of Personality and Social Psychology* 49 (1985): 481–91; Elsie M. J. Smith, "Ethnic Minorities: Life Stress, Social Support, and Mental Health Issues," *Counseling Psychologist* 13 (October 1985): 537–80; and Jay M. Uomoto, "Examination of Psychological Distress in Ethnic Minorities from a Learned Helplessness Framework," *Professional Psychology: Research and Practice* 17 (October 1986): 448–53.
22. Some of these characteristics are listed by Sue, *Counseling the Culturally Different.* A slightly different perspective is presented by two writers who try to focus on the similarities that exist in helping throughout different cultures; see Joseph G. Ponterrotto and Kevin F. Benesch, "An Organizational Framework for Understanding the Role of Culture in Counseling," *Journal of Counseling and Development* 66 (January 1988): 237–41.
23. For a good discussion of these, see Patricia Long, "Growing Up Military," *Psychology Today* 20 (December 1986): 30–37.

24. An excellent discussion of these and related counseling issues is given by Florence W. Kaslow and Richard I. Ridenour, eds., *The Military Family: Dynamics and Treatment* (New York: Guilford, 1984); see also Charles R. Figley and Hamilton I. McCubbin, *Stress and the Family: Coping with Catastrophe* (New York: Brunner/Mazel, 1983), vol. 2; and Thomas A. Harris, *Counseling the Serviceman and His Family* (Englewood Cliffs, N.J.: Prentice-Hall, 1964).
25. E.g., Overseas Christian Servicemen's Centers has a network of missionaries who minister to service personnel. For more information, write OCSC, P.O. Box 1268, Englewood, Colo. 80150.
26. For more information, contact Prison Fellowship, P.O. Box 17500, Washington, D.C. 20041.
27. This is the observation of Norman A. Scott, "Counseling Prisoners: Ethical Issues, Dilemmas, and Cautions," *Journal of Counseling and Development* 64 (December 1984): 272–73.
28. Allen K. Hess, "The Self-Imposed Death Sentence," *Psychology Today* 21 (June 1987): 50–53.
29. Scott M. Whiteley and Ray E. Hosford, "Counseling in Prisons," *Counseling Psychologist* 11 (1983): 27–34.
30. See, e.g., Irving B. Weiner and Allen Hess, *Handbook of Forensic Psychology* (New York: Wiley, 1987).
31. George C. Kandle and Henry H. Cassler, *Ministering to Prisoners and Their Families* (Englewood Cliffs, N.J.: Prentice-Hall, 1968); and Louis P. Carney, "The Counseling Perspective in Parole," *Counseling Psychologist* 11 (1983): 41–47.
32. JoAnn Cutler Friedrich, *The Pre-Menstrual Solution* (San Jose, Calif.: Arrow Press, 1987).
33. For additional information, counselors can call the PMS hot line number: 1-800-222-4PMS (in Wisconsin 608-833-4PMS); see also Greg J. Neimeyer and Shae Graham Kosch, "An Overview of Assessment and Treatment of Premenstrual Syndrome," *Journal of Counseling and Development* 66 (April 1988): 397–99.
34. David L. Schiedermayer, "Choices in Plague Time," *Christianity Today* 31 (7 August 1987): 20–22.
35. Sharon E. Mumper, "AIDS in Africa: Death Is the Only Certainty," *Christianity Today* 32 (8 April 1988): 36–39.
36. Russell T. Joffe and David R. Rubinow, "The Neuropsychiatric Symptoms of AIDS," *Harvard Medical School Mental Health Letter* 7 (January 1987): 8; John Patten, "Medical Facts about AIDS," *Family Therapy Networker* 12 (January-February 1988): 28; and C. Everett Koop, *Surgeon General's Report on Acquired Immune Deficiency Syndrome* (Washington, D.C.: U.S. Department of Health and Human Services, n.d.).
37. E. K. Nichols, *Mobilizing against AIDS: The Unfinished Story of the Virus* (Cambridge, Mass.: Harvard University Press, 1986).
38. Kevin Krajick, "Private Passions and Public Health," *Psychology Today* 22 (May 1988): 50–58.
39. Jimmie C. Holland and Susan Tross, "AIDS and Mental Health," *Harvard Medical School Mental Health Letter* 4 (July 1987): 4–5.
40. Lauren S. Kaplan, "AIDS and Guilt," *Family Therapy Networker* 12 (January-February 1988): 40–41, 80.

41. Paul Brand, "The AIDS Plague: What Now?" *Christian Herald* 109 (April 1986): 43–45.
42. Richard E. Price, Michael M. Omizo, and Victoria L. Hammett, "Counseling Clients with AIDS," *Journal of Counseling and Development* 65 (October 1986): 96–97; and S. F. Morin, K. A. Charles, and A. K. Malyon, "The Psychological Impact of AIDS on Gay Men," *American Psychologist* 39 (November 1984): 1288–93.
43. Susan Landers, "Practitioners and AIDS: Face-to-Face with Pain," *APA Monitor* 19 (January 1988): 1, 14; for a discussion of some of the ethical issues in counseling AIDS victims, see Lizbeth A. Gray and Anna K. Harding, "Confidentiality Limits with Clients Who Have the AIDS Virus," *Journal of Counseling and Development* 66 (January 1988): 219–23.
44. Landers, "Practitioners and AIDS."
45. Diego J. Lopez and George G. Getzel, "Helping Gay AIDS Patients in Crises," *Social Casework* 65 (September 1984): 387–94.
46. Paul Lightner, "AIDS: A Descriptive Analysis and Counseling Approach," Master's integration paper, Trinity Evangelical Divinity School, Deerfield, Ill., 1987.
47. J. Dunkel and S. Hatfield, "Countertransference Issues in Working with AIDS," *Social Work* (March-April 1986): 114–17.
48. Heb. 12:15.
49. Psalm 73.
50. 2 Cor. 12:7–10; 1 Pet. 1:5–7; Rom. 8:28; Heb. 12:11; Ps. 119:71; Rom. 5:3–5.
51. 2 Cor. 1:3–7.
52. John 9:1–41; Luke 13:1–5.
53. Brand, "The AIDS Plague."

Chapter 38 *Counseling the Counselor*

1. Joshua L. Liebman, *Peace of Mind* (New York: Simon & Schuster, 1946); the story is taken from Bob Benson and Michael W. Benson, *Disciplines for the Inner Life* (Waco, Tex.: Word, 1985), 156–57.
2. John 14:27.
3. Phil. 4:12.
4. Phil. 4:4–7.
5. Jerry Bridges, *The Practice of Godliness* (Colorado Springs: NavPress, 1983), 197.
6. 1 Pet. 5:7–9; James 4:7; Phil. 4:6–9.
7. Gal. 5:22; John 14:26–27.
8. Bridges, *The Practice of Godliness,* 201.
9. Richard Exley, *The Rhythm of Life* (Tulsa, Okla.: Harrison House, 1987), 41.
10. Ibid., 137.
11. John 12:8.
12. Henri J. M. Nouwen, *The Genesee Diary: Report from a Trappist Monastery* (Garden City, N.Y.: Doubleday-Image, 1976), 13.
13. Mark 1:32–35; Luke 9:10.
14. Mark 1:36–38.
15. Mark 1:38–39.
16. Exley, *The Rhythm,* 181.

17. Heb. 10:24–25.
18. 1 Cor. 10:12.
19. Luke 9:1–2.
20. Henri J. M. Nouwen, *Clowning in Rome: Reflections on Solitude, Celibacy, Prayer and Contemplation* (Garden City, N.Y.: Doubleday-Image, 1979), 53–54.
21. James 1:27.
22. John 17:15.
23. 1 John 1:8–9.
24. 1 Thess. 4:7, 11; Heb. 12:14; see also 1 Pet. 1:14–16.
25. Jerry Bridges, *The Pursuit of Holiness* (Colorado Springs: NavPress, 1978), 20.
26. Except for the periodic fund-raising letters that come from the college development office; fund raisers always seem to be able to find alumni!
27. Matt. 20:20–28.

AUTHOR'S NOTE ABOUT THE INDEX

According to one definition, an index is "an alphabetical list, placed at the end of a book, for the purpose of facilitating reference within the body of the text." A good index is accurate and designed to be useful.

With computers, it is relatively easy to select a word and quickly retrieve a listing of its every appearance within the book. Sometimes that computer list becomes the index. Such a listing might be complete, but I doubt that it would be helpful.

Consider, for example, a word like "anxiety." The following index does not cite every page on which "anxiety" appears in the text. Such a computer-type listing probably would include several hundred references, many of which refer to anxiety only in passing. Instead, I have tried to look at each reference to anxiety and include in the index only those citations that would be of greatest help counselors and students.

Preparing such an index, even with a computer's help, depends on the author's decision about what should be included and what should not. I decided, for example, to include references to the Holy Spirit; I did not include references to Satan—even though the devil's activities are mentioned in different places through the book. I included the names of most contemporary people who are mentioned in the text, but I chose not to include most historical names, names of politicians and entertainers, or references to biblical characters like Paul or Sampson. To a large extent, these were judgments on my part about what would be most helpful to the reader-counselor. I tried to make the best decisions.

Hopefully, the resulting index will be helpful in your work as a Christian counselor. That has been my goal in these final few pages, as it has been in the many pages that have gone before.

Index

D

U

V

W

Y

Gary R. Collins is a licensed psychologist with a Ph.D. in clinical psychology from Purdue University. He has published numerous scientific and popular articles, serves as a consulting editor to two professional journals, and is a contributing editor to *Christian Herald.* Dr. Collins is also the general editor for the Resources for Christian Counseling series published by Word, Inc. In addition to *Christian Counseling: A Comprehensive Guide,* his books include *The Magnificent Mind, How to Be a People Helper, Can You Trust Psychology?* and many others.

Dr. Collins was chairman of the division of counseling and professor of psychology at Trinity Evangelical Divinity School. Despite his writing and speaking engagements, he continues to teach on a part-time basis at Trinity.

He lives in northern Illinois with his wife, Julie, and their two daughters, Marilynn and Jan.

OTHER BOOKS BY GARY R. COLLINS

Search for Reality
Living in Peace
Man in Transition
Effective Counseling
Fractured Personalities
Man in Motion
Overcoming Anxiety
The Christian Psychology of Paul Tournier
How to Be a People Helper
The Rebuilding of Psychology
Helping People Grow
Psychology and Theology
Getting Started
The Sixty-Second Christian
Beyond Easy Believism
Innovations in Counseling
Getting Your Life out of Neutral
Can You Trust Psychology?